HEATH

Algebra 2

with Trigonometry

Clyde A. Dilley

Steven P. Meiring

John E. Tarr

Ross Taylor

D.C. Heath and Company

HEATH Lexington, Massachusetts Toronto

Authors

Clyde A. Dilley

Author in residence; formerly Professor of Education,
University of Toledo, Ohio; and formerly mathematics teacher
in Iowa and Illinois

Steven P. Meiring

Supervisor of Mathematics, State of Ohio;
formerly mathematics teacher in Indiana

John E. Tarr

Professor, University of Northern Iowa;
and Mathematics Teacher, Malcolm Price Laboratory School

Ross Taylor

Supervisor of Mathematics, Minneapolis Public Schools;
formerly mathematics teacher in Illinois

International Standard Book Number: 0-669-20853-1

1 2 3 4 5 6 7 8 9 0

CONTENTS

1 Real Numbers

Application: Distance to horizon *5*   **Calculator Extension:** Decimals for fractions *8*
Extension: Fields *33*   **Historical Note:** Biography of Gauss *23*

2 Linear Equations and Inequalities

Applications: Linear depreciation *43*, Automobile weight distribution *44*,
Highway expansion *44*, Doppler effect *45*, Area *49*, Acceleration *50*,
Boyle's and Charles' laws *50*, Point of no return *51*, Better buy *58*
Computer Applications: Solving equations *45*, Compound inequalities *66*
Extension: Statistics—Range *62*   **Historical Note:** Earth's circumference *73*

04349

3 Functions and Graphs

Applications: Technology—Robots *83*, Airmail postage *117*, Sales tax *122*
Extensions: Statistics—Measures of central tendency *88*, Statistics—Mean *103*, Statistics—Histogram *110*

4 Systems of Linear Equations and Inequalities

Applications: *140, 146, 151, 159, 163, 175*   **Extension:** Statistics—Dispersion *153*
Historical Note: Determinants *165*

5 Polynomials

Applications: Earth *190*, Cryptography *204*, Geometric problems *214*, *215*
Extensions: Classifying whole numbers *195*, Quadratic inequalities *216*
Historical Note: Exponents *211*

6 Rational Expressions

Applications: Significant digits *226*, Harmonic mean and arithmetic mean *239*
Calculator Extension: Number trick *240*   **Historical Note:** Egyptian fractions *244*
Biography: Benoit Mandelbrot *232*

7 Radicals and Irrationals

Applications: Falling bodies *270*, Volume *270*, Earth's gravitational field *293*, Mass *294*
Calculator Extensions: Roots *271*, Evaluating radical expressions *277*

8 Quadratic Functions and Complex Numbers

Applications: Geometry *308*, Turning velocity *309*, Projectiles *314*,
Stopping distance *314*, Maximums and minimums *349*
Extension: Complex number plane *328, 352*   **Biography:** Paul Erdos *315*
Historical Note: Terms for numbers *345*

9 Conic Sections

Applications: *372, 379*   **Historical Note:** Orbits of planets *380*
Extension: Lemniscate of Bernoulli *397*

10 Polynomial Functions

Application: Using a computer or graphing calculator *428*
Computer Extension: Evaluating cubic functions *429*
Historical Note: Fermat's last theorem *421*

11 Exponential and Logarithmic Functions

Applications: The Richter scale *458*, Sound intensity *458*, Compound interest *465, 467*, Basal metabolism *469*, Total cost *472*, Speed of telegraphic signals *472*, Depreciation *477*, Population growth or decay *478*, Radioactive carbon dating *479*
Extensions: Linear interpolation *459*, Using logarithms *473*
Historical Note: Logarithms *454*

12 Sequences and Series

Applications: *490, 496, 506, 511, 516*   **Calculator Extension:** Infinite sequences *492*
Computer Extension: Evaluating series *518*   **Extension:** Definition of sequences *497*
Biography: Mary Ellen Rudin *507*

13 Probability

Applications: Circular permutations *536*, Stirling's formula *537*, Blood groups *540*, Odds *551*
Extensions: Circle graphs *531*, Bar graphs and line graphs *562*

14 Statistics

Computer Extension: Standard deviation *583*   **Biography:** Martin Gardner *595*

15 Matrices

Applications: *613, 619*
Computer Extensions: Adding matrices *615*, A program for Cramer's rule *632*
Extension: Graphing ordered triples *622*   **Historical Note:** Matrices *632*

16 Circular Functions

Application: Population functions *679*
Calculator Extension: Degrees and radians *696*
Extensions: Counting civilizations *660*, Combining functions *673*
Biography: Roger Penrose *654*

17 Applications of Trigonometric Functions

Applications: *714, 721, 726*   **Calculator Extension:** Evaluating sines *728*
Extensions: Perpendicular components of vectors *723*,
Finding the sum of two vectors *733*
Biography: Emmy Noether *734*

18 Trigonometric Identities and Equations

Calculator Extensions: Acceleration of gravity *757*, Trigonometric equations *761*

CHAPTER 1

Real Numbers

Mathematics, long a common "language" on Earth, has been used to try to communicate with extraterrestrials. In 1974 a radio telescope beamed a three-minute message in binary (base two) numbers toward a star cluster in the constellation Hercules, 25,000 light years away. The brief message contained 1679 bits of information about life on Earth. It described our numbering system; listed the atomic numbers of hydrogen, carbon, nitrogen, oxygen, and phosphorus; and gave the chemical structure of DNA. The message also supplied a crude sketch of human beings that indicated our average height and said that there are four billion of us and that we inhabit the third planet from the sun.

LESSON 1-1

The Set of Real Numbers

Several of the sets of numbers used in mathematics, science, and technology are displayed below. The diagram at the right shows the relationships among the sets.

Counting numbers: 1, 2, 3, 4, 5, . . .

Whole numbers: 0, 1, 2, 3, 4, 5, . . .

Integers: . . . , $^-3$, $^-2$, $^-1$, 0, 1, 2, 3, . . .

Rational numbers: $-6, -\frac{7}{3}, 0, \frac{15}{47}, \frac{1}{2}, 12$

Irrational numbers: $\sqrt{2}, \pi, 4 + \sqrt{3}$

Real numbers: All of the above are real numbers.

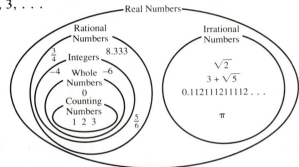

In Chapter 8, numbers that are not real numbers will be introduced. Until that point, we will concentrate on operations with the real numbers.

All real numbers are either rational or irrational.

Definitions: Rational and Irrational Numbers

A *rational number* is a number that can be expressed as the quotient of two integers.

An *irrational number* is a real number that cannot be expressed as the quotient of two integers.

We can prove, for example, that 0.5 and -6 are rational by showing that each is the quotient of two integers.

$$0.5 = \frac{1}{2} \qquad\qquad -6 = \frac{18}{-3}$$

Another important way of classifying real numbers is to consider how they can be written as decimals. Each real number can be represented by one of the following kinds of decimals.

Terminating decimals   0.125   **Repeating decimals**   1.3333 . . .

-2.146543 0.234234234 . . .

Nonrepeating, nonterminating decimals   0.12345678910111213 . . .

1.101001000100001 . . .

The portion of a decimal that repeats is called the **repetend.** A bar over the repetend indicates the repeating digits.

$$1.\overline{3} = 1.3333\ldots$$

$$0.0\overline{45} = 0.0045454545\ldots$$

$$1.0\overline{045} = 1.0045045045\ldots$$

Example 1 below shows that a quotient of two integers can be written as either a terminating or repeating decimal. Examples 2 and 3 show the converse. In light of these examples, rational and irrational numbers can also be defined as follows.

A *rational number* is a number that can be expressed as a terminating or a repeating decimal.

An *irrational number* is a number that can be expressed as a nonterminating, nonrepeating decimal.

Example 1   Show that $\dfrac{3}{4}$ and $\dfrac{5}{27}$ can be expressed as terminating or repeating decimals.

Solution   *Convert the fractions to decimals.* In the first case, a zero remainder eventually results and the decimal terminates. In the second case, remainders 5, 23, and 14 will keep repeating. Digits in the quotient will repeat the pattern 1, 8, 5. Thus the decimal is repeating.

$$\frac{3}{4} = \begin{array}{r} 0.75 \\ 4\overline{)3.00} \\ \underline{2\ 8} \\ 20 \\ \underline{20} \\ 0 \end{array} \qquad \frac{5}{27} = \begin{array}{r} 0.185 \\ 27\overline{)5.000} \\ \underline{2\ 7} \\ 230 \\ \underline{216} \\ 140 \\ \underline{135} \\ 5 \end{array}$$

$$\frac{3}{4} = 0.75 \qquad \frac{5}{27} = 0.\overline{185}$$

Example 2   Show that 1.3456 is the quotient of two integers.

Solution $1.3456 = 1\dfrac{3456}{10{,}000} = \dfrac{13{,}456}{10{,}000} = \dfrac{841}{625}$

Example 3   Show that $0.\overline{25}$ is the quotient of two integers.

Solution   Let $N = 0.252525\ldots$.

Then $100N = 25.252525\ldots$.

Subtracting the first equation $99N = 25$
from the second gives:

$$N = \frac{25}{99}$$

In this example two digits repeat. Therefore, we multiplied by 100. If one digit repeats, multiply by 10. If three digits repeat, multiply by 1000.

CLASSROOM EXERCISES

State whether the number is rational or irrational.

1. $\dfrac{5}{6}$ **2.** $2.\overline{345}$ **3.** $-0.1213141516\ldots$ **4.** -38.7

Write each rational number as a terminating or a repeating decimal.

5. $\dfrac{5}{8}$ **6.** $\dfrac{3}{7}$

Write each decimal as the quotient of two integers. Write the quotient as a simplified fraction.

7. 0.35 **8.** 2.76 **9.** $0.\overline{2}$

WRITTEN EXERCISES

 Indicate whether the number is rational or irrational.

1. $-\dfrac{3}{4}$ **2.** $-\dfrac{5}{8}$ **3.** -16 **4.** -9

5. $0.\overline{43}$ **6.** $0.\overline{403}$ **7.** $\sqrt{36}$ **8.** $\sqrt{9}$

9. $-0.121221222\ldots$ **10.** $0.121121112\ldots$ **11.** $5.389389389\ldots$ **12.** $-2.765765765\ldots$

13. $1 + \sqrt{3}$ **14.** $2 + \sqrt{7}$ **15.** $\sqrt{2} + \sqrt{2}$ **16.** $\sqrt{2} - \sqrt{2}$

Write each rational number as a terminating or a repeating decimal.

17. $\dfrac{5}{6}$ **18.** $\dfrac{7}{12}$ **19.** $\dfrac{2}{9}$ **20.** $\dfrac{4}{11}$

21. $\dfrac{3}{16}$ **22.** $\dfrac{39}{40}$ **23.** $\dfrac{61}{125}$ **24.** $\dfrac{9}{20}$

Write each decimal as the quotient of two integers. Write the quotient as a simplified fraction.

25. 0.64 **26.** 0.2 **27.** 4.555 **28.** 5.444

29. $4.\overline{5}$ **30.** $5.\overline{4}$ **31.** $0.\overline{75}$ **32.** $0.\overline{63}$

True or false?

33. Every real number can be written as a terminating decimal or a repeating decimal.

34. Every terminating decimal, repeating decimal, and nonterminating, nonrepeating decimal is a real number.

35. The sum of any two irrational numbers is an irrational number.

36. The sum of any two rational numbers is a rational number.

37. The sum of any two terminating decimals is a terminating decimal.

38. The product of any two irrational numbers is an irrational number.

Complete. You could use a calculator.

39. Write the decimals for $\frac{1}{7}, \frac{2}{7}, \frac{3}{7}$, and $\frac{4}{7}$. Describe the pattern.

40. Write the decimals for $\frac{37}{99}, \frac{43}{99}$, and $\frac{49}{99}$. Describe the pattern.

The average or (arithmetic mean) of two numbers always falls between the two numbers. Find the average of the two numbers and show that it is between the two numbers by writing all three numbers as fractions with the same denominator.

41. $\frac{3}{8}, \frac{1}{2}$ **42.** $\frac{1}{6}, \frac{1}{5}$ **43.** $2, 2\frac{1}{2}$ **44.** $\frac{2}{3}, \frac{3}{4}$

Exercises 41–44 illustrate that between any two rational numbers there is another rational number. Therefore, we say that the set of rational numbers is **dense**.

True or false?

45. The set of real numbers is dense.   **46.** The set of integers is dense.

47. There are infinitely many rational numbers between any two rational numbers.

48. The sum of a repeating decimal and a terminating decimal is a terminating decimal.

49. If a and b are positive integers and b is a power of 2, then $\frac{a}{b}$ can be written as a terminating decimal.

50. If $a = 0.\overline{1}$, $b = 0.\overline{2}$, and $c = 0.\overline{12}$, then c is between a and b.

51. If $a = 0.101101110 \ldots$ and $b = 0.101001000 \ldots$ then $a + b$ is an irrational number.

52. If $a = 0.101101110 \ldots$ and $b = 0.010010001 \ldots$ then $a + b$ is an irrational number.

53. Write $0.28363636 \ldots$ as the quotient of two integers.

*R*EVIEW EXERCISES

Simplify.

1. $-3 + 8$ **2.** $-3(8)$ **3.** $7.32 + (-10)$ **4.** $7.32(-10)$

5. $-6\frac{1}{4} + \left(-1\frac{1}{2}\right)$ **6.** $\left(-6\frac{1}{4}\right)\left(-1\frac{1}{2}\right)$ **7.** $12 - (-8)$ **8.** $13 - 21$

9. $-24.5 \div (-10)$ **10.** $-6\frac{2}{3} \div -2$ **11.** $(-2)^5$ **12.** $-\sqrt{121}$

LESSON 1-2

Algebraic Expressions

Eskimo hunters, lacking anything tall to climb, used a blanket to toss another hunter high into the air to search for game in the distance. The photo shows the reenactment of this event at a modern-day festival. The relationship between the viewing height and the distance to the horizon can be shown by data in a table or by algebraic notation.

Viewing height (ft)	6	24	54	96
Distance to horizon (mi)	3	6	9	12

Algebraic notation: For a viewing height of h feet above ground, the horizon is $\dfrac{\sqrt{6h}}{2}$ miles away.

Algebraic expressions are made up of four different kinds of symbols.

Variables	Numbers	Grouping symbols	Operation signs
$x \quad y \quad M$	$2 \quad 0 \quad -5$	$(\quad) \quad [\quad]$	$+ \quad - \quad \div \quad \sqrt{}$ exponents

When numbers are substituted for variables in an algebraic expression, the result is a numerical expression. The numerical expression can be simplified by carrying out the operations according to the following rules.

Order of Operations

1. Evaluate inside grouping symbols first.
2. Evaluate powers and roots next.
3. Do multiplications and divisions in order from left to right.
4. Do additions and subtractions in order from left to right.

Example 1 **Simplify.** $6 + 7(5 - 8)^3$

Solution *Evaluate inside grouping symbols.* $\quad 6 + 7(5 - 8)^3 = 6 + 7(-3)^3$

Raise to a power. $\qquad\qquad\qquad\qquad\quad = 6 + 7(-27)$

Multiply. $\qquad\qquad\qquad\qquad\qquad\quad = 6 + (-189)$

Add. $\qquad\qquad\qquad\qquad\qquad\qquad\quad = -183$

Example 2   **Simplify.** $10[3^2 - 4(1 + 2^3)]$

Solution   Simplify inside the innermost grouping symbols.

Cube 2.	$10[3^2 - 4(1 + 2^3)] = 10[3^2 - 4(1 + 8)]$
Add.	$= 10[3^2 - 4(9)]$

Simplify inside the other grouping symbols.

Square 3.	$= 10[9 - 4(9)]$
Multiply by 4.	$= 10[9 - 36]$
Subtract.	$= 10[-27]$
Multiply.	$= -270$

The bar used in writing a fraction is both a grouping symbol *and* an operation sign (division).

Example 3   **Substitute values from the table into the expression and simplify.**

$$\frac{a + bc^2}{d}$$

a	b	c	d
4	5	6	2

Solution   *Substitute.* $\dfrac{a + bc^2}{d} = \dfrac{4 + 5(6)^2}{2}$

Simplify above the fraction bar, which acts as a grouping symbol.

Square 6. $= \dfrac{4 + 5(36)}{2}$

Multiply. $= \dfrac{4 + 180}{2}$

Add. $= \dfrac{184}{2}$

Divide. $= 92$

Operation keys on a calculator or computer, such as the division and square root keys, only perform the operations. They do not act as grouping symbols. When keying expressions into a calculator or computer, it is sometimes necessary to key in pairs of parentheses that are not shown in the original expressions. For example,

Expression	**Calculator Keying Sequence**
$\sqrt{29 - 4}$	$($ 29 $-$ 4 $)$ $\sqrt{}$ $=$
$\dfrac{-5}{\sqrt{16} - 3}$	5 $^+\!/\!_-$ $\div$ $($ 16 $\sqrt{}$ $-$ 3 $)$ $=$

*C*LASSROOM EXERCISES

Simplify.

1. $12 + 18 - 6 - 4$

2. $(12 + 18) - 6 - 4$

3. $12 + 18 - (6 - 4)$

4. $(12 + 18) - (6 - 4)$

5. $\dfrac{7[4 + 2(3)]}{2}$

6. $(-1)^{14} - (-1)^{15}$

*W*RITTEN EXERCISES

A **Simplify.**

1. $10 - 6 + 2$

2. $15 - 10 + 3$

3. $2 + 5(3)$

4. $5 + 2(3)$

5. $5^2 + 25(3)$

6. $4^2 - 6(2)$

7. $3 - 7^2$

8. $(2 + 5)^2$

9. $(3 - 7)^2$

10. $2 + 5^2$

11. $30 - (8^2 - 6)$

12. $30 - 8^2 - 6$

13. $100 - 6^2 - 6$

14. $100 - (6^2 - 6)$

15. $2(3^2) + 11$

16. $3(2^3) + 12$

17. $\sqrt{11 + 5^2}$

18. $\sqrt{20 + 4^2}$

19. $\dfrac{3^2 - 2^3 + 17}{2 - 4}$

20. $\dfrac{4^2 - 2^2 + 8}{-7 + 2}$

21. $\dfrac{2(7 - 4) + 5(2)}{4^2 - 24}$

22. $\dfrac{3(9 - 4) + 2(3)}{4^2 - 3^2}$

23. $3(2 + 4[17 - 4(3)])$

24. $4[3 - 2(14 - 5(2))]$

Substitute and simplify.

a	*b*	*c*	*A*	*B*
2	-3	4	$\frac{1}{2}$	3

25. bc^a

26. $(bc)^a$

27. $(a + b)^B$

28. $a + bB$

29. $cA + aB$

30. $-(b + c)^a$

31. $\dfrac{a + b + c}{B}$

32. $\dfrac{a + bc}{a + B}$

33. $\dfrac{aB + c}{-cA}$

34. $\sqrt{a(c + A)}$

35. $\sqrt{a(Bc + A)}$

36. $b[B - A(a + c)]$

B **Simplify.**

37. $\dfrac{8 + \sqrt{4(3)^2}}{1 + 2(3)}$

38. $\dfrac{5^2 - \sqrt{7 + 3^2}}{6 - \dfrac{6}{2}}$

39. $\dfrac{[(3 - 1)^2]^3}{\sqrt{5^2 - 3^2}}$

40. $[9 - (2 + 5)]^3$

41. $9[5^2 - 3(1 + 3)^2]$

42. $4[5 - 4(2 - 3^3)]$

43. $[3 - (2 - 8)^2] - [5 + (6^2 - 2)]$

44. $(16 - 4)^2 - 5^3 \cdot [36 - (2 \cdot 3)^2]$

45. $[(5^2 - 4) - 3^3][6^2 - (5 + 2)^2]$

46. $4^3 - \sqrt{2 \cdot 3^2 + [-5 - (-7)]}$

47. $\dfrac{[2^4 - 3(2^3 + 1)]^2 - 1}{\sqrt{6^2 + 8^2}}$

48. $\dfrac{[(-3 - 5)^2 - 2^3] + [4^2 - 3^2]}{-(\sqrt{7^2 - 6^2})^2}$

C Assume that each variable represents a positive integer. State whether the expressions are equivalent or not equivalent. If they are not equivalent, show replacements for the variables that make the expressions unequal.

49. $a + bc$, $a + (bc)$ **50.** $(a + b)c$, $a + (bc)$ **51.** $(a + b)c$, $a + bc$

52. ab^c, $(ab)^c$ **53.** $\sqrt{a + b}$, $\sqrt{a} + \sqrt{b}$ **54.** $\sqrt{ab}$, $\sqrt{a} \cdot \sqrt{b}$

55. $\dfrac{a + b}{c}$, $\dfrac{a}{c} + \dfrac{b}{c}$ **56.** $(a + b)^c$, $a^c + b^c$ **57.** $a^b \cdot a^c$, a^{bc}

 EVIEW EXERCISES

Find the missing length in the right triangle using the Pythagorean theorem. (In a right triangle with legs a and b and hypotenuse c, $a^2 + b^2 = c^2$.)

1. 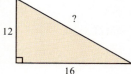 12, 16, ?

2.   1, 1

3.   2, ?, 1

4. Find the average of 25, 30, and 50.

𝒞ALCULATOR EXTENSION   Decimals for Fractions

The repetend of the decimal representation of $\dfrac{3}{23}$ has 22 digits, many more than a calculator can display. Here is a way to compute the repetend.

Divide 3 by 23. Re-enter the quotient dropping the last digit. Then multiply by 23. Change the sign of the product. Add it to the numerator 3 to find the remainder.

3 ÷ 23 =   0.130434782

0.13043478 × 23 =   2.99999994   +/− + 3 =   0.00000006

So, $\dfrac{3}{23} = 0.13043478 \dfrac{6}{23}$. Divide 6 by 23 to find the next digits.

Continue as often as necessary to find the repetend.

$$\frac{3}{23} = 0.\overline{1304347826086956521739}$$

Use the method to write the following fractions as repeating decimals.

1. $\dfrac{17}{23}$ **2.** $\dfrac{3}{17}$ **3.** $\dfrac{3}{19}$

LESSON 1-3

Order and the Number Line

The real numbers are **ordered.** Therefore, they can be matched to points on a line in the following way. One point on the line called the **origin** is selected and associated with the number 0. Then a second point is selected and associated with the number 1.

This choice of an origin and a unit distance (distance from 0 to 1) associates each real number with a point on the line. The point is called the **graph** of the real number. The real number is called the **coordinate** of the point. For example, 4 is associated with the point that is 4 units to the right of the origin, and -3 is associated with the point that is 3 units to the left of the origin. Similarly, 1.5 is associated with the point halfway between the points for 1 and 2.

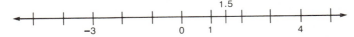

To locate irrational numbers, like $\sqrt{2}$, on the number line construct a right triangle, each of whose legs is 1 unit long. The length of the hypotenuse is $\sqrt{2}$. The point on the line that is $\sqrt{2}$ units from the origin can now be located using a compass. The coordinate of that point is $\sqrt{2}$.

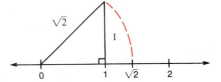

Since all real numbers can be graphed on the number line, the number line can be used to compare and order all real numbers.

$$-3 < 0 \qquad \sqrt{2} < 2$$

However, there are algebraic methods of comparing and ordering real numbers.

Here are two important properties of order.

Trichotomy Property

For all real numbers a and b, one and only one of these statements is true:
$$a < b, \qquad a = b, \qquad a > b.$$

Transitive Property of Order

For all real numbers a, b, and c, if $a < b$ and $b < c$, then $a < c$.

Example 1   **Arrange these numbers in order from least to greatest:**

$$0.8, \qquad \frac{5}{6}, \qquad \frac{\sqrt{3}}{2}.$$

Solution   Use a calculator to convert $\frac{5}{6}$ and $\frac{\sqrt{3}}{2}$ to decimals.

$$5 \boxed{\div} 6 \boxed{=} \; 0.83333 \qquad 3 \boxed{\sqrt{}} \boxed{\div} 2 \boxed{=} \; 0.866602$$

Answer   Since $0.8 < 0.8\overline{3}$ and $0.8\overline{3} < 0.86\ldots$, the order of the numbers from least to greatest is $0.8, \dfrac{5}{6}, \dfrac{\sqrt{3}}{2}$.

A third property can be derived from the Trichotomy Property and the Transitive Property of Order.

> For all nonnegative real numbers a and b,
> $$\text{if } a^2 < b^2, \text{ then } a < b.$$

A consequence of this property is a method of comparing two numbers without using a calculator.

$$\left(\frac{5}{6}\right)^2 = \frac{25}{36} \qquad \left(\frac{\sqrt{3}}{2}\right)^2 = \frac{3}{4} = \frac{27}{36}$$

$$\text{Since } \left(\frac{5}{6}\right)^2 < \left(\frac{\sqrt{3}}{2}\right)^2, \frac{5}{6} < \frac{\sqrt{3}}{2}.$$

A set can be described by either words, such as "the set of all positive integers," or listing the set's **elements** between braces like this:

$$\{1, 2, 3, 4, 5, \ldots\}$$

Sometimes a description of a set can be ambiguous because it may not be clear what the ellipsis ". . ." represents.

A more precise way of naming sets is **set-builder notation.** The set of all real numbers that are greater than 1 can be written in set-builder notation as follows:

$$\{x: x > 1\}$$

This notation is read:

The set of all real numbers x such that x is greater than 1.

The notation is called set-builder notation because the sentence "builds" the set by selecting the elements that belong to the set. Those elements that make the sentence true are in the set. Those elements that do not make it true are not in the set.

Since the points on the number line correspond to the real numbers, the number line can be used to draw the graph of a **subset** (a set contained within a set) of the set of real numbers.

Example 2 Graph these sets on a number line.

a. $\{x: x < 2\}$ b. $\{x: x > -1\}$ c. $\{x: x \text{ is an integer} \neq 0\}$

Solution   a.

Note that the open circle at 2 shows that 2 is a **boundary** of the set but is not included in the set.

b.   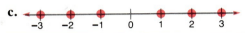   c.

𝒞LASSROOM EXERCISES

1. Which is greater, $\frac{3}{5}$ or $\frac{3}{4}$?

2. Which is greater, $\frac{13}{18}$ or 0.72?

Describe each set using set-builder notation.

3. The set of real numbers greater than -3.

4. The set of integers less than 3.

5.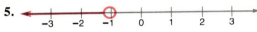

6.

Graph each set on a number line.

7. $\{x: x > -0.5\}$ **8.** $\{x: x = 3\}$ **9.** $\{x: x < 3\}$

𝒲RITTEN EXERCISES

 Arrange the numbers in order from least to greatest.

1. $\frac{1}{8}, \frac{1}{6}, \frac{1}{10}$

2. $\frac{3}{14}, \frac{3}{8}, \frac{3}{10}$

3. 0.806, 0.860, 0.81

4. 0.73001, 0.731, 0.73

5. $-\frac{3}{8}, -0.37$

6. $-\sqrt{3}, -1.73$

7. $-1.4, -\sqrt{2}$

8. $\frac{4}{11}, 0.36$

9. $\frac{7}{11}, 0.63$

10. $\frac{\sqrt{10}}{5}, \frac{3}{5}$

11. $\frac{\sqrt{14}}{5}, \frac{\sqrt{5}}{3}$

12. $\frac{\sqrt{11}}{6}, \frac{\sqrt{5}}{4}$

Use set-builder notation to describe each set.

13. The set of real numbers greater than 12.5.

14. The set of real numbers less than 22.7.

15. The set of real numbers less than $-\pi$.

16. The set of real numbers greater than $\sqrt{7}$.

17. $\{100, 101, 102, 103, \ldots\}$

18. $\{-10, -9, -8, -7, -6, \ldots\}$

19. $\{\ldots, -2, -1, 0, 1, 2\}$

20. $\{\ldots, 97, 98, 99, 100\}$

Use set-builder notation to describe each set.

21.

22.

23.

24.

Graph each set on a number line.

25. $\left\{x: x \text{ is an integer between } -2\frac{1}{2} \text{ and } 2\frac{1}{2}\right\}$ **26.** $\left\{x: x \text{ is an integer between } -1\frac{1}{2} \text{ and } 4\frac{1}{2}\right\}$

27. $\{x: x < 3\}$ **28.** $\{x: x < -2\}$ **29.** $\left\{x: x > -2\frac{1}{2}\right\}$ **30.** $\left\{x: x > 1\frac{1}{2}\right\}$

B **Write the numbers in order from least to greatest.**

31. $\dfrac{4}{5}, \dfrac{17}{5}, \sqrt{0.6}$ **32.** $\dfrac{\sqrt{11}}{4}, \dfrac{3}{4}, \sqrt{0.625}$ **33.** $\dfrac{\sqrt{3}}{2}, \dfrac{5}{6}, \dfrac{\sqrt{26}}{6}$

34. $\dfrac{\sqrt{26}}{3}, 1\dfrac{2}{3}, \sqrt{3}$ **35.** $\dfrac{3}{7}, \dfrac{3}{8}, \dfrac{4}{9}$ **36.** $\dfrac{5}{11}, \dfrac{5}{12}, \dfrac{6}{13}$

Use set-builder notation to describe each set.

37. The set of all integers greater than $-\pi$.

38. The set of integers less than π.

39. $\{0, 1, 2, 3, \ldots\}$ **40.** $\{\ldots, -6, -5, -4\}$

41.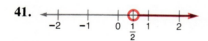

42.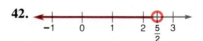

Graph each set on a number line.

43. $\{x: x \text{ is a positive even integer less than } 9\}$

44. $\{x: x \text{ is a positive prime number less than } 10\}$

C **True or false? If the statement is false, give an example to illustrate.**

45. If k is a positive integer, $\dfrac{2+k}{3+k}$ is between $\dfrac{2}{3}$ and 1.

46. If k is a positive integer, $\dfrac{5+k}{3+k} > \dfrac{5}{3}$.   **47.** If $\dfrac{a}{b} > 0$, then $\dfrac{a^2}{b^2} > \dfrac{a}{b}$.

48. If $0 < \dfrac{a}{b} < 1$, then $\dfrac{a^2}{b^2} < \dfrac{a}{b}$.

Ancient Greek mathematicians were aware that there are points on the line that have irrational-number coordinates. Use the Pythagorean theorem to find the length of each segment.

49. *a*

50. *e*

51. If the pattern continues, what is the letter of the segment that is 4 units long?

52. Show that between any two rational numbers there is another rational number.

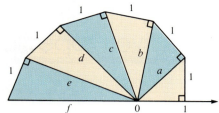

ℛEVIEW EXERCISES

Compute.

1. $3.9 + (-4.31)$

2. $-3.45 + (-4)$

3. $-4.2 (-100)$

4. $-3.7 (0.1)$

5. $2.8 \div (-100)$

6. $-0.45 \div (-0.1)$

7. $-0.34 - (-1)$

8. $0.032 \div 1.6$

9. $25.6 \div 0.0008$

10. $4\frac{1}{4} + \left(-3\frac{1}{2}\right)$

11. $-\frac{1}{2} + \frac{1}{3}$

12. $3.4 - (-2.8)$

𝒮elf-Quiz 1

1-1 **Write the following rational numbers as decimals.**

1. $\dfrac{9}{13}$

2. $\dfrac{7}{40}$

Write each decimal as a rational number in lowest terms.

3. 0.155

4. $0.\overline{42}$

1-2 **Simplify.**

5. $\dfrac{3(7-4)+6(5)}{2^4 - 7}$

6. $\dfrac{\sqrt{12^2 + 9^2}}{2(8-1)}$

Use the table of values to evaluate each expression.

7. $2eX + 3dY$

8. $(de + Y)^X$

d	*e*	*X*	*Y*
4	−1	2	$\frac{1}{3}$

1-3 **9.** Which real number is greatest, $\dfrac{\sqrt{5}}{3}$, $0.\overline{5}$, or $\dfrac{5}{11}$?

Use set-builder notation to describe these sets.

10. The set of integers greater than 9.

11.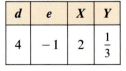

LESSON 1-4

The Commutative, Associative, and Distributive Properties

The basic properties of numbers and operations permit us to rearrange some computations so they can be done mentally.

$$(-36)(-48) + (-36)(48) = -36(-48 + 48)$$

$$(-298 - 159) + 198 = -159 + (-298 + 198)$$

$$\left(3 \times \frac{1}{4}\right)\left(4 \times \frac{1}{5}\right)\left(5 \times \frac{1}{6}\right)\left(6 \times \frac{1}{7}\right) = 3\left(\frac{1}{4} \times 4\right)\left(\frac{1}{5} \times 5\right)\left(\frac{1}{6} \times 6\right)\left(\frac{1}{7}\right)$$

The same basic properties allow us to simplify complicated algebraic expressions.

The following properties are used in arithmetic. These properties can be used both to simplify computations and to simplify algebraic expressions.

Commutative property of addition

For all real numbers a and b,　　$a + b = b + a$.

Commutative property of multiplication

For all real numbers a and b,　　$ab = ba$.

Associative property of addition

For all real numbers a, b, and c,　　$(a + b) + c = a + (b + c)$.

Associative property of multiplication

For all real numbers a, b, and c,　　$(ab)c = a(bc)$.

Distributive property of multiplication over addition

For all real numbers a, b, and c,

$$a(b + c) = ab + ac \quad \text{and} \quad (b + c)a = ba + ca.$$

Example 1　Show that this computation is a consequence of the distribution property.

$$\begin{array}{r} 45 \\ \times\ \ 6 \\ \hline 270 \end{array}$$

Solution　$45 \cdot 6 = (40 + 5)6$　　　*Definition of place value*

$\qquad\qquad = 40 \cdot 6 + 5 \cdot 6$　　*Distributive property*

$\qquad\qquad = 240 + 30$　　　　*Computation*

$\qquad\qquad = 270$　　　　　　*Computation*

Example 2 An easy way to multiply 57 by 25 is to divide 57 by 4 $\left(\text{multiply by } \dfrac{1}{4}\right)$, and then multiply by 100. Show that this shortened calculation is a consequence of the associative property of multiplication.

Solution $57 \cdot 25 = 57\left(\dfrac{1}{4} \cdot 100\right)$ *Computation*

$\qquad\qquad = \left(57 \cdot \dfrac{1}{4}\right) \cdot 100$ *Associative property of multiplication*

$\qquad\qquad = 14.25 \cdot 100 = 1425$ *Computation*

Example 3 **Simplify.** $3x + 2(7x + 5)$

Solution $3x + 2(7x + 5) = 3x + [2(7x) + 2(5)]$ *Distributive property*

$\qquad\qquad\qquad\quad = 3x + [(2 \cdot 7)x + 2(5)]$ *Associative property of multiplication*

$\qquad\qquad\qquad\quad = 3x + [14x + 10]$ *Computation*

$\qquad\qquad\qquad\quad = [3x + 14x] + 10$ *Associative property of addition*

$\qquad\qquad\qquad\quad = [3 + 14]x + 10$ *Distributive property*

$\qquad\qquad\qquad\quad = 17x + 10$ *Computation*

In Example 3 we used the distributive property to **combine the like terms** $3x$ and $14x$. Recall that like terms contain the same variable factors. The terms $7x^2$ and x^2 are like terms, but $2y^2$ and $2y$ are not like terms. Numbers are also like terms because they contain no variable factors.

*C*LASSROOM EXERCISES

Each of these equations contains an example of one of the real-number properties listed on page 14. State the property.

1. $(-6 + 4) + (-2 + 3) = -6 + [4 + (-2 + 3)]$

2. $6(-3) + 6(5) = 6(-3 + 5)$

3. $-2(-3) + [4(-3) + 5(2)] = -2(-3) + [5(2) + 4(-3)]$

4. $-12 + 2(-5(-13)) = -12 + (2(-5))(-13)$

Simplify.

5. $3x^2 + 2(5x + 3x^2)$

6. $-7(-2(3x + 1) + 4) + 9$

State the properties, in order, that are used in this simplification.

7. $2(r + 2s) + 3s = 2r + 4s + 3s$
$\qquad\qquad\qquad = 2r + (4s + 3s)$
$\qquad\qquad\qquad = 2r + (4 + 3)s$
$\qquad\qquad\qquad = 2r + 7s$

 RITTEN EXERCISES

 Each of these equations illustrates the use of one of the real-number properties listed on page 14. State which property.

1. $(-234 + 135) + (-246) = -234 + (135 + (-246))$

2. $-234(135 + (-246)) = -234(135) + (-234)(-246)$

3. $(234 + 135) + (-246) = -246 + (234 + 135)$

4. $(-234(-135))246 = -234(-135 \cdot 246)$

5. $-571 + 629 = 629 + (-571)$

6. $28(-7214) = -7214(28)$

7. $-413(76(-15)) = (-413(76))(-15)$

8. $-23 + (43 + (-91)) = (-23 + 43) + (-91)$

9. $-73(64) + 28(64) = (-73 + 28)64$

10. $-23 + 43 + (-91) = (-91) + (-23 + 43)$

It is sometimes useful to think of 999 as $(1000 + (-1))$. State the property that justifies the second step of each of these calculations.

11. $23(999) = 23(1000 + (-1))$
$\quad\quad = 23(1000) + 23(-1)$
$\quad\quad = 23,000 + (-23)$
$\quad\quad = 22,977$

12. $\frac{1}{2}(999) = \frac{1}{2}(1000 + (-1))$
$\quad\quad = \frac{1}{2}(1000) + \frac{1}{2}(-1)$
$\quad\quad = 500 + \left(-\frac{1}{2}\right)$
$\quad\quad = 499\frac{1}{2}$

State the properties, in order, that are used in these simplifications.

13. $7x + 5x = (7 + 5)x$
$\quad\quad = 12x$

14. $20x + 6x = (20 + 6)x$
$\quad\quad = 26x$

15. $5a + 3b + 2a = 5a + (3b + 2a)$
$\quad\quad = 5a + (2a + 3b)$
$\quad\quad = (5a + 2a) + 3b$
$\quad\quad = (5 + 2)a + 3b$
$\quad\quad = 7a + 3b$

16. $3(2r + s) + 2s = 6r + 3s + 2s$
$\quad\quad = 6r + (3s + 2s)$
$\quad\quad = 6r + (3 + 2)s$
$\quad\quad = 6r + 5s$

Simplify.

17. $5(a + b) + 3(2a + b)$

18. $6(a + 2b) + 2(3a + b)$

19. $2x^2 + 3y + 5x^2 + 4y$

20. $2x + 3y^2 + 4x + 2y^2$

21. $2 + 3(4 + 5(x + 3))$

22. $3 + 2(5 + 4(x + 3))$

23. $x(x + 5) + 5(x + 5)$

24. $2x(2x - 3) - 3(2x - 3)$

25. $2x(x + 5) + 3x^2 + 3x + 2$

26. $3x(x + 3) + 2x^2 + 7x + 10$

B **True or false? If the statement is false, give an example to illustrate.**

27. $a - b = b - a$ for all real numbers a and b.

28. $a \div b = b \div a$ for all real numbers a and b. $(a \neq 0, b \neq 0)$

29. $a + b = b + a$ for all irrational numbers a and b.

30. $(a + b) + c = a + (b + c)$ for all negative numbers a, b, and c.

31. $a(bc) = (ab)(ac)$ for all real numbers a, b, and c.

32. $a(b + c) = ab + c$ for all real numbers a, b, and c.

State the properties, in order, that are used in these simplifications.

33. $4(3 + 2(x + 5))$
$= 12 + 8(x + 5)$
$= 12 + (8x + 40)$
$= 12 + (40 + 8x)$
$= (12 + 40) + 8x$
$= 52 + 8x$

34. $x(x + 3) + 2(x + 5)$
$= (x^2 + x \cdot 3) + (2x + 10)$
$= (x^2 + 3x) + (2x + 10)$
$= [(x^2 + 3x) + 2x] + 10$
$= [x^2 + (3x + 2x)] + 10$
$= [x^2 + (3 + 2)x] + 10$
$= x^2 + 5x + 10$

Indicate a more efficient way to carry out these calculations.

35. $297(999)$

36. Multiplying by 125

37. $998 + 996 + 997$

38. Subtracting 196

C **Use the properties of real numbers to show each of the following.**

39. $a(b + c + d) = ab + ac + ad$

40. $(a + b)(c + d) = ac + bc + ad + bd$

41. $(a + b)^2 - b^2 = a(a + 2b)$

EVIEW EXERCISES

Compute.

1. $-\dfrac{3}{4} + \left(-\dfrac{3}{8}\right)$

2. $-4\dfrac{1}{4} + 2\dfrac{2}{3}$

3. $-\dfrac{3}{4}\left(-\dfrac{3}{5}\right)$

4. $-\dfrac{7}{4} \div \dfrac{2}{3}$

5. $-3.6(0.01)$

6. $-4.7 \div (-0.01)$

7. Find the missing length.

$\sqrt{75}$ 10   ?

8. Find the average of -7, -3, -6, and 4.

9. Find the perimeter and area of this rectangle.

10 cm
6 cm

10. Use set-builder notation to describe this set.

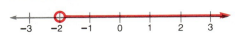

-3 -2 -1 0 1 2 3

The Closure, Identity, and Inverse Properties

The expansion of the known numbers from the whole numbers, to the integers, to the rational numbers, to the real numbers allows for the extended use of operations on these numbers. Real numbers can be used in many applications where whole numbers are inadequate.

Closure The sum of any two whole numbers is also a whole number. For this reason the set of whole numbers is said to be closed with respect to addition. Similarly, the set of whole numbers is closed with respect to multiplication.

$$3 + 4 = 7 \qquad 3 \times 4 = 12$$

whole numbers

However, the set of whole numbers is not closed with respect to either subtraction or division.

$$3 - 4 = -1 \qquad 3 \div 4 = \frac{3}{4}$$

not whole numbers

The set of integers is closed with respect to subtraction and the set of rational numbers is closed with respect to division (except by 0). Therefore, the set of real numbers is closed with respect to both subtraction and division, except for division by zero, which is not defined.

Closure Properties

For all real numbers a and b, $a + b$, ab, and $a - b$ are real numbers.

If $b \neq 0$, then $\dfrac{a}{b}$ is a real number.

Identities Adding zero to a real number and multiplying a real number by one do not change the number. Zero and one are called the **additive identity element** and **multiplicative identity element,** respectively.

Identity Properties

There are real numbers 0 and 1 such that for each real number a,
$$a + 0 = 0 + a = a \quad \text{and} \quad 1 \cdot a = a \cdot 1 = a.$$

Additive Inverses Certain pairs of real numbers have the sum 0. Such numbers are called **additive inverses** (or **opposites**).

5 and -5 are additive inverses. π and $-\pi$ are additive inverses.

$\frac{1}{2}$ and $-\frac{1}{2}$ are additive inverses. 0 is its own additive inverse.

Additive Inverse Property

For all real numbers a,

there exists a real number $-a$ such that $a + (-a) = 0$.

The existence of an additive inverse for each real number means that subtraction can be defined in terms of addition.

Definition: Subtraction of Real Numbers

For all real numbers a and b,

$$a - b = a + (-b).$$

Multiplicative Inverses Certain pairs of real numbers have the product 1. Such numbers are called **multiplicative inverses** (or **reciprocals**).

3 and $\frac{1}{3}$ are multiplicative inverses. π and $\frac{1}{\pi}$ are multiplicative inverses.

$-\frac{3}{4}$ and $-\frac{4}{3}$ are multiplicative inverses. 1 is its own multiplicative inverse.

Multiplicative Inverse Property

For each real number a, $a \neq 0$,

there exists a real number $\frac{1}{a}$ such that $a\left(\frac{1}{a}\right) = 1.$

The multiplicative inverse property allows division to be defined in terms of multiplication.

Definition: Division of Real Numbers

For all real numbers a and b, $b \neq 0$, $\frac{a}{b} = a\left(\frac{1}{b}\right).$

Since subtraction and division are defined in terms of addition and multiplication, the set of basic properties can be kept short. For example, there is no need to state a distributive property for multiplication over subtraction. Such a property can be proved as a theorem using the basic properties.

The closure, identity, and inverse properties allow us to justify the steps used in simplifying or expanding algebraic expressions.

Example 1   **Expand this product.** $(a + 3)(b + 2)$

Solution
$$\begin{aligned}
(a + 3)(b + 2) &= (a + 3)b + (a + 3)2 & &\textit{Distributive property}\\
&= (ab + 3b) + (a \cdot 2 + 3 \cdot 2) & &\textit{Distributive property}\\
&= ab + 3b + a \cdot 2 + 3 \cdot 2 & &\textit{Associative property of}\\
& & &\textit{addition}\\
&= ab + 3b + 2a + 3 \cdot 2 & &\textit{Commutative property}\\
& & &\textit{of multiplication}\\
&= ab + 3b + 2a + 6 & &\textit{Computation}
\end{aligned}$$

The example above shows precise explanations of the steps involved in expanding or simplifying an algebraic expression. In most instances such manipulations are done more quickly and efficiently with many details omitted from the written record.

Example 2   **Show that** $2(x - 1)$ **and** $\dfrac{4 - 4x}{2}$ **are additive inverses.**

Solution   Two expressions are additive inverses if their sum is 0.

$$\begin{aligned}
2(x - 1) + \frac{4 - 4x}{2} &= 2(x - 1) + \frac{1}{2}(4 - 4x)\\
&= (2x - 2) + (2 - 2x)\\
&= 0
\end{aligned}$$

Therefore, $2(x - 1)$ and $\dfrac{4 - 4x}{2}$ are additive inverses.

Example 3   **Simplify.** $2a - 3b - (b - a)$

Solution
$$\begin{aligned}
2a - 3b - (b - a) &= 2a + (-3b) + [-(b + (-a))]\\
&= 2a + (-3b) + (-1)(b + (-a))\\
&= 2a + (-3b) + (-b) + a\\
&= 3a + (-4b)\\
&= 3a - 4b
\end{aligned}$$

Example 4   Show that $\sqrt{2} - 1$ is the multiplicative inverse of $\sqrt{2} + 1$.

Solution   Two quantities are multiplicative inverses if their product is 1.

$$(\sqrt{2} - 1)(\sqrt{2} + 1) = (\sqrt{2})^2 + \sqrt{2} - \sqrt{2} - 1$$
$$= 2 + \sqrt{2} - \sqrt{2} - 1 = 2 - 1 = 1$$

Therefore, $\sqrt{2} - 1$ and $\sqrt{2} + 1$ are multiplicative inverses.

*C*LASSROOM EXERCISES

True or false? If the sentence is false, give an example to illustrate.

1. The set of integers is closed with respect to multiplication.

2. The set of integers is closed with respect to division with the restriction that division by 0 is not allowed.

3. The set of irrational numbers is closed with respect to multiplication.

4. The set of rational numbers has an additive identity element.

5. The set of irrational numbers has a multiplicative identity element.

6. The number -3 has a reciprocal. This means that there is a real number b such that $-3 \cdot b = 1$.

Each sentence is an example of one of the properties or definitions listed on pages 18 and 19. Name the property or definition.

7. $6 + \sqrt{2}$ is a real number.
8. $2x - 3y = 2x + (-3y)$
9. $1(3x + 4) = 3x + 4$

Simplify.

10. $3a - 5b - a + 3b$
11. $5x - (3y + 2x)$
12. $6x - 2(x + 3y)$

Expand.

13. $7(4a - 3b + 1)$
14. $(2x + 1)(x - 3)$
15. $(2a + 3b)(a - 5b)$

*W*RITTEN EXERCISES

A **State the property or definition from pages 18 and 19 that is illustrated by each statement.**

1. $0 + 17 = 17$

2. $-8\frac{2}{3} + 8\frac{2}{3} = 0$

3. $(17.6)(5.\overline{43})$ is a real number.

4. $48.\overline{7} + 0 = 48.\overline{7}$

5. $(\sqrt{2} + \pi)$ is a real number.

6. $\left(\frac{2}{2}\right)5 = 5$

7. $5.\overline{47} + (-5.\overline{47}) = 0$

8. $\left(5\frac{6}{17}\right)\left(7\frac{9}{13}\right)$ is a real number.

9. $\left(\frac{7}{8}\right)\left(\frac{8}{7}\right) = 1$

10. $1(\sqrt{15}) = \sqrt{15}$

True or false? If the statement is false, state a counterexample to show that it is false.

11. The set of integers is closed with respect to division.

12. The set of integers is closed with respect to subtraction.

13. The set of even numbers has an additive identity element.

14. The set of odd numbers has a multiplicative identity element.

15. If $\dfrac{a}{b}$ is a real number, $a \neq 0$, then $\left(\dfrac{a}{b}\right)\left(\dfrac{b}{a}\right) = 1$.

16. If $\sqrt{a}$ is a real number, then $\sqrt{a} + \left(-\sqrt{a}\right) = 0$.

17. The additive inverse of 1 is 0.
18. The additive inverse of -1 is -1.

19. The multiplicative inverse of -1 is -1.
20. The multiplicative inverse of 0 is 0.

Expand.

21. $5(x + 3y - 2)$
22. $3(a + 2b - 4)$

23. $-1(2x - 3y + 2)$
24. $-1(3a + 2b - 9)$

25. $(a + 2b)(2a + b)$
26. $(3a + b)(a + 3b)$

27. $(a + 3)^2$
28. $(2x + 5)^2$

29. $(n - 2)^2$
30. $(3n - 1)^2$

Simplify.

31. $7x + 2(x + 3)$
32. $12x + 3(x + 2)$

33. $5w - 9(w + 1)$
34. $7w - 8(w + 3)$

35. $6x + 4(x - 2)$
36. $4x + 6(x - 5)$

37. $8c - (c - 7)$
38. $9c - (c - 11)$

39. $3(a + 2) - 2(a - 2)$
40. $5(a - 3) - 2(a + 4)$

41. $6(b - 4) - 5(b + 4)$
42. $10(b + 5) - 8(b + 5)$

B 43. $1.2(a + 6) - 6(a + 1.2)$
44. $5.1(b - 0.5) + 3.1(0.2 + b)$

45. $\dfrac{2}{3}r + \dfrac{1}{6}(r - 3)$
46. $\dfrac{3}{4}s - \dfrac{1}{2}(5s + 1)$

47. $3.5w - (1 - w)$
48. $6.9t + 0.5(0.3 - t)$

49. $\dfrac{1}{5}(x - 4) - \dfrac{1}{10}(x + 1)$
50. $\dfrac{3}{8}(y + 2) - \dfrac{1}{4}(y - 2)$

True or false? If the statement is false, state a counterexample to show that it is false.

51. $\left(\sqrt{a} - \sqrt{b}\right)$ and $\left(\sqrt{b} - \sqrt{a}\right)$ are additive inverses.

52. $\dfrac{a}{b}$ and $-\dfrac{b}{a}$ are multiplicative inverses, where $a \neq 0$ and $b \neq 0$.

53. The set of odd numbers is closed with respect to both addition and multiplication.

54. The set of even numbers is closed with respect to both addition and multiplication.

C 55. The set of prime numbers is closed with respect to addition.

56. The set of prime numbers is closed with respect to multiplication.

57. The set of composite numbers is closed with respect to addition.

58. The set of composite numbers is closed with respect to multiplication.

Complete.

59. If $ab = -2$, what is the multiplicative inverse of a in terms of b?

60. Show that $0.\overline{27}$ and $3.\overline{6}$ are multiplicative inverses.

61. State the reason for each step.
$$
\begin{aligned}
3x + 7 + x &= 3x + (7 + x) \\
&= 3x + (x + 7) \\
&= 3x + x + 7 \\
&= 3x + 1x + 7 \\
&= (3 + 1)x + 7 \\
&= 4x + 7
\end{aligned}
$$

REVIEW EXERCISES

1. Find the average of -12, -8, 0, 4, and 6.

Find the perimeter and the area of the figure.

2.

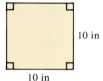

10 in

10 in

3.

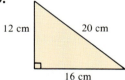

12 cm   20 cm

16 cm

4.

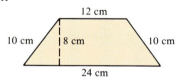

12 cm

10 cm   8 cm   10 cm

24 cm

HISTORICAL NOTE   BIOGRAPHY

Carl Friedrich Gauss (1777–1855) showed early signs of genius as a schoolboy. When asked to find the sum of the integers from 1 to 1000, he produced the answer almost immediately. As a young man he proved that a regular polygon of 17 sides could be constructed with straight-edge and compass. He was the first to make important discoveries about infinite series of numbers and contributed masterful work to many branches of algebra and geometry.

LESSON 1-6

Problem Solving—Finding Patterns

Problem: Find the sum of the integers from 1 to n.

To solve the problem we can try to find a pattern in simpler but related problems.

n	1	2	3	4	5
Sum of integers from 1 to n	1	3	6	10	15

Sometimes it is helpful to think of geometric representations of numbers to help find patterns.

$$1 + 2 + 3 + 4 + 5 \qquad 2(1 + 2 + 3 + 4 + 5) = 5(6)$$

In general, $2(1 + 2 + 3 + \ldots + n) = n(n + 1)$. So, the sum of the integers from 1 to n equals $\dfrac{n(n + 1)}{2}$.

Discovering a mathematical pattern is an **inductive** process that can help solve difficult problems. The discovered pattern in an organized set of data can be represented mathematically and used to predict other data.

Example 1 **Find a pattern.**
Write an equation for Q in terms of n.

n	1	2	3	4
Q	2	4	8	16

Solution Factor each value of Q. Write using exponents.

The value of n is the exponent for the corresponding power of 2.

n	1	2	3	4
Q	2	4	8	16
	2^1	2^2	2^3	2^4

$$Q = 2^n$$

In many problems no data are supplied. We can often generate our own data by solving simpler problems.

Example 2   **Write a formula for the sum S of the first n odd numbers.**

Solution   Solve simpler problems—find the sum of the first two odd numbers, the first three odd numbers, etc. Organize the data in a table for analysis.

Number of odd numbers	Sum	
2	$1 + 3 = 4$	
3	$1 + 3 + 5 = 9$	
4	$1 + 3 + 5 + 7 = 16$	Each sum is the square
5	$1 + 3 + 5 + 7 + 9 = 25$	of the number of odd numbers.

Answer $S = n^2$

Sometimes when a situation is represented mathematically, the mathematical expression can be simplified so that a pattern is revealed.

Example 3   **Write an algebraic expression to show why this trick works.**

Write down your age, multiply it by 2, add 5, and multiply the result by 50. Add the amount of change in your pocket (less than $1). From the result subtract the number of days in a year and add 115. The digits in the tens and ones places show the amount of change you added, and the digits in the thousands and hundreds places show your age.

Solution   Let a = the number of years in your age and c = the number of cents change in your pocket.

Expression: $(2a + 5)50 + c - 365 + 115$
Simplify. $= 100a + 250 + c - 250 = 100a + c$

Answer   The arithmetic is equivalent to multiplying your age by 100 and adding the amount of change in your pocket. Multiplying your age by 100 moves those digits to the thousands and hundreds place with zeros in the tens and ones places. Adding the change in your pocket to this result places those digits in the tens and ones places.

*C*LASSROOM EXERCISES

1. Find a pattern. Then use it to write the next three terms in the sequence.

$$5, 6, 8, 11, 15, \ldots$$

2. Find a pattern. Then write an equation for Q in terms of n.

n	1	2	3	4	5
Q	10	15	20	25	30

3. Write the nth term of the sequence $2, 6, 10, 14, 18, \ldots$.

RITTEN EXERCISES

A Find a pattern. Then use it to write the next three terms in each sequence.

1. 3, 7, 11, 15
2. 2, 7, 12, 17,
3. 10, 11, 13, 16, 20
4. 100, 102, 106, 112
5. 3, 6, 12, 24
6. 2, 6, 18, 54
7. $\frac{1}{2}, \frac{2}{3}, \frac{3}{4}, \frac{4}{5}$
8. $\frac{1}{8}, \frac{2}{9}, \frac{3}{10}, \frac{4}{11}$
9. 0.1, 0.02, 0.003
10. 0.1, 0.12, 0.121, 0.1212
11. 1, 4, 9, 16
12. 2, 5, 10, 17

Find a pattern and use it to complete the table. Then write an equation for Q in terms of n.

13.

n	1	2	3	4	10	20
Q	2	6	12	20	110	?

14.

n	1	2	3	4	10	20
Q	2	2	6	12	90	?

15.

n	1	2	3	4	10	20
Q	0	1	4	9	81	?

16.

n	1	2	3	4	10	20
Q	4	9	16	25	121	?

17.

n	1	2	3	4	10	20
Q	4	10	18	28	130	?

18.

n	1	2	3	4	10	20
Q	0	3	8	15	99	?

Write the nth term of each sequence.

19. 2, 4, 6, 8, 10, . . . , ___?___, . . .
20. 10, 11, 12, 13, 14, . . . , ___?___, . . .
21. 1, 4, 9, 16, 25, . . . , ___?___, . . .
22. 1, 8, 27, 64, 125, . . . , ___?___, . . .
23. 0, $\frac{1}{2}, \frac{2}{3}, \frac{3}{4}, \frac{4}{5}$, . . . , ___?___, . . .
24. 10, 20, 40, 80, 160, . . . , ___?___, . . .

Write a simplified algebraic expression for each puzzle. Let n represent the number.

25. Select a whole number. Double the number, add 5, multiply the sum by 5, and then subtract 20 from the product. In the result, the original number appears to the left of the digit 5.

26. Select a whole number. Add 5 to the number, multiply the sum by 5, double the result, and subtract 42. In the result, the original number appears to the left of the digit 8.

27. Select a whole number. Add 3 to the number, multiply the sum by 25, subtract 53 from the product, and then multiply the difference by 4. The result consists of the original number written to the left of "88."

28. Select a whole number. Multiply the number by 25, add 3 to the product, and then multiply the sum by 4. The result consists of the original number written to the left of "12."

29. Write an expression for the nth even number.

30. What is the sum of the first 100 even counting numbers. [*Hint:* Think about similar but simpler problems: $2 + 4$, $2 + 4 + 6$, etc.]

31. Write an algebraic expression for the sum of the first n even counting numbers.
$2 + 4 + 6 + \cdots + 2n$

32. Show that the expression from Exercise 31 gives the correct results when $n = 1$, $n = 2$, $n = 3$, and $n = 4$.

33. This table shows how many games must be played in a tournament in which each team plays one game with each of the other teams.

Number of teams	1	2	3	4	5
Number of games	0	1	3	6	10

   a. How many games must be played if there are 100 teams in the tournament?

   b. Write an algebraic expression for the number of games played if there are n teams in the tournament.

34. Lines are drawn so that they intersect all other lines previously drawn and the intersection points are counted. None of the lines are parallel, and all the points of intersection are unique.

Number of lines	1	2	3	4	5
Number of points of intersection	0	1	3	6	10

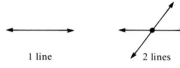

1 line   2 lines   3 lines

   a. How many points of intersection are there if 100 lines are drawn?

   b. Write an algebraic expression for the number of intersection points if n lines are drawn.

35. Use the expressions found in Example 2, Exercise 31, and the introduction to the lesson to show that the sum of the first n odd counting numbers and the first n even counting numbers is equal to the sum of the first $2n$ counting numbers.

36. T_1, T_2, T_3, and T_4 are the first four triangular numbers. Write a formula for T_n, the nth triangular number.

$T_1 = 1$ $T_2 = 3$ $T_3 = 6$ $T_4 = 10$

37. Explain why the situations in Exercises 33 and 34 have the same values in the tables and can be described using the same algebraic expression.

38. Explain why the expressions for the nth triangular number (Exercise 36), the sum of the first n positive integers (Introduction), the number of games when n teams enter a tournament (Exercise 33), and the number of points of intersection of n lines (Exercise 34) are so much alike.

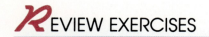 EVIEW EXERCISES

Compute.

1. $-3(-4) + 5(-2)$

2. $-6.1(-1000)$

3. $-4 - 10.6$

4. $-4 - \left(-2\frac{1}{3}\right)$

5. $-3\frac{1}{2} \div -1\frac{1}{2}$

6. $-\frac{1}{3} + \frac{-4}{-5}$

Find the perimeter and the area. Find the circumference and the area in terms of π.

7.
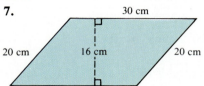
30 cm

20 cm   16 cm   20 cm

30 cm

8.

5 in.

9.

20 m

---

*S*elf-Quiz 2

1-4 **Name the property illustrated by each statement.**

1. $\sqrt{5} + 1.\overline{3}$ is a real number.

2. $(0.\overline{27})(3.\overline{6}) = 1$

3. $\left(\frac{3}{8} + \frac{5}{7}\right) + \frac{2}{7} = \frac{3}{8} + \left(\frac{5}{7} + \frac{2}{7}\right)$

4. $6x + (y + 1.5x) = 6x + (1.5x + y)$

5. $6x + 1.5x + y = (6 + 1.5)x + y$

1-4 **Simplify.**

6. $2(3 + 4(5 + x))$

7. $a(3b + c) + 2b(a + b)$

1-5 **Consider these values in answering the following questions.**

8. Which pair of numbers are additive inverses?

9. Which number is the additive identity?

10. Which pair of numbers are multiplicative inverses?

$-\frac{3}{2}$	$-\frac{2}{2}$	$-\frac{2}{3}$	$\frac{0}{2}$	$\frac{2}{2}$	2

1-6 **Write an equation for Q in terms of n.**

11.

n	1	2	3	4
Q	$\frac{1}{3}$	$\frac{1}{2}$	$\frac{3}{5}$	$\frac{2}{3}$

12.

n	1	2	3	4
Q	0	7	26	63

LESSON 1-7

Proof: Formal and Informal

Someone claims that the expression $x^2 + x + 41$ generates prime numbers for all whole number solutions for x.

$0^2 + 0 + 41 = 41$: a prime	$1^2 + 1 + 41 = 43$: a prime
$2^2 + 2 + 41 = 47$: a prime	$3^2 + 3 + 41 = 53$: a prime
$4^2 + 4 + 41 = 61$: a prime	$5^2 + 5 + 41 = 71$: a prime

The first 6 whole-number substitutions give primes. Does that *prove* the claim? The first 40 whole-number substitutions ($x = 0$ to $x = 39$) give primes. Are 40 examples enough to prove the claim? The answers to these questions are, of course, no. No number of examples is sufficient to prove the claim. But it takes only one counterexample to disprove it.

$$40^2 + 40 + 41 = 1681 = 41^2: \quad \text{not a prime}$$

The claim is wrong. The expression does not generate prime numbers for all whole-number substitutions.

A generalization must be proved before it can be accepted as true. Once a statement has been proved, it can be called a **theorem.** Algebraic proof relies on definitions of terms and on properties of numbers and operations.

A set of numbers that has the properties listed below is called a **field.** The set of real numbers is a field. These properties are also called **postulates** because they are accepted as true without proof.

Field Postulates of the Real-Number System

	Addition	*Multiplication*
Closure Property	For all real numbers a and b, $a + b$ is a real number.	For all real numbers a and b, ab is a real number.
Commutative Property	For all real numbers a and b, $a + b = b + a$.	For all real numbers a and b, $ab = ba$.
Associative Property	For all real numbers a, b, and c, $(a + b) + c = a + (b + c)$.	For all real numbers a, b, and c, $(ab)c = a(bc)$.
Identity Property	There is a real number 0, such that for each real number a, $a + 0 = 0 + a = a$.	There is a real number 1, such that for each real number a, $1 \cdot a = a \cdot 1 = a$.

Field Postulates (continued)

	Addition	**Multiplication**
Inverse Property	For each real number a, there is a real number $(-a)$ such that $$a + (-a) = -a + a = 0.$$	For each real number a, $a \neq 0$, there is a real number $\left(\dfrac{1}{a}\right)$ such that $$a\left(\frac{1}{a}\right) = \left(\frac{1}{a}\right)a = 1.$$
Distributive Property	For all real numbers a, b, and c, $$a(b + c) = ab + ac \quad \text{and} \quad (b + c)a = ba + ca.$$	

The field postulates are based on the meaning of equality and on the following properties of equality.

Properties of Equality

Reflexive Property

For each real number a, $a = a$.

Symmetric Property

For all real numbers a and b, if $a = b$ then $b = a$.

Transitive Property

For all real numbers a, b, and c, if $a = b$ and $b = c$, then $a = c$.

Substitution Property

For all real numbers a and b, if $a = b$, then a may be substituted for b in any sentence in which b occurs (or b for a in any sentence in which a occurs) without changing the truth or falseness of the sentence.

The following are some commonly used properties that can be derived from the field postulates. (The proof of one of these properties will be given in Example 1.)

For all real numbers a,

$$a \cdot 0 = 0 \cdot a = 0.$$
$$-(-a) = a.$$
$$(-1)a = a(-1) = -a.$$

For all real numbers a and b,

$$-(ab) = -ab = a(-b).$$
$$(-a)(-b) = ab.$$
$$-(a + b) = -a + (-b).$$

For all real numbers a and b, $b \neq 0$,

$$-\left(\frac{a}{b}\right) = \frac{-a}{b} = \frac{a}{-b}. \qquad \frac{-a}{-b} = \frac{a}{b}.$$

For all real numbers a, b, and c,

$$a(b - c) = ab - ac.$$

The proof in Example 1 is a formal proof. The proof in Example 2 is less formal and the other two proofs are examples of informal proofs. Compared to a formal proof, the informal proof has many gaps, but the gaps are such that only information familiar to the expected reader is omitted.

Example 1

Prove. For each real number a, $-(-a) = a$.

Solution

For each real number a,

1. $-a$ and $-(-a)$ are real numbers	*Additive inverse property*
2. $-(-a) = -(-a) + 0$	*Additive identity property*
3. $-a + a = 0$	*Additive inverse property*
4. $-(-a) = -(-a) + (-a + a)$	*Substitution (from 3 into 2)*
5. $-(-a) = (-(-a) + (-a)) + a$	*Associative property of addition*
6. $-(-a) + (-a) = 0$	*Additive inverse property*
7. $-(-a) = 0 + a$	*Substitution (from 6 into 5)*
8. $0 + a = a$	*Additive identity property*
9. $-(-a) = a$	*Transitive property (7 and 8)*

Therefore, for each real number a, $-(-a) = a$.

Example 2

Show that $2(x + y) + x = 3x + 2y$ for all real numbers x and y.

Solution

For all real numbers x and y.

$2(x + y) + x = 2x + 2y + x$	*Distributive property*
$= 2x + (2y + x)$	*Associative property of addition*
$= 2x + (x + 2y)$	*Commutative property of addition*
$= 2x + x + 2y$	*Associative property of addition*
$= 2x + 1x + 2y$	*Multiplicative identity property*
$= (2 + 1)x + 2y$	*Distributive property*
$= 3x + 2y$	*Computation*

Example 3

Show that if $n = 10t + 5$, then $n^2 = t(t + 1)100 + 25$.

Solution

Let $n = 10t + 5$. Then $n^2 = (10t + 5)^2$. Expanding the right side gives $100t^2 + 100t + 25$. Applying the distributive property gives $(t^2 + t)100 + 25$. Then applying the distributive property again gives the desired result: $n^2 = t(t + 1)100 + 25$.

Example 4

Show that the sum of two odd numbers is an even number.

Solution

Let $2n + 1$ and $2m + 1$ be odd numbers, where n and m are integers.

$$(2n + 1) + (2m + 1) = 2n + 2m + 2$$
$$= 2(n + m + 1)$$

Since the set of integers is closed with respect to addition and since n, m, and 1 are integers, the sum $n + m + 1$ is an integer, which we will call p. Therefore, $(2n + 1) + (2m + 1) = 2p$, an even number. Thus the sum of any two odd numbers is an even number.

CLASSROOM EXERCISES

1. State the reason for each step of the proof of this statement:

   For each real number x, $7x - x = 6x$.

   $7x - x = 7x - 1x$ _____?_____

   $= 7x + (-1x)$ _____?_____

   $= 7x + (-1)x$ For all a and b, $-(ab) = -ab$.

   $= (7 + (-1))x$ _____?_____

   $= 6x$ _____?_____

2. Show that the product of two even numbers is an even number.

WRITTEN EXERCISES

A **State the reason for each step of the proof.**

1. The product of any real number and 0 is 0.
   For each real number x,

   $0x = 0x + 0$

   $= 0x + (x + (-x))$

   $= 0x + x + (-x)$

   $= 0x + 1x + (-x)$

   $= (0 + 1)x + (-x)$

   $= 1x + (-x)$

   $= x + (-x)$

   $= 0$

2. The product of -1 and any number is the opposite of that number.
   For each real number x,

   $(-1)x = (-1)x + 0$

   $= (-1)x + (x + (-x))$

   $= (-1)x + x + (-x)$

   $= (-1)x + 1x + (-x)$

   $= (-1 + 1)x + (-x)$

   $= 0x + (-x)$

   $= 0 + (-x)$

   $= -x$

3. For each real number x, $10x - x = 9x$.
   For each real number x,

   $10x - x = 10x + (-x)$

   $= 10x + (-1x)$

   $= (10 + (-1))x$

   $= 9x$

4. For each real number x, $2(x + 2) - 4 = 4x$.
   For each real number x,

   $2(x + 2) - 4 = 2x + 4 - 4$

   $= 2x + 4 + (-4)$

   $= 2x + (4 + (-4))$

   $= 2x + 0$

   $= 2x$

5. Show that the sum of an odd number and an even number is odd.

6. Show that the sum of any two even numbers is even.

7. Show that the square of an even number is even.

8. Show that the product of an odd number and an even number is even.

9. Show that the square of an odd number is odd.

10. Show that the product of two odd numbers is odd.

11. Prove: For all real numbers a and b, $(-a) + (-b) = -(a + b)$.

12. Prove: For all real numbers a and b, $(-a)(-b) = ab$.

13. Prove: For all real numbers a, b, and c, $a(b - c) = ab - ac$.

 C

14. Suppose that the remainder is 4 when a number m is divided by 7, and the remainder is 5 when another number n is divided by 7. Show that the remainder is 2 when the sum $(m + n)$ is divided by 7.

15. For the numbers m and n in Exercise 14, state the remainder when the product mn is divided by 7.

 **EVIEW EXERCISES**

1. Find the perimeter and area of this figure.

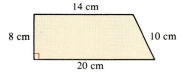
14 cm
8 cm   10 cm
20 cm

2. Express $\frac{3}{4}$ as a percent.

3. Express 45% as a fraction.

4. Express 6% as a decimal.

5. Express 0.15 as a percent.

 **XTENSION**   Fields

A system is a set of numbers and operations on the numbers. Consider the system made up of {0, 1, 2, 3, 4, 5, 6, 7, 8, 9} and the operations of addition and multiplication as defined below.

$a \oplus b$ = [the units digit of $a + b$] (For example, $7 \oplus 7 = 4$.)

$a \otimes b$ = [the units digit of ab] (For example, $8 \otimes 9 = 2$.)

This system has many but not all of the properties of a field. For example, it is closed with respect to the two operations. Both operations are commutative and associative. There are identity properties for both operations. Each element has an additive inverse. Multiplication is distributive over addition. However, some elements do not have multiplicative inverses. For example, the number 7 has a multiplicative inverse ($3 \otimes 7 = 1$), but the numbers 2, 4, 5, 6, and 8 do not.

Complete.

1. Consider the system made up of {0, 2, 4, 6, 8} and the two operations defined above. Is this system a field? What is the multiplicative identity element?

2. Is the set of rational numbers together with the usual addition and multiplication operations a field?

3. Is the set of irrational numbers together with the usual addition and multiplication operations a field?

CHAPTER SUMMARY

▶ **Vocabulary**

▶ A *rational number* is a number that can be expressed as the quotient of two integers. Rational numbers can be expressed as repeating decimals or terminating decimals.   [1-1]

▶ Real numbers that are not rational numbers are called *irrational numbers*. Irrational numbers can be expressed as nonterminating, nonrepeating decimals.   [1-1]

▶ Order of operations   [1-2]
  1. Evaluate inside grouping symbols first.
  2. Evaluate powers and roots next.
  3. Do multiplications and divisions in order from left to right.
  4. Do additions and subtractions in order from left to right.

▶ Trichotomy property   [1-3]

  For all real numbers a, b, one and only one of the following statements is true:

$$a < b, \quad a = b, \quad a > b.$$

▶ Transitive property of order   [1-3]
  For all real numbers a, b, and c,

$$\text{if } a < b \text{ and } b < c, \text{ then } a < c.$$

Field Postulates of the Real-Number System [1-4, 1-5, 1-7]

	Addition	*Multiplication*
Closure Property	For all real numbers a and b, $a + b$ is a real number.	For all real numbers a and b, ab is a real number.
Commutative Property	For all real numbers a and b, $a + b = b + a$.	For all real numbers a and b, $ab = ba$.
Associative Property	For all real numbers a, b, and c, $(a + b) + c = a + (b + c)$.	For all real numbers a, b, and c, $(ab)c = a(bc)$.
Identity Property	There is a real number 0, such that for each real number a, $a + 0 = 0 + a = a$.	There is a real number 1, such that for each real number a, $1 \cdot a = a \cdot 1 = a$.
Inverse Property	For each real number a, there is a real number $(-a)$ such that $a + (-a) = -a + a = 0$.	For each real number a, $a \neq 0$, there is a real number $\left(\dfrac{1}{a}\right)$ such that $a\left(\dfrac{1}{a}\right) = \left(\dfrac{1}{a}\right)a = 1$.
Distributive Property	For all real numbers a, b, and c, $a(b + c) = ab + ac$ and $(b + c)a = ba + ca$.	

▶ Definition of subtraction [1-5]

For all real numbers a and b, $a - b = a + (-b)$.

▶ Definition of division [1-5]

For all real numbers a and b, $b \neq 0$, $\dfrac{a}{b} = a\left(\dfrac{1}{b}\right)$.

Properties of Equality [1-7]

Reflexive Property

For each real number a, $a = a$.

Symmetric Property

For all real numbers a and b, if $a = b$ then $b = a$.

Transitive Property

For all real numbers a, b, and c, if $a = b$ and $b = c$, then $a = c$.

Substitution Property

For all real numbers a and b, if $a = b$, then a may be substituted for b in any sentence in which b occurs (or b for a in any sentence in which a occurs) without changing the truth or falseness of the sentence.

$\mathcal{C}$HAPTER REVIEW

1-1 **Objective:** To identify rational numbers and irrational numbers.

State whether the number is rational or irrational.

1. 5.12341234 . . .

2. 1.2112111211112 . . .

3. $-3\dfrac{2}{3}$

4. $2 + \sqrt{2}$

1-2 **Objective:** To substitute in algebraic expressions and simplify using the rules of order of operations.

Simplify.

5. $2(3^2) - 5(3) + 12$

6. $2(6 + 3(4)) - (10 - 3)$

Substitute and simplify.

x	y
5	2

7. $(xy^2)^2$

8. $\sqrt{(2y)^2 + (x - y)^2}$

1-3 **Objective:** To match sets of numbers with their number-line graphs.

9. Use set-builder notation to describe the graph.

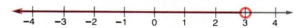

Graph each set on a number line.

10. $\{x: x \neq 1\}$

11. $\left\{ x: x \text{ is an integer between } -2\dfrac{1}{2} \text{ and } 2\dfrac{1}{2} \right\}$

1-4 **Objective:** To identify examples of the commutative, associative, and distributive properties and to use these properties to simplify algebraic expressions.

What property of real numbers is illustrated in the equation?

12. $3(4 + 5) = 3(4) + 3(5)$

13. $(-26 \cdot 25)4 = -26(25 \cdot 4)$

14. Simplify. $4a + 5b + 3(a + b)$

1-5 **Objective:** To identify examples of the closure, identity, and inverse properties and to use these properties to expand or simplify algebraic expressions.

15. Is the set of negative integers closed
   a. with respect to addition?
   b. with respect to multiplication?

16. What property is illustrated in the equation $5x + x = 5x + 1x$?

17. Expand. $(x + 2)(x - 3)$

18. Simplify. $2(x - 3) - (x + 2)$

1-6 **Objective:** To make generalizations and write algebraic expressions for them.

Identify the next number in each sequence.

19. 20, 24, 28, 32, __?__

20. 2, 8, 18, 32, 50, __?__

Use the variable *n* to write an expression for the *n*th term of each sequence.

21. 10, 12, 14, 16, 18, . . .

22. $\dfrac{1}{2}, \dfrac{2}{3}, \dfrac{3}{4}, \dfrac{4}{5}, \ldots$

1-7 **Objective:** To write simple formal and informal algebraic proofs.

23. Fill in the missing reasons in this proof:
For all real numbers x,
$4x + x = 5x$.

$$
\begin{aligned}
4x + x &= 4x + 1x &&\underline{\hspace{2cm}?\hspace{2cm}} \\
&= (4 + 1)x &&\underline{\hspace{2cm}?\hspace{2cm}} \\
&= 5x &&\text{Computation}
\end{aligned}
$$

24. Show that the sum of two multiples of 3 is also a multiple of 3.

✐HAPTER 1 SELF-TEST

1-1 **1.** Express as a repeating or a terminating decimal.

a. $\dfrac{6}{11}$

b. $\dfrac{21}{240}$

2. Identify as rational or irrational.

a. $5 + 0.\overline{6}$

b. π^3

3. True or false?

a. The product of two irrational numbers is always irrational.

b. The difference of a rational and an irrational number is always irrational.

1-2 **4.** Simplify. $(2 + 6)^2 \div 16 - 8$

5. Substitute and simplify.
$(a + b)^x - 12cy$

a	b	c	x	y
-1	4	$\dfrac{1}{3}$	2	0.5

6. Identify the greatest number.

a. $\dfrac{\sqrt{6}}{4}, 0.\bar{6}, \dfrac{5}{8}$

b. $-1\dfrac{1}{4}, \sqrt{11}, \dfrac{\pi}{2}$

7. Graph on a number line. $\{x : x < 2\}$

8. Use set-builder notation to describe the set of all real numbers less than $\sqrt{7}$.

9. Simplify.

a. $\dfrac{24s + 16t}{6}$

b. $2((x - 1) - 3) + 4(1 + (2 - x))$

10. Identify the property illustrated in each equation.

a. $(16 \cdot 3)\left(\dfrac{10}{3}\right) = 16\left(3\left(\dfrac{10}{3}\right)\right)$

b. $5.2x + 3.6x = (5.2 + 3.6)x$

11. True or false?

a. $\left(3 - \sqrt{2}\right)$ and $\dfrac{\left(\sqrt{2} + 3\right)}{7}$ are multiplicative inverses.

b. The set of numbers that are perfect squares is closed with respect to multiplication.

12. Identify the property illustrated in each equation.

a. $4\left(\dfrac{\sqrt{2}}{\sqrt{2}}\right) = 4$

b. $(9.\bar{3} + 4) + 0 = 9.\bar{3} + 4$

13. Write the next number in the pattern.

a. 0, 3, 8, 15, ___?___

b. $\dfrac{35}{4}, \dfrac{28}{5}, \dfrac{21}{6}, \dfrac{14}{7},$ ___?___

14. Write an equation for Q in terms of n.

a.

n	2	4	7	9
Q	5	9	15	19

b.

n	1	2	3	4
Q	2	8	18	32

15. Fill in the reasons for this proof:

For each real number x, $x + 2y + x = 2(y + x)$.

$$
\begin{aligned}
\text{For each real number } x, \quad x + 2y + x &= 2y + x + x \\
&= 2y + (x + x) \\
&= 2y + (1x + 1x) \\
&= 2y + (1 + 1)x \\
&= 2y + 2x \\
&= 2(y + x)
\end{aligned}
$$

16. Show that the product of two multiples of 5 is also a multiple of 5.

$\mathcal{P}$RACTICE FOR COLLEGE ENTRANCE TESTS

Choose the best answer to each question.

1. If $x = 0$ and $y = -5$, then $xy^2 + \dfrac{x^2}{y} = $ ___?___.

 A. 25 **B.** 10 **C.** 5 **D.** 0 **E.** -5

2. If $AC = 5$, $BD = 6$, and $AD = 8$, then $BC = $ ___?___.

 A. 1 **B.** 2 **C.** 3 **D.** 4 **E.** 5

3. What is the average (arithmetic mean) of -16, -4, 0, 8?

 A. -12 **B.** -4 **C.** -3 **D.** -2 **E.** 0

4. Which of the following numbers is the greatest?

 A. 0.121 **B.** 0.112 **C.** 0.1122 **D.** 0.1202 **E.** 0.12

5. If a and b are odd integers, which of the following must be true?

 I. $a + b$ is even. II. ab is odd. III. $\dfrac{a + b}{2}$ is odd.

 A. I only **B.** II only **C.** I and II only **D.** II and III only **E.** I, II, and III

6. There are eight teams in a football league. If each team plays each other exactly once, then how many games will there be in all?

 A. 7 **B.** 8 **C.** 28 **D.** 32 **E.** 56

7. If n is an integer, what is the sum of the next three consecutive even integers greater than $2n$?

 A. $6n + 12$ **B.** $6n + 10$ **C.** $6n + 8$ **D.** $6n + 6$ **E.** $6n + 4$

8. What is the expression for the total surface area of a rectangular solid with altitude b and with a square base a units on a side?

 A. $4ab$
 B. a^2b
 C. $a^2 + 2ab$
 D. $2a^2 + 2ab$
 E. $2a^2 + 4ab$

9. If operation $\boxed{X}$ is defined by the equation $a \boxed{X} b = a + b^2$, then $2 \boxed{X} 3 = $ ___?___.

 A. 7 **B.** 11 **C.** 12 **D.** 13 **E.** 25

10. Jane is now j years old. In two years Dick will be twice as old as Jane is then. In terms of j, how old was Dick two years ago?

 A. $2j$ **B.** $2j - 2$ **C.** $2j + 2$ **D.** $2j - 4$ **E.** $2j + 4$

11. If $x + 2x + 3x + 4x = 1 + 2 + 3 + 4$, then $x = $ ___?___.

 A. 0 **B.** 1 **C.** 2 **D.** 3 **E.** 4

CHAPTER 2

Linear Equations and Inequalities

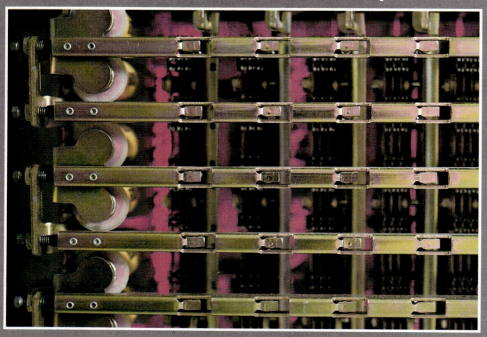

Linear equations arise in applications ranging from routing millions of long-distance telephone calls to devising the best mix of stocks and bonds in investment portfolios. Some of these problems consist of thousands of variables and thousands of equations that must be satisfied. Companies spend millions of dollars and use computers to decide how to distribute limited resources in the most efficient ways.

LESSON 2-1

Solving Linear Equations

One of the many contributions made to mathematics by the ancient Hindus is the method of solving equations by "inversion"—working backward from a given piece of information. For example, if four times a certain number is known to give a product of 42, we work backward from the result, dividing by four to obtain the number.

Linear equations in one variable (that is, equations that can be put in the form $ax + b = 0$ with $a \neq 0$) can be solved by applying the real-number properties and the following two properties of equality.

Addition Property of Equality

For all real numbers a, b, and c,   if $a = b$, then $a + c = b + c$.

Multiplication Property of Equality

For all real numbers a, b, and c,   if $a = b$, then $ac = bc$.

Example 1 **Solve.** $3(2x - 5) = 12 + 4x$

Solution

$$3(2x - 5) = 12 + 4x$$

Use the distributive property. $6x - 15 = 12 + 4x$

Add $-4x$ to both sides. $2x - 15 = 12$

Add 15 to both sides. $2x = 27$

Multiply both sides by $\frac{1}{2}$. $x = \dfrac{27}{2}$

Answer The solution set is $\left\{\dfrac{27}{2}\right\}$.

Example 2 **Solve.** $0.3a + 0.08 = 3.4$

Solution

$$0.3a + 0.08 = 3.4$$

Multiply both sides by 100. $30a + 8 = 340$

Add -8 to both sides. $30a = 332$

Multiply both sides by $\frac{1}{30}$. $a = \dfrac{332}{30}$

Simplify the fraction. $a = \dfrac{166}{15}$

Answer $\left\{\dfrac{166}{15}\right\}$

Example 3   Solve. $\frac{2}{3}(b + 9) = 2$

Solution

$$\frac{2}{3}(b + 9) = 2$$

Multiply both sides by 3. $2(b + 9) = 6$

Use the distributive property. $2b + 18 = 6$

Add -18 *to both sides.* $2b = -12$

Multiply both sides by $\frac{1}{2}$. $b = -6$

Answer $\{-6\}$

Example 4   Solve.

The value that business equipment loses as it gradually wears out is called *depreciation*. The Internal Revenue Service allows a business to deduct its depreciation as a business expense. One method of computing depreciation is linear. Suppose that the original cost of a piece of equipment is C dollars and that the equipment is depreciated over n years. Its value (V) after t years is given by the formula $V = C\left(1 - \frac{t}{n}\right)$. If a truck costing \$20,000 is depreciated over 8 years, when will it be worth \$7500?

Solution   Substitute 7500 for V, 20,000 for C, and 8 for n.

$$7500 = 20{,}000\left(1 - \frac{t}{8}\right)$$

Expand and simplify. $7500 = 20{,}000 - 2500t$

Subtract 20,000 from both sides. $-12{,}500 = -2500t$

Divide both sides by -2500. $5 = t$

Answer   The truck will be worth \$7500 after 5 years.

*C*LASSROOM EXERCISES

Solve.

1. $3x + 5 = 41$

2. $0.7y - 0.8 = 5.5$

3. $\frac{c}{4} + 3 = 9$

4. $5d - 3 = 2d + 8$

5. $\frac{2w}{5} + 2 = 11$

6. $q - 6 = 4q + 6$

7. $3(p - 4) = 5(p + 3)$

8. $\frac{3b - 5}{4} = 9$

9. $\frac{4t - 1}{3} = 6$

Use the formula given in Example 4 to solve the following problem.

10. A machine costing $18,000 is depreciated linearly over 10 yr. The owner wishes to sell the machine when its value depreciates to $11,700. After how many years will the machine be sold?

RITTEN EXERCISES

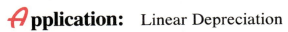

A Solve.

1. $4x + 5 = 33$

2. $5y + 4 = 34$

3. $0.6q - 0.24 = 0.6$

4. $0.4r - 0.26 = 0.7$

5. $\frac{t}{5} + 4 = 20$

6. $\frac{a}{3} + 7 = 11$

7. $4(b - 5) = 6$

8. $2(p - 6) = 5$

9. $7m + 5 = 9m - 2$

10. $5x + 2 = 8x - 2$

11. $\frac{5c}{3} + 4 = 9$

12. $\frac{3y}{2} + 1 = 7$

13. $2(a - 3) = 3(a - 4)$

14. $4(x - 1) = 3(x + 1)$

15. $\frac{5d - 3}{4} = 8$

16. $\frac{4w + 4}{5} = 4$

17. $\frac{2}{3}v + \frac{3}{4} = \frac{25}{12}$

18. $\frac{3}{4}T + \frac{2}{3} = \frac{35}{12}$

19. $25 + 3(x + 2) = 22$

20. $31 + 5(y + 7) = 41$

21. $5(2a + 3) = 7a + 12$

22. $3(4v + 7) = 7v + 11$

23. $0.4(H - 2) + 0.2 = 0.6$

24. $0.3(Q + 1) = Q - 2.5$

$\mathcal{A}$pplication: Linear Depreciation

Use the formula given in Example 4 to solve the following problems.

25. A machine costing $100,000 is depreciated linearly over 20 yr. The owner wants to sell the machine when its depreciated value is $40,000. After how many years will the machine be sold?

26. Office furniture costing $5000 is depreciated linearly over 5 yr. What will its value be in $3\frac{1}{2}$ yr?

27. After being depreciated linearly for 5 yr of an 8-yr depreciation schedule, a company car has a value of $3000. What was its original cost?

28. A building is depreciated linearly over 50 yr. After 40 yr, the depreciated value is $500,000. What was its original value?

𝒜pplication: Automobile Weight Distribution

The weight (W) of most cars is evenly distributed on the four tires. Suppose that A is the
area (in square inches) of each tire's contact
with the ground at a tire pressure P (in pounds
per square inch). Then

$$\frac{W}{4A} = P.$$

Use the formula to solve the following problems.

29. For safe operation, each tire of a car weighing 4200 lb should have 37.5 in.^{2}
   of area in contact with the ground. To what pressure should the tires be
   inflated?

30. The tire pressure in each tire of a 3000-lb car is 29.2 lb per in.^{2} What is the
   total tire area in contact with the ground? Round your answer to the nearest
   tenth.

B Solve.

31. $35 - 13x = 2(7x - 8)$

32. $1.5(2 - y) = 4.9y + 11$

33. $4[12 - 3(r + 2)] = -8(2 - r)$

34. $\frac{2}{3} + \frac{3}{4}(w + 1) = \frac{5}{6}$

35. $\frac{2}{5}t + 4 = \frac{1}{5}(8 - t)$

36. $\frac{1}{2}a + \frac{1}{3}a + \frac{1}{4}a = 26$

37. $8.3 + 1.9k = 0.3(2 - k)$

38. $\{13 - [12 - (11 - y)]\} = 1$

39. $\frac{1}{8}(7x + 5) = \frac{1}{10}(3x + 15) + 2$

40. $1.2(y - 0.6) = 6(0.3 - 0.1y)$

𝒜pplication: Highway Expansion

Engineers use the following formula to calculate the expansion of a two-lane highway on a hot day:

$$I = 0.000012L(T - t)$$

where I represents the expansion in feet, L represents the length of the highway
in feet, T represents the present temperature (in degrees Fahrenheit), and t represents the temperature when the highway was built.

Solve:

41. How much does 10,000 ft of highway expand at 80° F if the highway was built
   at 70°F?

42. What is the temperature if 5000 ft of highway built at 70°F expands 1.8 ft?

43. A 5000-ft highway expanded 2.1 ft on a day when the temperature was 90°F.
   What was the temperature when the highway was built?

*C*omputer Application: Solving Equations

A computer can solve this equation directly for X only if it is changed into the form X = . . .

$$0.7X - 3.988 = 0$$

However, computers can use systematic trials to approximate solutions of equations. As a simple example, consider this program for the above equation.

10 FOR X = −10 TO 10	Line 10 substitutes each integer from −10 to 10 for X
20 Y = 0.7 * X − 3.988	Line 20 computes the value of the left side of the given equation
30 PRINT "X = "; X, "Y = "; Y	
40 NEXT X	Line 40 loops back to line 10 for the next integer
50 END	

44. Run the program. How does it tell you that the solution is between 5 and 6?

45. Replace line 10 with the following to "narrow in" on the solution.

$$10 \text{ FOR X} = 5 \text{ to } 6 \text{ STEP } 0.1$$

State an approximation of the solution correct to the nearest tenth.

46. Write a new line 10 and compute an approximation of the solution to the nearest hundredth.

Write programs like the one above to find each solution to the nearest tenth.

47. 2.3X − 4.6 = 0

48. 0 = 0.6X + 0.38

49. 0.3X + 4.2 = 5X − 3.1

50. 2.4X − 0.15 = 4.1X + 4.56

ⓒ *A*pplication: The Doppler Effect

If you and a source of sound are moving toward each other, the pitch of the sound you hear is higher than the pitch of the emitted sound. The relationship between the two pitches is given by the formula

$$f' = f\left(1 + \frac{v}{760}\right)$$

where f' is the frequency (in cycles per second) of the sound heard, f is the frequency of the emitted sound, and v is the velocity in miles per hour at which you and the source are moving toward each other. If you and a source of sound are moving away from each other, the pitch of the sound heard is lower than the pitch of the emitted sound. The same formula can be used by assigning a negative value to the velocity. This change in pitch, called the *Doppler effect,* is very noticeable when a locomotive or automobile goes past you with its whistle or horn blowing.

51. A locomotive is traveling toward a crossing at 60 mph. The whistle is emitting a sound at 380 cycles per second. What frequency will a pedestrian at the crossing hear as the locomotive approaches the crossing? Travels away from the crossing? [Remember: $f' = f\left(1 + \dfrac{v}{760}\right)$]

52. A trumpeter on a platform is sounding a long "Concert A" note at 440 cycles per second. How fast would a bicycle rider have to be approaching the platform in order to hear the note as an A# (A sharp) at 466.2 cycles per second? Round your answer to the nearest whole number.

53. A problem given during the sixth century by Aryabhata states: "Tell me, as thou understandst the right method of inversion, which is the number which multiplied by 3, then increased by $\dfrac{3}{4}$ of the product, then divided by 7, diminished by $\dfrac{1}{3}$ of the quotient, multiplied by itself, diminished by 52, by the extraction of the square root, addition of 8, and division by 10 gives the number 2?"

To solve the problem, the scholar would simply have worked backward through the problem by using the inverse operation at each step: multiplying by 10, subtracting 8, squaring, etc. Find the number.

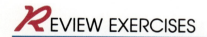 EVIEW EXERCISES

1. Find the perimeter and area of this triangle.

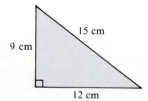

9 cm, 15 cm, 12 cm

2. Find the circumference and area of this circle. Use 3.14 as the value of π.

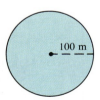

100 m

3. Find the perimeter and area of this trapezoid.

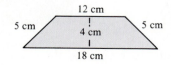

12 cm, 5 cm, 5 cm, 4 cm, 18 cm

4. Express $\dfrac{3}{5}$ as a percent.

5. Express 35% as a decimal.

6. Express 0.08 as a percent.

7. Express 110% as a fraction in simplest form.

Factor.

8. $ax - cx$

9. $mx + 3x$

LESSON 2-2

Literal Equations and Formulas

Equations and formulas containing several variables such as $ax + b = c$ and $lwh = V$ are called **literal equations.**

> **Definition: Literal Equation**
> A *literal equation* is an equation in which constants are represented by letters.

Usually letters from the first part of the alphabet are used as literal constants and letters from the last part of the alphabet are used as variables. In the equation $ax + by = c$, x and y are variables and a, b, and c are literal constants.

To solve a literal equation for a specific variable, transform it to an equivalent equation in which that variable is expressed in terms of other variables and constants. Techniques used to transform the given literal equation are the same as those used for solving any other equation.

Example 1   **Solve for x. $ax + b = c$, $a \neq 0$**

Solution

$$ax + b = c$$

Isolate the x-term. $ax = c - b$

Divide by a. $x = \dfrac{c - b}{a}$

Example 2   **Solve for x. $ax + b = cx + d$, $a \neq c$**

Solution

$$ax + b = cx + d$$

Collect x-terms. $ax - cx + b = d$

Collect terms not containing x. $ax - cx = d - b$

Use the distributive property. $(a - c)x = d - b$

Divide both sides by $(a - c)$. $x = \dfrac{d - b}{a - c}$

Example 3   **Solve for x. $m(x - n) = 3(r - x)$, $m \neq -3$**

Solution

$$m(x - n) = 3(r - x)$$

Expand. $mx - mn = 3r - 3x$

Collect x-terms and terms not containing x. $mx + 3x = 3r + mn$

Use the distributive property. $(m + 3)x = 3r + mn$

Divide both sides by $(m + 3)$. $x = \dfrac{3r + mn}{m + 3}$

Equations with more than one variable, such as formulas, can be treated as literal equations in solving for a particular variable.

Example 4   Solve for F. $C = \frac{5}{9}(F - 32)$

Solution $C = \frac{5}{9}(F - 32)$

Multiply both sides by $\frac{9}{5}$. $\frac{9}{5}C = F - 32$

Collect terms not containing F. $\frac{9}{5}C + 32 = F$

Use the symmetry property of equality. $F = \frac{9}{5}C + 32$

*C*LASSROOM EXERCISES

Solve for x.

1. $ax - b = c$

2. $\frac{x}{a} + b = 0$

3. $ax + bx = d$

4. $x + y = b(y - x)$

5. $c = \frac{1}{a}(x + y)b$

6. $a_1x + b_1y = a_2x + b_2y$

7. The formula for the area of a trapezoid is $A = \frac{h}{2}(b_1 + b_2)$. Solve for h.

*W*RITTEN EXERCISES

 Solve both equations for x.

1.a. $2x + 3 = 8$

b. $ax + b = c$

2.a. $3x + 2 = 9$

b. $rx + s = t$

3.a. $7x - 5 = 6$

b. $jx - k = m$

4.a. $5x - 6 = 7$

b. $px - q = r$

5.a. $2(x + 13) = 29$

b. $r(x + s) = t$

6.a. $7(x - 5) = 11$

b. $a(x - b) = c$

Solve for r.

7. $\frac{r}{s} = t$

8. $\frac{r}{a} = b + s$

9. $sr + tr = w$

10. $ar - br = c$

11. $\frac{r}{k} - h = j$

12. $\frac{r}{n} + s = t$

Solve for the indicated variable.

13. $ab + cw = d$, for w

14. $mx + pq = r$, for x

15. $c(t + e) = f$, for t

16. $a(b + r) = d$, for r

17. $\dfrac{x + y}{z} = w$, for x

18. $\dfrac{p + q}{r} = s$, for q

19. $ax + by = c$, for x

20. $cx - dy = e$, for y

21. $\dfrac{x}{b} = \dfrac{c}{d}$, for x

22. $\dfrac{a}{y} = \dfrac{c}{d}$, for y

$\mathscr{A}$pplications: Formulas

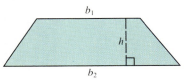

The formula for the area of a trapezoid is $A = \dfrac{h}{2}(b_1 + b_2)$.

23. Solve for b_1.

24. Solve for b_2.

The formula for the area of a triangle is $A = \dfrac{bh}{2}$.

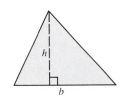

25. Solve for b.

26. Express the formula in terms of the constant 2.

The formula for the circumference of a circle is $C = \pi d$.

27. Express π in terms of C and d.

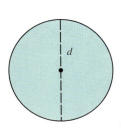

28. Solve for d.

The formula for simple interest is $i = prt$.

29. Solve for p.   30. Solve for t.

B 31. The formula for linear depreciation is $V = C\left(1 - \dfrac{t}{n}\right)$. (See page 42.)

    a. Solve for C.   **b.** Solve for t.

32. The formula for the Doppler effect is $f' = f\left(1 + \dfrac{v}{760}\right)$. (See pages 45 and 46.)

    a. Solve for f.   **b.** Solve for v.

33. The formula for the expansion (I) of a two-lane highway is $I = 0.000012L(T - t)$. (See page 44.)

    a. Solve for L.   **b.** Solve for T.   **c.** Solve for t.

34. The formula for the acceleration (a) of an object is

$$a = \frac{v_f - v_o}{t}$$

where v_o is the initial velocity, v_f is the final velocity, and t is the time.

    a. Solve for t.   **b.** Solve for v_f.   **c.** Solve for v_o.

 35. The relationship between temperature, pressure, and volume of a gas according to Boyle's and Charles' laws is given by the equation

$$\frac{P_1 V_1}{T_1} = \frac{P_2 V_2}{T_2}$$

where P_1, V_1, and T_1 and P_2, V_2, and T_2 are the initial and final pressures, volumes, and temperatures, respectively.

    a. Solve for V_2.   **b.** Solve for P_2.   **c.** Solve for T_2.

Solve for the indicated variables.

36. $F = \dfrac{Wv^2}{gr}$, for W and for g **37.** $F = k\dfrac{m_1 m_2}{d^2}$, for m_1 and for d^2

38. $S = \dfrac{a}{1 - r}$, for a and for r **39.** $I = \dfrac{E}{R + nr}$, for E, for R, and for r

EVIEW EXERCISES

Substitute and simplify.

a	b	c	x
3	-4	5	-10

[1-2]

  1. $bx + cx$ **2.** $ac + bc - (a + b)c$ **3.** $(a + b)^2 - (a^2 + b^2)$
  4. $ax^2 + bx + c$ **5.** $\sqrt{a^2 + b^2}$ **6.** $\sqrt{c^2 - b^2}$

Solve these percent problems.

  7. Write 125% as a decimal.   **8.** Write 0.03% as a decimal.

  9. Write 45% as a fraction in lowest terms.   **10.** Write 115% as a fraction in lowest terms.

 11. What is 75% of 200?   **12.** What is 200% of 75?

 13. What is 0.5% of 89?   **14.** What is 421.3% of 70?

 15. What percent is 12 of 20?   **16.** What percent is 20 of 12?

 17. What percent is 23 of 52?   **18.** What percent is 52 of 23?

 19. 10 is 8% of what number?   **20.** 8 is 10% of what number?

 21. Jane scored 85%, 80%, and 100% on her first three mathematics tests. What must she score on her next test in order to bring her average (mean) score to 88%?

Problem Solving: Writing Equations

Application: Point of No Return An important calculation for air flights over water is the
point of no return. It is the point at which there
is just enough fuel to return to the point of
departure.

A pilot takes off from an island in a plane with
an air speed of 500 mph, enough fuel for 4 hours,
and a tail wind of 100 mph. In 2 hours with the
help of the tail wind, the plane will travel 1200
miles. If the pilot must return against the wind,
the plane will run out of fuel after 800 mi. Clearly
it is important that the pilot *calculate* the point
of no return. This can be done by writing and
solving an equation. (See Exercise 24.)

Writing and solving equations is a powerful tool for solving problems in mathematics. Skill is required both in the writing and in the solving of an equation.
Before writing an equation with algebraic symbols, it is sometimes helpful to make
a table and write a word equation.

Here is a list of steps that can help you structure your thinking each time you
solve a problem.

Problem Solving Steps

1. Read the problem carefully, making sure that you understand the situation.
   Note which quantities are given and which quantities are requested.

2. Assign a variable to represent a quantity that is being sought. Then use the
   variable to write expressions for other quantities. A table can be used to organize the information.

3. Write a word equation that describes the problem situation.

4. Write an algebraic equation.

5. Solve the equation.

6. Answer the question asked in the problem.

7. Check the answers to see that they satisfy the original problem.

Example 1   **Solve.**

Carl took part in a 15-mile walk-athon to raise money for a charity. He walked partway at 5 mph and ran the rest of the way at 8 mph. He covered the whole route in 2 hours and 15 minutes. How much time did he spend running and how much time did he spend walking?

Solution   1. ***Read*** *the problem carefully. Note which quantities are given and which quantities are requested.*

Given: total distance, walking rate, running rate, and total time
Asked for: time running and time walking

2. ***Assign*** *a variable to represent one quantity requested.*

Let w = the number of hours walking.

Use the variable to write expressions for other quantities. A table can help to organize the information. Note that distance, rate, and time are related by the formula $d = rt$. Since w represents a number of hours, the time 2 h and 15 min must be represented as a number of hours (2.25 h).

	Rate (in mph)	Time (in hours)	Distance (in miles)
Walking	5	w	$5w$
Running	8	$2.25 - w$	$8(2.25 - w)$

3. ***Write*** *a word equation that describes the problem situation.*

There are two good possibilities:

Time walking + Time running = Total time
Distance walking + Distance running = Total distance

4. ***Write*** *an algebraic equation.*

Substitute algebraic expressions from the table for the words in the first word equation.

$$w + (2.25 - w) = 2.25$$

This equation is true for all real numbers, but it does not help solve the problem. We turn to the second word equation and substitute expressions from the table for the words.

$$5w + 8(2.25 - w) = 15$$

Example 1   (continued)

    5. *Solve* the equation.

$$5w + 8(2.25 - w) = 15$$
$$5w + 18 - 8w = 15$$
$$-3w + 18 = 15$$
$$-3w = -3$$
$$w = 1$$

    6. *Answer* the question asked in the problem.

        Since w = the number of hours walked, and $w = 1$, Carl walked for 1 h.

        Since $2.25 - w$ = the number of hours run, Carl ran for 1.25 h (1 h and 15 min).

    7. *Check* the answers to see that they satisfy the problem.

        If Carl walked for 1 h at 5 mph, he walked 5 mi. If he ran for 1.25 h at 8 mph, he ran 10 mi. The total is 15 mi, so the answer checks.

Example 2   **Solve.**

A print shop has three presses. The fastest press can print twice as many copies per hour as the slowest press. The third press can print 2000 fewer copies per hour than the fastest press. Together the presses can print 19,500 copies in an hour and a half. How many copies per hour can each press print?

Solution   Let n = the number of copies per hour printed by the slowest press.

	Rate (copies per hour)	Time (hours)	Work (copies)
Slowest press	n	1.5	$1.5n$
Fastest press	$2n$	1.5	$1.5(2n)$
Third press	$2n - 2000$	1.5	$1.5(2n - 2000)$

Word equation: $\begin{array}{c}\text{Copies from}\\\text{slow press}\end{array}$ + $\begin{array}{c}\text{Copies from}\\\text{fast press}\end{array}$ + $\begin{array}{c}\text{Copies from}\\\text{third press}\end{array}$ = $\begin{array}{c}\text{Total}\\\text{copies}\end{array}$

Equation:
$$1.5n + 1.5(2n) + 1.5(2n - 2000) = 19{,}500$$
$$1.5n + 3n + 3n - 3000 = 19{,}500$$
$$7.5n - 3000 = 19{,}500$$
$$7.5n = 22{,}500$$
$$n = 3000$$

Answer The slowest press prints n, or 3000 copies per hour.
The fastest press prints $2n$, or 6000 copies per hour.
The third press prints ($2n - 2000$), or 4000 copies per hour.

Check $1.5(3000 + 6000 + 4000) = 1.5(13{,}000) = 19{,}500$ It checks.

Example 3　**Solve.**

Painter A can paint a small auditorium in 6 h. Painter B can paint it in 8 h. If they work together, how long will it take them to paint the auditorium?

Solution　Let x = the number of hours the two painters require to paint the auditorium. Since painter A can paint the entire auditorium in 6 h, the hourly rate is $\frac{1}{6}$ of an auditorium per hour. Painter B's hourly rate is $\frac{1}{8}$ of an auditorium per hour. The amount of work done by a painter is the rate (in auditoriums per hour) times the number of hours worked.

	Rate (auditoriums per hour)	Time (hours)	Work (auditoriums painted)
Painter A	$\frac{1}{6}$	x	$\frac{1}{6}x$
Painter B	$\frac{1}{8}$	x	$\frac{1}{8}x$

Word equation:　Work done by painter A　$+$　Work done by painter B　$=$　Total work done

$$
\begin{aligned}
\textit{Equation:}\qquad \frac{1}{6}x \;+\; \frac{1}{8}x &= 1 \\
4x + 3x &= 24 \\
7x &= 24 \\
x &= \frac{24}{7}
\end{aligned}
$$

Multiply both sides by 24.

Answer　They can paint the auditorium in $\frac{24}{7}$ h (about 3 h and 26 min).

Check　(*By estimation.*) Since a fast painter can paint the auditorium in 6 h, two fast painters can paint it in 3 h. Similarly, two slow painters can paint the auditorium in 4 h. Therefore, one fast and one slow painter can paint the auditorium in between 3 h and 4 h. The answer seems reasonable.

𝓒LASSROOM EXERCISES

Write an equation for each problem and solve.

1. If n is the first of three consecutive integers whose sum is 120, then what are the integers?

2. The first of three gadget machines can produce g gadgets per day. A second machine can produce twice as many gadgets per day as the first. A third machine can produce 100 gadgets more per day than the first machine. If the three machines together can produce 900 gadgets per day, how many can each machine produce in a day?

Make a table and then solve the problem.

3. The cost of a student ticket for a school play is $2, and the cost of an adult ticket is $4. If 250 tickets are sold for a total amount of $800, how many student tickets and how many adult tickets are sold?

 RITTEN EXERCISES

 Write an equation for each problem and solve.

1. The sum of five consecutive integers is 65. What is the largest integer?

2. Find three consecutive odd integers such that the first plus three times the second, minus twice the third, is 44.

3. Two sides of an isosceles triangle are each 5 cm longer than the base. The perimeter of the triangle is 100 cm. What are the lengths of the sides and the base?

4. The second side of a triangle is twice as long as the first side, and the third side is 10 cm longer than the first side. If the perimeter is 70 cm, what are the lengths of the three sides?

5. If Wendy scored 75, 80, and 95 on her first three math tests, what must she score on the fourth test in order to have an average score of 85?

6. Attendance at the first three home football games of Central High School was 1300, 1400, and 1450, respectively. What must the attendance be at the next home game in order for the average attendance to reach 1500 per game?

7. A pump moves $(x + 500)$ gallons of water per hour. Another pump moves 250 fewer gallons of water per hour than the first pump. Together the two pumps can fill a 5500-gallon tank in one hour. How much water can the first pump move in an hour?

8. One machine makes $(2x + 50)$ products per hour and another machine makes 100 more products per hour. If the two machines together can make 850 products per hour, how many does each machine make?

9. Sue paints a room at the rate of $\frac{1}{10}$ room per hour, and Kelly paints the same room at the rate of $\frac{1}{8}$ room per hour. How long will it take them to paint the room together?

10. Neal mows the lawn at the rate of $\frac{1}{2}$ lawn per hour. Jeff mows the same lawn at the rate of $\frac{1}{3}$ lawn per hour. How long will it take them to mow the lawn together?

Make a table and then solve the problem.

11. Walking sometimes and running sometimes, Jill covered a total of 18 kilometers. She walked at a constant rate for 2 hours and ran at twice that rate for $\frac{1}{2}$ hour. What was her walking rate?

12. Erynn walked at a constant rate for 2 h and then bicycled at three times that rate for $\frac{1}{3}$ h. She traveled 12 km in all. What was her walking rate?

13. Busley Smythe drove at 85 km/h from Premley to Quimton and then at 75 km/h from Quimton to Ramsburg. The second part of the trip took 1 h more than the first part. The total trip was 875 km. How many hours did the trip from Premley to Quimton take?

14. Violet Carpenter drove at 80 km/h from Sandyville to Townsend and then at 60 km/h from Townsend to Union Center. The first part of the trip took 2 h more than the second part. The total trip was 860 km. How many hours did the trip from Townsend to Union Center take?

15. The total quota per work shift for two machines is 735 parts. Machine R can produce 50 parts per hour, and machine S can produce 80 parts per hour. Machine S is not available for the first three hours of the shift. How many hours does each machine work in order to produce the parts?

16. Machine A produces 200 parts per hour, and machine B produces 300 parts per hour. Machine B breaks down two hours before the end of a shift during which the two machines produce 2650 parts. How many hours did each machine work?

B Solve.

17. A custodian can set up chairs for a concert in 50 min. His assistant can do the same job in 75 min. How long does it take the custodian and his assistant to do the job together?

18. A military tanker left Stapleton Airport at 2:30 P.M. flying south at 575 mph. An hour and a half later, a bomber left the airport on the same course flying at 800 mph. At what time will the two planes meet for midair refueling?

19. Working by herself, April can distribute a batch of advertising posters in 6 h. Whitney can do the same job in 4 h. Annabeth, fastest of all, can do the job in 3 h. If all three girls work on the same job, how long will it take?

20. A motorboat's speed in calm water is 8 mph. The rate of the river current is 2 mph. The boat takes 4 h to go upstream from the dock to Royal Island and to return to the dock. How far is Royal Island from the dock?

21. It takes David 100 h to complete a given project. Benjamin can complete the same project in 80 h, and Sean can do it in 60 h. The project must be completed in 40 h. David can work on it full-time, but Benjamin cannot join in until after David has worked for 20 h. How many hours must Sean help to ensure that the job is completed on time?

22. Pipe A can fill a tank in 8 h. Pipe B can fill the same tank in 5 h. One hour after pipe A begins filling the tank, pipe B is also used for 2 h. If the tank begins filling at 10:00 A.M., when will it be filled?

23. A swimming pool can be filled in 7 h and drained in 12 h. At 9:00 A.M., the empty pool begins to fill. At 11:00 A.M., the drain is discovered open and is closed. At what time will the pool be filled?

24. Find the point of no return for the situation described in the opening paragraph on page 51.

 **R**EVIEW EXERCISES

1. Write $3.\overline{12}$ as a mixed number.

2. Write $\frac{2}{11}$ as a decimal.

[1–1]

Simplify.

[1–2]

3. $\sqrt{(3 + 4)^2} - \sqrt{3^2 + 4^2}$

4. $\dfrac{\frac{1}{2} - \frac{1}{3}}{\frac{1}{2} + \frac{1}{3}}$

5. $\$1000 + 12\frac{1}{2}\%$ of $\$4000$

Graph on a number line.

[1–3]

6. $\{x: x < 1.5\}$

7. $\{x: x > 2\}$

 **S**elf-Quiz I

2-1 **1.** Solve.
  a. $5(3x - 1) = 8 + 7x$ **b.** $\frac{4}{5}(y - 5) = 8 - y$ **c.** $1.5 + 0.6x = 0.3(2 - x)$

  2. The theoretical power in kilowatts (P) of a stream is given by $P = \dfrac{ch}{708}$, where c is the water volume in cubic feet per minute and h is the head (vertical fall) of water in feet. What vertical fall is needed to produce 2000 kilowatts of power for a stream flowing at a rate of 40,000 cubic feet per minute?

2-2 **3.** Solve for r.
  a. $A = p + prt$

  b. $L = \pi r + 6r$

  Solve.

2-3 **4.** One machine can mix 80 bags of cattle feed per hour. Another machine can mix 80 bags in 50 min. How long will it take to mix 400 bags if both machines are used?

LESSON 2-4

Linear Inequalities in One Variable

Application: Better Buy The junior class is sponsoring a dance and charging $2.00 admission. One band will play for $300 plus 40% of the ticket sales. Another band will play for $550. What minimum attendance would make the second band the better buy? We can decide by solving the following inequality, where A is the number of people attending the dance:

$300 minimum	+	40% of ticket sales	is more than	$550
300	+	0.4(2.00A)	>	550

Techniques for solving linear inequalities in one variable are much like those for solving linear equations. (See Classroom Exercise 5.)

If we begin with a true inequality such as $2 < 5$ and add the same quantity to both sides, the resulting inequalities are also true.

$2 < 5$	**True**	$2 < 5$	**True**
$2 + 4 < 5 + 4$	**True**	$2 + (-6) < 5 + (-6)$	**True**
$6 < 9$	**True**	$-4 < -1$	**True**

This illustrates the **addition property of inequality.**

Addition Property of Inequality

For all real numbers a, b, and c,
$$\text{if } a < b, \text{ then } a + c < b + c,$$
$$\text{and}$$
$$\text{if } a > b, \text{ then } a + c > b + c.$$

Multiplying both sides of a true inequality by a *positive number* also results in ; true inequality.

$2 < 5$	**True**
$2(4) < 5(4)$	**True**

However, multiplying both sides of a true inequality by a *negative number* results in a false inequality.

$$2 < 5 \qquad \textbf{True}$$
$$2(-3) < 5(-3) \qquad \textbf{False}$$

When multiplying by a negative number, we must reverse the **sense** of the inequality. (Greater than ($>$) and less than ($<$) are opposite senses.)

$2 < 5$ $-2 > -5$ **True**

  $\updownarrow$ **reversed** $\updownarrow$ **reversed**

$2(-3) > 5(-3)$ $-2(-1) < -5(-1)$ **True**

    $-6 > -15$ $2 < 5$ **True**

This illustrates the **multiplication property of inequality.**

Multiplication Property of Inequality

For all real numbers a, b, and c, $c > 0$,   if $a < b$, then $ac < bc$,
                                              and
                                     if $a > b$, then $ac > bc$.

For all real numbers a, b, and c, $c < 0$,   if $a < b$, then $ac > bc$,
                                                and
                                     if $a > b$, then $ac < bc$.

Linear inequalities in one variable can have infinitely many solutions. Solution sets may be described in two ways: set-builder notation or graphs.

Example 1   **Solve and graph.** $7(x - 2) < 4x - 8$

Solution $7(x - 2) < 4x - 8$

         Expand. $7x - 14 < 4x - 8$

         Add $-4x$ to both sides. $3x - 14 < -8$

         Add 14 to both sides. $3x < 6$

         Multiply both sides by $\frac{1}{3}$. $x < 2$

Answer $\{x : x < 2\}$

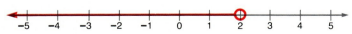

Example 2 **Solve and graph.** $\frac{1}{3}x - 5 > x + 3$

Solution

$$\frac{1}{3}x - 5 > x + 3$$

Multiply both sides by 3. $x - 15 > 3x + 9$

Add 15 to both sides. $x > 3x + 24$

Add $-3x$ to both sides. $-2x > 24$

Multiply both sides by $-\frac{1}{2}$. $x < -12$

Note that in the last step the sense of the inequality was reversed.

Answer $\{x\colon x < -12\}$

Example 3 **Solve and graph.** $x < x + 1$

Solution

$$x < x + 1$$

Add $-x$ to both sides. $0 < 1$

Since the inequality is transformed into a *true* inequality, the original inequality is true for all real numbers.

Answer $\mathscr{R}$ The solution set is the set of real numbers.

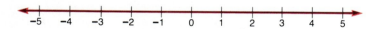

Example 4 **Solve.**

A plumber charges $10 for a home call plus $16 per hour for repair work. He rounds the time worked to the nearest quarter hour. How long did he work if a repair bill was less than $70?

Solution Let t = the number of hours worked. Then $10 + 16t < 70$

$$16t < 60$$
$$t < 3.75$$

Answer The plumber *charged for* fewer than 3.75 hours (3 hours and 45 minutes). Since he rounded the time worked to the nearest 15 minutes, he might have worked up to an additional $7\frac{1}{2}$ minutes. Thus, he *worked* less than 3 hours and 52.5 minutes.

Solve and graph.

1. $3x - 8 < 7$

2. $2x + 6 > 6x - 18$

3. $-5x + 7 < 1.4x - 17$

4. $\dfrac{2x + 5}{3} > 9$

5. Solve the junior-class dance problem given on page 58.

WRITTEN EXERCISES

 Solve and graph.

1. $2x - 3 > 6$

2. $3y - 6 > 3$

3. $4m + 5 < 3m + 7$

4. $2n + 1 < n + 4$

5. $\dfrac{2}{3}a - 1 > 5$

6. $\dfrac{3}{4}b + 2 > 5$

7. $2(r + 3) < 4r - 2$

8. $3(t - 2) < t + 2$

9. $1.2q - 0.4 < 0.8q + 1.6$

10. $1.5c + 3 < c + 5$

11. $\dfrac{3y + 4}{2} > 5$

12. $\dfrac{2w + 3}{4} > 5$

A pplications

Solve each problem using an inequality.

13. Company X pays its sales representatives a straight 10% commission. Company Y pays $60 per week plus 5% commission. For what amounts of sales will company X pay more money?

14. Company P pays its sales representatives a straight 10% commission. Company Q pays $75 per week plus 5% commission. For what amounts of sales will company P pay more money?

15. The Ace Garage assesses a $15 "shop charge" plus $20 per hour for labor. How many hours of labor did a repair take if the total charge was less than $85?

16. The Salty Nut Company charges $4 per pound plus $2 for handling for the nuts it sells by mail. How many pounds of nuts were sold if the total bill was more than $20?

 Solve and graph.

17. $5(x - 3) < 7(x + 6)$

18. $2(y + 7) < 4(y - 1)$

19. $\dfrac{1}{2}T + 1 > \dfrac{1}{5}T + 2$

20. $\dfrac{1}{4}Q + 2 > \dfrac{3}{8}Q + 3$

21. $\dfrac{2}{3}b + \dfrac{3}{4} < \dfrac{4}{5}b + \dfrac{5}{6}$

22. $\dfrac{3}{4}c + \dfrac{2}{3} < \dfrac{5}{6}c + \dfrac{4}{5}$

23. $-2t - 3 > -5t - 12$

24. $-3w - 8 > -6w - 17$

25. $-6(2 - r) < 18$

26. $15 < -3(1 - v)$

27. $\dfrac{9 - 2k}{5} > k - 1$

28. $\dfrac{2 - 3n}{4} > n + 4$

$\mathscr{A}$pplications

C **Use an inequality to solve the problem.**

29. A replacement part for Cara Hansen's automobile costs $22.50. The mechanic charges $25 per hour for making the repair. How many hours could the repair take if the total bill is under $100?

30. Six large packages weigh more than 10 small packages plus 30 pieces. What could a small package weigh if a large package weighs 500 g and a piece weighs 10 g?

31. If $a < b$ and $c < d$, prove that $a(c - d) > b(c - d)$.

32. If $0 < a < b$, prove that $\dfrac{1}{a} > \dfrac{1}{b}$.

33. What is the relationship in Exercise 32 between $\dfrac{1}{a}$ and $\dfrac{1}{b}$ if $a < 0 < b$? If $a < b < 0$?

 # $\mathscr{R}$EVIEW EXERCISES

State the property that corresponds to each sentence.   [1-4, 1-5]

1. $(987 + 126) + 13 = 13 + (987 + 126)$ 2. $45 + (-45) = 0$

3. $(483 \cdot 25) \cdot 4 = 483 \cdot (25 \cdot 4)$ 4. $5x + x = 5x + 1x$

Simplify.   [1-4, 1-5]

5. $2(2a + b) + 3(a + 2b)$ 6. $6(b - 3) - 3(a + 2b)$

7. $2x(3x - 2) - (4x - 5)$

Expand.   [1-5]

8. $(2a - 3b)^2$ 9. $(5x - 3)(2x + 1)$

 # $\mathscr{E}$XTENSION   Statistics Range

Each of these two sets of data has 10 scores and a mean of 20.

   Set 1: 14, 15, 17, 18, 19, 19, 22, 23, 26, 27
   Set 2: 7, 10, 13, 18, 19, 21, 24, 25, 30, 33

However, the scores in set 2 are more scattered than those in set 1. One measure of the dispersion is the **range**. The range of a set of data is the difference between the high and low scores.

1. State the range of each set.

2. Which set has the greater range?

LESSON 2-5

Compound Inequalities

Computer Application: PRINT Statements If you type this command, a computer will print 1.

Command	Display
PRINT 5 < 12	1

The computer printed 1 because the sentence that followed the word PRINT is true. If the sentence had been false, the computer would have printed 0. For example,

Command	Display
PRINT 9 = 3	0

Predict what a computer would print for each of these commands. Then test your predictions.

▶ PRINT 4 = 5   OR   4 < 5   ▶ PRINT 4 = 5   AND   4 < 5

▶ PRINT 4 = 5   OR   (3 > 2   AND   6 = 6)

A compound mathematical sentence states more than one condition. Consider this example:
$$x \leq 2$$
It is a simplified form of the compound sentence:
$$x < 2 \quad \text{or} \quad x = 2$$
A compound sentence linking two conditions with **"or"** is true whenever either condition (or both) is satisfied. The solutions of the above sentence are all real numbers less than 2 and the real number 2. Here is a number-line graph of the set of solutions. In this case, the boundary point is in the set. This fact is shown by the solid circle at 2.

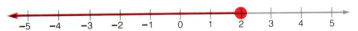

Consider this **compound inequality:**
$$-2 < x < 1$$
It is a simplified form of the compound sentence:
$$-2 < x \quad \text{and} \quad x < 1$$
A compound inequality linking two conditions with **"and"** is true only when both conditions are satisfied. The solutions of the above inequality include all real numbers between -2 and 1. In this example, the boundary points, -2 and 1, are not in the graph. This is shown by the open circles at those points.

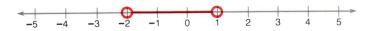

Example 1   **Solve and graph.** $1 \leqslant 2y + 3 < 7$

Solution

$$1 \leqslant 2y + 3 < 7$$
$$1 \leqslant 2y + 3 \quad \text{and} \quad 2y + 3 < 7$$
$$-2 \leqslant 2y \quad\quad\quad \text{and} \quad\quad\quad 2y < 4$$
$$-1 \leqslant y \quad\quad\quad\quad \text{and} \quad\quad\quad\quad y < 2$$

$$\{y : -1 \leqslant y < 2\}$$

Example 2   **Solve and graph.** $6 - 3a < 12$ or $2 - 5a > 12$

Solution

$$6 - 3a < 12 \quad \text{or} \quad 2 - 5a > 12$$
$$-3a < 6 \quad \text{or} \quad -5a > 10$$
$$a > -2 \quad \text{or} \quad a < -2$$

A concise way of writing $a > -2$ or $a < -2$ is $a \neq -2$.

Answer $\{a : a \neq -2\}$

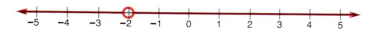

Example 3   **Solve.**

A college graduate is offered similar sales jobs by two companies. One company pays a straight commission of 10%. The other pays $148 per week plus 6% commission. What weekly sales will enable the graduate to earn at least as much from the first company as from the second?

Solution   Let x = the amount of weekly sales in dollars.

Word inequality:	Earnings from 1st company	are at least	earnings from 2nd company
Inequality:	$0.1x$	$\geqslant$	$148 + 0.06x$

$$0.04x \geqslant 148$$
$$x \geqslant 3700$$

Answer   For sales of $3700 or more, the graduate will earn at least as much from the first company as from the second company.

Check   10% of $3700 = $370 $148 + 6% of $3700 = $148 + $222 = $370

Earnings are equal for sales of $3700. For sales greater than $3700, the first company pays 10% commission, whereas the second company pays only 6%. The answer checks.

*C*LASSROOM EXERCISES

Rewrite as two expressions joined by "and" or "or."

1. $2m \geqslant 13$

2. $-2 < 3x < 6$

Rewrite as a single expression.

3. $y < 3$ and $y > 2$

4. $4w < -8$ or $4w = -8$

Graph.

5. $\{y: y \geqslant -1\}$

6. $\{x: -1 < x \leqslant 3\}$

Solve and graph.

7. $-4 < 4 - 2t < 6$

8. $2n - 3 \geqslant 4n + 5$

*W*RITTEN EXERCISES

A   **Write using the symbols $<, >, \leqslant, \geqslant$.**

1. x is less than -2 or equal to -2.

2. r is greater than 6 and less than 10.

3. y is less than $\frac{1}{2}$ or equal to $\frac{1}{2}$.

4. q is greater than $\frac{1}{2}$ and less than $\frac{3}{4}$.

5. a is less than 0 and greater than -5.

6. b is less than 5 and greater than 3.

Graph.

7. $2x < 8$

8. $3x > 9$

9. $-x \leqslant 3$

10. $-x \geqslant 4$

11. $0 \leqslant x - 3$

12. $0 \geqslant x + 2$

13. $0 \geqslant 2x + 3$

14. $0 \geqslant 2x - 5$

15. $1 < x < 3$

16. $-1 < x < 1$

17. $-2 \leqslant x \leqslant 2$

18. $4 \leqslant x < 5$

Solve and graph.

19. $5n + 3 \leqslant 3n + 5$

20. $4b + 2 \leqslant 2b + 6$

21. $0 < w + 2 < 5$

22. $3 < y + 1 < 5$

23. $5 \leqslant 2x + 1 \leqslant 11$

24. $5 \leqslant 3t + 2 \leqslant 14$

25. $6 > -3r > 3$

26. $6 > -2q > 2$

27. $9 < 3(m - 1) \leqslant 15$

28. $-8 \leqslant 2(k + 1) < -4$

29. $1 \geqslant \frac{1}{3}(4a - 1)$

30. $4 \geqslant \frac{1}{3}(5b + 2)$

B   **State a compound inequality for each of the graphs.**

31.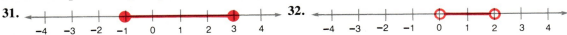

32.

33.

34.

35.

36.

Solve each compound sentence.

37. $5q \leq 9 + 4(2q - 1)$

38. $3(1 - 2t) \geq 7 + 6t$

39. $\frac{2}{3}(b - 1) \geq \frac{1}{4}(2 - b)$

40. $6(1 - 0.2k) \leq 0.4(k + 3)$

41. $6(1 - w) - 3 \leq 3(1 - 2w)$

42. $9(t - 1) \geq 4(3 + 2t) + t$

43. $2x + 5 < 4$ or $3(2 - x) < 6$

44. $\frac{2y}{5} - 1 < 0$ or $1 < \frac{2y + 1}{2}$

45. $8a - 2 \leq 5$ and $6(a - 1) > 18$

46. $2(c + 1) \geq 3(c - 1)$ and $\frac{2c}{5} - 2 \leq 0$

$\mathcal{A}$pplications

Solve.

47. Professor Klinowitz receives two estimates for the repair of his antique car. The first shop will charge $595 for parts plus $22.50 per hour for labor. A second shop offers to repair the car for $700 plus $19.00 per hour for labor. How many hours of labor must be involved in order to make the second estimate the cheaper?

48. Ms. Kranberg was offered two similar sales jobs. The first job paid $1200 per month plus 7% of her sales. The second job paid $1000 per month plus 12% of her amount of sales that exceeded $1500. How much must the sales be per month in order to make the second job pay more?

$\mathcal{C}$omputer Application: Compound Inequalities

The following is a computer program that can be used to solve compound inequalities such as

$$3x - 5 < 7 \quad \text{and} \quad 2x + 4 > 6$$

by repeated trials.

```
10 FOR X = −10 TO 10
20 LET X = 3 * X − 5:   LET Z = 2 * X + 4
30 PRINT X, Y, Z
40 NEXT X
50 END
```

Run the program and answer the questions.

49. How can you tell that all the numbers less than 4 are solutions of $3x - 5 < 7$?

50. What numbers are solutions of $2x + 4 > 6$?

51. What numbers are solutions of the compound inequality?

C **52. a.** Graph: $x < 2$ or $x < 4$.

    b. Write a simple inequality (not compound) that is equivalent to $x < 2$ or $x < 4$.

53. a. Graph: $x < 2$ and $x < 4$.

    b. Write a simple inequality (not compound) that is equivalent to $x < 2$ and $x < 4$.

Graph the following compound inequalities to explore whether the logical operations represented by "and" and "or" are distributive.

54. a. $x > 2$ and $(x < 1$ or $x > 4)$

    b. $(x > 2$ and $x < 1)$ or $(x > 2$ and $x > 4)$

55. a. $x < 4$ or $(x > 2$ and $x < 5)$

    b. $(x < 4$ or $x > 2)$ and $(x < 4$ or $x < 5)$

*R*EVIEW EXERCISES

State the value of x.

1.

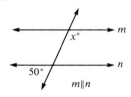

2.

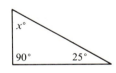

3.

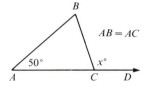

Substitute and simplify.

[1-2]

a	b	c	d
$\frac{1}{2}$	-1.5	2	$-\frac{1}{5}$

4. $a(b + c)$

5. ab^c

6. $(a + d)(a - d)$

7. $\dfrac{a + b}{c + d}$

8. $\dfrac{ab}{cd}$

9. $\dfrac{a + d}{b + c}$

Write Q in terms of n.

[1-6]

10.

n	1	2	3	4
Q	1	4	9	16

11.

n	1	2	3	4
Q	2	4	8	16

12.

n	1	2	3	4
Q	7	10	13	16

LESSON 2-6

Absolute Values in Inequalities

Application: Tolerance Tolerance is a term used to describe the "allowable difference" between the desired size of a product and the actual size that is acceptable. Certain components in the space program must be within a tolerance of 0.0001 in. This means that if the dimension of a part is specified as 5.030 in., then only parts within the range from 5.0299 in. to 5.0301 in. are acceptable.

If m is the actual measurement of the space component described above, then $(m - 5.030)$ is the difference between the actual size and the specified size. The value $(m - 5.030)$ is positive if the part is bigger than the specified size and negative if the part is smaller than the specified size. The tolerance can be expressed in terms of absolute value as

$$|m - 5.030| < 0.0001$$

Graphically, we might think of absolute value in terms of distance on the number line. The **absolute value** of a number x (which is written $|x|$) is the distance from the origin to the point with coordinate x.

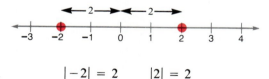

$$|-2| = 2 \qquad |2| = 2$$

A formal definition can be stated as follows:

For each real number a, $\qquad |a| = \begin{cases} a, \text{ if } a \geq 0 \\ -a, \text{ if } a < 0 \end{cases}$

An inequality containing the absolute value of a variable is equivalent to a compound inequality.

Absolute-Value Inequality Properties

For all real numbers a and x, $a > 0$,
$$|x| \leq a \text{ is equivalent to } -a \leq x \leq a;$$
$$|x| \geq a \text{ is equivalent to } x \leq -a \text{ or } x \geq a.$$

Example 1 **Graph.** $|x| < 3$

Solution According to the properties, $|x| < 3$ is equivalent to $-3 < x < 3$.

Answer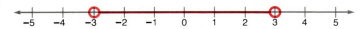

The graph of $|x| < 3$ contains all points that are within 3 units of the origin. In general, for $a > 0$, the graph of $|x| < a$ contains all points within a units of the origin.

Example 2 **Graph.** $|x| > 2$

Solution $|x| > 2$ is equivalent to $x < -2$ or $x > 2$.

Answer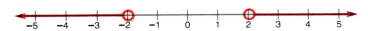

The points of the graph of $|x| > 2$ are more than 2 units from the origin. In general, for $a > 0$, the points of the graph of $|x| > a$ are more than a units from the origin.

Example 3 **Solve and graph.** $|x - 1| \leqslant 3$

Solution
$$|x - 1| \leqslant 3 \qquad\qquad \textit{Absolute-value inequality property}$$
$$-3 \leqslant x - 1 \leqslant 3$$
$$-3 \leqslant x - 1 \quad \text{and} \quad x - 1 \leqslant 3$$
$$-2 \leqslant x \qquad \text{and} \qquad x \leqslant 4$$
$$-2 \leqslant x \leqslant 4$$

Answer $\{x: -2 \leqslant x \leqslant 4\}$

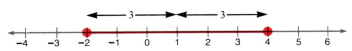

Graphically, $|x - 1|$ represents the distance between the point with coordinate x and the point with coordinate 1. The solutions of the inequality $|x - 1| \leqslant 3$ are numbers whose graphs are within 3 units of the point with coordinate 1. In general, for $a > 0$, the points of the graph of $|x - p| \leqslant a$ are *within* a units of the graph of p.

The graphical interpretation provides another way to determine the graphs of some absolute-value inequalities.

Example 4 **Solve using the graphical interpretation.** $|x - 4| < 2$

Solution Draw a number line and locate the point with coordinate 4.

Locate the boundary points 2 units to either side of 4. Solutions must be between these two points.

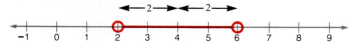

Answer $\{x: 2 < x < 6\}$

𝓒LASSROOM EXERCISES

Solve and graph.

1. $|x| \leqslant 2$

2. $|x| > 1$

3. $|x - 2| > 1$

Solve.

4. $|x + 3| < 2$

5. $|3x - 1| \geqslant 2$

6. $|2x + 3| > 0$

Use absolute value to write an inequality that describes each graph.

7.

8.
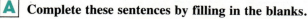

9.

𝐖RITTEN EXERCISES

[A] **Complete these sentences by filling in the blanks.**

1. If $|x| > 2$, then all points in the graph are ___(a)___ than _(b)_ units from _(c)_.
   (more/less)

2. If $|x| < 3$, then all points in the graph are ___(a)___ than _(b)_ units from _(c)_.
   (more/less)

3. If $|x - 2| < 3$, then all points in the graph are ___(a)___ than _(b)_ units from _(c)_.
   (more/less)

4. If $|x - 3| > 2$, then all points in the graph are ___(a)___ than _(b)_ units from _(c)_.
   (more/less)

Write as an absolute-value expression or sentence. Points A, B, and C have coordinates 3, -2, and x, respectively.

5. The distance between A and B.

6. The distance between C and A.

7. The distance between points C and B is less than 2.

8. The distance between points A and C is not less than 3.

Use absolute value to write an inequality that describes each graph.

9.
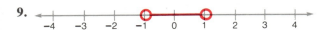

10.

11.

12.

13.

14.

15.

16.

Solve and graph.

17. $|x| = 5$

18. $|2x| = 5$

19. $|x - 3| = 4$

20. $|-x| = 2$

21. $|-x| < 2$

22. $|-x| \geq 1$

23. $|x - 2| > 2$

24. $|x - 1| > 1$

25. $|p - 100| < 3$

26. $|w - 50| < 4$

27. $|3y - 6| < 9$

28. $|3a - 9| < 6$

29. $|2b + 4| > 6$

30. $|2r + 6| > 4$

31. $|4(t + 1)| < 6$

32. $|4(v + 2)| < 10$

33. $|3 - d| < 2$

34. $|2 - q| \geq 1$

35. $\left|\dfrac{x+2}{3}\right| < 4$ **36.** $\left|\dfrac{x-3}{2}\right| > 1$ **37.** $|4x - 5| < -2$ **38.** $|7x - 1| > -3$

39. $\left|\dfrac{2}{3}x - 4\right| \geqslant 6$ **40.** $\left|4 - \dfrac{x}{2}\right| < 1$ **41.** $|x| > x$ **42.** $|x| \leqslant x$

C **43.** $|x - 2| + 2x < 4$ **44.** $|1 - x| + 3x > 7$
45. $1 < |x - 4| < 3$ **46.** $2 \leqslant |x + 1| \leqslant 5$

*R*EVIEW EXERCISES

Write an expression for the *n*th term of each sequence. [1-6]

1. 3, 6, 9, 12, 15, . . . **2.** 100, 110, 120, 130, . . .

3. $\dfrac{1}{2}, \dfrac{2}{4}, \dfrac{3}{8}, \dfrac{4}{16}, \dfrac{5}{32}, \ldots$

4. Write an algebraic expression for this puzzle, letting *n* represent the number. [1-6]
Then simplify the expression.
Think of a number. Multiply the number by 7, then multiply the product by 11, then multiply that product by 13. Then subtract the original number. Finally, divide by 1000, and the result is the original number.

*S*elf-Quiz 2

2-4 **1.** Solve and graph.

 a. $4(x - 0.3) > 0.5x + 5.8$ **b.** $5 - \dfrac{1}{3}y < -\dfrac{1}{4}y + 1$

 2. Use an inequality to solve.

 The Armchair Theater guarantees its major stars a $3000 minimum plus $2 a ticket. If tickets cost $7.50 each, what is the minimum attendance necessary to cover this expense?

2-5 **3.** Solve.

 a. $\dfrac{4n - 5}{12} \geqslant 1$ **b.** $2 \leqslant 4 - 0.5x < 6$

 4. Graph the solution.

 a. $x > 4$ or $x < -1$ **b.** $5 > 2x + 1 > 0$

2-6 **5.** Write $|x + 1| < 3$ as two inequalities.
 6. Solve and graph. $|3y - 2| \geqslant 4$
 7. Write an absolute-value inequality to describe this graph.

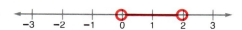

LESSON 2-7

Problem Solving: Using Drawings

Historical Note: *The Earth's Circumference* The ancient Greeks are renowned for both their theoretical and practical contributions to mathematics. Eratosthenes, a contemporary of Archimedes, devised this ingenious method of determining the earth's circumference.

At noon, during the summer solstice, Eratosthenes observed that a vertical rod cast no shadow in the city of Syene (present-day Aswan). In Alexandria, a distance of 5000 stadia directly north, a pillar was observed at the same time to cast a shadow making an angle of $7.2°$ with the vertical (or $\frac{1}{50}$ of $360°$). From this diagram, Eratosthenes concluded that $\frac{1}{50}$ of the earth's circumference intercepted an arc of 5000 stadia, and therefore wrote this proportion.

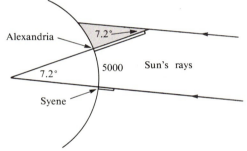

$$\frac{\text{Circumference}}{5000\,\text{stadia}} = \frac{1}{\frac{1}{50}}$$

$$\text{Circumference} = 250,000 \text{ stadia}$$

This measure of the circumference is so accurate that it implies a diameter that is only about 50 miles less than the known polar diameter.

Many problems can be made clearer using a figure. A figure should be as simple as possible. It should be carefully labeled with variable and numerical expressions that show the known relationships.

Example 1   **Solve.**

A farmer has 100 m of fencing to make a rectangular pen with three congruent rectangular subdivisions side by side. Each subdivision must be 3 m wide and at least 8 m long. What is the range of possible lengths of each subdivision?

Solution   Make a drawing. Let $x =$ the length in meters of each subdivision. Then

$$x \geq 8 \quad \text{and} \quad 4x + 6(3) \leq 100$$

Solving the last inequality gives:

$$4x + 18 \leq 100$$
$$4x \leq 82$$
$$x \leq 20.5$$

Thus, $8 \leq x \leq 20.5$

Answer   Each subdivision must be at least 8 m long and at most 20.5 m long.

Problems like Example 1 that ask for a range of values can be solved by using equations instead of inequalities. Equations are written and solved to find the **boundary conditions** (in Example 1, the boundary conditions are the greatest and least values). The question is then answered in terms of the boundary conditions.

Example 2   **Solve.**

A sculptor wishes to cut a steel bar and weld the pieces into a cubical framework with the greatest possible length. The bar is 16 ft (192 in.) long and has a square cross section 1.25 in. on each side. What is the length of the cube?

Solution   A sketch shows that there are 12 pieces to be cut and welded. If the length of the cube is x inches, the four vertical pieces are each x inches long and the 8 horizontal pieces are each $(x - 2(1.25))$ inches long.

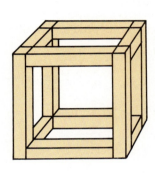
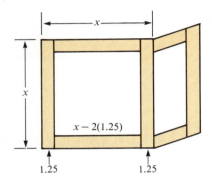

Word inequality: $\dfrac{\text{Vertical}}{\text{lengths}} + \dfrac{\text{Horizontal}}{\text{lengths}} \leq \dfrac{\text{Length}}{\text{of bar}}$

$$4x + 8(x - 2(1.25)) \leq 192$$

Since the problem asks for the greatest possible length (a boundary condition), solve only the equation part of the inequality.

$$4x + 8(x - 2(1.25)) = 192$$
$$4x + 8x - 20 = 192$$
$$12x - 20 = 192$$
$$12x = 212$$
$$x = 17\tfrac{2}{3}$$

Answer   The maximum length for the cube is $17\tfrac{2}{3}$ in.

See Classroom Exercise 2 and Written Exercise 15 for other ways of assembling the cube.

CLASSROOM EXERCISES

Solve.

1. The length of a rectangle is three times the width. The perimeter is at most 80 m. What are the possible lengths of the rectangle?

2. Suppose in Example 2 that the cube is built as shown in this figure. What is the maximum length of the cube?

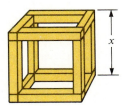

WRITTEN EXERCISES

 Solve by drawing a figure and writing an equation or inequality.

1. An architect's assistant has the task of constructing a wire model of a regular hexagonal prism. The prism's height must be twice the length of an edge of a base. Two 30-in. pieces of wire can be used to make the model. Determine the edge length and the height of the largest prism model that can be constructed.

2. A circle is contained within a square. The total length of the square's perimeter and the circle's circumference is L centimeters. What is the maximum radius of the circle?

3. A wire model is to be made of a pyramid with a square base. The triangular surfaces are congruent. The edges that meet at the top of the pyramid are twice the length of the edges of the base. What is the edge length of the largest model that can be made from 90 cm of wire?

4. The length, width, and height of a right rectangular prism are in the ratio 5:3:2. A wire model of the prism is made from 1 meter of wire. What are the dimensions, in centimeters, of the model?

5. The sides of a pentagon are each a different length. Starting with the shortest side, each successive side is 2 cm longer than the side that precedes it. What is the length of each side if the perimeter is 100 cm?

6. The sides of a quadrilateral are each a different length. Starting with the shortest side, each successive side is 3 cm longer than the preceding side. What is the length of each side if the perimeter is 100 cm?

7. Anne starts walking at 8 km/h. Fifteen minutes later Althea begins jogging along the same route at 12 km/h. How long will it take Althea to catch up to Anne?

8. Harry starts walking home from school at 5 mph. Ten minutes later, Les leaves school, running to catch up with Harry. How fast does Les have to run to catch up to Harry in 15 min?

9. An artist created a wire sculpture from a piece of wire that was 10 ft long ± 0.5 in. It consisted of a circle contained within a square. What was the maximum diameter of the circle?

10. The bases of an isosceles trapezoid are in the ratio 2:3. The nonparallel sides are 3 cm longer than the shorter base. How long (in centimeters) is each side if the perimeter is 1.5 m? [*Hint:* Let $2x$ represent the number of centimeters in the shorter base.]

11. The length of each side of a regular hexagon and the length of each side of a regular octagon are equal. If each side of the hexagon is increased by 3 cm, the two polygons will have the same perimeter. How long is each side of the octagon?

12. A 400-m track is built by placing a semicircular curve on each end of a rectangle. If the length of the rectangle is 1.5 times its width, what is the radius of each curve?

13. Five picture frames must be cut from a piece of molding 84 in. long. If the ratio of width to length of each frame must be 3:4, what are the largest frames that can be made?

14. A manufacturer has 3000 units in stock. Each unit presently sells for $5. Next month, the unit price will be increased by 10%. The manufacturer wants to sell at least $9500 worth over the next two months and at the end of the two months still retain 40% of the units in stock. What is the maximum number of units that can be sold this month?

15. Suppose that in the cube of Example 2, the top and bottom are cut and assembled as shown here. What is the length of the largest cube that can be constructed?

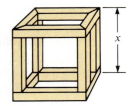

*R*EVIEW EXERCISES

State the value of x.

1.

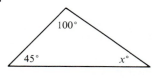

2.

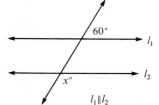

$l_1 \| l_2$

3.

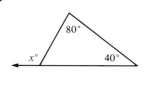

4. Show that the sum of two odd integers is even.   [1-7]

5. Show that a product of two multiples of 7 is also a multiple of 7.

CHAPTER SUMMARY

▶ **Vocabulary**

▶ Addition property of equality [2-1]

For all real numbers a, b, and c,   if $a = b$, then $a + c = b + c$.

▶ Multiplication property of equality [2-1]

For all real numbers a, b, and c,   if $a = b$, then $ac = bc$.

▶ To solve verbal problems: [2-3]

1. Read the problem carefully.

2. Assign a variable to represent a quantity that is being sought. Then use the variable to write expressions for the other quantities. A table can be used to organize the information.

3. Write a word equation.

4. Write an algebraic equation.

5. Solve the equation.

6. Answer the question asked in the problem.

7. Check the answers to see that they satisfy the original problem.

▶ Addition property of inequality [2-4]

For all real numbers a, b, and c,   if $a < b$, then $a + c < b + c$;
and if $a > b$, then $a + c > b + c$.

▶ Multiplication property of inequality [2-4]

For all real numbers a, b, and c, $c > 0$,   if $a < b$, then $ac < bc$;
and if $a > b$, then $ac > bc$.

For all real numbers a, b, and c, $c < 0$,   if $a < b$, then $ac > bc$;
and if $a > b$, then $ac < bc$.

▶ Definition of absolute value [2-6]

For each real number a, $\quad |a| = \begin{cases} a & \text{if } a \geq 0 \\ -a & \text{if } a < 0 \end{cases}$

▶ Absolute-value inequality properties [2-6]

For all real numbers a and x, $a > 0$,

$|x| \leq a$ is equivalent to $-a \leq x \leq a$;

$|x| \geq a$ is equivalent to $x \leq -a$ or $x \geq a$.

CHAPTER REVIEW

2-1   **Objective:**   To solve linear equations.

Solve.

1. $0.3x - 5 = 16$

2. $\dfrac{x + 1}{3} = 2(x - 4)$

3. A car worth $10,000 is depreciated linearly over 5 years. After how many years will it be worth $4000? [Use $V = C\left(1 - \dfrac{t}{n}\right)$, where C is the initial cost of the car that is depreciated over n years, and V is the value after it is depreciated t years.]

2-2   **Objective:**   To solve literal linear equations.

4. Solve for x: $ax - b = c$.

5. Solve for w: $P = 2w + 2l$.

6. The formula for the total surface area of a right circular cylinder is $S = 2\pi\,rh + 2\pi\,r^2$. Solve for h.

2-3   **Objective:**   To write and use equations to solve verbal problems.

Write an equation for this problem. Do not solve.

7. The length of a rectangle is 20 cm greater than the width (w). What are the length and width of the rectangle if the perimeter is 160 cm?

Solve using an equation.

8. Three times a number is 30 more than the number. What is the number?

9. A widget factory worked at half-capacity for two days and then at full-capacity for three days. If 1000 widgets were produced in the five days, what is the factory's daily capacity?

2-4   **Objective:**   To solve and graph linear inequalities.

Solve and graph.

10. $3x - 4 < 8$

11. $\dfrac{2x + 9}{5} > 3$

Solve using an inequality.

12. Jane has $100 in the bank, and she deposits $15 each week. In how many weeks will she have saved enough in her account to pay for a $200 bicycle?

2-5   **Objective:**   To solve and graph compound inequalities.

Solve and graph.

13. $-3 \geqslant x$

14. $3x - 5 \leqslant 5(x + 1)$

15. $12 < 2x + 8 < 18$

2-6 Objective: To solve and graph inequalities that contain absolute values.

16. Use absolute values to write an inequality that describes this graph.

Solve and graph.

17. $|x + 2| < 1$

18. $|2x - 6] > 2$

2-7 Objective: To use drawings to help solve problems.

Make a drawing and solve.

19. The two vertices of the hypotenuse of a right triangle are the endpoints of the diameter of a circle, and the third vertex is a point on the circle. If the diameter of the circle is 10 cm, write an inequality that represents the possibilities for the area of the triangle.

 HAPTER 2 SELF-TEST

2-1 Solve.

1. $3.2(x + 2) = 2(4 - 3.2x)$

2. $\frac{3}{2}w - 5 = \frac{7}{4}$

3. The sum of n consecutive numbers that increase in regular amounts from a beginning value of a to a greatest value z is determined by $S = \frac{n}{2}(a + z)$. Find the beginning value a if the sum of 29 numbers is 348 and the largest number is 199.

2-2 4. Solve for t: $ct + k = m$.

5. Solve for w: $b(aw - 1) = z$.

2-3 Write an equation for the problem and solve.

6. The sum of three consecutive even integers is 204. Find the smallest integer x.

7. If Juanita scored 75, 90, and 82 on her first three math tests, what must she score on her fourth test in order to bring her average (mean) score to 85?

2-4 Solve.

8. $5m - 3 > 2m + 4$

9. $2(1 - y) < 8$

10. $17(x - 4) + 25 < 6(3 + x)$

11. $-\frac{1}{2}t + 5 > \frac{3}{4}t - 7$

2-5 Solve and graph.

12. $3 \geqslant \frac{2k + 1}{5}$

13. $y + 1 < 4$ and $5 - y < 6$

14. $-3 < 2x + 1 < 5$

2-6 **15.** Write an inequality that describes this graph.

Solve and graph.

16. $|w + 3| > \dfrac{1}{2}$ **17.** $|2x - 1| \leqslant 3$

2-7 **Solve.**

18. A window opening is to be cut in the shape of a rectangle surmounted by a semicircle. If the window is to be 40 in. wide, what restriction should there be on the window's height (including the semicircle) so that the opening has an area of no more than $200(12 + \pi)$ in.^{2}?

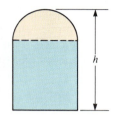

𝒫RACTICE FOR COLLEGE ENTRANCE TESTS

Each question consists of two quantities, one in column A and one in column B. Compare the two quantities and select one of the following answers.

   A if the quantity in column A is greater;
   B if the quantity in column B is greater;
   C if the two quantities are equal;
   D if the relationship cannot be determined from the information given.

Comments:

▶ Letters such as a, b, x, and y are variables that can be replaced by real numbers.
▶ A symbol that appears in both columns in a question stands for the same thing in column A as in column B.
▶ In some questions, information that applies to quantities in both columns is centered above the two columns.

Examples

Column A	Column B	Answers
$5 \cdot 2$	5^2	B
x	y	C
ac	bc	D

	Column A	Column B
1.	2^3	3^2
2.	$a(b + c)$	$ab + ac$
3.	$a = -3, b = -2$	
	$a^2 + b^2$	$(a + b)^2$
4.	Angle *ABC* is a right angle.	

	Column A	Column B
	x	$90 - y$
5.	$y > 10 - x$	
	x	y
6.	$\dfrac{1.25}{100}$	0.125
7.	$x > 10, y > 3$	
	x	y
8.	$(3 + 4)5$	$3 + 4 \cdot 5$
9.		

	Column A	Column B
	$x + y$	$180 - z$
10.	The average (mean) of 20, 30, and 40	The average (mean) of 10, 20, 30, and 40
11.	$0 < x < 1$	
	x	x^2
12.	$rs = 1, rt = 1$	
	s	t
13.	$5x - x$	5
14.	The distance from Allendale to Blue Ridge is 10 mi. The distance from Blue Ridge to Center City is 3 mi.	
	The distance from Allendale to Center City	15 mi
15.	The price of a stereo increased by 10% and then the new price increased by 10%	The price of a stereo increased by 20%

CHAPTER 3

Functions and Graphs

Accurate forecasting of storms
such as tornados, hurricanes,
and blizzards, is vital to industries
such as farming, fishing, and
transportation, and to human
welfare everywhere. One method
of weather forecasting requires
the forecaster to apply his or her
experience with past weather
patterns to present data. Another
method uses mathematics by
applying equations of fluid
dynamics to the present state of
the atmosphere so that future
states can be predicted.

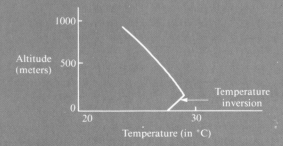

LESSON 3-1

Graphs and Relations

Technology: Robots Industrial robots use one of four coordinate systems in specifying movement of their operation arms: Cartesian, cylindrical, polar, or revolute. The motion ability of a robot is described by the "degree of freedom" that governs its movement—that is, the number of axes it uses or the number of independent types of movement it can make. To completely specify robot motion, *six* coordinates or angles of rotation are needed.

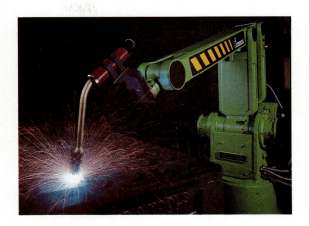

To locate a point on a line, only one number is needed. Each point on the line has a unique real-number **coordinate.** To locate a point on a plane, two numbers are required. One way to assign number pairs to points of the plane is to choose two perpendicular lines as **coordinate axes.** Their point of intersection, the **origin,** is designated (0, 0). By choosing a unit length for each axis and by specifying positive and negative directions, it is possible to assign each point on the plane a unique pair of real numbers.

The two numbers identify the location of a particular point by indicating its horizontal and vertical distances from the axes. Since we agree to indicate the horizontal distance first, the order of the numbers is important. We refer to the numbers as an **ordered pair.** The numbers of the pair are the **coordinates** of the point, and the point is the **graph** of the ordered pair.

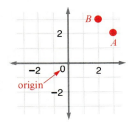

In the figure, the graph of the ordered pair (3, 2) is point *A*. The coordinates of point *B* are (2, 3). Note that (2, 3) and (3, 2) are different ordered pairs. Ordered pairs are equal when they have the same **first components** and the same **second components.**

Definition: Equality of Ordered Pairs

For all real numbers a, b, c, and d, $(a, b) = (c, d)$ if and only if $a = c$ and $b = d$.

We associate the first components of ordered pairs with the horizontal axis, usually designated the *x*-axis; and we associate the second component with the vertical axis, or *y*-axis. The axes divide the plane into four **quadrants** numbered I, II, III, and IV as shown in the figure. The axes are boundaries of the quadrants, but are not part of any quadrant.

Sets of ordered pairs are called **relations.**

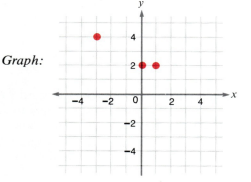

Definition: Relation

A *relation* is a set of ordered pairs.

If a relation consists of a few ordered pairs, it can be described by listing the pairs and by graphing.

List: {(1, 2), (−3, 4), (0, 2)}   *Graph:*

The set of *first components* of the ordered pairs of a relation is called the **domain** of the relation. The set of *second components* is called the **range** of the relation. In this relation, the domain is {−3, 0, 1} and the range is {2, 4}.

More efficient ways are used to describe a relation consisting of many ordered pairs. One way is to describe the relation in words. Another way is to use **set-builder notation.**

Words: The set of all ordered pairs of real numbers, such that the first component equals the second.

Set-builder notation: {(x, y): y = x}   The set-builder notation is read: "The set of ordered pairs *x, y* such that *y* is equal to *x.*"

Unless otherwise stated, we assume that the domain and range of a relation are the set of real numbers $\mathcal{R}$.

We can also graph relations consisting of infinitely many ordered pairs. To draw the graph of an infinite relation, plot enough points of the graph to be sure of its shape, and then complete the pattern.

Example 1   **Graph the relation $\{(x, y): y = x^2\}$, and state its domain and range.**

Solution   Select values for x and substitute into the equation to find the corresponding values of y. Choose positive, negative, and functional values for x.

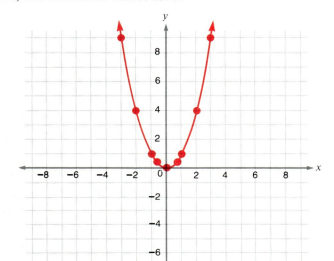

x	y
-3	9
-2	4
-1	1
$-\dfrac{1}{2}$	$\dfrac{1}{4}$
0	0
$\dfrac{1}{4}$	$\dfrac{1}{16}$
1	1
2	4
3	9

Answer   Domain: $\mathcal{R}$
Range: $\{y: y \geq 0\}$

Example 2   **Graph the relation $\{(x, y): y = 2\}$, and state its domain and range.**

Solution   Every ordered pair of this relation has a y-coordinate of 2. No condition is specified for the x-coordinate. Therefore, the set of x-coordinates includes all real numbers.

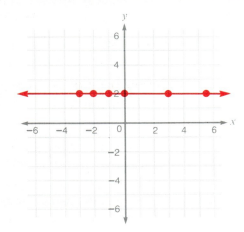

x	y
-3	2
-2	2
-1	2
0	2
3	2
5.5	2

Answer   Domain: $\mathcal{R}$
Range: $\{2\}$

LASSROOM EXERCISES

For each ordered pair, state the letter of the corresponding point on the graph.

1. $(2, -1)$ **2.** $(0, 3)$ **3.** $(-2, -1)$

State the coordinates of each point.

4. A **5.** D **6.** F

In which quadrant or on which axis is each point?

7. A **8.** B **9.** C

10. D **11.** F

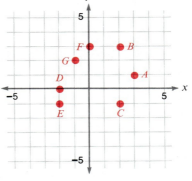

State the domain and range of each relation.

12. $\{(1, 2), (3, 4), (-3, -2), (-3, 0)\}$ **13.** $\{(x, y): y = |x|\}$

Graph each relation and state its domain and range.

14. $\{(2, -5)\}$ **15.** $\{(x, y): y = 3x\}$ **16.** $\{(x, y): x = y^2\}$

RITTEN EXERCISES

A **For each ordered pair, state the letter of the corresponding point on the graph.**

1. $(-2, 0)$ **2.** $(0, -2)$ **3.** $(0, 2)$

4. $(2, 0)$ **5.** $(-4, 1)$ **6.** $(-1, 4)$

State the coordinates of each point.

7. E **8.** G **9.** K

10. L **11.** F **12.** D

In which quadrant or on which axis is each point?

13. A **14.** C **15.** J

16. F **17.** K **18.** E

19. $(0, 100)$ **20.** $(100, 0)$

State the domain and range of each relation.

21. $\{(0, 3), (0, 5), (1, 7)\}$ **22.** $\{(3, 0), (5, 0), (7, 1)\}$

23. $\{(-3, 5), (-2, 5), (-1, 5)\}$ **24.** $\{(-1, -2), (-1, 0), (-1, 2)\}$

The domain for each of the following relations is {0, 1, 2}. State the range of each relation.

25. The set of ordered pairs whose second component is twice the first component.

26. The set of ordered pairs whose second component is half the first component.

27. $\{(x, y): y = 0.1x\}$

28. $\{(x, y): y = 10x\}$

29. $\{(x, y): y = 10 - x\}$

30. $\{(x, y): y = x + 0.1\}$

The domain of the following relations is $\{x: -3 < x < 3\}$. Graph each relation.

31. $\{(x, y): y = 2x + 1\}$

32. $\{(x, y): y = -3x - 2\}$

33. $\{(x, y): y = 1\}$

34. $\{(x, y): y = -2\}$

35. $\{(x, y): y = |x| + 2\}$

36. $\{(x, y): y = |x| - 2\}$

37. $\{(x, y): y = |x + 2|\}$

38. $\{(x, y): y = |x - 2|\}$

B Graph each relation and state its domain and range.

39. $\{(x, y): x = |y|\}$

40. $\{(x, y): x = y^3\}$

41. $\{(x, y): x + y = 0\}$

42. $\{(x, y): xy = 0\}$

43. $\left\{(x, y): \dfrac{x}{y} = 0\right\}$

44. $\{(x, y): x - y = 0\}$

45. $\left\{(x, y): \dfrac{y}{4} + \dfrac{y}{3} = 1\right\}$

46. $\{(x, y): xy = 12\}$

47. $\{(x, y): y = x^2 + 4\}$

48. $\{(x, y): x = y^2 + 4\}$

List the ordered pairs in each relation. Give the domain and range.

49. The first component of an ordered pair is the square of one of the following numbers, and the second component is a square root of the same number.

$$0, 1, 4, 9, 16$$

50. The first component of an ordered pair is the number of sides of one of the following polygons, and the second component is the number of diagonals of the same polygon.

triangle, square, pentagon, hexagon, octagon

51. The first component of an ordered pair is the number of digits in one of the following numbers, and the second component is the number of positive factors of the same number.

$$1, 2, 4, 8, 11, 12$$

C Graph the relation defined by each equation.

52. $|x| = |y|$

53. $|x| + |y| = 4$

54. $|x + y| = 4$

55. $x + y = y + x$

56. $x - y = y - x$

57. $\dfrac{x}{y} = \dfrac{y}{x}$

58. $xy = |xy|$

59. $\dfrac{4}{x} + \dfrac{3}{y} = 1$

Simplify.

1. $3(-2)^2 - 5(-2) + 3$

2. $3(4 - (-3)) - (2 - 8)$

3. $(6 - (-7)) - (-3) + 6 - (-7 - (-3))$

4. $16.34 + 0.07 - 4.1$

5. $3.14 \cdot 100^2$

6. $1000(1.1)^3$

7. Complete the following table for $y = \frac{1}{3}x + 3$.

x	-3	-2	-1	0	1	2	3
y	?	?	?	?	?	?	?

[1-1]

8. Complete the following table for $y = x^2$.

x	-3	-2	-1	0	1	2	3
y	?	?	?	?	?	?	?

$\mathcal{E}$XTENSION   Statistics: Measures of Central Tendency

At the right is the **frequency distribution** for student scores on an algebra test. The frequency 3 for the score 80 means that 3 students scored 80. In order to give a complete description of the results, all scores must be listed. But large masses of data are difficult to comprehend and work with. Therefore, we "summarize" the data in various ways. Commonly used summaries are three **measures of central tendency.** The **mode** is the most common score—in this case, 81. The **median** is the middle (or 13th) score, 83. The **mean** is the sum of the scores divided by the number of scores, 83.64.

Score	Frequency
80	3
81	5
82	4
83	3
84	0
85	3
86	3
87	0
88	2
89	0
90	2
Total 2091	25

For the frequency distribution given below, state the mean, median, and mode. (If a frequency distribution has an even number of scores, the median is midway between the two middle scores.)

Score	30	31	33	34	35	36	38	40	44
Frequency	1	3	3	4	2	6	4	1	2

LESSON 3-2

Functions

When you read a map, a blueprint, or a circuit diagram, you are using mathematics because these are examples of mathematical mappings. A map is any way of relating one set to another set. For example, in a geographical map, each of the infinitely many points on the earth's surface corresponds to just one of the infinitely many points on the map. Similarly, blueprints and circuit diagrams map characteristics of physical objects into a pattern on paper.

A useful way to represent a relation is to show it as an association, or **mapping,** from the elements of the domain to the elements of the range. Let relation P be defined as:

$$P = \{(2, 3), (2, 4), (1, 5), (-1, -2)\}$$

The representation of P as a mapping shows which elements of the domain and the range are paired.

Compare relation P with relation Q defined as: $Q = \{(2, 3), (1, 5), (-1, -2)\}$.

Relation Q has an important property that P does not have. In relation P, 2 is mapped to both 3 and 4. In relation Q, each element of the domain is mapped to only one element of the range. We can identify each ordered pair once the first component is known. In P, the second component is not uniquely determined by the first component. Relation Q is an example of a special kind of relation called a **function.**

Definition: Function

A relation is a *function* if and only if each element of the domain is paired with exactly one element of the range.

Example 1 Is $M = \{(x, y): y = x^2\}$ a function?

Solution Draw a mapping diagram of some of the ordered pairs in M.

Answer Each number in the domain is mapped to just one number in the range. Therefore, M is a function.

Example 2 Is $N = \{(x, y): x = y^2\}$ a function?

Solution Draw a mapping diagram of some ordered pairs in N.

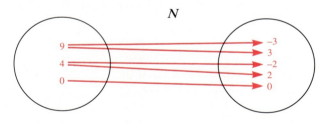

Answer Most numbers in the domain of N are mapped to two numbers in the range. Therefore, N is not a function.

The graphs of relations M and N can also be examined to determine whether the relations are functions.

$M = \{(x, y): y = x^2\}$

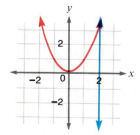

$N = \{(x, y): x = y^2\}$

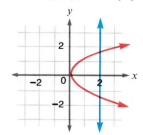

For relation M, any vertical line intersects the graph only once, illustrating that each element of the domain is matched with only one element of the range. There-fore, M is a function. For relation N, some vertical lines intersect the graph in more than one point. Elements of the domain are matched with more than one element of the range. Therefore, N is not a function. This method of determining whether a relationship is a function is called the **vertical-line test.**

Now consider relations R and S.

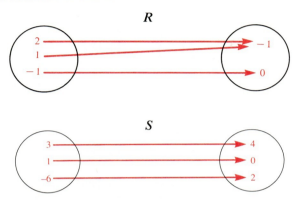

Both are functions since each number of the domain is matched with just one number of the range. Relation R maps both 2 and 1 to the same number, -1. Relation S, on the other hand, does not map more than one number of the domain to any number in the range. Relation S is an example of a **1-1 function** ("one-to-one function"). Relation R is not a 1-1 function.

Definition: 1-1 Function

A function is a *one-to-one function* if and only if each element of the range is paired with exactly one element of the domain.

Example 3 State the domain and range of the relation. Then state whether the relation is a function. If it is a function, state whether it is a 1-1 function.

$$
\begin{array}{ccc}
-2 & \longrightarrow & 3 \\
-1 & \longrightarrow & 0 \\
0 & \longrightarrow & -2 \\
1 & \longrightarrow & 7 \\
2 & \longrightarrow & -6
\end{array}
$$

Solution Domain: $\{-2, -1, 0, 1, 2\}$; Range: $\{-6, -2, 0, 3, 7\}$

Each number of the domain is mapped to just one number of the range, so the relation is a function. Each number of the range is paired to just one number in the domain, so the function is 1-1.

Example 4 State the domain and range of relation $A = \{(x, y): y = |x|\}$. Then state whether A is a function. If it is a function, state whether it is 1-1.

Solution Draw a graph of relation A. The graph passes the vertical-line test. Some numbers of the range are paired with two numbers in the domain. For example.

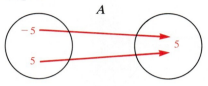

A

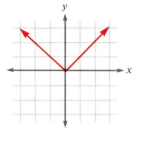

Answer Domain: Set of real numbers, $\mathcal{R}$
Range: Set of nonnegative real numbers, $\{y: y > 0\}$

Relation A is a function but is not a 1-1 function.

All functions must pass the vertical-line test. All 1-1 functions must also pass the **horizontal-line test.** That is, if a function is 1-1, each horizontal line crosses the graph in at most one point.

Not 1-1

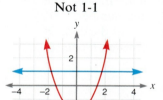

1-1

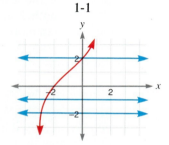

*C*LASSROOM EXERCISES

List the ordered pairs in each relation. State whether the relation is a function.

1.

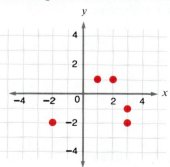

2.

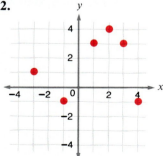

State the domain and the range of each relation. Then state whether the relation is a function. If so, state whether it is a 1-1 function.

3. $\{(0, 0), (4, 2), (4, -2)\}$

4. $\{(0, 0), (2, 4), (-2, 4)\}$

5.
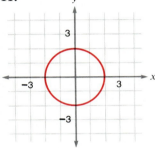

$3 \longrightarrow 7$
$-2 \longrightarrow 8$
$5 \longrightarrow 8$

6.

x	y
-2	5
-1	8
-1	9

7. $\{(x, y): y = 2x + 3\}$

8. $\{(x, y): x = |y|\}$

9. $\{(x, y): xy = 1\}$

10. $\{(x, y): x = 2\}$

11.
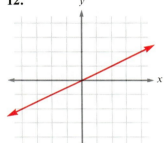

12.

WRITTEN EXERCISES

A List the ordered pairs in each relation. State whether the relation is a function.

1. Domain   Range
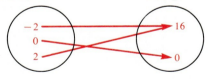

2. Domain   Range
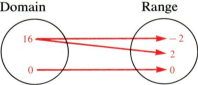

3. Domain   Range
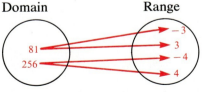

4. Domain   Range
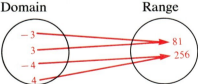

5. $\{(x, y): x$ is an integer $-3 \le x \le 3$ and y is the absolute value of $x.\}$

6. $\{(x, y): x$ is an integer $0 < x \le 4$ and y is a factor of $x.\}$

State the domain and range of each relation. State whether the relation is a function.

7. {(2, 3), (3, 4), (4, 5)}

8. {(3, 2), (4, 3), (5, 4)}

9. {(2, 3), (2, 4), (2, 5)}

10. {(3, 2), (3, 3), (3, 4)}

11.
2 $\longrightarrow$ 4
6 $\longrightarrow$ −5
3 $\longrightarrow$ 0
2 $\longrightarrow$ −1
0 $\longrightarrow$ 3

12.
−7 $\longrightarrow$ 19
−3 $\longrightarrow$ 12
2 $\longrightarrow$ −5
4 $\longrightarrow$ −5
6 $\longrightarrow$ −8

13.
56 $\longrightarrow$ −2
85 $\longrightarrow$ 17
56 $\longrightarrow$ 4
75 $\longrightarrow$ 8
93 $\longrightarrow$ 12

14.
102 $\longrightarrow$ 1
83 $\longrightarrow$ 2
64 $\longrightarrow$ 6
102 $\longrightarrow$ 1
15 $\longrightarrow$ 39

15.

x	y
−6	20
−1	10
4	0
7	−6
50	−92

16.

t	Q
−9	85
−3	13
1	5
6	40
9	85

17.

n	3	2	0	1	−2
S	6	1	3	4	5

18.

x	5	3	2	−1	−2
y	9	5	3	−3	−5

List the ordered pairs in each relation. State the domain and the range. State whether the relation is a function.

19.

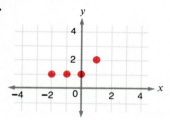

20.

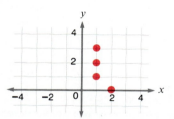

21.

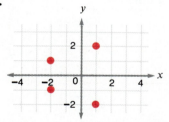

22.

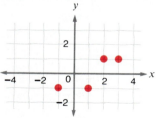

Graph each relation. State whether the relation is a function. If so, state whether it is a 1-1 function.

23. {(x, y): y = 2x + 3}

24. {(x, y): y = 3x + 2}

25. {(x, y): y = 2x − 3}

26. {(x, y): x = 3y − 2}

27. {(x, y): y = $\frac{1}{3}$x + 3}

28. {(x, y): y = $\frac{1}{2}$x + 2}

B **Graph each relation. State the domain and the range of each relation. State whether the relation is a function. If so, state whether it is a 1-1 function.**

29. {(x, y): x = y^3}

30. {(x, y): x = y^4}

31. {(x, y): x = 3}

32. {(x, y): y = 4}

List five number pairs in each relation and state whether the relation is a function.

33. $\{(x, y): x$ is an integer between -3 and 3 and $y = x^2\}$

34. $\{(x, y): x$ is a positive real number less than 3, and y is the greatest integer less than or equal to the number$\}$

35. $\{(x, y): x$ is an integer, $5 \leqslant x \leqslant 9$, and y is the number of factors of $x\}$

36. $\{(x, y): x$ and y are positive integers, $x < 5$, and $y < x\}$

$\mathcal{A}$pplications

Graph each relation and state whether the relation is a function.

37. The width of a rectangle is 2 cm.
$\{(l, A): l$ is the length of the rectangle in centimeters, and A is the area of the rectangle in square centimeters$\}$

38. An employee at the Hammond House is paid $5 per hour.
$\{(h, P): h$ is the number of hours worked, and P is the number of dollars paid$\}$

39. $\{(s, P): s$ is the length of a side of a square in centimeters, and P is the perimeter of the square in centimeters$\}$

40. $\{(s, A): s$ is the length of a side of a square in centimeters, and A is the area of the square in square centimeters$\}$

 41. If $(2, a)$ and $(2, b)$ are elements of a function, what can you conclude about a and b?

42. If $(c, 3)$ and $(d, 3)$ are elements of a function, what can you conclude about c and d?

43. If $(4, p)$ and $(4, q)$ are elements of a 1-1 function, what can you conclude about p and q?

44. If $(r, 5)$ and $(s, 5)$ are elements of a 1-1 function, what can you conclude about r and s?

$\mathcal{R}$EVIEW EXERCISES

Substitute $4\frac{1}{2}$ for a and $1\frac{2}{3}$ for b and simplify. [1-2]

1. $a + b$ **2.** $a - b$ **3.** ab **4.** $\dfrac{a}{b}$ **5.** $a^2 - b^2$

[1-2]

Substitute and simplify.

x_1	y_1	x_2	y_2
-4	5	-2	-1

6. $\dfrac{y_1 - y^2}{x_1 - x_2}$ **7.** $\sqrt{(x_2 - x_1)^2 + (y_2 - y_1)^2}$

Solve each equation for the indicated variable. [2-2]

8. $2x + 3y = 7$, for y **9.** $ax + by = c$, for y

Linear Functions

Equations used to define relations and functions can look very similar. However, the ordered pairs and graphs that satisfy these equations can be quite different. Each of the following equations contains first powers of x and y. Two of the equations represent functions. The graph of one of the equations is a straight line. With experience, you will be able to recognize the shape of a graph from its equation.

$$4|x| + 2|y| = 1 \qquad\qquad 2xy = 4 \qquad\qquad \frac{x}{4} + \frac{y}{2} = 1$$

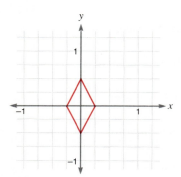 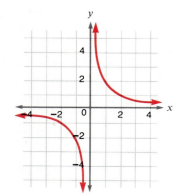 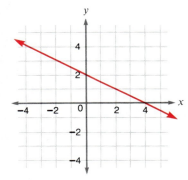

Mathematicians often use concise language and refer to a function only by its equation. Rather than saying, "Graph the function $\{(x, y): y = 3x - 1\}$," they say, "Graph the function $y = 3x - 1$." or "Graph the equation $y = 3x - 1$." We assume that the ordered pairs (x, y) satisfying the equation are to be graphed.

Example 1 **Graph.** $y = 3x - 1$

Solution The graph of the equation
$$y = 3x - 1$$
is the graph of the function
$$\{(x, y): y = 3x - 1\}.$$

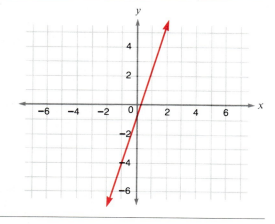

The graph of any equation of the form $y = mx + b$ is a straight line. Such an equation is called a **linear equation in two variables.** A function defined by a linear equation is called a **linear function.** The domain of a linear function is the set of real numbers unless otherwise specified.

Definition: Linear Function

A function is a *linear function* if and only if its equation can be written in the form

$$y = mx + b$$

If $m = 0$, $y = mx + b$ simplifies to $y = b$. If the equation of a function can be written in the form $y = b$, the function is called a **constant linear function.** Its graph is a horizontal line.

Example 2   Is $2x + 3y = 7$ a linear function?

Solution   Solve the equation for y. $2x + 3y = 7$
$$3y = 2x + 7$$
$$y = -\frac{2}{3}x + \frac{7}{3}$$

Answer   The equation can be written in the form $y = mx + b$ where $m = -\frac{2}{3}$ and $b = \frac{7}{3}$. Therefore, $2x + 3y = 7$ is a linear function.

Example 3   Is the function $x^2 - y + 1 = 0$ a linear function?

Solution   Solve the equation for y. $x^2 - y + 1 = 0$
$$y = x^2 + 1$$

Answer   The function is not a linear function since the equation cannot be written in the form $y = mx + b$.

Below are the graphs of two linear functions.

$$y = 3x + 2 \qquad\qquad\qquad y = 0.5x + 2$$

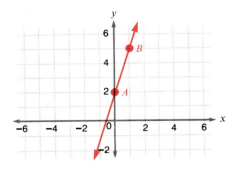
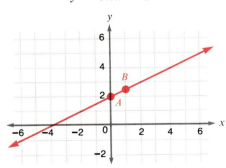

In both graphs, the lines cross the y-axis at the point (0, 2). The y-coordinate of that point is called the **y-intercept** of the graph. In both graphs, the y-intercept is 2.

Definition: *y*-Intercept

The *y-intercept* of a function is the *y*-coordinate of the point at which the graph crosses the *y*-axis. If the equation of a linear function is in the form $y = mx + b$, then b is the *y*-intercept.

Consider moving from point A to point B on each graph above; the x-coordinate changes by 1. On the first graph, the y-coordinate changes by 3. On the second graph, the y-coordinate changes by only 0.5. The change in y, relative to the change in x, is greater for the first graph than for the second. The ratio is a measure of the "steepness" of the lines.

The ratio of the change in y (written Δy and read "**delta y**") to the change in x (written Δx and read "**delta x**") is called the **slope** of the line.

Definition: Slope of a Line

If $x_1 \neq x_2$, the *slope* of the line through the points (x_1, y_1) and (x_2, y_2) is the ratio

$$\frac{\Delta y}{\Delta x} = \frac{y_2 - y_1}{x_2 - x_1} = \frac{y_1 - y_2}{x_1 - x_2}$$

If the equation of a linear function is in the form $y = mx + b$, m is the slope of the function.

Example 4 State the slope of the straight line that contains the points $(1, -1)$ and $(4, 5)$.

Solution *Substitute the coordinates of the two points into the slope formula.*

$$\frac{\Delta y}{\Delta x} = \frac{y_2 - y_1}{x_2 - x_1} = \frac{5 - (-1)}{4 - 1} = \frac{6}{3} = 2$$

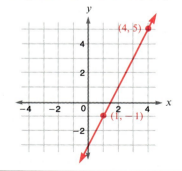

Answer The slope is 2.

Since the slope and y-intercept appear in the equation $y = mx + b$, that form is called the **slope-intercept form** of the equation of a linear function.

Definition: Slope-Intercept Form

The form $y = mx + b$ is called the *slope-intercept form* of a linear equation in two variables. The slope is m, and the y-intercept is b.

Example 5 State the slope and y-intercept of the line $2x + y + 1 = 0$.

Solution *Write the equation in slope-intercept form.*

$2x + y + 1 = 0$

$$y = -2x + (-1)$$

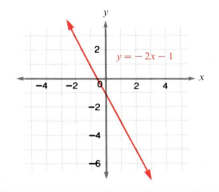

Answer The slope is -2, and the y-intercept is -1.

Compare the graphs in Examples 4 and 5. The graphs "slant" in opposite directions. In Example 4, the slope is positive: As x increases, so does y. In Example 5, the slope is negative: As x increases, y decreases.

Example 6 State the slope of each line.   **a.** $y = 2$ **b.** $x = 2$

Solution   **a.** $y = 2$ **b.** $x = 2$

$(x_1, y_1) = (1, 2)$ $(x_1, y_1) = (2, 2)$
$(x_2, y_2) = (4, 2)$ $(x_2, y_2) = (2, 5)$

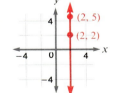

$\dfrac{\Delta y}{\Delta x} = \dfrac{2 - 2}{4 - 1} = \dfrac{0}{3} = 0$ $\dfrac{\Delta y}{\Delta x} = \dfrac{5 - 2}{2 - 2} = \dfrac{3}{0}$ undefined

Answer The horizontal line (a constant linear function) has a slope of 0. The vertical line (not a function) has no slope.

ℓLASSROOM EXERCISES

State whether the graph is the graph of a linear function.

1.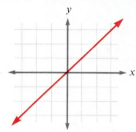

2.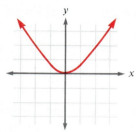

Graph each equation and state whether it defines a linear function.

3. $y = x + 3$

4. $x = -1$ (Consider this as an equation in two variables: $0y + x = -1$)

Transform each equation into the form $y = mx + b$. State the values of m and b.

5. $y = x - 5$ 1;

6. $2y + 2x = 6$

7. $5x - 2y + 6 = 0$

Compute $\dfrac{\Delta y}{\Delta x}$ for the two given points.

8. $(2, 4), (5, -2)$

9. $(-1, -3), (3, 4)$

State the slope and y-intercept of each line.

10. $y = 2x - 5$

11. $x + y = 3$

12. $y = x + 1$

13. $y = 0$

𝒲RITTEN EXERCISES

 State whether the graph is the graph of a linear function.

1.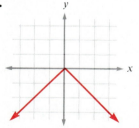

2.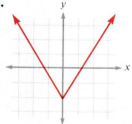

3.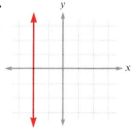

4.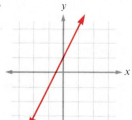

5.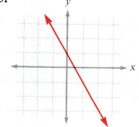

6.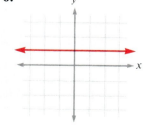

State whether the equation is a linear function.

7. $2x + 3y = 18$ **8.** $3y - 4x = 24$ **9.** $y = -2.5$

10. $y = 1.75$ **11.** $x = 6$ **12.** $x = -4$

13. $y = x^2 + 2x + 1$ **14.** $y = x^2 + 3x + 4$ **15.** $y = -\dfrac{4}{x}$

16. $y = \dfrac{6}{x}$ **17.** $x^2 = y^2$ **18.** $y^2 = 4x \cdot 2$

State the slope and y-intercept of each linear function.

19. $y = 3(x - 2)$ **20.** $y = 2(x - 3)$ **21.** $y = 7$

22. $y = -10$ **23.** $5x + 10y - 20 = 0$ **24.** $10x - 5y - 20 = 0$

25. $4x - 3y = 12$ **26.** $3x + 2y = 5$ **27.** $2(x - y) = 3(x + y)$

28. $6(x + y) = 3(x - y)$ **29.** $2(x + y) = 5(y + 1)$ **30.** $4(y - 2) = 7(x + 1)$

B **State whether the equation is a linear equation.**

31. $|y| = |-x|$ **32.** $y + x^2 = x^2 + 3x$

33. $x(y + 3) = y(x + 6)$ **34.** $2(-x) = 2(y - 4)$

35. $3(y + 1) - 2(x + 2)(x - 3) = 2x(4 - x)$ **36.** $5|x| - 4|y| = 20$

37. $5(y - 2) + (x + 1)(x + 2) = 5(2 - y) + (x + 3)(x + 4)$

Find the slope and y-intercept of each line.

38. $(x + 2)(x + 3) = (x - 2)(x - 3) + y$ **39.** $x(y + 3) + 4 = y(x + 2) + 7$

40. $x = my + b$ **41.** $y - y_0 = m(x - x_0)$
$\qquad\qquad\qquad\qquad\qquad$ (x_0 and y_0 are constants)

42. Suppose that $A(1, 2)$, $B(-1, -4)$, and $C(3, 8)$ are three points on a straight line. Show that the choice of the two points to use in the computation of the slope of the line does not affect the value of the slope.

43. Consider the function $\{(x, y): y = x^2\}$.

a. Complete this table of solutions.

x	0	2	4	6
y	?	?	?	?

b. Show that the slope changes depending on the ordered pairs selected.

The ordered pairs in each table belong to a linear function. Complete each table.

44.

x	-2	-1	0	?	1
y	-2	1	4	9	?

45.

x	1	4	10	?	7
y	5	2	-4	$\dfrac{3}{2}$	?

C State whether the pairs in each set are related by a linear equation.

46. $2 \rightarrow 2$
$6 \rightarrow 4$
$12 \rightarrow 7$

47. $0 \rightarrow 1$
$8 \rightarrow 3$
$15 \rightarrow 4$

48.

x	y
-1	3
2	6
0	2

49.

x	y
3	-2
9	2
-6	-8

Graph each equation. Write the two linear equations that describe the parts of the graph.

50. $y = |x + 2|$ **51.** $|y| = x + 2$

52. a. Show that the choice of an ordered pair to use as (x_1, y_1) does not affect the slope of the line through $(2, 3)$ and $(-3, 5)$.

b. Show that $\dfrac{y_2 - y_1}{x_2 - x_1} = \dfrac{y_1 - y_2}{x_1 - x_2}$.

53. Show that the slope of a line is independent of the selection of points (x_1, y_1) and (x_2, y_2) that are on the line. [*Hint:* Remember that if x_1 is a first component of an ordered pair that satisfies the equation $y = mx + b$, then the second component is $mx_1 + b$.]

54. A linear function has a slope of a and a y-intercept of b. What are two ordered pairs of the function?

55. A linear function has a slope of a and contains the point (p, q). What is the y-intercept of the function?

56. State another ordered pair of the function described in Exercise 55.

EVIEW EXERCISES

1. Is $0.\overline{123456789}$ a rational number? **2.** Is the number $1 + \sqrt{2}$ rational? [1-1]

3. Write $0.\overline{17}$ as a fraction.

Substitute $-\dfrac{1}{2}$ for x in the following expressions and simplify. [1-2]

4. $3x^2 + 5x + 12$ **5.** $\dfrac{x + 4}{x - 4}$

Substitute and simplify. [1-2]

a	b	c
-3	-4	5

6. $(a^2 + b^2) - (a + b)^2$ **7.** $(c^2 - a^2) - (c - a)^2$

8. $(c^2 - b^2) - (c - b)(c + b)$ **9.** $ab^2 - (ca)^2$

10. Write an expression for the average of -25, a, -10, 5, and b.

*S*elf-Quiz 1

3-1 **1.** List the domain and range of the relation.

$$A = \left\{ (0, -1), \left(4, \frac{1}{2}\right), (\pi, 10), \left(-0.1, \sqrt{2}\right) \right\}$$

Graph these relations for the domain $\{x: -4 \leqslant x \leqslant 4\}$.

2. $\{(x, y): x = 3 - y\}$ **3.** $\{(x, y): y = 2\,|x - 1|\}$

3-2 **Indicate whether the relation is a function. Then state the domain and range.**

4. $R = \left\{ (3, 4), \left(-2, \frac{1}{4}\right), (0, 4), \left(-\frac{1}{2}, 0\right) \right\}$

5. $S = \{(x, y): y^2 + 1 = x\}$

6.

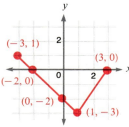

7.

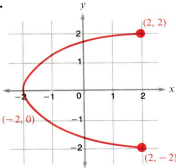

3-3 **State the slope and y-intercept of the line with the given equation.**

8. $3x - 2y = 12$ **9.** $2y + 1 = 0$ **10.** $5(x - y) = x + 10$

---

*E*XTENSION   Statistics: The Mean

Of the three measures of central tendency (mean, median, and mode) the mean has the greatest theoretical importance. One reason is that the mean is more easily described and operated on as a mathematical expression than either the median or the mode. If $a_1, a_2, a_3, \ldots, a_n$ are n scores, then the mean M is given by this formula

$$M = \frac{a_1 + a_2 + a_3 + \cdots + a_n}{n}$$

1. Suppose that 10 points are added to each score in a distribution. How is the mean affected?

2. Suppose each score of a distribution is doubled. How is the mean affected?

Equations of Lines

Consider the square $ABCD$.

1. The slopes of the parallel sides $\overline{AB}$ and $\overline{CD}$ are both $-\frac{1}{2}$. The slopes of the parallel sides $\overline{BC}$ and $\overline{DA}$ are both 2.

2. The slopes of the perpendicular sides $\overline{AB}$ and $\overline{BC}$ are $-\frac{1}{2}$ and 2. In fact, the slopes of any pair of perpendicular sides are $-\frac{1}{2}$ and 2. In each case, their product is -1.

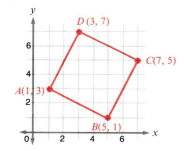

Recall these facts from geometry.

► Given a line and a point, there is one and only one line through the point parallel to the line.

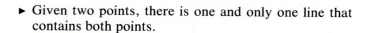

► Given a line and a point, there is one and only one line through the point perpendicular to the line.

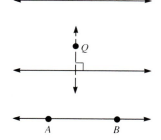

► Given two points, there is one and only one line that contains both points.

In each case, we can write the equation of the unique line satisfying the given condition. In doing so, we make use of two facts illustrated above. Lines that are **parallel** have equal slopes. Lines that are **perpendicular** have slopes that are negative reciprocals.

Definitions: Parallel and Perpendicular Lines

Two lines are *parallel* if and only if they have the same slopes or they both have undefined slopes.

Two lines are *perpendicular* if and only if their slopes are negative reciprocals (that is, the product of their slopes is -1) or one slope is 0 and the other is undefined.

Equal slopes—parallel lines

$y = 2x + 3$
$y = 2x - 1$

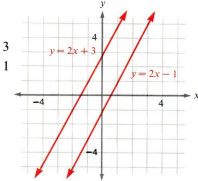

Negative reciprocal slopes—perpendicular lines

$y = \dfrac{3}{4}x - 1$

$y = -\dfrac{4}{3}x + 2$

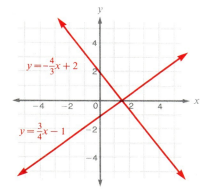

Example 1   Write an equation of the line parallel to $y = 3x - 1$ and passing through the point $(2, -5)$.

Solution   The slope of the given line is 3. Therefore, the slope of a parallel line is also 3. The slope-intercept equation of a line with slope 3 is

$$y = 3x + b$$

The coordinates of the point $(2, -5)$ must satisfy the equation

$$-5 = 3(2) + b$$
$$b = -11$$

Answer   The required line is $y = 3x - 11$.

Example 2   Write an equation of the line through $(-4, 3)$ that is perpendicular to the line $2x - y + 3 = 0$.

Solution   Write the equation of the given line in slope-intercept form.

$$2x - y + 3 = 0$$
$$y = 2x + 3$$

The slope of the given line is 2. Therefore, the slope of any perpendicular line is $-\dfrac{1}{2}$. The slope-intercept equation of a line with slope $-\dfrac{1}{2}$ is

$$y = -\frac{1}{2}x + b$$

The coordinates of the point $(-4, 3)$ must satisfy the equation.

$$3 = -\frac{1}{2}(-4) + b$$

$$b = 1$$

Answer   The required line is $y = -\dfrac{1}{2}x + 1$

In both Examples 1 and 2, the basic task was to write an equation of a line with a given slope through a given point. Since this is a frequent task, it is helpful to have a **point-slope form** of the equation of a line.

Suppose that we wish to write the equation of the line with slope m and passing through point (x_1, y_1). The slope-intercept form of the equation is

$$y = mx + b$$

The coordinates (x_1, y_1) satisfy the equation. So:

$$y_1 = mx_1 + b$$

and

$$b = y_1 - mx_1$$

Substituting this value of b in the first equation gives:

$$y = mx + (y_1 - mx_1)$$

or

$$y - y_1 = m(x - x_1)$$

Definition: Point-Slope Form

The *point-slope form* of a linear equation of the line with slope m and passing through the point (x_1, y_1) is

$$y - y_1 = m(x - x_1)$$

Example 3 shows how to write the equation of the unique line that passes through two given points.

Example 3 Write the slope-intercept equation of the line that passes through $(2, 5)$ and $(-1, 3)$.

Solution First, find the slope m.

$$\frac{\Delta y}{\Delta x} = \frac{y_2 - y_1}{x_2 - x_1} = \frac{3 - 5}{-1 - 2} = \frac{2}{3}$$

Next, substitute in the point-slope equation of a line.

$$y - y_1 = m(x - x_1)$$

$$y - 5 = \frac{2}{3}(x - 2)$$

$$y - 5 = \frac{2}{3}x - \frac{4}{3}$$

Answer
$$y = \frac{2}{3}x + \frac{11}{3}$$

Note that substituting $(-1, 3)$ into the point-slope equation of Example 3 leads to the same answer.

$$y - y_2 = m(x - x_2)$$

$$y - 3 = \frac{2}{3}(x - (-1))$$

$$y = \frac{2}{3}x + \frac{11}{3}$$

LASSROOM EXERCISES

State whether the two lines are parallel, perpendicular, or neither.

1. $y = x - 3$
$y = x + \frac{1}{3}$

2. $y = -\frac{2}{3}x + 4$
$y = \frac{3}{2}x + 4$

3. $y = 4$
$x = 4$

4. $y = x + 2$
$y = 2 - x$

5. $y = 2x - 3$
$y = 3 - 3x$

6. $5x + 6y = 12$
$6x - 5y = 5$

7. Write the slope-intercept equation of the line through the origin that is parallel to the line $y = -\frac{1}{2}x + 7$.

8. Write the slope-intercept equation of the line perpendicular to the line $y = \frac{2}{3}x + 4$ that passes through the origin.

9. Write the point-slope equation of the line with slope $-\frac{1}{4}$ that contains the point $(3, -1)$.

10. Write an equation of the line through the points $(3, 6)$ and $(-4, 5)$.

*W*RITTEN EXERCISES

A Write an equation of the line through the origin that is parallel to the given line.

1. $y = \frac{x}{2} + 6$

2. $y = \frac{x}{3} + 5$

3. $2y - 4x = 15$

4. $3y - 12x = 7$

Write an equation of the line through the origin that is perpendicular to the given line.

5. $y = \frac{x}{2} + 6$

6. $y = \frac{x}{3} + 5$

7. $2x + 3y = -18$

8. $4x - 5y = 10$

Write the equation of the line through $(4, 6)$ that is parallel to the given line.

9. $y = \frac{3}{2}x + 3$

10. $y = \frac{3}{4}x + 10$

11. $y = -\frac{3}{4}x + 5$

12. $y = -\frac{1}{2}x + 10$

Write the equation of the line through $(4, 6)$ that is perpendicular to the given line.

13. $y = \frac{2}{3}x - 7$

14. $y = -\frac{2}{3}x + 50$

15. $y = -\frac{3}{2}x + 20$

16. $y = \frac{3}{2}x - 8$

Write the slope-intercept equation of the line that contains the given points.

17. $(3, 2), (-1, 10)$

18. $(-5, 11), (3, -13)$

19. $(12, 3), (-6, -9)$

20. $(6, 10), (-3, -2)$

21. $(7, 3), (-2, 3)$

22. $(-3, 6), (-3, -1)$

23. Show that line AB is perpendicular to line CD.

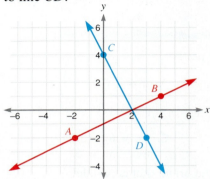

24. Show that line MN is parallel to line ST.

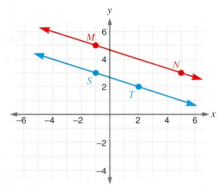

25. Show that line EF is parallel to line GH.

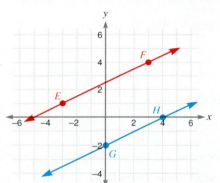

26. Show that line PQ is perpendicular to line UV.

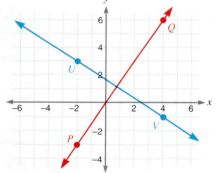

Write the slope-intercept equation that satisfies the given conditions.

27. Slope: $-\dfrac{3}{4}$, intercept: -1

28. Slope: 2, intercept: 4

29. Passes through $(3, 1)$ and $(0, 5)$

30. Passes through $(-2, 5)$ and $(4, 0)$

31. Parallel to $2y + 3x = 6$ and contains $(5, 1)$

32. Parallel to $3y + 8 = 2x$ and contains $(-1, -4)$

33. Perpendicular to $5 - x - 3y = 0$ and contains $(-2, 3)$

34. Perpendicular to $4x - y + 6 = 0$ and contains $(0, 1)$

35. Contains $(0, 0)$ and $(3, -4)$

36. Contains $(0, -3)$ and $\left(\dfrac{2}{3}, \dfrac{1}{2}\right)$

37. Perpendicular to $y = -5$ and contains $(4, -2)$

38. Perpendicular to $x = 3$ and contains $(-3, -4)$

The three points are vertices of a triangle. State whether the triangle is a right triangle.

39. $(1, 2), (0, -3), (-2, -1)$ **40.** $(2, 7), (-2, -1), (6, 5)$

41. Recall that the diagonals of a rhombus are perpendicular. Show that the points $(-2, 1), (3, 3), (5, 0)$, and $(-1, -2)$ are not the vertices of a rhombus.

Three points are *collinear* if they lie on the same line. If two lines share a common point and their slopes are equal, the lines are *coincident* (that is, they are the same line). Find the slopes of lines *AB* and *BC*, and state whether *A*, *B*, and *C* are collinear.

42. $A(-3, -3), B(2, 1), C(5, 4)$ **43.** $A(-3, -4), B(1, -1), C(5, 2)$

44. $A(-3, 5), B(-1, 1), C(2, 5)$ **45.** $A(3, 13), B(0, -8), C(-1, -15)$

Graph the following sets of data. State whether the pairs belong to a linear relationship. If so, write an equation that relates the data.

46.

x	4	6	-2	8
y	-1	4	-4	11

47.

S	-6	0	3	12
R	1	5	7	13

48.

t	v
0	0
2	-2
4	-8
7	$-\dfrac{49}{2}$

49.

K	C
283	10
275	2
269	-4
264	-9

C	F
0	32
40	104
100	212

Line *DE* is perpendicular to line *EF*. Find the value of k.

51. $D(1, -1); E(3, 1); F(2, k)$ **52.** $D(2, 2); E(1, 0); F(-5, k)$

53. $D(-3, -1); E(3, 3); F(k, 6)$

In the following equations, k is a constant called a *parameter*. A family of related lines occurs for different values of k. On the same set of axes, sketch graphs for each equation for these values of k: $\left\{-2, 0, \dfrac{4}{3}, 5\right\}$.

54. $y = kx + 4$ **55.** $3x - y = k$ **56.** $y - 3 = k(x + 2)$ **57.** $\dfrac{x}{k} + \dfrac{y}{4} = 1$

58. Show that a line whose equation is in the form $\dfrac{x}{a} + \dfrac{y}{b} = 1$ has:

     a. x-intercept a.   **b.** y-intercept b.   **c.** slope $-\dfrac{b}{a}$.

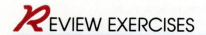
REVIEW EXERCISES

Graph on the number line.   [1-3]

1. $\{x: x > -2\}$

2. $\left\{x: -2 \leq x < \dfrac{1}{2}\right\}$

3. Describe the set of numbers shown on the graph using set-builder notation.

State the property of real numbers illustrated by each equation.

4. $3x + x = 3x + 1x$

5. $3x + 1x = (3 + 1)x$ [1-4, 1-5]

Simplify.

6. $3(x - 2) - (4 - x)$

7. $(3x^2 - 4x + 2) - (x^2 - 2x - 5)$ [1-4]

Expand and simplify.   [1-5]

8. $(2x + 3)(3x - 5)$

9. $(x - 9y)(x + 9y)$

EXTENSION   Statistics: A Histogram

In the study of statistics, the graph of a frequency distribution is called a **histogram.**

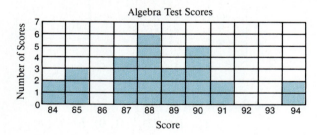

Use the histogram to answer these questions.

1. What is the mode (most common score)?

2. What is the median (middle score)?

3. What is the mean (arithmetic average)?

4. Graph the following frequency distribution. Then state its mode, median, and mean.

Score	10	13	15	18	20	23
Frequency	1	2	1	2	3	1

LESSON 3-5

Direct Variation

If an object travels at a constant speed of 60 km/h, the relationship between the time (t) in hours and the distance traveled (d) in kilometers is given by this formula:

$$d = 60t$$

Here is a table of values for the formula.

Time (h)	0	1	2	3	4	5
Distance (km)	0	60	120	180	240	300

Examination of the graph reveals an interesting relationship. When time is doubled, distance is also doubled. When time is tripled, distance is also tripled. This behavior is an example of **direct variation.**

Definition: Direct Variation

Two variables x and y are said to *vary directly* if and only if there is a **constant of variation** (or **constant of proportionality**) k, $k \neq 0$, such that $y = kx$.

If $x \neq 0$, $\dfrac{y}{x} = k$.

Example 1   **If y varies directly as x and $y = 5$ when $x = 4$, what is the value of x when $y = 12$?**

Solution   Since y varies directly as x, there is a constant k such that $y = kx$ or $\dfrac{y}{x} = k$.

Problems about direct variation can be solved in two ways.

Method 1. Find the value of k. Since $y = 5$ when $x = 4$,

$$5 = k \cdot 4$$

$$\frac{5}{4} = k$$

Use $k = \dfrac{5}{4}$ to solve for x when $y = 12$.

$$12 = \frac{5}{4}x$$

$$9.6 = x$$

Example 1   (continued)

Method 2. Since $k = \frac{5}{4} = \frac{12}{x}$, solve the proportion.

$$\frac{5}{4} = \frac{12}{x}$$
$$5x = 48$$
$$x = 9.6$$

Answer   When $y = 12$, $x = 9.6$.

A direct variation is a linear function with y-intercept equal to 0.

Example 2   **A worker earns \$7 per hour plus time and a half for overtime (hours worked in excess of 40 h per week). Do the worker's earnings vary directly as the time worked?**

Solution   Let t = the number of hours worked and e = the number of dollars earned. If the worker works 40 h or less in a week, then this equation relates t and e:

$$e = 7t$$

For $t \le 40$, e varies directly as t. Consider what happens if the worker works more than 40 hours per week. "Time and a half" overtime pay means that each hour in excess of 40 hours counts as $1\frac{1}{2}$ hours. Equivalently, the pay for each hour of overtime is $1\frac{1}{2}$ the base rate of \$7. Using the latter interpretation, the overtime pay rate is \$10.50 per hour. An equation that relates t to e for $t \ge 40$ is:

Earnings = Regular pay + Overtime pay

$$e \quad = \quad 7(40) \quad + 10.5(t - 40)$$
$$= 10.5t - 140$$

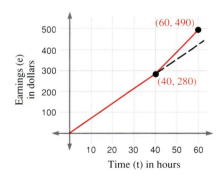

Answer   This equation is linear but is not a direct variation.

Note that the earnings for 25 h of work is \$175, whereas the earnings for 50 h (2 times as many hours) is \$385. The time is doubled, but the earnings are more than doubled. In this case, time and earnings do not vary directly.

The area and the radius of a circle are related by this formula: $A = \pi r^2$

The form of the equation $A = \pi r^2$ and the graph of ordered pairs (r, A) show that the function defined by the formula is not linear. The area does not vary directly as the radius.

r	$A = \pi r^2$
0	0
1	3.14
2	12.56
3	28.26

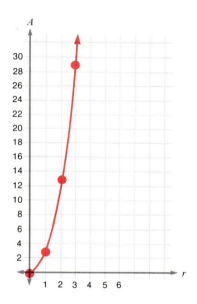

However, the area does vary directly as the square of the radius. This is easily seen if s is substituted for r^2 and the ordered pairs (s, A) are graphed.

r	$s = r^2$	$A = \pi s$
0	0	0
1	1	3.14
2	4	12.56
3	9	28.26

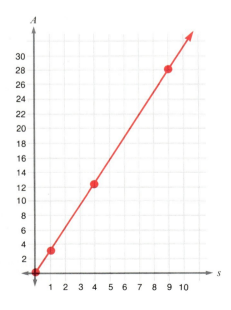

The slope of the line is π, and the y-intercept is 0. We say that the area varies directly as the square of the radius.

Example 3 **Find the constant of variation and write the equation relating the variables.**

The force (F) of the wind on a plane surface varies directly as the square of the wind velocity (w). The force is 2 pounds per square foot when the wind velocity is 20 miles per hour.

Solution Since F varies directly as the square of w, the constant of variation k must satisfy the relationship: $F = kw^2$

Substitute for F and w. $\quad 2 = k \cdot 20^2 \quad$ So, $k = \dfrac{1}{200}$.

Answer The equation relating F and w is $F = \dfrac{w^2}{200}$.

 LASSROOM EXERCISES

State whether the equation defines a direct variation. Give the constant of variation.

1. $y = 3x + 1$ **2.** $c = \pi d$ **3.** $E = 200r$ **4.** $C = 1.8F + 32$

5. Does the volume of a cube vary directly as the length of its edge?

6. Does the volume of a cube vary directly as the third power of its edge?

7. Suppose that x and y vary directly and that $y = 7$ when $x = 3$. What is the value of y when $x = 7$?

8. How much force does a 50-mph wind exert on a 4-ft by 8-ft plywood sheet? [*Hint:* See Example 3.]

 RITTEN EXERCISES

A **State whether the equation defines a direct variation.**

1. $y = 3x$ **2.** $y = \dfrac{1}{5}x$ **3.** $p = 5$ **4.** $p = 3q + 5$

Complete.

5. If $c = \pi d$, then c varies directly as ___?___. **6.** If $d = 2r$, then d varies directly as ___?___.

7. If $A = \pi r^2$, then A varies directly as ___?___. **8.** If $A = \dfrac{\pi}{4}d^2$, then A varies directly as ___?___.

9. If $A = s^2$, then s varies directly as ___?___. [*Hint:* Solve for s.]

10. If $A = \pi r^2$, then r varies directly as ___?___.

11. $V = \dfrac{4}{3}\pi r^3$ is the formula for the volume (V) of a sphere with radius r. Describe in words how the volume varies with respect to the radius. What is the constant of variation?

12. $A = 4\pi r^2$ is the formula for the area (A) of the surface of a sphere with radius r. Describe in words how the area varies with respect to the radius. What is the constant of variation?

Suppose the two variables vary directly.

13. If $y = 20$ when $x = 4$, what is the value of y when $x = 3$?

14. If $y = 20$ when $x = 5$, what is the value of y when $x = 3$?

15. If $y = 2$ when $x = 8$, what is the value of x when $y = 3$?

16. If $y = 3$ when $x = 15$, what is the value of x when $y = 2$?

17. If $d = 220$ when $t = 4$, what is the value of d when $t = 3$?

18. If $d = 1200$ when $t = 2$, what is the value of d when $t = 3$?

19. If $c = 4\pi$ when $r = 2$, what is the value of c when $r = 3$?

20. If $s = 6\pi$ when $r = 2$, what is the value of s when $r = 3$?

Solve.

21. Suppose y varies directly as the square of x. If $y = 24$ when $x = 2$, what is the value of y when $x = 3$?

22. Suppose y varies directly as the cube of x. If $y = 4$ when $x = 2$, what is the value of y when $x = 4$?

23. Suppose y varies directly as the square root of x. If $y = 30$ when $x = 25$, what is the constant of proportionality?

24. Suppose y varies directly as the square of x. If $y = 72$ when $x = 3$, what is the constant of proportionality?

B 25. Suppose r varies directly as s. If $r = 3$ when $s = \sqrt{3}$, what is the value of r when $s = 3$?

26. Suppose r varies directly as s. If $r = 3$ when $s = \sqrt{3}$, what is the value of s when $r = \sqrt{3}$?

27. Suppose p varies directly as the square of q. If $p = 4$ when $q = \sqrt{3}$, what is the value of q when $p = 48$?

28. Suppose p varies directly as the square of q. If $p = 4$ when $q = \sqrt{3}$, what is the value of p when $q = 3$?

29. The surface area (A) of a cube varies directly as the square of the length (e) of the edge of the cube. If the area is 37.5 cm^2 when the edge is 2.5 cm, what is the area when the edge is 3 cm?

30. The perimeter (P) of a semicircular region varies directly as the radius (r). If the perimeter is ($\pi + 2$) cm when the radius is 1 cm, what is the perimeter when the radius is 10 cm?

Graph the ordered pairs in each table. Then state whether these data represent a direct variation. If so, state the constant of variation.

31.

x	y
0	0
1	6
2.5	15
4	24
5.5	33

32.

r^2	A
1	1.5
4	6
9	13.5
16	24
25	37.5

33.

w	F
0	0
2	5
4	10
7	24.5
8	28

34.

a	P
1	16
2.5	34
3	40
4	52
5.25	67

Find the constant of variation and write the equation for the direct variation. Then answer the question.

35. A freely falling body falls 256 ft in 4 s. The distance fallen (d) varies directly as the square of the time (t). How long will it take the body to fall 1600 ft?

36. Power (w) in watts is proportional to the square of the current (a) in amperes. If the power of a radio station is 1000 watts when the current is 5 amperes, what must the current be in order for the power to be 36,000 watts?

C **37.** For vibrating strings of constant length, frequency of pitch (f) varies directly as the square root of the tension (T) on the string. A certain string vibrates 432 times per second under a tension of 16 lb. What tension on the string would double this frequency?

38. The surface area (S) of a sphere varies directly as the square of its radius (r). A sphere with a diameter of 28 cm has the surface area of 784π cm^2. What is the surface area of a sphere with a radius that is half as long?

39. The quantities in the table are related by some type of direct variation.

x	0	1	2	3
y	0	2	16	54

  a. Graph the (x, y) pairs.

  b. Graph the (x^2, y) pairs.   **c.** Graph the (x^3, y) pairs.

  d. Which of the three graphs is part of a straight line?

  e. What is the slope of that line?

  f. Write the equation showing the direct variation.

*R*EVIEW EXERCISES

Identify the next number in each sequence. [1-6]

1. 9, 13, 17, 21, __?__

2. 5, 10, 20, 40, 80 __?__

Give the area and the perimeter of each figure.

3.

6 cm
8 cm

4

10 cm
6 cm
8 cm

5.
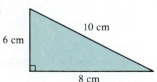
12 in.
10 in.
8 in.
24 in.
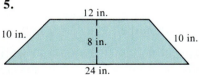
10 in.

6. In terms of π, what are the area and circumference of the circle?

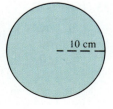
10 cm

7. What is the length of the hypotenuse of the triangle?

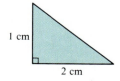
1 cm
2 cm

Step Functions

Application: Airmail Postage In 1988, the airmail postage from the United States to Europe was 45¢ per $\frac{1}{2}$ ounce or fraction of $\frac{1}{2}$ ounce. This means that the cost of a letter that weighs $\frac{1}{2}$ ounce or less is 45¢. The cost of a letter that weighs from a little more than $\frac{1}{2}$ ounce through 1 ounce costs 90¢. The graph shows the weight-cost relationship where c represents the cost in cents and w represents the weight in ounces for letters up to 2 ounces.

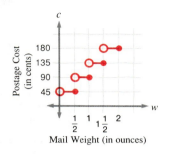

Mail Weight (in ounces)

The mail weight-cost relationship is an example of a **step function,** named for the shape of the graph.

An important step function is the **greatest integer function.** This function pairs a real number with the greatest integer that is less than or equal to the real number. The greatest integer of a real number x is denoted by $[x]$. For example,

$$[3.1] = 3 \qquad [3.95] = 3$$
$$[4] = 4 \qquad [-3.1] = -4$$

The graph of $y = [x]$ shows that this relationship is a step function.

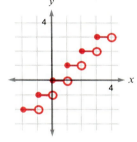

Example 1 True or false? For all real numbers x and y, $[x + y] = [x] + [y]$.

Solution Investigate this generalization for several values of x and y. Make a table of the results.

x	y	$x + y$	$[x + y]$	$[x] + [y]$
1.2	2.7	3.9	3	3
3.7	2.3	6.0	6	5
5	3	8	8	8
−2.5	−4.3	−6.8	−7	−8
−3.8	5.6	1.8	1	1

The table contains two counterexamples to the generalization.

Answer The generalization is false.

Example 2 Graph $y = 2[x] + 1$ for $-3 \leqslant x \leqslant 3$.

Solution For $-3 \leqslant x < -2$, $y = 2(-3) + 1 = -5$.
For $-2 \leqslant x < -1$, $y = 2(-2) + 1 = -3$.
For $-1 \leqslant x < 0$, $y = 2(-1) + 1 = -1$.
For $0 \leqslant x < 1$, $y = 2(0) + 1 = 1$.
For $1 \leqslant x < 2$, $y = 2(1) + 1 = 3$.
For $2 \leqslant x < 3$, $y = 2(2) + 1 = 5$.
For $x = 3$, $y = 2(3) + 1 = 7$.

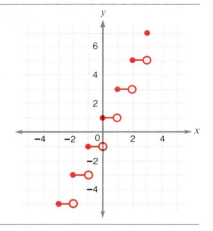

Often in applications, one quantity **depends** on another. For example, in a situation involving the length of time worked (t) and the take-home pay (p), take-home pay is determined by time worked. Therefore, t is considered to be the **independent variable** and p the **dependent variable.** Similarly, in a situation involving the weight of a package (w) and the cost of mailing the package (c), w is considered to be the independent variable and c the dependent variable. Customarily we choose the horizontal axis of the graph for the independent variable and the vertical axis for the dependent variable.

Example 3 **Graph the relationship between the length of time worked (t) and the take-home pay (p) at the rate of \$4 per hour. Time worked is rounded to the nearest half hour.**

Solution We consider t to be the independent variable and the horizontal axis the t-axis.

The function relating p to t is a step function. We assume that $\frac{1}{4}$ hour is rounded up to $\frac{1}{2}$ hour, $\frac{3}{4}$ hour is rounded up to 1 hour, etc.

For $t < \frac{1}{4}$, $p = 0$.

For $\frac{1}{4} \leqslant t < \frac{3}{4}$, $p = 2$.

For $\frac{3}{4} \leqslant t < \frac{5}{4}$, $p = 4$.

For $\frac{5}{4} \leqslant t < \frac{7}{4}$, $p = 6$.

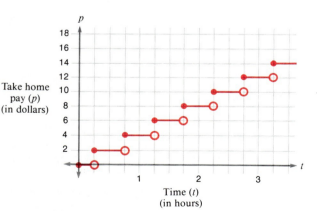

For computers, the greatest integer function [ ] is denoted by INT( ). A computer evaluates INT(X) as the greatest integer equal to or less than X.

$$INT(4.357) = 4 \qquad INT(106) = 106 \qquad INT(-17.8) = -18$$

This function enables computer users to round numbers to an appropriate place value rather than printing numbers to eight or more decimal places.

*C*LASSROOM EXERCISES

Simplify.

1. [3.99]
2. [6]
3. [−4.01]
4. INT(−5)
5. INT(6.88)

6. Graph $y = [x] + 3$

7. True or false? For all real numbers x and y, $[xy] \geq [x] \cdot [y]$.

8. Which variable is the independent variable? A car is driven m miles in t hours at the rate of 55 mph.

*W*RITTEN EXERCISES

 Simplify.

1. [2.7]
2. [4.8]
3. [0.79]
4. [0.93]

5. [10]
6. [50]
7. [−7.14]
8. [−7.01]

9. INT(−3)
10. INT(−8)
11. INT(2.99)
12. INT(−7.99)

Graph the equation for $-4 \leq x \leq 4$.

13. $y = [x] + 2$
14. $y = [x] - 2$
15. $y = [x + 2]$
16. $y = [x - 2]$

17. $y = 3[x]$
18. $y = 2[x]$
19. $Y = INT(3 * X)$
20. $Y = INT(2 * X)$

Simplify.

21. $\left[2\frac{1}{2}\right] \cdot [6]$
22. $\left[2\frac{1}{4}\right] \cdot [8]$
23. $[0.98] \cdot [100]$
24. $[0.8] \cdot [10]$

25. $[-0.8] \cdot [37.8]$
26. $[-1.4] \cdot [-7.9]$
27. $2.5 \cdot [6.1]$
28. $2.25 \cdot [8.2]$

*A*pplications

Write an equation that describes the relationship. Use [ ] notation.

29. When Cory Graff is asked his age, he always answers with his age on his most recent birthday. Let a represent his actual age and A represent the age he gives.

30. Whenever Susan Rains accumulates 50 pennies, she puts them in a coin wrapper. Let n represent her number of pennies and w represent the number of wrappers used.

Identify the independent variable and then write an equation for the dependent variable.

31. Jeffrey Dieken's total income (I) is the sum of his \$500 monthly salary and 5% of his sales dollars (S).

32. DeJood's Processing Company finds that its total expenses (E) are a fixed amount of \$1200 each month plus a variable amount of \$200 for each item processed. Let n represent the number of items processed.

33. Andrea Grindland found that the total repair bill (R) was \$25 for new parts plus \$15 per hour (h) for labor.

34. Frankhauser Inc. has repeat sales of \$25,000 each month and new sales averaging \$300 each working day. Let d represent the number of working days in the month and let S represent the total sales per month.

B **Indicate whether the statement is true for all real numbers, a, b, and c. If false, give a counterexample.**

35. $[a] + [b] = [b] + [a]$

36. $[a] - [b] = [a - b]$

37. $[a]([b] + [c]) = [ab] + [ac]$

38. $[a] = [|a|]$

39. $\dfrac{[a]}{2} = \left[\dfrac{a}{2}\right]$

40. $[a^2] = [a]^2$

41. $[a] + [b] \leqslant [a + b]$

42. $[a + b] + [c] = [a] + [b + c]$

Graph each pair of equations using the same coordinate system. Are the equations in each pair equivalent?

43. $y = \dfrac{[x]}{2}$

$y = \left[\dfrac{x}{2}\right]$

44. $y = \dfrac{1}{2} + [x]$

$y = \left[\dfrac{1}{2} + x\right]$

45. $y = [-x]$

$y = -[x]$

46. $y = \dfrac{12}{[x]}$, for $x \neq 0$

$y = \left[\dfrac{12}{x}\right]$, for $[x] \neq 0$

C **47.** The greatest integer function can be used to round each of these numbers to the *nearest integer*: $\{-2.6, -1.3, 0.5, 2, 4.7, 6.2, 7.9\}$. For what single value of n is INT$(X + n)$ the appropriate rounded value of x? (Remember that -2.6 rounds to -3, -1.3 rounds to -1, and so on.)

48. Write an expression that will round any number x to the nearest 10.

49. Write an expression that will round any number x to the nearest 100.

EVIEW EXERCISES

Use the variable *n* to write the *n*th term of each sequence.   [1-6]

1. 100, 103, 106, 109, 112, . . .   **2.** 2, 4, 8, 16, 32, . . .

Fill in the missing reasons in each proof.   [1-7]

3. $(3 + x) = (x + 3) + 2$ _____?_____

  $= x + (3 + 2)$ _____?_____

  $= x + 5$ _____?_____

4. $(a + c) + (-c) = a + (c + (-c))$ _____?_____

  $= a + 0$ _____?_____

  $= a$ _____?_____

5. Show that the product of two even numbers is a multiple of 4.   [1-7]

Use the Pythagorean theorem to find the following.

6. The diagonal of a
square with side 1.

7. The altitude of an
equilateral triangle
with side 2.

$\mathcal{S}$elf-Quiz 2

3-4 **1.** Write the equation for a line that passes through $(-1, 2)$ and is parallel
to $y = 3x + 5$.

2. Write the equation for a line that passes through $(3, 0)$ and is perpendicular
to $3x + 4y = 5$.

3-5 **3.** Suppose y varies directly as x. If $y = 24$ when $x = 14$, find y when
$x = 4$.

4. Describe how the surface area (S) of a cube varies with respect to the
length (e) of an edge.

3-6 **The greatest integer function is $y = [x]$. Simplify.**

5. $[-3.97]$ **6.** $[4.51]$

7. For $-4 \leq x \leq 4$, graph $y = \left[\frac{1}{2}x\right]$.

Write an equation for the dependent variable.

8. An atmosphere is a unit of pressure (P) equal to the pressure of the air
at sea level. The pressure experienced by scuba divers increases by 1
atmosphere for each 33 ft of depth (d) below sea level.

LESSON 3-7

Function Notation

Application: Sales Tax The city of Fulton has a 5% sales tax. This table can be used to find the tax, $t(x)$, on an item selling for x cents.

x	$t(x)$
0–10	0
11–30	1
31–50	2
51–70	3
71–90	4

x	$t(x)$
91–110	5
111–130	6
131–150	7
151–170	8
171–190	9

The tax on an item marked 75 cents is 4 cents since 75 is in the interval 71–90. Therefore, $t(75) = 4$.

The tax, $t(x)$, on an item selling for x cents can be found by using this equation:

$$t(x) = \left[\frac{x + 9}{20}\right].$$

For example: $t(241) = \left[\frac{241 + 9}{20}\right] = \left[\frac{250}{20}\right] = [12.5] = 12$

The symbol $t(x)$ is an example of a special notation for functions.

By convention, functions are usually denoted by the letters, f, g, h, F, G, and H. For example, one might write $f = \{(x, y): y = 2x - 1\}$ or $g = \{(x, y): y = [x]\}$.

We can think of a function as acting on a first component to give the second component. The notation $f(x)$ represents the result of applying function f to x. Read "$f(x)$" as "f of x."

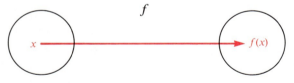

Using the above definitions for functions f and g gives these true statements.

$$f(3) = 2(3) - 1 = 5 \qquad g(3.4) = [3.4] = 3 \qquad g(-2.3) = [-2.3] = -3$$

Function notation is a relabeling of y as $f(x)$. This relabeling has two distinct advantages.

1. It shows that $f(x)$ depends on x; that is, x is the independent variable, and $f(x)$ is the dependent variable.

2. In a single symbol, it shows the first component of an ordered pair, the name of the function, and the second component of the ordered pair.

Name of function ————↓ ↓ ———— First component (independent variable)

$$\underbrace{f(x)}$$

————Second component (dependent variable)

We now have these equivalent ways of defining a function using set-builder notation.

$$f = \{(x, y): y = 3x + 4\} = \{(x, f(x)): f(x) = 3x + 4\}$$

Usually only the equation is written: $f(x) = 3x + 4$.

Example 1 Let $f(x) = 2x - 5$. Simplify each of these expressions.

a. $f(6)$ **b.** $f\left(-\frac{1}{2}\right)$ **c.** $f(a + 1)$ **d.** $f(3x - 2)$

Solution   **a.** $f(6) = 2(6) - 5 = 7$ **b.** $f\left(-\frac{1}{2}\right) = 2\left(-\frac{1}{2}\right) - 5 = -6$

c. $f(a + 1) = 2(a + 1) - 5 = 2a - 3$

d. $f(3x - 2) = 2(3x - 2) - 5 = 6x - 9$

Example 2 Let $f(x) = 2x^2$. Find x if $f(x) = 98$.

Solution $f(x) = 2x^2 = 98$

$x^2 = 49$

$x = 7$ or $x = -7$ *Answer* $\{-7, 7\}$

Function notation can be used to show a function of a function. After applying the function f to x, the function g is applied to that result, $f(x)$, to give $g(f(x))$.

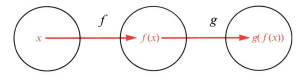

Example 3 Let $f(x) = 3x - 1$ and $g(x) = |x|$. Simplify $g(f(-2))$.

Solution   *Method 1.* The symbol $g(f(-2))$ shows that function g is acting on the number $f(-2)$. Therefore, first compute $f(-2)$.

$$f(-2) = 3(-2) - 1 = -7$$

Then substitute -7 for $f(-2)$ in $g(f(-2))$ and simplify.

$$g(f(-2)) = g(-7) = |-7| = 7$$

Method 2. Write an expression for $g(f(x))$. Since $f(x) = 3x - 1$, substitute $3x - 1$ for $f(x)$ in $g(f(x))$.

$$g(f(x)) = g(3x - 1) = |3x - 1|.$$

To simplify $g(f(-2))$, substitute -2 for x in $g(f(x)) = |3x - 1|$

$$g(f(x)) = |3x - 1|$$

$$g(f(-2)) = |3(-2) - 1| = |-7| = 7$$

*C*LASSROOM EXERCISES

Let the functions f, g, and h be defined by $f(x) = [x]$, $g(x) = -x + 2$, and $h(x) = |x|$.

Simplify.

1. $f(-2.3)$ 2. $g(-2.3)$ 3. $h(-2.3)$

4. $g(3a + 1)$ 5. $h(-5a)$ 6. $g(2x + 1)$

7. $f(g(2))$ 8. $h(f(-5.73))$ 9. $f(h(-0.8))$

10. $f(g(3a))$ 11. $h(g(2a + 1))$ 12. $g(h(f(-5.2)))$

13. True or false? For all real numbers a, $f(h(a)) = h(f(a))$. If it is false, give a counterexample

*W*RITTEN EXERCISES

 Let $f(x) = x^2$. **Simplify.**

1. $f(9)$ 2. $f(4)$ 3. $f(-4)$ 4. $f(-9)$

5. $f\left(\frac{1}{2}\right)$ 6. $f\left(\frac{1}{4}\right)$ 7. $f\left(\sqrt{3}\right)$ 8. $f\left(\sqrt{5}\right)$

Let $h(x) = x - 2$. **Simplify.**

9. $h(10)$ 10. $h(8)$ 11. $h(2)$ 12. $h(0)$

13. $h(-10)$ 14. $h(-8)$ 15. $h\left(\frac{1}{3}\right)$ 16. $h\left(\frac{1}{5}\right)$

Let $g(x) = 5x - 4$. **Solve.**

17. $g(x) = 26$ 18. $g(x) = 56$ 19. $g(x) = -10$ 20. $g(x) = -3$

Let $j(x) = x^2 - 3$. **Solve.**

21. $j(x) = 22$ 22. $j(x) = 6$ 23. $j(x) = 8$ 24. $j(x) = -1$

Let $F(x) = 3x$ and $G(x) = \frac{x}{3}$. **Simplify.**

25. **a.** $F(6)$ 26. **a.** $G(6)$ 27. **a.** $G(30)$ 28. **a.** $F(30)$
    b. $G(F(6))$ **b.** $F(G(6))$ **b.** $F(G(30))$ **b.** $G(F(30))$

Let $g(x) = x + 1$ and $h(x) = x + 2$. **Simplify.**

29. **a.** $g(h(10))$ 30. **a.** $g(h(0))$ 31. **a.** $g(h(a))$ 32. **a.** $g(h(a - 1))$
    b. $h(g(10))$ **b.** $h(g(0))$ **b.** $h(g(a))$ **b.** $h(g(a - 1))$

Let $f(x) = 4x$ and $F(x) = x + 4$. **Simplify.**

33. **a.** $f(F(-4))$ 34. **a.** $f(F(-1))$ 35. **a.** $f(F(-a))$ 36. **a.** $f(F(w^2))$
    b. $F(f(-4))$. **b.** $F(f(-1))$ **b.** $F(f(-a))$ **b.** $F(f(w^2))$

37. If $f(x) = 2x - 5$ and $0 < x < 4$, then $f(x)$ is between __?__ and __?__.

38. If $f(x) = \dfrac{x}{x-1}$ and $g(x) = \dfrac{1}{x}$, then $f(g(4)) = $ __?__.

39. If $f(x) = x^2 + kx + 2$ and $f(2) = 4$, then $k = $ __?__.

40. If $f(x) = x^2$, $g(x) = 3x$, and $h(x) = x - 3$, then $f(g(h(2))) = $ __?__.

41. Let $f(x) = 3x$ and $g(x) = 4x$. Show that $f(g(x)) = g(f(x))$ for all real numbers x.

42. Let $F(x) = 2x + 1$ and $G(x) = 3x - 2$. Show that $F(G(x)) \neq G(F(x))$ for all real numbers x.

43. Let $f(x) = 5x$ and $g(x) = |2x|$. Show that $f(g(x)) = g(f(x))$ for all real numbers x.

Using function notation, write the equation relating each set of data pairs.

44.
$$1 \xrightarrow{\;f\;} 4$$
$$3 \xrightarrow{\;f\;} 14$$
$$-2 \xrightarrow{\;f\;} -11$$

45.
$$-4 \xrightarrow{\;g\;} 1$$
$$5 \xrightarrow{\;g\;} \frac{11}{2}$$
$$0 \xrightarrow{\;g\;} 3$$

46.
$$10 \xrightarrow{\;h\;} -3$$
$$6 \xrightarrow{\;h\;} 1$$
$$-1 \xrightarrow{\;h\;} 8$$

47.
$$-6 \xrightarrow{\;j\;} 12$$
$$9 \xrightarrow{\;j\;} 2$$
$$3 \xrightarrow{\;j\;} 6$$

Complete.

48. If $f(x) = 2x$ and $g(f(x)) = x$, then $g(x) = $ __?__.

49. If $f(x) = 3x + 2$ and $g(f(x)) = x$, then $g(x) = $ __?__.

50. If $f(x) = x^2 + 2x$, then $f(a - 3) = $ __?__.

51. What is the range of function g? $g = \{(x, y): y = \dfrac{1}{x} - 2\}$

52. Consider the function defined by $f(x) = kx$ (where k is a constant). Prove that $f(a) + f(b) = f(a + b)$ for all real numbers a and b.

53. Consider the function defined by $g(x) = x^n$ (where n is a positive integer). Prove that $g(a) \cdot g(b) = g(ab)$ for all real numbers a and b.

*R*EVIEW EXERCISES

Solve and graph.   [2-4]

1. $2x - 3 < 6 - x$ **2.** $4 - 3x < 16$

3. $10 \leq 3x - 5 \leq 25$ **4.** $50 \leq 10 - 5x \leq 100$

5. $|x - 1| \leq 3$ **6.** $|x + 3| \geq 1$

Use absolute values to write an inequality that describes this graph.   [2-6]

7.

CHAPTER SUMMARY

▶ **Vocabulary**

▶ **Equality of ordered pairs**   [3-1]

For all real numbers a, b, c, and d,

$(a, b) = (c, d)$ if and only if $a = c$ and $b = d$.

▶ A *relation* is a set of ordered pairs.

▶ A relation is a *function* if and only if each element of the domain is paired with   [3-2]
exactly one element of the range.

▶ A relation is a *1-1 function* if and only if each element of the domain is associated
with a unique element of the range, and each element of the range is associated
with a unique element of the domain.

▶ A function is a *linear function* if and only if its equation can be written in the   [3-3]
form $y = mx + b$.

▶ Definition of slope

    If $x_1 \neq x_2$, the *slope* of the line through (x_1, y_1) and (x_2, y_2) is the ratio

$$\frac{\Delta y}{\Delta x} = \frac{y_2 - y_1}{x_2 - x_1} = \frac{y_1 - y_2}{x_1 - x_2}$$

▶ The slope of a horizontal line (a constant linear function) is 0.

▶ The slope of a vertical line (not a function) is undefined.

▶ The form $y = mx + b$ is called the *slope-intercept form* of a linear equation in   [3-3]
two variables. The slope is m, and the y-intercept is b.

▶ The *point-slope form* of a linear equation with slope m and passing through the   [3-4]
point (x_1, y_1) is $y - y_1 = m(x - x_1)$.

▶ The graphs of two linear functions are parallel if and only if their slopes are
equal. Two lines with undefined slopes are parallel.

▶ The graphs of two linear functions are perpendicular if and only if the product
of their slopes is -1. A line with zero slope and a line with undefined slope are
perpendicular.

▶ Two variables x and y are said to *vary directly* if and only if there is a constant   [3-5]
of variation, k, $k \neq 0$, such that $y = kx$. If $x \neq 0$, $\frac{y}{x} = k$.

𝒞HAPTER REVIEW

3-1 **Objective:** To graph relations.

    1. In which quadrant or on which axis is
each of these points?

      a. *A*   **b.** *B*   **c.** *C*   **d.** *D*

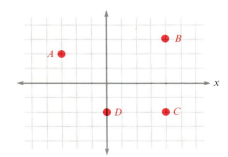

**Graph each relation and list
its domain and range.**

    2. $\{(3, 0), (3, -2), (-3, 2)\}$

    3. $\{(x, y): y = |x| - 1\}$

3-2 **Objective:** To identify functions.

    **Indicate whether each relation is a function. If so, state whether it is a 1-1
function.**

    4. $\{(3, 4), (3, 5), (3, 6)\}$ **5.**

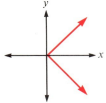

    6. $\{(x, y): x$ is a positive integer, and y
is a prime number less than $x\}$

    7. $\{(x, y): x + y = 3\}$

3-3 **Objectives:** To identify linear equations.
To find the slopes and y-intercepts of their graphs.
To use the slope-intercept form of linear equations.

8. Indicate whether $xy = 6$ is a linear equation.

9. Compute $\dfrac{\Delta y}{\Delta x}$ for these two points. $(4, -2)$, $(0, 2)$

10. Find the slope and y-intercept of the graph of $2x + 3y = 6$.

3-4 **Objectives:** To use the point-slope form of linear equations.
To use slopes to determine whether lines are parallel or perpendicular.

11. Write the equation of the line through the origin that is parallel to $y = \dfrac{2}{3}x - 3$.

12. Write the slope-intercept form of the line through the points $(3, -1)$ and $(-2, 5)$.

13. Write the equation of the line through $(2, -3)$ that is parallel to $x + y = 5$.

3-5 **Objective:** To solve direct-variation problems.

14. If $A = 4s^2$, then A varies directly as _____?_____.

15. Suppose that y varies directly as x. If $y = 12$ when $x = 4$, then what is the value of y when $x = 6$?

16. Suppose that y varies directly as the square of x. If $y = 100$ when $x = 5$, then what is the value of y when $x = 3$?

3-6 **Objectives:** To solve problems involving the greatest integer function.
To identify dependent and independent variables.

17. Simplify: $[-3.16]$.

18. Graph $y = 0.5 \cdot [x]$ for $-3 \leqslant x \leqslant 4$.

19. Simplify: $\left[4\dfrac{1}{2}\right] \cdot [10]$.

20. Identify the independent and dependent variables. Then write an equation for the dependent variable.

John started walking toward home from a distance of 10 mi at a rate of 4 mph. Let d be the distance from home and t be the number of hours from the time he started.

3-7 **Objective:** To apply function notation.

Let $f(x) = 5x$ and $g(x) = x + 2$. Simplify.

21. $f(10)$ 22. $f(g(10))$ 23. $g(f(10))$

CHAPTER 3 SELF-TEST

3-1   **1.** What is the domain of the relation $R = \{(3, -9), (4, -1), (0, 6), (-2, 5)\}$?

3-2,   **2.** True or false?
3-4
    a. All functions are relations, but not all relations are functions.

    b. A straight line with a zero slope does not have a y-intercept.

    c. $\{(1, 2), (3, 7), (-1, 2)\}$ is a function.

    d. $\{(3, 0), (-4, 4), (5, 3)\}$ is a 1-1 function.

3-3,   **3.** Write the slope-intercept form of the equation of the line.
3-4
    a. That passes through $(6, -1)$ and $(2, 1)$

    b. With slope 2 and x-intercept 5

3-4   **4.** Find the slope and y-intercept of the line $2(y - 6) = 3(1 - x)$.

    5. Given the line $2x = 3 + 5y$, find the slope of any line that is:

    a. perpendicular to the given line.

    b. parallel to the given line.

    6. Write the equation of the line with undefined slope that passes through the point $(4, -6)$.

3-5   **7.** If B varies directly as the square of r, find the constant of proportionality given that $B = \dfrac{9\pi}{2}$ when $r = 3$.

    8. W is directly proportional to the square root of s. If $W = 40$ when $s = 25$, what is W when $s = 36$?

3-6   **9.** If the step-function $y = [x - 2]$ has a domain of $-1 < x \le 3$, what is its range?

3-7   **10.** Graph $f(x) = 3x - 1$.

    11. Write an equation for the dependent variable. The shipping cost (c) is a $2.00 flat fee plus 50¢ for each pound (p) or fraction of a pound.

3-6,   **12.** Let $f(x) = 3 \cdot [x]$, $g(x) = 2x^2 - 1$, and $h(x) = 4x + 2$.
3-7
    Simplify.

        a. $f(-1.4)$ **b.** $g(-3)$

        c. $h(g(1))$ **d.** $f(h(x))$

PRACTICE FOR COLLEGE ENTRANCE TESTS

Compare the quantities in column A and column B. Select one of the following answers.

    A   if the quantity in column A is greater;
    B   if the quantity in column B is greater;
    C   if the two quantities are equal;
    D   if the relationship cannot be determined from the information given.

▶ Letters such as a, b, x, and y are variables that can be replaced by real numbers.

▶ A symbol that appears in a question stands for the same thing in column A as in column B.

▶ In some questions, information that applies to quantities in both columns is centered above the two columns.

	Column A	Column B
1.	$\dfrac{7}{16}$	$\dfrac{13}{32}$
2.	2456 rounded to the nearest hundred	2456 rounded to the nearest hundred
3.	$x < 0 < y$	
	$\lvert x + y \rvert$	$\lvert x \rvert + \lvert y \rvert$
4.	$\dfrac{1}{3}a = \dfrac{1}{2}b$	
	a	b
5.	The number of positive integer factors of 12	6
6.	$x > 0$ and $y > 0$	
	$x + y$	xy
7.	30% of $x = 15$	
	75% of x	40
8.	The number of prime numbers between 10 and 20	3
9.	$ab + ac$	$a(b + c)$
10.	$a > 0 > b$	
	$a^2 + b^2$	$(a + b)^2$

Column A	Column B

11.

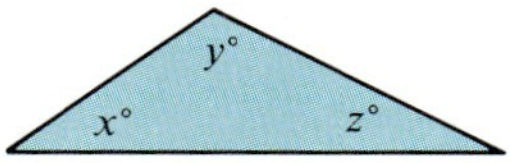

$x + y$ | $180 - z$

12. $AB > BC$

AC | BD

13. The area of a square with side $\sqrt{2}$

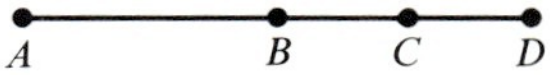

| The area of a square with diagonal 2

14. $x^3 + 10 = 0$

x^3 | 10

15.

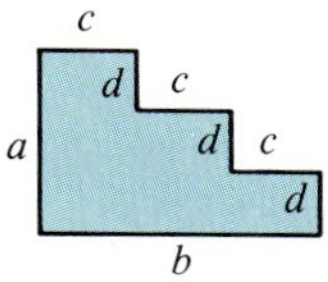

$a + b$ | $3(c + d)$

16. $xy > 0$

$|x + y|$ | $|x| + |y|$

17. The area of a square with side s | The area of a circle with radius $\dfrac{s}{2}$

18.

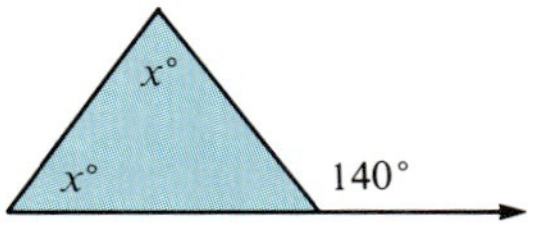

x | 60

19. $a > 0$ and $b > 0$

$2ab$ | $\dfrac{a^2 + b^2}{2}$

20. The hypotenuse of a right triangle with legs 3 and 5 | 6

21. $a < 0$

$-a$ | $\dfrac{1}{a}$

Column A	Column B

22.

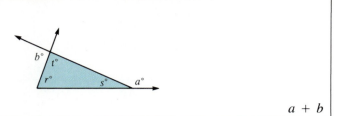

$r + s + t$ $a + b$

23. $AC > AB$

b c

24. $x^2 < y^2$

x y

$\mathcal{C}$UMULATIVE REVIEW (CHAPTERS 1–3)

1-1   **1.** State whether the number is rational or irrational.

      a. $4.\overline{9}$ **b.** $-\dfrac{5}{9}$

      c. $0.424242\ldots$ **d.** $6.01001000100001\ldots$

  2. Write each fraction as a terminating or a repeating decimal.

      a. $\dfrac{5}{8}$ **b.** $\dfrac{2}{11}$

  3. Write the decimal as the quotient of two integers. $1.\overline{6}$

1-2   **Simplify.**

  4. $9 + 2(7 - 1)^2$ **5.** $\dfrac{3(8 - 4)}{\sqrt{9 + 16}}$

  6. Substitute and simplify.

                 $bx^a + y$

a	b	x	y
2	$\dfrac{1}{8}$	4	-6

1-3 **7.** Arrange the numbers in order from least to greatest. $\frac{1}{6}, \frac{1}{8}, \frac{1}{3}$

8. Describe with set-builder notation the set of all real numbers greater than 9.

9. Graph on a number line. $\{x: x$ is a positive integer less than ten$\}$

1-4 **State the property illustrated.**

10. $a(bc) = (ab)c$ $\qquad\qquad$ **11.** $17y + 6y = (17 + 6)y$

12. Simplify. $6 + 2(4 + 3(x + 1))$

1-5 **State the property illustrated.**

13. $4.\overline{7} + (-4.\overline{7}) = 0$ $\qquad\qquad$ **14.** $4 + \sqrt{2}$ is a real number.

15. Simplify. $6w - (w - 3)$

1-6 **Find a pattern. Then use it to write the next three terms of each sequence.**

16. 3, 6, 12, 24, 48, . . .

17. 2, 3, 5, 9, 17, . . .

18. Write Q in terms of n.

n	1	2	3	4	5
Q	4	6	8	10	12

Write the nth term of the sequence.

19. $\frac{1}{3}, \frac{2}{4}, \frac{3}{5}, \frac{4}{6}, \frac{5}{7}, \ldots$ $\qquad\qquad$ **20.** 1, 8, 27, 64, . . .

1-7 **21.** Show that the square of an even number is even.

22. Show that the difference of two odd numbers is an even number.

2-1 **Solve**

23. $3(4x + 5) = 45 - 8x$

24. $0.6(x - 4) - 0.4 = 0.8$

25. The formula for the linear depreciation of equipment originally costing C dollars and depreciated for n years is $V = C\left(1 - \frac{t}{n}\right)$, where V is the value after t years. Find the original cost of equipment depreciated linearly for 8 years if its value is \$11,250 after 5 years.

2-2 **Solve for the indicated variable.**

26. $A = \frac{1}{2}bh$, for h

27. $A = 2s^2 + 4sh$, for h

2-3 **Make a table and then solve the problem.**

28. Jacoby ran the last 3 mi of a 6-mi race at a pace that was 2 minutes per mile slower than his pace for the first 3 mi. His time for the race was 39 min. What was his pace in minutes per mile for the first 3 mi?

29. Machines A and B were used to produce 875 parts. Machine A was used for 5 h. Machine B was used for only 4 h, but its rate was 50 more parts per hour than machine A. Find the rates of the two machines.

2-4 **Solve and graph.**

30. $-5t > 35$

31. $6(1 - x) < 30$

32. $\frac{3}{8}x + 1 > \frac{1}{4}x - 2$

2-5, 33. $-1 < x < 3$

34. $0 \geqslant 4x + 18$

35. $|y - 1| < 4$

2-6 36. State a compound inequality for this graph.

37. Use absolute value to write an inequality for this graph.

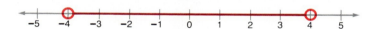

2-7 **Solve by drawing a figure and writing an equation.**

38. If each side of a square is decreased by 3 cm, it will have a perimeter equal to that of a regular pentagon, each of whose sides is 6 cm. Find the length of a side of the square.

39. A ranch hand is going to enclose a rectangular area for a vegetable patch. Three strands of barbed wire from a roll that is 198 ft long will be used to protect the patch from cattle. What size patch can be enclosed if the length must be double the width?

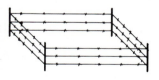

3-1 40. State the domain and range of this relation. $\{(6, 1), (-3, 4), (2, 5), (0, 1)\}$

41. Graph. $\{(x, y): x = |y|\}$

3-2 **State whether the relation is a function.**

42.

43. $\{(x, y): x \text{ is an integer between } -4 \text{ and } 4 \text{ and } y = x^2\}$

3-3 **44.** State the slope and y-intercept of the line $3x + 4y = 8$.

45. Is the equation $3x^2 + y = 6$ a linear equation?

3-4 **Write the equation of the line in slope-intercept form that:**

46. has $m = -2$ and $b = 5$.

47. is perpendicular to the line $y = \dfrac{2}{3}x + 4$ and passes through the point $(-4, 7)$.

48. passes through the points $(-3, 6)$ and $(2, 1)$.

3-5 **49.** Does the equation $y = -5x + 4$ define a direct variation?

50. If $V = \dfrac{4}{3}\pi r^3$, then V varies directly as __?__.

51. Suppose y varies directly as $\sqrt{x}$. If $y = 3$ when $x = 16$, what is the value of y when $x = 36$?

3-6 **52.** Simplify [6.4] where $y = [x]$ is the greatest integer function.

53. Graph $y = [x] - 2$ for $-3 \leqslant x \leqslant 3$.

54. Simplify $3.5 \cdot [9.7]$.

Identify the independent variable and then write an equation for the dependent variable.

55. Roger's income (I) per month is $350 plus 10% of his sales (S).

3-7 **Let** $f(x) = \dfrac{3}{4}x - 5$ **and** $g(x) = -2x$. **Simplify.**

56. $f(8)$ **57.** $g(a)$ **58.** $f(g(3))$

59. If $h(x) = x^2 - kx + 4$ and $h(1) = 7$, find k.

CHAPTER 4

Systems of Linear Equations and Inequalities

Systems of equations and inequalities are used to solve problems such as scheduling crude oil deliveries to refineries. The problems can be immensely complicated, often with thousands of variables.

Mathematicians think of these problems as multidimensional shapes called **polytopes.** Each corner of the shape is a possible solution, and the task is to find the best one without examining every corner.

The simplex method, devised in 1947, conducts a search along the edges of the surface for an efficient path to the optimal solution (solid line). In 1984, Dr. Narendra Karmarkar achieved a startling breakthrough in devising a technique that finds a solution path (dashed line) in a small fraction of the time previously required.

LESSON 4-1

Solving Linear Systems by Graphing

The Golden Gate Bridge was considered a marvelous engineering triumph. Without the aid of computer accuracy, the dimensions of the pieces were precalculated, and then the pieces were cut and fitted into place with no piece more than 15 cm off a perfect fit.

One of the most difficult mathematical problems faced in the design of the bridge involved the stresses and forces that would act on the towers. The solution of this problem required 33 simultaneous linear equations in as many variables.

Consider this **system** of two equations in two variables.

$$y = 2x - 1$$
$$y = -x + 5$$

The solution of this system is the set of ordered pairs that are solutions of *both* equations. One way of solving a system is to graph each equation. The graphed lines represent the solution sets of the individual equations of the system. Therefore, the intersection is the graph of the solution of the system.

The solution of the system is {(2, 3)}.

Check:

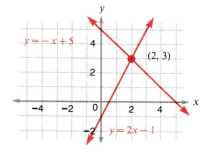

$y = 2x - 1$	$y = -x + 5$
$3 \stackrel{?}{=} 2(2) - 1$	$3 \stackrel{?}{=} -2 + 5$
$3 = 3$ Check.	$3 = 3$ Check.

In the above example, the two lines cross at exactly one point. The figures below show two other possibilities. The graphs may be parallel, or they may coincide.

$$y = \frac{1}{2}x - 1$$

$$y = \frac{1}{2}x + 2$$

$$y = x - 3$$
$$2y = 2x - 6$$

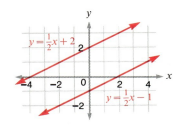

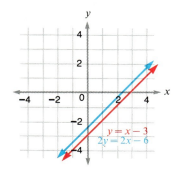

A system that has at least one solution is called **consistent.** If the graphs of the two lines are parallel, there is no solution of the system; the system is said to be **inconsistent.** If the graphs coincide, there are infinitely many solutions and the system is said to be **dependent.**

The possible relationships among a system, the slopes of the individual graphs, and the system's solutions are shown in the following table.

System	Slopes	Graphs	Solutions
Consistent and independent	Different	Lines intersect in a point	One
Inconsistent	Same	Lines are parallel	None
Consistent and dependent	Same	Lines coincide	Infinitely many

Even though a dependent system has infinitely many solutions, only certain ordered pairs satisfy the system. These pairs are described by listing either equation as a condition that the ordered pairs must satisfy.

Dependent System   **Solution Set**

$$y = x - 3$$
$$2y = 2x - 6$$

$$\{(x, y): y = x - 3\}$$

Example 1 **Solve by graphing.** $y = x - 3$
$y = -2x + 3$

Answer $\{(2, -1)\}$

Check $y = x - 3$ $y = -2x + 3$
$-1 \stackrel{?}{=} 2 - 3$ $-1 \stackrel{?}{=} -2(2) + 3$
$-1 = -1$ True $-1 = -1$ True

Solution

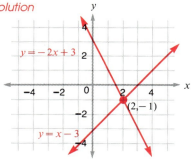

Example 2 **Solve by graphing.** $y = -x + 3$
$2x + 2y - 6 = 0$

The graphs coincide. Therefore, the system is dependent.

Answer $\{(x, y): y = -x + 3\}$

Solution

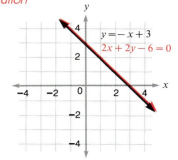

Example 3   **Solve.**

A rectangle is 3 cm longer than it is wide. If the perimeter is 42 cm, what are the length and width?

Solution   Let w = the width in centimeters, and l = the length in centimeters.

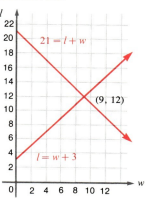

Equations:

length equals width plus 3

$$l = w + 3$$

perimeter equals 2 times length plus 2 times width

$$42 = 2l + 2w \quad \text{or} \quad 21 = l + w$$

System: $l = w + 3$
$21 = l + w$

Answer   The rectangle is 9 cm wide and 12 cm long.

Check   The length is 3 cm greater than the width, and the perimeter is 42 cm. That is, $2(9) + 2(12) = 42$.

LASSROOM EXERCISES

Solve by graphing. If there is no solution, write "inconsistent."

1. $2x + y = 1$
$3x + 2y = 5$

2. $x - 2y = 2$
$2x - y = -5$

3. $y = 2x - 3$
$y = 2x + 1$

4. $4x - 6y = 12$
$y = \frac{2}{3}x - 2$

Solve.

5. There are 5 more dimes than quarters in a child's bank. The total value of the dimes and quarters is $2.95. How many dimes and how many quarters are there?

RITTEN EXERCISES

A **Solve by graphing. If there is no solution, write "inconsistent." If the system is dependent, use set-builder notation to describe the solutions.**

1. $y = 2x + 2$
$y = \frac{1}{2}x + 5$

2. $y = \frac{1}{2}x + 1$
$y = 2x - 5$

3. $y = -2x + 4$
$y = x + 1$

4. $y = x - 1$
$y = -2x + 5$

5. $x - y = 3$
$x + y = 1$

6. $y - x = 3$
$y + x = 1$

7. $y = 5x + 1$
$1 = 5x - y$

8. $y = -2x + 2$
$2x + y = 4$

9. $3x - y = 3$
$2x - y = 1$

10. $\frac{1}{2}x + y = 4$
$x + \frac{1}{2}y = 5$

11. $\frac{1}{2}x + y = 3$
$x + 2y = 6$

12. $2x - y = 8$
$x - \frac{1}{2}y = 4$

Applications

Write two equations in two variables. Solve the system by graphing. Then answer the question.

13. A test sample of bolts contained twice as many defective bolts as good ones. If there were 6 more defective bolts than good ones, how many were defective?

14. On Wednesday, the Blue Cab Company had 3 times as many cabs in operation as those in the shop for repairs. If there were 16 more cabs on the street than in the shop, how many cabs were being repaired?

15. A parking lot has 28 cars in it. There are 10 more 4-door cars than 2-door cars in the lot. How many 4-door cars are in the lot?

16. There are 22 juniors and seniors in an advanced art class. There are 8 more seniors than juniors in the class. How many seniors are in the class?

17. The Sunshine Bakery delivered some loaves of bread and some pies. There were 6 more loaves of bread than pies. Each loaf of bread cost $1 and each pie cost $3. How many loaves of bread and how many pies were delivered if the bill was $38?

18. An electronics engineer assembled modules requiring either 3 or 4 integrated circuits each. Her total circuit supply was 36. She assembled 5 more 3-circuit modules than 4-circuit modules. How many 3-circuit modules did she assemble?

19. A solvent used to clean industrial parts requires $2\frac{1}{2}$ times as much chemical P as chemical Q. If 14 gal of solvent is needed, how much of each chemical is needed?

True or false?

20. The graphs of two linear equations intersect at the point (2, 3). The ordered pair (2, 3) is a solution of both equations.

21. The number pairs (10, 20) and (5, −5) are solutions of a system of two linear equations. The system is dependent.

22. The slopes of two lines are negative reciprocals of each other. The system is inconsistent.

23. If the graph of one equation is a vertical line and the graph of another equation is a horizontal line, then the system is inconsistent.

24. If the solution of a system of linear equations is (0, 0), then the *y*-intercept of each equation is 0.

25. The solution of a system of linear equations is (−100, −100). The slopes of both lines must be positive.

In the following systems, *k* is a constant. Determine the value(s) of *k* that fits the description of each system.

26. $y = \frac{1}{3}x + 6$
$y = kx + 2$
inconsistent

27. $x - 2y = 6$
$-2x + ky = -12$
dependent

28. $y = 5x - 13$
$y = kx + k$
consistent

29. $y = -7x + k$
$y = 2x + k$
consistent

30. $ky = x + 3$
$y = kx - 2$
inconsistent

31. $kx + ky = -28$
$x + y = 7$
dependent

 Suppose a system consists of three different equations of the form $ax + by = c$. Draw sketches representing all possible cases for each of these solution situations.

32. No solutions

33. Only one solution

34. Infinitely many solutions

The functions *f*, *g*, *h*, and *j* are linear. Use graphing to determine each answer.

35. $f(3) = 1$ $g(10) = 3$
$f(7) = 9$ $g(1) = 12$
$f(0) = -5$ $g(8) = 5$
Find *x* such that $f(x) = g(x)$.

36. $h(-0.5) = 9$ $j(10) = 8$
$h(6) = -4$ $j(0) = 3$
$h(4) = 0$ $j(-2) = 2$
Find *x* such that $h(x) = j(x)$.

 REVIEW EXERCISES

1. Write as a terminating or a repeating decimal.   2. Write as a quotient of integers.   [1-1]

a. $\frac{3}{16}$ b. $\frac{5}{33}$

a. 1.63   b. $0.\overline{41}$

Substitute and simplify using this table: [1-2]

x_1	y_1	x_2	y_2
4	−2	−2	6

3. $\frac{x_1}{x_2} + \frac{y_1}{y_2}$

4. $\frac{y_2 - y_1}{x_2 - x_1}$

5. $\sqrt{(x_2 - x_1)^2 + (y_2 - y_1)^2}$

6. Arrange the numbers $\frac{6}{11}, \frac{7}{12},$ and $\frac{8}{13}$ in order from least to greatest.   [1-3]

Use set-builder notation to describe each set.

7. The set of all real numbers greater than the square root of two

8. $\{10, 11, 12, 13, \ldots\}$

LESSON 4-2

Solving Systems by Substitution

The graph of this system of equations is shown at the right.

$$y = -5x - 0.3$$
$$y = 2x + 0.5$$

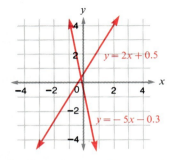

It is clear from the graph that there is just one point of intersection, but the coordinates of the point are not integers. Although we could estimate the solution from the graph, it is very difficult to determine it exactly. More precise methods are needed.

Consider the points that satisfy the equation $y = 3x$. Each y-coordinate is 3 times the corresponding x-coordinate.

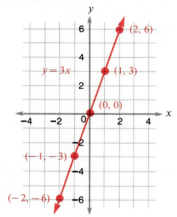

For the equation $y = x + 2$, each y-coordinate is 2 more than its paired x-coordinate.

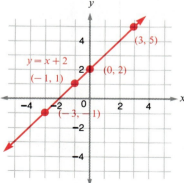

A point that lies on the intersection of the two graphs must have a y-coordinate that is *simultaneously* 3 times its x-coordinate *and* 2 more than its x-coordinate. We can impose the first condition ($y = 3x$) on the y in the second equation by substituting $3x$ for y in $y = x + 2$.

$$3x = x + 2$$
$$x = 1$$

The x-coordinate of the point that satisfies both equations is 1. The y-coordinate of that point can now be found by substituting 1 for x in either of the equations.

$$y = 3x = 3(1) = 3$$

The ordered pair that satisfies both equations is $(1, 3)$.

The technique used above is called **solving a system of equations by substitution.**

Example 1   **Solve by substitution.** $y = 3x - 1$
$$y = -x + 5$$

Solution   *Substitute $3x - 1$ for y in the second equation.*

$$3x - 1 = -x + 5$$
$$4x = 6$$
$$x = \frac{3}{2}$$

Any solution of the system must satisfy the condition $x = \frac{3}{2}$. Substitute $\frac{3}{2}$ for x in one of the original equations to find the corresponding value for y.

$$y = 3x - 1$$
$$y = 3\left(\frac{3}{2}\right) - 1$$
$$y = \frac{7}{2}$$

Answer $\left\{\left(\frac{3}{2}, \frac{7}{2}\right)\right\}$

Check   The solution should be checked in the other equation.

$$y = -x + 5$$
$$\frac{7}{2} \stackrel{?}{=} -\frac{3}{2} + 5$$
$$\frac{7}{2} = \frac{7}{2} \qquad \text{It checks.}$$

Through substitution, we eliminate one of the variables to get one linear equation in one variable that can then be easily solved. Examples 2 and 3 show the result when substitution is used on inconsistent or dependent systems.

Example 2   **Solve by substitution.** $y = 2x + 1$
$\qquad\qquad\qquad\qquad\qquad\qquad\quad\; y = 2x - 3$

Solution   *Substitute 2x + 1 for y in the second equation.* $2x + 1 = 2x - 3$
Subtract 2x from both sides. $\qquad\qquad\qquad\qquad 1 = -3$

Substitution has produced a false equation. Therefore, the assumption that an (x, y) pair exists that satisfies both equations simultaneously must also be false.
    Examining the two equations, we note that their graphs are parallel. The system is inconsistent, and there is no solution.

Answer $\emptyset$ (no solution)

Example 3   **Solve.** $2y = 4 - 6x$
$\qquad\qquad\qquad\qquad\quad\; 3y = 6 - 9x$

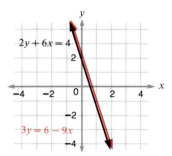

Solution   *Solve the first equation* $\qquad\quad 2y = 4 - 6x$
for y. $\qquad\qquad\qquad\qquad\quad y = 2 - 3x$

Substitute 2 − 3x for y $\quad 3(2 - 3x) = 6 - 9x$
in the second equation. $\qquad 6 - 9x = 6 - 9x$

$\qquad\qquad\qquad\qquad\qquad\qquad\; 6 = 6$

Substitution has produced a *true* equation. This implies that every x-value satisfies the equation and that for every x there is an (x, y) pair that satisfies the system. Graphing shows that the two lines coincide. The system is dependent, and there are infinitely many solutions.

Answer $\{(x, y): y = -3x + 2\}$

If substitution produces a false equation, the system is inconsistent and has no solutions. If the equation produced has no variables and is true, the system is dependent and has infinitely many solutions.

Example 4   **Solve.**

On a river, a boat travels 64 mi downstream in 2 h and returns 54 mi upstream in 3 h. What is the rate of the river's flow and the rate of the boat in still water?

Solution   Let w = the rate of the river's flow and b = the rate of the boat in still water. Then the rate of the boat downstream is $b + w$ and the rate of the boat upstream is $b - w$.

First, write equations.   Simplify both equations.

    rate · time = distance

    $(b + w) \cdot 2 = 64 \longrightarrow b + w = 32$

    $(b - w) \cdot 3 = 54 \longrightarrow b - w = 18$

Example 4 (continued)

Solve the first equation for b.	$b = 32 - w$
Substitute into the second equation.	$(32 - w) - w = 18$
	$32 - 2w = 18$
	$-2w = -14$
	$w = 7$
Substitute 7 for w in the first equation.	$b + 7 = 32$
Solve for b.	$b = 25$

Answer The rate of the river is 7 mph and the rate of the boat is 25 mph.

Check Downstream, the rate of the boat in miles per hour is $25 + 7 = 32$. In 2 h, the boat travels $2 \cdot 32$, or 64, mi. Upstream, the rate of the boat in miles per hour is $25 - 7$ or 18. In 3 h, the boat travels $3 \cdot 18$, or 54, mi. The answer checks.

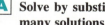LASSROOM EXERCISES

Solve by substitution.

1. $2x - y = 7$
$3x + 2y = 14$

2. $2y - 3x = 5$
$4y + 2x = -4$

3. $2y - 6x + 4 = 0$
$y = 3x + 1$

4. Tickets to a play are priced at $2.50 for students and $3.50 for adults. Thirty more student tickets than adult tickets were sold. If the total ticket sales were $1335, how many tickets of each kind were sold?

WRITTEN EXERCISES

A Solve by substitution. If the system is inconsistent, write '∅.' If there are infinitely many solutions, use set-builder notation to describe the solutions.

1. $y = x + 7$
$y = 2x + 9$

2. $y = x - 3$
$y = 2x - 8$

3. $y = x - 3$
$2x + y = 18$

4. $y = x + 4$
$2x + y = 1$

5. $y = 2x - 3$
$2x - y = 3$

6. $y = 3x - 5$
$3x - y = 5$

7. $y = 5x$
$10x - y = 6$

8. $y = 4x$
$y - 2x = 3$

9. $y = 3x$
$y - 3x = 2$

10. $y = 2x$
$2x - y = 3$

11. $y - 2x = 1$
$2y - 5x = 4$

12. $y - 3x = 7$
$2y - 7x = 17$

13. $x = 2y + 7$
$3x + 4y = 6$

14. $x = 4y - 4$
$2x + 10y = 1$

15. $x + y = 1$
$6x + 4y = 7$

16. $x + y = 4$
$3x + 5y = 15$

17. $2x - 3y = 6$
$3x + 3y = 19$

18. $3x + y = 3$
$3x + 4y = 7$

 **pplications**

Write two equations in two variables. Solve by substitution to answer the question.

19. Flying with the wind, an airplane takes 2 h to fly 360 mi from Amarillo to Dallas. Flying against the wind, the airplane takes 3 h to fly the same distance. What is the speed of the wind and the speed of the airplane in calm air?

20. Flying against the wind, it took a small plane 4 h to fly the 600 miles between Sacramento and Portland. On the return flight, it took 3 h to make the trip flying with the wind. What was the speed of the wind and the speed of the airplane in calm air, if each speed was constant?

21. The length of a rectangle is 3 cm more than the width. What are the dimensions of the rectangle if its perimeter is 41 cm?

22. A state trooper issued 37 more warnings than speeding tickets during one calendar year. How many speeding tickets were issued if 375 citations were issued in all?

B **23.** An adult pass for an amusement park costs $2 more than a child's pass. When 378 adult and 214 children's passes were sold, the total gate receipts were $2384. What was the cost of an adult pass?

24. A small package of nurps costs $0.75 and a large package costs $2.25. Fifty-six more small packages than large packages were sold, making the total sales $2253. How many large packages of nurps were sold?

25. The ones digit of a two-digit number is 4 more than the tens digit. If the digits are reversed, the resulting number is 7 times the sum of its digits. Find the original number.

26. The difference between the opening and closing stock market quotations for Azuki stock was $28\frac{1}{2}$ points. If the closing price had been 5 points higher, the closing price quotation would have been double the opening quotation. Find the opening and closing quotation prices for Azuki stock.

27. A canoe is paddled downstream in 2 h. The return trip takes 5 h. Find the rate of the canoe in still water if the rate of the stream's flow is 3 mph.

Solve by substitution.

28. $y = \frac{2}{3}x + 8$

$3x + 4y = 117$

29. $y = \frac{3}{4}x + 5$

$2x + 3y = 100$

30. $y = \frac{3}{8}x$

$5x - 6y = 66$

31. $y = \frac{2}{5}x$

$7y - 2x = 12$

32. $8x = 9y$

$12x - 6y = 5$

33. $20x = 9y$

$16x + 18y = 21$

 Solve for x and y. Express the solutions using a, b, c, and d.

34. $y = ax + b$

$y = cx + d$

35. $ay = bx$

$x + y = c$

36. $ax + by = c$

$x - y = d$

Solve by substitution.

37. $7y + 18xy = 30$

$13y - 18xy = 90$

38. $xy - x = 14$

$5 - xy = 2x$

39. $7x + xy = 30$

$3x - xy = 10$

 EVIEW EXERCISES

State the property or definition that is illustrated by each statement.

1. $243 \cdot 1 = 243$

2. $6 + 0 = 0 + 6$

3. $987 \cdot 37 + 13 \cdot 37 = (987 + 13) \cdot 37$

4. $(6.3 + 4.93) + 2.07 = 6.3 + (4.93 + 2.07)$

5. $43 \cdot \left(\frac{1}{43}\right) = 1$

6. $\pi \cdot \sqrt{3}$ is a real number.

[1-4, 1-5]

7. Find a pattern. Then use it to write the next three terms in the sequence.

$$\frac{1}{2}, \frac{2}{4}, \frac{3}{8}, \frac{4}{16}, \ldots$$

[1-6]

8. Write Q in terms of n.

n	2	3	4	5	6
Q	3	8	15	24	35

[1-6]

9. Write the nth term of this sequence.

$$5, 10, 15, 20, 25, \ldots$$

[1-6]

10. Write a simplified expression for this puzzle. Let n represent the number. Select a two-digit whole number. Multiply it by 7, and then multiply the result by 13. To that result add 10 times the original number. The result is a four-digit number with the original number as the first two digits and the last two digits.

[1-6]

Solving Systems Using Linear Combinations

Consider this system of two linear equations in two variables.

$$(1) \quad 2x + 3y = 11$$
$$(2) \quad 4x - y = -13$$

The solution of the system is $\{(-2, 5)\}$.

Suppose that both sides of equation (1) are multiplied by a nonzero constant, 3, and both sides of equation (2) are multiplied by a nonzero constant, -1.

$$(3) \quad 6x + 9y = 33$$
$$(4) \quad -4x + y = 13$$

Form a new equation (5) by adding the respective sides of equations (3) and (4).

$$(5) \quad 2x + 10y = 46$$

Equation 5 is called a **linear combination** of equations (1) and (2). Note that the pair $(-2, 5)$ that is the common solution of equations (1) and (2) is also a solution of the linear combination, equation (5).

$$2x + 10y = 46$$
$$2(-2) + 10(5) = 46$$
$$46 = 46$$

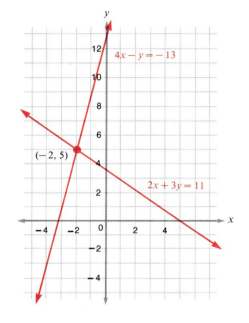

In general, any linear combination of the equations of a system produces another linear equation. The solutions of the new equation must also contain the solution of the original system. By selecting constants so that the linear combination is an equation in only one variable, we can solve the system. For example, in the system above we can multiply both sides of equation (2) by 3 and then add the respective sides of the equations.

$$
\begin{aligned}
2x + 3y &= 11 \\
12x - 3y &= -39 \\
\hline
14x \phantom{{}+3y} &= -28 \\
x \phantom{{}+3y} &= -2
\end{aligned}
$$

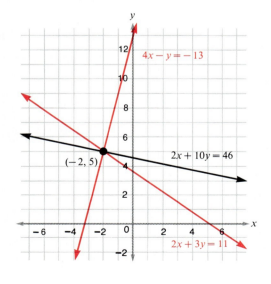

The graph of this equation is a vertical line containing the solution of the system. Since each point on this line has an x-coordinate of -2, we know the x-coordinate of the solution of the system.

Similarly, we can multiply both sides of the first equation of the system by -2 and add.

$$
\begin{array}{r}
-4x - 6y = -22 \\
\underline{4x - y = -13} \\
-7y = -35 \\
y = 5
\end{array}
$$

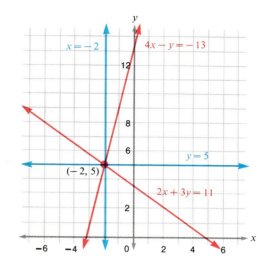

The graph of this equation is a horizontal line containing the solution of the system. Since each point on this line has a y-coordinate of 5, this gives the y-coordinate of the system. The solution of the system is the ordered pair $(-2, 5)$.

Example 1 Solve. $3x + 2y = 8$
$5x - 3y = 26$

Solution Transform each of the equations to change the coefficients of y to opposites. Multiply both sides of the first equation by 3 and both sides of the second equation by 2.

$$
\begin{array}{r}
9x + 6y = 24 \\
10x - 6y = 52
\end{array}
$$

Now add the left sides and the right sides to get this linear combination.

$$
\begin{array}{r}
19x = 76 \\
x = 4
\end{array}
$$

The y-value of the solution can be found in a similar way. Multiply both sides of the first equation by 5 and both sides of the second equation by -3. Then add.

$$
\begin{array}{r}
15x + 10y = 40 \\
-15x + 9y = -78 \\
19y = -38 \\
y = -2
\end{array}
$$

Answer $\{(4, -2)\}$

Check Substitute in the original equations.

$$
\begin{array}{ll}
3x + 2y = 8 & 5x - 3y = 26 \\
3(4) + 2(-2) \stackrel{?}{=} 8 & 5(4) - 3(-2) \stackrel{?}{=} 26 \\
12 - 4 = 8 \quad \text{True} & 20 + 6 = 26 \quad \text{True}
\end{array}
$$

To solve for the second variable, it is often easier to substitute the value found for the first variable into one of the original equations and then solve the resulting equation for the second variable.

Example 2 Solve. $2x + 3y = 17$
$5x + 8y = 20$

Solution *Multiply the first equation by 8, and the second by −3.*

$$16x + 24y = 136$$
$$\underline{-15x - 24y = -60}$$

Add.

$$x = 76$$

Substitute 76 for x in the first equation and solve for y.

$$2(76) + 3y = 17$$
$$3y = -135$$
$$y = -45$$

Answer $\{(76, -45)\}$

Check The check is left to the student.

Example 3 **Solve using linear combinations.** $2x + 5y = 7$
$-4x - 10y = -14$

Solution Multiply the first equation by 2 and then add.

$$4x + 10y = 14$$
$$\underline{-4x - 10y = -14}$$
$$0 = 0$$

Answer Since both variables are eliminated and the equation is true, the system is dependent. The solution is $\{(x, y): 2x + 5y = 7\}$.

*C*LASSROOM EXERCISES

Solve by writing a linear combination that has no *y*-term.

1. $2x - y = 7$
   $3x + 2y = 14$

2. $2y - 3x = 5$
   $4y + 2x = -4$

Solve by writing a linear combination that has no *x*-term.

3. $5x - 2y = 10$
   $4x + 2y = 8$

4. $3y + 4x = 7$
   $2y + 2x = 9$

Solve.

5. One press can print 400 more pages per hour than another press. Together, the two presses can print 11,400 pages in 3 h. What is the rate of each press in pages per hour?

RITTEN EXERCISES

A Solve using linear combinations.

1. $2x + 3y = 10$
   $x - 6y = -10$

2. $3x - 2y = 0$
   $x - 4y = -10$

3. $3x + 2y = 14$
   $9x - 5y = 31$

4. $4x - y = -5$
   $2x + 3y = -13$

5. $3x - 4y = 4$
   $2x + 4y = 56$

6. $5x + 3y = 73$
   $3x - 3y = 15$

7. $4x + 3y = 11$
   $4x + 5y = 5$

8. $5x + 6y = 5$
   $5x + 5y = 10$

Solve using linear combinations. Check by graphing the given equations.

9. $2x + 5y = 1$
   $3x - 10y = 19$

10. $3x + 4y = 7$
    $4x - 2y = 24$

11. $2x - 5y = -24$
    $3x + 2y = 2$

12. $5x - 2y = -25$
    $2x + 3y = 9$

13. $3x - 4y = -4$
    $6x - 2y = 1$

14. $5x - 3y = -1$
    $3x + 7y = 6$

15. $6x - 12y = 5$
    $9x - 16y = 6$

16. $12x - 8y = 1$
    $3x - 16y = 9$

Solve by writing two equations in two variables.

17. The sum of two numbers is 100. Their difference is 30. What are the numbers?

18. The sum of two numbers is 46. Twice their difference is 24. What are the numbers?

19. The quarters in a bank are worth 55 cents more than the dimes. If there are 5 more dimes than quarters, how many quarters are in the bank?

20. There are 5 more quarters than dimes in a pile. If the total value of the dimes and quarters is $6.50, how many dimes are there?

B Write each equation in the form $ax + by = c$, where a, b, and c are integers. Then solve the system using linear combinations.

21. $12(x + y) = 75$
    $3x + 2y = 15$

22. $16(x - y) = 22$
    $24x + 8y = 105$

23. $\frac{1}{2}x + \frac{2}{3}y = \frac{5}{6}$
    $\frac{5}{12}x + \frac{7}{12}y = \frac{3}{4}$

24. $\frac{x}{10} + \frac{y}{15} = \frac{1}{6}$
    $\frac{x}{4} - \frac{y}{8} = 1$

25. $3x - y = 5 - 3x$
    $3x - 3y = 8 - x$

26. $3(x + 2y) = 2 + 5y$
    $2(3x - y) = 8 - 5y$

pplications

Solve by writing two equations in two variables.

27. Machine P can produce 200 gears per hour, and machine Q can produce 300 gears per hour. Running a total of 7 h, the machines produced 1650 gears. How many hours did each machine run?

28. A small package of nurps weighs 20 g, and a large package weighs 120 g. Mrs. Murphy bought 13 packages of nurps and found that their total weight was 1060 g. How many packages of each size did she buy?

29. Mr. Kelley drove part of a trip at 85 km/h and part in a rain shower at 75 km/h. If the 335-km trip took 4 h, how long did the rain shower last?

30. Two small tubes and three large tubes of toothpaste cost $6.53, whereas three small tubes and two large tubes cost $5.82. What is the cost of one small tube of toothpaste?

31. Two numbers that are in the ratio of 5:4 have a sum of 24. What are the numbers?

32. The denominator of a fraction is 12 more than the numerator. If the numerator is doubled and 5 is added to the denominator, the resulting fraction is equal to 1. What is the original fraction?

33. An old addressing machine worked for 3 h and a new addressing machine worked for 4 h to put addresses on 50,400 envelopes. On another job, the old machine worked for 1 h and the new machine worked for 6 h to address 58,800 envelopes. How many envelopes does the new machine address per hour?

34. Salt solutions of 60% and 15% are mixed to produce a 450 cm^3 mixture of a 25% solution. How much of each solution is required?

35. Eighty pounds of 20% copper alloy are to be produced by melting down a bar of 12% alloy with another bar of 32% alloy. How much of each alloy is used?

[C] **Use linear combinations to reduce the system to two equations in two variables. Then solve the reduced system and find x, y, and z.**

36. $x + y + z = 3$
$x - y + z = 7$
$2x + y + z = 4$

37. $x + 2y + 3z = 16$
$x + y + 2z = 9$
$x - y + 2z = 5$

38. $2x + y - 2z = 1$
$4x - y + 3z = 5$
$6x + 2y - 4z = 3$

39. $3x + 2y + z = 4$
$6x + 6y - z = 18$
$9x - 10y - 2z = 19$

REVIEW EXERCISES

Solve.   [2-1]

1. $0.3x - 0.5 = 6.7$ **2.** $\dfrac{3x + 2}{4} = 5$ **3.** $\dfrac{1}{2}x - \dfrac{5}{6} = \dfrac{2}{3}x$

Solve each equation for the indicated variable.   [2-2]

4. $A = \dfrac{1}{2}bh$, for h **5.** $ax + by + c = 0$, for y

6. $V = c\left(1 - \dfrac{L}{N}\right)$, for L

Write an equation and solve.   [2-3]

7. If the sum of three consecutive integers is 147, what are the integers?

$\mathcal{S}$elf-Quiz 1

4-1 **1.** Solve by graphing. $\quad 3x - y = 10$
$$5x + 2y = 2$$

2. Write two equations in two variables. Solve the system by graphing.

Beryl has 20 records and tapes. She has 6 more records than tapes. How many records does she have?

4-2 **3.** Solve by substitution. $\quad y - 3x = 4$
$$3y + 2x = 1$$

4. Write two equations in two variables. Solve the system by substitution.

Moving with the current, a boat took 2 h to travel 10 mi downstream. The return trip against the current took 5 h. Find the rate of the boat in still water.

4-3 **5.** Solve using linear combinations. $\quad 5x + 4y = 6$
$$2x - 3y = 7$$

6. Write two equations in two variables. Solve the system by linear combinations.

A 30% potassium chloride solution is mixed with a 70% potassium chloride solution to make 200 mL of a 60% solution. How many milliliters of each solution are required?

$\mathcal{E}$XTENSION   Statistics: Dispersion

The following two sets of data have the same mean (60) and the same range (40).

Set 1	40	50	60	70	80	**Set 2**	40	60	79	80
		58	60				41		79	80
		59	63				41			80

However, the data in set 1 are grouped closely about the mean, whereas those in set 2 are **dispersed** away from the mean.

The mean for each of sets A, B, and C is 79.5, and the range is 28.

Set A: 65, 66, 69, 77, 84, 90, 92, 93
Set B: 64, 72, 77, 79, 82, 84, 86, 92
Set C: 66, 67, 72, 76, 83, 88, 90, 94

1. Arrange the data in sets A, B, and C as shown above (grouped by tens).

Estimate which set has the greater dispersion from the mean.

2. A or B? **3.** B or C? **4.** A or C?

LESSON 4-4

Determinants

Systems of equations are used to solve very complex problems in business, science, transportation, and communication. The problems may involve hundreds of equations in hundreds of variables. Finding solutions to such problems is humanly posssible only by developing generalized techniques suited to computer application.

All systems of two linear equations in two variables can be written in the form

$$a_1x + b_1y = c_1$$
$$a_2x + b_2y = c_2$$

By solving this general system, we can write formulas for finding x and y in terms of the constants a_1, b_1, c_1 and a_2, b_2, c_2. Multiplying both sides of the first equation by b_2 and both sides of the second equation by $-b_1$ gives

$$a_1b_2x + b_1b_2y = c_1b_2$$
$$-a_2b_1x - b_1b_2y = -c_2b_1$$

Adding these two equations gives

$$a_1b_2x - a_2b_1x = c_1b_2 - c_2b_1$$

Factoring the left side gives

$$(a_1b_2 - a_2b_1)x = c_1b_2 - c_2b_1$$

Asssuming that $a_1b_2 - a_2b_1 \neq 0$, we solve for x.

$$x = \frac{c_1b_2 - c_2b_1}{a_1b_2 - a_2b_1}$$

Similarly, we solve the system of equations for y.

$$y = \frac{a_1c_2 - a_2c_1}{a_1b_2 - a_2b_1}$$

To apply these formulas for finding x and y, a given system must first be rewritten in the form of the general system shown above. Using the coefficients and constants in these equations, the specific solution of the given system can be found by substitution.

General Solution of a System of Two Linear Equations in Two Variables

For all real numbers a_1, b_1, c_1, a_2, b_2, and c_2, the solution of the system

$$a_1x + b_1y = c_1$$
$$a_2x + b_2y = c_2$$

is

$$x = \frac{c_1b_2 - c_2b_1}{a_1b_2 - a_2b_1} \quad \text{and} \quad y = \frac{a_1c_2 - a_2c_1}{a_1b_2 - a_2b_1}$$

where $a_1b_2 - a_2b_1 \neq 0$.

Example 1 Use the formulas given above to solve this system.

$$2x - 3y = 7$$
$$x + 4y = 9$$

Solution Substitute 2, -3, and 7 for a_1, b_1, and c_1, respectively, and substitute 1, 4, and 9 for a_2, b_2, and c_2, respectively.

$$x = \frac{7 \cdot 4 - 9(-3)}{2 \cdot 4 - 1(-3)} \qquad y = \frac{2 \cdot 9 - 1 \cdot 7}{2 \cdot 4 - 1(-3)}$$

$$= \frac{28 + 27}{8 + 3} \qquad\qquad = \frac{18 - 7}{8 + 3}$$

$$= 5 \qquad\qquad\qquad = 1$$

Answer The solution is $\{(5, 1)\}$.

Check The check is left to the student.

The general solution of a system can be written and remembered more easily using **determinants.**

Definition: Determinant

A *determinant* is a real number represented by a square array of numbers.

For example, the following is a **second-order determinant** (*second order* because it has two rows and two columns).

Column 1 ———⟶ ⟵——— Column 2

$$\begin{vmatrix} 3 & -5 \\ 2 & 4 \end{vmatrix} \begin{matrix} \leftarrow\text{Row 1} \\ \leftarrow\text{Row 2} \end{matrix}$$

The value of a second-order determinant is computed by subtracting the products of the elements (numbers) on the two diagonals.

Definition: The Value of a Second-Order Determinant

$$\begin{vmatrix} a & b \\ c & d \end{vmatrix} = ad - cb$$

Example 2 Simplify each determinant.

a. $\begin{vmatrix} 2 & 0 \\ 3 & 7 \end{vmatrix}$ b. $\begin{vmatrix} -3 & 1 \\ 4 & -1 \end{vmatrix}$

Solution a. $\begin{vmatrix} 2 & 0 \\ 3 & 7 \end{vmatrix}$

$2 \cdot 7 - 3 \cdot 0 = 14$

b. $\begin{vmatrix} -3 & 1 \\ 4 & -1 \end{vmatrix}$

$-3(-1) - 4 \cdot 1 = -1$

The formulas for x and y in the general solution of a system are fractions. The denominators of these fractions are expressed by a determinant D called the **coefficient determinant.**

$$\begin{aligned} a_1 x + b_1 y &= c_1 \\ a_2 x + b_2 y &= c_2 \end{aligned} \qquad D = \begin{vmatrix} a_1 & b_1 \\ a_2 & b_2 \end{vmatrix} = a_1 b_2 - a_2 b_1$$

The numerators of the fractions for x and y are represented by determinants D_x and D_y, respectively.

$$D_x = \begin{vmatrix} c_1 & b_1 \\ c_2 & b_2 \end{vmatrix} = c_1 b_2 - c_2 b_1 \qquad D_y = \begin{vmatrix} a_1 & c_1 \\ a_2 & c_2 \end{vmatrix} = a_1 c_2 - a_2 c_1$$

Determinants D_x and D_y can be written by replacing the column of coefficients in D for variable x or variable y with the corresponding constant terms.

The formulas for x and y in the general solution of a system of two linear equations in two variables are usually written with determinants. This statement of the general solution is called **Cramer's rule.**

Cramer's Rule

For all real numbers a_1, b_1, c_1, a_2, b_2, and c_2, the solution of the system

$$\begin{aligned} a_1 x + b_1 y &= c_1 \\ a_2 x + b_2 y &= c_2 \end{aligned}$$

is

$$\left(\frac{D_x}{D}, \frac{D_y}{D} \right)$$

where $D \neq 0$. If $D = 0$, the system has no solution or infinitely many solutions.

Example 3   **Solve using Cramer's rule.** $2x = 23 + 3y$
$$-y = x + 1$$

Solution   *Write the system in the general form.*

$$2x - 3y = 23$$
$$-x - y = 1$$

Evaluate D, D_x, and D_y.

$$D = \begin{vmatrix} 2 & -3 \\ -1 & -1 \end{vmatrix} = -2 - 3 = -5$$

$$D_x = \begin{vmatrix} 23 & -3 \\ 1 & -1 \end{vmatrix} = -23 - (-3) = -20$$

$$D_y = \begin{vmatrix} 2 & 23 \\ -1 & 1 \end{vmatrix} = 2 - (-23) = 25$$

Apply Cramer's rule.

$$x = \frac{D_x}{D} = \frac{-20}{-5} = 4$$

$$y = \frac{D_y}{D} = \frac{25}{-5} = -5$$

Answer $\{(4, -5)\}$

Example 4   **Solve.**

One evening 76 people gathered to play doubles and singles table tennis. There were 26 games going on at one time. If a doubles game requires 4 players and a singles game requires 2 players, how many games of each kind were in progress at one time?

Solution   Let x = the number of doubles games and y = the number of singles games.

$$x + y = 26$$
$$4x + 2y = 76$$

Apply Cramer's rule to find x.

$$x = \frac{\begin{vmatrix} 26 & 1 \\ 76 & 2 \end{vmatrix}}{\begin{vmatrix} 1 & 1 \\ 4 & 2 \end{vmatrix}} = \frac{-24}{-2} = 12$$

Substitute 12 for x in the first equation and solve for y.

$$12 + y = 26$$
$$y = 14$$

Answer   There are 12 doubles games and 14 singles games.

Check   The check is left to the student.

*C*LASSROOM EXERCISES

Evaluate each determinant.

1. $\begin{vmatrix} -3 & -4 \\ 2 & 5 \end{vmatrix}$

2. $\begin{vmatrix} 4 & 0 \\ 5 & 1 \end{vmatrix}$

3. $\begin{vmatrix} 1 & 0 \\ 0 & 1 \end{vmatrix}$

Solve using Cramer's rule.

4. $3x - 2y = 5$
   $x + y = 4$

5. $5x = 7 + 11y$
   $y = 1 + x$

*W*RITTEN EXERCISES

A **Evaluate each determinant.**

1. $\begin{vmatrix} 2 & 3 \\ 5 & 4 \end{vmatrix}$

2. $\begin{vmatrix} 2 & 5 \\ 3 & 4 \end{vmatrix}$

3. $\begin{vmatrix} 3 & 4 \\ 2 & 5 \end{vmatrix}$

4. $\begin{vmatrix} 4 & 5 \\ 2 & 3 \end{vmatrix}$

5. $\begin{vmatrix} \frac{1}{2} & -\frac{1}{3} \\ 6 & 10 \end{vmatrix}$

6. $\begin{vmatrix} \frac{3}{4} & -\frac{2}{3} \\ 9 & 12 \end{vmatrix}$

7. $\begin{vmatrix} 10 & -6 \\ -5 & 7 \end{vmatrix}$

8. $\begin{vmatrix} -2 & 3 \\ 13 & -20 \end{vmatrix}$

Write D, D_x, and D_y for each system of equations. Evaluate each determinant.

9. $2x + 5y = 7$
   $3x + 9y = 1$

10. $4x + 5y = 6$
    $5x + 6y = 3$

11. $7x - 2y = 11$
    $5x + 3y = 6$

12. $6x + 7y = 2$
    $5x - 4y = 10$

13. $\frac{1}{2}x - 3y = 6$
    $\frac{2}{3}x - 8y = 10$

14. $\frac{3}{4}x - 9y = 15$
    $\frac{1}{3}x - 4y = 12$

Solve using Cramer's rule.

15. $5x - 3y = 2$
    $7x + 2y = 3$

16. $4x - 7y = 10$
    $6x + 2y = 7$

17. $5x + 8y = 3$
    $2x + 4y = 7$

18. $-2x + 9y = 5$
    $3x - 10y = 2$

19. $0.3x - 2.3y = 1.5$
    $0.2x - 0.5y = 2$

20. $0.6x - 1.4y = 3$
    $0.5x - 1.2y = 2.1$

21. $2x = 3y + 7$
    $7x + 5y = 8$

22. $4y = 6x + 9$
    $4x + 8y = 5$

23. $10x - 8y - 3 = 0$
    $9x - 7y - 12 = 0$

24. $11x - 5y - 8 = 0$
    $13x - 6y - 4 = 0$

25. $2(x - 3y) = 7$
    $3(2x + 4y) = 1$

26. $5(3x + y) = 2$
    $4(2x + 5y) = 9$

B **Solve.**

27. $\begin{vmatrix} 6x & 5 \\ 2x & 3 \end{vmatrix} = 12$

28. $\begin{vmatrix} 5x & -3 \\ 2x & 1 \end{vmatrix} = -11$

29. $\begin{vmatrix} 4x & 3x \\ 7 & 6 \end{vmatrix} = 15$

30. $\begin{vmatrix} 7 & 3x \\ 5 & -2 \end{vmatrix} = -x$

31. $\begin{vmatrix} 6 & 7 \\ -x & 3 \end{vmatrix} = 4$

32. $\begin{vmatrix} 2x & 7 \\ 2 & 3 \end{vmatrix} = x + 6$

**pplications**

For each problem, write two equations in two variables, solve the system using determinants, and answer the question.

33. When catering a wedding reception, the Purple Parrot charges a fixed amount plus a certain amount for each guest. The charge for 75 guests is $312.50 and the charge for 200 guests is $750. What are the fixed charge and the charge per guest?

34. King's Auto Repair charges for parts and labor when installing mufflers. Mandy Moore had Model 1030 installed on her car. The installment time was 0.4 h, and her bill was $41.75. Leah Lake had the same model muffler installed on her car, but the installation time was 0.6 h. Her bill was $49.75. What is the cost of a Model 1030 muffler and what is the labor charge per hour?

35. The Maxton Car Rental Company has a daily charge plus a charge per mile. Brad Brown rented a car for 2 days and drove 325 mi. His bill was $153.75. Geno Gray rented a car for 3 days, drove it 280 mi, and was charged $158.00. What are the daily charge and the charge per mile?

36. John Whitefeather needed $80,000 for a business venture. He borrowed some of the money from a relative and paid 5% interest. He borrowed the rest of the money from a finance company at an interest rate of 20%. His yearly interest payments on the two loans was $13,750. How much was borrowed from each source?

 37. The following system is inconsistent. Explain what happens when you attempt to solve an inconsistent system using Cramer's rule.

$$x + 3y = 8$$
$$2x + 6y = 5$$

38. The following system is dependent for all nonzero real values of k.

$$ax + by = c$$
$$kax + kby = kc$$

Show that $D = D_x = D_y = 0$.

EVIEW EXERCISES

Solve and graph on a number line.

1. $x + 0.4 < 0.6x + 2$ **2.** $3(x - 2) \geq x + 10$ [2-4]

3. $0 \leq 2x - 1 \leq 5$ **4.** $x < 10 - 3x < 40$ [2-5]

5. $|x - 3| < \dfrac{1}{2}$ **6.** $|2x - 1| > 3$ [2-6]

7. Write an absolute-value inequality to describe this graph.

LESSON 4-5

Third-Order Determinants

We need to expand our methods for evaluating determinants to include third- and higher-order determinants. This is a **third-order determinant.**

$$\begin{vmatrix} 2 & 0 & 1 \\ 3 & -1 & -2 \\ 4 & 5 & -3 \end{vmatrix}$$

In a determinant, each element is associated with a **minor.** The minor for an element is the determinant that remains after the row and column containing the element have been deleted.

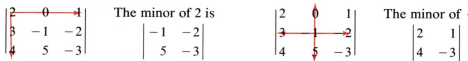

All determinants can be evaluated using expansion by minors.

Steps for Expanding a Determinant by Minors

1. Select any row or column.
2. Multiply each element of that row or column by its minor.
3. If the sum of the row number and the column number of the element is odd, multiply the product of step (2) by -1.
4. Add the products.

The position of an element in the chart at the right is indicated by a negative sign if the product of that element and its minor must be multiplied by -1 in step 3.

$$\begin{vmatrix} + & - & + \\ - & + & - \\ + & - & + \end{vmatrix}$$

Example 1   Evaluate this third-order determinant.

$$\begin{vmatrix} 4 & 2 & -1 \\ 1 & 0 & 3 \\ 2 & 1 & 3 \end{vmatrix}$$

Solution 1   Select a row or column, say column 1. Expand by minors.

$$\begin{vmatrix} 4 & 2 & -1 \\ 1 & 0 & 3 \\ 2 & 1 & 3 \end{vmatrix} \qquad 4\begin{vmatrix} 0 & 3 \\ 1 & 3 \end{vmatrix} = 4(0 \cdot 3 - 1 \cdot 3) = -12$$

Example 1 (continued)

$$\begin{vmatrix} 4 & 2 & -1 \\ 1 & 0 & 3 \\ 2 & 1 & 3 \end{vmatrix} \qquad 1\begin{vmatrix} 2 & -1 \\ 1 & 3 \end{vmatrix} = 1(2\cdot3 - 1(-1)) = 7$$

$$\begin{vmatrix} 4 & 2 & -1 \\ 1 & 0 & 3 \\ 2 & 1 & 3 \end{vmatrix} \qquad 2\begin{vmatrix} 2 & -1 \\ 0 & 3 \end{vmatrix} = 2(2\cdot3 - 0(-1)) = 12$$

According to the chart given with step (3), the second product must be multiplied by -1.

$$-1(7) = -7$$

$$\begin{vmatrix} + & - & + \\ - & + & - \\ + & - & + \end{vmatrix}$$

Add the products. $-12 + (-7) + 12 = -7$

Solution 2 Select a different row or column, say row 2. Find the product of each element of row 2 and its minor.

$$\begin{vmatrix} 4 & 2 & -1 \\ 1 & 0 & 3 \\ 2 & 1 & 3 \end{vmatrix} \qquad 1\begin{vmatrix} 2 & -1 \\ 1 & 3 \end{vmatrix} = 1(2\cdot3 - 1(-1)) = 7$$

$$\begin{vmatrix} 4 & 2 & -1 \\ 1 & 0 & 3 \\ 2 & 1 & 3 \end{vmatrix} \qquad 0\begin{vmatrix} 4 & -1 \\ 2 & 3 \end{vmatrix} = 0$$

$$\begin{vmatrix} 4 & 2 & -1 \\ 1 & 0 & 3 \\ 2 & 1 & 3 \end{vmatrix} \qquad 3\begin{vmatrix} 4 & 2 \\ 2 & 1 \end{vmatrix} = 3(4\cdot1 - 2\cdot2) = 0$$

The first and third products above must be multiplied by -1.
Add the products. $-7 + 0 + 0 = -7$

$$\begin{vmatrix} + & - & + \\ - & + & - \\ + & - & + \end{vmatrix}$$

Example 1 shows the fact that the value of the determinant is the same regardless of the row or column used in the computation. Solution 2 shows that we can simplify the computation by selecting a row or column with one or more zero elements.

Cramer's rule can be extended to systems of three equations in three variables. Consider the following system:

$$a_1x + b_1y + c_1z = d_1$$
$$a_2x + b_2y + c_2z = d_2$$
$$a_3x + b_3y + c_3z = d_3$$

The solution of the system of three equations in three variables is the set of **ordered triples** $\{(x, y, z)\}$:

$$x = \frac{D_x}{D}, \qquad y = \frac{D_y}{D}, \qquad z = \frac{D_z}{D}$$

where D is the coefficient determinant and $D \neq 0$.

$$D = \begin{vmatrix} a_1 & b_1 & c_1 \\ a_2 & b_2 & c_2 \\ a_3 & b_3 & c_3 \end{vmatrix}$$

The numerator of the fractions for x, y, and z are represented by determinants D_x, D_y, and D_z, respectively.

$$D_x = \begin{vmatrix} d_1 & b_1 & c_1 \\ d_2 & b_2 & c_2 \\ d_3 & b_3 & c_3 \end{vmatrix}, \qquad D_y = \begin{vmatrix} a_1 & d_1 & c_1 \\ a_2 & d_2 & c_2 \\ a_3 & d_3 & c_3 \end{vmatrix}, \qquad D_z = \begin{vmatrix} a_1 & b_1 & d_1 \\ a_2 & b_2 & d_2 \\ a_3 & b_3 & d_3 \end{vmatrix}$$

If $D = 0$, the system has no solution or infinitely many solutions.

Example 2 Use Cramer's rule to solve this system.
$$2x + y - z = 9$$
$$3x - 4y + z = 3$$
$$x - 3y + 2z = -4$$

Solution

$$D = \begin{vmatrix} 2 & 1 & -1 \\ 3 & -4 & 1 \\ 1 & -3 & 2 \end{vmatrix} = -10 \qquad D_x = \begin{vmatrix} 9 & 1 & -1 \\ 3 & -4 & 1 \\ -4 & -3 & 2 \end{vmatrix} = -30$$

$$D_y = \begin{vmatrix} 2 & 9 & -1 \\ 3 & 3 & 1 \\ 1 & -4 & 2 \end{vmatrix} = -10 \qquad D_z = \begin{vmatrix} 2 & 1 & 9 \\ 3 & -4 & 3 \\ 1 & -3 & -4 \end{vmatrix} = 20$$

$$x = \frac{D_x}{D} = \frac{-30}{-10} = 3, \qquad y = \frac{D_y}{D} = \frac{-10}{-10} = 1, \qquad z = \frac{D_z}{D} = \frac{20}{-10} = -2$$

Answer $\{(3, 1, -2)\}$

Check The check is left to the student.

𝒞LASSROOM EXERCISES

Write the minor of the given element for this determinant.
1. 4   **2.** -6 **3.** 2

$$\begin{vmatrix} 3 & 4 & -2 \\ 1 & 0 & 0 \\ 2 & -2 & -6 \end{vmatrix}$$

4. If the elements of the third row and their minors are used to evaluate the determinant above, indicate the products that are to be multiplied by -1.

5. What is the most efficient row or column to use in expanding the determinant above?

Evaluate each determinant.

6. $\begin{vmatrix} 3 & 2 & -1 \\ 4 & -3 & -2 \\ 1 & 2 & 1 \end{vmatrix}$

7. $\begin{vmatrix} -2 & -1 & -3 \\ -4 & -2 & -6 \\ 1 & 2 & 4 \end{vmatrix}$

8. $\begin{vmatrix} 1 & 0 & 0 \\ 0 & 1 & 0 \\ 0 & 0 & 1 \end{vmatrix}$

RITTEN EXERCISES

 Write the minor of the given element for this determinant. Evaluate the minor.

$\begin{vmatrix} 2 & 1 & 3 \\ 0 & 5 & 6 \\ 4 & 7 & \dfrac{1}{2} \end{vmatrix}$

1. 1   **2.** 2   **3.** 3   **4.** 4

5. 5   **6.** 6   **7.** 0   **8.** $\dfrac{1}{2}$

Evaluate each determinant.

9. $\begin{vmatrix} 0 & 1 & 2 \\ 2 & 1 & 2 \\ 3 & 2 & 1 \end{vmatrix}$

10. $\begin{vmatrix} 1 & 0 & 2 \\ 2 & 1 & 3 \\ 1 & 3 & 2 \end{vmatrix}$

11. $\begin{vmatrix} -2 & 3 & 5 \\ 4 & -1 & 3 \\ 5 & 0 & 6 \end{vmatrix}$

12. $\begin{vmatrix} 1 & 2 & -8 \\ 2 & 4 & 7 \\ 3 & 6 & 10 \end{vmatrix}$

13. $\begin{vmatrix} 1 & 2 & -4 \\ 1 & -3 & 4 \\ 1 & 5 & 8 \end{vmatrix}$

14. $\begin{vmatrix} 3 & 2 & 6 \\ -1 & -2 & 1 \\ -4 & 0 & 0 \end{vmatrix}$

Solve using Cramer's rule.

15. $\begin{aligned} 2x + 3y + 4z &= 3 \\ 4x - 2y - 3z &= 4 \\ 3x + y - 2z &= 10 \end{aligned}$

16. $\begin{aligned} x + 2y + 3z &= 11 \\ 2x - 2y - z &= 12 \\ 2x + 3y + z &= 5 \end{aligned}$

17. $\begin{aligned} x - y + z &= 7 \\ 2x - 3y - z &= 3 \\ 5x - 4y &= 6 \end{aligned}$

18. $\begin{aligned} x + y &= 10 \\ 2x - y - z &= 5 \\ 5x - 3y - 2z &= 8 \end{aligned}$

19. $\begin{aligned} 8x + 5y + 3z &= 7 \\ -2x + 3y - 2z &= 2 \\ 5x - 2y + z &= 7 \end{aligned}$

20. $\begin{aligned} 4x + 2y - z &= 1 \\ -5x + 6y - 3z &= 3 \\ x + y + z &= 11 \end{aligned}$

B Solve.

21. $\begin{vmatrix} 1 & 0 & 3 \\ 0 & x & 4 \\ 0 & 2 & 3 \end{vmatrix} = 7$

22. $\begin{vmatrix} 0 & 7 & 9 \\ x & 1 & 2 \\ 0 & 2 & 3 \end{vmatrix} = 24$

23. $\begin{vmatrix} x & 1 & 5 \\ x & 2 & 0 \\ 2 & 3 & 4 \end{vmatrix} = 4x$

𝓐pplications

Write a system of three equations in three variables for each problem and solve by Cramer's rule.

24. The measure of the largest angle of a triangle is equal to twice the sum of the measures of the other two angles. The sum of the measures of the smallest and largest angles is three times the measure of the remaining angle. Find the measures of the three angles.

25. Find a three-digit number such that the sum of its digits is 12, twice the hundreds digit equals the sum of the other two digits, and the units digit is two more than the sum of the tens and hundreds digits.

26. A metallurgist has three alloys available. Their composition by weight is given in the following table:

	Lead	Copper	Zinc
Alloy A	60%	20%	20%
Alloy B	20%	50%	30%
Alloy C	40%	10%	50%

How many kilograms of each alloy must the metallurgist melt and mix together in order to obtain 20.7 kg of a new alloy containing equal amounts by weight of the three metals?

C **27.** In drilling for oil, a "wildcatter" estimates that his drilling expenses E, in \$100,000's, are related to the depth x, in miles, of the well by the formula $E = a + bx + cx^2$, where a, b, and c are constants. The following costs were reported for drilling the well.

> Cost of 1 mile: \$ 400,000
> Cost of 2 miles: \$1,300,000
> Cost of 3 miles: \$3,000,000

Find the formula by determining a, b, and c and calculate the cost of drilling 4 miles.

28. Show that the technique for evaluating second-order determinants (see Lesson 4-4) is expansion by minors.

The value of a fourth-order determinant is found by following these steps.

1. Select any row or column.

2. Multiply each element of that row or column by its minor, a third-order determinant.

3. If the sum of the row number and the column number is odd, multiply the product of step (2) by -1.

4. Add the products.

Evaluate.

29.
$$\begin{vmatrix} 1 & 0 & 2 & 3 \\ 0 & 4 & 1 & -3 \\ 1 & 4 & 3 & -2 \\ -2 & -2 & 1 & 1 \end{vmatrix}$$

Solve using Cramer's rule.

30.
$$\begin{aligned} w - x - z &= 7 \\ 3w + y + 2z &= 10 \\ 2w - x - y &= 2 \\ 2x + 3y + 4z &= 6 \end{aligned}$$

REVIEW EXERCISES

1. State the missing reasons in this proof that $5x - 4x = x$.   [1-7]

$$5x - 4x = 5x + -(4x) \qquad \underline{\qquad ? \qquad}$$
$$= 5x + (-4)x \qquad \text{For all } a \text{ and } b, -(ab) = (-a)b.$$
$$= (5 + -4)x \qquad \underline{\qquad ? \qquad}$$
$$= 1x \qquad \text{Computation}$$
$$= x \qquad \underline{\qquad ? \qquad}$$

2. Show that the sum of two multiples of 5 is also a multiple of 5. $5x + 5y = 5(x + y)$ [1-7]

Solve by drawing a figure and writing an equation.   [2-7]

3. The two longest sides of a parallelogram are each 10 cm longer than each of the two shortest sides. What are the lengths of each of the sides if the perimeter is 100 cm?

4. The circumference of a path around a lake is 5 km. A cyclist moving at 20 km/h and a runner moving at 10 km/h each leave the same spot at the same time, going in opposite directions around the lake. How long will it take them to meet and how far will each have traveled from the starting point?

The domain of the following relations is $\{x: -4 \leqslant x \leqslant 4\}$. Graph each relation.   [3-1]

5. $\{(x, y): y = |x| + 1\}$
6. $\{(x, y): y = |x + 1|\}$

HISTORICAL NOTE   Determinants   Leibniz

The ideas on which determinants are based were the result of contributions from many mathematicians. A Japanese mathematician Seki Kowa (1683) improved on the Chinese method for solving systems of linear equations. His techniques were similar to those presently used to evaluate determinants.

Gottfried Wilhelm von Leibniz (1693) formally developed the theory of determinants and presented a notation for them. However, our modern vertical-line notation for determinants is credited to the Englishman Arthur Cayley (1841).

Working independently of others, Gabriel Cramer developed many of the ideas for determinants and in 1750 published the rule named in his honor.

Graphing Linear Inequalities in Two Variables

Consider the inequality in one variable

$$3(x - 1) < 12$$

and its graph. The solution of the boundary equation is the point 5. The possible substitutions for x in the inequality are divided by the boundary point into two sets: points in the graph and points not in the graph.

Consider the linear inequality in two variables

$$x + y \geq 3$$

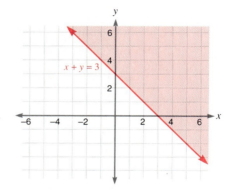

and its graph. The possible substitutions are ordered pairs (x, y). The corresponding boundary equation $x + y = 3$ is a linear function whose graph divides the xy-plane into points that are in the graph or not in the graph of the inequality.

The inequality given below is also linear in two variables.

$$y < 2x + 1$$

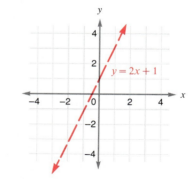

The solutions of the inequality are ordered pairs of real numbers that can be graphed in the coordinate plane. The **boundary** of the graph is the line $y = 2x + 1$. The boundary is not included in the graph because the solutions of the equation are not solutions of the inequality. Therefore, the boundary is drawn as a dashed line.

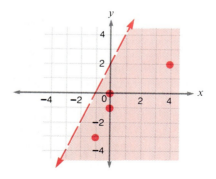

The ordered pairs $(0, 0)$, $(0, -1)$, $(-1, -3)$, and $(4, 2)$ are some solutions of the inequality. Note that the graphs of these solutions are on the same side of the boundary. In fact, each point on that side of the boundary is the graph of a solution. Therefore, we shade all points in that half-plane (all points below the boundary).

Example 1   **Graph.** $y \geq -x + 3$

Solution   Graph the boundary $y = -x + 3$ with a solid line because the points on the boundary are solutions of the inequality.

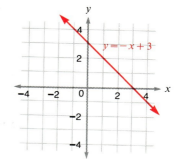

Test one point that is not on the boundary to determine which half-plane to shade. We choose the point $(0, 0)$.

$$y \geq -x + 3$$
$$0 \geq -0 + 3$$
$$0 \geq 3 \qquad \text{False}$$

Since $(0, 0)$ is not a solution, the solutions lie in the opposite half-plane; shade that half-plane.

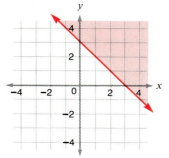

Example 2   **Graph the system.** $y \leq 3x - 1$
                                          $y > -2x + 1$

Solution   Graph $y \leq 3x - 1$ using arrows to show which half-plane is included.

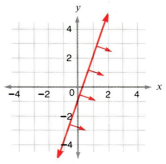

Graph $y > -2x + 1$ using arrows to show which half-plane is included.

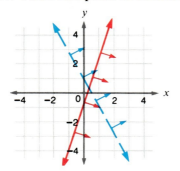

Shade the parts of the plane that are included in both graphs.

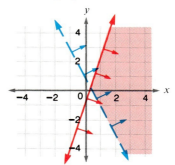

Example 3   **Graph.** $y < x$ or $y > 2x$

Solution   Graph each inequality using arrows to show the half-planes that are included in the graph.

Since the word "or" is used, the solutions of the compound inequality are ordered pairs that are solutions of at least one of the inequalities. Therefore, shade all parts of the plane that are in one or both individual graphs.

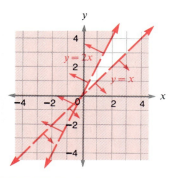

LASSROOM EXERCISES

Graph.

1. $y \geqslant -3x - 2$

2. $y \geqslant 2x - 3$
$y > x + 4$

3. $y > 2x + 1$ or $y < x - 3$

WRITTEN EXERCISES

A State whether the given ordered pair is a solution of the given inequality.

1. $(4, -2)$; $4y - 2x < 2$

2. $(-1, 6)$; $3x + 2y < 7$

3. $(3, 5)$; $y < 2x - 1$

4. $(-2, 1)$; $2y - 3x \leqslant -7$

5. $(4, 0)$; $x \geqslant 4y + 4$

6. $(-2, -3)$; $x - 5y > 13$

State whether the given ordered pairs is a solution of the given system.

7. $(5, 4)$; $-y + 2x < 7$
$3x + 2y > 4$

8. $(-1, 2)$; $4x + 1 > 2y$
$x + 3y < 6$

9. $(-2, 2)$; $y \leqslant 2x + 6$
$-1 < 3x - y$

10. $(0, 0)$; $y \leqslant 7x + 1$
$x > 3y - 2$

11. $(-4, 0.2)$; $y < 2x - 5$
$0.8 > 2x + y - 4$

12. $(0.5, 1.1)$; $3y - 4x < 1.5$
$8 - 2x > 3y$

State whether the boundary of each graph is a solid or a dashed line.

13. $y > 2x + 3$

14. $y \leqslant -2x + 6$

15. $y \geqslant 5x - 6$

16. $y < 6x - 8$

Graph.

17. $y \geqslant x - 4$

18. $y \geqslant 2x - 6$

19. $y < \frac{1}{3}x + 1$

20. $y < \frac{1}{2}x + 2$

21. $y \leqslant -2x + 6$

22. $y \leqslant -\frac{1}{2}x + 4$

23. $y > 3$

24. $x > 2$

Graph each system.

25. $x + y \leqslant 4$
$\quad\, y \geqslant x - 2$

26. $x - y \leqslant 5$
$\quad\, y \leqslant x + 3$

27. $y < x$
$\quad\, y > 2x$

28. $y < \frac{1}{2}x$
$\quad\, y > -2x$

29. $y < 4$
$\quad\, x > -2$

30. $y > 2$
$\quad\, x < -2$

31. $y \geqslant \frac{2}{3}x - 6$
$\quad\, y \leqslant -\frac{1}{2}x + 3$

32. $y \leqslant \frac{3}{4}x + 3$
$\quad\, y \geqslant -\frac{1}{3}x + 1$

Graph.

33. $y + \frac{1}{2}x \geqslant 4$ or $y \geqslant 2x$

34. $y \leqslant -2x + 4$ or $y \geqslant \frac{1}{2}x - 2$

35. $y < -1$ or $y > 2$

36. $x < -2$ or $x - 1 > 0$

37. $y - x > 3$ or $y < x - 3$

38. $y > \frac{1}{2}x$ or $y < \frac{1}{2}x - 2$

39. $y \leqslant -\frac{1}{2}x + 3$ or $y + 2x \leqslant 0$

40. $y + \frac{1}{3}x \leqslant 2$ or $y \leqslant x + 2$

B **41.** $y \leqslant -x + 3$ or $y \geqslant \frac{1}{2}x + \frac{3}{2}$ or $y \leqslant 2x - 6$

42. $y \geqslant \frac{1}{2}x + 3$ or $y \leqslant \frac{1}{2}x - 1$ or $y \leqslant -\frac{3}{2}x - 1$

43. $y + x \leqslant 2$ or $y \geqslant -x + 4$ or $y \leqslant \frac{1}{2}x - 2$ or $y \geqslant 2x + 1$

44. $|y| \geqslant 2$ and $|x| \leqslant 3$

45. $y \leqslant |x|$ and $x > -2$

46. $|y| < |x|$ and $|y| < 3$

47. $y \leqslant [x]$ and $|x| \leqslant 2$

Graph each system.

48. $y \geqslant x - 3$
$\quad\, y \leqslant -x + 3$
$\quad\, y \leqslant 7x + 3$

49. $y - 2x \geqslant 1$
$\quad\, y \geqslant -\frac{1}{2}x - 1$
$\quad\, y - \frac{1}{3}x \leqslant \frac{2}{3}$

50. $x + y \leqslant 3$
$\quad\, x - y \geqslant -1$
$\quad\, y \leqslant -1$

51. $y \geqslant \frac{1}{2}x - 2$
$\quad\, y \leqslant 2x + 1$
$\quad\, x - 1 \geqslant 0$

C Consider the graph of this system. $\quad y \geqslant x + 2$
$\qquad\qquad\qquad\qquad\qquad\qquad\quad\ y \leqslant x + k$

What values of k produce the following graphs?

52. A single line

53. No points

Consider the graph of $y \geqslant x + 2$ or $y \leqslant x + k$. What values of k produce the following graphs?

54. The entire plane

55. Two nonintersecting half-planes

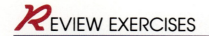

State whether each of the following relations is a function. [3-2]
If a relation is a function, state whether it is a one-to-one function.

1. $\{(x, y): x$ is a positive integer, and y is a factor of $x\}$

2. $\{(x, y): x$ is a positive integer, and y is the number of factors of $x\}$

3. $\{(x, y): y = 0.01x - 1000\}$

4. State whether $y = \dfrac{12}{x}$ is a linear equation. [3-3]

5. Write $3x + 4y = 12$ in the form $y = mx + b$. State the values of m and b. [3-3]

6. State the slope and y-intercept of $x - 4y + 10 = 0$. [3-3]

Write an equation in slope-intercept form for each of these situations. [3-4]

7. The line passes through $(3, 4)$ and has a slope of 2.

8. The line passes through $(-3, 6)$ and is parallel to $y = \dfrac{2}{3}x - 5$.

9. The line passes through $(0, -5)$ and is perpendicular to $y = 2x + 1$.

$\mathcal{S}$elf-Quiz 2

4-4 **1.** Evaluate the determinant.

$$\begin{vmatrix} 5 & -1 \\ 6 & 3 \end{vmatrix}$$

2. Solve using Cramer's rule.

$3x + 2y = 9$
$x - y = -1$

3. Solve. $\begin{vmatrix} 4x & 1 \\ -2x & 0 \end{vmatrix} = 10$

4-5 **4.** Write the expansion by minors of this determinant by the second row. Do *not* evaluate.

$$\begin{vmatrix} 9 & -1 & 2 \\ 4 & 0 & 3 \\ -5 & 7 & 1 \end{vmatrix}$$

5. Evaluate. $\begin{vmatrix} -2 & 0 & 1 \\ 3 & -1 & 0 \\ 0 & 6 & 4 \end{vmatrix}$

6. Solve using Cramer's rule.

$x + y + z = 2$
$2x - y = -1$
$-x + 2y - z = 7$

4-6 **7.** Graph the system.

$x + y < 5$
$y > x - 1$

8. Graph.

$y \geqslant 2x + 3$ or $y \leqslant 0$

LESSON 4-7

Linear Programming

The manager of a fast food restaurant is designing a rectangular "island" for a salad bar. First, she wrote inequalities for all of the constraints on the size of the island, such as cost of materials, amount of available space, number of salads to be offered, and so on. Then she graphed the length-width pairs that satisfy the inequalities. The graph is shown at the right. Her task now is to find the length-width pair that will provide the greatest perimeter so that as many people as possible can be served at one time.

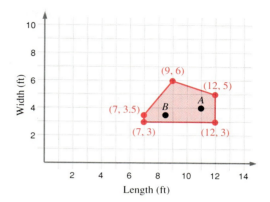

The formula for the perimeter of a rectangle is:

$$P = 2(l + w)$$

The coordinates of point A, for example, produce a perimeter of 30 feet.

$$P = 2(11 + 4) = 30$$

The coordinates of point B produce a perimeter of 24 feet.

$$P = 2(8.5 + 3.5) = 24$$

Since there are infinitely many points in the region, it is impossible to compute the perimeter for each of them. A more efficient method is needed. The **Maximum-Minimum Property** provides that method.

Maximum-Minimum Property

The *maximum* and *minimum* values of a linear function defined on a convex polygonal region occur at vertices of the region.

Using the Maximum-Minimum Property, the manager uses the function $P = 2(l + w)$ to compute the values of P for each vertex and then chooses the length-width pair giving the greatest perimeter as the dimensions of the island.

Points: (7, 3.5)	(7, 3)	(12, 3)	(12, 5)	(9, 6)
$P = 2(7 + 3.5)$	$P = 2(7 + 3)$	$P = 2(12 + 3)$	$P = 2(12 + 5)$	$P = 2(9 + 6)$
$P = 21$	$P = 20$	$P = 30$	$P = 34$	$P = 30$

The dimensions that give the greatest perimeter are length: 12 ft; width: 5 ft.

Two important points must be noted about the Maximum-Minimum Property.

1. The function defined on the region must be linear. That is, it must be possible to write it in the form $A = ax + by + c$.
2. The region must be **convex** and have a boundary that is a polygon. (A convex region has no "indentations.")

Convex polygonal regions

Not convex polygonal regions

Boundary is not a polygon.　　Region is not convex.

The mathematics used to solve problems involving the Maximum-Minimum Property is called **linear programming.**

Example 1 Let $A = 2x - y + 3$ be defined on the region shown in the graph.

Find the maximum value of A.

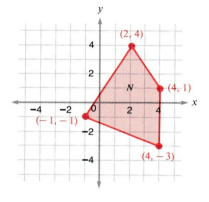

Solution Substitute the coordinates of the vertices into the defining equation and find the corresponding values of A.

$$A = 2x - y + 3$$
$$(-1, -1): A = 2(-1) - (-1) + 3 = 2$$
$$(2, 4): A = 2(2) - 4 + 3 = 3$$
$$(4, 1): A = 2(4) - 1 + 3 = 10$$
$$(4, -3): A = 2(4) - (-3) + 3 = 14$$

Answer The linear function assumes its maximum value, 14, at the point $(4, -3)$.

Example 2 **Solve.**

The Wheeler Manufacturing Company makes bicycles and tricycles. In order to meet demands of its retailers, the company must make at least 20 bicycles and 30 tricycles each day. At most, twice as many tricycles as bicycles can be made in a day. A total of only 90 bicycles and tricycles can be made each day. The profit on each bicycle is $17, and the profit on each tricycle is $21. How many bicycles and tricycles should be made in order to maximize the profits?

Example 2 (continued)

Solution   Let x = the number of bicycles and y = the number of tricycles.

Write inequalities for the constraints. $x \geqslant 20$ $y \leqslant 2x$
                                                    $y \geqslant 30$ $x + y \leqslant 90$

Write the profit (P) equation. $P = 17x + 21y$
Graph the system.

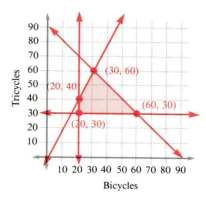

Substitute the coordinates of each vertex into the profit equation.

$P = 17(60) + 21(30)$ $P = 17(20) + 21(40)$
    $= 1650$ $= 1180$

$P = 17(20) + 21(30)$ $P = 17(30) + 21(60)$
    $= 970$ $= 1770$

Answer   To maximize profits, the company should manufacture 30 bicycles and 60 tricycles per day.

*e*LASSROOM EXERCISES

State whether the region is a convex polygonal region.

1.

2.

3.

4. Which of the pairs (3, 5) or (4, 7) produces the greater value of N? $N = 3x - y$

5. Find the minimum value of C and the point at which it occurs for the shaded region shown.

        $C = 5x - 2y$

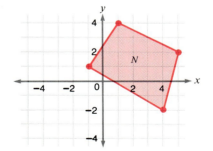

WRITTEN EXERCISES

 A State whether the region is a convex polygonal region.

1.   **2.**   **3.**   **4.**

Find the maximum value of *P* and the point at which it occurs for shaded region *M*.

5. $P = 4x - 3y$ **6.** $P = 3x + 2y$

7. $P = 2x + 5y$ **8.** $P = -2x + 4y$

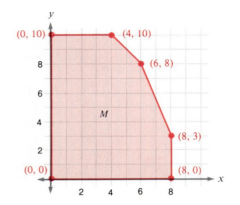

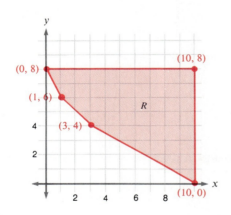

Find the minimum value of *C* and the point at which it occurs for shaded region *R*.

9. $C = 2x + 3y$ **10.** $C = 5x + 4y$

11. $C = 7x + 2y$ **12.** $C = 3x + 6y$

Find the maximum or minimum value of the linear function and the point at which it occurs for the given constraints.

13. Maximize $P = 10x + 12y$.
   Given: $x + y \leqslant 60$ $x \geqslant 0$
   $x \geqslant 2y$ $y \geqslant 0$

14. Maximize $R = 3x + y$.
   Given: $4x + 3y \leqslant 24$ $x \geqslant 0$
   $x + 2y \leqslant 11$ $y \geqslant 0$

15. Maximize $C = 6x + 4y$.
   Given: $3x + 2y \geqslant 18$ $x \geqslant 0$
   $6x + 10y \leqslant 60$ $y \geqslant 0$

16. Minimize $L = 10x + 12y$.
   Given: $x + y \leqslant 5$ $x \geqslant 0$
   $y \geqslant 3$

17. Maximize $S = 0.5x - 0.3y$.
   Given: $x - y \geqslant -2$ $x + y \geqslant -4$
   $2x - y \leqslant 4$

18. Minimize $T = 9x + 6y$.
   Given: $x + y \leqslant 7$ $x \geqslant 2$
   $3x + 4y \leqslant 24$ $y \geqslant 0$

*A*pplications

B Solve.

19. Alice and Arthur Campbell have decided to produce and sell dog food. In brand A they use 2 pounds of cereal for each pound of meat. In brand B they use 2 pounds of meat for each pound of cereal. They are starting with 100 pounds of meat and 140 pounds of cereal. They plan to charge $2 for a 3-pound package of brand A and $3 for a 3-pound package of brand B.

Let x be the number of packages of brand A sold and let y be the number of packages of brand B sold.

Write inequalities for these constraints.

    a. The amount of meat used.

    b. The amount of cereal used.

    c. Show that x and y cannot be negative.

    d. Graph the system of inequalities (**a, b, c**) and list the vertices of the polygon.

    e. Write an equation for the total revenue R from the sale of both brands.

    f. How many packages of each brand should they produce in order to maximize their revenue?

20. A small firm manufactures necklaces and bracelets and must decide how many bracelets (x) and necklaces (y) to make daily in order to maximize its profits. These facts must be considered:

	Bracelet	**Necklace**	**Possible Totals**
Number of units	x	y	24
Hours of labor	1	0.5	16
Profit per unit	$12	$9	P

Write inequalities expressing these constraints.

    a. The amount of labor used.

    b. The total number of necklaces and bracelets produced.

    c. Show that x and y cannot be negative.

    d. Graph the system of inequalities (**a, b, c**) and list the vertices of the polygon.

    e. Write an equation for the profit P from the sale.

    f. How many bracelets and how many necklaces should be made daily?

    g. If the profit on a necklace is $12 and the profit on a bracelet is $9, how many of each should be made daily in order to maximize profit?

21. A company manufactures two types of electric lawn edgers, one of which is cordless. The cord edger requires 2 work-hours to make, and the cordless model requires 4 work-hours. The company has only 800 work-hours to use in manufacturing each day, and the packing department can package only 300 edgers per day.

a. If the company sells the cord model for $40 and the cordless model for $50, how many of each type should it produce daily to maximize its revenue?

b. If the profit on the cord edger is $15 and the profit on the cordless edger is $18, how many of each type should the company sell daily to maximize its profit?

c. If the profit on each type of edger is $15, how many of each type should the company produce to maximize its profit? Can its profit be maximized at more than one point in this case?

C **22.** A firm manufactures bumper bolts and fender bolts for trucks. One machine can produce 130 fender bolts daily, and another machine can produce 120 bumper bolts daily. The combined number of fender bolts and bumper bolts that the packaging department can handle is 230 daily.

a. How many of each type of bolt should the firm produce daily in order to maximize its sales if fender bolts sell for $1 and bumper bolts sell for $2?

b. If the firm makes a 50¢ profit on each fender bolt and a 40¢ profit on each bumper bolt, how many bolts of each type should it produce daily for maximum profit?

c. If the increased price of producing the fender bolts of part (b) reduces the profit per fender bolt to 35¢, how many bolts of each type should the firm produce daily for maximum profit (the bumper-bolt profit remains at 40¢)?

d. If the profits on the bolts are changed so that the profit will be 50¢ on each type of bolt, can profit be maximized at more than one point? Explain.

$\mathcal{R}$EVIEW EXERCISES

1. If y varies directly as x and $y = 100$ when $x = 5$, what is the value of y when $x = 2$?   [3-5]

2. If y varies directly as the square of x and $y = 20$ when $x = 2$, what is the value of y when $x = 10$?   [3-5]

3. Graph $y = [x + 0.5]$ for $0 \leqslant x \leqslant 4$.   **4.** Simplify $[3.6] + [-5.2]$.   [3-6]

5. If y varies directly as the cube of x, is y a function of x?   [3-7]

6. Assume that r is the independent variable in the equation $A = \pi r^2$. Label the axes and sketch a graph of the function for $r \geqslant 0$.   [3-7]

Let $f(x) = 2x - 3$ and $g(x) = x^2$. Simplify.   [3-8]

7. $f(g(5))$ **8.** $g(f(5))$ **9.** $f(f(-2))$

CHAPTER SUMMARY

▶ **Vocabulary**

▶ Systems of Two Linear Equations in Two Variables   [4-1]

System	Slopes	Graphs	Solutions
Consistent and independent	Different	Lines intersect in a point.	One
Inconsistent	Same	Lines are parallel.	None
Consistent and dependent	Same	Lines coincide.	Infinitely many

▶ A *determinant* is a real number represented by a square array of numbers.   [4-4]

▶ Cramer's Rule   [4-4]

For all real numbers a_1, b_1, c_1, a_2, b_2, and c_2, the solution of the system

$$a_1x + b_1y = c_1$$
$$a_2x + b_2y = c_2$$

$$D = \begin{vmatrix} a_1 & b_1 \\ a_2 & b_2 \end{vmatrix} = a_1b_2 - a_2b_1,$$

$$D_x = \begin{vmatrix} c_1 & b_1 \\ c_2 & b_2 \end{vmatrix} = c_1b_2 - c_2b_1,$$

is $\left(\dfrac{D_x}{D}, \dfrac{D_y}{D}\right)$, where $D \neq 0$. If $D = 0$, the system has no solution or infinitely many solutions.

$$D_y = \begin{vmatrix} a_1 & c_1 \\ a_2 & c_2 \end{vmatrix} = a_1c_2 - a_2c_1$$

▶ A *minor* for an element of a determinant is the determinant that remains after the row and column containing the element have been deleted.   [4-5]

▶ A determinant is expanded by using the following steps.   [4-5]

1. Select any row or column.

2. Multiply each element of that row or column by its minor.

3. If the sum of the row number and the column number is odd, multiply the product of step (2) by -1.

4. Add the products.

▶ Cramer's rule applies to the third-order determinants as follows.   [4-5]

The solution of the system

$$a_1x + b_1y + c_1z = d_1$$
$$a_2x + b_2y + c_2z = d_2$$
$$a_3x + b_3y + c_3z = d_3$$

is the ordered triple $\left(\dfrac{D_x}{D}, \dfrac{D_y}{D}, \dfrac{D_z}{D}\right)$, where $D \neq 0$.

If $D = 0$, the system has no solution or infinitely many solutions.

▶ Maximum-Minimum Property   [4-7]

The *maximum* and *minimum* values of a linear function defined on a convex polygonal region occur at vertices of the region.

HAPTER REVIEW

4-1 **Objective:** To solve a system of linear equations in two variables by graphing.

State the number of solutions for a system of equations whose two graphs are described by each condition.

1. Two parallel lines   **2.** Two intersecting lines

3. One line

4. Solve by graphing. $x - 2y = 5$
$$3x + y = 1$$

4-2 **Objective:** To solve a system of linear equations in two variables by substitution.

Solve by substitution.

5. $4x + 3y = 19$ **6.** $x + 2y = -\dfrac{9}{2}$
$y = 5x$
$$2x - 4y = 15$$

Solve.

7. An airplane flew 600 mi in 3 h with a tail wind. Flying back against the same wind, the airplane flew 450 mi in 3 h. What was the speed of the wind and the speed of the airplane in still air?

4-3 **Objective:** To solve a system of linear equations in two variables using linear combinations.

Solve using linear combinations.

8. $-x + 4y = 7$ **9.** $5x + 2y = 4$
$2x - 3y = -9$ $-3x + 2y = -28$

4-4 Objectives: To evaluate second-order determinants.

To solve a system of linear equations in two variables using Cramer's rule.

Evaluate.

10. $\begin{vmatrix} -1 & 4 \\ 2 & 6 \end{vmatrix}$
11. $\begin{vmatrix} 8 & -4 \\ 5 & 9 \end{vmatrix}$
12. $\begin{vmatrix} \frac{1}{2} & -8 \\ -\frac{3}{4} & 12 \end{vmatrix}$

13. Evaluate the coefficient determinant D for this system.

$x + 4y = 6$

$3x - 2y = 1$

14. Solve using Cramer's rule. $5x - 2y = 4$

$2x + 8y = -5$

4-5 Objectives: To evaluate third-order determinants.

To solve a system of linear equations in three variables using Cramer's rule.

Write the minor of the element 5 for the following determinant and indicate whether this term of the expansion is to be multiplied by -1.

15. $\begin{vmatrix} 2 & -9 & 0 \\ 1 & 3 & 5 \\ -6 & 1 & 8 \end{vmatrix}$

16. Evaluate the determinant. $\begin{vmatrix} -4 & 2 & 1 \\ 0 & 6 & 3 \\ 1 & 1 & 0 \end{vmatrix}$

17. Solve. $\begin{vmatrix} x & 0 & 1 \\ 6 & 2 & -4 \\ 0 & 1 & 2 \end{vmatrix} = 30$

Express the x-value of the solution of this system in terms of the values of D_x and D.

18. $x + 4y - z = 4$

$2x - 3y + 4z = 3$

$-x + y + 2z = 2$

4-6 Objective: To graph a system of two inequalities in two variables.

Sketch the graph.

19. $y \geq x$

$y \leq -x + 4$

20. $x + 2y > 4$

$x - y < 1$

21. $y \geq \frac{1}{2}x + 1$ or $y \leq -\frac{1}{2}x - 3$

4-7 Objective: To use linear programming to solve problems involving maximum and minimum values.

22. Find the maximum and minimum values of $C = 4x - 2y$ on the shaded region shown.

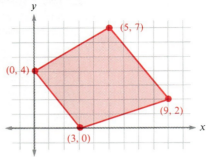

23. Find the maximum value of $R = 14 - x + 2y$ on the region defined by these inequalities.

$$x \leqslant 6 \qquad y \leqslant x + 4 \qquad y \geqslant 8 - x$$

*C*HAPTER 4 SELF-TEST

4-1 **1.** How many solutions does a system of two linear equations in two variables have if it is (a) dependent? (b) inconsistent?

2. A system of linear equations that has exactly one solution is a _____?_____ system.

3. Solve this system by graphing.

$$2x - y = 6$$
$$4x + 3y = 12$$

4-2 **Solve by substitution.**

4. $5x + 3y = -2$
   $\quad x = y + 2$

5. $2x + 3y = 7$
   $\quad 2x - 4y = -14$

6. In Exercise 5, what expression could be substituted for $2x$ in the second equation?

4-3 **Solve using linear combinations.**

7. $\quad 7x - 2y = 3$
   $-3x + y = 1$

8. $4x + 3y = 11$
   $\quad 3x + 5y = 11$

9. The diagram shows the graph of this system:

$$x - 2y = 4$$
$$2x + 3y = 6$$

What is true about the graph of any nonzero linear combination of the given equations?

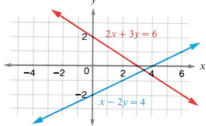

4-4 **Evaluate.**

10. $\begin{vmatrix} -2 & 9 \\ 1 & 4 \end{vmatrix}$

Solve.

11. $\begin{vmatrix} 3 & x \\ -5 & 2x \end{vmatrix} = 4$

12. Solve the system using Cramer's rule.

$$2x + y - 1 = 0$$
$$-6x + 2y + 23 = 0$$

4-5 **Evaluate.**

13. $\begin{vmatrix} 1 & -3 & 0 \\ 2 & 4 & -1 \\ 5 & 8 & 6 \end{vmatrix}$

List the minor of the element 2.

14. $\begin{vmatrix} 1 & 6 & -4 \\ 3 & 0 & 12 \\ -1 & 2 & 5 \end{vmatrix}$

15. Evaluate the coefficient determinant for this system.

$$x + 2y - z = 6$$
$$2x - y + z = 3$$
$$4x + y - 3z = 5$$

4-6 **Sketch the graphs.**

16. $\quad y \leqslant x + 4$

$\quad 2x + 3y \geqslant 13$

17. $x - 2y > 8 \quad$ or $\quad 3x + y < 6$

4-7 **18.** Find the maximum value of $R = 4x + 5y$ and where it occurs on the shaded region at the right.

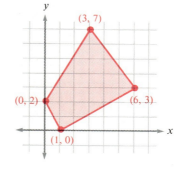

19. Find the maximum value of $C = 7x + 3y$ given these constraints:

$$x + 2y \leqslant 9$$
$$3x + y \leqslant 12$$

4-2, **Solve.**
4-3 **20.** Flying against the wind, an airplane takes 5 h to travel 900 mi. Flying with the same wind, the airplane takes 3 h for the return trip. What is the speed of the airplane in still air and the speed of the wind?

21. Six planks and four plunks cost $54, but three planks and ten plunks cost $87. Find the costs of a plank and a plunk.

Each question consists of two quantities, one in column A and one in column B.
Compare the two quantities and select one of the following answers.

A if the quantity in column A is greater;
B if the quantity in column B is greater;
C if the two quantities are equal;
D if the relationship cannot be determined from the information given.

	Column A	Column B
1.	$1 \cdot a$	$a + 0$
2.	The greatest common factor of 10 and 15	The least common multiple of 10 and 15
3.	$x > y - 5$ x	y
4.	The average of -1, 2, -3, and 4	The average of -1, 0, and 2
5.	$2(x + 3)$	$2x + 3$
6.	$1, -1, 1, -1, 1, -1, \ldots$ The sum of the first 100 terms of the sequence	The sum of the first 99 terms of the sequence
7.	$AB = BC$ a	c
8.	$\dfrac{1}{2} - \dfrac{1}{3}$	$\dfrac{1}{3} - \dfrac{1}{4}$
9.	$y = x - 3$ $2x + y = 12$ y	2
10.	The number of vertices of a pentagon	The number of diagonals of a pentagon
11.	$999 \cdot 1001$	1000^2

	Column A	Column B
12.	100 miles per hour	2 miles per minute
13.		
	$x + y$	180
14.	$x > y$	
	$x + y$	$x - y$
15.	$0 < x$	
	$\dfrac{1}{x}$	$\dfrac{1}{x^2}$
16.	$x - y = 10$ $x + z = 12$	
	The average of x and z	11
17.	The area of the triangle with vertices $(0, 0)$, $(0, 3)$, and $(4, 0)$	5
18.	$a < 0 < b$	
	ab	$a + b$
19.	2^4	4^2
20.	$10 < x < 100$ $1 < y < 10$	
	$\dfrac{x^2}{y}$	10,000
21.	The number of factors of 3 between 10 and 20	The number of prime numbers between 10 and 20
22.	The original price of an item	The price of an item after it has been increased by 10% and then decreased by 10%
23.	The circumference of a circle with radius 1	The perimeter of a regular hexagon with side 1
24.	$a = b + 5$	
	$b - a$	5

CHAPTER 5

Polynomials

Temperature changes affect the length of a wire between fixed points and, therefore, also affect the sag in the wire. The formula relating the length l of wire attached between two poles a distance d apart with a sag s in the wire is $l^2 = d^2 + 5.3s^2$. Using the linear coefficient of expansion of the wire, engineers calculate a sufficient sag in a wire to prevent it from snapping at low temperatures or sagging too low at high temperatures.

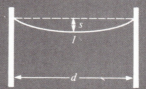

LESSON 5-1

Monomials

A **monomial** is a constant, a variable, or a product of constants and/or variables. These expressions are monomials.

$$-6 \qquad x \qquad 5x \qquad 2a^3 \qquad -3xy^4 \qquad \sqrt{3}$$

Note that monomials may contain exponents and recall the following definition.

Definition: Nonnegative Integer Exponents

For all real numbers x and all positive integers n,

$$x^n = \overbrace{x \cdot x \cdot x \cdot \ldots \cdot x}^{n \text{ factors}}$$

where x^n is called the nth *power* of x.
For all nonzero real numbers, $x^0 = 1$.

In a monomial, only 0 and positive integers can be used as exponents of variables. No monomial has a variable as an exponent, nor does it have a variable as the denominator of a fraction. A monomial may not have a variable in the radicand of a root. These expressions are not monomials.

$$3^a \qquad \frac{6}{x} \qquad x + y \qquad \sqrt{2x}$$

The constant factor of a monomial is called the **numerical coefficient,** or just the **coefficient** of the monomial. The **degree of a monomial** is the sum of the exponents of the variables. The degree of a constant is 0 because a constant such as 7 is equivalent to $7x^0$.

Here are some more examples of monomials.

Monomial	Coefficient	Degree
$-2x^3$	-2	3
a^3b^3	1	6
$-x$	-1	1
7	7	0

The definition of exponent and the commutative and associative properties of multiplication can be used to simplify the product of two monomials, as follows:

$$
\begin{aligned}
a^3b^2 \cdot a^4b^3 &= (a \cdot a \cdot a \cdot b \cdot b)(a \cdot a \cdot a \cdot a \cdot b \cdot b \cdot b) \\
&= (a \cdot a \cdot a \cdot a \cdot a \cdot a \cdot a)(b \cdot b \cdot b \cdot b \cdot b) \\
&= a^7b^5
\end{aligned}
$$

In the product a^7b^5, the exponent of a is the sum of the exponents of the a-factors, and the exponent of b is the sum of the exponents of the b-factors. This property is true for all positive-integer exponents m and n.

$$a^m \cdot a^n = \overbrace{(a \cdot a \cdot \ldots \cdot a)}^{m\,\text{factors}} \overbrace{(a \cdot a \cdot \ldots \cdot a)}^{n\,\text{factors}}$$

$$= \overbrace{a \cdot a \cdot \ldots \cdot a}^{m+n\,\text{factors}}$$

$$= a^{m+n}$$

This result can be stated as the following property.

Addition Property of Exponents

For each real number a, and for all nonnegative integers m and n,

$$a^m \cdot a^n = a^{m+n}.$$

Example 1   **Simplify.**   **a.** $x^2 \cdot x^5$ **b.** $cd^4 \cdot c^3d^2$

Solution   **a.** $x^2 \cdot x^5 = x^{2+5}$ **b.** $cd^4 \cdot c^3d^2 = (c \cdot c^3)(d^4 \cdot d^2)$

$\qquad\qquad\qquad = x^7$ $\qquad\qquad\qquad\qquad\qquad = c^{1+3} \cdot d^{4+2}$

$\qquad\qquad\qquad\qquad\qquad\qquad\qquad\qquad\qquad = c^4 \cdot d^6$

$\qquad\qquad\qquad\qquad\qquad\qquad\qquad\qquad\qquad = c^4d^6$

The definition of exponent and the real-number properties can also be used to simplify a monomial that is the power of a power. For example,

$$(x^3)^2 = x^3 \cdot x^3$$

$$= x^{3+3} \qquad (x^3 \text{ is used as a factor 2 times.})$$

$$= x^{3 \cdot 2}$$

$$= x^6$$

In this case the exponent of the simplified expression is the product of the exponents of the original powers. This relationship holds for all positive integers m and n.

$$(a^m)^n = \overbrace{a^m \cdot a^m \cdot \ldots \cdot a^m}^{n\,\text{factors}}$$

$$= \overbrace{a^{m+m+\ldots+m}}^{n\,\text{addends}}$$

$$= a^{mn}$$

This result can be stated as the following property.

Multiplication Property of Exponents

For each real number a, and all nonnegative integers m and n,

$$(a^m)^n = a^{mn}.$$

Example 2 **Simplify.** $(x^3)^4$

Solution $(x^3)^4 = x^{3 \cdot 4}$

$\qquad\qquad\quad = x^{12}$

The following property is also a consequence of the definition of exponents and the properties of real numbers.

Distributive Property of Exponents over Multiplication

For all real numbers a and b, and each nonnegative integer m,

$$(ab)^m = a^m b^m.$$

Example 3 **Simplify.** **a.** $(a^2b^3)^3$ **b.** $(-2ab)^2(3ab^2)$

Solution **a.** $(a^2b^3)^3 = (a^2)^3 \cdot (b^3)^3$ **b.** $(-2ab)^2(3ab^2) = ((-2)^2 a^2 b^2)(3ab^2)$

$\qquad\qquad\qquad = a^{2 \cdot 3}b^{3 \cdot 3}$ $\qquad\qquad\qquad\qquad\quad = 4 \cdot 3a^2ab^2b^2$

$\qquad\qquad\qquad = a^6 b^9$ $\qquad\qquad\qquad\qquad\quad = 12a^3 b^4$

Scientific notation is often used to simplify the task of writing very large numbers. A number is expressed in scientific notation when it is written as the product of a power of 10 and a number that is greater than or equal to 1 and less than 10.

Calculators and computers also use scientific notation to display large numbers, but only the power of 10 is shown. Calculators use a space before the power, while computers use the letter E.

Decimal notation	Scientific notation	Calculator display	Computer display
250,000	$2.5 \cdot 10^5$	2.5　5	2.5 E+5
48,700,000	$4.87 \cdot 10^7$	4.87　7	4.87 E+7
958,800,000,000	$9.588 \cdot 10^{11}$	9.588　11	9.588 E+11

Example 4   **Simplify. Write the answer in scientific notation.**
$$(2.3 \cdot 10^4)(4.5 \cdot 10^7)$$

Solution 1 $(2.3 \cdot 10^4)(4.5 \cdot 10^7) = (2.3 \cdot 4.5)(10^4 \cdot 10^7)$
$$= 10.35 \cdot 10^{11}$$
$$= (1.035 \cdot 10)10^{11}$$
Answer $= 1.035 \cdot 10^{12}$

Solution 2   Using a calculator:

Keying Sequence	**Display**
2.3 EXP 4 × 4.5 EXP 7 =	1.035 12

Answer $1.035 \cdot 10^{12}$

CLASSROOM EXERCISES

State the coefficient and the degree of the monomial.

1. $3xy^3$ **2.** -12 **3.** $-2a^2b^3c$

Simplify.

4. $(x^3)(x^5)$ **5.** $a \cdot a^4$ **6.** $3a^2b^2(2ab^3)$

7. $(x^3)^4$ **8.** $(5x^2)^3$ **9.** $(2a^2b^3)^3$

10. Write $3.04 \cdot 10^4$ in standard decimal notation.

Write in scientific notation.

11. 98,700   **12.** 3,456,000,000   **13.** $(3.6 \cdot 10^7)(9.9 \cdot 10^4)$

WRITTEN EXERCISES

A   **State whether the expression is a monomial.**

1. $3a$ **2.** $-5x$ **3.** $3 - a$ **4.** $-5 + x$

5. $\dfrac{a}{3}$ **6.** $\dfrac{x}{5}$ **7.** a^3 **8.** x^5

9. 3^a **10.** 5^x **11.** $\dfrac{3}{a}$ **12.** $\dfrac{5}{x}$

List the coefficient and the degree for the monomial.

13. $-3x^2$ **14.** $2a^3$ **15.** y^7 **16.** b^{10}

17. $17z$ **18.** $-25c$ **19.** 5 **20.** -6

21. $2x^3y^4$ **22.** $5a^4b^3$ **23.** $-xyz$ **24.** $-pqr^2$

Simplify.

25. $(x^2)(x^4)$ **26.** $(y^5)(y^{10})$ **27.** $(w^2)^4$ **28.** $(t^5)^{10}$

29. $(a^2b^3)^4$ **30.** $(a^4b^3)^2$ **31.** $(-7y)(9y^4)$ **32.** $(-4x^6)(-3x)$

33. $(2n)^3(3n)^2$ **34.** $(4r)^2(5r)^2$ **35.** $(8m^3)(3m)^2$ **36.** $(9d^2)(5d)^2$

Simplify. All exponents are positive integers.

37. $(3^a)(3^{2a})$ **38.** $(5^b)(5^3)$ **39.** $(x^m)(x^2)$ **40.** $(y^n)(y^{5n})$

41. $(x^2)^m$ **42.** $(y^a)^b$ **43.** $(2^{a+1})(2^3)$ **44.** $(5^{m-2})^3$

45. $(x^ay)^3$ **46.** $(x^by^3)^a$ **47.** $(-7a^{x+4})(6a^{x-4})$ **48.** $(3b^{y+1})(-2b^{2y-3})$

Write in standard decimal notation.

49. $6.32 \cdot 10^4$ **50.** $7.01 \cdot 10^7$ **51.** $5 \cdot 10^{10}$ **52.** $4 \cdot 10^8$

Write in scientific notation.

53. 200   **54.** 7000   **55.** 190,000   **56.** 82,000

57. 51,300,000,000,000   **58.** 394,000,000,000,000,000

59. $(3.2 \cdot 10^5)(3 \cdot 10^8)$ **60.** $(2.1 \cdot 10^{12})(4 \cdot 10^3)$

61. $(6.6 \cdot 10^8)(5 \cdot 10^{12})$ **62.** $(7.5 \cdot 10^5)(4 \cdot 10^{15})$

63. $(2 \cdot 10^6)(8.4 \cdot 10^6)$ **64.** $(9 \cdot 10^7)(1.2 \cdot 10^{19})$

State whether the number is positive or negative.

65. $(-2)^9$ **66.** $(-3)^8$ **67.** -2^8 **68.** -3^9

69. $((-2)^3)^5$ **70.** $((-3)^7)^3$ **71.** $(-2)^9(-3)^3$ **72.** $(-2)^7(-3)^6$

 73. Describe how to determine whether the product of several numbers is positive or negative. (See Exercises 65–72.)

74. Find the area of this triangle.   **75.** Find the volume of this prism.

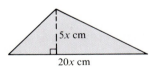

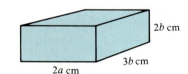

Simplify.

76. $-5t^0 \cdot 4t^7$ **77.** $(-x^4)^2(-x^2)^3$ **78.** $(a^3b^2)^3$

79. $(-3m^2n)(-4mn^2)^2$ **80.** $(-8y^3)(0.5y^2)^4$ **81.** $(-5st^2)(-r^2s)^3(-3r^4)$

82. $-(2x^3)(-3x)^2(-2x)^3$ **83.** $(6 \cdot 10^4)^3$ **84.** $(-2 \cdot 10^6)^5$

Application : The Earth

C Use scientific notation.

85. The estimated mass of the earth in tons is $5.833 \cdot 10^{21}$ tons.

  a. Express the estimated mass in pounds.

  b. Express the estimated mass in grams. (There are approximately $9 \cdot 10^5$ grams in one ton.)

86. The surface area of the earth is approximately $1.97 \cdot 10^8$ square miles.

  a. Express the approximate surface area in square feet. (There are approximately $3 \cdot 10^7$ square feet in a square mile.)

  b. Express the approximate surface area in square meters. (There are about $2.6 \cdot 10^6$ square meters in a square mile.)

87. The volume of the earth is approximately $3.12 \cdot 10^{11}$ cubic miles.

  a. Express the approximate volume in cubic meters. (There are approximately $4.2 \cdot 10^9$ cubic meters in a cubic mile.)

  b. It is estimated that there are about $8 \cdot 10^3$ grains of sand in a cubic centimeter. How many grains of sand would it take to make the entire earth of sand?

88. Show that $(x^m)^n = x^{mn}$, $x \neq 0$, is true for $m = 0$ or $n = 0$.

REVIEW EXERCISES

1. Graph on the number line. $\{x: x \text{ is between } -2 \text{ and } 2\}$ [1-3]
2. Write the set of numbers shown in the graph using set-builder notation.   [1-3]

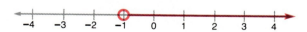

State the property of real numbers that is illustrated by the following.

3. $(x + 2) + 3x = 3x + (x + 2)$ [1-4]
4. $(17.3 \cdot 2.5)40 = 17.3(2.5 \cdot 40)$ [1-5]
5. Write Q in terms of n.   [1-6]

n	2	4	6	8	10
Q	12	16	20	24	28

Polynomials

A **polynomial** is a monomial or the sum of monomials. These are polynomials.

$$3x + 4y \qquad 5x^2 + 2x + 7 \qquad n^3 - 3 \qquad 2x$$

These are not polynomials.

$$\frac{1}{x + 1} \qquad \sqrt{a^2 + b^2}$$

The polynomial $3x + 4y$ is called a **binomial** because it has two **terms** (monomials). The polynomial $a + b + c$ is called a **trinomial** because it has three terms. If a term of a polynomial is written with a subtraction sign, the coefficient of that term is considered to be negative. For example, the coefficient of y in the polynomial $4x - 3y + 2z$ is -3, because the polynomial can be written as $4x + (-3)y + 2z$. The **degree of a polynomial** is the degree of the term (or terms) of highest degree.

Polynomial	Terms of highest degree	Degree of polynomial
$3x^2 + 5x - 7$	$3x^2$	2
$2a^2 + 3b^3 - 2a^2b^2$	$-2a^2b^2$	4
$x^3 + 2x^2y + 5y^2$	x^3 and $2x^2y$	3

The set of polynomials is closed with respect to addition and subtraction. That is, the sum or difference of two polynomials is a polynomial. The sum of two polynomials with like terms can be simplified.

Example 1 **Simplify.** $(2a + 3b - 1) + (4b - a + 3)$

Solution $\begin{aligned}(2a + 3b - 1) + (4b - a + 3) &= 2a + 3b - 1 + 4b - a + 3 \\ &= (2a - a) + (3b + 4b) + (-1 + 3) \\ &= a + 7b + 2\end{aligned}$

The difference of two polynomials with like terms can be simplified by changing the subtraction to addition. Instead of subtracting a polynomial, add its opposite. The opposite of a given polynomial consists of the opposites of the terms of the given polynomial. That is,

For all real numbers a and b, $-(a + b) = -a + (-b)$.

Example 2 **Simplify.** $(3x^2 + 2x - 8) - (x^2 + 5x - 3)$

  Solution $(3x^2 + 2x - 8) - (x^2 + 5x - 3)$

  $= 3x^2 + 2x - 8 + [-(x^2 + 5x - 3)]$ *Definition of subtraction*

  $= 3x^2 + 2x - 8 + [(-x^2) + (-5x) + (3)]$

  $= 2x^2 - 3x - 5$

Example 3 **Expand.** $3xy(2x^2 - xy + 3y^2)$

  Solution *Use the distributive property to expand the product.*

  $3xy(2x^2 - xy + 3y^2) = 3xy(2x^2) + 3xy(-xy) + 3xy(3y^2)$

  $= 6x^3y - 3x^2y^2 + 9xy^3$

Example 4 **Simplify.** $(8x^2 + x - 5) - 2(3x^2 - 2x + 4)$

  Solution $(8x^2 + x - 5) - 2(3x^2 - 2x + 4) = (8x^2 + x - 5) + (-2)(3x^2 - 2x + 4)$

  $= 8x^2 + x - 5 - 6x^2 + 4x - 8$

  $= (8x^2 - 6x^2) + (x + 4x) + (-5 - 8)$

  $= 2x^2 + 5x - 13$

*C*LASSROOM EXERCISES

State whether the expression is a polynomial.

1. $2ab$

2. $\dfrac{1}{x} + \dfrac{1}{y}$

3. $3x^2 + 2x + 7$

4. $\sqrt{2a - b}$

State the degree of the polynomial and the coefficient of the first-degree term.

5. $3x^2 - 5x + 6$

6. $a^2b + 3ab + 7a - 1$

Simplify.

7. $(3a^2 - 5a + 9) + (-a^2 - 3a - 5)$

8. $(2x^2y + 3xy^2) + (4xy^2 - 2x^2y)$

9. $(6 - 2y - 5y^2) - (3y^2 - 3y)$

10. $(3a - 2b + 5c) - (2b + 3a - 5c)$

Expand.

11. $2(x^2 - 6x + 9)$

12. $2x^2(3x - 2y + 1)$

13. $6a^2b(a^2b - ab^2)$

*W*RITTEN EXERCISES

 State whether the expression is a polynomial. If the answer is yes, state whether it is a monomial, binomial, trinomial, or other polynomial.

1. $2x + 3y$

2. $5x - 4y$

3. $7x^2 + \dfrac{1}{x}$

4. $x + \dfrac{3}{x}$

5. $\sqrt{x^2 + x}$

6. $\sqrt[3]{x^3 + x^2}$

7. $\dfrac{1}{2}y^3$

8. $\dfrac{1}{3}x^6$

9. $a^2 - 2a + 1$

10. $b^2 + 6b + 9$

11. $\dfrac{1}{x^2} + \dfrac{1}{8x} + \dfrac{1}{16}$

12. $\dfrac{1}{x^2} - \dfrac{1}{6x} + \dfrac{1}{9}$

13. $-7x^7 + 5x^5 - 3x^3 + x$

14. $10x^6 + 9x^4 + 8x^2 + 7$

Write the degree of the polynomial.

15. $3b + 5b^2 + 7$

16. $9rt + r^2t - 1$

17. 5

18. -3

19. $abc - ab^2$

20. $xyz^4 - y^5$

21. $(ab)^3 + a^2b^3$

22. $(xy)^4 - x^3y^4$

Write the polynomial in *descending order*. That is, write the term with the highest degree first, the term with the next highest degree second, and so on.

23. $ab + a^3 + 5b$

24. $10x + 5xy + 2y^3$

25. $x^2 - 5x - x^3 + 5$

26. $16 - a^5 + a^3 - 16a^4$

Simplify.

27. $(3a^2 + 2a) + (a^2 - a)$

28. $(5x^2 - 5) + (x^2 + 6)$

29. $(a^3 + a - 5) + (a^2 - a + 7)$

30. $(x^3 + 2x^2 + 3) + (x^2 - x - 3)$

31. $(4x^2 + 5x + 4) - (x^2 + x + 6)$

32. $(3x^2 + 7x + 5) - (x^2 + 9x + 2)$

33. $(x^2 - 6x - 5) - (x^2 + 5x - 7)$

34. $(x^2 - 2x - 4) - (x^2 - 8x + 3)$

35. $(x^2y + 2xy^2 + 4y^3) + (x^3 - x^2y - xy^2)$

36. $(a^3 - a^2b + 5ab^2) + 2(ab^2 + b^3)$

37. $(2a^2 + 3ab - b^2) - (3a^2 - 2ab + b^2)$

38. $2(4a^2 - 6ab + 3b^2) - (5a^2 + 2ab - 6b^2)$

39. $4(xy^2 - x^2y + xy + x^2) + (3xy + 5x^2y)$

40. $(a^3 - a^2b + 3ab) - (a^3 + a^2b - ab)$

41. $(3a^2b + 2ab^2 - 4b^3) - 4(a^2b + 2ab^2 - b^3)$

42. $6(ab + a^2b - ab^2 + b) + 5(a^2b - ab^2)$

43. $(ab - 4) - (a - 3) + (b + 5)$

44. $(x^2 - 3) + (8 - 2x^2) - (x^2 - 2)$

Expand.

45. $(x^2 - 3)2x^3$

46. $(y^3 + 4)5y^2$

47. $3x(x^2 - 2x + 1)$

48. $-2x(3x^2 + x - 5)$

49. $-x(x^3 - 2x)$

50. $7a(a^2 + 5)$

51. $a^2(3a^2 - 4)$

52. $2x^3(x^2 - 3)$

Find the area of the rectangle.

53.

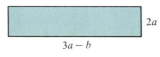

$2a$

$3a - b$

54.

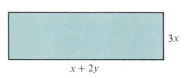

$3x$

$x + 2y$

Find the volume of the rectangular solid.

55.

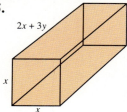

$2x + 3y$

x

x

56.

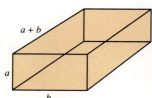

$a + b$

a

b

Simplify.

57. $6x(x + y) + 8x(x - y)$

58. $9y(x + y) + 8x(x - y)$

59. $2x^2(3x - 2y) + 8x(x^2 + xy)$

60. $2xy^2(x + 3y) + 5xy(y^2 - 2xy)$

61. $-10ab(b^2 - ab + 1) - 9b^2(a^2 - ab)$

62. $a^2(9a - 4b^2) - 2b^2(2a^2 + 7b)$

True or false? If the statement is false, give a counterexample to illustrate.

63. If the terms of a polynomial are arranged in a different order, the degree of the polynomial is unchanged.

64. The sum of any two binomials is a binomial.

65. The product of a monomial and a polynomial (not a monomial) never has more terms than the polynomial.

66. The product of a monomial and a polynomial (not a monomial) may have a higher degree than either the monomial or the polynomial.

67. The sum of two polynomials may have fewer terms than either polynomial.

68. The sum of two polynomials may be of a lower degree than either polynomial.

69. Every polynomial has an additive inverse that is a polynomial.

70. Every polynomial has a multiplicative inverse that is a polynomial.

Simplify where j, k, and n represent positive integers.

71. $y^j(y^2 - 3y^k)$

72. $x(x^n + x^{j+1})$

73. $-r(r^n - r^{j-1}) + r^2(r^{n-1} + r^j)$

74. $-y^2(y^j - y^{j-2}) + y^{2j}$

Write the degree of the expression.

75. $x^2y(x^4y^3 + xy + 100)$

76. $2x^3y^4(3x^5y^6 - 7xy^7)$

77. $abc(a + b + c)$

78. $a^{100}(b^{200} + c^{300})$

79. Find the total surface area of the figure in Exercise 55.

80. Find the total surface area of the figure in Exercise 56.

1. Give the next number in the sequence. [1-6]

$$1, -\frac{1}{2}, \frac{1}{4}, -\frac{1}{8}, \frac{1}{16}, \underline{\quad?\quad}$$

Use the variable _n_ to write an expression for the _n_th term of each sequence. [1-6]

2. 10, 15, 20, 25, 30, . . .

3. 20, 40, 80, 160, . . .

4. When an integer x is divided by 4, the remainder is 2. What is the remainder when $3x$ is divided by 4? [1-7]

Supply the reasons for these proofs. [1-7]

5. $2x + x = 2x + 1x$ —————?—————

       $= (2 + 1)x$ —————?—————

       $= 3x$ Computation

6. $8a + 5b + 3a = 8a + (5b + 3a)$ —————?—————

               $= (5b + 3a) + 8a$ —————?—————

               $= 5b + (3a + 8a)$ —————?—————

               $= 5b + (3 + 8)a$ —————?—————

               $= 5b + 11a$ —————?—————

$\mathcal{E}$XTENSION   Classifying Whole Numbers

The ancient Greeks classified whole numbers in many ways. One way was by the sum of the factors that are less than the given number.

If the sum of the factors is less than the number, the number is **defective;** if the sum is equal to the number, the number is **perfect;** and if the sum is greater than the number, the number is **abundant.** For example, the number 12 is abundant because $6 + 4 + 3 + 2 + 1 > 12$.

1. Classify the following whole numbers as defective, perfect, or abundant.

   a. 4   **b.** 6   **c.** 8   **d.** 28   **e.** 30   **f.** 128   **g.** 500

2. Euclid discovered the following fact about prime numbers and perfect numbers.

   If $2^n - 1$ is a prime number, then $(2^n - 1)2^{n-1}$ is a perfect number.

   a. Use this rule for $2 \le n \le 5$. What perfect numbers do you find?

   b. What is the next perfect number that can be found with this rule?

LESSON 5-3

Expanding Polynomials

Many patterns occur in the triangular arrangement of numbers called **Pascal's triangle**. Each number within the triangle is the sum of the two numbers above it in the preceding row. For example, 10 is $4 + 6$. Pascal's triangle can be applied to many problems, including expanding powers of binomials.

```
              1
            1   1
          1   2   1
        1   3   3   1
      1   4   6   4   1
    1   5   10   10   5   1
  1   6   15   20   15   6   1
```

The distributive properties can be used to **expand** the product of two polynomials. Then like terms can be combined to simplify the result.

Example 1   **Expand and simplify.** $(2x + 3)(4x - 1)$

Solution   *Apply the distributive property* $(2x + 3)(4x - 1)$
       (using $4x - 1$) as the common factor. $= 2x(4x - 1) + 3(4x - 1)$
       Expand the first term. $= 8x^2 - 2x + 3(4x - 1)$
       Expand the second term. $= 8x^2 - 2x + 12x - 3$
       Combine like terms. $= 8x^2 + 10x - 3$

The result of applying the distributive properties is that each term of one polynomial is multiplied by each term of the other polynomial and the products are added.

Example 2   **Expand and simplify.** $(a + b)^3$

Solution $(a + b)^3 = (a + b)(a + b)(a + b)$
            $= (a^2 + ab + ab + b^2)(a + b)$
            $= (a^2 + 2ab + b^2)(a + b)$
            $= a^3 + a^2b + 2a^2b + 2ab^2 + ab^2 + b^3$
            $= a^3 + 3a^2b + 3ab^2 + b^3$

Any power of a binomial can be expanded as in Example 2, but the task can be laborious. By examining expansions of increasing powers, we can identify patterns to simplify the task.

$$(x + y)^1 = x + y$$
$$(x + y)^2 = x^2 + 2xy + y^2$$
$$(x + y)^3 = x^3 + 3x^2y + 3xy^2 + y^3$$
$$(x + y)^4 = x^4 + 4x^3y + 6x^2y^2 + 4xy^3 + y^4$$
$$(x + y)^5 = x^5 + 5x^4y + 10x^3y^2 + 10x^2y^3 + 5xy^4 + y^5$$
$$(x + y)^6 = x^6 + 6x^5y + 15x^4y^2 + 20x^3y^3 + 15x^2y^4 + 6xy^5 + y^6$$

The following four patterns exist among the variables and exponents in the expansion of

$$(x + y)^n.$$

1. The degree of each term is n.

2. The first term is x^n. The exponent of x decreases by 1 in successive terms; x does not occur in the last term.

3. The y variable does not occur in the first term; y to the first power occurs in the second term. The exponent of y increases by 1 in successive terms.

Observe the pattern of the coefficients.

Power	Coefficients
1	1, 1
2	1, 2, 1
3	1, 3, 3, 1
4	1, 4, 6, 4, 1
5	1, 5, 10, 10, 5, 1
6	1, 6, 15, 20, 15, 6, 1

The coefficients are the numbers of Pascal's triangle.

4. The coefficient of each term is the corresponding number in the $(n + 1)$st row of Pascal's triangle.

Example 3   **Expand and simplify.** $(3a + 2b)^4$

Solution   Use Pascal's triangle to expand $(x + y)^4$.
$$(x + y)^4 = 1x^4 + 4x^3y + 6x^2y^2 + 4xy^3 + 1y^4$$
Substituting $3a$ for x and $2b$ for y, we then have the following.
$$(3a + 2b)^4 = 1(3a)^4 + 4(3a)^3(2b) + 6(3a)^2(2b)^2 + 4(3a)(2b)^3 + 1(2b)^4$$
$$= 81a^4 + 4(27a^3)(2b) + 6(9a^2)(4b^2) + 4(3a)(8b^3) + 16b^4$$
$$= 81a^4 + 216a^3b + 216a^2b^2 + 96ab^3 + 16b^4$$

Note that the final coefficients of the expanded polynomial $(3a + 2b)^4$ are *not* the constants from Pascal's triangle.

CLASSROOM EXERCISES

Expand and simplify.

1. $(3a - 5)(2a + 4)$

2. $(2m - 3n)(3m - 2n)$

3. $(x + 2)(x^2 - 3x + 1)$

4. $(x + y)^6$

5. $(2a + 4)^3$

6. $(2x - y)^4$

WRITTEN EXERCISES

A **Expand and simplify.**

1. $(2x - 3)(4x + 5)$

2. $(7x + 2)(5x - 1)$

3. $(x - 8y)(3x - 2y)$

4. $(2x - y)(5x - 2y)$

5. $(2a - 3b)(4c - 5d)$

6. $(3a - 2b)(5c - 4d)$

7. $(a + 3)(a^2 + 2a + 4)$

8. $(a + 4)(2a^2 + a + 3)$

9. $(xy + x)(xy^2 + y)$

10. $(x + y)(x^2y + xy^2)$

11. $(x - y + 2)(x + y - 3)$

12. $(x + y - 2)(x + y - 3)$

13. $(3a - b)(3a + b)$

14. $(4x + 9)(4x - 9)$

15. $(x - 2)(x^2 + 2x + 4)$

16. $(a + b)^3$

17. $(a + b)^4$

18. $(x + 2)(x^2 - 2x + 4)$

19. $(a + b)^6$

20. $(a + b)^7$

21. $(x + 3)^4$

22. $(x + 4)^3$

23. $(t - 5)^3$

24. $(w - 2)^5$

25. $(3 - s)^4$

26. $(4 - q)^3$

Write the area as a simple polynomial.

27.

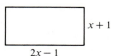
$x + 1$
$2x - 1$

28.

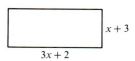
$x + 3$
$3x + 2$

29.

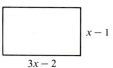
$x - 1$
$3x - 2$

30.

$3x - 2$
$4x + 3$

31.

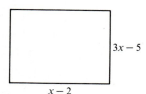
$3x - 5$
$x - 2$

Write the volume as a simple polynomial.

32.

$x + 2$

33.

$x - 2$

34.

$2x + 3$

35.

$3x + 2$

B Describe the pattern marked in Pascal's triangle. Give the missing number in the pattern.

36.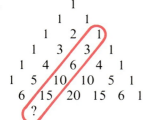

37.

38.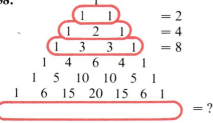

39.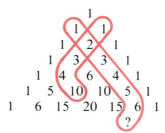

Expand and simplify.

40. $(2x + 1)^6$

41. $(y - 2x)^8$

42. $(r - 3t)^5$

43. $(x + 3b)^7$

44. $(2x + 3b)^5$

45. $(3a - 2b)^5$

46. $(4a + 2)^6$

47. $(10 - 1)^6$

48. $(3x - 2y)^4$

49. $(4a + 2b)^5$

50. $(5x + 2)^7$

51. $(10 + 1)^7$

C Let $P(x)$ be the simplified product of the polynomials $Q(x)$ and $R(x)$ that have q and r terms, respectively.

52. What is the greatest number of terms that $P(x)$ can have?

53. What is the least number of terms that $P(x)$ can have if:
   a. $q = 1, r > 2$?
   b. $q = r = 2$?
   c. $q = 2, r = 3$?

54. Suppose that $Q(x)$ and $R(x)$ are of degree a and b, respectively. What is the degree of $P(x)$?

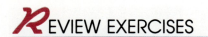

EVIEW EXERCISES

Solve. [2-1]

1. $3(x - 5) = 4(5 - x)$ **2.** $\dfrac{x - 3}{3} = x$ **3.** $0.4(y + 3) = y - 1.2$

Solve for the indicated variable. [2-2]

4. $V = \pi r^2 h$, for h **5.** $S = 2\pi r(r + h)$, for h

6. $ax + by = c$, for y

Solve by writing an equation. [2-3]

7. If 10 times a number equals 100 more than half of the result when 10 is subtracted from the number, what is the number?

Solve and graph on a number line.

8. $4 - x < 7$ **9.** $4x + 2 < 10$ [2-4]

10. $4 \leqslant 3x - 2 \leqslant 10$ **11.** $2x > 6$ or $x + 1 < 3$ [2-5]

12. $|x - 1| \leqslant 3$ [2-6]

13. Use absolute values to write an inequality that describes the graph. [2-6]

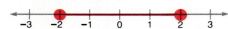

elf-Quiz 1

5-1 **Which of the following expressions are monomials?**

1. $x^2 - 1$ **2.** $\dfrac{2x}{7}$ **3.** $-\dfrac{3}{x^4}$ **4.** $\sqrt{2}x$

Give the degree of the monomial.

5. $3y^2$ **6.** $14xyz^3$ **7.** $0.2r^3 s$

Simplify.

8. $(2x)(-3y^2)$ **9.** $(1.5 \cdot 10^4)(4 \cdot 10^3)$ **10.** $(5ab^2)(2ab)^2$

5-2 **Give the degree of the polynomial.**

11. $7r^2 s - 3r^4$ **12.** $4xyz + 5x^2$

Simplify.

13. $(x^2 - 3x + 6) - (x^2 + 2x - 7)$ **14.** $4x(3x^2 - 5) + 2x(x^2 + 3)$

15. Expand. $2ab(3a - 5b^2)$

5-3 **Expand and simplify.**

16. $(x - 2y)(7x + 5y)$ **17.** $(7a - 2)(4a^2 - 5a + 1)$

18. $(3x - y)^3$

LESSON 5-4

Monomial Factors

Since $3 \cdot 6 = 18$, we say that 3 and 6 are **factors** of 18. If we factor *over the set of positive integers,* the set of all factors of 18 is $\{1, 2, 3, 6, 9, 18\}$. Five is not a factor of 18 over the set of positive integers, because there is no positive integer n such that $n \times 5 = 18$.

If we factor *over the set of integers,* the set of factors of 18 is

$$\{-18, -9, -6, -3, -2, -1, 1, 2, 3, 6, 9, 18\}.$$

Generally, we factor *over the set of positive integers* unless the context makes clear that another set of numbers is involved. The following are examples.

Factors of $6n$: $\{1, 2, 3, 6, n, 2n, 3n, 6n\}$
Factors of $3n^2$: $\{1, 3, n, 3n, n^2, 3n^2\}$

A **common factor** of two monomials is a monomial that is a factor of each given monomial. For example,

The common factors of $6n$ and $3n^2$ are $\{1, 3, n, 3n\}$.

The **greatest common factor (GCF)** is the common factor that is a multiple of each common factor. For example,

The greatest common factor of $6n$ and $3n^2$ is $3n$ because it is a multiple of every factor in the set of common factors $\{1, 3, n, 3n\}$.

Listing all factors to find the greatest common factor of two monomials can be tedious. The following examples illustrate a more efficient method.

Example 1   **State the greatest common factor of 108 and 120.**

Solution   *Write the **prime factorizations**.* $108 = 2^2 \cdot 3^3$
$120 = 2^3 \cdot 3 \cdot 5$

Consider each prime factor.

Powers of 2: 2^2 is the greatest power of 2 that is a common factor.
Powers of 3: 3 is the greatest power of 3 that is a common factor.

No other prime number is a common factor.

Answer   The greatest common factor of 108 and 120 is $2^2 \cdot 3 = 12$.

To find the greatest common factor of several monomials, write the product of each prime-number factor and each variable to the least degree that it appears in any monomial. (If a variable does not appear in each monomial, then the variable does not appear in the greatest common factor.)

Example 2   State the greatest common factor of $6ab^4c^2$ and $12a^2b^3cd$.

Solution $6ab^4c^2 = 2 \cdot 3 \cdot a \cdot b^4 \cdot c^2$

$12a^2b^3cd = 2^2 \cdot 3 \cdot a^2 \cdot b^3 \cdot c \cdot d$

$GCF = 2 \cdot 3 \cdot a \cdot b^3 \cdot c$

$= 6 \cdot a \cdot b^3 \cdot c$

Answer   The greatest common factor of $6ab^4c^2$ and $12a^2b^3cd$ is $6ab^3c$.

For polynomials, expanding and factoring are inverse operations. Expanding changes a product to a sum, and factoring changes a sum to a product. The distributive property is used in both operations. An important step in factoring a polynomial is to factor out the greatest common factor of the terms of the polynomial.

Example 3   Factor. $2x^3y + 6xy^3$

Solution   The greatest common factor of $2x^3y$ and $6xy^3$ is $2xy$.
Therefore,

$2x^3y + 6xy^3 = 2xy \cdot x^2 + 2xy \cdot 3y^2$

$= 2xy(x^2 + 3y^2)$

LASSROOM EXERCISES

State the greatest common factor.

1. 91, 133

2. 78, 143

3. $5x^3y$, $10xy^2$

4. $3a^2b^2$, $6a^3b$, $-9a^3b^3$

Factor.

5. $5x^3y + 10xy^2$

6. $3a^4b - 5bc^3$

7. $15tu^2 - 20u$

8. $6x^4yz + 15x^3y^2z$

RITTEN EXERCISES

A **List all positive integer factors of each number.**

1. 68

2. 63

3. 175

4. 75

List all integer factors of each number.

5. -21

6. -26

7. 28

8. 45

Write each number as the product of prime factors.

9. 42

10. 66

11. 90

12. 60

State the greatest common factor of each set of monomials.

13. $27xy$ and $36x$

14. $-8xy$ and $20y$

15. $-20xyz$ and $18x^2z^2$

16. $20xyz$ and $15yz^2$

17. $2ab$, $6abc$, and $4a^2c$

18. $3x^2y$, $6xy^2$, and $9xyz$

Factor each expression.

19. $5x + 10y$

20. $6x - 2y$

21. $7x^2 - 3x$

22. $5x^2 + 2x$

23. $5x^2 + 5x$

24. $3a^2 - 3a$

25. $18xy^2 - 12x^2y$

26. $16a^2b + 24ab^2$

27. $-30abc + 24bc - 18a^2b$

28. $8xy^2 + 28xyz - 4xy$

29. $15tu^2 + 21t^2u - 3tu$

30. $-10mn^3 + 4m^2n - 6mn^2$

31. $7a^2b^3 + 5ab^2 + 3a^2b^2$

32. $2a^3b^3 + 3a^3b^2 + 4a^2b$

33. $8a^2b^3c^4 - 12a^3b^2c^3$

34. $12ab^2c^3 + 16ac^4$

Factor the numerator and denominator of each expression.

35. $\dfrac{3x^2 - 6x}{8xy + 12y}$

36. $\dfrac{5x^2y + 6xy^2}{3xy - 7x^2y^2}$

37. $\dfrac{14a^2b^2 - 21a^2b}{6bc - 9c}$

38. $\dfrac{6ac - 10c}{9ab - 15b}$

B **Write a factored polynomial expression for each shaded area.**

39.

40.

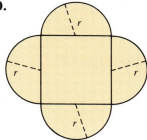

41.

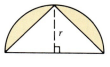

State whether each statement is true or false for all positive integers m, n, p, and q. If the answer is false, write a counterexample to illustrate.

42. If a number n has p positive integer factors, then n has $2p$ integer factors.

43. If a number n has p positive integer factors, then the number $2n$ has $2p$ positive integer factors.

44. If 2 is a factor of n, and 3 is a factor of n, then 6 is a factor of n.

45. If n has exactly 2 positive integer factors, then n is a prime number.

46. If n is a perfect square, then n has an odd number of positive integer factors.

47. If n has exactly 3 positive integer factors, then n is a square.

48. If n has exactly 4 positive integer factors, then n is a cube.

49. If a number n has p positive integer factors, then the number $3n$ has $3p$ positive integer factors.

C **50.** If m is a factor of n and n is a factor of p, then m is a factor of p.

51. If m is a factor of n and p is a factor of q, then mp is a factor of nq.

52. If m is a factor of n and p is a factor of q, then $m + p$ is a factor of $n + q$.

Factor each pair of expressions and state their greatest common factors.

53. $a^3b + a^2b^2$
$2a^2b + 4ab^2$

54. $12t^2u - 12tu^2$
$8tu^2 - 8u^3$

55. $6x^2yz + 12xy^2z + 18xyz$
$3x^2y + 3xy^3 + 9xy^2z$

56. $a^2bc + 2ab^2c + 3abc^2$
$3a^2b + 6ab^2 + 9abc$

Write a factored polynomial expression for each shaded area.

57.

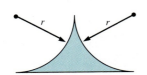

58.

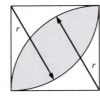

59.

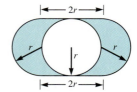

$\mathcal{R}$EVIEW EXERCISES

1. Graph $\{(x, y): y = |x + 1|\}$ and state its domain and range.　　　　[3-1]

State whether each of the following is a function. If it is a function, state whether it is a one-to-one function.　　　　[3-2]

2. $\{(2, 1), (3, 2), (4, 2)\}$

3. $\{(x, y): 2y + 3x = 6\}$

State whether each of the following is a linear function.　　　　[3-3]

4. $\{(x, y): y = 2x + 3\}$

5. $\{(x, y): y = |x|\}$

6. Write an equation of the line through $(0, 3)$ that is parallel to $y = \frac{1}{3}x + 12$.　　　　[3-4]

7. What is the slope of a line perpendicular to $y = -\frac{1}{3}x + 10$?　　　　[3-4]

$\mathcal{E}$XTENSION Cryptography

"Ultrasecure" cryptography systems are based on codes involving extremely large numbers—numbers having 100 to 200 digits. Such codes can be "broken" if the numbers can be factored, that is, written as the product of prime numbers. Therefore, factoring large numbers has received renewed interest from mathematicians. Using new techniques with computers that can perform hundreds of millions of operations per second, mathematicians were able to factor a 69-digit number in 38.3 minutes. Earlier-model computers and older techniques would have enabled mathematicians to factor the number in only 35,000 years!

LESSON 5-5

Factoring Binomials

Expanding the product $(a + b)(a - b)$ results in a binomial that is the difference of two squares $(a^2 - b^2)$. Starting with the difference of two squares and reversing the steps results in the factoring of the expression.

Factoring the Difference of Two Squares

For all real numbers a and b,
$$a^2 - b^2 = (a + b)(a - b)$$

Example 1 Factor. $16x^2 - y^4$

Solution *Rewrite as the difference of squares.* $16x^2 - y^4 = (4x)^2 - (y^2)^2$

Factor. $= (4x + y^2)(4x - y^2)$

Similarly, by expanding the following products, we can discover how to factor the sum or difference of two cubes.

$$(a + b)(a^2 - ab + b^2) = a(a^2 - ab + b^2) + b(a^2 - ab + b^2)$$
$$= a^3 - a^2b + ab^2 + a^2b - ab^2 + b^3$$
$$= a^3 + b^3$$
$$(a - b)(a^2 + ab + b^2) = a(a^2 + ab + b^2) - b(a^2 + ab + b^2)$$
$$= a^3 + a^2b + ab^2 - a^2b - ab^2 - b^3$$
$$= a^3 - b^3$$

Factoring the Sum or Difference of Two Cubes

For all real numbers a and b,
$$a^3 + b^3 = (a + b)(a^2 - ab + b^2)$$
and
$$a^3 - b^3 = (a - b)(a^2 + ab + b^2)$$

The similarity of $a^2 + b^2$ to $a^3 + b^3$, $a^3 - b^3$, and $a^2 - b^2$ leads some students to try to factor $a^2 + b^2$. But $a^2 + b^2$ cannot be factored over the real numbers.

Example 2 Factor. $8m^3 - n^3$

Solution $8m^3 - n^3 = (2m)^3 - n^3$

$$= (2m - n)((2m)^2 + 2mn + n^2)$$
$$= (2m - n)(4m^2 + 2mn + n^2)$$

Example 3 **Factor.** $x^6 + 27y^3$

Solution First rewrite the expression as the sum of two cubes.

$$x^6 + 27y^3 = (x^2)^3 + (3y)^3$$
$$= (x^2 + 3y)((x^2)^2 - 3x^2y + (3y)^2)$$
$$= (x^2 + 3y)(x^4 - 3x^2y + 9y^2)$$

Some polynomials can be **factored by grouping** terms containing common factors.

Example 4 **Factor.** $xy + 2y + 3x + 6$

Solution $xy + 2y + 3x + 6 = (xy + 2y) + (3x + 6)$
$$= y(x + 2) + 3(x + 2)$$
$$= (y + 3)(x + 2)$$

When factoring any polynomial, first look for common monomial factors. If there is a common monomial factor, factor it out: The remaining polynomial factor will be simpler, and recognizable forms will be seen more easily.

Example 5 **Factor.** $5a^3 - 20ab^4$

Solution $5a^3 - 20ab^4 = 5a(a^2 - 4b^4)$
$$= 5a(a + 2b^2)(a - 2b^2)$$

LASSROOM EXERCISES

Factor.

1. $x^2 - 9y^2$

2. $\dfrac{4a^2}{9} - b^2$

3. $c^3 + 8d^3$

4. $27a^3 - b^3$

5. $3ax^2 - 3ay^4$

6. $8m^3 - 18mn^2$

7. $6ab + 3b - 8a - 4$

8. $4x^2y^2 - 16x^2y - 8xy^2 + 32xy$

RITTEN EXERCISES

A **Factor. If the expression cannot be factored, write "simplest form."**

1. $9p^2 - q^2$

2. $25p^2 - q^2$

3. $16r^2 - 25s^2$

4. $9r^2 - 4s^2$

5. $\dfrac{4}{25}x^2 - \dfrac{9}{16}y^2$

6. $\dfrac{4}{9}x^2 - \dfrac{16}{25}y^2$

7. $a^6 - b^2$ **8.** $a^2 - b^4$ **9.** $3p^3 - 12pq^2$

10. $4q - 36p^2q$ **11.** $99a^2 - 11a^2b^2$ **12.** $11a^2b^2 - 44b^2$

13. $27 - p^3$ **14.** $q^3 - 27$ **15.** $8r^3 - 1$

16. $s^3 - 8$ **17.** $x^2 + 4$ **18.** $x^2 + 9$

19. $5x^3 - 5$ **20.** $6x^3 - 48$ **21.** $3a^3 - 81b^3$

22. $4a^3 - 108b^3$ **23.** $x^3 + 64$ **24.** $x^3 + 125$

25. $t^2 + u^2$ **26.** $p^2 + q^2$ **27.** $27a^3 + 8$

28. $8a^3 + 1$ **29.** $125ab^3 + a$ **30.** $64a^3b + b$

31. $2ax^3 + 16a$ **32.** $3ct^3 + 24c$ **33.** $ab + 2a + 3b + 6$

34. $ab + 3a + 2b + 6$ **35.** $ab + 5a - 4b - 20$ **36.** $ab - 6a + 3b - 18$

37. $x^2 + 5x + xy + 5y$ **38.** $y^2 + xy + 6y + 6x$ **39.** $3x + 4y^2 + xy + 12y$

40. $4x + 3y^2 + xy + 12y$ **41.** $abc - 6ac + 3bc - 18c$ **42.** $abc + 2ac - 5bc - 10c$

43. $a^2b + abc + 3ab^2 + 3b^2c$ **44.** $3a^2c + 3ac^2 + abc + bc^2$ **45.** $p - 2q + 2p^2 - 4pq$

46. $3t^2 - 6tu - t + 2u$ **47.** $3x^2 - 3xy + 6x - 6y$ **48.** $5ab - 10a + 15b^2 - 30b$

B Write as the product of three factors.

49. $a^4 - 16$ **50.** $w^4 - 81$ **51.** $b^3 + 3b^2 - 25b - 75$

52. $y^3 + y^2 - 36y - 36$ **53.** $R^4 + 8R$ **54.** $t^4 - 27t$

Write as the product of four factors.

55. $x^6 - 64$ **56.** $y^6 - 1$

57. $a^4 + 3a^3 - 16a^2 - 48a$ **58.** $3b^3 + 12b^2 - 27b - 108$

C Find the greatest common factor of each pair of expressions.

59. $a^2 - b^2$ and $a^3 - b^3$ **60.** $a^2 + b^2$ and $a^3 + b^3$ **61.** $a^2 - b^2$ and $a^3 + b^3$

62. $a^2 + b^2$ and $a^4 - b^4$ **63.** $a^3 - b^3$ and $(a - b)^3$ **64.** $a^4 - b^4$ and $a^6 - b^6$

REVIEW EXERCISES

1. If $V = \frac{4}{3}\pi r^3$, then V varies directly as __?__. [3-5]

2. Suppose that y varies directly as the square of x. If $y = 75$ when $x = 5$, what is the value of y when $x = 10$? [3-5]

Let $[x]$ represent the greatest integer function. [3-6]

3. Simplify $[2.3] \cdot [-4.2]$. **4.** Graph $y = 2\,[x]$ for $-2 \le x \le 2$.

5. Let $f(x) = x^2$ and $g(x) = x + 5$. Simplify $f(g(5))$. [3-7]

6. Let $f(x) = 2x + 3$ and $g(x) = \dfrac{x - 3}{2}$. Find $g(f(a))$. [3-7]

Factoring Trinomials

Studying particular cases can be a powerful means of discovering generalizations that can be applied to new problems. Consider the effect of signs in multiplying two binomials.

$$(x + 3)(x + 2) = x^2 + 5x + 6 \qquad (x - 3)(x + 2) = x^2 - x - 6$$
$$(x - 3)(x - 2) = x^2 - 5x + 6 \qquad (x + 3)(x - 2) = x^2 + x - 6$$

Given a trinomial $x^2 + bx + c$ that can be factored into two binomials $(x + q)(x + s)$, we can draw the following conclusions:

▶ If c and b are both positive then q and s are positive.

▶ If c is positive and b is negative then q and s are both negative.

▶ If c is negative then q is positive and s is negative or vice versa.

By expanding $(px + q)(rx + s)$, we can derive the factors of a trinomial of the form $ax^2 + bx + c$.

$$(px + q)(rx + s) = prx^2 + (qr + ps)x + qs$$
$$ax^2 + \qquad bx \qquad + c$$

Therefore, the task of factoring the trinomial $ax^2 + bx + c$ is a matter of finding the values of $p, q, r,$ and s such that

$$pr = a, \qquad (qr + ps) = b, \quad \text{and} \quad qs = c.$$

These values can be found using systematic trials.

Example 1 **Factor completely.** $10x^2 + 9x + 2$

Solution Let us assume that factors $(px + q)$ and $(rx + s)$ exist. Then

$$10x^2 + 9x + 2 = (px + q)(rx + s) = prx^2 + (qr + ps)x + qs$$

We must find the values of $p, q, r,$ and s such that

$$pr = 10, \qquad (qr + ps) = 9, \qquad \text{and} \qquad qs = 2.$$

Because all signs are positive, q and s are positive. These possibilities exist.

$$(10x + 2)(1x + 1) \qquad (5x + 2)(2x + 1)$$
$$(10x + 1)(1x + 2) \qquad (5x + 1)(2x + 2)$$

However, the first and last possibilities contain a binomial factor that has 2 as a factor. Since the terms of $10x^2 + 9x + 2$ do not have 2 as a common monomial factor, these possibilities can be eliminated. Of the remaining two, expanding the products identifies the correct factors.

$$(10x + 1)(1x + 2) = 10x^2 + 21x + 2$$
$$(5x + 2)(2x + 1) = 10x^2 + 9x + 2$$

Answer $10x^2 + 9x + 2 = (5x + 2)(2x + 1)$

Since the major task in factoring is to find the coefficients, we can save some effort by listing only the *coefficients* of the factors as we try the various possibilities.

Example 2 **Factor completely.** $6x^2 - 5x - 4$

Solution Factor pairs of 6 are 6 and 1, and 2 and 3. Factor pairs of -4 are 1 and -4, -1 and 4, and 2 and -2.

	p	q	r	s	pr	$qr + ps$	qs
1.	6	1	1	-4	6	-23	-4
2.	6	-4	1	1	6	2	-4
3.	6	2	1	-2	6	-10	-4
4.	6	-2	1	2	6	10	-4
5.	3	1	2	-4	6	-10	-4
6.	3	-4	2	1	6	-5	-4
7.	3	2	2	-2	6	-2	-4
8.	3	-2	2	2	6	2	-4

Answer $6x^2 - 5x - 4 = (3x - 4)(2x + 1)$

Several observations can reduce the effort required to factor a trinomial like the one in Example 2.

▶ Since the values of p, q, r, and s are selected to produce appropriate values of pr and qs, we need only compute $qr + ps$ for each pair of binomials.

▶ Since the required sum $qr + ps$ is -5, the binomial pair in line 1 can be eliminated as soon as it is noted that $|ps|$ is large compared to $|qr|$.

▶ Note that 2 is a factor of both p and q in lines 2, 3, and 4, and also that 2 is a factor of r and s in lines 5, 7, and 8, but 2 is not a factor of the original trinomial. Therefore, those possibilities may be ruled out without computing $qr + ps$.

▶ As soon as the correct factors are found in line 6, there is no reason to continue the list.

Example 3 **Factor completely.** $y^2 + 5y + 2$

Solution Compute $qr + ps$ for the possibilities of p, q, r, and s.

p	q	r	s	$qr + ps$
1	1	1	2	3
1	2	1	1	3

There are no other possibilities. In neither trial does $qr + ps = 5$.

Answer The polynomial $y^2 + 5y + 2$ is in simplest form.

Example 4 **Factor completely.** $12m^3 - 4m^2 - 8m$

Solution *First factor out the greatest common factor.*

Factor the trinomial.

$12m^3 - 4m^2 - 8m$

$= 4m(3m^2 - m - 2)$

$= 4m(3m + 2)(m - 1)$

In some cases, you may recognize a trinomial as a **perfect-square trinomial** (the square of a binomial). If so, factor it without going through the procedure shown in the previous examples.

Factoring a Perfect-Square Trinomial

For all real numbers a and b,

$$a^2 + 2ab + b^2 = (a + b)^2$$
$$a^2 - 2ab + b^2 = (a - b)^2$$

LASSROOM EXERCISES

Factor completely. If the expression cannot be factored, write "simplest form."

1. $x^2 + 2x - 3$
2. $y^2 + 7y + 12$
3. $x^2 - 7x + 10$
4. $15 + 2x - x^2$
5. $2a^2 + 7a - 4$
6. $6b^2 - 13b + 5$
7. $4a^2 + 12a + 9$
8. $3a^3 + 12a^2 + 12a$

RITTEN EXERCISES

A Factor completely. If the expression cannot be factored, write "simplest form."

1. $x^2 + 7x + 10$
2. $b^2 + 8b + 12$
3. $x^2 - 3x - 18$
4. $x^2 - 6x - 16$
5. $w^2 + 5w - 24$
6. $n^2 + n - 30$
7. $x^2 - 14x + 48$
8. $y^2 - 19y + 48$
9. $t^2 + 22t - 48$
10. $x^2 + 47x - 48$
11. $x^2 + 8x + 6$
12. $a^2 + 3a + 5$
13. $21 - 10x + x^2$
14. $24 + 10x + x^2$
15. $2 + z - z^2$
16. $3 - 2x - x^2$
17. $2x^2 + 7x + 3$
18. $3x^2 + 7x + 2$
19. $5x^2 + 13x - 6$
20. $7r^2 + 3r - 4$
21. $3x^2 + 11x - 6$
22. $3x^2 + 7x + 6$
23. $4y^2 + 8y + 3$
24. $4x^2 + 16x + 15$
25. $4x^2 - 11x - 3$
26. $4c^2 + c - 3$
27. $25 - x^2$
28. $9 - x^2$
29. $16 + a^2$
30. $36 + d^2$
31. $4x^2 + 20x + 9$
32. $9x^2 + 12x + 4$
33. $y^3 + 4y^2 - 12y$
34. $x^3 + 6x^2 - 16x$
35. $6x^2 - 11x - 10$
36. $6y^2 + 11y - 10$

B 37. $6x^3 + 59x^2y - 10xy^2$
38. $6x^2y - 59xy^2 - 10y^3$
39. $50x^3z - 40x^2z + 8xz$
40. $36x^3y - 87x^2y^2 + 45xy^3$
41. $27x^3y^2 - 90x^2y^2 + 75xy^2$
42. $24x^2y^2 - 34xy^3 + 12y^4$
43. $48x^2 - 62xy + 9y^2$
44. $4x^2 - 6xy - 9y^2$
45. $2x^6 + x^3 - 6$
46. $x^4 - xy^3$

C   47. $3x^{2n} + 14x^n - 24$ 48. $2x^{2n+1} - 17x^{n+1} + 8x$

49. $8x^{6n} - 6x^{3n} - 9$ 50. $x^{4n} - x^{2n} - 12$

51. $x^5 - x^3 - x^2 + 1$ 52. $4x^3 + 12x^2 - 9x - 27$

53. $x^{6n} - y^{6m}$ 54. $x^{16n} - 1$

$\mathcal{R}$EVIEW EXERCISES

1. Solve by graphing.   [4-1]
   $$y = 2x - 2$$
   $$x + y = 10$$

2. Solve by substitution.   [4-2]
   $$y = x + 4$$
   $$2x + y = 10$$

3. Solve by linear combinations.   [4-3]
   $$2x + 3y = 12$$
   $$3x - 2y = 5$$

4. Solve the system using Cramer's rule.   [4-4]
   $$3x + 4y = 8$$
   $$2x - 5y = 13$$

$\mathcal{S}$elf-Quiz 2

5-4   **Find the greatest common factor.**

     1. 48 and 120   2. $14x^2yz$ and $35xy^2$

5-5   **Factor.**

     3. $27x - 3x^2$ 4. $2a^2b^3 - 8a^3b + 12ab^2$

     5. $9x^2 - 4y^2$ 6. $a^2 - 3a + 2ab - 6b$

     7. $64x^3 - 1$ 8. $3r^4 - 3s^4$

5-6   9. $x^2 - 12x - 28$ 10. $12 - x - x^2$

     11. $5y^2 + 13y - 6$ 12. $7x^2y + 42xy + 63y$

     13. $x^3 - 6x^2 - 16x$ 14. $x^2 + xy - 2y^2$

$\mathcal{H}$ISTORICAL NOTE   Exponents

The power of modern mathematics depends to a large degree on its concise and unambiguous symbolism. Today it seems so natural to write a term like $5x^3$ that it is difficult to understand that the notation (first used by Descartes in 1637) evolved from many centuries of experimentation with more cumbersome notations.

Modern notation		*Some earlier forms*			
$5x^2$	5xx	$\frac{2}{5}$ $\overset{ii}{5}$	5Q	5.quad	5 $\diamond$
$5x^3$	5xxx	$\frac{3}{5}$ $\overset{iii}{5}$	5C	5.cub	5 $\square$

LESSON 5-7

Quadratic Equations

A second degree polynomial in one variable $ax^2 + bx + c$ (where a, b, and c are real numbers, $a \neq 0$) is called a **quadratic polynomial.** An equation that can be expressed in the form $P(x) = 0$ where $P(x)$ is a quadratic polynomial in x, is called a **quadratic equation.** The **standard form of a quadratic equation** in one variable is $ax^2 + bx + c = 0$, $a \neq 0$. The following are quadratic equations in one variable, not necessarily in standard form.

$$3x^2 + 2x - 5 = 0 \qquad 4x + 3 = x^2 \qquad 2x^2 = 0$$
$$(3a - 2)(4a + 1) = 1 \qquad 6b^2 + 2b = 3b^2 \qquad m^2 - 1 = 0$$

This equation is not quadratic since it is equivalent to $1 - x = 0$, a linear equation.

$$2x^2 + 1 = x + 2x^2$$

Many quadratic equations can be solved by applying the Zero-Product Property to the factored form of the equation.

Zero-Product Property

For all real numbers a and b,

$$ab = 0 \text{ if and only if } a = 0 \text{ or } b = 0.$$

Example 1   **Solve.** $x^2 - 3x = 0$

    Solution   *Factor the quadratic polynomial.*

       Apply the Zero-Product Property.

$$x^2 - 3x = 0$$
$$x(x - 3) = 0$$
$$x = 0 \quad \text{or} \quad x - 3 = 0$$
$$x = 0 \quad \text{or} \qquad x = 3$$

    Answer $\{0, 3\}$

Example 2   **Solve.** $x^2 + \dfrac{5}{2}x - 6 = 0$

    Solution   *Multiply both sides by 2.*

$$2\left(x^2 + \frac{5}{2}x - 6\right) = 2(0)$$
$$2x^2 + 5x - 12 = 0$$

       Factor.

$$(2x - 3)(x + 4) = 0$$

       Apply the Zero-Product Property.

$$2x - 3 = 0 \text{ or } x + 4 = 0$$
$$x = \frac{3}{2} \text{ or } \qquad x = -4$$

    Answer $\left\{\dfrac{3}{2}, -4\right\}$

Example 3   **Solve.** $4y^2 = 7y - 3$

Solution   *Write the equation in standard form.*

$$4y^2 - 7y + 3 = 0$$

Factor.

$$(4y - 3)(y - 1) = 0$$

$$4y - 3 = 0 \quad \text{or} \quad y - 1 = 0$$

$$y = \frac{3}{4} \quad \text{or} \quad y = 1$$

Answer $\left\{\frac{3}{4}, 1\right\}$

Example 4   **Solve.**

A field is in the shape of a rectangle. Its length is 4 rods greater than its width. Its area is 96 square rods. What are the dimensions of the field?

Solution   Let x = the width of the field in rods. Then $(x + 4)$ = the length of the field in rods. Since the field is in the shape of a rectangle, draw and label a rectangle.

$$\text{Length} \cdot \text{Width} = \text{Area}$$

$$(x + 4)x = 96$$

$$x^2 + 4x - 96 = 0$$

$$(x + 12)(x - 8) = 0$$

$$x + 12 = 0 \quad \text{or} \quad x - 8 = 0$$

$$x = -12 \quad \text{or} \quad x = 8$$

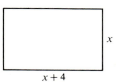

Since the width of a rectangle cannot be negative, the root -12 is discarded.

Answer   The width of the field is 8 rods, and the length $(x + 4)$ is 12 rods.

$\mathcal{C}$LASSROOM EXERCISES

1. Write this equation in standard form. $(x + 2)(x + 3) = 2$

2. State whether this equation is quadratic. $(x - 2)(x - 3) = (x + 1)^2$

Solve.

3. $(x - 3)(x + 2) = 0$

4. $x^2 + 5x + 6 = 0$

5. $(2y - 3)(3y + 2) = 0$

6. $4w^2 + w - 3 = 0$

7. $\frac{1}{2}x^2 - x - \frac{3}{2} = 0$

8. $2t^2 = 7t + 4$

 RITTEN EXERCISES

 Write these quadratic equations in standard form. Do not solve.

1. $2x + x^2 = 3$ 2. $5 + x^2 = 6x$
3. $(x + 1)(x + 6) = 2x$ 4. $(x + 2)(x + 6) = x$
5. $(x + 3)(x + 4) = x + 4$ 6. $(x + 3)(x + 5) = x + 3$

State whether the equation is quadratic. (Answer yes or no.)

7. $x^2 + 3x + 2 = x + 1$ 8. $x^2 - 3x + 4 = x + 9$
9. $(x + 3)(x + 4) = (x + 1)(x + 6)$ 10. $(x + 8)(x + 1) = (x + 2)(x + 4)$
11. $(2x - 1)(3x + 4) = (4x + 3)(x - 3)$ 12. $(2x + 3)(4x + 1) = (5x + 2)(x + 4)$

Solve.

13. $(2x - 5)(x + 2) = 0$ 14. $(2x - 7)(x + 3) = 0$ 15. $(4a + 7)(3a + 2) = 0$
16. $(3a + 8)(2a + 5) = 0$ 17. $y^2 - 5y - 14 = 0$ 18. $y^2 - 2y - 15 = 0$
19. $x^2 - 10x + 16 = 0$ 20. $x^2 - 8x + 15 = 0$ 21. $x^2 + 8x + 12 = 0$
22. $x^2 + 11x + 18 = 0$ 23. $a^2 + 7a - 18 = 0$ 24. $a^2 + 3a - 18 = 0$
25. $6c^2 + 7c = 0$ 26. $c^2 + 17c = 0$ 27. $x^2 + 5x = -6$
28. $x^2 + 5x = 6$ 29. $y^2 - 5 = 4y$ 30. $y^2 - 5 = -4y$

$\mathcal{A}$pplications

For each problem, write an equation that fits the situation, solve the equation, and answer the question.

31. The width of a rectangular mat is 7 ft less than its length. Its area is 60 ft². What is its width?

32. The length of a rectangular picture is 4 cm greater than its width. Find the width of the picture if its area is 60 cm².

33. The product of two numbers is -36. What are the two numbers if one is 13 more than the other? (Two answers)

34. Find two consecutive positive even integers whose product is 168.

35. Find the dimensions of a right triangle with sides of x, $(x + 7)$, and $(x + 8)$ centimeters, respectively.

 Solve. [*Hint:* First simplify the equation by "dividing out" a monomial factor or by clearing the equation of fractions.]

36. $6x^2 - 9x - 81 = 0$ 37. $48x^2 = 64x + 12$ 38. $5x^2 - \frac{11}{2}x - 3 = 0$

39. $\frac{1}{4}x^2 - 4x + 15 = 0$ 40. $x^2 - 2x + \frac{3}{4} = 0$ 41. $x^2 - 2x + \frac{8}{9} = 0$

42. $(x + 2)(x - 3) = (x - 4)(x + 5)$ 43. $(2x - 3)(x + 6) = x(x + 2)$
44. $(2x + 7)(x + 1) = (4x + 9)(x - 1)$ 45. $(5x + 2)(3x - 1) = 3(x^2 - 4x + 11)$

 **pplications**

Solve.

46. The horizontal sides of a square are made 3 cm longer and its vertical sides are made 4 cm shorter. The resulting rectangle has an area of 18 cm². What was the length of the original square?

47. A polygon with n sides has $\frac{1}{2}n(n - 3)$ diagonals. How many sides does a polygon with 65 diagonals have?

48. A pane of glass is 6 in. longer than it is wide. The pane was cut from a rectangular piece whose length and width were each 6 in. greater than the dimensions of the pane. The area of the rectangular piece was twice the area of the pane. What are the dimensions of the pane of glass?

49. A farmer has 40 rods of fence to enclose a rectangular area, using an existing fence as one side. The maximum area that can be enclosed in this manner is 200 square rods. Find the dimensions of the area enclosed.

50. The radius of a circle is 15 cm. By how much must the radius be decreased in order to reduce the original area by 104π cm²?

 51. A tile walk of uniform width is to be constructed with 1-ft wide square tiles around a swimming pool. The homeowner has 600 such tiles to enclose a pool that is 20 ft by 30 ft. What is the widest walk that can be constructed?

52. Find the dimensions of a rug that covers 60% of the floor of a room 16 ft by 20 ft and that is equidistant from the walls.

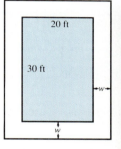

Solve.

53. $p^2(p - 1) - 3p(p - 1) - 4(p - 1) = 0$

54. $x^2(x + 3) = 4(x + 3)$

55. Why is it poor practice to divide both sides of an equation by a variable?

$\mathcal{R}$EVIEW EXERCISES

1. Evaluate this determinant.

$$\begin{vmatrix} 3 & 6 & 2 \\ 1 & -2 & 3 \\ 0 & 4 & 2 \end{vmatrix}$$

2. Solve this system using Cramer's rule. [4-5]

$$x + y = 5$$
$$x - z = -4$$
$$2x - y + z = 11$$

The function $P = 2x - 3y$ **is defined on the shaded region.**

3. State the point in the shaded region that produces the maximum value of P.

4. State the point in the shaded region that produces the minimum value of P.

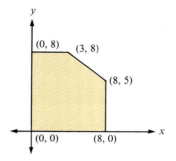

$\mathcal{E}$XTENSION   Quadratic Inequalities

Quadratic inequalities in one variable can be solved using a property similar to the Zero-Product Property for Equalities. It states that if the product of two real numbers is greater than 0, the two numbers are both positive or are both negative; if the product of two real numbers is negative, then one is positive and one is negative.

Zero-Product Property for Inequalities

For all real numbers a and b,

   if $ab > 0$, then $(a > 0$ and $b > 0)$ or $(a < 0$ and $b < 0)$;

   if $ab < 0$, then $(a < 0$ and $b > 0)$ or $(a > 0$ and $b < 0)$.

Sample   **Solve and graph.** $x^2 + x - 6 > 0$

Factor. $(x + 3)(x - 2) > 0$

Apply the zero-product property for inequalities.

$(x + 3 > 0 \text{ and } x - 2 > 0)$ or $(x + 3 < 0 \text{ and } x - 2 < 0)$

$(x > -3 \text{ and } x > 2)$ or $(x < -3 \text{ and } x < 2)$

$x > 2$ or $x < -3$

The solution set is $\{x: x > 2 \text{ or } x < -3\}$.

Solve. Graph on the number line.

1. $x^2 - x - 6 < 0$

2. $y^2 - 7y + 10 > 0$

3. $x^2 + 10x + 16 \leq 0$

4. $r^2 + 2r - 15 \geq 0$

5. $x^2 - 5x > 0$

6. $x^2 + 6x + 9 \leq 0$

7. What are the dimensions of a square for which the number of square units is less than the number of units in the perimeter?

CHAPTER SUMMARY

▶ **Vocabulary**

▶ Definition of nonnegative integer exponents   [5-1]

For all real numbers x and all positive integers n, where x^n is called the nth *power* of x.

$$x^n = \overbrace{x \cdot x \cdot x \cdot \ldots \cdot x}^{n\text{ factors}}$$

For all nonzero real numbers, $x^0 = 1$.

▶ Properties of exponents   [5-1]

For all real numbers a and b and for all nonnegative integers m and n,

$$a^m \cdot a^n = a^{m+n}, \quad (a^m)^n = a^{mn}, \quad (ab)^m = a^m b^m.$$

▶ For real numbers a and b, $\quad -(a + b) = -a + (-b)$.   [5-2]

▶ To multiply two polynomials, multiply each term of one polynomial by each term of the other polynomial. Then add the products.   [5-3]

▶ The expansion of $(x + y)^n$ has $n + 1$ terms.   [5-3]

1. The degree of each term is n.

2. The first term is x^n. The exponent of x decreases by 1 in successive terms; x does not occur in the last term.

3. The y variable does not occur in the first term; y to the first power occurs in the second term. The exponent of y increases by 1 in successive terms.

4. The coefficient of each term is the corresponding number from the $(n + 1)$st row of Pascal's triangle.

▶ Pascal's triangle   [5-3]

```
            1
          1   1
        1   2   1
      1   3   3   1
    1   4   6   4   1
  1   5  10  10   5   1
1   6  15   ...
```

▶ For all real numbers a and b, [5-5]

$$a^2 - b^2 = (a + b)(a - b)$$
$$a^3 + b^3 = (a + b)(a^2 - ab + b^2)$$
$$a^3 - b^3 = (a - b)(a^2 + ab + b^2)$$
$a^2 + b^2$ cannot be factored over the real numbers.

▶ General strategy for factoring [5-5, 5-6]

1. Factor out the greatest common monomial factor.

2. If the remaining polynomial factor has two terms, determine whether it can be factored as the difference of two squares or the sum or difference of two cubes.

3. If the remaining factor has four terms, determine whether it can be factored by grouping.

4. If the remaining factor has three terms, determine whether it can be factored into the product of two binomials.

▶ Zero-Product Property [5-7]

For all real numbers a and b,

$$ab = 0 \text{ if and only if } a = 0 \text{ or } b = 0.$$

*C*HAPTER REVIEW

5-1 **Objective:** To recognize and simplify monomials.

1. State whether the expression is a monomial.

   a. $\sqrt{5x}$ **b.** $17x^2yz^3$ **c.** $\dfrac{12}{x + 1}$ **d.** $a + b$ **e.** 3

2. Identify the degree of each monomial.

   a. $-\dfrac{1}{3}$ **b.** $8xy$ **c.** $0.2a^2b^2$ **d.** 5^2st^5

3. Simplify.   **a.** $(5x^2)(3x)^2$ **b.** $(4.1 \cdot 10^{18})(3 \cdot 10^{15})$

5-2 **Objectives:** To recognize polynomials.
                To simplify sums and differences of polynomials, and products of monomials and polynomials.

4. State whether the expression is a polynomial.

   a. $\dfrac{17}{x^2 + 3x + 4}$ **b.** 0.9 **c.** $3n^4 - 1$ **d.** $\sqrt{5x^3} - 2x + 12$

5. State the degree of this polynomial. $3ab^2 - 15a^3bc + \dfrac{5}{2}a^2b^2c^2$

6. Simplify.   **a.** $(x^3 + 2x - 3) - (x^2 - 2x + 4)$ **b.** $2x(3x + 4) - 3(x + 5)$

218   Chapter 5   Polynomials

5-3 **Objective:** To multiply polynomials.

 7. Expand and simplify.

   a. $(a + 2b)(3a - 4b)$ **b.** $(x + 2y)^4$

 8. Express the volume of this cube as a polynomial.

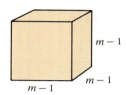

5-4 **Objective:** To factor out the greatest common factor of the terms of a polynomial.

 9. State the greatest common factor of $4r^2s^3t$ and $6prs^2$.

 10. Factor.

   a. $18mn^3 - 3m^2n$ **b.** $12x^2yz^2 + 48x^3y^2z - 16x^4y^3$

5-5 **Objective:** To factor binomials.

 Factor.

 11. $9p^2 - q^2$ **12.** $64x^3 - 1$

 13. $2m^4 - 8n^4$ **14.** $20xy - 3 + 4y - 15x$

5-6 **Objective:** To factor trinomials.

 Factor.

 15. $5x^2 + x - 4$ **16.** $12x^2 + 5 - 17x$ **17.** $18xy^2 + 11xyz + xz^2$

5-7 **Objective:** To solve quadratic equations by factoring.

 Solve.

 18. $x^2 + 9 = 6x$ **19.** $2x^2 + 5x - 3 = 0$

$\mathcal{C}$HAPTER 5 SELF-TEST

5-1 **State whether the expression is a monomial. If it is a monomial, give its degree.**

 1. $13a^3b^3$ **2.** $\dfrac{7}{xy^2}$

 Simplify.

 3. $(5x^2)(3xy)^3$ **4.** $(5.3 \cdot 10^{14})(4 \cdot 10^6)$

 5. What is the degree of this polynomial?
 $$4mn^2 - 9m^3n + 7n$$

5-2 **Simplify.**

 6. $x(y^2 + 5xy) + 2xy(3x - 2y)$ **7.** $2(a^2b - 4ab^2) - 7(ab^2 + 3a^2b)$

5-3   **8.** $2x(x - 3y)^2$ **9.** $(r - 2s)^4$

        10. Find the surface area of this cube.

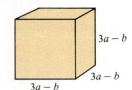

$3a - b$

$3a - b$

$3a - b$

5-4   **Factor.**

        11. $7xy - 42xy^2$ **12.** $20a^2b - 15a^3b^2$

5-5,   **Factor.**

5-6   **13.** $9x^2 - t^2$ **14.** $2ab^2 - b^2 + 6a - 3$

        15. $2y^3 - 16$ **16.** $2x^2 - 5xy + 3y^2$

5-7   **Solve.**

        17. $y^2 - 9y - 36 = 0$ **18.** $(x + 2)(x + 4) = 15$

        19. Find two consecutive positive integers whose product is 156.

        20. The hypotenuse of a right triangle is 10 in. longer than the shorter leg and 5 in. longer than the longer leg. Find the length of each side of the triangle.

𝒫RACTICE FOR COLLEGE ENTRANCE TESTS

Choose the best answer for each question.

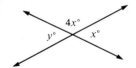

$4x°$

$y°$ $x°$

 1. If the two lines intersect as shown, what is the value of y?

     A. 20   **B.** 30   **C. 36**   **D.** 40   **E.** 45

 2. Of the following numbers, which is the greatest?

     A. 0.0111   **B.** 0.1001   **C.** 0.101   **D.** 0.1011   **E.** 0.11

 3. A triangle with sides 6, 8, and 10 has the same perimeter as a square with sides of length __?__.

     A. 4   **B.** 6   **C.** 8   **D.** 10   **E.** 12

 4. If $x - 10 = 4$, then $x - 12 = $ __?__.

     A. 2   **B.** 6   **C.** 8   **D.** 14   **E.** 16

 5. If $x + y = 10$ and $x - y = 6$, what is the value of $x^2 - y^2$?

     A. 16   **B.** 36   **C.** 60   **D.** 64   **E.** 104

 6. If $x - a = 6$ and $a - y = 8$, then $x - y = $ __?__.

     A. -2 **B.** 2   **C.** 4   **D.** 7   **E.** 14

 7. If $|x + 2| = |x - 2|$, then $x = $ __?__.

     A. -4 **B.** -2 **C.** 0   **D.** 2   **E.** 4

8. If a jar contains 8 jelly beans, some red and some green, which of the following could be the ratio of red beans to green beans?

   A. 1:2   **B.** 1:3   **C.** 1:4   **D.** 1:5   **E.** 1:6

9. If $x + y = 6$, what is the value of $x^2 + y^2$?

   A. 9   **B.** 18   **C.** 24   **D.** 36

   E. It cannot be determined from the information given.

10. In triangle ABC, if $AB = AC$, what is the value of x?

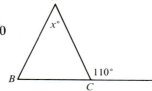

   A. 30   **B.** 40   **C.** 60   **D.** 70

   E. It cannot be determined from the information given.

11. If $ab + 5a + 3b + 15 = 24$ and $a + 3 = 6$, then $b + 5 = $ ___?___ .

   A. 4   **B.** 5   **C.** 6   **D.** 8   **E.** 12

12. If the surface area of a cube is numerically equal to the volume, what is the length of a side?

   A. 2   **B.** 3   **C.** 4   **D.** 6

   E. It cannot be determined from the information given.

13. If the product of two positive numbers is 24 and the difference of the two numbers is 10, then the average of the two numbers is ___?___ .

   A. 5   **B.** 5.5   **C.** 7   **D.** 12.5

   E. It cannot be determined from the information given.

14. Which of the following is the closest approximation to $\dfrac{6{,}932{,}715}{35{,}187}$?

   A. 200   **B.** 500   **C.** 700   **D.** 2000   **E.** 5000

15. If the remainder is 2 when a number n is divided by 7, what is the remainder when $3n$ is divided by 7?

   A. 2   **B.** 3   **C.** 4   **D.** 5   **E.** 6

16. What is the area of the shaded region in the figure?

   A. $(4 - \pi)r^2$ **B.** $2r^2(4 - \pi)$ **C.** $4r(2 - \pi)$

   D. $\left(\dfrac{2 - \pi}{2}\right)r^2$ **E.** $r(r - 2\pi)$

17. If $a = 10 + k$ and $b = 10 - k$, then $a^2 + b^2 = $ ___?___ .

   A. $100 - k^2$ **B.** $100 + k^2$ **C.** 200   **D.** $2(100 + k^2)$

   E. $2(100 + 20k + k^2)$

18. If $ab = 5$ and $a^2 + b^2 = 25$, then $(a + b)^2 = $ ___?___ .

   A. 15   **B.** 20   **C.** 25   **D.** 30   **E.** 35

CHAPTER 6

Rational Expressions

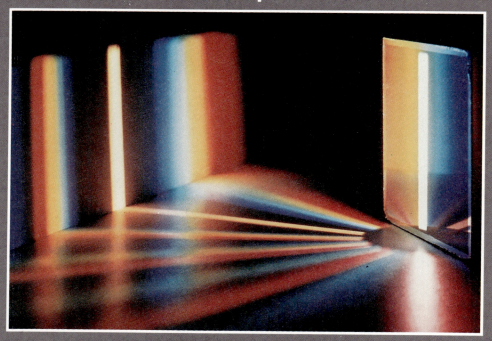

Since the early 1800's, physicians have known that light has wave characteristics. The wavelength λ (the Greek letter lambda) can be computed from the quotient (or rational expression) $\frac{v}{f}$ where v is the velocity and f is the frequency. For visible light, the velocity is about 3×10^8 meters per second and the frequency is about 5×10^{14} Hertz (cycles per second). Therefore,

$$\lambda = \frac{v}{f} = \frac{3 \times 10^8 \, \text{m/s}}{5 \times 10^{14} \, \text{Hz}} = 6 \times 10^{-7} \, \text{m} = 0.0006 \, \text{mm}$$

Thus the wavelength is a little more than half of a thousandth of a millimeter.

As light waves pass through a large number of very narrow slits, the waves spread from each slit. In certain directions, waves of one wavelength reinforce each other causing the bright bands of color in the photo above.

LESSON 6-1

Negative Exponents

Applications in sciences like electronics, nuclear physics, computer science, and physical chemistry involve some very small measurements. For example, the rest mass of an electron is

$$0.0000000000000000000000000000009109 \text{ kg}$$

In scientific notation, the mass of an electron can be written as

$$9.109 \cdot 10^{-31}.$$

The expansion of the concept of exponent to include negative exponents enables scientists to work accurately and efficiently with such small numbers.

Quotients of powers suggest a property of exponents comparable to a property of multiplying powers. For example, facts like $\frac{10^5}{10^3} = 10^2$ suggest the following property of exponents.

Subtraction Property of Exponents

For each real number a, $a \neq 0$, and for all positive integers m and n,

$$\text{if } m > n, \text{ then } \frac{a^m}{a^n} = a^{m-n}.$$

Now consider the extension of the property to the case in which m is less than n, that is, where the exponent in the denominator is greater than the exponent in the numerator.

$$\frac{10^3}{10^5} = 10^{3-5} = 10^{-2}$$

But,
$$\frac{10^3}{10^5} = \frac{1}{10^2}$$

We can make these two statements consistent by defining **negative exponents**.

Definition: Negative Exponents

For each nonzero real number a and for each positive integer n, $a^{-n} = \frac{1}{a^n}$.

For example, $4^{-3} = \frac{1}{4^3}$.

The following properties can now be extended to include all integral exponents.

Properties of Exponents

For all nonzero real numbers a and b, and for all integers m and n,

$$a^m \cdot a^n = a^{m+n} \qquad \frac{a^m}{a^n} = a^{m-n} \qquad (a^m)^n = a^{mn} \qquad a^n b^n = (ab)^n$$

Example 1   **Write without using exponents.**

         a. 3^{-2}   **b. $5^2 \cdot 5^{-3}$**   **c. $(4^{-2})^3$**   **d. $5^{-3} \cdot 2^{-3}$**

Solution   **a.** $3^{-2} = \dfrac{1}{3^2} = \dfrac{1}{9}$

         b. $5^2 \cdot 5^{-3} = 5^{2+(-3)} = 5^{2-3} = 5^{-1} = \dfrac{1}{5}$

         c. $(4^{-2})^3 = 4^{(-2)(3)} = 4^{-6} = \dfrac{1}{4^6} = \dfrac{1}{4096}$

         d. $5^{-3} \cdot 2^{-3} = (5 \cdot 2)^{-3} = 10^{-3} = \dfrac{1}{10^3} = \dfrac{1}{1000} = 0.001$

Example 2   **Write using positive exponents.** $\dfrac{1}{x^{-2}}, x \neq 0$

Solution $\dfrac{1}{x^{-2}} = \dfrac{1}{\dfrac{1}{x^2}} = 1 \cdot \dfrac{x^2}{1} = x^2$

Example 3   **Write without using fractions.** $\dfrac{x^4 y^2}{x^7 y^3}, x \neq 0, y \neq 0$

Solution $\dfrac{x^4 y^2}{x^7 y^3} = \dfrac{x^4}{y^7} \cdot \dfrac{y^2}{y^3} = x^{4-7} y^{2-3} = x^{-3} y^{-1}$

We can express numbers between 0 and 1 in scientific notation using negative exponents.

    $0.000032 = 3.2 \cdot 0.00001 = 3.2 \cdot 10^{-5}$ $0.0000000000562 = 5.62 \cdot 10^{-11}$

Example 4   **Simplify. Write in scientific notation.** $(4 \cdot 10^{-4})(3.5 \cdot 10^{-6})$

Solution $(4 \cdot 10^{-4})(3.5 \cdot 10^{-6}) = (4 \cdot 3.5)(10^{-4} \cdot 10^{-6})$

                              $= 14 \cdot 10^{-10}$

                              $= (1.4 \cdot 10^1)(10^{-10})$

                              $= 1.4 \cdot 10^{-9}$

Simplify.

1. 2^{-3}
2. 10^{-5}
3. 4^{-4}
4. $\dfrac{1}{3^{-2}}$
5. $6^2 \cdot 6^{-4}$

6. $\dfrac{1}{3^{-3}}$
7. $\dfrac{2}{2^{-3}}$
8. $\dfrac{3^{-3}}{3}$
9. $2^{-2} \cdot 5^{-2}$
10. $(2^{-2})^{-3}$

Write using positive exponents.

11. x^{-3}
12. xy^{-2}
13. $\dfrac{1}{a^{-4}}$
14. $\dfrac{1}{ab^{-3}}$

Write without using fractions.

15. $\dfrac{1}{x^2}$
16. $\dfrac{1}{3y^4}$
17. $\dfrac{a^3}{b^{12}}$
18. $\dfrac{x^3y}{x^2y^3}$

Write in scientific notation.

19. 0.000067
20. 0.000000314
21. $(3 \cdot 10^{-5})(4 \cdot 10^{-6})$
22. $\dfrac{(5.4 \cdot 10^{-15})}{(9 \cdot 10^{-9})}$

RITTEN EXERCISES

A **Write without using exponents.**

1. 4^{-2}
2. 5^{-1}
3. 6^0
4. $(-2)^0$

5. $\left(\dfrac{2}{3}\right)^{-3}$
6. $\left(\dfrac{3}{2}\right)^{-2}$
7. $\dfrac{2^3}{2^{-3}}$
8. $\dfrac{3^2}{3^{-2}}$

9. $\left(-\dfrac{1}{2}\right)^{-3}$
10. $\left(-\dfrac{1}{3}\right)^{-2}$
11. $\dfrac{2^{-1}}{3}$
12. $\dfrac{3^{-1}}{4}$

13. $2^{-3} \cdot 3^2$
14. $3^{-2} \cdot 2^3$
15. $5^{-3} \cdot 5^5$
16. $7^{-4} \cdot 7^6$

17. $4^{-10} \cdot 4^7$
18. $6^{-8} \cdot 6^5$
19. $\dfrac{3^7}{3^{10}}$
20. $\dfrac{2^7}{2^{12}}$

21. $2^{-4} \cdot 5^{-4}$
22. $2^{-2} \cdot 3^{-2}$
23. $(10^{-3})^{-4}$
24. $(10^{-4})^2$

Write using positive exponents.

25. a^{-7}
26. a^{-5}
27. a^2b^{-3}
28. $a^{-2}b^3$

29. $xy^{-1}z^2$
30. $x^{-1}y^2z^{-3}$
31. $\dfrac{x}{y^{-2}}$
32. $\dfrac{x^2}{y^{-1}}$

Write without using fractions. (Assume that no denominators are zero.)

33. $\dfrac{x^4y^2}{xy^5}$
34. $\dfrac{x^4y^2}{x^6y}$
35. $\dfrac{4}{x^2y^3}$
36. $\dfrac{6}{x^3y^2}$

37. $\dfrac{a^2b^3}{a^{-4}b}$
38. $\dfrac{a^{-2}b}{a^{-4}b^3}$
39. $\dfrac{8a^4b^6}{2a^4b^7}$
40. $\dfrac{8a^4b^6}{4a^7b^6}$

Write in scientific notation.

41. $(2 \cdot 10^8)(3.1 \cdot 10^{-12})$

42. $(3 \cdot 10^7)(2.5 \cdot 10^{-15})$

43. $(4 \cdot 10^{-4})(5 \cdot 10^{-10})$

44. $(5 \cdot 10^{-5})(8 \cdot 10^{-7})$

45. $\dfrac{(6.8 \cdot 10^{-8})}{(4 \cdot 10^6)}$

46. $\dfrac{(7.5 \cdot 10^{-6})}{(5 \cdot 10^9)}$

47. $\dfrac{(3.2 \cdot 10^{-7})}{(8 \cdot 10^{-4})}$

48. $\dfrac{(4.5 \cdot 10^{-8})}{(5 \cdot 10^{-6})}$

B pplication: Significant Digits

Scientists and engineers use scientific notation to indicate the number of **significant digits** in a measurement number. For example, $6.321 \cdot 10^6$ has four significant digits: 6, 3, 2, and 1. The number 4.20 has three significant digits, whereas 4.2 has only two significant digits.

When scientists multiply measurements, they round the product so that it does not have more significant digits than the factor with the fewest significant digits.

Example
$$(6.32 \cdot 10^{-3})(4.19 \cdot 10^{-5}) = 26.4808 \cdot 10^{-8}$$
$$= 2.64808 \cdot 10^{-7}$$
$$\approx 2.65 \cdot 10^{-7}$$

Simplify. Write the result in scientific notation and round to the appropriate number of significant digits.

49. $(3.45 \cdot 10^{-6})(4.193 \cdot 10^{-8})$

50. $(6.07 \cdot 10^{-15})(3.6 \cdot 10^8)$

51. $\dfrac{6.670 \cdot 10^{-11}}{3.1 \cdot 10^{-4}}$

52. $\dfrac{2.5 \cdot 10^3}{9.3 \cdot 10^8}$

53. The density of air is $1.293 \cdot 10^{-6}$ kg/cm^3. What is the mass (in kilograms) of the air in a room whose volume is $4 \cdot 10^7$ cm^3?

54. The density of helium is $1.78 \cdot 10^{-7}$ kg/cm^3. What is the mass (in kilograms) of the helium in a balloon whose volume is $3 \cdot 10^8$ cm^3?

55. The mass of methane in a $3 \cdot 10^3$-cm³ container is known to be $2.151 \cdot 10^{-3}$ kg. What is the density of methane in kilograms per cubic centimeter?

56. The volume of the Red Sea is approximately $8.64 \cdot 10^{15}$ ft³. If the area of its surface is about $4.8 \cdot 10^{12}$ ft², what is its average depth?

 Given that $y = 3^x$, describe the values of x that make each condition true. If there is no solution, write $\emptyset$.

57. $y > 81$ **58.** $y < \dfrac{1}{3}$ **59.** $y = 1$

60. $y < 0$ **61.** $y > \dfrac{1}{27}$ **62.** $0 < y \le \dfrac{1}{9}$

Given that $y = 2^{-x}$, describe the values of x that make each condition true. If there is no solution, write $\emptyset$.

63. $y < 2$ **64.** $y = 1$ **65.** $y \ge 8$

66. $y < 0$ **67.** $\dfrac{1}{8} \le y \le 8$ **68.** $0 < y \le 32$

 EVIEW EXERCISES

1. Simplify $4x(x + 3) + 5(x + 2)$.   [1-4]

What property of real numbers does each equation illustrate?

2. $c(a + b) = (a + b)c$ [1-4]

3. $\dfrac{3}{4} \cdot \dfrac{4}{3} = 1$ [1-5]

4. Expand $(2x + 3)(x + 5)$.   [1-5]

5. Write Q in terms of n.   [1-6]

n	1	2	3	4
Q	1	3	5	7

6. Write R in terms of m.

m	1	2	3	4
R	1	-1	-3	-5

      [1-6]

7. Write the next number in the sequence.   [1-6]
$$\dfrac{1}{1}, \dfrac{2}{2}, \dfrac{3}{4}, \dfrac{4}{8}, \dfrac{5}{16}, \underline{\quad ? \quad}$$

Use the variable n to write an expression for the nth term in each sequence.

8. 1, 4, 7, 10, 13, . . .

9. $1 \cdot 2, 2 \cdot 3, 3 \cdot 4, 4 \cdot 5, . . .$

10. Show that a product of two even numbers is even.   [1-7]

Simplifying Rational Expressions

Bubbles are spherical instead of cubic or cylindrical because the sphere is the solid that contains a given volume with the least surface. A measure of the "efficiency" of a solid is the ratio of its volume V to its surface area S. The ratio for a sphere is

$$\frac{V}{S} = \frac{\frac{4}{3}\pi r^3}{4\pi r^2} = \frac{1}{3}r$$

Notice that the expression $\dfrac{\frac{4}{3}\pi r^3}{4\pi r^2}$ is the quotient of two polynomials. The quotient of two polynomials is called a **rational algebraic expression** or a **rational expression**. These are rational expressions:

$$\frac{3+x}{4-y} \qquad \frac{7}{2a+b} \qquad \frac{x^2-3x+4}{x+3}$$

These are not rational expressions because either the numerator or the denominator is not a polynomial:

$$\frac{3+\sqrt{x}}{7} \qquad \frac{4}{\sqrt{x+y}}$$

Recall that 1 is a polynomial. Therefore, each polynomial is a rational expression since it is the quotient of itself and 1. For example, $x + y$ can be written as the quotient $\dfrac{x+y}{1}$.

A fraction is expressed in **lowest terms** (or **simplest form**) when its numerator and denominator have no common factors other than 1 or -1.

$$\frac{273}{567} = \frac{13 \cdot 21}{27 \cdot 21} = \frac{13}{27} \cdot \frac{21}{21} = \frac{13}{27} \cdot 1 = \frac{13}{27}$$

To write a fraction in lowest terms, we use the following property.

For all real numbers a, b, and c, $b \neq 0$, $c \neq 0$,

$$\frac{ac}{bc} = \frac{a}{b}.$$

Example 1   **Simplify.** $\dfrac{6x^3y}{3x^2y^2}$, $x \neq 0$, $y \neq 0$

Solution   *Rewrite the numerator and denominator in terms of their GCF.* $\dfrac{6x^3y}{3x^2y^2} = \dfrac{3x^2y \cdot 2x}{3x^2y \cdot y}$

Divide both the numerator and denominator by the GCF. $= \dfrac{2x}{y}$, $x \neq 0$, $y \neq 0$

The denominator of a rational expression may not equal zero. Restrictions on the variable to prevent this possibility should be determined *before* the expression is simplified.

Example 2   **Simplify.** $\dfrac{12ab - 3bc + 6b}{3b}$

Solution   *Factor.* $\dfrac{12ab - 3bc + 6b}{3b} = \dfrac{3b(4a - c + 2)}{3b \cdot 1}$ Restriction: $b \neq 0$

Simplify. $= \dfrac{4a - c + 2}{1}$

$= 4a - c + 2, \quad b \neq 0$

Example 3   **Simplify.** $\dfrac{(x - 3)}{(x + 2)(x - 3)}$

Solution $\dfrac{(x - 3)}{(x + 2)(x - 3)} = \dfrac{1 \cdot (x - 3)}{(x + 2)(x - 3)}$ Restriction: $x \neq -2, x \neq 3$

$= \dfrac{1}{x + 2}, x \neq -2, x \neq 3$

Example 4   **Simplify.** $\dfrac{7x - 21}{x^2 - x - 6}$

Solution $\dfrac{7x - 21}{x^2 - x - 6} = \dfrac{7(x - 3)}{(x + 2)(x - 3)}$

$= \dfrac{7}{x + 2}, x \neq -2, x \neq 3$

Example 5   **Simplify.** $\dfrac{2 - x}{x^2 - 4}$

Solution $\dfrac{2 - x}{x^2 - 4} = \dfrac{-1(x - 2)}{(x + 2)(x - 2)}$ Restrictions: $x \neq -2, x \neq 2$

$= \dfrac{-1}{x + 2}, x \neq -2, x \neq 2$

In the first step, -1 was factored from the numerator so that all factors were written in descending powers of x. This made it easier to recognize common factors in the numerator and denominator.

A fraction in which either the numerator or the denominator or both are fractions is called a **complex fraction**.

Example 6 **Simplify.** $\dfrac{\dfrac{a}{b} + \dfrac{b}{a}}{\dfrac{a}{b} - \dfrac{b}{a}}$ Restrictions: $a \neq 0,\ b \neq 0,\ |a| \neq |b|$

Solution Multiply the numerator and denominator of the complex fraction by the least common multiple of the denominators within the fraction. Then simplify.

$$\frac{\dfrac{a}{b} + \dfrac{b}{a}}{\dfrac{a}{b} - \dfrac{b}{a}} = \frac{\left(\dfrac{a}{b} + \dfrac{b}{a}\right)ab}{\left(\dfrac{a}{b} - \dfrac{b}{a}\right)ab} = \frac{a^2 + b^2}{a^2 - b^2},\ a \neq 0,\ b \neq 0,\ |a| \neq |b|$$

$\mathcal{C}$LASSROOM EXERCISES

Simplify each fraction, stating necessary restrictions.

1. $\dfrac{12a^2b^3}{8ab^4}$

2. $\dfrac{2xy^2 - 4x^2y}{6xy}$

3. $\dfrac{(x + 2)(x - 3)}{x + 2}$

4. $\dfrac{x^2 - 9}{x - 3}$

5. $\dfrac{y - 3}{(3 - y)(2 + y)}$

6. $\dfrac{x^2 - x - 20}{5 - x}$

$\mathcal{W}$RITTEN EXERCISES

 For each expression, (a) list the greatest common factor of the numerator and denominator, (b) state necessary restrictions on the variables, and (c) simplify the expression.

1. $\dfrac{6x^3y}{4xy^5}$

2. $\dfrac{10xy^5}{8x^2y^2}$

3. $\dfrac{ab + b^2}{3b}$

4. $\dfrac{a^2 + ab}{2b}$

5. $\dfrac{a^2b^2 + ab^2}{a^2b}$

6. $\dfrac{a^2b - ab^2}{ab^2}$

7. $\dfrac{(a - 2)(a + 3)}{(a + 3)(a + 2)}$

8. $\dfrac{(a + 4)(a - 1)}{(a - 4)(a + 4)}$

Simplify. Assume that denominators are not zero.

9. $\dfrac{2x + 6y}{4x}$

10. $\dfrac{3x + 9y}{6y}$

11. $\dfrac{x - y}{y - x}$

12. $\dfrac{x + y}{y + x}$

13. $\dfrac{2x + 6y}{x + 3y}$

14. $\dfrac{3x + 9y}{x + 3y}$

15. $\dfrac{a + b}{b + a}$

16. $\dfrac{a - b}{b - a}$

17. $\dfrac{(x + 3)(x - 4)}{(x - 8)(x + 3)}$

18. $\dfrac{(x + 3)(x - 4)}{(x - 4)(x + 6)}$

19. $\dfrac{x^2 - 16}{x + 4}$

20. $\dfrac{x^2 - 25}{x + 5}$

21. $\dfrac{x + 5}{x^2 + 7x + 10}$

22. $\dfrac{x + 3}{x^2 + 6x + 9}$

23. $\dfrac{w^2 - 2w}{w^2 - w - 2}$

24. $\dfrac{w^2 - 2w}{w^2 - 3w + 2}$

25. $\dfrac{2x - 1}{(1 + 2x)(1 - 2x)}$ **26.** $\dfrac{(a - b)(2a - b)}{(b - 2a)(b - a)}$ **27.** $\dfrac{(y - z)(y + z)}{(z - y)(z + y)}$ **28.** $\dfrac{1 - 3a}{(3a - 1)(1 - 3a)}$

29. $\dfrac{4x^2 - 9}{3 - 2x}$ **30.** $\dfrac{x^2 + 5x + 6}{3 + x}$ **31.** $\dfrac{x^2 - 6x - 7}{1 + x}$ **32.** $\dfrac{a^2 - 5a - 14}{a - 7}$

Complete each table. State whether the two expressions are equivalent. Recall that two expressions are equivalent if they both result in the same value for each *admissible* value.

33.

x	$\dfrac{x^2 + x}{x}$	$x + 1$
10	?	?
0	?	?
−1	?	?

34.

x	$\dfrac{x^2 + 3x - 10}{x^2 + x - 20}$	$\dfrac{x + 5}{x + 1}$
9	?	?
4	?	?
−2	?	?

B For each rational expression, state the value(s) of the variable (a) for which the expression equals 0, and (b) for which the expression is undefined.

35. $\dfrac{x^2 - x - 6}{x^2 + 10x + 16}$ **36.** $\dfrac{x^2 - 3x + 2}{x^2 - 7x + 10}$ **37.** $\dfrac{x^2 - 2x - 24}{x^2 - 4x - 32}$ **38.** $\dfrac{x^2 + x - 12}{x^2 + 3x - 18}$

39. $\dfrac{x^2 + 6x + 8}{x^2 + x - 2}$ **40.** $\dfrac{a^2 - 4a - 12}{a^2 - 4a + 3}$ **41.** $\dfrac{b^2 - 4}{b^2 - b - 6}$ **42.** $\dfrac{y^2 + y - 12}{9 - y^2}$

43. $\dfrac{d^2 - 5d + 6}{d^2 + 5d + 6}$ **44.** $\dfrac{x^2 - 2x - 15}{10 - 7x + x^2}$ **45.** $\dfrac{a^2 - 3a}{12 - 7a + a^2}$ **46.** $\dfrac{2m^2 - 5m - 3}{6 + 5m - m^2}$

47. $\dfrac{3x^2 - 2x - 1}{x^2 - 1}$ **48.** $\dfrac{4y^2 + 6y + 2}{4y^2 - 4}$ **49.** $\dfrac{x^2 - y^2}{y^2 - x^2}$ **50.** $\dfrac{3a^2 + a - 2}{2a^2 - a - 3}$

Simplify these complex fractions. Assume that denominators are nonzero.

51. $\dfrac{\dfrac{1}{a} - \dfrac{1}{b}}{\dfrac{1}{a} + \dfrac{1}{b}}$ **52.** $\dfrac{\dfrac{1}{a} - \dfrac{1}{b}}{\dfrac{1}{b} - \dfrac{1}{a}}$ **53.** $\dfrac{\dfrac{1}{x} + \dfrac{2}{3x}}{\dfrac{3}{x} + \dfrac{4}{3x}}$ **54.** $\dfrac{1 + \dfrac{2}{x}}{1 + \dfrac{4}{x}}$

55. $\dfrac{1 + \dfrac{2}{x}}{x + 2}$ **56.** $\dfrac{2 + \dfrac{1}{x + 2}}{2 + \dfrac{5}{x}}$ **57.** $\dfrac{x^{-1} - y^{-1}}{x^{-1} + y^{-1}}$ **58.** $\dfrac{a^{-2} - b^{-2}}{a^{-1} + b^{-1}}$

59. $\dfrac{a^{-1} + b^{-1}}{a^{-2} - b^{-2}}$ **60.** $\dfrac{1 - 3x^{-1}}{1 + 4x^{-1}}$ **61.** $\dfrac{3 - y^{-1}}{y^{-1} - 3}$ **62.** $\dfrac{ab^{-2}}{a^{-2}b}$

C Explain how the graphs of these pairs of equations are alike and how they are different.

63. $y = \dfrac{x^2}{x}$

$y = x$

64. $y = \dfrac{x^2 - 1}{x + 1}$

$y = x - 1$

65. $y = \dfrac{x^2 - 3x + 2}{x^2 - 5x + 6}$

$y = \dfrac{x - 1}{x - 3}$

Solve for the indicated variable.   [2-2]

1. $v = v_0 + at$, for a

2. $A = \frac{1}{2}h(b_1 + b_2)$, for b_2

Solve.

3. When 12 is subtracted from 5 times a number and the result is divided by 2, the quotient equals the original number. What is the number?   [2-3]

4. If the length of a rectangle is 12 more than the width and the perimeter is 10 times the width, what are the length and width?

Solve and graph on a number line.

5. $\dfrac{5 - 3x}{2} < 10$

6. $0 \leqslant 3x + 6 \leqslant 18$ [2-4, 2-5]

7. $|x - 1| < 2$

8. $|x - 1| < 2$ [2-6]

9. Use absolute value to write an inequality that describes the graph.   [2-6]

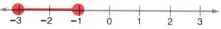

IOGRAPHY   Benoit Mandelbrot

"The rare scholars who are nomads by choice are essential to the intellectual welfare of the settled disciplines," says Benoit Mandelbrot; and he is surely such a nomad. He has contributed to linguistics, economics, physiology, and physics. He has taught economics at Havard, engineering at Yale, and physiology at Einstein College of Medicine. He has also been a research fellow in psychology at Harvard. He is best known for the development of fractal geometry, one of the most important developments in twentieth-century mathematics. Fractals have to do with irregularities and utilize the fact that large-scale irregularities are often echoed in finer details, just as the shape of a broccoli head is echoed in each floret. Fractals are closely related to nature. They have been used to generate lifelike computer pictures resembling moss, seaweed, roots, snails, and jellyfish. They have been used in the movie industry to create alien planets, as in *Star Trek II: The Wrath of Khan* and in *Return of the Jedi*. They have proven to be of value in studying turbulence and disorder and the way things meld together, branch apart, or shatter. Mandelbrot is currently Professor of the Practice of Mathematics at Harvard University.

LESSON 6-3

Multiplying and Dividing Rational Expressions

Rational expressions have the same relationships to polynomials as rational numbers have to integers. Both the set of integers and the set of polynomials are closed with respect to addition, subtraction, and multiplication but not to division. A set of numbers that is closed with respect to division (except division by zero) is the set of rational numbers. A set of polynomials that is closed with respect to division (except division by zero) is the set of rational expressions.

To find the product of rational expressions, multiply the numerators and multiply the denominators.

Definition: Multiplication of Fractions

For all real numbers a, b, c, and d, $b \neq 0$, $d \neq 0$, $\dfrac{a}{b} \cdot \dfrac{c}{d} = \dfrac{ac}{bd}$.

The following example illustrates the techniques for simplifying products of rational expressions.

Example 1   **Simplify.** $\dfrac{4(x-3)}{x+4} \cdot \dfrac{x-2}{2(x-3)}, \; x \neq -4, \; x \neq 3$

Solution 1   *Multiply. Leave the product in factored form.*
$$\frac{4(x-3)}{x+4} \cdot \frac{x-2}{2(x-3)} = \frac{4(x-3)(x-2)}{2(x+4)(x-3)}$$

Factor the GCF from both the numerator and denominator.
$$= \frac{2(x-3) \cdot 2(x-2)}{2(x-3) \cdot (x+4)}$$

Divide the numerator and denominator by $2(x-3)$.
$$= \frac{2(x-2)}{x+4}, \, x \neq -4, x \neq 3$$

Solution 2   The numerators and denominators of two rational expressions can be divided by the same factors *before* multiplication.

Divide a numerator and a denominator by 2.
$$\frac{4(x-3)}{x+4} \cdot \frac{x-2}{2(x-3)} = \frac{2(x-3)}{x+4} \cdot \frac{x-2}{1(x-3)}$$

Divide a numerator and a denominator by $(x-3)$.
$$= \frac{2}{x+4} \cdot \frac{x-2}{1}$$

Multiply.
$$= \frac{2(x-2)}{x+4}, \, x \neq -4, x \neq 3$$

To divide rational expressions, multiply by the reciprocal of the divisor.

Example 2 **Simplify this quotient.** $\dfrac{(a-2)^2}{b^2} \div \dfrac{6a-12}{4b}$, $b \neq 0$, $a \neq 2$

Solution *Apply the definition of division.*

$$\dfrac{(a-2)^2}{b^2} \div \dfrac{6a-12}{4b} = \dfrac{(a-2)^2}{b^2} \cdot \dfrac{4b}{6a-12}$$

Factor.

$$= \dfrac{(a-2)^2}{b^2} \cdot \dfrac{4b}{6(a-2)}$$

Divide both the numerator and denominator by the GCF: $2b(a-2)$.

$$= \dfrac{(a-2)}{b} \cdot \dfrac{2}{3}$$

Multiply.

$$= \dfrac{2(a-2)}{3b}, \, b \neq 0, \, a \neq 2$$

$\mathcal{C}$LASSROOM EXERCISES

Simplify. State any necessary restrictions on the variables.

1. $\dfrac{10x}{9y} \cdot \dfrac{3xy}{5}$

2. $\dfrac{10x}{9y} \div \dfrac{5}{3xy}$

3. $\dfrac{4(x-y)}{(x+y)} \cdot \dfrac{(x+y)^2}{2(x-y)}$

4. $\dfrac{4(x-y)}{x+y} \div \dfrac{2(x-y)}{(x+y)^2}$

RITTEN EXERCISES

 Simplify. State any necessary restrictions on the variables.

1. $\dfrac{w}{x} \cdot \dfrac{y}{z}$

2. $\dfrac{p}{q} \cdot \dfrac{r}{s}$

3. $\dfrac{w}{x} \div \dfrac{y}{z}$

4. $\dfrac{p}{q} \div \dfrac{r}{s}$

5. $\dfrac{8x^2}{9y} \div \dfrac{6x}{y^4}$

6. $\dfrac{4x^3}{5y^2} \div \dfrac{10x^4}{3y^4}$

7. $\dfrac{8x^2}{9y} \div \dfrac{6x^4}{y}$

8. $\dfrac{4x^3}{5y^2} \cdot \dfrac{10x^4}{3y^4}$

9. $\dfrac{x}{x-2} \cdot \dfrac{x-2}{x+2}$

10. $\dfrac{p-2}{p+2} \cdot \dfrac{p+2}{p+4}$

11. $\dfrac{2(x+2)}{3x} \div \dfrac{4(x-2)}{9x}$

12. $\dfrac{3(x-2)}{8x} \div \dfrac{x+2}{12x}$

13. $\dfrac{5x+10y}{3x-6y} \cdot \dfrac{6x-12y}{3x+14y}$

14. $\dfrac{2x-y}{6x+3y} \cdot \dfrac{8x+4y}{6x-3y}$

15. $\dfrac{a^2+ab}{b} \div \dfrac{ab+b^2}{a}$

16. $\dfrac{a^2-ab}{b} \div \dfrac{ab-b^2}{a}$

17. $\dfrac{a^2+ab}{b} \cdot \dfrac{ab+b^2}{a}$

18. $\dfrac{a^2-ab}{b} \cdot \dfrac{ab+b^2}{a}$

Complete the table for each rectangle. Assume that all rational expressions are defined and not equal to zero.

19.

	Width (cm)	Length (cm)	Area (cm²)
a.	$\dfrac{a^2}{a+2}$	$\dfrac{a+2}{a}$	?
b.	$\dfrac{b-1}{b}$	?	$\dfrac{b-1}{b+2}$
c.	?	$\dfrac{(c+3)^2}{c^2}$	$\dfrac{c+3}{c}$

20.

	Width (cm)	Length (cm)	Area (cm²)
a.	$\dfrac{r}{r-1}$	$\dfrac{r-1}{r}$	?
b.	$\dfrac{s-1}{s+2}$	?	$\dfrac{s}{s+2}$
c.	?	$\dfrac{t^2-9}{t+2}$	$t+3$

B Complete each table for the missing time, rate, or distance.

21.

	Time (h)	Rate (km/h)	Distance (km)
a.	$\dfrac{x-1}{x+2}$	?	$\dfrac{x^2-1}{x^2+4x+4}$
b.	?	$\dfrac{x+1}{x-2}$	$\dfrac{x^2-1}{x^2-4}$
c.	$\dfrac{x^2+5x+6}{x^2+2x-8}$	$\dfrac{x-2}{x+3}$	?
d.	$\dfrac{x^2-3x-4}{x^2-7x+10}$	$\dfrac{x-5}{x-4}$	?

22.

	Time (h)	Rate (km/h)	Distance (km)
a.	$\dfrac{x-2}{x-6}$	?	$\dfrac{x^2+3x-10}{x^2-8x+12}$
b.	?	$\dfrac{x+3}{x-4}$	$\dfrac{x^2-9}{x^2-x-12}$
c.	$\dfrac{x^2+6x+8}{x^2-4x+3}$	$\dfrac{x-3}{x+2}$	?
d.	$\dfrac{x^2-9x+20}{x^2-3x-18}$	$\dfrac{x+3}{x-5}$	?

Simplify. State any necessary restrictions.

23. $\dfrac{x^2+5x+6}{x^2-7x+12} \cdot \dfrac{x^2-6x+9}{x^2+6x+8}$

24. $\dfrac{x^2-2x-3}{x^2+5x+6} \cdot \dfrac{x^2+8x+15}{x^2+2x-15}$

25. $\dfrac{x^2-2x-8}{x^2+2x-15} \div \dfrac{x^2-5x+4}{x^2+6x+5}$

26. $\dfrac{x^2+4x+3}{x^2+2x-8} \div \dfrac{x^2+3x+2}{x^2-4}$

C **27.** $\dfrac{\dfrac{a}{b}\cdot\dfrac{b}{c}}{\dfrac{c}{d}}$

28. $\dfrac{\dfrac{a}{b}\div\dfrac{b}{c}}{\dfrac{c}{d}}$

29. $\dfrac{\dfrac{a}{b}}{\dfrac{b}{c}\cdot\dfrac{c}{d}}$

30. $\dfrac{\dfrac{a}{b}}{\dfrac{b}{c}\div\dfrac{c}{d}}$

31. Let a, b, and c be positive real numbers such that no two of the numbers are equal. Is $\dfrac{a+b}{b+c}$ always, sometimes, or never equal to $\dfrac{a}{c}$?

32. Let $x=\dfrac{rs}{r+s}$ and $y=\dfrac{rs}{r-s}$. Show that $\dfrac{y^2-x^2}{y^2+x^2}=\dfrac{2rs}{r^2+s^2}$.

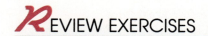

REVIEW EXERCISES

1. In which quadrant is each of these points?
   a. A
   b. B
   c. C
   d. D

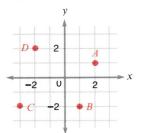

   [3-1]

2. Graph $\{(x, y): y = |x| + 1\}$ and state the domain and range.

For each relation, state whether it is a function. If it is a function, state whether it is a one-to-one function.   [3-2]

3. $\{(1, 5), (2, 5), (3, 10)\}$

4. $\{(x, y): x$ is a positive integer, and y is a factor of $x\}$

5. State whether $y = \dfrac{x}{10}$ is a linear equation.

6. Find the slope and y-intercept of $2x - 3y = 24$.   [3-3]

7. What is the slope of the line perpendicular to $y = \dfrac{1}{2}x - 6$?   [3-4]

8. Write the equation of the line through $(0, 5)$ that is parallel to $y = 2x + 3$.   [3-4]

9. Suppose that y varies directly as the square of x. If $y = 100$ when $x = 5$, what is the value of y when $x = 15$?   [3-5]

Self-Quiz 1

6-1 Write using positive exponents.

1. $\left(\dfrac{3}{4}\right)^{-1}$

2. $x^{-3}y^2$

3. $\dfrac{a^{-5}}{b^{-4}c^2}$

Write without using fractions.

4. $\dfrac{x^2y^4}{x^3y}$

5. $\dfrac{10m^5n^{-7}}{5m^5n^{-9}}$

6. $\dfrac{3 \cdot 10^5}{5 \cdot 10^{-3}}$

6-2 Simplify.

7. $\dfrac{3x + 12y}{6xy}$

8. $\dfrac{a^2 - b^2}{b - a}$

9. $\dfrac{x^2 - xy - 2y^2}{x^2 + 2xy + y^2}$

6-3 Simplify.

10. $\dfrac{3x^2 - x}{3(y + 1)} \cdot \dfrac{4y + 4}{6x - 2}$

11. $\dfrac{15m^4}{8n} \div \dfrac{5m^2}{2n^3}$

12. $\dfrac{x^2 - 4}{x + 3} \div \dfrac{x + 2}{2x + 6}$

LESSON 6-4

Adding and Subtracting Rational Expressions

Rational expressions can be added and subtracted in the same way as fractions are added and subtracted. The following definition states how to add two real numbers with the same denominator.

Definition: Addition of Fractions with Like Denominators

For all real numbers a, b, and c, $c \neq 0$, $\dfrac{a}{c} + \dfrac{b}{c} = \dfrac{a+b}{c}$.

The same definition is used to simplify the sum of two rational expressions such as $\dfrac{3x}{x+1} + \dfrac{2}{x+1}$, $x \neq -1$; that is, $\dfrac{3x}{x+1} + \dfrac{2}{x+1} = \dfrac{3x+2}{x+1}$.

To add rational expressions with different denominators, change them to equivalent expressions with common denominators. Generally, the simplest denominator to use is the **least common denominator (LCD)**. The least common denominator is the polynomial of least degree and with the least positive constant factor that has each denominator as a factor.

Example 1   State the least common denominator. $\dfrac{1}{2x}$, $\dfrac{1}{4xy}$, $\dfrac{1}{3x^2}$

Solution   *Write the prime factorization of each denominator.*

$$2x = 2 \cdot x$$
$$4xy = 2^2 \cdot x \cdot y$$
$$3x^2 = 3 \cdot x^2$$

Form the LCD by choosing the greatest power of each prime factor.

$$2^2 \cdot 3 \cdot x^2 \cdot y = 12x^2y$$

Example 2   State the least common denominator. $\dfrac{3}{2(x-3)^2}$, $\dfrac{5}{8(x-3)}$, $\dfrac{7}{5(x-2)}$

Solution   *Write the prime factorization of each denominator.*

$$2(x-3)^2 = 2(x-3)^2$$
$$8(x-3) = 2^3(x-3)$$
$$5(x-2) = 5(x-2)$$

Form the LCD by choosing the greatest power of each prime factor.

$$2^3 \cdot 5 \cdot (x-3)^2 \cdot (x-2) = 40(x-3)^2(x-2)$$

Example 3   Simplify. $\dfrac{3}{4y} - \dfrac{5}{6y^2}$, $y \neq 0$

Solution   *Change to fractions with the LCD, $12y^2$, as denominator.*

$$\dfrac{3}{4y} - \dfrac{5}{6y^2} = \dfrac{3 \cdot 3y}{4y \cdot 3y} - \dfrac{5 \cdot 2}{6y^2 \cdot 2}$$

$$= \dfrac{9y}{12y^2} - \dfrac{10}{12y^2}$$

$$= \dfrac{9y - 10}{12y^2}, \ y \neq 0$$

Example 4   Simplify. $\dfrac{3}{x - 5} + \dfrac{5}{x^2 - 25}$, $x \neq 5$, $x \neq -5$

Solution $\dfrac{3}{x - 5} + \dfrac{5}{x^2 - 25} = \dfrac{3}{x - 5} + \dfrac{5}{(x - 5)(x + 5)}$, LCD $= (x - 5)(x + 5)$

$$= \dfrac{3(x + 5)}{(x - 5)(x + 5)} + \dfrac{5}{(x - 5)(x + 5)}$$

$$= \dfrac{3(x + 5) + 5}{(x - 5)(x + 5)}$$

$$= \dfrac{3x + 20}{x^2 - 25}, \ x \neq 5, x \neq -5$$

Example 5   Simplify. $\dfrac{5}{x - y} - \dfrac{4}{y - x}$, $x \neq y$

Solution $\dfrac{5}{x - y} - \dfrac{4}{y - x} = \dfrac{5}{x - y} - \dfrac{-1 \cdot 4}{-1(y - x)}$

$$= \dfrac{5}{x - y} - \dfrac{-4}{x - y}$$

$$= \dfrac{5 - (-4)}{x - y}$$

$$= \dfrac{9}{x - y}, \ x \neq y$$

*e*LASSROOM EXERCISES

State the least common denominator of the fractions.

1. $\dfrac{1}{4xy^2}, \dfrac{1}{6x^2y}$

2. $\dfrac{1}{2x}, \dfrac{1}{x + 2}$

3. $\dfrac{1}{x^3(x + 1)}, \dfrac{1}{x(x + 1)^2}$

Simplify. State all restrictions on the domains of the variables.

4. $\dfrac{2}{3x} + \dfrac{1}{6x}$

5. $\dfrac{5a}{b^2} + \dfrac{3}{a^2b}$

6. $\dfrac{a}{a - 1} - \dfrac{1}{a(a - 1)}$

WRITTEN EXERCISES

A State the least common denominator.

1. $\dfrac{3}{4ab^2}, \dfrac{5}{6ab}$

2. $\dfrac{5}{8a^2b^2}, \dfrac{1}{6ab^2}$

3. $\dfrac{10}{x}, \dfrac{7}{x+2}$

4. $\dfrac{8}{x-2}, \dfrac{12}{x}$

5. $\dfrac{x+2}{x+4}, \dfrac{x+3}{x-3}$

6. $\dfrac{x-4}{x+2}, \dfrac{x+1}{x+5}$

Simplify. State any necessary restrictions.

7. $\dfrac{5}{a} + \dfrac{3}{b}$

8. $\dfrac{7}{a} + \dfrac{2}{b}$

9. $\dfrac{b}{a} - \dfrac{a}{b}$

10. $\dfrac{x}{y} - \dfrac{y}{x}$

11. $\dfrac{5}{ab^2} + \dfrac{3}{a^2b}$

12. $\dfrac{2}{a^2b} + \dfrac{4}{ab}$

13. $\dfrac{7}{x} - \dfrac{2}{x+3}$

14. $\dfrac{5}{x} - \dfrac{7}{x+2}$

15. $\dfrac{8}{x+2} + \dfrac{3}{x-2}$

16. $\dfrac{6}{x+3} + \dfrac{2}{x-3}$

17. $\dfrac{x}{x+2} - \dfrac{x}{x+3}$

18. $\dfrac{x}{x+3} - \dfrac{x}{x+2}$

19. $\dfrac{2x}{x-4} - \dfrac{1}{x-3}$

20. $\dfrac{3a}{a-5} - \dfrac{2}{a-1}$

21. $\dfrac{4}{ab} - 1$

22. $\dfrac{5}{xy} - 2$

23. $\dfrac{5}{9-x} - \dfrac{4}{x-9}$

24. $\dfrac{7}{3-a} - \dfrac{2}{a-3}$

B 25. $\dfrac{1}{n+1} + \dfrac{1}{n(n+1)}$

26. $\dfrac{1}{n} + \dfrac{1}{n(n-1)}$

27. $\dfrac{1}{n-1} - \dfrac{1}{n(n-1)}$

28. $\dfrac{1}{a} + \dfrac{1}{b} - \dfrac{1}{ab}$

29. $\dfrac{a}{b} + \dfrac{b}{a} + 2$

30. $1 + \dfrac{1}{a} + \dfrac{1}{a^2}$

31. $1 + \dfrac{1}{1+a} + \dfrac{1}{1+2a}$

32. $\dfrac{6}{x} + \dfrac{1}{x^2} - \dfrac{3}{x^3}$

33. $a - 4 + \dfrac{16}{a+4}$

34. $\dfrac{2}{x+3} - \dfrac{x}{x^2+6x+9}$

35. $\dfrac{2w^2}{2w^2-w-1} - \dfrac{w}{w-1}$

36. $\dfrac{b}{a^2-ab} - \dfrac{a}{b^2-ab}$

Application: The Harmonic Mean and the Arithmetic Mean

The arithmetic mean A of a set of n numbers may be found by dividing the sum of the numbers by n. The arithmetic mean of 2, 4, and 6 is

$$\frac{2+4+6}{3} = \frac{12}{3} = 4.$$

Give the arithmetic mean in simplest form.

37. 2, 4

38. $3, \dfrac{1}{3}$

39. $\dfrac{1}{3}, \dfrac{1}{4}$

40. a, b

41. $a, \dfrac{1}{a}$ $(a \neq 0)$

42. $\dfrac{1}{a}, \dfrac{1}{b}$ $(a \neq 0, b \neq 0)$

C The **harmonic mean** H of a set of n numbers may be found by dividing n by the sum of the reciprocals of the numbers. The harmonic mean of 2, 4, and 6 is

$$\frac{3}{\frac{1}{2}+\frac{1}{4}+\frac{1}{6}} = \frac{3}{\frac{11}{2}} = \frac{36}{11}.$$

Give the harmonic mean in simplest form. Assume that all variables are nonzero.

43. 2, 4

44. 1, 2, 3

45. $\dfrac{1}{2}, \dfrac{1}{4}$

46. a, b

47. a, b, c

48. $\dfrac{1}{a}, \dfrac{1}{b}$

49. Let m and n be two positive numbers. Prove that $H \leq A$ for the harmonic mean H and the arithmetic mean A. [*Hint:* Assume that $H > A$ and show that a contradiction results.]

50. In Exercise 49, when will $H = A$?

 EVIEW EXERCISES

Let [x] represent the greatest integer function.

1. Simplify $[4.7] \cdot [-2.7]$.

2. Graph $y = -[x]$ for $-2 \leq x \leq 2$.　　　　[3-6]

Let $f(x) = 5x$ and $g(x) = x^2 - 100$. Simplify.

3. $f(g(5)) = \underline{}$

4. $g(f(5)) = \underline{}$　　　　[3-7]

5. State whether this system has 0, 1, or infinitely many solutions.　　　　[4-1]

$$y = 2x + 5$$
$$y = 3x + 5$$

6. Solve by graphing.

$$y = \frac{1}{3}x$$　　　　[4-1]

$$x + y = 8$$

7. Solve by substitution.

$$y = 2x + 5$$　　　　[4-2]

$$4x + 3y = 5$$

8. Solve by linear combinations.

$$4x + 4y = 12$$　　　　[4-3]

$$2x + 3y = 6$$

 ALCULATOR EXTENSION A Number Trick

On a calculator enter a four-digit number all of whose digits are alike (for example, 7777). Divide that number by the sum of the four digits. Repeat using a different digit. Compare the results and explain what you found.

LESSON 6-5

Solving Fractional Equations

You can use fractional equations to solve problems about rates $\left(\dfrac{130\text{ miles}}{3\text{ hours}}\right.$ for a train, $\dfrac{3\text{ rooms}}{4\text{ days}}$ for a painter, $\dfrac{135\text{ words}}{2\text{ minutes}}$ for a typist, etc.$\left.\right)$ Fractions can be eliminated from equations by multiplying both sides of the equation by the least common denominator of the fractions. We have already used this technique with an equation that has a variable in the numerator of a fraction.

To solve the fractional equation $\dfrac{m}{5} + \dfrac{1}{3} = \dfrac{m+1}{6}$, multiply both sides by the LCD, 30.

$$30\left(\frac{m}{5} + \frac{1}{3}\right) = 30\left(\frac{m+1}{6}\right)$$

Then simplify.
$$6m + 10 = 5m + 5$$
$$m = -5$$

Multiplying both sides of an equation by a nonzero constant is an example of an **equivalent transformation**, that is, a transformation that results in an equation equivalent to the original. However, multiplying both sides of an equation by a variable may introduce new roots. This is an example of a **nonequivalent transformation**. For example,

The only root of this equation is 3. $\qquad\qquad 2m = 6$
Now multiply both sides by m. $\qquad\qquad\quad 2m^2 = 6m$
$$2m^2 - 6m = 0$$
$$2m(m - 3) = 0$$
$$2m = 0 \quad \text{or} \quad m - 3 = 0$$
$$m = 0 \quad \text{or} \qquad m = 3$$

The roots of the final equation are 0 and 3. We gained a root by multiplying both sides of the equation by a variable.

Multiplying both sides of an equation by a variable may transform an equation into a more desirable form, but the roots of the new equation should be checked in the original equation since a nonequivalent transformation may have occurred. Also note the restrictions on the values of the variables. Even though these numbers may appear as roots of the transformed equation, they cannot be roots of the original equation.

Example 1 **Solve.** $x + \dfrac{3x}{x - 2} = \dfrac{6(x - 1)}{x - 2}$

Solution The restriction on the value of x is: $x \neq 2$.

$$x + \frac{3x}{x - 2} = \frac{6(x - 1)}{x - 2}$$

Multiply both sides by $(x - 2)$. $(x - 2)\left(x + \dfrac{3x}{x - 2}\right) = (x - 2)\left(\dfrac{6(x - 1)}{x - 2}\right)$

Simplify.

$$x^2 - 2x + 3x = 6x - 6$$
$$x^2 + x = 6x - 6$$
$$x^2 - 5x + 6 = 0$$
$$(x - 3)(x - 2) = 0$$
$$x = 3 \quad \text{or} \quad x = 2$$

Check The roots of the transformed equation are 3 and 2, but 2 cannot be a root of the original equation. Substitute 3 in the original equation.

$$x + \frac{3x}{x - 2} = \frac{6(x - 1)}{x - 2}$$

$$3 + \frac{3(3)}{3 - 2} \stackrel{?}{=} \frac{6(3 - 1)}{3 - 2}$$

$$12 = 12 \quad \text{It checks.}$$

Answer {3} (The only root of the equation is 3.)

Example 2 **Solve.** $\dfrac{1}{3} + \dfrac{1}{y} = \dfrac{4}{3y^2}$

Solution The restriction on the value of y is $y \neq 0$.

$$\frac{1}{3} + \frac{1}{y} = \frac{4}{3y^2}$$

$$3y^2\left(\frac{1}{3} + \frac{1}{y}\right) = 3y^2\left(\frac{4}{3y^2}\right)$$

$$y^2 + 3y = 4$$
$$y^2 + 3y - 4 = 0$$
$$(y + 4)(y - 1) = 0$$
$$y = -4 \quad \text{or} \quad y = 1$$

Check The check is left to the student.

Answer {-4, 1} (The roots are -4 and 1.)

*C*LASSROOM EXERCISES

Solve.

1. $\dfrac{x}{3} + \dfrac{x}{4} = 7$

2. $\dfrac{2}{x} + \dfrac{3}{x} = 5$

3. $\dfrac{3}{a} + \dfrac{1}{5} = 2$

4. $\dfrac{3x}{(x - 1)} = \dfrac{3}{(x - 1)}$

5. $\dfrac{3}{2} + \dfrac{1}{y} = \dfrac{5}{2y^2}$

6. $\dfrac{x}{x - 3} + \dfrac{1}{(x - 4)} = \dfrac{1}{(x - 3)(x - 4)}$

WRITTEN EXERCISES

A | **Give the least positive factor that will clear the equation of fractions. Do not solve.**

1. $\dfrac{2(x + 3)}{5} = \dfrac{3x + 4}{4}$

2. $\dfrac{3(x - 4)}{6} = \dfrac{x + 5}{5}$

3. $\dfrac{5}{n} - \dfrac{4}{2n^2} = \dfrac{3}{4n}$

4. $\dfrac{2}{3n} + \dfrac{5}{n^2} = \dfrac{8}{6n}$

5. $\dfrac{4}{x^2 - 9} + \dfrac{7}{x - 3} = \dfrac{9}{x + 3}$

6. $\dfrac{8}{x^2 - 16} + \dfrac{2}{x + 4} = \dfrac{7}{x - 4}$

7. A student gave -1 and 6 as solutions of the following equation. Was the student correct? Explain. $\dfrac{x}{x - 3} + \dfrac{2}{x + 1} = \dfrac{8x}{(x - 3)(x + 1)}$

8. A student gave -2 and 3 as solutions of the following equation. Was the student correct? Explain. $\dfrac{x}{x - 3} + \dfrac{4x - 15}{(x - 2)(x - 3)} = \dfrac{3}{x - 2}$

Solve and check. If there are no solutions, write $\emptyset$.

9. $\dfrac{x + 7}{5} = \dfrac{x + 4}{4}$

10. $\dfrac{x + 3}{6} = \dfrac{x + 2}{5}$

11. $\dfrac{3}{8}x + \dfrac{1}{2} = \dfrac{3}{4}x$

12. $\dfrac{5x}{6} + \dfrac{1}{3} = \dfrac{1}{2}x$

13. $\dfrac{a}{2} + \dfrac{(a + 1)}{3} = \dfrac{(a + 2)}{4}$

14. $\dfrac{a}{4} + \dfrac{(a + 1)}{3} = \dfrac{(a + 2)}{3}$

15. $\dfrac{a}{2} - \dfrac{(a + 1)}{3} = \dfrac{(2a + 7)}{6}$

16. $\dfrac{a}{4} - \dfrac{(a + 2)}{4} = \dfrac{(3a - 7)}{8}$

17. $\dfrac{5}{x} + 3 = \dfrac{7}{x}$

18. $\dfrac{2}{x} + 5 = \dfrac{6}{x}$

19. $\dfrac{6}{x + 3} + 5 = \dfrac{1}{x + 3}$

20. $\dfrac{7}{x + 5} + 3 = \dfrac{13}{x + 5}$

21. $1 + \dfrac{4}{x} = \dfrac{5}{x^2}$

22. $1 + \dfrac{1}{x} = \dfrac{6}{x^2}$

23. $\dfrac{3}{x - 2} = \dfrac{1}{x + 2}$

24. $\dfrac{5}{x - 3} = \dfrac{3}{x + 1}$

25. $x + \dfrac{5}{x} = 6$

26. $\dfrac{x + 2}{x} + \dfrac{x}{x - 2} = 2$

B | 27. $\dfrac{x}{x - 2} = \dfrac{3}{x - 3} - \dfrac{2}{(x - 3)(x - 2)}$

28. $\dfrac{2x}{x - 7} + \dfrac{x}{x - 1} = \dfrac{14}{x - 7} + \dfrac{1}{x - 1} + 1$

29. $\dfrac{x}{x - 1} = \dfrac{2}{x + 1} + \dfrac{2}{x^2 - 1}$

30. $\dfrac{x}{x - 2} + \dfrac{6}{(x - 2)(x + 5)} = \dfrac{2}{x - 2}$

31. $\dfrac{1}{x} + \dfrac{3}{x + 1} = \dfrac{-3}{x^2 + x}$

32. $\dfrac{x + 7}{x^2 - x - 6} = \dfrac{2}{x - 3} - \dfrac{1}{x + 2}$

33. $\dfrac{4}{(x - 1)(x + 1)^2} = \dfrac{1}{x - 1} - \dfrac{1}{x + 1} - \dfrac{2}{(x + 1)^2}$

34. $\dfrac{6}{x^2 - 1} = \dfrac{1}{2} + \dfrac{1}{1 - x}$

35. $\dfrac{x}{x - 2} - \dfrac{1 - x}{2} = x + 1$

36. $\dfrac{x}{x - 5} = \dfrac{2}{x - 3} + \dfrac{4}{(x - 3)(x - 5)}$

C | 37. $\dfrac{4}{(x - 3)(x + 1)} = \dfrac{1}{x - 3} - \dfrac{1}{x + 1}$

38. $\dfrac{x}{x + 1} = \dfrac{8}{x - 8} - \dfrac{9x}{x^2 - 7x - 8}$

39. $\dfrac{x}{x + a} + \dfrac{3a}{x - a} = \dfrac{5ax + a^2}{x^2 - a^2}$

40. $\dfrac{x - a}{x - 2a} + \dfrac{x + 2a}{x - a} = \dfrac{x^2}{x^2 - 3ax + 2a^2}$

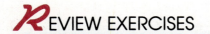

1. Evaluate this determinant. [4-4]

$$\begin{vmatrix} 0 & -1 \\ 4 & 5 \end{vmatrix}$$

2. List the determinants D, D_x, D_y, [4-5] and D_z for this system of equations.

$$\begin{aligned} x + y - z &= 4 \\ x - y &= -3 \\ 2x + 4z &= -12 \end{aligned}$$

3. Graph this system. [4-6]

$$y > \frac{1}{2}x - 2$$

$$x \le 3$$

4. Graph $y > x - 1$ or $x + y < 3$. [4-6]

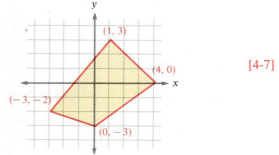

Consider functions in two variables defined on the region shown here. [4-7]

5. Find the minimum value of $S = x - 2y$ on the shaded region.

6. Find the maximum value of $P = x + 3y$ on the shaded region.

HISTORICAL NOTE   Egyptian Fractions

Our system of writing fractions as the ratio of two integers is Babylonian in origin. A rival method, the Egyptian system, was dominant at least until the time of Archimedes (about 287 to 212 B.C.). Egyptians used a bar over an integer to represent the reciprocal of that number (for example, $\overline{5} = \frac{1}{5}$). With some exceptions, their system expressed any fractional number as a sum of unit fractions without repetition.

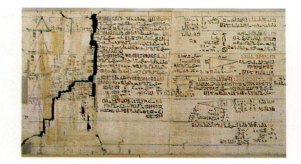

$$\frac{5}{6} = \overline{2} + \overline{3} \qquad \frac{2}{9} = \overline{9} + \overline{12} + \overline{36}$$

Finding a combination of unit fractions to represent numbers such as $\frac{5}{11}$ or $\frac{4}{13}$ can be quite a challenge.

   The Egyptians made the following helpful observation in working with unit fractions: If n is a positive integer, then

$$\frac{1}{n} = \frac{1}{(n + 1)} + \frac{1}{n(n + 1)}.$$

Find the Egyptian fractions for $\frac{5}{11}$ and $\frac{4}{13}$.

LESSON 6-6

Solving Problems Using Fractional Equations

A **fractional equation** is an equation with a variable in the denominator of a fraction. Problems such as this one generate fractional equations.

For the first 15 mi of a marathon, a runner ran with the race leaders at a constant rate. In order to break away from the pack she increased her speed by 10% for the next 5 mi. Then she slowed to her original pace and completed the final 6.2 mi. Her time for the race was 2 h 36 min (2.6 h). At what rate did the runner run most of the race?

Let r = the runner's original rate in miles per hour. Then her faster rate was $r + 0.1r = 1.1r$ miles per hour.

	Distance (mi)	Rate (mph)	Time (h)
Slower rate	21.2	r	$\dfrac{21.2}{r}$
Faster rate	5	$1.1r$	$\dfrac{5}{1.1r}$

Running rates for the problem are expressed in miles per hour and distances are expressed in miles. Therefore, the time at each rate and the total time must be expressed in hours (2 h, 34.2 min = 2.57 h).

$$\underset{\substack{\text{Time at}\\\text{slower rate}}}{\dfrac{21.2}{r}} \;+\; \underset{\substack{\text{Time at}\\\text{faster rate}}}{\dfrac{5}{1.1r}} \;=\; \underset{\substack{\text{Total}\\\text{time}}}{2.57}$$

Multiply both sides of the equation by 1.1r (the LCD) to eliminate denominators.

$$1.1r\left(\frac{21.2}{r} + \frac{5}{1.1r}\right) = 1.1r(2.57)$$

$$23.32 + 5 = 2.827r$$

$$2.827r = 28.32$$

$$r \approx 10.0$$

The runner ran most of the race at a rate of about 10 mph (6-min miles). Her fastest rate was about 11 mph (about 5.45-min miles).

The following examples show how to solve other problems that result in fractional equations.

Example 1 Solve.

A painter can paint an area in 3 h that would take her apprentice 4 h to paint. If they can paint a small home together in 12 h, how long should it take the painter working alone?

Solution Let t = the time (h) for the painter alone to paint the home. Let $\frac{4}{3}t$ = the time (h) for the apprentice to paint the home alone.

If the painter can do the job in t hours, her rate is $\frac{1}{t}$ job per hour. Similarly, the rate of her apprentice is $\frac{1}{\frac{4}{3}t}$ or $\frac{3}{4t}$ jobs per hour.

	Time worked (in hours)	Rate (in jobs per hour)	Work (in jobs)
Painter	12	$\frac{1}{t}$	$12 \cdot \frac{1}{t}$
Apprentice	12	$\frac{3}{4t}$	$12 \cdot \frac{3}{4t}$
Together	12	$\frac{1}{12}$	$12 \cdot \frac{1}{12}$

Word equation: $\begin{array}{c}\text{Work done by}\\\text{master painter}\end{array} + \begin{array}{c}\text{Work done by}\\\text{apprentice}\end{array} = \text{Total work}$

Equation: $12 \cdot \frac{1}{t} \quad + \quad 12 \cdot \frac{3}{4t} \quad = 12 \cdot \frac{1}{12}$

$$\frac{12}{t} + \frac{36}{4t} = 1$$

$$\frac{12}{t} + \frac{9}{t} = 1$$

Multiply both sides by 1. $\quad 12 + 9 = t$

$$t = 21$$

Answer The painter could paint the house in 21 h. (The apprentice could paint the house in $\frac{4}{3}(21)$, or 28 h.)

Example 2   Solve.

A boat takes twice as long to travel 10 mi upstream as it does to travel 7 mi downstream in a river that flows at 5 mph. At what speed does the boat travel in still water?

Solution   When the boat is going upstream, the rate of the boat is decreased by the rate of the river's current. When the boat is going downstream, the rate of the boat is increased by the rate of the river's current.

Let r = the boat's rate in still water, $r - 5$ = the rate going upstream, and $r + 5$ the rate going downstream.

	Distance (mi)	Rate (mph)	Time (h)
Upstream	10	$r - 5$	$\dfrac{10}{r - 5}$
Downstream	7	$r + 5$	$\dfrac{7}{r + 5}$

Word equation: Time upstream $= 2 \cdot$ (Time downstream)

Equation:
$$\frac{10}{r - 5} = 2\left(\frac{7}{r + 5}\right)$$

Multiply both sides by $(r - 5)(r + 5)$.

$$10(r + 5) = 14(r - 5)$$
$$10r + 50 = 14r - 70$$
$$120 = 4r$$
$$r = 30$$

Answer   The boat travels at 30 mph in still water.

eLASSROOM EXERCISES

A computer operator can enter the company weekly payroll information into a computer in 1 h. With the help of another operator, the data can be entered in 24 min. How long would it take the second operator to enter the data alone?

1. What is the time in minutes for the first operator to enter the data?

2. What is the rate of the first operator in data entry jobs per minute?

3. Let t be the time in minutes for the second operator to enter the data. What is the rate of the second operator in data entry jobs per minute?

4. What fraction of the data entry job does the first operator do in 24 min? the second operator?

5. Write an equation that relates the amount of work done by each operator to the total entry job (1 job). Solve the equation and the problem.

 Complete the table that organizes the information and then write an equation that fits the problem. Do *not* solve the equation.

1. A sales representative drove at a constant rate for 100 km. In order to arrive home on schedule, the last 60 km of the trip were driven at a constant rate that was 20% faster than the first part of the trip. What were the two rates if the total time for the trip was 3 h?

	Rate	Time	Distance
First part	r	?	100
Second part	$1.2r$	?	60

2. A cyclist pedaled 50 km at a constant rate and another 55 km at a rate that was 10% faster. The total trip took 5 h. What were the rates for the two parts of the trip?

	Rate	Time	Distance
First part	r	?	50
Second part	$1.1r$	?	55

3. Machine A and machine B each produce the same product, but machine B produces at half the rate of machine A. Working together for a total of 4 hours, each machine produces 200 products. What is the rate of each machine?

	Rate	Time	Products
Machine A	r	?	200
Machine B	?	?	200

4. Carrie types 25% more words per minute than Jack. First Carrie typed 280 words, and then Jack typed 160 words. If their total typing time was 12 min, what was the typing rate for each typist?

	Rate	Time	Words
Jack	r	?	160
Carrie	?	?	280

Solve.

5. A nut mixture is made from two kinds of nut. One kind of nut costs twice as much per pound as the other type. Ten dollars worth of the less expensive nuts is mixed with $8 worth of the more expensive nuts to make 7 lb of the mixture. What is the price per pound of each kind of nut?

	Price per pound	**Pounds**	**Cost**
Less expensive nuts	p	?	10
More expensive nuts	?	?	?

6. A lawn seed mixture is made from two types of seed. One seed is three times as expensive as the other. Ten dollars worth of the less expensive seed is mixed with $15 worth of the more expensive seed to make a 10-lb mixture. What is the cost per pound of each seed type?

	Cost per pound	**Amount**	**Cost**
Less expensive seeds	c	?	10
More expensive seeds	?	?	15

7. One data entry operator can complete a job in 8 h and another can complete the job in 12 h. How long will it take both operators to complete the job together?

8. One pump can fill a tank 10 h and another pump can fill the same tank in 15 h. How long will it take the pumps working together to fill the tank?

9. Doug's typing rate is 10% faster than Carol's. First Doug typed 330 words, and then Carol typed 270 words. Their total typing time was 19 min. What were their typing rates?

10. One pump works at a rate that is 20% faster than another pump. First the slower pump put 9100 gal of fuel into a storage tank, and then the faster pump put in 3900 gal. Nineteen hours were required to fill the 13,000-gal tank. What was the rate of each pump in gallons per hour?

11. If two resistances r_1 and r_2 are connected in parallel, the total resistance R of the circuit can be found using the formula $\dfrac{1}{R} = \dfrac{1}{r_1} + \dfrac{1}{r_2}$. Find two resistances, one 3 ohms more than the other, that produce a total resistance of 2 ohms when connected in parallel.

12. The total resistance of a parallel circuit is 4 ohms, and one resistance is 6 ohms less than the other. What are the two resistances? (See Exercise 11.)

13. When an object travels *equal distances* at *different rates*, the average rate for the entire distance is the harmonic mean of the two rates. The harmonic mean of two numbers, a and b, is given by the formula

$$H = \dfrac{2}{\dfrac{1}{a} + \dfrac{1}{b}}.$$

A sales representative drove half of his route at 60 km/h and the other half at 30 km/h. What was the average rate for the entire route? Check your answer by assuming that the entire route was 120 km long.

14. A delivery service drove half the distance at 60 km/h and the other half at 40 km/h. What was the average rate for the entire distance? Check your answer by assuming that the entire distance was 240 km. (See Exercise 13.)

Solve.

B 15. A design engineer ran an engine test at an initial rate (revolutions per minute) for 4500 revolutions and then ran it at twice that rate for another 5400 revolutions. The engine test lasted for 4 min. What was the initial rate of the engine (rpm)? How long was it run at that rate?

16. Ice cream has 2.25 times as many calories per cup as orange juice. In 100 cups of punch made of orange juice and ice cream, 9600 calories came from the orange juice and 5400 calories came from the ice cream. How many calories are in a cup of orange juice? How many cups of orange juice were used in the punch?

17. The formula $\dfrac{1}{R} = \dfrac{1}{r_1} + \dfrac{1}{r_2} + \dfrac{1}{r_3}$ can be used to find the total resistance R for three resistances (r_1, r_2, r_3) connected in parallel. One resistance is 3 times the smallest resistance and the third resistance is 2 ohms more than the smallest resistance. What are the three resistances if the total resistance is 2 ohms?

18. The total resistance in a circuit with three resistances connected in parallel is 6 ohms. The first resistance is twice the second. The second resistance is 6 ohms more than the third. What are the three resistances? (Use the formula in Exercise 17.)

19. The harmonic mean H of three numbers, x_1, x_2, and x_3, can be found using the formula $H = \dfrac{3}{\dfrac{1}{x_1} + \dfrac{1}{x_2} + \dfrac{1}{x_3}}$.

The harmonic mean of three positive numbers is 12. The first number is 4 times the second number and the third number is 2 less than the second number. What are the three numbers?

20. A truck travels 250 mi from Dallas to Houston. Half the route is driven at a rate r_1 and half at a different rate r_2. On the return trip, the truck is driven half the time at rate r_1 and half the time at rate r_2. Show that the return trip took less time than the trip going.

REVIEW EXERCISES

1. Write the product in scientific notation. $(6.5 \cdot 10^6)(4 \cdot 10^6)$ [5-1]

Simplify.   [5-1, 5-2]

2. $(3x^2)(5x)^2$ **3.** $(x^2 - 3x + 4) + 2(x^2 + 5x - 3)$

4. $2x(x - 3) - (x^2 - 3x + 4)$

Expand.   [5-3]

5. $(x + 3)(2x - 5)$ **6.** $(x + y)^4$

7. State the greatest common factor of $6a^3bc$ and $15a^2b^2c$.   [5-4]

8. Factor $6x^3 - 9x^2 + 15x$.   [5-4]

Self-Quiz 2

6-4   **Simplify.**

1. $\dfrac{4x}{x + 2} + \dfrac{8}{x + 2}$ **2.** $\dfrac{5b}{2a} - \dfrac{3b^2}{ab}$ **3.** $\dfrac{5}{y - 1} - \dfrac{2}{y + 1}$

6-5   **Solve.**

4. $\dfrac{b}{4} - 1 = \dfrac{2b}{3}$ **5.** $y + 2 = \dfrac{15}{y}$ **6.** $\dfrac{x}{x - 2} - \dfrac{1}{x + 2} = \dfrac{4}{x^2 - 4}$

6-6   **Solve.**

7. A transmission assembly line can be operated at a 20% faster rate when 5 extra workers are added. During an 8-h period, 1445 transmissions were assembled, 510 of them at the faster rate. What is the normal assembly rate of the transmission line?

LESSON 6-7

Inverse Variation

A traveler wishing to go from Toledo to Cincinnati, a distance of about 200 miles could choose various modes of transportation. The relationship between the rate r and the time t for the trip is given by the formula

$$t = \frac{200}{r}.$$

The graph of the relation is not linear. As r increases, t decreases toward zero; and as r decreases toward zero, t increases.

Rate (mph)	0.25	0.5	1	2	10	20	100	200	400	800
Time (h)	800	400	200	100	20	10	2	1	0.5	0.25

If r is doubled, then t is halved. If r is multiplied by 4, then t is multiplied by $\frac{1}{4}$. This type of relationship is an example of **inverse variation.**

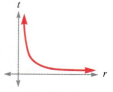

Definition: Inverse Variation

Two quantities x and y vary inversely if and only if there is a constant k, $k \neq 0$, such that $y = \frac{k}{x}$ or $xy = k$.

The constant k is called the **constant of inverse variation** or just the **constant of variation**. In most practical problems, the constant of variation is positive.

The figure below shows the graph of an inverse variation. The graph is in the first and third quadrants when $k > 0$.

The graph of an inverse variation is in the second and fourth quadrants when $k < 0$.

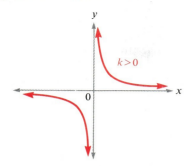

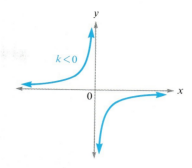

Example 1 Solve.

In an experiment, the volume V of a gas was determined to be 100 mL when the pressure P on the gas was 150 kPa (kilopascals). When the pressure was increased to 200 kPa, the volume decreased to 80 mL. Do the volume and pressure vary inversely?

Solution First instance: $PV = 150(100) = 15,000$.
Second instance: $PV = 200(80) = 16,000$.

Answer The product of the pressure and the volume is not constant, so the relationship is not an inverse variation.

Example 2 Solve.

The experiment in Example 1 is repeated, but this time the temperature is kept constant. Some of the data are given below. Do the volume and pressure vary inversely?

Pressure (kPa)	100	150	200	250
Volume (mL)	150	100	75	60

Solution In each instance, $PV = 15,000$.

Answer Since the product of the pressure and the volume is constant in all measured cases, the relationship appears to be an inverse variation.

Example 3 Complete.

The measure of the central angle m of a regular polygon varies inversely as the number of sides n. Express this relationship in an equation.

Solution Since m and n vary inversely, their product is constant.

Answer $mn = k$ or $m = \dfrac{k}{n}$ or $n = \dfrac{k}{m}$ [*Note:* The value of k is 360.]

If x and y vary inversely, then $\quad x_1y_1 = k \quad$ and $\quad x_2y_2 = k$.

Therefore, $\qquad\qquad\qquad\qquad x_1y_1 = x_2y_2 \quad$ and $\quad \dfrac{x_1}{x_2} = \dfrac{y_2}{y_1}$.

This formula gives the relationship for two ordered pairs of an inverse relation.

If (x_1, y_1) and (x_2, y_2) are two pairs of an inverse relation, then

$$x_1y_1 = x_2y_2 \quad \text{and} \quad \dfrac{x_1}{x_2} = \dfrac{y_2}{y_1}.$$

Example 4   Solve.

Suppose y varies inversely as x. If $y = 7$ when $x = 5$, what is the value of y when $x = 9$?

Solution   Since $x_1y_1 = x_2y_2$, $5 \cdot 7 = 9y_2$ and $\dfrac{35}{9} = y_2$.

Answer $\dfrac{35}{9}$

Example 5   Solve.

The force of gravitational attraction F between two bodies with equal masses varies inversely as the square of the distance between their centers. If d_1 represents the present distance between the centers of the moon and earth, what relative distance separating the two bodies would make the force of attraction nine times as much?

Solution   Since the force of attraction F varies inversely as the square of the distance, the inverse relationship is expressed by $F = \dfrac{g}{d^2}$, where g is the gravitational constant of variation. For two different positions of the earth and moon,

$$\dfrac{f_1}{F_2} = \dfrac{d_2{}^2}{d_1{}^2}.$$

Let F_1 represent the force of attraction for the present distance d_1. We are looking for a relative distance d_2 at which $F_2 = 9F_1$.

Substitute $9F_1$ for F_2. $\qquad \dfrac{F_1}{9F_1} = \dfrac{d_2{}^2}{d_1{}^2}$

Simplify. $\qquad\qquad\qquad\quad \dfrac{1}{9} = \dfrac{d_2{}^2}{d_1{}^2}$

$$d_2{}^2 = \dfrac{d_1{}^2}{9}$$

$$d_2 = \sqrt{\dfrac{d_1{}^2}{9}} = \dfrac{d_1}{3}$$

Answer   The distance between the centers would have to be $\dfrac{1}{3}$ the present distance d_1.

LASSROOM EXERCISES

Do x and y vary inversely?

1.

x	1	2	3	4	6	12
y	12	6	4	3	2	1

2.

x	12	24	36	48	60
y	1	2	3	4	5

3. Suppose that y varies inversely as x, and that $y = 7$ when $x = 3$. What is the value of y when $x = 9$?

4. Suppose that y varies inversely as the square of x, and that $y = 7$ when $x = 3$. What is the value of y when $x = 9$?

5. If 8 stamping machines can complete a job order in 5 h, how much time is required to do the same job if 2 machines are shut down, assuming that each machine works at the same rate?

WRITTEN EXERCISES

A Do x and y vary inversely?

1.

x	1	2	4	5	10	20
y	20	10	5	4	2	1

2.

x	1	2	3	6	9	18
y	18	9	6	3	2	1

3.

x	1	2	3	4	5	6
y	12	11	10	9	8	7

4.

x	32	28	24	20	16	14
y	16	14	12	10	8	7

5.

x	36	33	30	27	24	21
y	12	11	10	9	8	7

6.

x	10	11	12	13	14	15
y	10	9	8	7	6	5

7.

x	10	8	6	5	4	2
y	0.2	0.25	$0.\overline{3}$	0.4	0.5	1

8.

x	1	2	3	4	5	6
y	3	$\frac{3}{2}$	1	$\frac{3}{4}$	$\frac{3}{5}$	$\frac{1}{2}$

Suppose that a varies inversely as b. Find the constant of variation.

9. $a = 2$ when $b = 10$

10. $a = 3$ when $b = 8$

11. $a = \frac{1}{3}$ when $b = \frac{3}{8}$

12. $a = \frac{1}{2}$ when $b = \frac{4}{3}$

Suppose that p and q vary inversely, and that $p = 3$ when $q = 6$. Find the value of p for each value of q.

13. $q = 12$ **14.** $q = 18$ **15.** $q = 2$ **16.** $q = 3$

Suppose that r varies inversely as s, and that $r = 0.1$ when $s = 0.6$. Find the value of r for each value of s.

17. $s = 6$ **18.** $s = 60$ **19.** $s = 0.02$ **20.** $s = 0.3$

Suppose that t varies inversely as the square of w, and that $t = 4$ when $w = 3$. Find the value of t for each value of w.

21. $w = 4$ **22.** $w = 5$ **23.** $w = 10$ **24.** $w = 8$

*A*pplications

Write an equation for each problem. Solve the equation and answer the question.

25. The drama club has 20 members. Working at the same rate, each member addressed promotional flyers for a production in 45 min. If only 15 members had addressed the flyers, how many minutes would each person have had to work?

26. The organizers of a contest decided to divide the prize money equally among 100 winners, with each receiving $50. If they had decided to have only 4 winners, how much would each have received?

27. A regular decagon (10 sides) and a regular dodecagon (12 sides) have the same perimeter. If each side of the decagon is 36 cm long, how long is each side of the dodecagon?

28. A regular dodecahedron (12 faces) and a regular icosahedron (20 faces) have the same surface area. If each face of the dodecahedron has an area of 400 cm^2, what is the area of each face of the icosahedron?

For right circular cones of constant volume, height (h) varies inversely as the square of the radius (r) of the base.

29. If $h = 25$ cm when $r = 4$ cm, what is h when $r = 10$ cm?

30. If $h = 36$ cm when $r = 5$ cm, what is h when $r = 15$ cm?

31. If $h = 25$ cm when $r = 4$ cm, what is h when $r = 100$ cm?

32. If $h = 36$ cm when $r = 5$ cm, what is r when $h = 9$ cm?

B | Solve.

33. Flying into a headwind from Jacksonville to Tallahassee, a light plane had a ground speed of 140 mph and took 1 h and 12 min to make the trip. Flying with a tailwind, the plane took only 56 min for the return trip. What was the ground speed for the Tallahassee-to-Jacksonville flight?

34. A plane took 3 h and 50 min flying from Washington, D.C., to Los Angeles into a headwind and only 3 h and 20 min on the return trip flying with a tailwind. If the ground speed was 600 mph on the Washington-to-Los Angeles flight, what was the ground speed on the Los Angeles-to-Washington flight?

$\mathcal{A}$pplication: Levers

If two objects on a lever are balanced, their masses and their distances from the fulcrum vary inversely. $m_1d_1 = m_2d_2$

35. A 2-kg object that is 20 cm from the fulcrum balances a 4-kg object. How far is the 4-kg object from the fulcrum?

36. A rock placed 30 cm from the fulcrum balances a 15-kg mass placed 9 cm farther from the fulcrum. What is the mass of the rock?

37. A 5-kg rock balances a 17-kg rock. The rock of lesser mass is 12 cm farther from the fulcrum. How far is each rock from the fulcrum?

38. One object has a mass that is 60 g greater than another object. They balance when one object is 10 cm from the fulcrum and the other is 40 cm from the fulcrum. What is the mass of each object?

$\mathcal{A}$pplication: Dimensional Analysis

When you compute with measurements, you can treat the units in the same ways you treat the numbers. For example, substitute 60 miles per hour for r and 3 hours for t in the distance formula $d = rt$.

$$d = rt$$

$$d = 60\frac{\text{mi}}{\text{h}} \cdot 3h$$

Regroup the numbers and the units.

$$d = (60 \cdot 3)\left(\frac{\text{mi}}{\text{h}} \cdot h\right)$$

Divide both the numerator and denominator by h.

$$d = 180\,\text{mi}$$

This technique is especially useful when converting from one unit to another.

Example Convert 60 miles per hour to an equivalent unit in feet per seconds.

$$60\frac{\text{mi}}{\text{h}} = \left(60\frac{\text{mi}}{\text{h}}\right)\left(\frac{1\,\text{h}}{3600\,\text{s}}\right)\left(\frac{5280\,\text{ft}}{1\,\text{mi}}\right)$$

$$= \left(60 \cdot \frac{1}{3600} \cdot 5280\right)\left(\frac{\text{mi}}{\text{h}} \cdot \frac{\text{h}}{\text{s}} \cdot \frac{\text{ft}}{\text{mi}}\right)$$

$$= 88\,\text{ft/s}$$

Notice that the **conversion fractions** $\frac{1\,\text{h}}{3600\,\text{s}}$ and $\frac{5280\,\text{ft}}{1\,\text{mi}}$ were chosen so that the given units divide out and the desired units remain.

Solve.

39. A car was driven at 50 miles per hour for 12 minutes. How many miles were driven?

40. Consider the formula $s = \frac{1}{2}gt$. If g is measured in feet per second, and t is measured in seconds, in what unit is s measured?

41. Convert 432 inches to feet.

42. Convert 0.03 kilometers to meters.

Use a calculator.

43. Light travels about 183,000 miles per second. Express that rate in miles per year?

44. A bicyclist rode 7 miles in 18 minutes. At that rate, how many feet will be ridden in 5 minutes?

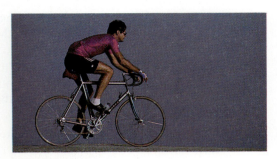

C **Suppose that the square of p varies inversely as the square of q.**

45. If $p = 6$ when $q = 8$, what is p when $q = 16$?

46. If $p = 6$ when $q = 8$, what is q when $p = 4$?

Express the answer in terms of a and b.

47. If x varies inversely as y^2, and $x = a$ when $y = b$, what is x when $y = 2b$?

48. If y varies inversely as x^2, and $x = a$ when $y = b$, what is y when $x = 3a$?

49. If x^2 varies inversely as y^2, and $x = a$ when $y = b$, what is y when $x = 4a$?

50. A varies inversely as B, and B varies inversely as the square of C. Write an equation to show how A varies with respect to C.

*R*EVIEW EXERCISES

Factor.   [5-5, 5-6]

1. $2x^2 - 18$ **2.** $x^3 + 8$

3. $2x^4 - 54x$ **4.** $x^2 - 3x - 18$

5. $2x^2 + 9x - 5$ **6.** $3 + 2x - x^2$

Solve by factoring.   [5-7]

7. $x^2 + 9 = 6x$ **8.** $x^2 + 3x = 28$

9. $3x^2 = 2x + 1$ **10.** $x(x - 2) = 7(2 - x)$

11. $2a^2 - 7a + 5 = 0$ **12.** $2a^2 - 5a + 3 = 0$

13. $3a^2 + 2a - 8 = 0$ **14.** $3a^2 - 10a - 8 = 0$

15. $4a^2 - 4a - 15 = 0$ **16.** $4a^2 - 8a - 21 = 0$

CHAPTER SUMMARY

▶ **Vocabulary**

▶ **Definition of Negative Exponents** [6-1]

For each real number a, $a \neq 0$, and for each integer n, $\qquad a^{-n} = \dfrac{1}{a^n}$

▶ **Properties of Exponents** [6-1]

For all real numbers a and b, $a \neq 0$, $b \neq 0$, and for all integers m and n,

$$a^m \cdot a^n = a^{m+n} \qquad \frac{a^m}{a^n} = a^{m-n} \qquad (a^m)^n = a^{mn} \qquad a^m b^m = (ab)^m$$

▶ For all real numbers a, b, and c, $b \neq 0$, $cd \neq 0$, $\qquad \dfrac{ac}{bc} = \dfrac{a}{b}$ [6-2]

▶ **Definition of Multiplication of Fractions** [6-3]

For all real numbers a, b, c, and d, $b \neq 0$, $d \neq 0$,

$$\frac{a}{b} \cdot \frac{c}{d} = \frac{ac}{bd}$$

▶ **Definition of Division of Fractions** [6-3]

For all real numbers a, b, c, and d, $b \neq 0$, $c \neq 0$, $d \neq 0$,

$$\frac{a}{b} \div \frac{c}{d} = \frac{ad}{bc}$$

▶ **Definition of Addition of Fractions with Like Denominators** [6-4]

For all real numbers a, b, and c, $c \neq 0$, $\qquad \dfrac{a}{c} + \dfrac{b}{c} = \dfrac{a+b}{c}$

▶ **Definition of Inverse Variation** [6-7]

Two quantities x and y vary inversely if and only if there is a constant k, $k \neq 0$,

such that $y = \dfrac{k}{x}$ or $xy = k$.

CHAPTER REVIEW

6-1 **Objective:** To use negative integer exponents.

Write without negative exponents.

1. $\dfrac{3x^{-2}}{y^{-1}}$

2. $\left(\dfrac{-1}{4}\right)^{-2}$

Write without fractions.

3. $\dfrac{12m^2n^3}{-3m^3n^2}$

4. $\dfrac{b^2c}{a^2b^2c^3}$

5. $\dfrac{6 \cdot 10^{-3}}{2 \cdot 10^{-5}}$

6. The mass of $5 \cdot 10^3$ cm^3 of helium at one atmosphere of pressure is $8.9 \cdot 10^{-1}$ g. Find the density of helium in g/cm^3.

6-2 **Objective:** To simplify rational expressions.

Simplify, listing any restrictions on the variables.

7. $\dfrac{xy^2 - x^2y}{2xy}$

8. $\dfrac{3y^2 - 6y}{y^2 - 4}$

9. $\dfrac{1 - \dfrac{1}{x}}{1 + \dfrac{1}{x}}$

6-3 **Objective:** To simplify products and quotients of rational expressions.

Simplify, listing any restrictions on the variables.

10. $\dfrac{3x^2}{y} \cdot \dfrac{5y^3}{6x}$

11. $\dfrac{7a^4b}{c^2} \div \dfrac{14a^4b^2}{c^3}$

12. $\dfrac{5x + 10}{x - 3} \cdot \dfrac{x^2 - 9}{x^2 + 4x + 4}$

13. $\dfrac{2w + 8}{w + 1} \div \dfrac{w + 4}{w^2 + w}$

6-4 **Objective:** To simplify sums and differences of rational expressions.

State the least common denominator.

14. $\dfrac{1}{x^2}, \quad \dfrac{5}{x + 2}, \quad -\dfrac{3}{2x}$

Write as a simplified rational expression. List any restrictions on the variables.

15. $\dfrac{5}{2xy^2} - \dfrac{5}{x^2y}$

16. $\dfrac{1}{a + 4} - \dfrac{2}{a} + 3$

6-5 **Objective:** To solve fractional equations.

Solve.

17. $\dfrac{8}{2y + 1} = \dfrac{3}{y - 1}$

18. $\dfrac{5}{a - 1} - \dfrac{3}{1 - a} = 4$

Solve and check. Write Ø if there are no roots.

19. $\dfrac{4}{x - 2} - x = 1$

20. $\dfrac{3}{(x^2 - 16)} = \dfrac{2}{(x - 4)} - \dfrac{2}{(x + 4)}$

6-6 Objective: To solve problems using fractional equations.

21. Two resistances r_1 and r_2 are connected in parallel, giving an effective total resistance R of 20 ohms. If one resistance is 30 ohms more than the other, find the two resistances.

22. A canoe takes 1 h longer to be paddled 9 mi upstream than 14 mi downstream. If the stream flows at 2 mph, find the rate at which the canoe can be paddled in still water.

6-7 Objective: To solve problems involving inverse variation.

23. F varies inversely as the square of r. Find F when $r = 5$, if $F = 100$ when $r = 6$.

24. Two masses m_1 and m_2 balance when placed on a lever at respective distances d_1 and d_2. If mass m_1 is tripled, at what distance from the fulcrum will m_2 balance this additional mass?

 **CHAPTER 6 SELF-TEST**

6-1 Write without exponents.

1. $(2^{-3})^2$

2. $\dfrac{4^{-8}}{4^{-6}}$

Write in scientific notation.

3. $\dfrac{6.3 \cdot 10^{-4}}{9 \cdot 10^8}$

Write using positive exponents.

4. $a^{-4}b^2$

5. $\dfrac{r^{-2}s}{3t^{-3}}$

Write without using fractions.

6. $\dfrac{5x^2}{x^6}$

7. $\dfrac{-4}{bc^3}$

6-2 Simplify.

8. $\dfrac{7x + 14xy}{7x}$

9. $\dfrac{y^2 - 36}{y - 6}$

10. $\dfrac{a^2 + 5a - 6}{a^2 - a}$

6-3 Simplify, listing any restrictions on the variables.

11. $\dfrac{5x^2}{y^2} \cdot \dfrac{7y}{x}$

12. $\dfrac{b(a + b)}{a} \div \dfrac{(a + b)^2}{a^2}$

13. $\dfrac{3x + 6}{x^3} \cdot \dfrac{x^2}{x + 2}$

6-4 14. $\dfrac{4}{x - 1} - \dfrac{2}{x}$

15. $\dfrac{9}{2ab} + \dfrac{5}{b^2}$

16. $\dfrac{5y - 1}{y + 4} - \dfrac{1 + 2y}{y + 4}$

6-5 Solve.

17. $\dfrac{6}{x} + 4 = \dfrac{2}{x}$

18. $\dfrac{1}{x - 1} + \dfrac{2}{x + 3} = \dfrac{7}{(x - 1)(x + 3)}$

19. $y + 3 = \dfrac{4}{y}$

6-6 Solve.

20. A rocket traveled 100 km at one rate and another 75 km at a rate that was 50% faster. The rocket traveled for 30 s. Find the original speed of the rocket.

6-7 21. Suppose that R is inversely proportional to the square of s. If $R = 16$ when $s = 3$, find R when $s = 6$.

22. If 6 members of a street crew can complete a job in 1 h and 15 min, how long would the job take 5 crew members to complete?

$\mathcal{P}$RACTICE FOR COLLEGE ENTRANCE TESTS

Choose the best answer for each question.

1. If n is divided by 5, the remainder is 3. What is the remainder when $3n$ is divided by 5?

   A. 0   **B.** 1   **C.** 2   **D.** 3   **E.** 4

2. $\dfrac{1}{2} - \dfrac{1}{3} + \dfrac{1}{4} - \dfrac{1}{5} = \underline{}$.

   A. $\dfrac{13}{60}$ **B.** $\dfrac{7}{30}$ **C.** $\dfrac{1}{4}$ **D.** $\dfrac{4}{15}$ **E.** $\dfrac{17}{60}$

3. If $x^3 = -1$, then $x(x + 1) = \underline{}$.

   A. -1 **B.** 0   **C.** 1   **D.** 2   **E.** It cannot be determined from the given information.

4. If $a = 4p$ and $b = \dfrac{8p}{1 + 16p}$, then what is b in terms of a?

   A. $\dfrac{2a}{1 + 4a}$ **B.** $\dfrac{4a}{1 + 8a}$ **C.** $\dfrac{8a}{1 + 16a}$ **D.** $\dfrac{16a}{1 + 32a}$ **E.** $\dfrac{32a}{1 + 64a}$

5. If $\dfrac{x}{y} = -2$, then $\dfrac{x^2}{y^2} + \dfrac{y^2}{x^2} = \underline{}$.

   A. $2\dfrac{1}{4}$ **B.** $3\dfrac{3}{4}$ **C.** $4\dfrac{1}{4}$ **D.** $5\dfrac{3}{4}$ **E.** $6\dfrac{1}{4}$

6. Susan scored 80, 84, and 92 on her first three algebra tests. What must she score on her fourth test in order to have an average of 85?

   A. 81   **B.** 82   **C.** 83   **D.** 84   **E.** 85

7. If there are six teams in a soccer league and each of them plays each of the other teams once, how many games will be played in all?

   A. 10   **B.** 12   **C.** 15   **D.** 30   **E.** 36

8. What is the ratio of the area of the large square to the area of the shaded square?

A. $\sqrt{2}:1$ **B.** $2:1$ **C.** $2\sqrt{2}:1$ **D.** $4:1$ **E.** $4\sqrt{2}:1$

9. $\dfrac{\dfrac{1}{a} + \dfrac{1}{b}}{\dfrac{1}{ab}} = \underline{}$ $(a \neq 0, b \neq 0)$

A. $\dfrac{ab}{a+b}$ **B.** $\dfrac{a+b}{ab}$ **C.** $\dfrac{ab}{a^2+b}$ **D.** $\dfrac{1}{a+b}$ **E.** $a+b$

10. If $x = \dfrac{1}{a}$ and $y = \dfrac{1}{a+2}$, what is the average of x and y?

A. $\dfrac{1}{2a}$ **B.** $\dfrac{2a+2}{a(a+2)}$ **C.** $\dfrac{2a+1}{a(a+2)}$ **D.** $\dfrac{a+1}{a(a+2)}$ **E.** $\dfrac{2a+1}{2a(a+2)}$

11. If the sum of two positive consecutive integers is s, what is the value of the smaller integer in terms of s?

A. $\dfrac{s}{2} - 2$ **B.** $\dfrac{s-1}{2}$ **C.** $\dfrac{s}{2} - 1$ **D.** $\dfrac{s+1}{2}$ **E.** $\dfrac{s}{2} + 1$

12. A restaurant sells an average of h hamburgers per day at c cents per hamburger. What is the amount of money in dollars received for hamburgers in a 30-day period?

A. $3000hc$ **B.** $\dfrac{3000h}{c}$ **C.** $\dfrac{10h}{3c}$ **D.** $\dfrac{3hc}{10}$ **E.** $\dfrac{3h}{10c}$

*C*UMULATIVE REVIEW (Chapters 4–6)

4-1   **1.** How many solutions does a system of two linear equations in two variables have if the system is:

     a. Dependent?   **b.** Independent and consistent?   **c.** Inconsistent?

   2. Solve by graphing. $2x - y = 5$
$$x + 4y = -2$$

4-2   **3.** What expression should be substituted for x in the first equation in order to solve this system by substitution?
$$4x + 3y = 15$$
$$x - 2y = 1$$

   4. Solve by substitution. $3x + y = 11$
$$2x - 3y = 11$$

4-3 **5.** Solve by linear combination. $5x + 4y = 9$
$$3x - 2y = 1$$

Solve by writing a system of two equations in two variables.

6. Two phone volunteers handled a total of 290 calls during a charity drive. One volunteer took 10 more calls per hour than the second volunteer but worked 2 h less. If the volunteer who worked longer took calls for 7 h, how many calls per hour did each volunteer take?

7. Evaluate. $\begin{vmatrix} 6 & 5 \\ -2 & 4 \end{vmatrix}$

4-4 **8.** Solve using Cramer's rule. $8x + y = 1$
$$2x - 3y = 10$$

9. List the minor of the element 1. $\begin{vmatrix} 2 & -7 & 4 \\ 3 & 5 & 0 \\ 0 & 2 & 1 \end{vmatrix}$

4-5 **10.** Evaluate. $\begin{vmatrix} 4 & 0 & 1 \\ -5 & 1 & 3 \\ -2 & 7 & 0 \end{vmatrix}$

11. Solve using Cramer's rule. $x + y - z = 4$
$$x + 2y + z = 5$$
$$2x - y = 1$$

4-6 **Graph.**

12. $x + y < 4$ **13.** $2x + y > 5$ or $x - y < 7$
$$y > x$$

4-7 **14.** Find the maximum and minimum values of $R = 7x + 5y$, and where those values occur on the shaded region.

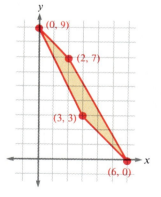

5-1 **Simplify.**

15. $(w^6)(w^4)$ **16.** $(2y^5)(-4y^3)$ **17.** $(3x^2)^3$

5-2 **18.** What is the degree of this polynomial? $7a - 3a^2b + 9b^2$

19. Simplify. $(12x^2 - 8x + 1) - (5x^2 + 2x - 10)$

5-2, **Expand and simplify.**
5-3

20. $3x(x - y) + 2y(y - x)$ **21.** $(z + 4)(z^2 - 4z + 16)$

5-3 **22.** Write the volume of the cube as a simple polynomial.

$b - 1$

5-4 **23.** State the GCF of $14a^2b^3$ and $16a^3b$.

Factor.

5-5, **24.** $9a^2b - 3ab$ **25.** $5mn^2 + 30m^2n - 10mn$ **26.** $4s^2 - 25$
5-6   **27.** $a^3 - 64a$ **28.** $y^2 + 9y + 8$ **29.** $4x^2 - 12x + 9$

5-7 **Solve.**

30. $(5y - 3)(y + 4) = 0$ **31.** $x^2 - x = 30$

32. The height of a parallelogram is 4 in. less than twice the length of the base. Find the length of the base of the parallelogram if its area is 126 in.².

6-1 **33.** Write without using exponents. $(2^{-3})^2$

34. Write using positive exponents. $x^3 \cdot x^{-5}$

35. Write without using fractions. $\dfrac{a^2b^3}{a^4b^4}$

Simplify. State all restrictions on the variables.

6-2 **36.** $\dfrac{3x + 9}{5x + 15}$ **37.** $\dfrac{x^2 + 5x}{x^2 + 4x - 5}$ **38.** $\dfrac{x^2 - 14x + 48}{2x - 12}$

6-3 **39.** $\dfrac{5a^2}{9b} \cdot \dfrac{12b^2}{20a^2}$ **40.** $\dfrac{xy^3}{8} \div \dfrac{x^2y}{4}$ **41.** $\dfrac{2m + n}{8m - 4n} \cdot \dfrac{6m - 3n}{8m + 4n}$

6-4 **42.** $\dfrac{4x}{x + 2} + \dfrac{8}{x + 2}$ **43.** $\dfrac{b}{b - 1} - \dfrac{1}{b(b - 1)}$ **44.** $\dfrac{2}{x + 1} + \dfrac{1}{x - 1}$

Solve.

6-5 **45.** $\dfrac{4}{y - 1} = \dfrac{2}{y + 3}$ **46.** $\dfrac{1}{w} + 4 = \dfrac{9}{w}$ **47.** $\dfrac{a}{a - 2} = \dfrac{8}{a + 2} + \dfrac{7}{(a + 2)(a - 2)}$

6-6 **48.** A nut mixture is made from two kinds of nuts. One kind costs 3 times as much per pound as the other. A clerk mixes $10 worth of the less expensive nuts with $15 worth of the more expensive nuts to make a 10-lb mixture. What is the cost per pound of each kind of nut?

6-7 **49.** Suppose p varies inversely as q. If $p = 16$ when $q = \dfrac{7}{2}$, find p when $q = 14$.

50. What size mass placed 8 cm from the fulcrum of a lever will balance a mass of 12 g placed 6 cm from the fulcrum?

CHAPTER 7

Radicals and Irrationals

It has been said that if air were clear enough, you could see the St. Louis Arch from the top of the Sears Tower in Chicago. Do you think this statement is true?

A formula for estimating the distance d (in kilometers) to the horizon from a height h (in meters) above the ground is

$$d = 3.53\sqrt{h}.$$

How tall would the Sears Tower have to be in order for you to see the St. Louis Arch, a distance of about 420 km?

LESSON 7-1

Roots

A law enforcement officer uses the formula $s = \sqrt{12.5d}$ to estimate the speed s in miles per hour that a car was traveling from the distance d in feet that it skidded in coming to a halt on wet asphalt. It is easy to show that a car that skidded 50 feet was not exceeding the 35 mph speed limit.

$$s = \sqrt{12.5(50)} = \sqrt{625} = 25$$

Recall that 625 is the square of 25 and of -25, and that 25 and -25 are the **square roots** of 625. We write:

$$25^2 = 625 \quad \text{and} \quad (-25)^2 = 625$$
$$\sqrt{625} = 25 \quad \text{and} \quad -\sqrt{625} = -25$$

The symbol $\sqrt{625}$ is read as **"the principal square root of 625"** or just **"the square root of 625,"** and $-\sqrt{625}$ is read as **"the negative square root of 625."** If a is a positive real number, $\sqrt{a}$ is a positive real number. Negative real numbers do not have real-number square roots. The square root of zero is zero.

Similarly, since $4^3 = 64$, 64 is the cube of 4, and 4 is the **cube root** of 64.

$$\sqrt[3]{64} = 4$$

The symbol $\sqrt[3]{64}$ is read as **"the principal cube root of 64"** or just **"the cube root of 64."** Each real number has exactly one real-number cube root.

$$(-3)^3 = -27, \quad \text{so} \ \sqrt[3]{-27} = -3 \qquad 0^3 = 0, \quad \text{so} \ \sqrt[3]{0} = 0$$

Definition: The *n*th Root

For all real numbers a and b, and all positive integers n, if $a^n = b$, then a is an nth root of b. A positive nth root of b is written $\sqrt[n]{b}$ and a negative nth root of b is written $-\sqrt[n]{b}$.

The symbol $\sqrt[n]{b}$ (read as "the nth root of b"), called a **radical**, is used to indicate the principal nth root of b. The symbol n is called the **index**, $\sqrt{}$ is a **radical sign**, b is the **radicand**, and the bar over the radicand is a grouping symbol called the **vinculum**. When no index is written, the radical sign indicates a square root.

$$\text{index} \longrightarrow \quad \sqrt[n]{81} \quad \longleftarrow \text{vinculum}$$
$$\text{radical sign} \longrightarrow \qquad \longleftarrow \text{radicand}$$

Numbers such as $\sqrt{23}$, $\sqrt[3]{35}$, and $\sqrt[5]{10}$ are irrational numbers and cannot be written as terminating or repeating decimals. However, it is possible to approximate irrational numbers as closely as desired using decimals. These **rational approximations** can be found using a scientific calculator or using a less sophisticated calculator for successive trials. The method of *successive trials* uses this property.

For all positive real numbers a, b, and c and all integers n,
$$\text{if } a^n < b < c^n, \text{ then } a < \sqrt[n]{b} < c.$$

Example 1   Use a calculator and successive trials to compute $\sqrt[3]{53}$ to the nearest tenth.

Solution $3^3 = 27$ and $4^3 = 64$, so $3 < \sqrt[3]{53} < 4$.

Try 3.5: $3.5^3 = 42.875$,   so $3.5 < \sqrt[3]{53} < 4$.

Try 3.7: $3.7^3 = 50.653$,   so $3.7 < \sqrt[3]{53} < 4$.

Try 3.8: $3.8^3 = 54.872$,   so $3.7 < \sqrt[3]{53} < 3.8$.

Try 3.75: $3.75^3 = 52.734375$,   so $3.75 < \sqrt[3]{53} < 3.8$.

Answer $\sqrt[3]{53}$ is 3.8 to the nearest tenth.

Example 2   Find a rational approximation of $\sqrt{43}$ to the nearest hundredth.

Solution   Use divide-and-average and a calculator.

Locate $\sqrt{43}$ between successive integers. $6 < \sqrt{43} < 7$

Estimate $\sqrt{43}$ to tenths. $\sqrt{43} \approx 6.5$

Divide 43 by 6.5.
$$6.5\overline{)43.0000} \quad \text{(quotient } 6.615\text{)}$$

Average the divisor and quotient. $\dfrac{6.5 + 6.615}{2} \approx 6.558$

Divide 43 by 6.558.
$$6.558\overline{)43.000} \quad \text{(quotient } 6.557\text{)}$$

Answer $\sqrt{43}$ is between 6.557 and 6.558. It is 6.56 to the nearest hundredth.

*C*LASSROOM EXERCISES

True or false?

1. $\sqrt{49} = 7$

2. $\sqrt{49} = -7$

3. $-\sqrt{49} = 7$

4. $\sqrt[3]{27} = 3$

5. $\sqrt[3]{27} = -3$

6. $\sqrt[3]{-27} = -3$

7. $\sqrt[3]{\dfrac{1}{8}} = \dfrac{1}{2}$

8. $\sqrt{\dfrac{1}{4}} = \dfrac{1}{2}$

9. For each real number a between 0 and 1, $a < \sqrt{a}$.

Simplify. If the symbol does not represent a real number, state "not real."

10. $\sqrt{36}$ **11.** $-\sqrt{64}$ **12.** $\sqrt{-100}$ **13.** $\sqrt[3]{8}$ **14.** $\sqrt[3]{-8}$

15. Find a rational approximation of $\sqrt{92}$ to the nearest tenth.

 RITTEN EXERCISES

A State whether the symbol represents a real number (answer yes or no).

1. $\sqrt{3}$ **2.** $\sqrt{5}$ **3.** $-\sqrt{16}$ **4.** $-\sqrt{25}$

5. $\sqrt{-9}$ **6.** $\sqrt{-4}$ **7.** $\sqrt[3]{6}$ **8.** $\sqrt[3]{9}$

9. $\sqrt[3]{-27}$ **10.** $\sqrt[3]{-8}$ **11.** $-\sqrt[3]{-2}$ **12.** $-\sqrt[3]{-4}$

State whether the number is rational or irrational.

13. $\sqrt{4}$ **14.** $\sqrt{5}$ **15.** $\sqrt{8}$ **16.** $\sqrt{9}$

17. $\sqrt[3]{24}$ **18.** $\sqrt[3]{27}$ **19.** $\sqrt[3]{-1}$ **20.** $\sqrt[3]{-18}$

21. $\sqrt[4]{36}$ **22.** $\sqrt[4]{81}$ **23.** $\sqrt[5]{20}$ **24.** $-\sqrt[5]{-1}$

True or false?

25. $\sqrt{9} = -3$ **26.** $\sqrt{16} = -4$ **27.** $-\sqrt{2} = \sqrt{-2}$ **28.** $\sqrt{-3} = -\sqrt{3}$

29. $\sqrt{\dfrac{1}{9}} = \dfrac{1}{3}$ **30.** $\sqrt{\dfrac{1}{25}} = \dfrac{1}{5}$ **31.** $\sqrt[3]{-64} = -4$ **32.** $\sqrt[3]{-1000} = -10$

Simplify.

33. $\sqrt{81}$ **34.** $\sqrt{121}$ **35.** $-\sqrt{\dfrac{4}{25}}$ **36.** $-\sqrt{\dfrac{9}{16}}$

37. $-\sqrt[3]{\dfrac{1}{8}}$ **38.** $-\sqrt[3]{\dfrac{1}{64}}$ **39.** $\sqrt[3]{-\dfrac{8}{27}}$ **40.** $\sqrt[3]{-\dfrac{27}{64}}$

41. $\sqrt[4]{81}$ **42.** $\sqrt[4]{16}$ **43.** $\sqrt[5]{-32}$ **44.** $\sqrt[5]{-1}$

Find a rational approximation to the nearest tenth.

45. $-\sqrt{70}$ **46.** $-\sqrt{110}$ **47.** $\sqrt[3]{20}$ **48.** $\sqrt[3]{40}$

If A is an approximation to $\sqrt{N}$, then $A_1 = \dfrac{1}{2}\left(A + \dfrac{N}{A}\right)$ is a better approximation.

Verify this statement by using a calculator to complete the tables.

49.

N	A	A_1	A^2	$A_1{}^2$
70	8	?	?	?

50.

N	A	A_1	A^2	$A_1{}^2$
20	4	?	?	?

pplications

The time in seconds that it takes an object to fall h meters is given by this formula:

$$t = \sqrt{\frac{h}{5}}$$

Use a calculator to find the time (to the nearest tenth of a second) for an object to fall each distance.

51. 3 m   **52.** 28 m   **53.** 150 m   **54.** 8534 m

B   **55.** What is the edge of a cube with a volume of 1,000,000 cm³?

56. What is the edge of a square with an area of 1,000,000 cm²?

57. The largest lake in Florida is Lake Okeechobee. Its area is 700 mi². If the lake were in the shape of a square, how long would each side of the square be (to the nearest mile)?

58. The volume of the water in the Pacific Ocean is about 167,000,000 mi³. If the water were in a container in the shape of a cube, how long would each edge of the cube be (to the nearest mile)?

The *geometric mean* of two positive numbers is the principal square root of their product. Find the geometric mean of the two numbers.

59. 2 and 72   **60.** $\frac{1}{2}$ and 800   **61.** 3 and 5   **62.** a and b

True or false? If the statement is false, state a counterexample.

63. If x is a real number and $x^2 = 2$, then $x = \sqrt{2}$.

64. If a and b are positive real numbers and $a > b$, then $\sqrt{a} > \sqrt{b}$.

65. If a is a positive real number, then $a > \sqrt{a}$.

66. If a is a real number and $a > 1$, then $a > \sqrt{a}$.

67. If a is a real number and $a > 1$, then $\sqrt{a} > \sqrt[3]{a}$.

68. If a is a real number and $0 < a < 1$, then $\sqrt{a} > \sqrt[3]{a}$.

 **Express as a single radical.**

69. $\sqrt{\sqrt[3]{7}}$

70. $-\sqrt[3]{\sqrt{2}}$

71. $\dfrac{\sqrt[3]{25}}{\sqrt{5}}$

72. Show that $\sqrt{\sqrt[3]{n^2}} = \sqrt[3]{n}$ for $n > 0$.

73. Explain why $\sqrt[4]{36} = \sqrt{6}$.

$\mathcal{R}$EVIEW EXERCISES

1. State whether each number is rational or irrational. [1-1]

    a. $7.191919\ldots$ **b.** $\sqrt{3}$ **c.** $-1\dfrac{2}{3}$ **d.** $1.010010001\ldots$

2. Substitute and simplify. [1-2]
$$\sqrt{(x_1 - x_2)^2 + (y_1 - y_2)^2}$$

x_1	y_1	x_2	y_2
3	4	-1	7

3. Simplify $2\sqrt{3} + 5\sqrt{3}$. [1-4]

4. Find the next number in the sequence. [1-6]
$$1, \sqrt{2}, \sqrt{3}, 2, \sqrt{5}, \sqrt{6}, \sqrt{7}, \sqrt{8}, \ldots$$

5. Use the variable n to write an expression for the nth term of the sequence. [1-6]
$$\dfrac{1}{2}, \dfrac{2}{4}, \dfrac{3}{8}, \dfrac{4}{16}, \dfrac{5}{32}, \ldots$$

 $\mathcal{C}$ALCULATOR EXTENSION   Roots

Here is a technique for calculating the nth root of a number on any calculator without using the root key.

To calculate an approximation of $\sqrt[n]{x}$ for any positive integer n:

1. Choose any number as an estimate g for $\sqrt[n]{x}$. (Any number will do, but the closer to the actual value the faster the process works.)

2. Raise g to the $(n - 1)$ power, using the $\boxed{\times}$ and $\boxed{=}$ keys or the power key.

3. Divide x by the result of step 2.

4. Multiply g by $n - 1$ and add to the result in step 3.

5. Divide the sum in step 4 by n. This is a better estimate of $\sqrt[n]{x}$.

6. Repeat steps 1–5, using the result of step 5 as the new estimate g. Continue until you get the same result (step 5) twice in a row. That value is a good approximation to $\sqrt[n]{x}$.

▶ Use the above technique to compute $\sqrt[6]{300}$ to the nearest tenth.

▶ Can the above technique be used to compute square roots?

Simplifying Radicals

The **inverse** of an ordered pair (a, b) is the ordered pair (b, a). The inverse of a set of ordered pairs contains the inverse of each of the individual ordered pairs of the set. For example, the inverse of $\{(2, 3), (-4, 1)\}$ is $\{(3, 2), (1, -4)\}$. Consider the square function set $A = \{(x, y): y = x^2\}$. The inverse of A can be written in set-builder notation by interchanging x and y in the equation for A.

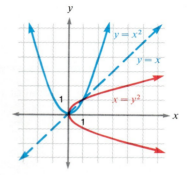

$$\{(x, y): x = y^2\}$$

The graphs of A and its inverse are shown. Note that each graph is the reflection of the other about the line $y = x$. Set A is a function. Is its inverse also a function?   No

The graphs of the **power functions** (functions with equations of the form $y = x^n$, for positive integers n) and their inverses make apparent necessary restrictions in simplifying radical expressions. The graphs of the cube power function and its inverse are shown at the right.

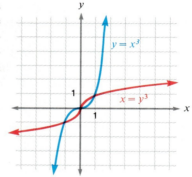

The inverses of the square and cube power functions show two important differences.

1. The inverse of the square function is not a function. The inverse of the cube function is a function.

2. The domain of the inverse of the square function is the set of nonnegative real numbers. The domain of the inverse of the cube function is the set of all real numbers.

To define a square-root function, we "separate" the inverse of the square function into two subsets, each of which is a function. The two subsets of $x = y^2$ are

$$\{(x, y): x = y^2, y \geq 0\} \quad \text{and} \quad \{(x, y): x = y^2, y < 0\}.$$

The first function is the **principal square-root function** and is written $\{(x, y): y = \sqrt{x}\}$. The second function is the **negative square-root function** and is written $\{(x, y): y = -\sqrt{x}\}$.

$$\{(x, y): y = \sqrt{x}\}$$ $$\{(x, y): y = -\sqrt{x}\}$$

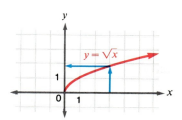   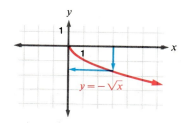

Note these two important characteristics of the square-root functions.

The domain of each of the square-root functions is the set of nonnegative real numbers.

The range of the principal square-root function is the set of nonnegative real numbers. The range of the negative square-root function is the set of nonpositive real numbers.

A consequence of the first characteristic is the fact that $\sqrt{x}$ does not always represent a real number. For example, $\sqrt{x}$ does not represent a real number if $x < 0$: $\sqrt{-17}$ and $\sqrt{-4}$ are not real numbers. On the other hand, $\sqrt{-x}$ does represent a real number if $x \leq 0$: $\sqrt{-(-16)} = 4$. In order to apply the properties of real numbers to radicals, we must know that those radicals represent real numbers. Therefore, we state **restrictions** on the radicands so that they do not represent negative numbers.

Real Numbers	Restrictions
$\sqrt{n}$	$n \geq 0$
$\sqrt{ab}$	$ab \geq 0$
$\sqrt{x^2}$	None (since $x^2 \geq 0$ for every x)

No such restrictions are necessary for variables in cube-root radicands, since the domain of the cube-root function is the set of all real numbers.

A consequence of the second characteristic above is that we must often use absolute values in expressions involving square roots. For example,

$$\sqrt{x^2} = |x|$$

For negative values of x, without the absolute values, we would get false sentences such as $\sqrt{(-2)^2} = -2$. Similarly, we must write:

$$-\sqrt{x^2} = -|x|$$

This complication does not arise for the cube-root function, since its range is the set of all real numbers.

From the graphs below, note the similarities among inverses of all *even* power functions and among inverses of all *odd* power functions.

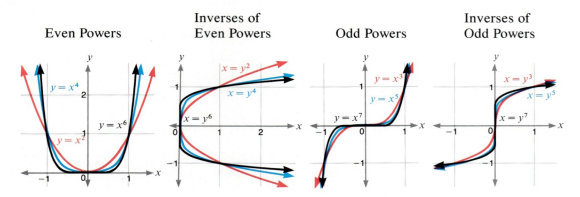

Even Powers   Inverses of Even Powers   Odd Powers   Inverses of Odd Powers

In stating generalizations about nth roots of real numbers, it is often necessary to distinguish between roots with odd indexes and those with even indexes.

For each real number a and each positive *odd* integer n, $\sqrt[n]{a^n} = a$.
For each real number a and each positive *even* integer n, $\sqrt[n]{a^n} = |a|$.

$$\sqrt[5]{(-2)^5} = -2 \qquad \sqrt[3]{x^3} = x \qquad \sqrt[4]{(-2)^4} = |-2| = 2 \qquad \sqrt[4]{x^4} = |x|$$

Example 1 **Simplify and state restrictions needed to ensure that the radicand is not negative.**

a. $\sqrt{x^2}$ **b.** $\sqrt[3]{-27x^3}$ **c.** $\sqrt{25x^4}$ **d.** $\sqrt[6]{x^6}$ **e.** $\sqrt[4]{x^3}$

Solution **a.** $\sqrt{x^2} = |x|$ **b.** $\sqrt[3]{-27x^3} = \sqrt[3]{(-3x)^3} = -3x$

c. $\sqrt{25x^4} = \sqrt{(5x^2)^2} = 5x^2$ **d.** $\sqrt[6]{x^6} = |x|$

e. $\sqrt[4]{x^3}$ is in simplest form.   Restriction: $x \geqslant 0$

The following property is used to simplify radicals. An nth-degree radical is in simplest form if the radicand contains no factors that can be expressed as nth powers.

Multiplication Property of Radicals

For all real numbers a and b *for which the radicals are defined*, and all positive integers n,

$$\sqrt[n]{ab} = \sqrt[n]{a} \cdot \sqrt[n]{b}.$$

Example 2   Simplify.   a. $\sqrt{48}$ b. $\sqrt{6} \cdot \sqrt{2}$

Solution   a. $\sqrt{48} = \sqrt{16 \cdot 3}$ b. $\sqrt{6} \cdot \sqrt{2} = \sqrt{12}$
$\qquad\qquad = \sqrt{16} \cdot \sqrt{3}$ $\qquad\qquad\quad = \sqrt{4 \cdot 3}$
$\qquad\qquad = 4\sqrt{3}$ $\qquad\qquad\qquad = \sqrt{4} \cdot \sqrt{3}$
$\qquad\qquad\qquad\qquad\qquad\qquad\qquad = 2\sqrt{3}$

Example 3   Simplify. State necessary restrictions. $\sqrt{8x^3}$

Solution $\sqrt{8x^3} = \sqrt{4x^2 \cdot 2x}$
$\qquad\qquad = \sqrt{4x^2} \cdot \sqrt{2x}$
$\qquad\qquad = 2|x|\sqrt{2x}, \; x \geqslant 0$

Example 4   Simplify. $\sqrt[3]{-54a^5b^4}$

Solution $\sqrt[3]{-54a^5b^4} = \sqrt[3]{-27a^3b^3} \cdot \sqrt[3]{2a^2b}$
$\qquad\qquad\qquad = -3ab\sqrt[3]{2a^2b}$

LASSROOM EXERCISES

Simplify. State restrictions where necessary.

1. $\sqrt{50}$ 2. $\sqrt{48}$ 3. $\sqrt[3]{16}$ 4. $\sqrt[4]{96}$

5. $\sqrt{a^2}$ 6. $-\sqrt{b^4}$ 7. $\sqrt{x^2y^3}$ 8. $\sqrt{-a^3b^4}$

9. $\sqrt[3]{a^6b^4}$ 10. $\sqrt{6x^3} \cdot \sqrt{3x^2}$ 11. $\sqrt{2a^3} \cdot \sqrt{12a^2b}$ 12. $-\sqrt[3]{x^6}$

RITTEN EXERCISES

A   **State any restrictions on the variables. If no restrictions are necessary, write "none."**

1. $\sqrt{a}$ 2. $\sqrt[3]{a}$ 3. $-\sqrt[3]{a}$ 4. $-\sqrt{a}$

5. $\dfrac{3}{\sqrt[3]{b}}$ 6. $\dfrac{3}{\sqrt{b^2}}$ 7. $\sqrt[4]{a^2b}$ 8. $\sqrt[4]{ab^2}$

Simplify. Assume all variables are positive. If the expression cannot be simplified, write "simplest form."

9. $\sqrt{20}$ 10. $\sqrt{28}$ 11. $\sqrt[3]{24}$ 12. $\sqrt[3]{40}$

13. $\sqrt{15}$ 14. $\sqrt{30}$ 15. $\sqrt[3]{-54}$ 16. $\sqrt[3]{-128}$

17. $\sqrt{a^2b^3}$ 18. $\sqrt{a^3b^2}$ 19. $\sqrt[3]{a^2b^3}$ 20. $\sqrt[3]{a^3b^2}$

21. $\dfrac{\sqrt{r}}{t}$ 22. $\dfrac{\sqrt{t}}{r}$ 23. $\sqrt[3]{p^{17}q^{18}}$ 24. $\sqrt[3]{p^{15}q^{16}}$

Simplify. State restrictions where necessary. If an expression cannot be simplified, write "simplest form."

25. $\dfrac{\sqrt[4]{x^8}}{y-2}$ **26.** $\dfrac{\sqrt[4]{x^{16}}}{y-3}$ **27.** $\dfrac{\sqrt{y^7}}{2x}$ **28.** $\dfrac{\sqrt{y^{11}}}{3x}$

29. $\sqrt{8x}\cdot\sqrt{6x}$ **30.** $\sqrt{18a}\cdot\sqrt{10a^3}$ **31.** $\sqrt{2c^2}\cdot\sqrt{4c^3}$

32. $\sqrt{5y^4}\cdot\sqrt{10y^3}$ **33.** $\sqrt{12a^7}\cdot\sqrt{15a^4}$ **34.** $\sqrt{12c^5}\cdot\sqrt{5c^3}$

 35. $\sqrt{10xy^3}\cdot\sqrt{15xy^4}$ **36.** $\sqrt[3]{9p^5q}\cdot\sqrt[3]{6p^4q}$ **37.** $\sqrt[4]{3r^2t^3}\cdot\sqrt[4]{2r^2t}$

38. $\dfrac{\sqrt[3]{(x+2)^3}}{x+2}$ **39.** $\sqrt{a^2+4a+4}$ **40.** $\sqrt{a^2-b^2}$

State the restrictions that are necessary to ensure that each expression represents a real number.

41. $\sqrt{-4xy}$ **42.** $\sqrt{5+t}$ **43.** $\sqrt{5-t}$ **44.** $\sqrt{5+t^2}$

45. $\sqrt{5-t^2}$ **46.** $\sqrt[3]{7-m}$ **47.** $\sqrt[4]{(x+y)^2}$ **48.** $\sqrt{x^2-y^2}$

Solve for x.

49. $x^2=72$ **50.** $x^2=72a^2b$ **51.** $x^2-90ab^2=0$ **52.** $x^3-200r^4t^7=0$

Simplify. Assume that n is a positive integer and values of the variables are such that each expression represents a real number.

53. $\sqrt[n]{a^{n+2}}$ **54.** $\sqrt[n]{x^{2n}}$ **55.** $\sqrt[n]{b^{n-2}}$ **56.** $\dfrac{\sqrt[n]{ab}}{\sqrt[n]{a^{n-2}}}$

C | **57.** Solve the equation for x: $x^2-2x=4m^2n-1$.

58. State whether the equation is true for all real numbers a and b. If the equation is false, give a counterexample. $\sqrt{a^2}+\sqrt{2ab}+\sqrt{b^3}=\sqrt{(a+b)^2}$

59. Find x^4 if $x=\sqrt{1+\sqrt{1+\sqrt{1}}}$.

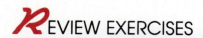 EVIEW EXERCISES

1. Solve $\dfrac{x}{2}+\dfrac{x}{3}=10$. [2-1]

2. Solve $a=\pi r^2$ (where $a>0$ and $r>0$) for r. [2-2]

Solve and graph on a number line. [2-4,

3. $5-2x<8$ **4.** $6\le 3x+9\le 21$ **5.** $|x-3|<1$ **6.** $|x+2|>1$ 2-5,

2-6]

$\mathcal{S}$elf-Quiz 1

7-1 **True or false?**

1. $-\sqrt{\dfrac{25}{36}}=-\dfrac{5}{6}$ **2.** $-\sqrt[3]{-64}=4$ **3.** If $x<0$, then $\sqrt{x^2}=-x$.

Simplify. State any restrictions where necessary.

4. $-\sqrt{\dfrac{144}{9}}$ **5.** $\sqrt[3]{-\dfrac{1}{125}}$ **6.** $\sqrt{48}$ **7.** $\sqrt[3]{54a^4}$

7-2   **8.** $\sqrt{x^2y^4}$ **9.** $\sqrt[3]{4a^8b^{12}}$ **10.** $\dfrac{-\sqrt{8r^4}}{8r}$ **11.** $\sqrt[4]{8a^2b} \cdot \sqrt[4]{4a^3b^3}$

 ℰALCULATOR EXTENSION   *Evaluating Radical Expressions*

Many calculators have two keys for finding roots, the $\boxed{\sqrt{x}}$ key and the $\boxed{\sqrt[x]{y}}$ key. The $\boxed{\sqrt{x}}$ key is used for square roots and the $\boxed{\sqrt[x]{y}}$ key is used to determine a root with any index x.

Radical Expression	Keying Sequence	Display
$\sqrt{39}$	39 $\boxed{\sqrt{x}}$ $\boxed{=}$	6.244998
$\sqrt[3]{0.047}$	0.047 $\boxed{\sqrt[x]{y}}$ 3 $\boxed{=}$	0.3608826

Evaluate these expressions to the nearest hundredth.

1. $2.4 - \sqrt{12}$ **2.** $\dfrac{51.2}{\sqrt{89}}$ **3.** $\sqrt[3]{\dfrac{47}{4}}$ **4.** $2\sqrt[5]{61} + 11$ **5.** $\sqrt[3]{-0.065}$

State whether each pair of expressions is equivalent.

6. $(5 + \sqrt{2})(3 - \sqrt{2})$,   **7.** $17\sqrt{11} - 3\sqrt{5}$,   **8.** $\dfrac{5}{\sqrt[3]{5}}$, $\sqrt[3]{5}$ **9.** $\sqrt[4]{3} \cdot \sqrt[3]{2}$, $\sqrt[12]{27 \cdot 16}$
$13 - 2\sqrt{2}$ $14\sqrt{6}$

ℬIOGRAPHY   Tom Lehrer

Tom Lehrer has been successful both as a mathematician and as a musician. A child prodigy in mathematics, he entered Harvard at age fifteen and at age seventeen was teaching courses as a graduate student. While a student, he wrote songs, including one entitled "New Math," and performed for parties and produced three successful records. He worked as a mathematician for an electronics firm and for the National Security Agency; and he taught mathematics courses at Harvard, Massachusetts Institute of Technology, and Wellesley College. He wrote songs for the television program "That Was the Week That Was" and for the Children's Television Workshop. He also performed at the *hungry i* in San Francisco. In 1980, his popular musical *Tom Foolery* opened. Mr. Lehrer currently teaches courses in mathematics and in musicals in Santa Cruz, California.

LESSON 7-3

Computing with Radicals

Is this triangle a right triangle?
Using a calculator, we find

$$a^2 + b^2 = (5.9282032)^2 + (5.7320508)^2$$
$$= 35.143593 + 32.856406$$
$$= 67.999999$$

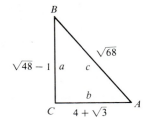

Because of rounding errors in the calculator approximations, we cannot use these computations to confirm whether the Pythagorean theorem is satisfied. We need exact methods of computation to check whether $68 = (\sqrt{48} - 1)^2 + (4 + \sqrt{3})^2$.

Sums and differences of radical expressions can be simplified by applying the basic properties of real numbers. The sum of two radicals cannot be simplified if the radicals have different indexes or different radicands.

$$\sqrt{5} + \sqrt[3]{5} \qquad \text{cannot be simplified (indices are different)}$$
$$\sqrt{11} + \sqrt{7} \qquad \text{cannot be simplified (radicands are different)}$$

It is important that the radicals are written in simplest form before attempting to add or subtract them. For example, it may not appear that $\sqrt{2} + \sqrt{8}$ can be further simplified. But $\sqrt{8}$ is equivalent to $2\sqrt{2}$, so

$$\sqrt{2} + \sqrt{8} = \sqrt{2} + 2\sqrt{2} = (1 + 2)\sqrt{2} = 3\sqrt{2}.$$

Example 1 **Simplify.** $(3 + \sqrt{2}) - (5 + 3\sqrt{8})$

Solution $(3 + \sqrt{2}) - (5 + 3\sqrt{8}) = (3 + \sqrt{2}) - (5 + 3 \cdot 2\sqrt{2})$
$$= 3 + \sqrt{2} - 5 - 6\sqrt{2}$$
$$= (3 - 5) + (\sqrt{2} - 6\sqrt{2})$$
$$= -2 - 5\sqrt{2}$$

Example 2 **Simplify.** $\sqrt{5} + \sqrt[3]{5} + 2\sqrt[3]{135} - \sqrt{20}$

Solution $\sqrt{5} + \sqrt[3]{5} + 2\sqrt[3]{135} - \sqrt{20} = \sqrt{5} + \sqrt[3]{5} + 2\sqrt[3]{27 \cdot 5} - \sqrt{4 \cdot 5}$
$$= \sqrt{5} + \sqrt[3]{5} + 2 \cdot 3\sqrt[3]{5} - 2\sqrt{5}$$
$$= \sqrt{5} + \sqrt[3]{5} + 6\sqrt[3]{5} - 2\sqrt{5}$$
$$= 7\sqrt[3]{5} - \sqrt{5}$$

The following example demonstrates how to expand the product of polynomials that contain radicals.

Example 3 Expand and simplify. $(2 + \sqrt{13})(3 - \sqrt{13})$

$$(2 + \sqrt{13})(3 - \sqrt{13}) = 2(3 - \sqrt{13}) + \sqrt{13}(3 - \sqrt{13})$$
$$= 6 - 2\sqrt{13} + 3\sqrt{13} - (\sqrt{13})^2$$
$$= 6 + \sqrt{13} - 13$$
$$= \sqrt{13} - 7$$

Example 4 Is $1 + \sqrt{3}$ a root of $x^2 - 2x - 2 = 0$?

Solution
$$x^2 - 2x - 2 = 0$$

Substitute $1 + \sqrt{3}$ for x. $(1 + \sqrt{3})^2 - 2(1 + \sqrt{3}) - 2 \overset{?}{=} 0$

Simplify. $1 + 2\sqrt{3} + (\sqrt{3})^2 - 2 - 2\sqrt{3} - 2 \overset{?}{=} 0$

$$1 + 3 - 2 - 2 \overset{?}{=} 0$$
$$0 = 0 \quad \text{True}$$

Answer Yes, $(1 + \sqrt{3})$ satisfies the equation and is a root.

*C*LASSROOM EXERCISES

Simplify.

1. $3\sqrt{7} + 2\sqrt{7} - 6\sqrt{7}$
2. $(2 - 3\sqrt{5}) - (1 - 7\sqrt{5})$
3. $4\sqrt{2}(\sqrt{8} - 3\sqrt{6})$

Expand and simplify.

4. $(3 + \sqrt{2})(3 - \sqrt{2})$
5. $(2 + \sqrt{5})(1 - \sqrt{3})$

*W*RITTEN EXERCISES

A **Simplify. If the expression cannot be simplified, write "simplest form."**

1. $\sqrt{3} + \sqrt{3} + \sqrt{3}$
2. $\sqrt{2} + \sqrt{2} + \sqrt{2} + \sqrt{2}$
3. $\sqrt{5} + \sqrt{10} + 2\sqrt{5}$
4. $\sqrt{3} + \sqrt{6} + 4\sqrt{3}$
5. $\sqrt{12} + \sqrt{75}$
6. $\sqrt{18} + \sqrt{50}$
7. $\sqrt{20} + \sqrt{10} + \sqrt{80}$
8. $\sqrt{40} + \sqrt{10} + \sqrt{30}$
9. $5 + \sqrt[3]{5}$
10. $\sqrt[3]{6} + \sqrt{6}$
11. $\sqrt[3]{40} + \sqrt[3]{24}$
12. $\sqrt[3]{32} + \sqrt[3]{16}$
13. $(2 + \sqrt{3}) + (4 + \sqrt{5})$
14. $(1 + \sqrt{6}) + (3 + \sqrt{10})$
15. $(5 - \sqrt[3]{6}) + (2 + 3\sqrt[3]{6})$
16. $(3 + \sqrt[3]{7}) + (10 - 4\sqrt[3]{7})$
17. $\sqrt{54} - \sqrt{24}$
18. $\sqrt{63} - \sqrt{28}$
19. $(3 - \sqrt[3]{5}) - (1 - \sqrt[3]{5})$
20. $(5 - \sqrt[3]{6}) - (2 - \sqrt[3]{6})$
21. $\sqrt{2}(\sqrt{2} + \sqrt{3})$
22. $\sqrt{3}(\sqrt{3} + \sqrt{5})$
23. $\sqrt{6}(\sqrt{10} + \sqrt{21})$
24. $\sqrt{10}(\sqrt{15} + \sqrt{14})$

Expand and simplify.

25. $(\sqrt{5} + \sqrt{6})(\sqrt{5} + \sqrt{2})$ **26.** $(\sqrt{2} + \sqrt{3})(\sqrt{5} + \sqrt{3})$ **27.** $(\sqrt{10} + \sqrt{2})(\sqrt{2} + \sqrt{5})$

28. $(\sqrt{6} + \sqrt{3})(\sqrt{3} + \sqrt{2})$ **29.** $(2 + \sqrt{2})(3 + \sqrt{2})$ **30.** $(5 + \sqrt{3})(2 + \sqrt{3})$

31. $(\sqrt{10} - 2)(\sqrt{10} + 2)$ **32.** $(\sqrt{6} + 1)(\sqrt{6} - 1)$ **33.** $(\sqrt{8} - \sqrt{7})^2$

34. $(\sqrt{7} - \sqrt{6})^2$ **35.** $(x - \sqrt{7})(x + \sqrt{7})$ **36.** $(x + \sqrt{5})(x - \sqrt{5})$

B | **State whether the given number is a root of the given equation.**

37. $3 + \sqrt{6}; x^2 + 3 = 6x$ **38.** $4 + \sqrt{6}; x^2 + 10 = 8x$ **39.** $2 - \sqrt{3}; x^2 + 1 = 4x$

40. $4 - \sqrt{2}; x^2 + 14 = 8x$ **41.** $4 + \sqrt{10}; x^2 + 5 = 8x$ **42.** $2 + \sqrt{2}; x^2 - 4x + 2 = 0$

Simplify. Assume that each variable is a nonnegative number.

43. $(x - 4 - \sqrt{3})(x - 4 + \sqrt{3})$ **44.** $(x + 3 + \sqrt{3})(x + 3 - \sqrt{3})$ **45.** $(7 - \sqrt{25a}) - (3 - \sqrt{a})$

46. $(\sqrt{xy^2} + 4) + (12 - 3\sqrt{x})$ **47.** $\sqrt[3]{x^4y} + 2\sqrt{xy} - \sqrt[3]{xy}$ **48.** $(\sqrt{m} + \sqrt{n})(\sqrt{m} + \sqrt{n})$

49. $(a + \sqrt{6})(a - 2\sqrt{6})$ **50.** $(\sqrt[3]{a} + \sqrt[3]{b})(\sqrt[3]{a^2} - \sqrt[3]{ab} + \sqrt[3]{b^2})$

51. Show that the triangle in the lesson introduction is a right triangle.

C | **Show that the given number is a root of the given equation. Substitute and simplify.**

52. $2 + \sqrt[3]{4}; x^3 = 12 + 12\sqrt[3]{4} + 12\sqrt[3]{2}$ **53.** $1 + \sqrt{2}; x^3 - 5x^2 + 5x + 3 = 0$

54. Show that $\sqrt{\sqrt[3]{a}} = \sqrt[3]{\sqrt{a}}$ for $a \geqslant 0$.   **55.** Show that $\sqrt[3]{\sqrt{b}} \cdot \sqrt[3]{\sqrt{b}} = \sqrt[3]{b}$ for $b \geqslant 0$.
[*Hint:* See Exercise 54.]

 EVIEW EXERCISES

1. State whether each relation defines a function.   [3-2]

    a. $\{(x, y): y = x^2\}$ **b.** $\{(x, y): y^2 = x\}$ **c.** $\{(x, y): y = \sqrt{x}\}$

2. Find the slope and y-intercept of $3x + 2y = 12$.   [3-3]

3. Which of the following are linear equations?   [3-3]

    a. $y = \dfrac{x}{2}$ **b.** $y = \dfrac{2}{x}$ **c.** $y = |x|$

4. Write an equation of the line through the origin that is parallel to $2x + 3y = 10$.   [3-4]

5. Write an equation of the line through $(0, 5)$ that is perpendicular to the line   [3-4]
    $y = \dfrac{1}{2}x - 3$.

6. Suppose that y varies directly as x. If $y = 36$ when $x = 12$, what is the value   [3-5]
    of y when $x = 9$?

7. Suppose that y varies directly as the square of x. If $y = 100$ when $x = 5$, what   [3-5]
    is the value of y when $x = 3$?

Let $f(x) = 2x - 3$ and $g(x) = x^2$.   [3-7]

8. $g(f(5)) = \underline{\ \ ?\ \ }$ **9.** $f(g(5)) = \underline{\ \ ?\ \ }$ [3-7]

LESSON 7-4

Dividing Radicals

Before the age of calculators and computers, finding decimal approximations for these two irrational numbers represented different levels of difficulty.

$$\frac{1}{\sqrt{2}} \qquad \frac{\sqrt{2}}{2}$$

In each calculation, the first step was to find an approximation of $\sqrt{2}$ in a table (it is 1.414214). In the calculation $\frac{1}{\sqrt{2}}$, 1 is then divided by 1.414214, a formidable task. Evaluating $\frac{\sqrt{2}}{2}$ as $\frac{1.414214}{2} = 0.707107$ was relatively easy. Since $\frac{1}{\sqrt{2}}$ is equivalent to $\frac{\sqrt{2}}{2}$, mathematicians learned how to transform expressions with radicals in the denominator into equivalent expressions with rational numbers in the denominators in order to simplify the calculations.

Today, these two computations are equally simple using a calculator. However, we still need to know how to transform expressions with radical denominators in order to standardize results and to simplify formulas.

A radical expression is in simplest form if the following conditions are satisfied.

Simplest Form of a Radical with Index n

1. There are no perfect nth powers in the radicand.
2. There are no radicals in the denominator of a fraction.
3. There are no fractions in the radicand.

Lesson 7-2 covered the techniques needed to ensure that condition 1 is satisfied. Now consider condition 2. To write $\frac{1}{\sqrt{7}}$ in simplest form, the denominator must be changed to a rational number. To get a rational denominator, multiply both the numerator and denominator by $\sqrt{7}$. The result is an equivalent expression in simplest form. This process is called **rationalizing the denominator**.

$$\frac{1}{\sqrt{7}} = \frac{1 \cdot \sqrt{7}}{\sqrt{7} \cdot \sqrt{7}}$$
$$= \frac{\sqrt{7}}{7}$$

Example 1 Rationalize the denominator. $\dfrac{1}{\sqrt{x^3}}$, $x > 0$

Solution $\dfrac{1}{\sqrt{x^3}} = \dfrac{1}{x\sqrt{x}} = \dfrac{1 \cdot \sqrt{x}}{x\sqrt{x} \cdot \sqrt{x}} = \dfrac{\sqrt{x}}{x^2}, x > 0$

Example 2 Simplify. $\dfrac{14y}{\sqrt[3]{7y^2}}$, $y \neq 0$

Solution Multiply by an appropriate fraction to make the radicand a perfect cube.

$$\dfrac{14y}{\sqrt[3]{7y^2}} = \dfrac{14y \cdot \sqrt[3]{7^2y}}{\sqrt[3]{7y^2} \cdot \sqrt[3]{7^2y}} = \dfrac{14y \cdot \sqrt[3]{7^2y}}{\sqrt[3]{7^3y^3}} = \dfrac{14y \sqrt[3]{49y}}{7y} = 2\sqrt[3]{49y}, y \neq 0$$

The product of binomials containing square-root radicals can be a rational number.

$$(2 - \sqrt{3})(2 + \sqrt{3}) = 2^2 - (\sqrt{3})^2 = 4 - 3 = 1$$

Binomials of the form $(a + \sqrt{b})$ and $(a - \sqrt{b})$, where a and b are rational numbers, are called **conjugates** of each other. The product of conjugates is a rational number.

$$(a + \sqrt{b})(a - \sqrt{b}) = a^2 - b$$

irrational conjugates   rational number

This property of conjugates can be used to rationalize binomial denominators.

Example 3 Simplify. $\dfrac{3}{1 - \sqrt{2}}$

Solution $\dfrac{3}{1 - \sqrt{2}} = \dfrac{3(1 + \sqrt{2})}{(1 - \sqrt{2})(1 + \sqrt{2})} = \dfrac{3(1 + \sqrt{2})}{1 - 2} = \dfrac{3(1 + \sqrt{2})}{-1} = -3(1 + \sqrt{2})$

Now consider the third condition for a radical to be in simplest form. These examples suggest a division property of radicals that corresponds to the multiplication properties given in Lesson 7-2.

$$\sqrt{\dfrac{36}{9}} = \sqrt{4} = 2 \quad \text{and} \quad \dfrac{\sqrt{36}}{\sqrt{9}} = \dfrac{6}{3} = 2 \quad \text{So,} \quad \sqrt{\dfrac{36}{9}} = \dfrac{\sqrt{36}}{\sqrt{9}}$$

Division Property of Radicals

For all real numbers a and b, $(b \neq 0)$, *for which the radicals are defined* and for each positive integer n,

$$\sqrt[n]{\dfrac{a}{b}} = \dfrac{\sqrt[n]{a}}{\sqrt[n]{b}}.$$

In the above property, if the index n is even, then both a and b must be nonnegative.

Example 4 illustrates two ways of simplifying a fractional radical.

Example 4 **Simplify.** $\sqrt[3]{\dfrac{2}{5}}$

Solution 1   Change to the quotient of two radicals.

$$\sqrt[3]{\frac{2}{5}} = \frac{\sqrt[3]{2}}{\sqrt[3]{5}}$$

$$= \frac{\sqrt[3]{2} \cdot \sqrt[3]{5^2}}{\sqrt[3]{5} \cdot \sqrt[3]{5^2}}$$

$$= \frac{\sqrt[3]{50}}{5}$$

Solution 2   Change to an equivalent fraction with a perfect cube as its denominator.

$$\sqrt[3]{\frac{2}{5}} = \sqrt[3]{\frac{2 \cdot 5^2}{5 \cdot 5^2}}$$

$$= \sqrt[3]{\frac{50}{125}}$$

$$= \frac{\sqrt[3]{50}}{\sqrt[3]{125}}$$

$$= \frac{\sqrt[3]{50}}{5}$$

$\mathcal{C}$LASSROOM EXERCISES

Simplify. State restrictions where necessary.

1. $\dfrac{1}{\sqrt{3}}$
2. $\dfrac{5}{\sqrt[3]{2}}$
3. $\dfrac{1}{\sqrt[3]{2}}$
4. $\dfrac{1}{\sqrt{a^5}}$
5. $\dfrac{3x^2}{\sqrt{x}}$

6. $\dfrac{1}{1+\sqrt{3}}$
7. $\sqrt{\dfrac{3}{4}}$
8. $\sqrt{\dfrac{1}{a}}$
9. $\sqrt[3]{\dfrac{2}{7}}$
10. $\sqrt[3]{\dfrac{1}{y}}$

$\mathcal{W}$RITTEN EXERCISES

A Simplify.

1. $\dfrac{2}{\sqrt{2}}$
2. $\dfrac{3}{\sqrt{3}}$
3. $\dfrac{\sqrt{2}}{\sqrt{6}}$
4. $\dfrac{\sqrt{3}}{\sqrt{6}}$
5. $\dfrac{\sqrt{5}}{\sqrt{6}}$

6. $\dfrac{\sqrt{2}}{\sqrt{5}}$
7. $\sqrt{\dfrac{5}{9}}$
8. $\sqrt{\dfrac{7}{4}}$
9. $\sqrt{\dfrac{16}{3}}$
10. $\sqrt{\dfrac{9}{5}}$

11. $\dfrac{\sqrt{5}}{2\sqrt{3}}$
12. $\dfrac{\sqrt{7}}{3\sqrt{2}}$
13. $\dfrac{\sqrt[3]{3}}{\sqrt[3]{4}}$
14. $\dfrac{\sqrt[3]{11}}{\sqrt[3]{16}}$
15. $\sqrt[3]{\dfrac{15}{64}}$

16. $\sqrt[3]{\dfrac{7}{8}}$
17. $\sqrt[3]{\dfrac{1}{9}}$
18. $\sqrt[3]{\dfrac{3}{4}}$
19. $\dfrac{5}{\sqrt[3]{4}}$
20. $\dfrac{4}{\sqrt[3]{9}}$

21. $\dfrac{\sqrt[3]{18}}{\sqrt[3]{9}}$
22. $\dfrac{\sqrt[3]{20}}{\sqrt[3]{4}}$
23. $\dfrac{5}{3-\sqrt{2}}$
24. $\dfrac{2}{4-\sqrt{3}}$
25. $\sqrt[4]{\dfrac{3}{8}}$

26. $\sqrt[4]{\dfrac{4}{9}}$
27. $\sqrt[5]{\dfrac{20}{81}}$
28. $\sqrt[5]{\dfrac{5}{16}}$
29. $\dfrac{\sqrt[4]{3}}{\sqrt[4]{27}}$
30. $\dfrac{\sqrt[4]{2}}{\sqrt[4]{8}}$

Simplify. State restrictions where necessary.

31. $\dfrac{4}{\sqrt{x^7}}$

32. $\dfrac{2}{\sqrt{x^8}}$

33. $\dfrac{4xy}{\sqrt{x^2y}}$

34. $\dfrac{3xy}{\sqrt{xy^2}}$

35. $\dfrac{10x^2y^2}{\sqrt{5xy^8}}$

36. $\dfrac{12x^2y^2}{\sqrt{3x^2y}}$

37. $\sqrt{\dfrac{5}{x}}$

38. $\sqrt{\dfrac{3}{y}}$

39. $\sqrt{\dfrac{x}{5}}$

40. $\sqrt{\dfrac{y}{7}}$

41. $\dfrac{\sqrt[3]{x}}{\sqrt[3]{y}}$

42. $\dfrac{\sqrt[3]{x^2}}{\sqrt[3]{y^2}}$

43. $\sqrt[3]{\dfrac{3x^2}{5y^4}}$

44. $\sqrt[3]{\dfrac{2x}{25y^5}}$

45. $\sqrt[4]{\dfrac{x}{y^2}}$

46. $\sqrt[4]{\dfrac{x^2}{y}}$

B **47.** $\sqrt[5]{\dfrac{x^4}{y^6}}$

48. $\sqrt[5]{\dfrac{x^8}{y^3}}$

49. $\dfrac{1}{2 - \sqrt{x}}$

50. $\dfrac{3}{5 - \sqrt{x^3}}$

51. $\dfrac{x - y}{\sqrt{x} - \sqrt{y}}$

52. $\sqrt{\dfrac{3}{x + 4}}$

53. $\sqrt{\dfrac{8 - x}{7 + x}}$

54. $\sqrt{\dfrac{y - 2}{y + 1}}$

Example 5 Solve. $2x + \sqrt{2}x = 10$

Solution

$$2x + \sqrt{2}x = 10$$

Combine like terms. $$(2 + \sqrt{2})x = 10$$

Divide both sides by $(2 + \sqrt{2})$.

$$x = \dfrac{10}{2 + \sqrt{2}}$$

Rationalize the denominator.

$$= \dfrac{10(2 - \sqrt{2})}{(2 + \sqrt{2})(2 - \sqrt{2})}$$

Simplify.

$$= \dfrac{10(2 - \sqrt{2})}{4 - 2}$$

$$= \dfrac{10(2 - \sqrt{2})}{2}$$

$$= 5(2 - \sqrt{2})$$

Answer $\{5(2 - \sqrt{2})\}$ or $\{10 - 5\sqrt{2}\}$

Solve.

55. $3x - \sqrt{7}x = 6$

56. $3t + \sqrt{3}t = 18$

57. $\sqrt{7}s - 2s = 12$

58. $\sqrt{11}r - 3r = 26$

59. $5a = \sqrt{7}a + 6$

60. $6y = \sqrt{6}y - 5$

61. $\sqrt{5}p - \sqrt{3}p = 8$

62. $\sqrt{6}b + \sqrt{3}b = 9$

63. $\sqrt{7}k - \sqrt{6} = \sqrt{3}k$

64. $\sqrt{11}j + \sqrt{6} = \sqrt{5}j$

C Explain the difference in the methods of rationalizing each of the denominators of the two expressions.

65. $\dfrac{3}{\sqrt{x-y}}, \dfrac{3}{\sqrt{x}-\sqrt{y}}$

66. $\dfrac{2}{\sqrt[3]{x-1}}, \dfrac{2}{\sqrt[3]{x}-1}$

Replace each expression with a single radical.

67. $\sqrt{\sqrt{2}}$

68. $\sqrt{\sqrt[3]{4}}$

69. $\sqrt{\sqrt[3]{a^2}}$

70. $\sqrt[3]{\sqrt{a^2}}$

71. Compare Exercises 69 and 70. Do the results indicate anything about the order of operations when a radicand is a radical?

72. Use graphs to show the regions of the coordinate plane in which each of these radicals is defined.

a. $\sqrt{\dfrac{y}{x+y}}$

b. $\sqrt{\dfrac{x-y}{x}}$

c. $\sqrt{\dfrac{x-y}{x+y}}$

EVIEW EXERCISES

1. Solve by substitution. $y = 2x + 5$
$3x - 2y = 8$ [4-2]

2. Solve by linear combinations. $3x + 5y = 26$
$2x - 3y = -8$ [4-3]

3. Jane has 35 coins worth a total of $5.00. If the coins consist only of dimes and quarters, how many of them are dimes and how many are quarters?   [4-3]

4. Write D, D_x, and D_y for this system. $4x + y = 10$
$3x - 5y = 0$ [4-4]

5. Graph $x + y \geq -2$ or $y < \dfrac{1}{2}x$.   [4-6]

elf-Quiz 2

7-3 **Simplify.**

1. $\sqrt{128} - \sqrt{32}$

2. $(4 - \sqrt[3]{81}) - (\sqrt{9} + 2\sqrt[3]{24})$

3. $(\sqrt{3} - 5)^2$

4. Is $(1 + \sqrt{2})$ a root of the equation $x^2 - 2x - 1 = 0$?

7-4 **Simplify. State restrictions where necessary.**

5. $\dfrac{\sqrt[3]{2}}{\sqrt[3]{9}}$

6. $\dfrac{2 + \sqrt{6}}{2 - \sqrt{2}}$

7. $-\sqrt{\dfrac{9}{7}}$

8. $\sqrt[3]{\dfrac{a^5}{4b}}$

Solve.

9. $\sqrt{2x} = 1 - 3x$

The Distance Between Two Points

The distance between two points on a horizontal line is the absolute value of the difference between their x-coordinates. The absolute value ensures that the distance is not negative. We write the distance between points E and F as $d(E, F)$ or EF.

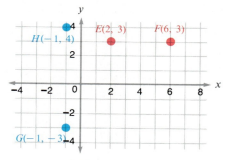

$$EF = |6 - 2| = 4$$

Similarly, the distance between two points on a vertical line is the absolute value of the difference between their y-coordinates.

$$GH = |-3 - 4| = 7$$

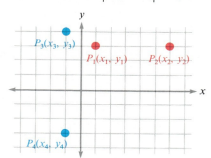

In general, for points $P_1(x_1, y_1)$ and $P_2(x_2, y_2)$, if $y_1 = y_2$, then $P_1P_2 = |x_1 - x_2|$.

For points $P_3(x_3, y_3)$ and $P_4(x_4, y_4)$, if $x_3 = x_4$, then $P_3P_4 = |y_3 - y_4|$.

If two points are not on the same horizontal or vertical line, the Pythagorean theorem is used to find the distance between them.

The Pythagorean Theorem

If a and b are the legs of a right triangle and c is the hypotenuse, then
$$a^2 + b^2 = c^2.$$

Consider two points $P_1(x_1, y_1)$ and $P_2(x_2, y_2)$:

$$(P_1P_2)^2 = |x_2 - x_1|^2 + |y_2 - y_1|^2$$
$$= (x_2 - x_1)^2 + (y_2 - y_1)^2$$

Therefore,

$$P_1P_2 = \sqrt{(x_2 - x_1)^2 + (y_2 - y_1)^2}$$

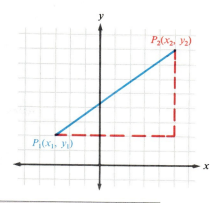

This equation is called the **distance formula**.

The Distance Formula

For points $P_1(x_1, y_1)$ and $P_2(x_2, y_2)$,
$$P_1P_2 = \sqrt{(x_2 - x_1)^2 + (y_2 - y_1)^2}.$$

Example 1   **Find the distance between $A(-2, 5)$ and $B(6, -4)$.**

Solution $AB = \sqrt{(6 - (-2))^2 + (-4 - 5)^2}$
$= \sqrt{8^2 + (-9)^2}$
$= \sqrt{64 + 81}$
$= \sqrt{145}$

Answer   The distance between A and B is $\sqrt{145}$.

Example 2   **Prove that point $M(1, 3)$ is equidistant from point $A(-3, -2)$ and point $B(5, 8)$.**

Solution $MA = \sqrt{(-3 - 1)^2 + (-2 - 3)^2} = \sqrt{16 + 25} = \sqrt{41}$
$MB = \sqrt{(5 - 1)^2 + (8 - 3)^2} = \sqrt{16 + 25} = \sqrt{41}$

Answer $MA = MB$. Therefore, M is equidistant from A and B.

In Example 2, point M is equidistant from points A and B, and is also *on* segment AB $(\overline{AB})$. This means that point M is the **midpoint** of $\overline{AB}$. Note that the x-coordinate of point M is the average of the x-coordinates of the endpoints A and B of the segment. Similarly, the y-coordinate of the midpoint is the average of the y-coordinates of the endpoints. This illustrates the **midpoint formula**.

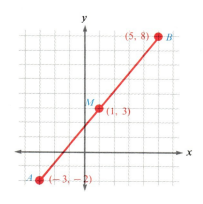

The Midpoint Formula

If the coordinates of point A are (x_1, y_1) and the coordinates of point B are (x_2, y_2), then the coordinates of the midpoint of $\overline{AB}$ are

$$\left(\frac{x_1 + x_2}{2}, \frac{y_1 + y_2}{2} \right).$$

Example 3 Given point $A(0, 3)$ and point $B(6, 6)$, write an equation of the perpendicular bisector of segment AB.

Solution First, find the coordinates of M, the midpoint of $\overline{AB}$.

$$M: \left(\frac{0 + 6}{2}, \frac{3 + 6}{2} \right) = (3, 4.5)$$

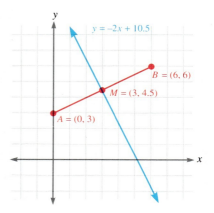

The slope of the perpendicular bisector of segment AB is the negative reciprocal of the slope of $\overline{AB}$.

$$\text{slope of } \overline{AB} = \frac{6 - 3}{6 - 0} = \frac{1}{2}$$

Therefore, the slope of the perpendicular bisector of $\overline{AB}$ is -2.

The equation of the perpendicular bisector is of the form $y = -2x + b$. Since the midpoint $(3, 4.5)$ is on the perpendicular bisector, its coordinates must satisfy the equation.

$$4.5 = -2(3) + b$$
$$10.5 = b$$

Answer $y = -2x + 10.5$

$\mathcal{C}$LASSROOM EXERCISES

1. Given $A(-1, -4)$ and $B(5, 5)$, find AB.

2. What is the distance between the point $(-2, 6)$ and the origin?

3. Use the distance formula to find the distance between (x_1, y_1) and (x_1, y_2).

4. Give the coordinates of the midpoint of the segment joining $C(3, 4)$ and $D(-2, -5)$.

5. The midpoint of a line segment AB is at $C(4, 6)$. If point A has coordinates $(-8, 4)$, find the coordinates of point B.

WRITTEN EXERCISES

A | Find the distance between the points.

1. B and E
2. A and B
3. A and E
4. G and F
5. G and H
6. E and H
7. A and F
8. D and G
9. C and E
10. B and D
11. B and H
12. D and H

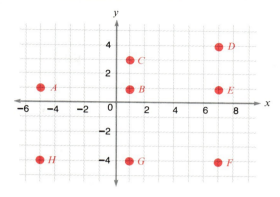

Find the distance between the points.

13. (2, 3) and (4, 0)
14. (4, 2) and (8, 0)
15. (-12, 4) and (12, 11)
16. (6, 8) and (14, -7)
17. (5, 12) and (5, -3)
18. (7, 12) and (-3, 12)
19. (0, 0) and (0.4, 0.3)
20. (0.6, 0.8) and (0, 0)

The vertices of a triangle are given. Determine whether the triangle is isosceles.

21. A(5, 2), B(5, 8), C(10, 5)
22. P(0, 0), Q(5, 12), R(9, 9)
23. S(6, 8), T(0, 0), U(9, 4)
24. D(2, 8), E(4, 8), R(3, 2)

Find the midpoint of the segment joining the two points.

25. A and B
26. C and D
27. A and C
28. B and D
29. C and E
30. B and E

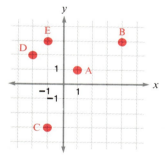

B | Write an equation for the perpendicular bisector of $\overline{AB}$.

31. A(4, 1), B(6, 3)
32. A(2, 2), B(6, 4)
33. A(-4, 1), B(-2, 5)
34. A(0, -2), B(4, -4)

Triangle ABC has vertices A(1, 2), B(3, 8), and C(9, 4).

35. Find the length of sides $\overline{AB}$, $\overline{BC}$, and $\overline{AC}$.
36. What kind of triangle is ABC?
37. E(2, 5) is on side $\overline{AB}$. Find the lengths of $\overline{AE}$ and $\overline{EB}$.
38. How is point E related to side $\overline{AB}$?
39. F(6, 6) is on side $\overline{BC}$. Find the lengths of $\overline{BF}$ and $\overline{FC}$.
40. How is point F related to side $\overline{BC}$?
41. How does the length of $\overline{EF}$ compare to the length of side $\overline{AC}$?

Triangle *DEF* has vertices *D*(2, 1), *E*(10, 7), and *F*(7, 11).

42. Find the length of side $\overline{DF}$.

43. Point *G* is the midpoint of side $\overline{DE}$. Find the coordinates of *G*.

44. Point *H* is the midpoint of side $\overline{EF}$. Find the coordinates of *H*.

45. Find the length of $\overline{GH}$.

46. How does the length of $\overline{GH}$ compare to the length of side $\overline{DF}$?

 47. Describe two ways to determine whether three given points are vertices of a right triangle.

48. **a.** Select one of these methods to determine whether triangle *DEF* described above is a right triangle.

    b. Which method did you use? Why?

49. Triangle *ABC* has vertices $A(x_1, y_1)$, $B(x_2, y_2)$, and $C(x_3, y_3)$. The midpoint of $\overline{AB}$ is point *D* and the midpoint of $\overline{BC}$ is point *E*. Prove that the length of *DE* is one-half the length of side *AC*.

50. $\overline{AB}$ has endpoints $A(x_1, y_1)$ and $B(0, 0)$.

    a. Use the distance formula to express the length of $\overline{AB}$ as a radical.

    b. Write an equation stating that the radical in part (a) equals 5.

    c. Write an equivalent equation for your answer to part (b) without using a radical.

    d. Sketch the graph of all the possible locations of point *A* in the coordinate plane.

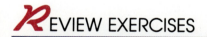
REVIEW EXERCISES

1. Evaluate this determinant.

$$\begin{vmatrix} 3 & 0 & 2 \\ 3 & 2 & -4 \\ 0 & 1 & 5 \end{vmatrix}$$

[4-5]

2. Simplify. Express the result in scientific notation.

$$(4.2 \cdot 10^5)(3 \cdot 10^{10})$$

[5-1]

Expand and simplify.

3. $2x(x - 3) - (x^2 + 4x - 5)$.   [5-2]

4. $(a + 3b)(2a - 5b)$.   [5-3]

Factor completely.

5. $2a^2b + 6ab + 8ab^2$ 6. $ab + 2b + 3a + 6$ [5-4]

7. $4x^2 - 9$ 8. $5a^2 - 5b^2$ [5-5]

9. $x^2 - 5x - 24$ 10. $2x^2 + 5x + 3$ [5-6]

Solve

11. $x^2 + 36 = 12x$ 12. $12 + 3x - x^2 = 0$ [5-7]

LESSON 7-6

Radical Equations

These equations have radicands that contain variables. They are known as **radical equations**.

$$\sqrt{x^2 + 1} - \sqrt{10} = 0 \qquad \sqrt{y + 2} - y = -4$$

If you have a new kind of equation to solve, try to transform it into a form that you already know how to solve. The general strategy is to isolate the radical on one side of the equation. Then raise each side of the equation to the appropriate power in order to eliminate the radical.

For example, to solve the equation: $\sqrt{x + 1} - 2 = 0$

Isolate the radical on one side. $\sqrt{x + 1} = 2$

Then square both sides of the equation to eliminate the radical. $x + 1 = 4$

Then solve. $x = 3$

Squaring both sides of an equation is not an equivalence transformation. Consider the equation $x = 7$. It has one solution, 7. If we square both sides of the equation we get $x^2 = 49$, which has two solutions, 7 and -7. The transformed equation is not equivalent to the original equation.

Because the final equation may have roots that are not roots of the original equation, it is important to check possible roots carefully. The possible root of 3 for the equation $\sqrt{x + 1} - 2 = 0$ given above must be checked.

$$\sqrt{x + 1} - 2 \stackrel{?}{=} 0$$
$$\sqrt{3 + 1} - 2 \stackrel{?}{=} 0$$
$$2 - 2 = 0 \quad \text{It checks. The answer is } \{3\}.$$

Example 1 Solve. $9 + \sqrt{x - 2} = 4$

Solution
$$9 + \sqrt{x - 2} = 4$$
$$\sqrt{x - 2} = -5$$
$$(\sqrt{x - 2})^2 = (-5)^2$$
$$x - 2 = 25$$
$$x = 27$$

Check
$$9 + \sqrt{x - 2} = 4$$
$$9 + \sqrt{27 - 2} \stackrel{?}{=} 4$$
$$9 + \sqrt{25} \stackrel{?}{=} 4$$
$$9 + 5 = 4 \quad \text{False}$$

Answer ∅ (There are no solutions.)

In the solution of Example 1, we might have observed that the equation $\sqrt{x - 2} = -5$ could not have any real roots because the principal square root of a real number is never negative. Since this equation has no real roots, neither does the original equation $9 + \sqrt{x - 2} = 4$.

When the radicals have indexes greater than 2, both sides of the equation should be raised to the appropriate power.

Example 2   Solve. $\sqrt[3]{2x - 1} = -3$

Solution

$$\sqrt[3]{2x - 1} = -3$$

Cube both sides. $(\sqrt[3]{2x - 1})^3 = (-3)^3$

$$2x - 1 = -27$$
$$2x = -26$$
$$x = -13$$

Check $\sqrt[3]{2x - 1} = -3$

$$\sqrt[3]{2(-13) - 1} \overset{?}{=} -3$$
$$\sqrt[3]{-27} \overset{?}{=} -3$$
$$-3 = -3 \quad \text{True}$$

Answer $\{-13\}$

In some situations, you may have to square both sides of the equation more than once to eliminate radicals that contain variables.

Example 3   Solve. $\sqrt{1 + 5y} = 1 + 3\sqrt{y}$

Solution

$$\sqrt{1 + 5y} = 1 + 3\sqrt{y}$$

Square both sides. $1 + 5y = 1 + 6\sqrt{y} + 9y$

Isolate the radical term. $-4y = 6\sqrt{y}$

Simplify. $-2y = 3\sqrt{y}$

Square both sides. $4y^2 = 9y$

Write in standard form. $4y^2 - 9y = 0$

Factor. $y(4y - 9) = 0$

Solve. $y = 0 \quad \text{or} \quad 4y - 9 = 0$

$$y = 0 \quad \text{or} \quad y = \frac{9}{4}$$

Check $\sqrt{1 + 5y} = 1 + 3\sqrt{y}$

$$\sqrt{1 + 5(0)} \overset{?}{=} 1 + 3\sqrt{0}$$

$$1 = 1 \quad \text{True}$$

$\sqrt{1 + 5y} = 1 + 3\sqrt{y}$

$$\sqrt{1 + 5\left(\frac{9}{4}\right)} \overset{?}{=} 1 + 3\sqrt{\frac{9}{4}}$$

$$\sqrt{\frac{49}{4}} \overset{?}{=} 1 + 3\left(\frac{3}{2}\right)$$

$$\frac{7}{2} = 1 + \frac{9}{2} \quad \text{False}$$

Answer $\{0\}$

---

*C*LASSROOM EXERCISES

Solve. If there are no real roots, write Ø.

1. $3 + \sqrt{x + 2} = 0$ **2.** $2x + \sqrt{x} = 3$ **3.** $\sqrt{2x + 1} = 5$ **4.** $\sqrt{t} + \sqrt{t - 2} = 2$

A Solve. If there are no real roots, write ∅.

1. $\sqrt{t - 2} = 3$
2. $\sqrt{t + 4} = 5$
3. $\sqrt{2x + 3} = 4$

4. $\sqrt{2x - 5} = 4$
5. $\sqrt{a + 1} + 3 = 5$
6. $\sqrt{a + 5} + 6 = 10$

7. $\sqrt{2c + 1} + 7 = 3$
8. $\sqrt{3c + 2} + 8 = 5$
9. $p = \sqrt{4p - 3}$

10. $p = \sqrt{6p - 8}$
11. $y = \sqrt{y + 22} - 2$
12. $y = \sqrt{y + 9} - 7$

13. $\sqrt{3 + \sqrt{x + 2}} = 3$
14. $\sqrt{2 + \sqrt{x - 3}} = 2$
15. $\sqrt{5 + \sqrt{a + 2}} = 2$

16. $\sqrt{4 + \sqrt{a + 3}} = 1$
17. $\sqrt{k + \sqrt{3k + 6}} = 2$
18. $\sqrt{k + \sqrt{6k + 1}} = 3$

19. $\sqrt[3]{5x + 7} = 3$
20. $\sqrt[3]{4x - 4} = 2$
21. $\sqrt[3]{3x - 1} + 8 = 4$

22. $\sqrt[3]{2x + 9} + 7 = 6$
23. $\sqrt{5 + \sqrt[3]{6x + 11}} = 2$
24. $\sqrt[3]{21 + \sqrt{5x + 1}} = 3$

B 25. $1 + \sqrt{x} = \sqrt{2x + 2}$
26. $1 + \sqrt{y} = \sqrt{2y + 1}$
27. $\sqrt{2a - 2} - \sqrt{a} = 1$

28. $\sqrt{2t - 7} - \sqrt{t} = 1$
29. $\sqrt{3b + 1} - \sqrt{b - 4} = 3$
30. $\sqrt{2c + 7} - \sqrt{c} = 2$

31. Find all points that have y-coordinate 2 and that are 13 units from the point (4, 14).

32. Find all points that have equal coordinates and that are 13 units from the point (2, −5).

33. Find all points that have opposite coordinates and that are 10 units from the point (0, 2).

Application: Earth's Gravitational Field

The strength (G) of the Earth's gravitational field at various points can be determined by using a physical pendulum and this formula.

$$T = 2\pi \sqrt{\frac{I}{mRG}}$$

34. For a given pendulum $I = 1.25 \cdot 10^6$ g-cm², $m = 500$ g and $R = 50$ cm. At one point on Earth the time T of one vibration is 1.42 s. What is the value of G?

C Solve.

35. $\sqrt{x} + \sqrt{2x + 1} = \sqrt{3x + 13}$
36. $\sqrt{x + 4} + \sqrt{2x + 31} = \sqrt{x + 39}$

37. $\sqrt{4x + 7} + \sqrt{6x + 6} = \sqrt{20x + 26}$
38. $\sqrt{12x + 17} + 2 = \sqrt{3x + 27}$

39. **a.** Find the equation of the set of all points (x, y) that are equidistant from the points (2, 3) and (2, 7)

b. Show that the set of points defined in part (a) is the perpendicular bisector of the segment joining the two given points.

$\mathcal{A}$pplication: Mass

The mass m (in grams) of an object traveling at velocity v (in meters per second) is greater than its mass at rest m_0. This change is usually not noticeable unless an object is traveling at velocities near the speed of light $c \approx 3 \cdot 10^8$ m/s. At such velocities, an object's mass can be determined by the formula:

$$m = \frac{m_0}{\sqrt{1 - \dfrac{v^2}{c^2}}}$$

If the mass of an object at rest is 10 g, find its mass at these velocities.

40. $\dfrac{1}{10}c$ **41.** $\dfrac{1}{3}c$ **42.** $\dfrac{1}{2}c$ **43.** $\dfrac{4}{5}c$ **44.** $\dfrac{99}{100}c$

45. Use your calculator to state decimal approximations for the answer to Exercises 40–44 to the nearest hundredth.

$\mathcal{R}$EVIEW EXERCISES

1. Write without negative exponents. $3x^{-1}y^{-2}$ [6-1]

2. Write without using fractions. $\dfrac{6ab^2}{2a^2c^2}$, $a \neq 0$, $c \neq 0$ [6-1]

Simplify.

3. $\dfrac{x^2 - 3x}{3x}$, $x \neq 0$ **4.** $\dfrac{a^2 - b^2}{a - b}$, $a \neq b$ [6-2]

5. $\dfrac{3ab}{4c} \cdot \dfrac{2c^2}{a}$, $a \neq 0$, $c \neq 0$ **6.** $\dfrac{2a}{3b} \div \dfrac{3c}{4a}$, $a \neq 0$, $b \neq 0$, $c \neq 0$ [6-3]

7. $\dfrac{3}{x} + \dfrac{4}{y}$, $x \neq 0$, $y \neq 0$ **8.** $\dfrac{x - 1}{x} - \dfrac{x + 1}{x^2}$, $x \neq 0$ [6-4]

$\mathcal{S}$elf-Quiz 3

7-5

1. Show that the point $P(3, 1)$ is twice as far from point $A(-7, -5)$ as it is from point $B(8, 4)$.

2. Show that the triangle with vertices $A(2, -2)$, $B(6, 2)$, and $C(4 - 2\sqrt{3}, 2\sqrt{3})$ is equilateral.

3. Find the midpoint of the segment that joins $P(9, 2)$ and $Q(4, -6)$.

7-6   **Solve. If there are no real roots, write $\emptyset$.**

4. $3x - \sqrt{5} = \dfrac{1}{2}$ **5.** $\sqrt{7x} - 3 = 2x$

6. $\sqrt{2y - 3} - 4 = 0$ **7.** $\sqrt[3]{3y - 1} - 2 = 0$

8. $\sqrt{y + 4} - \sqrt{2y - 6} = 1$ **9.** $\sqrt{7 + \sqrt{3x - 5}} = 2$

LESSON 7-7

Rational Exponents

Fractional exponents have been defined so that the addition and multiplication properties of exponents are unchanged. For example, consider the square of $3^{\frac{1}{2}}$.

$$(3^{\frac{1}{2}})^2 = 3^{\frac{1}{2} \cdot 2} = 3^1 = 3$$

Since $3^{\frac{1}{2}}$ is the positive number whose square is 3, then $3^{\frac{1}{2}} = \sqrt{3}$.

If the addition property of exponents is unchanged, then

$$a^{\frac{1}{3}} \cdot a^{\frac{1}{3}} = a^{\frac{2}{3}} \qquad \text{But, } a^{\frac{1}{3}} \cdot a^{\frac{1}{3}} = \sqrt[3]{a} \cdot \sqrt[3]{a} = (\sqrt[3]{a})^2$$

Therefore, $a^{\frac{2}{3}}$ must be defined to equal $(\sqrt[3]{a})^2$. In general, rational exponents are defined as follows.

Definition: Unit Fraction Exponents

For each real number a for which the radical represents a real number, and for each positive integer n,

$$a^{\frac{1}{n}} = \sqrt[n]{a}.$$

Definition: Rational Exponents

For all positive integers m and n, and all real numbers a for which the radical represents a real number,

$$a^{\frac{m}{n}} = (\sqrt[n]{a})^m = \sqrt[n]{a^m}.$$

All properties of exponents previously developed for integer exponents can be shown to hold for rational exponents.

Properties of Rational Exponents

For all rational numbers r and s and all real numbers a and b, $a \neq 0$, $b \neq 0$, the following properties hold.

Addition property	$a^r a^s = a^{r+s}$
Subtraction property	$\dfrac{a^r}{a^s} = a^{r-s}$
Distributive property of raising to a power over multiplication	$(ab)^r = a^r b^r$
Multiplication property	$(a^r)^s = a^{rs}$

Example 1   Write in exponential notation.

      a. $\sqrt{7}$ **b.** $\dfrac{1}{\sqrt[5]{10}}$ **c.** $\sqrt[3]{2x}$ **d.** $\sqrt[5]{2x-1}$

Solutions **a.** $\sqrt{7} = 7^{\frac{1}{2}}$ **b.** $\dfrac{1}{\sqrt[5]{10}} = 10^{-\frac{1}{5}}$ **c.** $\sqrt[3]{2x} = (2x)^{\frac{1}{3}}$ **d.** $\sqrt[5]{2x-1} = (2x-1)^{\frac{1}{5}}$

Example 2   Write as a radical expression in simplest form.

      a. $3m^{\frac{1}{2}}, m \geqslant 0$ **b.** $6^{-\frac{1}{3}}$ **c.** $(x-1)^{\frac{1}{7}}$

Solutions **a.** $3m^{\frac{1}{2}} = 3\sqrt{m}, m \geqslant 0$ **b.** $6^{-\frac{1}{3}} = \dfrac{1}{6^{\frac{1}{3}}} = \dfrac{1}{\sqrt[3]{6}}$ or $\dfrac{\sqrt[3]{36}}{6}$ **c.** $(x-1)^{\frac{1}{7}} = \sqrt[7]{x-1}$

Example 3   Simplify.

      a. $25^{\frac{1}{2}}$ **b.** $(-8)^{\frac{1}{3}}$ **c.** $4^{-\frac{1}{2}}$

Solutions **a.** $25^{\frac{1}{2}} = \sqrt{25} = 5$ **b.** $(-8)^{\frac{1}{3}} = \sqrt[3]{-8} = -2$ **c.** $4^{-\frac{1}{2}} = \dfrac{1}{4^{\frac{1}{2}}} = \dfrac{1}{\sqrt{4}} = \dfrac{1}{2}$

Example 4   Write in radical form. $7^{\frac{3}{4}}$

Solution $7^{\frac{3}{4}} = (\sqrt[4]{7})^3 = \sqrt[4]{7^3}$

Example 5   Simplify. $(\sqrt{5})^{\frac{2}{3}}$

Solution Since $\sqrt{5}$ is positive, $(\sqrt{5})^{\frac{2}{3}} = (5^{\frac{1}{2}})^{\frac{2}{3}}$

$$= 5^{\frac{1}{2} \cdot \frac{2}{3}} = 5^{\frac{1}{3}} = \sqrt[3]{5}.$$

    Expressions can be transformed to equivalent expressions by simplifying fractional exponents or by changing them to a mixed-number form.

Example 6   Write as a radical expression in simplest form. $2x^{\frac{9}{4}}, x \geqslant 0$

Solution 1 $2x^{\frac{9}{4}} = 2\sqrt[4]{x^9}$

              $= 2x^2\sqrt[4]{x}, x \geqslant 0$

Solution 2 $2x^{\frac{9}{4}} = 2x^{2\frac{1}{4}}$

              $= 2x^{(2+\frac{1}{4})}$

              $= 2x^2 \cdot x^{\frac{1}{4}}$

              $= 2x^2\sqrt[4]{x}, x \geqslant 0$

Write in exponential form.

1. $\sqrt{3}$

2. $\sqrt[3]{a}$

3. $(\sqrt[3]{6})^2$

Write in radical form. Simplify, if possible.

4. $2^{\frac{1}{5}}$

5. $-32^{\frac{1}{4}}$

6. $x^{\frac{4}{3}}$

RITTEN EXERCISES

 Write in the form 2^r, where r is a rational number.

1. $\sqrt[3]{2}$

2. $\sqrt{2}$

3. $\sqrt{2^3}$

4. $\sqrt[3]{2^2}$

5. $\dfrac{1}{\sqrt{2}}$

6. $\dfrac{1}{\sqrt[3]{2}}$

7. $\dfrac{1}{\sqrt[7]{2^{13}}}$

8. $\dfrac{1}{\sqrt[5]{2^{11}}}$

Write in exponential form.

9. $\sqrt[4]{3}$

10. $\sqrt[6]{10}$

11. $\sqrt[3]{-5}$

12. $\sqrt[5]{-3}$

13. $\sqrt[5]{13^3}$

14. $\sqrt[7]{5^2}$

15. $\dfrac{1}{\sqrt[3]{3^4}}$

16. $\dfrac{1}{\sqrt[8]{11^7}}$

Write in radical form. Simplify, if possible.

17. $3^{\frac{1}{2}}$

18. $5^{\frac{1}{2}}$

19. $64^{\frac{1}{3}}$

20. $8^{\frac{1}{3}}$

21. $7^{-\frac{1}{4}}$

22. $11^{-\frac{1}{5}}$

23. $-2^{-\frac{1}{3}}$

24. $-4^{-\frac{1}{3}}$

Write as radical expressions in simplest form. Assume all variables are nonnegative.

25. $x^{\frac{4}{3}}$

26. $x^{\frac{5}{4}}$

27. $3x^{\frac{5}{2}}$

28. $3x^{\frac{3}{2}}$

29. $2y^{\frac{2}{4}}$

30. $5y^{\frac{4}{8}}$

31. $2a^{\frac{6}{5}}$

32. $3a^{\frac{7}{3}}$

Simplify.

33. $64^{\frac{1}{2}}$

34. $16^{\frac{1}{4}}$

35. $9^{\frac{3}{2}}$

36. $8^{\frac{2}{3}}$

37. $27^{\frac{2}{3}}$

38. $81^{\frac{3}{4}}$

39. $\dfrac{1}{\sqrt[4]{4^2}}$

40. $\dfrac{1}{\sqrt[3]{8^2}}$

41. $\sqrt[4]{5^5}$

42. $\sqrt[3]{5^4}$

43. $\sqrt[5]{7^7}$

44. $\sqrt[6]{7^7}$

B Write in the form 5^r, where r is a rational number.

45. $(\sqrt{5})^7$ **46.** $(\sqrt[3]{5})^7$ **47.** $\sqrt[3]{25}$ **48.** $\sqrt{125}$

49. $\dfrac{1}{5}$ **50.** 1 **51.** $\dfrac{1}{\sqrt{5}}$ **52.** $\dfrac{1}{\sqrt[3]{25}}$

Write in simplest radical form. State restrictions where necessary.

53. $x^{\frac{1}{3}}$ **54.** $x^{-\frac{1}{2}}$ **55.** $x^{\frac{7}{2}}$

56. $x^{-\frac{3}{8}}$ **57.** $25x^{\frac{3}{2}}$ **58.** $(25x)^{\frac{3}{2}}$

59. $\left(\dfrac{8}{x}\right)^{-\frac{1}{2}}$ **60.** $8x^{\frac{2}{3}}$ **61.** $(2-x)^{\frac{1}{2}}$

62. $(3-x)^{-\frac{1}{2}}$ **63.** $(1-2x)^{\frac{1}{4}}$ **64.** $(5+4x)^{-\frac{2}{3}}$

C **65.** Which is larger, $\sqrt[3]{4}$ or $\sqrt{3}$? [*Hint:* Change the radicals to equivalent radicals with the same index.]

66. Simplify $\dfrac{\sqrt{6}}{\sqrt[4]{2}}$. **67.** Simplify $\dfrac{x-36}{\sqrt{x}-6}$.

68. Write in simplest form.
$$\sqrt[n]{x^n y^{n+2} z^{3n}},\ n>0,\ x\geq 0,\ y\geq 0,\ z\geq 0$$

REVIEW EXERCISES

Solve.

1. $\dfrac{1}{10}+\dfrac{1}{x}=\dfrac{1}{2}$ **2.** $\dfrac{10}{x-1}+\dfrac{1}{1-x}=1, x\neq 1$ [6-5]

3. The total resistance of a circuit consisting of two resistances connected in parallel is 100 ohms. If one of the resistances is 500 ohms, what is the other? $\left(\dfrac{1}{R}=\dfrac{1}{r_1}+\dfrac{1}{r_2}\right)$ [6-6]

4. One painter takes 6 h to paint a room and another painter takes 8 h to paint the same room. How long will it take both of them working together to paint the room? [6-6]

5. If y varies inversely as x and the value of $y=10$ when $x=3$, what is the value of y when $x=5$? [6-7]

6. If y varies inversely as the square of x and $y=4$ when $x=5$, what is the value of y when $x=2$? [6-7]

298 Chapter 7 Radicals and Irrationals

HAPTER SUMMARY

▶ **Vocabulary**

▶ For all real numbers a and b, and all positive integers n, if $a^n = b$, then a is the nth root of b. A positive nth root of b is written $\sqrt[n]{b}$ and a negative nth root of b is written $-\sqrt[n]{b}$.   [7-1]

▶ For each real number a and each positive integer n,
  if n is odd, then $\sqrt[n]{a^n} = a$; if n is even, then $\sqrt[n]{a^n} = |a|$.   [7-2]

▶ **The Multiplication Property of Radicals**   [7-2]
  For all real numbers a and b for which the radicals are defined and all positive integers n, $\sqrt[n]{ab} = \sqrt[n]{a} \cdot \sqrt[n]{b}$.

▶ **The Division Property of Radicals**   [7-4]
  For all real numbers a and b, $b \neq 0$, for which the radicals are defined, and
  for each positive integer n,

$$\sqrt[n]{\frac{a}{b}} = \frac{\sqrt[n]{a}}{\sqrt[n]{b}}.$$

▶ **The Distance Formula**   [7-5]
  For points $P_1(x_1, y_1)$ and $P_2(x_2, y_2)$, $P_1P_2 = \sqrt{(x_2 - x_1)^2 + (y_2 - y_1)^2}$.

▶ If the coordinates of point A are (x_1, y_1) and the coordinates of point B are (x_2, y_2), then the coordinates of the *midpoint* of $\overline{AB}$ are $\left(\dfrac{x_1 + x_2}{2}, \dfrac{y_1 + y_2}{2}\right)$.   [7-5]

▶ For all positive integers m and n, and all real numbers a for which the radical represents a real number, $a^{\frac{m}{n}} = (\sqrt[n]{a})^m = \sqrt[n]{a^m}$.   [7-7]

CHAPTER REVIEW

7-1 **Objective:** To recognize and write rational and irrational numbers.

1. State whether each is a rational number.

   a. $\sqrt[3]{-50}$ b. $-\sqrt{\dfrac{49}{4}}$ c. $-\sqrt{-36}$

2. Simplify.

   a. $\sqrt[5]{243}$ b. $-\sqrt{169}$ c. $\sqrt[3]{\dfrac{8}{27}}$

3. Find a rational approximation to the nearest tenth.
   a. $\sqrt{60}$ b. $\sqrt[3]{19}$

7-2 **Objective:** To simplify radicals.

Simplify, stating any necessary restrictions.

4. $\sqrt{180}$ 5. $\sqrt{4x^2y^3}$

6. $\sqrt[3]{\dfrac{56a^5b^4}{27c^6}}$ 7. $\sqrt{15x} \cdot \sqrt{35xy}$

7-3 **Objective:** To compute with radicals.

Simplify.

8. $\sqrt{45} + \sqrt{20} - \sqrt{80}$ 9. $(3\sqrt[3]{16} - 2) - (1 - \sqrt[3]{128})$

10. $(\sqrt{12} + 3)(\sqrt{18} - 1)$

11. State whether $3 - \sqrt{7}$ is a root of the equation $x^2 - 6x + 2 = 0$.

7-4 **Objectives:** To rationalize denominators of rational expressions.
To write quotients of radicals in simplest form.

Write in simplest radical form.

12. $\dfrac{5}{\sqrt[3]{16}}$ 13. $\dfrac{6ab^2}{\sqrt{2ab}}, \ a > 0, \ b > 0$

14. $\dfrac{5\sqrt{x}}{1 + \sqrt{x}}, \ x \geqslant 0, \ x \neq 1$

Write in simplest form, stating any necessary restrictions.

15. $\sqrt[3]{\dfrac{3}{4}}$ 16. $\dfrac{\sqrt{5x^3}}{\sqrt{12y}}$

Solve, writing roots in simplest form.

17. $\sqrt{3}y = 1 + 2y$ 18. $2x^2 - 7 = 0$

7-5 **Objective:** To apply the formula for the distance between two points and the midpoint formula.

19. Find the distance between points $S(-3, 1)$ and $T(5, 4)$.

20. The vertices of a triangle are $A(4, -2)$, $B(-5, 0)$, and $C(-2, 5)$. Which sides of triangle ABC are congruent?

21. Find the coordinates of the midpoint of the segment joining the points $P(2, 3)$ and $Q(-6, 4)$.

7-6 **Objective:** To solve equations containing radicals.

Solve.

22. $1 + \sqrt{5x} = 4$ **23.** $\sqrt[3]{x + 3} - 1 = 2$ **24.** $\sqrt{3x - 3} = 1 - \sqrt{x}$

7-7 **Objective:** To interpret rational-number exponents.
To write radical expressions in exponential form and vice versa.

Write, using rational exponents.

25. $\dfrac{5}{\sqrt[5]{6}}$

26. $\sqrt[3]{(8a)^2}$

27. $(\sqrt[4]{49xy^3})^2$, $x \geq 0$, $y \geq 0$

Write as a radical in simplest form, stating any necessary restrictions.

28. $(x^2 - 4)^{\frac{1}{2}}$ **29.** $12^{\frac{2}{3}}$ **30.** $4a^{\frac{7}{4}}$

$\mathcal{C}$HAPTER 7 SELF-TEST

7-1 **1.** Identify the number as rational, irrational, or not real.

  a. $-\sqrt[5]{-1}$ **b.** $\sqrt[4]{-\dfrac{64}{81}}$ **c.** $-\sqrt{18}$

2. Find a rational approximation for $\sqrt[3]{29}$ to the nearest tenth.   3.1

7-2 **Simplify, if possible.**

  3. $\sqrt[3]{24}$ **4.** $-\sqrt{50}$ **5.** $\sqrt{x^2 - y^2}$

Simplify, stating any necessary restrictions.

  6. $\sqrt[3]{a^{14}b^9}$ **7.** $\sqrt{12x} \cdot \sqrt{6x^3}$

7-3 **Simplify.**

  8. $\sqrt[3]{54} - \sqrt{32} - \sqrt[3]{16} + \sqrt{98}$ **9.** $3\sqrt{2}(\sqrt{32} - \sqrt{48})$

  10. State whether $(1 - \sqrt{5})$ is a root of $x^2 - 2x - 4 = 0$.

7-4 **Write in simplest form. State restrictions where necessary.**

11. $-\dfrac{6}{2\sqrt{18}}$

12. $\dfrac{15xy}{\sqrt[3]{25x^3y}}$

13. $\sqrt[5]{-\dfrac{1}{8a^3}}$

14. $\sqrt{\dfrac{3x^2}{x-1}}$

7-5 **15.** Find the distance between points $P(-1, 4)$ and $Q(-6, -6)$.

16. Find the coordinates of the midpoint of the segment joining $S(1, 7)$ and $T(-2, -3)$.

7-6 **Solve. Express the answer in simplest form.**

17. $\sqrt{3} - \sqrt{5x} = x$

18. $\sqrt[3]{2x^2 - 15} = 1$

19. $\sqrt{x + 2} = 3 + \sqrt{x}$

7-7 **20.** Express $\dfrac{1}{\sqrt[3]{7^2}}$ in exponential form.

21. Express $(x + 1)^{\frac{4}{3}}$ in simplest radical form.

Simplify.

22. $(\sqrt[4]{8})^3$

23. $\sqrt[3]{(-27)^2}$

$\mathcal{P}$RACTICE FOR COLLEGE ENTRANCE TESTS

Each question consists of two quantities, one in column A and one in column B. Compare the two quantities and select one of the following answers:

　A if the quantity in column A is greater;
　B if the quantity in column B is greater;
　C if the two quantities are equal;
　D if the relationship cannot be determined from the information given.

Comments:

▶ Letters such as a, b, x, and y are variables that can be replaced by real numbers.

▶ A symbol that appears in both columns in a question stands for the same thing in column A as in column B.

▶ In some questions, information that applies to quantities in both columns is centered in the two columns.

	Column A	Column B
1.	$\sqrt[3]{3}$	$\sqrt{2}$
2.	$\dfrac{1}{2 - \sqrt{2}}$	$\dfrac{2 + \sqrt{2}}{2}$
3.	$x > 0$ $\sqrt{x}$	$\dfrac{x}{2}$

	Column A	Column B
4.	$a > 0, b > 0$	
	$\sqrt{a+b}$	$\sqrt{a} + \sqrt{b}$
5.	The diagonal of a square with side 2	3
6.	The hypotenuse of a right triangle with legs 1 and 4	The hypotenuse of a right triangle with legs 2 and 3
7.	$\sqrt{0.01}$	$\sqrt[3]{0.001}$
8.	$0 < x < 1$	
	x	$\sqrt{x}$
9.	$a < 0 < b$	
	a^2	b^2
10.	$\sqrt{x^6}$	$\lvert x^3 \rvert$
11.	$x + y = 10$ $\sqrt{xy} = 3$	
	$\sqrt{x} + \sqrt{y}$	4
12.	$a > 1$	
	a^{-3}	$a^{-\frac{1}{3}}$
13.	For questions 13 and 14, refer to the following definition of $\boxed{x}$, where x is any real number. $\boxed{x} = x^2 + x + 1$	
	1	$\boxed{-1}$
14.	0	$\boxed{x}$
15.	$2y = 16 - 2x$	
	The average (mean) of x and y	4
16.	The smaller circle is tangent to the four sides of the square. The larger circle contains all vertices of the square.	
	The area of the smaller circle	The area of the shaded region between the circle

CHAPTER 8

Quadratic Functions and Complex Numbers

A complex number is a linear combination of the real number 1 and the nonreal number $\sqrt{-1}$. For example $4(1) + 3(\sqrt{-1})$ is a complex number. Complex numbers have applications in many fields including electronics and nuclear physics.

Complex numbers can be graphed by using the real part as the first component and the nonreal part as the second component.

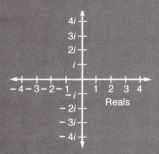

The above photograph is a computer generated graph of a set of complex numbers called the Mandelbrot set, named for Benoit B. Mandelbrot, who discovered it. The Mandelbrot set has been called the most complex object in mathematics.

LESSON 8-1

Quadratic Equations

One problem facing designers of highways is to determine the maximum speed limits for curved entrance and exit ramps. The force on the turning car can be expressed by the formula

$$F = \frac{Wv^2}{32r}$$

When we substitute values for the acceptable force F, the weight W of a car, and the turning radius r, the formula becomes a quadratic equation that can be used to find the maximum velocity v at which the car can go through the turn without skidding.

A **general quadratic equation** in x has the form $ax^2 + bx + c = 0$ $(a \neq 0)$. Any quadratic equation can be transformed into this form and is then said to be written in **standard form.** For example,

Quadratic: $x^2 = x + 2 \rightarrow x^2 - x - 2 = 0; a = 1, b = -1, c = -2$

Not
Quadratic: $(x + 2)^2 = x^2 \rightarrow 0x^2 + 4x + 4 = 0; a = 0$

A quadratic equation with no x-term, like $2x^2 - 50 = 0$, is called a **pure quadratic equation.** Any pure quadratic equation that has real roots can be solved by factoring and by using the zero-product property. For example, consider the equation $x^2 = k$, where $k \geqslant 0$.

$$x^2 = k$$
$$x^2 - k = 0$$
$$x^2 - \left(\sqrt{k}\right)^2 = 0$$
$$\left(x - \sqrt{k}\right)\left(x + \sqrt{k}\right) = 0$$
$$x = \sqrt{k} \text{ or } x = -\sqrt{k}$$

The last sentence is often abbreviated:

$x = \pm \sqrt{k}$ ("x equals the positive or negative square root of k").

This example leads to the following property.

The Square Root Property of Equations

For all real numbers m and n, $n \geqslant 0$,

$$\text{if } m^2 = n, \text{ then } m = \pm \sqrt{n}.$$

This property can be used directly to solve any pure quadratic equation. Some other quadratic equations may be given in a form that permits the same solution process to be used.

Example 1   Solve. $x^2 - 12 = 0$

Solution $x^2 - 12 = 0$

$$x^2 = 12$$

$$x = \pm\sqrt{12} = \pm 2\sqrt{3}$$

Answer $\{\pm 2\sqrt{3}\}$ (The roots are $2\sqrt{3}$ and $-2\sqrt{3}$.)

Example 2   Solve. $(x + 3)^2 = 7$

Solution $(x + 3)^2 = 7$

$$x + 3 = \pm\sqrt{7}$$

$$x = -3 \pm \sqrt{7}$$

Answer $\{-3 \pm \sqrt{7}\}$ (The roots are $-3 + \sqrt{7}$ and $-3 - \sqrt{7}$.)

The equation in Example 2 is not a pure quadratic equation. Expressing the equation in standard form, we have:

$$(1) \qquad (x + 3)^2 = 7$$

$$(2) \quad x^2 + 6x + 9 = 7$$

$$(3) \quad x^2 + 6x + 2 = 0 \,(\text{standard form})$$

Equation 3 is not factorable over the rational numbers. However, the example shows that such an equation can be solved if it can be written in the following form:

$$(x + d)^2 = k$$

This form requires the left side of the equation to be the square of a binomial and the right side to be a constant. The procedure used to produce this form is called **completing the square.**

Example 3   Solve. $x^2 - 6x + 4 = 0$

Solution   The left side of the equation is not a perfect square. First, change it into a perfect square and then solve.

Remove the constant from the left side.	$x^2 - 6x = -4$
Add the number to both sides that makes the left side a perfect square. (Complete the square.)	$x^2 - 6x + 9 = -4 + 9$
Factor and simplify.	$(x - 3)^2 = 5$
Apply the square root property of equations.	$x - 3 = \pm\sqrt{5}$
Solve.	$x = 3 \pm \sqrt{5}$

Answer $\{3 \pm \sqrt{5}\}$ (The roots are $3 + \sqrt{5}$ and $3 - \sqrt{5}$.)

Example 4 Solve by completing the square. $2x^2 - 16x + 9 = 0$.

Solution   *Multiply both sides of the equation by $\frac{1}{2}$, so that the coefficient of x^2 is 1.*

$$x^2 - 8x + \frac{9}{2} = 0$$

Isolate the x^2 and x-terms on the left side of the equation.

$$x^2 - 8x = -\frac{9}{2}$$

Complete the square by adding 16 (the square of half the coefficient of x) to both sides.

$$x^2 - 8x + 16 = -\frac{9}{2} + 16$$

Factor, simplify, and solve for x.

$$(x - 4)^2 = \frac{23}{2}$$

$$x - 4 = \pm \sqrt{\frac{23}{2}}$$

$$x - 4 = \pm \frac{\sqrt{46}}{2}$$

$$x = 4 \pm \frac{\sqrt{46}}{2}$$

Answer $\left\{ 4 \pm \dfrac{\sqrt{46}}{2} \right\}$

*C*LASSROOM EXERCISES

State whether the equation is quadratic.

1. $2x^2 + x = x^2 + 3$

2. $(x - 1)^2 = x^2 + 5x$

Solve by applying the square root property of equations.

3. $y^2 - 3 = 0$

4. $(a - 2)^2 = 8$

Solve by completing the square.

5. $x^2 + 6x - 5 = 0$

6. $3x^2 - 2x - 6 = 0$

Solve.

7. A rectangle is 4 m longer than it is wide. Find the dimensions of the rectangle if its area is 117 m².

*W*RITTEN EXERCISES

 A **Write each equation in standard form. Then state whether the equation is quadratic.**

1. $(x + 3)^2 = (x - 1)^2$ **2.** $(x - 4)^2 = (x + 2)^2$ **3.** $(2x + 3)^2 = 2x^2 + 3$ **4.** $(3x + 2)^2 = 3x^2 + 5$
5. $x^2 + 3x = 3x + 5$ **6.** $x^2 + 2x = 2x - 6$ **7.** $(2r + 3)^2 = (r + 1)^2$ **8.** $(2n + 3)^2 = (n - 2)^2$

Write the equation in the form $(x + d)^2 = k$, where d and k are constants.

9. $x^2 + 6x + 9 = 0$ 10. $x^2 + 4x + 4 = 5$ 11. $x^2 + 8x = 5$ 12. $x^2 + 2x = 20$

13. $x^2 - 4x + 2 = 0$ 14. $x^2 - 10x + 7 = 0$ 15. $2x^2 = 8x - 8$ 16. $2x^2 = 5 - 3x$

Solve. If there is no real-number solution, write $\emptyset$.

17. $(a + 3)(a - 2) = 1$ 18. $(b - 2)(b + 2) = b$ 19. $k^2 - 7 = 0$

20. $x^2 - 6 = 0$ 21. $(t - 2)^2 = 5$ 22. $(v - 3)^2 = 2$

23. $(x + 3)^2 = -1$ 24. $(y + 2)^2 = -4$ 25. $d^2 + 10d + 25 = 10$

26. $h^2 - 10h + 25 = 15$ 27. $a^2 - 6a + 9 = -3$ 28. $b^2 - 8b + 16 = -5$

29. $c^2 + 6c = 11$ 30. $g^2 + 8g = 16$ 31. $x^2 - 9x = -7$

32. $x^2 - 3x = -1$ 33. $t^2 + 7t + 4 = 0$ 34. $w^2 - 7w + 8 = 0$

𝓐pplications

Write an equation for each problem. Solve the equation and answer the question.

35. A rectangle is 4 m longer than it is wide. What are its dimensions if the area of the rectangle is 6 m²?

36. One positive number is 6 more than another positive number. What are the two numbers if their product is 9?

37. The parallel bases of a trapezoid are, respectively, 5 cm longer than the height and 11 cm longer than the height. Find the lengths of the parallel bases if the area of the trapezoid $\left(A = \frac{1}{2}h(b_1 + b_2) \right)$ is 3 cm².

38. A parallelogram with an area of 8 cm² has a base that is 4 cm longer than its height. Find the length of the base.

B Solve.

39. $2 - 5x - x^2 = 0$ 40. $9x + 3 = x^2$ 41. $5x^2 + 7x + 2 = 0$

42. $4x^2 + 6x - 1 = 0$ 43. $2x^2 + 6x - 3 = 0$ 44. $3x^2 + 6x - 4 = 0$

45. $3x^2 + 5x + 1 = 0$ 46. $x(2x + 3) = 1$ 47. $7x(x - 1) = 5 - x$

48. $\dfrac{x^2}{2} - x - 2 = 0$ 49. $\dfrac{x^2}{4} + \dfrac{x}{2} - 3 = 0$ 50. $\dfrac{2x^2}{3} + \dfrac{x}{2} - 2 = 0$

𝓐pplications

Write an equation for each problem. Solve the equation and answer the question.

51. The base of a triangle is 2 cm greater than the altitude. What is the base if the area of the triangle is 5 cm²?

52. The side of a square is 4 cm longer than the side of a smaller square. The sum of the areas of the squares is 17 cm². What are the lengths of the sides of the squares?

53. One leg of a right triangle is 35 cm shorter than the other. The hypotenuse is 10 cm longer than the longer leg. What are the dimensions of the triangle?

54. One leg of a right triangle is 1 cm longer than the other and the hypotenuse is 3 cm longer than the shorter leg. What is the perimeter of the triangle?

 𝒜pplication: Turning Velocity

The formula $F = \dfrac{Wv^2}{32r}$ can be used to find the maximum velocity v (in feet per second) at which a car weighing W pounds can go through a turn of radius r feet without skidding. For a 2000-lb, rubber-tired car on dry concrete, $F = 1400$.

Find the maximum velocity for turns of the given radius.

55. 35 ft   **56.** 140 ft

57. 78.75 ft   **58.** 560 ft

59. Can a speeding car weighing 2000 lb safely go 60 mph through an unbanked turn with a radius of 300 ft? [*Hint:* 60 mph = 88 ft/s.]

60. A square is inscribed in a semicircle of radius r as shown. Show that segment
$$a = \left(1 - \frac{\sqrt{5}}{5}\right)r.$$

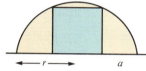

ℛEVIEW EXERCISES

1. Write $0.\overline{14}$ as a fraction.   [1-1]

For each equation below, state the corresponding property of real numbers.   [1-4]

2. $(236 \cdot 25) \cdot 4 = 236 \cdot (25 \cdot 4)$ **3.** $1 + 1776 = 1776 + 1$

4. $237 \cdot 49 + 237 \cdot 51 = 237(49 + 51)$ **5.** $\sqrt{2} \cdot 1 = \sqrt{2}$

6. $\sqrt{5} - \sqrt{5} = 0$ [1-5]

x	2	4	6	8
Q	8	14	20	26

7. Write Q in terms of x.   [1-6]

8. Use the variable n to write an expression for the nth term of this sequence.   [1-6]
$$-1, 1, -1, 1, -1, 1, \ldots$$

9. Fill in the missing reasons for this shortcut in computation.   [1-7]

$$
\begin{aligned}
(992 + 187) + 8 &= (187 + 992) + 8 &&\underline{\qquad ? \qquad} \\
&= 187 + (992 + 8) &&\underline{\qquad ? \qquad} \\
&= 187 + 1000 &&\text{Computation} \\
&= 1187 &&\text{Computation}
\end{aligned}
$$

LESSON 8-2

The Quadratic Formula

Completing the square can be used to solve quadratic equations such as:

$$\frac{9}{4}x^2 + \frac{3}{17}x + \pi = 0$$

$$1037w^2 - 65w + 14 = 0$$

$$\sqrt{7}y^2 - 2y - 10.49 = 0$$

However, individual steps might be computationally difficult. The mathematician seeks ways to apply algebra to solve equations of the same type efficiently. A general formula that can be applied to any quadratic equation makes the task of solving the equations above much simpler.

Every quadratic equation in one variable can be written in the form $ax^2 + bx + c = 0$, where a, b, and c are real numbers, $a \neq 0$. When that general equation is solved by completing the square, the result is a formula for the roots of every quadratic equation.

$$ax^2 + bx + c = 0$$

Multiply both sides by $\frac{1}{a}$.

$$x^2 + \frac{b}{a}x + \frac{c}{a} = 0$$

Add $-\frac{c}{a}$ to both sides.

$$x^2 + \frac{b}{a}x = -\frac{c}{a}$$

Complete the square.

$$x^2 + \frac{b}{a}x + \frac{b^2}{4a^2} = -\frac{c}{a} + \frac{b^2}{4a^2}$$

Factor and simplify.

$$\left(x + \frac{b}{2a}\right)^2 = \frac{b^2 - 4ac}{4a^2}$$

Apply the square root property of equations.

$$x + \frac{b}{2a} = \pm\sqrt{\frac{b^2 - 4ac}{4a^2}}$$

Simplify.

$$x + \frac{b}{2a} = \pm\frac{\sqrt{b^2 - 4ac}}{2a}$$

Add $-\frac{b}{2a}$ to both sides.

$$x = -\frac{b}{2a} \pm \frac{\sqrt{b^2 - 4ac}}{2a}$$

Simplify.

$$x = \frac{-b \pm \sqrt{b^2 - 4ac}}{2a}$$

The equation in the last step is a formula for the roots of any quadratic equation in one variable in terms of its coefficients a, b, and c when expressed in standard form.

The Quadratic Formula

The roots of $ax^2 + bx + c = 0$, $a \neq 0$, are:

$$\frac{-b + \sqrt{b^2 - 4ac}}{2a} \quad \text{and} \quad \frac{-b - \sqrt{b^2 - 4ac}}{2a}.$$

The quadratic formula can be used to solve any quadratic equation in one variable.

Example 1   **Solve.** $x^2 + 3x - 4 = 0$

Solution   *Substitute 1 for a, 3 for b, and −4 for c in the quadratic formula.*

$$x = \frac{-b \pm \sqrt{b^2 - 4ac}}{2a}$$

$$x = \frac{-3 \pm \sqrt{3^2 - 4(1)(-4)}}{2(1)}$$

Simplify.

$$x = \frac{-3 \pm \sqrt{9 + 16}}{2}$$

$$x = \frac{-3 \pm \sqrt{25}}{2}$$

$$x = \frac{-3 \pm 5}{2}$$

$$x = \frac{-3 + 5}{2} \quad \text{or} \quad x = \frac{-3 - 5}{2}$$

$$x = 1 \quad \quad \text{or} \quad x = -4$$

Answer $\{-4, 1\}$

Check   *Check each solution.*

$$x^2 + 3x - 4 = 0 \quad\quad\quad\quad x^2 + 3x - 4 = 0$$
$$(-4)^2 + 3(-4) - 4 \stackrel{?}{=} 0 \quad\quad (1)^2 + 3(1) - 4 \stackrel{?}{=} 0$$
$$16 - 12 - 4 = 0 \;\; \text{It checks.} \quad\quad 1 + 3 - 4 = 0 \;\; \text{It checks.}$$

Example 2   **Solve.** $3x^2 - 5x = 7$

Solution   *Change the equation to standard form.*

$$3x^2 - 5x - 7 = 0$$

Substitute 3 for a, −5 for b, and −7 for c in the quadratic formula.

$$x = \frac{-(-5) \pm \sqrt{(-5)^2 - 4(3)(-7)}}{2(3)}$$

$$x = \frac{5 \pm \sqrt{25 + 84}}{6}$$

$$x = \frac{5 \pm \sqrt{109}}{6}$$

Answer $\left\{ \dfrac{5 \pm \sqrt{109}}{6} \right\}$

Check   The check is left to the student.

Example 3   Solve. $2x^2 - x + 5 = 0$

Solution   *Substitute 2 for a, −1 for b, and 5 for c in the quadratic formula.*

$$x = \frac{-(-1) \pm \sqrt{(-1)^2 - 4(2)(5)}}{2(2)}$$

Simplify.

$$x = \frac{1 \pm \sqrt{1 - 40}}{4}$$
$$= \frac{1 \pm \sqrt{-39}}{4}$$

Answer $\emptyset$ (There are no real roots; $\sqrt{-39}$ is not a real number.)

Example 4   Solve.

The formula $h = v_0 t - 5t^2$ gives the height h in meters of an object t seconds after it has been projected vertically upward at v_0 meters per second. How long after an object is projected upward at the rate of 50 m/s will it be at a height of 100 m?

Solution   From the given information, $v_0 = 50$ and $h = 100$. We are to find t in the formula $h = v_0 t - 5t^2$.

$$100 = 50t - 5t^2$$

Multiply both sides by $\frac{1}{5}$. $20 = 10t - t^2$

Write in standard form. $t^2 - 10t + 20 = 0$

Apply the quadratic formula.
$$t = \frac{-(-10) \pm \sqrt{(-10)^2 - 4(1)(20)}}{2(1)}$$

$$t = \frac{10 \pm \sqrt{100 - 80}}{2}$$

$$t = \frac{10 \pm \sqrt{20}}{2} = \frac{10 \pm 2\sqrt{5}}{2} = 5 \pm \sqrt{5}$$

Answer   The object will be 100 m high at two distinct times: $\left(5 - \sqrt{5}\right)$ s (≈ 2.76 s) after launch on its way up and $\left(5 + \sqrt{5}\right)$ s (≈ 7.24 s) after launch on its way down.

*C*LASSROOM EXERCISES

Write the equation in standard form and state the values of a, b, and c.

1. $2x(x + 3) = 5$

2. $x(2x + 1) - 3x = 5x + 4$

3. $x^2 - x - 2 = 0$

4. $3y(2y - 5) = 7$

Solve.

5. $x^2 + 3x - 9 = 0$

6. $x^2 - 5x = 4$

7. $2x^2 = 3 + 7x$

8. $y^2 - 7y - 2 = 3$

9. The sum of the first n positive integers is given by the formula $S = \frac{n(n + 1)}{2}$. If $S = 91$, what is n?

RITTEN EXERCISES

A **Write the equation in standard form and list the values of a, b, and c.**

1. $x^2 + 2.5x = 3$ **2.** $x^2 - 3.2x = 4$ **3.** $(x + 4)^2 - 3x = 0$ **4.** $(x + 5)^2 - x = 0$

5. $\dfrac{x^2 + 4}{2} = 10x$

6. $\dfrac{x^2 + 6}{3} = 9x$

7. $(x + 7)(x + 5) = x + 3$

8. $(x + 2)(x + 10) = 7x + 5$

Solve. Write all roots in simplest form. If there are no real roots, write $\emptyset$.

9. $2x^2 + 7x + 6 = 0$ **10.** $2x^2 + 13x + 6 = 0$ **11.** $y^2 + 5y + 1 = 0$

12. $y^2 + 3y + 1 = 0$ **13.** $p^2 - 6p - 4 = 0$ **14.** $p^2 - 5p - 5 = 0$

15. $r^2 - 4r = 2$ **16.** $r^2 - 6r = 2$ **17.** $t^2 - 8t = 6$

18. $t^2 - 10t = 3$ **19.** $3n^2 + 5n - 3 = 0$ **20.** $3n^2 + 2n - 3 = 0$

21. $d^2 = d - 4$ **22.** $d^2 = d - 6$ **23.** $6q^2 + 23q - 4 = 0$

24. $6q^2 - 5q - 4 = 0$ **25.** $2v^2 + 3v + 3 = 0$ **26.** $3v^2 + 5v + 6 = 0$

27. $2h^2 + 3h - 3 = 0$ **28.** $3h^2 + 5h - 6 = 0$ **29.** $2w^2 - 3w + 3 = 0$

30. $3w^2 - 5w + 6 = 0$ **31.** $2g^2 - 3g - 3 = 0$ **32.** $3g^2 - 5g - 6 = 0$

B **33.** $\left(\dfrac{1}{2}\right)x^2 + 2x - 3 = 0$ **34.** $\left(\dfrac{1}{4}\right)x^2 - x - 1 = 0$ **35.** $x^2 = 2(1 - 3x)$

36. $2x^2 + \sqrt{3}x - 4 = 0$ **37.** $3x^2 + \sqrt{15}x + 1 = 0$ **38.** $8 + \sqrt{3}x - 3x^2 = 0$

Find the length of each side of the right triangle.

39.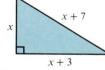

40.

41.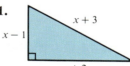

42.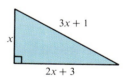

Solve.

43. The center one third of a 120-m by 80-m lawn remains to be mowed as shown in the diagram. What are the dimensions of the uncut portion?

44. Find the dimensions of a rectangle whose area is 66 in.^{2} and whose perimeter is 35 in.

45. The monthly revenue of the Griggs Gear Company for a particular gear is given by the formula $R = 600p - 5p^2$, where p is the price in dollars of the gear. At what price will the company's revenue be $16,000, assuming the gear price should be kept above $50?

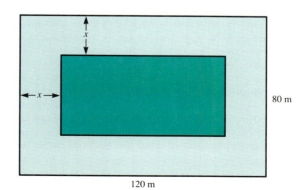

46. A stop sign with edges 35 cm in length is to be cut from a square sheet of metal. What size square is required?

$\mathcal{A}$pplication: Projectiles

The formula $h = v_0t - 5t^2$ gives the height h in meters of an object t seconds after it has been projected vertically upward at v_0 m/s. An object is projected upward at 60 m/s.

Find the time the object is at the given height.

47. 180 m **48.** 100 m **49.** 60 m **50.** 40 m

$\mathcal{A}$pplication: Stopping Distance

The distance d that it takes a driver to stop a car is related to the speed of the car. The formula $d = s + \dfrac{s^2}{20}$ gives the approximate distance (in feet) required to stop a car traveling at s miles per hour.

Find the speed of a car corresponding to each stopping distance.

51. 6.25 ft **52.** 15 ft **53.** 40 ft **54.** 100 ft

$\mathcal{A}$pplication: Roots of Quadratic Equations

C **True or false? If the statement is false, write an example to illustrate.**

55. If $x^2 + 10x + c = 0$ and $c < 0$, the equation has two roots.

56. If $x^2 + 10x + c = 0$ and $c > 0$, the equation has two roots.

57. If $x^2 + bx + 9 = 0$ and $b > 6$, the equation has two roots.

58. If $x^2 + bx + 9 = 0$ and $b < -6$, the equation has two roots.

59. Show that the sum of two roots of the quadratic equation $ax^2 + bx + c = 0$ is $-\dfrac{b}{a}$.

60. Show that the product of the roots of the quadratic equation $ax^2 + bx + c = 0$ is $\dfrac{c}{a}$.

61. Show that the sum of the reciprocals of the roots of $ax^2 + bx + c = 0$ is $-\dfrac{b}{c}$.

Use your calculator to find the roots of these equations to the nearest hundredth.

62. $3x^2 + 4x - 2 = 0$ **63.** $5x^2 + 8x - 12 = 0$

64. $2x^2 - 4x - 7 = 0$ **65.** $3.1x^2 + 1.7x - 4.3 = 0$

REVIEW EXERCISES

[2-2]

1. Solve for r: $V = \frac{4}{3} \pi r^3$, $V \geq 0$, $r \geq 0$.

Write an equation and solve.

[2-3]

2. In five years, Jane will be twice as old as she was ten years ago. How old is she now?

3. If the lengths of the sides of a triangle are three consecutive even integers and the perimeter is 120 cm, what are the lengths of the three sides?

Solve. Graph the solution on a number line.

[2-4, 2-5, 2-6]

4. $3 - 5x > 18$

5. $-6 \leq 2x \leq 10$

6. $|x - 1| > 2$

Draw a picture and solve.

7. The longer base of a trapezoid is twice as long as the shorter base. The shorter base is 10 cm longer than each of the two nonparallel sides. If the perimeter is 100 cm, what are the lengths of the four sides?

8. What is the ratio of the area of the circle inscribed in a square with side s to the area of the circle circumscribed about the square?

BIOGRAPHY   Paul Erdös

Most mathematicians today know who Paul Erdös is, and a great many have had first-hand-communications with him, either in person or by mail. He is certainly the most prolific mathematician in the world, having written or coauthored over 1000 papers—all substantial and many monumental. In a year, he may publish more than most good mathematicians do in a lifetime. He maintains contact with many mathematicians by mail, writing over 1500 letters per year. But his most important service is cross-pollination: carrying ideas from one mathematician to another. He has no family, no home, no possessions, and no job—he prefers absolute independence so that he can continually move from place to place, staying only as long as it is productive to do so.

LESSON 8-3

Complex Numbers

When negative numbers were first studied, they were not considered important because they had no real interpretations. Eventually, significant applications of negative numbers were discovered and negative numbers became accepted as "real" numbers.

Four hundred years ago mathematicians began to use $\sqrt{-1}$ as though it were a number. To distinguish it and similar numbers from real numbers, the term "imaginary" number was used. Today, imaginary numbers are recognized as having many important applications in the solutions of problems in science and engineering.

The pure quadratic equation $x^2 + 1 = 0$ has no solution if we are restricted to the set of real numbers. No real number squared equals -1.

$$x^2 + 1 = 0$$
$$x^2 = -1$$
$$x = \pm\sqrt{-1}$$

However, this need not mean that such an equation has *no* solution. It simply means that the solutions are not real numbers.

Mathematicians invented a nonreal number, called the **imaginary number** i, to solve equations resulting in the square root of a negative number.

Definition: The Imaginary Number i

Let $i = \sqrt{-1}$ and $i^2 = -1$.

The invention of one imaginary number quickly led to other imaginary numbers. For example, $i + i = 2i$. The number i was identified as the imaginary unit of a new set of numbers. Any number of the form ai, were a is real, $a \neq 0$, is called a **pure imaginary number.** The term $0i$ is defined to equal 0.

Some properties of pure imaginary numbers are similar to those of real numbers. For example, multiplication of a real number and i is commutative and multiplication of pure imaginary numbers is both commutative and associative.

Example 1   **Simplify.**   **a.** $(2i)(3i)$ **b.** $(2i)^2$ **c.** $(-i)(i)$

Solution   **a.** $(2i)(3i) = (2 \cdot 3)i^2 = 6(-1) = -6$

b. $(2i)^2 = 4i^2 = 4(-1) = -4$ **c.** $(-i)(i) = -i^2 = -(-1) = 1$

The square root of any negative real number can be written as the product of i and the square root of the opposite of the real number. For example, $\sqrt{-5} = i\sqrt{5}$.

Definition: Square Root of a Negative Number

If a is a positive real number, then $\sqrt{-a} = i\sqrt{a}$.

When simplifying square root radicals with negative radicands, it is important to follow these steps.

1. First write the radical as the product of i and a real number.
2. Simplify the product using the techniques for simplifying real radicals (Chapter 7) and the properties of pure imaginary numbers.

Example 2   **Simplify.** $(\sqrt{-8})(\sqrt{-25})$

Solution $(\sqrt{-8})(\sqrt{-25}) = (i\sqrt{8})(i\sqrt{25}) = (\sqrt{8})(\sqrt{25})i^2 = (2\sqrt{2})(5)(-1) = -10\sqrt{2}$

Example 2 shows that the property $\sqrt{a} \cdot \sqrt{b} = \sqrt{ab}$ does not hold when both a and b are negative.

The sum of a real number and a pure imaginary number is neither a real number nor a pure imaginary number. The sum represents a new number called a **complex number.**

Definition: Complex Number

A *complex number* is a number of the form $a + bi$, where a and b are real numbers and i is the imaginary unit.

The real part of the number $a + bi$ is a and the imaginary part of the number is bi.

Each of the following is a complex number.

$$3 + 2i \qquad 3 - 2i \qquad (3 - 2i = 3 + (-2)i)$$
$$-8 + \sqrt{3}i \qquad 7 \qquad (7 = 7 + 0i)$$
$$5i \qquad (5i = 0 + 5i)$$

Real numbers are complex numbers in which the imaginary part is zero. Pure imaginary numbers are complex numbers in which the real part is zero. The complex numbers that are not real are **imaginary numbers.**

Complex numbers $(a + bi)$

Real numbers
$(a + bi, b = 0)$

Imaginary numbers
$(a + bi, b \neq 0)$

Pure imaginary numbers
$(a + bi, a = 0, b \neq 0)$

Two complex numbers are equal if and only if their real parts are equal and their imaginary parts are equal.

Definition: Equality of Complex Numbers

For all complex numbers $a + bi$ and $c + di$,

$$a + bi = c + di \text{ if and only if } a = c \text{ and } b = d.$$

For example, $2 + 3i = \dfrac{10}{5} + (7 - 4)i$ but $2 + 3i \neq 3 + 2i$.

Complex numbers are not ordered. For example, $2 + 3i$ and $3 + 2i$ are not equal. But, also, $2 + 3i$ is not greater than nor less than $3 + 2i$.

Definition: Absolute Value of a Complex Number

The absolute value of a complex number $a + bi$ is $|a + bi| = \sqrt{a^2 + b^2}$.

The absolute value of a complex number is a nonnegative real number.

Example 3 Simplify. **a.** $|6 + 8i|$ **b.** $|5 + 0i|$

Solution **a.** $|6 + 8i| = \sqrt{6^2 + 8^2} = \sqrt{100} = 10$ **b.** $|5 + 0i| = \sqrt{5^2 + 0^2} = \sqrt{25} = 5$

Example 4 Solve. $x^2 - 4x + 29 = 0$

Solution *Use the quadratic formula.*
$$x = \frac{-(-4) \pm \sqrt{(-4)^2 - 4 \cdot 1 \cdot 29}}{2 \cdot 1}$$

$$= \frac{4 \pm \sqrt{16 - 116}}{2} = \frac{4 \pm \sqrt{-100}}{2}$$

$$= \frac{4 \pm 10i}{2} = 2 \pm 5i$$

Answer $\{2 + 5i, \, 2 - 5i\}$

Example 4 illustrates an important point: All quadratic equations have solutions in the set of complex numbers.

*C*LASSROOM EXERCISES

Simplify, using i for $\sqrt{-1}$.

1. $\sqrt{-2}$ **2.** $\sqrt{-\dfrac{4}{9}}$ **3.** $\sqrt{-2} \cdot \sqrt{-2}$ **4.** $\sqrt{-3} \cdot \sqrt{-5}$

5. $(3i)(5i)$ **6.** i^3 **7.** i^{10} **8.** i^{13}

Write each number as a complex number in the form $a + bi$, where a and b are real numbers.

9. $5i - 2$ **10.** $-4i$ **11.** 3

Simplify.

12. $|2 + 5i|$ **13.** $|-2 - 5i|$ **14.** $|6 + 0i|$

Solve. Write the solutions in the form $a + bi$.

15. $x^2 + 2x + 8 = 0$ **16.** $-2x^2 = 3x + 7$

 RITTEN EXERCISES

A **Simplify, using i for $\sqrt{-1}$.**

1. $\sqrt{-5}$ **2.** $\sqrt{-3}$ **3.** $-\sqrt{-100}$ **4.** $-\sqrt{-25}$

5. $\sqrt{-2} \cdot \sqrt{-8}$ **6.** $\sqrt{-3} \cdot \sqrt{-12}$ **7.** $\sqrt{-5} \cdot \sqrt{20}$ **8.** $\sqrt{2} \cdot \sqrt{-32}$

9. $\sqrt{-3} \cdot \sqrt{2}$ **10.** $\sqrt{-5} \cdot \sqrt{3}$ **11.** $\sqrt{-\frac{2}{3}} \cdot \sqrt{-\frac{3}{10}}$ **12.** $\sqrt{-\frac{3}{8}} \cdot \sqrt{-\frac{2}{9}}$

13. $(2i)(10i)$ **14.** $(4i)(3i)$ **15.** $(2i)(2i)(2i)$ **16.** $(3i)(3i)(3i)$

17. $(3i)^2$ **18.** $(4i)^2$ **19.** $(-5i)(7i)$ **20.** $(-3i)(11i)$

Write each number as a complex number in the form $a + bi$, where a and b are real numbers.

21. $-3i + 2$ **22.** $7i - 3$ **23.** $2i$ **24.** $6i$

25. 7 **26.** 10 **27.** $\sqrt{-5}$ **28.** $\sqrt{-10}$

Find the absolute value of each number.

29. $5 + 12i$ **30.** $8 + 6i$ **31.** -5 **32.** -7

33. $2i$ **34.** $8i$ **35.** $-2 - 3i$ **36.** $-3 - 2i$

Solve. Write the solutions in the form $a + bi$.

37. $x^2 + 3x + 4 = 0$ **38.** $x^2 - 2x + 4 = 0$ **39.** $2x^2 + x + 3 = 0$ **40.** $3x^2 - x + 1 = 0$

41. $5x^2 - 4x + 1 = 0$ **42.** $4x^2 + 3x + 5 = 0$ **43.** $x^2 - 2x + 5 = 0$ **44.** $x^2 + 4x + 6 = 0$

B **Simplify. Assume that $a > 0$, $b > 0$. Use i for $\sqrt{-1}$.**

45. $\sqrt{-a} \cdot \sqrt{-b}$ **46.** $-\sqrt{a} \cdot \sqrt{-b}$ **47.** $\left(\sqrt{-a}\right)^2$ **48.** $\sqrt{-2} \cdot \sqrt{-ab}$

49. $\sqrt{-48a} \cdot \sqrt{-27b}$ **50.** $\left(-\sqrt{-b}\right)^3$ **51.** $\sqrt[3]{-a} \cdot \sqrt[3]{-b}$ **52.** $-\sqrt[3]{12a} \cdot \sqrt[3]{-18b}$

Simplify.

53. i^9 **54.** i^{18} **55.** i^{36} **56.** i^{99}

57. $-i^{11}$ **58.** $(-i)^{11}$ **59.** $-i^{13} \cdot i^{15}$ **60.** $i^{21}(-i)^9$

True or false? If the statement is false, give an example to illustrate. [Note: a, b, c, and d are real numbers.]

61. If $a + bi = c + di$, then $|a + bi| = |c + di|$

62. If $|a + bi| = |c + di|$, then $a + bi = c + di$.

63. If $|a + bi| = |c + di|$, then $|a| + |b|i = |c| + |d|i$.

64. If $|a + bi| = c + di$, then $d = 0$

Solve for x and y, where x and y are real numbers.

65. $x + 3\sqrt{-2} = 3\sqrt{2} + yi$

66. $|x + xi| = \sqrt{6}$

C **Let n be a positive integer. Simplify.**

67. i^{4n+3}

68. $(i^{2n+1})^2$

69. $i^{3n-1}i^{n+1}$

70. i^{2n+2}, n odd

71. i^{2n-1}, n even

72. $\dfrac{i^{4m}}{i^{4n}}$, m an integer, $m > n$

73. Show that if $b = 0$, then $|a + bi| = |a|$.

$\mathcal{R}$EVIEW EXERCISES

1. State the domain and range of $\{(x, y): |y| = x\}$. [3-1]
2. State whether $\{(x, y): x^2 = y^2\}$ is a function. [3-2]
3. Find the slope and y-intercept of $3x - 2y = 10$. [3-3]
4. State whether $\{(x, y): xy = 12\}$ is a linear function. [3-3]
5. Write the equation of the line through the origin that is perpendicular to $y = 2x - 3$. [3-4]
6. Suppose that y varies directly as x. If $y = 20$ when $x = 12$, what is the value of y when $x = 9$? [3-5]
7. If $A = \pi r^2$, then A varies directly as $\underline{\quad?\quad}$. [3-5]
8. Simplify: $[-2.5] \cdot [2.5]$. [3-6]

Let $f(x) = x^2$ and $g(x) = 10 - x$. Simplify. [3-7]

9. $f(g(-2))$

10. $g(f(-2))$

$\mathcal{S}$elf-Quiz 1

8-1 **Write in the form $(x + d)^2 = k$.**

    1. $x^2 - 12x + 3 = 0$ **2.** $x^2 + 5x = 1$

8-1, **Solve. Write $\emptyset$ if there is no real solution.**
8-2
    3. $(2x + 3)^2 = 25$ **4.** $y(y + 4) = 8$ **5.** $3x^2 - 8x + 6 = 0$

8-3 **Simplify.**

    6. $(2i)(4i)$ **7.** $\sqrt{-8} \cdot \sqrt{-32}$ **8.** $|7 - 24i|$

Write each complex number in the form $a + bi$, where a and b are real numbers.

    9. $3i - 4$ **10.** 8 **11.** $2i$

Solve.

    12. $x^2 - 4x + 5 = 0$ **13.** $\dfrac{5}{2}x^2 - x + 5 = 0$

LESSON 8-4

Addition and Subtraction of Complex Numbers

Application: Impedance Current in an electrical circuit can be obstructed by different parts of the circuit: resistors (R), capacitors (C), and inductances (L).

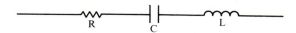

Impedance Z is the total effective resistance (in ohms) of the circuit. The impedance is the sum of the resistance from resistors and the reactance from capacitors X_C and inductances X_L of each part of the circuit. The effective resistance (in ohms) is represented by a real number. The effective reactance (in ohms) is represented by a pure imaginary number.

For a circuit with a resistance R of 6 ohms and a reactance of 8 ohms, the impedance Z is expressed as a complex number:

$$Z = 6 + 8i$$

with a value in ohms of $|Z| = \sqrt{6^2 + 8^2} = 10$.

Addition of complex numbers is defined as follows.

Definition: Addition of Complex Numbers

For all real numbers a, b, c, and d,

$$(a + bi) + (c + di) = (a + c) + (b + d)i.$$

Since the set of real numbers is closed with respect to addition, $(a + c)$ and $(b + d)$ are real numbers. Therefore, $(a + c) + (b + d)i$ is a number in the form $(x + yi)$ where x and y are real numbers. The set of complex numbers is closed with respect to addition.

Example 1   Show that addition of complex numbers is commutative.

Solution $(a + bi) + (c + di) = (a + c) + (b + d)i$ *Definition of addition of complex numbers*

$\qquad\qquad\qquad = (c + a) + (d + b)i$ *Commutative property of addition of real numbers*

$\qquad\qquad\qquad = (c + di) + (a + bi)$ *Definition of addition of complex numbers*

The additive identity element of the set of complex numbers is 0. That is, the sum of a complex number $a + bi$ and 0 is $a + bi$.

$$(a + bi) + 0 = (a + bi) + (0 + 0i)$$
$$= (a + 0) + (b + 0)i$$
$$= a + bi$$

The set of complex numbers also has a property similar to the additive inverse property of real numbers.

The Additive Inverse Property of Complex Numbers

For each complex number z, there is a complex number $- z$ such that
$$z + (-z) = 0.$$
If $z = a + bi$, then $-z = -(a + bi) = -a - bi$.

Subtraction of complex numbers is defined as follows.

Definition: Subtraction of Complex Numbers

For all complex numbers w and z, $w - z = w + (-z)$,
$$\text{if } w = a + bi \text{ and } z = c + di, \text{ then}$$
$$w - z = (a + bi) - (c + di) = (a - c) + (b - d)i.$$

Example 2   **Simplify.**   **a. $(2 - 3i) + (5 + 4i)$**   **b. $(4 + 3i) - (3 - 5i)$**

Solution   **a.** $(2 - 3i) + (5 + 4i) = (2 + 5) + (-3 + 4)i = 7 + 1i = 7 + i$
b. $(4 + 3i) - (3 - 5i) = (4 - 3) + (3 - (-5))i = 1 + 8i$

Example 3   **Simplify.**   **a. $(2 + 4i) + (2 - 4i)$**   **b. $(2 + 4i) - (2 - 4i)$**

a. $(2 + 4i) + (2 - 4i) = (2 + 2) + (4 + (-4))i = 4$
b. $(2 + 4i) - (2 - 4i) = (2 - 2) + (4 - (-4))i = 8i$

In Example 3, the complex numbers $2 + 4i$ and $2 - 4i$ are called **complex conjugates.**

Definition: Complex Conjugates

For all real numbers a and b,
$$a + bi \text{ and } a - bi \text{ are complex conjugates.}$$

Part (a) of Example 3 illustrates that the sum of a complex number and its complex conjugate is a real number. Part (b) illustrates that the difference of complex conjugates, $b \neq 0$, is a pure imaginary number.

Simplify.

1. $(5 - 3i) + (4 - 2i)$
2. $(4 + 2i) - (5 - 1i)$
3. $(5 - 2i) + (5 + 2i)$
4. $(6 - 3i) - (6 + 3i)$
5. $\left(2 - \sqrt{-4}\right) + \left(6 + \sqrt{-9}\right)$
6. $\left(3 - \sqrt{-2}\right) - \left(4 + \sqrt{-2}\right)$

State the complex conjugate of each complex number.

7. $3 + 7i$
8. $4 - 2i$
9. 8
10. $3i$

11. Simplify both sides of the following equation to illustrate that addition of complex numbers is associative.

$$((2 + 3i) + (4 + 5i)) + (6 + 7i) = (2 + 3i) + ((4 + 5i) + (6 + 7i))$$

WRITTEN EXERCISES

A **Simplify.**

1. $(5 + 3i) + (7 + 9i)$
2. $(2 + 7i) + (8 + 3i)$
3. $(-6 + 5i) + (8 - 10i)$
4. $(4 - 5i) + (-10 + 6i)$
5. $(12 + 3i) + (12 - 3i)$
6. $(7 - 4i) + (-7 - 4i)$
7. $\left(\pi + \sqrt{2}i\right) + \left(\pi + \sqrt{2}i\right)$
8. $\left(\sqrt{3} + \pi i\right) + \left(\sqrt{3} + \pi i\right)$
9. $\left(7 + \sqrt{-10}\right) + \left(8 + \sqrt{-40}\right)$
9. $\left(6 + \sqrt{-28}\right) + \left(12 + \sqrt{-7}\right)$

Write the additive inverse of each number.

11. $2 - 3i$
12. $5 - 2i$
13. $-2 + 10i$
14. $-3 + 8i$
15. $5i$
16. $7i$
17. $-\dfrac{2}{3}$
18. $-\dfrac{1}{4}$

Simplify.

19. $(10 + 12i) - (2 + 3i)$
20. $(5 + 9i) - (3 + 7i)$
21. $(5 + 5i) - (2 - 2i)$
22. $(4 + 4i) - (3 - 3i)$
23. $(7 - 3i) - 10$
24. $(6 - 5i) - 7$
25. $-5i - (2 - 2i)$
26. $-3i - (3 - i)$
27. $\left(\sqrt{6} + \sqrt{-5}\right) - \left(\sqrt{24} + \sqrt{-45}\right)$
28. $\left(\sqrt{12} + \sqrt{-44}\right) - \left(\sqrt{3} + \sqrt{-99}\right)$

Write the complex conjugate of each number.

29. $2 -$
30. $3 - 5i$
31. $-2 + 10i$
32. $-5 + 2i$
33. 7
34. 6
35. $-\sqrt{2}i$
36. $-\sqrt{3}i$

Show that the set of complex numbers has the following properties.

37. Closure for subtraction. (Show that $(a + bi) - (c + di)$ is a complex number.)
38. A complex number and its complex conjugate have the same absolute value.

In electricity, impedance (measured in ohms) is the sum of resistance represented by a real number and reactance represented by a pure imaginary number. For example, if the resistance is 4 ohms and the reactance is 3 ohms, the impedance is $4 + 3i$. The value of the impedance is $|4 + 3i|$ ohms.

39. Simplify $|4 + 3i|$ ohms.

40. a. Find the impedance when the resistance is 12 ohms and the reactance is 5 ohms.

  b. Find the value of the impedance.

41. a. Find the impedance when the resistance is 15 ohms and the reactance is 8 ohms.

  b. Find the value of the impedance.

42. The total impedance of a circuit comes from two sources of impedances, $12 + 9i$ and $12 + 3i$.

  a. What is the total impedance?

  b. What is the value of the total impedance?

  c. What is the value of the impedance from each source?

  d. Can the value of the total impedance be found by adding the values of the individual impedances?

C Let $\bar{z}$ denote the complex conjugate of the complex number $z = a + bi$.

43. How is the sum of the conjugates of two complex numbers z_1 and z_2 related to the conjugate of their sum?

44. Show that $\overline{z_1 - z_2} = \overline{z_1} - \overline{z_2}$.

REVIEW EXERCISES

1. Does this system have 0, 1, or infinitely many solutions?
$$y = 5x - 2$$
$$10x - 2y = 4$$
[4-1]

Solve.

2. $y = x - 5$
   $3x + 2y = 10$

3. $2x + 3y - 24 = 0$
   $5x + 4y - 60 = 0$
[4-3]

4. Evaluate this determinant.
$$\begin{vmatrix} -3 & 1 \\ -10 & 2 \end{vmatrix}$$
[4-4]

5. Write D, D_x, D_y, D_z for this system.
$$x + y + z = 12$$
$$x - y \quad\quad = 10$$
$$2x \quad\quad - 3z = 0$$
[4-5]

6. Graph $x \geqslant 2$ or $y > \dfrac{1}{2}x - 2$.
[4-6]

Multiplication and Division of Complex Numbers

Using the quadratic formula to solve the equation $x^2 - 6x + 13 = 0$ gives $3 + 2i$ as one of the roots. To check this root, we substitute in the original equation.

$$(3 + 2i)^2 - 6(3 + 2i) + 13 \stackrel{?}{=} 0$$

Treat $(3 + 2i)$ as a binomial and simplify the left side of the equation:

$$9 + 12i + 4i^2 - 18 - 12i + 13 \stackrel{?}{=} 0$$

$$0 = 0 \quad \text{It checks.}$$

Complex numbers can be multiplied as though they were binomials.

$$(3 + 2i)(4 + 5i) = 3 \cdot 4 + 3 \cdot 5i + 2i \cdot 4 + 2i \cdot 5i$$

$$= 12 + 15i + 8i + 10i^2$$

$$= 12 + 15i + 8i - 10$$

$$= (12 - 10) + (15 + 8)i = 2 + 23i$$

Definition: Multiplication of Complex Numbers

For all complex numbers $a + bi$ and $c + di$,

$$(a + bi)(c + di) = (ac - bd) + (ad + bc)i.$$

Example 1 Simplify each product using the definition of multiplication.

 a. $(3 - 5i)(1 + 2i)$ b. $2(3 + 4i)$

Solution a. $(3 - 5i)(1 + 2i) = (3 \cdot 1 - (-5)2) + (3 \cdot 2 + (-5)1)i = 13 + 1i = 13 + i$

 b. $2(3 + 4i) = (2 + 0i)(3 + 4i) = (6 - 0) + (8 + 0)i = 6 + 8i$

Example 2 Simplify each product using the definition of multiplication.

 a. $2i(3i)$ b. $3(4)$ c. $(2 - 6i)(2 + 6i)$

Solution a. $2i(3i) = (0 + 2i)(0 + 3i) = (0 - 6) + (0 + 0)i = -6$

 b. $3(4) = (3 + 0i)(4 + 0i) = (12 - 0) + (0 + 0)i = 12$

 c. $(2 - 6i)(2 + 6i) = (4 - (-36)) + (12 + (-12))i = 40$

Example 2 shows that the definition of multiplication of complex numbers is consistent with the definitions for multiplying pure imaginary numbers and for multiplying real numbers. Part (c) shows that the product of complex conjugates is a real number.

Complex numbers have multiplication properties similar to those for real numbers. For example, multiplication of complex numbers is commutative, associative, and distributive over addition. The identity element for multiplication is $1 + 0i$, or simply 1. Each complex number z, except 0, has a multiplicative inverse or reciprocal, $\dfrac{1}{z}$. However, an expression for a complex number is not considered to be in simplest form if it has i in the denominator.

Example 3 Simplify. $\dfrac{3}{5i}$

Solution Multiply both numerator and denominator by i.

$$\frac{3}{5i} = \frac{3i}{5i^2} = \frac{3i}{-5}$$

$$= -\frac{3i}{5}$$

Since each complex number z except 0 has a multiplicative inverse, division by z, $z \neq 0$, can be defined as multiplying by the multiplicative inverse of z.

Definition: Division of Complex Numbers

For all complex numbers w and z ($z \neq 0$),

$$\frac{w}{z} = w\left(\frac{1}{z}\right).$$

The quotient of two imaginary numbers can be simplified by multiplying both the numerator and the denominator by the complex conjugate of the denominator.

Example 4 Simplify. $\dfrac{2 + 3i}{4 + i}$

Solution Multiply both numerator and denominator by the complex conjugate of $(4 + i)$.

$$\frac{2 + 3i}{4 + i} = \frac{(2 + 3i)(4 - i)}{(4 + i)(4 - i)}$$

$$= \frac{(8 + 3) + (12 - 2)i}{16 + 1}$$

$$= \frac{11 + 10i}{17}$$

$$= \frac{11}{17} + \frac{10}{17}i$$

CLASSROOM EXERCISES

Simplify.

1. $(2 + 6i)(3 - 5i)$ 2. $3(4 - 8i)$ 3. $\dfrac{5i}{4 + 3i}$ 4. $\dfrac{6 + i}{3 - 2i}$

5. Show that multiplication of complex numbers is commutative.

WRITTEN EXERCISES

A **Simplify.**

1. $(3 + 2i)(4 + 5i)$
2. $(5 + 3i)(2 + 2i)$
3. $(5 + 4i)(97 - 2i)$
4. $(8 + 4i)(2 - 3i)$
5. $(-2 + 3i)(1 - i)$
6. $(-3 + 6i)(2 - i)$
7. $(-5 - 10i)(-3 - 2i)$
8. $(-6 - 4i)(-2 - 8i)$
9. $(4 + 0i)(6 - 9i)$
10. $(3 + 0i)(7 - 2i)$
11. $(0 + 2i)(4 - 3i)$
12. $(0 + 7i)(2 - 9i)$
13. $(5 - 6i)(5 + 6i)$
14. $(4 + 9i)(4 - 9i)$
15. $(10 + i)(-10 + i)$
16. $(8 + 3i)(-8 + 3i)$
17. $(2 + 7i)^2$
18. $(5 + 4i)^2$

Write the reciprocal of each number in the form $a + bi$.

19. $3 + 2i$
20. $4 + 3i$
21. $5 - i$
22. $1 - 4i$

23. $2 + 0i$
24. $6 + 0i$
25. $0 + 10i$
26. $0 + 8i$

Simplify. Write in the form $a + bi$.

27. $\dfrac{5 + 3i}{2 - 4i}$
28. $\dfrac{6 + 2i}{3 - 5i}$
29. $\dfrac{4 + 3i}{6 + 2i}$
30. $\dfrac{1 + 7i}{5 + 2i}$

31. $\dfrac{4}{2 + 5i}$
32. $\dfrac{3}{3 + 2i}$
33. $\dfrac{5i}{1 - i}$
34. $\dfrac{2i}{2 - i}$

35. $\dfrac{5}{3i}$
36. $\dfrac{7}{2i}$
37. $\dfrac{1 - 4i}{5i}$
38. $\dfrac{3 - i}{4i}$

39. Show that the product of complex conjugates is a real number.

40. Show that the set of complex numbers is closed with respect to multiplication. (Show that $(a + bi)(c + di)$ is a complex number.)

B 41. Show that the set of complex numbers is closed with respect to division (divisor not equal to 0).

42. Show that $1 + 0i$ is the multiplicative identity element for the set of complex numbers.

Solve.

43. $(x + 2i)(2 + 4i) = -14 - 8i$
44. $(x + i)(3 - 2i) = 14 - 5i$
45. $(3 + xi)(-6 - 4i) = 2 - 42i$
46. $(2 + 5i)x = 5 - 3i$
47. $x + yi = (4 + 5i)^2$
48. $(x + yi)(2 - i) = 3 + 7i$
49. $\dfrac{2 - xi}{4 + 2i} = 1 + i$
50. $\dfrac{3 + 2i}{1 + xi} = -\dfrac{5}{17} + \dfrac{14}{17}i$

C 51. For what numbers of the form $(x + yi)$ does $(x + yi) = \sqrt{-i}$? [*Hint:* Square both sides.]

52. Show that multiplication is distributive over addition in the set of complex numbers.

Let $\bar{z}$ denote the conjugate of $z = a + bi$.

53. Show that $\bar{z}_1 \cdot \bar{z}_2 = \overline{z_1 \cdot z_2}$.

54. Show that if z is a root of the equation $x^2 + 3x + k = 0$, k a real number, then its conjugate $\bar{z}$ is also a root.

EVIEW EXERCISES

Simplify.

1. $(10a^2)(2b^3)$
2. $(3 \cdot 10^{10})(4.5 \cdot 10^5)$ [5-1]
3. $(x^2 - 3x + 4) - (x^2 + 4x - 4)$
4. $2x(x - 5) + 3(x - 5)$ [5-2]

Expand and simplify.

5. $(a + b)^3$
6. $(x - 2)^4$ [5-3]
7. $(a + b)(a^2 - ab + b^2)$
8. $(a - 2b)(2a + 5b)$
9. Factor completely: $3x^3 - 12x^2 + 6x$.   [5-4]

$\mathcal{E}$XTENSION   The Complex-Number Plane

Each complex number $a + bi$ is identified by the ordered pair of numbers (a, b). Therefore, complex numbers can be represented graphically as points in the complex-number plane. The horizontal axis is the real-number line, and the vertical axis is the pure imaginary-number line.

Point O represents the complex number $0 + 0i$.

Point A represents the complex number $2 + i$.

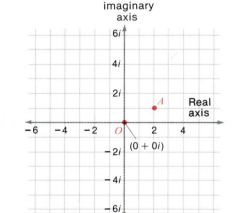

Addition of two complex numbers can be illustrated graphically. Graph the following numbers using the same set of axes.

1. $B(1 + 3i)$ 2. $C(2 + i) + (1 + 3i)$

3. Prove that quadrilateral $ABOC$ is a parallelogram by showing that opposite sides have the same length.

4. How is the absolute value of the sum of $2 + i$ and $1 + 3i$ related to the length of the diagonal OC?

328   Chapter 8   Quadratic Functions and Complex Numbers

LESSON 8-6

The Discriminant

In the quadratic formula $x = \dfrac{-b \pm \sqrt{b^2 - 4ac}}{2a}$, the expression $b^2 - 4ac$ determines several characteristics of the roots of the original quadratic equation. Because this expression ($b^2 - 4ac$) discriminates among the number and kind of roots, it is called the **discriminant** D of the quadratic equation $ax^2 + bx + c = 0$, where a, b, and c are rational numbers.

For discriminant $D = b^2 - 4ac$

Condition	Roots r_1 and r_2
$D = 0$	Equal and rational
$D > 0$ and D a perfect square	Unequal and rational
$D > 0$ and D not a perfect square	Unequal and irrational
$D < 0$	Unequal and not real (complex conjugates)

Recall that if r_1 and r_2 are roots of a quadratic equation, the equation can be written in the following form:

$$(x - r_1)(x - r_2) = 0.$$

If $r_1 = r_2$, the two factors are alike and the root is called a **double root.** An important generalization that we can now state is:

If the domain of the variable is the set of complex numbers, every quadratic equation in one variable has two roots or one double root.

Example 1   State the number and kind of roots of each equation.

     a. $x^2 + 6x - 2 = 0$ b. $x^2 + 6x = 0$

     c. $x^2 + 6x + 9 = 0$ d. $x^2 + 6x + 13 = 0$

Solution   Find the value of the discriminant for each equation.

     a. $b^2 - 4ac = 6^2 - 4(1)(-2) = 36 + 8 = 44$ two unequal irrational roots

     b. $b^2 - 4ac = 6^2 - 4(1)(0) = 36 - 0 = 36$ two unequal rational roots

     c. $b^2 - 4ac = 6^2 - 4(1)(9) = 36 - 36 = 0$ one double rational root

     d. $b^2 - 4ac = 6^2 - 4(1)(13) = 36 - 52 = -16$ two unequal imaginary roots

Example 2 Find the values of k for which $2x^2 + kx + 8 = 0$ has a double root.

Solution The equation will have a double root when the discriminant is 0.

$$b^2 - 4ac = 0$$
$$k^2 - 4(2)(8) = 0$$
$$k^2 - 64 = 0$$
$$k^2 = 64$$
$$k = \pm\sqrt{64}$$
$$k = \pm 8$$

Answer The equation will have a double root when $k = 8$ or $k = -8$.

Some equations that are not second degree can still be solved by quadratic techniques if they are **quadratic in form.** Consider the equation
$$x^4 - 3x^2 - 4 = 0.$$
This fourth-degree equation has the form of a quadratic equation. To show that form more clearly:

Substitute y for x^2.	$y^2 - 3y - 4 = 0$
Factor.	$(y - 4)(y + 1) = 0$
	$y = 4$ or $y = -1$

Replacing y with x^2, we have a sentence that is equivalent to the original fourth-degree equation,

$$x^2 = 4 \qquad \text{or} \quad x^2 = -1$$
$$x = \pm\sqrt{4} = \pm 2 \quad \text{or} \quad x = \pm\sqrt{-1} = \pm i$$

The solution set of $x^4 - 3x^2 - 4 = 0$ is $\{2, -2, i, -i\}$.

Example 3 Solve. $x + 2\sqrt{x} - 8 = 0$

Solution *Substitute y for $\sqrt{x}$.*

$$y^2 + 2y - 8 = 0$$
$$(y + 4)(y - 2) = 0$$
$$y = -4 \quad \text{or} \quad y = 2$$

Replace y with $\sqrt{x}$.

$$\sqrt{x} = -4 \quad \text{or} \quad \sqrt{x} = 2$$
$$x = 4$$

No number satisfies the condition $\sqrt{x} = -4$ because the principal square root of any number is nonnegative.

Answer {4}

Check *Check the solution in the original equation.*
$$x + 2\sqrt{x} - 8 = 0$$
$$4 + 2\sqrt{4} - 8 \stackrel{?}{=} 0$$
$$0 = 0 \text{ It checks.}$$

CLASSROOM EXERCISES

State the number and kind of roots for each equation.

1. $x^2 - 4x + 4 = 0$

2. $2x^2 + 5x - 7 = 0$

3. $5x^2 = 2x - 8$

4. For what values of k will the roots of $-x^2 + 9x + 3k = 0$ be real?

Make a substitution and write an equation to show that each equation is quadratic in form.

5. $x^4 - 5x^2 + 4 = 0$ 6. $x^4 - 4x^2 = 0$ 7. $x - 9\sqrt{x} + 8 = 0$ 8. $x^{\frac{2}{3}} + 5x^{\frac{1}{3}} + 6 = 0$

9.–12. Solve the equations in Exercises 5–8.

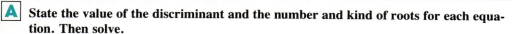

WRITTEN EXERCISES

A   **State the value of the discriminant and the number and kind of roots for each equation. Then solve.**

1. $x^2 + 3x + 3 = 0$

2. $x^2 + 2x + 2 = 0$

3. $x^2 - 3x + 3 = 0$

4. $x^2 - 2x + 2 = 0$

5. $16x^2 + 24x + 9 = 0$

6. $9x^2 + 24x + 16 = 0$

7. $6x^2 + x - 15 = 0$

8. $9x^2 - 9x - 10 = 0$

9. $0.6x^2 + 2.5x + 2 = 0$

10. $0.4x^2 + 3.5x + 7 = 0$

11. $\frac{1}{2}x^2 + \frac{4}{3}x - \frac{5}{6} = 0$

12. $\frac{1}{3}x^2 + \frac{3}{4}x + \frac{27}{64} = 0$

Make a substitution and write an equation to show that each equation is quadratic in form.

13. $h^4 - 2h^2 + 1 = 0$

14. $n^4 - 10n^2 + 9 = 0$

15. $x - 9\sqrt{x} + 14 = 0$

16. $x - 7\sqrt{x} + 12 = 0$

17. $\sqrt{x} - 6\sqrt[4]{x} + 8 = 0$

18. $\sqrt{x} - 7\sqrt[4]{x} + 12 = 0$

19. $k^8 - 17k^4 + 16 = 0$

20. $a^8 - 82a^4 + 81 = 0$

21. $x^{\frac{2}{3}} - x^{\frac{1}{3}} - 2 = 0$

22. $c^{\frac{2}{5}} + c^{\frac{1}{5}} - 2 = 0$

23.–32. Solve the equations in Exercises 13–22.

Solve for k. Use inequalities where necessary. Write $\emptyset$ if there is no real value of k.

33. $x^2 + 6x + k = 0$ has a double root.

34. $x^2 - 8x + k = 0$ has a double root.

35. $x^2 + 6x + k = 0$ has two real roots.

36. $x^2 - 8x + k = 0$ has two real roots.

B   **True or false? If the statement is false, write an example to illustrate.**

37. If the discriminant is negative, there is no solution.

38. If the discriminant is positive, there is a double root.

39. If the discriminant is zero, the root is $-\dfrac{b}{2a}$.

40. If the discriminant is negative, the sum of the roots is a real number.

41. If the discriminant is positive, the difference of the roots is an irrational number.

42. If the discriminant is positive, the product of the roots is a rational number.

Solve

43. $(x^2 - 3x)^2 + 6(x^2 - 3x) - 40 = 0$

44. $(x^2 + 2x)^2 - 2(x^2 + 2x) - 3 = 0$

45. $\dfrac{1}{t^2} - \dfrac{13}{t} + 36 = 0$

46. $\dfrac{1}{x^2} - \dfrac{9}{x} + 18 = 0$

47. $\sqrt[3]{v^2} + 5\sqrt[3]{v} + 6 = 0$

48. $\sqrt[3]{x^2} + \sqrt[3]{x} - 12 = 0$

49. $\sqrt{\dfrac{b + 3}{b - 1}} - 6\sqrt{\dfrac{b - 1}{b + 3}} = 1$

50. $w^2 + 6w - 6\sqrt{w^2 + 6w - 2} + 3 = 0$

 51. Show that if $x^2 + bx + c = 0$ has a double root and b and c are integers, then b is an even number.

52. Show that if $x^2 + bx + c = 0$ and c is negative, then there are two real roots.

The generalization about the number and kind of roots determined by the discriminant $b^2 - 4ac$ assumes that a, b, and c are *rational* numbers. Solve these equations in which some of the coefficients are not rational numbers.

53. $x^2 - \sqrt{8}x + 2 = 0$

54. $x^2 - 4ix - 4 = 0$

55. $x^2 - 3ix + 10 = 0$

56. $\sqrt{5}x^2 + 6ix - 5\sqrt{5} = 0$

57. $x^2 - 6ix = 0$

58. $ix^2 + 3x - 2i = 0$

 EVIEW EXERCISES

Factor completely.

1. $x^3 - 8$

2. $ac + ad - bc - bd$

3. $2x^2 - 8$

4. $4a^2 - 16b^2$

5. $14 + 5x - x^2$

6. $x^2 - x - 20$

Solve by factoring.

7. $x^2 + 35 = 12x$

8. $3x^2 + 20x = 7$

9. $2x^2 - 7x + 6 = 0$

*S*elf-Quiz 2

8-4, **Simplify.**
8-5

1. $(6 + 2i) + (-1 + 3i)$

2. $\left(\dfrac{3}{4} - 4i\right) - \left(\dfrac{5}{2} + i\right)$

3. $(1 + 4i)(3 - i)$

4. $(2 + 3i)^2$

5. $\dfrac{3 + 5i}{1 - i}$

6. $\dfrac{8}{2 + 2i}$

8-5 **7.** Find b such that $(b + 2i)(1 - i) = 1 + 3i$.

8-6 **State the number and kind of roots of each equation.**

8. $4x^2 - x + 5 = 0$

9. $3x^2 + 6x = 5$

10. Find the value(s) of k such that this equation has two unequal real roots.

$$x^2 - kx + 4 = 0$$

11. Solve. $x^4 - 5x^2 - 36 = 0$

332   Chapter 8   Quadratic Functions and Complex Numbers

Quadratic Functions

The solutions of a quadratic equation in x and y are the (x, y) number pairs that satisfy the equation. The set of these solutions of the quadratic equation form a **quadratic function.**

Definition: Quadratic Function

A quadratic function is the set of ordered pairs (x, y) defined by the equation
$$y = ax^2 + bx + c,$$
where a, b, and c are real numbers and $a \neq 0$.

In the defining equation, the term ax^2 is called the **quadratic term,** bx is called the **linear term,** and c is called the **constant term.** The form $y = ax^2 + bx + c$ is called the **standard form of a quadratic function.**

The simplest quadratic function is $y = x^2$. It serves as a standard against which other quadratic functions may be compared. The graph of $y = x^2$ is shown here. The domain of $y = x^2$ is the set of all real numbers, and the range is the set of all nonnegative real numbers.

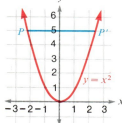

The graphs of all quadratic functions have this basic shape and are called **parabolas.** The **vertex** is the lowest point of a parabola that opens upward. The vertex for the function $y = x^2$ is the point $(0, 0)$. At the vertex, the parabola changes direction from downward to upward or vice versa.

The vertical line through the vertex is called the **axis of symmetry** of the parabola. The axis of symmetry of $y = x^2$ is $x = 0$. The axis of symmetry can be considered a line of reflection (like a mirror). For each point P of the parabola, other than the vertex, there is a matching point P' that is the **reflection image** of the point P about the axis of symmetry. The axis of symmetry is the perpendicular bisector of the segment joining P and P'.

Example 1   Show that $y = 2(3x - 1)^2 + 5$ defines a quadratic function.

Solution $y = 2(3x - 1)^2 + 5$

$\qquad = 2(9x^2 - 6x + 1) + 5$

$\qquad = 18x^2 - 12x + 2 + 5$

$\qquad = 18x^2 - 12x + 7$

Answer   Since the equation can be written in the form $y = ax^2 + bx + c$, where $a = 18$, $b = -12$, and $c = 7$, it defines a quadratic function.

Example 2   Graph the quadratic functions defined by these equations on the same pair of axes. Describe the similarities and differences among the graphs.

  a. $y = x^2$ **b.** $y = 3x^2$ **c.** $y = \frac{1}{3}x^2$

Solution   These functions have the general form $y = ax^2$. In each case, the vertex is $(0, 0)$, the axis of symmetry is $x = 0$, and the graph opens upward. The domain of each function is the set of real numbers, and the range is the set of nonnegative real numbers. The rate at which any parabola opens (rises) is determined by the coefficient of x^2. The greater the absolute value of this constant, the more narrow appearing the parabola is. A small absolute value for this constant produces a wider appearing parabola.

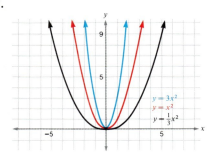

Example 3   Graph the quadratic functions defined by these equations and describe the similarities and differences among the graphs.

  a. $y = -x^2$ **b.** $y = -3x^2$ **c.** $y = -\frac{1}{3}x^2$

Solution   Each vertex is $(0, 0)$, each axis of symmetry is $x = 0$, and the domain of each function is the set of real numbers. In this case the negative coefficients of x^2 cause the graphs to open downward. The range is the set of nonpositive real numbers. The rate at which the parabola opens is again determined by the coefficient of x^2.

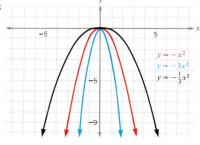

𝑒 LASSROOM EXERCISES

Write each equation in the form $y = ax^2 + bx + c$.

1. $y = 6 - 3x - 2x^2$ **2.** $y = 3(x - 2)^2$ **3.** $y = 4(x + 1)^2 - (2x + 3)^2$

4. Which of the equations in Exercises 1–3 do not define quadratic functions?

5. Does the parabola $y = x^2$ cross the line $x = 1,000,000$?

6. Does the parabola $y = -5x^2$ cross the line $x = 1,000,000$?

7. Does the parabola $y = -x^2$ cross the line $y = 10$?

8. Is 10 in the range of $y = 20x^2$?

9. State the vertex and axis of symmetry of $y = 2x^2$.

10. Which of these graphs are "inside" the graph of $y = x^2$?

  a. $y = 3x^2$ **b.** $y = \frac{1}{2}x^2$ **c.** $y = -2x^2$ **d.** $y = 13x^2$

 RITTEN EXERCISES

 State whether the equation defines a quadratic function. If the equation is quadratic, write it in standard form.

1. $x^2 + 5x = y$
2. $3x^2 - 2x = y$
3. $3y = 6x^2 + 9 - 3x$

4. $2y = 8x + 6x^2 - 2$
5. $2x + 3y = y + 5x + 2$
6. $3x + 4y = y + 7x + 6$

Graph the equations using the same set of axes.

7. a. $y = x^2$
b. $y = 3x^2$
c. $y = \frac{1}{4}x^2$

8. a. $y = x^2$
b. $y = 4x^2$
c. $y = \frac{1}{2}x^2$

9. a. $y = -x^2$
b. $y = -3x^2$
c. $y = -\frac{1}{2}x^2$

10. a. $y = -x^2$
b. $y = -2x^2$
c. $y = -\frac{1}{3}x^2$

State the vertex and axis of symmetry of each parabola.

11. $y = 2x^2$
12. $y = 20x^2$
13. $y = -\frac{1}{2}x^2$
14. $y = -\frac{1}{10}x^2$

State the number of points at which the parabola and line intersect.

15. $y = x^2$
$x = 100$

16. $y = x^2$
$x = 78$

17. $y = 100x^2$
$x = -10$

18. $y = 100x^2$
$x = -100$

19. $y = \frac{1}{2}x^2$
$y = 100$

20. $y = \frac{1}{2}x^2$
$y = 50$

21. $y = -50x^2$
$y = 10$

22. $y = -50x^2$
$y = 5$

23. $y = -\frac{1}{10}x^2$
$y = 0$

24. $y = \frac{1}{10}x^2$
$y = 0$

25. $y = -\frac{1}{10}x^2$
$y = -5$

26. $y = \frac{1}{10}x^2$
$y = -5$

27. Which of these graphs is "inside" the graph of $y = x^2$?
  a. $y = 0.4x^2$
  b. $y = 3x^2$?

28. Which of these graphs is "inside" the graph of $y = -x^2$?
  a. $y = 2x^2$
  b. $y = -1.1x^2$

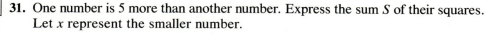 pplications

Write each quadratic function in the form $y = ax^2 + bx + c$.

29. The sum of two numbers is 26. Express their product P. Let x represent the smaller number and $26 - x$ the larger number.

30. The difference of two numbers is 17. Express their product P. Let x represent the smaller number and $x + 17$ the larger number.

B **31.** One number is 5 more than another number. Express the sum S of their squares. Let x represent the smaller number.

32. One number is twice another number. Express the difference D of their squares. Let x represent the smaller number.

33. A rectangular rose garden is enclosed by a 36-ft-long decorative fence. Express the area A of the garden in square feet.

34. The perimeter of a rectangular reflecting pool is 40 m. Express the area A of the pool in square meters.

35. An automobile dealer sells 40 cars of a certain model each month at $8000 each. For each $150 decrease in price, the dealer will sell one more car. Express the dealer's monthly sales amount S for that model of car. (Let x represent the number of price decreases.)

36. A television cable service has 4000 subscribers at a monthly charge of $8 each. For each $1 increase in the monthly charge, the company will lose 300 customers. Express the monthly income I for the cable service. (Let x represent the number of price increases.)

C For each function, state the range corresponding to the given domain.

37. $y = x^2$

$\{x: -3 \leqslant x \leqslant 3\}$

38. $y = 5x^2$

$\{x: -2 \leqslant x \leqslant 2\}$

39. $y = -\frac{1}{2}x^2$

$\{x: -6 \leqslant x \leqslant 6\}$

For each function, state the domain corresponding to the given range.

40. $y = -x^2$

$\{y: -81 \leqslant y \leqslant 0\}$

41. $y = \frac{1}{3}x^2$

$\{y: 0 \leqslant y \leqslant 24\}$

42. $y = -4x^2$

$\{y: -22 \leqslant y \leqslant 0\}$

Complete.

43. Can a nonvertical, nonhorizontal line $y = mx$ intersect the parabola $y = ax^2$ at only one point? Justify your answer.

44. Show that a parabola $y = ax^2$ will always intersect a vertical line no matter how sharply the parabola rises and no matter how far the vertical line is from the axis of symmetry of the parabola.

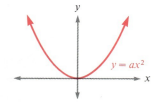

REVIEW EXERCISES

1. Write without negative exponents: $3ab^{-1}c^{-2}$. [6-1]

2. Write without using fractions: $-\dfrac{3x}{y^2}$. [6-1]

Simplify. Assume that no denominator is zero.

[6-2, 6-3, 6-4]

3. $\dfrac{1}{\dfrac{1}{a} + \dfrac{1}{b}}$

4. $\dfrac{a^2b - ab^2}{2ab}$

5. $\dfrac{3x^2}{2} \div \dfrac{5x}{3}$

6. $\dfrac{x}{x-2} \cdot \dfrac{2x-4}{x^2}$

7. $\dfrac{1}{x^2} - \dfrac{1}{x}$

8. $\dfrac{1}{x-1} - \dfrac{1}{x^2-1}$

Equations of the Form $y = a(x - h)^2$

Surfaces, made by rotating a parabola about its axis of symmetry, have the property that rays emanating from a central point and reflecting from the surface are sent out in parallel rays (for example, a spotlight). Rays from distant sources striking a parabolic surface (for example, an antenna or a sound dish) will be reflected to a central point, where their effect is amplified.

Some forms of quadratic equations show important characteristics of their parabolas. One of those forms is $y = a(x - h)^2$. We can examine the effect of h in the equation by setting $a = 1$ and graphing equations with different values of h on the same pair of axes.

These three equations are graphed at the right.

If $h = 0$, $y = (x - 0)^2 = x^2$.

If $h = 3$, $y = (x - 3)^2$.

If $h = -2$, $y = (x - (-2))^2 = (x + 2)^2$.

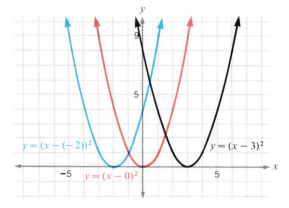

The three graphs are congruent and open upward. Each graph has a different vertex and a different axis of symmetry.

Equation	Vertex	Axis of symmetry
$y = (x - 0)^2$	$(0, 0)$	$x = 0$
$y = (x - 3)^2$	$(3, 0)$	$x = 3$
$y = (x - (-2))^2$	$(-2, 0)$	$x = -2$

The graphs illustrate the following pattern.

> For each real number h, the graph of $y = (x - h)^2$ has vertex $(h, 0)$ and axis of symmetry $x = h$.

In general, subtracting h from x shifts the graph of $y = x^2$ to the right h units when $h > 0$. The graph is shifted $|h|$ units to the left when $h < 0$.

Example 1 Graph these equations on the same pair of axes and describe patterns among the graphs and equations.

a. $y = \frac{1}{2}(x - 2)^2$ b. $y = -\frac{1}{2}(x - 2)^2$

c. $y = 3(x - 2)^2$ d. $y = -3(x - 2)^2$

Solution In the equation $y = a(x - h)^2$, the coefficient a determines how the parabola opens. When a is positive, the graph opens upward. When a is negative, the graph opens downward. When $|a|$ is small (a is close to 0), the graph "rises (falls) slowly." The graph "narrows" as $|a|$ increases. Each graph has vertex (2, 0) and axis of symmetry $x = 2$.

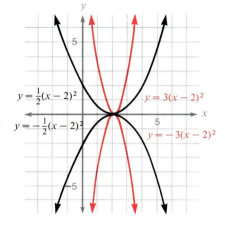

For parabolas of the form $y = a(x - h)^2$, the value of a determines the "width" and whether the graph opens upward or downward.

Graphs of Equations of the Form $y = a(x - h)^2$

For all real numbers h and a, the graph of $y = a(x - h)^2$ has vertex $(h, 0)$ and axis of symmetry $x = h$. The graph opens upward if $a > 0$ and downward if $a < 0$. The graph narrows as $|a|$ increases.

Example 2 Describe the graph of $y = 2(x + 4)^2$. Then sketch the graph.

Solution Since $h = -4$, the vertex is $(-4, 0)$ and the axis of symmetry is $x = -4$.

Since $a = 2$, the graph opens upward.

x	y
-6	8
-5	2
-4	0
-3	2
-2	8
-1	18

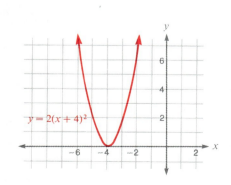

Example 3   State the vertex, the axis of symmetry, and whether the graph opens upward or downward.

$$y = 4x - 2x^2 - 2$$

Solution   *Write in standard form.* $y = -2x^2 + 4x - 2$

Factor -2 *from each term.* $= -2(x^2 - 2x + 1)$

Factor the trinomial. $= -2(x - 1)^2$

Answer   Since the value of h is 1, the vertex is $(1, 0)$, and the axis of symmetry is $x = 1$. Since the value of $a < 0$, the graph opens downward.

*C*LASSROOM EXERCISES

Write each equation in the form $y = a(x - h)^2$. State the values of a and h.

1. $\frac{1}{2}y = (x - 5)^2$ **2.** $y = x^2 + 6x + 9$ **3.** $y = 3x^2 - 30x + 75$ **4.** $y + 4 = 4x - x^2$

Sketch the graph of each equation. Identify the vertex and the axis of symmetry, and state whether the graph opens upward or downward.

5. $y = 2(x - 3)^2$ **6.** $y = -(x + 2)^2$ **7.** $y - 16 = x^2 + 8x$

*W*RITTEN EXERCISES

   Write each equation in the form $y = a(x - h)^2$.

1. $(x - 2)^2 = y$ **2.** $(x + 3)^2 = y$ **3.** $2y = 6(x + 10)^2$

4. $4y = 2(x - 5)^2$ **5.** $y = x^2 - 10x + 25$ **6.** $y = x^2 + 8x + 16$

7. $y = 6x^2 + 12x + 6$ **8.** $y = 5x^2 + 20x + 20$ **9.** $y = -x^2 + 20x - 100$

10. $y = -x^2 + 14x - 49$ **11.** $y - 18 = 2x^2 + 12x$ **12.** $y - 3 = 3x^2 - 6x$

Identify the vertex and the axis of symmetry, and state whether the graph opens upward or downward. Do not graph.

13. $y = \frac{1}{2}(x - 6)^2$ **14.** $y = \frac{1}{3}(x - 8)^2$ **15.** $y = -8(x - 100)^2$

16. $y = 10(x - 150)^2$ **17.** $y = 150(x + 3)^2$ **18.** $y = -3(x + 17)^2$

19. $y = -2x^2 - 2 + 4x$ **20.** $v = 2 + 2x^2 - 4x$ **21.** $y = 6x - 3(x^2 + 1)$

22. $y = -6x + 3(x^2 + 1)$ **23.** $y + x^2 = -9 - 6x$ **24.** $y + 8x + x^2 + 16 = 0$

Sketch these equations on the same set of axes.

25. a. $y = (x - 3)^2$ **26. a.** $y = (x - 2)^2$ **27. a.** $y = (x + 4)^2$ **28. a.** $y = (x + 3)^2$

b. $y = -\frac{1}{4}(x - 3)^2$ **b.** $y = \frac{1}{2}(x - 2)^2$ **b.** $y = (x + 2)^2$ **b.** $y = (x + 1)^2$

c. $y = 2(x - 3)^2$ **c.** $y = -\frac{1}{6}(x - 2)^2$ **c.** $y = (x - 4)^2$ **c.** $y = (x - 1)^2$

Write each equation in the form $y = a(x - h)^2$ and then graph.

29. $y = 2x^2 + 12x + 18$ **30.** $y = 3x^2 - 12x + 12$ **31.** $y = \frac{1}{2}x^2 - 4x + 8$

32. $y = \frac{1}{4}x^2 - x + 1$ **33.** $y = 2x - x^2 - 1$ **34.** $y = -32 - 16x - 2x^2$

35. $y + 9 = 3x - \frac{1}{4}x^2$ **36.** $y + 12 = -\frac{1}{3}x^2 - 4x$ **37.** $y + 8 + \frac{1}{2}x^2 = 4x$

True or false? If the statement is false, give an example to illustrate. The equations $y = a_1(x - h_1)^2$ and $y = a_2(x - h_2)^2$ define quadratic functions.

38. If $a_1 = a_2$, the graphs are identical.

39. If $a_1 = a_2$, the graphs are congruent.

40. If $a_1 = -a_2$, the graphs are congruent.

41. If $a_1 = a_2$ and $h_1 = h_2$, the graphs are identical.

42. If $a_1 = a_2$ and $h_1 > h_2$, the graphs intersect in one point.

43. If $a_1 \neq a_2$ and $h_1 = h_2$, the graphs intersect in one point.

44. If $a_1 > a_2$ and $h_1 \neq h_2$, the graphs intersect in two points.

45. If $0 < a_1 < a_2$ and $h_1 \neq h_2$, the graphs intersect in two points.

C **Write an equation in the form $y = a(x - h)^2$ that defines each quadratic function and its graph.**

46. Vertex at $(15, 0)$; congruent to $y = 2x^2$; opens upward.

47. Axis of symmetry $x = -2$; congruent to $y = -3x^2$; opens downward.

48. Vertex at $(10, 0)$; includes $(8, -2)$.   **49.** Includes $(6, 12)$ and $(3, 3)$.

 EVIEW EXERCISES

1. Simplify, listing restrictions on the variable: [6-5]

2. Solve: $\frac{1}{x^2} = \frac{1}{2x} + 3$.   [6-5]

3. A runner ran 6 km at a constant rate and then 4 km at a rate 50% faster. If the runner ran the total distance in 52 min, what was the original rate?   [6-6]

4. A painter can paint a house in 40 h. The painter and an apprentice working together can paint the house in 25 h. How long would it take the apprentice working alone to paint the house?   [6-6]

5. If volume varies inversely as pressure and the volume is 1000 cm^3 when the pressure is 0.5 atmosphere, what is the volume when the pressure is 0.2 atmosphere?   [6-7]

6. If b varies inversely as a, and $b = 20$ when $a = 10$, find b when $a = 2$.   [6-7]

Equations of the Form $y - k = a(x - h)^2$

To explore the effect of the constant k in the equation $y - k = a(x - h)^2$, let us first consider the simplest case, $y - k = x^2$. The ordered pairs below satisfy quadratic equations for three different values of k.

$y = x^2$

x	y
−3	9
−2	4
−1	1
0	0
1	1
2	4
3	9

$y - 4 = x^2$

x	y	
−3	13	= 9 + 4
−2	8	= 4 + 4
−1	5	= 1 + 4
0	4	= 0 + 4
1	5	= 1 + 4
2	8	= 4 + 4
3	13	= 9 + 4

$y + 5 = x^2$

x	y	
−3	8	= 9 − 5
−2	3	= 4 − 5
−1	−4	= 1 − 5
0	−5	= 0 − 5
1	−4	= 1 − 5
2	3	= 4 − 5
3	8	= 9 − 5

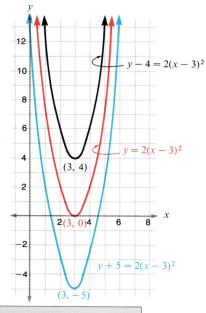

The graph of each quadratic equation is a parabola. The effect of k in the equation $y - k = x^2$ is to shift the parabola $y = x^2$ up k units when $k > 0$, and down $|k|$ units when $k < 0$.

Now, consider a more general situation by examining the graphs of these three equations.

$$y = 2(x - 3)^2$$
$$y - 4 = 2(x - 3)^2$$
$$y + 5 = 2(x - 3)^2$$

The vertices of the three parabolas are, respectively, $(3, 0)$, $(3, 4)$, and $(3, -5)$. In each case, the vertex is $(3, k)$.

Graphs of Equations of the Form $y - k = a(x - h)^2$

For all real numbers $a \neq 0$, h, and k, the graph of $y - k = a(x - h)^2$ is a parabola with the following properties:

Vertex: (h, k) *Axis of symmetry:* $x = h$
Graph: opens upward if $a > 0$ and downward if $a < 0$, narrows as $|a|$ increases.

Example 1 Sketch the graph of $y + 1 = -3(x - 2)^2$.

Solution The vertex is at $(h, k) = (2, -1)$.

The axis of symmetry is at $x = 2$.
The graph opens downward, since $a = -3$.
The graph is narrower than the graph of
$\quad y = x^2$, since $|a| = 3$.

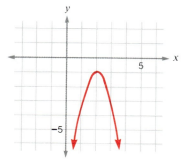

Example 2 Determine the vertex and axis of symmetry. Then sketch the graph.

$$y = -\frac{x^2}{2} + 4x - 5$$

Solution

Multiply both sides by -2 to make the coefficient of x^2 equal to 1.

Complete the square.

Factor the trinomial. Simplify.

Multiply both sides by $-\frac{1}{2}$.

Subtract 3 from both sides.

$$y = -\frac{x^2}{2} + 4x - 5$$
$$-2y = x^2 - 8x + 10$$
$$-2y = (x^2 - 8x + 16) - 16 + 10$$
$$-2y = (x - 4)^2 - 6$$
$$y = -\frac{1}{2}(x - 4)^2 + 3$$
$$y - 3 = -\frac{1}{2}(x - 4)^2$$

Answer The parabola has vertex $(4, 3)$ and axis of symmetry $x = 4$, and opens downward. Determine the coordinates of a few additional points to sketch the graph accurately.

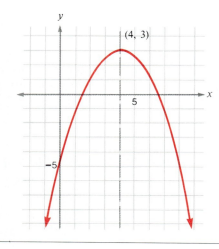

Much information can be determined about the graph of an equation in the form $y - k = a(x - h)^2$. We can transform any quadratic equation into that form by completing the square.

Example 3 Write $y = 2x^2 - 4x + 7$ in the form $y - k = a(x - h)^2$.

Solution *Multiply both sides of the equation by $\frac{1}{2}$ so that the coefficient of x^2 is 1.*

$$\frac{y}{2} = x^2 - 2x + \frac{7}{2}$$

Group the quadratic and linear terms in x.

$$\frac{y}{2} = (x^2 - 2x) + \frac{7}{2}$$

Add and subtract 1 to make a perfect-square trinomial.

$$\frac{y}{2} = (x^2 - 2x + 1) - 1 + \frac{7}{2}$$

Factor the trinomial. Simplify.

$$\frac{y}{2} = (x - 1)^2 + \frac{5}{2}$$

Multiply both sides by 2 to make the coefficient of y equal to 1.

$$y = 2(x - 1)^2 + 5$$

Subtract 5 from both sides.

$$y - 5 = 2(x - 1)^2$$

$\mathcal{C}$LASSROOM EXERCISES

Write each equation in the form $y - k = a(x - h)^2$. Identify a, h, and k.

1. $y = 3(x - 2)^2 - 5$ **2.** $y = x^2 - 6x + 9$

3. $y = -2x^2 + 16x - 35$ **4.** $y = 3x^2 - 8x - 7$

5–8. Sketch the graph of each equation in Exercises 1–4. Identify the vertex and axis of symmetry, and state whether the graph opens upward or downward.

$\mathcal{W}$RITTEN EXERCISES

 Write each equation in the form $y - k = a(x - h)^2$.

1. $2y + 6 = (x + 2)^2$ **2.** $2y - 4 = 6(x + 5)^2$ **3.** $y = 3(x - 6)^2 + 9$

4. $y = 4x(x - 8)^2 + 12$ **5.** $y + 5 = x^2 + 4x + 4$ **6.** $y - 4 = x^2 - 4x + 4$

7. $y - 6 = 2x^2 - 24x + 72$ **8.** $y + 2 = 3x^2 - 24x + 48$ **9.** $y = 4 - x^2$

10. $y = 1 - 2x^2$ **11.** $y = x^2 - 5x + 1$ **12.** $y = x^2 - 3x + 10$

13. $y = 4x^2 - 16x - 3$ **14.** $y = 2x^2 - 12x - 7$ **15.** $y = 2x^2 + 4x + 5$

16. $y = 12x - 3x^2 - 14$ **17.** $y = \left(\frac{1}{2}\right)x^2 + 5x + 4$ **18.** $y = \left(\frac{1}{3}\right)x^2 + 2x + 2$

Identify the vertex and the axis of symmetry, and state whether the graph opens upward or downward. Do not graph.

19. $y - 10 = -8(x - 12)^2$

20. $y - 100 = -5(x - 3)^2$

21. $y + 2 = \frac{1}{2}(x - 5)^2$

22. $y - 5 = \frac{1}{3}(x + 2)^2$

23. $y = 2x^2 - 4x + 6$

24. $y = -2x^2 - 20x - 53$

25. $y + 3 = -\frac{1}{10}(x + 5)^2$

26. $y + 8 = -6(x - 7)^2$

27. $y = x^2 + 7x + 8.25$

28. $y = x^2 - 5x - 9.25$

29. $y = 3x^2 - 18x + 100$

30. $y = 2x^2 - 16x + 100$

Sketch the three graphs on the same set of axes.

31.a. $y - 1 = (x - 3)^2$

  b. $y + 3 = (x + 2)^2$

  c. $y + 2 = (x + 4)^2$

32.a. $y + 1 = 2(x - 2)^2$

  b. $y + 1 = -\frac{1}{2}(x - 2)^2$

  c. $y + 1 = \frac{1}{3}(x - 2)^2$

33.a. $y - 2 = 3(x + 3)^2$

  b. $y - 2 = -\frac{1}{4}(x + 3)^2$

  c. $y - 2 = -2(x + 3)^2$

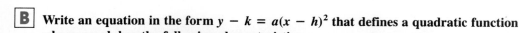

B Write an equation in the form $y - k = a(x - h)^2$ that defines a quadratic function whose graph has the following characteristics.

34. Vertex at $(2, -3)$; congruent to $y = 5x^2$; opens upward.

35. Vertex at $(100, 50)$; congruent to $y = \frac{1}{10}x^2$; opens downward.

36. Vertex at $(-50, 25)$; congruent to $y = -2(x + 1)^2$; opens upward.

37. Axis of symmetry $x = 5$; congruent to $y = x^2$; includes $(5, 6)$; opens downward.

38. Axis of symmetry $x = 10$; includes $(9, 8)$, $(10, 9)$, and $(11, 8)$.

39. Vertex at $(3, 6)$; includes $(6, 7)$.

Determine the value(s) of k such that the graph of the function is tangent to the line $y = 4$.

40. $y = -x^2 + 2x + k$

41. $y = x^2 - 4kx + 8$

Write each equation in the form $y - k = a(x - h)^2$ and graph the equation.

42. $y = x^2 + 6x + 7$

43. $y = x^2 + 4x + 7$

44. $y = 2x^2 - 16x + 29$

45. $y = -\frac{1}{2}x^2 + 4x - 4$

46. $y + 2x = \frac{1}{3}x^2 + 5$

47. $y + x + 4 = -\frac{1}{4}x^2$

C The equations $y - k_1 = a_1(x - h_1)$ and $y - k_2 = a_2(x - h_2)$ define two quadratic functions. Under the following conditions, at how many points do their graphs intersect?

48. $a_1 = a_2, k_1 = k_2, h_1 \neq h_2$

49. $a_1 = a_2, h_1 = h_2, k_1 \neq k_2$

50. $h_1 = h_2, k_1 = k_2, a_1 \neq a_2$

Determine the value(s) of k such that the graph of the function intersects the line $y = -1$ at two points.

51. $y = x^2 + 2x + k$

52. $y = -x^2 - kx - 5$

REVIEW EXERCISES

Simplify. State restrictions on the variables.

1. $-\sqrt{144}$

2. $\sqrt[3]{-\dfrac{1}{27}}$

3. $\sqrt{72}$

4. $\sqrt{a^5b^2}$ [7-1, 7-2]

5. $(3 + \sqrt{2})(3 - \sqrt{2})$

6. $\sqrt{18} + \sqrt{8} - \sqrt{50}$

7. $\dfrac{3ab}{\sqrt{a^2b}}$

8. $\dfrac{12}{3 + \sqrt{3}}$ [7-3, 7-4]

Self-Quiz 3

8-7 1. Write the equation $2(y - 1) = (2x - 3)^2$ in the form $y = ax^2 + bx + c$.

2. Graph these equations on the same pair of axes. $y = 2x^2, \; y = -\dfrac{1}{2}x^2$

3. Which of the parabolas $y = 10x^2$ and $y = -5x^2$ will intersect the lines?
   a. $x = 10$ **b.** $y = -3$

8-8 4. Write the equation $y + 18 = (x + 2)^2 + (x + 8)^2$ in the form $y = a(x - h)^2$ and state the values of a and h.

8-8,   **Identify the vertex and the axis of symmetry, and state whether the graph opens**
8-9   **upward or downward.**

5. $y = 2x - 1 - x^2$

6. $y = 5\left(x + \dfrac{3}{2}\right)^2$

7. $2y - 4 = -\left(x + \dfrac{5}{2}\right)^2$

8-9 8. Write the equation $y = -2x^2 - 4x + 1$ in the form $y - k = a(x - h)^2$.

9. Write an equation in the form $y - k = a(x - h)^2$ for a parabola that has its vertex at $(-1, 2)$, is congruent to the parabola $y = -x^2$, and opens downward.

HISTORICAL NOTE   Terms for Numbers

The terms **real number** and **imaginary number** were first used in 1637 by French mathematician René Descartes. Imaginary numbers were once considered curiosities of no practical value. Karl Friedrich Gauss demonstrated their importance to mathematical theory and coined the term **complex number** in 1832. Around 1900, the practicality of complex numbers was established in the solution of electrical problems by a German-born American engineer, Charles Steinmetz.

René Descartes

LESSON 8-10

Maximum and Minimum Values

The path followed by a projectile is parabolic if factors such as air resistance are negligible. The launch angle determines the height and range achieved by the projectile. The theoretical angle for achieving maximum range (in a vacuum) is 45°. However, for projectiles fired long distances (such as 50 miles), air resistance becomes a determining factor. When launched at 60°, a projectile achieves a greater maximum height and can go above the troposphere into the less dense stratosphere. Owing to decreased air resistance, the projectile achieves a greater range when launched at 60° than at 45°.

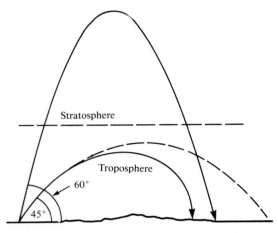

If the graph of a quadratic function defined by the equation $f(x) = ax^2 + bx + c$ opens upward, a **minimum value** of $f(x)$ occurs at the vertex. There is no maximum value. If the graph of a quadratic function opens downward, a **maximum value** of $f(x)$ occurs at the vertex. There is no minimum value.

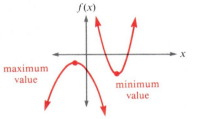

Example 1 Determine the maximum or minimum for the function $f(x) = 4 - 3x - x^2$.

Solution *Write in standard form.*

$$f(x) = -x^2 - 3x + 4$$
$$-f(x) = (x^2 + 3x) - 4$$

Complete the square to find the vertex.

$$-f(x) = \left(x^2 + 3x + \frac{9}{4}\right) - \frac{9}{4} - 4$$

$$-f(x) = \left(x + \frac{3}{2}\right)^2 - \frac{25}{4}$$

$$f(x) = -1\left(x + \frac{3}{2}\right)^2 + \frac{25}{4}$$

$$f(x) - \frac{25}{4} = -1\left(x + \frac{3}{2}\right)^2 \quad \text{The vertex is } \left(-\frac{3}{2}, \frac{25}{4}\right).$$

Answer Since the coefficient of the quadratic term is negative, the graph opens downward and a *maximum* of $\frac{25}{4}$ occurs at the vertex.

Example 2   **Determine the value at which the maximum or minimum occurs for**
$y = 4x^2 - 16x + 1.$

Solution   Since the coefficient of x^2 is positive, the graph opens upward, and a *minimum* occurs at the vertex.

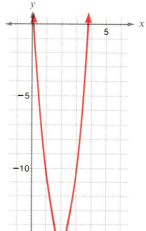

Complete the square to find the vertex.

$$y = 4x^2 - 16x + 1$$

$$\frac{1}{4}y = x^2 - 4x + \frac{1}{4}$$

$$\frac{1}{4}y = (x^2 - 4x + 4) - 4 + \frac{1}{4}$$

$$\frac{1}{4}y = (x - 2)^2 - \frac{15}{4}$$

$$y = 4(x - 2)^2 - 15$$

$$y + 15 = 4(x - 2)^2$$

The vertex is $(2, -15)$.

Answer   The minimum of -15 occurs for the value $x = 2$.

Example 3   **Solve.**

An object is projected upward from the ground with an initial velocity of v_0 feet per second. Its distance $d(t)$ in feet above the ground after t seconds is given by the formula $d(t) = v_0 t - 16t^2$. What is the maximum height reached by an object shot straight up with an initial velocity of 240 ft/s?

Solution   Substituting into the formula gives:

$$d(t) = 240t - 16t^2$$

$$d(t) = -16t^2 + 240t.$$

Write in the form $y - k = a(x - h)^2$ by completing the square.

$$-\frac{1}{16}d(t) = t^2 - 15t$$

$$-\frac{1}{16}d(t) = t^2 - 15t + \frac{225}{4} - \frac{225}{4}$$

$$-\frac{1}{16}d(t) = \left(t - \frac{15}{2}\right)^2 - \frac{225}{4}$$

$$d(t) = -16\left(t - \frac{15}{2}\right)^2 + 900$$

$$d(t) - 900 = -16\left(t - \frac{15}{2}\right)^2$$

The vertex is $\left(\frac{15}{2}, 900\right)$.

Answer   The maximum height reached is 900 ft.

Example 4   **Solve.**

A doughnut shop usually sells 600 dozen doughnuts each day at a price of $1.60 per dozen. Because of an increase in the cost of labor and ingredients, the owner decides that prices must be raised. From past experience the owner knows that each $0.10 increase in price will decrease the number of doughnuts sold by 25 dozen per day. How much should the owner raise the price to maximize the daily income?

Solution   Let x = the number of $.10 increases in the price per dozen. Then $1.60 + 0.10x$ = the cost per dozen in dollars, and $600 - 25x$ = the number of dozen sold. Let y = the number of dollars of income.

Equation: Income = (price per dozen)(number of dozens)

$$y = (1.60 + 0.10x)(600 - 25x)$$
$$= 960 - 40x + 60x - 2.5x^2$$
$$= -2.5x^2 + 20x + 960$$

Write in the form $y - k = a(x - h)^2$ to find the vertex.

$$\frac{y}{-2.5} = x^2 - 8x - 384$$

$$\frac{y}{-2.5} = x^2 - 8x + 16 - 16 - 384$$

$$\frac{y}{-2.5} = (x - 4)^2 - 400$$

$$y = -2.5(x - 4)^2 + 1000$$

$$y - 1000 = -2.5(x - 4)^2$$

The vertex is (4, 1000).

Answer   The income will be maximized if there are 4 raises in price of $.10 each. Therefore, the price should be raised $.40.

*C*LASSROOM EXERCISES

State whether the function has a maximum or minimum. Then identify the maximum or minimum and the x-value for which it occurs.

1. $y - 7 = 2\left(x + \frac{3}{2}\right)^2$ **2.** $0 = x^2 + 6x - 3 + y$

3. A gardener wishes to enclose the maximum rectangular area possible within 24 m of fencing. What are the dimensions of the garden?

 RITTEN EXERCISES

 State whether the function has a maximum, a minimum, neither, or both.

1. $y = 20x^2 - 15x - 10$ **2.** $y = -20x^2 + 15x + 10$ **3.** $y - 7 = -2(x + 9)^2$

4. $y - 6 = 3(x - 8)^2$ **5.** $y + 5x^2 = 2x + 7$ **6.** $y + 3x^2 = 6x + 4$

7. $4y - 8 = 3(x + 20)^2 - 4$ **8.** $3y + 9 = 12(x + 7)^2 + 6$ **9.** $y + x^2 = (x + 3)^2$

10. $y + 4x(x + 3) = (2x + 1)^2$ **11.** $y = (x + 2)^2 - x(x + 4)$ **12.** $y + x^2 + 6x = (x + 3)^2$

For each function, state (a) the maximum or minimum, and (b) the value at which the maximum or minimum occurs.

13. $y - 10 = 2(x + 3)^2$ **14.** $y + 10 = 2(x - 3)^2$ **15.** $f(x) + 12.3 = -2(x - 5)^2$

16. $f(x) - 7.7 = -3(x + 6)^2$ **17.** $h(t) - 50.6 = -0.1(t - 2.3)^2$ **18.** $h(t) + 9.4 = -0.6(t + 3.2)^2$

19. $p = q^2 - 8q + 10$

20. $g = h^2 + 8h - 10$

21. $g(r) = r^2 + 5r - 8$

22. $f(b) = b^2 - 7b + 2$

23. $y = 5x^2 + 10x + 100$

24. $y = 2x^2 + 20x + 25$

25. $y = -3x^2 + 12x - 2$

26. $y = -4x^2 + 16x - 1$

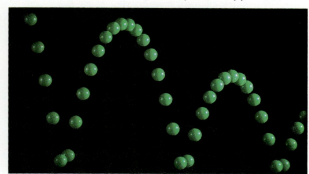

 A pplications: Maximums and Minimums

27. Standing on the roof of a building 160 ft above the ground, Klaus threw a ball upward with a speed of 48 ft/s. The formula $h = 160 + 48t - 16t^2$ gives the height in feet h of the ball relative to the ground after t seconds.

   a. What is the maximum height reached by the ball?

   b. After how many seconds did the ball reach its maximum height?

   c. After how many seconds did the ball strike the ground?

28. Scouts used a slingshot to launch a small rock upward from a cliff 250 ft above the river. The initial velocity was 320 ft/s. The formula $h = 250 + 320t - 16t^2$ gives the height in feet h of the rock relative to the river after t seconds.

   a. What is the maximum height reached by the rock?

   b. After how many seconds did the rock reach its maximum height?

   c. After how many seconds did the rock strike the river?

B **29.** A rancher has 20 m of chicken wire to make a rectangular chicken pen using the barn for one side of the pen. What are the dimensions of the pen that will contain the greatest area?

30. A long sheet of copper 32 cm wide is to be made into a rain gutter by turning up vertical strips along each side. How many centimeters should be turned up at each side in order to give a gutter with the largest cross-sectional area?

31. An independent telephone company has 4000 subscribers, each having a monthly charge of $16. It estimates that it can add 500 new customers for each $1 decrease in the monthly charge. What monthly charge will give the largest monthly income? What is that income?

32. A television set manufacturer can sell 1000 sets per month for $500 each. Marketing research indicates that the company can sell 50 more sets per month for each $10 decrease in price. What price per set will give the greatest monthly sales? What is that sales amount?

33. The rate of photosynthesis in a certain plant depends on the intensity of light x according to the formula $R(x) = 270x - 90x^2$.

   a. Find the value of the intensity that maximizes the rate.

   b. What is the maximum rate value?

34. The orange yield y from a grove of orange trees is given by $y = x(800 - x)$, where x is the number of orange trees per acre.

   a. How many trees per acre will give the greatest yield?

   b. What is the greatest yield?

35. Sensitivity S to a drug depends on the dosage size x according to the formula $S = 1000x - x^2$.

   a. What dosage size maximizes the sensitivity?

   b. What is the maximum sensitivity?

   c. What dosage sizes produce zero sensitivity?

36. Meixner, Inc. manufactures garden tools. They estimate that their daily profit P in dollars depends on the number of tools n produced according to the formula $P = -0.01n^2 + 8n - 700$.

   a. How many garden tools should be produced in order to get the greatest profit?

   b. What is the maximum profit?

   c. Sketch a graph of the function.

   d. What are the break-even points? ($P = 0$)

   e. Interpret the P-intercept. ($n = 0$)

37. The Bleisteiner Company manufactures laboratory scales for pharmacies. They found that their monthly profit P depends on the selling price s according to the formula $P = -1.4s^2 + 980s - 115{,}550$, where P and s are measured in dollars.

    a. At what selling price is the profit greatest?

    b. What is the maximum profit?

    c. Graph the function. What are the break-even points (where $P = 0$)?

    d. Interpret the P-intercept (where $s = 0$).

C **38.** The owner of an apartment building with 50 units has found that if the rent for each unit is \$360 per month, all of the units will be filled. But one unit will become vacant for each \$10 increase in the monthly rent. What monthly rent would maximize the monthly income? What is the maximum income?

39. A travel agent charges \$50 per person for a tour if 30 people go on the tour. For each additional person (in excess of 30), the charge is reduced \$1 per person. What number of people would maximize the revenue for the travel agent? What is the maximum revenue?

40. The Garden City Nursery wants to fence a rectangular plot of land into four equal sections for different varieties of shrubs. The plot is to be subdivided with three fences parallel to the sides. What is the maximum area that can be enclosed with 200 m of available fencing?

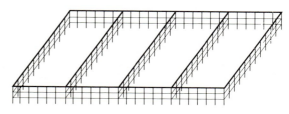

41. Show that if P is the perimeter of a rectangle, the maximum possible area is that of a square whose side is $\dfrac{P}{4}$ and whose area is $\dfrac{P^2}{16}$.

42. The height in feet of an object t seconds after it has been projected upward from the ground is given by the formula $h(t) = v_0 t - 16t^2$, where v_0 is the initial velocity (in feet per second). Determine the initial velocity required for the object to reach a maximum height of 100 ft.

*R*EVIEW EXERCISES

1. Find the distance between $(2, 3)$ and $(-5, 4)$.   [7-5]

2. Find the midpoint of the segment joining $(3, 5)$ and $(-2, 1)$.   [7-5]

Solve.

3. $x + \sqrt{x} = 2$ **4.** $\sqrt{2x - 3} = 5$ **5.** $\sqrt{5 + \sqrt{x - 5}} = 4$ [7-6]

6. Write in radical form: $5^{\frac{2}{3}}$.   **7.** Write using rational exponents: $\dfrac{1}{\sqrt[3]{2}}$.   [7-7]

EXTENSION   The Complex-Number Plane

Refer to the graph at the right. Point A is the graph of the number $2 + 3i$.

1. Which labeled point is the graph of the complex conjugate of $2 + 3i$?

2. Which other labeled points are complex conjugates of each other?

3. How are the graphs of complex conjugates related to each other?

4. Which labeled point is the additive inverse of $2 + 3i$?

5. Which other labeled points are additive inverses of each other?

6. How are the graphs of additive inverses related to each other?

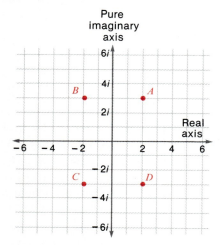

CHAPTER SUMMARY

▶ **Vocabulary**

general quadratic equation	[page 305]	double root	[page 329]
quadratic equation	[page 305]	quadratic in form	[page 330]
standard form (of a quadratic equation)	[page 305]	quadratic function	[page 333]
		quadratic term	[page 333]
pure quadratic equation	[page 305]	linear term	[page 333]
completing the square	[page 306]	constant term	[page 333]
quadratic formula	[page 311]	standard form of a quadratic function	[page 333]
imaginary number	[page 316]		
pure imaginary number	[page 316]	parabola	[page 333]
complex number	[page 317]	vertex	[page 333]
absolute value of a complex number	[page 318]	axis of symmetry	[page 333]
		reflection image	[page 333]
complex conjugates	[page 322]	minimum value	[page 346]
discriminant	[page 329]	maximum value	[page 346]

▶ The equation $ax^2 + bx + c = 0$, $a \neq 0$, is called the *general quadratic equation in x*. A quadratic equation with no *x*-term is called a *pure quadratic equation*. [8-1]

▶ The Square Root Property of Equations
For all real numbers m and n, $n \geq 0$, if $m^2 = n$, then $m = \sqrt{n}$ or $m = -\sqrt{n}$.

▶ The Quadratic Formula [8-2]
The roots of the quadratic equation $ax^2 + bx + c = 0$, $a \neq 0$, are
$$\frac{-b + \sqrt{b^2 - 4ac}}{2a} \text{ and } \frac{-b - \sqrt{b^2 - 4ac}}{2a}.$$

▶ A *complex number* is a number of the form $a + bi$, where a and b are real numbers and i is the imaginary unit. [8-3]

▶ Equality of Complex Numbers
For all complex numbers $a + bi$ and $c + di$,
$a + bi = c + di$ if and only if $a = c$ and $b = d$.

▶ Absolute Value of a Complex Number
The absolute value of a complex number $a + bi$ is
$$|a + bi| = \sqrt{a^2 + b^2}.$$

▶ Addition of Complex Numbers [8-4]
For all real numbers a, b, c, and d,
$$(a + bi) + (c + di) = (a + c) + (b + d)i.$$

▶ The Additive Inverse Property of Complex Numbers
For each complex number z, there is a complex number $-z$ such that
$z + (-z) = 0$. If $z = a + bi$, then $-z = -(a + bi) = -a - bi$.

▶ Subtraction of Complex Numbers
For all complex numbers w and z, $w - z = w + (-z)$.
If $w = a + bi$ and $z = c + di$, then $w - z = (a + bi) - (c + di)$
$$= (a - c) + (b - d)i.$$

▶ Complex Conjugates
For all real numbers a and b, $a + bi$ and $a - bi$ are *complex conjugates*.

▶ Multiplication of Complex Numbers [8-5]
For all complex numbers $a + bi$ and $c + di$,
$$(a + bi)(c + di) = (ac - bd) + (ad + bc)i.$$

▶ Division of Complex Numbers   [8-5]
For all complex numbers w and z, $z \neq 0$, $\dfrac{w}{z} = w\left(\dfrac{1}{z}\right)$.

▶ If $ax^2 + bx + c = 0$, and the discriminant $D = b^2 - 4ac$, where a, b, and c [8-6]
are rational, then:

Condition	Roots r_1 and r_2
$D = 0$	Equal and rational
$D > 0$ and D a perfect square	Unequal and rational
$D > 0$ and D not a perfect square	Unequal and irrational
$D < 0$	Unequal and not real (complex conjugates)

▶ A quadratic function is the set of ordered pairs (x, y) defined by the equation   [8-7]
$y = ax^2 + bx + c$, where a, b, and c are real numbers and $a \neq 0$.

▶ For all real numbers $a \neq 0$, h, and k, the graph of $y - k = a(x - h)^2$ is a   [8-8,
parabola with the following properties.   8-9]
   Vertex: (h, k) Axis of symmetry: $x = h$
   Graph: opens upward if $a > 0$ and downward if $a < 0$,
          narrows as $|a|$ increases.

▶ If the graph of a quadratic function $f(x) = ax^2 + bx + c$ opens upward, a   [8-10]
minimum value of $f(x)$ occurs at the vertex. If the graph opens downward, a
maximum value of $f(x)$ occurs at the vertex.

$\mathcal{C}$HAPTER REVIEW

8-1 **Objective:** To write quadratic equations in standard form.

**Identify whether the equation is quadratic. If it is, write it in standard form
and state the values of a, b, and c.**
   1. $(x + 5)^2 = (3 - x)^2$ **2.** $2x(x - 3) = 5$

8-1 **Objective:** To solve quadratic equations by completing the square.
   3. Write $x^2 - 12x + 30 = 0$ in the form $(x + d)^2 = k$.
   4. Solve: $y^2 - 6y = 23$.

8-2 **Objective:** To apply the quadratic formula to second-degree equations in
                one variable.

Solve.
   5. $6x^2 - 11x - 7 = 0$ **6.** $x^2 - 5x = 7$ **7.** $9w^2 = 4(3w - 1)$

8-3 Objective: To simplify expressions containing imaginary numbers.

Simplify.

8. $\sqrt{-6} \cdot \sqrt{-24}$ **9.** $\sqrt{-\dfrac{25}{9}}$ **10.** $(4i)(3)(2i)$ **11.** $(2i)^5$

Solve.

12. $x^2 = -81$ **13.** $4t^2 + 288 = 0$

8-3 Objective: To apply the properties of complex numbers.

14. Find x, a real number, if $\dfrac{7}{2} + 3xi = \dfrac{\sqrt{49} - 6i}{2}$.

15. Simplify: $|3 - 2i|$.

16. Solve: $x^2 - 4x + 5 = 0$.

8-4 Objective: To simplify sums and differences of complex numbers.

Simplify.

17. $5 - (2 + 3i)$ **18.** $\left(4 - \sqrt{5}i\right) + \left(\dfrac{5}{2} + 2\sqrt{5}i\right)$

8-5 Objective: To simplify products and quotients of complex numbers.

Simplify.

19. $(8 - i)(3 + 2i)$ **20.** $\dfrac{6 + 2i}{1 + i}$

21. Solve: $(x + 2i)(5 - i) = -8 + 12i$.

8-6 Objective: To use the discriminant to identify the number and kind of roots of a quadratic equation.

State the number and kind of roots.

22. $x^2 - 6x - 27 = 0$ **23.** $2x^2 + 5x + \left(\dfrac{13}{4}\right) = 0$

24. Find the value(s) of k for which $3x^2 + 6x - k = 0$ has real roots.

Objective: To solve equations that are quadratic in form.

Solve.

25. $y^4 + 2y^2 - 8 = 0$ **26.** $x^{\frac{2}{3}} + 7x^{\frac{1}{3}} - 8 = 0$

8-7 Objective: To identify quadratic functions and write their equations in standard form.

State whether the equation defines a quadratic function of x. If so, write it in standard form.

27. $y - 3 = (2x - 1)^2 - 4x^2$ **28.** $(x - 4)^2 - 5 = 4(5 - 2x) + y$

Objective: To graph quadratic functions.

Graph on the same set of axes.

29. a. $y = -x^2$ **b.** $y = x^2$ **c.** $y = 2x^2$

30. State the number of points of intersection of the parabola and line.
$$y = -3x^2, \qquad y = -3$$

8-8 **Objective:** To identify and apply characteristics of the graphs of quadratic equations with the form $y = a(x - h)^2$.

31. Identify the vertex and the axis of symmetry, and state whether the graph of the parabola opens upward or downward.
$$y = 6x - 3 - 3x^2$$

32. True or false? The graph of $y = a_1(x - h_1)^2$ is congruent to the graph of $y = a_2(x - h_2)^2$ if $a_1 = a_2$ and $h_1 \neq h_2$.

33. Graph: $y = -\dfrac{1}{2}(x + 4)^2$.

8-9 **Objective:** To identify and apply characteristics of the graphs of quadratic equations with the form $y - k = a(x - h)^2$.

34. Which of these parabolas are congruent?

   a. $y - 3 = -2(x - 1)^2$ **b.** $y + 3 = -2(x - 1)^2$

   c. $y - 3 = 2(x - 1)^2$ **d.** $y + 3 = 2(x + 1)^2$

35. Which of the parabolas in Exercise 34 have the same vertex?

36. Write the equation in the form $y - k = a(x - h)^2$ of the quadratic function with axis of symmetry $x = -1$, congruent to $y = x^2$, opening downward, and tangent to the line $y = 3$.

8-10 **Objective:** To determine the maximum or minimum values of a quadratic function.

37. Find the maximum value of the function $f(x) = 1 - 16x - 4x^2$.

38. For what value of x does $y = x^2 - 5x + 3$ have its minimum?

39. The height in feet of a football from the ground t seconds after being kicked is given by the formula $h(t) = 80t - 16t^2$. Find the maximum height that the football attains.

$\mathcal{C}$HAPTER 8 SELF-TEST

8-1   **1.** Write in standard form: $5x(1 - x) = \dfrac{3 + 2x}{4}$.

      2. Write in the form $(x + d)^2 = k$: $2x^2 - 4x + 1 = 0$.

8-1, **Solve.**

8-2   **3.** $(x + 7)^2 = 8$ **4.** $x^2 - 2\sqrt{2}x - 7 = 0$ **5.** $6x^2 - 19x + 15 = 0$

8-3 **Simplify.**

6. $\sqrt{-6} \cdot \sqrt{-15} + 2\sqrt{10}$ **7.** $(-2i)^3$ **8.** i^{10}

8-3 **9.** Find real numbers x and y such that $2x + 8i = -14 - 3yi$.

8-3, **Solve.**
8-4,
8-5 **10.** $x^2 - 6x + 21 = 0$.   **11.** $x^2 + 4x + 6 = 0$

Simplify.

12. $|3 + i|$ **13.** $(5i)^2 + 3i^4 - 1$

14. $\dfrac{4}{(1 + 2i)}$ **15.** $3(5 + 2i) - (4 + 6i)$ **16.** $i^3 - i$

17. Show that $3 - 2i$ is a root of the equation $x^2 - 6x + 13 = 0$.

8-6 **18.** Use the discriminant to identify the number and kind of roots of $4x^2 - 12x + 9 = 0$.

19. Find the value(s) of k such that $2x^2 - 6x + k = 0$ has imaginary roots.

20. Solve: $x - 7\sqrt{x} - 8 = 0$.

8-7 **State whether the equation represents a quadratic function. If so, state whether the graph opens upward or downward.**

21. $x^2 - y = 2x^2 + 4$ **22.** $y = (x + 2)(-x + 1)$

Let $y = ax^2$, $y = bx^2$, and $y = cx^2$ be parabolas.

23. What is the relationship between a and b if the graph of $y = bx^2$ is "inside" that of $y = ax^2$?

24. What is the relationship between a and c if the graph of $y = cx^2$ opens in the direction opposite to that of $y = ax^2$?

8-8 **25.** Write the quadratic equation $2x^2 - y = 6(2x - 3)$ in the form $y = a(x - h)^2$.

8-8, **Graph.**
8-9
26. $y = -x^2 - 4x - 4$ **27.** $y = x^2 + 2x - 3$

For each set of parabolas in Exercises 28 and 29, state which of the following statements are true.

    a. The three parabolas are congruent.

    b. The three parabolas have the same vertex.

    c. The three parabolas have the same axis of symmetry.

    d. The three parabolas open in the same direction.

28. $y = (x - 2)^2$ **29.** $y = (x - 1)^2$
       $y + 1 = 3(x - 2)^2$ $y + 2 = 3(x + 5)^2$
         $y = -(x - 2)^2$ $y = \dfrac{1}{2}x^2$

8-9 **30.** Write the equation of the parabola that has an axis of symmetry $x = -1$ and passes through $(-3, 10)$ and $(-1, 2)$.

8-10 **31.** State whether the function $y = 1 - 4x - 2x^2$ has a maximum or a minimum value and state this value.

Solve.

32. A farmer with 300 yd of fencing wishes to enclose a rectangular area as large as possible, using an existing fence as one side. What is the maximum area that can be fenced?

33. Find a number which when added to its square gives the smallest possible sum. Then, state the sum.

$\mathcal{P}$RACTICE FOR COLLEGE ENTRANCE TESTS

Choose the best answer for each problem.

1. If $i^2 = -1$ and $z = 1 + 3i$, then $z^2 = $ _?_ .

    A. -8 **B.** $-8 + 6i$ **C.** $-9 + 3i$ **D.** $-9 + 7i$ **E.** $10 + 6i$

2. If $i^n = i$, then which of the following is a possible value of n?

    A. 23   **B.** 24   **C.** 25   **D.** 26   **E.** 27

3. Which of the following graphs could represent $y = ax^2 + bx + c = 0$, where $b^2 - 4ac = 0$?

A.
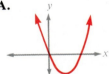

B.
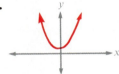

C.
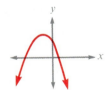

D.
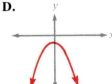

E.
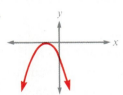

4. If $z = a + bi$ and $\bar{z} = a - bi$, then $z \cdot \bar{z} = $ _?_ .

    A. $a^2 - b^2$ **B.** $(a^2 - b^2) - 2abi$ **C.** $(a^2 - b^2) + abi$

    D. $(a^2 + b^2) - 2abi$ **E.** $a^2 + b^2$

5. If $z = a + bi$ and $\bar{z} = a - bi$, where $a \neq 0$ and $b \neq 0$, then which of the following are real numbers?

$$\text{I. } z + \bar{z} \qquad \text{II. } z - \bar{z} \qquad \text{III. } z \cdot \bar{z}$$

A. I only
B. I and II only
C. III only
D. I and III only
E. I, II, and III

6. If $z = 1 + i$, then $z^3 = $ ___?___.

A. $-2 + 2i$ **B.** $-1 + 3i$ **C.** $-3 + i$ **D.** $-4 + 2i$ **E.** $-2 + 4i$

7. Which of the following properties hold for complex numbers?

I. If $a = b$, then $a^2 = b^2$. II. If $ab = 0$, then $a = 0$ or $b = 0$. III. $a > b$ or $a = b$ or $a < b$.

A. I and II only
B. II only
C. I and III only
D. II and III only
E. I, II, and III

8. The roots of the equation $3x^2 + 2x - 8 = 0$ are ___?___.

A. Equal and rational
B. Unequal and rational
C. Unequal and irrational
D. Unequal and nonreal
E. Equal and nonreal

9. For what values of k will $3x^2 + kx + 12 = 0$ have a double rational root?

A. 6
B. 6 and -6
C. 12
D. 12 and -12
E. No values

10. If $f(x) = 2x^2 - 5$ and $0 < x < 4$, then $f(x)$ is between which of the following pairs of numbers?

A. -10 and 22
B. -5 and 27
C. -5 and 59
D. 0 and 22
E. 0 and 27

11. Which of the following could represent the equation $y = ax^2 + bx + c$ if $b^2 - 4ac < 0$?

A.

B.
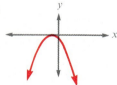
C.
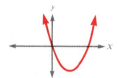

D.
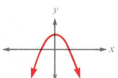
E.
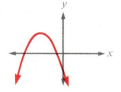

12. The function defined by $y = 40x - 5x^2$ has a maximum value when $x = $ ___?___.

A. 0
B. 2
C. 4
D. 6
E. 8

CHAPTER 9

Conic Sections

The orbit of a comet is a conic section: an ellipse, parabola, or hyperbola. A comet in an elliptical orbit follows a path with the sun at one focus and returns periodically to the vicinity of the sun. Comets in parabolic and hyperbolic orbits are not bound to our solar system. These comets pass our sun and then head into space, never to return.

The most famous comet in an elliptical orbit is Halley's comet named in honor of Edmund Halley. Halley was the first to recognize the similarity in the orbits of comets observed in 1531, 1607, and 1682. He concluded that the observations were of the same comet, one that orbited the sun every 75 years in an elongated elliptical orbit. Halley predicted this comet would return to the vicinity of the sun in 1758. The comet was first observed again on December 25, 1758.

Halley's comet has returned during this century in 1910 and in 1985–1986.

Circles and Translations

Four curves, the circle, the parabola, the ellipse, and the hyperbola, are called the **conic sections.** The words *conic section* may be traced back to the early Greek scholars such as Apollonius (third to second century B.C.). They are derived from the fact that each conic section is the intersection of a plane and a right circular cone. (See Lesson 9-5.)

The circle has been used throughout history in art and architecture because of the beauty of its form and the ease of its construction. The Romans were the first to recognize the importance of a semicircular arch in architecture. They used semicircular arches and domes extensively in building bridges, aqueducts, city gates, and trumphal monuments.

Each conic section has a second-degree equation and is defined in terms of the distance of its points from fixed points and/or lines. Perhaps the simplest of the conic sections is the **circle.**

Definition: Circle

A *circle* is the set of all points in a plane such that the distance (**radius**) from a given point (**center** of the circle) is constant.

We can derive an equation of the circle that has point (h, k) as its center and r as its radius by using the distance formula. Let (x, y) be the coordinates of a general point on the circle.

The distance between (h, k) and (x, y) equals r.

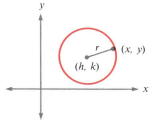

$$\sqrt{(x - h)^2 + (y - k)^2} = r$$

Squaring both sides of the equation, we get the following.

General Equation of a Circle

The general equation of a circle with center (h, k) and radius r.
$$(x - h)^2 + (y - k)^2 = r^2$$

Example 1   **Write an equation of the circle with center $(-3, 4)$ and radius 7.**

Solution   Substitute -3 for h, 4 for k, and 7 for r in the general equation of a circle.

$$(x - (-3))^2 + (y - 4)^2 = 7^2$$
$$(x + 3)^2 + (y - 4)^2 = 49$$

Answer   The equation of the circle is $(x + 3)^2 + (y - 4)^2 = 49$.

Example 2   **Graph. $(x - 2)^2 + (y + 3)^2 \leqslant 16$**

Solution   The graph of the equation $(x - 2)^2 + (y + 3)^2 = 16$ is a circle with center $(2, -3)$ and radius 4. The circle is drawn with a solid line since it is included in the graph.

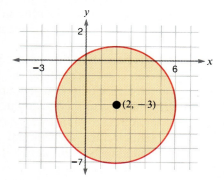

The remainder of the plane is separated into two regions. One of those regions is the graph of the **quadratic inequality** $(x - 2)^2 + (y + 3)^2 < 16$.

Choose a representative point in one of the regions and determine whether that point is a solution. We choose the point $(0, 0)$.

$$(0 - 2)^2 + (0 + 3)^2 < 16$$
$$4 + 9 < 16 \qquad \text{True}$$

The point $(0, 0)$ is in the graph, so all points inside the circle are in the graph.

If the center of a circle is the origin, then $h = 0$ and $k = 0$, and the equation of the circle is

$$x^2 + y^2 = r^2.$$

The graph of the following equation is a circle with radius 5 and center at the origin.

$$x^2 + y^2 = 25$$

If we substitute $x - 3$ for x and $y + 2$ for y, we get the equation of a circle with radius 5 and center at $(3, -2)$:

$$(x - 3)^2 + (y + 2)^2 = 25.$$

Graphically, the effect of substituting $x - 3$ for x and $y + 2$ for y is to shift the circle 3 units to the right and 2 units down.

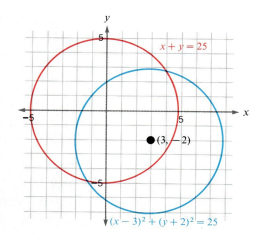

In general, substituting $x - h$ for x and $y - k$ for y shifts a graph h units horizontally and k units vertically. This kind of transformation is called a **translation**. A translation shifts each point of a given graph to a different location *without* changing the shape of the graph.

Example 3 Complete.
The graph of the equation
$(x + 5)^2 + (y - 3)^2 = 16$
is a translation of the circle with radius 4 centered at the origin. State the substitutions used to make the translation. Sketch both circles.

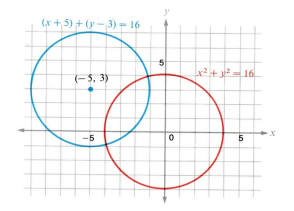

Solution The equation of the circle with radius 4 centered at the origin is $x^2 + y^2 = 16$. The substitutions used to change the equation to $(x + 5)^2 + (y - 3)^2 = 16$ are $x + 5$ for x and $y - 3$ for y.

LASSROOM EXERCISES

State the center and radius of each circle.

1. $x^2 + y^2 = 81$
2. $(x + 2)^2 + (y - 5)^2 = 7^2$
3. $x^2 = 25 - (y - 4)^2$

Write an equation of the circle with the given center and radius.

4. Center: (3, 4)
   Radius: 1
5. Center: (0, 6)
   Radius: 5
6. Center: (1, −1)
   Radius: 2

7. Graph $x^2 + y^2 = 36$
8. Graph $x^2 + (y - 3)^2 \geqslant 4$
9. Substitute $(x + 3)$ for x and $(y + 3)$ for y in Exercise 7 and graph the result.

WRITTEN EXERCISES

Write an equation in the form $(x - h)^2 + (y - k)^2 = r^2$ for each circle.

1. Center: (2, 3)
   Radius: 4
2. Center: (4, 2)
   Radius: 3
3. Center: (−3, 4)
   Radius: 2
4. Center: (3, −2)
   Radius: 4

5. Center: (4, −3)
   Radius: $\sqrt{2}$
6. Center: (−4, 2)
   Radius: $\sqrt{3}$
7. Center: (0, 0)
   Radius: $\sqrt{10}$
8. Center: (0, 0)
   Radius: $\sqrt{15}$

Graph.

9. $(x - 5)^2 + (y - 1)^2 = 9$
10. $(x - 1)^2 + (y - 5)^2 = 16$
11. $(x + 5)^2 + (y + 1)^2 \leq 9$
12. $(x + 1)^2 + (y + 5)^2 \geq 16$
13. $(x + 1)^2 + (y - 5)^2 = 1$
14. $(x - 5)^2 + (y + 1)^2 = 4$
15. $x^2 + (y - 1)^2 = 4$
16. $(x - 2)^2 + y^2 = 9$
17. $(x - 1)^2 + (y - 2)^2 < 16$
18. $(x + 3)^2 + (y + 2)^2 > 25$
19. $(x + 3)^2 + (y - 1)^2 \geq 4$
20. $(x - 2)^2 + (y + 2)^2 \geq 25$

Identify the center and radius of each circle.

21. $(x - 10)^2 + (y + 6)^2 = 25$
22. $(x + 10)^2 + (y - 6)^2 = 25$
23. $(x - 4)^2 + (y - 15)^2 = 7$
24. $(x - 20)^2 + (y + 3)^2 = 5$
25. $4(x - 2)^2 + 4y^2 - 36 = 0$
26. $3x^2 + 3(y - 8)^2 - 48 = 0$

Write the general equation or inequality for each graph.

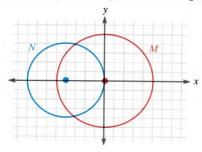
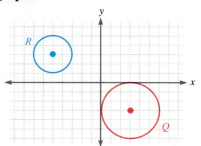

27. Circle M 28. Circle N 29. Circle Q 30. Circle R

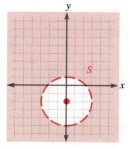
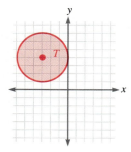

31. Region S 32. Region T

Identify the substitutions that translate the graph of the first equation to the graph of the second. Then graph both equations on the same set of axes.

33. $x^2 + y^2 = 16$
    $(x - 2)^2 + (y + 3)^2 = 16$

34. $x^2 + y^2 = 9$
    $(x + 3)^2 + (y - 2)^2 = 9$

35. $x^2 + y^2 = 4$
    $(x + 4)^2 + y^2 = 4$

36. $x^2 + y^2 = 25$
    $x^2 + (y + 3)^2 = 25$

37. $y = x^2$
    $y - 2 = (x - 3)^2$

38. $y = x^2$
    $y - 4 = (x - 2)^2$

B 39. $y = \frac{1}{4}x^2$

   $y + 2 = \frac{1}{4}(x + 3)^2$

40. $y = -\frac{1}{4}x^2$

   $y + 4 = -\frac{1}{4}(x + 2)^2$

41. $y = 2|x|$
    $y - 3 = 2|x + 4|$

Solve.

42. A circle with center (2, 3) passes through the point (5, 7).

   a. What is the radius of the circle?

   b. Write an equation of the circle.

   c. Is the point $(-3, 3)$ on the circle?

43. A circle with center (2, 3) passes through the point (4, 7).

   a. What is the radius of the circle?

   b. Write an equation of the circle.

   c. Is the point (5, 6) inside, outside, or on the circle?

44. A circle with center (2, 3) passes through the point (10, 9). State whether each of these points is inside, outside, or on the circle.

   a. (13, 3)   **b.** (9, 10)   **c.** (2, 13)   **d.** $(-4, -5)$

 The equation: $x^2 + y^2 - 8x + 2y + 8 = 0$

is equivalent to: $(x^2 - 8x + 16) + (y^2 + 2y + 1) = 9$

and to: $(x - 4)^2 + (y + 1)^2 = 3^2$

The graph of each of the above equations is a circle with center $(4, -1)$ and radius 3.

Identify the center and radius of each of these circles.

45. $(x^2 + 6x + 9) + (y^2 - 8y + 16) = 49$ **46.** $x^2 + 8x + y^2 + 4y - 5 = 0$

47. $x^2 + y^2 - 20x - 6y + 108 = 0$ **48.** $x^2 + y^2 - 2y - 15 = 0$

49. Determine an equation of the circle with center $(-4, 3)$ and tangent to the y-axis.

50. The points (6, 0) and $(0, -4)$ are the endpoints of a diameter of a given circle. Determine the equation of the circle.

EVIEW EXERCISES

1. State whether this system has 0, 1, or infinitely many solutions. $y = 2x - 6$ [4-1]

$$x = \frac{1}{2}y + 3$$

2. Solve by substitution.

   $2y - 5 = x$

   $2x + 3y = 15$

3. Solve by linear combinations.   [4-2,

   $4x + 5y = 32$ 4-3]

   $5x - 2y = 7$

4. Solve, using Cramer's rule.   [4-4]

   $x + 2y = 10$

   $2x - 3y = -8$

5. Graph. $x + y \le 5$ or $x - y > 2$ [4-6]

6. What is the maximum value of the function $C = 2x - y$ on the region in the graph?   [4-7]

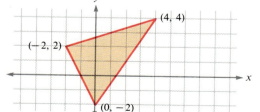

LESSON 9-2

The Parabola

The **parabola** is a second-degree curve that can be defined in terms of the distance of a point on the graph from a given point called the **focus** and from a given line called the **directrix**.

Definition: Parabola

A *parabola* is the set of all points in a plane that are the same distance from a given point (focus) as they are from a given line (directrix).

The equation of a parabola having directrix $y = 2$ and focus $(1, 4)$, can be found using the distance formula. Let $P(x, y)$ be a general point of the parabola.

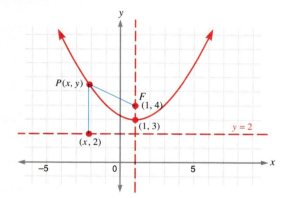

Distance of P from directrix	is equal to	Distance of P from focus
$\lvert y - 2 \rvert$	$\overset{\text{to}}{=}$	$\sqrt{(y - 4)^2 + (x - 1)^2}$

This equation of the parabola can be transformed to the standard form

$$y - k = a(x - h)^2$$

by squaring both sides and simplifying.

$$(\lvert y - 2 \rvert)^2 = (y - 4)^2 + (x - 1)^2$$
$$y^2 - 4y + 4 = y^2 - 8y + 16 + (x - 1)^2$$
$$4y - 12 = (x - 1)^2$$
$$4(y - 3) = (x - 1)^2$$
$$y - 3 = \frac{1}{4}(x - 1)^2$$

From this equation in standard form, we can determine that the **vertex** of the parabola is $(1, 3)$, the axis of symmetry is $x = 1$, and the parabola opens upward. Note that the axis of symmetry passes through the focus and that the vertex is the point on the axis of symmetry midway between the focus and the directrix.

Consider a parabola with vertex at the origin and focus $F(0, p)$. It can be shown (see Exercise 34) that the equation of the parabola is

$$4py = x^2 \quad \text{or} \quad y = \frac{1}{4p}x^2.$$

The segment through the focus, parallel to the directrix, and joining two points of the parabola is called the **latus chord.** It can be shown that the length of the latus chord is $|4p|$. (See Exercise 35.)

In the general case, the equation of the parabola is:

$$y - k = a(x - h)^2$$

The coefficient a equals $\dfrac{1}{4p}$ for the parabola having vertex $V(h, k)$, focus $F(h, k + p)$, directrix $y = k - p$ and latus chord of length $|4p|$.

The following table summarizes information about a parabola with a vertical line of symmetry.

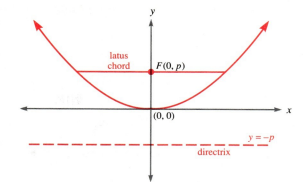

Given: Equation in the Form $4p(y - k) = (x - h)^2, p \neq 0.$

Vertex:	(h, k)
Axis of symmetry:	$x = h$
Focus:	$(h, k + p)$
Directrix:	$y = k - p$
Length of latus chord:	$|4p|$
Directrix:	Opens upward if $p > 0$ Opens downward if $p < 0$

Example 1   Given the parabola $y - 4 = \dfrac{1}{8}(x + 1)^2.$ State the following:

 a. vertex.
 b. axis of symmetry.
 c. focus.
 d. directrix.
 e. Use the latus chord to sketch the graph.

Solution   Rewrite the equation as
$$8(y - 4) = (x + 1)^2.$$
Then $4p = 8$ or $p = 2.$

 a. Vertex $V(h, k)$: $(-1, 4)$
 b. Axis of symmetry $x = h$: $x = -1$
 c. Focus $F(h, k + p)$: $(-1, 6)$
 d. Directrix $y = k - p$: $y = 2$
 e. Plot V and F. Through F, sketch the latus chord with length $|4p| = 8.$ Sketch the graph.

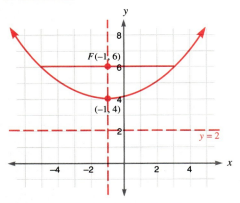

If $(x - h)$ and $(y - k)$ are interchanged in the standard equation of a parabola, we have

$$x - h = a(y - k)^2 \quad \text{or} \quad 4p(x - h) = (y - k)^2 \text{ where } 4p = \frac{1}{a}.$$

The axis of symmetry is a horizontal line, and the directrix is a vertical line. The graph opens left when $p < 0$ and right when $p > 0$. The focus is $F(h + p, k)$, and the directrix is $x = h - p$.

Example 2 Sketch the parabola with the standard equation $x - 2 = -\frac{1}{2}y^2$. State the vertex, focus, and directrix.

Solution Rewrite the equation as

$$-2(x - 2) = (y - 0)^2. \text{ Then}$$

$$4p = -2 \text{ or } p = -\frac{1}{2}.$$

Vertex $V(h, k)$: $(2, 0)$

Focus $F(h + p, k)$: $\left(2 + \left(-\frac{1}{2}\right), 0\right)$

or $\left(\frac{3}{2}, 0\right)$

Directrix $x = h - p$: $x = 2 - \left(-\frac{1}{2}\right)$

or $x = \frac{5}{2}$

Plot V and F and construct latus chord of length $|4p| = |-2| = 2$. Sketch the graph.

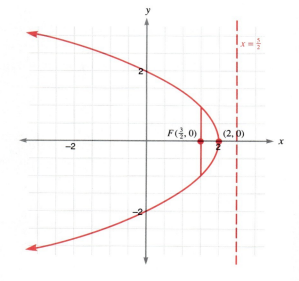

Example 3 Solve.

A doorway of a museum is in the shape of a parabola 3 m high at the center and 2.4 m wide at the base. Find the approximate height of the doorway 1 m horizontally from the center of the door.

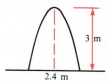

Solution Select axes so that one is the axis of symmetry and the other contains the points where the doorway intersects the floor. Label the vertex and the two points at the bottom of the doorway.

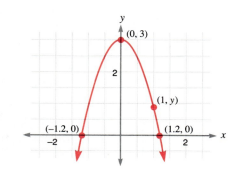

Example 3 (continued)

Substitute known values into the equation of a parabola, using $(h, k) = (0, 3)$ and $(x, y) = (1.2, 0)$

$$y - k = a(x - h)^2$$
$$0 - 3 = a(1.2 - 0)^2$$
$$-3 = 1.44a$$
$$a = -\frac{25}{12}$$

The point of the doorway that is 1 m horizontally from the center of the door is $(x, y) = (1, y)$. Substituting known values in the equation of a parabola gives:

$$y - k = a(x - h)^2$$
$$y - 3 = -\frac{25}{12}(1 - 0)^2$$
$$y = \frac{11}{12} \approx 0.9$$

Answer   The desired height is about 0.9 m.

*C*LASSROOM EXERCISES

Given the equation of the parabola $x - 2 = \frac{1}{16}(y + 3)^2$.

1. State the vertex and the direction the parabola opens.
2. State the value of $4p$ and the focus.
3. State the equations of the axis of symmetry and the directrix.
4. What is the length of the latus chord?
5. Sketch the graph.

Consider point $P(x, y)$ on a vertical parabola that has focus $F(4, 3)$ and directrix $y = 1$. Let D be a point on the directrix such that $\overline{PD}$ is perpendicular to the directrix.

6. State the vertex of the parabola.
7. Use the distance formula to write the length of $\overline{PF}$.
8. State the length of PD.
9. Set the lengths of $\overline{PF}$ and $\overline{PD}$ equal to each other and then write the equation of the parabola in standard form.

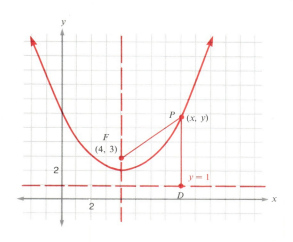

 For each equation, state the vertex, axis of symmetry, focus, and directrix. Then sketch the graph.

1. $y + 1 = \frac{1}{4}(x - 8)^2$ **2.** $x + 2 = \frac{1}{12}(y - 6)^2$ **3.** $y = 3x^2 - 6x + 1$

4. $x = 2y^2 + 8y + 11$ **5.** $y = -x^2 + 6x - 7$ **6.** $x = -y^2 + 4y - 1$

$P(x, y)$ **is a point on the parabola with the given directrix and focus** F. **Segment** PD **is perpendicular to the directrix.**

a. Write the standard equation of the parabola.

b. State the axis of symmetry of the parabola.

c. State the vertex of the parabola.

7.

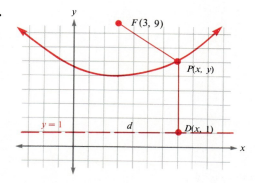

8.

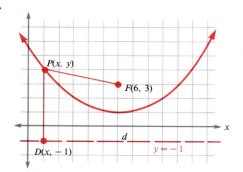

9.

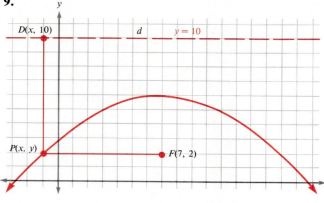

10.

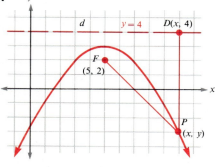

11.

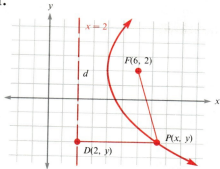

12.

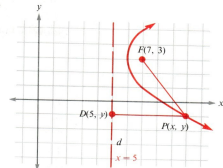

13.

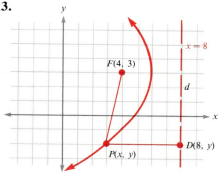

14.

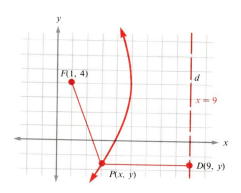

The focus and directrix of a parabola are given. Write the standard equation of the parabola, sketch the graph and label the coordinates of the vertex.

15. Focus: (10, 10)
Directrix: $x = 4$

16. Focus: (10, 10)
Directrix: $x = -4$

17. Focus: $(-10, -10)$
Directrix: $x = -4$

18. Focus: (10, 10)
Directrix: $y = 4$

19. Focus: (10, 10)
Directrix: $y = -4$

20. Focus: $(-10, -10)$
Directrix: $y = -4$

Graph.

21. $y - 2 \leq 3(x + 1)^2$ **22.** $y - 4 > 2(x + 2)^2$ **23.** $y + 1 > \frac{1}{2}(x - 2)^2$ **24.** $y + 1 \leq \frac{1}{3}(x - 3)^2$

B Write the standard equation of the parabola that meets these conditions.

25. Focus: (3, 0)

Vertex: (1, 0)

26. Directrix: $y = -1$

Vertex: (0, 2)

27. Vertex (1, 4), vertical axis of symmetry, passes through (3, 3).

[*Hint:* Write the equation in standard form and substitute.]

𝒜pplications

Solve.

28. A cable of a suspension bridge is in the shape of a parabola. The supporting towers are 1280 m apart and rise 166 m above the roadway. The lowest point of the cable is 2 m above the roadway. Find the approximate length of each supporting rod (from the cable to the roadway) that is 40 m from its nearest tower. [*Hint:* Draw the parabola on a coordinate system with its vertex at (0, 2).]

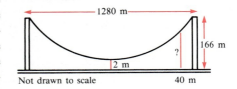

Not drawn to scale

29. The dimensions of a parabolic reflector are given in the diagram. How far from the vertex is the focus of the parabola?

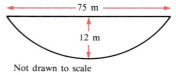

C 30. A ball thrown obliquely into the air reaches a greatest height of 12 m and lands 60 m away. Its path is a parabola.

   a. Write an equation that describes the parabola. Let *y* represent the height of the ball in meters and let *x* represent the horizontal distance in meters of the ball from the place it was thrown.

   b. What is the height of the ball when its horizontal distance from the starting point is 50 m?

   c. About how far has the ball traveled horizontally when it is 10 m high?

31. A floodgate across a river is 75 m wide and 12 m deep at the center. It is parabolic in shape.

   a. Write an equation for the parabola.

   b. Find the floodgate's depth every 15 m.

32. The cable supporting a suspension bridge hangs in the shape of a parabola if the bridge is uniformly loaded. The towers that support a particular bridge are 100 ft high and 300 ft apart. The lowest point of the cable is 30 ft above the roadway. Determine the equation of the parabola in the form

$$y^2 = 4px.$$

33. Show that all parabolas of the form $y^2 = 2dx + d^2$, where d is a constant, have the same focus.

34. Show that $4py = x^2$ is the equation of a parabola with focus $F(0, p)$ and directrix $y = -p$.

35. For the parabola in Exercise 34, show that the length of the latus chord is $|4p|$.

EVIEW EXERCISES

Simplify.   [5-1,
1. $(2ab^2)(3a)^2$ **2.** $3x(x - 3) - 4(x + 2)$ 5-2]
3. Expand and simplify: $(2x - 3)(x + 5)$.   [5-3]
4. What is the greatest common factor of $12x^2y$ and $18xy$?   [5-4]

Factor completely.   [5-5,
5. $25x^2 - 4$ **6.** $3x^2 + 7x - 6$ 5-6]
7. Solve: $x^2 + 12 = 7x$.   [5-7]
8. Write an expression for the area of the shaded region and factor it completely.   [5-4]

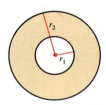

Self-Quiz 1

9-1 **1.** Write an equation for the circle with center $(-5, 2)$ and radius 6.

2. Graph: $x^2 + (y - 1)^2 < 4$.

3. What substitution(s) will translate the graph of $x^2 + y^2 = 16$ to that of a congruent circle with center $(2, 3)$?

4. Write the equation of the circle that has center $(-1, 10)$ and passes through $(3, 3)$.

9-2 **5.** Write the standard equation for the parabola with focus $(4, 2)$ and directrix $x = -2$.

6. State the vertex, axis of symmetry, focus, and directrix of the parabola
$y - 2 = \frac{1}{2}(x + 1)^2$.

7. Graph: $y + 1 = \frac{1}{2}(x - 3)^2$.

LESSON 9-3

The Ellipse

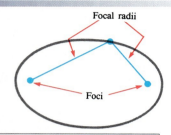

Focal radii

Foci

An **ellipse** is a second-degree curve defined in terms of the distance from two given points called **foci**. The distances from the points of the ellipse to the foci are called **focal radii**.

Definition: Ellipse

An *ellipse* is the set of all points in a plane such that the sum of the distances (focal radii) from two given points (foci) is constant.

Suppose that the foci of an ellipse are $F(-4, 0)$ and $F'(4, 0)$ and that the sum of the focal radii is 10. Then the distance formula can be used to generate the equation of the ellipse. Let (x, y) be the coordinates of any point P on the ellipse.

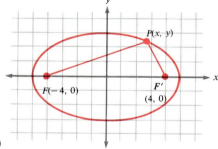

$$\underset{\text{Distance from } P \text{ to } F}{\underline{\sqrt{(x - (-4))^2 + (y - 0)^2}}} + \underset{\text{Distance from } P \text{ to } F'}{\underline{\sqrt{(x - 4)^2 + (y - 0)^2}}} = 10$$

$$\sqrt{(x + 4)^2 + y^2} = 10 - \sqrt{(x - 4)^2 + y^2}$$

Isolate one radical.

Square both sides.

$$x^2 + 8x + 16 + y^2 = 100 - 20\sqrt{(x - 4)^2 + y^2} + x^2 - 8x + 16 + y^2$$

Simplify.

$$16x - 100 = -20\sqrt{(x - 4)^2 + y^2}$$

Divide both sides by 4.

$$4x - 25 = -5\sqrt{(x - 4)^2 + y^2}$$

Square both sides.

$$16x^2 - 200x + 625 = 25(x^2 - 8x + 16 + y^2)$$

Simplify.

$$225 = 9x^2 + 25y^2$$

Divide both sides by 225.

$$1 = \frac{x^2}{25} + \frac{y^2}{9}$$

The standard equation for an ellipse with foci at $(-4, 0)$ and $(4, 0)$ and with the sum of the focal radii equal to 10 is

$$\frac{x^2}{25} + \frac{y^2}{9} = 1.$$

Note these facts for the ellipse $\frac{x^2}{25} + \frac{y^2}{9} = 1$.

1. The denominator of the x^2 term is the square of half of the sum of the focal radii.

$$25 = \left(\frac{1}{2} \cdot 10\right)^2$$

2. The difference between the two denominators is the square of the distance from the origin to either focus.

$$25 - 9 = 4^2$$

Using this information, we can write a general equation of an ellipse centered at the origin with foci on the x-axis.

Definition: Standard Equation for an Ellipse

The standard equation for an ellipse with foci $(-c, 0)$ and $(c, 0)$ and with the sum of the focal radii equal to $2a$ is:

$$\frac{x^2}{a^2} + \frac{y^2}{b^2} = 1, \quad \text{where } b^2 = a^2 - c^2.$$

In a similar manner, we can write a general equation of an ellipse centered at the origin with foci on the y-axis by interchanging x and y.

$$\frac{y^2}{a^2} + \frac{x^2}{b^2} = 1, \quad \text{where } b^2 = a^2 - c^2$$

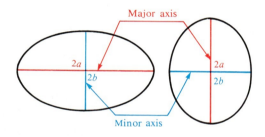

Note these relationships for ellipses:

1. $a > b$ and $a > c$.
2. The length of the **major axis** is $2a$.
3. The length of the **minor axis** is $2b$. The endpoints of the major and minor axes are called the **vertices** of the ellipse.
4. An ellipse has two axes of symmetry, the lines containing the major and minor axes. The intersection of the axes of symmetry is the **center** of the ellipse.

Example 1   Graph the ellipse and identify the foci.

$$\frac{x^2}{16} + \frac{y^2}{12} = 1$$

Solution   From the standard equation for an ellipse, $\frac{x^2}{a^2} + \frac{y^2}{b^2} = 1$, the equation is that of an ellipse with $a^2 = 16$, $b^2 = 12$, and $c^2 = 16 - 12 = 4$. Therefore, $a = 4$, $b = 2\sqrt{3}$, and $c = 2$. Since $c = 2$, the foci are $(-2, 0)$ and $(2, 0)$.

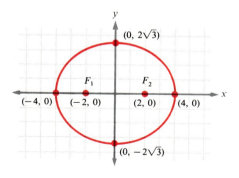

Example 2   Write the standard equation for the ellipse that has foci at $(0, -3)$ and $(0, 3)$ and crosses the x-axis at $(-2, 0)$ and $(2, 0)$.

Solution   The fact that the foci are at $(0, -3)$ and $(0, 3)$ implies that $c = 3$ and that the general equation of the ellipse is $\dfrac{y^2}{a^2} + \dfrac{x^2}{b^2} = 1$.

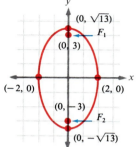

Since the ellipse crosses the x-axis at $(-2, 0)$ and $(2, 0)$, $b = 2$. Then $b^2 = 4$ and $c^2 = 9$.

Because $a^2 = b^2 + c^2$, $a^2 = 13$.

The equation of the ellipse is $\dfrac{y^2}{13} + \dfrac{x^2}{4} = 1$.

Example 3   Sketch the graph. $\dfrac{(y - 3)^2}{25} + \dfrac{(x + 2)^2}{9} = 1$

Solution   The graph of the given equation is the graph of the following ellipse translated 2 units to the left and 3 units up.

$$\frac{y^2}{25} + \frac{x^2}{9} = 1$$

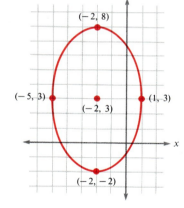

Note these characteristics of the graph of this equation.

1. The foci are on the y-axis.
2. $a = 5$. The major axis is a vertical segment 10 units long.
3. $b = 3$. The minor axis is a horizontal segment 6 units long.
4. The center of the ellipse is $(0, 0)$.

The translation shifts the center of the ellipse to $(-2, 3)$. The lengths of the major and minor axes are not changed by the translation. Therefore, the vertices on the major axis are $(-2, 8)$ and $(-2, -2)$, and the vertices on the minor axis are $(-5, 3)$ and $(1, 3)$. Once these points are located, the graph can be sketched easily.

$\mathcal{C}$LASSROOM EXERCISES

1. Graph the ellipse and identify the foci: $\dfrac{x^2}{289} + \dfrac{y^2}{225} = 1$.

F_1 and F_2 are the foci of the ellipses shown. State the values of a, b, and c, and then write the standard equation of the ellipse.

2.

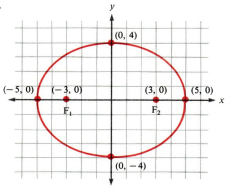

3.

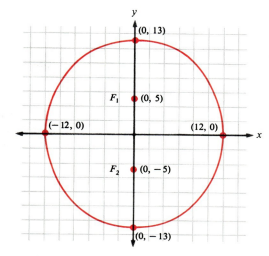

WRITTEN EXERCISES

A Write the standard equation for each ellipse.

1.

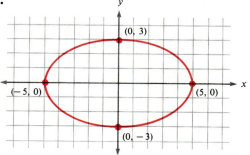

2.

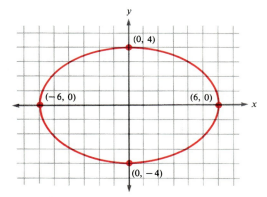

3.

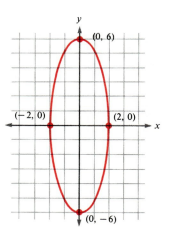

4.

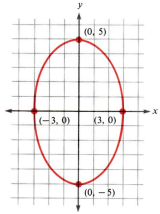

Write a standard equation for each ellipse.

5. Center: (0, 0)
Major axis: 12 units on the
x-axis
Minor axis: 10 units on the
y-axis

6. Center: (0, 0)
Major axis: 10 units on the
x-axis
Minor axis: 6 units on the
y-axis

7. Center: (0, 0)
Major axis: 30 units on the
y-axis
Minor axis: 6 units on the
x-axis

8. Foci: (−3, 0) and (3, 0)
Sum of focal radii: 10

9. Foci: (0, −6) and (0, 6)
Sum of focal radii: 20

10. Foci: (0, −2) and (0, 2)
Sum of focal radii: 8

11. Center: (0, 0)
Foci: (0, −8) and (0, 8)
Vertices: (0, −10) and
(0, 10)

12. Center: (0, 0)
Foci: (0, −3) and (0, 3)
Vertices: (0, −5) and
(0, 5)

13. Foci: (−12, 0) and (12, 0)
Vertices: (0, −5) and
(0, 5)

14. Foci: (−4, 0) and (4, 0)
Vertices: (0, −3) and
(0, 3)

15. Center: (3, 4)
Foci: (3, 9) and (3, −1)
Vertices: (3, 17) and
(3, −9)

16. Center: (12, 4)
Foci: (12, 19) and (12, −11)
Vertices: (12, 21) and
(12, −13)

17. Center: (−2, 4)
Vertices: (−2, 7), (−2, 1), (3, 4),
and (−7, 4)

18. Center: (3, −6)
Vertices: (3, −10), (3, −2), (−2, −6),
and (8, −6)

Sketch the graph of each ellipse or region. Identify the coordinates of the vertices, the foci, and the center.

19. $\dfrac{y^2}{25} + \dfrac{x^2}{9} = 1$

20. $\dfrac{y^2}{100} + \dfrac{x^2}{64} = 1$

21. $\dfrac{x^2}{25} + \dfrac{y^2}{9} \leq 1$

22. $\dfrac{x^2}{100} + \dfrac{y^2}{64} \leq 1$

23. $\dfrac{(x-2)^2}{169} + \dfrac{(y-4)^2}{144} = 1$

24. $\dfrac{(x-4)^2}{289} + \dfrac{(y-6)^2}{225} = 1$

25. $\dfrac{y^2}{169} + \dfrac{(x+5)^2}{144} \leq 1$

26. $\dfrac{(y+5)^2}{289} + \dfrac{x^2}{225} \leq 1$

27. $36x^2 + 16y^2 = 576$

28. $64x^2 + 4y^2 = 256$

29. $49x^2 + 196y^2 = 9604$

30. $81x^2 + 121y^2 = 9801$

*A*pplication: Graphing Conic Sections

B Graphing calculators and computer graphing programs can be used to graph the conic sections. In order to use some of these graphing devices, it is often necessary to enter equations in the form "$y = \cdots$." So to graph the circle $x^2 + y^2 = 36$, you would have to solve the equation for y.

$$y = \sqrt{36 - x^2} \quad \text{and} \quad y = -\sqrt{36 - x^2}$$

To view the entire graph, you would need to enter both equations.

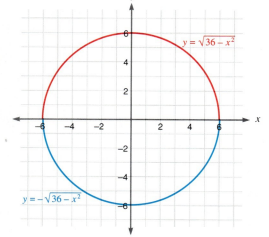

State the equations required to view the graphs of these conics on some graphing devices.

31. $(x - 1)^2 + y^2 = 12$

32. $x = 9 - y^2$

33. $y = 4(x + 2)^2$

34. $x - 3 = \dfrac{1}{2}(y - 4)^2$

35. $\dfrac{x^2}{4} + \dfrac{y^2}{9} = 1$

36. $4(x + 1)^2 + 25(y - 2)^2 = 100$

*A*pplications

Solve.

37. A railroad bridge has a semielliptical arch that is 30 m wide at the base and 9 m high at the center. The railroad bed runs 1.5 m above the centerpoint of the arch. Find the length of the support from the arch to the railbed 3 m from the end of the bridge.

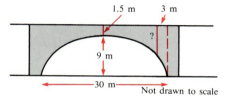

[*Hint:* Write an equation for an ellipse centered at (0, 0). What is the y-coordinate of the point at the bottom of the support?]

38. Show that the area of the circle whose diameter joins the foci of an ellipse is equal to the difference in areas of those circles that have the ellipse's major and minor axes as diameters, respectively.

39. A water channel is semielliptical in cross section. The width of the channel is 100 ft and its maximum depth is 25 ft. Marker buoys are to be placed on both sides of the channel to indicate a minimum depth of 15 ft. How far from either bank should these buoys be placed?

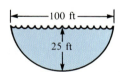

40. A metal building is constructed in the shape of a semielliptical cylinder 16 m across and 6 m high. How close to either wall can a person who is 2 m tall stand erect?

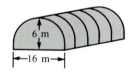

C An ellipse can be defined as a set of points that are related to a point (called the focus) and a line (called the directrix) in a certain way. The ratio of the distances from a point on the ellipse to the focus and to the directrix is a constant (called the *eccentricity*) between 0 and 1. If P is a point (x, y) on the ellipse, F is the focus, d is the directrix, and e is the eccentricity. Then

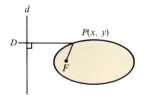

$$\dfrac{PF}{PD} = e, \quad 0 < e < 1.$$

Write an equation for each ellipse. Use the distance formula. The simplified equation should be free of radicals.

41. Focus: (8, 6)
Directrix: $x = 2$
Eccentricity: $\dfrac{1}{2}$

42. Focus: (11, 0)
Directrix: $x = 3$
Eccentricity: $\dfrac{3}{5}$

43. Focus: (0, 0)
Directrix: $y = 6$
Eccentricity: $\dfrac{1}{5}$

44. Focus: (0, 0)
Directrix: $y = 6$
Eccentricity: $\dfrac{4}{5}$

45. The area of an ellipse whose major and minor axes are $2a$ and $2b$ in length is πab. Find the difference between the area of the ellipse and that of the largest inscribed circle. What happens to this difference as the length of the minor axis approaches that of the major axis?

EVIEW EXERCISES

1. Write without using negative integer exponents: $6a^{-1}b^{-2}c^2$.   [6-1]

Simplify. State any restrictions on the variables.

2. $\dfrac{2y - 12xy^2}{3xy}$

3. $\dfrac{3a}{5b} \div \dfrac{10b}{9a}$

4. $\dfrac{1}{1-a} - \dfrac{1}{a-1}$ [6-2, 6-3, 6-4]

5. Solve: $\dfrac{1}{3} - \dfrac{1}{x} = \dfrac{1}{12}$.   [6-5]

6. If resistances of 100 ohms and 200 ohms are connected in parallel, what is the total resistance of the circuit?   [6-6]

7. If y varies inversely as the square of x, and $y = 100$ when $x = 5$, what is the value of y when $x = 50$?   [6-7]

ISTORICAL NOTE   Orbits of Planets

In the early years of astronomy, it was thought that the moon and planets move in circular orbits. This belief was supported in part by crude observations and in part by the philosophical position that since the universe is perfect, the path of heavenly bodies must be the most perfect of figures, circles. As more accurate data became available, astronomers found that the orbits are not circular and tried to explain the orbits in terms of combinations of circles. After years of great effort, Johann Kepler (1571–1630) was able to show that the orbits of the planets are ellipses and that the sun is at one of the foci of the ellipses.

The Hyperbola

The **hyperbola** is a second-degree curve whose graph consists of two symmetric branches. It can be defined in terms of the *difference* of the distances from two given points, called **foci**.

The hyperbola appears as the edges of the shadow cast on a wall by a lampshade. It is useful in military applications and in sound ranging.

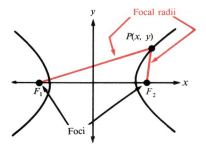

Definition: Hyperbola

A *hyperbola* is the set of all points in a plane such that the absolute value of the difference of the distances (**focal radii**) from two given points (**foci**) is constant.

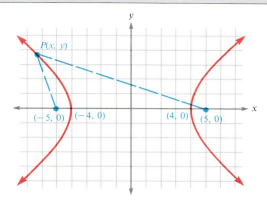

Suppose that the foci of a hyperbola are $F_1(-5, 0)$ and $F_2(5, 0)$ and that $P(x, y)$ is any point on the graph. If the absolute value of the difference of the focal radii is 8, then

$$|PF_1 - PF_2| = 8$$

or

$$\left|\sqrt{(x + 5)^2 + (y - 0)^2} - \sqrt{(x - 5)^2 + (y - 0)^2}\right| = 8$$

Eliminating radicals and simplifying gives this equation of the hyperbola.

$$\frac{x^2}{4^2} - \frac{y^2}{3^2} = 1$$

Careful examination of the equation shows these characteristics:

$$\frac{x^2}{4^2} - \frac{y^2}{3^2} = 1$$

1. The x-intercepts are 4 and -4. The points $(4, 0)$ and $(-4, 0)$ are called the **vertices** of the hyperbola.

2. The domain includes all real numbers except those between -4 and 4.

3. There are no y-intercepts.

Note, too, the relationship among the constants:

$$5^2 - 4^2 = 3^2$$

where 5 is half the distance between the foci, and 4 is half the absolute value of the difference between focal radii.

These values suggest the standard equation of a hyperbola.

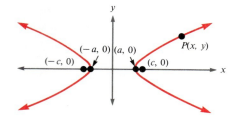

Definition: Standard Equation of a Hyperbola

The standard equation of a hyperbola with foci $(-c, 0)$ and $(c, 0)$ whose focal radii differ by $2a$ is

$$\frac{x^2}{a^2} - \frac{y^2}{b^2} = 1, \quad \text{where } b^2 = c^2 - a^2.$$

Similarly the standard equation of a hyperbola with foci $(0, -c)$ and $(0, c)$ whose focal radii differ by $2a$ is

$$\frac{y^2}{a^2} - \frac{x^2}{b^2} = 1.$$

Now consider the rectangle centered at the origin with length $2a$ and width $2b$. The lines formed by extending the diagonals of the rectangle are called **asymptotes** of the hyperbola. Each branch of the hyperbola lies entirely within one of the regions determined by the asymptotes. As x increases in absolute value, the graph of the hyperbola becomes progressively closer to the asymptotes. The slope of one asymptote is $\frac{b}{a}$, and the slope of the other is $-\frac{b}{a}$. Therefore, the equations of the asymptotes are

$$y = \frac{b}{a}x \quad \text{and} \quad y = -\frac{b}{a}x.$$

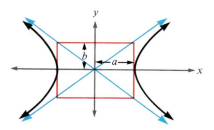

In the case in which the foci are on the y-axis, the equations of the asymptotes are

$$y = \frac{a}{b}x \quad \text{and} \quad y = -\frac{a}{b}x.$$

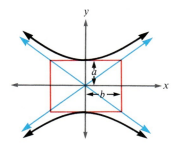

Example 1   Sketch a graph of the hyperbola, including the asymptotes and foci.

$$\frac{x^2}{64} - \frac{y^2}{36} = 1$$

Solution   The equation is that of a hyperbola with foci on the x-axis:

$$\frac{x^2}{a^2} - \frac{y^2}{b^2} = 1.$$

Therefore, $a^2 = 64$ and $b^2 = 36$. Since $c^2 = a^2 + b^2$, $c^2 = 100$. Therefore, $a = 8$, $b = 6$, and $c = 10$. The foci are $(-10, 0)$ and $(10, 0)$, and the vertices are $(-8, 0)$ and $(8, 0)$.

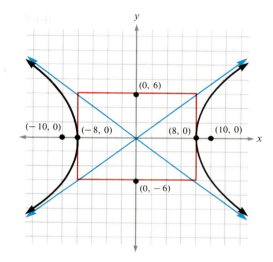

Example 2   Write the equation of the hyperbola with foci $(0, -4)$ and $(0, 4)$ and whose focal radii differ by 6. Sketch the graph, including asymptotes, and state the equations of the asymptotes.

Solution   The equation is that of a hyperbola with foci on the y-axis:

$$\frac{y^2}{a^2} - \frac{x^2}{b^2} = 1$$

Since the focal radii differ by 6, $2a = 6$. Therefore, $a = 3$ and $a^2 = 9$. Since $c = 4$, $c^2 = 16$. Since $b^2 = c^2 - a^2$, $b^2 = 7$.

Answer   *Equation:* $\dfrac{y^2}{9} - \dfrac{x^2}{7} = 1$

The slopes of the asymptotes are

$$\pm\frac{3}{\sqrt{7}} = \frac{3\sqrt{7}}{7} \quad \text{and} \quad \frac{-3\sqrt{7}}{7}.$$

Asymptotes:

$$y = \frac{3\sqrt{7}}{7}x \quad \text{and} \quad y = -\frac{3\sqrt{7}}{7}x$$

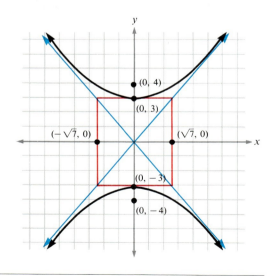

The simplest equations of hyperbolas are of the form $xy = k$, where k is a nonzero real number. These hyperbolas have the x-axis and the y-axis as asymptotes. The hyperbola is in the first and third quadrants when $k > 0$ and in the second and fourth quadrants when $k < 0$.

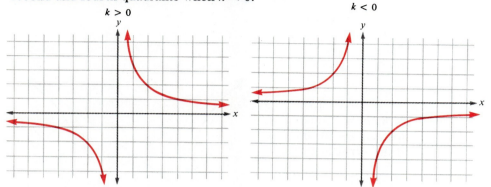

Note that the domain of $xy = k$ is the set of real numbers except 0. The graph is symmetric with respect to the origin. It is also symmetric with respect to the lines $y = x$ and $y = -x$.

ℓLASSROOM EXERCISES

Give the values of *a*, *b*, and *c* for the hyperbolas pictured. Then write the standard equation of each hyperbola.

1.

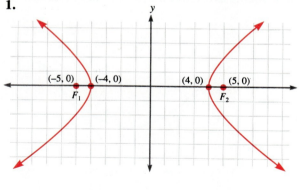

2.

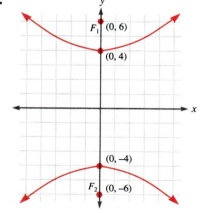

Sketch the graph, including foci and asymptotes. Write the equations of the asymptotes.

3. $\dfrac{x^2}{25} - \dfrac{y^2}{16} = 1$

4. $\dfrac{y^2}{12} - \dfrac{x^2}{8} = 1$

5. Sketch the graph of $y = \dfrac{1}{x}$.

6. Sketch the graph of $xy + 4 = 0$.

WRITTEN EXERCISES

A Write the standard equation of each hyperbola.

1.

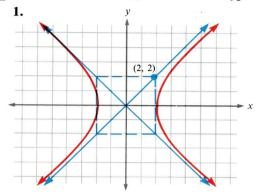

(2, 2)

2.

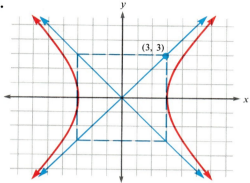

(3, 3)

3.

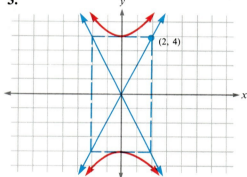

(2, 4)

4.

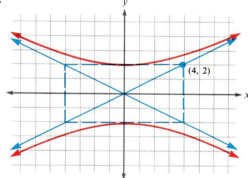

(4, 2)

5.

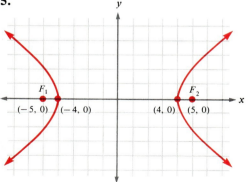

F_1 (−5, 0) (−4, 0) (4, 0) (5, 0) F_2

6.

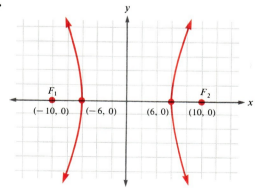

F_1 (−10, 0) (−6, 0) (6, 0) (10, 0) F_2

Write the standard equation of each hyperbola.

7.

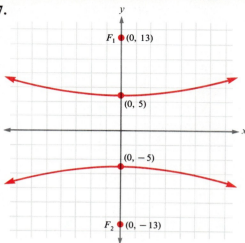

8.

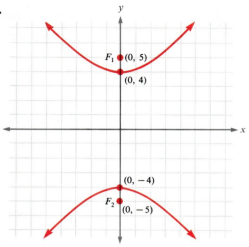

Sketch the graph of each hyperbola or region, including foci and asymptotes.

9. $\dfrac{x^2}{3^2} - \dfrac{y^2}{6^2} = 1$

10. $\dfrac{x^2}{6^2} - \dfrac{y^2}{3^2} = 1$

11. $\dfrac{x^2}{25} - \dfrac{y^2}{4} \geqslant 1$

12. $\dfrac{x^2}{4} - \dfrac{y^2}{36} \geqslant 1$

13. $\dfrac{y^2}{8^2} - \dfrac{x^2}{6^2} = 1$

14. $\dfrac{y^2}{12^2} - \dfrac{x^2}{5^2} = 1$

15. $\dfrac{y^2}{9} - \dfrac{x^2}{7} \leqslant 1$

16. $\dfrac{y^2}{4} - \dfrac{x^2}{21} \leqslant 1$

Sketch these graphs.

17. $xy = 10$

18. $xy = 15$

19. $xy = -18$

20. $xy = -8$

Write the equations of the hyperbolas with the stated conditions.

21. Foci: $(0, 6)$ and $(0, -6)$
    Difference of focal radii: 8

22. Foci: $(0, 7)$ and $(0, -7)$
    Difference of focal radii: 10

23. Foci: $(10, 0)$ and $(-10, 0)$
    Difference of focal radii: 12

24. Foci: $(8, 0)$ and $(-8, 0)$
    Difference of focal radii: 10

B Sketch the graph of each hyperbola or region, including foci and asymptotes. Write the equations of the asymptotes.

25. $\dfrac{x^2}{9} = \dfrac{y^2}{36} + 1$

26. $x^2 - y^2 = 16$

27. $\dfrac{x^2}{10^2} - \dfrac{y^2}{5^2} = -1$

28. $\dfrac{x^2}{9} - \dfrac{y^2}{16} = 4$

29. $25x^2 - 16y^2 \leqslant 400$

30. $\dfrac{y^2}{12} - \dfrac{x^2}{8} > 1$

31. $y^2 - 4x^2 = 9$

32. $y = \pm\sqrt{4 + x^2}$

Sketch the graph.

33. $20 - xy = 0$

34. $xy + 36 = 0$

35. $x = -\dfrac{12}{y}$

36. $(x - 2)(y - 4) = 12$

37. $y = \dfrac{8}{x}$

38. $x + \dfrac{y}{16} = 0$

39. $y = \dfrac{1}{x - 1}$

40. $y - 3 = \dfrac{2}{x}$

C Each of the following hyperbolas is to be translated to the given center. Write the equation of the translated hyperbola, sketch, and label the vertices and asymptotes. Write the equations of the asymptotes.

41. $y^2 - \dfrac{x^2}{4} = 1$

Translated center: $(-2, 2)$

42. $4y^2 - 9x^2 = 36$

Translated center: $(-2, 3)$

43. $\dfrac{x^2}{25} - \dfrac{y^2}{144} = 1$

Translated center: $(5, 1)$

44. $\dfrac{y^2}{9} - \dfrac{x^2}{16} = 4$

Translated center: $(-3, 3)$

A hyperbola can be defined as a set of points that are related to a point (called the focus) and a line (called the directrix) in a certain way. The ratio of the distances from a point of the hyperbola to the focus and to the directrix is a constant (called the *eccentricity*) greater than 1. If P is a point (x, y) on the hyperbola, F the focus, d the directrix, and e the eccentricity, then $\dfrac{PF}{PD} = e$, $e > 1$.

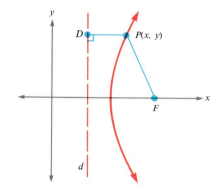

Write an equation for each hyperbola. Use the distance formula. The simplified equation should not contain radicals.

45. Focus: $(8, 0)$
Directrix: $x = 2$
Eccentricity: 2

46. Focus: $(0, 6)$
Directrix: $y = 2$
Eccentricity: 3

47. Focus: $(0, 0)$
Directrix: $y = 10$
Eccentricity: $\dfrac{5}{4}$

EVIEW EXERCISES

Simplify. State any restrictions on the variables.

1. $-\sqrt{\dfrac{4}{9}}$

2. $\sqrt{12a^3}$

3. $\sqrt{\dfrac{2}{5b}}$

4. $8^{-\frac{2}{3}}$

5. Substitute $1 + \sqrt{3}$ for x and simplify: $x^2 - 2x + 1$.

6. Rationalize the denominator: $\dfrac{3}{1 + \sqrt{2}}$.

7. What is the distance between $(2, -1)$ and $(-5, -3)$?

8. Solve: $\sqrt[3]{3x + 2} = -4$.

9. If the volume of a cube is 216 cm^3, what is the surface area?

10. Write in exponential notation. $\sqrt[4]{3 - x}$

11. Write in simplest radical form. **a.** $-32^{\frac{1}{4}}$ **b.** $6y^{\frac{6}{4}}$

[7-1, 7-2, 7-4, 7-7]
[7-3]

[7-4]

[7-5]
[7-6]

[7-7]
[7-7]

LESSON 9-5

Conic Sections

Curves and surfaces associated with the conic sections are studied for their natural beauty and also for practical reasons. Cylindrical objects (tubes, bolts, rods) are easily created by rotating machinery. Pressure containers such as boilers and vacuum chambers are cylindrical or spherical because those shapes resist pressure better than others.

Cooling towers are hyperboloid because the two-way "saddle" curvature provides a large surface area that resists weight and wind loads. Parabolas and ellipses are ideally suited for their focusing characteristics in radio-telescope dishes and whisper galleries.

It is fascinating that each of the conic curves is a special case of the same general second-degree equation.

General Second-Degree Equation in *x* and *y*

where A, B, and C are not all equal to zero.
$$Ax^2 + Bxy + Cy^2 + Dx + Ey + F = 0$$

The following table lists the relationship between A and C for each conic section described by the general equation when $B = 0$.

$Ax^2 + Bxy + Cy^2 + Dx + Ey + F = 0,$ $B = 0$	
Conic Section	*Values of A and C*
Parabola	$AC = 0, A \neq C$
Circle	$A = C$
Ellipse	$AC > 0, A \neq C$
Hyperbola	$AC < 0$

If $B \neq 0$, the equation is the general equation of a conic section whose axes of symmetry are *not parallel* to the coordinate axes. The simplest example is that of $xy = n$, where $n \neq 0$. If a quadratic equation in two variables, x and y, has no xy-term, the conic section can be identified by transforming the equation into one of the standard forms given above. If there is an xy-term, the curve can be identified by graphing.

The circle, parabola, ellipse, and hyperbola are called conic sections because each is the intersection of a plane with a cone. The angle of the plane relative to the cone determines which of the figures is formed.

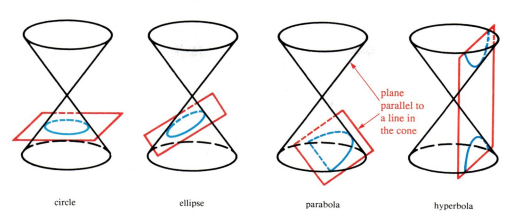

circle   ellipse   parabola   hyperbola

The standard forms of the equations of the conic sections with axes parallel to the coordinate axes are listed in the following table.

Conic Section	Standard Form of the Equation
Parabola	$y - k = a(x - h)^2$ or $x - h = a(y - k)^2$
Circle	$(x - h)^2 + (y - k)^2 = r^2$
Ellipse	$\dfrac{(x - h)^2}{a^2} + \dfrac{(y - k)^2}{b^2} = 1$ or $\dfrac{(y - k)^2}{a^2} + \dfrac{(x - h)^2}{b^2} = 1$
Hyperbola	$\dfrac{(x - h)^2}{a^2} - \dfrac{(y - k)^2}{b^2} = 1$ or $\dfrac{(y - k)^2}{a^2} - \dfrac{(x - h)^2}{b^2} = 1$

Example 1 Transform this equation into a standard form and sketch the graph of the conic section.
$$3(y - 2) + (x - 3)^2 = 0$$

Solution The equation has a quadratic term in x but not in y. Therefore, the conic section is a parabola with axis of symmetry parallel to the y-axis.

$$3(y - 2) + (x - 3)^2 = 0$$
$$3(y - 2) = -(x - 3)^2$$
$$y - 2 = -\frac{1}{3}(x - 3)^2$$

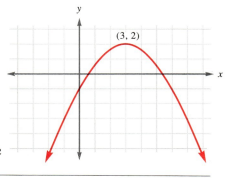

Example 2 **Identify the conic section and then transform the equation into a standard form.**

$$4x^2 + 8x + 3y^2 = 8$$

Solution The equation is quadratic in both x and y with no xy-term. Since $4x^2$ and $3y^2$ agree in sign, the equation is that of an ellipse.

To transform the equation into standard form, divide both sides of the equation by 4 to make the coefficient of x^2 equal to 1.

$$x^2 + 2x + \frac{3}{4}y^2 = 2$$

Complete the square in x.
$$x^2 + 2x + 1 + \frac{3}{4}y^2 = 2 + 1$$

$$(x + 1)^2 + \frac{3}{4}y^2 = 3$$

Divide both sides by 3 to make the constant term equal to 1.
$$\frac{(x + 1)^2}{3} + \frac{y^2}{4} = 1$$

Example 3 **Sketch the graph of $xy - x + 2y + 1 = 0$.**

Solution Solve the equation for y.

$$xy - x + 2y + 1 = 0$$
$$y(x + 2) = x - 1$$
$$y = \frac{x - 1}{x + 2}$$

Rewrite the numerator in terms of the denominator to eliminate the variable:

$$y = \frac{x + 2 - 3}{x + 2}$$

$$y = \frac{x + 2}{x + 2} - \frac{3}{x + 2}$$

$$y = 1 - \frac{3}{x + 2}$$

$$y - 1 = -\frac{3}{x + 2}$$

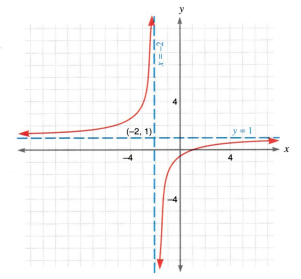

The graph of this equation is a translation of the graph of the hyperbola $y = -\dfrac{3}{x}$. Its center is the point $(-2, 1)$. Therefore, its asymptotes are $x = -2$ and $y = 1$.

Identify these conic sections.

1. $5x^2 + 2x + 3y - 5 = 0$

2. $8x^2 - 3y^2 - 4x - 4y + 7 = 0$

Write in standard form.

3. $x^2 + y + 2x = 0$

4. $x^2 + y^2 + 4x + 6y - 3 = 0$

WRITTEN EXERCISES

A | **Classify each of these conic sections as a parabola, circle, ellipse, or hyperbola.**

1. $\dfrac{(x-1)^2}{4^2} - \dfrac{(y-3)^2}{5^2} = 1$

2. $\dfrac{(x-1)^2}{4^2} + \dfrac{(y-3)^2}{5^2} = 1$

3. $y - 3 = 4(x-1)^2$

4. $(x-1)^2 + (y-3)^2 = 5^2$

5. $y^2 - x - 3 = 0$

6. $xy - 12 = 0$

7. $x^2 + y^2 - 2x - 6y - 6 = 0$

8. $5x^2 - 10x - y + 8 = 0$

9. $4x^2 + y^2 + 24x - 4y + 36 = 0$

10. $x^2 - 9y^2 - 4x + 54y - 86 = 0$

11. $x^2 - y^2 - 4x - 6y = 0$

12. $4x^2 + y^2 + 16x + 6y + 21 = 0$

Write an equivalent equation in the form $Ax^2 + By^2 + Cx + Dy + E = 0, A \geq 0$.

13. $(x+2)^2 + (y+1)^2 = 3^2$

14. $(x+3)^2 + (y+2)^2 = 1$

15. $\dfrac{(x+2)^2}{3^2} + \dfrac{(y+1)^2}{4^2} = 1$

16. $\dfrac{(x+2)^2}{3^2} - \dfrac{(y+1)^2}{4^2} = 1$

17. $\dfrac{(x-2)^2}{3^2} - \dfrac{(y+1)^2}{4^2} = 1$

18. $\dfrac{(x-4)^2}{4^2} + \dfrac{(y+3)^2}{3^2} = 1$

19. $y - 2 = 3(x+4)^2$

20. $x - 5 = 2(y-3)^2$

Write an equivalent equation in standard form for a circle, parabola, ellipse, or hyperbola. Sketch the graph of the conic and label key points such as vertices and centers.

21. $x^2 + y^2 + 4x + 8y + 11 = 0$

22. $x^2 + y^2 + 6x + 10y + 30 = 0$

23. $x^2 - y^2 - 6x + 4y + 1 = 0$

24. $4x^2 + 9y^2 + 36y = 0$

25. $\dfrac{6}{x} = y$

26. $x = \dfrac{-8}{y}$

27. $x^2 + 4y^2 - 24y + 20 = 0$

28. $4x^2 - 9y^2 - 36y - 72 = 0$

29. $3y^2 - x - 30y + 78 = 0$

30. $2x^2 + 4x + y = 0$

B | **Sketch each graph or inequality.**

31. $y - 3 = \dfrac{1}{x-1}$

32. $y = -4 + \dfrac{2}{x+2}$

33. $y = \dfrac{x+2}{x+(-1)}$

34. $xy + x - 3y + 1 = 0$

35. $25x^2 + y^2 + 100x + 6y + 84 \leq 0$

36. $x^2 + 25y^2 + 4x + 150y + 204 \geq 0$

37. $x^2 - y^2 - 4 \leq 0$

38. $x^2 - y^2 - 4x + 4y - 4 \geq 0$

39. $xy \leq 16$

40. $(x-3)(y-5) \leq 16$

41. A plane and cone can intersect in seven different ways. List the possible intersections.

C Sketch the intersection of the graphs.

42. $\dfrac{(x-5)^2}{5^2} + \dfrac{(y-3)^2}{3^2} \leqslant 1$

and

$\dfrac{x^2}{5^2} + \dfrac{(y-3)^2}{3^2} \leqslant 1$

43. $\dfrac{(x-4)^2}{2^2} + \dfrac{(y-4)^2}{4^2} \leqslant 1$

and

$(x-4)^2 + (y-10)^2 \geqslant 4^2$

44. $xy \leqslant 9$
and
$xy \geqslant -9$

*R*EVIEW EXERCISES

Solve.

1. $(x-3)^2 = 5$

2. $2x^2 - 6x + 3 = 0$

[8-1, 8-2]

Simplify.

3. $(5i)^2$

4. $|3 - 4i|$

[8-3, 8-4]

5. $(3 - 2i) - (7 - 3i)$

6. $\dfrac{10 + 5i}{2 - i}$

[8-5]

Solve.

7. $x^4 + 8 = 6x^2$

8. $\dfrac{1}{x} + x = 5$

[8-6]

*S*elf-Quiz 2

9-3 **1.** Give the coordinates of the vertices and foci of the ellipse $\dfrac{y^2}{36} + \dfrac{x^2}{16} = 1$.

2. Sketch the graph of the ellipse $25x^2 + 4y^2 = 100$.

3. Write the equation of the ellipse with foci $(6, 0)$ and $(-6, 0)$ and with the sum of its focal radii 20.

9-4 **4.** Sketch the graph of $\dfrac{x^2}{4} - \dfrac{y^2}{9} = 1$.

5. Give the coordinates of the vertices and foci of the hyperbola $\dfrac{y^2}{25} - \dfrac{x^2}{16} = 1$.

6. Sketch the graph of $4 + xy = 0$.

9-5 **7.** Identify these conic sections.

    a. $x^2 - y^2 + 3x - 4y + 1 = 0$ **b.** $4x^2 + 9y^2 + 36x - 4 = 0$

    c. $12xy - 4y - 6 = 0$ **d.** $5x^2 + 5y^2 - 10x + 20y = 0$

8. Write equation 7(d) in standard form.

9. Sketch the graph of $9x^2 + 16y^2 \leqslant 144$.

Nonlinear Systems of Equations

The depth of a well in feet can be computed by dropping a stone and measuring the time it takes to hear the splash.

Suppose the splash is heard 4 s after a stone has been dropped. Part of that 4 s is the length of time it takes the stone to fall to the water. This time t in seconds is determined by the formula $d = 16t^2$, where d is the distance in feet. The remainder of the time $(4 - t)$ is the length of time it takes for the sound of the splash to travel back to our ears. The speed of sound in air is about 1100 ft/s, $d = 1100(4 - t)$.

Therefore the following system of equations can be solved to determine the approximate depth of the well.

$$d = 16t^2$$
$$d = 1100(4 - t)$$

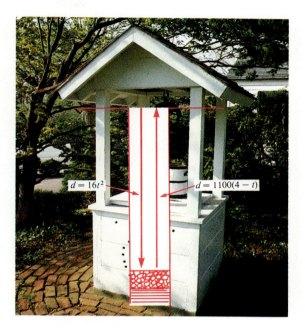

If one of the equations in a system of two or more equations is nonlinear, the system is considered to be a **nonlinear system**. Nonlinear systems can be solved by the techniques used for linear systems.

The figures below show some of the possibilities for linear-quadratic systems or quadratic-quadratic systems.

Linear-quadratic systems   **Quadratic-quadratic systems**

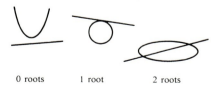

0 roots   1 root   2 roots

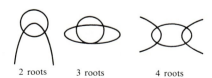

2 roots   3 roots   4 roots

A sketch of a graph is an aid to understanding a system. However, roots of these systems can seldom be determined exactly from a graph. Therefore, algebraic methods are required. Substitution and linear combinations are frequently used.

Example 1 Solve. $y = (x - 1)^2$
$$y = 2x - 3$$

Solution   A sketch of the graphs suggests that the system has one real solution.

Solve for x by substituting $2x - 3$ for y in the first equation.

$$2x - 3 = (x - 1)^2$$
$$2x - 3 = x^2 - 2x + 1$$
$$0 = x^2 - 4x + 4$$
$$0 = (x - 2)^2$$
$$x = 2$$

Substitute 2 for x in the linear equation and solve for y.

$$y = 2(2) - 3$$
$$y = 1$$

Answer $\{(2, 1)\}$

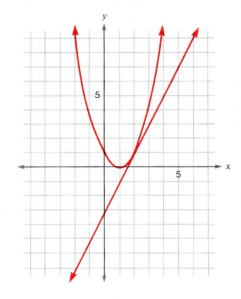

Example 2 **Find all real-number solutions by the method of linear combinations.**
$$x^2 + y^2 = 9$$
$$2x^2 + 3y^2 = 22$$

Solution   A sketch of the graphs shows that there are four real roots of the system.

Multiply both sides of the first equation by -2. Then add the sides of the two equations.

$$-2x^2 - 2y^2 = -18$$
$$\underline{2x^2 + 3y^2 = \quad 22}$$
$$y^2 = \quad 4$$
$$y = \quad \pm 2$$

Substitute 2 for y in the first equation and solve for the corresponding values of x.

$$x^2 + (2)^2 = 9$$
$$x^2 = 5$$
$$x = \pm\sqrt{5}$$

Substituting -2 for y in the first equation will also produce $\pm\sqrt{5}$ for x.

Answer $\{(\sqrt{5}, 2), (-\sqrt{5}, 2), (\sqrt{5}, -2), (-\sqrt{5}, -2)\}$

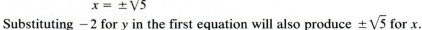

Example 3 Find all real-number solutions.

$$\frac{x^2}{16} - \frac{y^2}{9} = 1$$

$$y = 2x - 1$$

Solution   A sketch of the graphs suggests that the system has no real-number solutions.

Substitute $2x - 1$ for y.

$$\frac{x^2}{16} - \frac{(2x-1)^2}{9} = 1$$

$$9x^2 - 16(2x-1)^2 = 144$$

$$9x^2 - 16(4x^2 - 4x + 1) = 144$$

$$-55x^2 + 64x - 160 = 0$$

Evaluate the discriminant.

$$b^2 - 4ac = 64^2 - 4(-55)(-160)$$

$$= 4096 - 35{,}200$$

$$= -31{,}104$$

Since the discriminant is negative, there are no real roots of the equation.

Answer   ∅ (There are no real-number solutions of the system.)

*C*LASSROOM EXERCISES

Find all real-number solutions. If there are none, write ∅.

1. $\dfrac{x^2}{25} + \dfrac{y^2}{9} = 1$
   $x + y = 8$

2. $xy = 6$
   $y = -3x + 1$

3. $x^2 + y^2 = 25$
   $\dfrac{x^2}{36} + \dfrac{y^2}{25} = 1$

*W*RITTEN EXERCISES

  Find all real-number solutions. Sketch the graphs and label the solutions of the system.

1. $x^2 + y^2 = 25$
   $y = \dfrac{4}{3}x$

2. $x^2 + y^2 = 100$
   $y = \dfrac{3}{4}x$

3. $\dfrac{x^2}{8} + \dfrac{y^2}{18} = 1$
   $y = \dfrac{3}{2}x$

4. $\dfrac{x^2}{12} + \dfrac{y^2}{4} = 1$
   $y = \dfrac{1}{3}x$

5. $y - 2 = (x - 3)^2$
   $y = x + 1$

6. $y - 3 = (x - 2)^2$
   $y = x + 3$

7. $xy = 6$
   $y = x + 1$

8. $xy = 8$
   $y = x + 2$

9. $\dfrac{x^2}{16} - \dfrac{y^2}{4} = 1$
   $6y = x + 4$

10. $\dfrac{x^2}{36} - \dfrac{y^2}{9} = 1$

$4y = x + 6$

11. $y - 2 = (x - 4)^2$

$y = 2x - 7$

12. $y - 1 = (x + 4)^2$

$y = 4x + 13$

13. $y + 5 = \dfrac{1}{2}x^2$

$x^2 + y^2 = 25$

14. $y + 10 = \dfrac{1}{2}x^2$

$x^2 + y^2 = 100$

15. $x^2 + y^2 = 64$

$(x - 4)^2 + y^2 = 16$

16. $x^2 + y^2 = 36$

$(x - 3)^2 + y^2 = 9$

17. $\dfrac{x^2}{8^2} - \dfrac{y^2}{8^2} = 1$

$x^2 + y^2 = 136$

18. $\dfrac{x^2}{4^2} - \dfrac{y^2}{4^2} = 1$

$x^2 + y^2 = 34$

B **19.** $\dfrac{(x - 1)^2}{4} + \dfrac{(y - 3)^2}{25} = 1$

$2y - 5x = 11$

20. $\dfrac{(x - 4)^2}{36} + \dfrac{(y - 1)^2}{25} = 1$

$5x - 6y = 44$

Graph both inequalities. Shade the real-number solutions of the system of inequalities. If there are none, write $\emptyset$.

21. $x^2 + y^2 \leqslant 36$

$x^2 + y^2 \geqslant 16$

22. $(x - 4)^2 + (y - 4)^2 \leqslant 16$

$x^2 + (y - 4)^2 \leqslant 16$

23. $\dfrac{(x - 6)^2}{4^2} + \dfrac{(y - 2)^2}{3^2} \leqslant 1$

$\dfrac{(x - 6)^2}{3^2} + \dfrac{(y - 2)^2}{3^2} \geqslant 1$

24. $x^2 + y^2 \leqslant 25$

$xy \geqslant 16$

Solve, using a system of equations.

25. Two circles are tangent to each other, the smaller circle inside the larger. The area between the circles is 18 cm². If the lengths of the radii differ by 2 cm, find each radius.

26. A rectangle has an area of 60 cm². What are the length and width of the rectangle if the diagonal is 13 cm?

27. What are the dimensions of a rectangle that has a diagonal of $\sqrt{20}$ cm and an area of 10 cm²?

28. Express the width w of a rectangle solely in terms of the area A and perimeter P.

29. Find two positive numbers such that the sum of their squares is 225 and the difference of their squares is 63.

C **30.** Show that it is possible for a nonvertical line $y = mx$, $m \neq 0$, to intersect the upper branch of a hyperbola $\dfrac{y^2}{a^2} - \dfrac{x^2}{b^2} = 1$ at just one point.

31. Find the equation of the line tangent to the circle $x^2 + y^2 = 8$ at the point $(-1, \sqrt{7})$.

32. Determine the value of k such that the line $y = x + k$ is tangent to the parabola $y^2 = 4x$.

33. Find the radius of a circle $x^2 + y^2 = r^2$ that is tangent to both branches of the hyperbola $xy = 1$.

34. Solve the problem given in the opening paragraph of this lesson.

EVIEW EXERCISES

1. Graph these equations on the same set of axes and describe patterns among the graphs and equations. State the vertex and axis of symmetry for each graph.

[8-7, 8-8]

   a. $y = 2x^2$ **b.** $y = -\dfrac{1}{2}(x + 3)^2$ **c.** $y = -2(x - 3)^2$

2. Write this equation in the form $y - k = a(x - h)^2$.

[8-9]

$$y = 3x^2 + 6x + 5$$

For the function $y + 5 = (x + 3)^2$, state:

[8-9, 8-10]

3. the vertex.   **4.** the axis of symmetry.

5. whether the graph opens upward or downward.

6. State whether it has a maximum or a minimum and its value.

XTENSION   The Lemniscate of Bernoulli

A curve known as the *lemniscate of Bernoulli* has been used to define curves in the design of highway interchanges. Its general equation is made up of quadratic terms and is defined geometrically by a locus relative to a hyperbola.

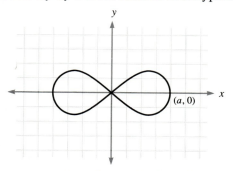

$$(x^2 + y^2)^2 = a^2(x^2 - y^2)$$

    It was named for the Swiss mathematician Jacques Bernoulli (1654–1705) who was the first to study it.

CHAPTER SUMMARY

▶ Vocabulary

▶ A *circle* is the set of all points in a plane such that the distance (radius) from a given point (center of the circle) is constant.   [9-1]

The standard equation of a circle with center (h, k) and radius r is
$$(x - h)^2 + (y - k)^2 = r^2.$$

▶ A *parabola* is the set of all points in a plane that are the same distance from a given point (focus) as they are from a given line (directrix).   [9-2]

The standard form of the equation of a parabola is
$$y - k = a(x - h)^2.$$

▶ An *ellipse* is the set of all points in a plane such that the sum of the distances (focal radii) from two given points (foci) is constant.   [9-3]

The equation of an ellipse with the sum of focal radii equal to $2a$, where $a > b$ and $b^2 = a^2 - c^2$, is
$$\frac{x^2}{a^2} + \frac{y^2}{b^2} = 1 \text{ for foci } (-c, 0) \text{ and } (c, 0).$$

The standard form of the equation of an ellipse with center (h, k) is
$$\frac{(x - h)^2}{a^2} + \frac{(y - k)^2}{b^2} = 1.$$

▶ A *hyperbola* is the set of all points in a plane such that the absolute value of the difference of the distances (focal radii) from two given points (foci) is constant.   [9-4]

The equation of a hyperbola with the difference of focal radii equal to $2a$, where $b^2 = c^2 - a^2$, is
$$\frac{x^2}{a^2} - \frac{y^2}{b^2} = 1 \text{ for foci } (-c, 0) \text{ and } (c, 0).$$

The equations of the asymptotes are $y = \dfrac{b}{a}x$ and $y = -\dfrac{b}{a}x$.

The standard form of the equation of a hyperbola with center (h, k) is
$$\frac{(x - h)^2}{a^2} - \frac{(y - k)^2}{b^2} = 1.$$

▶ Equations of the form $xy = n$, $n \neq 0$, also define hyperbolas whose asymptotes are the coordinate axes.

▶ General Second Degree Equation in x and y [9-5]
$$Ax^2 + Bxy + Cy^2 + Dx + Ey + F = 0.$$

If $B = 0$, then the conic section can be determined by the relationship between A and C.

Conic Section	Values of A and C
Parabola	$AC = 0, A \neq C$
Circle	$A = C$
Ellipse	$AC > 0, A \neq C$
Hyperbola	$AC < 0$

HAPTER REVIEW

9-1   **Objective:**   To write equations of circles, given identifying characteristics.
1. Write an equation of the circle with center $(-5, 1)$ and radius 2.
2. Write an equation of the circle with center $(4, -3)$ and tangent to the y-axis.

     Objective: To graph circles and circular regions.
3. Graph $(x - 1)^2 + (y - 3)^2 \leq 2^2$.
4. Write the substitutions required to translate the graph of $x^2 + y^2 = 9$ to that of a congruent circle with center $(-4, -3)$.

9-2   **Objective:**   To write and graph equations of parabolas, given their identifying characteristics.
5. Write an equation of the parabola with focus $(0, 2)$ and directrix $y = 1$.
6. Graph the parabola $x = \dfrac{1}{2}(y - 2)^2$.

     Objective: To identify properties of parabolas from their equations.
7. Identify the vertex, axis of symmetry, focus, directrix, length of latus chord, and direction of the parabola $y + 3 = \dfrac{1}{4}(x - 1)^2$.

9-3 **Objective:** To write and graph equations of ellipses, given their identifying characteristics.

8. Write an equation of the ellipse with foci $(\sqrt{7}, 0)$ and $(-\sqrt{7}, 0)$ and minor axis from $(0, 3)$ to $(0, -3)$.

9. Graph the ellipse $\dfrac{(x-1)^2}{9} + \dfrac{y^2}{16} = 1$.

Objective: To identify properties of ellipses from their equations.

10. Identify the vertices and foci of the ellipse $16x^2 + 4y^2 = 64$.

9-4 **Objective:** To write and graph equations of hyperbolas, given their identifying characteristics.

11. Graph the hyperbola $\dfrac{y^2}{4} - x^2 = 1$.

12. Graph the hyperbola $xy - 3 = 0$.

13. Write an equation of the hyperbola with vertices $(3, 0)$ and $(-3, 0)$ and foci $(5, 0)$ and $(-5, 0)$.

Objective: To identify properties of hyperbolas from their equations.

14. Write the equations of the asymptotes of the hyperbola $\dfrac{x^2}{2} - \dfrac{y^2}{8} = 1$.

9-5 **Objective:** To identify conics from their general second-degree equations.

15. Identify these conic sections.

a. $x^2 - y^2 = 4$
b. $4x^2 - 16x + y - 3 = 0$
c. $x^2 + 9y^2 - 2x + 18y + 4 = 0$
d. $16 - x^2 - y^2 = 0$

Objective: To rewrite equations of conics in standard form.

16. Identify the conic section, and then write an equivalent equation for it in standard form.

a. $9x^2 - 4y^2 - 18x - 16y - 43 = 0$
b. $x^2 - 4y + 6x + 17 = 0$
c. $4x^2 + 4y^2 + 40x + 99 = 0$

9-6 **Objective:** To solve nonlinear systems of two equations in two variables.

Find all real-number solutions.

17. $\dfrac{x^2}{4} - \dfrac{y^2}{8} = 1$
$y = x - 2$

18. $9x^2 + y^2 = 32$
$y = 3x$

19. $x^2 - y^2 = 1$
$4x^2 + y^2 = 4$

20. $x^2 + y^2 = 5^2$
$xy = 12$

400   Chapter 9   Conic Sections

Solve.

21. The sum of the circumferences of two circles is 22π cm. The sum of the areas of the circles is 65π cm^2. Find the radius of each circle.

HAPTER 9 SELF-TEST

9-1   **1.** Write an equation of the circle with radius 5 and center $(-1, 2)$.

    2. Graph $x^2 + (y - 3)^2 \leqslant 9$.

9-2   **3.** State the substitutions that translate the parabola $y = 2x^2$ into the congruent parabola that has a vertex of $(-4, 5)$ and that opens upward.

    4. Write an equation of the parabola with focus $(-3, 1)$ and directrix $y = -1$.

    5. Graph $y - 4 = \frac{1}{2}(x + 1)^2$.

9-3   **6.** Write an equation of the ellipse with major axis 8, minor axis 6, center at the origin, and foci on the x-axis.

    7. Identify the foci of the ellipse $\dfrac{x^2}{8^2} + \dfrac{y^2}{6^2} = 1$.

    8. Graph $\dfrac{(x + 2)^2}{4} + \dfrac{y^2}{9} = 1$.

9-4   **9.** Write an equation of the hyperbola with foci $(0, 6)$ and $(0, -6)$ and whose focal radii differ by 10.

    10. Graph $16 + 4xy = 0$.   **11.** Graph $9x^2 - 16y^2 = 144$.

9-5   **Identify the conic section.**

    12. $3x^2 + 3y^2 - 6x + 1 = 0$ **13.** $9x^2 + y^2 - 18x + 2y + 4 = 0$

    14. $4y^2 + x - 8y + 12 = 0$ **15.** $4x^2 - 4y^2 = 20$

    16. Write the equation of the conic section $9x^2 - y^2 - 18x - 4y - 76 = 0$ in standard form.

9-6   **Solve each system for real roots.**

    17. $x^2 + y^2 = 20$ **18.** $x^2 - y^2 = 12$

         $x + y = 2$ $x = y^2$

Solve.

19. Find two positive numbers such that the sum of their squares is 185 and the difference of their squares is 57.

20. The sum of the squares of two numbers is 5. The sum of the numbers is -3. What are the two numbers?

21. The sum of two numbers is -3, and the difference of their squares is 21. What are the numbers?

Choose the best answer.

1. In the figure at the right, the small square is inscribed in the circle, and the circle is inscribed in the large square. What is the ratio of the area of the small square to the area of the shaded region?

   A. 1:2   **B.** 1:$\sqrt{2}$ **C.** 1:1   **D.** $\sqrt{2}$:1   **E.** 2:1

2. An equation for the circle that passes through (3, 2) and has its center at the origin is ___?___.

   A. $x^2 + y^2 = \sqrt{5}$ **B.** $x^2 + y^2 = 5$ **C.** $x^2 + y^2 = \sqrt{13}$

   D. $x^2 + y^2 = 13$ **E.** $x^2 + y^2 = 25$

3. If $(-1, 2)$ is one end of a line segment and (4, 0) is the midpoint, then the other endpoint is ___?___.

   A. $(9, -2)$ **B.** $\left(\frac{3}{2}, \frac{1}{2}\right)$ **C.** $(-6, 4)$ **D.** $(8, 1)$ **E.** $(-1, -2)$

4. What is the area of the triangle with vertices $(-2, 0)$, (2, 3), and $(2, -3)$?

   A. 10   **B.** 12   **C.** 15   **D.** 16   **E.** 24

5. Which of the following is an equation of the circle that has center $(-3, 5)$ and is tangent to the y-axis?

   A. $(x - 3)^2 + (y + 5)^2 = 9$ **B.** $(x - 3)^2 + (y + 5)^2 = 25$

   C. $(x - 5)^2 + (y + 5)^2 = 25$ **D.** $(x + 3)^2 + (y - 5)^2 = 9$

   E. $(x + 3)^2 + (y - 5)^2 = 25$

6. Which equation represents the graph below?

   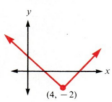

   (4, −2)

   A. $y + 2 = |x + 4|$ **B.** $y + 2 = |x - 4|$ **C.** $y + 2 = |x| - 4$

   D. $y - 2 = |x + 4|$ **E.** $y - 2 = |x - 4|$

7. Which is the set of all ordered pairs (x, y) that satisfies the system?

   $$x^2 + y^2 = 1$$
   $$x^2 - y^2 = 1$$

   A. $\{(1, 0), (-1, 0)\}$ **B.** $\{(0, 1), (0, -1)\}$ **C.** $\emptyset$

   D. $\{(1, 1), (-1, -1)\}$ **E.** $\{(1, 0), (-1, 0), (0, 1), (0, -1)\}$

8. If a right triangle is rotated 360° about one of its legs, the solid generated is ___?___.

A. a sphere   **B.** a cylinder   **C.** two cones

D. a cylinder and a cone   **E.** a cone

9. The figure at the right shows an ellipse inscribed in a circle. The area of the ellipse is given by the formula $A = \pi ab$. If $a = 4$ and $b = 3$, what is the area of the shaded region?

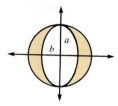

A. 3π **B.** 4π **C.** 7π **D.** 9π **E.** 12π

10. Triangle ABC is an equilateral triangle with sides of length 1. Circular arcs AB, BC, and CA are drawn with centers C, A, and B, respectively. What is the perimeter of the figure formed by the circular arcs AB, BC, and CA?

A. $\frac{1}{3}\pi$ **B.** $\frac{2}{3}\pi$ **C.** π **D.** $\frac{3}{2}\pi$ **E.** 2π

11. $\overline{AB}$ is a diameter of the circle with center O and radius 1. Arcs AO and OB are semicircles. What is the total length of arcs AO and OB?

A. $\frac{1}{4}\pi$ **B.** $\frac{1}{2}\pi$ **C.** π **D.** 2π **E.** 4π

$\mathcal{C}$UMULATIVE REVIEW (CHAPTERS 7–9)

7-1 **True or false?**

1. $-\sqrt{\dfrac{25}{36}} = -\dfrac{5}{6}$

2. $-\sqrt[3]{-64}$ is not a real number.

Simplify. State any necessary restrictions.

7-1, **3.** $\sqrt{144}$ **4.** $\sqrt[3]{a^4 b^6}$ **5.** $\sqrt{63} - \sqrt{28} + \sqrt{7}$

7-2,
7-3 **6.** Expand and simplify: $(2 + \sqrt{3})(5 - \sqrt{3})$.

Simplify.

7-4   **7.** $\dfrac{20}{2\sqrt{5}}$ **8.** $-\dfrac{12xy}{\sqrt[3]{9xy^2}}$, $x \neq 0$, $y \neq 0$ **9.** $\sqrt{\dfrac{5x}{18y}}$, $x \geq 0$, $y > 0$

7-5   **10.** Find the distance between $P(-6, 5)$ and $Q(2, 1)$.

       11. Triangle ABC has vertices at $A(-2, -2)$, $B(1, -6)$, and $C(5, 0)$. Determine whether the triangle is isosceles.

Solve.

7-6   **12.** $\sqrt[3]{1 - 2x} = 3$ **13.** $\sqrt{x + 6} = x$

7-7   **14.** Write in exponential notation: $\sqrt[5]{x - 7}$.

Write in simplest radical form.

15. $12^{-\frac{1}{3}}$ **16.** $4x^{\frac{3}{2}}$ **17.** $5y^{-\frac{1}{2}}$

8-1   **18.** Write the equation $(x - 9)^2 = (2x + 5)^2$ in standard quadratic form.

Solve.

8-1,   **19.** $y^2 - 18 = 0$ **20.** $(x + 4)^2 = 48$ **21.** $4x^2 - 12x - 7 = 0$

8-2   **22.** The sum S of the first n positive integers is given by the formula $S = \dfrac{n(n + 1)}{2}$. Find n if $S = 105$.

Simplify.

8-3   **23.** $(5i)(-9i)$ **24.** $\sqrt{-27} \cdot \sqrt{-6}$ **25.** $|-2 + 6i|$

       26. Solve: $x^2 - 8x + 41 = 0$.

Simplify.

8-4   **27.** $(7 - 9i) + (2i - 4)$ **28.** $(14 - i) - (-5 + 3i)$

8-5   **29.** $(2 - 3i)(1 + 4i)$ **30.** $(6 + 2i)^2$ **31.** $\dfrac{1 - i}{3i}$

8-6   **State the number and kind of roots of the equation.**

       32. $4x^2 - x - 5 = 0$ **33.** $x^2 + 4x + 13 = 0$ **34.** $9x^2 - 12x + 4 = 0$

Solve.

       35. $x^4 + 3x^2 - 4 = 0$ **36.** $y - 4\sqrt{y} + 3 = 0$

8-7   **37.** State the number of points at which the parabola $y = 4x^2$ and the line $y = 0$ intersect.

       38. Graph these equations on the same set of axes.

$$y = x^2, \quad y = -x^2, \quad y = \frac{1}{4}x^2$$

8-8 **39.** State the vertex and axis of symmetry, and tell whether the graph opens upward or downward. Do not graph.

$$y = \frac{1}{4}(x - 2)^2$$

True or false?

40. The graphs of the parabolas $y = (x - 4)^2$ and $y = (x + 2)^2$ are congruent.

8-9 **41.** Sketch the graph of the following parabola.

$$y - 1 = (x + 3)^2.$$

42. Write $y = 3x^2 - 6x + 4$ in the form $y - k = a(x - h)^2$.

8-10 **State the maximum or minimum value for the function and where it occurs.**

43. $f(x) = -x^2 + 6x - 4$ **44.** $g(x) = x^2 + 3x - 1$

9-1 **45.** Write the equation of a circle with center $(-4, 3)$ and radius 6.

46. Graph: $(x - 2)^2 + (y - 1)^2 = 4$.

9-2 **Write the standard equation of the parabola described.**

47. Focus: $(-4, 4)$ **48.** Focus: $(0, 2)$
      Directrix: $y = 0$ Vertex: $(0, -2)$

49. Graph: $(y - 3) = 2(x + 5)^2$.

9-3 **Write the standard equation of the ellipse described.**

50. Foci: $(0, 3)$ and $(0, -3)$ **51.** Center: $(0, 0)$
      Sum of focal radii: 8   Major axis: 6 units on the x-axis
                                         Minor axis: 2 units on the y-axis

52. Graph: $\dfrac{x^2}{25} + \dfrac{y^2}{9} = 1$.

9-4 **53.** Write the standard equation of the hyperbola with foci $(-5, 0)$ and $(5, 0)$, and with the difference of the focal radii equal to 8.

Sketch the graph of each of these hyperbolas.

54. $\dfrac{x^2}{1} - \dfrac{y^2}{4} = 1$ **55.** $xy = 8$

9-5 **Identify the conic of each of these equations.**

56. $x^2 - 9y^2 + 4x - 18y + 10 = 0$ **57.** $9x^2 + 4y^2 + 36x = 0$

58. Sketch the graph:

$$x^2 + y^2 - 8x + 4y = 0.$$

9-6 **Solve the system.**

59. $xy = 6$ **60.** $x^2 + y^2 = 9$ **61.** $x^2 - 4y^2 = 16$
      $y = x - 1$ $y = x^2 + 3$ $x^2 + y^2 = 21$

CHAPTER 10

Polynomial Functions

The tools of the mathematician are relations and functions. Through them, mathematicians can analyze complex physical systems and apply powerful ideas to solve difficult problems. For example, theoretical physicists are mathematicians who explore, using the equations of quantum mechanics, the strange nuclear world populated by quarks and gluons. Experimental physicists use particle accelerators to test the mathematical theories.

Polynomial Functions

Polynomials and numbers have much in common. In fact, our decimal place-value notation is an abbreviation for a lengthier expanded polynomial notation. For example,

$$3425 = 3 \cdot 10^3 + 4 \cdot 10^2 + 2 \cdot 10 + 5.$$

Like integers, polynomials can be added, subtracted, multiplied, and divided. Like the set of integers, the set of polynomials is closed with respect to addition, subtraction, and multiplication, but not with respect to division.

A **polynomial in one variable** is an expression that is equivalent to

$$a_n x^n + a_{n-1} x^{n-1} + a_{n-2} x^{n-2} + \cdots + a_2 x^2 + a_1 x + a_0,$$

where the coefficients a_n, a_{n-1}, . . ., a_0 are complex numbers, $a_n \neq 0$, and n is a nonnegative integer. The term a_0 is the **constant term** of the polynomial, but it can be considered the coefficient of x^0. The above form is called the **standard form of the polynomial.**

Polynomials in one variable	*Not polynomials in one variable*
$2y - 3$	$x^3 - \sqrt{x}$ ($\sqrt{x}$ cannot be written as x^n with n an integer)
$4x^2 + 3x - 8$	$3x + \dfrac{1}{x} + 6$ ($\dfrac{1}{x}$ cannot be written as x^n with n a positive integer)
$\dfrac{1}{5}x^4 - \sqrt{6}$	$2xy - 3z + 8x^2$ (contains three variables)

The **degree of a polynomial in one variable** is the degree of the term of the highest degree when the polynomial is written in standard form. The **leading coefficient** of the polynomial is the coefficient of the term with the highest degree.

Polynomial	Degree	Leading coefficient
$2x - 5$	1	2
$4x - 3x^2 + 1$	2	-3
$a_n x^n + a_{n-1} x^{n-1} + \cdots + a_1 x + a_0$	n	a_n

A polynomial of degree 0 is a **constant**. A polynomial of degree 1 is a **linear polynomial**. Polynomials of degrees 2 and 3 are **quadratic** and **cubic polynomials,** respectively.

A **polynomial function** is a function P whose values are defined by a polynomial.

$$P(x) = a_n x^n + a_{n-1} x^{n-1} + \cdots + a_2 x^2 + a_1 x + a_0$$

The value $P(b)$ can be computed by substituting b for x in the polynomial and simplifying.

Example 1 Find $P(4)$ if $P(x) = 2x^4 - x^3 - 5x^2 + 3x + 6$.

Solution $P(4) = 2(4^4) - 4^3 - 5(4^2) + 3(4) + 6$

$\qquad\qquad = 512 - 64 - 80 + 12 + 6$

$\qquad\qquad = 386$

Evaluating a polynomial term by term as in Example 1 can be time-consuming. We can evaluate more simply by factoring the polynomial in a special way.

$$2x^4 - x^3 - 5x^2 + 3x + 6$$

Factor x from the first four terms. $(2x^3 - 1x^2 - 5x + 3)x + 6$

Factor x from the first three terms. $((2x^2 - 1x - 5)x + 3)x + 6$

Factor x from the first two terms. $(((2x - 1)x - 5)x + 3)x + 6$

The last expression is called the **nested form** of the polynomial. For any value of x, this form can be efficiently computed using the calculator keys $\boxed{\text{STO}}$ (store in memory) and $\boxed{\text{RCL}}$ (recall from memory). On some calculators, these keys may be labeled $\boxed{\text{M in}}$ (or $\boxed{\text{M +}}$) and $\boxed{\text{MR}}$.

Sequence: Enter 2, multiply by x, add -1, multiply by x, add -5, multiply by x, add 3, multiply by x, and add 6.

For $x = 4$, the keying sequence is:

$4 \boxed{\text{STO}}$

$\boxed{(}\ \boxed{(}\ \boxed{(}\ 2\ \boxed{\times}\ \boxed{\text{RCL}}\ \boxed{+}\ 1\ \boxed{\text{+/-}}\ \boxed{)}\ \boxed{\times}\ \boxed{\text{RCL}}\ \boxed{+}\ 5\ \boxed{\text{+/-}}\ \boxed{)}\ \boxed{\times}\ \boxed{\text{RCL}}\ \boxed{+}\ 3\ \boxed{)}$

$\boxed{\times}\ \boxed{\text{RCL}}\ \boxed{+}\ 6\ \boxed{=}$

This same procedure can be used with paper and pencil in a method called **synthetic substitution.** Here is another method of solving Example 1.

1. Write the value of x. Write the coefficients of the polynomial in *descending powers* of x.

$$4\,\rfloor \quad 2 \quad -1 \quad -5 \quad 3 \quad 6$$

2. Write the first coefficient below the line, multiply it by 4, and write the product under the next coefficient.

$$4\,\rfloor \quad 2 \quad -1 \quad -5 \quad 3 \quad 6$$
$$\underline{\qquad\qquad 8 \qquad\qquad}$$
$$\quad\; 2$$

3. Add this to the next coefficient, multiply the sum by 4, and write the product under the next coefficient.

$$\begin{array}{r|rrrrr} 4 & 2 & -1 & -5 & 3 & 6 \\ & & 8 & 28 & & \\ \hline & 2 & 7 & & & \end{array}$$

4. Repeat, until you write the product under the constant term and add the constant term.

$$\begin{array}{r|rrrrr} 4 & 2 & -1 & -5 & 3 & 6 \\ & & 8 & 28 & 92 & 380 \\ \hline & 2 & 7 & 23 & 95 & 386 \leftarrow P(4) \end{array}$$

The last sum, 386, is the value of $P(4)$.

Note that $P(x)$ *must be written in descending powers of* x. If a power of x is missing, the coefficient 0 must be inserted in its place. An nth-degree polynomial has $(n + 1)$ coefficients.

Example 2 Use synthetic substitution to compute $P(-3)$ if $P(x) = x^5 + 2x - 5x^3 + 7$.

Solution Rewrite $P(x)$ in standard form including the missing terms with zeros as coefficients.

$P(x) = x^5 + 0x^4 - 5x^3 + 0x^2 + 2x + 7$

Now use synthetic substitution to compute $P(-3)$.

$$\begin{array}{r|rrrrrr} -3 & 1 & 0 & -5 & 0 & 2 & 7 \\ & & -3 & 9 & -12 & 36 & -114 \\ \hline & 1 & -3 & 4 & -12 & 38 & -107 \leftarrow P(-3) \end{array}$$

Example 3 Sketch the graph of $f(x) = x^3 - 2x^2 + 3x - 1$.

Solution Use synthetic substitution or a calculator to compute $f(x)$ for some values of x.

x	-3	-2	-1	0	1	2	3
$f(x)$	-55	-23	-7	-1	1	5	17

Plot the points and connect them with a smooth curve.

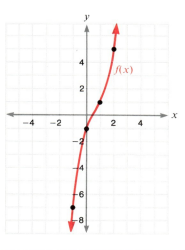

$\mathcal{C}$LASSROOM EXERCISES

State whether the expression is a polynomial in one variable.

1. $2a^3$

2. $\dfrac{1}{x^2}$

3. $4x^5 - 2x^3 + x^2 - 7x - \dfrac{1}{2}$

State the degree of the polynomial.

4. $16a^5 - 6$

5. $-2x + x^2 - 5 - x^2$

6. $4x^2 + 3x$

Use synthetic substitution to evaluate the polynomial for the given values.
$P(x) = 3x^3 - 2x^2 + 4x - 7$

7. $P(2)$

8. $P(-3)$

9. $P(0)$

Use an appropriate method to evaluate the polynomial for the given values.
$f(x) = 2x^5 - 2x^2 + 4x - 2$

10. $f(3)$

11. $f(0)$

12. $f\left(\dfrac{1}{2}\right)$

$\mathcal{W}$RITTEN EXERCISES

 State whether the expression is a polynomial in one variable.

1. $x^2 + 3x + 1 + \dfrac{5}{x}$

2. $5x - 6 + 2\sqrt{x} + \dfrac{7}{x^2}$

3. $\sqrt{2}x^4 + x$

4. $\pi x^3 + 13$

5. $x^2y + xy^2$

6. $xy^2 + xy$

State the degree of the polynomial.

7. $10x^2 + 5x^3 - 2$

8. $7 - 3x^3 + 2x^5$

9. $5x - 3x^4 + 1$

10. $7x - 2x^3 + 1$

11. $3x^4 - x - 3x^4$

12. $x^3 + 5x^2 - x^3$

Write the polynomial in standard form.

13. $5(x + 3)$

14. $-7(x^2 - 2)$

15. $3 + x - x^2$

16. $5 - x^2 + x$

17. $x(3x^3 - 1)$

18. $x^3 + x^2(5 - x)$

Use synthetic substitution to evaluate the polynomial $g(x) = x^3 + 3x^2 - 4x - 6$ for the given values.

19. $g(3)$

20. $g(2)$

21. $g(10)$

22. $g(-10)$

23. $g(-5)$

24. $g(5)$

Use synthetic substitution to find $P(2)$ for each polynomial.

25. $P(x) = 2x^3 - 4x - 6$

26. $P(x) = -3x^3 + 2x + 1$

27. $P(x) = x^4 - x^3 + x^2 - x + 1$

28. $P(x) = x^5 + x^4 - x^3 - x^2 + x - 1$

29. $P(x) = 4x^4 - x^2$

30. $P(x) = 5x^2 - x$

Use a calculator to evaluate the function for integer values of x, $-4 \leq x \leq 4$. Then graph the function.

31. $f(x) = x^3 + 3x^2 - 4x - 12$

32. $P(x) = x^3 - 3x^2 - x + 3$

33. For what three integer values of x is synthetic substitution or a calculator an *inefficient* method of evaluating a polynomial.

Use an appropriate method to compute values of the function. Then graph the function for the given domain.

34. $f(x) = x^4 - 10x^2 + 9$
$-4 \leq x \leq 4$

35. $h(x) = x^4 - 2x^3 - 5x^2 + 6x$
$-4 \leq x \leq 4$

36. $g(x) = 4x^3 + 4x^2 + x$
$-1 \leq x \leq 1$ $\left[\textit{Note: Find } g\left(-\frac{1}{2}\right) \text{ and } g\left(\frac{1}{2}\right). \right]$

37. $p(x) = 10x^3 - 12x^2 - 10x + 3$
$-2 \leq x \leq 2$

38. $f(x) = -x^4 + 5x^2 - 6$
$-4 \leq x \leq 4$

39. $g(x) = -2x^3 + 3x - 4$
$-3 \leq x \leq 3$

40. $h(x) = x^5 - x + 1$
$-3 \leq x \leq 3$

41. $p(x) = -x^2 - x + 2$
$-4 \leq x \leq 4$

Let $f(x) = x^3 - 2x^2 + 9x - 18$. Evaluate.

42. $f(3i)$

43. $f(-3i)$

44. $f\left(\sqrt{3}\right)$

45. Use an appropriate method to compute values of the function. Then graph the function for the given domain.
$$f(x) = x^5 - 2x^4 + 4x^3 - 8x^2 + 3x - 6, \quad -5 \leq x \leq 5$$

46. Let $P(x) = -2x^3 + 4x - 5$. Use synthetic substitution to find $P(a)$ and $P(-a)$.

REVIEW EXERCISES

1. Simplify and express in scientific notation: $(4.5 \cdot 10^4)(3 \cdot 10^{10})$. [5-1]

2. Simplify: $(x^2 - 3x + 4) - (x^2 + 5x - 6)$. [5-2]

3. Expand: $(x + 2)^3$. [5-3]

4. Write an expression in factored form for the surface area of this rectangular solid. [5-4]

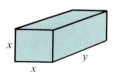

Factor completely. [5-4, 5-5, 5-6]

5. $ac + ad + bc + bd$

6. $2a^2 - 18b^2$

7. $5x^2 + 16x + 3$

8. Solve: $x^2 + 6x = 7$. [5-7]

The Remainder and Factor Theorems

To determine the remainder when one integer is divided by another, it is usually necessary to use long division.

$$
\begin{array}{r}
34 \\
17\overline{)593} \\
-51 \\
\hline
83 \\
-68 \\
\hline
\end{array}
$$

To divide one polynomial by another polynomial of the form $(x - r)$, it is usually not necessary to use long division to determine the remainder.

$15 \leftarrow$ remainder

Each polynomial in x can be divided by any other polynomial in x of lesser degree. Of particular interest is the quotient when a polynomial $P(x)$ is divided by a binomial $(x - r)$, where r is a real number. For example, let $P(x) = 3x^4 + 2x^3 - 5x^2 - x + 7$ and $r = 2$.

Long division

$$
\begin{array}{r}
3x^3 + 8x^2 + 11x + 21 \longleftarrow \text{quotient} \\
\text{divisor} \longrightarrow x - 2\overline{)3x^4 + 2x^3 - 5x^2 - x + 7} \longleftarrow \text{dividend} \\
\underline{3x^4 - 6x^3} \\
8x^3 - 5x^2 \\
\underline{8x^3 - 16x^2} \\
11x^2 - x \\
\underline{11x^2 - 22x} \\
21x + 7 \\
\underline{21x - 42} \\
49 \longleftarrow \text{remainder}
\end{array}
$$

The long division shows that the quotient is $3x^3 + 8x^2 + 11x + 21$ and the remainder is 49. That is,

$$P(x) = (x - 2)(3x^3 + 8x^2 + 11x + 21) + 49.$$

Substituting 2 for x in the above equation gives

$$P(2) = 0 + 49 = 49.$$

That is, $P(2)$ is the remainder when $P(x)$ is divided by $(x - 2)$.

This result can be generalized as the **Remainder Theorem.**

The Remainder Theorem

For each polynomial $P(x)$, of degree $n \geq 1$, and each real number r, there is a polynomial $Q(x)$, of degree $n - 1$, such that $P(x) = (x - r)Q(x) + P(r)$.

The long-division process can be simplified considerably. First, the variables can be omitted, leaving only the coefficients.

$$
\begin{array}{r}
3 +\ \ 8 + 11 + 21 \\
-2\overline{\smash{)}3 + 2 -\ \ 5 -\ \ 1 + 7} \\
\underline{-6} \\
8 \\
\underline{-16} \\
11 \\
\underline{-22} \\
21 \\
\underline{-42} \\
49
\end{array}
$$

Second, rewriting the terms that are brought down can be omitted.

Next, write 2 instead of -2 as the divisor. This makes it appear as if we are dividing by r and allows us to add, instead of subtract, at each step. Also, we can collapse the division into four lines.

$$
\begin{array}{r}
3 +\ \ 8 + 11 + 21 \\
2\overline{\smash{)}3 + 2 -\ \ 5 -\ \ 1 + 7} \\
\underline{6\quad 16\quad 22\quad 42} \\
8 + 11 + 21 + 49
\end{array}
$$

Finally, noting the repetition in the top and bottom rows, delete the top row and write both quotients and remainder in the bottom row.

$$
\begin{array}{r|rrrrr}
2 & 3 + 2 -\ \ 5 -\ \ 1 + 7 \\
& \quad 6\quad 16\quad 22\quad 42 \\
\hline
& 3 + 8 + 11 + 21 + 49
\end{array}
$$

The first four terms of the bottom row are the coefficients of the quotient and the last term is the remainder.

Quotient: $3x^3 + 8x^2 + 11x + 21$ Remainder: 49

These simplified division steps are precisely the same as those used in synthetic substitution. This process is referred to as **synthetic division.**

Example 1   Use synthetic division to divide $3x^4 - 2x^2 + 7x - 9$ by $(x - 3)$.

Solution

$$
\begin{array}{r|rrrrr}
3 & 3 & 0 & -2 & 7 & -9 \\
& & 9 & 27 & 75 & 246 \\
\hline
& 3 & 9 & 25 & 82 & 237
\end{array}
$$

Answer $3x^4 - 2x^2 + 7x - 9 = (x - 3)(3x^3 + 9x^2 + 25x + 82) + 237$

Example 2   Use synthetic division to divide $-2x^3 - 4x^2 + x + 3$ by $(x + 2)$.

Solution

$$
\begin{array}{r|rrrr}
-2 & -2 & -4 & 1 & 3 \\
& & 4 & 0 & -2 \\
\hline
& -2 & 0 & 1 & 1
\end{array}
$$

Answer $-2x^3 - 4x^2 + x + 3 = (x + 2)(-2x^2 + 1) + 1$

An immediate consequence of the Remainder Theorem is the **Factor Theorem.** Synthetic division and the factor theorem provide a method for finding binomial factors $(x - r)$ of higher-degree polynomials.

The Factor Theorem

For each polynomial $P(x)$, of degree $n \geq 1$, and each real number r, $(x - r)$ is a factor of $P(x)$ if and only if $P(r) = 0$.

Example 3 Is $(x - 5)$ a factor of $x^4 - 4x^3 - 9x^2 + 16x + 20$?

Solution

$$
\begin{array}{r|rrrrr}
5 & 1 & -4 & -9 & 16 & 20 \\
  &   & 5 & 5 & -20 & -20 \\
\hline
  & 1 & 1 & -4 & -4 & 0
\end{array}
$$

$P(5) = 0$, so $(x - 5)$ is a factor of $x^4 - 4x^3 - 9x^2 + 16x + 20$.

$\mathcal{C}$LASSROOM EXERCISES

Use synthetic division to divide each polynomial by the given binomial. Write the quotient and the remainder.

1. $2x^4 - 3x^3 + 5x^2 - 2x + 6$; $x - 3$

2. $4x^3 - 4x + 6$; $x + 2$

Use the factor theorem to determine whether the given binomial is a factor of the given polynomial.

3. $x^4 + 3x^3 - 11x^2 + 4$; $x - 2$

4. $-x^3 - 3x^2 + 4x + 6$; $x + 3$

$\mathcal{W}$RITTEN EXERCISES

 Use synthetic division to divide each polynomial $P(x)$ by the given binomial $(x - r)$. Write the quotient and the remainder.

1. $P(x) = x^3 - 7x^2 + x + 10$; $x - 2$

2. $P(x) = x^3 + 3x^2 + 10x + 5$; $x - 3$

3. $P(x) = 2x^3 - 5x^2 + 3x - 7$; $x + 3$

4. $P(x) = 3x^3 - 7x^2 + 5x - 2$; $x + 2$

5. $P(x) = 5x^3 + 7x^2 + 8$; $x + 2$

6. $P(x) = 4x^3 + 2x + 10$; $x + 3$

7. $P(x) = 2x^4 + 5x^3 + 8x^2$; $x - 4$

8. $P(x) = 5x^4 + 6x^3 + 10x^2$; $x - 5$

9. $P(x) = x^4 + 10x^3 - 8x - 80$; $x + 10$

10. $P(x) = x^4 + 10x^3 - 8x - 80$; $x - 2$

11. $P(x) = x^5 + 2x^4 - 3x^3 + 4x^2 - 5x + 2$; $x - 1$

12. $P(x) = 3x^5 - 8x^4 + 2x^3 - 10x^2 + x - 6$; $x - 10$

Use the factor theorem to determine whether the given binomial is a factor of $P(x) = x^3 - 9x^2 + 26x - 24$.

13. $x - 2$

14. $x - 4$

15. $x - 1$

16. $x - 3$

Use the factor theorem to determine whether the given binomial is a factor of
$P(x) = x^3 + 2x^2 - 25x - 50$.

17. $x + 2$ **18.** $x - 2$ **19.** $x - 5$ **20.** $x + 3$

Simplify each expression.

21. $\dfrac{x^4 + 6x^3 + 8x^2 + 5x + 20}{x + 4}$

22. $\dfrac{x^4 + 5x^3 + 6x^2 + 32x + 10}{x + 5}$

23. $\dfrac{x^5 - 9x^4 + 18x^3 + 5x^2 - 29x - 6}{x - 6}$

24. $\dfrac{x^5 - 3x^4 - 5x^3 + 16x^2 - 11x + 24}{x - 3}$

25. $\dfrac{x^5 + 2x^4 - 12x - 24}{x + 2}$

26. $\dfrac{x^5 + 4x^4 + 6x + 24}{x + 4}$

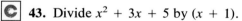 Write each polynomial in the form $(x - r)Q(x) + P(r)$.

27. $P(x) = x^3 + 5x^2 - 6x - 8; r = 2$ **28.** $P(x) = 3x^2 - 10x + 15; r = 5$
29. $P(x) = 5x^3 + 6x - 20; r = 4$ **30.** $P(x) = 4x^4 - 37x^2 + 10; r = -3$

Find the remainder when the polynomial $P(x)$ is divided by $(x - r)$.

31. $P(x) = 3x^2 + 5x + 7; r = 10$ **32.** $P(x) = 8x^2 + 6x + 2; r = -10$

Given r, find $P(r)$ for $P(x) = ax^5 + bx^4 + cx^3 + dx^2 + ex + f$.

33. $r = 1$ **34.** $r = -1$ **35.** $r = 0$ **36.** $r = 10$

Determine the value of k necessary to meet the given condition.

37. $(x - 2)$ is a factor of $3x^3 - x^2 - 11x + k$.
38. $(x + 3)$ is a factor of $2x^5 + 5x^4 + x^3 + kx^2 - 14x + 3$.
39. When $8x^3 - 4x^2 - 7x + k$ is divided by $(x - 1)$, the remainder is 5.
40. When $kx^3 - x^2 + 2x - 30$ is divided by $(x - 2)$, the remainder is 2.
41. $(x + 1)$ is a factor of $-x^4 + kx^3 - x^2 + kx + 10$.
42. When $x^3 + kx^2 + 2x + 5$ is divided by $(x + k)$, the remainder is 7.

43. Divide $x^2 + 3x + 5$ by $(x + 1)$.

    a. Express the result as a quotient and remainder.

    b. Express the result as a quotient plus a fraction having $(x + 1)$ as its denominator.

    c. Express the result as a quotient plus a series of terms having denominators $x, x^2, x^3, \ldots .$ [*Hint:* Use synthetic division for coefficients 1, 3, 5, 0, 0, 0, ...]

44. Divide $5x^2 - 9x - 1$ by $(x - 2)$.

    a. Express the result as a quotient and remainder.

    b. Express the result as a quotient plus a fraction having $(x - 2)$ as its denominator.

    c. Express the result as a quotient plus a series of terms having denominators $x, x^2, x^3, \ldots$

The synthetic-division process determines the quotient and remainder when a polynomial $P(x)$ is divided by a binomial in the form $(x - r)$. Describe how to change the process to fit these circumstances.

45. The leading coefficient of the binomial divisor is not 1. Show that $(2x + 1)$ is a factor of $P(x) = 6x^3 - 9x^2 - 10x - 2$.

46. The divisor is a factorable quadratic polynomial. Show that $(x^2 - x - 6)$ is a factor of $P(x) = x^5 - x^4 - 4x^3 - 3x^2 - 11x + 6$.

 EVIEW EXERCISES

1. Write without using fractions: [6-1]

Simplify. (Assume that no denominator is zero.)

2. $\dfrac{1}{\dfrac{1}{a} + \dfrac{1}{b}}$
    3. $\dfrac{x + 3}{2x - 6} \cdot \dfrac{x^2 - 3x}{3x + 9}$
    4. $\dfrac{1}{x^2} - \dfrac{2}{3}x$ [6-2, 6-3, 6-4]

5. Solve: $\dfrac{1}{2x - 1} + \dfrac{1}{3} = \dfrac{4}{6x - 3}$. [6-5]

6. One painter works 20% faster than another. Together, they can paint a house in 36 h. How long would it take each painter working alone to paint the house? [6-6]

7. If y varies inversely as x and $y = 100$ when $x = 5$, then what is the value of y when $x = 25$? [6-7]

$\mathcal{S}$elf-Quiz 1

10-1 Express the polynomial in standard form and state its degree and leading coefficient.

    1. $(2x - 7)(3 - x)^2$ **2.** $-(7 - a + a^2)(3a^2 + 4)$

    Let $P(x) = x^3 + 2x^2 - 3x + 7$. Use synthetic substitution to find the following.

    3. $P(-1)$ **4.** $P(2)$

    5. Plot integer values of $f(x) = x^4 - 3x^2$ for the domain $\{x: -2 \leqslant x \leqslant 2\}$. Then sketch the graph of the function for all real numbers.

10-2   **6.** Use synthetic division to divide $2x^3 - 4x - 5$ by $(x + 1)$.

    7. Find the remainder when $x^5 - 4x^4 + x^3 + 2x^2 + 7x + 1$ is divided by $(x - 2)$.

    8. Show that $(x + 3)$ is a factor of $P(x)$.
$$P(x) = 2x^5 + 5x^4 - 3x^3 - 4x^2 - 11x + 3.$$

LESSON 10-3

Roots of a Polynomial Equation

A dictionary gives two definitions for the word "root" in mathematics:

▶ a quantity that when multiplied by itself a specified number of times produces a given quantity.

For example, $-\frac{1}{2} + \frac{\sqrt{3}}{2}i$ is a cube root of 1.

▶ a quantity that when substituted for an unknown quantity will satisfy an equation.

For example, $-\frac{1}{2} + \frac{\sqrt{3}}{2}i$ is a root of $x^3 = 1$.

Consider the polynomial $P(x)$ such that $P(x) = x^3 - 2x^2 - 5x + 6$. Synthetic division will show that $(x - 3)$, $(x - 1)$, and $(x + 2)$ are factors of $P(x)$ and that 3, 1, and -2 are roots of the equation $P(x) = 0$.

$$x^3 - 2x^2 - 5x + 6 = (x - 3)(x - 1)(x + 2)$$

This *third*-degree polynomial factors into *three* linear factors. That is, the degree and the number of factors is the same. This fact is a specific case of the **Fundamental Theorem of Algebra.**

The Fundamental Theorem of Algebra

Each nth-degree polynomial, $n \geq 1$, can be factored into n linear factors.

For example, $x^4 - 2x^3 - 3x^2 + 8x - 4 = (x - 2)(x + 2)(x - 1)(x - 1)$.

By zero-product property, the roots of the *equation*

$$x^4 - 2x^3 - 3x^2 + 8x - 4 = 0$$

are 2, -2, and 1. Since $(x - 1)$ appears twice as a factor, 1 is said to be a root with **multiplicity** 2. When the idea of multiplicity of roots is used, the Fundamental Theorem of Algebra is equivalent to the following.

The Fundamental Theorem of Algebra

Every polynomial equation of degree n has exactly n roots, where a root with multiplicity k is counted as k roots.

Each nth-degree polynomial equation has at least one root and at most n distinct roots. For example, $x^3 - 5x^2 + 8x - 6 = (x - 3)(x^2 - 2x + 2)$

$$= (x - 3)(x - 1 - i)(x - 1 + i).$$

Therefore, the roots of $x^3 - 5x^2 + 8x - 6 = 0$ are 3, $(1 + i)$, and $(1 - i)$.

Note that the imaginary roots are in conjugate pairs. In general:

Imaginary Root Theorem

Imaginary roots of polynomial equations with real coefficients occur in conjugate pairs.

Similarly, the roots of $x^2 - 4x + 1 = 0$ are $\left(2 + \sqrt{3}\right)$ and $\left(2 - \sqrt{3}\right)$.

Quadratic Root Theorem

Quadratic roots of the form $a + \sqrt{b}$, where a and b are rational and $\sqrt{b}$ is irrational, of polynomial equations with rational coefficients occur in conjugate pairs.

Finally, note the relationship of integer roots to the constant term. Since $P(x)$ is the product of the factors $(x - r_1), (x - r_2), \ldots, (x - r_m)$, where $r_1, \ldots, r_m$ are the roots of $P(x) = 0$, integer roots must be factors of the constant term, a_0. For example, integer roots of $x^3 - 2x^2 - 5x + 6 = 0$ must be factors of 6: $\{\pm 1, \pm 2, \pm 3, \pm 6\}$.

Example 1   Write an equation in standard form that has only $-1, -2, 2,$ and 3 as roots.

Solution $(x + 1)(x + 2)(x - 2)(x - 3) = 0$ has the given roots.

By expanding, we can write the equation $x^4 - 2x^3 - 7x^2 + 8x + 12 = 0$.

Example 2   Solve. $x^3 - 6x^2 + 12x - 8 = 0$

Solution   The possible integer roots of the equation are factors of -8. Use synthetic division to determine whether any of the numbers $\{\pm 1, \pm 2, \pm 4, \pm 8\}$ is a root of the equation.

$$
\begin{array}{r|rrrr}
-2 & 1 & -6 & 12 & -8 \\
   &   & -2 & 16 & -56 \\
\hline
   & 1 & -8 & 28 & -64 \\
\end{array}
\qquad
\begin{array}{r|rrrr}
2 & 1 & -6 & 12 & -8 \\
  &   & 2 & -8 & 8 \\
\hline
  & 1 & -4 & 4 & 0 \\
\end{array}
$$

$$P(-2) = -64 \qquad\qquad P(2) = 0$$

Since 2 is a root of the equation, the equation factors to

$$(x - 2)(x^2 - 4x + 4) = 0.$$

The quadratic factor can be factored by inspection as $(x - 2)(x - 2)$. The given equation is equivalent to

$$(x - 2)^3 = 0.$$

Since $(x - 2)$ appears as a factor 3 times, 2 is a root with multiplicity 3.
A cubic equation has 3 roots, therefore all roots have been found.

Answer $\{2\}$ (The equation has one real root, 2, with multiplicity 3.)

Example 3 Solve. $x^4 + x^3 - 2x^2 - 6x - 4 = 0$

Solution Let $P(x) = x^4 + x^3 - 2x^2 - 6x - 4$. Possible integer roots are ± 1, ± 2, and ± 4. Use synthetic division to determine whether any of these numbers is a root.

$$
\begin{array}{r|rrrrr}
1 & 1 & 1 & -2 & -6 & -4 \\
  &   & 1 & 2 & 0 & -6 \\
\hline
  & 1 & 2 & 0 & -6 & -10 \\
\end{array}
\qquad P(1) = -10
$$

$$
\begin{array}{r|rrrrr}
-1 & 1 & 1 & -2 & -6 & -4 \\
   &   & -1 & 0 & 2 & 4 \\
\hline
   & 1 & 0 & -2 & -4 & 0 \\
\end{array}
\qquad P(-1) = 0
$$

Since $P(-1) = 0$, -1 is a root and the given polynomial can be factored as

$$(x + 1)(x^3 + 0x^2 - 2x - 4).$$

The remaining roots of $P(x) = 0$ are also roots of the **depressed equation:**

$$Q(x) = x^3 + 0x^2 - 2x - 4 = 0.$$

Test for roots of $Q(x)$ by synthetic division. Try 2.

$$
\begin{array}{r|rrrr}
2 & 1 & 0 & -2 & -4 \\
  &   & 2 & 4 & 4 \\
\hline
  & 1 & 2 & 2 & 0 \\
\end{array}
$$

Since $Q(2) = 0$, then 2 is a root of $Q(x)$. Thus, $P(x)$ can be factored as

$$(x + 1)(x - 2)(x^2 + 2x + 2).$$

To solve the depressed equation, $x^2 + 2x + 2 = 0$, use the quadratic formula.

$$x = \frac{-2 \pm \sqrt{2^2 - 4(1)(2)}}{2} = \frac{-2 \pm \sqrt{-4}}{2} = -1 \pm i$$

Answer $\{-1, 2, -1 + i, -1 - i\}$ (The equation has two real roots, -1 and 2, and two imaginary roots, $-1 \pm i$.)

$\mathcal{C}$LASSROOM EXERCISES

1. Write an equation in standard form that has -1 and 1 as roots with multiplicity 1, and 3 as a root with multiplicity 2.

Solve.

2. $x^3 - 4x^2 + 9x - 10 = 0$ 3. $x^3 - 7x + 6 = 0$ 4. $x^4 - x^3 - 4x^2 - 2x - 12 = 0$

$\mathcal{W}$RITTEN EXERCISES

 Write a fourth-degree equation in standard form that has the following roots.

1. $-1, 1, -3, 3$
2. $-2, 2, -4, 4$
3. $-1, 1, -2, 0$
4. $-1, 1, 2, 0$
5. $-1, -2, -3, -4$
6. $-2, -3, -4, -5$

Write a fifth-degree equation in factored form that has integer coefficients and the following roots. Multiplicities greater than one are shown in parentheses.

7. -3, 1 (two), 4 (two)

8. -2, 0, 2 (three)

9. $\frac{1}{2}$, -1 (four) [*Hint:* If $x - \frac{1}{2} = 0$, then $2x - 1 = 0$.]

10. $-\frac{2}{3}$ (two), 5 (two), $\frac{7}{2}$

Solve. [*Remember:* **Possible integer roots are factors of the constant term.**]

11. $x^3 + 3x^2 - 4x - 12 = 0$

12. $x^3 - 2x^2 - 9x + 18 = 0$

13. $x^3 - x^2 - 14x + 24 = 0$

14. $x^3 - 5x^2 - 2x + 24 = 0$

15. $x^4 - 20x^2 + 64 = 0$

16. $x^4 - 26x^2 + 25 = 0$

17. $x^3 - 3x + 2 = 0$

18. $x^3 - 3x^2 + 4 = 0$

Solve. [*Note:* **Some roots are irrational numbers.**]

19. $x^3 - 8x^2 + 16x - 8 = 0$

20. $x^3 - 7x^2 + 12x - 6 = 0$

21. $x^3 - 3x^2 - 8x + 24 = 0$

22. $x^3 - 2x^2 - 6x + 12 = 0$

23. $x^3 + 6x^2 + 10x + 3 = 0$

24. $x^3 + 10x^2 + 27x + 10 = 0$

Solve. [*Note:* **Some roots are imaginary numbers.**]

25. $x^3 - 2x^2 + 4x - 8 = 0$

26. $x^3 - 4x^2 + x - 4 = 0$

27. $x^3 - 3x^2 + 6x - 4 = 0$

28. $x^3 - 4x^2 + 7x - 6 = 0$

29. $x^3 + 7x^2 + 16x + 30 = 0$

30. $x^3 + 8x^2 + 22x + 20 = 0$

B True or false? In each equation, r and s represent integers.

31. A root of the equation $x^3 + rx^2 + sx + 8 = 0$ could be 5.

32. A root of the equation $x^3 + rx^2 + sx + 10 = 0$ could be -5.

33. If t is the only root of $x^3 + 4x^2 + sx + 18 = 0$, then t is a root of multiplicity 3.

34. If $(2 + i)$ is a root of $x^3 + rx^2 + sx + 6 = 0$, then $(-2 - i)$ is also a root of the equation.

35. If $(3 - i)$ is a root of $x^3 + rx^2 + sx + 6 = 0$, then $(3 + i)$ is also a root of the equation.

36. If $\left(2 + \sqrt{3}\right)$ is a root of $x^3 + rx^2 + sx + 12 = 0$, then $\left(2 - \sqrt{3}\right)$ is also a root of the equation.

C The following is a statement of the rational root theorem.

The Rational Root Theorem

If p and q are integers and $\frac{p}{q}$ is a rational-number solution of a polynomial equation $a_n x^n + a_{n-1} x^{n-1} + \cdots + a_1 x + a_0 = 0$ with integer coefficients, then p is a factor of a_0 and q is a factor of a_n.

For example, the only possible rational roots of $2x^3 - 15x^2 + 24x + 15 = 0$ are $\pm 1, \pm 3, \pm 5, \pm 15, \pm \frac{1}{2}, \pm \frac{3}{2}, \pm \frac{5}{2},$ and $\pm \frac{15}{2}.$

Use the rational root theorem to list all possible rational roots of each equation. Assume that r and s represent integers.

37. $2x^3 + rx^2 + sx + 5 = 0$ **38.** $4x^3 + rx^2 + sx + 6 = 0$

Solve.

39. $12x^3 - 32x^2 + 25x - 6 = 0$ **40.** $10x^3 - 49x^2 + 68x - 20 = 0$

41. $8x^3 - 28x^2 + 14x + 15 = 0$ **42.** $4x^4 - 37x^2 + 9 = 0$

REVIEW EXERCISES

1. Give a rational approximation to $\sqrt[3]{4}$ correct to the nearest tenth.   [7-1]

2. Simplify: $\sqrt{18x^2}.$ **3.** Simplify: $\sqrt{50} - \sqrt{32}.$ [7-2, 7-3]

4. Rationalize the denominator and state restrictions on the variable: $\dfrac{x}{\sqrt[3]{x}}.$ [7-4]

5. Simplify: $\sqrt[3]{\dfrac{3}{4}}.$ [7-4]

6. Find the perimeter of the triangle with vertices $(0, 0)$, $(6, 0)$, and $(3, 4)$.   [7-5]

7. Solve. $\sqrt{x + 2} = x.$ **8.** Simplify. $(-32)^{\frac{3}{5}}.$ [7-6, 7-7]

HISTORICAL NOTE   "Fermat's Last Theorem"

A statement scribbled in the margin of a book by French mathematician Pierre de Fermat shortly before his death has haunted mathematicians for 300 years. He claimed to have discovered a truly marvelous proof that there are no integer solutions (other than zero) for equations of the form $x^n + y^n = z^n$ where n is an integer, $n > 2$.

Now, West German mathematician Gerd Faltings has proved that certain equations, including those of Fermat, have at most a finite number of rational solutions. Using nothing more than paper and pencil and 18 months in which he thought of little else, Faltings has achieved a result sought for decades. While not solving the Fermat problem completely, this proof establishes that there are, at most, a finite number of solutions to Fermat's Theorem.

Falting's proof is an achievement that mathematicians liken to the four-minute mile. This breakthrough promises many more significant discoveries to follow.

Roots of Equations and the Graphs of Polynomial Functions

A graphing program was used to graph the equation

$$f(x) = 2x^2 - 8x - 7.$$

The picture shows that the roots are not whole numbers. The computer then printed the table of values for $2x^2 - 8x - 7$ when x has values from 4 through 5. The table and graph both show that one solution of the equation is between 4.7 and 4.8.

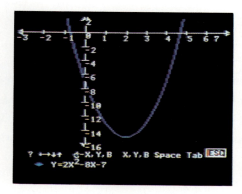

x	$2x^2 - 8x - 7$
4	-7
4.1	-6.18
4.2	-5.32
4.3	-4.42
4.4	-3.48
4.5	-2.5
4.6	-1.48
4.7	-0.42
4.8	0.68
4.9	1.82
5	3

Recall that the x-intercept of the graph of a function f is a root of the equation $f(x) = 0$. For example, if f is the function such that $f(x) = x^3 - 2x^2 - x + 2$, then the graph of f crosses the x-axis at the points $(-1, 0)$, $(1, 0)$, and $(2, 0)$. The roots of the equation $0 = x^3 - 2x^2 - x + 2$ are the x-intercepts, -1, 1, and 2.

If the equation $f(x) = 0$ has no real roots, then the graph of f does not intersect the x-axis. For example, $0 = x^2 + 4$ has two imaginary roots, and the graph of the function $f(x) = x^2 + 4$ lies entirely above the x-axis.

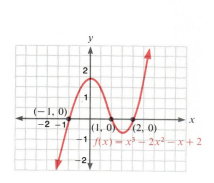

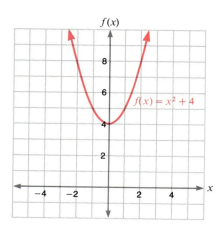

Now consider functions that are tangent to the x-axis. The graph of $f(x) = x^2 + 4x + 4$ is tangent to the x-axis at the point $(-2, 0)$. The equation $f(x) = 0$ has the root -2 with multiplicity 2.

The graph of $f(x) = x^3 + x^2 - 5x + 3$ crosses the x-axis at $(-3, 0)$ and is tangent to the x-axis at $(1, 0)$. The equation $f(x) = 0$ has -3 as a root, and 1 as a root with multiplicity 2.

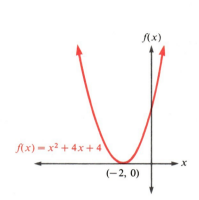

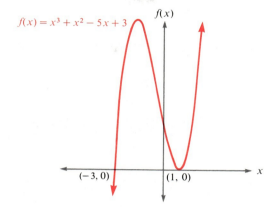

In the graph of a polynomial function $f(x)$, a root corresponding to a point of tangency to the x-axis has an even multiplicity.

The relationships between the roots and x-intercepts of graphs of polynomial functions can be used to locate roots of polynomial equations. For example, consider the equation

$$3x^3 - x^2 - 9x + 3 = 0.$$

Compute the value of the related polynomial function for some integer values of x and graph those points.

$$f(x) = 3x^3 - x^2 - 9x + 3$$
$$f(-2) = -7 \qquad f(0) = 3$$
$$f(-1) = 8 \qquad f(1) = -4$$
$$f(2) = 5$$

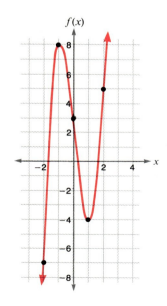

Because the graphs of the polynomial functions are **continuous** (smooth, without "jumps"), we know that the graph must cross the x-axis between $x = -2$ and $x = -1$, between $x = 0$ and $x = 1$, and again between $x = 1$ and $x = 2$. These are particular illustrations of the **Location Theorem.**

The Location Theorem

If f is a polynomial function such that $f(a) > 0$ and $f(b) < 0$, then there is a real number c between a and b such that $f(c) = 0$.

The Location Theorem does not say that there is just one x-intercept between a and b. The graph may intersect the x-axis several times. For the function shown on the right, there are five real numbers, $c_1, c_2, c_3, \ldots$, between a and b, such that $f(c_1) = 0$, $f(c_2) = 0$, $f(c_3) = 0, \ldots$

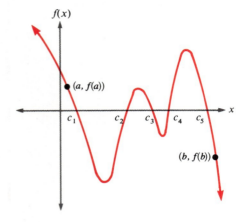

The Location Theorem makes no statement about f if $f(a)$ and $f(b)$ are both positive or both negative. There may be one or more intercepts, or there may be none.

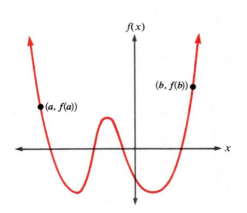

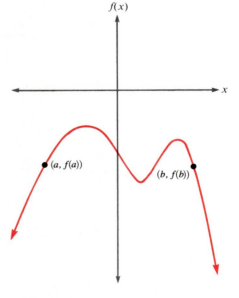

In some cases, the Fundamental Theorem of Algebra can be used with the Location Theorem to determine exactly the number of roots between values of a and b. For example, for $f(x) = x^3 - x^2 - 9x + 3$, we determined that there were roots between -2 and -1, between 0 and 1, and between 1 and 2. By the Fundamental Theorem of Algebra, we know that a cubic equation has at most three roots. So there is exactly one root in each of the intervals.

Example 1 Each graph is that of a cubic function.

a.
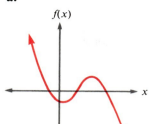

b.
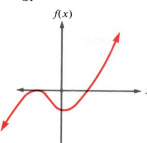

c.
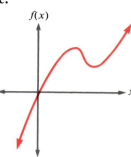

Describe the roots of the corresponding cubic equation.

Solution **a.** The graph crosses the x-axis three times, so the cubic equation has three real roots.

b. The graph is tangent to the x-axis at one point and crosses it at another point. The point of tangency determines a multiple root with even multiplicity. Therefore, the cubic equation has two real roots, one of them a root with multiplicity 2.

c. The graph crosses the x-axis at one point. Therefore, the cubic equation has one real root and two imaginary roots.

Example 2 **Locate the real roots of this equation between consecutive integers.**
$$6x^4 - x^3 - 43x^2 + 7x + 7 = 0$$

Solution Let $f(x) = 6x^4 - x^3 - 43x^2 + 7x + 7$. Then compute values of the function for integer values of x.

x	-3	-2	-1	0	1	2	3
$f(x)$	112	-75	-36	7	-24	-63	100

Since $f(x)$ changes from positive to negative between $x = -3$ and $x = -2$, there is a root between -3 and -2. Similarly, there are roots between -1 and 0, 0 and 1, and 2 and 3. The equation is fourth degree and has at most four roots. Therefore, each of the roots has been located between consecutive integers.

Answer The real roots are between -3 and -2, between -1 and 0, between 0 and 1, and between 2 and 3.

Example 3 Examine the graph of the function. Describe the roots.

$$f(x) = x^5 - x^4 - 3x^3 + 3x^2 - 4x + 4$$

Solution Use a graphing calculator or computer graphing software to graph the function.

Answer Since the degree of f is 5, there are 5 complex roots. The graph intersects the x-axis at -2, 1, and 2; therefore, there are three real roots of -2, 1, and 2. Since the graph has no points tangency, there are no roots with even number multiplicities. There are two imaginary roots.

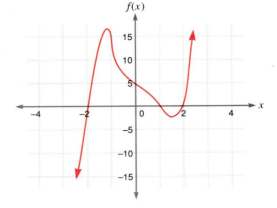

𝒞LASSROOM EXERCISES

Each of these graphs is of a fourth-degree function. Describe the roots of the corresponding equation.

1.

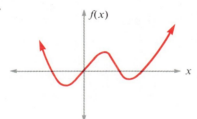

2.

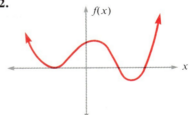

3. The table shows values of the function $f(x) = 12x^3 + 16x^2 - 3x - 4$. What can you conclude about the real roots of $f(x) = 0$?

x	-3	-2	-1	0	1	2	3
$f(x)$	-175	-30	3	-4	21	150	455

4. Locate the real roots of this equation between consecutive integers.

$$2x^3 - 3x^2 - 16x + 24 = 0$$

 Each graph is that of a cubic function f. Describe the roots of $f(x) = 0$.

1.
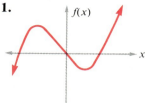

2.
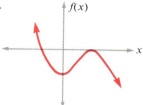

3.
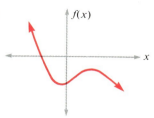

4.
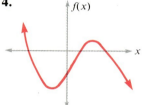

5.
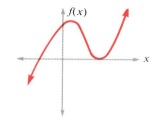

6.
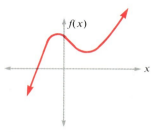

A table of values of function f is given. What can you conclude about the real roots of $f(x) = 0$?

7. $f(x) = 16x^3 + 44x^2 + 4x - 15$

x	-4	-3	-2	-1	0	1	2
$f(x)$	-351	-63	25	9	-15	49	297

8. $f(x) = -8x^3 + 20x^2 + 34x - 21$

x	-2	-1	0	1	2	3	4
$f(x)$	55	-27	-21	25	63	45	-77

9. $f(x) = 15x^4 - x^3 + 15x^2 - x - 2$

x	-3	-2	-1	0	1	2	3
$f(x)$	1378	308	30	-2	26	288	1318

10. $f(x) = 2x^4 - 5x^2 + 2$

x	-3	-2	-1	0	1	2	3
$f(x)$	119	14	-1	2	-1	14	119

Evaluate the function for integer values of the domain $-2 \leqslant x \leqslant 2$. What can you conclude about the real roots of the function?

11. $18x^3 - 27x^2 - 8x + 12 = 0$

12. $8x^3 + 12x^2 - 2x - 3 = 0$

13. $8x^3 + 4x^2 - 18x - 9 = 0$

14. $18x^3 + 27x^2 - 18x - 12 = 0$

15. $8x^3 - 4x^2 - 2x + 1 = 0$

16. $8x^3 + 4x^2 - 2x - 1 = 0$

17. $2x^3 - x^2 - 4x + 2 = 0$

18. $2x^3 + x^2 - 6x - 3 = 0$

19. $8x^3 - 12x^2 + 6x - 1 = 0$

20. $8x^3 - 36x^2 + 54x - 27 = 0$

B **Sketch a graph of a third-degree function f that meets the given conditions.**

21. The roots of $f(x) = 0$ are -1, 2, and 3; $f(0) = 2$.

22. The roots of $f(x) = 0$ are -1 and 2 with multiplicity 2; $f(0) = 2$.

23. The root of $f(x) = 0$ is 1 with multiplicity 3; $f(0) = -2$.

24. Why will a polynomial equation with real coefficients and of odd degree always have at least one real root?

25. Let f be a polynomial function. Show by example that the equation $f(x) = 0$ can have a multiple root at a value other than a point of tangency of $y = f(x)$ to the x-axis.

 26. For what values of k will the graph of $f(x) = x^4 - 2x^2 + k$ not intersect the x-axis? $k > 1$

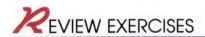 **pplication:** Using a Computer or Graphing Calculator

Examine each graph on a computer or graphing calculator. Describe the roots of $f(x) = 0$.   **29.** $\{-4, -2, 1, 2\}$

27. $f(x) = x^3 - 6x^2 + 5x + 12$ $\{-1, 3, 4\}$ **28.** $f(x) = x^3 + 2x^2 + 4x + 8$

29. $f(x) = x^4 + 3x^3 - 8x^2 - 12x + 16$ **30.** $f(x) = x^4 + 2x^3 - x^2 + 2x - 3$

31. $f(x) = x^5 + x^4 - 3x^3 - 3x^2 - 4x - 4$ **32.** $f(x) = x^5 - 4x^4 + 2x^3 - 2x^2 + x - 1$

Use the Rational Root Theorem to solve each equation. (See the Rational Root Theorem on page 420.)

33. $18x^3 - 27x^2 - 8x + 12 = 0$
[*Hint:* See Exercise 11 for the location of the roots.]

34. $8x^3 + 12x^2 - 2x - 3 = 0$
[*Hint:* See Exercise 12.]

35. $8x^3 - 4x^2 - 2x + 1 = 0$
[*Hint:* See Exercise 15.]

36. $8x^3 - 12x^2 + 6x - 1 = 0$
[*Hint:* See Exercise 19.]

*R*EVIEW EXERCISES

Solve.

1. $(x - 3)^2 = 5$ **2.** $3x^2 - 4x = 5$ [8-1, 8-2]

Simplify.   [8-3, 8-4,

3. $(2i)^2(3i)$ **4.** $(4 + 3i) + (3 + 4i) - (3 - 2i)$ **5.** $\dfrac{3 + 2i}{4 - 3i}$ 8-5]

6. State the number and kind of roots: $x^2 + 2x + 5 = 0$.   [8-6]

Solve.

7. $x^4 - 2x^2 - 3 = 0$ **8.** $x - 12\sqrt{x} + 20 = 0$ [8-6]

9. State whether the equation $y - 3 = (x - 4)^2$ defines a quadratic function in x. If so, write the equation in standard form.   [8-7]

$\mathcal{S}$elf-Quiz 2

10-3 **1.** Write an equation of least degree in standard form that has these numbers as roots: $-1, 3$ (multiplicity of two).

2. Given that 4 is a root of $x^3 - 5x^2 + 2x + 8 = 0$, find the depressed equation and other roots.

3. Solve. $x^3 + x^2 - 5x - 5 = 0$.

10-4 **4.** The graph shown here is that of a fourth-degree polynomial function P. Describe the roots of $P(x) = 0$.

5. Locate the roots of the equation between consecutive integers.
$$8x^3 + 20x^2 - 2x - 5 = 0$$

6. Sketch a third-degree polynomial function P with y-intercept 4 such that $P(x) = 0$ has roots -3, 1, and 5.

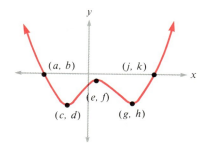

$\mathcal{C}$OMPUTER EXTENSION   Evaluating Cubic Functions

The following computer program evaluates the cubic function
$$y = ax^3 + bx^2 + cx + d$$
for integer values of x from -2 to 2. This information can be used to locate the real roots of the cubic equation
$$ax^3 + bx^2 + cx + d = 0.$$

```
10 PRINT "ENTER VALUES OF A, B, C, AND D ";
20 PRINT "SEPARATED BY COMMAS."
30 INPUT A, B, C, D
40 FOR X = -2 TO 2
50 Y = A * X ↑ 3 + B * X ↑ 2 + C * X + D
60 PRINT X, Y
70 NEXT X
80 END
```

1. Use the program to check your answers to Exercises 11–20 on page 427. Does the program help you to locate all the roots?

2. If you were not able to locate all the real roots between consecutive integers, change line 40 to read
$$\text{40 FOR X} = -2 \text{ TO 2 STEP 0.25}$$
and rerun the program.

3. *Bonus:* Solve the following equation. [*Hint:* Change line 40.]
$$100x^3 + 100x^2 - 69x + 9 = 0$$

Inverse Functions

The graph of the function $y = (x - 1)^2$ is shown below. It can be reflected about a line in various ways. If x is replaced by $-x$, the resulting graph (in blue) is the reflection of the original graph about the y-axis. If y is replaced by $-y$ in the original equation, the resulting graph (in red) is the reflection of the original graph about the x-axis. Note how the points of each pair of graphs are symmetrically placed about the line of reflection.

   If x and y are interchanged in the original equation, the resulting graph (in green) is the reflection of the original graph about another line, $y = x$.

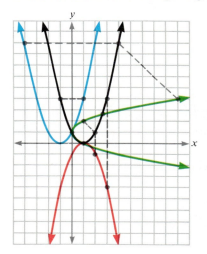

Consider relations R and Q, each consisting of just three ordered pairs.

$$R = \{(2, 3), (-4, 1), (6, 3)\}$$
$$Q = \{(3, 2), (1, -4), (3, 6)\}$$

Each pair of one relation is the corresponding pair of the other relation with the first and second coordinates interchanged. Relations R and Q are called **inverse relations.** Note that the graph of R is the reflection about the line $y = x$ of the graph of Q, and vice versa.

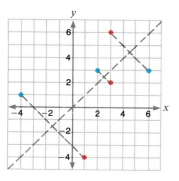

If a relation is defined by an equation in x and y, the inverse of that relation can be defined by interchanging x and y in the original equation.

For example, the equations $y = x^2$ and $x = y^2$ define inverse relations. The graphs of inverses are reflections about the line $y = x$.

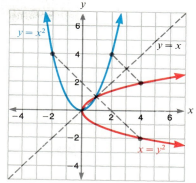

In the example above, $y = x^2$ defines a function, but $x = y^2$ does not define a function. Of special interest in mathematics are inverses of functions that are themselves functions.

Consider the linear function f defined by $y = 3x$. The inverse is defined by $x = 3y$ or $y = \frac{1}{3}x$. In this case, the inverse of f is also a function and is denoted f^{-1}. (The "-1" is not an exponent.) The symbol f^{-1} is read as "f inverse" or "the inverse of f" and is used only when the inverse of a function f is also a function.

Recall that a relation is a 1–1 function if and only if each element of the domain is matched with a unique element of the range, and each element of the range is matched with a unique element of the domain. Only 1–1 functions have inverses that are also functions.

$y = x^2$ is not a 1–1 function. $y = 3x$ is a 1–1 function.

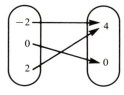

The inverse $x = y^2$ is not a function.   The inverse $y = \frac{1}{3}x$ is also a function.

Example 1   Let $f(x) = 3x + 2$. Is the inverse of f a function? If so, write its defining equation.

Solution   The function f is defined by the equation $y = 3x + 2$. The inverse of f is defined by the equation $x = 3y + 2$. Solving for y gives $y = \frac{1}{3}x - \frac{2}{3}$. This equation is the equation of a linear function.

Answer   The inverse of function f is the function $f^{-1}(x) = \frac{1}{3}x - \frac{2}{3}$.

Example 2 Each of these equations defines a function. State whether each function has an inverse function.

a. $y = |x|$

b. $y = x^3$

c. $y = 3$

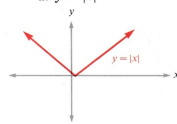

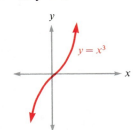

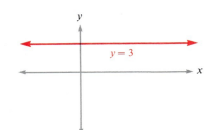

Solution

a. The function defined by $y = |x|$ is not a 1–1 function. Therefore, its inverse $x = |y|$ is not a function.

b. The function $y = x^3$ is a 1–1 function. Therefore, its inverse $y = \sqrt[3]{x}$ is a function.

c. The function $y = 3$ is not a 1–1 function. Therefore, its inverse $x = 3$ is not a function.

An important property of inverse functions f and f^{-1} is that $f(f^{-1}(x)) = x$ and $f^{-1}(f(x)) = x$. For example, $f(x) = 4x$ and $f^{-1}(x) = \dfrac{x}{4}$ define inverse functions. Applying f to a member of its domain b gives $f(b) = 4b$. Then applying f^{-1} to $4b$ gives $f^{-1}(4b) = \dfrac{4b}{4} = b$. The inverse of f "undoes" what f "does," and vice versa.

Example 3 State whether f and g are inverse functions. $f(x) = 2x - 5$

$$g(x) = \frac{1}{2}x + 5$$

Solution For a number b in the domain of f, $f(b) = 2b - 5$. Then

$$g(2b - 5) = \frac{1}{2}(2b - 5) + 5 = b + \frac{5}{2}.$$

Answer Since $g(f(b)) \neq b$, f and g are not inverse functions.

𝒞LASSROOM EXERCISES

1. Are f and g inverses? $f(x) = 2x$ $g(x) = \dfrac{1}{2}x$

2. Are g and h inverses? $g(x) = \dfrac{x + 1}{2}$ $h(x) = 2x + 1$

3. Write a defining equation of the inverse of f: $f(x) = 4 - 3x$.

State whether the inverse of each of the following functions is a function.

4.

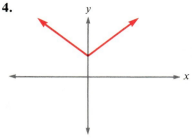

5.

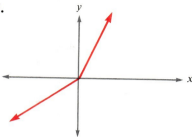

6. $f(x) = x^4$

7. $g(x) = [x]$

*W*RITTEN EXERCISES

A Show that f and g are inverses.

1. $f(x) = 3x + 6$

$g(x) = \frac{1}{3}x - 2$

2. $f(x) = 2x - 6$

$g(x) = \frac{1}{2}x + 3$

3. $f(x) = \frac{2}{3}x - 12$

$g(x) = \frac{3}{2}x + 18$

4. $f(x) = \frac{3}{4}x + 12$

$g(x) = \frac{4}{3}x - 16$

5. $f(x) = x^2, x \geqslant 0$

$g(x) = \sqrt{x}, x \geqslant 0$

6. $f(x) = x^4, x \geqslant 0$

$g(x) = \sqrt[4]{x}, x \geqslant 0$

State whether f and g are inverse functions.

7. $f(x) = -2x + 4$

$g(x) = -\frac{1}{2}x + 2$

8. $f(x) = -2x + 6$

$g(x) = -\frac{1}{2}x + 3$

9. $f(x) = [x + 1]$

$g(x) = [x - 1]$

10. $f(x) = [2x]$

$g(x) = \left[\frac{1}{2}x\right]$

11. $f(x) = -x$

$g(x) = -x$

12. $f(x) = \sqrt{|x|}$

$g(x) = x^2$

Write a defining equation for f^{-1}.

13. $f(x) = 3x + 15$

14. $f(x) = 4x + 12$

15. $f(x) = \frac{1}{3}x + 3$

16. $f(x) = \frac{1}{2}x + 2$

17. $f(x) = -3x - 18$

18. $f(x) = -6x - 18$

19. $f(x) = 8 - 6x$

20. $f(x) = 6 - 8x$

21. $f(x) = \frac{x + 2x}{3}$

22. $f(x) = \frac{x + 2}{3x}$,

$x \neq 0, f(x) \neq \frac{1}{3}$

23. $f(x) = \frac{1}{x}, x \neq 0,$

$f(x) \neq 0$

24. $f(x) = -\frac{1}{x}, x \neq 0,$

$f(x) \neq 0$

State whether the inverse of each of the following relations is a function.

25.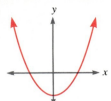

26.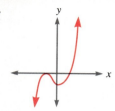

27.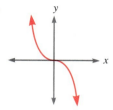

28.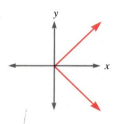

29.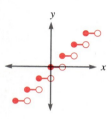

30.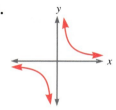

B Each of the following relations f defines a function. (a) Graph f and its inverse relation using the same set of axes. Label the graphs. (b) Is the inverse relation also a function?

31. $f = \left\{ (x, y)\colon y = \frac{2}{3}x + 6 \right\}$

32. $f = \left\{ (x, y)\colon y = \frac{1}{3}x - 3 \right\}$

33. $f = \{(x, y)\colon y = x^2, x \geq 0, y \geq 0\}$

34. $f = \{(x, y)\colon y = x^3 + 2\}$

35. $f = \left\{ (x, y)\colon y = \frac{12}{x}, x \neq 0, y \neq 0 \right\}$

36. $f = \left\{ (x, y)\colon y = -\frac{6}{x}, x \neq 0, y \neq 0 \right\}$

37. $f = \{(x, y)\colon y = -x\}$

38. $f = \{(x, y)\colon y = x^5\}$

C Find the value of k so that functions f and g are inverses.

39. $f(x) = 3x + k$

40. $f(x) = k - 2x$

41. $f(x) = \dfrac{x + 1}{x}, x \neq 0$

$g(x) = \frac{1}{3}x + 1$

$g(x) = kx - k^2$

$g(x) = \dfrac{1}{x - k}, x \neq k$

42. Write the defining equations of two 1–1 functions f and g such that $f(g(x)) = x$ but $g(f(x)) \neq x$.

ℛEVIEW EXERCISES

1. Write an equation in the form $(x - h)^2 + (y - k)^2 = r^2$ for the circle with center $(4, -5)$ and radius 3. [9-1]

2. For the parabola with focus $(3, 6)$ and directrix $y = 2$, write an equation in standard form, sketch the graph, and label the coordinates of the vertex. [9-2]

3. Write the equation in standard form of the ellipse with center $(5, -3)$, major axis 10 units on the y-axis, and minor axis 6 units on the x-axis. [9-3]

4. Sketch a graph of the hyperbola $\dfrac{x^2}{16} - \dfrac{y^2}{9} = 1$ including asymptotes and foci.   [9-4]
Write equations of the asymptotes.

5. Write an equivalent equation in standard form for a circle, parabola, ellipse,   [9-5]
or hyperbola. Sketch the graph of the conic and label key points such as
vertices and center.

$$x^2 + 4x - y^2 + 6y - 6 = 0$$

$\mathcal{C}$HAPTER SUMMARY

▶ **Vocabulary**

polynomial in one variable	[page 407]	polynomial function	[page 408]
constant term	[page 407]	nested form	[page 408]
standard form of a polynomial	[page 407]	synthetic substitution	[page 408]
degree of a polynomial	[page 407]	synthetic division	[page 413]
leading coefficient	[page 407]	multiplicity	[page 417]
constant	[page 407]	depressed equation	[page 419]
linear polynomial	[page 407]	continuous	[page 422]
quadratic polynomial	[page 407]	inverse functions	[page 430]
cubic polynomial	[page 407]		

▶ **The Remainder Theorem**   [10-2]

For each polynomial $P(x)$ of degree $n \geq 1$ and each real number r, there is a
polynomial $Q(x)$ of degree $n - 1$, such that $P(x) = (x - r)Q(x) + P(r)$.

▶ **The Factor Theorem**   [10-2]

For each polynomial $P(x)$, of degree $n \geq 1$ and each real number r, $(x - r)$
is a factor of $P(x)$ if and only if $P(r) = 0$.

▶ **The Fundamental Theorem of Algebra**   [10-3]

Each nth-degree polynomial, $n \geq 1$, can be factored into n linear factors.

or

Every polynomial equation of degree n has exactly n roots, where a root of
multiplicity k is counted as k roots.

▶ **Imaginary Root Theorem**   [10-3]

Imaginary roots of polynomial equations with real coefficients occur in conjugate pairs.

▶ **Quadratic Root Theorem**   [10-3]

Quadratic roots of the form $a + \sqrt{b}$, where a and b are rational and $\sqrt{b}$ is
irrational, of polynomial equations with rational coefficients occur in conjugate pairs.

▶ The Rational Root Theorem [10-3]

  If p and q are integers and $\frac{p}{q}$ is a rational-number solution of a polynomial
  equation $a_nx^n + a_{n-1}x^{n-1} + \cdots + a_1x + a_0 = 0$ with integer coefficients,
  then p is a factor of a_0 and q is a factor of a_n.

▶ The Location Theorem [10-4]

  If f is a polynomial function such that $f(a) > 0$ and $f(b) < 0$, then there is a
  real number c between a and b such that $f(c) = 0$.

▶ In the graph of a polynomial function $f(x)$, a root corresponding to a point of [10-4]
  tangency to the x-axis has an even multiplicity.

▶ Functions f and g are *inverse functions* if and only if $f(g(x)) = g(f(x)) = x$ for [10-5]
  all numbers x in the domains of both f and g.

 HAPTER REVIEW

10-1 **Objective:** To use appropriate terminology in referring to polynomials.

  Let $P(x) = 2x - 7 + 4x^2 - x^3$.

  1. Write the polynomial in standard form, state the degree, and state the
  leading coefficient.

  2. State the coefficient of the given term.

  a. the quadratic term. **b.** the linear term.

  Objective: To evaluate polynomials by synthetic substitution.

  3. Evaluate the polynomial $f(x) = 4x^3 - 2x^2 + 5x - 3$ for the value
  $f(-1)$.

  4. Graph $f(x) = -2x^3 + 3x^2 - 2$ for integer values of x, $-2 \leqslant x \leqslant 2$.
  Then complete the graph.

10-2 **Objective:** To apply the remainder and factor theorems.

  5. Use synthetic division to determine the quotient and remainder when
  $2x^4 - x^3 + 5x^2 + 7x - 4$ is divided by $(x + 1)$.

  6. Show that $(x - 1)$ is a factor of $x^{14} - 2x^8 + 1$.

10-3 **Objective:** To apply the Fundamental Theorem of Algebra.

  7. How many roots (real and imaginary) does the equation have?
  $$x^8 - 5x^2 - 2x + 1 = 0$$

  8. Write an equation in standard form that has 3 as a root, -1 as a root
  with multiplicity two, and no other roots.

  Objective: To find roots of polynomial equations by synthetic substitution.

  9. Find all roots of the equation $x^4 + 2x^3 - 7x^2 - 8x + 12 = 0$.

10-4 **Objective:** To use the graph of $y = f(x)$ to describe the roots of $f(x) = 0$.

Describe the roots of the equation $f(x) = 0$ given the graph of $y = f(x)$ and its degree.

10. degree 3

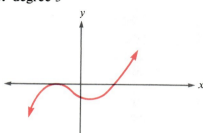

11. degree 4

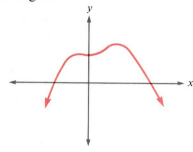

12. Locate the roots of $12x^3 - 16x^2 - 41x + 15 = 0$ between consecutive integers.

10-5 **Objective:** To identify and define inverse functions.

13. Show that $f(x) = \frac{1}{3}x - 2$ and $g(x) = 3x + 6$ are inverse functions.

14. Write the equation that defines the inverse of $f(x) = x^3 - 1$.

CHAPTER 10 SELF-TEST

10-1 **1.** Write the polynomial $(4 - a^2)(a^2 + a - 1)$ in standard form. State its degree and leading coefficient.

2. Compute $P(3)$ if $P(x) = -2x^3 + 5x^2 + 7x + 6$.

3. Graph the function $f(x) = x^3 - 3x + 2$ for the domain $-3 \leqslant x \leqslant 3$.

10-2 **4.** Find the value of k such that $(x - 2)$ is a factor of the polynomial $x^5 + x^4 - 4x^3 - 4x^2 - 8x + k$.

5. Find the remainder when $x^5 + x^2 - 3$ is divided by $(x + 1)$.

6. Show that $(x - 1)$ is a factor of $x^3 - x^2 - 4x + 4$.

10-3 **7.** Write an equation of least degree in standard form having as roots -2 with multiplicity 2, and 1.

8. Find all roots of $x^3 + x^2 - x + 2 = 0$ given that -2 is a root.

10-4 **9.** There is one real root r of the equation $2x^3 - 3x^2 + 8x - 12 = 0$. Locate r between consecutive integers.

10. Sketch a graph of a third-degree polynomial function f such that the equation $f(x) = 0$ has roots of -2, 1, and 4 and such that $f(0) = -2$.

10-5 **11.** Write the defining equation for the inverse of the function defined by $f(x) = x^3$.

12. Let g and g^{-1} be inverse functions. If g is defined by the equation $g(x) = 4x - 1$, evaluate $g^{-1}(-5)$.

13. Show that $f(x) = \dfrac{1}{6}x + \dfrac{5}{6}$ and $g(x) = 6x - 5$ are inverse functions.

$\mathcal{P}$RACTICE FOR COLLEGE ENTRANCE TESTS

Choose the best answer.

1. If $f(x) = 2x - 3$ and $0 < x < 5$, then $f(x)$ is between ___?___.

   A. -3 and 0 **B.** -3 and 7 **C.** -3 and 10

   D. 0 and 7 **E.** 0 and 10

2. If $f(x) = (x + 1)^2$ and $g(x) = x - 1$, then $f(g(5)) = $ ___?___.

   A. 16 **B.** 17 **C.** 25 **D.** 35 **E.** 36

3. For which function graphed below is the inverse also a function?

   A.   **B.**   **C.**

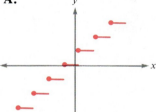 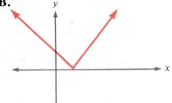 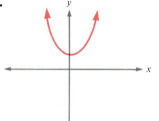

   D.   **E.**

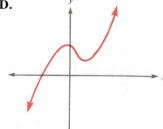 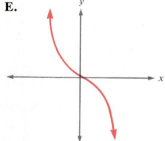

4. If $f(x) = 5x - 1$, then the y-intercept of $y = f(x + 2)$ is ___?___.

   A. -1 **B.** 1 **C.** 2 **D.** 9 **E.** 11

5. If $f(x) = 3x + 2$, and $g(f(x)) = x$, then $g(x) = $ ___?___.

   A. $\dfrac{x-2}{3}$ **B.** $\dfrac{x}{3} - 2$ **C.** $\dfrac{1}{3x+2}$ **D.** $\dfrac{3}{x} - 2$ **E.** $\dfrac{1}{3x-2}$

6. If $f(x) = x^3 + x^2 + x + k$ and $f(-2) = 0$, then $k = $ ___?___.

   A. -6 **B.** -2 **C.** 0 **D.** 2 **E.** 6

7. If $f(x) = x^2 - 2x + 1$, then $f(a + 1) =$ ___?___.

   A. $a^2 - 2a$ **B.** $a^2 - 1$ **C.** a^2 **D.** $a^2 + 1$ **E.** $a^2 + 2a$

8. If $f(x) = x^3 - x$, then the set of all x for which $f(x) = -f(x)$ is ___?___.

   A. $\{0\}$ **B.** $\{-1, 0\}$ **C.** $\{-1, 0, 1\}$ **D.** $\{-1, 1\}$ **E.** $\{0, 1\}$

9. This is a graph of $y = f(x)$.

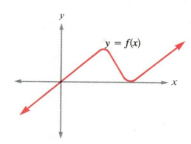

Which of the following could be the graph of $y = f(-x)$?

A.
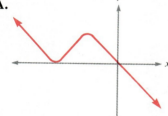

B.
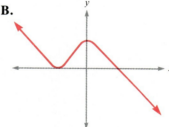

C.
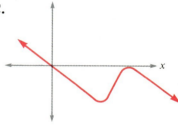

D.
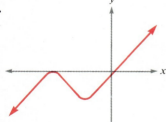

E.
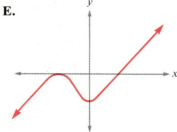

10. If $(x - 2)$ is a factor of $x^3 - 4x^2 + kx + 6$, then $k =$ ___?___.

   A. -2 **B.** -1 **C.** 0 **D.** 1 **E.** 2

11. If $f(x) = x + 1$, $g(x) = x^2$, and $h(x) = 3x$, then $f(g(h(-2))) =$ ___?___.

   A. 3 **B.** 9 **C.** 13 **D.** 25 **E.** 37

12. If $f(a - 1) = a^2 - a$, then $f(x) =$ ___?___.

   A. $x^2 - x$ **B.** $x^2 + x$ **C.** x^2 **D.** $x^2 - 1$ **E.** $x^2 + 1$

CHAPTER 11

Exponential and Logarithmic Functions

The Gateway Arch in St. Louis is an example of a mathematical function applied to architecture. The arch has the shape of an inverted, weighted catenary curve. Inverted means the curve is projected upward to form an arch. Weighted means that the lower sections of the legs are larger than the upper sections. The catenary curve is particularly suitable for the construction of arches because the force of the arch's weight is transferred directly through its legs into the ground.

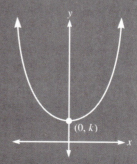

A catenary curve is the shape formed by a chain freely suspended between two supports. Any catenary curve can be represented by an exponential

function of the form $y = \frac{k}{2}\left(e^{\frac{x}{k}} + e^{\frac{-x}{k}}\right)$ where k is the y-intercept.

LESSON 11-1

Exponential Functions

This table shows some ordered pairs of the **exponential function** $y = 2^x$. Its domain is the set of real numbers, $\mathcal{R}$.

x	−2	−1	0	1	2
2ˣ	0.25	0.5	1	2	4

Definition: Exponential Function

For all real numbers x and for all positive real numbers b, $b \neq 1$, the equation $y = b^x$ defines an *exponential function* with base b.

An exponential function can have any positive number except 1 as its base. Figure 1 shows the graphs of some exponential functions with bases greater than 1. Figure 2 shows the graphs of some exponential functions with bases between 0 and 1.

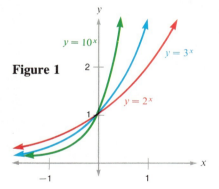

Figure 1

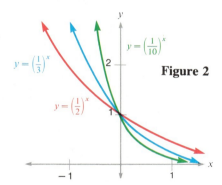

Figure 2

Note these facts about the graphs of exponential functions:

1. All graphs contain the point (0, 1).
2. Each graph approaches the x-axis asymptotically.
3. The domain of each function is the set of real numbers.
4. The range of each function is the set of positive real numbers.
5. The functions with bases greater than 1 are **increasing** functions, called *growth functions*. (f is an increasing function if, for each a and b in the domain of f, whenever $a > b$, then $f(a) > f(b)$.)
6. The functions with bases between 0 and 1 are **decreasing** functions, called *decay functions*. (f is a decreasing function if, for each a and b in the domain of f, whenever $a > b$, then $f(a) < f(b)$.)

The domain of each function includes irrational numbers. Therefore, expressions such as 2^π and $3^{\sqrt{2}}$ have meaning. We shall not give a formal definition of irrational exponents. However, we will approximate an irrational power of a base by rational powers. For example, since 3.1 is an approximation of π, $2^{3.1}$ is an approximation of 2^π. Since 3.14 is a better approximation of π, $2^{3.14}$ is a better approximation of 2^π.

An **exponential equation** is an equation with the variable in an exponent. Some exponential equations can be solved using the following property.

Equality Property of Exponential Functions

For all positive real numbers b, $b \neq 1$, and all real numbers a and c,

$$b^a = b^c \text{ if and only if } a = c.$$

Example 1 **Solve.** $2^{x+4} = 8^x$

Solution *Express both sides in terms of the same base.* $\qquad 2^{x+4} = (2^3)^x$

Simplify exponents. $\qquad 2^{x+4} = 2^{3x}$

Apply the equality property of exponential functions. $\qquad x + 4 = 3x$

Solve. $\qquad 4 = 2x$

$\qquad x = 2$ $\qquad$ *Check* $\quad 2^{2+4} \overset{?}{=} 8^2$

Answer $\{2\}$ $\qquad\qquad\qquad\qquad\qquad\qquad\qquad 64 = 64 \qquad$ True!

Example 2 **Use the graph of $y = 3^x$ to estimate the solution of $3^x = 7$ to the nearest tenth.**

Solution The points on the graph are ordered pairs in which the first component is the exponent of the base 3 and the second component is the value of 3 raised to that power. Therefore, to solve $3^x = 7$ for x, draw a horizontal line through 7, intersecting the graph at point P. Draw a vertical line through P and read its intersection with the x-axis. $x \approx 1.8$

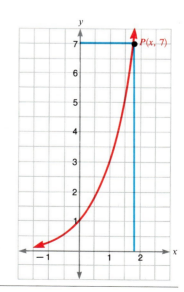

Answer $\{1.8\}$

$\mathscr{C}$LASSROOM EXERCISES

1. Which of these are not graphs of exponential functions of the form $y = b^x$? Explain.

a.

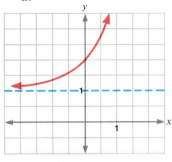

b.

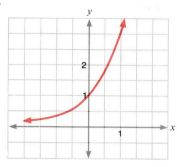

c.

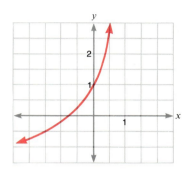

2. Solve: $3^x = \left(\frac{1}{9}\right)^{-2}$.

$\mathscr{W}$RITTEN EXERCISES

 Copy and complete the table for each of the given exponential functions. Use radicals if necessary.

x	-2	$-\frac{3}{2}$	-1	$-\frac{1}{2}$	0	$\frac{1}{2}$	$\frac{2}{3}$	1	$\frac{3}{2}$	2
y	?	?	?	?	?	?	?	?	?	?

1. $y = 3^x$ **2.** $y = 4^x$ **3.** $y = \left(\frac{1}{3}\right)^x$ **4.** $y = \left(\frac{1}{4}\right)^x$ **5.** $y = \left(\frac{5}{2}\right)^x$ **6.** $y = 2.2^x$

Graph the two functions for the domain $\{x: -2 \leqslant x \leqslant 2\}$. You could use a graphing calculator or computer graphing program.

7. a. $y = 3x$

    b. $y = \left(\frac{1}{3}\right)^x$

8. a. $y = 4^x$

    b. $y = \left(\frac{1}{4}\right)^x$

9. a. $y = 5^x$

    b. $y = \left(\frac{1}{5}\right)^x$

10. a. $y = 2^x$

    b. $y = \left(\frac{1}{2}\right)^x$

Use the graph of $y = 5^x$ (see Exercise 9) to estimate the solution of each equation to the nearest tenth.

11. $5^x = 6.9$ **12.** $5^x = 11$ **13.** $5^x = 3$ **14.** $5^x = 0.5$

Use the graph of $y = 4^x$ (see Exercise 8) to estimate the solution of each equation to the nearest tenth.

15. $4^x = 9$ **16.** $4^x = 12$ **17.** $4^x = 0.33$ **18.** $4^x = 0.5$

Solve.

19. $3^x = 3^{1.2}$

20. $5 = 5^{2.6}$

21. $3^x = \sqrt{3}$

22. $5^x = \sqrt{5}$

23. $3^x = \dfrac{1}{9}$

24. $5^x = \dfrac{1}{5}$

25. $3^{x+2} = 27$

26. $5^{x+3} = 25$

27. $3^{2x+1} = \dfrac{1}{81}$

28. $5^{3x-1} = 125$

29. $9^x = 27^{x+1}$

30. $25^{x+1} = 125^x$

31. $2^x = 4^{x+3}$

32. $6^{3x+2} = 36^x$

33. $100^{3x} = 10^{x+1}$

34. $100^{4x-3} = 1000^x$

35. $6^{4x-3} = 36^{x+1}$

36. $4^{3x+1} = 8^{x-1}$

B **37.** $\left(\dfrac{1}{2}\right)^x = 16$

38. $(0.01)^{2x} = 10{,}000$

39. $4^x = 2\sqrt{2}$

40. $\left(\sqrt{5}\right)^{1-x} = 625$

41. $\left(\sqrt[3]{6}\right)^x = \sqrt[5]{36}$

42. $\left(\sqrt{2}\right)^x = \dfrac{1}{4}$

Graph the three functions using the same set of axes. You could use a graphing calculator or computer graphing program.

43. a. $y = 2^x$

44. a. $y = 3^x$

45. a. $y = \left(\dfrac{1}{3}\right)^x$

    b. $y = 2^{x+3}$

    b. $y = 3^{x+2}$

    b. $y = 2 + \left(\dfrac{1}{3}\right)^x$

    c. $y = 2^{x-1}$

    c. $y = 3^{x-3}$

    c. $y + 2 = \left(\dfrac{1}{3}\right)^x$

46. a. $y = \left(\dfrac{1}{2}\right)^x$

47. a. $y - 2 = 2^{x+3}$

48. a. $y - 3 = 3^{x+2}$

    b. $y = 3 + \left(\dfrac{1}{2}\right)^x$

    b. $y + 2 = 2^{x-3}$

    b. $y + 3 = 3^{x-3}$

    c. $y - 1 = \left(\dfrac{1}{2}\right)^x$

    c. $y - 2 = \left(\dfrac{1}{2}\right)^{x-3}$

    c. $y - 3 = \left(\dfrac{1}{3}\right)^{x-3}$

C Each graph is congruent to $y = 2^x$. Match the graphs with their equations. Then state whether the function is increasing or decreasing.

49. $y = 2^x$

50. $y = -(2^x)$

51. $y = 2^{-x}$

52. $y = -(2^{-x})$

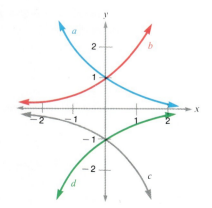

State whether the graph of the given function is congruent to the graph of $y = 7^x$.

53. $y = \left(\dfrac{1}{7}\right)^x$

54. $y = 7^{x+1}$

55. $y = 7^{-x}$

56. $y = -(7^x)$

57. $y = 49^{\frac{x}{2}}$

58. $y = 7^{\frac{x}{2}}$

REVIEW EXERCISES

1. Write the product in scientific notation: $(3 \cdot 10^8)(3.6 \cdot 10^3)$. [5-1]

2. Simplify: $3(x - 2) - x(3 - x) - (x + 3)$. [5-2]

3. Write an expression in expanded form for the volume of this cube. [5-3]

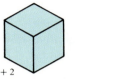

$a + 2$

Factor completely. [5-4,

4. $10ab^2 - 5abc$

5. $2n^2 - 18$

6. $3x^2 + x - 4$ 5-5,
5-6]

7. Solve: $x^2 + 5x = 6$. [5-7]

8. Write an expression for the volume of the spherical shell shown in the figure. Then factor the expression completely. [*Hint:* The formula for the volume of a sphere is $V = \dfrac{4}{3}\pi r^3$.] [5-5]

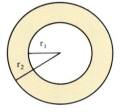

HISTORICAL NOTE Fractional Exponents

Just as mathematicians found it worthwhile to expand the concept of exponents to include zero and negative integers, they also found it worthwhile to include all rational numbers.

The English mathematician Isaac Newton (1642–1727) extended the exponent symbolism in 1676 by stating that since aa and aaa are written a^2 and a^3, so $\sqrt{a}$ and $\sqrt{a^3}$ could be written $a^{\frac{1}{2}}$ and $a^{\frac{3}{2}}$.

However, the use of exponents and the development of the symbols evolved over a period of time with contributions from various earlier mathematicians.

LESSON 11-2

Logarithmic Functions

Recall that a relation and its inverse are related in the following ways.

▶ An equation of the inverse can be obtained by interchanging the variables in the equation of the relation.

▶ If the ordered pair (a, b) is in the relation then the ordered pair (b, a) is in the inverse.

▶ The graph of the inverse is the reflection of the graph of the relation about the line $y = x$.

The equations, ordered pairs, and graphs shown here illustrate the relationship between the cubing function and its inverse.

	f	f^{-1}
Equations:	$y = x^3$	$x = y^3$
Number pairs (sample):	(2, 8)	(8, 2)
	(3, 27)	(27, 3)
	(4, 64)	(64, 4)

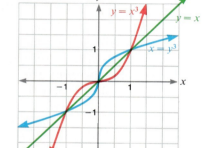

The base-2 exponential function $y = 2^x$ has an inverse defined by the equation $x = 2^y$. The inverse is called the **base-2 logarithmic function**. We write $y = \log_2 x$ which is read, "y equals log base 2 of x" or "y equals the base-2 logarithm of x."

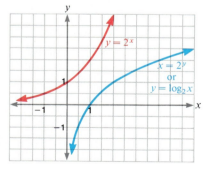

Comparing the two equations for the base-2 logarithm function, $x = 2^y$ and $y = \log_2 x$, we see that the exponent y in the first equation is the base-2 logarithm of x in the second equation.

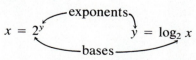

Substituting $\log_2 x$ for y in the first equation, we get $x = 2^{\log_2 x}$.

Each exponential function $y = b^x$ has an inverse function that is a logarithmic function.

Definition: Logarithmic Function

For all positive real numbers x and b, $b \neq 1$, there is a real number y such that $y = \log_b x$ if and only if $x = b^y$.

Here is the graph of an exponential function $y = b^x$ with *base greater than 1* and its inverse $y = \log_b x$. Note that the graph of a function and the graph of its inverse are reflections of each other about the line $y = x$.

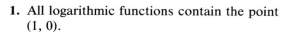

Recalling facts about exponential functions (page 444), we note these corresponding facts about logarithmic functions from the graph.

1. All logarithmic functions contain the point $(1, 0)$.
2. The graph of the function approaches the y-axis asymptotically.
3. The domain is the set of positive real numbers.
4. The range is the set of all real numbers.
5. The logarithmic functions (with $b > 1$) are increasing.

Logarithmic notation or exponential notation can be used to express the same relationship. Use whichever is more convenient.

Exponential notation $2^3 = 8$ $10^4 = 10{,}000$ $3^{-2} = \dfrac{1}{9}$

Logarithmic notation $3 = \log_2 8$ $4 = \log_{10} 10{,}000$ $-2 = \log_3 \dfrac{1}{9}$

Example 1   Write in logarithmic form.

   a. $7^2 = 49$

   b. $\left(\dfrac{1}{2}\right)^4 = \dfrac{1}{16}$

   c. $10^{0.477} \approx 3$

Solution   a. $\log_7 49 = 2$

   b. $\log_{\frac{1}{2}} \dfrac{1}{16} = 4$

   c. $\log_{10} 3 \approx 0.477$

Example 2   Write in exponential form.

   a. $\log_{10} 1000 = 3$

   b. $\log_{\frac{1}{2}} 8 = -3$

   c. $\log_{10} 1.197 \approx 0.07891$

Solution   a. $10^3 = 1000$

   b. $\left(\dfrac{1}{2}\right)^{-3} = 8$

   c. $10^{0.07891} \approx 1.197$

The following properties of logarithmic functions are useful in simplifying expressions.

Properties of Logarithmic Functions

I. For all positive real numbers x, y, and b, $b \neq 1$,

$$\text{if } \log_b x = \log_b y, \text{ then } x = y.$$

II. For all real numbers x and all positive real numbers b, $b \neq 1$,

$$\log_b b^x = x.$$

III. For all positive real numbers x and b, $b \neq 1$,

$$b^{\log_b x} = x.$$

Recall that inverse functions "undo" each other. That is, for inverse functions f and f^{-1}, $f^{-1}(f(x)) = x$ and $f(f^{-1}(x)) = x$. Since exponential functions and logarithmic functions are inverses, Properties II and III above are consequences of that general statement.

Example 3   Simplify.

   a. $3^{\log_3 4}$ **b.** $\log_5 5^6$ **c.** $\log_b b$ **d.** $\log_b 1$

Solution   **a.** Apply Property III from above. $3^{\log_3 4} = 4$

   b. Apply Property II from above. $\log_5 5^6 = 6$

   c. Substitute b^1 for b and then apply Property II. $\log_b b^1 = 1$

   d. Let $y = \log_b 1$. Then $b^y = 1$ and $y = 0$. Therefore, $\log_b 1 = 0$.

Note from parts (c) and (d) in Example 3 the following two properties.

Properties of Logarithmic Functions

For all positive real numbers b, $b \neq 1$,

   IV. $\log_b b = 1$ V. $\log_b 1 = 0$

These properties are equivalent to the following exponential properties: $b^1 = b$ $b^0 = 1$.

Example 4   Solve. $\log_2 16 = x$

Solution   *Change to exponential notation.* $2^x = 16$

   Change to the same base. $2^x = 2^4$

   Apply the equality property of exponential functions. $x = 4$

Answer $\{4\}$

Example 5   Solve. $\log_{3x} 324 = 2$

Solution   *Change to exponential form.* $(3x)^2 = 324$

$$9x^2 = 324$$
$$x^2 = 36 \qquad x = \pm 6$$

Answer   The base of a logarithmic function cannot be negative. {6}

*C*LASSROOM EXERCISES

Write in logarithmic form.

1. $6^3 = 216$

2. $25^{\frac{1}{2}} = 5$

Write in exponential form.

3. $\log_3 81 = 4$

4. $\log_{16} 4 = 0.5$

Simplify.

5. $5^{\log_5 2}$ **6.** $7^{\log_7 5}$ **7.** $\log_5 5^7$ **8.** $\log_b b^c$

*W*RITTEN EXERCISES

A   **Write in logarithmic form.**

1. $2^5 = 32$ **2.** $2^6 = 64$ **3.** $10^8 = 100,000,000$

4. $10^3 = 1000$ **5.** $7^4 = 2401$ **6.** $7^3 = 343$

Write in exponential form.

7. $\log_2 1024 = 10$ **8.** $\log_2 512 = 9$ **9.** $\log_{10} 7 \approx 0.845$

10. $\log_{10} 8 \approx 0.903$ **11.** $\log_7 12 \approx 1.277$ **12.** $\log_7 25 \approx 1.654$

Solve.

13. $\log_2 16 = x$ **14.** $\log_2 8 = x$ **15.** $\log_3 x = 4$

16. $\log_3 x = 5$ **17.** $x = \log_7 7$ **18.** $x = \log_7 1$

19. $\log_{10} x = 2$ **20.** $\log_{10} x = 4$ **21.** $\log_x 25 = 2$

22. $\log_x 64 = 3$ **23.** $x = 6^{\log_6 3}$ **24.** $x = 8^{\log_8 5}$

25. $\log_{2x} 27 = 3$ **26.** $\log_{2x} 64 = 3$ **27.** $\log_{10} 2x = 3$

28. $\log_{10} 4x = 2$ **29.** $\log_2 (3x + 2) = 4$ **30.** $\log_2 (2x - 1) = 3$

Graph f and f^{-1} using the same set of axes.

31. $f(x) = 2^x$ **32.** $f(x) = 3^x$

B   **Graph the three functions using the same set of axes. You could use a graphing calculator or computer graphing program.**

33. a. $y = \log_2 x$ **34. a.** $y = \log_2 x$ **35. a.** $y = \log_2 x$ **36. a.** $y = \log_2 x$

    b. $y = \log_3 x$ **b.** $y = -\log_2 x$ **b.** $y = \log_2 4x$ **b.** $y = \log_2 x + 2$

    c. $y = \log_4 x$ **c.** $y = \log_2 (-x)$ **c.** $y = 4 \log_2 x$ **c.** $y = \log_2 (x + 2)$

Solve. Use logarithmic notation to express the solutions.

37. $7^x = 3$ **38.** $5^{2x-1} = 132$ **39.** $3^{\frac{x}{4}} = 6$ **40.** $2^{\frac{1-x}{3}} = 10$

Use the fact that $\log_2 10 \approx 3.322$ and $\log_{10} 2 \approx 0.301$ to solve the equations.

41. $\log_2 x = 4.322$ **42.** $\log_{10} x = 1.301$ **43.** $10^{-0.301} = x$ **44.** $2^{-3.322} = x$

 45. Prove that $\log_b b^x = x$, $b > 1$. [*Hint:* Let $y = b^x$ and apply the definition of a logarithmic function.]

46. Prove that $b^{\log_b x} = x$, $b > 1$.

REVIEW EXERCISES

1. Write without negative exponents: $3x^{-2}y^{-1}$.   [6-1]

Simplify, listing any restrictions on the variables.   [6-2,
6-3,
2. $\dfrac{(a+b)^2}{a^2-b^2}$ **3.** $\dfrac{4x}{5y} \cdot \dfrac{15y}{x^3}$ **4.** $\dfrac{1}{x^2} - \dfrac{1}{3x} + \dfrac{1}{3}$ 6-4]

5. Solve: $\dfrac{1}{10} = \dfrac{1}{r} + \dfrac{1}{100}$.   [6-5]

6. If a 200-ohm and a 300-ohm resistance are connected in parallel, what is the   [6-6]
total resistance of the circuit? [*Hint:* Use the formula $\dfrac{1}{R} = \dfrac{1}{r_1} + \dfrac{1}{r_2}$.]

7. If y varies inversely as x, and $y = 20$ when $x = 5$, find y when $x = 25$.   [6-7]

Self-Quiz 1

11-1 **1.** Complete the table for the exponential function $y = 9^x$.

x	2	1	$\dfrac{1}{2}$	0	$-\dfrac{1}{2}$	-1
y	?	?	?	?	?	?

Graph the function $y = 3^x$. **Estimate the solution of each equation to the nearest tenth.**

2. $3^x = 17$ **3.** $3^x = 0.25$

Solve.

4. $6^{2x-1} = \dfrac{1}{36}$ **5.** $4^x = \sqrt{2}$

11-2 **6.** Write in logarithmic form.   **a.** $5^4 = 625$ **b.** $8 = \left(\dfrac{1}{2}\right)^{-3}$

7. Write in exponential form.   **a.** $\log_3 243 = 5$ **b.** $\log_{10} 0.0001 = -4$

8. Solve. $\log_2 2\sqrt{2} = x$.

450   Chapter 11   Exponential and Logarithmic Functions

Simplifying Logarithmic Expressions

$2^0 = 1$
$2^1 = 2$
$2^2 = 4$
$2^3 = 8$
$2^4 = 16$
$2^5 = 32$
$2^6 = 64$
$2^7 = 128$
$2^8 = 256$
$2^9 = 512$
$2^{10} = 1024$
$2^{11} = 2048$
$2^{12} = 4096$

Here is a powers of two table.
You can use the table to perform computations.

$$32^2 = (2^5)^2 = 2^{10} = 1024$$
$$\sqrt[3]{4096} = \sqrt[3]{2^{12}} = 2^4 = 16$$
$$32 \cdot 64 = 2^5 \cdot 2^6 = 2^{11} = 2048$$

Since the equations $y = \log_b x$ and $x = b^y$ are equivalent, familiar properties of exponents that were used in the computations above can be restated in terms of logarithms.

Properties: Exponents and Logarithms

For all admissible real values of b, m, and n,

Exponents

$b^m \cdot b^n = b^{m+n}$

$\dfrac{b^m}{b^n} = b^{m-n}$

$(b^m)^n = b^{mn}$

Logarithms

VI. $\log_b (mn) = \log_b m + \log_b n,\ m > 0,\ n > 0$

VII. $\log_b \left(\dfrac{m}{n}\right) = \log_b m - \log_b n,\ m > 0,\ n > 0$

VIII. $\log_b (m^n) = n(\log_b m),\ m > 0$

To prove Property VI, we start with the facts:

$$m = b^{\log_b m} \quad \text{and} \quad n = b^{\log_b n}.$$

Then
$$mn = (b^{\log_b m})(b^{\log_b n})$$
$$= b^{\log_b m + \log_b n}.$$

So
$$\log_b (mn) = \log_b b^{\log_b m + \log_b n}$$
$$= \log_b m + \log_b n.$$

The other two properties, Properties VII and VIII, can be proved in similar ways (Exercises 61 and 62).

Example 1   Use the fact that $\log_2 5 \approx 2.322$ to find approximations for the following.

  a. $\log_2 40$ **b.** $\log_2 25$

Solution   **a.** $\log_2 40 = \log_2 (5 \cdot 8)$ **b.** $\log_2 25 = \log_2 (5^2)$

$\qquad\qquad\quad = \log_2 5 + \log_2 8$ $\qquad\qquad\quad = 2 \log_2 5$

$\qquad\qquad\quad = \log_2 5 + \log_2 2^3$ $\qquad\qquad\quad \approx 2(2.322)$

$\qquad\qquad\quad \approx 2.322 + 3$ $\qquad\qquad\quad \approx 4.644$

$\qquad\qquad\quad \approx 5.322$

Check   (By estimation)

40 is between 2^5 and 2^6.   25 is between 2^4 and 2^5.

The answer seems reasonable.   The answer seems reasonable.

Example 2   Write in expanded form (that is, write as a linear combination of logarithms of single variables.)

$$\log_b \left(\frac{x}{y}\right)^z$$

Solution $\log_b \left(\dfrac{x}{y}\right)^z = z \log_b \left(\dfrac{x}{y}\right)$

$\qquad\qquad\qquad\quad = z \left(\log_b x - \log_b y\right)$

$\qquad\qquad\qquad\quad = z \log_b x - z \log_b y$

Example 3   Write as a single logarithm. $-\log_{10} 2 + \log_{10} a + 2 \log_{10} t$

Solution $-\log_{10} 2 + \log_{10} a + 2 \log_{10} t = -\log_{10} 2 + \log_{10} a + \log_{10} t^2$

$\qquad\qquad\qquad\qquad\qquad\qquad\quad = -\log_{10} 2 + \log_{10} at^2$

$\qquad\qquad\qquad\qquad\qquad\qquad\quad = \log_{10} \dfrac{at^2}{2}$

*C*LASSROOM EXERCISES

Use the facts that $\log_{10} 2 \approx 0.3010$ and $\log_{10} 3 \approx 0.4771$ to find a decimal value for each expression.

1. $\log_{10} 6$ **2.** $\log_{10} 9$ **3.** $\log_{10} \dfrac{3}{2}$ **4.** $\log_{10} 8$

Write in expanded form.

5. $\log_b \pi r^2$

  6. $\log_2 \sqrt{ab}$

Write as a single logarithm.

7. $\log_{10} P + \log_{10} r + \log_{10} t$

  8. $2 \log_5 x - \log_5 y$

RITTEN EXERCISES

A Use these facts to find a decimal value for each expression.

$$\log_7 5 \approx 0.82709 \qquad \log_7 6 \approx 0.92078$$

1. $\log_7 12$

2. $\log_7 10$

3. $\log_7 25$

4. $\log_7 36$

5. $\log_7 \dfrac{5}{2}$

6. $\log_7 \dfrac{6}{5}$

7. $\log_7 \dfrac{1}{5}$

8. $\log_7 \dfrac{1}{6}$

9. $\log_7 \sqrt{6}$

10. $\log_7 \sqrt[3]{6}$

11. $\log_7 \dfrac{2}{5}$

12. $\log_7 \dfrac{5}{6}$

Write in expanded form. Simplify when possible.

13. $\log_4 xy$

14. $\log_2 \dfrac{x}{y}$

15. $\log_{10} \dfrac{M}{N}$

16. $\log_6 3R$

17. $\log_7 \dfrac{xy}{z}$

18. $\log_5 \dfrac{y}{xz}$

19. $\log_3 \sqrt[5]{a}$

20. $\log_9 b^3$

21. $\log_b (2^t b)$

22. $\log_b (b^2 a^5)$

23. $\log_6 \dfrac{x^2}{6}$

24. $\log_3 \sqrt{5xy}$

25. $\log_4 \dfrac{1}{16y^2}$

26. $\log_{10} \dfrac{100}{rs}$

27. $\log_2 \dfrac{1}{8x^3}$

28. $\log_3 \sqrt[3]{\dfrac{3v}{4\pi}}$

Write as a single logarithm.

29. $\log_5 x - \log_5 y$

30. $\log_{10} 100 + \log_{10} a + \log_{10} b$ **31.** $2\log_7 r + \log_7 \pi$

32. $\dfrac{1}{2}\log_b x - \log_b z$

33. $3\log_c w - 2\log_c v$

34. $\log_6 b + \log_6 h - \log_6 2$

35. $\dfrac{1}{2}\log_{10} x + 1$ [*Hint:* Rewrite 1 as a log.]

36. $3\log_4 M - 2$ [*Hint:* Rewrite 2 as a log.]

37. $\log_a \pi + 2\log_a r + \log_a h - \log_a 3$

38. $\log_e 2 + \log_e \pi + \dfrac{1}{2}\log_e l - \dfrac{1}{2}\log_e g$

B Indicate whether the following equations are true or false for all admissible values
of *m*, *n*, and *p*. All logarithms are to the base, *b*, $b \neq 1$.

39. $\log(mn) - \log m = \log n$

40. $\dfrac{\log(mn)}{\log n} = m$

41. $\dfrac{\log m^p}{\log m} = p$

42. $\log(m - n) = \dfrac{\log m}{\log n}$

43. $\log\left(\dfrac{m}{n}\right) + \log n = \log m$

44. $(\log m) \cdot (\log n) = \log(m + n)$

45. $\log m - (\log n + \log p) = \log \dfrac{m}{np}$

46. $\log m^2 = (\log m)^2$

47. $\log\left(\dfrac{1}{m}\right) = -\log m$

48. $\log(m + n) = \log m + \log n$

Solve.

49. $\log_5 2 + \log_5 7 = \log_5 x$

50. $\log_5 x + \log_5 8 = \log_5 12$

51. $\log_5 18 - \log_5 9 = \log_5 x$

52. $\log_5 21 - \log_5 x = \log_5 7$

53. $\log_5 10 = \log_5 x + \log_5 2$

54. $\log_5 (x + 2) + \log_5 3 = \log_5 15$

55. $\log_8 (x - 6) - \log_8 5 = \log_8 6$

56. $\log_9 9^x = 3$

C 57. $\log_{10} (2x + 3) - \log_{10} x = \log_{10} 4$

58. $\log_7 (x - 2) + \log_7 x = \log_7 15$

59. $\log_4 (x + 2) + \log_4 (x - 3) = \log_4 4x$

60. $\log_5 (x + 3) + \log_5 (x + 4) = \log_5 (2x + 6)$

Prove these properties.

61. $\log_b \left(\dfrac{m}{n} \right) = \log_b m - \log_b n$

62. $\log_b (m^n) = n \log_b m$

63. If $\log_e i = \log_e I - \dfrac{Rt}{L}$, show that $i = Ie^{-\frac{Rt}{L}}$.

*R*EVIEW EXERCISES

1. Give a rational approximation of $\sqrt{10}$ to the nearest tenth. [7-1]

Simplify. State restrictions on variables where necessary. [7-2, 7-3, 7-4]

2. $\sqrt{50a^2}$　　　　**3.** $\sqrt{18} + \sqrt{8}$　　　　**4.** $\dfrac{2}{2 + \sqrt{2}}$　　　　**5.** $\sqrt[3]{\dfrac{125}{9}}$

6. What is the surface area of a cube whose volume is 1000 cm³? [7-4]

7. What is the distance between the points (2, 1) and (4, −3)? [7-5]

8. Solve:　$\sqrt{3x + 4} = x$. [7-6]

9. Write in radical form and simplify if possible:　$16^{\frac{1}{3}}$. [7-7]

*H*ISTORICAL NOTE　Logarithms

Logarithms were invented by Scotsman John Napier in the seventeenth century to simplify very lengthy paper-and-pencil computations in astronomy. Until the advent of electronic calculators and computers, logarithms continued to be a major timesaver in computation. Most computations used base-10 logarithms since the decimal system is based on 10.

LESSON 11-4

Common Logarithms

Base-10 logarithms are called **common logarithms.** The notation for common logarithms is simplified by omitting the designation of the base, writing log x for $\log_{10} x$.

A calculator with a ⬛log⬛ key will compute the common logarithm of any positive number. If such a calculator is not available, common logarithms of numbers betweeen 1 and 10 can be found correct to four decimal places in the tables on page 769. The following example shows how to use the tables.

Example 1   **Use the tables on page 769 to find the decimal value of log 2.16 correct to four decimal places.**

Solution   Find the first two digits (21) in the n-column. Then read across the 21-row to the 6-column.

n	0	1	2	3	4	5	6	7	8	9
20	3010	3032	3054	3075	3096	3118	3139	3160	3181	3201
21	3222	3243	3263	3284	3304	3324	3345	3365	3385	3404
22	3424	3444	3464	3483	3502	3522	3541	3560	3579	3598

Answer   log 2.16 ≈ 0.3345

If we know the common logarithms of numbers between 1 and 10, we can use those logarithms and our knowledge of scientific notation to write the logarithms of any other positive numbers.

Example 2   **Use the fact that log 2 ≈ 0.3010 to write the common logarithms of the following numbers.**

     a. 20   **b. 2,000,000**   **c. 0.002**

Solution   **a.** $20 = 2 \cdot 10^1 \approx 10^{0.3010} \cdot 10^1 = 10^{1.3010}$
           Therefore, log 20 ≈ 1.3010.

           b. $2{,}000{,}000 = 2 \cdot 10^6 \approx 10^{0.3010} \cdot 10^6 = 10^{6.3010}$
           Therefore, log 2,000,000 ≈ 6.3010.

           c. $0.002 = 2 \cdot 10^{-3} \approx 10^{0.3010} \cdot 10^{-3} = 10^{0.3010 - 3}$
           Therefore, log 0.002 ≈ 0.3010 − 3 = −2.6990.

Example 2 illustrates a close relationship between scientific notation and common logarithms. When a number is written in scientific notation, the power of ten determines the integer part of the logarithm and the factor between one and ten determines the decimal part. This means that the decimal parts repeat in a cycle, as shown in Example 3.

Example 3 Graph the ordered pairs (x, y), where y is the *fraction part* of the common logarithm of x for values of x from 1 to 1000.

Solution Use the tables of common logarithms on page 769.

x	log x	y
1	0	0
2	0.301	0.301
3	0.477	0.477
4	0.602	0.602
.		
.		
.		
8	0.903	0.903
9	0.954	0.954

x	log x	y
10	1	0
20	1.301	0.301
30	1.477	0.477
40	1.602	0.602
.		
.		
.		
80	1.903	0.903
90	1.954	0.954

x	log x	y
100	2	0
200	2.301	0.301
300	2.477	0.477
400	2.602	0.602
.		
.		
.		
800	2.903	0.903
900	2.954	0.954

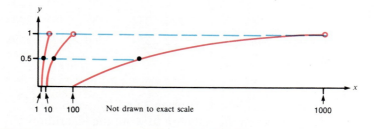

Not drawn to exact scale

A table of logarithms for the numbers 1 to 9.99 can be used to determine the logarithm for any nonnegative number. Express the number in scientific notation $a \times 10^n$. Use n for the integer part of the logarithm. Find the logarithm of a in the table for the decimal part.

Example 4 State the consecutive integer powers of 10 that bound x, if log $x = 2.9$.

Solution The logarithm of x is between the whole numbers 2 and 3. Therefore, x is between 10^2 and 10^3.

Example 5 State the consecutive integer powers of 10 that bound x, if log $x = -0.1$.

Solution The logarithm of x is between -1 and 0.

Answer x is between 10^{-1} and 10^0.

Negative common logarithms are sometimes written with the decimal part positive and the integer part negative. For example, $\log x = -3.6690$ can be rewritten as $\log x = 0.3010 - 4$. From this expression we can see that
$$x = 10^{(0.3010 - 4)} = 10^{0.3010} \cdot 10^{-4} = 2 \cdot 10^{-4}.$$

 ## CLASSROOM EXERCISES

Use a calculator or the tables on page 769 to find the decimal values for the common logarithms of the given numbers correct to four decimal places.

1. 4.32   2. 6.5   3. 7

Use the values given in the table at the right to express each logarithm in decimal notation.

$\log 1 = 0$
$\log 2 \approx 0.3010$
$\log 3 \approx 0.4771$

4. $\log 3{,}000$ 5. $\log 0.03$ 6. $\log 6$

Solve, using the table of values above.

7. $\log x = 6.4771$ 8. $\log x = 0.3010 - 2$ 9. $\log x = -4.5229$

 ## WRITTEN EXERCISES

A Use a calculator or the tables on page 769 to find the decimal approximation for the common logarithm of the given number. Write the approximation correct to four decimal places.

1. 5.16   2. 7.49   3. 6   4. 5

5. 4.02   6. 2.08   7. 6,000,000   8. 5,000,000

9. 402,000   10. 20,800   11. 0.006   12. 0.00005

Show that the sum of logarithms (a) and (b) to the nearest thousandth equals logarithm (c) to the nearest thousandth.

13. a. $\log 2$ 14. a. $\log 3$ 15. a. $\log 4$ 16. a. $\log 2.5$
    b. $\log 2.5$ b. $\log 2$ b. $\log 2$ b. $\log 3$
    c. $\log 5$ c. $\log 6$ c. $\log 8$ c. $\log 7.5$

Show that the product (a) to the nearest thousandth equals the logarithm (b) to the nearest thousandth.

17. a. $2 \log 3$ 18. a. $3 \log 2$ 19. a. $3 \log 3$ 20. a. $2 \log 4$
    b. $\log 9$ b. $\log 8$ b. $\log 27$ b. $\log 16$

Solve.

21. $\log 6.23 = x$ 22. $\log 2.89 = x$ 23. $\log 623 = x$

24. $\log 28.9 = x$ 25. $\log 62{,}300{,}000 = x$ 26. $\log 289{,}000{,}000 = x$

27. $\log 0.623 = x$ 28. $\log 0.289 = x$ 29. $\log 0.0000623 = x$

30. $\log 0.000289 = x$ **31.** $\log x = 0.6911$ **32.** $\log x = 0.8621$

33. $\log x = 2.6911$ **34.** $\log x = 3.8621$ **35.** $\log x = 0.6991 - 1$

36. $\log x = 0.6911 - 3$ **37.** $\log x = -2.3089$ **38.** $\log x = -3.1379$

B **39.** $10^{0.4116} = x$ **40.** $10^{3.4116} = x$ **41.** $10^{6.4116} = x$

42. $10^x = 8.06$ **43.** $10^x = 7,090,000$ **44.** $10^x = 0.00049$

Let $a = \log x$ and $b = \log y$. Write each expression without logs.

45. $\log \left(\dfrac{x^4}{y} \right)$ **46.** $\log \left(\dfrac{y}{x^3} \right)$ **47.** $\log \left(\dfrac{10^x}{y^2} \right)$ **48.** $\log \left(\dfrac{0.1}{\sqrt{10xy}} \right)$

Solve.

49. If $\log x = 1.3909$, find $\log 10x$.   **50.** If $\log y = 0.5211 - 2$, find $\log 1000y$.

51. If $60 = 10^{1.7782}$, find $\log \sqrt{60}$.   **52.** If $4.5 = 10^{0.6532}$, find $\log (4.5)^{10}$.

C **53.** Find $\log 100z - \log z$.   **54.** Find $\log \left(\dfrac{x}{10} \right) - \log x^2 + \log 1000x$.

55. If $A = 10x^2$, then $\log A = $ ___?___ .   **56.** If $P = \dfrac{x^{-3}}{1000}$, then $\log P = $ ___?___ .

ℛpplication: The Richter Scale

Magnitudes of earthquakes are measured on the Richter scale on the basis of the equation $R = \log \left(\dfrac{I}{I_0} \right)$, where R is the Richter scale number, I is the intensity of the earthquake, and I_0 is the standard minimum intensity that is used to measure underground vibrations.

57. On September 19, 1985, there was an earthquake in Mexico City measuring 7.8 on the Richter scale. How many times the intensity I_0 was the intensity of that quake? [*Hint:* Let $I = kI_0$ and solve for k.]

58. What is the ratio of the intensity of an earthquake measuring 8 on the Richter scale to the intensity of an earthquake measuring 5 on the Richter scale?

ℛpplication: Sound Intensity

59. The intensity level of a sound (the amount of energy in the sound waves) is given by the equation $\beta = 10 \log \left(\dfrac{I}{I_0} \right)$, where β is the intensity level in decibels of a sound of intensity I and I_0 is the lowest intensity that can be detected by the human ear. The loudest rock music has an intensity of about 110 decibels. How many times I_0 is that?

# REVIEW EXERCISES

Solve.

1. $(x + 2)^2 = 10$

2. $2x^2 - 7 = 2x$

[8-1, 8-2]

Simplify.

3. $i^3(3i)^2$ **4.** $|2 + 3i|$ **5.** $(-7 - 2i) - (2 - 3i) + (6 + 4i)$ **6.** $\dfrac{4}{3 + 2i}$

[8-3, 8-4, 8-5]

7. State the number and kinds of roots of $x^2 + 2x - 5 = 0$.

[8-6]

8. Solve: $x - 6\sqrt{x} - 40 = 0$.

[8-6]

9. If the equation $y - 3 = 3x^2 - (x + 1)^2$ defines a quadratic function, write it in standard form.

[8-7]

State the vertex and axis of symmetry, and indicate whether the graph opens upward or downward.

[8-8, 8-9]

10. $y - 3 = \dfrac{1}{2}(x + 5)^2$

11. $y = -2x^2 + 4x - 4$

12. State whether the function $y = -3x^2 - 6x + 1$ has a maximum or minimum value and give this value.

[8-10]

EXTENSION   Linear Interpolation

Consider a square root table, part of which is shown at the right. Using this table, we can find an approximation of $\sqrt{3.1}$ or $\sqrt{3.2}$ to three decimal places. However, we can also use the table to find approximations of square roots of values between the given values of n such as 3.14. A process for doing this is called **linear interpolation.**

n	$\sqrt{n}$
3.0	1.732
3.1	1.761
3.2	1.789

To use linear interpolation to find $\sqrt{3.14}$, we write the following proportion.

$$\frac{0.04}{0.1} = \frac{x}{0.028}$$

$$x \approx 0.011$$

Answer: $\sqrt{3.14} \approx 1.761 + 0.011$

≈ 1.772

n	$\sqrt{n}$
3.1	1.761
3.14	?
3.2	1.789

Use linear interpolation and the table above to find approximations of the following square roots.

1. $\sqrt{3.17}$

2. $\sqrt{3.03}$

Use linear interpolation and the tables of common logarithms (page 769) to find approximations of the following logarithms.

3. log 2.425

4. log 2468

Natural Logarithms

Using a calculator, we find

$$\left(1 + \frac{1}{1}\right)^1 = 2, \left(1 + \frac{1}{2}\right)^2 = 2.25, \left(1 + \frac{1}{3}\right)^3 = 2.\overline{370}, \left(1 + \frac{1}{4}\right)^4 \approx 2.441, \cdots \left(1 + \frac{1}{10}\right)^{10} \approx 2.594,$$

$$\cdots \left(1 + \frac{1}{1000}\right)^{1000} \approx 2.717, \cdots \left(1 + \frac{1}{100}\right)^{100} \approx 2.705, \cdots \left(1 + \frac{1}{1,000,000}\right)^{1,000,000} \approx 2.718, \cdots$$

As the value of n gets larger, the value of $\left(1 + \frac{1}{n}\right)^n$ gets closer and closer to, but never greater than, the number e (≈ 2.7182818). This very important number is given the name e for the Swiss mathematician Leonard Euler.

The number e is an irrational number 2.7182818 . . . that arises in many applications of mathematics. Base-e logarithms are called **natural logarithms.** To simplify notation and to distinguish natural logarithms from common logarithms, we write **ln x** to represent $\log_e x$.

$$\ln e^3 = 3 \qquad \ln e^{-4} = -4$$

The following decimal approximations of powers of e will be useful in the work with natural logarithms.

$$e^4 \approx 54.598 \qquad e^3 \approx 20.086 \qquad e^2 \approx 7.389 \qquad e^1 \approx 2.718$$
$$e^0 = 1 \qquad e^{-1} \approx 0.368 \qquad e^{-2} \approx 0.135 \qquad e^{-3} \approx 0.050$$

Example 1 **State the consecutive integers that bound the natural logarithm.**
 a. ln 15 **b. ln 1.5** **c. ln 0.15**

Solution **a.** 15 is between e^2 and e^3. Therefore, ln 15 is between 2 and 3.
 b. 1.5 is between e^0 and e^1. Therefore, ln 1.5 is between 0 and 1.
 c. 0.15 is between e^{-2} and e^{-1}. Therefore, ln 0.15 is between -2 and -1.

Decimal values of natural logarithms for the numbers 1 to 10 can be found in the tables on page 770 or computed by using the $\boxed{\ln}$ key on a calculator. To use the tables to find the natural logarithms of numbers greater than 10 or less than 1, write the number in scientific notation and use the fact that ln 10 ≈ 2.30259.

For example:

$$220 = 2.2 \cdot 10^2 \qquad\qquad 0.022 = 2.2 \cdot 10^{-2}$$
$$\ln 220 = \ln 2.2 + 2 \ln 10 \qquad \ln 0.022 = \ln 2.2 - 2 \ln 10$$
$$\approx 0.7885 + 2(2.30259) \qquad \approx 0.7885 - 2(2.30259)$$
$$\approx 5.3937 \qquad\qquad\qquad \approx -3.8167$$

Every positive number can be written as an exponential with any positive number except 1 as the base. For example, 16 can be written as

$$2^4 \qquad 4^2 \qquad \approx 10^{1.2041} \qquad \approx e^{2.7726}$$

Equivalently, every positive number has a logarithm to any positive number base (except 1).

$$\log_2 16 = 4 \qquad \log_4 16 = 2 \qquad \log 16 \approx 1.2041 \qquad \ln 16 \approx 2.7726$$

It is possible to calculate the logarithm of a number to *any* base using a calculator that has only a particular logarithm function. The following theorem states a relationship between logarithms of different bases.

The Change-of-Base Theorem

For all positive real numbers a and b (except 1) and any positive real number x,

$$\log_a x = \frac{\log_b x}{\log_b a}.$$

Proof:

$$x = a^{\log_a x}$$
$$\log_b x = \log_b a^{\log_a x}$$
$$\log_b x = (\log_a x)(\log_b a)$$
$$\frac{\log_b x}{\log_b a} = \log_a x$$

Example 2   Use base-10 logarithms to compute $\log_4 8$.

Solution   Use the change-of-base theorem.

$$\log_a x = \frac{\log_b x}{lob_b a}$$

$$\log_4 8 = \frac{\log 8}{\log 4} \approx \frac{0.9031}{0.6021} \approx 1.5$$

You can also use the change-of-base theorem to solve equations using natural logarithms if you do not have access to a calculator.

Example 3   Solve $\ln x = 5.9915$ without using the $\boxed{e^x}$ key on a calculator.

Solution $\log_e x = \dfrac{\log x}{\log e}, e \approx 2.71828$

$$5.9915 \approx \frac{\log x}{0.4343}$$

$$2.6021 \approx \log x$$

$$400.0 \approx x$$

Answer   {400}

Solve.

1. $\ln x = -1$ **2.** $\ln(-1) = x$ **3.** $\ln 7.389 = x$

4. Use base-10 logarithms to compute $\log_3 12$.

RITTEN EXERCISES

A Use a calculator or the tables on page 770 to find the natural logarithm of each number.

1. 4.82   **2.** 5.48   **3.** 7.3   **4.** 8.9

5. 71.6   **6.** 22.4   **7.** 0.51   **8.** 0.26

Show that the sum of the natural logarithms (a) and (b) is the logarithm (c). Use the tables on page 770.

9. a. $\ln 3$ **10. a.** $\ln 3$ **11. a.** $\ln 5$ **12. a.** $\ln 5$

b. $\ln 4$ **b.** $\ln 6$ **b.** $\ln 4$ **b.** $\ln 6$

c. $\ln 12$ **c.** $\ln 18$ **c.** $\ln 20$ **c.** $\ln 30$

Show that the product (a) equals the logarithm (b).

13. a. $3 \ln 2$ **14. a.** $2 \ln 3$ **15. a.** $2 \ln 4$ **16. a.** $3 \ln 3$

b. $\ln 8$ **b.** $\ln 9$ **b.** $\ln 16$ **b.** $\ln 27$

Solve.

17. $\ln 2.5 = x$ **18.** $\ln 2.1 = x$ **19.** $\ln e = x$ **20.** $\ln 1 = x$

21. $\ln x = 2.1883$ **22.** $\ln x = 2.2555$ **23.** $\ln x = 1.206$ **24.** $\ln x = 1.292$

25. $\ln 95.1 = x$ **26.** $\ln 56.2 = x$ **27.** $\ln x = 3.9927$ **28.** $\ln x = 4.4474$

B Complete.

29. Use $\ln 6$ and $\ln 4$ to find $\log_4 6$.

30. Use $\ln 7$ and $\ln 3$ to find $\log_3 7$.

31. Use $\ln 5$ and $\ln 15$ to find $\log_5 15$.

32. Use $\ln 4$ and $\ln 20$ to find $\log_4 20$.

33. Use $\log 8$ and $\log 6$ to find $\log_6 8$.

34. Use $\log 7$ and $\log 2$ to find $\log_2 7$.

Write a logarithmic equation, using natural logarithms, for the given equation.

35. $C = \pi d$ **36.** $S = 2\pi rh$ **37.** $S = 4\pi r^2$ **38.** $A = \left(\frac{s^2}{4}\right)\pi 3$

39. $V = \frac{1}{3}bh$ **40.** $V = \left(\frac{4}{3}\right)\pi r^3$ **41.** $t = 2\pi \sqrt{\frac{l}{g}}$ **42.** $A = \left(\frac{h}{2}\right)(b_1 + b_2)$

C In the graph at the right, the area of the shaded region is $\ln a$ $(a > 1)$. The region is bounded by the hyperbola $y = \dfrac{1}{x}$, the x-axis, and two vertical lines $(x = 1$ and $x = a)$. [If $0 < a < 1$, the area is $-\ln a$.]

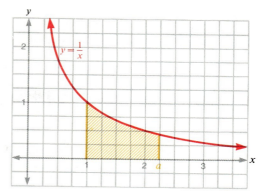

Find the area of the shaded region in each graph.

43.

44.

45.

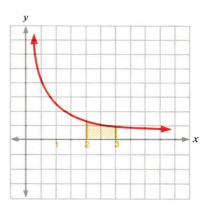

46.

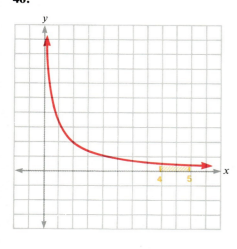

47.

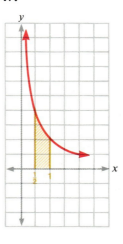

48.

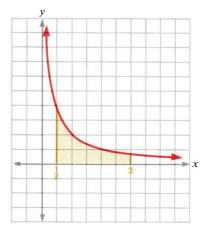

1. Write the equation of a circle with center $(2, -3)$ and radius 4.   [9-1]

2. Write the substitution required to translate the graph of $x^2 + y^2 = 16$ to that of a congruent circle with center $(-5, 4)$.   [9-1]

3. Write the equation for the parabola with focus $(0, 4)$ and directrix $y = 0$.   [9-2]

4. Identify the vertex and axis of symmetry of the parabola $y - 5 = 2(x + 3)^2$.   [9-2]

5. Graph the parabola $y + 4 = 2x^2$.   [9-2]

6. Write the equation of the ellipse with minor axis from $(0, 3)$ to $(0, -3)$ and major axis from $(5, 0)$ to $(-5, 0)$.   [9-3]

*S*elf-Quiz 2

Use the following logarithms to answer Exercises 1-3.

$$\log_{12} 2 \approx 0.2789 \qquad \log_{12} 5 \approx 0.6477 \qquad \log_{12} 9 \approx 0.8842$$

11-3   **Evaluate.**

1. $\log_{12} 18$ 2. $\log_{12} \dfrac{5}{9}$ 3. $\log_{12} 3$

4. Write $\log_a \sqrt{\dfrac{x}{y}}$ in expanded form.

Write as a single logarithm.

5. $\log_3 x - \log_3 y - \log_3 2$ 6. $3 \log_7 a + \dfrac{1}{2} \log_7 b$

11-4   **Use a calculator or the tables on page 769 to find the decimal value of each logarithm.**

7. $\log 40.2$ 8. $\log 0.94$

Solve.

9. $\log 753 = x$ 10. $x = 10^{1.4216}$

11. $\log x = 0.5563 - 1$ 12. $10^x = 923$

11-5   **Use a calculator or the tables on page 770 to find the natural logarithm of each number.**

13. 6.1 14. 1.9

Solve.

15. $\ln x = 1.5$ 16. $\ln e^2 = x$

17. Evaluate $\log_6 38$ by using $\log 38$ and $\log 6$.

Exponential Equations

Application: Compound Interest When a principal P is invested at **compound interest,** the interest earned is added to the principal at regular intervals. This makes the amount earning interest greater, thus making the interest earned in a given period greater than that earned during each preceding period. Money grows faster at compound interest.

The formula for compound interest is $A = P\left(1 + \frac{r}{n}\right)^{nt}$, where A is the amount to which the principal P will grow, r is the yearly rate of interest, t is the number of years that the principal is invested, and n is the number of compounding periods in a year.

Suppose that we have $1000 invested at 8% interest, compounded quarterly, and we wish to know how many years it will take for the $1000 to double in value. We can solve this problem by substituting into the compound-interest formula.

$$2000 = 1000\left(1 + \frac{0.08}{4}\right)^{4t}$$
$$2 = (1.02)^{4t}$$

How can we solve an equation with the variable in the exponent? We could use a calculator to find various powers of 1.02 and estimate the value of $4t$ that makes the expression $(1.02)^{4t}$ close to 2. Since $(1.02)^{35} \approx 2$, $4t \approx 35$, and $t \approx 8.75$. It will be useful to develop a systematic method for solving these exponential equations.

An exponential equation is an equation in which a variable appears in an exponent. An exponential equation can be transformed into a polynomial equation by using either common or natural logarithms.

Example 1 **Solve to the nearest hundredth.** $9^x = 50$

Solution *Take the logarithm of each side.*

$$\log(9^x) = \log 50 \qquad\qquad \ln(9^x) = \ln 50$$
$$x \log 9 = \log 50 \qquad\qquad x \ln 9 = \ln 50$$
$$x = \frac{\log 50}{\log 9} \qquad\qquad x = \frac{\ln 50}{\ln 9}$$
$$\approx \frac{1.6990}{0.9542} \qquad\qquad \approx \frac{3.9120}{2.1972}$$
$$\approx 1.7804 \qquad\qquad \approx 1.7804$$

Answer $\{1.78\}$

Check Since 50 is between 9^1 and 9^2, the answer is reasonable.

Example 2 Solve.

If $1000 is invested at 8% compounded quarterly, in how many years will the investment double?

Solution Use the formula $A = P\left(1 + \dfrac{r}{n}\right)^{nt}$, where A is the amount to which P dollars will grow invested at rate r compounded n times each year for t years.

Substitute.

$$2000 = 1000\left(1 + \frac{0.08}{4}\right)^{4t}$$

Divide both sides by 1000.

$$2 = (1.02)^{4t}$$

Take the logarithm of each side.

$$\log 2 = \log(1.02^{4t})$$
$$\log 2 = 4t \log 1.02$$
$$4t = \frac{\log 2}{\log 1.02}$$
$$4t \approx 35.003$$
$$t \approx 8.7508$$

Answer The computed value of t is slightly greater than 8.75. However, since the interest is compounded at the *end of a quarter,* it will take 9 years for the investment to double.

Example 3 Solve. $25^{2x} = 5^{x^2 - 12}$

Solution *Replace 25 by 5^2.*

$$(5^2)^{2x} = 5^{x^2 - 12}$$
$$5^{4x} = 5^{x^2 - 12}$$
$$4x = x^2 - 12$$
$$x^2 - 4x - 12 = 0$$
$$(x - 6)(x + 2) = 0$$
$$x = 6 \text{ or } x = -2$$

Answer $\{6, -2\}$

Example 4 Solve to the nearest hundredth. $5^{x+2} = 7^{x-2}$

Solution *Take the logarithm of each side.*

$$\ln 5^{x+2} = \ln 7^{x-2}$$
$$(x + 2)\ln 5 = (x - 2)\ln 7$$
$$(x + 2)1.6094 \approx (x - 2)1.9459$$
$$0.3365x \approx 7.1106$$
$$x \approx 21.13$$

Answer $\{21.13\}$

Check (using a calculator) $5^{21.13+2} \stackrel{?}{=} 7^{21.13-2}$

$$1.47 \cdot 10^{16} = 1.47 \cdot 10^{16} \quad \text{It checks.}$$

CLASSROOM EXERCISES

Solve.

1. $7^x = 55$

2. $9^{2x} = 27^{3x-4}$

WRITTEN EXERCISES

A Solve to the nearest hundredth.

1. $7^x = 60$
2. $5^x = 60$
3. $6^{2x} = 300$
4. $4^{3x} = 700$
5. $9^{x-2} = 892$
6. $8^{x-3} = 243$
7. $3^x = 2^{x+1}$
8. $3^{x+1} = 4^x$
9. $e^x = 10^{x-2}$
10. $e^x = 10^{x-3}$
11. $4^{3x+1} = 6^{x+2}$
12. $4^{x+2} = 6^{3x+1}$

Application: Compound Interest

Solve. Use the formula $A = P\left(1 + \dfrac{r}{n}\right)^{nt}$.

13. For how many years must $1000 be invested at 12% compounded annually in order for the investment to grow to $3000?

14. For how many years must $200 be invested at 12% compounded annually in order for the value of the investment to reach $1000?

15. For how many years must $1000 be invested at 12% compounded monthly in order for the value of the investment to reach $3000?

16. For how many years must $200 be left on deposit at 12%, compounded monthly, to grow to $1000?

17. Sancha Gomez invested $1000 for her grandson to use for college expenses. The money was invested for 20 years, compounded annually. What was the interest rate if the value of the investment was $2500 at the end of 20 years?

18. Rich Parsons invested $800, compounded annually, for 20 years for his retirement. What was the interest rate if the value of the investment was $2400 after the 20 years?

19.–20. In exercises 17 and 18, what would be the values of the investment after 30 years?

B Find the coordinates to the nearest tenth of the point at which the graphs intersect.

21. $y = 2^x$
$y = 3^{x-1}$

22. $y = 2^{x-1}$
$y = 3^x$

23. $y = 2^{x-2}$
$y = 3^{1-x}$

24. $y = 2^{x-1}$
$y = 3^{2-x}$

25. $y = 5x$
$y = 2^{x+3}$

26. $y = 6^x$
$y = 3^{x+2}$

Solve these literal equations. Remember that e is the base of the natural logarithms.

27. Solve $y = cx^n$ for n.

28. Solve $y = be^t$ for t.

29. Solve $pV^n = k$ for n.

30. Solve $u = ae^{-bv}$ for v.

31. Solve $\ell = ar^{n-1}$ for n.

32. Solve $S = a\left(\dfrac{1 - r^n}{1 - r}\right)$ for n.

33. Solve $i = Ie^{-\frac{Rt}{L}}$ for t.

34. Solve $i = \left(\dfrac{E}{R}\right)e^{-\frac{t}{RC}}$ for C.

Solve without using logarithm tables.

35. $3^x = 9^{2x-5}$

36. $4^x = 8^{2x+1}$

37. $9^{2x+1} = 27^{x-1}$

38. $3^x \cdot 9^5 = 27^{x+1}$

39. $2^{x^2+1} = 4^{x+2}$

40. $2^{x+2} = 4^{x^2+1}$

41. Write the solution of $5^{x-1} = 3^{2-x}$ in terms of common logarithms.

42. Write the solution of $10^{y+2} = e^{y+4}$ in terms of natural logarithms.

43. Use common logarithms and the quadratic formula to express the solution of $4^{x^2} = 7^{x+2}$.

44. Solve $t^{\log t} = 10,000$.

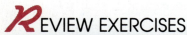

REVIEW EXERCISES

1. Write the equation of the hyperbola with vertices $(8,0)$ and $(-8, 0)$ and foci $(10, 0)$ and $(-10, 0)$. [9-4]

Graph the hyperbola. [9-4]

2. $xy = 9$

3. $\dfrac{x^2}{9} - \dfrac{y^2}{4} = 1$

4. What type of conic is defined by the equation $3y^2 = 2x^2 + 6$? [9-5]

5. Write an equivalent equation for the conic $x^2 - 4x + y^2 = 0$ in standard form. Identify the graph and its characteristics. [9-5]

Solve the system. [9-6]

6. $y = (x + 2)^2$
$x + y = 4$

7. $x^2 + y^2 = 25$
$y - x = 5$

8. The sum of the squares of two numbers is 100. The difference between the numbers is 2. What are the numbers? [9-6]

Logarithmic Equations

Application: Basal Metabolism For various mammals, the following table lists representative weights W in pounds and their basal metabolism M in calories per pound per day.

	Mouse	Guinea pig	Chicken	Cat	Dog	Human	Pig	Cow	Elephant
W	0.045	0.88	4.0	6.2	30	132	370	970	7300
M	72	39	25	23	16	11.4	9.5	5.9	5.5

To help find an equation relating W and M, the *logarithms* of each pair of data are plotted on the graph.

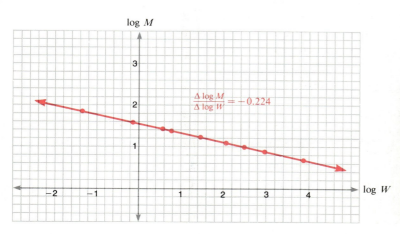

The graph indicates a linear relationship between log M and log W. From the graph we can determine that the slope $\dfrac{(\triangle \log M)}{(\triangle \log W)}$ is -0.224 and the intercept of the vertical axis is 1.55 or log 35.5. Using the slope-intercept form for a linear relationship, we can write

$$\log M = -0.224 \log W + \log 35.5.$$

This logarithmic equation expresses the relationship between the weight and metabolism of any mammal listed in the table.

Equations that involve logarithms of expressions containing variables are called **logarithmic equations.** Logarithmic equations can be solved using properties of equations and properties of logarithms and exponents. One technique for solving a logarithmic equation is to write the equation as an equality of two powers with the same base.

Example 1 **Solve.** $\log_3 (x + 1) + \log_3 (x + 3) = 1$

Solution *Apply the addition property of logarithms.*

$$\log_3 (x + 1)(x + 3) = 1$$

Write each side as a power of 3.

$$3^{\log_3 (x+1)(x+3)} = 3^1$$

Simplify.

$$(x + 1)(x + 3) = 3$$
$$x^2 + 4x + 3 = 3$$
$$x^2 + 4x = 0$$
$$x(x + 4) = 0$$
$$x = 0 \quad \text{or} \quad x = -4$$

The value -4 makes both $x + 1$ and $x + 3$ negative. The domain of the logarithmic function does not include negative numbers.

Answer $\{0\}$ *Check* $\log_3 (0 + 1) + \log_3 (0 + 3) \overset{?}{=} 1$

$$0 + 1 = 1 \qquad \text{It checks.}$$

Another technique for solving a logarithmic equation is to write the equation as an equality of two logarithms with the same base.

Example 2 **Solve.** $\dfrac{\log (7x - 12)}{\log x} = 2$

Solution *Multiply each side by log x.*

$$\log (7x - 12) = 2 \log x$$
$$\log (7x - 12) = \log x^2$$
$$7x - 12 = x^2$$
$$x^2 - 7x + 12 = 0$$
$$(x - 3)(x - 4) = 0$$
$$x = 3 \quad \text{or} \quad x = 4$$

Answer $\{3, 4\}$

Check $\dfrac{\log (7 \cdot 3 - 12)}{\log 3} \overset{?}{=} 2$ $\qquad$ $\dfrac{\log (7 \cdot 4 - 12)}{\log 4} \overset{?}{=} 2$

$\dfrac{\log 9}{\log 3} \overset{?}{=} 2$ $\qquad\qquad$ $\dfrac{\log 16}{\log 4} \overset{?}{=} 2$

$\log 9 \overset{?}{=} 2 \log 3$ $\qquad\qquad$ $\log 16 \overset{?}{=} 2 \log 4$

$\log 9 = \log 3^2 \quad$ It checks. $\qquad$ $\log 16 = \log 4^2 \quad$ It checks.

Example 3   **Solve for x. $y = 4 + \ln x$**

Solution
$$y = 4 + \ln x$$
$$y - 4 = \ln x$$
$$e^{y-4} = x$$
$$x = e^{y-4}$$

Example 4   **Solve to the nearest hundredth. $\log\,(\log x) = -0.4089$**

Solution
$$\log\,(\log x) = -0.4089$$
$$\log x = 10^{-0.4089}$$
$$\log x \approx 0.39$$
$$x \approx 10^{0.39}$$
$$x \approx 2.45$$

Answer $\{2.45\}$

$\mathcal{C}$LASSROOM EXERCISES

Solve.

1. $\log\,(x + 2) = 1$

2. $\log x + \log 2 - 1 = 0$

3. $\dfrac{\log 3x}{\log x} = 2$

4. $\log\,(\log x) = 1$

$\mathcal{W}$RITTEN EXERCISES

 Solve.

1. $\log_4 (x - 5) = 1$

2. $\log_3 (x - 4) = 1$

3. $\log_6 (2x + 3) = 2$

4. $\log_5 (3x - 2) = 2$

5. $\log_3 (2x + 5) = \log_3 (4x - 2)$

6. $\log_4 (3x + 5) = \log_4 (x + 8)$

7. $\log_2 (x - 4) + \log_2 (x - 2) = 3$

8. $\log_2 (x - 3) + \log_2 (x - 5) = 3$

9. $2 \log_7 x = \log_7 (6x - 8)$

10. $2 \log_5 x = \log_5 (7x - 12)$

11. $\dfrac{\log 8}{\log x} = 3$

12. $\dfrac{\log 64}{\log x} = 3$

13. $\log\,(\log x) = 0$

14. $\log\,(\log x) = \log 2$

15. $\log\,(\log x) = \log 3$

16. $\log\,(\log x) = -1$

Solve for c.

17. $\log c = a$

18. $\log c = r$

19. $\log c + \log 2 = s$

20. $\log c + \log 3 = t$

21. $\log c - \log a = d$

22. $\log c - \log p = q$

23. $\ln c = a$

24. $\ln c = r$

25. $\ln c = 2 + j$

Complete.

26. If $\ln V = \ln l + w + \ln h$, express V in terms of l, w, and h.
27. If $\log n = 4 \log r - \log s$, express n in terms of r and s.
28. If $\log s = \log g + 2 \log t - \log 2$, express s in terms of g and t.
29. If $\log A = \log 4 + \log \pi + 2 \log r$, express A in terms of π and r.

$\mathcal{A}$pplication: Total Cost

The total cost C in dollars of producing n products at a factory is given by the equation $C = 500 + 100 \log (n + 10)$.

Find the cost of producing the given number of products.

30. 0   31. 1   32. 90   33. 100
34. 900   35. 1000   36. 180   37. 200

38. Does the cost vary directly as the number of products produced?
39. Does the cost vary directly as the logarithm of the number of products produced?
40. How many products can be produced for $800?
41. State the equation, without logarithms, that relates the metabolism M to the weight W in the introduction to this section.

$\mathcal{A}$pplication: Speed of Telegraphic Signals

The speed of signals s in a submarine telegraphic cable is given by the formula $s = \left(\dfrac{r}{t}\right)^2 \log \left(\dfrac{t}{r}\right)$, where r is the radius of the core of the cable and t is the thickness of the covering of the cable.

Given the following values of t and r, find s.

42. $t = \dfrac{1}{2}$ and $r = \dfrac{1}{20}$ 43. $t = \dfrac{1}{4}$ and $r = \dfrac{1}{20}$

44. $t = \dfrac{1}{8}$ and $r = \dfrac{1}{20}$

45. Assume that the radius of the core remains constant at $\dfrac{1}{20}$ and that the thickness of the covering continues to decrease. At what value of t is the speed of the signal equal to 0? How does this value compare to the value of the radius r?

46. Use your answers to Exercises 42–45 to graph values of s and t for $0.05 \le t \le 1$. Use your graph to describe how the speed of the signal is affected by the thickness of the covering.

47. Solve $x^{\log x} = \dfrac{100}{x}$.   48. Solve $n = 10 \log \left(\dfrac{I_1}{I_2}\right)$ for I_1.

REVIEW EXERCISES

1. Write the polynomial $(x + 2)(3x - 5)$ in standard form.   [10-1]
2. Use synthetic substitution to evaluate $f(2)$ if $f(x) = x^3 - 2x^2 - 3x + 4$.   [10-1]
3. Use synthetic division to divide $x^3 - 6x^2 + 13x - 10$ by $x - 2$.   [10-2]
4. Use synthetic division to determine whether $x + 1$ is a factor of the polynomial $2x^4 + 2x^3 + x^2 - 2x - 3$.   [10-2]

Self-Quiz 3

Solve.

11-6   **1.** $e^{x^2} - 55 = 0$ **2.** $4^{x-1} = 20$ **3.** $3^{x^2} \cdot 9^{2x} = 243$

     4. If \$1000 is invested at 8.1% compounded annually, how many years does it take the investment to double in amount? [*Remember:* $A = P\left(1 + \dfrac{r}{n}\right)^{nt}$.]

11-7   **5.** $\log_6 (x + 3) - \log_6 (x - 2) = 1$ **6.** $2 \log (x - 4) = \log (28 - 4x)$

     7. Solve $\log c + \log t = 2$ for c.

     8. The total cost in dollars of producing n products is given by the formula $C = 200 + 50 \log (n + 20)$. If the total cost was \$300, how many products were produced?

EXTENSION   Using Logarithms

One test of newly designed super computers is to have the computer search for large prime numbers. In 1980, a computer found that $2^{44,494} - 1$ is prime. At that time this was the largest known prime. Logarithms can be used to approximate that number.

Let $2^{44,497} = m \times 10^c$ where m is a real number between 1 and 10 and c is an integer.

Then $44,497 \cdot \log 2 = \log m + c \cdot \log 10 = \log m + c$

$$13,394.9317 \approx \log m + c$$

$$c = 13,394 \text{ and } \log m \approx 0.9317$$

$$m \approx 8.545$$

So, $2^{44,947} - 1 \approx 8.545 \cdot 10^{13,394}$ This number has 13,395 digits.

In 1985, an even larger prime number was found during testing of a new Cray super computer. The number is $2^{216,091} - 1$. Approximate this prime number by the above technique.

Problem Solving: Growth and Decay

Exponential functions are used to describe growth in which the rate of change is not constant. Interest on bank accounts, radioactive decay, biological growth, and the spread of infectious diseases are examples of growth in which the amount of change depends on the amount of material present.

The equation that describes these processes of growth is

$$P = P_0 e^{kt},$$

where P is the population at time t, P_0 is the initial population, and k is a constant for the particular growth situation.

If $k > 0$, the equation represents **exponential growth** that begins slowly but increases rapidly with time.

Exponential Growth

$$P = P_0 e^{kt}, k > 0$$

If $k < 0$, the equation represents **exponential decay** (negative growth) that begins rapidly but decreases slowly with time.

Exponential Decay

$$P = P_0 e^{kt}, k < 0$$

Exponential Growth

$$P = P_0 e^{kt}, k > 0$$

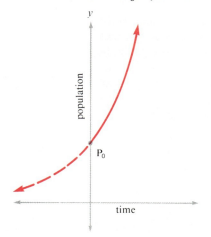

Exponential Decay

$$P = P_0 e^{kt}, k < 0$$

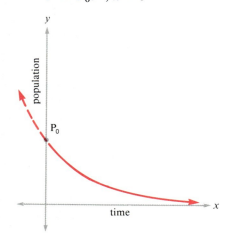

An example of exponential growth is compounding interest instantaneously. The formula for compound interest is $A = P\left(1 + \dfrac{r}{n}\right)^{nt}$. Consider what happens to A as n (the number of compounding periods in a year) increases. Let P, r, and t each equal 1 in order to concentrate on the effect of n as it increases in value.

$$A = \left(1 + \frac{1}{n}\right)^n$$

As n increases, the value of the expression on the right side of the equation approaches the irrational number e. (See page 460.) When n becomes infinitely large, we say that the interest is **compounded instantaneously** or **compounded continuously**.

In general for principal P, rate r, and time t, the value of A when interest is compounded instantaneously is given by the formula $A = Pe^{rt}$.

Example 1   Solve.

When Rachel Roberts was born eighteen years ago, her grandparents deposited $4000, compounded instantaneously, in a savings account to help pay for her college expenses. If there is now $12,000 in the account, what rate of interest has the money been earning?

Solution

	$A = Pe^{rt}$
Substitute in the formula.	$12{,}000 = 4000e^{18r}$
Divide each side by 4000.	$3 = e^{18r}$
Take the natural logarithm of each side.	$\ln 3 = \ln e^{18r}$
	$\ln 3 = 18r$
Use a calculator or table to find $\ln 3$.	$1.0986 \approx 18r$
	$r \approx 0.061$

Answer   The money has been earning interest at the rate of 6.1% per year.

An example of exponential decay is radioactive decay. Atoms of radioactive isotopes are not stable. Over time, they emit radiation and change to different atoms. For example, in three years, half the atoms in 100 g of polonium-208 (that is, polonium with atomic mass number 208) disintegrate, leaving 50 g of polonium-208 and 50 g of lead-204. Half the remaining 50 g of polonium will further disintegrate after three more years. In each three-year period the amount of radioactive material is reduced by one half. Therefore, this material is said to have a three-year **half-life.**

A general formula for radioactive decay is

$$N = N_0 e^{-kt},$$

where N is the amount of material at the end of a time period, N_0 is the amount of material at the beginning of the time period, k is a constant unique to the material, and t is the time.

Example 2   Solve.

For a particular radioactive material, 300 g of the material will decay to 150 g in 2 years. Find the value of k for this material.

Solution

Substitute in the formula.	$N = N_0 e^{-kt}$
	$150 = 300 e^{-2k}$
Divide by 300.	$0.5 = e^{-2k}$
Take the natural logarithm of each side.	$\ln 0.5 = -2k$
Use a calculator or table to solve.	$0.6931 \approx 2k$
	$k \approx 0.347$

Answer   The value of k for the given material is about 0.347.

LASSROOM EXERCISES

Find the value of k in the formula $R = Se^{kt}$ given the following values of R, S, and t.

1. $R = 300$, $S = 75$, $t = 5$
2. $R = 75$, $S = 300$, $t = 5$

3. State whether a growth or decay situation is described in Exercises 1 and 2.

WRITTEN EXERCISES

A Use the formula $A = Pe^{rt}$ to find the amount A if $1000 is invested at the given rate for the given period of time.

1. 10% for 5 years   **2.** 12% for 6 years   **3.** 20% for 5 years

4. 24% for 6 years   **5.** 10% for 10 years   **6.** 12% for 12 years

Find the principal P if the value of the investment A is $1000 after being compounded instantaneously under the given conditions.

7. 10% for 5 years   **8.** 12% for 5 years

9. 10% for 20 years   **10.** 12% for 20 years

For each given rate, find the number of years (t) it takes for an investment to double its value.

11. 8%   **12.** 9%   **13.** 12%   **14.** 18%

Use the formula $N = N_0 e^{-kt}$ to find the value of k for these substances.

15. 100 g remain from 500 g of a substance after 50 years

16. 100 g remain from 500 g of a substance after 100 years

17. 450 g remain from 500 g of a substance after 100 years

18. 450 g remain from 500 g of a substance after 50 years

*A*pplications

The value V of an object that depreciates 10% each year can be found using the formula $V = V_0(0.9)^t$, where V_0 is the value when $t = 0$, and t is the number of years.

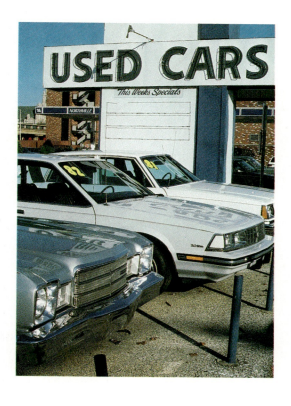

Solve.

19. After how many years will a $500 object have a depreciated value of less than $250?

20. After how many years will an $800 object have a depreciated value of less than $200?

21. After how many years will a $500 object have a depreciated value of less than $50?

22. After how many years will an $800 object have a depreciated value of less than $8?

B **23.** The temperature of a body surrounded by a medium at a different temperature is given by the equation

$$T = T_0 e^{kt}.$$

Where T_0 is the initial difference in temperatures, T is the difference in temperatures at time t hours, and k is a constant depending on various physical factors and units. During a power failure, a freezer originally at $-10°$ F begins to warm up in a room at $80°$ F. How long will it take the temperature in the freezer to reach $32°$ F? (Assume that $k = -0.0342$.)

24. According to Halley's law, the atmospheric pressure P in inches of mercury is related to the height h in miles above sea level by the equation $P = 29.92e^{-\frac{h}{5}}$. At what height will the pressure become 18.5 in. of mercury?

25. A vacuum pump can remove 2% of the gas contained in a chamber with each stroke. If the pump makes one stroke every 2 s, how long will it take the pump to remove 95% of the gas present in the chamber? Use the formula $P = P_0 e^{-kt}$.

26. An overweight person (110-kg mass) decides to go on a diet. Assume that the formula $M = M_0(0.9)^t$ holds, where M is the person's mass after t months of dieting and M_0 is the mass at $t = 0$.

    a. What is the dieter's mass after one month?

    b. How many months must the dieter stay on the diet in order to get below 75 kg?

$\mathcal{A}$pplication: Population Growth or Decay

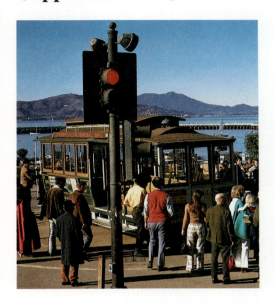

A population growing at a constant rate is described by the formula

$$P = P_0(1 + r)^t,$$

where P is the population after t decades, P_0 is the population at time 0, and r is the rate of growth per decade expressed as a decimal.

Solve.

27. Between 1970 and 1980, California grew at the rate of 18.5% per decade. Estimate and predict the population in California in 1980 and 1990 if its population in 1970 was about 20,000,000. (Assume a constant rate of growth.)

28. Recently, an ecological disaster occurred in the North Sea, A rise in water temperature and a heavy concentration of pollutants caused a blue-green algae to spread over a 60-mile-long area killing marine life. If the algae doubled every 20 hours, then what was its rate of growth per hour? (Use the formula given in Exercise 27.)

[C] 29. The formula $D = D_0 b^t$ gives the relationship between a cooling object and the time it has been cooling, where:

D = the difference between the temperature of the object being cooled and the temperature of the medium surrounding it;

D_0 = the value of D when $t = 0$;

t = the number of units of time; and

b = a constant that depends on the object's material and shape.

The temperature of a metal ball is 160° C. The ball is left to cool in a room where the temperature is 23°C.

a. What is the value of D_0?

b. After one minute, the temperature of the ball is 146°C. What is the value of b rounded to the nearest hundredth?

c. What is the temperature of the ball after 5 min?

𝒜 pplication: Radioactive Carbon Dating

Professor Willard Libby of the University of California at Los Angeles was awarded the Nobel prize in chemistry for discovering a method of determining the date of death of a once-living object. Living tissue contains two kinds of carbon atoms, radioactive carbon A and stable carbon B, and the ratio of A to B is approximately constant. When an organism dies, the law of natural radioactive decay applies to A. By comparing the amounts of A and B in a sample of a once-living object, a chemist can determine what percent of the carbon A has decayed. The length of time it takes half of an amount of material to decay is called the half-life of the material. Knowing that the half-life of carbon A is 5500 years, the chemist can determine how long the object has been dead.

30. The formula for radioactive decay is $N = N_0 e^{-kt}$.

   a. Show that the time of half-life (time for half of the material to decay) is $\dfrac{0.6931}{k}$.

   b. If 3% of a certain radioactive element decays in 1 h, determine its half-life.

31. It is determined that the amount of radioactive isotope of carbon in a piece of charcoal is only 15% of its original amount and that the half-life of that isotope is 5500 years. When did the tree from which the charcoal came die?

32. The present size of a colony of bacteria at time t is related to the initial size of the colony when $t = 0$ by the formula $N = N_0 e^{kt}$. If there are 1000 bacteria present initially and the number increases by 20% every half hour, how many bacteria will be present after 24 hours? [*Hint:* First solve for k to the nearest 0.001.]

𝑅 EVIEW EXERCISES

1. Locate the roots of the equation $2x^3 - x^2 - 10x + 5 = 0$ between consecutive integers. [10-4]

2. Sketch a graph of a third-degree function f that meets these conditions: the roots of $f(x) = 0$ are -1, 1, and 2; $f(0) = -2$. [10-4]

3. Let $f(x) = \dfrac{1}{x}$, $x \neq 0$. Does f have an inverse f^{-1}? [10-5]

HAPTER SUMMARY

▶ **Vocabulary**

▶ Definition of an exponential function   [11-1]

For all real numbers x and for all positive real numbers b, $b \neq 1$, the equation $y = b^x$ defines an exponential function with base b.

▶ f is an *increasing* function if, for each a and b in the domain of f, whenever   [11-1]
$a > b$, $f(a) > f(b)$. f is a *decreasing* function if for each a and b in the domain of f, whenever $a > b$, $f(a) < f(b)$.

▶ The Equality Property of Exponential Functions   [11-1]

For all positive real numbers b, $b \neq 1$, $b^x = b^y$ if and only if $x = y$.

▶ Definition of a logarithmic function   [11-2]

For all positive real numbers x and b, $b \neq 1$, there is a real number y such that $y = \log_b x$ if and only if $x = b^y$.

▶ Properties of Logarithmic Functions   [11-2,
                                                                             11-3]
For all positive real numbers b, $b \neq 1$, and all admissible real values of x, y, m, and n:

   I. If $\log_b x = \log_b y$, then $x = y$

  II. $\log_b b^x = x$

 III. $b^{\log_b x} = x$, $x > 0$

 IV. $\log_b b = 1$

  V. $\log_b 1 = 0$

 VI. $\log_b (mn) = \log_b m + \log_b n$.

VII. $\log_b \left(\dfrac{m}{n}\right) = \log_b m - \log_b n$.

VIII. $\log_b (m^n) = n(\log_b m)$

▶ The Change-of-Base Theorem

[11-5]

For all positive real numbers a and b (except 1) and any positive real number x,

$$\log_a x = \frac{\log_b x}{\log_b a}.$$

▶ The Compound-Interest Formula: $A = P\left(1 + \dfrac{r}{n}\right)^{nt}.$

[11-6]

▶ The Formula for Exponential Growth: $P = P_0 e^{kt}, \ k > 0.$

[11-8]

▶ The Formula for Exponential Decay: $P = P_0 e^{kt}, \ k < 0.$

$\mathcal{C}$HAPTER REVIEW

11-1   **Objective:**   To graph exponential functions.

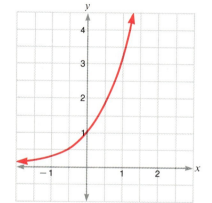

1. Graph $y = 2^x$ and $y = \left(\dfrac{1}{2}\right)^x$ for $\{x: -3 \leqslant x \leqslant 3\}$ on the same set of axes.

2. Copy the given graph of $y = 3^x$.

   Sketch the graph of $y = 3^{x-2}$ on the same set of axes.

Objective: To solve simple exponential equations.

3. Use the graph in Question 2 to estimate the solutions.

   a. $3^{-1.5} = y$ **b.** $3^x = 4$

4. Solve.

   a. $5^x = \dfrac{1}{25}$ **b.** $2^{x+2} = 8$

11-2   **Objective:**   To rewrite an equation in exponential form as an equation in logarithmic form and vice versa.

5. Write in logarithmic form.

   a. $7^5 = 16,807$ **b.** $81 = \left(\dfrac{1}{3}\right)^{-4}$

6. Write in exponential form.

   a. $\log_{10} 398 = 2.6$ **b.** $\log_{25} 5 = \dfrac{1}{2}$

Objective: To solve simple logarithmic equations.

Solve.

7. $\log_3 x = 4$ **8.** $\log_x 9 = 2$ **9.** $x = \log_5 \sqrt[3]{5}$

Objective: To recognize characteristics of the graph of a logarithmic function.

Let $y = \log_b x$ be the equation of a logarithmic function. True or false?

10. The domain of x is the set of real numbers.

11. The value of b must be a positive real number not equal to 1.

12. The logarithm of a number is always positive.

13. The graph of $y = \log_b x$ passes through the point $(0, 1)$.

11-3 **Objective:** To use properties of logarithms to simplify or evaluate expressions.

14. Given $\log_8 4 \approx 0.6667$ and $\log_8 12 \approx 1.1950$, find the following.

    a. $\log_8 3$ **b.** $\log_8 \sqrt{12}$

Write in expanded form. Simplify when possible.

15. $\log_b \left(\dfrac{x}{yz} \right)$ **16.** $\log (100w^3)$

Objective: To use properties of logarithms to solve logarithmic equations.

Solve for x.

17. $\log_4 x + 2 \log_4 9 = \log_4 27$ **18.** $\log_7 7^{x+1} = 3$

11-4 **Objective:** To use a table of common logarithms to simplify or evaluate expressions.

19. What is the difference between $\log 623$ and $\log 6.23$?

Use the tables on page 769 to solve for x.

20. $x = \log 49.2$ **21.** $\log x = 0.6721$ **22.** $x = 10^{2.1761}$

11-5 **Objective:** To use a table of natural logarithms to simplify or evaluate expressions.

Use the tables on page 770 to solve for x.

23. $\ln 3.4 = x$ **24.** $\ln x = 1.1442$

25. Write an expression for $\log_4 25$ in terms of natural logarithms.

11-6 **Objective:** To solve exponential equations.

Solve.

26. $5^x = 40$ **27.** $8^{2x} = 16^{x+1}$

28. Solve $s = k \cdot 3^t$ for t.

29. Find the number of years it will take at an annual inflation rate of 20% for an $80,000 house to triple in value.

11-7 Objective: To solve logarithmic equations.

Solve.

30. $3 \log_4 (x - 1) = \log_4 64$

31. $\dfrac{\log x^2}{\log x} = 1$

32. Solve $\ln P = \ln (P_0 \, e^{rt})$ for t.

11-8 Objective: To solve problems that are applications of exponential (logarithmic) growth or decay.

Solve.

33. For how many years must $1000 be compounded continuously at 11% to grow to $10,000?

34. The half-life of a radioactive element is the time required for half of the material to disintegrate into another element. If radium-226 decays according to the equation $A = A_0 e^{-0.000428t}$, where A_0 is the original amount, A is the amount of radioactive material remaining at time t, and t is the number of years, determine the half-life of radium-226.

$\mathcal{C}$HAPTER 11 Self-Test

11-1
1. a. State the domain and range of the exponential function $y = a^x$, $a > 0$.

b. Is y an increasing or decreasing function?

2. Sketch the graph of $y = 2^x$.

3. Between what two consecutive integers does x lie if $5^x = 72$?

11-2
4. Express $64^{\frac{1}{3}} = 4$ in logarithmic form.

5. Express $\log_6 \dfrac{1}{36} = -2$ in exponential form.

Solve.

6. $7^{\log_7 4} = x$

7. $\log_4 x = \dfrac{3}{2}$

11-3 **Given $\log_5 3 \approx 0.6826$ and $\log_5 6 \approx 1.1133$, find the following.**

8. a. $\log_5 2$

b. $\log_5 9$

9. Solve $\log_4 x = \log_4 5 - \log_4 20$.

10. Write $\log_b \dfrac{xy}{z^2}$ in expanded form.

11-4 **Use the tables on page 769 to find x.**

11. $\log 452 = x$

12. $\log x = 1.9009$

13. Given ln 1.2 $\approx$ 0.1823, find ln (1.44e). [*Hint:* $(1.2)^2 = 1.44$.]

14. Write an expression for $\log_8 24$ in terms of base-10 logarithms.

Solve.

15. $4^{x+1} = 8^x$

16. For how many years must $5000 be invested at 4%, compounded annually, in order to double in amount?

17. Solve $y = 4 + \ln x$ for x.   **18.** Solve: $\dfrac{\log 64}{\log x} = 2$.

19. The World Future Society indicates that the number of robots is increasing by 30% per year. They predict that there will be about 35,000 installed robots in 6 years. Use the formula $P = P_0(1 + r)^t$, where P_0 is the present amount, r is the constant growth rate per year, and t is the time in years, to find how many robots there are now.

20. Half of the original 200 g of a radioactive element remains undecayed after 3 h. If the element decays according to the equation $N = N_0 e^{kt}$, where N_0 is the original amount of the element present and t is time in hours, find the constant k.

$\mathcal{P}$RACTICE FOR COLLEGE ENTRANCE TESTS

Choose the best answer to each question.

1. If $f(x) = 10^{2x-3}$, then $f(3) = $ __?__ .

   A. 10   **B.** 100   **C.** 1000   **D.** 10,000   **E.** 100,000

2. If $b > 0$ and $b \neq 1$, then the graph of the function $y = \log_b x$ must contain which point?

   A. (1,0)   **B.** (0, 1)   **C.** (1, 1)   **D.** (b, 0)   **E.** (0, b)

3. If $0 < b < 1$, then the function $y = b^x$ is __?__ .

   A. increasing for all x

   B. decreasing for all x

   C. decreasing for $x < 0$ and increasing for $x > 0$

   D. increasing for $x < 0$ and decreasing for $x > 0$

   E. constant

4. If x and y are integers and $\log_3 81 = 2^x 3^y$, then $xy = $ __?__ .

   A. 0   **B.** 1   **C.** 2   **D.** 3   **E.** 4

5. If $2^{-x} = \left(\dfrac{1}{16}\right)$, then $\log_2 x = $ __?__ .

   A. 0   **B.** 1   **C.** 2   **D.** 3   **E.** 4

6. If $9^{2x} = 27$, then $x = \underline{\ ?\ }$.

   A. $\dfrac{2}{3}$ **B.** $\dfrac{3}{4}$ **C.** $\dfrac{4}{3}$ **D.** $\dfrac{3}{2}$ **E.** $\dfrac{9}{4}$

7. If $10^x = 100^{x+1}$, then $x = \underline{\ ?\ }$.

   A. -2 **B.** -1 **C.** 0 **D.** 1 **E.** 2

8. $\log_5 \sqrt[3]{5} = \underline{\ ?\ }$.

   A. $-\dfrac{1}{3}$ **B.** $-\dfrac{1}{5}$ **C.** $\dfrac{1}{5}$ **D.** $\dfrac{1}{3}$ **E.** $\dfrac{3}{5}$

9. If $2^x + 2^x + 2^x + 2^x = 2^k$, then $x = \underline{\ ?\ }$.

   A. $\dfrac{k}{2}$ **B.** $2k$ **C.** $k + 2$ **D.** $2 - k$ **E.** $k - 2$

10. If for all x, $f(x) = a^x$ and $f(x - 2) = \dfrac{1}{a}$, then $x = \underline{\ ?\ }$.

   A. -3 **B.** -2 **C.** -1 **D.** 1 **E.** 2

11. If $\ln 3 \approx 1.1$, then $\ln 81 \approx \underline{\ ?\ }$.

   A. 1.2 **B.** 1.5 **C.** 2.2 **D.** 3.3 **E.** 4.4

12. If $\log 2 \approx 0.301$, then $\log 50 \approx \underline{\ ?\ }$.

   A. 1.091 **B.** 1.301 **C.** 1.505 **D.** 1.699 **E.** 1.903

13. If $f(x) = (x - 2)^2$, which of the following could be the graph of $f(-x)$?

   A. 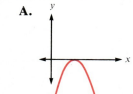   **B.** 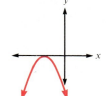   **C.**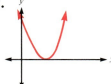

   D.    **E.**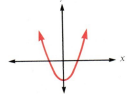

CHAPTER 12

Sequences and Series

Many natural objects have spiral shapes. There are spirals in the seeds in the head of a sunflower, in the scales of a pine cone, and in the webs of some spiders. Most galaxies of the universe are spirals. The spiral in the chambered nautilus is a logarithmic spiral.

A logarithmic spiral can be generated by rotating a ray about its vertex and moving a point along the ray away from the vertex. As the amount of rotation increases in an arithmetic sequence and the distance of the point from the vertex increases in an exponential sequence, the moving point traces a logarithmic spiral as shown.

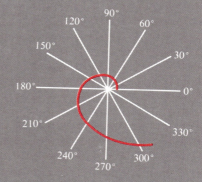

LESSON 12-1

Sequences

A Counting Problem Suppose that a pair of rabbits develops from birth to maturity in one month. At maturity, a pair of rabbits can produce another pair of rabbits in another month. Each new pair matures and then produces young pairs at the same rate as the older pair, while the older pair continues to produce a pair of new rabbits each month. If no rabbits die, this table shows the number of pairs of rabbits at the beginning of each month.

Month	1	2	3	4	5	6	7
Pairs of rabbits at beginning of month	1	1	2	3	5	8	13

The numbers of pairs of rabbits in the table above form a **sequence.**

Definition: Sequence

A *sequence* is a function defined on the positive integers or on a subset of consecutive positive integers starting with 1.

The first seven number pairs above can be listed as this sequence.

$$\{(1, 1), (2, 1), (3, 2), (4, 3), (5, 5), (6, 8), (7, 13)\}$$

However, usually only the second components of the pairs are listed as the sequence:

$$1, 1, 2, 3, 5, 8, 13$$

The numbers in the sequence are called **terms** of the sequence. The first term is 1, and the sixth term is 8. The terms of a sequence can be denoted using a sequence variable and subscripts.

$$t_1, t_2, t_3, t_4, \ldots, t_n$$

A sequence that has a last term is called a **finite sequence.** A sequence that does not have a last term is called an **infinite sequence.** The **ellipsis,** ". . .", is often used to show that a sequence is infinite.

Finite sequences	*Infinite sequences*
1, 3, 5, 7, 9	1, 3, 5, 7, . . .
2, 4, 8, 16, 32, 64, 128	2, 4, 8, 16, . . .
t_1, t_2, t_3, t_4	$t_1, t_2, t_3, \ldots$

Listing the terms of an infinite sequence and using the ellipsis ". . ." to indicate that "the pattern continues" assumes that both the writer and the reader identify the same pattern. To avoid possible ambiguity, an **explicit definition** is used to state the relationship between a term t_n of a sequence and the number n of that term. For example, "$t_n = 2n - 1$ for each positive integer n" is an explicit definition of a sequence.

Example 1 State the 1st, 2nd, 3rd, and 24th terms of the sequence $t_n = 2n - 1$.

Solution $t = 2n - 1$ $t_1 = 2(1) - 1 = 1$ $t_3 = 2(3) - 1 = 5$

$\qquad\qquad\qquad\qquad\quad t_2 = 2(2) - 1 = 3 \qquad t_{24} = 2(24) - 1 = 47$

Answer   The first three terms are 1, 3, and 5. The 24th term is 47.

In the following sequence, the difference of successive terms is constant. The **constant difference** d is 3.

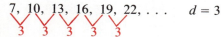

$$7,\ 10,\ 13,\ 16,\ 19,\ 22,\ \ldots \qquad d = 3$$

differences   3   3   3   3   3

A sequence with a constant difference is called an **arithmetic sequence** (or **arithmetic progression**).

Arithmetic sequence	*Constant difference*
$0, \dfrac{1}{2}, 1, \dfrac{3}{2}, 2, \dfrac{5}{2}, 3, \ldots$	$\dfrac{1}{2}$
$15, 10, 5, 0, -5, -10, \ldots$	-5

The terms of a general arithmetic sequence can be written using the first term and the constant or **common difference.**

a_1	a_2	a_3	a_4	$\ldots$	a_n
a_1	$a_1 + d$	$a_1 + 2d$	$a_1 + 3d$	$\ldots$	$a_1 + (n - 1)d$

Definition of an Arithmetic Sequence

For each positive integer n, the sequence with first term a_1 and nth term a_n is an arithmetic sequence if and only if $a_n = a_1 + (n - 1)d$.

Example 2 Write the 20th term of the arithmetic sequence 6, 10, 14, 18, ...

Solution
$$a_n = a_1 + (n - 1)d$$
$$a_{20} = 6 + (20 - 1)4 = 6 + (19)4 = 82$$

The terms of an arithmetic sequence that are between two given terms are called **arithmetic means** of the given terms. Consider this sequence:

$$5, 12, 19, 26, 33, \ldots$$

The numbers 12 and 19 are the two arithmetic means between 5 and 26.

A single arithmetic mean between two numbers is called *the* arithmetic mean of the two numbers. The arithmetic mean of two numbers is sometimes called the *average* of the two numbers.

Example 3   **Find the three arithmetic means between 12 and -8.**

Solution   Since there are to be three arithmetic means, let $a_1 = 12$ and $a_5 = -8$. Then a_2, a_3, and a_4 are the three arithmetic means. First, find the difference d between successive terms.

$$a_5 = a_1 + (n - 1)d$$
$$-8 = 12 + (5 - 1)d$$
$$-8 = 12 + 4d$$
$$d = -5$$

Compute the means.
$$a_2 = a_1 + d = 12 + (-5) = 7$$
$$a_3 = a_2 + d = 7 + (-5) = 2$$
$$a_4 = a_3 + d = 2 + (-5) = -3$$

Example 4   **Solve.**

At the end of a year, a certain company gives each of its employees a bonus depending on the number of years the employee has worked for the company. First-year employees are given $500. Employees with more than one year of service are given $500 plus 4% (of $500) for each additional year of service. What is the year-end bonus for an employee who has worked for the company for 7 years?

Solution   The year-end bonuses form an arithmetic sequence with $a_1 = 500$ and $d = 0.04(500) = 20$, and we are to find the 7th term.

$$a_n = a_1 + (n - 1)d$$
$$a_7 = 500 + (7 - 1)20$$
$$= 620$$

Answer   The bonus for a 7-year employee is $620.

*C*LASSROOM EXERCISES

State the 1st and 15th terms of each sequence.

1. $t_n = 3n + 1$

2. $t_n = \sqrt[n]{n}$

3. $t_n = \dfrac{n}{n + 2}$

State whether each of the following sequences is an arithmetic sequence. If it is, state the common difference d.

4. $a_n = -2n + 5$

5. $a_n = n^2$

6. $a_n = 4n + 1$

7. Find the 15th term of the arithmetic sequence $-3, 1, 5, 9, \ldots$.

8. Find the three arithmetic means between 5 and 15.

 RITTEN EXERCISES

A State the 1st and 10th terms of each sequence.

1. $t_n = 5n$

2. $t_n = -2n + 1$

3. $t_n = 2n^2$

4. $t_n = n^3$

5. 2, 4, 6, 8, . . .

6. 12, 9, 6, 3, . . .

7. 1, 4, 9, 16, . . .

8. 1, 2, 4, 8, . . .

State whether each of the following sequences is an arithmetic sequence.

9. 3, 6, 12, 24, . . .

10. 2, 6, 18, 54, . . .

11. 3, 6, 9, 12, . . .

12. 2, 6, 10, 14, . . .

13. $\frac{1}{2}, \frac{2}{3}, \frac{3}{4}, \frac{4}{5}, \ldots$

14. $\frac{1}{2}, \frac{2}{3}, \frac{5}{6}, 1, \ldots$

15. $a_n = -4n + 10$

16. $a_n = -5n + 20$

Find the indicated term for each arithmetic sequence.

17. $a_n = 27 + 5n; a_{10}$

18. $a_n = 5 + 27n; a_{10}$

19. $a_n = -5 + 0.2n; a_{100}$

20. $a_n = -3 + 0.1n; a_{100}$

21. $a_n = -2n + 50; a_{20}$

22. $a_n = -3n + 500; a_{30}$

23. 5, 6, 7, 8, . . . ; a_{100}

24. $-17, -16, -15, -14, \ldots ; a_{100}$

25. 7, 10, 13, 16, . . . ; a_{15}

26. 5, 9, 13, 17, . . . ; a_{15}

27. 27, 25, 23, 21, . . . ; a_{25}

28. 35, 32, 29, 26, . . . ; a_{25}

Write the first three terms of the arithmetic sequence containing the given terms.

29. $a_4 = 7$ and $a_6 = 15$

30. $a_4 = 13$ and $a_6 = 23$

31. $a_8 = -20$ and $a_{11} = -26$

32. $a_8 = -11$ and $a_{11} = -17$

Find the arithmetic mean between the given numbers.

33. $-8, 10$

34. $-12, 4$

35. 58, 72

36. 83, 95

Find the three arithmetic means between the given numbers.

37. 20, 32

38. 13, 21

39. $-2, -3$

40. $-4, -6$

*A*pplications

Use arithmetic sequences to answer the following questions.

41. In a game of Zonko, Concetta started with 6 points, and then she lost $\frac{1}{2}$ point each play for 10 straight plays. What was her score after 10 plays?

42. At the beginning of the year, Scott could jog 6 laps. He was able to increase the amount by 2 laps each week. How many laps could he jog after 12 weeks?

Complete.

43. Customers entering a store were given a ticket with a number. The first customer got number 0214, the second customer got 0216, the third customer 0218, and so on. The numbers on the tickets formed an arithmetic sequence.

    a. If the sequence continues, what number will the 10th customer get?

    b. What is a_{48}?

    c. Which customer got ticket number 0400?

    d. If the last customer got ticket number 1664, how many customers entered the store?

Write an expression for the nth term of each of the following arithmetic sequences.

44. 2, 5, 8, 11, . . .   45. 3, 7, 11, 15, . . .   46. 7, 4, 1, −2, . . .

For each arithmetic sequence, find the requested information.

47. 7, 10, 13, 16, . . .

    a. What is a_{200}?

    b. Which term of the sequence is 967?

    c. Which term of the sequence is 1966?

    d. Write the equation in slope-intercept form that relates n and a_n.

48. The 10th and 12th terms of an arithmetic sequence are 11 and 14, respectively.

    a. What is d?

    b. What is a_1?

    c. What is a_{234}?

    d. How many terms of the sequence are negative?

49. The 100th and 200th terms of an arithmetic sequence are 83 and 103, respectively.

    a. What is the first term?

    b. What is a_{150}?

    c. What is a_{345}?

    d. Write the equation in slope-intercept form that relates n and a_n.

50. Gourmet Flora offers you a job with a choice of two salary increase plans. With Plan A, you receive an annual salary of $10,000 and an annual increase of $1000. With Plan B, you receive a semiannual salary of $5000 and a semiannual increase of $250. Which plan should you choose? How much money will you receive over five years for each of the plans?

51. The 25th term of an arithmetic sequence is 100. The $(25 + p)$-term of the sequence is $(100 + q)$.

   a. What is d in the sequence?

   b. What is a_1?

   c. Write the equation in slope-intercept form that relates n and a_n.

   d. What is a_{26}?

52. Seven equally-spaced, vertical supports are required in the construction of a ski ramp. The lengths of the shortest and longest supports must be 1 ft and 5 ft, respectively. What are the lengths of the other supports?

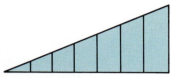

53. Show that an arithmetic progression is part of a linear function. State the slope and vertical-axis intercept.

*R*EVIEW EXERCISES

Solve.   [8-1,

   1. $(x - 3)^2 = 5$ **2.** $x^2 = 2x + 5$ 8-2]

Simplify.   [8-3,

   3. $(2i)^3$ **4.** $|3 - 4i|$ **5.** $(4 - 3i) - (5 + 6i)$ 8-4,

                                                                                                      8-5]
   6. $(6 + 2i)(3 - i)$ **7.** $\dfrac{(1 + i)}{(1 - i)}$

   8. State the number and kind of roots for $x^2 + 6x + 6 = 0$.   [8-6]

   9. Solve: $x^4 - 2x^2 - 3 = 0$.   [8-6]

---

*C*ALCULATOR EXTENSION   Infinite Sequences

We have defined x^0 as 1 $(x \neq 0)$. With the calculator you can do computations that support the definition. For example, start with any positive number x and repeatedly compute the square root.

$$x \; \boxed{\sqrt{}} \; \boxed{\sqrt{}} \; \boxed{\sqrt{}} \; \ldots$$

The numbers displayed on the calculator are $x^{\frac{1}{2}}, x^{\frac{1}{4}}, x^{\frac{1}{8}}, x^{\frac{1}{16}}, \ldots$. These numbers approach x^0.

1. Enter the number 2 on a calculator. How many times must you press the square root key to get a display of 1?

2. For what value of x does it take 20 steps for your calculator to display 1?

3. What is the maximum number of steps to display 1 for any number x you can enter on your calculator?

LESSON 12-2

Geometric Sequences

Suppose that a sheet of paper 0.001 in. thick is torn in half and one piece is placed on top of the other. Next, the two pieces are torn in half and the four resulting pieces placed one on top of the other. Then, the four pieces are torn in half and the resulting eight pieces are stacked. If the process of tearing and stacking is continued, the heights of the stacks are given by this sequence:

$$0.001, 0.002, 0.004, 0.008, \ldots$$

In the sequence above, the first term is 0.001. Each term after the first term is two times the preceding term.

$$0.001, \quad 0.002, \quad 0.004, \quad 0.008, \quad 0.016, \ldots$$
$$\times 2 \qquad \times 2 \qquad \times 2 \qquad \times 2$$

This sequence is an example of a **geometric sequence.** In general, a geometric sequence is a sequence in which the ratio of any term to the preceding term is constant. That constant is called the **common ratio.** The common ratio of the geometric sequence above is 2.

The following are examples of other geometric sequences. The first two are finite sequences, and the last is an infinite sequence.

Geometric sequence	Common ratio
$3, -6, 12, -24, 48, -96$	-2
$2, 1, \dfrac{1}{2}, \dfrac{1}{4}, \dfrac{1}{8}, \dfrac{1}{16}, \dfrac{1}{32}$	$\dfrac{1}{2}$
$4, 20, 100, 500, 2500, \ldots$	5

The terms of the general geometric sequence whose first term is a_1, with a common ratio r, are

$$a_1, a_1 r, a_1 r^2, a_1 r^3, \ldots, a_1 r^{n-1}.$$

Using the notation above, we can now state a definition of a geometric sequence.

Definition of a Geometric Sequence

For each positive integer n, and for each real number r, $r \neq 0$, the sequence with first term a_1 and nth term a_n is a geometric sequence if and only if $a_n = a_1 r^{n-1}$.

Example 1   Write the first four terms of this sequence.

$$a_n = 6\left(-\frac{1}{2}\right)^{n-1} \text{ for each positive integer } n$$

Solution $a_1 = 6\left(-\frac{1}{2}\right)^{1-1} = 6\left(-\frac{1}{2}\right)^0 = 6 \cdot 1 = 6$

$a_2 = 6\left(-\frac{1}{2}\right)^{2-1} = 6\left(-\frac{1}{2}\right)^1 = 6\left(-\frac{1}{2}\right) = -3$

$a_3 = 6\left(-\frac{1}{2}\right)^{3-1} = 6\left(-\frac{1}{2}\right)^2 = 6\left(\frac{1}{4}\right) = \frac{3}{2}$

$a_4 = 6\left(-\frac{1}{2}\right)^{4-1} = 6\left(-\frac{1}{2}\right)^3 = 6\left(-\frac{1}{8}\right) = -\frac{3}{4}$

Example 2   The first three terms of a geometric sequence are 5, 15, and 45. Find the fourth term.

Solution   Find r by dividing the second term by the first. $r = \frac{a_2}{a_1} = \frac{15}{5} = 3$

$$a_4 = a_3 r = 45(3) = 135$$

The terms of a geometric sequence between two given terms are called the **geometric means** of the two given terms. Therefore, 4 and 8 are the two geometric means of 2 and 16 for the sequence 2, 4, 8, 16.

Example 3   Find the two geometric means between 2 and $-\frac{1}{4}$.

Solution   Let $a_1 = 2$ and $a_4 = -\frac{1}{4}$.

Since $a_4 = a_1 r^3$, solve to find r.

$$-\frac{1}{4} = 2r^3 \quad \text{so} \quad r = -\frac{1}{2}$$

The two geometric means are a_2 and a_3.

$a_2 = a_1\left(-\frac{1}{2}\right) = 2\left(-\frac{1}{2}\right) = -1$ $\qquad$ $a_3 = a_2\left(-\frac{1}{2}\right) = -1\left(-\frac{1}{2}\right) = \frac{1}{2}$

A single geometric mean between two numbers is called the **geometric mean** or the **mean proportional**. For example, if a, b, and c are successive terms of a geometric sequence, then b is the geometric mean of a and c. It follows from the definition of a geometric sequence that

$$\frac{b}{a} = \frac{c}{b} \quad \text{and} \quad b^2 = ac. \quad \text{Therefore, } b = \sqrt{ac} \quad or \quad b = -\sqrt{ac}.$$

Since b^2 is positive, a and c are both positive or both negative, there is no single geometric mean of a positive number and a negative number.

Example 4   Solve.

Suppose that a small puncture in a space capsule allows 5% of the air to escape each second. What percent of the air will remain in the capsule 6 s after the puncture?

Solution   Let the amount of air in the capsule before the puncture be represented by 1 (100%). Then the amount 1 s after the puncture is 0.95 and the amount 2 s after the puncture will be $(0.95)(0.95)$, or $(0.95)^2$.

The amounts of air left in the capsule each second (starting with the time of the puncture) form a geometric sequence.

$$1, 0.95, (0.95)^2, (0.95)^3, \ldots$$

To answer the question, we must find the 7th term of the sequence.

$$a_7 = a_1 r^6$$
$$= 1(0.95)^6$$
$$\approx 0.735$$

Answer   After 6 s, approximately 73.5% of the air will remain.

---

*C*LASSROOM EXERCISES

State whether each equation defines a geometric sequence. If it does, state the common ratio r.

1. $a_n = 3(2)^{n-1}$ **2.** $a_n = 5n$ **3.** $a_n = 3^n$

Find the 5th term of each of the following geometric sequences.

4. $10, 5, 2.5, \ldots$ **5.** $a_n = 4\left(-\dfrac{1}{2}\right)^n$

6. Find the geometric mean of 3 and 12.

---

*W*RITTEN EXERCISES

 State whether each sequence is a geometric sequence, arithmetic sequence, or other kind of sequence.

1. $\dfrac{1}{2}, 2, 8, 32, \ldots$ **2.** $\dfrac{1}{6}, 2, 24, 288, \ldots$ **3.** $\dfrac{1}{2}, 2, 10, 60, \ldots$ **4.** $\dfrac{1}{6}, \dfrac{1}{3}, 1, 4, \ldots$

5. $\dfrac{1}{2}, 2, 3\dfrac{1}{2}, 5, \ldots$ **6.** $\dfrac{1}{6}, 2, 3\dfrac{5}{6}, 5\dfrac{2}{3}, \ldots$ **7.** $a_n = 12 + n$ **8.** $a_n = 4n + 5$

9. $a_n = 5 \cdot 2^n$ **10.** $a_n = 5 + 2^n$ **11.** $a_n = 2 + 5^n$ **12.** $a_n = 2 \cdot 5^n$

Write the fifth term of each geometric sequence.

13. 8, 24, 72, . . .

14. 3, 12, 48, . . .

15. 5, − 10, 20, . . .

16. − 4, 12, − 36, . . .

17. $a_n = -2 \cdot 3^n$

18. $a_n = \left(\frac{1}{2}\right)4^n$

19. $a_n = 0.1(-3)^n$

20. $a_n = 3(-2)^n$

Find the geometric mean of the given numbers.

21. 4 and 25

22. 2 and 32

23. $\frac{1}{2}$ and $\frac{1}{8}$

24. $\frac{1}{4}$ and $\frac{1}{9}$

B **Find the two geometric means between the given numbers.**

25. 4 and 108

26. 3 and 192

27. − 3 and − 192

28. − 3 and 192

pplications

Solve.

29. A bouncing metal ball reaches heights on successive bounces according to this geometric sequence: in cms:

    300, 270, 243, 218.7, 196.83 cm, . . .

What is the height of the ball after 6 bounces if its height is 300 cm after one bounce?

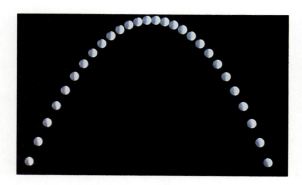

30. A $100,000 machine is depreciated 20% each year. The depreciated values form this geometric sequence:

    $100,000, $80,000, $64,000, $51,200, $40,960, . . .

What is the depreciated value of the machine after 5 yr if its value after 1 yr is $80,000?

31. The interest on Melanie Reed's $10,000 investment is compounded annually. The investment's values form this geometric sequence:

    $10,000, $10,850, $11,772.25, $12,770.89, $13,858.59, . . .

a. At what interest rate was the money invested?

b. Write an expression in the form $10,000b^t$ to show the value of the investment after 20 yr.

c. Use a calculator to evaluate your expression.

32. In the opening paragraph, the heights of the stacks of paper form this geometric sequence:

    0.001, 0.002, 0.004, 0.008, . . .

Write an expression in the form $0.001b^t$ to show the height of the stack after 50 tears.

33. In the opening paragraph, suppose that the area of the original piece of paper was 1 m², or 10,000 cm². The areas of the pieces of paper in the stacks form this geometric sequence:

$$10,000 \text{ cm}^2, \; 5000 \text{ cm}^2, \; 2500 \text{ cm}^2, \; 1250 \text{ cm}^2, \ldots$$

Write an expression in the form $10,000b^t$ to show the size of each piece of paper after 50 tears. Use a calculator to evaluate your expression.

Solve for x. Write ∅ if there is no solution.

34. The geometric mean of 3 and x is 4.
35. The geometric mean of 3 and 4 is x.
36. The geometric mean of -3 and x is 4.
37. The geometric mean of 3 and x is -4.

C **38.** The half-life of tungsten–176 is 80 min. In the first 80 min, half of the tungsten–176 will disintegrate to a nonradioactive substance. In the next 80 min, half of the remaining tungsten–176 will disintegrate. How long will it take for $\dfrac{1}{64}$ of the original tungsten–176 to remain?

39. A tank of 20% chlorine solution is emptied of one fourth its volume and is refilled with pure water. If this is done four times, assuming mixing after each refilling, what is the final concentration of the chlorine mixture?

40. The successive distances traveled by a weight attached to an oscillating spring are 90 cm, 60 cm, 40 cm, ... How far will the weight travel on its sixth oscillation?

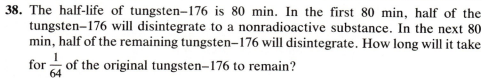 XTENSION   Definitions of Sequences

For the sequence 1, 3, 5, 7, 9, . . . an **explicit definition** is: For each positive integer n, $t_n = 2n - 1$. An explicit definition states the relationship between a term of a sequence (t_n) and the number of that term (n).

   A **recursive definition** of a sequence states the first term and then states how each other term is related to its preceding term. In the sequence above, the first term is 1, and each other term is 2 more than its preceding term. A recursive definition of the sequence is:

$$t_1 = 1$$

$$t_{n+1} = t_n + 2, \text{ for each positive integer } n$$

Write the first four terms of each sequence. State whether the sequence is a geometric sequence, arithmetic sequence, or other kind of sequence. (Assume n is a positive integer.)

1. $t_1 = 5$
$t_{n+1} = 2t_n + 10$

2. $t_1 = 256$
$t_{n+1} = \sqrt{t_n}$

3. $t_1 = 256$
$t_{n+1} = \dfrac{1}{4}t_n$

Write both a recursive definition and an explicit definition for each of the following sequences.

4. 5, 2, -1, -4, -7, . . .

5. 5, -15, 45, -135, 405, . . .

REVIEW EXERCISES

1. Graph on the same set of axes.   [8-7]

    a. $y = x^2$ **b.** $y = \frac{1}{2}x^2$ **c.** $y = -\frac{1}{2}x^2$

2. Graph: $y = 2(x - 3)^2$ [8-8]

Write equations for the following in the form $y - k = a(x - h)^2$.   [8-9]

3. The quadratic function with vertex (4, 5), opening downward, and congruent to $y = \frac{1}{4}x^2$.

4. The quadratic function with vertex (6, − 4), opening upward, and congruent to $y = 2x^2$.

Find the maximum or minimum values of these functions and state whether they are maximum or minimum.   [8-10]

    5. $y - 5 = 2(x + 4)^2$ **6.** $y = 4x - x^2$

Self-Quiz 1

12-1 **1.** State the 1st and 9th terms of the sequence with each of the following definitions.

    a. $t_n = 3 - 2n$ **b.** $t_n = \dfrac{n}{n + 1}$

  2. Write the indicated term of each arithmetic sequence.

    a. $a_n = 4 + \left(\dfrac{3}{4}\right)n;\ a_{20}$ **b.** 24, 26, 28, . . . ; a_{25}

  3. Write the first three terms of the arithmetic sequence containing the terms $a_5 = 4$ and $a_7 = -2$.

  4. Find the two arithmetic means between − 1 and 4.

12-1, **5.** State whether the sequence is arithmetic, geometric, or other.
12-2

    a. 1, 3, 6, 10, . . .   **b.** 8, − 4, 2, − 1, . . .   **c.** − 12, − 4, 4, 12, . . .

12-2 **6.** Write the fifth term of each geometric sequence.

    a. 16, 12, 9, . . .   **b.** $a_2 = -1,\ r = 3$

  7. Write the geometric mean of 4 and 36.

12-1, **8.** The front row of an auditorium has 37 seats. Each row after the first has
12-2   3 more seats than the preceding row. Which row has 100 seats?

  9. An item of business equipment originally costs $8000. At the end of the first year and for each year thereafter, it depreciates 20% in value. How much is the equipment worth at the beginning of the fourth year?

LESSON 12-3

Series

Seven basketball teams play in a round-robin tournament (each team plays each other team once). How many games will be played?

Let the 7 teams be represented by the letters A, B, C, . . . , G. Then the game between team A and team B can be represented by a pair of letters, AB (or BA). Now we can systematically list all the possible games.

AB, AC, AD, AE, AF, AG	6 games
BC, BD, BE, BF, BG	5 games
CD, CE, CF, CG	4 games
DE, DF, DG	3 games
EF, EG	2 games
FG	1 game

The total number of games is
$$1 + 2 + 3 + 4 + 5 + 6.$$

The sum of the terms of a sequence is frequently of interest in mathematics and in applications of mathematics.

Definition: Series

A **series** is the indicated sum of the terms of a sequence.

Given any sequence such as:
$$1, 1, 2, 3, 5, 8$$
another sequence $S_1, S_2, S_3, \ldots$ can be constructed in which the general term S_n is the indicated sum of the first n terms of the given sequence.

$$S_1 = 1 \qquad\qquad S_4 = 1 + 1 + 2 + 3$$

$$S_2 = 1 + 1 \qquad\quad S_5 = 1 + 1 + 2 + 3 + 5$$

$$S_3 = 1 + 1 + 2 \quad\; S_6 = 1 + 1 + 2 + 3 + 5 + 8$$

Each of the indicated sums $S_1, S_2, S_3, S_4, S_5,$ and S_6 is a series. The simplified sum of the series for any value of n is called the **value** of the series. For example, the value of S_5 is 12.

The indicated sum of the terms of an arithmetic sequence is called an **arithmetic series.** The indicated sum of the terms of a geometric sequence is called a **geometric series.**

Arithmetic series	*Geometric series*
$1 + 3 + 5 + 7 + 9 + 11$	$2 + 4 + 8 + 16 + 32 + 64$
$20 + 15 + 10 + 5 + 0 + (-5)$	$8 + (-4) + 2 + (-1) + \dfrac{1}{2}$

Example 1 Given the arithmetic sequence 1, 3, 5, 7, 9, 11, . . . , write the series S_7. Then state its value.

Solution $S_7 = 1 + 3 + 5 + 7 + 9 + 11 + 13 = 49$

A series consisting of many terms may be awkward to express. The expression for a series can be shortened by omitting some of the addends.

$$2 + 4 + 6 + \cdots + 50$$

Enough terms from the beginning of the series must be listed to indicate how the series continues. For a finite series, the last term should also be indicated.

Sigma notation (Σ-notation) permits us to express a series even more efficiently. The Greek letter Σ is equivalent to S (for sum).

The series $2 + 4 + 6 + \cdots + 50$ can be written in Σ-notation as follows.

$$\sum_{k=1}^{25} 2k \qquad \text{Read as: "The sum from } k = 1 \text{ to } k = 25 \text{ of } 2k\text{"}$$

The notation indicates that each term of the series is of the form $2k$. The letter k is called the **index of summation.** The terms of the series are formed by substituting integer values for k from $k = 1$ (the lower index) to $k = 25$ (the upper index).

Example 2 Write in expanded form. Then state the value.   **a.** $\displaystyle\sum_{k=1}^{6} 3k$ **b.** $\displaystyle\sum_{k=4}^{7} (k + 1)^2$

Solution   **a.** $\displaystyle\sum_{k=1}^{6} 3k = (3 \cdot 1) + (3 \cdot 2) + (3 \cdot 3) + (3 \cdot 4) + (3 \cdot 5) + (3 \cdot 6) = 63$

   b. $\displaystyle\sum_{k=4}^{7} (k + 1)^2 = (4 + 1)^2 + (5 + 1)^2 + (6 + 1)^2 + (7 + 1)^2 = 174$

Example 3 Use Σ-notation to express the series $3^2 + 4^2 + 5^2 + \cdots + 100^2$.

Solution Each addend is of the form k^2. The first term of the series occurs for $k = 3$ and the last for $k = 100$.

$$3^2 + 4^2 + 5^2 + \cdots + 100^2 = \sum_{k=3}^{100} k^2$$

The choice of k as the index of summation is arbitrary. Other letters can also be used. The series of Example 3 could have been expressed

$$\sum_{i=3}^{100} i^2 \quad \text{or} \quad \sum_{j=3}^{100} j^2.$$

Moreover, there are alternative sigma expressions that can be used to express the same series.

$$\sum_{j=1}^{98} (j + 2)^2 = \sum_{k=4}^{101} (k - 1)^2 = 3^2 + 4^2 + 5^2 + \cdots + 100^2$$

Example 4 Use Σ-notation to express the series $1 + 3 + 5 + 7 + 9 + 11 + 13 + 15$.

Solution Each addend is of the form $(2k - 1)$. The first term of the series occurs for $k = 1$ and the last for $k = 8$.

$$(2 \cdot 1 - 1) + (2 \cdot 2 - 1) + (2 \cdot 3 - 1) + \cdots + (2 \cdot 7 - 1) + (2 \cdot 8 - 1)$$

Answer $\sum_{k=1}^{8} (2k - 1)$ One of many alternate answers is $\sum_{i=0}^{7} (2i + 1)$.

𝒞LASSROOM EXERCISES

Identify each series as arithmetic, geometric, or other.

1. $3 + 6 + 12 + 24 + 48$

2. $1 + 4 + 9 + 16 + 25 + 36$

3. Write the series S_6 for the sequence 2, 5, 8, 11, 14, 17, 20, 23. Then state the value.

Write each series in expanded form. Then state the value.

4. $\displaystyle\sum_{k=1}^{4} (5k)$

5. $\displaystyle\sum_{k=1}^{7} (2^k)$

6. $\displaystyle\sum_{k=1}^{6} (3k + 1)$

𝒲RITTEN EXERCISES

A **Identify each series as arithmetic, geometric, or other.**

1. $\dfrac{1}{2} + \dfrac{1}{3} + \dfrac{1}{4} + \cdots + \dfrac{1}{100}$

2. $\dfrac{7}{10} + \dfrac{7}{100} + \dfrac{7}{1000} + \cdots + \dfrac{7}{10^n}$

3. $5 + 8 + 11 + 14 + \cdots + 302$

4. $2 + 5 + 11 + 23 + \cdots + 6143$

5. $8 + 4 + 2 + 1 + \cdots + \dfrac{1}{64}$

6. $100 + 96 + 92 + 88 + \cdots + 0$

Write the series S_5 for each sequence. Then state the value of the series.

7. 2, 4, 8, 16, . . .

8. 3, 6, 12, 24, . . .

9. 4, 2, 0, −2, . . .

10. 1, 3, 5, 7, . . .

11. 1, 2, 3, 1, 2, 3, . . .

12. 5, −5, 5, −5, 5, . . .

Write each series in expanded form. Then state the value of the series.

13. $\displaystyle\sum_{k=1}^{3} 6k$ **14.** $\displaystyle\sum_{j=1}^{3} (3 - j)$ **15.** $\displaystyle\sum_{i=1}^{4} (2 - i)$ **16.** $\displaystyle\sum_{k=4}^{9} 1^k$ **17.** $\displaystyle\sum_{k=0}^{3} 4 \cdot 2^k$ **18.** $\displaystyle\sum_{k=0}^{3} 2 \cdot 4^k$

Write each series in Σ-notation.

19. $2 + 4 + 6 + 8 + 10$ **20.** $3 + 6 + 9 + 12 + 15$ **21.** $2 + 4 + 8 + 16 + 32$

22. $7 + 14 + 28 + 56$ **23.** $3 + 9 + 27 + 81 + 243$ **24.** $5 + 15 + 45 + 135$

25. $6 + 8 + 10 + 12 + \cdots + 100$ **26.** $9 + 12 + 15 + \cdots + 300$

27. $1 + \dfrac{1}{2} + \dfrac{1}{3} + \dfrac{1}{4} + \cdots + \dfrac{1}{100}$ **28.** $7 + \dfrac{7}{2} + \dfrac{7}{3} + \dfrac{7}{4} + \cdots + \dfrac{7}{100}$

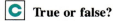 **Identify each series as arithmetic, geometric, or other.**

29. $\displaystyle\sum_{k=1}^{100} \dfrac{1}{2}k$ **30.** $\displaystyle\sum_{k=1}^{100} - k$ **31.** $\displaystyle\sum_{j=1}^{100} \dfrac{j - 1}{j + 1}$ **32.** $\displaystyle\sum_{j=1}^{100} (j - 5)$

33. $\displaystyle\sum_{i=1}^{100} 3 \cdot 2^i$ **34.** $\displaystyle\sum_{i=1}^{100} 3\left(\dfrac{1}{2}\right)^i$ **35.** $\displaystyle\sum_{k=1}^{100} \dfrac{k^2 - 1}{k + 1}$ **36.** $\displaystyle\sum_{k=1}^{100} (k + 2)^2$

A definition is given for each sequence. Find the value of S_4 for each sequence.

37. $a_n = 2n - 1$ **38.** $a_n = 5^n$ **39.** $a_n = \left(\dfrac{1}{2}\right)^n$ **40.** $a_n = \dfrac{1}{n}$

C   **True or false?**

41. $\displaystyle\sum_{k=1}^{10} (2 + k) = 2 + \sum_{k=1}^{10} k$ **42.** $\displaystyle\sum_{k=1}^{10} 2k = 2\sum_{k=1}^{10} k$

43. $\displaystyle\sum_{k=1}^{10} k^2 = \left(\sum_{k=1}^{10} k\right)^2$ **44.** $\displaystyle\sum_{j=1}^{10} (27 - j) = 270 - \sum_{j=1}^{10} j$

For each real number a and positive integer n, show that:

45. $\displaystyle\sum_{k=1}^{n} (a + k) = na + \sum_{k=1}^{n} k$ **46.** $\displaystyle\sum_{k=1}^{n} ak = a\sum_{k=1}^{n} k$ **47.** $\displaystyle\sum_{k=1}^{n-1} k(k + 1) = \sum_{i=2}^{n} i(i - 1)$

$\mathcal{R}$EVIEW EXERCISES

1. Write the equation of the circle with center $(3, 4)$ and radius 5.   [9-1]

2. Write the equation of the parabola with focus $(4, 0)$ and directrix $x = -4$.   [9-2]

3. Write the equation of the ellipse with foci $(4, 0)$ and $(-4, 0)$ and vertices $(5, 0)$ and $(-5, 0)$.   [9-3]

4. Sketch a graph of this hyperbola $\dfrac{y^2}{9} - \dfrac{x^2}{4} = 1$ including the asymptotes and   [9-4]

   foci. Write equations of the asymptotes.

5. Classify the conic $4x^2 - 16 - y^2 + 6y = 9$ as a parabola, circle, ellipse, or   [9-5]
   hyperbola.

LESSON 12-4

Arithmetic Series

A grocer wants to display canned goods by stacking them as shown here, so that there are 10 rows of cans with 3 cans in the top row. To find the number of cans needed, we need to compute the value of the arithmetic series

$$3 + 5 + 7 + 9 + 11 + 13 + 15 + 17 + 19 + 21.$$

If the series is written in increasing order and in decreasing order, the terms can be paired vertically and added.

$$S_{10} = 3 + 5 + 7 + 9 + 11 + 13 + 15 + 17 + 19 + 21$$
$$S_{10} = 21 + 19 + 17 + 15 + 13 + 11 + 9 + 7 + 5 + 3$$
$$2S_{10} = 24 + 24 + 24 + 24 + 24 + 24 + 24 + 24 + 24 + 24$$
$$2S_{10} = 10(24) = 240$$
$$S_{10} = 120$$

This procedure suggests a method of deriving a general formula for the value of an arithmetic series.

Let S_n be the value of the arithmetic series with first term a_1, common difference d, and last term a_n. The terms of the arithmetic series can be generated by starting with the first term and repeatedly adding d, or by starting with the last term and repeatedly subtracting d. Therefore,

$$S_n = a_1 + (a_1 + d) + (a_1 + 2d) + \cdots + (a_1 + (n - 1)d)$$
$$S_n = a_n + (a_n - d) + (a_n - 2d) + \cdots + (a_n - (n - 1)d)$$

Adding the members of the two equations gives:

$$2S_n = (a_1 + a_n) + (a_1 + a_n) + (a_1 + a_n) + \cdots + (a_1 + a_n)$$

where the term $(a_1 + a_n)$ occurs n times. Therefore,

$$2S_n = n(a_1 + a_n)$$

and

$$S_n = \frac{n(a_1 + a_n)}{2}.$$

Since $a_n = a_1 + (n - 1)d$, the final equation above can be written in terms of a_1.

$$S_n = \frac{n[a_1 + (a_1 + (n - 1)d)]}{2} = \frac{n[2a_1 + (n - 1)d]}{2}$$

Value of an Arithmetic Series

For an arithmetic series in which a_1 is the first term, d is the common difference, a_n is the last term, and S_n is the value of the series,

$$S_n = \frac{n(a_1 + a_n)}{2} \quad \text{and} \quad S_n = \frac{n[2a_1 + (n-1)d]}{2}.$$

Example 1 Find the sum of the first 15 odd numbers.

Solution Let $a_1 = 1$, $n = 15$, and $d = 2$ in the formula $S_n = \dfrac{n[2a_1 + (n-1)d]}{2}$.

$$S_{15} = \frac{15[2(1) + (15-1)2]}{2} = 225$$

Answer The sum of the first 15 odd numbers is 15^2, or 225.

The result in Example 1 suggests this interesting theorem (see Exercise 39):

The sum of the first n positive odd integers is n^2.

A related theorem (see Exercise 40) is:

The sum of the first n positive integers is $\dfrac{n(n+1)}{2}$.

Example 2 Find the value of the series $18 + 21 + 24 + \cdots + 90$.

Solution To find n, substitute in the formula:

$a_n = a_1 + (n-1)d$

$90 = 18 + (n-1)3$

$25 = n$

To find S_n, substitute in the formula:

$$S_n = \frac{n(a_1 + a_n)}{2}$$

$$S_{25} = \frac{25(18 + 90)}{2} = 1350$$

Answer The value of the series is 1350.

Example 3 The value of an arithmetic series is 248. The first of the 8 terms of the series is 17. What is the last term of the series?

Solution Substitute in the formula.

$$S_n = \frac{n(a_1 + a_n)}{2}$$

$$248 = \frac{8(17 + a_n)}{2}$$

$$248 = 4(17 + a_n)$$

$$45 = a_n$$

Answer The last term of the series is 45.

Example 4 Solve.

Mrs. Kline assembles carburetors at an automobile plant. On her first day she assembled 15 carburetors. Each day after that for 6 days, her production increased by 3 carburetors per day. How many carburetors did she assemble in her first 7 days?

Solution The total number of carburetors is the sum of the first 7 terms of an arithmetic series with 15 as the first term and 3 as the common difference.

$$S_n = \frac{n[2a_1 + (n-1)d]}{2} \qquad S_7 = \frac{7[2(15) + (7-1)3]}{2} = 168$$

Answer Mrs. Kline assembled 168 carburetors.

$\mathcal{C}$LASSROOM EXERCISES

Find the value of each series.

1. $\sum_{k=1}^{7} (k+4)$ **2.** $\sum_{k=1}^{5} 2k$ **3.** $\sum_{j=1}^{6} j^2$ **4.** $5 + 10 + 15 + 20 + \cdots + 75$

5. Find the sum of the first 20 even numbers.

$\mathcal{W}$RITTEN EXERCISES

A **Find the sum of the indicated number of terms of each arithmetic sequence.**

1. $3, 6, 9, 12, \ldots ; n = 8$

2. $4, 8, 12, 16, \ldots ; n = 10$

3. $\frac{1}{2}, 1, 1\frac{1}{2}, 2, \ldots ; n = 11$

4. $\frac{1}{3}, \frac{2}{3}, 1, \frac{4}{3}, \ldots ; n = 14$

5. $-100, -98, -96, \ldots ; n = 20$

6. $-150, -147, -144, \ldots ; n = 30$

7. $47, 52, 57, 62, \ldots ; n = 50$

8. $35, 41, 47, 53, \ldots ; n = 100$

Find the value of each series.

9. $7 + 10 + 13 + 16 + \cdots + 184$

10. $19 + 26 + 33 + 40 + \cdots + 432$

11. $119 + 123 + 127 + \cdots + 295$

12. $119 + 122 + 125 + \cdots + 296$

13. $\sum_{k=1}^{40} k$ **14.** $\sum_{j=1}^{24} (j+1)$ **15.** $\sum_{i=1}^{30} (3i+17)$ **16.** $\sum_{k=1}^{20} (3k+17)$

17. $\sum_{i=1}^{50} \left(\frac{1}{2}i - 20\right)$ **18.** $\sum_{k=1}^{100} \left(\frac{1}{5}k - 10\right)$ **19.** $\sum_{j=1}^{10} (10 - j)$ **20.** $\sum_{j=1}^{20} (40 - 2j)$

21. Find the sum of the first 50 positive:

    a. odd integers.   **b.** even integers.   **c.** integers.

22. Find the sum of the first 75 positive:

    a. odd integers.   **b.** even integers.   **c.** integers.

$\mathcal{A}$ pplications

Solve.

23. Kim Hua decided to do one more pushup in her exercise program each day than she had done the previous day. The first day she did 10 pushups.

    a. How many pushups did Kim do on the 20th day?

    b. How many pushups did Kim do altogether in the 20 days?

24. Kris Begay vowed to study $\frac{1}{4}$ h more each day than the previous day. The first day she studied $1\frac{1}{4}$ h.

    a. How many hours did Kris study on the 10th day?

    b. How many hours did Kris study altogether in the 10 days?

25. Teresa Osborn decided to spend 10 min more jogging each day than she did the previous day. The first day she jogged 15 min.

    a. How many minutes did Teresa jog on the 7th day?

    b. How many minutes did Teresa jog altogether in the 7 days?

26. Kurt Green promised to practice the piano 5 min more each day than he did the previous day. The first day he practiced 10 min.

    a. How many minutes did Kurt practice on the 15th day?

    b. How many minutes did Kurt practice altogether in the 15 days?

B 27. A stack of logs had 4 logs in the top row and 13 logs in the bottom row. Each row below the top row had one more log than the row just above it. How many logs were in the stack?

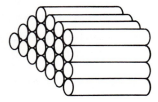

28. A diamond pattern was made from individual square tiles as shown. If the pattern was 27 tiles wide at the widest point, how many tiles were used in all?

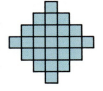

Find the required information for each of the following arithmetic series.

29. $S_n = 2920$, $a_1 = 20$, $n = 7$

    a. $a_n = ?$ **b.** $d = ?$

30. $n = 50$, $a_1 = 10$, $a_{50} = 20$

    a. $S_n = ?$ **b.** $d = ?$

31. $S_n = 100$, $a_1 = 15$, $a_n = 35$

    a. $n = ?$ **b.** $d = ?$

32. $S_n = 30,400$, $n = 100$, $d = 6$

    a. $a_1 = ?$ **b.** $a_{100} = ?$

33. $S_n = 306$, $a_1 = 5$, $d = \frac{1}{5}$

    a. $n = ?$ **b.** $a_n = ?$

34. $S_n = 23$, $n = 46$, $d = \frac{1}{5}$

    a. $a_1 = ?$ **b.** $a_{46} = ?$

35. A cannonball dropped from a cliff fell 16 ft during the first second, 48 ft during the second second, and 80 ft during the third second.

    a. How far does the cannonball fall during the 8th second?

    b. How high is the cliff if it strikes the ground at the end of the 9th second?

36. Plastic pipe is shipped in bundles with a hexagonal cross section as shown. Determine how many lengths of pipe are in a bundle with 9 pipes on a side.

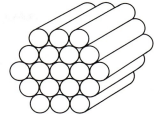

Solve for x.

37. $\displaystyle\sum_{k=1}^{x} (2k + 5) = 520$ **38.** $\displaystyle\sum_{k=1}^{20} (3k + x) = 1455$

39. Show that the sum of the first n positive odd integers is n^2.

40. Show that the sum of the first n positive integers is $\dfrac{n(n + 1)}{2}$.

EVIEW EXERCISES

1. Use synthetic substitution to evaluate $f(2)$, where $f(x) = x^3 - 4x^2 + 3$.   [10-1]

2. Use synthetic division to divide $x^3 - x + 4$ by $(x - 2)$. Write the quotient and the remainder.   [10-2]

3. Write a fourth-degree equation in factored form that has -1, 1, and 3 (multiplicity 2) as roots.   [10-3]

${\mathcal B}$IOGRAPHY   Mary Ellen Rudin

Mary Ellen Rudin registered at the University of Texas with no idea of what she should major in. She went to the mathematics registration table simply because it had the shortest line! She went on to get her Ph.D. and has authored more than 70 research papers, primarily in topology. A mother of four, she was never career oriented but pursued mathematics because she enjoyed it. She has been an invited speaker dozens of times in the United States, Canada, Czechoslovakia, Hungary, Italy, and the Soviet Union. She became vice-president of the American Mathematical Society in 1981 and in the same year became a professor of mathematics at the University of Wisconsin at Madison. Says Dr. Rudin, "Math is obviously something that women should be able to do very well. It's very intuitive. You don't need a lot of machinery, and you don't need a lot of physical strength. You just need stamina, and women often have a great deal of stamina."

LESSON 12-5

Geometric Series

In a certain city, two scoundrels concoct a rumor at 9:00 A.M. During the next 10 min, each of them tells the rumor to three other people in the city. Then the two scoundrels leave the city. During the next 10 min, each of the six people remaining in the city tells the rumor to three additional people who have not heard it. By 11:00 A.M., every person in the city has heard the rumor. We can use this information to compute the population of the city.

The number of additional people who knew the rumor at each 10-min interval forms a geometric sequence.

Time	Additional people who knew the rumor
9:00	2
9:10	$2 \cdot 3$
9:20	$2 \cdot 3^2$
9:30	$2 \cdot 3^3$
9:40	$2 \cdot 3^4$
$\cdots$	$\cdots$

The population of the city is the value of a geometric series.

$$S_n = \sum_{k=1}^{n} a_1 r^{k-1},$$

where $a_1 = 2$, $r = 3$, and $n = 13$. (See Exercise 27.)

To find a general formula for the value of a geometric series S_n, we first write the series in expanded form:

(1) $\qquad S_n = a_1 + a_1 r + a_1 r^2 + \cdots + a_1 r^{n-2} + a_1 r^{n-1}.$

Next, we multiply both sides by $-r$:

(2) $\qquad -rS_n = -a_1 r - a_1 r^2 - \cdots - a_1 r^{n-2} - a_1 r^{n-1} - a_1 r^n.$

Adding (1) and (2) gives:

$$S_n - rS_n = a_1 - a_1 r^n$$

$$S_n(1 - r) = a_1 - a_1 r^n$$

$$S_n = \frac{a_1 - a_1 r^n}{1 - r} \qquad r \neq 1.$$

Since $a_n = a_1 r^{n-1}$, $a_n r = a_1 r^n$. Substituting $a_n r$ for $a_1 r^n$ in the formula, we have:

$$S_n = \frac{a_1 - a_n r}{1 - r} \qquad r \neq 1.$$

The general formula for the value of a geometric series S_n can be stated as follows.

Value of a Geometric Series

For a geometric series in which a_1 is the first term, a_n is the last term, r is the common ratio, $r \neq 1$, and S_n is the value of the series,

$$S_n = \frac{a_1 - a_1 r^n}{1 - r} \quad \text{and} \quad S_n = \frac{a_1 - a_n r}{1 - r}.$$

Example 1   State the value of this series in exponential notation.

$$4 + 4 \cdot 3^1 + 4 \cdot 3^2 + \cdots + 4 \cdot 3^6$$

Solution   Let $a_1 = 4$, $a_n = 4 \cdot 3^6$, and $r = 3$ in this formula.

$$S_n = \frac{a_1 - a_n r}{1 - r} = \frac{4 - 4 \cdot 3^6 \cdot 3}{1 - 3} = \frac{4(1 - 3^7)}{-2} = 2(3^7 - 1)$$

Example 2   State the sum of the first 10 terms of this sequence in exponential notation.

$$1, 2, 4, 8, \ldots$$

Solution   Divide any term by the preceding term to find r.

$$r = \frac{2}{1} = 2$$

Substitute 1 for a_1, 2 for r, and 10 for n in this formula.

$$S_n = \frac{a_1 - a_1 r^n}{1 - r} = \frac{1 - 1(2^{10})}{1 - 2} = 2^{10} - 1$$

Example 3   Evaluate. $\displaystyle\sum_{k=1}^{8} \left(\frac{1}{2}\right)^k$

Solution   The first term of this geometric series is $\frac{1}{2}$, $r = \frac{1}{2}$, and $n = 8$. Substitute those values in this formula.

$$S_n = \frac{a_1 - a_1 r^n}{1 - r}$$

$$S_8 = \frac{\dfrac{1}{2} - \left(\dfrac{1}{2}\right)\left(\dfrac{1}{2}\right)^8}{1 - \dfrac{1}{2}} = \frac{255}{256}$$

Answer   The sum of the powers of $\frac{1}{2}$ from $\left(\frac{1}{2}\right)^1$ to $\left(\frac{1}{2}\right)^8$ is $\frac{255}{256}$.

LASSROOM EXERCISES

Give the value of each series.

1. $\displaystyle\sum_{k=1}^{6} \left(\frac{1}{4}\right)^k$

2. $6 + 2 + \dfrac{2}{3} + \dfrac{2}{9} + \cdots + \dfrac{2}{81}$

3. Find the sum of the eight powers of 2 from 2^0 to 2^7: 1, 2, 4, ...

RITTEN EXERCISES

A State the value of each series in exponential notation.

1. $6 + 12 + 24 + \cdots + 3 \cdot 2^{10}$

2. $14 + 28 + 56 + \cdots + 7 \cdot 2^{10}$

3. $5 + 15 + 45 + \cdots + 5 \cdot 3^{20}$

4. $2 + 6 + 18 + \cdots + 2 \cdot 3^{20}$

5. $8 + 4 + 2 + \cdots + \left(\dfrac{1}{2}\right)^{45}$

6. $32 + 16 + 8 + \cdots + \left(\dfrac{1}{2}\right)^{47}$

7. $-3 + 9 - 27 + 81 - \cdots + 3^{24}$

8. $2 - 4 + 8 - 16 + \cdots + 2^{33}$

State the sum of the first n terms of each geometric sequence in exponential notation.

9. $5, 10, 20, 40, \ldots ; n = 6$

10. $3, 6, 12, 24, \ldots ; n = 8$

11. $32, 8, 2, \dfrac{1}{2}, \ldots ; n = 15$

12. $3, 1, \dfrac{1}{3}, \dfrac{1}{9}, \ldots ; n = 13$

13. $2, -4, 8, -16, \ldots ; n = 20$

14. $-5, 15, -45, 135, \ldots ; n = 30$

15. $-1, -\dfrac{1}{2}, -\dfrac{1}{4}, -\dfrac{1}{8}, \ldots ; n = 100$

16. $-1, -\dfrac{1}{3}, -\dfrac{1}{9}, -\dfrac{1}{27}, \ldots ; n = 50$

Evaluate.

17. $\displaystyle\sum_{k=1}^{6} 7 \cdot 10^k$

18. $\displaystyle\sum_{k=1}^{7} 9 \cdot 10^k$

19. $\displaystyle\sum_{i=1}^{3} 20^i$

20. $\displaystyle\sum_{k=1}^{3} 11^k$

21. $\displaystyle\sum_{k=1}^{5} \left(\frac{1}{2}\right)^k$

22. $\displaystyle\sum_{j=1}^{4} \left(\frac{1}{3}\right)^j$

23. $\displaystyle\sum_{i=1}^{6} (-2)^i$

24. $\displaystyle\sum_{k=1}^{4} (-3)^k$

B 25. According to legend, the inventor of the game of chess made the following request to his grateful king: 1 grain of wheat for the first square on the chess board, 2 grains for the second square, 4 grains for the next, and so on, doubling the number of grains of wheat for each subsequent square. If there are 64 squares on a chess board:

  a. What is the last term of the series for the total request? $1 + 2 + 4 + \cdots + \underline{\ ?\ }$

  b. Use Σ-notation to express the sum.

  c. Simplify the sum using exponential notation.

Applications

Solve.

26. A champion bullfrog leaps in a geometric sequence, each succeeding jump $\frac{2}{3}$ of the previous jump.

   If the frog's first leap is 27 ft, find the distance the frog has covered after 5 leaps.

27. Solve the problem described in the lesson opener. What is the population of the city?

28. A grade-school class is convinced to try this recess time plan for 6 days; 3 min on the 1st day, 6 min on the 2nd day, 12 min on the 3rd day, doubling the time each day. How does this plan compare in total recess time to the normal 30 min per day for the 6-day period?

29. A vacuum pump draws off $\frac{1}{3}$ of the remaining air in a vacuum chamber each 30 s. What fraction of air has been removed after 3 min?

30. A tennis ball is dropped on a sidewalk from a height of 256 cm. Each time the ball bounces, it rises to $\frac{3}{4}$ of the previous height. How far has the ball traveled when it strikes the sidewalk the 5th time?

Use this information to complete Exercises 31–42.

$2^{20} = 1,048,576 \qquad 3^{13} = 1,594,323 \qquad 2^{21} = 2,097,152 \qquad 3^{14} = 4,782,969$

State the value of each series. Do not use exponential notation.

31. $1 + 2 + 4 + \cdots + 2^{20}$

32. $1 + 3 + 9 + \cdots + 3^{13}$

33. $1 - 2 + 4 - \cdots + 2^{20}$

34. $1 - 3 + 9 - \cdots - 3^{13}$

35. $-1 + 2 - 4 + \cdots - 2^{20}$

36. $-1 + 3 - 9 + \cdots + 3^{13}$

37. $\displaystyle\sum_{k=1}^{20} 10 \cdot 2^k$

38. $\displaystyle\sum_{k=1}^{13} 2 \cdot 3^k$

39. $\displaystyle\sum_{k=1}^{21} 10 \cdot 2^k$

40. $\displaystyle\sum_{k=1}^{14} 2 \cdot 3^k$

41. $\displaystyle\sum_{k=1}^{21} 10(-2)^k$

42. $\displaystyle\sum_{k=1}^{14} 2(-3)^k$

43. A geometric series with 20 terms and ratio 2 has a value of 6,291,450. What is the first term of the series?

44. A geometric series with 13 terms and ratio 3 has a value of 3,985,805. What is the first term of the series?

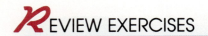

REVIEW EXERCISES

[11-1]

1. Graph the three functions on the same set of axes for the domain $\{x: -2 \leqslant x \leqslant 2\}$.

   a. $y = 2^x$ **b.** $y = 4^x$ **c.** $y = \left(\frac{1}{2}\right)^x$

2. Solve: $5^x = \dfrac{1}{25}$.   [11-1]

3. Write $2^4 = 16$ in logarithmic form.   [11-2]

4. Solve: $\log_x 64 = 2$.   [11-2]

5. If $\log_{10} 2 \approx 0.3010$, give an approximation for $\log_{10} 8$.   [11-3]

6. Solve: $\log_2 10 + \log_2 x = \log_2 16$.   [11-3]

Given log 3 $\approx$ 0.4771. Find an approximation for these expressions.   [11-4]

7. log 90   **8.** $\log\left(\frac{1}{9}\right)$

Self-Quiz 2

12-3   1. State whether the series is arithmetic, geometric, or other.

      a. $6 + 12 + 18 + 24 + \cdots + 36$

      b. $16 + 4 + 1 + \dfrac{1}{4} + \cdots + \dfrac{1}{256}$

      2. Write in expanded form and state the value of $\displaystyle\sum_{k=2}^{5} (1 - k)$.

      3. Write this series in Σ-notation.

$$5 + \frac{5}{2} + \frac{5}{3} + \frac{5}{4} + \cdots + \frac{5}{11}$$

12-4   4. Find the sum of the 50 terms of the sequence 27, 30, 33, 36, . . . , 174.

      5. Find the value of this series: $\displaystyle\sum_{k=1}^{50} (2k - 1)$.

      6. The value of an arithmetic series with 40 terms is 3020. The first term is -22.

       a. Find the 40th term.   **b.** Find the common difference.

12-5   7. Find the sum of the first six terms of the geometric sequence $6, 3, \dfrac{3}{2}, \dfrac{3}{4}, \ldots$

      8. Evaluate: $\displaystyle\sum_{k=1}^{6} 3 \cdot 2^k$.

LESSON 12-6

Infinite Geometric Series

A Mathematical Fable A hare chasing a tortoise reduces the distance between the two animals by one half in one half-minute. During the next quarter-minute, the hare reduces the remaining distance by one half. In the next eighth-minute, the remaining distance is reduced by one half again, and so on.

The number of minutes needed for the hare to catch the tortoise is given by the **infinite geometric series:**

$$\frac{1}{2} + \frac{1}{4} + \frac{1}{8} + \frac{1}{16} + \cdots$$

Here is another example of an infinite geometric series.

$$3 + 9 + 27 + 81 + \cdots$$

These infinite series can be written in Σ-notation as follows, where ∞ is the symbol for infinity and indicates that the index grows infinitely large.

$$\sum_{k=1}^{\infty} (3^k) \qquad \sum_{k=1}^{\infty} \left(\frac{1}{2}\right)^k$$

One method of studying the behavior of an infinite series is to consider the **partial sums** of the series. The first five partial sums of the infinite geometric series $\sum_{k=1}^{\infty} (3^k)$ are:

S_1: 3 $= 3$	S_4: 3 + 9 + 27 + 81 $= 120$
S_2: 3 + 9 $= 12$	S_5: 3 + 9 + 27 + 81 + 243 $= 363$
S_3: 3 + 9 + 27 $= 39$	

In a geometric series with $r > 1$ and $a_1 > 0$, the terms in the sequence of partial sums increase rapidly and eventually become infinitely large. If there is no real number that is the value of the infinite series, we say that the series **diverges.**

Now consider partial sums of the infinite geometric series $\sum_{k=1}^{\infty} \left(\frac{1}{2}\right)^k$.

$$S_1: \frac{1}{2} = \frac{1}{2} \qquad S_2: \frac{1}{2} + \frac{1}{4} = \frac{3}{4} \qquad S_3: \frac{1}{2} + \frac{1}{4} + \frac{1}{8} = \frac{7}{8}$$

$$S_4: \frac{1}{2} + \frac{1}{4} + \frac{1}{8} + \frac{1}{16} = \frac{15}{16} \qquad S_5: \frac{1}{2} + \frac{1}{4} + \frac{1}{8} + \frac{1}{16} + \frac{1}{32} = \frac{31}{32}$$

In a geometric series with $0 < r < 1$ and $a_1 > 0$, the partial sums increase, but they do not grow infinitely large. If there is a real number that is the value of the infinite series, we say that the series **converges.** For $\sum_{k=1}^{\infty} \left(\frac{1}{2}\right)^k$ the value of the infinite series is 1. So, the hare catches the rabbit in 1 minute.

The examples above illustrate that, in general, the infinite geometric series

$$a_1 + a_1r + a_1r^2 + a_1r^3 + \cdots$$

converges (has a value) only when $|r| < 1$. To determine the value of an infinite series, consider the formula for the nth partial sum.

$$S_n = \frac{a_1 - a_1r^n}{1 - r}$$

Since $|r| < 1$, the values of r^n get close to zero as the values of n become very large. Therefore, the values of a_1r^n also get close to zero. This means that the value of

$$S_n = \frac{a_1 - a_1r^n}{1 - r} \quad \text{approaches} \quad S = \frac{a_1}{1 - r}.$$

Value of an Infinite Geometric Series

The value S of an infinite geometric series with first term a_1 and common ratio r, $|r| < 1$, is given by the formula
$$S = \frac{a_1}{1 - r}.$$

Example 1   State the value of the infinite series $1 + \dfrac{1}{2} + \dfrac{1}{4} + \dfrac{1}{8} + \dfrac{1}{16} + \cdots$.

Solution   This is an infinite geometric series with $a_1 = 1$ and $r = \dfrac{1}{2}$.

$$S = \frac{a_1}{1 - r} = \frac{1}{1 - \frac{1}{2}} = 2$$

Example 2   Express the repeating decimal $0.\overline{3}$ as a common fraction.

Solution   The repeating decimal $0.\overline{3}$ is equivalent to this infinite geometric series:

$$\frac{3}{10} + \frac{3}{10^2} + \frac{3}{10^3} + \frac{3}{10^4} + \cdots .$$

Therefore, $a_1 = \dfrac{3}{10}$ and $r = \dfrac{1}{10}$.

$$S = \frac{a_1}{1 - r} = \frac{\frac{3}{10}}{1 - \left(\frac{1}{10}\right)} = \frac{1}{3}$$

Example 3 **Solve.**

A ball is dropped from a height of 50 in. Each time the ball bounces it rebounds to $\frac{3}{5}$ its previous maximum height. What is the total distance traveled by the ball before it comes to rest?

Solution   The downward distances on successive bounces form an "infinite" geometric sequence with $a_1 = 50$ and $r = \frac{3}{5}$.

$$S = \frac{50}{1 - \frac{3}{5}} = 125$$

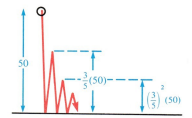

The upward distances form an "infinite" geometric sequence with $a_1 = 30$ and $r = \frac{3}{5}$.

$$S = \frac{30}{1 - \frac{3}{5}} = 75$$

Answer   The total distance traveled is 125 in. + 75 in. = 200 in.

LASSROOM EXERCISES

State whether the infinite geometric series converges.

1. $1 + \frac{1}{3} + \frac{1}{9} + \frac{1}{27} + \cdots$

2. $1 - \left(\frac{2}{3}\right) + \frac{4}{9} - \left(\frac{8}{27}\right) - \cdots$

Find the value of each infinite series.

3. $4 + 1 + \frac{1}{4} + \frac{1}{16} + \frac{1}{64} + \cdots$

4. $1 - 0.9 + 0.81 - 0.729 + \cdots$

5. Write $0.\overline{5}$ as an infinite series. Then evaluate the series.

WRITTEN EXERCISES

A **State whether the infinite geometric series converges.**

1. $\frac{1}{8} + \frac{1}{4} + \frac{1}{2} + 1 + \cdots$

2. $\frac{1}{64} + \frac{1}{16} + \frac{1}{4} + \cdots$

3. $1 + \frac{1}{2} + \frac{1}{4} + \frac{1}{8} + \cdots$

4. $1 + \frac{1}{4} + \frac{1}{16} + \frac{1}{64} + \cdots$

5. $1 - 2 + 4 - 8 + \cdots$

6. $1 - 4 + 16 - 64 + \cdots$

7. $1 - \frac{1}{2} + \frac{1}{4} - \frac{1}{8} + \cdots$

8. $1 - \frac{1}{4} + \frac{1}{16} - \frac{1}{64} + \cdots$

Find the value of each infinite series.

9. $6 + 2 + \dfrac{2}{3} + \cdots$

10. $6 + 3 + \dfrac{3}{2} + \cdots$

11. $100 + 10 + 1 + \cdots$

12. $100 + 20 + 4 + \cdots$

13. $\dfrac{3}{4} + \dfrac{3}{8} + \dfrac{3}{16} + \cdots$

14. $\dfrac{2}{3} + \dfrac{1}{3} + \dfrac{1}{6} + \cdots$

15. $9 + 6 + 4 + \cdots$

16. $16 + 12 + 9 + \cdots$

17. $1 - \dfrac{1}{2} + \dfrac{1}{4} - \dfrac{1}{8} + \cdots$

18. $1 - \dfrac{1}{3} + \dfrac{1}{9} - \dfrac{1}{27} + \cdots$

19. $7 + \dfrac{7}{2} + \dfrac{7}{4} + \dfrac{7}{8} + \cdots$

20. $7 - \dfrac{7}{2} + \dfrac{7}{4} - \dfrac{7}{8} + \cdots$

21. $\displaystyle\sum_{k=1}^{\infty} 10\left(\dfrac{1}{2}\right)^k$

22. $\displaystyle\sum_{k=1}^{\infty} 12\left(\dfrac{1}{3}\right)^k$

23. $\displaystyle\sum_{k=1}^{\infty} 10\left(-\dfrac{1}{2}\right)^k$

24. $\displaystyle\sum_{k=1}^{\infty} 12\left(-\dfrac{1}{3}\right)^k$

25. $\displaystyle\sum_{k=1}^{\infty} 23\left(\dfrac{1}{100}\right)^k$

26. $\displaystyle\sum_{k=1}^{\infty} 32\left(\dfrac{1}{100}\right)^k$

Write each repeating decimal as an infinite series. (Show three terms.) Then express the value as a common fraction.

27. $0.\overline{4}$

28. $0.\overline{8}$

29. $0.\overline{9}$

30. $0.\overline{6}$

31. $0.\overline{23}$

32. $0.\overline{32}$

33. $0.\overline{124}$

34. $0.\overline{214}$

 pplications

B Solve.

35. A metal ball is dropped from a height of 200 cm and bounces to $\dfrac{9}{10}$ its previous height.

   a. What height does it reach following the 100th bounce?

   b. What is the total distance traveled by the ball before it comes to rest?

36. Draw a rectangle. Then follow these steps.

   Step 1.   Shade one fourth the region inside the rectangle.

   Step 2.   Shade one fourth the unshaded region.

   Step 3.   Shade one fourth the unshaded region.

   a. If you continue to shade the rectangle in the same manner, what fraction of the rectangle is shaded in the 100th step?

   b. What fraction of the rectangle remains unshaded after the 100th step?

   c. How much of the rectangle is shaded if the steps are continued endlessly?

   d. How much of the rectangle remains unshaded if the steps are continued endlessly?

37. A parent pushing a small child in a swing causes the child to travel 21 ft for each arc the swing passes through. When the swing comes to a gradual rest, the length of each arc is 85% that of the previous one. How far does the child swing before coming to a rest?

38. Once set in motion, a yo-yo rises to $\frac{8}{10}$ its previous height each time it returns. How far does the yo-yo travel before coming to rest if the length of its string is 1 m? How much farther will the yo-yo travel if it rises to $\frac{9}{10}$ its previous height each time it returns?

39. The first six terms of the *Fibonacci sequence* are 1, 1, 2, 3, 5, 8. Each successive term is the sum of the two preceding terms. Use a calculator to determine what happens to the ratios of successive terms:

$$\frac{1}{1}, \frac{2}{1}, \frac{3}{2}, \frac{5}{3}, \cdots$$

40. A weight attached to a spring is in its rest position. If the spring is stretched by pulling the weight 40 cm below its rest position and released, the weight will oscillate back and forth past the rest position until it comes to a gradual stop. Each time the weight passes the rest position it will move a distance equal to $\frac{3}{5}$ of the previous displacement. How far will the weight travel?

at rest

40 cm

C **41.** Successive squares within squares are formed by joining the midpoints of the sides. The area is shaded as shown. If this process is continued indefinitely, what fraction of the largest square will be shaded?

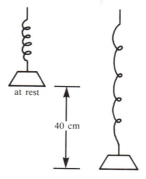

42. Find the sum of the altitudes $h, h_1, h_2, \ldots$ if the sequence of altitudes is continued indefinitely.

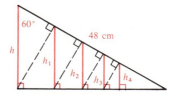

$60°$ 48 cm

h h_1 h_2 h_3 h_4

43. Suppose that an infinite tree is structured as follows. The trunk is 100 cm long. At the end of one year two branches are formed. At the end of the next year each branch grows two more branches. The pattern continues with twice as many branches formed each year. The length of the new branch is half the length of the previous branch, that is, 50 cm, 25 cm, 12.5 cm, and so on. The branches are vertical, horizontal, or 45° from vertical or horizontal as shown.

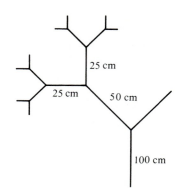

a. What is the length of each branch formed in the 50th year?

b. How many branches are formed in the 50th year?

c. What is the height of the infinite tree?

d. How close to the ground do the tips of the branches get?

$\mathcal{R}$EVIEW EXERCISES

Solve.

1. $\ln e^2 = x$　　　　　　　　　　　　　　**2.** $\ln x = 0$　　　　　　　　　　　[11-5]

3. $1.08^x = 2$ (If a calculator is available, simplify the solution. If not, write the solution in computational form.)　　　　　　　　　　　[11-6]

4. How many years must $1000 be invested at 10%, compounded annually, in order for the value of the investment to reach $2500?　　　　　　　[11-6]

5. $\log_5 (x + 3) = 2$　　　　　　　　　　**6.** $\log a + \log 4 = 3$　　　　[11-7]

$\mathcal{C}$OMPUTER EXTENSION　Evaluating Series

FOR-NEXT loops are ideal for computing values of a finite series that is expressed in Σ-notation. The following program evaluates

$$\sum_{k=1}^{10} (2k - 1).$$

```
10 FOR K = 1 TO 10
20 X = 2 * K - 1
30 Y = Y + X
40 NEXT K
50 PRINT Y
60 END
```

1. Use the program to evaluate $\sum\limits_{k=1}^{10} (2k - 1)$.　　**2.** Rewrite the program to evaluate $\sum\limits_{k=1}^{100} (2k - 1)$.

3. Rewrite the program to evaluate $\sum\limits_{k=1}^{30} \left(\frac{1}{2}\right)^k$.

CHAPTER SUMMARY

▶ A *sequence* is a function defined on the positive integers or on a subset of consecutive positive integers starting with 1. [12-1]

▶ For each positive integer n, the sequence with first term a_1 and nth term a_n is an *arithmetic sequence* if and only if $a_n = a_1 + (n - 1)d$. [12-1]

▶ For each positive integer n, and for each real number r, $r \neq 0$, the sequence with first term a_1 and nth term a_n is a geometric sequence if and only if $a_n = a_1 r^{n-1}$. [12-2]

▶ A *series* is the indicated sum of the terms of a sequence. [12-3]

▶ For an arithmetic series in which a_1 is the first term, d is the common difference, a_n is the last term, and S_n is the value of the series: [12-4]

$$S_n = \frac{n(a_1 + a_n)}{2} \quad \text{and} \quad S_n = \frac{n[2a_1 + (n-1)d]}{2}.$$

▶ For a geometric sequence in which a_1 is the first term, a_n is the last term, r is the common ratio ($r \neq 1$), and S_n is the value of the series: [12-5]

$$S_n = \frac{a_1 - a_1 r^n}{1 - r} \quad \text{and} \quad S_n = \frac{a_1 - a_n r}{1 - r}.$$

▶ The value of an infinite geometric series with first term a_1 and common ratio r, $|r| < 1$, is given by the formula [12-6]

$$S = \frac{a_1}{1 - r}.$$

12-1 **Objective:** To write the terms of a sequence from the given definition.

Write the 1st and 8th terms of the sequence.

1. $t_n = 2^n - 1$ **2.** $t_n = -2n + 4$

Objective: To write the terms of an arithmetic sequence.

State whether the sequence is an arithmetic sequence.

3. 9, 27, 81, 243, . . .   **4.** $a_n = n^2$

Write the indicated term for each arithmetic sequence.

5. 1, 4, 7, 10, . . . ; a_{19} **6.** $a_4 = 14$ and $a_8 = 30$; a_1

7. Write the three arithmetic means between 2 and 8.

12-2 **Objective:** To write the terms of a geometric sequence.

State whether the sequence is a geometric sequence, arithmetic sequence, or other kind of sequence.

8. $a_n = -6 + 7n$ **9.** $\dfrac{1}{2}, \dfrac{1}{4}, \dfrac{1}{8}, \dfrac{1}{16}, \ldots$

10. $\dfrac{1}{18}, \dfrac{1}{3}, 2, \ldots$ **11.** $a_n = 200(0.1)^n$

12. Find the geometric mean of $\dfrac{1}{9}$ and 16.

13. The population of Drewsville was 8000 in 1940. If the population has been decreasing by 10% each 10 years, what was the population in 1980?

12-3 **Objective:** To express a series in expanded form or Σ-notation and to determine the value of the series.

14. Write the series S_5 for the sequence 1, 4, 9, 16, ...

15. Write the series $\displaystyle\sum_{k=1}^{4} (3k + 2)$ in expanded form.

16. Write the series $9 + 18 + 27 + \cdots + 63$ in Σ-notation.

17. Find the value of the series $\displaystyle\sum_{k=1}^{4} \dfrac{(k - 1)}{(k + 1)}$.

12-4 **Objective:** To apply the formulas $S_n = \dfrac{n(a_1 + a_n)}{2}$ and $S_n = \dfrac{n}{2}[2a_1 + (n - 1)d]$.

Find the value of each series.

18. S_9 for the sequence 12, 20, 28, 36, . . .

19. $10 + 21 + 32 + 43 + \cdots + 1099$ **20.** $\displaystyle\sum_{k=1}^{20} 3k$

21. It took 9 days for a survivor of a desert accident to escape from the desert on foot. If the survivor covered 16 mi the first day and $1\frac{1}{2}$ fewer mi each succeeding day, how many miles were covered in the 9 days?

12-5 **Objective:** To apply the formulas $S_n = \dfrac{a_1 - a_1 r^n}{1 - r}$ and $S_n = \dfrac{a_1 - a_n r}{1 - r}$.

State the value in exponential notation.

22. S_7 for the sequence $4, 2, 1, \frac{1}{2}, \ldots$

23. $\displaystyle\sum_{k=1}^{4} 5 \cdot 10^k$

State the value.

24. S_7 for the series $2 - 4 + 8 - 16 + \cdots + 128$

25. $\displaystyle\sum_{k=1}^{4} 81 \left(\frac{1}{3}\right)^k$

12-6 **Objective:** To determine whether an infinite geometric series has a finite sum and to determine the value if it exists.

State whether the infinite series converges.

26. $\dfrac{4}{10} + \dfrac{4}{100} + \dfrac{4}{1000} + \dfrac{4}{10,000} + \cdots$

27. $\dfrac{1}{16} + \dfrac{1}{8} + \dfrac{1}{4} + \dfrac{1}{2} + \cdots$

Find the value of the infinite series.

28. $18 + 12 + 8 + \dfrac{16}{3} + \cdots$

29. $\displaystyle\sum_{k=1}^{\infty} \left(\frac{5}{6}\right)^k$

30. The tip of a pendulum swings through an initial distance of 30 cm. On each succeeding swing, the tip covers $\frac{2}{3}$ the distance of the previous swing. Through what total distance does the tip move?

$\mathcal{C}$HAPTER 12 SELF-TEST

12-1 **Find the indicated term of the given sequence.**

    1. Find t_5 given that $t_n = 3n^2$.

    2. Find a_{10} given that $a_n = n^2 + 4$.

12-1, **Identify the sequence or series as arithmetic, geometric, or other.**
12-2

    3. $1, 3, 7, 15, 31, \ldots$

    4. $16, 40, 100, 250, 625, \ldots$

    5. $\displaystyle\sum_{k=1}^{40} (k + 17)$

    6. $\displaystyle\sum_{k=1}^{20} 3k$

12-1 **7.** Write the explicit definition of the arithmetic sequence $8, 10, 12, 14, 16, \ldots$.

    8. Find the three arithmetic means between 1 and 17.

12-2 **9.** Find the geometric mean of 14 and 56.

10. The fifth term of a geometric sequence is $\frac{16}{3}$. If the ratio between terms of the sequence is $\frac{2}{3}$, then what is the first term?

12-3 **11.** Give the value of S_4 for the sequence 1, 4, 9, 16, 25, 36.

12. Write $\sum\limits_{k=1}^{5} (-2k)$ in expanded form.

12-4 **13.** The second term of an arithmetic series of 20 terms is 5. If the common difference between terms of the series is 3, then what is the value of the series?

12-4 **Determine the value of the series.**

14. $3 + 6 + 9 + \cdots + 300$

15. An arithmetic series where $a_1 = 2$, $a_n = 14$, and $n = 20$

Solve.

16. Logs are stacked in the manner shown here. If the total number of logs is 105, how many logs are in the bottom row?

12-5 **17.** In an eating competition, a contestant consumed 64 grapes in the first minute. During each additional minute, the contestant ate $\frac{3}{4}$ as many grapes as in the previous minute. About how many grapes were eaten in 6 minutes?

12-5, **Find the value of each series.**
12-6

18. $\sum\limits_{k=1}^{6} 3 \cdot 2^k$

19. $9 + \frac{9}{4} + \frac{9}{16} + \frac{9}{64} + \cdots$

12-6 **20.** Write the repeating decimal $0.\overline{42}$ as a common fraction.

$\mathscr{P}$RACTICE FOR COLLEGE ENTRANCE TESTS

Choose the best answer to each question.

1. The Central High School basketball team has 12 players in uniform for each game, all of them juniors or seniors. Which of the following could not be the ratio of seniors who are in uniform for a game?

   A. 1:1   **B.** 2:1   **C.** 3:1   **D.** 4:1   **E.** 5:1

2. The first term of a finite sequence is 1. Each successive term is the product of the preceding term and -1. Which of the following is the set of all possible sums of the sequence?

A. $\{0\}$ **B.** $\{1\}$ **C.** $\{0, 1\}$ **D.** $\{-1, 1\}$ **E.** $\{-1, 0, 1\}$

3. $S_5 = \left(\frac{1}{2}\right) + \left(\frac{1}{4}\right) + \left(\frac{1}{8}\right) + \left(\frac{1}{16}\right) + \left(\frac{1}{32}\right)$, then $2(1 - S_5) = $ _?_ .

A. $\frac{1}{4}$ **B.** $\frac{1}{8}$ **C.** $\frac{1}{16}$ **D.** $\frac{1}{32}$ **E.** $\frac{1}{64}$

4. If the first two terms of a sequence are 1 and 2 and each succeeding term is the product of the preceding two terms, then what is the sixth term in the sequence?

A. 16   **B.** 32   **C.** 64   **D.** 128   **E.** 256

5. A deck of cards in the seven colors of the rainbow is arranged in this repeating pattern: red, orange, yellow, green, blue, indigo, violet, red, orange, yellow, ... What is the color of the 50th card in the deck?

A. Red   **B.** Orange   **C.** Blue   **D.** Indigo   **E.** Violet

6. A student council has a 4-day fundraising drive for famine relief. Twice as much money was raised each day as on the previous day, and the total amount raised was $300. How much was raised on the first day?

A. $10   **B.** $15   **C.** $20   **D.** $25   **E.** $30

7. If $\displaystyle\sum_{k=1}^{8} k + x = \sum_{k=1}^{10} k$, then $x = $ _?_ .

A. 17   **B.** 18   **C.** 19   **D.** 20   **E.** 21

8. There are eight teams in a basketball league, and during the regular season each team plays each of the other teams twice. How many games are played in all during the regular league season?

A. 49   **B.** 56   **C.** 64   **D.** 112   **E.** 128

9. A square piece of paper is repeatedly folded in half until the area of the exposed side is $\frac{1}{64}$ of the original area. How many times will the paper have been folded?

A. 4   **B.** 5   **C.** 6   **D.** 7   **E.** 8

10. If $n = \dfrac{a}{18} + \dfrac{a}{18} + \dfrac{a}{18}$, the least positive integer a for which n is an integer is _?_ .

A. 3   **B.** 6   **C.** 8   **D.** 12   **E.** 18

11. $\displaystyle\sum_{k=1}^{10} k = $ _?_ .

A. 45   **B.** 50   **C.** 55   **D.** 100   **E.** 110

$\mathcal{C}$UMULATIVE REVIEW (CHAPTERS 10–12)

10-1 **1.** Use synthetic substitution to find $f(-3)$ for the polynomial function $f(x) = x^4 - 8x^3 + 4x^2 - x + 1$.

2. What is the degree of the polynomial in Exercise 1?

10-2 **3.** What is the remainder when $P(x) = 2x^3 + x^2 - 6x + 9$ is divided by $x + 2$?

4. Show that $x - 3$ is a factor of $P(x) = 4x^3 - 11x^2 - 5x + 6$.

5. For what value of k is $x - 2$ a factor of $f(x) = x^4 - 6x^2 + k$?

10-3 **6.** Solve: $x^3 - 2x^2 - 5x + 6 = 0$.

7. Write a fourth-degree equation in factored form with these roots: -2, 3, and 4 (multiplicity two).

8. What is the minimum number of real roots that a fifth-degree polynomial equation $P(x) = 0$ with real coefficients can have?

10-4 **9.** If $f(x) = 8x^3 - 12x^2 - 26x + 15$, use the following table to locate the roots of $f(x) = 0$ between consecutive integers.

x	-2	-1	0	1	2	3
$f(x)$	-45	21	15	-15	-21	45

10-5 **10.** State the inverse of $g = \{(2, 3), (-1, 4), (5, 0)\}$.

11. Write the defining equation of the inverse of $f(x) = 5x - 1$.

11-1 **Sketch the graph.**

12. $y = 2^x$

13. $y = \left(\dfrac{1}{2}\right)^x$

Is the function increasing or decreasing?

14. $y = 2^x$

15. $y = 2^{-x}$

16. $y = -2^x$

Solve.

17. $4^{x+2} = 64$

18. $9^{2x-1} = 81$

11-2 **Write in logarithmic form.**

19. $5^4 = 625$

20. $10^6 = 1,000,000$

Write in exponential form.

21. $\log_6 36 = 2$

22. $\log_4 8 = 1.5$

11-3 **Write in expanded form.**

23. $\log_3 x^2 y$

11-3 **Write as a single logarithm.**

24. $\dfrac{1}{2} \log_6 x - \log_6 y$

524 Chapter 12 Sequences and Series

11-4 **Use this fact in Exercises 25–27: log 5 = 0.6990.**

    25. Evaluate.

        a. log 500   **b.** log 25

    Solve.

    26. $10^{0.6990} = x$ **27.** $\log x = 1.6990$

11-5 **28.** $\ln x = 1$ **29.** $\ln 34 = x$

11-6 **30.** $3^x = 100$ **31.** $10^x = 6^{x+2}$

    32. $9^{x+1} = 27^{x-1}$ **33.** Solve for t: $A = e^{rt}$.

11-7 **34.** $\log (x + 3) = 1$ **35.** $\log_6 x + \log_6 (x - 1) = 1$

11-8 **36.** A radioactive material decays according to the formula $N = N_0 e^{-kt}$. Find the decay constant k if 40 g of an original 200 g remain undecayed after 3 years.

12-1 **State the 3rd and 8th terms of each sequence.**

    37. $t_n = 2^n - 1$ **38.** 60, 30, 20, 15, 12, . . .

    Find the indicated term of each arithmetic sequence.

    39. $a_n = 4 + 9n$; a_{10} **40.** 20, 19.5, 19, 18.5, 18, . . . ; a_{24}

12-2 **41.** State whether the sequence $\frac{1}{3}, 2, 3\frac{2}{3}, 5\frac{1}{3}, \ldots$, is arithmetic, geometric, or other.

    Find the 7th term of each geometric sequence.

    42. $18, -36, 72, -144, \ldots$ **43.** $a_n = \left(\frac{2}{3}\right)^n$

12-3 **44.** Given the sequence 18, 15, 12, 9, . . . , write the series S_6 and state its value.

    Write each series in expanded form and state its value.

    45. $\displaystyle\sum_{k=1}^{4} (7 - 2k)$ **46.** $\displaystyle\sum_{k=0}^{5} 10^k$

12-4 **Find the value of each series.**

    47. $20 + 24 + 28 + \ldots + 56$ **48.** $\displaystyle\sum_{k=1}^{10} (k + 6)$

12-5 **State the value of each series.**

    49. $8 + 2 + \frac{1}{2} + \frac{1}{8} + \frac{1}{32} + \frac{1}{128}$ **50.** $\displaystyle\sum_{k=1}^{6}$

12-6 **51.** Express the repeating decimal $0.\overline{15}$ as a common fraction.

    52. Find the value of the infinite series $12 + 3 + \frac{3}{4} + \frac{3}{16} + \ldots$.

CHAPTER 13

Probability

Robots—reprogrammable, multifunctional manipulators that move materials, parts, or tools through variable programmed motions—are being used to automate factory production throughout the industrial world. Robots allow humans to escape from boring, hazardous, or repetitive tasks that require exacting precision.

Whether parts are produced by robots or humans, however, there is always a possibility that some parts are defective. Frequently, it is impossible or impractical to test every part—the test may destroy the part or the test may be very expensive. Thus the manufacturers must decide what percent of the parts should be tested. Probability theory is used in making these sampling decisions.

A Counting Principle

In this lesson you will learn how to determine systematically the number of possible ways in which a task can be performed.

Suppose a travel agent offers a number of different tours to Egypt. The cost of a tour depends on the number of days you stay (10, 14, or 17 days), the season of the year in which you travel, and whether you take an optional Nile cruise. The **tree diagram** shows the total number of tours that can be taken. For each trip-length branch there are four season branches. For each length-season branch there are two cruise branches.

The path in red is a 14-day tour in the spring with a Nile cruise.

There are 24 paths, each one representing a different tour. Note that 24 is the product of 3, 4, and 2, the number of choices, respectively, for the three components of a tour. This example illustrates the Fundamental Counting Principle.

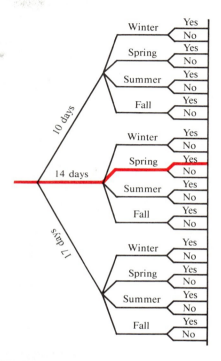

Fundamental Counting Principle

If one event can occur in m ways and a second event can occur in n ways, the pair of events can occur in mn ways.

This principle can be generalized to include multiple events that can occur in n_1, n_2, n_3, . . . n_k ways. The collection of k events can occur in a total of $n_1 \cdot n_2 \cdot n_3 \cdot . . . . \cdot n_k$ ways.

Example 1   Use the Fundamental Counting Principle to solve this problem.

Each Sunday a newspaper publishes a list of 15 bestselling fiction books and 10 bestselling nonfiction books. In how many different ways can one fiction book and one nonfiction book be selected from the list?

Solution   A fiction book can be selected in 15 ways and a nonfiction book can be selected in 10 ways. A fiction book and a nonfiction book can be selected in 15 · 10, or 150 ways.

Example 2 **Solve.**

A pizza parlor offers these toppings for pizza: sausage, pepperoni, onion, mushroom, and green pepper. A pizza can be made with any combination of the toppings or with no topping. How many different kinds of pizza can be made?

Solution For each topping one of two decisions must be made: include or do not include. For example, if the following decisions are made, a sausage-onion pizza is the result.

sausage	pepperoni	onion	mushroom	green pepper
yes	no	yes	no	no

The total number of decisions is $2 \cdot 2 \cdot 2 \cdot 2 \cdot 2$.

Answer There are 32 different kinds of pizza.

LASSROOM EXERCISES

1. In the example of the Egyptian tour, how many choices are there for a person who has only a two-week vacation that must be taken in the winter?

2. In Example 1, suppose that 5 of the nonfiction books are biographies. How many choices are there of a fiction book and a biography?

3. An automobile is available in 6 colors, 2 body styles, and 3 engine sizes. How many choices are available to a customer?

WRITTEN EXERCISES

A **Solve.**

1. A baseball team has 6 pitchers and 3 catchers. How many different pitcher-catcher combinations are there?

2. There are 4 roads from Carleton to Washington and 6 roads from Washington to Hareton. How many Carleton-Washington-Hareton routes are there?

3. There are 56 girls and 48 boys at a dance. In how many different ways can a girl-boy couple be formed for dancing?

4. Twenty-five students were nominated for student council president and eighteen other students were nominated for secretary. How many different president-secretary pairs are possible?

5. James has 4 pairs of trousers, 5 shirts, and 2 pairs of boots. How many outfits can he wear?

6. An ice-cream shop has 10 flavors of ice cream, 5 kinds of syrup, and 3 toppings. How many different sundaes can be made with one scoop of ice cream, one syrup, and one topping?

7. In a club election 4 students run for president, 3 for vice-president, 5 for secretary, and 3 for treasurer. How many possible outcomes are there for the election?

8. A menu at a small restaurant offers 4 appetizers, 3 salads, 6 entrees, and 3 desserts. How many four-course dinners are available?

9. How many subscripted variables a_{ij} can be formed if i can be replaced by 1, 2, 3, or 4 and j can be replaced by 1, 2, or 3?

10. There are 16 caddies available for 12 golfers. How many golfer-caddie combinations are possible?

11. A coin is flipped ten times. How many different sequences of heads and tails (such as HHHTTHTTHT) are possible? Write your answer in exponential notation.

12. A die is rolled ten times. How many different sequences of outcomes (such as 1, 3, 6, 3, 5, 4, 2, 1, 4, 3) can occur? Write your answer in exponential notation.

13. How many three-digit numbers are even? [*Hint:* How many different digits may be used in the hundreds place? tens place? ones place?]

14. How many three-digit numbers have three different digits?

B **Karla has 15 mysteries, 12 science-fiction books, and 8 sports books in her collection.**

15. In how many ways can Karla's friend Dave borrow one science-fiction book and one sports book?

16. In how many ways can Dave borrow one book of each kind?

17. In how many ways can Dave borrow 2 mysteries?

18. Flags are made by sewing three colored sections together. Five colors are available and adjacent sections must have different colors. How many different flags can be made?

19. A flag is made by selecting a colored background, one of the symbols ▼ ★ ● ◆ ♣, and a color for the symbol. There are six colors to choose from, and the symbol and background must be different colors. How many different flags can be made?

20. In how many different ways can 10 questions on a true-false test be answered if a student answers every question? if some questions may be left unanswered?

21. Ten people were invited to a party. How many different sets of guests might show up or not show up? [*Hint:* Each guest has two choices: show up or not show up.]

22. In how many ways can 6 multiple-choice questions be answered if each question has 4 choices and each question is answered? if some questions are left unanswered?

23. There are 16 caddies available for 12 golfers. How many golfer-caddie combinations are there if some golfers prefer not to have a caddie?

24. A red die and a green die are tossed. How many different outcomes are possible? Each outcome is a "red-green" pair of numbers.

25. A license plate contains 3 letters followed by 3 digits. How many different license plates can be formed?

26. How many license plates can be formed (see Exercise 25) if the letters I and O are not used?

27. A gift shop assembles fruit baskets containing apples, oranges, and pears. There are from 1 to 8 apples, 1 to 6 oranges, and 1 to 5 pears in each basket. How many different selections of fruit are possible?

28. In Exercise 27, how many different selections of fruit are possible if a selection must contain apples and oranges, but not necessarily pears?

29. One of a club's rules requires that at least one of the club's 8 members be inside the clubhouse at all times. How many different selections of members can satisfy this rule of the club?

$\mathcal{R}$EVIEW EXERCISES

Simplify. State restrictions on the variables.

1. $\sqrt[3]{-64}$

2. $\sqrt{20a^2b^3}$

3. $(2 + \sqrt{3})^2$

4. $\sqrt[3]{54} - \sqrt[3]{16}$

5. $\dfrac{1 - x}{1 - \sqrt{x}}$

6. $\dfrac{6x}{\sqrt[3]{3x^2}}$

7. Find the distance between $(-8, 6)$ and $(4, 1)$.

8. Solve: $\sqrt{x - 3} = x - 3$.

9. Write using rational exponents: $\sqrt{2} + \sqrt[3]{5}$.

[7-1, 7-2, 7-3, 7-4], [7-5] [7-6] [7-7]

ℰXTENSION Circle Graphs

Circle graphs show how parts are related to the whole. This circle graph was made using the following data about undergraduate degrees conferred in the United States in 1986.

238,160	in business
93,703	in social sciences
64,535	in health
95,953	in engineering
87,221	in education

Total number of degrees = 987,823

Using the number of degrees in its central angle, a pie-shaped sector of the circle is drawn so that its size is proportional to the number of undergraduate degrees it represents.

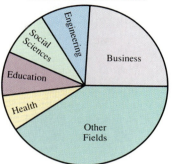

Distribution of Undergraduate Degrees Granted in the United States

For example,

$$\frac{\text{business degrees}}{\text{total degrees}} = \frac{238160}{987823} \approx 24.1\%$$

There are 360° in a circle and 24.1% of 360 ≈ 87. Therefore, the sector for business should be drawn with a central angle of 87°. Similarly, central angles are computed and sectors are drawn for each of the other categories.

1. Compute the percent and central angle for each of the other sectors of this circle graph.

2. In 1986, 288,567 masters degrees were conferred. Of these, 76,353 were in education, 67,137 in business, 21,661 in engineering, 18,624 in health, and 10,465 in social sciences. Make a circle graph showing the distribution of masters degrees. Put the sectors in the same order as in the graph for undergraduate degrees so that the two graphs can be easily compared.

3. Survey your classmates to learn what they plan to do after graduation from high school. Draw a circle graph of the results.

Permutations

Mathematicians first became interested in counting the ways in which an event can occur when they began to study probability in the period 1770–1870. In such counting, products of consecutive integers like

$$12 \cdot 11 \cdot 10 \cdot 9 \cdot 8 \cdot 7 \cdot 6 \cdot 5 \cdot 4 \cdot 3 \cdot 2 \cdot 1$$

occur frequently. These products take too much space to write out, so shorter symbols were invented. Some of the symbols suggested by mathematicians are shown.

Year	Mathematician	Year
1774	Basedow	12*
1808	Legendre	$\Gamma(13)$
1811	Gauss	$\Pi(12)$
1816	Kramp	12!
1827	Jarrett	⌊12
1838	DeMorgan	[12]
1841	Weierstrauss	12⌐
1855	Carmichael	$\overline{12}$

Two of the notations (12! and ⌊12) continued to be used into the twentieth century. Of those, 12! is now the accepted notation.

Suppose that 7 people are to be arranged in a line for a photograph. The first person in line can be chosen in 7 ways. The second person can be chosen from among the 6 remaining people. The third person can be chosen in 5 ways, and so on.

$$\underline{\quad}\ \underline{\quad}\ \underline{\quad}\ \underline{\quad}\ \underline{\quad}\ \underline{\quad}\ \underline{\quad}$$
$$\uparrow\quad\uparrow\quad\uparrow\quad\uparrow\quad\uparrow\quad\uparrow\quad\uparrow$$
$$7\quad 6\quad 5\quad 4\quad 3\quad 2\quad 1$$

By the Fundamental Counting Principal the total number of arrangements of the 7 people is $7 \cdot 6 \cdot 5 \cdot 4 \cdot 3 \cdot 2 \cdot 1$, or 5040. Each arrangement of the people is called a **permutation**.

Definition: Permutation

A *permutation* of a number of objects is any arrangement of the objects in a definite order.

Example 1 How many permutations are there of 4 people selected from a group of 35?

Solution The first person can be selected in 35 ways. Then the next can be selected in 34 ways, the third can be selected in 33 ways, and the fourth can be selected in 32 ways.

$$\underline{\quad}\ \underline{\quad}\ \underline{\quad}\ \underline{\quad}$$
$$\uparrow\quad\uparrow\quad\uparrow\quad\uparrow$$
$$35\quad 34\quad 33\quad 32$$

Answer By the Fundamental Counting Principle the total number of permutations is $35 \cdot 34 \cdot 33 \cdot 32$, or 1,256,640.

The symbol $_{35}P_4$ is used to represent "the number of permutations of 35 things taken 4 at a time."

$$_{35}P_4 = 35 \cdot 34 \cdot 33 \cdot 32$$

The number of permutations of 7 things taken 7 at a time is

$$_7P_7 = 7 \cdot 6 \cdot 5 \cdot 4 \cdot 3 \cdot 2 \cdot 1.$$

The product $7 \cdot 6 \cdot 5 \cdot 4 \cdot 3 \cdot 2 \cdot 1$ is written as 7! (read "seven **factorial**").

Definition: Factorial Notation

For each positive integer n, $n! = n(n - 1)(n - 2) \cdots 3 \cdot 2 \cdot 1.$
Also, $0! = 1.$

Applying factorial notation to our permutations gives:

$$_7P_7 = 7 \cdot 6 \cdot 5 \cdot 4 \cdot 3 \cdot 2 \cdot 1 = 7!$$

$$_{35}P_4 = \frac{35 \cdot 34 \cdot 33 \cdot 32 \cdot 31 \cdot 30 \cdot 29 \cdot \ldots \cdot 3 \cdot 2 \cdot 1}{31 \cdot 30 \cdot 29 \cdot \ldots \cdot 3 \cdot 2 \cdot 1} = \frac{35!}{31!}$$

In general, we have the following definition of permutation notation.

Definition: $_nP_r$ Notation

For all positive integers n and r, where $r \leqslant n$, the number of permutations of n things taken r at a time is

$$_nP_r = \frac{n!}{(n - r)!}.$$

Example 2   **How many permutations are there of 5 cards taken from a deck of 52 cards?**

Solution   The number of permutations of 52 cards taken 5 at a time is $_{52}P_5$, or $\dfrac{52!}{(52 - 5)!}$.

$$\frac{52!}{(52 - 5)!} = \frac{52 \cdot 51 \cdot 50 \cdot 49 \cdot 48 \cdot 47 \cdot 46 \cdot \ldots \cdot 3 \cdot 2 \cdot 1}{47 \cdot 46 \cdot 45 \cdot \ldots \cdot 3 \cdot 2 \cdot 1}$$

$$= 52 \cdot 51 \cdot 50 \cdot 49 \cdot 48$$

$$= 311{,}875{,}200$$

Answer   There are 311,875,200 permutations of 5 cards selected from a deck of 52 cards.

Example 3   In how many ways can a president, vice-president, secretary, and treasurer be elected from a club with 30 members?

Solution   If we assume that no person can hold two offices and that all members are eligible for all offices, this problem involves the number of permutations of 30 people taken 4 at a time.

$$_{30}P_4 = \frac{30!}{(30-4)!} = \frac{30 \cdot 29 \cdot 28 \cdot 27 \cdot 26 \cdot 25 \cdot \ldots \cdot 3 \cdot 2 \cdot 1}{26 \cdot 25 \cdot 24 \cdot \ldots \cdot 3 \cdot 2 \cdot 1} = 30 \cdot 29 \cdot 28 \cdot 27$$

$$= 657,720$$

Answer   There are 657,720 ways.

Now consider the question, "In how many ways can the letters of the word BOOT be arranged?" There are $_4P_4$ arrangements of the four letters of the word BOOT. Not all of those arrangements look different, however. Using subscripts temporarily to distinguish the O's, we see that O_1, T, O_2, B and O_2, T, O_1, B are both counted but look the same. For each arrangement of the letters with O's in one order, there is a matching arrangement with the O's interchanged. Since there are $_2P_2$ arrangements of the O's, we must divide $_4P_4$ by $_2P_2$ to obtain the number of *visibly* different arrangements of the letters. Therefore, there are $\frac{_4P_4}{_2P_2} = \frac{4!}{2!} = 12$ distinguishable arrangements of the letters of the word BOOT.

Permutations with Repetitions

For all positive integers n and r, where $r \leq n$, the number of distinguishable permutations of n objects, r of which are alike, is

$$\frac{_nP_n}{_rP_r} = \frac{n!}{r!}.$$

Generally, if there are r_1 objects of one kind, r_2 of a second kind, and so on, there are $\frac{n!}{r_1!r_2!\cdots}$ distinguishable permutations of n things.

Example 4   How many distinguishable permutations are there of the letters in MISSISSIPPI?

Solution   There are 11 letters including 4 I's, 4 S's, and 2 P's. Therefore, there are $\frac{_{11}P_{11}}{_4P_4 \cdot _4P_4 \cdot _2P_2} = \frac{11!}{4!4!2!}$ distinguishable permutations.

Answer   There are 34,650 distinguishable permutations of the letters in the word MISSISSIPPI.

Simplify.

1. 6!

2. $\frac{8!}{5!}$

3. $\frac{8!}{4!2!}$

4. 0! + 1! + 2!

5. How many 4-digit numbers can be formed from the digits 1–9 if a digit can be used only once? more than once?

6. How many distinguishable permutations are there of the letters of the word MISSISSIPPI if the M must always come first?

WRITTEN EXERCISES

 Simplify.

1. 6! − 2!

2. 5! + 3!

3. $\frac{6!}{3!}$

4. $\frac{8!}{4!}$

5. 4!0!

6. (0 · 4)!

7. $\frac{8!}{5!3!}$

8. $\frac{10!}{8!2!}$

9. $\frac{9!}{(9-3)!}$

10. $\frac{10!}{(10-2)!}$

11. $_6P_3$

12. $_7P_5$

13. $(_8P_3)(_4P_2)$

14. $(_6P_3)(_7P_4)$

15. $\frac{_7P_7}{_4P_4}$

16. $\frac{_8P_5}{_6P_3}$

In how many different ways can the letters of these words be arranged?

17. MERCY

18. OXYGEN

19. DUNGEON

20. REFLECT

21. FOLLOW

22. REFEREE

Solve.

23. How many three-digit numbers can be formed from 1, 2, 3, 4, 5?

24. How many three-digit numbers can be formed from 1, 2, 3, 4, 5 if each digit is used at most once?

25. How many three-digit numbers can be formed using these digit cards?

26. How many three-digit numbers can be formed using these digit cards?

| 1 | 1 | 1 | 2 | 2 | 2 | 3 | 3 | 3 |

B **27.** How many batting orders are there for the 9 players starting a baseball game?

28. How many batting orders are there for 9 baseball players if the three best hitters are placed in the 1st, 4th, and 5th positions?

29. In how many ways can 3 men and 3 women be seated in a row for a photograph?

30. In how many ways can 3 men and 3 women be seated in a row if a woman is to be at each end?

31. In how many ways can 3 men and 3 women be seated in a row if the men and women must alternate?

32. In walking from his home to school, Ramon must go 6 blocks south and 4 blocks west. One route is SSWWSWSWSS. How many different 10-block routes are possible?

33. It is 10 blocks from A to B. How many 10-block routes are there from A to B? How many of the routes go through C? through D?

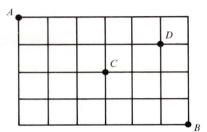

C *A*pplication: Circular Permutations

A circular permutation is an arrangement of elements in a circular pattern. Consider 5 people seated around a table. Since there is no "first place" at the table, all of these arrangements of the people are indistinguishable.

So long as the order is maintained, the circular arrangement will be the same. In general, n elements arranged in a circle can be depicted in n indistinguishable ways. Therefore, we must divide the $n!$ linear permutations by n to obtain the correct number of circular permutations.

$$\frac{n!}{n} = \frac{n(n-1)(n-2)\cdot\ldots\cdot 3\cdot 2\cdot 1}{n} = (n-1)!$$

Solve.

34. In how many ways can 6 people be seated around a circular table?

35. In how many ways can 8 dishes be arranged on a lazy-susan revolving platter?

36. A bracelet has 7 charms. How many arrangements of the charms are possible? [*Hint:* Flipping the bracelet over does not produce a new bracelet arrangement.]

37. In how many ways can 5 keys be arranged on a key chain? [See the hint in Exercise 36.]

Application: Stirling's Formula

Stirling's formula gives an estimate of $n!$ that is quite accurate for large values of n.

For large n,

$$n! \approx \left(\frac{n}{e}\right)^n \cdot \sqrt{2\pi n}.$$

38. Use Stirling's formula to compute 11!. Check the accuracy of your answer by computing 11! directly by multiplication.

REVIEW EXERCISES

Solve.

1. $(x + 3)^2 = 2$ **2.** $x^2 + 2x = 4$ **3.** $x^2 + 81 = 0$ [8-1,
8-2
8-3]

Simplify. [8-4,
8-5]

4. $(-8 + 2i) - (3 + 6i) + (5 + 5i)$ **5.** $\dfrac{5}{3 + 4i}$

Solve. [8-6]

6. $x^4 + 5x^2 = 36$ **7.** $\sqrt{x} + 2 = x$

8. Write $y + (x + 3)^2 = x^2 + 3$ in the form $y = ax^2 + bx + c$ and state whether or not it defines a quadratic function. [8-7]

9. Sketch the three graphs using the same set of axes. [8-8]

   a. $y = (x + 2)^2$ **b.** $y = \frac{1}{2}(x + 2)^2$ **c.** $y = -(x + 2)^2$

10. Find the maximum or minimum value of $y = 100 + 60x - 5x^2$, state whether it is a maximum or minimum, and state the value of x at which it occurs. [8-10]

LESSON 13-3

Combinations

Consider the difference between selecting a four-member committee and selecting four officers—a president, vice-president, secretary, and treasurer. Selecting officers involves permutations. These two slates of officers are different even though the same people are included.

Smith: president	Brown: president
Cooper: vice president	Cooper: vice president
Martin: secretary	Martin: secretary
Brown: treasurer	Smith: treasurer

However, selecting a four-member committee does not involve permutations since order among the commitee members is not important. Such unordered sets are called **combinations**.

Definition: Combination

A *combination* is a selection of objects considered without regard to their order.

Suppose that a club has 30 members. The number of possible slates of 4 officers is $_{30}P_4$, the number of permutations of 30 things taken 4 at a time. The number of 4-member committees is the number of combinations of 30 things taken 4 at a time and is denoted $_{30}C_4$.

Consider how $_{30}P_4$ and $_{30}C_4$ are related. We could form the 4-member permutations as follows. Select a 4-member combination and form its $_4P_4$ permutations. Then select another 4-member combination and form its $_4P_4$ permutations. Continue until all 4-member combinations have been selected. At that time all 4-member permutations will have been formed, too. Using the Fundamental Counting Principle, we have

$$_{30}P_4 = {}_{30}C_4 \cdot {}_4P_4, \quad \text{or} \quad {}_{30}C_4 = \frac{{}_{30}P_4}{{}_4P_4} = \frac{30!}{(30-4)!4!}.$$

This example illustrates the following definition of combination notation.

Definition: $_nC_r$ Notation

For all positive integers n and r, where $r \leq n$, the number of combinations of n things taken r at a time is

$$_nC_r = \frac{{}_nP_r}{{}_rP_r} = \frac{n!}{(n-r)!r!}.$$

Example 1   Simplify. $_8C_5$

Solution $_8C_5 = \dfrac{8!}{(8-5)!5!} = \dfrac{8!}{3!5!} = \dfrac{8 \cdot 7 \cdot 6}{3 \cdot 2 \cdot 1} = 56$

Example 2   **How many 5-card hands can be formed from a deck of 52 cards?**

Solution   The order of the cards is not important. Therefore, we must find the number of combinations

$$_{52}C_5 = \frac{52!}{(52-5)!5!}$$

$$= \frac{52 \cdot 51 \cdot 50 \cdot 49 \cdot 48}{5 \cdot 4 \cdot 3 \cdot 2 \cdot 1} = 2{,}598{,}960$$

Example 3   **Solve.**

How many ways are there to select 3 juniors and 4 seniors from a school chorus with 10 freshmen, 15 sophomores, 18 juniors, and 20 seniors to sing in an all-city chorus?

Solution   The 3 juniors can be selected in $_{18}C_3$ ways.
The 4 seniors can be selected in $_{20}C_4$ ways.
The juniors and seniors can be selected in $_{18}C_3 \cdot {_{20}C_4}$ ways.

$$_{18}C_3 \cdot {_{20}C_4} = \frac{18!}{(18-3)!3!} \cdot \frac{20!}{(20-4)!4!}$$

$$= \frac{18 \cdot 17 \cdot 16}{3 \cdot 2 \cdot 1} \cdot \frac{20 \cdot 19 \cdot 18 \cdot 17}{4 \cdot 3 \cdot 2 \cdot 1} = 3{,}953{,}520$$

$\mathcal{C}$LASSROOM EXERCISES

Convert to factorial notation and simplify.

1. $_6C_4$ **2.** $_6C_2$ **3.** $_8C_3$

State whether each situation involves permutations or combinations.

4. A hand of 5 cards **5.** A baseball-team batting order

6. A team of 6 chosen from 12 people **7.** The answers to a multiple-choice test

8. How many 13-card hands can be formed from a 52-card deck? Use factorials to express your answer.

$\mathcal{W}$RITTEN EXERCISES

 Convert to factorial notation and simplify.

1. $_7C_3$ **2.** $_7C_4$ **3.** $_9C_6$

4. $_{10}C_5$ **5.** $(_4C_2)(_3C_2)$ **6.** $(_8C_5)(_3C_3)$

A bag contains 8 red, 6 blue, and 4 green marbles. In how many ways can these draws be made?

7. 6 marbles

8. 4 marbles

9. 6 marbles, all blue

10. 4 marbles, all green

11. 5 marbles, 3 red and 2 blue

12. 5 marbles, 2 red and 3 blue

13. 3 marbles, 1 of each color

14. 6 marbles, 2 of each color

In how many ways can the following committees be formed from a group of 10 seniors and 7 juniors?

15. 3 seniors and 2 juniors

16. 2 seniors and 3 juniors

17. 5 seniors

18. 5 seniors and 1 junior

Solve.

19. On a 10-item test, in how many ways can a person get 9 items correct and 1 item wrong?

20. A track coach has to choose 4 of her 7 runners to send to a state competition. If we assume that the runners are equally fast, how many 4-runner teams could the coach select?

 21. In how many ways can Amy invite 3 girls and 4 boys to a party from a group of 8 girls and 9 boys, if her friend Kyle must be one of the boys?

22. From a deck of 52 cards, how many 5-card hands have all cards from one suit? all cards one color?

23. There are 25 telephones in an office building. How many different 2-phone connections can be made among the phones?

24. There are 10 points in a plane, no 3 of which are collinear. How many triangles can be formed having the given points as vertices?

25. In Exercise 24, suppose that one of the points must be a vertex of every triangle. How many triangles can be formed?

$\mathcal{A}$pplication: Blood Groups

According to the ABO blood classification system, each person has one of four possible blood types. The blood type is determined by a pair of genes such as A–A or A–O in which one gene (A, B, or O) is contributed by each parent.

The four possible blood types are called A, B, O, and AB. If the two genes are of the same type, the person has that type of blood. If the two genes are different, the dominant gene determines the blood type. Both A and B are dominant over O. (This means, for example, that a person with A–O genes will have A-type blood.) A person with one A gene and one B gene has AB-type blood.

26. List the possible combinations of pairs of genes (Father's gene, Mother's gene) that determine a person's blood type.

27. Determine the pairs from your previous list that decide each blood type.

The 12-member Faultless Tennis Club is hosting a series of singles and doubles matches with the 16-member Racketeers Club.

28. How many different singles matches can be played?

29. How many different doubles matches can be played?

Solve for n.

30. $_nC_2 = 36$

31. $_nC_8 = 4(_nC_7)$

C **32.** If $_nP_r = 110$ and $_nC_r = 55$, find n and r.

33. Use the formula $_nC_r = \dfrac{n!}{(n-r)!\,r!}$ to show that $_nC_r = {}_nC_{n-r}$.

34. Show that $_{n+1}C_r = {}_nC_r + {}_nC_{r-1}$ (Pascal's Rule).

*R*EVIEW EXERCISES

1. Write an equation in the form $(x - h)^2 + (y - k)^2 = r^2$ for the circle with center $(4, 3)$ and radius 5. [9-1]

2. Write the equation in standard form of the ellipse with center $(0, 0)$, major axis 6 units long on the x-axis, and minor axis 4 units long on the y-axis. [9-3]

3. Sketch the graph of $x^2 - y^2 = 16$. [9-4]

*S*elf-Quiz 1

13-1 **Solve.**

   1. A coin is flipped 4 times. For how many outcomes is the number of heads equal to or greater than the number of tails? [*Hint:* Make a tree diagram.]

13-2, **Simplify.**
13-3
   2. $_7P_3$ **3.** $_{10}C_7$

   Solve.

   4. Three people get into a van with 8 seats. In how many ways can they seat themselves?

   5. A man enters a room with 12 people whom he does not know. He must meet 5 people in order to appear sociable. How many different groups of 5 people could he select to meet?

Probability

The mathematical origin of probability arose from the need to "divide the stakes" at the end of a game of chance where there was no "absolute" winner. In the sixteenth century, mathematicians like Cordano and Galileo wrote rules for specific games of chance. In 1654, George Brassin, a courtier of Louis XIV of France, noticed that their theoretical reasoning on the division did not agree with his observations. He proposed the problem to two mathematicians, Blaise Pascal and Pierre de Fermat. The ensuing correspondence between these two men is regarded as the starting point of the theory of **probability.**

If three coins are flipped, there are 8 possible **outcomes**.

$$H, H, H \quad H, H, T \quad H, T, H \quad H, T, T$$
$$T, H, H \quad T, H, T \quad T, T, H \quad T, T, T$$

The set of all possible outcomes of an experiment is called a **sample space.** A subset of a sample space is called an **event.** The following are examples of events for the sample space above.

Event	Outcomes
Tossing exactly 2 heads:	H, H, T H, T, H T, H, H
Tossing 3 tails:	T, T, T
Tossing 3 alike:	H, H, H T, T, T

If all outcomes in a sample space are equally likely, we can define the probability of an event as follows.

Definition: Probability of an Event

The *probability of an event* is the ratio of the number of outcomes in the event to the number of outcomes in the sample space.

The probability of an event E is denoted by $P(E)$.

Example 1   In the sample space above, what is the probability of each of these events?

    a. Exactly 1 tail   **b.** At least 1 tail

Solution   **a.** $P(1 \text{ tail}) = \dfrac{\text{outcomes with 1 tail}}{\text{outcomes in sample space}} = \dfrac{3}{8}$

           b. $P(\text{at least 1 tail}) = \dfrac{\text{outcomes with 1 or more tails}}{\text{outcomes in sample space}} = \dfrac{7}{8}$

Example 2 Two dice are tossed. State the probability of each event.

   a. The sum is 7.   **b.** The sum is not 7.
   c. The sum is 13.   **d.** The sum is less than 13.

Solution There are 6 numbers on each die. The sample space has 6^2, or 36 outcomes.

Sample space

(1, 1) (1, 2) (1, 3) (1, 4) (1, 5) (1, 6)
(2, 1) (2, 2) (2, 3) (2, 4) (2, 5) (2, 6)
(3, 1) (3, 2) (3, 3) (3, 4) (3, 5) (3, 6)
(4, 1) (4, 2) (4, 3) (4, 4) (4, 5) (4, 6)
(5, 1) (5, 2) (5, 3) (5, 4) (5, 5) (5, 6)
(6, 1) (6, 2) (6, 3) (6, 4) (6, 5) (6, 6)

a. The outcomes with sum 7 are:

$$(1, 6), (2, 5), (3, 4), (4, 3), (5, 2), (6, 1)$$

$$P(\text{sum} = 7) = \frac{6}{36} = \frac{1}{6}$$

b. The 6 outcomes listed in part (a) have sum 7. The remaining 30 outcomes in the sample space have sums different from 7.

$$P(\text{sum} \neq 7) = \frac{30}{36} = \frac{5}{6}$$

c. There are 0 outcomes with sum 13.

$$P(\text{sum} = 13) = \frac{0}{36} = 0$$

d. All 36 outcomes have a sum less than 13.

$$P(\text{sum} < 13) = \frac{36}{36} = 1$$

The event in part (a) of Example 2 contained the outcomes of the sample space with sum 7. The event in part (b) contained all other outcomes of the sample space. Such events are called **complements**.

Definition: Complement of an Event

Event A is the *complement* of event B with respect to sample space S if and only if A and B include all outcomes of S, and A and B have no outcomes in common. The complement of A is denoted $\overline{A}$.

The diagram at the right shows a sample space S with event A and its complement $\overline{A}$.

An event and its complement are examples of **mutually exclusive events**.

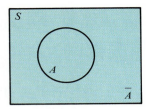

Definition: Mutually Exclusive Events

Two events A and B are *mutually exclusive* if and only if they have no outcomes in common.

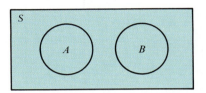

A and B are mutually exclusive.

Example 2 also illustrates several basic properties of probability.

Basic Properties of Probability

For every event E of a sample space S:

I $0 \leqslant P(E) \leqslant 1$
II If $E = S$, then $P(E) = 1$.
III If $\overline{E} = S$, then $P(E) = 0$.
IV $P(\overline{E}) = 1 - P(E)$

Property II indicates that the probability of an event that is certain to occur is 1. Property III indicates that the probability of an event that cannot occur is 0.

If two events A and B of the same sample space are mutually exclusive, the probability that one or the other occurs is the sum of the probabilities that either occurs. The probability that both A and B occur is 0.

Joint Probabilities of Mutually Exclusive Events

If A and B are mutually exclusive events, then
$$P(A \text{ or } B) = P(A) + P(B);$$
$$P(A \text{ and } B) = 0.$$

Example 3 **Two cards are drawn from a deck of cards at random. What is the probability that both are diamonds?**

Solution The sample space contains $_{52}C_2$ outcomes. The event has $_{13}C_2$ outcomes.

$$P(\text{two diamonds}) = \frac{_{13}C_2}{_{52}C_2} = \frac{78}{1326} = \frac{1}{17}$$

Example 4 **Two cards are drawn from a deck at random. What is the probability that the two cards are red or that the two cards are black?**

Solution The sample space contains $_{52}C_2$, or 1326 outcomes. Two red cards can occur in $_{26}C_2$, or 325 ways.

$$P(2 \text{ red}) = \frac{325}{1326}$$

Two black cards can occur in 325 ways.

$$P(2 \text{ black}) = \frac{325}{1326}$$

Answer $P(2 \text{ red or 2 black}) = \dfrac{325}{1326} + \dfrac{325}{1326} = \dfrac{25}{51}.$

*C*LASSROOM EXERCISES

1. What is the probability of an event that is certain to occur?
2. What is the probability of an event that cannot occur?
3. If $P(E) = \dfrac{3}{8}$, what is $P(\overline{E})$?
4. What is the probability of getting a sum of 7 or 11 by rolling two dice?
5. The mixed marbles in a jar consist of 5 red, 6 blue, and 3 green marbles. What is the probability of drawing 2 green marbles without looking?

*W*RITTEN EXERCISES

 The mixed marbles in a jar consist of 4 red, 5 blue, and 6 green marbles. Three marbles are drawn by someone who is blindfolded. State the probability of each event.

1. 3 red
2. 3 blue
3. 2 blue and 1 green
4. 2 red and 1 green
5. 1 of each color
6. 3 of one color

One card is drawn at random from a deck of 52 cards. State the probability of each event.

7. An ace
8. A red card
9. A black king
10. An ace, two, or three
11. The card is neither a king nor a queen.
12. The card is neither the king of spades nor the queen of hearts.

Two letters are selected at random from the word EXPONENT. Find the probability that:

13. both are vowels.   **14.** both are consonants.

15. one letter is a vowel and the other is a consonant.

16. the first letter selected is a vowel, and the second is a consonant.

17. Darlene tosses two dice. The probability of getting a sum of 7 is $\frac{1}{6}$. The probability of getting a sum of 10 is $\frac{1}{12}$. The probability of getting both at the same time is 0. What is the probability that:

    a. she will not get a 7?

    b. she will get a 7 or a 10?

    c. she will get neither a 7 nor a 10?

18. Devin plans to ask permission to buy a new jacket. He knows his parents will say "yes," "maybe," or "no." He estimates the probability that they will say "yes" at 0.15 and that they will say "maybe" as 0.25. What is the probability that:

    a. they will say "no"?

    b. they will say "yes" or "maybe"?

    c. they will not say "no"?

B   **19.** A pair of dice is tossed. What is the probability that the sum is even?

20. Ten cans of soup are randomly arranged in a row on a shelf. Two of the cans are tomato soup. What is the probability that the two cans of tomato soup are next to each other?

Four coins are flipped. What is the probability of each event?

21. 4 heads   **22.** 3 heads and 1 tail

23. 2 heads and 2 tails   **24.** At most 2 heads

25. At least 1 tail

26. The probability that the weather will turn colder, $P(C)$, is 0.6. The probability that it will snow, $P(S)$, is 0.8. The probability that it will turn colder and snow, $P(C \text{ and } S)$ is 0.4.

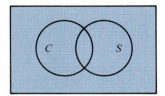

    a. Explain why the events C and S are *not* mutually exclusive.

    b. What is the probability that it will turn colder but not snow? [*Hint:* Assign probability to areas of the diagram.]

    c. What is the probability that it will snow but not turn colder?

    d. What is the probability that it will neither snow nor turn colder?

27. Explain the difference between complementary events and mutually exclusive events.

Each of six couples takes a basket lunch to a picnic. At the picnic each couple selects a basket at random. State the probability of each event.

28. Each couple will select their own basket.

29. Exactly five of the couples will select their own baskets.

30. Exactly four of the couples will select their own baskets.

31. Exactly three of the couples will select their own baskets.

32. Four cards are drawn from a deck of 52 cards. State the probability of getting one of each suit.

REVIEW EXERCISES

Write the general equation or inequality for each graph.   [9-1]

1.

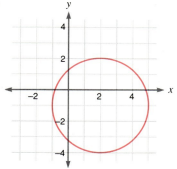

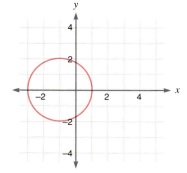

3. For the parabola $y + 2 = \frac{1}{4}(x + 1)^2$, state the vertex, axis of symmetry, focus, and directrix. Then sketch the graph.   [9-2]

4. For $x^2 + y^2 - 24x - 10y = 0$, write an equivalent equation in standard form for a circle, parabola, ellipse, or hyperbola. Sketch the graph of the conic and label key points such as the center and vertices.   [9-5]

Sketch the graphs of both equations. Solve the system.   [9-6]

5. $xy = -12$
   $x + y = 1$

6. $y^2 - x^2 = 1$
   $x^2 + y^2 = 7$

Independent and Dependent Events

The probability of a computer for an airline reservation system being "down" (inoperative) at any given time is 0.001. The airline found that it could reduce the probability of the computer being down by installing a second backup computer operating in parallel with but independent of the first computer. The probability of both computers being down at the same time is $(0.001)^2$, or 0.000001. In this lesson you will learn how to determine the probabilities of independent events.

The occurrence of two or more events may or may not be related. Consider these two experiments.

Experiment 1
Draw a card from a deck of 52 cards. Replace the card. Then draw another card from the deck. What is the probability that the first card is an ace and the second card is a face card (king, queen, or jack)?

Experiment 2
Draw a card from a deck of 52 cards. Do *not* replace the card. Then draw another card from the deck. What is the probability that the first card is an ace and the second card is a face card?

In Experiment 1 the sample space contains 52^2 outcomes since there are 52 outcomes for each draw. The first event (drawing an ace) can occur in 4 ways, and the second (drawing a face card) can occur in 16 ways. Therefore, the two events can occur in $4 \cdot 16$ ways.

$$P(\text{ace and then face card}) = \frac{4 \cdot 16}{52^2} = \frac{4}{52} \cdot \frac{16}{52}$$

Note that: $P(\text{ace and then face card}) = P(\text{ace}) \cdot P(\text{face card}).$

In Experiment 2 there are only 51 cards in the deck on the second draw. Therefore, the sample space contains $52 \cdot 51$ outcomes. In this experiment,

$$P(\text{ace and then face card}) = \frac{4 \cdot 16}{52 \cdot 51}$$

and $P(\text{ace and then face card}) \neq P(\text{ace}) \cdot P(\text{face card}).$

In Experiment 1 the two events are not affected by each other. Such events are called **independent events**.

Definition: Independent Events

Two events A and B are *independent* if and only if

$$P(A \text{ and then } B) = P(A) \cdot P(B).$$

The events in Experiment 2 are **dependent events**. When computing the probability of a compound event, it is necessary to know whether the simple events that make up the compound event are independent. If two events A and B are independent, then $P(A \text{ and then } B)$ is the product of $P(A)$ and $P(B)$. However, if B depends on A, then $P(A \text{ and then } B)$ is the product of $P(A)$ and $P(B$ after A has occurred$)$.

Example 1   If 2 marbles are drawn at random from a bag containing 5 black and 8 white marbles, what is the probability that both are black?

Solution   The two events (drawing single black marbles) are dependent. On the first draw, $P(\text{black}) = \dfrac{5}{13}$.

On the second draw, given that the first draw was black, $P(\text{black}) = \dfrac{4}{12}$.

$$P(\text{black and then black}) = \frac{5}{13} \cdot \frac{4}{12} = \frac{5}{39}$$

Example 2   Solve.

Odds-makers determined that the probability of the Rhinos beating the Tigers in any game was $\dfrac{3}{5}$. What is the probability of the Tigers winning all 3 games of a series?

Solution   We assume that the outcome of any game is independent of the outcome of any other game. Let T represent a Tiger win and R represent a Rhino win.

$$\text{Since } P(R) = \frac{3}{5}, P(T) = \frac{2}{5}.$$

$$P(T \text{ and then } T \text{ and then } T) = P(T) \cdot P(T) \cdot P(T)$$

$$= \frac{2}{5} \cdot \frac{2}{5} \cdot \frac{2}{5}$$

$$= \frac{8}{125}$$

Answer   The probability of the Tigers winning 3 games in a row against the Rhinos is $\dfrac{8}{125}$.

Example 3 A coin was flipped 8 times and landed heads up each time. What is the probability that the coin will land heads up on the ninth flip?

Solution Each flip of a coin is an independent event (that is, the coin doesn't "remember" what happened on the previous flips). If the coin is a fair coin (heads and tails are equally likely), the probability of heads is $\frac{1}{2}$ on each flip.

Answer The probability of heads on the ninth flip is $\frac{1}{2}$.

*C*LASSROOM EXERCISES

1. A fruit dish contains 5 peaches and 4 apples. Margo and Katrina each choose a piece of fruit at random. What is the probability that both of the girls choose apples?

2. A pair of dice is tossed. What is the probability that both dice land 6 up?

*W*RITTEN EXERCISES

 Suppose events A and B are independent. Find $P(A$ and then $B)$.

1. $P(A) = 0.4$
   $P(B) = 0.6$

2. $P(A) = 0.8$
   $P(B) = 0.2$

3. $P(A) = 1.0$
   $P(B) = 0.1$

4. $P(A) = 0.0$
   $P(B) = 0.7$

5. $P(A) = 0.5$
   $P(B) = 0.5$

6. $P(A) = 0.6$
   $P(B) = 0.6$

7. $P(A) = 0.9$
   $P(B) = 0.0$

8. $P(A) = 0.9$
   $P(B) = 1.0$

A coin is flipped and then a die is tossed. Find the probability of each event.

9. A head and a 3

10. A tail and a 4

11. H and a number greater than 3

12. T and a number greater than 4

13. T and a number less than 3

14. H and a number less than 4

15. T and an odd number

16. H and an even number

Two cards are dealt from a 52-card deck. Find each probability.

17. A spade and then a club

18. A king and then a queen

19. A spade and then a spade

20. A king and then a king

21. Red and then red

22. Red and then black

A bag contains 20 green and 30 red marbles. Two marbles are drawn at random. Find each probability.

23. Both green

24. Both red

25. Red and then green

26. Green and then red

Every time Jena shoots a free throw in a basketball game, the probability that she will score a point is 0.8. Find each probability when Jena shoots two free throws.

27. Both miss   **28.** Both good   **29.** Good and then miss   **30.** Miss and then good

The weather bureau forecasts the chance of rain on any one of the next three days to be 30%.

31. What is the probability that it will rain tomorrow?

32. What is the probability that it will not rain on any of the three days?

33. What is the probability that it will rain on each of the three days?

34. What is the probability that it will rain on at least one of the three days?

*A*pplication: Odds

The **odds** of an event occurring in an experiment is the ratio of the number of successes to the number of failures. For example, consider rolling a die. The possible outcomes are 1, 2, 3, 4, 5, and 6. The odds in favor of rolling a 6 on a die are 1:5, since there is 1 success and there are 5 failures. The odds of rolling an even number are 3:3 or 1:1 since there are the same number of successes as failures.

35. In rolling a pair of dice, what are the odds against getting 7 as the sum?

36. In tossing two coins, what are the odds in favor of getting two heads?

37. If the probability of success in an experiment is $\frac{2}{3}$, what are the odds of success?

38. If the odds against success in an experiment are 3:4, what is the probability of failure?

B Data kept on two machines show the following record of breakdowns.

	Machine A	Machine B
Number of days breakdowns occurred	10	15
Number of days with no breakdowns	70	75

On a given day, what is the probability of each of the following?

39. Machine A breaks down.   **40.** Machine B breaks down.

41. Machine B does not break down.   **42.** Neither machine breaks down.

43. At least one of the machines breaks down.   **44.** Exactly one of the machines breaks down.

The probabilities of *A* and *B* in sample space *S* are given in the diagram (for example, $P(B) = 0.6$).

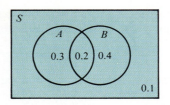

45. Find $P(A \text{ and } B)$.   **46.** Find $P(A \text{ and } \overline{B})$.

47. Find $P(B \text{ and } \overline{A})$.   **48.** Find $P(\overline{A} \text{ and } \overline{B})$.

49. Find $P(\overline{A \text{ and } B})$.   **50.** Find $P(\overline{A} \text{ and } \overline{B})$.   **51.** Are *A* and *B* independent events?

In playing a board game, a die is rolled three times. Find each probability.

52. $P(\text{all 6's})$ **53.** $P(\text{all 1's})$ **54.** $P(1, 1, 2)$ **55.** $P(\text{sum of 4})$

 The Birthday Problem A classical problem in the study of probability is "The Birthday Problem": How many randomly selected people must be gathered so that the probability of at least 2 of them having the same birthday exceeds 0.5? (Assume a 365-day year by neglecting February 29 as a possibility.)

56. What is the probability that 2 people have the same birthday?

57. What is the probability that in a group of 5 people at least 2 will have the same birthday? [*Hint:* Find the probability that they all have different birthdays. This question concerns the complement of that event.]

58. Answer the Birthday Problem. Use a calculator.

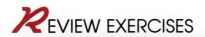EVIEW EXERCISES

1. Use synthetic division to evaluate $f(2)$ for $f(x) = x^3 - 3x^2 + 6$.   [10-1]

2. Use synthetic division to divide $2x^3 - 6x^2 + 3x - 10$ by $x - 3$. Write the quotient and remainder.   [10-2]

3. Solve $x^3 + 6x^2 - x - 6 = 0$. [*Hint:* Possible integer solutions are factors of the constant term.]   [10-3]

4. Describe the roots of the third-degree equation $f(x) = 0$, given this graph of $y = f(x)$.   [10-4]

5. Write the defining equation for the inverse of $g(x) = -2x - 3$.   [10-5]

6. If $f(x) = 2x - 5$, write a defining equation for f^{-1}.   [10-5]

7. State whether $f(x) = 2x + 4$ and $g(x) = \frac{1}{2}x + 2$ are inverse functions.   [10-5]

LESSON 13-6

The General Addition Principle of Probability

In Lesson 13-4 we noted that if A and B are mutually exclusive events, then $P(A \text{ or } B) = P(A) + P(B)$. Now consider a case in which A and B have outcomes in common. If two dice are rolled, the sample space consists of 36 outcomes. Let A be the set of outcomes with 5 as the first number and let B be the set of outcomes with 5 as the second number. Events A and B have one outcome in common, $(5, 5)$.

$$
\begin{array}{ccccccc}
 & & & & & B & \\
 & (1,1) & (1,2) & (1,3) & (1,4) & (1,5) & (1,6) \\
 & (2,1) & (2,2) & (2,3) & (2,4) & (2,5) & (2,6) \\
 & (3,1) & (3,2) & (3,3) & (3,4) & (3,5) & (3,6) \\
 & (4,1) & (4,2) & (4,3) & (4,4) & (4,5) & (4,6) \\
A & (5,1) & (5,2) & (5,3) & (5,4) & (5,5) & (5,6) \\
 & (6,1) & (6,2) & (6,3) & (6,4) & (6,5) & (6,6)
\end{array}
$$

$$P(A) = \frac{6}{36} \qquad P(B) = \frac{6}{36} \qquad P(A \text{ and } B) = \frac{1}{36} \qquad P(A \text{ or } B) = \frac{11}{36}$$

Note that $P(A \text{ or } B) = \dfrac{11}{36} = \dfrac{6}{36} + \dfrac{6}{36} - \dfrac{1}{36} = P(A) + P(B) - P(A \text{ and } B)$.

This example illustrates the **General Addition Principle of Probability**.

General Addition Principle of Probability

For any two events A and B in sample space S,
$$P(A \text{ or } B) = P(A) + P(B) - P(A \text{ and } B).$$

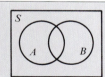

Example 1 In the toss of two dice, find the probability of a double or a sum of 4.

Solution $P(\text{double}) = \dfrac{6}{36} \qquad P(\text{sum of 4}) = \dfrac{3}{36} \qquad P(\text{double and sum of 4}) = \dfrac{1}{36}$

Therefore, by the General Addition Principle,
$P(\text{double or sum of 4})$

$$= P(\text{double}) + P(\text{sum of 4}) - P(\text{double and sum of 4})$$

$$= \frac{1}{6} + \frac{3}{36} - \frac{1}{36} = \frac{8}{36} = \frac{2}{9}$$

Example 2   In a group of 25 students, 14 play tennis, 16 play golf, and 3 students play neither. What is the probability that a given student plays both tennis and golf?

Solution $P(\text{tennis}) = \dfrac{14}{25}$ $P(\text{golf}) = \dfrac{16}{25}$

Since 3 students play neither tennis nor golf, 22 play one or the other or both.

Therefore, $P(\text{tennis or golf}) = \dfrac{22}{25}$.

By the General Addition Principle,

$$P(\text{tennis or golf}) = P(\text{tennis}) + P(\text{golf}) - P(\text{tennis and golf})$$

Substituting gives

$$\frac{22}{25} = \frac{14}{25} + \frac{16}{25} - P(\text{tennis and golf})$$

$$P(\text{tennis and golf}) = \frac{8}{25}.$$

Check   Use a diagram.
The answer checks.

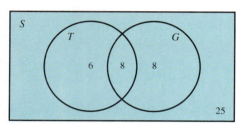

*C*LASSROOM EXERCISES

A pair of dice is tossed. What is the probability of each of the following events?

1. A sum of 7

2. 5 on at least one die

3. A sum of 7, and 5 on at least one die

4. A sum of 7, or 5 on at least one die

Both the boys' and girls' basketball teams from Hudson High are playing their arch rivals from Conant High. Experts estimate that for each team the probability of winning is $\dfrac{1}{2}$.

5. What is the probability of both Hudson High teams winning?

6. What is the probability of at least one Hudson High team winning?

RITTEN EXERCISES

A Three marbles are randomly selected from a jar containing 5 red, 7 blue, and 4 green marbles. State the probability of each event.

1. 3 red
2. 3 blue
3. 3 red or 3 blue
4. 3 red or 3 green
5. At least 2 green
6. At most 2 blue

A coin is flipped 4 times. State the probability of each event.

7. Exactly 3 alike (3 H or 3 T)
8. Exactly 2 tails
9. Exactly 3 alike and at least 2 tails
10. Exactly 3 alike or exactly 2 tails

In a club with 30 members, 18 are girls, 6 are left-handed, and 3 are left-handed girls. One club member is randomly selected. State the probability of each event.

11. Boy
12. Right-handed member
13. Right-handed girl
14. Left-handed boy
15. Right-handed boy or left-handed girl
16. Right-handed girl or left-handed boy

B In a group of 50 students, 35 are enrolled in algebra, 20 are enrolled in a language, and 10 are enrolled in neither. One student is selected at random. State the probability that the student is:

17. enrolled in both algebra and a language.
18. enrolled in either algebra or a language.
19. enrolled in algebra but not in a language.
20. enrolled in a language but not in algebra.
21. enrolled in algebra or in a language but not in both.
22. not enrolled in both algebra and a language.

Let A represent the event of an algebra student being selected and L represent the event of a language student being selected.

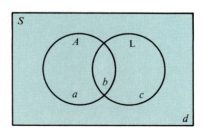

23. Copy the diagram and write the probabilities in regions a, b, c, and d.
24. Are events A and L independent? Explain.
25. Does $P(A \text{ or } L)$ equal $P(A) + P(L) - P(A \text{ and } L)$? Explain.
26. Does $P(\overline{A} \text{ and } \overline{L})$ equal $P(\overline{P \text{ or } L})$? Explain.

C 27. Under what circumstances is this statement true?

$$P(A \text{ or } B) = P(A) + P(B) - P(A) \cdot P(B)$$

28. Events A, B, and C are shown in the diagram. Write a formula for $P(A$ or B or $C)$ in terms of $P(A)$, $P(B)$, $P(C)$, $P(A$ and $B)$, $P(A$ and $C)$, $P(B$ and $C)$, and $P(A$ and B and $C)$.

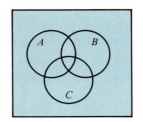

29. Find $P(A$ or B or $C)$ if $P(A) = 0.5$, $P(B) = 0.5$, $P(C) = 0.5$, $P(A$ and $B) = 0.35$, $P(A$ and $C) = 0.25$, $P(B$ and $C) = 0.25$, and $P(A$ and B and $C) = 0.2$.

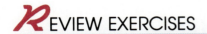EVIEW EXERCISES

1. Graph using the same set of axes.   [11-1]

    a. $y = 2x$ **b.** $y = \left(\dfrac{1}{2}\right)^x$

2. Solve: $\log_2 64 = x$.   [11-2]

Use the fact that $\log 2 \approx 0.3010$ and $\log 3 \approx 0.4771$ to find approximations for these logs.   [11-3, 11-4, 11-5]

3. $\log 8$ **4.** $\log \dfrac{2}{3}$ **5.** $\log 0.09$ **6.** $\log_2 3$

7. Solve $\ln a - \ln b = 2$ for a.   [11-7]

$\mathcal{S}$elf-Quiz 2

13-4   **1.** In a box of 18 calculators, 4 calculators have dead batteries and 2 of the remaining calculators are broken. What is the probability of each of the following?

        a. Selecting a working calculator

        b. Selecting a calculator that can be used if replacement batteries are available

  2. Two dice are tossed. What is the probability of getting a sum greater than 5?

13-5   **3.** There are 20 mixed chocolates in a box of candy. Cedric likes all but 5 of them. If Cedric randomly selects two chocolates, what is the probability that he will select 2 chocolates he doesn't like?

  4. A and B are the only two possible outcomes of an experiment. $P(A) = 0.6$ and $P(B) = 0.5$.

        a. Are A and B mutually exclusive events?

        b. What is $P(A$ and $B)$?

13-6   A number is selected at random from 1 to 100. State the probability.

    5. The number is odd.   **6.** The number is divisible by 5.

    7. The number is even or divisible by 5.   **8.** The number is divisible by 5 or by 3.

LESSON 13-7

The Binomial Theorem

In Lesson 5-3 you learned how to expand the powers of a binomial using Pascal's triangle to give you the coefficients. For example, to expand

$$(x + y)^5$$

use the numbers in the 6th row of Pascal's triangle in order as coefficients.

$$1x^5 + 5x^4y + 10x^3y^2 + 10x^2y^3 + 5xy^4 + 1y^5$$

Pascal's Triangle

```
           1
         1   1
       1   2   1
     1   3   3   1
   1   4   6   4   1
 1   5  10  10   5   1
1  6  15  20  15   6   1
```

This method, however, does not allow us to write the general expansion of the nth power of a binomial. We need a way of expressing the coefficients in algebraic symbols. The language of combinations provides a way of doing this.

Consider the values of $_5C_n$ for $n = 5$ to 0.

$$_5C_5 = 1 \quad _5C_4 = 5 \quad _5C_3 = 10 \quad _5C_2 = 10 \quad _5C_1 = 5 \quad _5C_0 = 1$$

These are the numbers in the 6th row of Pascal's triangle and are, then, the coefficients in the expansion $(x + y)^5$. We can write that the expansion as follows:

$$(x + y)^5 = {}_5C_5x^5 + {}_5C_4x^4y + {}_5C_3x^3y^2 + {}_5C_2x^2y^3 + {}_5C_1xy^4 + {}_5C_0y^5$$

It is easy to see how combinations enter into the expansion of a binomial. Expanding the power of a binomial is simply a matter of finding the ways of selecting one of the letters from the binomials in the product.

$$(x + y)^5 = (x + y)(x + y)(x + y)(x + y)(x + y)$$

For example, the term x^5 comes from selecting x from each of the five binomials. There is $_5C_5$ (or 1) way of selecting the five x's. The term $5x^4y$ comes from selecting x from four of the binomials. There are $_5C_4$ (or 5) ways of selecting the four x's. Similarly, there are $_5C_3$ (or 10) ways of selecting the three x's for the term $10x^3y^2$.

The **binomial theorem** is a formal way of stating the general rule for expanding any power of a binomial.

The Binomial Theorem

For all positive integers n,

$$(a + b)^n = {}_nC_na^n + {}_nC_{n-1}a^{n-1}b + {}_nC_{n-2}a^{n-2}b^2 + \cdots + {}_nC_1ab^{n-1} + {}_nC_0b^n$$

The 4th term in the expansion of $(a + b)^5$ contains a^2b^3. In any given term of the expansion of $(a + b)^5$

the power of b is one less than the number of the term,
the power of a is $5 -$ (the power of b).

So, for the rth term in the expansion of $(a + b)^n$

the power of b is $r - 1$,
the power of a is $n - (r - 1)$.

The coefficient of the 4th term in the expansion of $(a + b)^5$ is $_5C_{5-4+1} = {}_5C_2$. The coefficient of the rth term in the expansion of $(a + b)^n$ is $_nC_{n-r+1}$, which is equal to $_nC_{n-(r-1)}$. Since $_nC_p = {}_nC_{n-p}$, the coefficient of the rth term equals $_nC_{r-1}$.

From the discussion above, we have the following rule.

The rth term in the expansion of $(a + b)^n$ where $r < n$ is $_nC_{r-1}a^{n-(r-1)}b^{r-1}$.

In combinations, $_nC_{r-1} = \dfrac{n!}{(n-(r-1))!(r-1)!}$.

Example 1   Find the 5th term of $(x + y)^7$.

Solution   Substitute 7 for n, 5 for r, x for a, and y for b in the expression
$$_nC_{r-1}a^{n-(r-1)}b^{r-1}.$$

$$_7C_{5-1}x^{7-(5-1)}y^{5-1} = {}_7C_4x^3y^4 = \frac{7!}{(7-4)!4!}x^3y^4 = 35x^3y^4$$

The binomial expansion can be used to describe a certain class of probability experiments called **binomial trials.**

Characteristics of Binomial Trials

▶ The experiment is composed of n repeated trials.
▶ Each trial has two possible outcomes, "success" and "failure."
▶ The trials are independent.

An example of a binomial trial is flipping a coin 4 times. Each trial is one flip of the coin. On each trial there are two possible outcomes, heads or tails. Each flip of the coin is unaffected by other flips (the trials are independent). If heads is designated as "success" and tails as "failure", then the expansion of $(S + F)^4$ describes the probabilities of all possible outcomes of the 4 flips.

$$(S + F)^4 = \quad S^4 \quad + \quad 4S^3F \quad + \quad 6S^2F^2 \quad + \quad 4SF^3 \quad + \quad F^4$$

4 heads	3 heads and 1 tail	2 heads and 2 tails	1 head and 3 tails	4 tails

There is 1 way to get 4 heads, 4 ways to get 3 heads and 1 tail, 6 ways to get 2 heads and 2 tails, 4 ways to get 1 head and 3 tails, and 1 way to get 4 tails. The total number of ways for success and failure is the sum of the coefficients,

$1 + 4 + 6 + 4 + 1 = 16$. So the probabilities are respectively $\frac{1}{16}$, $\frac{4}{16} = \frac{1}{4}$, $\frac{6}{16} = \frac{3}{8}$, $\frac{4}{16} = \frac{1}{4}$, and $\frac{1}{16}$.

Another way to get the probabilities for the 4 flips of the coin is to substitute the probability of a success, $\frac{1}{2}$, for S and the probability of a failure, $\frac{1}{2}$, for F. Then the product of the powers of S and F in each term is $\left(\frac{1}{2}\right)^4$ or $\frac{1}{16}$. When $\frac{1}{16}$ is multiplied by the coefficient in each term the same probabilities result.

Another illustration of a binomial trial is a two-team game such as baseball or checkers. In such games there are two possible outcomes—a team (player) may win or not win—and the outcome of one game does not affect the outcome of another game.

Example 2   Solve.

When Angie plays checkers with Carla, the probability of Angie winning any game is $\frac{2}{3}$. If they play 5 games, what is the probability that Angie will win 4 games?

Solution   Let "success" represent Angie winning a game. The expansion of the binomial $(S + F)^n$ where $n = 5$, $S = \frac{2}{3}$, and $F = \frac{1}{3}$ describes the probabilities of all possible outcomes of a 5-game series. The term with S^4F represents 4 wins for Angie and 1 win for Carla. This term is the 2nd term of the expansion ($r = 2$).

$$_5C_{2-1}S^{5-(2-1)}F^{2-1} = {}_5C_1\left(\frac{2}{3}\right)^4\left(\frac{1}{3}\right) = \frac{5!}{(5-1)!\,1!}\left(\frac{2}{3}\right)^4\left(\frac{1}{3}\right)$$

$$= 5\left(\frac{2}{3}\right)^4\left(\frac{1}{3}\right)$$

$$= 5\left(\frac{16}{81}\right)\left(\frac{1}{3}\right)$$

$$= \frac{80}{243}$$

Answer   The probability that Angie will win exactly 4 games is $\frac{80}{243}$ or about 0.33.

Example 3 In Example 2, what is the probability that Angie will win *at least* 4 games?

Solution To win at least 4 games, Angie must win 5 games or 4 games. The probability of winning 4 games $\left(\dfrac{80}{243}\right)$ is given in Example 2. The probability of winning 5 games can be found by substituting 5 for n, $\dfrac{2}{3}$ for S, $\dfrac{1}{3}$ for F, and 1 for r.

$$_5C_0S^5F^0 = \frac{5!}{(5-0)!0!}\left(\frac{2}{3}\right)^5\left(\frac{1}{3}\right)^0 = 1\left(\frac{32}{243}\right)(1) = \frac{32}{243}$$

Answer The probability of winning at least 5 games is $\dfrac{80}{243} + \dfrac{32}{243} = \dfrac{112}{243}$, or about 0.46.

*C*LASSROOM EXERCISES

1. Expand $(x + y)^4$.

State whether the problem involves a binomial trial. If it does not involve a binomial trial, state the reason. If it involves a binomial trial, solve the problem.

2. A coin is flipped 4 times. What is the probability of 2 heads and 2 tails?

3. Four cards are selected from a deck without replacement. What is the probability of getting 3 aces?

4. Assume that a baseball player's batting average is the probability of the player getting a hit. What is the probability of a player with a 0.200 batting average getting 2 hits in 5 times at bat?

*W*RITTEN EXERCISES

A 1. Use combinations to expand $(x + y)^7$.   2. Use combinations to expand $(x + y)^6$.

Write the indicated term in the expansion of $(a + b)^{10}$.

3. 3rd term   4. 9th term   5. 10th term   6. 4th term

Write the indicated term in the expansion of $(a + b)^{100}$.

7. 2nd term   8. 100th term   9. 98th term   10. 3rd term

A coin is flipped five times. Find each probability.

11. Exactly 2 heads   12. 3 or more heads   13. Exactly 4 heads   14. Exactly 5 heads

A die is tossed three times. Find each probability.

15. Exactly one 6   16. Exactly two 6's   17. At least two 6's

18. No more than one 6   19. No more than two 6's   20. At least one 6

Every time Jeremy shoots a free throw during basketball practice, the probability he makes the shot is $\frac{3}{4}$. He takes 10 shots.

Find each probability. Use exponents to express answers.

21. Makes exactly 7 shots

22. Makes exactly 8 shots

23. Makes 7 or more shots

24. Makes 8 or more shots

25. Makes fewer than 3 shots

26. Makes fewer than 4 shots

B In an agricultural research laboratory, daisies injected with plant hormone KZ3 showed rapid growth 30% of the time. (The probability that a randomly selected daisy injected with KZ3 shows rapid growth is 0.3.) One hundred daisies are injected with KZ3.

Find each probability. Use exponents and factorial notation to express answers.

27. Exactly 30 daisies show rapid growth.

28. Exactly 30 daisies do not show rapid growth.

29. Fewer than four daisies show rapid growth.

30. More than 95 daisies show rapid growth.

The medical history of thousands of patients contracting a certain disease shows that 90% of the patients suffer loss of hair. In one week 6 patients entered a clinic with the disease.

Find each probability.

31. All 6 patients will suffer hair loss.

32. Exactly 5 patients will suffer hair loss.

33. Five of 6 patients will suffer hair loss.

34. Fewer than 3 of the patients will suffer hair loss.

C 35. If 100 coins are flipped, which is more likely to occur—exactly 50 heads or more than 50 heads? Explain.

36. Suppose 8 coins are flipped. Make a table to indicate the probability of each of the following events: 0 heads, 1 head, 2 heads, . . ., 8 heads.

37. A student takes a multiple-choice quiz with five questions, each question having five choices. Make a table that indicates the probability that the student will guess all five correctly, at least four correctly, at least three correctly, at least two correctly, at least one correctly, at least none correctly.

EVIEW EXERCISES

1. Write the sixth term of the sequence $a_n = \left(\frac{1}{3}\right)9^n$. [12,2]

2. Find the value of $40 + 45 + 50 + 55 + \cdots + 100$. [12-4]

3. Find the value of the infinite series. $1 + \frac{1}{3} + \frac{1}{9} + \frac{1}{27} + \cdots$ [12-5]

$\mathcal{E}$XTENSION   Bar Graphs and Line Graphs

Bar graphs are used to present data and show relationships. The bar graph below shows the 1984 median income of men and women based on their education.

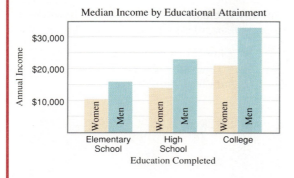

Line graphs are also used to present data and show relationships. They are useful for showing trends or changes, especially over time. The dots in the line graph at the right represent the number of graduates in 1920, 1930, etc. The lines connecting the dots help us visualize trends, but they do not represent actual data. If the data for each year (instead of for each ten years) were plotted, the graph would present more information; but the trends might become less obvious. When reading a line graph, remember that the lines between dots do not represent actual data.

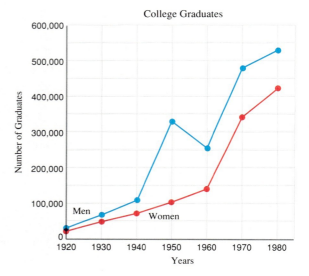

1. Draw a bar graph to represent the data that is shown in the line graph above.

2. This table shows numbers of potential college graduates, that is, numbers of men and women who had graduated from high school 4 years prior to the listed date. The numbers represent thousands.

	1920	1930	1940	1950	1960	1970	1980
Men	108	246	486	467	680	1,326	1,554
Women	151	315	580	613	735	1,346	1,601

Use this table and the data from the line graph above to compute the percents of potential graduates, men and women, who actually graduated from college in the given years. Draw a line graph of the percentages.

CHAPTER SUMMARY

▶ **Vocabulary**

▶ **Fundamental Counting Principle**   **[13-1]**

      If one event can occur in m ways and a second event can occur in n ways, the pair of events can occur in mn ways

▶ A *permutation* of a number of objects is any arrangement of the objects in a   **[13-2]** definite order.

▶ **Definition of Factorial Notation**

      For each positive integer n, $n! = n(n - 1)(n - 2) \cdot \ldots \cdot 3 \cdot 2 \cdot 1$.
Also, $0! = 1$.

▶ **Definition of $_nP_r$ Notation**

      For all positive integers n and r, where $r \leq n$, the number of permutations of n things taken r at a time is

$$_nP_r = \frac{n!}{(n - r)!}.$$

▶ **Permutations with Repetitions**

      For all positive integers n and r, where $r \leq n$, the number of distinguishable permutations of n objects, r of which are alike, is

$$\frac{_nP_n}{_rP_r} = \frac{n!}{r!}.$$

▶ A *combination* is a selection of objects considered without regard to their order.   **[13-3]**

▶ **Definition of $_nC_r$ Notation**

      For all positive integers n and r, where $r \leq n$, the number of combinations of n things taken r at a time is

$$_nC_r = \frac{_nP_r}{_rP_r} = \frac{n!}{(n - r)!r!}$$

▶ The *probability of an event* is the ratio of the number of outcomes in the event   **[13-4]** to the number of outcomes in the sample space.

▶ Event A is the *complement* of event B with respect to sample space S if and only if A and B include all outcomes of S, and A and B have no outcomes in common. The complement of A is denoted $\overline{A}$.

▶ Two events A and B are *mutually exclusive* if and only if they have no outcomes in common.

▶ Basic Properties of Probability

For every event E of sample space S:

1. $0 \leqslant P(E) \leqslant 1$
2. If $E = S$, then $P(E) = 1$.
3. If $\overline{E} = S$, then $P(E) = 0$.
4. $P(\overline{E}) = 1 - P(E)$

▶ Two events A and B are *independent* if and only if   [13-5]
$$P(A \text{ and then } B) = P(A) \cdot P(B).$$

▶ General Addition Principle of Probability   [13-6]

For any two events A and B in sample space S,
$$P(A \text{ or } B) = P(A) + P(B) - P(A \text{ and } B).$$

▶ The Binomial Theorem   [13-7]

For all positive integers n,
$$(a + b)^n = {_nC_n}a^n + {_nC_{n-1}}a^{n-1}b + {_nC_{n-2}}a^{n-2}b^2 + \cdots$$
$$+ {_nC_1}ab^{n-1} + {_nC_0}b^n$$

▶ The rth term in the expansion of $(a + b)^n$ where $r < n$ is ${_nC_{r-1}}a^{n-(r-1)}b^{r-1}$.

▶ Characteristics of Binomial Trials

The experiment is composed of n repeated trials.

Each trial has two possible outcomes, "success" and "failure."

The trials are independent.

$\mathcal{C}$HAPTER REVIEW

13-1 **Objective:** To systematically count the number of ways in which an event or a combination of events can occur.

Solve.

1. A new teacher has 3 sport coats, 8 ties, and 5 pairs of slacks. How many different outfits can he wear consisting of coat, tie, and slacks?

2. How many three-digit numbers are:

   a. greater than 300?
   b. greater than 300 and have three different digits?

3. A frankfurter can be ordered with 4 kinds of topping: sauerkraut, mustard, onion, or relish. In how many different ways can a frankfurter be ordered if at least one kind of topping is ordered?

13-2 Objective: To determine the number of permutations of a set of objects with and without repetitions using factorial notation.

Simplify.

4. $0! + 4!$

5. $\dfrac{8 \cdot 7 \cdot 6!}{10!}$

6. $_9P_3$

7. $\dfrac{_{12}P_3}{_6P_3}$

Solve.

8. In how many ways can a talent-show producer arrange a 10-act show if one particular act must open the show and another must close the show?

9. How many distinguishable permutations are there of the letters in the word ABRACADABRA?

13-3 Objective: To determine the number of combinations of a set of objects.

Express in factorial notation and simplify.

10. $_8C_5$

11. $(_4C_1)(_{10}C_2)$

12. A coin bag contains 8 buffalo-head nickles and 20 Jefferson-head nickels. In how many ways can 4 Jefferson-head nickels be drawn?

13. A production run of windshield wipers consists of 92 good wipers and 4 defective wipers. In how many ways can a sample of 3 wipers contain 2 good wipers and 1 defective wiper?

13-4 Objective: To determine the probability of an event or its complement. To determine the compound probability of mutually exclusive events.

Find the probability of each event.

14. A yellow marble is drawn at random from a jar with 4 green, 6 black, and 2 yellow marbles.

15. A coin flipped three times gives exactly two heads or exactly two tails.

16. Three cards drawn without replacement from a 52-card deck are all the same suit.

13-5 Objective: To identify dependent and independent events and determine their probabilities.

17. $P(X) = 0.4$, $P(Y) = 0.6$, and $P(X \text{ and } Y) = 0.15$. Are the events X and Y dependent or independent?

Solve.

18. A coin is flipped 5 times. What is the probability the flips were H, T, T, H, T in that order?

19. The probability that the Townsend Turkeys can defeat the Charleston Cougars at basketball is 0.6 in each game. What is the probability that Charleston wins both games it plays with Townsend during the season but loses to Townsend in the tournament?

13-6 **Objective:** To determine the probability of compound events using the General Addition Principle of Probability.

20. Two dice are tossed. What is the probability that the sum is greater than 8 or the faces show a double?

21. In a television survey of 60 students, 40 said they watch the B-team, 25 said they watch wrestling, and 50 said they watch either wrestling or the B-team. What is the probability that a student watches both wrestling and the B-team?

13-7 **Objective:** To apply binomial trials to determine the probability of an event.

22. Write the sixth term of the expansion of $(a + b)^9$.

23. The probability that a thumbtack falls point up is $\frac{2}{5}$. If a thumbtack is dropped 5 times, what is the probability that it will fall point up at least 3 times?

CHAPTER 13 SELF-TEST

13-1
1. If three separate events can occur in 12, 9, and 5 ways, respectively, in how many ways can the three events occur together?

2. How many 4-digit numbers have 1 or 2 in the thousands place and 5 in the units place?

13-2
3. In how many ways can 8 runners finish 1st, 2nd, or 3rd in a 100-m dash?

4. How many distinguishable permutations are there of the letters of START?

5. $_{10}P_3$ 6. $0! + 5!$ 7. $_6C_2$

13-3
8. How many committees of 3 seniors and 2 juniors can be formed from a group of 15 seniors and 12 juniors?

13-4
9. A jar contains 5 red, 8 green, and 3 orange tokens. What is the probability of getting a red and then an orange token in two random draws from the jar without replacement?

10. A pair of dice is tossed. What is the probability that the sum is odd or the faces show a double?

13-5
11. The probability that an event occurs is 0.4. What is the probability that the complement of the event occurs on each of two successive trials

13-6
12. A class of 24 students has 12 students who play Ping-Pong and 9 students who play in the band. Seventeen students play Ping-Pong or play in the band. What is the probability that a randomly chosen student plays Ping-Pong and is in the band?

13. If $P(A) = 0.36$, $P(B) = 0.45$, and $P(A \text{ or } B) = 0.81$, how do you know that the events A and B are independent?

14. Find the 4th term of the expansion of $(x + y)^{12}$.

15. A coin is flipped six times. What is the probability that exactly four heads occur?

$\mathcal{P}$RACTICE FOR COLLEGE ENTRANCE TESTS

Choose the best answer to each question.

1. If 20 people attend a gathering and each person shakes hands with each of the other persons at the gathering, how many handshakes are there in all?

    A. 19   **B.** 20   **C.** 190   **D.** 200   **E.** 380

2. One box contains 2 red marbles and 4 blue marbles. A second box contains 3 red marbles and 2 blue marbles. What is the probability that a blindfolded person drawing 1 marble from each box will pick 2 red marbles?

    A. $\dfrac{1}{5}$ **B.** $\dfrac{3}{10}$ **C.** $\dfrac{2}{5}$ **D.** $\dfrac{1}{2}$ **E.** $\dfrac{3}{10}$

3. What is the probability that a baseball player with a .300 batting average will get exactly 1 hit in 5 times at bat?

    A. $(0.3)(0.7)^4$ **B.** $(0.3)^4(0.7)$ **C.** $5(0.3)^5$ **D.** $5(0.3)^4(0.7)$ **E.** $5(0.3)(0.7)^4$

4. What is the probability that 4 cards drawn from a 52-card deck without replacement will be aces? (The deck contains 4 aces.)

    A. $\dfrac{1}{52^4}$ **B.** $\dfrac{4}{42^4}$ **C.** $\dfrac{1}{48!}$ **D.** $\dfrac{4!48!}{52!}$ **E.** $\dfrac{48!}{52!}$

5. What is the probability that an 80% free-throw shooter will make exactly 1 out of 2 shots?

    A. 0.04   **B.** 0.08   **C.** 0.16   **D.** 0.32   **E.** 0.64

6. A club has 10 members. How many different slates of officers (president, vice president, and secretary) can be selected?

    A. 120   **B.** 240   **C.** 360   **D.** 600   **E.** 720

7. If 2 fair dice are tossed, what is the probability that the sum of the number of dots on the top faces will be 7?

    A. $\dfrac{1}{9}$ **B.** $\dfrac{5}{36}$ **C.** $\dfrac{1}{6}$ **D.** $\dfrac{7}{36}$ **E.** $\dfrac{2}{9}$

8. How many 3-digit numbers are there in which all 3 digits are different?

    A. 504   **B.** 648   **C.** 720   **D.** 729   **E.** 810

CHAPTER 14

Statistics

During election campaigns politicians need accurate feedback about how voters are reacting to their messages. This feedback is obtained by polling small samples of the total voting population. The techniques of selecting proper samples and analyzing the data obtained from the samples are determined by mathematicians specializing in statistics.

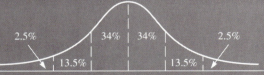

The data are sometimes analyzed using the normal curve.

Displaying Data

The data displayed in this cartoon are accurate. However, the picture distorts the message. The picture actually makes the 1986 debt appear to be eight times as big as the 1980 debt. (Why?)

Data can be organized and displayed in many ways to make the information understandable and useful. One simple way of displaying data is the **line plot**.

Davis Cup Tennis Competition Winners			
Country	Number of wins	Country	Number of wins
Australia	26	Italy	1
Czechoslovakia	1	South Africa	1
France	6	Sweden	3
Great Britain	9	United States	28

First, draw a number line. Then place an X above 26 to indicate that Australia won 26 times, place an X above 1 to indicate that Czechoslovakia won once, etc.

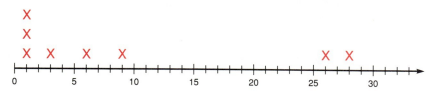

The line plot is a visual aid in understanding how the data are related. It is apparent that 1 win occurs most often (3 times), that most countries have fewer than 9 wins, and that 2 countries have more than twice as many wins as the others.

The number that occurs most often in a set of numbers (in this example it is 1) is called the **mode** for that set. If no number is repeated, the set has no mode. If two or more numbers each occur with the same greatest frequency, each one is a mode. For example,

1, 2, 2, 2, 3, 5, 7, 9	has a mode of 2,
2, 3, 6, 7, 9, 11, 12	has no mode,
and 1, 2, 2, 2, 3, 4, 6, 6, 6, 7, 9	has two modes, 2 and 6.

When data are to be presented to the public, the most common displays are circle graphs, bar graphs, and line graphs. A circle graph is used to show how parts of a whole compare to each other and to the whole. A bar graph is used to show how several related quantities compare to each other. A line graph is used to show how a given quantity changes as another quantity (often time) changes.

The stem-and-leaf-plot is another way to organize data. Here is how to make a **stem-and-leaf plot** of the ages of Presidents at their first inauguration.

Ages of Presidents at Their First Inauguration (I) and at Their Death (D)								
	I	**D**		**I**	**D**		**I**	**D**
Washington	57	67	Buchanan	65	77	Coolidge	51	60
J. Adams	61	90	Lincoln	52	56	Hoover	54	90
Jefferson	57	83	A. Johnson	56	66	F. Roosevelt	51	63
Madison	57	85	Grant	46	63	Truman	60	88
Monroe	58	73	Hayes	54	70	Eisenhower	62	78
J. Q. Adams	57	80	Garfield	49	49	Kennedy	43	46
Jackson	61	78	Arthur	50	56	L. Johnson	55	64
Van Buren	54	79	Cleveland	47	71	Nixon	56	
W. H. Harrison	68	68	B. Harrison	55	67	Ford	61	
Tyler	51	71	McKinley	54	58	Carter	52	
Polk	49	53	T. Roosevelt	42	60	Reagan	69	
Taylor	64	65	Taft	51	72	Bush	64	
Fillmore	50	74	Wilson	56	67			
Pierce	48	64	Harding	55	57			

For Washington's age, 5 is the stem and 7 is the leaf. Write the stem to the left of a vertical line and the leaf to the right.

```
5 | 7
```

For J. Adams's age the stem is 6 and the leaf is 1.

```
5 | 7
6 | 1
```

Enter the remaining data. If a stem is already written, write only the new leaf.

```
4 | 9 8 6 9 7 2 3
5 | 7 7 7 8 7 4 1 0 2 6 4 0 5 4 1 6 5 1 4 1 5 6 2
6 | 1 1 8 4 5 0 2 1 9
```

It is clear that the largest number of presidents were inaugurated in their fifties and that two more were in their sixties than in their forties.

For further analysis the leaves could be ordered.

```
4 | 2 3 6 7 8 8 9
5 | 0 0 1 1 1 1 2 2 4 4 4 4 5 5 5 6 6 6 7 7 7 7 8
6 | 0 1 1 1 2 4 5 8 9
```

Now it is apparent that only two Presidents were in their early forties, only three in their late sixties, and that 51, 54, and 57 are modes.

Both the line plot and the stem-and-leaf plot have some resemblance to bar graphs. Another kind of data display using bars is the **frequency histogram.**

Frequency table	
Test score	Number of students
83	||
84	||||
85	ⵉⵉⵉ
86	|||
87	ⵉⵉⵉ ||
88	||
89	||||
90	|

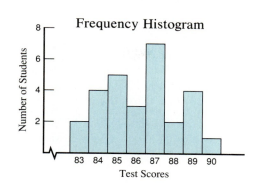

If the number of scores is great, the data can be grouped.

Test score	Number of students
74.5–79.5	ⵉⵉⵉ ⵉⵉⵉ ||
79.5–84.5	ⵉⵉⵉ ⵉⵉⵉ ⵉⵉⵉ |
84.5–89.5	ⵉⵉⵉ ⵉⵉⵉ ⵉⵉⵉ ⵉⵉⵉ
89.5–94.5	ⵉⵉⵉ |||

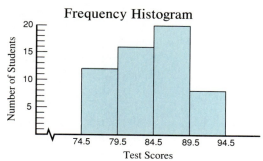

ℓLASSROOM EXERCISES

1. Make a line plot and stem-and-leaf plot for the ages of Presidents at their deaths.
2. Find the mode for the ages of the Presidents at their deaths.

Which is most appropriate for displaying the data, a circle, bar, or line graph?

3. The average cost of a one-family home from 1949 through 1989
4. The part of a family budget spent on housing
5. The average cost of a one-family home in each of the states
6. Number of members of Congress from various political parties to show relative strength of the parties
7. Times of the sunrise in a given location over a year
8. Expenditures of a state in a given year to compare the amounts spent by various agencies
9. Cost of first-class postage for a one-ounce letter from 1950 to the present

Signers of the Declaration of Independence					
Delegate and state	Born	Died	Delegate and state	Born	Died
Adams, John (MA)	1735	1826	Lynch, Thomas, Jr. (SC)	1749	1779
Adams, Samuel (MA)	1722	1803	McKean, Thomas (DE)	1734	1817
Bartlett, Josiah (NH)	1729	1795	Middleton, Arthur (SC)	1742	1787
Braxton, Carter (VA)	1736	1797	Morris, Lewis (NY)	1726	1798
Carroll, Charles (MD)	1737	1832	Morris, Robert (PA)	1734	1806
Chase, Samuel (MD)	1741	1811	Morton, John (PA)	1724	1777
Clark, Abraham (NJ)	1726	1794	Nelson, Thomas (VA)	1738	1789
Clymer, George (PA)	1739	1813	Paca, William (MD)	1740	1799
Ellery, William (RI)	1727	1820	Paine, Robert Treat (MA)	1731	1814
Floyd, William (NY)	1734	1821	Penn, John (NC)	1741	1788
Franklin, Benjamin (PA)	1706	1790	Read, George (DE)	1733	1798
Gerry, Elbridge (MA)	1744	1814	Rodney, Caesar (DE)	1728	1784
Gwinnett, Burton (GA)	1735	1777	Ross, George (PA)	1730	1779
Hall, Lyman (GA)	1724	1790	Rush, Benjamin (PA)	1745	1813
Hancock, John (MA)	1737	1793	Rutledge, Edward (SC)	1749	1800
Harrison, Benjamin (VA)	1726	1791	Sherman, Roger (CT)	1721	1793
Hart, John (NJ)	1711	1779	Smith, James (PA)	1719	1806
Hewes, Joseph (NC)	1730	1779	Stockton, Richard (NJ)	1730	1781
Heyward, Thomas, Jr. (SC)	1746	1809	Stone, Thomas (MD)	1743	1787
Hooper, William (NC)	1742	1790	Taylor, George (PA)	1716	1781
Hopkins, Stephen (RI)	1707	1785	Thorton, Matthew (NH)	1714	1803
Hopkinson, Francis (NJ)	1737	1791	Walton, George (GA)	1741	1804
Huntington, Samuel (CT)	1731	1796	Whipple, William (NH)	1730	1785
Jefferson, Thomas (VA)	1743	1826	Williams, William (CT)	1731	1811
Lee, Francis Lightfoot (VA)	1734	1797	Wilson, James (PA)	1742	1798
Lee, Richard Henry (VA)	1732	1794	Witherspoon, John (NJ)	1723	1794
Lewis, Francis (NY)	1713	1802	Wolcott, Oliver (CT)	1726	1797
Livingston, Philip (NY)	1716	1778	Wythe, George (VA)	1726	1806

 1. Make a line plot of the year of birth for signers of the Declaration of Independence through William Hooper (first 20 names in the alphabetical list).

2. Make a line plot of the year of birth for signers of the Declaration of Independence starting with Robert Treat Paine (last 20 names in the alphabetical list).

3. Make a stem-and-leaf plot of the year of birth for the signers of the Declaration of Independence through Philip Livingston (first half of the alphabetical list). Let the stem have three digits (173 for 1735, etc.).

4. Make a stem-and-leaf plot of the year of birth for the signers of the Declaration of Independence starting with Thomas Lynch, Jr. (second half of the list). Let the stem have three digits (174 for 1749, etc.).

5. Make a histogram for the data in Exercise 3. The date scale will be decades—1700's, 1710's, 1720's, etc.

6. Make a histogram for the data in Exercise 4. The date scale will be decades—1700's, 1720's, 1730's, etc.

Olympic Games Gold Medal Winners in 200-Meter Dash			
Men (1896–1988)		Women (1948–1988)	
Country	Number of times	Country	Number of times
U.S.A.	14	U.S.A.	4
Canada	2	E. Germany	3
Italy	2	Australia	2
USSR	1	Netherlands	1
Jamaica	1	Poland	1

7. Make a line plot of the number of gold medal winners in the men's 200-meter dash in the Olympic Games.

8. Make a line plot of the number of gold medal winners in the women's 200-meter dash in the Olympic Games.

Indianapolis 500 Auto Race (selected years)			
Year	Winner	Time (h: min)	Speed (mph)
1919	Howard Wilcox	5:41	88
1929	Ray Keech	5:07	98
1939	Wilbur Shaw	4:21	115
1949	Bill Holland	4:07	121
1959	Roger Ward	3:40	136
1969	Mario Andretti	3:11	157
1979	Rick Mears	3:08	159

9. Make a line graph of the winning times (h: min) in the Indianapolis 500. Describe the trend. Use the graph to estimate the winning time in 1964 and 1989. The actual winning time in 1964 was 3:23 (by A. J. Foyt). Why is it reasonable for your estimate to differ from the actual winning time?

10. Make a line graph of the speeds (mph) of the winners in the Indianapolis 500. Describe the trend. Use the graph to estimate the winner's speed in 1974 and 1984. The winner's actual speed in 1974 was 159 mph (by Johnny Rutherford). Why is it reasonable for your estimate to differ from the actual speed?

11. Make a line plot showing the test scores.

12. Make a stem-and-leaf plot of the test scores.

13. Group the data by fives—71–75, 76–80, 81–85, and so on. Then make a histogram of the test scores.

14. Group the data by tens—70–79, 80–89, 90–99. Then make a histogram of the test scores.

15. Make a histogram of Jennifer's and Alexander's test scores. Make two bars for each chapter—one for Jennifer and one for Alexander. Describe how you can easily tell from the graph which student scored higher on a particular test.

Distribution of Test Scores			
Score	Frequency	Score	Frequency
97	2	81	1
96	2	80	2
91	1	79	1
87	4	78	1
85	3	77	1
84	1	75	1
83	2	71	1

Jennifer's and Alexander's Test Scores (% correct)									
Chapter	1	2	3	4	5	6	7	8	9
Jennifer	80	82	78	85	90	92	90	85	92
Alexander	90	92	88	90	84	82	84	78	80

16. **a.** What is the mode of Jennifer's scores?

b. What is the mode of Alexander's scores?

c. What is the mode of Jennifer's and Alexander's scores?

This frequency histogram represents the number of racers at a bike race grouped by age.

17. What percent of the racers are 20–40?

18. The Senior Division is 50 and above. What percent of the racers are seniors?

19. The cost of entering the race is $8.00, but seniors (50–70) and juniors (10–20) get a $3.00 discount. What is the total revenue for the race?

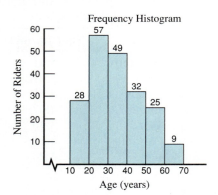

Frequency Histogram

REVIEW EXERCISES

Solve.

1. $y^2 + 10y = 24$

2. $x^2 - 3x - 5 = 0$ [8-1, 8-2]

Simplify.

3. $(2i)^3$

4. $|3 + 4i|$ [8-3]

5. $(4 + 3i) - (5 - 2i)$

6. $\dfrac{2 + i}{1 + i}$ [8-4, 8-5]

LESSON 14-2

Describing Data: Median and Range

These are the yearly salaries of the nine employees of a small company.

President:	$200,000
Bookkeeper:	$ 30,000
Foreman:	$ 25,000
Laborers (6):	$ 15,000

During salary negotiations, the president claimed that the average salary is $38,333 while the other workers claimed that the average salary is $15,000. Both were correct. The word *average* has several meanings all referring to a "center" of the data. The $15,000 salary is the middle salary since 4 employees have salaries less than or equal to it and 4 employees have salaries greater than or equal to it. This "middle" number is one **measure of central tendency** called the **median.**

Definition: Median

The *median* of an ordered set of numbers is the middle number of the set. If a set has an even number of members, the median is midway between the two middle numbers.

The median divides the set so that half of the members are less than or equal to the median and half are greater than or equal to the median. The set can be further subdivided by the **lower quartile** and the **upper quartile** as shown in Example 1.

Example 1 **Find the median and quartiles of this set:**
{32, 34, 35, 35, 35, 37, 39, 40, 41, 41, 42, 50, 57}.

Solution First, find the median. Next, find the median of the numbers to the left of the median. This is the lower quartile. Then find the median of the numbers to the right of the median. This is the upper quartile.

32, 34, 35, 35, 35, 37, 39, 40, 41, 41, 42, 50, 57

↑ 35 lower quartile   ↑ median   ↑ 41.5 upper quartile

The median and the lower and upper quartiles divide a set into approximately equal quarters.

Two measures of the amount of dispersion of the data are the **range** and the **interquartile range.**

Definitions: Range

The *range* of a set of data is the difference between the largest and smallest number in the set.

Interquartile Range

The *interquartile range* of a set of data is the difference between the upper quartile and the lower quartile.

All of these numbers can be shown in a **box-and-whisker plot.** The following is a box-and-whisker plot of the data in Example 1.

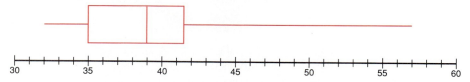

The ends of the box show the quartiles, the line in the box shows the median, and the extreme ends of the whiskers show the smallest and largest numbers in the set. The length of the box shows the interquartile range, and the overall length of the plot shows the range.

Example 2 State the a. median, b. quartiles, c. interquartile range, and d. range of the set shown on the plot below.

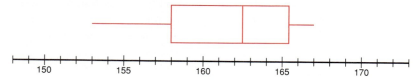

Solution
  a. median : 162.5
  b. lower quartile : 158
     upper quartile : 165.5
  c. interquartile range : 165.5 − 158 = 7.5
  d. range : 167 − 153 = 14

LASSROOM EXERCISES

State the a. median, b. quartiles, c. interquartile range, and d. range of each set of data.
  1. {9, 9, 11, 16, 16, 16, 16, 17, 18, 18, 20, 20, 25}

2.

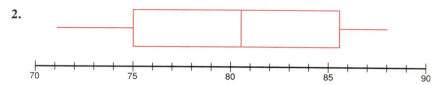

3. Draw a box-and-whisker plot of the data in Exercise 1.

RITTEN EXERCISES

Find the median in each set of numbers.

1. {18, 16, 10, 13, 17, 15, 11, 20, 12, 12, 14, 16, 18}
2. {44, 46, 49, 42, 48, 41, 45, 47, 43, 43, 42, 43, 49}
3. {99, 96, 96, 94, 95, 97, 98, 100, 102, 97, 95, 97}
4. {38, 36, 33, 34, 32, 31, 32, 33, 33, 34, 37, 39}

For each set of data, a. find the median, b. find the lower and upper quartiles, c. find the range, d. find the interquartile range, and e. draw a box-and-whisker plot.

5. {80, 82, 82, 83, 85, 87, 89, 91, 92, 94, 95, 95, 95}
6. {22, 22, 22, 23, 24, 26, 26, 28, 28, 28, 28, 29, 30}

7.

Score	60	61	63	64	66	68	69
Frequency	2	5	5	11	20	6	1

(50 scores in all)

8.

Score	51	52	53	54	55	56	59
Frequency	4	8	16	9	6	4	3

(50 scores in all)

For each box-and-whisker plot, find the a. median, b. the lower and upper quartiles, c. the interquartile range, and d. the range.

9.

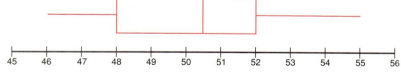

10.

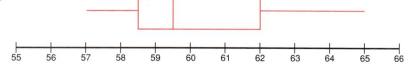

B Refer to the tables in the previous lesson. Find the a. median, b. lower and upper quartiles, c. interquartile range, d. range and e. draw a box-and-whisker plot for each.

11. Age of United States Presidents at the time of their first inauguration
12. Age of United States Presidents at the time of their death
13. Year the signers of the Declaration of Independence were born
14. Year the signers of the Declaration of Independence died
15. Determine the number of pages for each chapter of this book. Find the median number of pages, upper and lower quartiles, interquartile range, and the range. Draw a box-and-whisker plot.
16. Find the number of written exercises in each lesson of the first two chapters of this book. For each of these chapters, find the median number of exercises, upper and lower quartiles, interquartile range, and range. Draw a box-and-whisker plot.

C State which of these statistics—median, upper and lower quartiles, interquartile range, range—are affected under the following circumstances:

17. A number larger than any of the others and a number smaller than any of the others are put in the set of data.
18. Each number in the set of data is increased by 2.
19. Each number in the set of data is doubled in size.
20. Each number in the set of data is duplicated, so there are then twice as many numbers in the set.

REVIEW EXERCISES

1. State the number and kind of roots in: $x^2 + 5x + 2 = 0$. [8-6]
2. Write the equation in the form $(y - k) = a(x - h)^2$ of the quadratic function with vertex (3, 1) that opens upward and is congruent to $y = 2x^2$. [8-9]
3. Write an equation of a circle with center $(4, -3)$ and radius 5. [9-1]
4. Write an equation of a parabola with focus (2, 0) and directrix $x = 0$. [9-2]
5. Write an equation of an ellipse with minor axis from $(-3, 0)$ to (3, 0) and major axis from $(0, -5)$ to (0, 5). [9-3]
6. Write equations of the asymptotes of the hyperbola $\frac{x^2}{25} - \frac{y^2}{16} = 1$. [9-4]
7. Identify the conic section and write an equivalent equation for it in standard form: $4x^2 + 9y^2 - 16x - 18y - 11 = 0$. [9-5]
8. Find all of the real number solutions of this system of equations. [9-6]
$$x^2 + y^2 = 8$$
$$x + y = 4$$

Describing Data:
Mean and Standard Deviation

The median is a measure of central tendency that is not affected by the large size of one of the numbers. If there are five numbers in a set, the median is the third largest, no matter what the numbers are. For example, the median of each of these sets is 20. The median is not affected by the extreme values in the second set.

18, 19, 20, 21, 22   0, 10, 20, 100, 2456

The **mean,** on the other hand, is a measure of central tendency that depends on all the numbers and not merely on their position in a line. (The mean is sometimes referred to as the *arithmetic mean,* the *arithmetic average,* or simply the *average.*)

Definition: Mean

The *mean* of a set of numbers is the sum of the numbers divided by the number of numbers in that set.

Using Σ-notation we can write a formula for the mean μ of a set of n numbers x_i. (μ is the Greek letter mu.)

$$\mu = \frac{\sum_{i=1}^{n} x_i}{n}$$

The index is often omitted so that the formula is written as

$$\mu = \frac{\Sigma x}{n}$$

Example 1   **Compute the mean of 2, 5, 5, 5, 9, 16.**

Solution $\Sigma x = 2 + 5 + 5 + 5 + 9 + 16 = 42$

Since there are six numbers, $n = 6$. Therefore, $\dfrac{\Sigma x}{n} = \dfrac{42}{6} = 7$.

Answer   The mean is 7.

One way to measure the **dispersion,** or scattering, of a set of data is to compute the **mean absolute deviation** of *each* number x from the mean.

$$\text{mean absolute deviation} = \frac{\Sigma |x - \mu|}{n}$$

For the data in Example 1, the mean absolute deviation is

$$\frac{|-5| + |-2| + |-2| + |-2| + |2| + |9|}{6} = \frac{22}{6} \approx 3.7$$

A second and more common way of describing the dispersion is to find the mean of the squares of the deviations. The mean squared deviation is called the **variance.** The square root of the variance is the **standard deviation.**

The formulas for the variance σ^2 and standard deviation σ are

$$\sigma^2 = \frac{\Sigma(x - \mu)^2}{n} \qquad \sigma = \sqrt{\frac{\Sigma(x - \mu)^2}{n}}$$

(σ is the lowercase Greek letter *sigma*.)

Example 2 **Compute the variance and the standard deviation of this set.**
         10, 12, 17, 19, 25, 27, 30

Solution **1.** Compute the mean. $\mu = 20$

2. Compute the deviation of each score from the mean by subtracting the mean from the scores.

$10 - 20 = -10 \qquad 12 - 20 = -8 \qquad 17 - 20 = -3 \qquad 19 - 20 = -1$

$25 - 20 = 5 \qquad\quad 27 - 20 = 7 \qquad\quad 30 - 20 = 10$

3. Compute the sum of the squares of the deviations.

$\Sigma(x - \mu)^2 = (-10)^2 + (-8)^2 + (-3)^2 + (-1)^2 + 5^2 + 7^2 + 10^2 = 348$

4. Divide the sum of squares by n and compute the square root of that quotient.

$$\sigma^2 = \frac{\Sigma(x - \mu)^2}{n}$$

$$= \frac{348}{7} \approx 49.7$$

$$\sigma \approx \sqrt{49.7} \approx 7.05$$

Answer The variance is 49.7 and the standard deviation is 7.05.

Example 3 **The mean of an IQ test is 100, and the standard deviation is 15. Darcy scored 1.21 standard deviations above the mean. What is the measure of her IQ?**

Solution IQ measure = mean + deviation
         $= 100 + 1.21(15)$
         $= 100 + 18.15$
         $= 118.15$

Answer Darcy's IQ measure was about 118.

e LASSROOM EXERCISES

Compute the mean, mean absolute deviation, variance, and standard deviation of this set of test scores.

         10, 12, 13, 13, 13, 14, 23

 Compute the median, mean, mean absolute deviation, variance, and standard deviation for each set of numbers.

1. {12, 13, 14, 15, 16, 17, 18} **2.** {5, 5, 8, 9, 9, 10, 10}

3. {7, 7, 8, 12, 14, 14, 14, 14, 15, 15} **4.** {12, 12, 13, 13, 13, 13, 15, 19, 20, 20}

5. {12, 13, 17, 22, 22, 23, 25, 26} **6.** {23, 25, 27, 27, 32, 32, 36, 38}

On a 20-point quiz, the mean score is 12, and the standard deviation is 4. Find the score that is

7. 5 points above the mean. **8.** 2 standard deviations above the mean.

9. 1.5 standard deviations below the mean. **10.** 2 points below the mean.

11. 0.25 standard deviations above the mean. **12.** 1 point above the mean.

13. 3 points below the mean. **14.** 1 standard deviation below the mean.

15. Can more than half of the scores be above the mean? **16.** Can any of the scores be 20?

 Compute the mean, variance, and standard deviation.

17. {26, 27, 29, 29, 29, 31, 32, 33, 36, 37, 37, 38}

18. {26, 26, 27, 27, 30, 30, 30, 30, 37, 40, 40, 41}

Describe what happens to the mean and standard deviation of a set of numbers under these conditions.

19. 5 is added to each number in the set. **20.** 1 is subtracted from each number in the set.

21. Each number in the set is divided by 2. **22.** Each number in the set is multiplied by 3.

American League Home Run Champions		
1920–1924	**1940–1944**	**1960–1964**
54 Babe Ruth	41 Hank Greenberg	40 Mickey Mantle
59 Babe Ruth	37 Ted Williams	61 Roger Maris
39 Ken Williams	36 Ted Williams	48 Harmon Killebrew
41 Babe Ruth	34 Rudy York	45 Harmon Killebrew
46 Babe Ruth	22 Nick Etten	49 Harmon Killebrew

Without calculating, estimate which of the above three sets of data has the

23. largest mean. **24.** smallest mean.

25. greatest standard deviation. **26.** least standard deviation.

C **27.** Calculate the mean and standard deviation for two of the sets of data. Compare the two sets in terms of their mean and standard deviation.

28. Collect the data for the American League home run champions from 1980–1984 by referring to a recent almanac. Compare the mean and standard deviation of 1980–1984 with 1920–1924, 1940–1944, and 1960–1964.

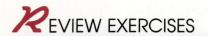
1. Compute $P(2)$ if $P(x) = x^3 - 4x^2 + 5x - 7$. [10-1]

2. Find the remainder when $x^4 - 3x^3 + x - 5$ is divided by $x - 1$. [10-2]

3. Find all the roots of $x^3 - 5x^2 + 5x + 3$, given that 3 is a root. [10-3]

4. A table of values of function f is given. What can you conclude about the roots of $f(x) = 0$? [10-4]

x	-3	-2	-1	0	1	2	3
$f(x)$	-877	-236	15	50	-17	-32	149

5. Let f and f^{-1} be inverse functions. If f is defined by the equation $f(x) = 3x + 2$, find $f^{-1}(-8)$. [10-5]

Self-Quiz 1

Entertainers of the Past		
Born	**Died**	**Name**
1906	1964	Allen, Gracie
1900	1971	Armstrong, Louis
1894	1974	Benny, Jack
1873	1921	Caruso, Enrico
1919	1965	Cole, Nat "King"
1923	1965	Dandridge, Dorothy
1899	1974	Ellington, Duke
1922	1969	Garland, Judy
1936	1959	Holly, Buddy
1926	1962	Monroe, Marilyn
1924	1963	Washington, Dinah
1896	1977	Waters, Ethel

14-1

1. Make a line plot of the year of birth of the entertainers.

2. Make a stem-and-leaf plot of the year of death of the entertainers. Use 3-digit numbers in the stems.

3. State the most appropriate type of graph for displaying the price of one gallon of gasoline from 1970 to the present to show trends.

4. What is the median of the set of numbers {2, 10, 7, 4, 3}?

14-2 **Exercises 5 and 6 refer to the box-and-whisker plot.**

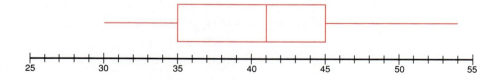

5. What is the median? 6. What is the interquartile range?

14-3 **Exercises 7 and 8 refer to the set {1, 3, 5, 6, 6, 10, 12, 13}.**

7. Find the mean. 8. Find the standard deviation.

The computer program below computes the mean and standard deviation of any set of N numbers. Lines 40 through 70 form a loop that computes the sum of the N numbers. Line 80 computes the mean. Lines 100 through 120 form a loop that computes $\Sigma(x - \mu)^2$, and line 130 computes the standard deviation.

```
10 INPUT "HOW MANY ITEMS ARE THERE ?"; N
20 DIM ITEM (N)
30 SUM = 0
40 FOR I = 1 TO N
50    INPUT "ITEM    "; ITEM (I)
60    SUM = SUM + ITEM (I)
70 NEXT I
80 MEAN = SUM/N
90 SUM = 0
100 FOR I = 1 TO N
110    SUM = SUM + (ITEM(I) − MEAN) ∧ 2
120 NEXT I
130 STDEV = SQR (SUM/N)
140 PRINT "THE MEAN IS    "; MEAN
150 PRINT "THE STANDARD DEVIATION IS    ";
    STDEV
160 END
```

1. Use the program to compute the mean and standard deviation for these sets of numbers.

   a. {4, 6, 8, 10}

   b. {4, 4, 6, 6, 8, 8, 10, 10}

   c. {4, 4, 4, 6, 8, 10, 10, 10}

   d. {4, 6, 6, 6, 8, 8, 8, 10}

2. Insert this line into the program.

   145 PRINT "THE VARIATION IS   "; SUM/N

   Use the modified program to compute the mean, variation, and standard deviation of these sets of numbers.

   a. {8, 9, 10, 11, 12}

   b. {6, 8, 10, 12, 14}

   c. {2, 6, 10, 14, 18}

   d. {0, 5, 10, 15, 20}

3. Use the program to help you find several sets of 5 numbers whose mean is 25 and whose standard deviation is close to 10.

Scatter Plots

The table shows the number of innings pitched (IP) and the number of strikeouts (SO) by 13 of the leading pitchers in the American League in a recent year.

American League Pitching					
Pitcher	**IP**	**SO**	**Pitcher**	**IP**	**SO**
Plesac	79	89	Eckersley	116	113
Thigpen	89	52	Jones, D.	91	87
Key	261	161	Eichorn	128	96
Viola	252	197	Williams, M.	109	129
Clemens	282	256	Saberhagen	257	163
Henneman	97	75	Morris	266	208
Mohorcic	99	48			

Examining the data shows that the number of strikeouts tended to increase with the number of innings pitched, but there is not a perfect relationship. (For example, Viola was third in strikeouts but was fifth in innings pitched.)

Very few relationships among real world data are strictly linear. However, many relationships are near enough to being linear that linear functions can be used to make reasonable predictions about them. A first step in determining whether a relationship can be approximated by a linear function is to graph the ordered pairs in a **scatter plot**. Here is a scatter plot of the data in the above table.

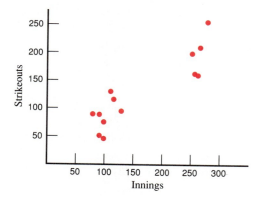

The scatter plot shows that as the number of innings increases, the number of strikeouts tends to increase. In other words, there is a *positive association* between innings pitched and strikeouts.

These scatter plots show *negative associations* between variables. (One quantity tends to decrease as the other increases.)

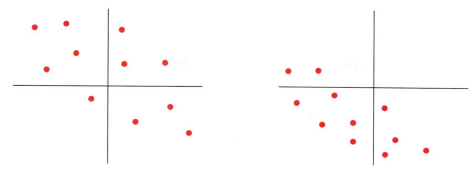

These scatter plots show no association.

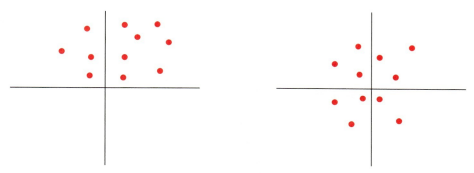

Here is the scatter plot of the pitched inning and strikeout data with a line drawn among the points. The line, called the **fitted line,** is the line that best fits the points of the plot. The fitted line can be used to predict the number of strikeouts for a given number of innings pitched. For example, we can predict that a pitcher who pitched 200 innings would probably have about 159 strikeouts. The accuracy of the prediction depends on how widely scattered the points of the plot are about the line.

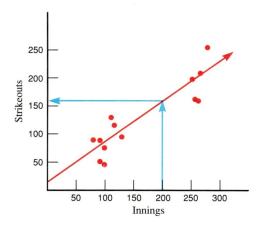

Here is one way to fit a line to a scatter plot.

Example   **Fit a line to the points of the scatter plot given above.**

Solution   1. Draw two vertical lines to separate the points of the plot into three sets. Each set should contain, as nearly as possible, the same number of points. In particular, put the same number of points in the two outside sets.

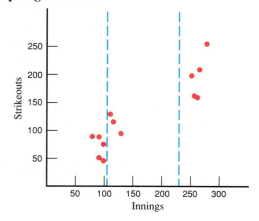

2. Locate the point in each section that represents the median of both the x values and the y values.

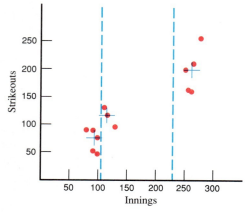

3. Align a ruler with the two outside median points. Then slide it one third of the way toward the middle median point. This is the fitted line.

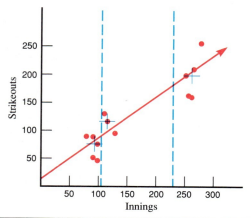

A more sophisticated algebraic technique can be used to produce the line of best fit, called the **regression line.** An important statistic, called the **correlation coefficient,** measures the dispersion of data points about the regression line. The correlation coefficient r varies from -1 to 1. For $r > 0$, the association between variables is positive (the slope of the fitted line is positive). A negative correlation coefficient indicates a negative association.

The absolute value of the correlation coefficient indicates the degree of the dispersion of the data points about the fitted line. The greater the absolute value, the closer the data points are to the fitted line; correlation coefficients of -1 and $+1$ indicate perfect linear relationships. Therefore, the greater the absolute value of r, the more accurately the fitted line can be used in making predictions. A correlation coefficient of zero does not mean that there is no relationship between variables, merely that the degree of linear relationship is zero.

$r = 0.9$ 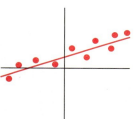 $r = -0.7$ 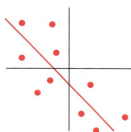 $r = 0.1$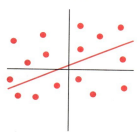

Here are some examples of typical correlation coefficients.

Between IQ test scores of identical twins	0.9
Between academic aptitude-test scores and college grades	0.4 to 0.6
Between a person's income and the number of letters in that person's name	0
Between the size of a wheat crop and the price per bushel of wheat	-0.8
Between a person's waking hours and that person's sleeping hours	-1.0

$\mathcal{C}$LASSROOM EXERCISES

Match the correlation coefficients with the scatter plots.

a.    b.    c. 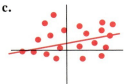   d.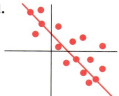

1. 0.3   **2.** 0.9   **3.** -0.5 **4.** -1

Pitching Records						
Name	**Games started**	**Games completed**		**Name**	**Games started**	**Games completed**
Cooper	45	17		Gently	37	14
Washington	40	12		Carver	37	9
Duke	40	11		Shoover	36	7
Silver	39	15		Schultz	36	12
Carpenter	38	18		Yanks	36	6
Ruiz	38	9		Able	36	10
Holt	37	10				

5. Make a scatter plot of these data. **6.** Fit a line to the data points.

7. Use your fitted line to predict how many games a pitcher would complete if he started 40 games.

RITTEN EXERCISES

 1. Use the height/mass data in the table.
  a. Make a scatter plot.
  b. Fit a line to the data points.
  c. Use your fitted line to predict Johnson's mass if Johnson's height is known to be 165 cm.
  d. Use your fitted line to predict Kelly's height if Kelly's mass is known to be 60 kg.

Name	Height (cm)	Mass (kg)
Gonzales	178	73
Hernandez	173	66
McGee	160	45
Miller	172	52
Olson	157	48
Ramarez	180	80
Rodriquez	183	86
Schilling	170	55
Valenzuela	185	86
Washington	160	50

2. Use the test score data in the table.
  a. Make a scatter plot.
  b. Fit a line to the data points.
  c. Use your fitted line to predict Lettow's physics score if Lettow's mathematics score is 85.
  d. Use your fitted line to predict Anderson's mathematics score if Anderson's physics score is 65.

Name	Mathematics score	Physics score
Bleisteiner	95	98
Frazell	90	80
Gleisman	70	80
Green	50	75
Meixner	60	70
Moore	50	60
Schuller	80	85
Smith	75	70
Waller	95	92
Witt	80	80

3. Use the basketball scoring data in the table.
  a. Make a scatter plot.
  b. Fit a line to the data points.
  c. Use your fitted line to predict Elmore's total points if Elmore made 158 free throws.
  d. Use your fitted line to predict Riggins's free throw if Riggins's total points are 692.

Player	Free throws	Total points
Chievous	244	821
Gilliam	185	903
Grayer	142	605
Hawkins	169	788
Hopson	215	958
Manning	165	860
Queenan	191	720
Robinson	202	903
White	165	711
Williams	156	802

4. Use the data of when these first ladies were born and married.
  a. Make a scatter plot.
  b. Fit a line to the data points.
  c. Use the fitted line to predict when a first lady born in 1920 was married.
  d. Describe how the means of the two columns could be used to predict when a first lady was married if the year she was born is known.

Name	Born	Married
Jaqueline Bouvier	1929	1953
Nancy Davis	1923	1952
Mamie Doud	1896	1916
Lou Henry	1875	1899
Anna Roosevelt	1884	1905
Pat Ryan	1912	1940
Rosalynn Smith	1928	1946
Lady Bird Taylor	1912	1934
Bess Wallace	1885	1919
Betty Warren	1918	1948

Match the correlation coefficients with the scatter plots.

5. 0.8   **6.** 0.2   **7.** −0.3   **8.** −0.7

a. 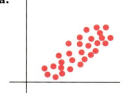 **b.** 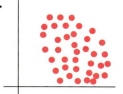   **c.** 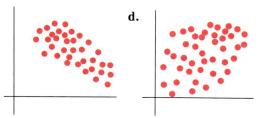 **d.**

B **9.** Use the information found in Lesson 14-1 for the age at inauguration and age at death of United States Presidents.

  a. Make a scatter plot.
  b. Fit a line to the data points.
  c. Estimate the correlation coefficient. (Positive or negative? Near 1, 0 or −1?)
  d. Is age at inauguration a good indicator of a President's age at death?

10. Use the information found in Lesson 14-1 for the year the signers of the Declaration of Independence were born and died.

   a. Make a scatter plot. **b.** Fit a line to the data.

   c. Estimate the correlation coefficient. (Near 1, 0, or -1?)

   d. Is the date a signer of the Declaration of Independence was born a good indicator of the year a signer died?

   e. Which has a higher correlation coefficient, a. the years a signer of the Declaration of Independence was born and died or b. the ages of a signer when he signed the Declaration of Independence and when he died?

 11. Gather the following information from the first ten chapters of the book: number of pages in each chapter and number of Written Exercises in each chapter.

   a. Make a scatter plot of the data. **b.** Draw a line of best fit.

   c. Use the line to predict the number of Written Exercises in Chapter 11 knowing it has 46 pages.

12. Gather the following information from the first ten chapters of this book: number of Classroom Exercises in each chapter and number of Written Exercises in each chapter.

   a. Make a scatter plot of the data. **b.** Draw a line of best fit.

   c. Use the line to predict the number of Written Exercises in a chapter with 50 Classroom Exercises.

   d. Use the line to predict the number of Classroom Exercises in a chapter with 125 Written Exercises.

Give an example of two numbers associated with people that would be correlated in the following way. (Numbers could include height, age, distance from school, body temperature, pulse rate, blood pressure, etc.)

13. correlation coefficient near 1.0   14. correlation coefficient near -1.0

15. correlation coefficient near 0

EVIEW EXERCISES

1. Solve: $3^{x+2} = \dfrac{1}{27}$.   [11-1]

2. Write in exponential form: $\log_{10} 1000 = 3$.   [11-2]

3. Given $\log_{10} 5 \approx 0.699$, find $\log_{10} 125$.   [11-3]

4. If $\log 457 \approx 2.66$, then $\log 4.57 \approx ?$.   [11-4]

5. Write an expression for $\ln 25$ in terms of $\log_{10}$.   [11-5]

6. Find the number of years it will take an investment of $1000 invested at 8% interest compounded annually to double in value.   [11-6]

7. Solve $\log x - \log a = b$ for x.   [11-7]

8. How many years will it take $1000 compounded continuously at 12% to grow to $5000?   [11-8]

LESSON 14-5

The Normal Distribution

Many kinds of measurements such as the heights of people, IQ scores, and milk production are distributed continuously within a given range. If the numbers in these frequency distributions are not grouped, the graphs of the distributions are smooth curves called **frequency curves.**

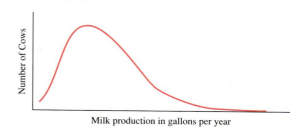

Many of these distributions are approximations of the **normal distribution.**

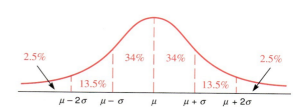

The normal distribution is the most important frequency distribution. Its graph is called the **normal curve** and has these properties.

▶ It is a bell-shaped curve that has the horizontal axis as the asymptote at both ends.

▶ The *y* value of the highest point is the mean, median, and mode.

▶ It is symmetric about the vertical line through the highest point.

▶ 68% of all numbers in the distribution lie within one standard deviation of the mean, and 95% lie within two standard deviations of the mean.

Example 1   Heights of a certain kind of tree are normally distributed with a mean of 35 feet and a standard deviation of 7 feet. What percent of the trees are

     a. between 35 and 42 feet tall?   **b.** more than 49 feet tall?

     c. between 28 and 42 feet tall?

Solution   Sketch and label a graph of the distribution. The answers can be read from the graph.

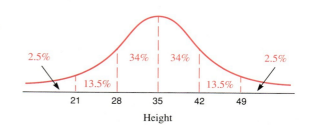

Answers   **a.** 34%   **b.** 2.5%   **c.** 68%

Example 2   Suppose that IQ scores are normally distributed with a mean of 100 and a standard deviation of 15. What is the probability that a randomly selected person will have an IQ score between 115 and 130?

Solution   Sketch and label a graph of the distribution.

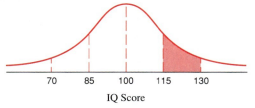

IQ Score

Answer   The probability is 0.135.

An important property of any number in a normal distribution is its deviation from the mean expressed in terms of the standard deviation. We often convert all scores to **standard scores** or *z* **scores**. The formula for making this conversion is:

$$z = \frac{x - \mu}{\sigma}$$

For example, if the height of a tree in Example 1 is 39 feet, its *z*-score is

$$z = \frac{39 - 35}{7} = 0.57$$

This means that the tree is 0.57 standard deviations above the mean. A *z* score of −1 means that the score is 1 standard deviation below the mean. The *z* score of the mean of a normal distribution is 0. The set of all *z* scores of a normal distribution is called the **standard normal distribution.**

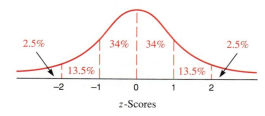

z-Scores

Example 3   The lifetimes of frosted light bulbs are normally distributed with a mean lifetime of 1200 hours and a standard deviation of 140 hours. The mean lifetime of a 20-bulb sample checked by a quality control engineer is 910 hours. What should she conclude?

Solution   Compute the *z* score of the sample.

$$z = \frac{x - \mu}{\sigma} = \frac{910 - 1200}{140} \approx -2.07$$

Answer   95% of the bulbs manufactured should have lifetimes within two standard deviations of 1200 hours. Fewer than 5% of the bulbs should have lifetimes as small as 910 hours. The *z* score of the mean of a normal distribution is 0. There probably is something wrong in the manufacturing process. The engineer should check another sample to be sure.

CLASSROOM EXERCISES

In a large high school, grade point averages are normally distributed with a mean of 2.2 and a standard deviation of 0.75.

1. Karla's grade point average is in the upper 2.5%. State what you know about her grade point average.
2. What is the z score of a grade point average of 1.75?
3. What is the probability that a grade point average is 2.95 or less?

WRITTEN EXERCISES

 A set of measurements is normally distributed. State the percent of objects in the set that are

1. greater than the mean.
2. less than the mean.
3. more than 2 standard deviations above the mean.
4. more than 2 standard deviations below the mean.
5. within 1 standard deviation of the mean.
6. within 2 standard deviations of the mean.
7. between 1 and 2 standard deviations above the mean.
8. between 1 and 2 standard deviations from the mean.
9. more than 1 standard deviation from the mean.
10. more than 1 standard deviation below the mean.

A set of measurements is normally distributed. How many standard deviations from the mean is an object that is in the

11. lowest 2.5%.	12. highest 2.5%.
13. highest 16%.	14. lowest 16%.
15. highest 84%.	16. highest 97.5%.
17. 5% farthest from the mean.	18. middle 68%.

The length of the leaves of a certain species of plants is known to be normally distributed with a mean of 7 cm and standard deviation of 2 cm. State the number of standard deviations from the mean for leaves of the following lengths.

19. 5 cm	20. 9 cm	21. 8 cm	22. 6 cm
23. 1 cm	24. 7.5 cm	25. 13 cm	26. 6.5 cm

A leaf is randomly chosen from the species of plant described above. Give the probability if its length is

27. between 7 cm and 9 cm.
28. between 9 cm and 11 cm.

29. between 5 cm and 3 cm.

30. between 5 cm and 7 cm.

31. at least 5 cm.

32. less than 5 cm.

33. between 5 cm and 9 cm.

34. between 3 cm and 7 cm.

35. less than 11 cm.

36. more than 11 cm.

 The scores on a test administered to 10,000 students have a mean of 50 and a standard deviation of 10. Find the z score of each student whose score is given.

37. Ashley 55

38. Nicole 40

39. David 50

40. Neal 70

41. Jessica 47

42. Darnell 58

A manufacturer of nurps knows that their lifetimes are normally distributed. Under normal usage, the mean lifetime is 150 days, and the standard deviation is 25 days. Nurps are manufactured on four assembly lines—A, B, C, D. Tests are run on nurps from each assembly line. Describe how the manufacturer might use the results of the tests.

43. On line A, the nurp tested wore out in 125 days.

44. On line B, the nurp tested wore out in 175 days.

45. On line C, the nurp tested wore out in 99 days.

46. On line D, the nurp tested wore out in 201 days.

47. Explain why a manufacturer might test the lifetime of a nurp even though the test destroys the nurp.

48. Explain why a manufacturer might test the lifetime of nurps very infrequently.

 The manufacturer of an auto part knows that the lifetimes of the parts are normally distributed with a mean of 60,000 miles and a standard deviation of 15,000 miles.

49. Why might the manufacturer be willing to give a full money-back guarantee on the part to the original owner of the car?

50. Why might the manufacturer be willing to give a full money-back guarantee on the part for up to 30,000 miles?

51. Why might the manufacturer be willing to give a full money-back guarantee on the part for up to 60,000 miles?

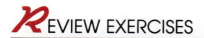
REVIEW EXERCISES

1. For the arithmetic sequence 1, 5, 9, 13, $\cdots$ write a_{10}.   [12-1]

2. For the geometric sequence 2, 20, 200, 200, $\cdots$, write a_8.   [12-2]

3. Write the series $1 + 3 + 5 + \cdots + 21$ in Σ notation.   [12-3]

4. Find S_{10} for the sequence 10, 13, 16, 19, $\cdots$.   [12-4]

5. State the value of S_8 in exponential notation: $1 - 3 + 9 - 27 + \cdots$.   [12-5]

[12-6]

6. Find the value of the infinite series $1 + \dfrac{1}{3} + \dfrac{1}{9} + \dfrac{1}{27} + \cdots$.

$\mathcal{S}$elf-Quiz 2

14-4
1. Make a scatter plot.
2. Fit a line to the data points.
3. Use your fitted line to predict the home run distance to right field if the distance to left field is 335 feet.

Home Run Distance (tens of feet)		
Team	**Left Field**	**Right Field**
Braves	33	33
Cubs	35.5	35.3
Astros	34	34
Expos	32.5	32.5
Red Sox	31.5	30.2
Tigers	34	32.5
Twins	34.3	32.7
Indians	32	32

14-5 The heights of mature plants of a certain species in Franklin County, Alabama, are known to be normally distributed with a mean of 33 cm and a standard deviation of 8 cm.

4. What is the z score of a plant with a height of 45 cm?
5. Approximately what percent of the plants are between 25 cm and 41 cm in height?

$\mathcal{B}$IOGRAPHY Martin Gardner

Martin Gardner became interested in mathematics and magic while in high school. He regularly wrote articles for a magazine devoted to magic, but planned on becoming a physicist. At the University of Chicago, however, he became intrigued with philosophy and earned his bachelor's degree in that field. His interest in mathematics continued, but he never took a formal mathematics course after high school. After college graduation, he became a writer for a children's magazine. He also wrote fictional articles and articles on magic, science, and mathematics. His special talent lay in his ability to present complex ideas in a clear, logical, understandable way. He became best known as the author of the Mathematical Games column for *Scientific American*. Since he lacked a strong mathematical background, he had to do a great deal of research for each article, but he felt this helped him present explanations that were understandable to nonmathematicians.

Using Random Numbers—Sampling and Simulation

A manufacturer of steel bolts wants to be very sure that the bolts are the desired size without going to the expense of inspecting every one.

A candidate for the U.S. Senate wants to know well before the election how the voters are responding to her stated position on defense spending.

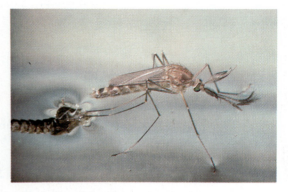

A scientist wants to know how a new chemical affects a certain species of mosquito.

A botanist wants to study the effects of acid rain on corn and wheat fields in the Midwest.

In each of these examples, someone wants to know a property of a large population without actually testing every member of the population. In each case, the answer can be found by examining a sample of the population.

When a sample is selected to represent a population, it is important that the sample be sufficiently large and that it be representative of the whole population. That is, the sample must be a **random sample.** A sample that is not random is **biased.**

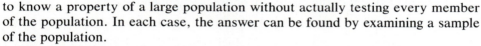

Definition: Random Sample

A procedure for selecting samples is a random sampling procedure if each sample of the population of the same size has exactly the same probability of being selected. A sample selected by a random sampling procedure is *a random sample*.

It is difficult to keep subtle biases out of the sample selection process. One tool that helps randomize selections is a table of random numbers. Here is a small table of random numbers with 4 rows and 45 columns.

Random Number Table								
02553	02462	91241	84863	32640	21097	47725	73359	50205
08310	03698	03164	52132	91175	51989	19008	25397	10093
01419	89118	61698	27769	21330	50393	52284	42579	60566
29867	19019	17771	26029	87898	41735	36039	55235	36199

Example 1 Use the table of random numbers to select 10 people from a group of 75.

Solution 1. Assign a number to each of the people in the group, say 00–74.

2. Enter the table at some random point, say row 2 column 6.

Random Number Table								
02553	02462	91241	84863	32640	21097	47725	73359	50205
08310	03698	03164	52132	91175	51989	19008	25397	10093
01419	89118	61698	27769	21330	50393	52284	42579	60566
29867	19019	17771	26029	87898	41735	36039	55235	36199

3. Starting at that point, separate the digits that follow into groups of two. The first few groups reading across are:

03 69 80 31 64 52 13 29 11 75 51 98 91 90 08

4. Discard numbers greater than 74 because they are not among the numbers used to identify people in the group. If a duplication had occurred, it would be discarded. The remaining ten numbers indicate the ten people in the sample.

Answer The sample contains the people numbered 03, 08, 11, 13, 29, 31, 51, 52, 64, and 69.

Computers also can be used to generate random numbers. When the command RND(X) (where X is any positive integer) is entered, the computer generates a random number between 0 and 1. Here is a program that can be used to select the sample in Example 1.

```
10 FOR X = 1 TO 15
20 PRINT INT(75 * RND(X))
30 NEXT X
40 END
```

Lines 10 and 30 instruct the computer to generate 15 numbers. This is done so that after duplications are discarded, there should be at least 10 different random numbers. In line 20, the random numbers are multiplied by 75 to spread them out between 0 and 75. The INT function discards the decimal portions of the random numbers, leaving integers 0 to 74. After discarding duplications, the first 10 numbers identify the people in the sample.

Random number tables or generators can also be used to simulate probability experiments as simple as tossing a die or a coin or as complex as dealing bridge hands. Here is a computer program to simulate tossing a pair of dice 50 times and calculating each of the sums.

```
10 FOR I = 1 TO 50
20 PRINT INT(6 * RND(I) + 1) + INT(6 * RND(I + 1) + 1)
30 NEXT I
40 END
```

RND(I) is a random number associated with one die, and RND(I + 1) is a second random number associated with the other die.

Example 2   A student takes a 20-question multiple-choice test involving 4 possible answers to each question. Design a computer simulation to determine the probability that the student will get at least half of the answers right by guessing.

Solution   **1.** Have the computer pick a random number from 1–4 as the correct answer Q for each question.

2. Have the computer pick another random number from 1–4 as the guessed answer A to each question.

3. If A = Q, have the computer print "C" for correct.

4. Repeat steps 1–3 twenty times to represent the length of the test.

Here is the program.

```
        ┌──→ 10 FOR I = 1 TO 20
        │    20 LET Q = INT(4 * RND(I) + 1)        ← step 1
step 4 ─┤    30 LET A = INT(4 * RND(I + 1) + 1) ← step 2
        │    40 IF A = Q THEN PRINT "C";           ← step 3
        └──→ 50 NEXT I
             60 END
```

Run the program 50 times, counting the number of trials T in which 10 or more C's occur. Write the experimental probability $\frac{T}{50}$.

Answer   The probability that a student will guess 10 or more answers correctly is very small—less than 0.02.

LASSROOM EXERCISES

A student wishing to approximate the average height of the 325 girls in her high school used the 22 girls in her chemistry class as a sample.

1. State whether the method of sampling was a good one. State your reasons.

2. Describe a better method of selecting the sample.

3. Describe how to use a random number table to simulate tossing a coin 10 times.

Random Number Table								
02553	02462	91241	84863	32640	21097	47725	73359	50205
08310	03698	03164	52132	91175	51989	19008	25397	10093
01419	89118	61698	27769	21330	50393	52284	42579	60566
29867	19019	17771	26029	87898	41735	36039	55235	36199

WRITTEN EXERCISES

A Suppose the 1000 students in a school are numbered from 000 to 999. Use the random number table to select a sample of 5 students to participate in an experiment. Give the numbers of the students selected using the procedures given.

1. Start in row 4, column 6. Pick 3-digit numbers. Read down. The first two numbers selected are 190 and 629.

2. Start in row 4, column 4. Pick 3-digit numbers. Read down. The first two numbers selected are 671 and 246.

3. Start in row 1, column 7. Pick 3-digit numbers. Read across. The first two numbers selected are 246 and 291.

4. Start in row 2, column 9. Pick 3-digit numbers. Read across. The first two numbers selected are 980 and 316.

5. Start in row 3, column 12. Pick 3-digit numbers. Read diagonally down and to the right. The first two numbers selected are 174 and 426.

6. Start in row 2, column 20. Pick 3-digit numbers. Read diagonally down and to the right. The first two numbers selected are 227 and 670.

A random sample of ten 2-digit numbers is to be selected from the random number table in order to get an estimate of the number of prime numbers in the set of 100 numbers from 00 to 99. Draw a sample of ten using the procedure given and determine the decimal fraction of prime numbers in the sample.

7. Start in row 1, column 11. Pick 2-digit numbers. Read down.

8. Start in row 1, column 16. Pick 2-digit numbers. Read down.

9. Start in row 1, column 21. Pick 2-digit numbers. Read down.

10. Start in row 1, column 26. Pick 2-digit numbers. Read down.

11. Would you expect the answers in Exercises 7–10 (above) to be the same even though different samples are drawn?

12. The actual fraction of prime numbers in the set of numbers 00 to 99 is 0.25. How accurate do you feel the sample results in Exercises 7–10 are in predicting the result?

Use the random number table in an experiment to predict the number of heads you expect to get when ten coins are tossed. Pick ten 1-digit numbers using the procedures below. Let even numbers represent heads and odd numbers represent tails. Find the number of heads in each sample.

13. Start in row 1, column 21. Read across.
14. Start in row 2, column 21. Read across.
15. Start in row 3, column 21. Read across.
16. Start in row 4, column 21. Read across.
17. Start in row 1, column 31. Read across.
18. Start in row 2, column 31. Read across.
19. Start in row 3, column 31. Read across.
20. Start in row 4, column 31. Read across.

21. The best estimate of the number of heads obtained when ten coins are tossed is 5. How accurate do you feel the sample results in Exercises 13–20 were in predicting the result?

22. Would you expect the answers in Exercises 13–20 (above) to be the same, even though different samples are drawn?

B Use the random number table in an experiment to predict the probability of getting one head and one tail when two coins are tossed. Pick ten 2-digit numbers using the procedures below. Let even digits represent heads and odd digits represent tails. (For example, 32 would be one tail and one head; 68 would be two heads.) Find the decimal fraction of favorable outcomes (one head and one tail) in each sample.

Random Number Table								
02553	02462	91241	84863	32640	21097	47725	73359	50205
08310	03698	03164	52132	91175	51989	19008	25397	10093
01419	89118	61698	27769	21330	50393	52284	42579	60566
29867	19019	17771	26029	87898	41735	36039	55235	36199

23. Start in row 1, column 26. Pick 2-digit numbers. Read across.

24. Start in row 2, column 26. Pick 2-digit numbers. Read across.

25. Start in row 3, column 26. Pick 2-digit numbers. Read across.

26. Start in row 4, column 26. Pick 2-digit numbers. Read across.

27. Based on the results in Exercises 23–26, estimate the probability of getting one head and one tail when two coins are tossed.

Use the random number table to simulate tossing three coins to determine the probability of getting two heads and one tail. (For example, 232 would be two heads and one tail; 459 would be one head and two tails.)

28. Draw a sample of twenty 3-digit numbers, starting in row 1, column 11. Read down. Find the fraction of favorable outcomes (2 heads, 1 tail).

29. Draw a sample of twenty 3-digit numbers, starting in row 1, column 31. Read down. Find the fraction of favorable outcomes (2 heads, 1 tail).

30. Based on the results in Exercises 28–29, estimate the probability of getting two heads and one tail when three coins are tossed.

C 31. Devise an experiment to use a sample of ten numbers to predict the number of prime numbers from 100 to 199. Pick 3-digit numbers in your sample. Describe your experiment and the results.

32. Devise an experiment to use a sample of twenty numbers to estimate the probability of getting all heads when four coins are tossed. Describe your experiment and the results.

REVIEW EXERCISES

1. A pizza can be ordered with six different kinds of topping: mushroom, sausage, hamburger, anchovy, onion, and pepperoni. In how many ways can a pizza be ordered with 0 to 6 toppings?   [13-1]

2. How many different numbers contain exactly one of each of the digits 1, 2, 3, 4, 5?   [13-2]

3. Simplify $_6C_4$.   [13-3]

4. Two dice are tossed. What is the probability that the sum is a multiple of 3?   [13-4]

5. A bag contains 4 red marbles and 6 green marbles. 2 marbles are drawn at random. What is the probability that the first will be red and the second will be green?   [13-5]

6. In a class of 30 geometry students, 14 are boys, 20 are tenth graders, and 6 are both. What is the probability that a girl in the geometry class is a tenth grader?   [13-6]

7. A coin is flipped six times. What is the probability of exactly three heads?   [13-4]

CHAPTER SUMMARY

▶ **Vocabulary**

line plot	[page 569]	variance	[page 580]
mode	[page 569]	standard deviation	[page 580]
stem-and-leaf plot	[page 570]	scatter plot	[page 584]
frequency histogram	[page 571]	fitted line	[page 585]
measure of central tendency	[page 575]	regression line	[page 587]
median	[page 575]	correlation coefficient	[page 587]
lower quartile	[page 575]	frequency curve	[page 591]
upper quartile	[page 575]	normal distribution	[page 591]
range	[page 576]	normal curve	[page 591]
interquartile range	[page 576]	standard score (z-score)	[page 592]
box-and-whisker plot	[page 576]	standard normal distribution	[page 592]
mean	[page 579]	random sample	[page 596]
dispersion	[page 579]	biased (sample)	[page 596]
mean absolute deviation	[page 579]		

▶ Data can be organized and displayed with a line plot, a stem-and-leaf plot, and a frequency histogram.   [14-1]

▶ The mode of a set of data is the number (or numbers) that occurs with greatest frequency. [14-1]

▶ A set of data can be described by its center, or central tendency, and its dispersion. [14-2]

▶ The median is a measure of central tendency. It is the middle number of an ordered set of numbers. If a set has an even number of members, the median is midway between the two middle numbers. [14-2]

▶ The lower quartile is the median of the numbers below the median of a set of data. The upper quartile is the median of the numbers above the median. The median and quartiles divided the set into approximately equal quarters. [14-2]

▶ The range and interquartile range are measures of dispersion of a set of data. The range is the difference between the largest and smallest numbers. The interquartile range is the difference between the upper and lower quartiles. [14-2]

▶ The box-and-whisker plot makes evident the extreme values, the quartiles, the median, the range, and the interquartile range. [14-2]

▶ The mean is another measure of central tendency. It is the sum of the numbers divided by the number of numbers in the set. [14-3]

▶ The standard deviation σ is another measure of dispersion. [14-3]

$$\sigma = \sqrt{\frac{\Sigma(x - \mu)^2}{n}}$$

where x refers to each number in the set, μ is the mean, and n is the number of numbers.

▶ Scatter plots display data involving two variables. They show whether there is a positive or negative association, or no association between the variables. [14-4]

▶ The greater the association (positive or negative) between two variables, the more nearly points can be represented by a straight line called the line of best fit, or the regression line. The correlation coefficient measures the dispersion of the points about the regression line. [14-4]

▶ Many measurements, such as the heights of people, are distributed continuously within a given range. In a normal distribution, the mean, median, and mode are equal, the numbers are equally distributed above and below the mean, 68% of all numbers in the distribution lie within one standard deviation of the mean, and 95% lie within two standard deviations of the mean. [14-5]

▶ A random sample is one that is selected by a procedure in which each sample of the same size has exactly the same probability of being selected. [14-6]

CHAPTER REVIEW

14-1 **Objective:** To display data using a line plot, stem-and-leaf plot, and frequency histogram.

1. Make a line plot of the World Series winners.
2. Make a frequency histogram of the World Series winners.
3. What is the mode of the numbers of times the teams won the World Series?

Baseball World Series Winners 1960's and 1970's	
Pittsburgh Pirates	3
New York Yankees	4
Los Angeles Dodgers	2
St. Louis Cardinals	2
Baltimore Orioles	2
Detroit Tigers	1
New York Mets	1
Oakland Athletics	3
Cincinnati Reds	2

14-2 **Objective:** To describe data using the median, quartiles, range, and interquartile range.

4. Find the median of the numbers in the set.
   {2, 3, 6, 10, 9, 3, 8, 2, 10, 12}

Exercises 5–7 refer to {20, 20, 21, 23, 25, 27, 28, 29, 29, 34}.

5. Find the median.
6. Find the lower and upper quartiles.
7. Find the range.

Objective: To use a box-and-whisker plot to describe data.

8. Find the median.
9. Find the range.
10. Find the interquartile range.

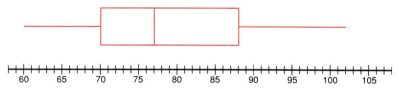

14-3 **Objective:** To describe data using the mean, mean absolute deviation, variance, and standard deviation.

11. Find the mean of a set of ten numbers consisting of seven 20's and three 12's.

Exercises 12–14 refer to the set {6, 9, 11, 11, 14, 15}.

12. Find the mean.
13. Find the variance.
14. Find the standard deviation.

14-4 **Objective:** To describe data using scatter plots, fitted lines, and correlation coefficients.

15. Make a scatter plot of the years of birth and death of U.S. vice presidents (from the table given).

16. Fit a line to the data points.

17. Use your fitted line to predict the year a vice president died, knowing he was born in 1824.

18. Describe the correlation coefficient between preschool children's ages in months and their weights in pounds. (Positive or negative? Near 1, −1, or 0?)

14-5 **Objective:** To analyze data that are normally distributed.

Exercises 19–22 refer to a set of data that are normally distributed with mean 60 and standard deviation 8.

19. Sketch a graph of the frequency distribution.

20. What percent of the data are between 52 and 68?

21. What percent of the data are less than 44?

22. What is the z score of 72?

U. S. Vice Presidents 1789–1881		
	Born	**Died**
John Adams	1735	1826
Thomas Jefferson	1743	1826
Aaron Burr	1756	1836
George Clinton	1739	1812
Elbridge Gerry	1744	1814
Daniel Tompkins	1774	1825
John Calhoun	1782	1859
Martin Van Buren	1782	1862
Richard Johnson	1780	1850
John Tyler	1790	1862
George Dallas	1792	1864
Millard Fillmore	1800	1874
William King	1786	1853
John Breckinridge	1821	1875
Hannibal Hamlin	1809	1891
Andrew Johnson	1808	1875
Schuyler Colfax	1823	1885
Henry Wilson	1812	1875
William Wheeler	1819	1887
Chester Arthur	1829	1886

14-6 **Objective:** To use random numbers in sampling and simulation.

Random Number Table			
81147	37083	52905	18510
40991	38799	43317	55973
20262	05088	73423	94535

23. The 100 members of a club are numbered 00 to 99. A sample of 5 persons is chosen using the random number table, starting in row 1, column 1 and reading across. What are the numbers of the persons chosen for the sample?

The random number table can be used to simulate tossing coins. Even numbers represent heads, and odd numbers represent tails. How many heads are in each of these samples of ten?

24. Start in row 1, column 1. Read across.

25. Start in row 1, column 6. Read down.

CHAPTER 14 SELF-TEST

14-1   **Exercises 1–7 refer to the table of vice presidents in the Chapter Review.**

1. Make a stem-and-leaf plot of the dates of birth of the vice presidents. Use 3-digit numbers in the stems.

2. Make a frequency histogram of the dates of birth data of the vice presidents, grouping the dates in two-decade intervals—1730–1749, 1750–1769, 1770–1789, 1790–1809, 1810–1829.

14-2
3. What is the median year of birth of the vice presidents?

4. What is the median year of death of the vice presidents?

5. What are the lower and upper quartiles of the years of death of the vice presidents?

6. What is the range of the years of death of the vice presidents?

7. Make a box-and-whisker plot of the years of death of the vice presidents.

14-3   **Exercises 8–10 refer to the set {12, 13, 16, 17, 20, 21, 25, 25, 25, 26}.**

8. What is the arithmetic mean of the ten numbers?

9. What is the variance of the numbers?

10. What is the standard deviation of the numbers?

11. The mean of a set of 50 numbers is 8.5. If the sum of the first 49 numbers in the set is 400, what is the last number in the set?

12. The variances of the numbers in two sets are 16 and 64 respectively. What is the ratio of the standard deviations of the numbers in the two sets?

14-4   **Exercises 13–16 refer to the table of height (in cm) and mass (in kg) of children in a preschool.**

13. Make a scatter plot of the height/mass data.

14. Fit a line to the data points.

15. A child of height 95 cm joins the preschool. Estimate the child's mass.

16. A child with mass 16.5 kg joins the preschool. Estimate the child's height.

17. The correlation coefficient between the scores of two tests (X and Y) is −0.9. If a person scored well above average on test X, estimate the person's performance on test Y.

Name	Height	Mass
Alexander	99	15
Amy	91	14
Ashley	107	18
Brad	84	12
Brittany	92	15
David	100	17
Elizabeth	92	16
Fran	90	14
Jason	105	16
Jennifer	99	16
Jessica	102	18
John	93	14
Kim	93	15
Ryan	96	18
Scott	96	15

14-5 Exercises 18–22 refer to the scores on a 100-item achievement test in geography. The scores are normally distributed with mean of 55 and standard deviation of 10.

18. In a graph of the frequencies of the test scores, where does the peak (maximum) occur?

19. What percent of the scores are between 45 and 65?

20. What scores are in the upper 2.5% of all the scores?

21. What is the z score of 40?

22. If a person had a z score of 3, what was the actual score on the test?

14-6 Exercises 23–26 use the random number table.

Random Number Table			
71304	36221	06234	00291
76845	28753	35966	95502
37444	80345	61595	08781
38650	73788	41926	96224

23. Students in a class of 25 are given identification numbers from 01 through 25. Three students are to be randomly selected to form a committee. What are the identification numbers of those selected if 2-digit numbers are selected from the random number table starting in row 1, column 1, reading down and disregarding those not in the 01–25 range?

24. What students are selected (in Exercise 23) if you start selecting in row 1, column 1 and read across?

The random number table can be used to simulate tossing a die. Only the 1, 2, 3, 4, 5, and 6 are used; the others are disregarded. Estimate the number of even numbers obtained when a die is rolled 12 times.

25. Start in row 1, column 6. Read down.

26. Start in row 2, column 1. Read across.

$\mathcal{P}$RACTICE FOR COLLEGE ENTRANCE TESTS

Choose the best answer to each question.

1. A student achieved an average of 90 on four tests. If the student scored 88, 96, and 92 on the first three tests, what was the student's score on the fourth test?

   A. 82   **B.** 84   **C.** 86   **D.** 88   **E.** 90

2. On a school bus are 100 eleventh graders and 40 members of the band. If a total of 125 students are either eleventh graders or members of the band, how many eleventh graders are in the band?

   A. 5   **B.** 10   **C.** 15   **D.** 20   **E.** 25

3. Of 80 cars in a used-car lot, $\frac{4}{5}$ are at least two years old and $\frac{3}{4}$ are priced at over $3000. What is the minimum number of cars that are at least two years old and priced over $3000?

A. 44   B. 48   C. 52   D. 56   E. 60

4. If the average of A and B is 20, the average of B and C is 24, and the average of A, B, and C is 18, what is the average of A and C?

A. 10   B. 14   C. 18   D. 22   E. 26

5. A jar contains six marbles, some red and some white. Which of the following could not be the ratio of white marbles to red marbles?

A. $1 : 5$ B. $1 : 2$ C. $1 : 1$ D. $2 : 1$ E. $3 : 1$

6. How many 2-digit numbers are there with an odd first digit and an even second digit?

A. 16   B. 20   C. 24   D. 25   E. 30

7. If two fair six-sided dice are rolled, what is the probability of obtaining a sum greater than 8?

A. $\frac{1}{6}$ B. $\frac{2}{9}$ C. $\frac{5}{18}$ D. $\frac{1}{3}$ E. $\frac{7}{18}$

8. If $2x + 2y + 2z = 144$, what is the average of x, y and z?

A. 16   B. 20   C. 24   D. 30   E. 36

9. If the ratio of seniors to underclass students in a high school calculus class is $4 : 1$, what percent of the class are seniors?

A. 60%   B. 64%   C. 72%   D. 75%   E. 80%

10. If the average of five test scores is 85 and the average of the top four of those scores is 90, what is the lowest score?

A. 60   B. 65   C. 70   D. 75   E. 80

11. In a class of 30 students, $\frac{3}{5}$ are girls and $\frac{1}{3}$ are over 15 years old. What is the maximum possible ratio of the number of boys under 16 to the number of girls under 16?

A. $1 : 1$ B. $5 : 4$ C. $3 : 2$ D. $4 : 3$ E. $2 : 1$

12. Twenty-five students took a test that was scored from 0 to 100. If only 20 of the students scored over 80, what was the highest possible average score for the 25 students?

A. 88   B. 90   C. 92   D. 95   E. 96

CHAPTER 15

Matrices

In the social sciences, one of the primary applications of **matrices** is in the construction of models of real-world situations. Businesses must collect, store, and analyze large amounts of data. Often, those data are arranged in tables. For example, a building contractor records the number of units of various products needed for the construction of five home styles.

House Style	Number of units of product used		
	Lumber	Siding	Roofing
Ranch	15	12	9
Duplex	25	18	7
Split-level	19	15	6
Colonial	20	17	6
Contemporary	50	42	20

LESSON 15-1

Matrices and Their Sums

Employees traveling on company business must submit a record of their expenses in a table like the following.

Daily expenses

	Day 1	Day 2	Day 3
Hotel/motel	$38	$45	$ 0
Meals/tips	20	30	10
Car rental	85	0	0
Gasoline	15	8	4
Miscellaneous	3	4	0

When these and other data are to be analyzed, the words "get in the way." Therefore, only the array of numbers is used.

$$\begin{bmatrix} 38 & 45 & 0 \\ 20 & 30 & 10 \\ 85 & 0 & 0 \\ 15 & 8 & 4 \\ 3 & 4 & 0 \end{bmatrix}$$

So long as the users of the data understand what each number refers to, the labels are not needed.

A rectangular array of numbers arranged in rows and columns like the one above is called a **matrix** (plural: matrices). The rows of a matrix are numbered from top to bottom, and the columns from left to right.

	Column 1	Column 2	Column 3	Column 4
Row 1	2	4	-1	12
Row 2	1	5	3	-15
Row 3	-2	-3	-6	24

The number of rows and the number of columns are called the **dimensions** of a matrix. The dimensions of the above matrix are 3×4 ("three by four"). When the dimensions are stated, it is understood that the number of rows is given first and the number of columns second. Uppercase letters with or without subscripts stating the dimensions are used to name matrices. For example, the above matrix can be named A or $A_{3 \times 4}$.

Here are the general 3×4 matrix and matrix $A_{3 \times 4}$.

$$\begin{bmatrix} a_{11} & a_{12} & a_{13} & a_{14} \\ a_{21} & a_{22} & a_{23} & a_{24} \\ a_{31} & a_{32} & a_{33} & a_{34} \end{bmatrix} \quad \begin{bmatrix} 2 & 4 & -1 & 12 \\ 1 & 5 & 3 & -15 \\ -2 & -3 & -6 & 24 \end{bmatrix}$$

Each entry in a matrix is called an **element of the matrix.** An element is identified by its row and column numbers. For example, 4 is the element in the first row and second column. Lowercase letters with subscripts indicating the row and column numbers identify the element at any particular location in the matrix. For example, the element a_{32} is -3 in matrix $A_{3 \times 4}$. The general expression for an element is a_{ij}, where i is a positive integer less than or equal to the number of rows and j is a positive integer less than or equal to the number of columns.

Example 1   **Identify these elements of A.**

       a. a_{23} **b.** a_{31}

$$A = \begin{bmatrix} 3 & 7 & -2 \\ -4 & 0 & 5 \\ 6 & -8 & 1 \end{bmatrix}$$

Solution   **a.** $a_{23} = 5$ **b.** $a_{31} = 6$

Example 2   **Label these elements of B with the variable b and subscripts.**

       a. -4 **b.** 0

$$B = \begin{bmatrix} 3 & 6 & -2 \\ \dfrac{1}{2} & 7 & 0 \\ -3 & 9 & \dfrac{3}{4} \\ -6 & -4 & 1 \end{bmatrix}$$

Solution   **a.** $b_{42} = -4$ **b.** $b_{23} = 0$

A matrix with one row is called a **row matrix.** A matrix with one column is called a **column matrix.** Row and column matrices are also called **vectors.** A matrix with n rows and n columns is called a **square matrix of order n.**

For two matrices with the *same dimensions,* elements in the same row and the same column are called **corresponding elements.**

Definition: Corresponding Elements

If A and B are $m \times n$ matrices, then a_{ij} and b_{ij} are corresponding elements for all $i \leq m$ and $j \leq n$.

Two matrices with the same dimensions are **equal** if and only if their corresponding elements are equal.

$$\begin{bmatrix} 1 & 2 \\ 4 & 5 \end{bmatrix} \neq \begin{bmatrix} 2 & 1 \\ 4 & 5 \end{bmatrix} \qquad \begin{bmatrix} 3 & 4 & -2 \\ 5 & 0 & -1 \end{bmatrix} = \begin{bmatrix} 3 & 4 & -2 \\ 5 & 0 & -1 \end{bmatrix} \qquad [3 \quad 1 \quad -2] \neq \begin{bmatrix} 3 \\ 1 \\ -2 \end{bmatrix}$$

Definition: Equal Matrices

For any $m \times n$ matrices A and B, $A = B$ if and only if $a_{ij} = b_{ij}$ for all $i \leq m$ and $j \leq n$.

Example 3   Let $A = \begin{bmatrix} 3 & 0 & 8 \\ -2 & 5 & 0 \\ 4 & 1 & -6 \end{bmatrix}$ and $B = \begin{bmatrix} x+4 & 0 & 8 \\ -2 & y-8 & 0 \\ 4 & 1 & 2z \end{bmatrix}$

Find x, y, and z such that $A = B$.

Solution   Since corresponding elements must be equal, $x + 4 = 3$, $y - 8 = 5$, and $2z = -6$.

Answer $x = -1$, $y = 13$, and $z = -3$

Matrices with the same dimensions can be added by adding corresponding elements.

Definition: Addition of Two Matrices

If A and B are $m \times n$ matrices with elements a_{ij} and b_{ij}, respectively, then $A + B$ is the $m \times n$ matrix whose elements are $a_{ij} + b_{ij}$.

Example 4   Write the sum of $\begin{bmatrix} 2 & 3 & -1 \\ -4 & 4 & 0 \end{bmatrix}$ and $\begin{bmatrix} 5 & 2 & 1 \\ 2 & -5 & 7 \end{bmatrix}$.

Solution $\begin{bmatrix} 2 & 3 & -1 \\ -4 & 4 & 0 \end{bmatrix} + \begin{bmatrix} 5 & 2 & 1 \\ 2 & -5 & 7 \end{bmatrix} = \begin{bmatrix} 2+5 & 3+2 & -1+1 \\ -4+2 & 4+(-5) & 0+7 \end{bmatrix}$

$$= \begin{bmatrix} 7 & 5 & 0 \\ -2 & -1 & 7 \end{bmatrix}$$

ℓLASSROOM EXERCISES

In matrix A at the right, identify these elements.

$$A = \begin{bmatrix} 3 & 4 & -1 & 2 \\ -5 & -2 & 0 & 1 \\ -3 & 7 & 9 & -6 \end{bmatrix}$$

1. a_{31} 2. a_{12}

For matrix A above, identify these elements using the letter a and subscripts.

3. 0   4. 7   5. 2   6. -5

7. State the dimensions of matrix A above.

8. Find x and y such that $C = D$.

$$C = \begin{bmatrix} 2 & -4 \\ 5 & y \end{bmatrix} \quad D = \begin{bmatrix} x & -4 \\ 5 & -2 \end{bmatrix}$$

9. Simplify.

$$\begin{bmatrix} 3 & -2 & 5 \\ 0 & 4 & 2 \end{bmatrix} + \begin{bmatrix} 4 & -3 & -5 \\ 0 & -2 & 5 \end{bmatrix}$$

*W*RITTEN EXERCISES

 Identify these elements in matrix A.

1. a_{23} **2.** a_{32} **3.** a_{22}

4. a_{33} **5.** a_{31} **6.** a_{14}

$$A = \begin{bmatrix} 1 & 5 & -1 & -2 \\ 4 & 2 & 0 & -5 \\ -3 & 6 & 4 & 3 \end{bmatrix}$$

Label these elements of matrix B with the variable b and subscripts.

7. 5   **8.** -5 **9.** -4

10. 6   **11.** 0   **12.** -3

$$B = \begin{bmatrix} 4 & -5 & 2 & -2 \\ 0 & 1 & -1 & 6 \\ 5 & -4 & 3 & -3 \end{bmatrix}$$

State the dimensions of each matrix.

13. $\begin{bmatrix} 0 & 1 & 0 \\ 3 & 2 & 0 \\ 5 & 2 & -1 \end{bmatrix}$ **14.** $\begin{bmatrix} 2 & -2 \\ 0 & 3 \end{bmatrix}$ **15.** $\begin{bmatrix} 1 & 5 \\ 5 & 2 \\ 3 & -7 \end{bmatrix}$ **16.** $\begin{bmatrix} 6 & 6 & 0 & 3 \\ -2 & -3 & 1 & 3 \end{bmatrix}$

17. $[4 \quad 1 \quad 4]$ **18.** $\begin{bmatrix} 0 \\ 1 \\ 1 \end{bmatrix}$ **19.** $\begin{bmatrix} 0 & 0 & 0 & 0 \\ 0 & 0 & 0 & 0 \\ 0 & 0 & 0 & 0 \end{bmatrix}$ **20.** $\begin{bmatrix} 1 & 0 & 0 \\ 0 & 1 & 0 \\ 0 & 0 & 1 \\ 0 & 0 & 0 \end{bmatrix}$

Solve for each variable.

21. $\begin{bmatrix} 2x + 3 & -5 \\ 6 & -8 \\ 7z & \frac{1}{2} \end{bmatrix} = \begin{bmatrix} x & -5 \\ 2y + 3 & -8 \\ -7 & -\frac{1}{2}z \end{bmatrix}$ **22.** $\begin{bmatrix} 5 & 3x - 2 \\ 2y + 1 & 8 \\ 4 & -2 \end{bmatrix} = \begin{bmatrix} 5 & x \\ 10 & 8 \\ 2z & -z \end{bmatrix}$

23. $\begin{bmatrix} 4 & 2x + 9 & 10 \\ y - 2 & -4 & 8 \\ 5 & 10 & 6z - 1 \end{bmatrix} = \begin{bmatrix} 4 & -2x + 3 & 10 \\ 2 - y & -4 & 8 \\ 5 & 10 & z + 2 \end{bmatrix}$

24. $\begin{bmatrix} -5 & 5x - 8 & 4 \\ 3 & 8 & y - 3 \\ 10 & 3z + 5 & 12 \end{bmatrix} = \begin{bmatrix} -5 & 2x + 3 & 4 \\ 3 & 8 & 5y - 6 \\ 10 & -3z + 5 & 12 \end{bmatrix}$

Simplify.

25. $\begin{bmatrix} 1 & 2 & \frac{1}{2} \\ 3 & -2 & 8 \end{bmatrix} + \begin{bmatrix} -4 & -2 & \frac{1}{2} \\ 7 & -2 & -3 \end{bmatrix}$

26. $\begin{bmatrix} 7 & -2 & 10 \\ \frac{1}{3} & 4 & -9 \end{bmatrix} + \begin{bmatrix} -7 & -2 & 10 \\ 1 & -4 & 9 \end{bmatrix}$

27. $\begin{bmatrix} 5 & 2 \\ 4 & -8 \\ \frac{2}{3} & \frac{1}{2} \end{bmatrix} + \begin{bmatrix} 5 & -2 \\ \frac{1}{4} & 4 \\ \frac{1}{3} & 3 \end{bmatrix}$

28. $\begin{bmatrix} \frac{3}{4} & \frac{5}{8} \\ 0 & -2 \\ 6 & 7 \end{bmatrix} + \begin{bmatrix} \frac{1}{4} & 3\frac{1}{8} \\ -\frac{1}{3} & 2 \\ -5 & -8 \end{bmatrix}$

𝒜pplications

The Jamestown Furniture Company, operating from two plants, produces tables and chairs. Matrix A summarizes its production for one week with row 1 representing tables, row 2 representing chairs, column 1 representing their large plant, and column 2 representing their small plant. Matrix B gives the production for the second week, and matrix C the production for the third and fourth weeks combined.

$$A = \begin{bmatrix} 100 & 40 \\ 500 & 280 \end{bmatrix} \qquad B = \begin{bmatrix} 80 & 40 \\ 440 & 320 \end{bmatrix}$$

$$C = \begin{bmatrix} 100 & 50 \\ 600 & 280 \end{bmatrix}$$

29. How many chairs were produced in the large plant in the first week?

30. How many tables were produced in the large plant in the first week?

31. How many tables were produced in the small plant in the third and fourth weeks?

32. How many chairs were produced in the small plant in the third and fourth weeks?

33. How many chairs were produced in the second week?

34. How many tables were produced in the second week?

35. Write a matrix that describes the total production for the first two weeks.

36. Write a matrix that describes the total production for the four weeks.

37. How many tables were produced at the large plant during the four-week period?

38. How many chairs were produced at the small plant during the four-week period?

39. If six chairs are usually sold with each table, should the production of tables or the production of chairs be increased?

In an agricultural experiment, three groups of plants were used. Group I had a high-nitrogen test plot. Group II had an average-nitrogen test plot. Group III had a low-nitrogen test plot. Matrix A represents the average height (in centimeters) and mass (in grams) of the plants at the beginning of the experiment. Matrix B shows the average heights and masses after two weeks and matrix C after four weeks. Column 1 represents heights and column 2 represents masses. Row 1 represents Group I, row 2 represents Group II, and row 3 represents Group III.

$$A = \begin{bmatrix} 6.2 & 1.3 \\ 6.3 & 1.4 \\ 6.2 & 1.4 \end{bmatrix} \quad B = \begin{bmatrix} 9.4 & 2.5 \\ 9.2 & 2.4 \\ 6.9 & 1.6 \end{bmatrix} \quad C = \begin{bmatrix} 16.2 & 4.0 \\ 12.1 & 3.1 \\ 7.3 & 1.6 \end{bmatrix}$$

40. Write matrix X to show the average plant growth during the first two weeks of the experiment. $(A + X = B)$

41. Write matrix Y to show the average plant growth during the last two weeks of the experiment. $(B + Y = C)$

42. Write matrix Z to show the average plant growth during the four-week experiment. $(A + Z = C)$

43. Show that $X + Y = Z$ in Exercises 40–42.

44. Explain the meaning of a negative entry in X, Y, or Z (see Exercises 40–42).

45. Use matrix P and matrix Q to show that $P + Q = Q + P$.

$$P = \begin{bmatrix} 2 & 3 & -4 \\ 5 & -2 & 1 \end{bmatrix} \quad Q = \begin{bmatrix} -2 & -10 & 6 \\ 4 & 3 & -1 \end{bmatrix}$$

46. Write matrix D such that $M + D = M$ if $M = \begin{bmatrix} 1 & -2 & 3 \\ -4 & 10 & \frac{1}{2} \end{bmatrix}$

47. Prove that if $A = \begin{bmatrix} a_{11} & a_{12} \\ a_{21} & a_{22} \end{bmatrix}$ and $B = \begin{bmatrix} b_{11} & b_{12} \\ b_{21} & b_{22} \end{bmatrix}$, then $A + B = B + A$.

48. Prove that if $R = [r_{11} \quad r_{12} \quad r_{13}]$, $S = [s_{11} \quad s_{12} \quad s_{13}]$, and $T = [t_{11} \quad t_{12} \quad t_{13}]$, then $(R + S) + T = R + (S + T)$.

REVIEW EXERCISES

1. Use synthetic substitution to evaluate $f(-3)$ for the given polynomial. $f(x) = x^3 + 2x^2 + x + 5$.   [10-1]

2. Use synthetic division to divide $3x^3 - 4x^2 + 12$ by $(x + 2)$. Write the quotient and the remainder.   [10-2]

3. Solve $x^3 + 2x^2 - 13x + 10 = 0$. [Remember that possible integral roots are factors of the constant term.]   [10-3]

4. Locate the real roots of $2x^3 - 3x^2 - 12x + 18 = 0$ between consecutive integers.   [10-4]

5. Let $f(x) = 10 - 2x$. Write the defining equation for f^{-1}.   [10-5]

LESSON 15-2

Matrix Multiplication

Store A of Solar Appliances, Inc., has 20 washing machines, 10 dryers, and 40 televisions in stock. Store B has 15 washers, 12 dryers, and 30 TV's in stock. The inventories of the stores can be represented by matrix S. The values of the appliances are \$250 for a washer, \$190 for a dryer, and \$340 for a TV. Matrix V represents these values.

$$S = \begin{bmatrix} 20 & 10 & 40 \\ 15 & 12 & 30 \end{bmatrix} \qquad V = \begin{bmatrix} 250 \\ 190 \\ 340 \end{bmatrix}$$

The total value of the inventory at each store can be expressed by a 2×1 matrix T in which t_{11} is the value of the inventory at store A and t_{21} is the value of the inventory at store B.

$$T = \begin{bmatrix} 20(250) + 10(190) + 40(340) \\ 15(250) + 12(190) + 30(340) \end{bmatrix} = \begin{bmatrix} 20,500 \\ 16,230 \end{bmatrix}$$

There are two kinds of multiplication that involve matrices: multiplication of a matrix by a matrix, as illustrated above, and multiplication of a matrix by a real number.

The multiplication of a real number and a matrix is called **scalar multiplication.** The real number is called a **scalar.** The product of a scalar and a matrix is obtained by multiplying each element of the matrix by the scalar.

$$3 \begin{bmatrix} -1 & 0 \\ 4 & 5 \end{bmatrix} = \begin{bmatrix} 3(-1) & 3(0) \\ 3(4) & 3(5) \end{bmatrix} = \begin{bmatrix} -3 & 0 \\ 12 & 15 \end{bmatrix}$$

Definition: Scalar Multiplication

For any scalar c, a real number, and any $m \times n$ matrix A with elements a_{ij}, the product of c and A is the $m \times n$ matrix whose elements are ca_{ij}.

The inventory example given in the lesson introduction is an example of multiplying two matrices. Two matrices can be multiplied only if the number of *columns* of the first matrix is equal to the number of *rows* of the second matrix.

An example of matrix multiplication is the multiplication of a 1×3 matrix by a 3×2 matrix.

$$[a \quad b \quad c] \cdot \begin{bmatrix} u & x \\ v & y \\ w & z \end{bmatrix} = [au + bv + cw \quad ax + by + cz]$$

Each element in the row of the first matrix is multiplied by an element in the column of the second matrix. The product is a 1×2 matrix. The product has as many rows as the first matrix and as many columns as the second matrix.

If the factors are reversed so that the product is of a 3×2 matrix times a 1×3 matrix, the product is not defined.

Next, consider the multiplication of a 2×3 matrix by a 3×2 matrix.

$$\begin{bmatrix} a_1 & b_1 & c_1 \\ a_2 & b_2 & c_2 \end{bmatrix} \cdot \begin{bmatrix} x_1 & y_1 \\ x_2 & y_2 \\ x_3 & y_3 \end{bmatrix}$$

Each row of the first matrix is multiplied by *each* column of the second matrix. The product of a row by a column is a single real-number element in the product matrix.

1st row $\times$ 1st column is the element in the 1st row and the 1st column.

$$\begin{bmatrix} a_1 & b_1 & c_1 \\ a_2 & b_2 & c_2 \end{bmatrix} \cdot \begin{bmatrix} x_1 & y_1 \\ x_2 & y_2 \\ x_3 & y_3 \end{bmatrix} = \begin{bmatrix} a_1x_1 + b_1x_2 + c_1x_3 & \\ & \end{bmatrix}$$

1st row $\times$ 2nd column is the element in the 1st row and the 2nd column.

$$\begin{bmatrix} a_1 & b_1 & c_1 \\ a_2 & b_2 & c_2 \end{bmatrix} \cdot \begin{bmatrix} x_1 & y_1 \\ x_2 & y_2 \\ x_3 & y_3 \end{bmatrix} = \begin{bmatrix} a_1x_1 + b_1x_2 + c_1x_3 & a_1y_1 + b_1y_2 + c_1y_3 \\ & \end{bmatrix}$$

2nd row $\times$ 1st column is the element in the 2nd row and the 1st column.

$$\begin{bmatrix} a_1 & b_1 & c_1 \\ a_2 & b_2 & c_2 \end{bmatrix} \cdot \begin{bmatrix} x_1 & y_1 \\ x_2 & y_2 \\ x_3 & y_3 \end{bmatrix} = \begin{bmatrix} a_1x_1 + b_1x_2 + c_1x_3 & a_1y_1 + b_1y_2 + c_1y_3 \\ a_2x_1 + b_2x_2 + c_2x_3 & \end{bmatrix}$$

2nd row $\times$ 2nd column is the element in the 2nd row and the 2nd column.

$$\begin{bmatrix} a_1 & b_1 & c_1 \\ a_2 & b_2 & c_2 \end{bmatrix} \cdot \begin{bmatrix} x_1 & y_1 \\ x_2 & y_2 \\ x_3 & y_3 \end{bmatrix} = \begin{bmatrix} a_1x_1 + b_1x_2 + c_1x_3 & a_1y_1 + b_1y_2 + c_1y_3 \\ a_2x_1 + b_2x_2 + c_2x_3 & a_2y_1 + b_2y_2 + c_2y_3 \end{bmatrix}$$

The product has as many rows as the first matrix and as many columns as the second matrix.

𝒞LASSROOM EXERCISES

Perform the indicated operations.

1. $3\begin{bmatrix} -2 & -1 \\ 5 & 0 \end{bmatrix}$

2. $[3 \quad 4 \quad 0] \cdot \begin{bmatrix} -2 \\ 5 \\ 1 \end{bmatrix}$

3. $\begin{bmatrix} 2 & -1 & 3 \\ 5 & 1 & 0 \end{bmatrix} \cdot \begin{bmatrix} -3 & 4 & 3 \\ 1 & 1 & 1 \\ 2 & -1 & 0 \end{bmatrix}$

4. Let $A = \begin{bmatrix} -2 & -1 \\ 5 & 0 \end{bmatrix}$ and $B = \begin{bmatrix} 2 & 1 \\ -5 & 0 \end{bmatrix}$. For what number k does $kB = A$?

 Use the following matrices for Exercises 1–12.

$$P = [3 \quad 5 \quad 7] \qquad Q = \begin{bmatrix} 5 & -1 & 0 \\ 3 & 7 & -2 \end{bmatrix} \qquad R = \begin{bmatrix} 6 \\ 0 \\ -3 \end{bmatrix} \qquad S = \begin{bmatrix} -2 & 3 \\ 7 & 8 \\ 6 & -10 \end{bmatrix}$$

State whether the indicated product is defined.

1. $5P$ 2. $\frac{1}{3}Q$ 3. $0R$ 4. $-7S$ 5. PQ 6. RS

7. PS 8. QR 9. RP 10. QS 11. PR 12. SQ

Write each product as a matrix.

13. $4\begin{bmatrix} 1 & 2 \\ 3 & 4 \end{bmatrix}$

14. $6\begin{bmatrix} -1 & 2 \\ 3 & -4 \end{bmatrix}$

15. $\frac{1}{2}\begin{bmatrix} 2 & 8 \\ -6 & -10 \end{bmatrix}$

16. $\frac{1}{3}\begin{bmatrix} 3 & 12 \\ -18 & 6 \end{bmatrix}$

17. $[1 \quad 2 \quad 3] \cdot \begin{bmatrix} 3 \\ 2 \\ 1 \end{bmatrix}$

18. $[-1 \quad 0 \quad 1] \cdot \begin{bmatrix} -1 \\ 0 \\ 1 \end{bmatrix}$

19. $\begin{bmatrix} 1 & 2 & -1 \\ 2 & -2 & 0 \end{bmatrix} \cdot \begin{bmatrix} 2 \\ 4 \\ 6 \end{bmatrix}$

20. $\begin{bmatrix} 0 & -3 & 7 \\ 6 & -2 & 1 \end{bmatrix} \cdot \begin{bmatrix} 5 \\ 1 \\ -2 \end{bmatrix}$

21. $\begin{bmatrix} 5 & 6 & \frac{1}{2} \\ -2 & 7 & 0 \end{bmatrix} \cdot \begin{bmatrix} 2 & -3 \\ -2 & 2 \\ 6 & 4 \end{bmatrix}$

22. $\begin{bmatrix} 7 & \frac{1}{3} & -1 \\ 9 & 0 & 2 \end{bmatrix} \cdot \begin{bmatrix} 2 & -1 \\ 9 & 6 \\ -1 & 4 \end{bmatrix}$

𝒜pplications

Solve.

23. The purchase prices and delivery costs (in dollars per unit) for sod, herbicide, and fertilizer used in lawn care are given in this table.

	Sod	Herbicide	Fertilizer
Purchase	8	3	2
Delivery	2	1	0.5

The table of costs (in dollars) can be represented by the matrix

$$C = \begin{bmatrix} 8 & 3 & 2 \\ 2 & 1 & 0.5 \end{bmatrix}.$$

   a. The supplier announces a 10% discount on both purchase and delivery of these items. Write a discount matrix D.

   b. Write a matrix W for the new costs.

24. The Owens Appliance Company has two retail stores, A and B. Their inventory for the numbers of stoves, refrigerators, washers, and dryers is given in this table.

	Stoves	Refrigerators	Washers	Dryers
Store A	7	12	10	10
Store B	15	6	8	6

Stoves are $350 each, refrigerators $625 each, washers $450 each, and dryers $425 each.

a. Write a 2 × 4 inventory matrix V.

b. Write a 4 × 1 matrix U for the unit values.

c. Calculate VU to find the value of the inventory at each store.

25. Beckman's Television Company has two retail stores, A and B. The number of television sets they have in stock is given in this table.

	5″ TV	9″ TV	13″ TV	19″ TV
Store A	10	20	25	6
Store B	8	15	20	10

A 5″ TV set costs $140, a 9″ TV set $120, a 13″ TV set $350, and a 19″ TV set $450.

a. Write a 2 × 4 matrix Y for the inventory.

b. Write a 4 × 1 matrix L for the unit values.

c. Calculate YL to find the value of the inventory at each store.

B

26. Products A and B are made from plastic, steel, and glass. The number of units of each raw material needed for each product is given in this table.

	Plastic	Steel	Glass
Product A	5	1	10
Product B	5	8	2

Because of transportation costs to the company's two plants, X and Y, the unit costs of the raw materials (in dollars) are different. The following table gives the unit costs.

	Plant X	Plant Y
Plastic	10	12
Steel	25	20
Glass	8	6

a. Write a matrix for raw materials needed.

b. Write a matrix for the costs.

c. Use matrix multiplication to find the total cost of producing each of the products at each of the plants.

d. Describe the meaning of the rows and columns in the product matrix.

27. A chair manufacturer produces four styles of chairs and has orders for 500 of style A, 1000 of style B, 3000 of style C, and 4000 of style D. The number of units of material needed to manufacture each style is given in this table.

	Wood	Filler	Fabric	Springs
Style A	10	2	5	0
Style B	10	5	10	4
Style C	5	5	10	8
Style D	5	8	15	10

a. Write a 1×4 matrix for the number ordered of each style.

b. Use matrix multiplication to find the total number of units of each material needed.

c. Suppose wood costs the manufacturer $5 per unit, filler $6 per unit, fabric $3 per unit, and springs $4 per unit. Write a 4×1 matrix for the costs of the materials.

d. Use matrix multiplication to find the cost of materials in manufacturing each chair style.

e. Use matrix multiplication to find the cost of materials to fill all the orders.

C Solve for x and y.

28. $\begin{bmatrix} 2 & 3 \\ -1 & 4 \\ 0 & 0 \end{bmatrix} \cdot \begin{bmatrix} x \\ y \end{bmatrix} = \begin{bmatrix} 2 \\ -12 \\ 0 \end{bmatrix}$

29. $\begin{bmatrix} 2 & 4 & -1 \\ -1 & 0 & 5 \end{bmatrix} \cdot \begin{bmatrix} 2x + 1 \\ 4 \\ x + y \end{bmatrix} = \begin{bmatrix} 12 \\ 11 \end{bmatrix}$

30. Show that $AB \neq BA$ for $A = \begin{bmatrix} 1 & 2 \\ 3 & 4 \end{bmatrix}$ and $B = \begin{bmatrix} 2 & 3 \\ -1 & 4 \end{bmatrix}$.

*R*EVIEW EXERCISES

1. Solve: $4^x = \dfrac{1}{2}$. [11-1]

2. Write $\log_{10} 100{,}000 = 5$ in exponential form. [11-2]

Use the fact that $\log 2 \approx 0.3010$ and $\log 3 \approx 0.4771$ to approximate the following logarithms. [11-3, 11-4,

3. $\log 1.5$ **4.** $\log 60$ **5.** $\log_2 3$ 11-5]

6. For how many years must $1000 be invested at 12% compounded quarterly before the value of the investment is $2000? [11-6]

7. Solve $\log a + \log b = c$ for a. [11-7]

8. For how many years must $1000 be invested at 12% compounded instantaneously before the value of the investment is $2000? [Use the formula $A = Pe^{rt}$.] [11-8]

*S*elf-Quiz 1

$$\text{Let } A = \begin{bmatrix} 2 & 9 \\ -4 & 3 \\ 0 & -5 \end{bmatrix} \quad \text{and} \quad B = \begin{bmatrix} -1 & 4 & 2 \\ 0 & 3 & -8 \\ 6 & 7 & 5 \end{bmatrix}.$$

15-1 **1.** Identify these elements in matrix A.

   a. a_{31} **b.** a_{12} **c.** a_{21}

2. Label these elements of matrix B with the variable b and subscripts.

   a. 3   **b.** -8 **c.** 6

3. What are the dimensions of matrix A?

4. Let $C = \begin{bmatrix} 2 & -8 & -4 \\ 0 & -6 & 16 \\ -12 & -14 & -10 \end{bmatrix}.$

Find these sums if they are defined.

   a. $B + C$ **b.** $A + C$

15-2 **5.** For what number k does $kB = C$?

6. Let $D = \begin{bmatrix} 0 & 6 \\ 1 & -1 \end{bmatrix}.$

Find these products if they are defined.

   a. AD **b.** DA **c.** BA

---

*E*XTENSION Graphing Ordered Triples

By using a third axis (the z-axis) perpendicular to both the x-axis and the y-axis, we can assign each ordered triple of real numbers to a point in three-dimensional space. For example, point A is the graph of the ordered triple $(2, 3, 4)$ and point B is the graph of $(2, -4, -2)$.

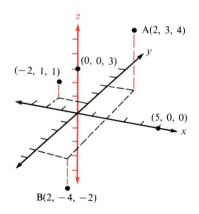

Sketch a set of axes and graph each of the points.

1. $A: (2, 0, 3)$ **2.** $B: (0, 0, 0)$

3. $C: (0, 0, 6)$ **4.** $D: (4, 3, 2)$

5. $E: (-2, 0, -4)$ **6.** $F: (0, -3, 0)$

7. Describe the graph of $x + y + z = 5$.

Properties of Matrices

There are many similarities between the system of matrices and the system of real numbers. For example, consider the matrix sum shown at the right.

$$\begin{bmatrix} 3 & -2 \\ 5 & 2 \end{bmatrix} + \begin{bmatrix} 0 & 0 \\ 0 & 0 \end{bmatrix} = \begin{bmatrix} 3 & -2 \\ 5 & 2 \end{bmatrix}$$

A matrix whose elements are all zero is an identity element for addition and is called a **zero matrix**.

Consider these two matrices: $\quad A = \begin{bmatrix} 2 & 0 \\ 3 & 0 \end{bmatrix}$ and $B = \begin{bmatrix} 0 & 0 \\ 9 & -8 \end{bmatrix}$.

Their product $\begin{bmatrix} 2 & 0 \\ 3 & 0 \end{bmatrix} \cdot \begin{bmatrix} 0 & 0 \\ 9 & -8 \end{bmatrix} = \begin{bmatrix} 0 & 0 \\ 0 & 0 \end{bmatrix}$ is the 2×2 zero matrix, Z.

This example shows that matrix multiplication does not have a zero-product property that corresponds to that of the real numbers.

$$A \times B = Z \quad \text{but} \quad A \neq Z \quad \text{and} \quad B \neq Z$$

Definition: Zero Matrix

An $m \times n$ matrix whose elements are all zero is called the zero matrix and is denoted $Z_{m \times n}$, or just Z.

Example 1 Find a matrix B such that $A + B = Z$. $A = \begin{bmatrix} -3 & 8 \\ 5 & -1 \end{bmatrix}$

Solution The desired matrix must be 2×2.

$$\begin{bmatrix} -3 & 8 \\ 5 & -1 \end{bmatrix} + \begin{bmatrix} w & x \\ y & z \end{bmatrix} = \begin{bmatrix} 0 & 0 \\ 0 & 0 \end{bmatrix}$$

Therefore, $\begin{matrix} -3 + w = 0 & 8 + x = 0 \\ 5 + y = 0 & -1 + z = 0 \end{matrix}$ and $\begin{matrix} w = 3 & x = -8 \\ y = -5 & z = 1 \end{matrix}$

Answer $B = \begin{bmatrix} 3 & -8 \\ -5 & 1 \end{bmatrix}$

In Example 1, since $A + B = Z$, B is called the **additive inverse** of A and is denoted $-A$. Notice that $b_{ij} = -a_{ij}$.

Definition: Additive Inverse of a Matrix

For each matrix $A_{m \times n}$, there is a matrix $-A_{m \times n}$, the *additive inverse* of A, such that $A + (-A) = Z$.

The additive inverse of a matrix allows us to define subtraction of matrices.

Definition: Subtraction of Matrices

For all matrices A and B with the same dimensions,
$$A - B = A + (-B).$$

Example 2 Find values of x, y, and z such that $A - B = C$.

$$A = \begin{bmatrix} x & 5 \\ -2 & 4 \\ 1 & -5 \end{bmatrix} \quad B = \begin{bmatrix} 2 & -1 \\ y & 3 \\ 0 & z \end{bmatrix} \quad C = \begin{bmatrix} 1 & 6 \\ -3 & 1 \\ 1 & -7 \end{bmatrix}$$

Solution By the definitions of subtraction and addition of matrices, $c_{ij} = a_{ij} - b_{ij}$. Therefore, $x - 2 = 1$, $-2 - y = -3$, and $-5 - z = -7$.

Answer Solving gives $x = 3$, $y = 1$, and $z = 2$.

If we apply the definitions of matrix addition, zero matrix, and additive inverse of a matrix, each of the following properties can be proved.

Properties of Matrix Addition

For all matrices A, B, and C of dimension $m \times n$:

1. $A + B$ is an $m \times n$ matrix.   Closure Property
2. $A + B = B + A$ Commutative Property
3. $(A + B) + C = A + (B + C)$ Associative Property
4. There is a unique $m \times n$ matrix Z such that
   $$A + Z = A \quad \text{and} \quad Z + A = A.$$ Identity Property
5. There is a unique $m \times n$ matrix $-A$ such that
   $$A + (-A) = Z \quad \text{and} \quad (-A) + A = Z.$$ Inverse Property

---

Example 3 Show that addition of matrices is commutative.

Solution Let a_{ij} and b_{ij} be corresponding elements in $m \times n$ matrices A and B, respectively. The corresponding elements of $A + B$ and $B + A$ are $a_{ij} + b_{ij}$ and $b_{ij} + a_{ij}$, respectively. Since a_{ij} and b_{ij} are real numbers, and addition of real numbers is commutative, $a_{ij} + b_{ij} = b_{ij} + a_{ij}$. Since corresponding elements of $A + B$ and $B + A$ are equal, $A + B = B + A$. Therefore, addition of matrices is commutative.

Matrix multiplication has some of the same properties as multiplication of real numbers. However, as noted in Lesson 15-2, multiplication of matrices is not always defined. If we restrict our work to square matrices, multiplication is still not commutative. In general, $AB \neq BA$.

The $n \times n$ square matrix with 1's on the **main diagonal** (upper left to lower right) and other entries 0 is the $n \times n$ **multiplicative identity matrix**. The $n \times n$ multiplicative identity matrix is written $I_{n \times n}$, or just I when no confusion results.

$$I_{2 \times 2} = \begin{bmatrix} 1 & 0 \\ 0 & 1 \end{bmatrix} \qquad I_{3 \times 3} = \begin{bmatrix} 1 & 0 & 0 \\ 0 & 1 & 0 \\ 0 & 0 & 1 \end{bmatrix} \qquad I_{4 \times 4} = \begin{bmatrix} 1 & 0 & 0 & 0 \\ 0 & 1 & 0 & 0 \\ 0 & 0 & 1 & 0 \\ 0 & 0 & 0 & 1 \end{bmatrix}$$

Consider the products IA and AI, where $I = \begin{bmatrix} 1 & 0 \\ 0 & 1 \end{bmatrix}$ and $A = \begin{bmatrix} 3 & 2 \\ -1 & 4 \end{bmatrix}$.

$$IA = \begin{bmatrix} 1 & 0 \\ 0 & 1 \end{bmatrix} \cdot \begin{bmatrix} 3 & 2 \\ -1 & 4 \end{bmatrix} = \begin{bmatrix} 3 & 2 \\ -1 & 4 \end{bmatrix}$$

$$AI = \begin{bmatrix} 3 & 2 \\ -1 & 4 \end{bmatrix} \cdot \begin{bmatrix} 1 & 0 \\ 0 & 1 \end{bmatrix} = \begin{bmatrix} 3 & 2 \\ -1 & 4 \end{bmatrix}$$

Since $IA = AI = A$, multiplication by I is commutative. The following is a summary of square-matrix multiplication properties.

Square-Matrix Multiplication Properties

For all $n \times n$ square matrices A, B, and C and each real number k:

1. AB is an $n \times n$ matrix.   Closure Property
2. $(AB)C = A(BC)$ Associative Property
3. $A(B + C) = AB + AC$ and   Distributive Property
   $(B + C)A = BA + CA$
4. $IA = AI = A$ Identity Property
5. $ZA = AZ = Z$ Zero-Product Property
6. $k(A + B) = kA + kB$ Scalar Distributive Property
7. $k(AB) = (kA)B = A(kB)$

Example 4   Simplify I^2A, where $I^2 = I \times I$.

Solution   By the identity property, $I \times I = I$. Therefore, $I^2A = IA = A$.

1. Solve: $x - \begin{bmatrix} 2 & 3 \\ -1 & 4 \\ -2 & 0 \end{bmatrix} = \begin{bmatrix} -1 & 2 \\ -1 & 5 \\ 3 & -6 \end{bmatrix}$.

2. Simplify.   **a.** AI **b.** $A - A$ **c.** A^2Z

3. Show that scalar multiplication is distributive over the sum of two $m \times n$ matrices.

WRITTEN EXERCISES

 For Exercises 1–24, let $A = \begin{bmatrix} 2 & 5 \\ 6 & -8 \end{bmatrix}$ $I = \begin{bmatrix} 1 & 0 \\ 0 & 1 \end{bmatrix}$ $Z = \begin{bmatrix} 0 & 0 \\ 0 & 0 \end{bmatrix}$ $B = \begin{bmatrix} 7 & 4 \\ 5 & 3 \end{bmatrix}$.

Express each matrix in terms of its elements. If there is no such matrix, write "undefined."

1. $-A$ **2.** $-B$ **3.** $A - B$ **4.** $B - A$

5. $A - A$ **6.** $B - B$ **7.** $B - Z$ **8.** $A - Z$

9. AI **10.** BI **11.** IA **12.** IB

13. ZB **14.** ZA **15.** $Z + I$ **16.** $Z - I$

17. AB **18.** A^2 **19.** B^2 **20.** BA

21. $4A$ **22.** $3B$ **23.** $(-A)^2$ **24.** $(-B)^2$

Let $P, Q, R, I,$ and Z be 2×2 matrices. Indicate whether these statements are true or false.

25. $P(QR) = (PQ)R$ for all $P, Q,$ and R.   **26.** $PQ = QP$ for all P and Q.

27. $RI = R$ for all R.   **28.** $RZ = Z$ for all R.

29. If $PX = Z$, then $X = Z$.   **30.** $P + Z = P$ for all P.

31. $P + (Q + R) = (P + Q) + R$ for all $P, Q,$ and R.

32. $(P + Q)^2 = P^2 + 2PQ + Q^2$ for all P and Q.

33. $(P - R)(P + R) = P^2 - R^2$ for all P and R.

34. $IQ = Q$ for all Q.

35. $(P + Q)(P + R) = P^2 + P(Q + R) + QR$

36. $(P + Q)(Q + R) = P(Q + R) + Q(Q + R)$

37. For 3×2 matrices A, B, and C, show that if $A + C = B + C$, then $A = B$.

38. For 3×2 matrices A and B, show that if $A - B = A$, then $B = \begin{bmatrix} 0 & 0 \\ 0 & 0 \\ 0 & 0 \end{bmatrix}$.

B Let $A = \begin{bmatrix} 1 & 2 & -3 \\ 3 & -2 & 1 \\ 0 & 4 & 6 \end{bmatrix}$, $B = \begin{bmatrix} 3 \\ 0 \\ 2 \end{bmatrix}$, $C = \begin{bmatrix} 1 & -1 \\ 4 & -2 \\ 6 & 0 \end{bmatrix}$, and $D = \begin{bmatrix} 2 & 3 \\ -4 & 1 \end{bmatrix}$.

Compute if possible. Write "undefined" if the product is not defined.

39. AB **40.** BA **41.** CD **42.** DC

43. B^2 **44.** C^2 **45.** CA **46.** AC

47. $4A$ **48.** $2D^2$ **49.** $(2D)^2$ **50.** ABC

Solve for x, y, and z.

51. $\begin{bmatrix} 2x + 3 & 8 \\ -4 & -1 \end{bmatrix} - \begin{bmatrix} 10 & 6 \\ 3y - 1 & -5 \end{bmatrix} = \begin{bmatrix} 7 & 4z - 5 \\ 8 & 4 \end{bmatrix}$

52. $\begin{bmatrix} 5x - 6 & 7 \\ 2y + 2 & z \end{bmatrix} - \begin{bmatrix} x & -2 \\ y & 3z + 1 \end{bmatrix} = \begin{bmatrix} 6 & 9 \\ 5y & 3z \end{bmatrix}$

C **53.** $\begin{bmatrix} x \\ 2x \\ z \end{bmatrix} - \begin{bmatrix} y \\ 3y \\ 3z \end{bmatrix} = \begin{bmatrix} 8 \\ 24 \\ 2 \end{bmatrix}$

54. $\begin{bmatrix} 2x + 3 \\ 5x - 2 \\ y \end{bmatrix} + \begin{bmatrix} 3y \\ 2y + 4 \\ z \end{bmatrix} = \begin{bmatrix} 4 \\ 10 \\ -5 \end{bmatrix}$

55. Prove that multiplication is associative for all 2×2 matrices.

56. Prove that $rA + sA = (r + s)A$ for all real numbers r and s and for all 2×3 matrices A.

 EVIEW EXERCISES

Write the first five terms of the following sequences.

1. The arithmetic sequence with $a_6 = 50$ and $a_8 = 60$ [12-1]

2. $a_n = 3(-2)^{n-1}$ [12-2]

3. Write the series $1 + 4 + 9 + 16 + 25 + 36 + 49$ using Σ notation.   [12-3]

Find the value of each series.

4. $\displaystyle\sum_{k=1}^{5} 2k$ **5.** $100 + 98 + 96 + 94 + \cdots + 50$ [12-3, 12-4]

6. $\displaystyle\sum_{k=1}^{6} 0.3(0.1)^{k-1}$ **7.** $1 + \dfrac{4}{5} + \dfrac{16}{25} + \dfrac{64}{125} + \cdots$ [12-5, 12-6]

LESSON 15-4

Other Applications of Matrices

A **network** is a set of points (vertices) connected by arcs. Examples of networks are pipeline systems, highway systems, and airline routes. A **directed network** is one that indicates the direction of flow on each arc. Networks can be described by matrices. This translation from geometric to matrix representation allows numerical analyses to be performed.

Here is a network and its matrix. The 2 in the first row and second column represents the two paths from A to B. The 0 in the first row and third column shows that there is no path directly from A to C. The 1 in the third row and third column shows that there is one path from C to C.

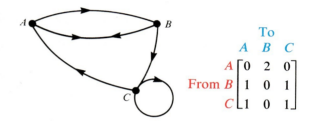

$$\begin{array}{c}\text{From} \end{array}\begin{array}{c} \\ A \\ B \\ C \end{array}\begin{array}{c}\quad\quad\text{To}\\ A\quad B\quad C\\ \begin{bmatrix} 0 & 2 & 0 \\ 1 & 0 & 1 \\ 1 & 0 & 1 \end{bmatrix}\end{array}$$

Example 1 **Write the matrix for this network.**

Solution The 1 in the first row and first column represents one path from point A to itself. The 2 in the first row and second column represents the two paths from A to B. The other elements of the matrix are found in a similar way.

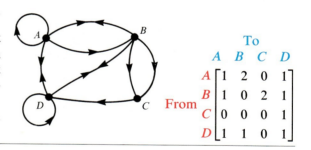

$$\begin{array}{c}\text{From} \end{array}\begin{array}{c} \\ A \\ B \\ C \\ D \end{array}\begin{array}{c}\quad\quad\quad\text{To}\\ A\quad B\quad C\quad D\\ \begin{bmatrix} 1 & 2 & 0 & 1 \\ 1 & 0 & 2 & 1 \\ 0 & 0 & 0 & 1 \\ 1 & 1 & 0 & 1 \end{bmatrix}\end{array}$$

Transformations of points in the coordinate plane such as reflections about the y-axis can be represented by matrices. A **point matrix** is a 2×1 matrix whose elements are the coordinates of a point.

Point matrix A $\begin{bmatrix} 3 \\ 1 \end{bmatrix}$ Point matrix B $\begin{bmatrix} -2 \\ 2 \end{bmatrix}$ Point matrix C $\begin{bmatrix} 0 \\ -1 \end{bmatrix}$

When a point matrix is multiplied by a 2×2 matrix, the product is a point matrix.

$$\underset{\substack{\text{Matrix}\\ T}}{\begin{bmatrix} -1 & 0 \\ 0 & 1 \end{bmatrix}} \cdot \underset{\substack{\text{Point}\\ \text{matrix } A}}{\begin{bmatrix} 3 \\ 1 \end{bmatrix}} = \underset{\substack{\text{Point}\\ \text{matrix } TA}}{\begin{bmatrix} -3 \\ 1 \end{bmatrix}}$$

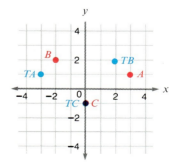

Multiplying by matrix $T = \begin{bmatrix} -1 & 0 \\ 0 & 1 \end{bmatrix}$ reflects points about the y-axis.

$$\underset{T}{\begin{bmatrix} -1 & 0 \\ 0 & 1 \end{bmatrix}} \cdot \underset{B}{\begin{bmatrix} -2 \\ 2 \end{bmatrix}} = \underset{TB}{\begin{bmatrix} 2 \\ 2 \end{bmatrix}} \qquad \underset{T}{\begin{bmatrix} -1 & 0 \\ 0 & 1 \end{bmatrix}} \cdot \underset{C}{\begin{bmatrix} 0 \\ -1 \end{bmatrix}} = \underset{TC}{\begin{bmatrix} 0 \\ -1 \end{bmatrix}}$$

The points TA, TB, and TC are the **reflection images** about the y-axis of the points A, B, and C.

The multiplication of several points by a **transformation matrix** can be simplified by combining the point matrices into a single matrix.

Example 2   Graph the image of triangle DEF under the transformation represented by the matrix $\begin{bmatrix} 1 & 0 \\ 0 & -1 \end{bmatrix}$.

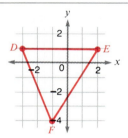

Solution   Transform the triangle by finding the images of the vertices.

$$\underset{T}{\begin{bmatrix} 1 & 0 \\ 0 & -1 \end{bmatrix}} \cdot \underset{D \quad E \quad F}{\begin{bmatrix} -3 & 2 & -1 \\ 1 & 1 & -4 \end{bmatrix}} = \underset{TD \quad TE \quad TF}{\begin{bmatrix} -3 & 2 & -1 \\ -1 & -1 & 4 \end{bmatrix}}$$

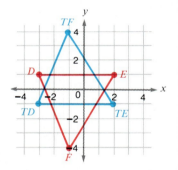

Example 3   Graph the image of square $ABCD$ under the transformation represented by matrix T.

$$T = \begin{bmatrix} 2 & 2 \\ -2 & 3 \end{bmatrix}$$

Solution

$$\underset{T}{\begin{bmatrix} 2 & 2 \\ -2 & 3 \end{bmatrix}} \cdot \underset{A \quad B \quad C \quad D}{\begin{bmatrix} 1 & -1 & -1 & 1 \\ 1 & 1 & -1 & -1 \end{bmatrix}}$$

$$= \underset{TA \quad TB \quad TC \quad TD}{\begin{bmatrix} 4 & 0 & -4 & 0 \\ 1 & 5 & -1 & -5 \end{bmatrix}}$$

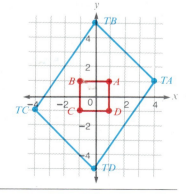

1. Write the matrix for the network shown here.

2. Find the images of the points $A(-3, 1)$, $B(2, 5)$, and $C(6, -2)$ under the transformation $T = \begin{bmatrix} 0 & 1 \\ 1 & 0 \end{bmatrix}$.

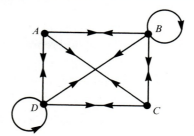

A Write a matrix for each directed network.

1.

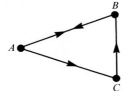

2.

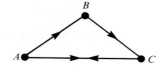

3.

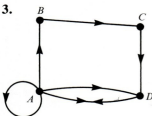

4.

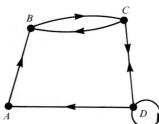

Matrix $T = \begin{bmatrix} 0 & 1 \\ 1 & 0 \end{bmatrix}$ represents a reflection transformation. Find the image of each point under the transformation.

5. $\begin{bmatrix} 2 \\ 5 \end{bmatrix}$ **6.** $\begin{bmatrix} -3 \\ -1 \end{bmatrix}$ **7.** $\begin{bmatrix} 0 \\ -4 \end{bmatrix}$ **8.** $\begin{bmatrix} 6 \\ 0 \end{bmatrix}$

Find and graph the image of each figure under transformation T above.

9.

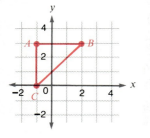

10.

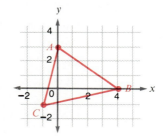

B 11. Transformation T above reflects points about what line?

Let $S = \begin{bmatrix} -2 & 3 \\ 1 & 4 \end{bmatrix}$ and $R = \begin{bmatrix} -1 & 0 \\ 0 & -1 \end{bmatrix}$ **represent transformations.**

12. Graph the image of the square with vertices $(1, 1)$, $(-1, 1)$, $(-1, -1)$, and $(1, -1)$ under the transformation represented by matrix S.

13. Graph the triangle with vertices $(3, 0)$, $(0, 3)$, and $(0, 0)$ and its image under transformation R on the same pair of axes.

14. Describe transformation R.

15. Graph the image of the triangle given in Exercise 13 under transformation R^2.

16. Describe transformation R^2.

17. Draw a directed network that is represented by this matrix.

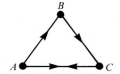

$$\begin{array}{c} \text{To} \\ \begin{array}{ccc} R & S & T \end{array} \\ \text{From } \begin{array}{c} R \\ S \\ T \end{array} \begin{bmatrix} 0 & 2 & 1 \\ 0 & 1 & 2 \\ 1 & 1 & 1 \end{bmatrix} \end{array}$$

C Matrix $M = \begin{bmatrix} 0 & 1 & 1 \\ 0 & 0 & 1 \\ 1 & 0 & 0 \end{bmatrix}$ **represents the directed network.**

18. Write the matrix that shows the number of ways to move from one point to another by following *two arcs* of the directed network. For example, there is one way of getting from C to B using two arcs. There is no way of getting from B to C using two arcs.

19. Compute M^2.

20. How do the matrices in Exercises 18 and 19 compare?

21. What does the matrix $M + M^2$ represent?

$\mathcal{R}$EVIEW EXERCISES

1. How many even three-digit numbers are there?   [13-1]

2. How many permutations are there of the first six letters of the alphabet?   [13-2]

3. In how many ways can an executive committee of three persons be selected from a club with eight members?   [13-3]

4. When two dice are tossed, what is the probability of a sum of three?   [13-4]

5. What is the probability that a 70% free-throw shooter will make the first of two free throws and miss the second?   [13-5]

6. When two dice are tossed, what is the probability that the numbers shown have a product that is even?   [13-6]

7. If a coin is flipped five times, what is the probability of getting at least four heads?   [13-7]

LESSON 15-5

Inverse of a Square Matrix

Recall that each real number except zero has a multiplicative inverse. The product of a number and its inverse is 1, the identity element for multiplication. Similarly, some square matrices have inverses. The product of an $n \times n$ matrix A and its inverse (denoted A^{-1}) is the $n \times n$ identity matrix I. For example, consider matrix A and matrix B. Since $AB = I$, $B = A^{-1}$.

$$A = \begin{bmatrix} 1 & 1 \\ 0 & 1 \end{bmatrix} \qquad B = \begin{bmatrix} 1 & -1 \\ 0 & 1 \end{bmatrix} \qquad \underset{A}{\begin{bmatrix} 1 & 1 \\ 0 & 1 \end{bmatrix}} \cdot \underset{B}{\begin{bmatrix} 1 & -1 \\ 0 & 1 \end{bmatrix}} = \underset{I}{\begin{bmatrix} 1 & 0 \\ 0 & 1 \end{bmatrix}}$$

We can determine the **inverse** of the general 2×2 matrix.

Let

$$A = \begin{bmatrix} a_1 & b_1 \\ a_2 & b_2 \end{bmatrix} \quad \text{and} \quad A^{-1} = \begin{bmatrix} x_1 & y_1 \\ x_2 & y_2 \end{bmatrix}.$$

Then $AA^{-1} = I$.

$$\begin{bmatrix} a_1 & b_1 \\ a_2 & b_2 \end{bmatrix} \cdot \begin{bmatrix} x_1 & y_1 \\ x_2 & y_2 \end{bmatrix} = \begin{bmatrix} 1 & 0 \\ 0 & 1 \end{bmatrix}$$

Therefore,

$$\begin{bmatrix} a_1x_1 + b_1x_2 & a_1y_1 + b_1y_2 \\ a_2x_1 + b_2x_2 & a_2y_1 + b_2y_2 \end{bmatrix} = \begin{bmatrix} 1 & 0 \\ 0 & 1 \end{bmatrix}.$$

The matrix equation above is equivalent to these two systems.

$$\begin{array}{ll} a_1x_1 + b_1x_2 = 1 & a_1y_1 + b_1y_2 = 0 \\ a_2x_1 + b_2x_2 = 0 & a_2y_1 + b_2y_2 = 1 \end{array}$$

The solutions of the systems are:

$$x_1 = \frac{b_2}{a_1b_2 - a_2b_1} \qquad y_1 = \frac{-b_1}{a_1b_2 - a_2b_1} \qquad x_2 = \frac{-a_2}{a_1b_2 - a_2b_1} \qquad y_2 = \frac{a_1}{a_1b_2 - a_2b_1}$$

Therefore,

$$A^{-1} = \begin{bmatrix} x_1 & y_1 \\ x_2 & y_2 \end{bmatrix} = \begin{bmatrix} \dfrac{b_2}{a_1b_2 - a_2b_1} & \dfrac{-b_1}{a_1b_2 - a_2b_1} \\ \dfrac{-a_2}{a_1b_2 - a_2b_1} & \dfrac{a_1}{a_1b_2 - a_2b_1} \end{bmatrix}.$$

The denominators of the entries in A^{-1} are identical. Recall from Chapter 4 that this denominator is the value of the determinant:

$$\begin{vmatrix} a_1 & b_1 \\ a_2 & b_2 \end{vmatrix} = a_1b_2 - a_2b_1.$$

The determinant $\begin{vmatrix} a_1 & b_1 \\ a_2 & b_2 \end{vmatrix}$ is the **determinant of matrix** A (denoted det A).

Therefore, $\qquad A^{-1} = \dfrac{1}{\det A} \begin{bmatrix} b_2 & -b_1 \\ -a_2 & a_1 \end{bmatrix}$, where det $A \neq 0$.

Definition: Inverse of a 2 × 2 Matrix

For each 2 × 2 matrix A, where $A = \begin{bmatrix} a_1 & b_1 \\ a_2 & b_2 \end{bmatrix}$, $A^{-1} = \dfrac{1}{\det A} \begin{bmatrix} b_2 & -b_1 \\ -a_2 & a_1 \end{bmatrix}$,

where $\det A \neq 0$.

Example 1　Find the inverse of matrix $A = \begin{bmatrix} 2 & 5 \\ -1 & 3 \end{bmatrix}$.

Solution　Compute $\det A$.　$\begin{vmatrix} 2 & 5 \\ -1 & 3 \end{vmatrix} = 2 \cdot 3 - (-1)5 = 11$

Apply the formula for the inverse of a 2 × 2 matrix.

$$A^{-1} = \frac{1}{11} \begin{bmatrix} 3 & -5 \\ 1 & 2 \end{bmatrix}$$

Answer　$A^{-1} = \begin{bmatrix} \dfrac{3}{11} & -\dfrac{5}{11} \\ \dfrac{1}{11} & \dfrac{2}{11} \end{bmatrix}$　*Check*　$\begin{bmatrix} 2 & 5 \\ -1 & 3 \end{bmatrix} \cdot \begin{bmatrix} \dfrac{3}{11} & -\dfrac{5}{11} \\ \dfrac{1}{11} & \dfrac{2}{11} \end{bmatrix} = \begin{bmatrix} 1 & 0 \\ 0 & 1 \end{bmatrix}$

A system of equations can be written as a matrix equation.

System	*Matrix equation*
$ax + by = c$	$\begin{bmatrix} a & b \\ d & e \end{bmatrix} \cdot \begin{bmatrix} x \\ y \end{bmatrix} = \begin{bmatrix} c \\ f \end{bmatrix}$
$dx + ey = f$	

The matrix $\begin{bmatrix} a & b \\ d & e \end{bmatrix}$ is called the **coefficient matrix** of the system.

A matrix equation of the form $A \begin{bmatrix} x \\ y \end{bmatrix} = \begin{bmatrix} a \\ b \end{bmatrix}$ can be solved using the inverse of A.

Example 2　Solve this system for x and y using the inverse of the coefficient matrix.

$$2x + 3y = 10$$
$$5x - 4y = -2$$

Solution　Write the system as a matrix equation.　$\begin{bmatrix} 2 & 3 \\ 5 & -4 \end{bmatrix} \cdot \begin{bmatrix} x \\ y \end{bmatrix} = \begin{bmatrix} 10 \\ -2 \end{bmatrix}$

Compute the inverse of the coefficient matrix.

$$\begin{bmatrix} 2 & 3 \\ 5 & -4 \end{bmatrix}^{-1} = \begin{bmatrix} \dfrac{4}{23} & \dfrac{3}{23} \\ \dfrac{5}{23} & -\dfrac{2}{23} \end{bmatrix}$$

Example 2 (continued)

Multiply both sides of the matrix equation by the inverse matrix.

$$\begin{bmatrix} \dfrac{4}{23} & \dfrac{3}{23} \\[2mm] \dfrac{5}{23} & -\dfrac{2}{23} \end{bmatrix} \cdot \begin{bmatrix} 2 & 3 \\ 5 & -4 \end{bmatrix} \cdot \begin{bmatrix} x \\ y \end{bmatrix} = \begin{bmatrix} \dfrac{4}{23} & \dfrac{3}{23} \\[2mm] \dfrac{5}{23} & -\dfrac{2}{23} \end{bmatrix} \cdot \begin{bmatrix} 10 \\ -2 \end{bmatrix}$$

$$\begin{bmatrix} x \\ y \end{bmatrix} = \begin{bmatrix} \dfrac{34}{23} \\[2mm] \dfrac{54}{23} \end{bmatrix} \qquad x = \dfrac{34}{23} \text{ and } y = \dfrac{54}{23}$$

Answer $\left\{ \left(\dfrac{34}{23}, \dfrac{54}{23} \right) \right\}$

Example 3 **Consider transformation T, where $T = \begin{bmatrix} 1 & 0 \\ 0 & -1 \end{bmatrix}$.**

If TP is the image of P under T, find the matrix that transforms TP back to P.

Solution Let R be the required transformation. Then $R \cdot TP = P$. Therefore, $R = T^{-1}$.
Compute T^{-1}.

$$T^{-1} = \dfrac{1}{\begin{vmatrix} 1 & 0 \\ 0 & -1 \end{vmatrix}} \cdot \begin{bmatrix} -1 & 0 \\ 0 & 1 \end{bmatrix} = -1 \cdot \begin{bmatrix} -1 & 0 \\ 0 & 1 \end{bmatrix}$$

Answer $T^{-1} = \begin{bmatrix} 1 & 0 \\ 0 & -1 \end{bmatrix}$

Check $T^{-1}T \begin{bmatrix} x \\ y \end{bmatrix} = \begin{bmatrix} 1 & 0 \\ 0 & -1 \end{bmatrix} \cdot \begin{bmatrix} 1 & 0 \\ 0 & -1 \end{bmatrix} \cdot \begin{bmatrix} x \\ y \end{bmatrix} = \begin{bmatrix} 1 & 0 \\ 0 & 1 \end{bmatrix} \cdot \begin{bmatrix} x \\ y \end{bmatrix} = \begin{bmatrix} x \\ y \end{bmatrix}$ It checks.

Note in Example 3 that T is its own inverse. Recall from Example 2 in Lesson 15-4 that T reflects points about the x-axis. Reflecting a point about the x-axis and then reflecting the image about the x-axis gives the original point.

$\mathcal{C}$LASSROOM EXERCISES

1. State whether the matrix $\begin{bmatrix} 0 & 1 \\ 1 & 0 \end{bmatrix}$ is its own inverse.

2. Find A^{-1} for $A = \begin{bmatrix} 2 & -4 \\ -1 & 3 \end{bmatrix}$.

3. Solve this system using the inverse of the coefficient matrix. $3x + 2y = 12$

$$4x + 5y = -3$$

A State whether the given pair of matrices are inverses.

1. $\begin{bmatrix} 1 & 3 \\ 4 & 13 \end{bmatrix}, \begin{bmatrix} 13 & -3 \\ -4 & 1 \end{bmatrix}$

2. $\begin{bmatrix} 1 & 3 \\ 2 & 7 \end{bmatrix}, \begin{bmatrix} 7 & -3 \\ -2 & 1 \end{bmatrix}$

3. $\begin{bmatrix} 2 & 4 \\ 3 & 1 \end{bmatrix}, \begin{bmatrix} -\dfrac{1}{10} & \dfrac{2}{5} \\ \dfrac{3}{10} & -\dfrac{1}{5} \end{bmatrix}$

4. $\begin{bmatrix} 3 & 6 \\ 2 & 1 \end{bmatrix}, \begin{bmatrix} -\dfrac{1}{9} & \dfrac{2}{3} \\ \dfrac{2}{9} & -\dfrac{1}{3} \end{bmatrix}$

5. $\begin{bmatrix} 4 & 8 \\ 5 & 5 \end{bmatrix}, \begin{bmatrix} \dfrac{1}{4} & -\dfrac{2}{5} \\ -\dfrac{1}{4} & \dfrac{1}{5} \end{bmatrix}$

6. $\begin{bmatrix} 2 & 6 \\ 3 & 5 \end{bmatrix}, \begin{bmatrix} \dfrac{5}{8} & -\dfrac{3}{4} \\ -\dfrac{3}{8} & \dfrac{1}{4} \end{bmatrix}$

Find the inverse of each matrix.

7. $\begin{bmatrix} 1 & 2 \\ 1 & 3 \end{bmatrix}$

8. $\begin{bmatrix} 1 & 6 \\ 1 & 5 \end{bmatrix}$

9. $\begin{bmatrix} -\dfrac{1}{22} & \dfrac{4}{11} \\ \dfrac{3}{22} & -\dfrac{1}{11} \end{bmatrix}$

10. $\begin{bmatrix} 1 & -\dfrac{1}{2} \\ 2 & -\dfrac{3}{2} \end{bmatrix}$

Find the determinant of each matrix and state whether the given matrix has an inverse.

11. $\begin{bmatrix} -2 & 3 \\ 4 & -6 \end{bmatrix}$

12. $\begin{bmatrix} 2 & -8 \\ -3 & 12 \end{bmatrix}$

13. $\begin{bmatrix} 0 & 0 \\ 5 & 9 \end{bmatrix}$

14. $\begin{bmatrix} 4 & 0 \\ 7 & 0 \end{bmatrix}$

Solve the system for x and y using the inverse of the coefficient matrix.

15. $4x - 3y = 3$
$6x + 9y = 0$

16. $6x - 2y = 5$
$15x + 6y = 7$

17. $\dfrac{1}{3}x - \dfrac{3}{4}y = 7$
$\dfrac{4}{3}x + \dfrac{3}{8}y = 1$

18. $\dfrac{3}{4}x + \dfrac{1}{3}y = -2$
$\dfrac{1}{2}x - \dfrac{2}{3}y = -4$

19. $3x + 5y = 0$
$2x - 3y = 19$

20. $3x + 2y = 0$
$2x + 3y = -4$

B Find the inverse of each matrix.

21. $\begin{bmatrix} 1 & 0 \\ 0 & k \end{bmatrix}, k \neq 0$

22. $\begin{bmatrix} k & 0 \\ 0 & k \end{bmatrix}, k \neq 0$

23. $\begin{bmatrix} 0 & k \\ k & 0 \end{bmatrix}, k \neq 0$

24. $\begin{bmatrix} 1 & k \\ 0 & 1 \end{bmatrix}$

25. $\begin{bmatrix} k & 1 \\ 1 & 0 \end{bmatrix}$

26. $\begin{bmatrix} k & 1 \\ 1 & 1 \end{bmatrix}, k \neq 1$

27. $\begin{bmatrix} k & 1 \\ 1 & k \end{bmatrix}$, $k \neq -1$, $k \neq 1$ **28.** $\begin{bmatrix} 0 & 1 \\ 0 & k \end{bmatrix}$, $k \neq 0$

 29. Are these matrices inverses? $\begin{bmatrix} 1 & 2 & 3 \\ 1 & 5 & 4 \\ 1 & 6 & 5 \end{bmatrix}$, $\begin{bmatrix} \dfrac{1}{2} & 4 & -\dfrac{7}{2} \\ -\dfrac{1}{2} & 1 & -\dfrac{1}{2} \\ \dfrac{1}{2} & -2 & \dfrac{3}{2} \end{bmatrix}$

30. Solve this system for x, y, and z using the inverse of the coefficient matrix. (See Exercise 29.)

$$x + 2y + 3z = 1$$
$$x + 5y + 4z = -6$$
$$x + 6y + 5z = -7$$

 REVIEW EXERCISES

1. Refer to the table of Signers of the Declaration of Independence on page 572. Make a stem-and-leaf plot of the year of death for the signers through Philip Livingston. Let the stem have three digits (182 for 1826, etc).   [14-1]

2. State the median, lower and upper quartiles, interquartile range, and range for the set: [14-2]
$$\{18, 22, 19, 15, 25, 9, 12, 35, 39\}$$

3. Compute the mean, mean absolute variance, variance, and standard deviation for these package weights.   [14-3]
$$11, 9, 5, 7, 11, 6, 11, 12, 14, 14$$

4. Use the data of points scored and minutes played per game.

Minutes	35	30	38	28	36	32	25	34	30	35	32	28	25	20
Points	15	10	25	8	18	10	22	20	15	20	15	16	10	8

  [14-4]

  a. Make a scatter plot of the data.   **b.** Fit a line to the data points.   [14-4]
  c. Use your fitted line to predict the number of points scored if a player plays 40 minutes.

5. The scores on a biology test are normally distributed with mean 65 and standard deviation 13. Give the probability of a score being   [14-5]
  a. between 52 and 78.   **b.** above 91.   **c.** between 39 and 65.   **d.** below 52.

6. Use the random number table on page 596 to choose twenty 2-digit numbers. Determine the percentage of even numbers.   [14-6]
  a. Start in row 1, column 1. Read down.   **b.** Start in row 1, column 21. Read down.

$\mathcal{S}$elf-Quiz 2

Let $A = \begin{bmatrix} 1 & -2 \\ 3 & 4 \end{bmatrix}$ and $B = \begin{bmatrix} 0 & 1 \\ 5 & -1 \end{bmatrix}$.

15-3 **1.** Show that $(2A)B = 2(AB)$.

2. Let $C = \begin{bmatrix} 0.4 & 0.2 \\ -0.3 & 0.1 \end{bmatrix}$. Show that $AC = I$.

Let X, Y, Z, and I be $n \times n$ matrices. Indicate whether these statements are true or false.

3. If $XY = YX$ for all X, then Y must be Z or I.

4. It is possible for $XY = Z$ with $X \neq Z$ and $Y \neq Z$.

5. X^2 is equal to the matrix in which each element of X is squared.

6. If $2Y + X = Z$, then $Y = -\frac{1}{2}X$.

15-4 **7.** Write the matrix for the network shown here.

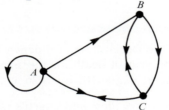

Matrix $T = \begin{bmatrix} 0 & 1 \\ 1 & 0 \end{bmatrix}$ represents a reflection transformation.

8. Find the image of the points $A(3, 2)$, $B(-1, 0)$, and $C(-3, -3)$ under the transformation.

15-5 State whether the given matrices are inverses.

9. $\begin{bmatrix} 1 & 0 \\ 0 & 1 \end{bmatrix}, \begin{bmatrix} 0 & 1 \\ 1 & 0 \end{bmatrix}$

10. $\begin{bmatrix} 6 & -2 \\ 5 & -3 \end{bmatrix}, \begin{bmatrix} \frac{3}{8} & -\frac{1}{4} \\ \frac{5}{8} & -\frac{3}{4} \end{bmatrix}$

Find the inverse of each matrix.

11. $\begin{bmatrix} 5 & -5 \\ 5 & 5 \end{bmatrix}$

12. $\begin{bmatrix} 5 & 5 \\ 4 & 6 \end{bmatrix}$

13. $\begin{bmatrix} -1 & \frac{3}{5} \\ 1 & -\frac{2}{5} \end{bmatrix}$

Solve the system for x and y using the inverse of the coefficient matrix.

14. $5x + 4y = -1$
     $2x - y = 10$

15. $\frac{1}{3}x + 5 = \frac{2}{3}y$

   $\frac{1}{2}x + \frac{1}{3}y = \frac{1}{2}$

LESSON 15-6

Solving Systems of Equations Using Matrices

The method of solving a system of equations using the inverse of the matrix of coefficients is ideal for computer use. A more efficient method for paper-and-pencil work involves operating on the rows of a matrix as you do on the equations themselves when using the linear combinations method (see Lesson 4-3).

Here is an outline of the method. First, write the matrix of the system (called the **augmented matrix**). Then transform that matrix using the **elementary row operations** until you obtain 1's on the "diagonal" and 0's for the other coefficients. Finally, write the system for that matrix. The solution of this system is obvious.

System	Augmented Matrix	Equivalent "Diagonal" Matrix	Equivalent System
$x + y + z = 3$	$\begin{bmatrix} 1 & 1 & 1 & 3 \\ 1 & -1 & 1 & 7 \\ 2 & 1 & 1 & 4 \end{bmatrix}$	$\begin{bmatrix} 1 & 0 & 0 & 1 \\ 0 & 1 & 0 & -2 \\ 0 & 0 & 1 & 4 \end{bmatrix}$	$x = 1$
$x - y + z = 7$			$y = -2$
$2x + y + z = 4$			$z = 4$

The elementary row operations are the same as the operations used to solve a system by the linear combinations method.

Elementary Row Operations

If the matrix of a system of equations is transformed by the following operations, the resulting matrix represents a system that is equivalent to the original system.

a. Interchange two rows.
b. Multiply a row by a nonzero constant.
c. Multiply any row by a constant and add it to another row.

Example Solve the system given above using elementary row operations.

Solution Write the matrix of the system.

$$\begin{bmatrix} 1 & 1 & 1 & 3 \\ 1 & -1 & 1 & 7 \\ 2 & 1 & 1 & 4 \end{bmatrix}$$

Subtract row 1 from row 3 to get 2 zeros in the bottom row.

$$\begin{bmatrix} 1 & 1 & 1 & 3 \\ 1 & -1 & 1 & 7 \\ 1 & 0 & 0 & 1 \end{bmatrix}$$

Example (continued)

Subtract row 1 from row 2 to get 2 zeros in the middle row.

$$\begin{bmatrix} 1 & 1 & 1 & 3 \\ 0 & -2 & 0 & 4 \\ 1 & 0 & 0 & 1 \end{bmatrix}$$

Divide row 2 by -2.

$$\begin{bmatrix} 1 & 1 & 1 & 3 \\ 0 & 1 & 0 & -2 \\ 1 & 0 & 0 & 1 \end{bmatrix}$$

Subtract row 3 from row 1.

$$\begin{bmatrix} 0 & 1 & 1 & 2 \\ 0 & 1 & 0 & -2 \\ 1 & 0 & 0 & 1 \end{bmatrix}$$

Subtract row 2 from row 1.

$$\begin{bmatrix} 0 & 0 & 1 & 4 \\ 0 & 1 & 0 & -2 \\ 1 & 0 & 0 & 1 \end{bmatrix}$$

The diagonal matrix represents this system:

$$\begin{bmatrix} 0 & 0 & 1 & 4 \\ 0 & 1 & 0 & -2 \\ 1 & 0 & 0 & 1 \end{bmatrix}$$

$$z = 4$$
$$y = -2$$
$$x = 1$$

Answer $\{(1, -2, 4)\}$

Check The check is left to the student.

Note that the sequence of operations used in the example is not unique. There are many other ways of transforming the given matrix to the desired matrix.

*C*LASSROOM EXERCISES

1. Suppose that the matrix of a system is reduced to: What is the solution of the system? $\{(-2, 3)\}$ $\begin{bmatrix} 1 & 0 & -2 \\ 0 & 1 & 3 \end{bmatrix}$

2. Solve this system using elementary row operations on an augmented matrix. $\{(-1, 3)\}$

$$2x + y = 1$$
$$x - y = -4$$

*W*RITTEN EXERCISES

 Solve each system using elementary row operations on an augmented matrix.

1. $x + y = 8$
   $2x - y = 7$

2. $2x - y = -7$
   $x + 2y = 4$

3. $3x - y = 4$
   $2x + y = 1$

4. $2x + y = 8$
$x - 2y = 4$

5. $\frac{1}{2}x - y = 1$
$x - \frac{1}{2}y = 5$

6. $2x - \frac{1}{2}y = -9$
$\frac{1}{2}x + y = 0$

7. $x + y + z = 4$
$x - y - z = 0$
$x + y - z = -2$

8. $x + y + z = 1$
$x - y - z = 7$
$-x + y - z = -5$

9. $x + 2y + z = 4$
$2x - y + z = 5$
$x + y - 2z = -5$

10. $3x - y + z = 8$
$x + y + z = -2$
$-x - y + 2z = -1$

11. $2x - y + z = 2$
$x + y + z = 2$
$x - 3y + z = -2$

12. $x - 2y + z = -1$
$x + y - 3z = -4$
$2x - y - z = -5$

13. $x + y = 4$
$x + z = 0$
$y + z = 2$

14. $2x + 4y + z = 3$
$x - 2y + z = 1$
$2x + 2y - z = \frac{1}{2}$

15. $2x + y - z = 5$
$2z + y = \frac{1}{2}x$
$x - z = -\frac{1}{2}y$

16. $5x - 3y + z = 0$
$2z - 2x = 4y$
$3x = -y + 4z$

17. $w + x + y + z = 5$
$w - x - y + 2z = 5$
$-w + x + y - z = -3$
$2w - x - y - z = 1$

18. $a_1x + b_1y = c_1$
$a_2x + b_2y = c_2$

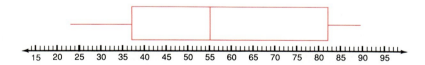

1. State the median, upper and lower quartiles, interquartile range, and range of the set shown on the plot below.

A set of scores is normally distributed with mean 125 and standard deviation 16.

2. What is your score if you are in the
  a. top 2.5%?   **b.** bottom 50%?

3. How many standard deviations from the mean is a score of
  a. 93?   **b.** 133?

4. What is the z-score of the following scores?
  a. 117   **b.** 149

5. What is your score if your z-score is
  a. -2.5?   **b.** 1.25?

CHAPTER SUMMARY

▶ **Vocabulary**

matrix	[page 609]	additive inverse of a matrix	[page 622]
dimensions	[page 609]	multiplicative identity matrix I	[page 624]
element of a matrix	[page 610]	directed network	[page 627]
row matrix	[page 610]	point matrix	[page 627]
column matrix	[page 610]	reflection image	[page 627]
vector	[page 610]	transformation matrix	[page 627]
square matrix of order n	[page 610]	inverse of a matrix	[page 631]
corresponding elements	[page 610]	determinant of a matrix	[page 631]
equal matrices	[page 610]	coefficient matrix	[page 632]
scalar multiplication	[page 615]	augmented matrix	[page 637]
zero matrix Z	[page 622]	elementary row opeations	[page 637]

▶ Given an $m \times n$ matrix A and an $n \times p$ matrix B, the matrix AB is an $m \times p$ **[15-2]**
matrix C with elements c_{ij} given by the formula
$$c_{ij} = a_{i1}b_{1j} + a_{i2}b_{2j} + \cdots + a_{in}b_{nj}.$$

▶ Properties of Matrix Addition   **[15-3]**

For all matrices A, B, and C of dimensions $m \times n$:

1. $A + B$ is an $m \times n$ matrix.   Closure Property
2. $A + B = B + A$ Commutative Property
3. $(A + B) + C = A + (B + C)$ Associative Property
4. There is a unique $m \times n$ matrix Z such that   Identity Property
   $A + Z = A$ and $Z + A = A$.
5. There is a unique $m \times n$ matrix $-A$ such   Inverse Property
   that $A + (-A) = Z$ and $(-A) + A = Z$.

▶ Square-Matrix Multiplication Properties   **[15-3]**

For all $n \times n$ square matrices A, B, and C and each real number k:

1. AB is an $n \times n$ matrix.   Closure Property
2. $(AB)C = A(BC)$ Associative Property
3. $A(B + C) = AB + AC$ and   Distributive Property
   $(B + C)A = BA + CA$
4. $IA = AI = A$ Identity Property
5. $ZA = AZ = Z$ Zero-Product Property
6. $k(A + B) = kA + kB$ Scalar Distributive Property
7. $k(AB) = (kA)B = A(kB)$

▶ An $m \times n$ matrix whose elements are all zero is called the *zero matrix* and is denoted $Z_{m \times n}$ or just Z. [15-3]

▶ Inverse of a 2×2 Matrix [15-5]

For each 2×2 matrix A, where $A = \begin{bmatrix} a_1 & b_1 \\ a_2 & b_2 \end{bmatrix}$, $A^{-1} = \dfrac{1}{\det A} \begin{bmatrix} b_2 & -b_1 \\ -a_2 & a_1 \end{bmatrix}$, where $\det A \ne 0$.

$\mathcal{C}$HAPTER REVIEW

15-1 Objective: To introduce matrix terminology.

$$A = \begin{bmatrix} 1 \\ 5 \\ -9 \\ 0 \end{bmatrix} \qquad B = \begin{bmatrix} 4 & -2 \\ 3 & 6 \end{bmatrix} \qquad C = \begin{bmatrix} 7 & 8 & -1 \end{bmatrix} \qquad D = \begin{bmatrix} -5 & 2 \\ 0 & 4 \end{bmatrix}$$

1. Which matrix is a row matrix?
2. Which matrix is a column matrix?
3. What are the dimensions of matrix A?
4. Identify these elements.

    a. a_{31} **b.** b_{22} **c.** c_{13} **d.** d_{12}

5. Label these elements of matrix B using the variable b and subscripts.

    a. -2 **b.** 4 **c.** 6

Objective: To find the sum of two matrices.

6. Find $B + D$.

15-2 Objective: To find the product of a matrix and a scalar.

7. Given $X = \begin{bmatrix} 7 & 1 \\ -3 & 4 \\ 0 & 2 \end{bmatrix}$, find $-3X$.

8. Solve this matrix equation for x and y. $2 \begin{bmatrix} 4 & x \\ -1 & 5 \end{bmatrix} = \begin{bmatrix} 8 & 5 \\ y & 10 \end{bmatrix}$

Objective: To find the product of two matrices.

9. If defined, what are the dimensions of the product of the matrices?

    a. $A_{4 \times 5} B_{5 \times 2}$ **b.** $C_{2 \times 1} D_{2 \times 3}$

10. Let $A = \begin{bmatrix} 1 & 4 \\ -2 & 3 \end{bmatrix}$ and $B = \begin{bmatrix} 0 & -1 & 2 \\ 5 & 6 & -3 \end{bmatrix}$. Find these products.

    a. AB **b.** A^2

15-3 **Objective:** To apply the properties of matrix addition and matrix multiplication.

11. For 2×2 matrices, write these matrices.   **a.** I **b.** Z

12. Write the additive inverse of $B = \begin{bmatrix} 6 & -4 & 12 \end{bmatrix}$.

13. Simplify these matrix expressions for $n \times n$ matrices.

   a. $A - 2A$ **b.** IB **c.** ZI **d.** $I + Z$

15-4 **Objective:** To use matrices to solve problems.

14. Write a 3×3 matrix for this network.

15. Suppose $P = \begin{bmatrix} 2 & 0 & -3 \\ -4 & 5 & 2 \end{bmatrix}$ repre- sents the coordinates of the vertices of triangle ABC. Graph the image of the triangle under the transformation $T = \begin{bmatrix} -1 & 0 \\ 0 & 1 \end{bmatrix}$.

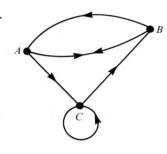

15-5 **Objective:** To determine the inverse of a square matrix.

16. Find the inverse: $B = \begin{bmatrix} 1 & 2 \\ -1 & 3 \end{bmatrix}$.

Objective: To solve a 2×2 system of two linear equations in two variables using the inverse of the coefficient matrix.

17. Write this matrix equation as a system of two equations.

$$\begin{bmatrix} 1 & 2 \\ 2 & -1 \end{bmatrix} \cdot \begin{bmatrix} x \\ y \end{bmatrix} = \begin{bmatrix} 3 \\ 10 \end{bmatrix}$$

18. Solve this system for x and y using the inverse of the co- efficient matrix.

$$2x - 3y = 7$$
$$x + y = 1$$

Objective: To solve a system of equations using the augmented matrix.

Solve each system using elementary row operations on an augmented matrix.

19. $x + y + z = 0$
    $2x + y - z = 2$
    $2x + 2y + z = 5$

20. $2x + y - z = -2$
    $x - y + 2z = -3$
    $-3x + 2y - 2z = 10$

$\mathcal{C}$HAPTER 15 SELF-TEST

15-1 1. What are the dimensions of $A = \begin{bmatrix} 2 & -11 & 0 \\ 9 & 6 & 5 \end{bmatrix}$?

2. Write a general 1×4 row matrix B using elements b_{ij}.

3. Identify the elements c_{22} and c_{31} of $C = \begin{bmatrix} 0 & 6 & -1 \\ 7 & -8 & 4 \\ 5 & 2 & 3 \end{bmatrix}$.

4. Find the sum of A (defined in Exercise 1) and D if

$$D = \begin{bmatrix} 4 & 2 & 4 \\ -7 & 3 & -6 \end{bmatrix}.$$

15-2 **5.** Write the product $6 \begin{bmatrix} 1 & 2 \\ -3 & 5 \end{bmatrix}$ as a matrix.

6. What are the dimensions of the matrix product AC, where A and C are defined in Exercises 1 and 3?

7. Find QP if $Q = \begin{bmatrix} 1 & 0 \\ 2 & -1 \\ 0 & 5 \end{bmatrix}$ and $P = \begin{bmatrix} 1 & 0 & 0 \\ -1 & 2 & 1 \end{bmatrix}.$

15-3 **8.** Find $D - 2A$, where D and A are defined in Exercises 1 and 4.

9. Write the 3×3 identity matrix for multiplication.

10. Solve for x, y, and z: $x \begin{bmatrix} 2 & 5 \\ y & 1 \end{bmatrix} = \begin{bmatrix} 4 & z \\ 6 & 2 \end{bmatrix}.$

11. Solve: $3Y - [9 \quad 0 \quad -4] = [6 \quad 3 \quad -8].$

12. Simplify these $n \times n$ matrix expressions.

a. $A(B + Z)$ **b.** $I(B - I)$

15-4 **13.** Write a 4×4 matrix for this network.

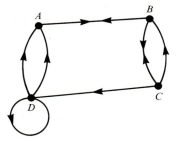

14. Find the coordinates of the point $P = \begin{bmatrix} 2 \\ 3 \end{bmatrix}$

under the transformation $\begin{bmatrix} 1 & -1 \\ -1 & 1 \end{bmatrix}.$

15-5 **15.** Find the inverse of the matrix $A = \begin{bmatrix} 0 & 2 \\ 4 & 1 \end{bmatrix}.$

16. Write this system as a matrix equation. $\begin{aligned} 2x - 3y &= 6 \\ 4x + 2y &= 7 \end{aligned}$

17. Given that the inverse of $\begin{bmatrix} 2 & -3 \\ 1 & -1 \end{bmatrix}$ is $\begin{bmatrix} -1 & 3 \\ -1 & 2 \end{bmatrix}$, use the inverse matrix

to solve this system for x and y. $\begin{bmatrix} 2 & -3 \\ 1 & -1 \end{bmatrix} \cdot \begin{bmatrix} x \\ y \end{bmatrix} = \begin{bmatrix} 4 \\ 5 \end{bmatrix}$

15-6 **18.** Solve using elementary row operations on an augmented matrix:

$$\begin{aligned} 2x + 3y &= 8 \\ x - y &= -1 \end{aligned}$$

Choose the best answer.

1. $461^2 - 2 \cdot 461 \cdot 361 + 361^2 = \underline{}$.

   A. 10,000   **B.** 82,200   **C.** 120,321   **D.** 167,421   **E.** 342,842

2. If $4\frac{3}{4} = 3 + \frac{x}{12}$, then $x = \underline{}$.

   A. 9   **B.** 12   **C.** 15   **D.** 18   **E.** 21

3. A monkey ate $\frac{1}{3}$ of a pile of coconuts. Another monkey ate $\frac{1}{3}$ of the remainder of the pile. If 12 coconuts were left, how many coconuts were in the original pile?

   A. 18   **B.** 27   **C.** 36   **D.** 54   **E.** 108

4. If $x = \frac{1}{a} + \frac{1}{b}$, then $\frac{1}{x} = \underline{}$.

   A. $a + b$ **B.** $\frac{1}{a+b}$ **C.** $\frac{a}{b} + \frac{b}{a}$ **D.** $\frac{a+b}{ab}$ **E.** $\frac{ab}{a+b}$

5. If n is an odd integer, then which of the following must be odd?

   A. $n^2 + 1$ **B.** $(n + 1)^2$ **C.** $n(n + 2)$ **D.** $n(n + 1)$ **E.** $(n-1)(n+1)$

6. If $3x - 5 = 10k$, then $\frac{3x}{5} - 1 = \underline{}$.

   A. k **B.** $2k$ **C.** $3k$ **D.** $4k$ **E.** $5k$

7. If the average of x, 36, and 60 is $3x$, then $x = \underline{}$.

   A. 12   **B.** 20   **C.** 24   **D.** 32   **E.** 48

8. $\frac{1}{2} - \frac{1}{3} + \frac{1}{4} - \frac{1}{5} = \underline{}$.

   A. $\frac{1}{6}$ **B.** $\frac{11}{60}$ **C.** $\frac{1}{5}$ **D.** $\frac{13}{60}$ **E.** $\frac{7}{30}$

9. What is the ratio of the number of multiples of 4 between 1 and 49 to the number of multiples of 5 between 1 and 49?

   A. 3:4   **B.** 4:5   **C.** 1:1   **D.** 4:3   **E.** 5:4

10. If there are six teams in a volleyball league and each team plays every other team exactly once, how many games will there be in all?

    A. 12   **B.** 15   **C.** 24   **D.** 30   **E.** 36

11. Which number is the closest approximation to $\frac{12}{13} + \frac{7}{8}$?

    A. 1   **B.** 2   **C.** 19   **D.** 21   **E.** 40

CUMULATIVE REVIEW (CHAPTERS 13–15)

13-1
1. How many four-digit numbers consist entirely of even digits?

2. An airplane has 6 pilots, 4 copilots, and 3 navigators available for an unscheduled flight. How many different flight crews can be chosen for the flight?

13-2
3. How many ways can the five finalists of a contest be selected for the first through fifth places?

4. How many distinguishable ways can the letters of the word PARAL-LEL be arranged?

Simplify

13-2,
13-3
5. $\frac{12!}{8!}$ 6. $\frac{7!}{4!3!}$ 7. $_{10}P_2$ 8. $_9C_3$

13-3
9. How many tennis games must be played so that every one of 12 players competes against every other player?

10. An urn contains 12 black and 10 white marbles. In how many ways can 2 black and 2 white marbles be drawn?

13-4
11. One card is drawn from a deck of 52 playing cards. What is the probability that the card drawn is:

  a. a ten?   **b.** not an ace?

12. Two numbers are selected from the set of numbers {1, 4, 9, 16, 25, 36}. What is the probability that:

  a. both numbers are odd?   **b.** the sum of the drawn numbers is even?

13-5
13. A coin is flipped and a die is tossed. What is the probability that the outcome is a head and a number less than a 3?

14. There are 3 red and 9 green marbles in a bag. What is the probability of drawing at random without replacing a green and then another green marble?

13-6
15. A card is drawn from a deck of 52 playing cards. What is the probability of getting an ace or a black card?

16. Slips of paper are numbered from 1 through 20 and placed in a fish bowl. One slip is drawn at random from the bowl. What is the probability that the number drawn is odd or greater than 12?

13-7 **17.** Find the 6th term in the expansion of $(a + b)^8$.

18. A die is tossed four times. Find the probability that there are exactly two 3's.

14-1 **19.** Make a stem-and-leaf plot of the year of birth of the people listed. Use 3-digit numbers in the stems.

14-2 **20.** Find the median of the years of birth of the people listed.

21. Find the interquartile range of the years of birth of the people listed.

22. Make a box-and-whisker plot of the years of birth of the people listed.

14-3 **Exercises 23 and 24 refer to the set:**
$R = \{10, 12, 12, 12, 12, 13, 13, 14, 14, 18\}$

23. What is the mean of the numbers in R?

People		
Name	**Born**	**Died**
Alexandre Archipenko	1887	1964
Elizabeth Arden	1881	1966
Desi Arnaz	1917	1986
Fred Astaire	1899	1967
Josephine Baker	1906	1975
Faith Baldwin	1893	1978
Bernard Baruch	1870	1965
Count Basie	1904	1984
John Belushi	1949	1982
Jack Benny	1894	1974
Ingrid Bergman	1918	1982
Eubie Blake	1883	1983
Pearl Buck	1892	1973
Billie Burke	1885	1970
Maria Callas	1923	1977
Rachel Carson	1907	1964
Willa Cather	1876	1947
Carlos Chavez	1899	1978
Agatha Christie	1890	1976
George Cohan	1878	1942

24. What is the standard deviation of the numbers in R?

14-4 **25.** Make a scatter plot of the years of birth and death for the people listed above.

26. Fit a line to the data points.

14-5 **27.** What is the z-score of 20 in a set of numbers that are normally distributed with mean 25 and standard deviation 4?

14-6 **28.** These random numbers were drawn in an experiment simulating tossing coins: 76 29 77 48 92 01 07 59 66 36 72 86 04 09 56 82 51 99 47 63. Even digits represent heads; odd digits represent tails. Based on the results of the experiment, what percent of the time do we get a head on the first coin and a tail on the second coin?

14-1

$$\text{Let } A = \begin{bmatrix} -6 & 4 & 0 \\ 1 & -2 & 9 \end{bmatrix} \text{ and } B = \begin{bmatrix} 3 & -4 & 12 \\ 0 & 7 & 2 \end{bmatrix}.$$

29. Find $A + B$

30. What are the dimensions of $A + B$?

31. Identify these elements in matrix B.   **a.** b_{13} **b.** b_{21}

32. Find the value of x and y if $\begin{bmatrix} 3x & 4 & 0 \\ 1 & -2 & y+1 \end{bmatrix} = A$.

15-2 **33.** Find k such that $k \begin{bmatrix} 4 & 2 \\ -3 & 8 \end{bmatrix} = \begin{bmatrix} -12 & -6 \\ 9 & -24 \end{bmatrix}$.

34. Find the product: $\begin{bmatrix} 8 & -2 \\ 5 & 3 \end{bmatrix} \cdot \begin{bmatrix} 0 & -4 \\ 6 & 1 \end{bmatrix}$.

35. The matrix [30 24 15 6 25] represents the number of coats of different styles in a store's inventory. If the retail value of each style coat is given by matrix A, write a matrix for the total retail value of the store's cost inventory.

$$A = \begin{bmatrix} 90 \\ 60 \\ 72 \\ 48 \\ 100 \end{bmatrix}$$

15-3 **Find the matrix X satisfying these equations.**

36. $X + \begin{bmatrix} 2 & -9 \\ 0 & 6 \end{bmatrix} = Z$

37. $\begin{bmatrix} 5 & -3 \\ 1 & 8 \end{bmatrix} - \begin{bmatrix} -2 & 4 \\ 7 & 0 \end{bmatrix} = X$

38. $3X = \begin{bmatrix} 0 & -6 \\ -15 & 6 \end{bmatrix}$

39. $X = \begin{bmatrix} 0 & 1 & 0 \\ 1 & 0 & 0 \\ 0 & 0 & 1 \end{bmatrix} \cdot \begin{bmatrix} 1 & 0 & 0 \\ 0 & 1 & 0 \\ 0 & 0 & 1 \end{bmatrix}$

15-4 **40.** The diagram at the right represents the railroad service between cities A, B, C, and D. Write a 4 × 4 matrix to represent the network.

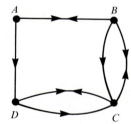

41. The vertices of a triangle are given by the matrix $\begin{bmatrix} 2 & -3 & 0 \\ -1 & 4 & -5 \end{bmatrix}$. Write the matrix for the images of these vertices under the transformation $T = \begin{bmatrix} 2 & 0 \\ 0 & 1 \end{bmatrix}$.

15-5 **42.** Find D^{-1} if $D = \begin{bmatrix} 6 & 1 \\ -1 & 2 \end{bmatrix}$.

43. Write a matrix equation and use it to solve this system.

$4x - 3y = 2$
$5x + 2y = 14$

15-6 **44.** Use an augmented matrix to solve the system in Exercise 43.

CHAPTER 16

Circular Functions

The predator-prey relationship between two animals can cause the relative sizes of their populations to vary consistently in a repeating pattern. The number of Canadian lynxes increases and declines according to the number of hares in the local ecological system. Italian mathematician Vito Volterra was the first to formulate equations that model this periodic-function behavior. The model assumes a continuous predator population constantly in search of a continuous prey population.

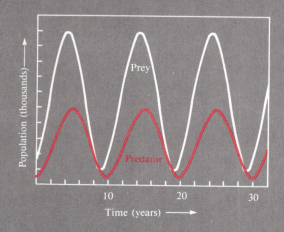

The Wrapping Function

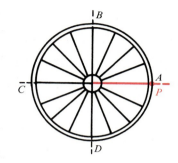

Consider point P on a wheel that is rotating in the counterclockwise direction on a fixed axle. The radius of the wheel is 1 unit. Recall that the circumference of a circle is $2\pi r$. Therefore, the whole circumference is 2π, one half the circumference is π, and one fourth the circumference is $\frac{\pi}{2}$.

This table describes the location of P for various rotations.

Distance P is rotated counterclockwise	$\frac{\pi}{2}$	π	$\frac{3\pi}{2}$	2π	$\frac{5\pi}{2}$	4π	6π
Location of P	B	C	D	A	B	A	A

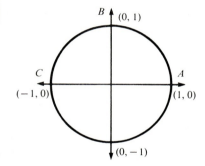

The circle shown at the right with its center at the origin of a coordinate system and with radius one unit is called the **unit circle.** Imagine a number line tangent to the unit circle with the point 0 of the number line coinciding with the point $A(1, 0)$ of the unit circle. If the number line is "wrapped" around the unit circle as shown in the figure, the point $\frac{\pi}{2}$ of the number line will fall on the point $B(0, 1)$ of the circle, the point π of the number line will fall on the point $C(-1, 0)$ of the circle, and the point 2π of the number line will fall on the point $A(1, 0)$ of the circle. If we wrap the number line around the circle a second time, the point $\frac{5\pi}{2}$ of the number line will fall on the point $B(0, 1)$ of the circle, and so on.

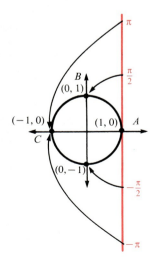

In a similar manner, we can wrap the negative part of the number line around the unit circle, as shown in the figure. In this way, each real number is mapped onto a point of the unit circle. The function that maps the real numbers onto the points of the unit circle is called the **wrapping function** and is denoted by W. For example, $W\left(\frac{\pi}{2}\right) = (0, 1)$, $W(\pi) = (-1, 0)$, $W\left(-\frac{\pi}{2}\right) = (0, -1)$, and so on.

Example 1   In which quadrant is each of the following points?

 a. $W(1)$ b. $W\left(-\dfrac{3\pi}{4}\right)$ c. $W\left(\dfrac{\pi}{4} + 2\pi\right)$

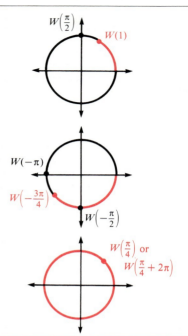

Solution   a. $\pi \approx 3.14$, so $\dfrac{\pi}{2} \approx 1.57$. Since $0 < 1 < \dfrac{\pi}{2}$,
$W(1)$ is in the first quadrant.

 b. Since $-\pi < -\dfrac{3\pi}{4} < -\dfrac{\pi}{2}$, $W\left(-\dfrac{3\pi}{4}\right)$ is in the third quadrant.

 c. Since $0 < \dfrac{\pi}{4} < \dfrac{\pi}{2}$, $W\left(\dfrac{\pi}{4}\right)$ is in the first quadrant.

 $W\left(\dfrac{\pi}{4} + 2\pi\right)$ is one full circumference beyond $W\left(\dfrac{\pi}{4}\right)$. Therefore, $W\left(\dfrac{\pi}{4} + 2\pi\right)$ is the same point as $W\left(\dfrac{\pi}{4}\right)$. $W\left(\dfrac{\pi}{4} + 2\pi\right)$ is in the first quadrant.

Consider point $A(m, n)$ on the unit circle with its center at the origin of a coordinate system having axes j and k.

Then

$$m^2 + n^2 = 1.$$

Point $B(-m, n)$ is the reflection of A about the vertical axis k. Point B is also on the unit circle since

$$(-m)^2 + n^2 = 1.$$

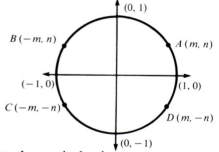

This fact means that the unit circle is symmetric with respect to the vertical axis. Similarly, $D(m, -n)$ and $C(-m, -n)$ are points on the unit circle and the unit circle is symmetric with respect to the horizontal axis j and with respect to the origin.

Example 2   Suppose $W(a) = (m, n)$. State one real number that is mapped onto each of the following points.

 a. $(m, -n)$

 b. $(-m, n)$

 c. $(-m, -n)$

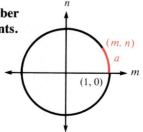

Example 2 (continued)

Solution   **a.** The unit circle is symmetric about the axes and the point (m, n) is a units from the point $(1, 0)$ counterclockwise along the circle. Thus, the point $(m, -n)$ is a units from the point $(1, 0)$ in the clockwise direction.

$$W(-a) = (m, -n)$$

b. The point $(-m, n)$ is half the circumference (π units) beyond the point $(m, -n)$ in the positive (counterclockwise) direction.

$$W(\pi - a) = (-m, n)$$

c. The point $(-m, -n)$ is π units beyond point (m, n) in the positive direction.

$$W(\pi + a) = (-m, -n)$$

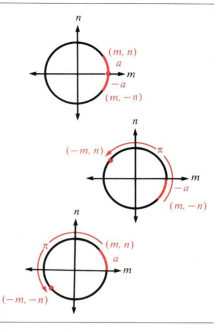

Suppose that W maps a real number x onto a point P of the unit circle. Since the circumference of the unit circle is 2π, W also maps the numbers $x + 2\pi$, $x + 4\pi$, $x + 6\pi$, etc., as well as $x - 2\pi$, $x - 4\pi$, etc., onto point P. The function W is an example of a **periodic function**.

Definition: Periodic Function

A function $y = f(x)$ is a *periodic function* if and only if there is a real number p such that for each x in the domain of f,

$$f(x + p) = f(x).$$

The smallest value of p is called **the fundamental period** of f or simply **the period** of f.

The fundamental period of the wrapping function W is 2π. That is,

$$W(x + k2\pi) = W(x) \quad \text{for } k \text{ an integer.}$$

Example 3   **Find the value of x between 0 and 2π such that $W(x) = W\left(\dfrac{11\pi}{2}\right)$.**

Solution   Since W is periodic with period 2π,

$$W\left(\frac{11\pi}{2}\right) = W\left(\frac{3\pi}{2} + 4\pi\right) = W\left(\frac{3\pi}{2}\right).$$

Answer $x = \dfrac{3\pi}{2}$

CLASSROOM EXERCISES

State the quadrant in which each point lies.

1. $W(1)$ **2.** $W(-1)$ **3.** $W\left(\dfrac{3\pi}{4}\right)$ **4.** $W\left(2\pi - \dfrac{\pi}{4}\right)$

$P\left(\dfrac{\sqrt{2}}{2}, \dfrac{\sqrt{2}}{2}\right)$ **is a point on the unit circle. State the reflection of P about each of the following.**

5. The vertical axis **6.** The horizontal axis **7.** The origin

Suppose that $W(1) = (j, k)$.

8. State three other positive numbers that are mapped onto (j, k) by W.

9. State three negative numbers that are mapped onto (j, k) by W.

WRITTEN EXERCISES

A **Determine the quadrant in which each point lies. If a point lies on an axis, state which axis, vertical or horizontal.**

1. $W(0.5)$ **2.** $W(0.75)$ **3.** $W(-2)$ **4.** $W(-1.5)$

5. $W\left(1 + \dfrac{\pi}{2}\right)$ **6.** $W\left(1 - \dfrac{\pi}{2}\right)$ **7.** $W\left(-\dfrac{3\pi}{4}\right)$ **8.** $W\left(\dfrac{3\pi}{4}\right)$

9. $W(1 - \pi)$ **10.** $W(\pi + 1)$ **11.** $W\left(\dfrac{\pi}{2} + \pi\right)$ **12.** $W\left(\dfrac{3\pi}{2} - \dfrac{\pi}{2}\right)$

13. Let $W(x) = \left(\dfrac{3}{4}, \dfrac{4}{5}\right)$. State the coordinates of each point.

    a. $W(x + 2\pi)$ **b.** $W(-x)$ **c.** $W(x + \pi)$ **d.** $W(\pi - x)$

14. Let $W\left(\dfrac{\pi}{6}\right) = \left(\dfrac{\sqrt{3}}{2}, \dfrac{1}{2}\right)$. State the coordinates of each point.

    a. $W\left(\dfrac{7\pi}{6}\right)$ **b.** $W\left(-\dfrac{\pi}{6}\right)$ **c.** $W\left(-\dfrac{5\pi}{6}\right)$ **d.** $W\left(\dfrac{5\pi}{6}\right)$

State one solution of each equation.

15. Let $W\left(\dfrac{\pi}{3}\right) = \left(\dfrac{1}{2}, \dfrac{\sqrt{3}}{2}\right)$.

    a. $W(x) = \left(-\dfrac{1}{2}, \dfrac{\sqrt{3}}{2}\right)$

    b. $W(x) = \left(-\dfrac{1}{2}, -\dfrac{\sqrt{3}}{2}\right)$

16. Let $W\left(-\dfrac{\pi}{6}\right) = \left(\dfrac{\sqrt{3}}{2}, -\dfrac{1}{2}\right)$

    a. $W(x) = \left(-\dfrac{\sqrt{3}}{2}, \dfrac{1}{2}\right)$

    b. $W(x) = \left(\dfrac{\sqrt{3}}{2}, \dfrac{1}{2}\right)$

17. Let $W(3) = (j, k)$. State four other positive numbers that are mapped onto (j, k) by W.

18. Let $W\left(\dfrac{3\pi}{4}\right) = (m, n)$. State four negative numbers that are mapped onto (m, n) by W.

19. Let $W(-1) = (r, s)$. State four other negative numbers that are mapped onto (r, s) by W.

20. Let $W(1) = (a, b)$. Write an expression for all numbers that are mapped onto (a, b) by W.

State whether each graph is the graph of a periodic function. If a function is periodic, state the fundamental period.

21.

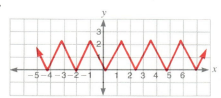

22.

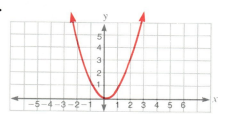

23.

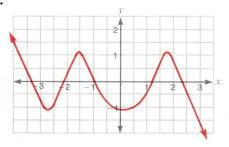

24.

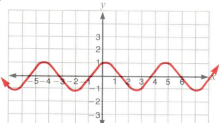

Suppose that the number line is wrapped around the square as shown in the figure. Let R be the function that maps the real numbers onto the points of the square. State the coordinates of each point.

25. $R(1)$ **26.** $R(2)$

27. $R(3)$ **28.** $R(4)$

29. $R(4.5)$ **30.** $R(-1.4)$

31. $R(17.3)$ **32.** $R(-41.1)$

33. Is R periodic? If so, state the fundamental period.

34. Suppose that $R(x) = (j, k)$. Let First and Second be functions such that First $(x) = j$ and Second$(x) = k$. State each value.

    a. First(2)   **b.** Second(3)   **c.** First(-3.2)   **d.** Second(-6.5)

Simplify. State restrictions on the variables. [7-1–7-4]

1. $\sqrt{12a^2b^3}$

2. $\sqrt{32} - \sqrt{18}$

3. $\sqrt{2}\left(\sqrt{2a} + \sqrt{b^2}\right)$

4. $\dfrac{\sqrt{10xy}}{\sqrt{4x}}$

5. $\sqrt{9x^2y^4}$

6. $\sqrt{3x}\left(\sqrt{6y} - \sqrt{3x}\right)$

Solve. [7-6]

7. $\sqrt{2x} + 4 = x$

8. $\sqrt{y + 2} = y - 4$

9. Write using rational exponents. [7-7]

$$\sqrt[3]{5} + \frac{1}{\sqrt{6}}$$

10. Find the length of the longer diagonal.

11. Find the length of the shorter diagonal.

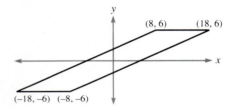

BIOGRAPHY Roger Penrose

Roger Penrose is a gentle-mannered, humble, playful geometrician, who is Visiting Professor of Mathematics at Rice University. In 1965, he proved that Einstein's work leads to the conclusion that there are infinitely dense and hot points in space, which led to the search for black holes. He has done much work on non-periodic tiling—tilings which leave no gaps and are not purely repetitive. This has led to new understandings of crystals, formerly thought to be periodically structured. He is currently working on artificial intelligence. Penrose tries to construct beautiful mathematical pictures of reality because "beautiful things are more likely to be true." He says, "Research in mathematics is like archaeology. One looks at aerial photographs and can see from the shapes of the hills that there is some kind of structure there. Then, if you have a strong intuitive feeling, you go and dig, and lo and behold, you find there is some actual thing that was there all the time. So you dig it out and start piecing it together."

LESSON 16-2

The Sine and Cosine Functions

Recall that the wrapping function W maps each real number x onto a point $W(x)$ of the unit circle. Using W allows two important mathematical functions, **cosine** (abbreviated **cos**) and **sine** (abbreviated **sin**), to be defined. The cosine function maps the real number x onto the first coordinate of the point $W(x)$, and the sine function maps the real number x onto the second coordinate of the point $W(x)$. If $W(x)$ is the point P (j, k), then $\cos x = j$ and $\sin x = k$.

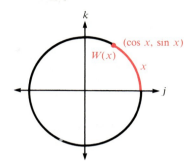

Definition: The Sine and Cosine Functions

For each real number x, let $P(j, k)$ be the point that is x units from $(1, 0)$ in the counterclockwise direction along the circle $j^2 + k^2 = 1$. Then cosine is the function such that $\cos x = j$, and sine is the function such that $\sin x = k$.

Cosine and sine are called **circular functions** because of their relationship to the unit circle. It follows from the definitions of the unit circle, wrapping function, cosine, and sine that the domain of both circular functions is the set of real numbers $\mathcal{R}$ and their range is $\{y: -1 \le y \le 1\}$.

Values of cosine and sine can be determined by examining the wrapping function and the unit circle. Since $\dfrac{\pi}{2}$ is one fourth the circumference of the unit circle, the wrapping function maps $\dfrac{\pi}{2}$ onto the point $B(0, 1)$. Therefore,

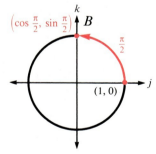

$\cos \dfrac{\pi}{2} = 0$ and $\sin \dfrac{\pi}{2} = 1$.

Example 1 Find each value.

   a. $\cos \pi$

   b. $\sin \pi$

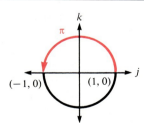

Solution W maps π onto point $C(-1, 0)$.

Answer   **a.** $\cos \pi = -1$ **b.** $\sin \pi = 0$

Since the wrapping function W is periodic with period 2π, both cosine and sine are also periodic with period 2π. That is,

$$\cos (x + k2\pi) = \cos x \text{ and } \sin (x + k2\pi) = \sin x, \text{ for all integers } k.$$

Example 2 Find $\sin \dfrac{9\pi}{2}$.

Solution Subtract multiples of 2π from $\dfrac{9\pi}{2}$ until reaching a value between 0 and 2π.

$$\sin \frac{9\pi}{2} = \sin \left(\frac{\pi}{2} + 4\pi\right) = \sin \frac{\pi}{2} = 1$$

The figure below shows in which quadrants $\sin x$ and $\cos x$ are positive and negative.

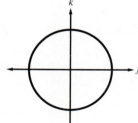

Quadrant II $\cos x < 0$
$\dfrac{\pi}{2} < x < \pi$ $\sin x > 0$

$\cos x > 0$ Quadrant I
$\sin x > 0$ $0 < x < \dfrac{\pi}{2}$

Quadrant III $\cos x < 0$
$\pi < x < \dfrac{3\pi}{2}$ $\sin x < 0$

$\cos x > 0$ Quadrant IV
$\sin x < 0$ $\dfrac{3\pi}{2} < x < 2\pi$

Since $\cos x$ and $\sin x$ are coordinates of a point on the unit circle, the following equation is an immediate consequence of the definition of the unit circle. (Note that $\cos^2 x$ means $(\cos x)^2$ and $\sin^2 x$ means $(\sin x)^2$.)

Basic Identity

For each real number x, $\sin^2 x + \cos^2 x = 1$.

Example 3 Let $\sin x = -\dfrac{1}{2}$. Find $\cos x$.

Solution $\sin^2 x + \cos^2 x = 1$, so $\left(-\dfrac{1}{2}\right)^2 + \cos^2 x = 1$

$$\frac{1}{4} + \cos^2 x = 1$$

$$\cos^2 x = \frac{3}{4}$$

$$\cos x = \pm \frac{\sqrt{3}}{2}$$

The symmetries of the unit circle lead to the following properties.

For each real number x,

I. $\cos(-x) = \cos x$

II. $\sin(-x) = -\sin x$

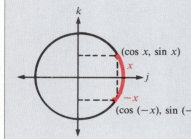

(cos x, sin x)

x

$-x$

(cos (−x), sin (−x))

III. $\cos(\pi - x) = -\cos x$

IV. $\sin(\pi - x) = \sin x$

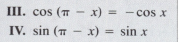

(cos (π − x), sin (π − x))

x

(cos x, sin x)

x

V. $\cos(\pi + x) = -\cos x$

VI. $\sin(\pi + x) = -\sin x$

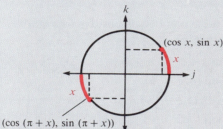

(cos x, sin x)

x

x

(cos (π + x), sin (π + x))

Example 4   Given $\sin \dfrac{\pi}{3} = \dfrac{\sqrt{3}}{2}$ and $\cos \dfrac{\pi}{3} = \dfrac{1}{2}$, find each of the following.

     a. $\sin \dfrac{2\pi}{3}$ **b.** $\sin \dfrac{4\pi}{3}$ **c.** $\sin \dfrac{5\pi}{3}$

     d. $\cos \dfrac{2\pi}{3}$ **e.** $\cos \dfrac{4\pi}{3}$ **f.** $\cos \dfrac{5\pi}{3}$

Solution   **a.** $\sin \dfrac{2\pi}{3} = \sin\left(\pi - \dfrac{\pi}{3}\right) = \sin \dfrac{\pi}{3} = \dfrac{\sqrt{3}}{2}$

     b. $\sin \dfrac{4\pi}{3} = \sin\left(\pi + \dfrac{\pi}{3}\right) = -\sin \dfrac{\pi}{3} = -\dfrac{\sqrt{3}}{2}$

     c. $\sin \dfrac{5\pi}{3} = \sin -\dfrac{\pi}{3} = -\sin \dfrac{\pi}{3} = -\dfrac{\sqrt{3}}{2}$

     d. $\cos \dfrac{2\pi}{3} = \cos\left(\pi - \dfrac{\pi}{3}\right) = -\cos \dfrac{\pi}{3} = -\dfrac{1}{2}$

     e. $\cos \dfrac{4\pi}{3} = \cos\left(\pi + \dfrac{\pi}{3}\right) = -\cos \dfrac{\pi}{3} = -\dfrac{1}{2}$

     f. $\cos \dfrac{5\pi}{3} = \cos -\dfrac{\pi}{3} = \cos \dfrac{\pi}{3} = \dfrac{1}{2}$

LASSROOM EXERCISES

1. State the values of $\sin \frac{3\pi}{2}$ and $\cos \frac{3\pi}{2}$.   2. Given $\cos x = \frac{1}{3}$, find $\sin x$.

Let $\cos x = 0.23$. Evaluate.

3. $\cos (-x)$ 4. $\cos (\pi - x)$ 5. $\cos (\pi + x)$ 6. $\cos (x + 2\pi)$

Let $\sin x = 0.55$. Evaluate.

7. $\sin (-x)$ 8. $\sin (\pi - x)$ 9. $\sin (\pi + x)$ 10. $\sin (x + 2\pi)$

WRITTEN EXERCISES

A Use the figure. State whether each of these numbers is positive or negative.

1. $\sin 0.75$
2. $\sin 5.5$
3. $\cos 2.5$
4. $\cos 4.2$
5. $\sin (2.5 + \pi)$
6. $\sin (4.2 + \pi)$
7. $\cos (0.75 + \pi)$
8. $\cos (5.5 + \pi)$
9. $\sin (-5.5)$
10. $\sin (-2.5)$
11. $\cos (-0.75)$
12. $\cos (-5.5)$
13. $\sin (-0.75 + 2\pi)$
14. $\cos (5.5 - 4\pi)$

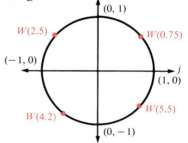

Given $\sin \frac{\pi}{6} = \frac{1}{2}$ and $\cos \frac{\pi}{6} = \frac{\sqrt{3}}{2}$, use the following properties to state the value of each expression.

> For each real number x,
>
> **I.** $\cos (-x) = \cos x$ **III.** $\cos (\pi - x) = -\cos x$ **V.** $\cos (\pi + x) = -\cos x$
> **II.** $\sin (-x) = -\sin x$ **IV.** $\sin (\pi - x) = \sin x$ **VI.** $\sin (\pi + x) = -\sin x$

15. $\sin \left(-\frac{\pi}{6}\right)$
16. $\sin \frac{5\pi}{6}$
17. $\sin \frac{13\pi}{6}$
18. $\sin \frac{7\pi}{6}$

19. $\sin \left(\frac{\pi}{6} + 10\pi\right)$
20. $\sin \left(\frac{\pi}{6} - \pi\right)$
21. $\sin \left(\frac{\pi}{6} - 2\pi\right)$
22. $\sin \left(3\pi - \frac{\pi}{6}\right)$

23. $\cos \frac{5\pi}{6}$
24. $\cos \left(-\frac{\pi}{6}\right)$
25. $\cos \frac{7\pi}{6}$
26. $\cos \frac{13\pi}{6}$

27. $\cos \left(\frac{\pi}{6} - \pi\right)$
28. $\cos \left(\frac{\pi}{6} + 10\pi\right)$
29. $\cos \left(3\pi - \frac{\pi}{6}\right)$
30. $\cos \left(\frac{\pi}{6} - 2\pi\right)$

Find sin *x* or cos *x* as indicated.

31. Given sin *x* = 0.6, find cos *x*.

32. Given sin *x* = 0.8, find cos *x*.

33. Given sin *x* = $-\dfrac{12}{13}$, find cos *x*.

34. Given sin *x* = $-\dfrac{15}{17}$, find cos *x*.

35. Given cos *x* = $\dfrac{2}{3}$, find sin *x*.

36. Given cos *x* = $\dfrac{\sqrt{7}}{4}$, find sin *x*.

37. Given cos *x* = $\dfrac{\sqrt{15}}{4}$, find sin *x*.

38. Given cos *x* = $\dfrac{2}{5}$, find sin *x*.

B **True or false for all values of *a* and *b*? If the statement is false, give an example.**

39. sin *a* = sin (−*a*)

40. sin *a* = −sin (−*a*)

41. cos (−*a*) = −cos *a*

42. cos *a* = cos (π − *a*)

43. sin *a* = cos $\left(a - \dfrac{\pi}{2}\right)$

44. cos *a* = sin $\left(a + \dfrac{\pi}{2}\right)$

45. sin (*a* + *b*) = sin *a* + sin *b*

46. sin² *a* + cos² *b* = 1

47. If sin *a* = 1, then *a* = $\dfrac{\pi}{2}$.

48. If cos *a* = 1, then *a* = 0.

C **Represent *all* the values of *x* for each equation. If there is no solution, write ∅.**

49. sin 2 = 0.91
sin *x* = 0.91

50. sin 2 = 0.91
sin *x* = −0.91

51. cos 2 = −0.42
cos *x* = −0.42

52. cos 2 = −0.42
cos *x* = 0.42

53. sin $\dfrac{\pi}{2}$ = 1
sin *x* = $\dfrac{\pi}{2}$

54. cos 1.4 = 0.17
sin *x* = 0.17

55. Suppose that *f*(*x* + *a*) = *f*(*x*) and *f*(*x* + *b*) = *f*(*x*) for all numbers *x*. What can you say about each of the following?

  a. *f*

  b. *a* and *b*

  c. *f*(*a* + *b*)

ℝEVIEW EXERCISES

1. Graph (*x* + 1)² + (*y* − 2)² ≤ 3². [9-1]

2. Identify the vertex, axis of symmetry, focus, directrix, and direction of the parabola *y* + 4 = $-\dfrac{1}{2}(x - 3)^2$. [9-2]

3. Write an equation of the ellipse with foci (−3, 0) and (3, 0) and with the sum of the focal radii equal to 2√10. [9-3]

4. Graph the hyperbola $\dfrac{x^2}{2} - \dfrac{y^2}{8} = 1$ [9-4]

5. Identify the conic section, and then write an equivalent equation for the conic section in standard form. [9-5]

    a. $16x^2 + 9y^2 + 64x + 18y - 71 = 0$

    b. $16x^2 - 9y^2 - 64x - 18y - 89 = 0$

Find all real-number solutions. [9-6]

6. $y + 4 = x^2$ **7.** $xy = 18$ **8.** $\dfrac{x^2}{4^2} + \dfrac{y^2}{3^2} = 1$

    $x^2 + y^2 = 1$ $(x - 3)(y + 1) = 18$ $\dfrac{x^2}{4^2} - \dfrac{y^2}{3^2} = 1$

$\mathcal{E}$XTENSION   Counting Civilizations

For years, scientists have been sending radio signals into space hoping to make contact with distant civilizations. Sound waves, radio signals, and electrical current are examples of periodic phenomena that can be described and studied using the sine and cosine functions.

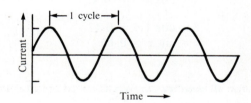

Sinusoidal Alternating Current

    Astronomer Frank Drake of Cornell University has formulated an equation for the possible number of extraterrestrial civilizations in our galaxy which are capable of sending messages that our radio telescopes might "hear." The estimated number N of such civilizations is given by the formula

$$N = R^* F_p N_p F_1 F_i F_c L$$

where

    R^* = the average rate in stars per year of star formation in our galaxy
    F_p = the fraction of stars having planets
    N_p = the number of suitable planets per planetary system
    F_1 = the fraction of planets on which life starts
    F_i = the fraction of life that evolves to intelligence
    F_c = the fraction of intelligent species to develop the means of communication
    L = the longevity (in years) of the technological phase of such a society

    Drake and other scientists have determined a value for N between 10^5 and 10^6 which is equivalent to about one such civilization per million stars.

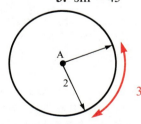

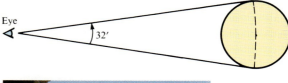

61. The latitude of Philadelphia is 40° N. If we assume that the earth is a sphere of radius 4000 mi, how far is Philadelphia from the equator?

62. Barcelona, Spain, is 488 mi due south of Paris, France. If the latitude of Paris is 48° N, find the latitude of Barcelona.

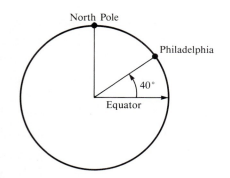

*R*EVIEW EXERCISES

1. Write the four arithmetic means between 10 and 30. [12-1]

2. Write the eighth term of the geometric sequence 16, 8, 4, 2, ... [12-2]

3. For the geometric sequence 3, 6, 12, 24, . . . , write the series S_{10} in Σ notation. [12-3]

4. Find the value of the series $\displaystyle\sum_{k=1}^{10} (2k - 1)$. [12-4]

5. Find the value of the series S_{10} for the sequence 10, 14, 18, 22, ... [12-4]

6. Find the value of $\displaystyle\sum_{k=1}^{12} 5k$. [12-4]

7. Express S_9 in exponential notation for the sequence $1, \dfrac{1}{3}, \dfrac{1}{9}, \dfrac{1}{27}, \dfrac{1}{81}, \ldots$. [12-5]

8. Find the value of the infinite series $\displaystyle\sum_{k=1}^{\infty} \left(\frac{2}{3}\right)^k$. [12-6]

*C*ALCULATOR EXTENSION   Degrees and Radians

If your calculator operates in both degree and radian modes, the trigonometric function keys can be used to convert from degrees to radians and vice versa. For example, to change 35° to radians:

a. Put the calculator in degree mode.

b. Enter 35°.

c. Press the $\boxed{\text{sin}}$ key.

d. Change to radian mode.

e. Press the $\boxed{\text{sin}^{-1}}$ key.

[*Note:* You could also use the $\boxed{\text{cos}}$ and $\boxed{\text{cos}^{-1}}$ keys or the $\boxed{\text{tan}}$ and $\boxed{\text{tan}^{-1}}$ keys.]

1. Convert 35° to radians. **2.** Convert 1 radian to degrees.

3. Convert 2 radians to degrees. (The answer is not 65.4°.)

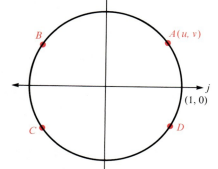

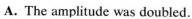

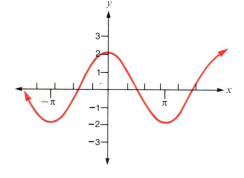

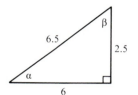

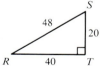

9. Angle *P*

10. Angle *R*

11. Angle *X*

12. Angle *Y*

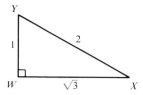

Find sin *A* and sin *B* for each triangle. Simplify all radicals.

13.

14.
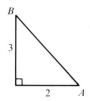

15.

16.

17.
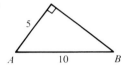

18.
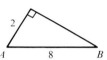

State the value to four significant digits. Use a scientific calculator or the tables on pages 771–775.

19. $\sin 12°$ **20.** $\sin 42°$ **21.** $\cos 80°$ **22.** $\cos 70°$

23. $\tan 75°$ **24.** $\tan 85°$ **25.** $\sec 165°$ **26.** $\sec 95°$

27. $\csc 110.5°$ **28.** $\csc 152.2°$ **29.** $\cot 27.4°$ **30.** $\cot 72.4°$

State the value of θ to the nearest tenth degree, $0° < θ < 90°$.

31. $\sin θ = 0.8511$ **32.** $\sin θ = 0.3854$ **33.** $\cos θ = 0.9228$

34. $\cos θ = 0.5250$ **35.** $\tan θ = 0.7454$ **36.** $\tan θ = 0.2642$

State the value of α to the nearest tenth degree, $90° < α < 180°$.

37. $\sin α = 0.3062$ **38.** $\sin α = 0.8175$ **39.** $\cos α = -0.8465$

40. $\cos α = -0.9942$ **41.** $\tan α = -7.5449$ **42.** $\tan α = -1.1021$

B | **In triangle *ABC*, *C* = 90°. Solve.**

43. $\tan A = \sqrt{2}; a = 10$
    Find *b*.

44. $\sin A = \frac{1}{4}; a = 3$
    Find *b*.

45. $b = 7; c = 10$
    Find csc *B*.

46. $a = 5; b = 12$
    Find sin *A*.

47. $\cos B = \frac{2}{3}; a = 5$
    Find *c*.

48. $a = 4; c = 6$
    Find tan *B*.

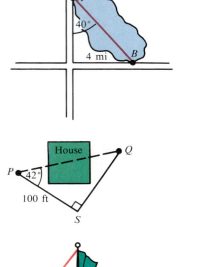

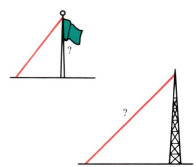

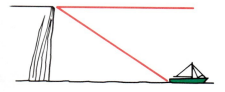

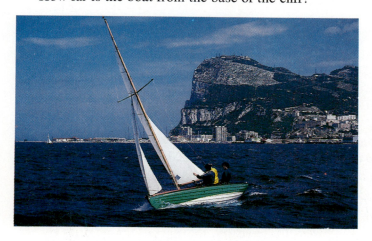

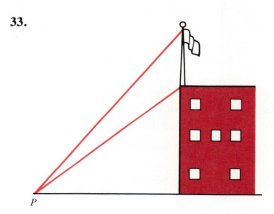

 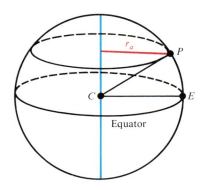

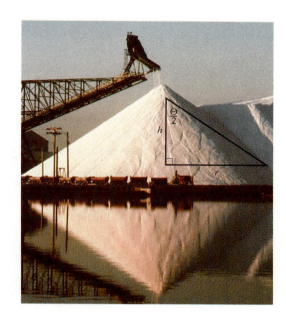

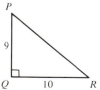

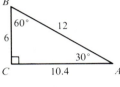

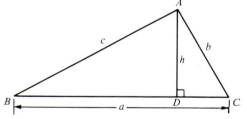

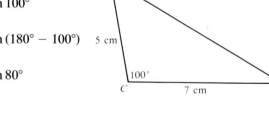

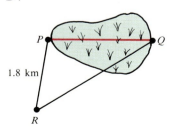

Example 4   State the radian measure of a central angle in a circle with radius 4 that intercepts an arc of length $\dfrac{2\pi}{3}$.

Solution $s = r\theta$ $\dfrac{2\pi}{3} = 4\theta$ $\theta = \dfrac{\pi}{6}$

Answer   The measure of the angle is $\dfrac{\pi}{6}$.

Note that if $r = 1$, then $s = \theta$. Therefore, in the unit circle, the number of radians in a central angle is the same as the real number that indicates the length of the arc. Thus the same relationship exists between degrees and radians as between degree measures and arc lengths.

$$\frac{\text{radians}}{\text{degrees}} = \frac{\pi}{180}$$

Example 5   What is the radian measure of a 50° angle?

Solution   Write a proportion and solve.

$$\frac{\theta}{50} = \frac{\pi}{180}$$

$$\theta = \frac{50\pi}{180} = \frac{5\pi}{18}$$

Answer   The radian measure of a 50° angle is $\dfrac{5\pi}{18}$ (about 0.87).

*C*LASSROOM EXERCISES

Evaluate.

1. cos 270°   **2.** sin 180°   **3.** sin −45°   **4.** cos 60°

5. State the radian measure of A.

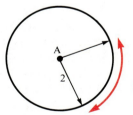

Copy and complete the table of equivalent radian and degree measures.

	6.	**7.**	**8.**	**9.**	**10.**	**11.**	**12.**
Degrees	60	45	27	?	?	?	2
Radians	?	?	?	$\dfrac{\pi}{6}$	$\dfrac{3\pi}{4}$	2	?

 Evaluate.

1. sin 30°   **2.** cos 60°   **3.** cos 45°   **4.** sin 135°

5. tan 90°   **6.** tan 45°   **7.** cos 30°   **8.** sin 60°

9. Graph $y = \sin \theta$ for values of θ between 0° and 360°.
10. Graph $y = \cos \theta$ for values of θ between 0° and 360°.

State the radian measure of the angle in each figure.

11.   **12.**   **13.**   **14.**

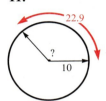   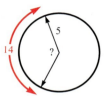

Find the degree measure equivalent to the given radian measure.

15. $\dfrac{\pi}{6}$ **16.** $\dfrac{\pi}{3}$ **17.** $\dfrac{\pi}{600}$ **18.** $\dfrac{\pi}{300}$

19. $-\dfrac{\pi}{2}$ **20.** $-\dfrac{\pi}{4}$ **21.** 3π **22.** 5π

23. 2   **24.** 3   **25.** 0.2   **26.** 0.3

Find the radian measure equivalent to the given degree measure.

27. 10°   **28.** 20°   **29.** $\pi°$ **30.** $18\pi°$

31. 400°   **32.** 450°   **33.** $-40°$ **34.** $-80°$

35. $\dfrac{360°}{\pi}$ **36.** $\dfrac{180°}{\pi}$ **37.** $d°$ **38.** $g°$

39. Consider $y = \sin \theta$, with domain the set of all degree measures θ.
   a. State the coordinates of the θ-intercepts of the function.
   b. State the values of θ where maximums occur.
   c. State the values of θ where minimums occur.
   d. State the values of θ where $y = \dfrac{1}{2}$.
   e. Sketch the graph of $y = \sin \theta$ for θ between $-360°$ and 1080°.

40. Consider $y = \cos \theta$ with domain the set of all degree measures θ.

    a. State the coordinates of the θ-intercepts of the function.

    b. State the values of θ where maximums occur.

    c. State the values of θ where minimums occur.

    d. State the values of θ where $y = \dfrac{1}{2}$.

    e. Sketch the graph of $y = \cos \theta$ for θ between $-270°$ and $990°$.

41. Consider $y = \tan \theta$ with domain the set of all degree measures θ.

    a. State the coordinates of the θ-intercepts.

    b. State the fundamental period.

    c. State the values of θ where $\tan \theta$ is undefined.

    d. Sketch the graph of $y = \tan \theta$ for θ between $-270°$ and $270°$.

42. Consider $y = \sec \theta$ with domain the set of all degree measures θ.

    a. State the values of θ where $y = 1$.

    b. State the fundamental period.

    c. State the values of θ where $\sec \theta$ is undefined.

    d. Sketch the graph of $y = \sec \theta$ for θ between $-270°$ and $270°$.

B   **For each function, the domain is the set of all degree measures θ. State (a) the fundamental period, (b) the coordinates of the θ-intercepts (if any), (c) the values of θ where maximums occur, (d) the amplitude, and (e) the coordinates of the y-intercept.**

43. $y = 3 \sin\theta$ **44.** $y = 4 \cos\theta$ **45.** $y = \sin 3\theta$ **46.** $y = \cos 4\theta$

47. $y = \cos 180\theta$ **48.** $y = \sin 90\theta$ **49.** $y = -4 \cos 100\theta$ **50.** $y = -\dfrac{1}{2} \cos 200\theta$

51. $y = 3 + \sin 360\theta$ **52.** $y = 5 + \cos 360\theta$ **53.** $y = 2 - \sin 3\theta$ **54.** $y = 4 - \cos 4\theta$

55. $y = 300 \sin(-90\theta)$ **56.** $y = -300 \sin 90\theta$ **57.** $y = \dfrac{\sin 0.1\theta}{100}$ **58.** $y = \dfrac{\sin 100\theta}{10}$

C   **59.** Seen from Earth, the sun subtends at the eye an angle of about 32 minutes (1 minute is $\dfrac{1}{60}$ of a degree). If the sun is 93,000,000 miles from Earth, find its diameter.

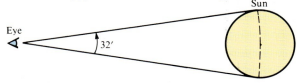

60. A person with normal vision can read print without eyestrain if it subtends at the eye an angle of 10 minutes. What is the smallest-sized print that should be used on a screen if the screen will be viewed from a distance of 8 ft?

61. The latitude of Philadelphia is 40° N. If we assume that the earth is a sphere of radius 4000 mi, how far is Philadelphia from the equator?

62. Barcelona, Spain, is 488 mi due south of Paris, France. If the latitude of Paris is 48° N, find the latitude of Barcelona.

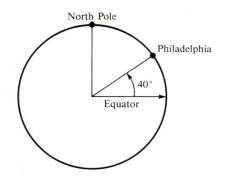

REVIEW EXERCISES

1. Write the four arithmetic means between 10 and 30.   [12-1]

2. Write the eighth term of the geometric sequence 16, 8, 4, 2, ...   [12-2]

3. For the geometric sequence 3, 6, 12, 24, . . . , write the series S_{10} in Σ notation.   [12-3]

4. Find the value of the series $\displaystyle\sum_{k=1}^{10} (2k - 1)$.   [12-4]

5. Find the value of the series S_{10} for the sequence 10, 14, 18, 22, ...   [12-4]

6. Find the value of $\displaystyle\sum_{k=1}^{12} 5k$.   [12-4]

7. Express S_9 in exponential notation for the sequence $1, \dfrac{1}{3}, \dfrac{1}{9}, \dfrac{1}{27}, \dfrac{1}{81}, \ldots$ [12-5]

8. Find the value of the infinite series $\displaystyle\sum_{k=1}^{\infty} \left(\dfrac{2}{3}\right)^k$.   [12-6]

CALCULATOR EXTENSION   Degrees and Radians

If your calculator operates in both degree and radian modes, the trigonometric function keys can be used to convert from degrees to radians and vice versa. For example, to change 35° to radians:

a. Put the calculator in degree mode.

b. Enter 35°.

c. Press the ☐ sin ☐ key.

d. Change to radian mode.

e. Press the ☐ sin⁻¹ ☐ key.

[*Note:* You could also use the ☐ cos ☐ and ☐ cos⁻¹ ☐ keys or the ☐ tan ☐ and ☐ tan⁻¹ ☐ keys.]

1. Convert 35° to radians.   2. Convert 1 radian to degrees.

3. Convert 2 radians to degrees. (The answer is not 65.4°.)

CHAPTER SUMMARY

▶ **Vocabulary**

▶ A function $y = f(x)$ is a *periodic function* if and only if there is a real number   [16-1]
p such that for each x in the domain of f,

$$f(x + p) = f(x).$$

The smallest value of p is called the *fundamental period* of f or simply the
period of f.

▶ Definition of the sine and cosine functions   [16-1,]

For each real number x, let $P(j, k)$ be the point that is x units from $(1, 0)$ in   16-2]
the counterclockwise direction along the circle $j^2 + k^2 = 1$. Then cosine is
the function such that $\cos x = j$, and sine is the function such that
$\sin x = k$.

▶ Equation of the unit circle   [16-2]

For each real number x, $\sin^2 x + \cos^2 x = 1$.

▶ Properties of $\sin x$ and $\cos x$ [16-2]

For each real number x:

  I. $\cos(-x) = \cos x$ **III.** $\cos(\pi - x) = -\cos x$ **V.** $\cos(\pi + x) = -\cos x$
  II. $\sin(-x) = -\sin x$ **IV.** $\sin(\pi - x) = \sin x$ **VI.** $\sin(\pi + x) = -\sin x$

▶ For all real numbers x, y, and b, $b \neq 0$, the *amplitude* of $y = b \sin x$ and   [16-4]
$y = b \cos x$ is $|b|$.

▶ For all real numbers, x, y, and c, $c \neq 0$, the *period* of $y = \sin cx$ and   [16-5]
$y = \cos cx$ is $\dfrac{2\pi}{|c|}$.

▶ For all values of x for which the denominator is not 0,   [16-6]

$$\tan x = \frac{\sin x}{\cos x} \qquad \cot x = \frac{\cos x}{\sin x} \qquad \sec x = \frac{1}{\cos x} \qquad \csc x = \frac{1}{\sin x}$$

▶ The Arccosine function   [16-7]

For real numbers x and y, $-1 \leq x \leq 1$ and $0 \leq y \leq \pi$, there is a function $y = \text{Cos}^{-1} x$ such that $x = \cos y$.

▶ The Arcsine function   [16-7]

For real numbers x and y, $-1 \leq x \leq 1$ and $-\dfrac{\pi}{2} \leq y \leq \dfrac{\pi}{2}$, there is a function $y = \text{Sin}^{-1} x$ such that $x = \sin y$.

▶ The Arctangent function   [16-7]

For real numbers x and y, $-\dfrac{\pi}{2} \leq y \leq \dfrac{\pi}{2}$, there is a function $y = \text{Tan}^{-1} x$ such that $x = \tan y$.

▶ Definition of sine and cosine functions on degree measures   [16-8]

If θ is the degree measure of a central angle of the unit circle with one side of the angle on the positive horizontal axis, $\cos \theta$ is the first coordinate and $\sin \theta$ the second coordinate of the intersection of the other side of the angle and the unit circle.

▶ Definition of a radian   [16-8]

If a central angle of a circle with radius r intercepts an arc of length s, the measure of the angle is $\dfrac{s}{r}$ radians.

▶ $1° = \dfrac{\pi}{180}$ radians (about 0.0175 radian)   1 radian $= \left(\dfrac{180}{\pi}\right)°$ (about 57.3°)   [16-8]

*C*HAPTER REVIEW

16-1 **Objectives:** To use the wrapping function W to map real numbers onto points of the unit circle.

To use symmetries of the unit circle to determine coordinates of points on the unit circle.

1. State the coordinates of each point.

   a. $W\left(\dfrac{\pi}{2}\right)$ **b.** $W(2\pi)$

2. Points B, C, and D are reflection images of point A about the vertical axis, origin, and horizontal axis, respectively. State the coordinates of the following points.

   a. B **b.** C **c.** D

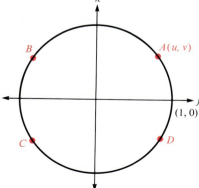

16-2 Objective: To apply some properties of the cosine and sine functions.

3. State the fundamental period of the cosine and sine functions.

4. In which quadrant are both sin x and cos x negative?

Let cos $x = \dfrac{4}{5}$ and sin $x = \dfrac{3}{5}$. Evaluate each expression.

5. $\cos(-x)$ **6.** $\sin(x + \pi)$ **7.** $\cos(\pi - x)$ **8.** $\sin(x + 4\pi)$

9. Let $\sin x = \dfrac{2}{5}$. Find cos x.

16-3 Objective: To evaluate the sine and cosine function for special values.

10. Copy and complete the table.

x	$\dfrac{\pi}{4}$	$\dfrac{\pi}{3}$	$\dfrac{5\pi}{6}$	$\dfrac{7\pi}{4}$	$\dfrac{9\pi}{2}$	8π
sin x	?	?	?	?	?	?
cos x	?	?	?	?	?	?

11. Write all solutions for $0 \leqslant x \leqslant 2\pi$.

     a. $\cos x = \dfrac{1}{2}$ **b.** $\sin x \leqslant \dfrac{\sqrt{2}}{2}$

16-4 Objective: To describe the graphs of the sine and cosine functions.

12. State the maximum and minimum values of $y = 2 + \cos x$.

13. State the period and the amplitude of the function $y = 5 + \sin x$

14. Sketch the graph of $y = 1 + \sin x$ for $0 \leqslant x \leqslant 2\pi$.

16-5 Objective: To sketch the graphs of $y = b \sin cx$ and $y = b \cos cx$ and to describe the characteristics of those graphs.

Sketch the graph of the function for $-\pi \leqslant x \leqslant \pi$.

15. $y = 3 \sin x$ **16.** $y = \cos 2x$

17. Write an equation for this graph.

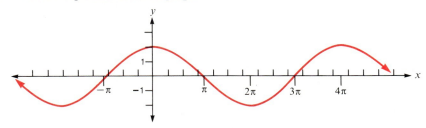

18. State the period, the amplitude, and the maximum and minimum values of the function $y = 2 \sin 3x$.

16-6 **Objective:** To describe the characteristics of the tangent, cotangent, secant, and cosecant functions.

19. Let $\sin b = \dfrac{7}{25}$ and $\cos b = -\dfrac{24}{25}$.

Evaluate.

    a. $\tan b$ **b.** $\cot b$ **c.** $\sec b$ **d.** $\csc b$

20. Copy and complete the table. Write *undefined* if the value does not exist.

x	$\dfrac{\pi}{6}$	$\dfrac{\pi}{4}$	$\dfrac{\pi}{3}$	$\dfrac{\pi}{2}$	$\dfrac{2\pi}{3}$	$\dfrac{3\pi}{4}$	π
$\tan x$	$\dfrac{\sqrt{3}}{3}$	?	?	?	?	?	?
$\cot x$	?	1	?	?	?	?	?
$\sec x$	?	?	2	?	?	?	?
$\csc x$	?	?	?	1	?	?	?

21. State the fundamental period of $y = \tan x$.

22. State the range of $y = \sec x$.

16-7 **Objective:** To evaluate the inverse circular functions and to learn their characteristics.

Evaluate.

23. $\text{Arctan}\left(-\sqrt{3}\right)$ **24.** $\text{Sin}^{-1} 1$ **25.** $\cos\left(\text{Sin}^{-1}\left(-\dfrac{\sqrt{2}}{2}\right)\right)$

26. Sketch the graph of $y = \text{Sin}^{-1} x$.
27. State the domain of $y = \text{Arccos } x$.

16-8 **Objectives:** To determine values of circular functions of degree measures.
To convert degree measure to radian measure and vice versa.

Evaluate.

28. $\sin 30°$ **29.** $\cos 30°$

30. $\tan 45°$ **31.** $\sin 120°$

Find the degree measure that corresponds to each of these radian measures.

32. $\dfrac{\pi}{4}$ radians   **33.** $-\dfrac{2\pi}{3}$ radians

Find the radian measure that corresponds to each of these degree measures.

34. $135°$

35. $-50°$

36. State the radian measure of the angle in this figure.

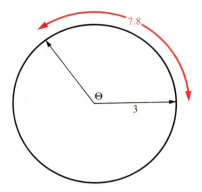

Solve.

37. A large tractor wheel has a diameter of 5 ft. When the wheel turns through an angle of 288°, how far will the tractor move?

*C*HAPTER 16 SELF-TEST

16-1, 16-2

1. Points C and D are $W(2)$ and $W(-1.2)$, respectively.
State whether these numbers are positive or negative.

    a. $\sin 2$

    b. $\cos (-1.2)$

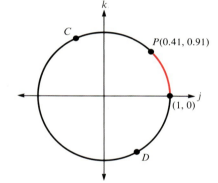

2. In the figure, x is the distance from $(1, 0)$ to point P.

    Evaluate.

    a. $\sin x$

    b. $\cos x$

3. Given $\cos \dfrac{\pi}{3} = \dfrac{1}{2}$, find the value of $\cos \left\{ \dfrac{\pi}{3} + 7\pi \right\}$.

True or false?

4. $\cos (-b) = \cos b$, for all b.

5. $0 \leqslant \sin^2 x \leqslant 1$, for every x.

16-3   **Solve for $0 \leqslant x \leqslant 2\pi$.**

6. $\cos x = -\dfrac{\sqrt{2}}{2}$

7. $\sin x = \dfrac{\sqrt{3}}{2}$

8. $\cos \dfrac{\pi}{6} = \sin x$

16-4   **9.** State the maximum value of $y = 4 + \sin x$.

16-5   **10.** State the period of $y = 3 \cos 4x$.

       11. State the amplitude of $y = 1 + 2 \sin x$.

16-5, 16-6   **Sketch the graph for $0 \leqslant x \leqslant 2\pi$.**

12. $y = 3 + \cos x$

13. $y = \sin 2x$

14. $y = \cot x$

16-6   **15.** Suppose that $\sin a = \dfrac{4}{5}$ and $\dfrac{\pi}{2} < a < \pi$. Evaluate $\tan a$.

      16. Suppose that $\sin x = -\dfrac{\sqrt{5}}{3}$ and $\cos x = \dfrac{2}{3}$.
        Evaluate.

        a. $\cot x$ **b.** $\sec x$

      17. State the period of the cosecant function.

      Evaluate.

      18. $\sin 45°$ **19.** $\cos 150°$

16-7   **Evaluate.**

      20. Arccos 0   **21.** $\text{Sin}^{-1}\left(-\dfrac{1}{2}\right)$

16-8   **Change to degree measure.**

      22. $\dfrac{3\pi}{4}$ radians   **23.** 2 radians

      Change to radian measure.

      24. $240°$ **25.** $-35°$

      Solve.

      26. A pendulum bob is suspended on a 30-ft wire. When the pendulum swings through an angle of 15°, how far does the bob travel?

$\mathcal{P}$RACTICE FOR COLLEGE ENTRANCE TESTS

Choose the best answer.

  1. Which of these choices best describes the change made to the cosine curve, $f(x) = \cos x$ for $-\pi \leqslant x \leqslant \pi$, to obtain the curve graphed below?

     A. The amplitude was doubled.

     B. The period was doubled.

     C. The graph was shifted up one unit.

     D. The graph was shifted $\dfrac{\pi}{2}$ units to the left.

     E. The graph was reflected about the x-axis.

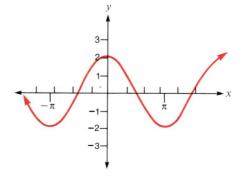

2. If an equilateral triangle is rotated 360° around one of its altitudes as an axis, then the figure generates a __?__.

A. sphere   **B.** cone   **C.** cylinder   **D.** prism   **E.** pyramid

3. An angle measure of 45° is equivalent to an angle measure of __?__ radians.

A. $\dfrac{\pi}{8}$ **B.** $\dfrac{\pi}{6}$ **C.** $\dfrac{\pi}{4}$ **D.** $\dfrac{\pi}{3}$ **E.** $\dfrac{\pi}{2}$

4. If $f(x) = \sin x$, then the set of all x for which $f(-x) = f(x)$ is __?__.

  A. the set of all real numbers   **B.** $\{0\}$ **C.** $\emptyset$

  D. the set of all multiples of $\dfrac{\pi}{2}$ **E.** the set of all multiples of π

5. Let n be any integer. For what values of x does $\sin x$ have minimum values?

A. $n\left(\dfrac{\pi}{2}\right)$ **B.** $\dfrac{\pi}{2} + n2\pi$ **C.** $\dfrac{3\pi}{2} + n2\pi$ **D.** $n\pi$ **E.** $\pi + n2\pi$

6. Let n be any integer. The set of all x for which $\cos(-x) = -\cos x$ is __?__.

A. $\mathcal{R}$ **B.** $\left\{\dfrac{\pi}{2} + n\pi\right\}$ **C.** $\left\{\dfrac{\pi}{2} + 2n\pi\right\}$ **D.** $\emptyset$ **E.** $\{n\pi\}$

7. If $-\pi \le x \le 0$ and $\cos x = \dfrac{1}{2}$, then $\sin x = $ __?__.

A. $-\dfrac{1}{2}$ **B.** $-\dfrac{\sqrt{2}}{2}$ **C.** $\dfrac{\sqrt{2}}{2}$ **D.** $-\dfrac{\sqrt{3}}{2}$ **E.** $\dfrac{\sqrt{3}}{2}$

8. If $\sin x = 0.2$, then $\sin(x + \pi) = $ __?__.

A. -0.2 **B.** 0.2 **C.** -0.8 **D.** 0.8 **E.** 0.96

9. For what value of k does $\cos kx$ have period π?

A. $\dfrac{1}{2}$ **B.** 1 **C.** 2 **D.** $\dfrac{\pi}{2}$ **E.** π

10. What is the amplitude of $y - 3 = 5 \sin 2(x - \pi)$?

A. 2 **B.** 3 **C.** π **D.** 5 **E.** 10

11. If $0 \le x \le \pi$ and $\sin x = \cos x$, then $x = $ __?__.

A. π **B.** 0 **C.** $\dfrac{\pi}{4}$ **D.** 1 **E.** $\dfrac{\pi}{2}$

12. Let n be any integer. For what values of x is $\tan x$ undefined?

A. $\left\{n\left(\dfrac{\pi}{2}\right)\right\}$ **B.** $\left\{\dfrac{\pi}{2} + n\pi\right\}$ **C.** $\{n\pi\}$ **D.** $\left\{\dfrac{\pi}{2} + 2n\pi\right\}$ **E.** $\{2n\pi\}$

CHAPTER 17

Applications of Trigonometric Functions

Speleology is the scientific study of caves. Scientists as well as amateur spelunkers explore caves to study their natural formations, flora, and fauna. Mapping a cave is an important part of its study. Due to the three-dimensional topography of a cave, mapping is a challenging surveying task. Equipped with a hand compass, measuring tape, and mountaineering skills, the surveyor takes an exhaustive set of measurements, which are later analyzed with the help of trigonometry to create a map of the cave.

LESSON 17-1

Trigonometric Ratios

The Simplon Tunnel, between Italy and Switz-
erland, is 12 miles long. Finished in 1906, this
tunnel through the Alps was bored from both
ends. When the headings came together, they
were found to be in exact alignment horizontally and only 4 inches out of line vertically. A
precise use of trigonometry enabled engineers
to cut through the mountain with this degree
of accuracy.

Important modern applications of the circular functions concern problems involving periodic behavior in areas such as optics, sound, electromagnetism, and high-
frequency technology. However, historically the circular functions were first defined
in terms of triangles and used to solve problems of surveying and astronomy. These
functions were called **trigonometric functions.** For all practical purposes, the trigonometric functions are the same as the circular functions.

Consider right triangle ABC with angle C the
right angle.

The **hypotenuse** of the right triangle is segment AB. Its length is c.

The **leg opposite** angle A is segment BC. Its
length is a.

The **leg adjacent** to angle A is segment AC.
Its length is b.

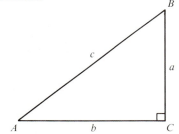

The measure of angle A is A, the measure of angle B is B, and the measure of

angle C is 90°, or $\frac{\pi}{2}$ radians. Throughout this chapter, we will use degrees to express

all angle measures.

The trigonometric ratios are defined as follows.

$$\sin A = \frac{\text{leg opposite angle } A}{\text{hypotenuse}} = \frac{a}{c} \qquad \csc A = \frac{\text{hypotenuse}}{\text{leg opposite angle } A} = \frac{c}{a}$$

$$\cos A = \frac{\text{leg adjacent to angle } A}{\text{hypotenuse}} = \frac{b}{c} \qquad \sec A = \frac{\text{hypotenuse}}{\text{leg adjacent to angle } A} = \frac{c}{b}$$

$$\tan A = \frac{\text{leg opposite angle } A}{\text{leg adjacent to angle } A} = \frac{a}{b} \qquad \cot A = \frac{\text{leg adjacent to angle } A}{\text{leg opposite angle } A} = \frac{b}{a}$$

Note that $\sin A = \cos B$, $\tan A = \cot B$, and $\sec A = \csc B$. Angles A and B are complementary. The pairs of functions sine and cosine, tangent and cotangent, and secant and cosecant are called **cofunctions.**

Cofunction Property

If f and g are trigonometric cofunctions and θ is the degree measure of an acute angle, then $f(\theta) = g(90° - \theta)$.

Example 1   **Find the values of the six trigonometric functions for angle A and for angle B. Compute the values correct to four significant digits.**

Solution $\sin A = \cos B = \dfrac{4}{5} = 0.8000$

$\cos A = \sin B = \dfrac{3}{5} = 0.6000$

$\tan A = \cot B = \dfrac{4}{3} = 1.333$

$\cot A = \tan B = \dfrac{3}{4} = 0.7500$

$\sec A = \csc B = \dfrac{5}{3} = 1.667$

$\csc A = \sec B = \dfrac{5}{4} = 1.250$

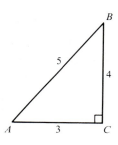

Example 2   **Compute $\sin 45°$.**

Solution   Draw right triangle ABC with angle $A = 45°$.

Angle B is also $45°$, and triangle ABC is isosceles. Let $a = b = 1$.

Use the Pythagorean theorem to compute the value of c.

$$c^2 = 1^2 + 1^2 = 2$$
$$c = \sqrt{2}$$

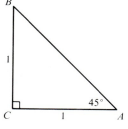

Answer $\sin 45° = \dfrac{1}{\sqrt{2}} = \dfrac{\sqrt{2}}{2}$

In Example 2, the length of each leg of the right triangle was selected to be 1. However, any length could have been used. For example, let $a = b = 3$. Then $c = 3\sqrt{2}$, and $\sin 45° = \dfrac{3}{3\sqrt{2}} = \dfrac{\sqrt{2}}{2}$.

Values of the trigonometric functions for angles from 0° to 90° can be found using a scientific calculator or tables like the ones given on pages 771–775. The table gives the values of the functions to four significant digits for angle measures given in tenths of degrees.

Example 3 **Use the tables on pages 771–775 to find these values.**
   a. tan 18.2°
   b. sin 71.3°

Solution **a.** Since 18.2° is found on the left side of the table, use the column labels at the top. The number in the "tangent" column and the "18.2°" row is 0.3288.

Angle	sin	cos	tan	cot	sec	csc	
18.0°	0.3090	0.9511	0.3249	3.078	1.051	3.236	72.0°
18.1°	0.3107	0.9505	0.3269	3.060	1.052	3.219	71.9°
18.2°	0.3123	0.9500	0.3288	3.042	1.053	3.202	71.8°
18.3°	0.3140	0.9494	0.3307	3.024	1.053	3.185	71.7°

Answer tan 18.2° ≈ 0.3288

b. Since 71.3° is found on the right side of the table, use the column labels at the bottom. The number in the "sine" column and the "71.3°" row is 0.9472.

18.6°	0.3190	0.9478	0.3365	2.971	1.055	3.135	71.4°
18.7°	0.3206	0.9472	0.3385	2.954	1.056	3.119	71.3°
18.8°	0.3223	0.9466	0.3404	2.938	1.056	3.103	71.2°
18.9°	0.3239	0.9461	0.3424	2.921	1.057	3.087	71.1°
19.0°	0.3256	0.9455	0.3443	2.904	1.058	3.072	71.0°
	cos	*sin*	*cot*	*tan*	*csc*	*sec*	*Angle*

Answer sin 71.3° ≈ 0.9472

Note that the table is constructed to take advantage of cofunctions. The table indicates values of the trigonometric functions for angles from 0° to 45°. Then the column labels for cofunctions are reversed and the same entries (in reverse order) indicate the values of the trigonometric functions for angles from 45° to 90°. In this way, both sin 19° and cos 71°, for example, are given by a single entry in the table.

Example 4   **Find the value of θ, to the nearest tenth degree, that satisfies this equation.**

$$\tan \theta = 0.3437$$

Solution   In the tangent column, find the number closest in value to 0.3437. That table entry is 0.3443. Read the corresponding angle from the row-heading.

Answer $\theta = 19.0°$ to the nearest tenth degree.

A scientific calculator can be used to find the measure of an angle when the value of one of its trigonometric functions is given. For example, to find A when the $\tan A = 1.871$, use the keying sequence 1.871 [INV] [tan] to get $\approx 61.9°$.

$\mathcal{C}$LASSROOM EXERCISES

1. In Example 1, $\tan A \approx 1.333$. What is the measure of angle A to the nearest tenth degree?

2. In Example 1, what is the measure of angle B to the nearest tenth degree?

Use the triangle shown at the right to answer the following.

3. What is $\sin \alpha$? (α is the Greek letter alpha.)

4. What is $\tan \beta$? (β is the Greek letter beta.)

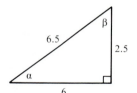

$\mathcal{W}$RITTEN EXERCISES

 Find the values of the six trigonometric functions for the given angle. State the value to four significant digits.

1. Angle A

2. Angle B

3. Angle R

4. Angle S

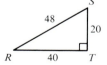

5. Angle D

6. Angle F

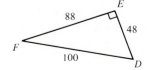

7. Angle L

8. Angle M

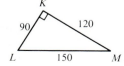

9. Angle P

10. Angle R

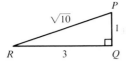

11. Angle X

12. Angle Y

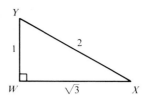

Find sin A and sin B for each triangle. Simplify all radicals.

13.

14.

15.

16.

17.

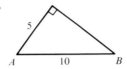

18.

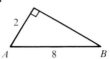

State the value to four significant digits. Use a scientific calculator or the tables on pages 771–775.

19. $\sin 12°$ **20.** $\sin 42°$ **21.** $\cos 80°$ **22.** $\cos 70°$

23. $\tan 75°$ **24.** $\tan 85°$ **25.** $\sec 165°$ **26.** $\sec 95°$

27. $\csc 110.5°$ **28.** $\csc 152.2°$ **29.** $\cot 27.4°$ **30.** $\cot 72.4°$

State the value of θ to the nearest tenth degree, $0° < \theta < 90°$.

31. $\sin \theta = 0.8511$ **32.** $\sin \theta = 0.3854$ **33.** $\cos \theta = 0.9228$

34. $\cos \theta = 0.5250$ **35.** $\tan \theta = 0.7454$ **36.** $\tan \theta = 0.2642$

State the value of α to the nearest tenth degree, $90° < \alpha < 180°$.

37. $\sin \alpha = 0.3062$ **38.** $\sin \alpha = 0.8175$ **39.** $\cos \alpha = -0.8465$

40. $\cos \alpha = -0.9942$ **41.** $\tan \alpha = -7.5449$ **42.** $\tan \alpha = -1.1021$

B | **In triangle ABC, $C = 90°$. Solve.**

43. $\tan A = \sqrt{2}$; $a = 10$ **44.** $\sin A = \dfrac{1}{4}$; $a = 3$ **45.** $b = 7$; $c = 10$

    Find b.   Find b.   Find $\csc B$.

46. $a = 5$; $b = 12$ **47.** $\cos B = \dfrac{2}{3}$; $a = 5$ **48.** $a = 4$; $c = 6$

    Find $\sin A$.   Find c.   Find $\tan B$.

Use the definitions of the trigonometric functions and cofunctions to solve the following. Express the answer in terms of p and q.

49. $\tan 23° = \dfrac{p}{q}$

$\cot 23° = ?$
$\cot 67° = ?$

50. $\sin 59° = p$

$\csc 59° = ?$
$\cos 31° = ?$

51. $\sec 17° = p$

$\cos 17° = ?$
$\csc 73° = ?$

52. $\cos 2° = p$

$\sin 88° = ?$
$\sec 2° = ?$

53. $\cot 83° = \dfrac{p}{q}$

$\tan 7° = ?$
$\cot 7° = ?$

54. $\csc 70° = q$

$\sec 20° = ?$
$\cos 20° = ?$

 Express the answer in terms of t and u.

55. $\cos 42° = t$

$\sin 42° = ?$
$\sin 48° = ?$
$\cos 48° = ?$
$\tan 48° = ?$

56. $\cot 36° = \dfrac{t}{u}$

$\tan 36° = ?$
$\tan 54° = ?$
$\cot 54° = ?$
$\sin 36° = ?$

57. $\sec 6° = u$

$\csc 84° = ?$
$\sin 84° = ?$
$\cos 84° = ?$
$\tan 84° = ?$

58. In right triangle ABC, $C = 90°$ and $\sin A = x$. Find $\sec A$ and $\tan B$.

EVIEW EXERCISES

1. Use synthetic substitution to evaluate $f(2)$ when
$f(x) = x^4 - 4x^3 + x - 6$. [10-1]

2. Use synthetic division to find the quotient and remainder when
$x^3 - 5x^2 + 4x + 6$ is divided by $x - 1$. [10-2]

3. For what value of k is $x - 3$ a factor of $x^3 - 4x^2 + kx + 3$? [10-2]

4. Write an equation in standard form that has -2 as a root, 1 as a root with
multiplicity 2, and no other roots. [10-3]

5. Find all roots of the equation
$x^3 - 7x + 6 = 0$. [10-3]

6. Here is a graph of $y = f(x)$. Describe the
roots of the equation $f(x) = 0$. [10-4]

[10-5]

7. Write the inverse of the function
$f(x) = -x + 6$.

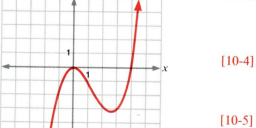

LESSON 17-2

Applications of Right Triangles

If one side and one acute angle or two sides of a right triangle are known, the other sides and angles can be computed using trigonometry. Finding the unknown measures of a triangle is called **solving the triangle.**

Consider the triangle shown at the right. First find B. Angle A and angle B are complementary. Therefore,

$$B = 90° - 37° = 53°.$$

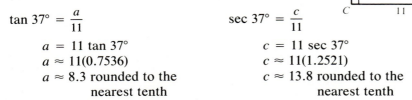

Next, find a.

$$\tan 37° = \frac{a}{11}$$

$$a = 11 \tan 37°$$
$$a \approx 11(0.7536)$$
$$a \approx 8.3 \text{ rounded to the}$$
$$\text{nearest tenth}$$

Finally, find c.

$$\sec 37° = \frac{c}{11}$$

$$c = 11 \sec 37°$$
$$c \approx 11(1.2521)$$
$$c \approx 13.8 \text{ rounded to the}$$
$$\text{nearest tenth}$$

In the above example, we used the tangent 37° instead of the cotangent, and we used the secant 37° instead of the cosine to avoid long divisions. But what if we did use $\cot 37° = \frac{11}{a}$ and $\cos 37° = \frac{11}{c}$? If we use a scientific calculator, we can easily compute $\frac{11}{\cot 37°}$ to get a, and $\frac{11}{\cos 37°}$ to get c.

$$37 \boxed{\tan} \boxed{1/x} \boxed{1/x} \boxed{\times} 11 \boxed{=} \rightarrow a \approx 8.3$$
$$\underbrace{\qquad\qquad\qquad}_{\cot 37}$$

$$37 \boxed{\cos} \boxed{1/x} \boxed{\times} 11 \boxed{=} \rightarrow c \approx 13.8$$

Many practical problems can be solved by identifying right triangles in the situations and solving those right triangles. A sketch or drawing is usually helpful in setting up an appropriate triangle that involves a right angle.

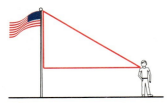
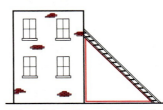

When solving practical problems, draw a figure. Then identify a right angle and a right triangle associated with that angle. Label the known sides and angles of the right triangle. Assign variables to unknown sides and angles, and then solve for the desired unknowns.

Example 1   A support cable for a 50-ft tower is to make a 60° angle with the ground. How long must the cable be?

Solution   Sketch a figure.

$$\sin 60° = \frac{50}{x}$$

$$x \sin 60° = 50$$

$$x(0.8660) \approx 50$$

$$x \approx \frac{50}{0.8660}$$

$$x \approx 57.74$$

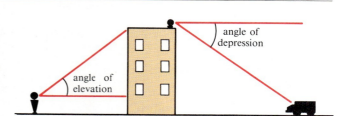

Answer   The cable must be 58 feet to the nearest foot.

Many applications of trigonometry involve an **angle of elevation** or an **angle of depression.** In each case the angle includes a horizontal ray and a ray from the observer to the object observed. Angles of elevation or depression have measures between 0° and 90°.

Example 2   Solve.

An airplane at a constant altitude of 30,000 ft is flying horizontally toward an observer on the ground. The angle of elevation at one time was 40°. One minute later the angle of elevation was 60°. What is the ground speed of the airplane?

Solution   Draw a figure.

$$\cot 40° = \frac{a}{30,000}$$

$$a = 30,000 \, (\cot 40°)$$

$$a \approx 30,000(1.192)$$

$$a \approx 35,800 \text{ rounded to the nearest } 100$$

$$\cot 60° = \frac{b}{30,000}$$

$$b = 30,000(\cot 60°)$$

$$b \approx 30,000(0.5774)$$

$$b \approx 17,300 \text{ rounded to the nearest } 100$$

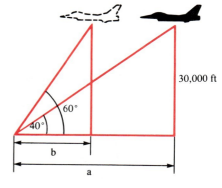

The distance traveled in one minute $\approx$ 35,800 ft $-$ 17,300 ft $=$ 18,500 ft.

$$\text{The rate} \approx \frac{18,500(60)}{5280} \approx 210.2$$

Answer   The rate in miles per hour is about 210.

1. Solve right triangle *ABC*.
   Give answers to the nearest tenth.

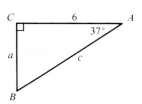

2. Draw a right triangle for the following problem. Label known sides and angles. Solve the
   problem.

   A kite is on 2000 ft of string. The string makes an angle of 57° with the horizontal.
   About how high is the kite above the ground? Round your answer to the nearest
   hundred feet.

RITTEN EXERCISES

A Solve each right triangle. Give answers to the nearest tenth.

1.
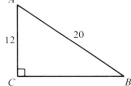

2.
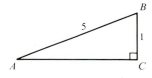

3.
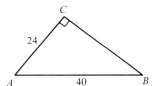

Solve each right triangle. Give answers to the nearest tenth.

4.
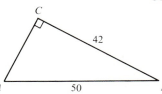

5.
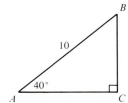

6.
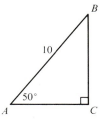

In triangle *PQR*, *R* = 90°. Sides *p*, *q*, and *r* are opposite angles *P*, *Q*, and *R*, respectively. Use the given information to find the measure of the side or angle. Give answers
to the nearest tenth.

7. *P* = 25°; *p* = 2
   Find *r*.

8. *Q* = 35°; *q* = 3
   Find *r*.

9. *P* = 73.8°; *q* = 2
   Find *p*.

10. *Q* = 27.3°; *p* = 11
    Find *r*.

11. *p* = 36; *q* = 40
    Find *Q*.

12. *p* = 36; *q* = 90
    Find *Q*.

$\mathcal{A}$pplications

Solve.

13. A north-south road and an east-west road touch the shores of a lake at points A and B. From point A the line of sight to point B makes a 40° angle with the north-south road. B is known to be 4 mi from the intersection of the roads.

    a. How far is A from the intersection?

    b. How far is it across the lake from A to B?

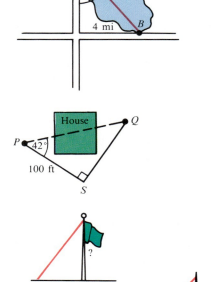

14. Points P and Q are on opposite sides of a house. Point S is found 100 ft from P so that angle S is 90° and angle P is 42°.

    a. How far is P from Q?

    b. How far is S from Q?

15. A flagpole casts a 24-ft shadow when the angle of elevation of the sun is 60°. What is the height of the pole?

16. A supporting cable is attached to the top of an 80-ft tower. How long is the cable if it forms a 70° angle with the ground?

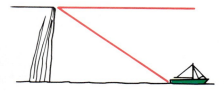

17. From a cliff 200 ft above the sea, the angle of depression to a sailboat is 20°. How far is the boat from the base of the cliff?

18. From a raft, the angle of elevation to the top of a tower is 5°. The tower is known to be 30 m high. How many meters is the raft from the tower?

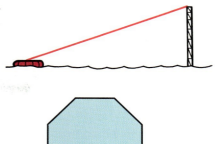

19. Each side of a regular octagon is 20 cm long.

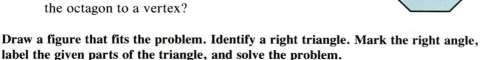

    a. What is the shortest distance from the center of the octagon to a side?

    b. What is the distance from the center of the octagon to a vertex?

Draw a figure that fits the problem. Identify a right triangle. Mark the right angle, label the given parts of the triangle, and solve the problem.

20. When an airplane is directly over a 30-m radio tower, an observer 3000 m from the tower determines that the angle of elevation of the plane is 23.5°. How high is the plane above the tower?

21. When an airplane is 3000 m above a 30-m radio tower, the angle of depression to the LaPorte Bridge is 23.5°. How far is the bridge from the radio tower?

22. A 6-ft person casts a 5-ft shadow. What is the angle of elevation of the sun?

23. When the angle of elevation of the sun is 10°, how long is the shadow cast by a 6-ft person?

24. A 12-ft ladder leans against a building. It forms an angle between 55° and 75° with the ground. What are the minimum and maximum heights above the ground where the ladder could touch the building?

25. A 10-ft-long board helps to brace a wall. The board touches the wall between 6 ft and 8 ft above the ground. What are the minimum and maximum angles that the board can form with the ground?

26. A satellite is 1000 miles above the earth. A laser beam aimed at the satellite misses its target by 0.7°. By how many miles does it miss the target?

27. A laser beam is directed at a target 200 mi away but it misses by 0.2°. By how many miles does it miss the target?

B **28.** What is the measure of the acute angle formed by the x-axis and the line $y = 2x - 4$?

29. What is the measure of the acute angle formed by the intersecting lines $y = 3x + 4$ and $y = 2x - 1$? [*Hint:* Find the measures of the angles formed by each line and the horizontal line through their intersection.]

30. Two adjacent sides of a rectangle are 5 cm and 8 cm, respectively.

    a. What is the measure of the angle formed by a diagonal and an 8-cm side?

    b. What is the measure of the angle formed by a diagonal and a 5-cm side?

    c. What is the measure of the acute angle formed by the intersecting diagonals?

31. A trapezoid has two right angles, a height of 6 cm, and parallel bases that are 5 cm and 10 cm long, respectively.

    a. What is the measure of the angle formed by the longer diagonal and a base?

    b. What is the measure of the angle formed by the shorter diagonal and a base?

Solve.

32. The angle of elevation from point A to the top of a mountain is 28°. From point B, 2 km farther away, the angle of elevation is 23°. How much higher than point A is the mountain peak? Refer to the drawing.

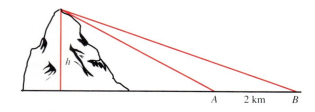

33.

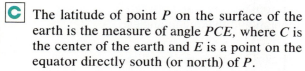

From point P, 50 m from a building, the angle of elevation to the base of a flagpole is 40.5° and the angle of elevation to the top of the flagpole is 45.3°. What is the height of the flagpole?

C The latitude of point P on the surface of the earth is the measure of angle PCE, where C is the center of the earth and E is a point on the equator directly south (or north) of P.

Find the radius r_a of the latitude through the given city. Assume that the radius of the earth is 6400 km (to the nearest 100 km).

34. Detroit, Michigan; 42.3°N

35. Nome, Alaska; 64.5°N

36. Laredo, Texas; 27.5°N

37. London, U.K.; 51.5°N

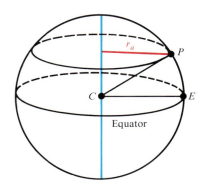

38. In a circle of radius r, chord AB subtends an inscribed angle θ. Show that the length of chord AB is $2r \sin \theta$.

39. Sand dropped from the top of a conveyor belt forms a conical heap or a "sand-tip." The volume of a cone is given by the formula

$$V = \frac{1}{3}\pi r^2 h.$$

In the right triangle, $\tan \dfrac{\theta}{2} = \dfrac{r}{h}$.

Therefore, $h = \dfrac{r}{\tan\dfrac{\theta}{2}}$.

In a sand-tip, the volume and radius have the following relationship:

$$V = 0.68r^3.$$

Substitute to find the value of the sand-tip angle.

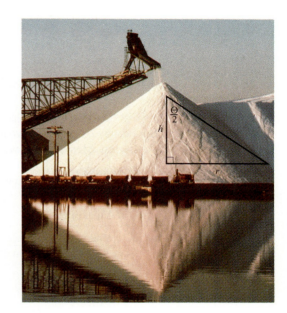

ℛEVIEW EXERCISES

1. Graph both functions on the same set of axes over the domain $\{x: -2 \leqslant x \leqslant 2\}$. $y = 2^x$ $y = \left(\dfrac{1}{2}\right)^x$ [11-1]

2. Write $10^4 = 10,000$ in logarithmic form.   **3.** Solve: $\log_{10} 5x = 3$.   [11-2]

4. If $\log_{10} 2 \approx 0.3010$, then $\log_{10} 8 \approx \underline{\ ?\ }$.   **5.** Solve: $\log_5 x + \log_5 2 = \log_5 20$.   [11-3]

𝒮elf-Quiz 1

17-1   **1.** Find the values of the six trigonometric functions of θ.

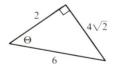

   2. State the value to four significant digits.

     a. $\tan 54°$ **b.** $\cos 14.5°$

   3. State the value of θ to the nearest tenth degree if $\sin \theta = 0.4173$.

17-2   **4.** Solve triangle PQR.

   5. A kite held aloft by a stiff wind is at the end of a 250-ft string. If the string makes an angle of 58° with the ground, find the height of the kite above the ground.

LESSON 17-3

The Law of Sines

In any triangle the longest side is opposite the largest angle, and the shortest side is opposite the smallest angle. This observation led mathematicians to wonder whether the side of a triangle varies directly with the angle opposite that side. This table suggests that in any triangle the ratio $\dfrac{\text{side}}{\text{sine of opposite angle}}$ is constant for each of the three sides.

Ratios of Measures

side	angle	$\dfrac{\text{side}}{\text{angle}}$	$\dfrac{\text{side}}{\text{sine of angle}}$	$\dfrac{\text{side}}{\text{tangent of angle}}$
a	A	0.200	12.0	10.4
b	B	0.173	12.0	6.93
c	C	0.133	12.0	undefined

d	D	0.243	16.2	9.52
e	E	0.278	16.2	15.4
f	F	0.143	16.2	-5.00

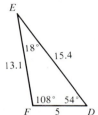

Every triangle can be "partitioned" into right triangles. For example, draw altitude AD to divide triangle ABC into two right triangles.

$$\text{area} = \frac{1}{2}(\text{base})(\text{height}) = \frac{1}{2}ah$$

$$\frac{h}{c} = \sin B$$

So, $h = c \sin B$.

Substituting $c \sin B$ for h gives: $\text{area} = \dfrac{1}{2}a(c \sin B) = \dfrac{1}{2}ac \sin B$.

In a similar manner the following relationships can be established.

$$\text{area} = \frac{1}{2}ab \sin C \qquad \text{area} = \frac{1}{2}bc \sin A$$

Area of a Triangle

For any triangle ABC, the area is one half the product of any two sides multiplied by the sine of the included angle.

The three expressions for the area of triangle ABC must be equal. Therefore,

$$\frac{1}{2}bc \sin A = \frac{1}{2}ac \sin B = \frac{1}{2}ab \sin C.$$

Multiplying each expression by $\frac{2}{abc}$ gives the **law of sines.**

Law of Sines

For any triangle ABC, where a, b, and c are the lengths of the sides opposite angles, A, B, and C, respectively,

$$\frac{\sin A}{a} = \frac{\sin B}{b} = \frac{\sin C}{c}.$$

The lengths of the sides of a triangle are proportional to the sines of the measures of the opposite angles.

Note that the derivation given of the law of sines assumed that the angles of the triangle are acute. However, the law of sines can be derived using obtuse triangles or right triangles. To find the sine of an obtuse angle using the tables on pages 771–775, use the following formula from Chapter 16:

$$\sin \theta = \sin (180° - \theta).$$

Example 1 **State the area of triangle ABC.**

Solution area $= \frac{1}{2}ab \sin C$

$= \frac{1}{2} \cdot 5 \cdot 7 \cdot \sin 100°$

$= \frac{1}{2} \cdot 5 \cdot 7 \cdot \sin (180° - 100°)$

$= \frac{1}{2} \cdot 5 \cdot 7 \cdot \sin 80°$

$\approx \frac{35}{2}(0.9848)$

≈ 17.23

Answer The area of triangle ABC is 17 cm² to the nearest square centimeter.

The law of sines can be used to solve triangles in which the given data are:

▶ The measures of two angles and the length of a side.
▶ The lengths of two sides and the measure of an angle opposite one of the sides.

Example 2   Solve triangle XYZ.

Solution   Solve for Z.

$$\frac{\sin 35°}{12} = \frac{\sin Z}{15}$$

$$\frac{15 \sin 35°}{12} = \sin Z$$

$$\frac{15(0.5736)}{12} \approx \sin Z$$

$$\sin Z \approx 0.7170 \quad Z \approx 46° \text{ (to the nearest degree)}$$

Solve for Y. $Y \approx 180° - 35° - 46° = 99°$ (to the nearest degree)

Solve for y.

$$\frac{\sin 35°}{12} = \frac{\sin 99°}{y}$$

$$\sin 99° = \sin(180° - 99°) = \sin 81°$$

$$\frac{\sin 35°}{12} = \frac{\sin 81°}{y}$$

$$y = \frac{12 \sin 81°}{\sin 35°} \approx \frac{12(0.9877)}{0.5736} \approx 21$$

Answer $Z \approx 46°$, $Y \approx 99°$, $y \approx 21$

Example 3   Solve.

First Street and Random Road meet at an angle of 80°. How far apart are two people if one person is on First Street 250 ft from the intersection and the other person is on Random Road 250 ft from the intersection?

Solution   Since the triangle is isosceles, the angles at A and B are both 50° angles.

$$\frac{\sin 80°}{x} = \frac{\sin 50°}{250}$$

$$x = \frac{250 \sin 80°}{\sin 50°}$$

$$x \approx \frac{250(0.9848)}{0.7660} \approx 321$$

Answer   The people are about 321 ft apart to the nearest foot.

𝑒LASSROOM EXERCISES

1. Find the area of triangle ABC if $a = 10$ cm, $b = 14$ cm, and $C = 57°$.

2. Solve for z in this triangle.

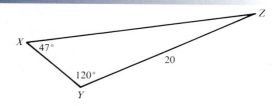

RITTEN EXERCISES

A **Find the area of triangle _ABC._**

1. $b = 10\,\text{m}; c = 7\,\text{m};$
   $A = 15°$

2. $a = 9\,\text{in.}; c = 10\,\text{in.};$
   $B = 160°$

3. $a = 3\,\text{in.}; c = 12\,\text{in.};$
   $B = 150°$

4. $a = 12\,\text{cm}; b = 6\,\text{cm};$
   $C = 90°$

5. $a = 10\,\text{cm}; b = 8\,\text{cm};$
   $C = 90°$

6. $a = 7\,\text{m}; c = 5\,\text{m};$
   $A = 65°; C = 40°$

7. $a = 9\,\text{m}; b = 8.3\,\text{m};$
   $A = 70°; B = 60°$

8. $b = 10\,\text{cm};$
   $c = 10\,\text{cm}; B = 25°;$
   $C = 25°$

Solve the triangle. Use appropriate units for the answers.

9. $a = 2\,\text{cm}; b = 2.1\,\text{cm};$
   $A = 70°$

10. $a = 2\,\text{cm}; b = 2.1\,\text{cm};$
    $B = 70°$

11. $b = 5\,\text{m}; c = 10\,\text{m};$
    $C = 115°$

12. $c = 5\,\text{m}; b = 10\,\text{m};$
    $B = 125°$

13. $b = 7.4\,\text{ft}; A = 120°;$
    $B = 40°$

14. $a = 20\,\text{ft}; A = 120°;$
    $B = 40°$

15. $b = 10\,\text{cm}; A = 80°;$
    $C = 30°$

16. $c = 10\,\text{cm}; A = 75°;$
    $B = 65°$

pplications

Solve.

17. Points _A_ and _C_ are at opposite ends of a lake. Point _B_ is 2.4 km from _A_. The measures of angles _B_ and _C_ are 70° and 30°, respectively. How far is point _A_ from point _C_?

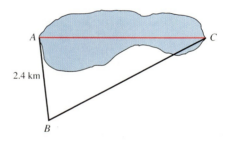

18.

Point _A_ is at the top of a hill, and point _B_ is at the foot of the hill. Point _C_ is 1500 m from _B_ on level ground. Angles _A_ and _B_ are 22° and 15°, respectively. How far is point _A_ from point _B_?

B 19. Points _P_ and _Q_ are at opposite ends of a field. Point _R_ is 1.8 km from _P._ Angles _P_ and _R_ are 102.5° and 48.8°, respectively. How far is _Q_ from _P_?

20. The angle of elevation from point A to point B is 24°. The angle of elevation from point C to point B is 56.5°. Find the length of $\overline{BC}$ if $\overline{AC}$ is 0.8 km long.

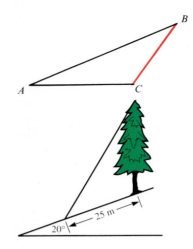

21. A pine tree stands on a 20° slope. From a point 25 m down the slope the angle of elevation to the top of the tree is 60°. How tall is the tree?

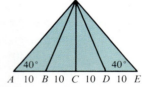

22. In triangle AEF, the measures of angles A and E are 40°. The lengths of segments AB, BC, CD, and DE are each 10 cm.

   a. What is the length of $\overline{AF}$? of $\overline{FE}$?

   b. $\overline{FC}$ is perpendicular to $\overline{AE}$. What is the length of $\overline{FC}$?

   c. What is the measure of angle FBC? of angle AFB?

   d. Do angles AFB, BFC, CFD, and DFE have equal measures?

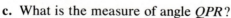

23. In triangle PQU, the measures of angles Q and U are 50°. The length of $\overline{QU}$ is 40 cm. The measures of angles QPR, RPS, SPT, and TPU are equal.

   a. What is the length of $\overline{QP}$? of $\overline{UP}$?

   b. $\overline{PS}$ is perpendicular to $\overline{QU}$. What is the length of $\overline{PS}$?

   c. What is the measure of angle QPR?

   d. What is the measure of $\overline{RS}$? of $\overline{QR}$?

   e. Do segments QR, RS, ST, and TU have equal measure?

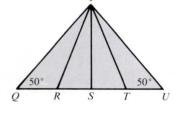

C **24.** In triangle ABC, prove that $\dfrac{\sin A + \sin B}{a + b} = \dfrac{\sin A}{a}$.

25. In triangle ABC, prove that $\dfrac{\sin A - \sin B}{a - b} = \dfrac{\sin C}{c}$.

26. If θ is a central angle expressed in radians, show that the shaded area in the figure is given by the formula

$$\frac{1}{2}r^2(\theta - \sin \theta).$$

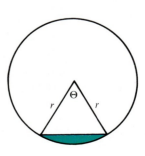

REVIEW EXERCISES

1. If $\log_{10} 3 \approx 0.4771$, find $\log_{10} 900$. [11-4]

2. Solve $5^x = 100$. Write the solution using logarithms. (If a calculator is available, simplify the solution.) [11-6]

3. For how many years must $1000 be invested at 15% compounded annually before the value of the investment is $4000? [11-6]

4. Solve: $\log_2 (x - 2) = 3$.

5. Solve for a: $\log a + \log b = c$. [11-7]

6. Use the formula $A = Pe^{rt}$ to express the value of $500 invested at 15% for 6 years compounded instantaneously. [11-8]

7. After 30 years, 100 g remain from 400 g of a substance. Use the formula $N = N_0e^{-kt}$ to find the value of k. [11-8]

EXTENSION   Perpendicular Components of Vectors

A quantity, such as a force or a velocity, that has both magnitude and direction can be represented graphically by an arrow or *vector*. For example, suppose a child pulls a wagon with a force of 40 newtons and the wagon handle makes an angle of 30° above the horizontal. The diagram on the right shows how this force is represented as a vector. The vertical component of the force is 40 · sin 30° newtons (or $40 \cdot \dfrac{1}{2}$ or 20 newtons). The horizontal component of the vector is 40 · cos 30° newtons.

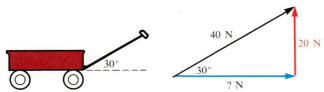

1. In the example above, what is the force (to the nearest whole newton) pulling the wagon horizontally?

2. A box is being dragged across a floor with a rope making an angle of 45° with the floor. If the force on the rope is 100 newtons (N), what force is actually pulling the box horizontally across the floor?

3. A plane flies at 500 miles per hour in a direction 70° east of north. At what rate is the plane moving (a) to the north? (b) to the east?

4. The tension on a waterski rope is 200 N when the skier is directly behind the boat. What will be the tension when the skier swings out so that the rope makes an angle of 60° with the direction line of the boat?

LESSON 17-4

Solving Triangles—Special Cases

Three pieces of information do not always define just one triangle. For example,

▸ It has sides of 2 cm, 5 cm, and 9 cm.
▸ It has angles of 30°, 60°, and 90°.
▸ It has sides of 4 in. and 5 in., and an angle of 30° opposite the shorter side.

Attempts to construct the triangles above would result in no solutions, infinitely many solutions, and two solutions, respectively.

Consider this problem: Given $A = 40°$, $a = 3$, and $b = 12$, solve the triangle.
Using the law of sines gives:
$$\frac{\sin 40°}{3} = \frac{\sin B}{12}$$
$$\sin B = 4 \sin 40° \approx 4(0.6428) \approx 2.57$$

Since 2.57 is not in the range of the sine function, the equation has no solution. This means that there is no triangle that satisfies the conditions of the problem. A figure shows the reason.

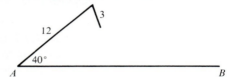

In solving triangles in which two sides and the angle opposite one of those sides are given, there may be no solutions, one solution, or two solutions. Before solving the problem, draw a figure to determine how many solutions exist. The figure's sides should be close to scale and the figure's angles close to actual size.

Example 1 Solve triangle ABC given $A = 42°$, $a = 8$, and $c = 10$.

Solution Find $c \sin A$.

The product $c \sin A$ is the value of the altitude of the right triangle with $A = 42°$ and $c = 10$. If this value is more than a, there is no solution. If this value is equal to a, there is one solution. If this value is less than a, there may be two solutions.

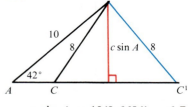

$$c \sin A \approx 10(0.6691) \approx 6.7$$

The drawing shows that there are two solutions for C.

$$\frac{\sin C}{10} = \frac{\sin 42°}{8}$$

$$\sin C \approx \frac{10(0.6691)}{8} \approx 0.8364$$

$$C \approx 57° \quad \text{or} \quad C \approx 123°$$

Example 1 (continued)

Solve for B. $B \approx 180° - 42° - 57° = 81°$

   $\text{or } B \approx 180° - 42° - 123° = 15°$

Solve for b. $b = \dfrac{10 \sin 81°}{\sin 57°}$ or $b = \dfrac{10 \sin 15°}{\sin 123°}$

   $b \approx 12$ $\qquad\qquad b \approx 3$

Answer   One solution is $C \approx 57°$, $B \approx 81°$, and $b \approx 12$. The other solution is $C \approx 123°$, $B \approx 15°$, and $b \approx 3$.

Example 2   **Solve.**

A large tree was partially blown down in a heavy windstorm. To keep the tree from falling further, an 18-m cable was attached to it 12 m from its base and to a steel stake in the ground. The cable makes a 40° angle with the ground. How far is the stake from the base of the tree?

Solution   A drawing shows that there are two triangles with the given conditions. However, the physical situation requires that triangle ABC must have an obtuse angle at C.

Solve for C. $\dfrac{\sin A}{a} = \dfrac{\sin C}{c}$

   $\dfrac{\sin 40°}{12} = \dfrac{\sin C}{18}$

   $\sin C = \dfrac{3}{2} \sin 40°$

   $\sin C \approx 1.5(0.6428)$

   $\sin C \approx 0.9642$

   $C \approx 105°$

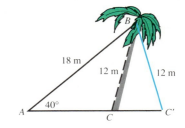

Solve for B. $B = 180° - 105° - 40° = 35°$

Solve for b. $b = \dfrac{12 \sin B}{\sin A} \approx \dfrac{12(0.5736)}{0.6428} \approx 11$

Answer   The stake is about 11 m from the base of the tree.

*C*LASSROOM EXERCISES

Draw a figure and state the number of solutions.

1. $A = 120°$, $a = 12$, $b = 12$
2. $A = 40°$, $a = 9$, $b = 10$
3. $A = 30°$, $a = 6$, $b = 12$
4. $A = 65°$, $a = 14$, $b = 15$

RITTEN EXERCISES

A Solve the triangle. There may be no solution, one solution, or two solutions.

1. In triangle ABC, $A = 130°$, $a = 10$, $b = 6$.

2. In triangle DEF, $D = 140°$, $d = 20$, $e = 18$.

3. In triangle JKL, $J = 20°$, $j = 10$, $k = 100$.

4. In triangle LMN, $L = 10°$, $l = 10$, $m = 50$.

5. In triangle BMW, $B = 30°$, $b = 7$, $m = 9$.

6. In triangle AMC, $C = 40°$, $c = 8$, $a = 10$.

In triangle ABC, find the desired angle or side.

7. $A = 22°$; $a = 10$; $b = 15$.
   Find B.

8. $B = 34°$; $b = 10$; $a = 12$.
   Find A.

9. $C = 15.5°$; $c = 20$; $b = 30$.
   Find A.

10. $A = 18.5°$; $a = 20$; $c = 25$.
    Find B.

11. $B = 24.3°$; $b = 30$; $a = 40$.
    Find c.

12. $B = 28.7°$; $b = 30$; $a = 50$.
    Find c.

B Draw a figure and state the number of solutions.

13. $A = 30°$; $a = 15$; $b = 20$

14. $A = 30°$; $a = 20$; $b = 20$

15. $A = 30°$; $a = 30$; $b = 20$

16. $A = 30°$; $a = 100$; $b = 20$

Solve the triangle.

17. In triangle PQR, $P = 80°$, $p = 30$, $q = 27$. 18. In triangle RST, $R = 15°$, $s = 80$, $r = 100$.

19. In triangle BCD, side b is 6 cm and side d is 8 cm. The sine of angle B is $\frac{3}{4}$.
    a. What is the measure of angle D?
    b. What is the length of side c?

20. In triangle KLM, side k is 8 cm and side m is 12 cm. The sine of angle K is $\frac{2}{3}$.

    a. What is the measure of angle M?
    b. What is the length of side l?

pplications

Solve.

21. From the top of a tower T, the angle of depression to point B is 20.8° and the angle of depression to point A is 31.2°. Points A and B are 100 m apart.

    a. How far is A from T?
    b. What is the height of the tower?
    c. How far is A from the base of the tower?

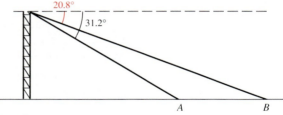

22. From the top of tower *T*, the angle of depression to point *B* is 20.8° and the angle of depression to point *A* is 31.2°. Points *A* and *B* are 100 m apart.

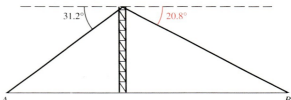

a. How far is *A* from *T*?

b. What is the height of the tower?

c. How far is *A* from the base of the tower?

 23. In triangle *ABC*, *A* = 52°, *b* = 48, and there are two solutions for the triangle. For what values of *a* is this possible?

24. In triangle *RST*, *R* = 50° and *r* = 100.

    a. What is the maximum value of *s* if the triangle exists?

    b. What is the minimum value of *s* if *S* is an obtuse angle?

    c. What is the maximum value of *s* if *S* is an obtuse angle?

EVIEW EXERCISES

Write the first three terms of each sequence defined below. [12-1]

1. $t_n = n^3 - 1$ **2.** $t_n = 10^{2-n}$

3. State whether the sequence defined by $t_n = 2n + 5$ is an arithmetic sequence. [12-1]

4. State the 20th term of the arithmetic sequence 50, 54, 58, 62, ... [12-1]

5. Write the fourth term of the geometric sequence defined by [12-2]

$a_n = 1024\left(\frac{1}{2}\right)^n.$

6. State the geometric mean of 2 and 32. [12-2]

7. Write the series $1 + 3 + 5 + \cdots + 15$ in Σ notation. [12-3]

$\mathcal{S}$elf-Quiz 2

17-3   **1.** Find the area of the triangular sail shown.

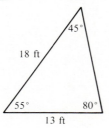

2. Solve triangle *ABC*, given $A = 41°$, $C = 73°$, $c = 8$.

3. Show that the law of sines gives the same value for *x* as the tangent function applied to the right triangle shown here.

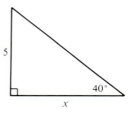

17-4   Solve the triangle, if possible. Write "none" if there is no solution. If there are two solutions, give both.

4. In triangle *RST*, $R = 52°$, $s = 7$, $r = 8$.

5. In triangle *KLM*, $M = 75°$, $l = 11$, $m = 9$.

$\mathcal{C}$ALCULATOR EXTENSION   Evaluating Sines

The value of sin *x* can be found to any degree of precision by the following infinite series:

$$\sin x = x - \frac{x^3}{3!} + \frac{x^5}{5!} - \frac{x^7}{7!} + \cdots .$$

Use the series above and a calculator to compute

$$\sin \frac{\pi}{6}$$

to six decimal places. Check your answer by using the sin key on your calculator. [*Note:* Study your calculator manual to find how the calculator is programmed to compute values of sin *x* or factorials.]

LESSON 17-5

The Law of Cosines

If angle C is a right angle, then $c^2 = a^2 + b^2$.

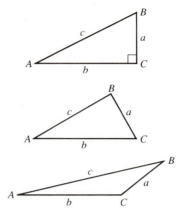

However, if angle C is an acute angle, then c^2 is less than $a^2 + b^2$. How much less depends on the measure of angle C and on the lengths of a and b.

If angle C is an obtuse angle, then c^2 is greater than $a^2 + b^2$.

Suppose that side a, side b, and angle C are given for triangle ABC. If angle C is a right angle, the triangle can be solved using the Pythagorean theorem and the trigonometric functions.

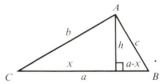

Let angle C be an acute angle. Then $c^2 = h^2 + (a - x)^2$.

But $h = b \sin C$ and $x = b \cos C$.

Therefore,
$$c^2 = (b \sin C)^2 + (a - b \cos C)^2$$
$$= b^2 \sin^2 C + a^2 - 2ab \cos C + b^2 \cos^2 C$$
$$= b^2(\sin^2 C + \cos^2 C) + a^2 - 2ab \cos C.$$

Since $\sin^2 C + \cos^2 C = 1$, $c^2 = a^2 + b^2 - 2ab \cos C$.

Similar arguments show that: $\quad a^2 = b^2 + c^2 - 2bc \cos A$ and
$$b^2 = a^2 + c^2 - 2ac \cos B.$$

The same result is obtained if C is an obtuse angle.

Law of Cosines

For any triangle ABC where A, B, and C are the measures of angles A, B, and C, respectively, and a, b, and c are the measures of the sides opposite angles A, B, and C, respectively,

$a^2 = b^2 + c^2 - 2bc \cos A \qquad b^2 = a^2 + c^2 - 2ac \cos B$
$c^2 = a^2 + b^2 - 2ab \cos C$

The law of cosines can be used to solve triangles in which the given data are:

▶ The lengths of three sides.

▶ The lengths of two sides and the measure of the included angle.

Tables of trigonometric functions contain values for angles from 0° to 90°. If the cosine of an angle greater than 90° is required, the following formulas from Chapter 16 can be used.

$$\cos(180° - θ) = -\cos θ \qquad \cos(90° + θ) = -\sin θ$$

Example 1   **In triangle XYZ, find the length of side ZY.**

Solution   *Use the law of cosines.*

$$x^2 = 5^2 + 15^2 - 2 \cdot 5 \cdot 15 \cdot \cos 130°$$
$$= 25 + 225 - 150 \cos 130°$$
$$= 250 - 150 \cos(180° - 50°)$$
$$= 250 - 150(-\cos 50°)$$
$$\approx 250 - 150(-0.6428)$$
$$\approx 346.42$$
$$x \approx 18.6$$

Answer   The length of side ZY is about 18.6.

Example 2   **Solve triangle XYZ.**

Solution   *Use the law of cosines to find X.*

$$11^2 = 8^2 + 15^2 - 2(8)(15)(\cos X)$$
$$121 = 64 + 225 - 240 \cos X$$
$$\cos X = 0.7000$$
$$X \approx 45.6° \text{ (to the nearest tenth degree)}$$

Use the law of sines to solve for Y.

$$\frac{\sin Y}{8} \approx \frac{\sin 45.6°}{11}$$

$$\sin Y \approx \frac{8 \sin 45.6°}{11}$$

$$\approx 0.5196$$

$$Y \approx 31.3° \text{ (to the nearest tenth degree)}$$

Solve for Z.

$$Z \approx 180° - 45.6° - 31.3° = 103.1° \text{ (to the nearest tenth degree)}$$

Answer $X \approx 46°$, $Y \approx 31°$, and $Z \approx 103°$ (to the nearest degree)

CLASSROOM EXERCISES

1. Find c to the nearest tenth unit.

2. Find B to the nearest tenth degree.

WRITTEN EXERCISES

A In triangle ABC, sides a, b, and c are opposite angles A, B, and C, respectively. Find the side or angle measure.

1. $b = 10$; $c = 20$; $A = 30°$. Find a.

2. $b = 30$; $c = 40$; $A = 50°$. Find a.

3. $a = 25$; $b = 20$; $C = 80°$. Find c.

4. $a = 35$; $b = 60$; $C = 75°$. Find c.

5. $a = 6$; $c = 8$; $B = 150°$. Find b.

6. $a = 4$; $c = 6$; $B = 165°$. Find b.

7. $a = 5$; $b = 6$; $c = 7$. Find A.

8. $a = 6$; $b = 7$; $c = 8$. Find A.

9. $a = 12$; $b = 5$; $c = 13$. Find C.

10. $a = 15$; $b = 8$; $c = 17$. Find C.

11. $a = 5$; $b = 6$; $c = 10$. Find B.

12. $a = 8$; $b = 4$; $c = 10$. Find B.

Find the side measure.

13. In triangle DEF, $d = 4$, $e = 3$, $\cos F = \dfrac{5}{6}$. Find f.

14. In triangle FGH, $f = 5$, $g = 6$, $\cos H = \dfrac{7}{15}$. Find h.

15. In triangle JKL, $j = 4$, $k = 3$, $\cos L = -\dfrac{5}{6}$. Find l.

16. In triangle LMN, $l = 5$, $m = 6$, $\cos N = -\dfrac{7}{15}$. Find n.

17. In triangle PQR, $p = 5$, $q = 10$, $\cos R = 0$. Find r.

18. In triangle RST, $r = 3$, $s = 6$, $\cos T = 0$. Find t.

Find the cosine of each angle in the given triangle.

19. In triangle WXY, $w = 2$, $x = 3$, $y = 4$.

20. In triangle ACE, $a = 8$, $c = 7$, $e = 12$.

21. In triangle BDF, $b = 10$, $d = 10$, $f = 12$.

22. In triangle HJL, $h = 29$, $j = 21$, $l = 20$.

23. In triangle KMP, $k = 40$, $m = 41$, $p = 9$.

24. In triangle NQT, $n = 6$, $q = 8$, $t = 6$.

B Use the law of sines or the law of cosines to find the side measure.

25. In triangle BAM, $B = 100°$, $A = 50°$, $b = 10$. Find m.

26. In triangle ALR, $A = 40°$, $l = 2$, $r = 1$. Find a.

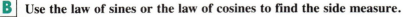

𝒜pplications

Solve.

27. The lengths of adjacent sides of a parallelogram are 6 cm and 8 cm. The length of a diagonal is 12 cm.

    a. What are the measures of the angles of the parallelogram?

    b. What is the length of the other diagonal?

28. The lengths of adjacent sides of a parallelogram are 4 cm and 8 cm. The length of a diagonal is 6 cm.

    a. What are the measures of the angles of the parallelogram?

    b. What is the length of the other diagonal?

29. The adjacent sides of a parallelogram are 5 cm and 10 cm, and they form an angle of 60°.

    a. What are the lengths of the diagonals of the parallelogram?

    b. What is the area of the parallelogram?

30. Points A and B are 60 ft apart on the bank of a river. Point P is on the opposite bank.

    a. How far is A from P?

    b. How far is B from P?

    c. What is the width of the river?

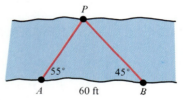

31. One ship leaves port on a heading of 10.5°, and another ship leaves on a heading of 123.8°. When one ship has gone 550 km, the other has gone 800 km. How far apart are the two ships at that time?

32. A regular pentagon with a perimeter of 60 cm is inscribed in a circle. What is the radius of the circle?

33. A regular octagon is inscribed in a circle with a radius of 10 cm. What is the perimeter of the octagon?

C 34. Two airplanes at different altitudes fly over a radio beacon at the same time. One is flying on a course of 82° at 700 km/h. The other is on a course of 222° at 500 km/h. How far apart are the two planes one-half hour later?

35. An airplane on a course of 325° flies 600 km/h over a navigational marker at 12:30 P.M. At 1:00 P.M. another plane at the same altitude flies 400 km/h over the marker on a course of 15°. At 1:30 P.M., how far apart will the planes be if they maintain their courses and speeds?

36. Derive the law of cosines for an obtuse angle C in triangle ABC.

𝓡EVIEW EXERCISES

1. Find the value of S_{10} for the sequence 10, 15, 20, 25, . . .   [12-4]

2. An arithmetic series consisting of 21 terms has a first term of 20 and a last term of 80. Find the value of the series.   [12-4]

3. Find the value of $\sum_{k=1}^{10} 4(k + 1)$. [12-4]

4. For the sequence $9, 3, 1, \frac{1}{3}, \ldots$, express S_9 in exponential notation. [12-5]

5. Find $\sum_{k=1}^{8} 3(0.1)^k$. [12-5]

6. Find the value of the infinite series $1 + \frac{1}{3} + \frac{1}{9} + \frac{1}{27} + \cdots$. [12-6]

$\mathcal{E}$XTENSION Finding the Sum of Two Vectors

The following example illustrates how the laws of cosines and sines can be used to find the *resultant* or *sum* of two vectors. Suppose a ship in the Atlantic steams to the east at a speed of 20 knots through the water, crossing the Gulf Stream, which is flowing in a northeasterly direction at a rate of 5 knots. In the diagram the tail of the current vector is placed at the tip of the ship's velocity vector. The sum of those two vectors is the resultant velocity vector of the ship, represented by the dashed arrow.

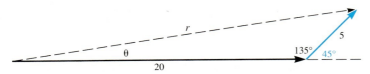

The length r of the resultant vector can be computed using the law of cosines.

$$r^2 = 5^2 + 20^2 - 2 \cdot 5 \cdot 20 \cdot \cos 135° \approx 25 + 400 - 200 \cdot (-0.707)$$
$$\approx 425 + 141 = 566$$
$$r \approx \sqrt{566} \approx 23.8$$

Then the angle θ can be computed using the law of sines.

$$\frac{\sin \theta}{5} = \frac{\sin 135°}{17} \quad \text{So, } \sin \theta \approx \frac{(5 \cdot 0.707)}{17} \approx 0.2079 \text{ and } \theta \approx 12°$$

Therefore, the resultant velocity of the ship is 23.8 knots in a direction 12° north of east.

When the vectors are perpendicular, the problem simplifies to one involving the Pythagorean theorem and trigonometric ratios.

1. If a plane flies north at a speed of 120 miles per hour in a 50-mile-per-hour crosswind from the West, what are its ground speed and direction?

2. An object is acted on by a 100-newton force in an easterly direction and a 50-newton force in a direction 30° west of north. Compute the magnitude and direction of the resultant force.

$\mathcal{C}$HAPTER SUMMARY

▶ **Vocabulary**

▶ The trigonometric values are defined as follows: [17-1]

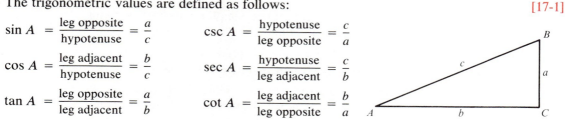

$$\sin A = \frac{\text{leg opposite}}{\text{hypotenuse}} = \frac{a}{c} \qquad \csc A = \frac{\text{hypotenuse}}{\text{leg opposite}} = \frac{c}{a}$$

$$\cos A = \frac{\text{leg adjacent}}{\text{hypotenuse}} = \frac{b}{c} \qquad \sec A = \frac{\text{hypotenuse}}{\text{leg adjacent}} = \frac{c}{b}$$

$$\tan A = \frac{\text{leg opposite}}{\text{leg adjacent}} = \frac{a}{b} \qquad \cot A = \frac{\text{leg adjacent}}{\text{leg opposite}} = \frac{b}{a}$$

▶ If f and g are trigonometric cofunctions and θ is the degree measure of an acute angle, then $f(\theta) = g(90° - \theta)$.   [17-1]

▶ Finding the unknown measures of a triangle is called *solving the triangle*.   [17-2]

▶ Area of a triangle   [17-3]

    For any triangle ABC, the area is one half the product of any two sides multiplied by the sine of the included angle.

▶ Law of sines   [17-3]

    For any triangle ABC, where a, b, and c are the lengths of the sides opposite angles A, B, and C, respectively,

$$\frac{\sin A}{a} = \frac{\sin B}{b} = \frac{\sin C}{c}.$$

▶ The lengths of the sides of a triangle are proportional to the sines of the measures of the opposite angles.   [17-3]

▶ Law of cosines   [17-5]

For any triangle ABC, where A, B, and C are the measures of angles A, B, and C, respectively, and a, b, and c are the measures of the sides opposite angles A, B, and C, respectively,

$$a^2 = b^2 + c^2 - 2bc \cos A$$
$$b^2 = a^2 + c^2 - 2ac \cos B$$
$$c^2 = a^2 + b^2 - 2ab \cos C$$

$\mathcal{C}$HAPTER REVIEW

17-1   **Objective:** To evaluate the six trigonometric functions as defined for the angles of a right triangle.

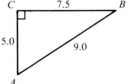

  1. Write the six trigonometric ratios for angle A in lowest terms.

  2. Use a calculator or the tables on pages 771–775 to evaluate these expressions.

    a. $\sin 81°$ **b.** $\cos 19.8°$ **c.** $\tan 36.5°$

  3. Find the angle θ to the nearest tenth degree that satisfies each expression, $0° < \theta < 90°$.

    a. $\tan \theta = 0.4417$ **b.** $\sin \theta = 0.8870$

17-2 Objective: To solve right triangles.

Use the given information to determine the measure of the indicated angle or side of triangle PQR, $R = 90°$.

4. $P = 23°$; $q = 5$.   **5.** $Q = 47°$; $r = 8$.   **6.** $p = 7$; $q = 3$.
Find r.   Find q.   Find Q.

7. Express side b of right triangle ABC as the product of a and a trigonometric function of angle B.

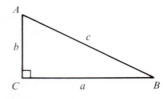

8. To determine the height of the cloud cover, an airport searchlight is trained vertically on the clouds above the airport. From a distance of 3000 ft, the angle of elevation to the point illuminated by the searchlight is 25°. Find the height of the cloud cover to the nearest 100 ft.

17-3 Objective: To apply the law of sines to solve any triangle.

9. Find the area of triangle KLM.

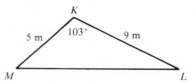

10. To the nearest tenth degree, find angle A of triangle ABC if $a = 4$, $b = 3$, and $B = 36°$.

11. Two forest rangers in fire towers at points A and B spot a fire at point C, noting angles A and B, respectively. If the fire towers are 1.5 km apart, how far is the fire from the tower at A?

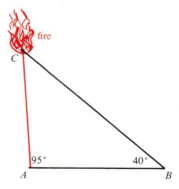

17-4 Objective: To solve triangles in which applications of the law of sines can result in two, one, or no solutions.

Solve the triangle, if possible. If there is no solution, write "none." If there are two solutions, list both.

12. In triangle PQR, $P = 60°$, $p = 10$, $q = 14$.

13. In triangle XYZ, $Y = 37°$, $y = 16$, $z = 21$.

17-5 Objective: To apply the law of cosines to solve triangles.

14. In triangle *KLM,* find *L* if $k = 5$, $l = 7$, and $m = 6$.

15. A regular pentagon with 10-in. sides is inscribed in a circle of radius *r.* Use the law of cosines to find *r.*

$\mathcal{C}$HAPTER 17 SELF-TEST

17-1 Identify the trigonometric function of angle *B* equal to the given ratio.

1. $\dfrac{3}{5}$ **2.** $\dfrac{5}{4}$

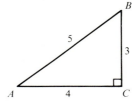

Use the tables on pages 771–775 to find the value of each expression.

3. tan 71°   **4.** cos 19.3°

5. Given $\sin\theta = 0.7716$ and $0° < \theta < 90°$, find θ.

17-2 Given right triangle *ABC*.

6. Find *c.*

7. Find *a.*

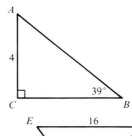

Given right triangle *EFG*.

8. Find angle *F*.

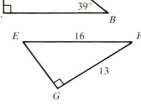

Solve.

9. The angle of elevation from the top of a building to the top of a nearby tower is 32°. The building is 110 ft high and the tower is 800 ft from the base of the building. How high is the tower from the ground?

10. A 14-in. long brace is used to support an 8-in. wide shelf. Find the angle that the brace makes with the wall.

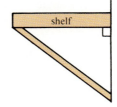

17-3 **11.** Find the area of triangle PQR if $p = 5$, $q = 8$, and $R = 74°$.

12. Given triangle DEF, write an expression for side e in terms of the given information. (Do not solve.)

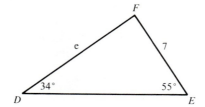

17-4 **Find the measure of the angle if possible. Write "none" if there is no solution. Find all solutions.**

13. For triangle MNP, $m = 12$, $n = 11.5$, $N = 110°$. Find angle M.

14. For triangle ABC, $b = 8$, $c = 6$, $C = 45°$. Find angle B.

17-5 **15.** Find side c of triangle ABC given $a = 5$, $b = 4$, $C = 35°$.

16. Two adjacent sides of a parallelogram are 6 cm and 10 cm. If the included angle is 120°, find the length of the longer diagonal.

*P*RACTICE FOR COLLEGE ENTRANCE TESTS

Choose the best answer.

1. In the right triangle in the figure, the cosine of angle B is __?__.

 A. $\dfrac{3}{5}$ **B.** $\dfrac{3}{4}$ **C.** $\dfrac{4}{5}$

 D. $\dfrac{5}{4}$ **E.** $\dfrac{5}{3}$

2. In triangle ABC, $AB = BC = DC$. The measure of angle A is 70°. What is the measure of angle ABD?

 A. 75°   **B.** 80°   **C.** 85°

 D. 90°   **E.** 95°

3. In triangle PQR, if the tangent of angle Q is $\dfrac{4}{3}$ and $PQ = 24$, then $RQ = $ __?__.

 A. 27   **B.** 30   **C.** 32   **D.** 36   **E.** 40

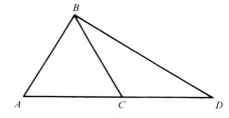

4. In triangle PQR, the sine of angle R is equal to ___?___.

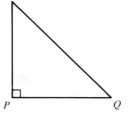

I. $\dfrac{PQ}{RQ}$ II. $\dfrac{RP}{RQ}$ III. The cosine of angle Q

A. I only   **B.** II only   **C.** III only
D. I and III   **E.** II and III

5. $1 - \cos^2 x - \sin^2 x = $ ___?___.
   A. -2 **B.** -1 **C.** 0 **D.** 1 **E.** 2

6. What angle does the line $y = 4 - x$ make with the x-axis?
   A. $30°$ **B.** $45°$ **C.** $60°$ **D.** $120°$ **E.** $145°$

7. If AB is a diameter of the circle and $\tan A = \dfrac{5}{12}$, then $\cos A = $ ___?___.

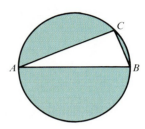

   A. $\dfrac{5}{13}$ **B.** $\dfrac{7}{12}$ **C.** $\dfrac{12}{17}$

   D. $\dfrac{12}{13}$ **E.** $\dfrac{13}{17}$

8. If $\sin x = \sin (x + 90°)$, and $0° \leq x \leq 90°$, then $x = $ ___?___.
   A. $30°$ **B.** $45°$ **C.** $60°$ **D.** $75°$ **E.** $90°$

9. When $90° < x < 180°$, which of the following could possibly be $\cos x$?
   A. -1 **B.** $-\dfrac{1}{2}$ **C.** 0 **D.** $\dfrac{1}{2}$ **E.** 1

10. If a diagonal of a rectangle is twice the width, what is the measure of the acute angle formed by the intersection of two diagonals?
   A. $30°$ **B.** $40°$ **C.** $45°$ **D.** $50°$ **E.** $60°$

11. If $0° \leq x \leq 90°$ and $\sin x \leq \cos x$, then ___?___.
   A. $0° \leq x \leq 30°$ **B.** $0° \leq x \leq 45°$ **C.** $0° \leq x \leq 60°$
   D. $30° \leq x \leq 90°$ **E.** $45° \leq x \leq 90°$

12. In the figure at the right, the square is inscribed in the circle, which has a radius of 1. What is the area of the shaded region between the square and the circle?

   A. $\pi - 2$ **B.** $\pi - \sqrt{2}$ **C.** $\pi - 2\sqrt{2}$
   D. $2\pi - 4$ **E.** $2\pi - 2\sqrt{2}$

CHAPTER 18

Trigonometric Identities and Equations

Radio emissions from space and orbits of celestial bodies are examples of periodic phenomena that can be represented mathematically as the sum of a series of sine and cosine functions. If f is a continuous periodic function, then constants A_i and B_i can be found so that approximations to $f(x)$ can be computed from the equation:

$$f(x) \approx A_0 + (A_1 \cos x + B_1 \sin x) + (A_2 \cos 2x + B_2 \cos 2x) + \cdots$$

This branch of mathematics is known as Fourier analysis, named for a French mathematician who was a friend of Napoleon.

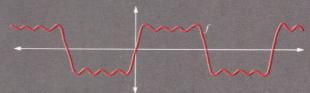

LESSON 18-1

Proving Identities

Consider the relationship of the graph of the sum of two functions to the graphs of the individual functions.

For example, consider the graphs of $f(X) = \sin^2 X$ and $g(X) = \cos^2 X$, where X is an angle measure. The graphs are congruent to each other and are periodic, each with period 360°.

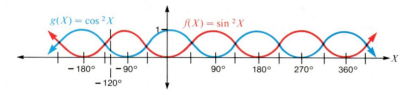

To obtain the graph of $h(X) = \sin^2 X + \cos^2 X$, we can add the second coordinate values that correspond to $f(X)$ and $g(X)$ for any particular degree measure X.

For example, for $X = -120°$, $f(-120°) = (\sin(-120°))^2 = \left(-\dfrac{\sqrt{3}}{2}\right)^2 = \dfrac{3}{4}$,

$$g(-120°) = (\cos(-120°))^2 = \left(-\dfrac{1}{2}\right)^2 = \dfrac{1}{4}.$$

$$\text{Thus, } h(-120°) = \dfrac{3}{4} + \dfrac{1}{4} = 1.$$

For $-180°$, $-90°$, $0°$, $90°$, $180°$, etc., the values of $\sin^2 X$ and $\cos^2 X$ are 0 or 1 and their sum is always 1. It appears that the graph of $h(X)$ is the horizontal line $h(X) = 1$.

An equation that is true for all elements of its domain is called an **identity.** For example, $2x + 3x = 5x$ and $aa = a^2$ are algebraic identities over the set of complex numbers. There are eight **basic trigonometric identities.**

Basic Trigonometric Identities

For all angle measures X for which the functions are defined,

1. $\tan X = \dfrac{\sin X}{\cos X}$ 2. $\cot X = \dfrac{\cos X}{\sin X}$ 3. $\sec X = \dfrac{1}{\cos X}$

4. $\csc X = \dfrac{1}{\sin X}$ 5. $\cot X = \dfrac{1}{\tan X}$ 6. $\sin^2 X + \cos^2 X = 1$

7. $1 + \tan^2 X = \sec^2 X$ 8. $1 + \cot^2 X = \csc^2 X$

Is the following equation an identity for all admissible angle measures X?

$$\tan X + \cot X = \sec X \csc X$$

One way to prove that $\tan X + \cot X = \sec X \csc X$ is an identity is to use known identities to transform one side of the equation into the other side.

Start with one side of the identity in question.	$\tan X + \cot X$
Substitute $\dfrac{\sin X}{\cos X}$ for $\tan X$ and $\dfrac{\cos X}{\sin X}$ for $\cot X$.	$= \dfrac{\sin X}{\cos X} + \dfrac{\cos X}{\sin X}$
Simplify the sum.	$= \dfrac{\sin^2 X + \cos^2 X}{\cos X \sin X}$
Substitute 1 for $\sin^2 X + \cos^2 X$.	$= \dfrac{1}{\cos X \sin X}$
Factor.	$= \dfrac{1}{\cos X} \cdot \dfrac{1}{\sin X}$
Substitute $\sec X$ for $\dfrac{1}{\cos X}$ and $\csc X$ for $\dfrac{1}{\sin X}$.	$= \sec X \csc X$

Since the left side of the identity in question has been transformed into the right side, the identity is proved.

Steps for Proving Identities

▶ Start with one side of the identity in question.

▶ Make substitutions using known trigonometric identities.

▶ Simplify sums, differences, products, and quotients.

▶ The proof is complete when the other side of the identity in question is derived.

Example   Prove that $\sin X \tan X = \sec X - \cos X$ is an identity.

Solution

Start with one side of the identity in question.	$\sec X - \cos X$
Substitute $\dfrac{1}{\cos X}$ for $\sec X$.	$= \dfrac{1}{\cos X} - \cos X$
Simplify the difference.	$= \dfrac{1 - \cos^2 X}{\cos X}$
Substitute $\sin^2 X$ for $1 - \cos^2 X$.	$= \dfrac{\sin^2 X}{\cos X}$
Factor.	$= \sin X \cdot \dfrac{\sin X}{\cos X}$
Substitute $\tan X$ for $\dfrac{\sin X}{\cos X}$.	$= \sin X \cdot \tan X$

Since one side of the equation in question was transformed into the other, the identity is proved.

CLASSROOM EXERCISES

Prove that each equation is an identity for all admissible values.

1. $\csc X - \sin X = \cos X \cot X$

2. $\dfrac{\sin X}{1 - \cos X} = \dfrac{1 + \cos X}{\sin X}$

WRITTEN EXERCISES

A **Prove that each equation is an identity for all admissible values.**

1. $\tan X + \dfrac{\sin X}{\cos X} = 2 \tan X$

2. $\dfrac{\cos X}{\sin X} + \cot X = \dfrac{2 \cos X}{\sin X}$

3. $(\sin X + \cos X)^2 = 1 + 2 \sin X \cos X$

4. $(\sin X - \cos X)^2 = 1 - 2 \sin X \cos X$

5. $\sin X (\csc X - \sin X) = \cos^2 X$

6. $\cos X(\sec X - \cos X) = \sin^2 X$

7. $\dfrac{1 + \cot^2 X}{1 + \tan^2 X} = \cot^2 X$

8. $\dfrac{1 + \tan^2 X}{1 + \cot^2 X} = \tan^2 X$

9. $\sin^2 X = 1 - \dfrac{1}{\sec^2 X}$

10. $\cos^2 X = 1 - \dfrac{1}{\csc^2 X}$

11. $\sin X \csc X - \cos^2 X = \sin^2 X$

12. $\cos X \sec X - \sin^2 X = \cos^2 X$

13. $\dfrac{\sin^2 X}{\csc X} + \dfrac{\cos^2 X}{\csc X} = \sin X$

14. $\dfrac{\cos^2 X}{\sec X} + \dfrac{\sin^2 X}{\sec X} = \cos X$

15. $\tan X \cos X = \sin X$

16. $\cot X \sin X = \cos X$

17. $\tan X(\cot X + \tan X) = \sec^2 X$

18. $\cot X(\tan X + \cot X) = \csc^2 X$

B **19.** $\dfrac{\cos X}{1 - \sin X} + \dfrac{\cos X}{1 + \sin X} = 2 \sec X$

20. $\dfrac{\sin X}{1 + \cos X} + \dfrac{\sin X}{1 - \cos X} = 2 \csc X$

21. $\sin X \cos X \tan X = 1 - \cos^2 X$

22. $\sin X \cos X \tan X \cot X \sec X \csc X = 1$

23. $\sec X \cos X + \dfrac{\tan X}{\cot X} = \sec^2 X$

24. $\sin X \cot X \csc X = \dfrac{1}{\tan X}$

C **25.** $\dfrac{\sin X}{1 - \csc X} - \dfrac{\sin X}{1 + \csc X} = -2 \cot^2 X$

26. $\dfrac{\sin X}{\csc X} + \dfrac{\cos X}{\sec X} + \dfrac{\tan X}{\cot X} = \sec^2 X$

REVIEW EXERCISES

1. If $f(x) = x^4 - x^2 + 2x - 4$, use synthetic substitution to evaluate $f(2)$. [10-1]

2. Use synthetic division to determine the quotient and remainder when $x^3 - 6x^2 - 2x + 12$ is divided by $x + 1$. [10-2]

3. Write an equation in standard form that has 0 as a root, -1 as a root with multiplicity two, and no other roots. [10-3]

4. Sketch the graph of a third degree function f such that $f(0) = 2$ and the roots of $f(x) = 0$ are -1, 1, and 3. [10-4]

5. Write the equation that defines the inverse function of $f(x) = \dfrac{x - 5}{2}$. [10-5]

Cosine of a Sum or Difference

To test whether the circular functions are distributive over sums and differences, we can check an example.

$$\cos(30° + 60°) \overset{?}{=} \cos 30° + \cos 60°$$

$$\cos 90° \overset{?}{=} \cos 30° + \cos 60°$$

$$0 \overset{?}{=} \frac{\sqrt{3}}{2} + \frac{1}{2}$$

This counterexample shows that, in general, the cosine and other circular functions are not distributive over sums and differences. That is, for most angles X and Y,

$$\cos(X - Y) \neq \cos X - \cos Y.$$

However, a formula can be derived for the cosine of a difference. Consider angles X and Y and their difference, $X - Y$.

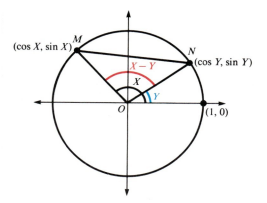

By the distance formula, the length of segment MN is:

$$\sqrt{(\cos X - \cos Y)^2 + (\sin X - \sin Y)^2}.$$

Apply the law of cosines to triangle MNO.

$$(MN)^2 = (OM)^2 + (ON)^2 - 2(OM)(ON)\cos(X - Y)$$

$$(\cos X - \cos Y)^2 + (\sin X - \sin Y)^2 = 1^2 + 1^2 - 2(1)(1)\cos(X - Y)$$

Expand the left side and simplify the right side:

$$(\cos^2 X - 2\cos X \cos Y + \cos^2 Y) + (\sin^2 X - 2\sin X \sin Y + \sin^2 Y)$$
$$= 2 - 2\cos(X - Y).$$

Rearrange terms:

$$(\cos^2 X + \sin^2 X) + (\cos^2 Y + \sin^2 Y) - 2\cos X \cos Y - 2\sin X \sin Y$$
$$= 2 - 2\cos(X - Y).$$

Replace $\cos^2 X + \sin^2 X$ by 1 and $\cos^2 Y + \sin^2 Y$ by 1:

$$1 + 1 - 2\cos X \cos Y - 2\sin X \sin Y = 2 - 2\cos(X - Y).$$

Subtract 2 from both sides and divide through by -2:

$$\cos X \cos Y + \sin X \sin Y = \cos(X - Y).$$

The last equation is the *formula for the cosine of a difference.*

Cosine of a Difference

For all angles with measures X and Y,

$$\cos (X - Y) = \cos X \cos Y + \sin X \sin Y$$

Example 1   **Evaluate. $\cos 15°$**

Solution $15° = 45° - 30°$

$\cos 15° = \cos (45° - 30°)$

$\quad\quad = \cos 45° \cos 30° + \sin 45° \sin 30°$

$\quad\quad = \left(\dfrac{\sqrt{2}}{2}\right)\left(\dfrac{\sqrt{3}}{2}\right) + \left(\dfrac{\sqrt{2}}{2}\right)\left(\dfrac{1}{2}\right)$

$\quad\quad = \dfrac{\sqrt{6}}{4} + \dfrac{\sqrt{2}}{4}$

$\quad\quad = \dfrac{\sqrt{6} + \sqrt{2}}{4}$

Example 2   **Simplify. $\cos (180° - X)$**

Solution $\cos (180° - X) = \cos 180° \cos X + \sin 180° \sin X$

$\quad\quad\quad\quad\quad\quad = -1 \cdot \cos X + 0 \cdot \sin X$

$\quad\quad\quad\quad\quad\quad = -\cos X$

The figure at the right illustrates the result of Example 2.

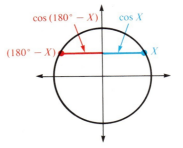

A formula for the cosine of a sum can be derived from the formula for the cosine of a difference.

$\cos (X + Y) = \cos (X - (-Y))$

$\quad\quad\quad\quad = \cos X \cos (-Y) + \sin X \sin (-Y)$

Since

$\quad \cos (-Y) = \cos Y$ and $\sin (-Y) = -\sin Y$,

$\cos (X + Y) = \cos X \cos Y - \sin X \sin Y$.

Cosine of a Sum

For all angles with measures X and Y,

$$\cos (X + Y) = \cos X \cos Y - \sin X \sin Y.$$

Example 3   Simplify. $\cos (90° + X)$

Solution $\cos (90° + X) = \cos 90° \cos X - \sin 90° \sin X$
$$= 0 \cdot \cos X - 1 \cdot \sin X$$
$$= - \sin X$$

The figure at the right illustrates the result of Example 3.

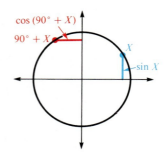

Formulas like those in Examples 2 and 3 can be used to reduce the cosine of any angle to the cosine or sine of an angle between 0° and 90°. Such formulas are called **reduction formulas.**

The following are the most useful reduction formulas for the cosine function.

Cosine Reduction Formulas

For any angle with measure X,

$$\cos (90° + X) = - \sin X \qquad \cos (90° - X) = \sin X$$
$$\cos (180° + X) = - \cos X \qquad \cos (180° - X) = - \cos X$$

Example 4   **Reduce cos 158°, that is, express cos 158° as the sine or cosine of an angle between 0° and 90°.**

Solution

Method 1		*Method 2*
$158° = 180° - 22°$		$158° = 90° + 68°$
$\cos 158° = \cos (180° - 22°)$		$\cos 158° = \cos (90° + 68°)$
$\cos 158° = - \cos 22°$	or	$\cos 158° = - \sin 68°$

In Example 4, the two methods give answers that differ considerably in appearance.

However, recall that $\sin X = \cos (90° - X)$.

Therefore, $- \sin 68° = - \cos (90° - 68°)$
$$= - \cos (22°).$$

The two answers are equivalent.

CLASSROOM EXERCISES

1. Evaluate cos 15° using the fact that 15° = 60° − 45°.

2. Simplify cos (270° + X) using the formula for the cosine of a sum.

3. Reduce cos 105°.   4. Use radicals to express cos 105° exactly.

WRITTEN EXERCISES

 Use radicals to express the numbers exactly.

1. cos 75° [*Hint:* 75° = 45° + 30°.]   2. cos 165° [*Hint:* 165° = 120° + 45°.]

3. cos 195° [*Hint:* 195° = 240° − 45°.]   4. cos 255° [*Hint:* 255° = 300° − 45°.]

5. cos 345°   6. cos 285°   7. cos (−75°)

8. cos (−15°)   9. cos 375°   10. cos 525°

Simplify using the formula for the cosine of a difference or sum.

11. cos (0° − X)   12. cos (X − 180°)   13. cos (X − 360°)

14. cos (360° − X)   15. cos (X + 360°)   16. cos (180° + X)

17. cos (90° + X)   18. cos (X + 270°)   19. cos (X − 90°)

20. cos (X − 270°)   21. cos (90° − X)   22. cos (270° + X)

Write each number as cos 12°, −cos 12°, sin 12°, or −sin 12°.

23. cos 168°   24. cos 192°   25. cos 348°   26. cos 372°

27. cos 78°   28. cos 102°   29. cos 258°   30. cos 282°

True or false?

31. cos (A + B) = cos A + cos B for all angles A and B.

32. cos (A − B) = cos A − cos B for all angles A and B.

33. cos (X + 180°) = cos (180° + X) for all angles X.

34. cos (X − 180°) = −cos (180° − X) for all angles X.

35. cos (X + 90°) = sin X for all angles X.

36. cos (− X) = −cos X for all angles X.

37. cos (90° − X) = sin X for all angles X.

38. cos (X − 90°) = sin X for all angles X.

The cosine of a difference or sum and the reduction formulas can also be stated in terms of real numbers x. For example, cos (π + x) = −cos x corresponds to the formula cos (180° + X) = −cos X.

B Find the exact values. Use radicals as necessary.

39. $\cos \dfrac{7\pi}{12}$
40. $\cos \dfrac{5\pi}{12}$
41. $\cos \dfrac{17\pi}{12}$
42. $\cos \dfrac{19\pi}{12}$

Express as a sine or cosine of a real number between 0 and $\dfrac{\pi}{2}$.

43. $\cos \dfrac{19\pi}{10}$
44. $\cos \dfrac{11\pi}{10}$
45. $\dfrac{7\pi}{10}$
46. $\cos \dfrac{9\pi}{10}$

Express as a sine or cosine of a real number between 0 and $\dfrac{\pi}{4}$.

47. $\cos \dfrac{2\pi}{5}$
48. $\cos \dfrac{3\pi}{5}$
49. $\cos \dfrac{7\pi}{5}$
50. $\cos \dfrac{8\pi}{5}$

C Simplify.

51. $\dfrac{\cos (X_1 - X_2)}{\cos X_1 \cos X_2}$
52. $\dfrac{\cos (X_1 - X_2)}{\sin X_1 \sin X_2}$
53. $\dfrac{\cos (X_1 + X_2)}{\sin X_1 \cos X_2}$
54. $\dfrac{\cos (X_1 + X_2)}{\cos X_1 \sin X_2}$

55. $\cos 12° \cos 27° - \sin 12° \sin 27°$
56. $\cos 83° \cos 23° + \sin 83° \sin 23°$
57. $\cos 97° \cos 7° + \sin 97° \sin 7°$
58. $\cos 300° \cos 60° - \sin 300° \sin 60°$

REVIEW EXERCISES

1. Graph $y = 3^x$ and $y = \left(\dfrac{1}{3}\right)^x$ on the same set of axes over the domain $\{x: -2 \leqslant x \leqslant 2\}$. [11-1]

Solve. [11-2, 11-3, 11-5]

2. $\log_2 x = 3$
3. $\log_5 5^x = 4$
4. $\ln 3 + \ln x = \ln 12$

5. How many years will it take an investment of $1000 invested at 15% compounded annually to be worth $5000? [11-6]

6. Solve for k: $\log k + \log 2 = 3$. [11-7]

7. Write an expression for the amount if $1000 is invested at 12% compounded instantaneously for 6 years. [11-8]

Self-Quiz 1

18-1 Prove the identity for all admissible values.

1. $\sec X - \dfrac{\tan X}{\csc X} = \cos X$
2. $\dfrac{\sin X}{1 + \cos X} + \dfrac{1 + \cos X}{\sin X} = 2 \csc X$

18-2 Use radicals to express the numbers exactly.

3. $\cos 315°$
4. $\cos (-165°)$

18-3 State each expression as a sine or cosine of an angle between 0° and 90°.

5. $\cos 290°$
6. $\cos 155°$

748 Chapter 18 Trigonometric Identities and Equations

LESSON 18-3

Sine of a Sum or Difference

Two observers d miles apart simultaneously sighted an airplane as shown in the figure. The angles of elevation were X and Y. The height h of the airplane in miles is given by a formula that involves the sine of the sum of two angles:

$$h = d\left(\frac{\sin Z \cdot \sin Y}{\sin(Z + Y)}\right) \quad \text{where } Z = 180° - X.$$

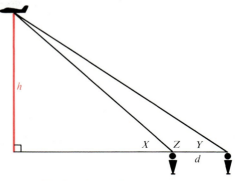

The formula for the sine of a sum can be derived from the formula for the cosine of a difference. Recall that sine and cosine are cofunctions. Therefore,

$$\sin(90° - X) = \cos X \quad \text{and} \quad \cos(90° - X) = \sin X.$$

We write sine $(X + Y)$ in terms of the cosine and then apply the formula for the cosine of a difference.

$$
\begin{aligned}
\sin(X + Y) &= \cos(90° - (X + Y)) \\
&= \cos((90° - X) - Y) \\
&= \cos(90° - X)\cos Y + \sin(90° - X)\sin Y \\
&= \sin X \cos Y + \cos X \sin Y
\end{aligned}
$$

Sine of a Sum

For all angles with measures X and Y,

$$\sin(X + Y) = \sin X \cos Y + \cos X \sin Y.$$

By replacing Y by $-Y$ in the formula for the sine of a sum, we can derive the formula for $\sin(X - Y)$.

$$
\begin{aligned}
\sin(X - Y) &= \sin(X + (-Y)) \\
&= \sin X \cos(-Y) + \cos X \sin(-Y)
\end{aligned}
$$

Since $\sin(-Y) = -\sin Y$ and $\cos(-Y) = \cos Y$, we have the formula for the sine of a difference.

Sine of a Difference

For all angles with measures X and Y,

$$\sin(X - Y) = \sin X \cos Y - \cos X \sin Y.$$

Example 1   **Show that 360° is a period of the sine function.**

Solution $\sin(360° + X) = \sin 360° \cos X + \cos 360° \sin X$
$$= 0 \cdot \cos X + 1 \cdot \sin X$$
$$= \sin X$$

Since for all X, $\sin(360° + X) = \sin X$, the sine is periodic with period 360°.

Example 2   **Reduce $\sin(90° + X)$.**

Solution $\sin(90° + X) = \sin 90° \cos X + \cos 90° \sin X$
$$= 1 \cdot \cos X + 0 \cdot \sin X$$
$$= \cos X$$

Example 3   **Use radicals to express $\sin 15°$ exactly.**

Solution $\sin 15° = \sin(45° - 30°)$
$$= \sin 45° \cos 30° - \cos 45° \sin 30°$$
$$= \frac{\sqrt{2}}{2}\left(\frac{\sqrt{3}}{2}\right) - \frac{\sqrt{2}}{2}\left(\frac{1}{2}\right)$$
$$= \frac{\sqrt{6}}{4} - \frac{\sqrt{2}}{4}$$
$$= \frac{\sqrt{6} - \sqrt{2}}{4}$$

The following are reduction formulas for the sine function.

Sine Reduction Formulas

$\sin(90° + X) = \cos X$ $\qquad\qquad$ $\sin(90° - X) = \cos X$

$\sin(180° + X) = -\sin X$ $\qquad\quad$ $\sin(180° - X) = \sin X$

The following figures illustrate the reduction formulas.

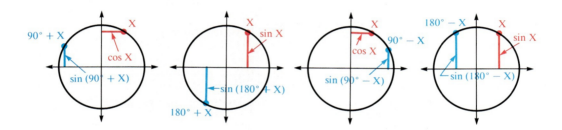

Example 4 **Reduce sin 550°.**

Solution $\sin 550° = \sin (360° + 190°)$

$$= \sin (190°)$$
$$= \sin (180° + 10°)$$
$$= -\sin 10°$$

*C*LASSROOM EXERCISES

Complete.

1. If $\sin X = 0.3314$, then $\sin (-X) = \underline{}$.
2. If $\sin X = 0.1258$, then $\sin (180° + X) = \underline{}$.
3. Reduce $\sin 290°$.
4. Use radicals to express $\sin 105°$ exactly.

*W*RITTEN EXERCISES

A **Use radicals to express the numbers exactly.**

1. $\sin 165°$
   [*Hint:* $165° = 120° + 45°$.]
2. $\sin 75°$
   [*Hint:* $75° = 45° + 30°$.]
3. $\sin 255°$
   [*Hint:* $255° = 300° - 45°$.]
4. $\sin 195°$
   [*Hint:* $195° = 240° - 45°$.]

5. $\sin 285°$ 6. $\sin 345°$ 7. $\sin (-15)°$
8. $\sin (-75°)$ 9. $\sin 555°$ 10. $\sin 645°$

Simplify, using the formula for the sine of a difference or sum.

11. $\sin (X - 180°)$ 12. $\sin (0° - X)$ 13. $\sin (360° - X)$
14. $\sin (X - 360°)$ 15. $\sin (180° + X)$ 16. $\sin (X + 360°)$
17. $\sin (X + 270°)$ 18. $\sin (90° + X)$ 19. $\sin (X - 270°)$
20. $\sin (X - 90°)$ 21. $\sin (270° - X)$ 22. $\sin (90° - X)$

Write each number as sin 7°, −sin 7°, cos 7°, or −cos 7°.

23. $\sin 353°$ 24. $\sin (-7°)$ 25. $\sin 173°$ 26. $\sin 97°$
27. $\sin 83°$ 28. $\sin 263°$ 29. $\sin 187°$ 30. $\sin 277°$

Reduce to a sine or cosine of an angle between 0° and 45°.

31. $\sin 80°$ 32. $\sin 252°$ 33. $\sin (-92°)$ 34. $\sin (-71°)$
35. $\sin 358°$ 36. $\sin 406°$ 37. $\sin 275°$ 38. $\sin 204°$

Suppose $\sin T = \dfrac{4}{5}$ and $0° < T < 90°$. Simplify.

39. $\sin(-T)$ **40.** $\sin(180° - T)$ **41.** $\sin(360° - T)$ **42.** $\sin(T + 180°)$

43. $\sin(90° + T)$ **44.** $\sin(90° - T)$ **45.** $\sin(270° + T)$ **46.** $\sin(T - 90°)$

B The sine of a difference or sum and the reduction formulas can also be stated in terms of a real number x. For example, $\sin(\pi - x) = \sin x$ corresponds to the formula $\sin(180° - X) = \sin X$.

Find the exact values. Use radicals as necessary.

47. $\sin \dfrac{5\pi}{12}$ **48.** $\sin \dfrac{7\pi}{12}$ **49.** $\sin \dfrac{19\pi}{12}$ **50.** $\sin \dfrac{17\pi}{12}$

Express as a sine or cosine of a real number between 0 and $\dfrac{\pi}{2}$.

51. $\sin \dfrac{15\pi}{14}$ **52.** $\sin \dfrac{9\pi}{14}$ **53.** $\sin\left(-\dfrac{9\pi}{14}\right)$ **54.** $\sin \dfrac{19\pi}{14}$

Express as a sine or cosine of a real number between 0 and $\dfrac{\pi}{4}$.

55. $\cos \dfrac{5\pi}{6}$ **56.** $\sin\left(-\dfrac{5\pi}{6}\right)$ **57.** $\sin \dfrac{11\pi}{8}$ **58.** $\sin \dfrac{5\pi}{8}$

Simplify.

59. $\dfrac{\sin(X_1 - X_2)}{\sin X_1 \sin X_2}$ **60.** $\dfrac{\sin(X_1 - X_2)}{\sin X_1 \cos X_2}$ **61.** $\dfrac{\sin(X_1 + X_2)}{\cos X_1 \cos X_2}$ **62.** $\dfrac{\sin(X_1 + X_2)}{\sin X_1 \cos X_2}$

63. $\sin 2° \cos 20° + \cos 2° \sin 20°$ **64.** $\sin 185° \cos 197° + \cos 185° \sin 197°$

65. $\sin 7° \cos 40° - \cos 7° \sin 40°$ **66.** $\sin 70° \cos 355° - \cos 70° \sin 355°$

C Complete.

67. Derive a formula for $\tan(X + Y)$ in terms of $\tan X$ and $\tan Y$. [*Hint:* Use $\sin(X + Y)$ and $\cos(X + Y)$.]

68. Derive a formula for $\tan(X - Y)$ in terms of $\tan X$ and $\tan Y$.

REVIEW EXERCISES

1. Write the first four terms of the sequence defined by $t_n = 10 \cdot 5^{n-1}$.   [12-1]

2. Write a_{10} for the sequence 7, 11, 15, 19, ...   [12-1]

3. Find the geometric mean of 1 and 10,000.   [12-2]

4. Write the series $1 + 3 + 5 + \cdots + 21$ in Σ notation.   [12-3]

5. Find $\displaystyle\sum_{k=1}^{10} (2k + 1)$.   **6.** Simplify: $\displaystyle\sum_{k=1}^{8} 6 \cdot (0.1)^k$.   [12-4, 12-5]

7. State the value of the infinite series $1 + \dfrac{1}{4} + \dfrac{1}{16} + \dfrac{1}{64} + \cdots$.   [12-6]

Double-Angle and Half-Angle Formulas

Since the graph of the cosine function is not linear, there is no linear relation between cos $2X$ and cos X. We cannot compute cos $2X$ simply by doubling cos X. However, a formula for cos $2X$ and other important identities can be derived from the formulas for the sine and cosine of a sum or difference. If $X = Y$ in the formula for the cosine of a sum, we obtain the following:

$$\cos (X + Y) = \cos X \cos Y - \sin X \sin Y$$
$$\cos (X + X) = \cos X \cos X - \sin X \sin X$$
$$\cos 2X = \cos^2 X - \sin^2 X.$$

Recall that $\cos^2 X = 1 - \sin^2 X$ and $\sin^2 X = 1 - \cos^2 X$. Substituting in the above equation gives these two identities.

$$\cos 2X = 1 - 2 \sin^2 X$$
$$\cos 2X = 2 \cos^2 X - 1$$

If $X = Y$ in the formula for the sine of a sum, then

$$\sin (X + Y) = \sin X \cos Y + \cos X \sin Y$$
$$\sin (X + X) = \sin X \cos X + \cos X \sin X$$
$$\sin 2X = 2 \sin X \cos X.$$

These identities are called **double-angle formulas.**

Double-Angle Formulas for the Sine and Cosine

For all angle measures X,

$$\cos 2X = \cos^2 X - \sin^2 X = 1 - 2 \sin^2 X = 2 \cos^2 X - 1$$
$$\sin 2X = 2 \sin X \cos X$$

The **half-angle formulas** for the sine and cosine may be derived from the double-angle formulas by replacing $2X$ by X and X by $\frac{X}{2}$ and then solving for $\sin \frac{X}{2}$ or $\cos \frac{X}{2}$. (See Exercise 45.)

Half-Angle Formulas for the Sine and Cosine

For all angles X,

$$\sin \frac{X}{2} = \pm \sqrt{\frac{1 - \cos X}{2}}, \quad \cos \frac{X}{2} = \pm \sqrt{\frac{1 + \cos X}{2}}.$$

The choice of which sign to use with the radical will depend on the value of $\frac{X}{2}$ and the trigonometric function for that angle.

Example 1 Given $\sin X = \frac{3}{4}$ and $0° \leqslant X \leqslant 90°$, find $\sin 2X$.

Solution First, find the values of $\cos X$.

Since $\sin^2 X + \cos^2 X = 1$, $\cos^2 X = 1 - \sin^2 X$

$$= 1 - \left(\frac{3}{4}\right)^2$$

$$= \frac{7}{16}$$

Therefore, $\qquad\qquad\qquad \cos X = \pm \frac{\sqrt{7}}{4}$

Since $0° \leqslant X \leqslant 90°$, $\cos X = \frac{\sqrt{7}}{4}$.

Substitute $\frac{3}{4}$ for $\sin X$ and $\frac{\sqrt{7}}{4}$ for $\cos X$ in $\sin 2X = 2 \sin X \cos X$.

$$\sin 2X = 2 \sin X \cos X$$

$$= 2\left(\frac{3}{4}\right)\left(\frac{\sqrt{7}}{4}\right)$$

$$= \frac{3\sqrt{7}}{8}$$

Example 2 Find $\cos 15°$, using a half-angle formula.

Solution Since $15° = \frac{1}{2}(30°)$, substitute $30°$ for X in the half-angle formula.

$$\cos 15° = \cos \frac{30°}{2} = \pm \sqrt{\frac{1 + \cos 30°}{2}}$$

$$= \pm \sqrt{\frac{1 + \frac{\sqrt{3}}{2}}{2}}$$

$$= \pm \sqrt{\frac{2 + \sqrt{3}}{4}}$$

$$= \pm \frac{\sqrt{2 + \sqrt{3}}}{2}$$

Answer Since $0° < 15° < 90°$, $\cos 15°$ is positive, $\cos 15° = \frac{\sqrt{2 + \sqrt{3}}}{2}$.

CLASSROOM EXERCISES

Write as a single trigonometric function.

1. $2 \sin 18° \cos 18°$

2. $2 \cos^2 22.5° - 1$

3. $\sqrt{\dfrac{1 - \cos 140°}{2}}$

4. $-\sqrt{\dfrac{1 + \cos 320°}{2}}$

Let $a = \sin X$ and $b = \cos X$ for $0° < X < 45°$. **Express these functions in terms of** a **and** b.

5. $\cos 2X$

6. $\sin \dfrac{X}{2}$

7. $\sin 2X$

WRITTEN EXERCISES

A **Suppose** $0° < X < 90°$. **Find** $\sin 2X$ **and** $\cos 2X$.

1. $\sin X = \dfrac{3}{5}$

2. $\sin X = \dfrac{12}{13}$

3. $\cos X = \dfrac{1}{3}$

4. $\cos X = \dfrac{1}{5}$

Suppose $90° < X < 180°$. **Find** $\sin 2X$ **and** $\cos 2X$.

5. $\sin X = \dfrac{5}{6}$

6. $\sin X = \dfrac{4}{5}$

7. $\cos X = -\dfrac{12}{13}$

8. $\cos X = -\dfrac{3}{5}$

Suppose $180° < X < 270°$. **Find** $\sin 2X$ **and** $\cos 2X$.

9. $\sin X = -\dfrac{1}{2}$

10. $\sin X = -\dfrac{2}{3}$

11. $\cos X = -\dfrac{2}{3}$

12. $\cos X = -\dfrac{1}{2}$

Suppose $90° < X < 180°$. **Find** $\sin \dfrac{X}{2}$ **and** $\cos \dfrac{X}{2}$.

13. $\sin X = \dfrac{24}{25}$

14. $\sin X = \dfrac{15}{17}$

15. $\cos X = -\dfrac{7}{9}$

16. $\cos X = -\dfrac{1}{9}$

Suppose $0° < X < 90°$. **Find** $\sin \dfrac{X}{2}$ **and** $\cos \dfrac{X}{2}$.

17. $\sin X = \dfrac{12}{13}$

18. $\sin X = \dfrac{3}{5}$

19. $\cos X = \dfrac{1}{8}$

20. $\cos X = \dfrac{7}{18}$

Suppose $270° < X < 360°$. **Find** $\sin 2X$ **and** $\cos 2X$. **Give answers to the nearest hundredth.**

21. $\sin X = -0.1$

22. $\sin X = -0.2$

23. $\cos X = 0.3$

24. $\cos X = 0.4$

Use double-angle or half-angle formulas to simplify each expression.

25. $2 \cos^2 8° - 1$

26. $2 \cos^2 32° - 1$

27. $2 \sin 10° \cos 10°$

28. $2 \sin 40° \cos 40°$

29. $\cos^2 124° - \sin^2 124°$

30. $\cos^2 170° - \sin^2 170°$

31. $\sqrt{\dfrac{1 - \cos 70°}{2}}$

32. $\sqrt{\dfrac{1 - \cos 110°}{2}}$

33. $\sqrt{\dfrac{1 + \cos 112°}{2}}$

34. $\sqrt{\dfrac{1 + \cos 170°}{2}}$

35. $\sqrt{\dfrac{1 + \cos 4°}{2}}$

36. $\sqrt{\dfrac{1 + \cos 88°}{2}}$

37. a. Use the difference formula to find $\cos (45° - 30°)$.

  b. Use the half-angle formula to find $\cos \left(\dfrac{30°}{2}\right)$.

  c. Show that the answers to parts (a) and (b) are the same.

38. a. Use the sum formula to find $\cos (45° + 30°)$.

  b. Use the half-angle formula to find $\cos \left(\dfrac{150°}{2}\right)$.

  c. Show that the answers to parts (a) and (b) are the same.

39. a. Use the sum formula to find $\sin (60° + 45°)$.

  b. Use the half-angle formula to find $\sin \left(\dfrac{210°}{2}\right)$.

  c. Show that the answers to parts (a) and (b) are the same.

40. a. Use the difference formula to find $\sin (150° - 135°)$.

  b. Use the half-angle formula to find $\sin \left(\dfrac{30°}{2}\right)$.

  c. Show that the answers to parts (a) and (b) are the same.

41. Suppose that $\sin X = -\dfrac{5}{6}$ and $\cos X = \dfrac{\sqrt{11}}{6}$.

  a. Find $\sin 2X$. **b.** Find $\cos 2X$. **c.** Show that $\sin^2 2X + \cos^2 2X = 1$.

42. Suppose that $\cos X = \dfrac{1}{9}$.

  a. Find $\sin \dfrac{X}{2}$. **b.** Find $\cos \dfrac{X}{2}$. **c.** Show that $\sin^2 \dfrac{X}{2} + \cos^2 \dfrac{X}{2} = 1$.

 43. Use the double-angle formulas for the sine and cosine to derive the half-angle formulas for the sine and cosine.

44. a. Derive a formula for $\tan 2X$ in terms of $\tan X$. [*Hint:* Use the formula for $\sin 2X$ and $\cos 2X$.]

  b. Derive a formula for $\tan \dfrac{X}{2}$ from the formulas for $\sin \dfrac{X}{2}$ and $\cos \dfrac{X}{2}$. The formula should be free of radicals and expressed in terms of $\sin X$ and $\cos X$.

*R*EVIEW EXERCISES

Sketch the graph of $y = 2 \cos x$ over the domain $\{x: -2\pi \leqslant x \leqslant 2\pi\}$. Then state the following. [16-3, 16-4, 16-5]

  1. $\cos \left(-\dfrac{\pi}{2}\right)$ **2.** $\cos \dfrac{\pi}{3}$ **3.** The period   **4.** The amplitude

  5. The maximum and minimum values

  6. The values of x at which the maximum and minimum values occur

Find the value of sin *a*, cos *a*, tan *a*, cot *a*, sec *a*, and csc *a*. Suppose *a* is a real number [16-6]
between 0 and $\frac{\pi}{2}$.

7. $\sin a = \frac{3}{5}$

8. $\csc a = 2$

9. A radian measure of $\frac{\pi}{3}$ is equivalent to a degree measure of __?__. [16-7]

10. A degree measure of 135° is equivalent to a radian measure of __?__.

$\mathcal{S}$elf-Quiz 2

18-3   **Use radicals to express the numbers exactly.**

1. $\sin 315°$

2. $\sin (135° + 30°)$

**State each expression as a sine or cosine of an angle measure between 0°
and 45°.**

3. $\sin 156°$

4. $\sin 330°$

18-4   **Let $\sin X = \frac{3}{5}$ and $\cos X = \frac{4}{5}$. Evaluate.**

5. $\sin 2X$

6. $\cos \frac{X}{2}$

Use double-angle or half-angle formulas to simplify each expression.

7. $\cos^2 15° - \sin^2 15°$

8. $\sqrt{\dfrac{1 - \cos 70°}{2}}$

$\mathcal{C}$ALCULATOR EXTENSION   Acceleration of Gravity

The approximation of the acceleration of a falling object due to Earth's
gravity that is generally used is 9.8 m/s². However, the acceleration due to
gravity varies according to the latitude of the falling object. A more accurate value
is

$$g = 9.78039(1 + 0.005288 \sin \theta - 0.000006 \sin^2 2\theta).$$

1. Find the value of *g* at your present
   latitude.

2. At what latitude is *g* greatest? Least?

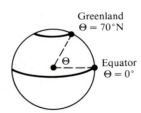

Greenland
$\Theta = 70°N$

Equator
$\Theta = 0°$

LESSON 18-5

Solving Equations

Trigonometric equations arise in many practical applications such as in the design of internal combustion engines, where the linear motion of the piston is converted to the circular motion of the crankshaft. The relationship between the displacement d of the piston from the top of the cylinder and time T is expressed by the trigonometric equation where k and θ are constants

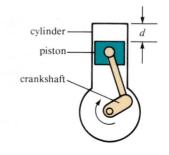

$$d = |k \sin \theta T|$$

that depend on the radius of the crankshaft and the speed of the engine.

Trigonometric equations can have many solutions. For example, an identity such as $\sin^2 X + \cos^2 X = 1$ has each angle measure as a solution. Other equations such as $\cos X = 2$ have no solutions. Since the trigonometric functions are periodic, an equation with at least one solution has infinitely many solutions. Solutions of such equations are usually stated in one of two ways: (1) as angles only for the interval $0° \leq X < 360°$ or (2) as angles between $0°$ and $360°$ plus integer multiples of the fundamental period of the function.

Example 1   Solve. $\cos 2X + \cos X = 0$ Describe *all* solutions of the equation, using general notation.

Solution
$$\cos 2X + \cos X = 0$$

Substitute for $\cos 2X$. $\qquad\qquad (2 \cos^2 X - 1) + \cos X = 0$

Write in standard quadratic form. $\qquad 2 \cos^2 X + \cos X - 1 = 0$

Factor. $\qquad\qquad\qquad\qquad (2 \cos X - 1)(\cos X + 1) = 0$

$$2 \cos X - 1 = 0 \qquad \text{or} \qquad \cos X + 1 = 0$$

$$\cos X = \frac{1}{2} \qquad \text{or} \qquad \cos X = -1$$

$$X = 60° \quad \text{or} \qquad X = 300° \quad \text{or} \qquad\qquad X = 180°$$

Answer $\{X : X = 60° + k360° \quad \text{or} \quad X = 180° + k360° \quad \text{or} \quad X = 300° + k360°, k \text{ an integer}\}$

In Example 1, the answer $X = 180° + k360°$ is often written as $(2k + 1)180°$, k an integer.

If an equation contains more than one trigonometric function, it can usually be solved by rewriting it as an equation in only one function.

Example 2   Solve. $3 \cos^2 X - 3 \sin^2 X = 0$ for $0° \leqslant X < 360°$

Solution
$$3 \cos^2 X - 3 \sin^2 X = 0$$

Divide both sides by 3.
$$\cos^2 X - \sin^2 X = 0$$

Substitute for $\cos^2 X$.
$$1 - \sin^2 X - \sin^2 X = 0$$
$$2 \sin^2 X = 1$$
$$\sin^2 X = \frac{1}{2}$$
$$\sin X = \pm \frac{\sqrt{2}}{2}$$

Answer $\{45°, 135°, 215°, 315°\}$

Recall that multiplying both sides of an equation by a variable or squaring both sides may introduce roots that are not roots of the original equation. Therefore, checking roots is important. Similarly, dividing both sides of an equation by a variable may result in "lost" roots. Possible lost roots are values that make the divisor equal to zero. Those values should be checked in the original equation to determine whether they are roots.

Example 3   Solve. $\sin X + \cos X = 1$ for $0° \leqslant X < 360°$

Solution
$$\sin X + \cos X = 1$$
$$\cos X = 1 - \sin X$$

Square both sides.
$$\cos^2 X = 1 - 2 \sin X + \sin^2 X$$

Replace $\cos^2 X$ *by* $1 - \sin^2 X$.
$$1 - \sin^2 X = 1 - 2 \sin X + \sin^2 X$$
$$2 \sin^2 X - 2 \sin X = 0$$
$$\sin^2 X - \sin X = 0$$
$$\sin X (\sin X - 1) = 0$$
$$\sin X = 0 \qquad \text{or} \qquad \sin X = 1$$
$$X = 0° \quad \text{or} \quad X = 180° \quad \text{or} \quad X = 90°$$

Checking shows that $180°$ is not a solution of the original equation.

Answer $\{0°, 90°\}$

C LASSROOM EXERCISES

Solve for $0° \leqslant X < 360°$.

1. $\cos X = -1$ **2.** $\tan X = 1$ **3.** $2 \sin^2 X - 1 = 0$ **4.** $\cos^2 X = 2$

 RITTEN EXERCISES

 One solution is given for each equation. Describe *all* solutions of the equation, using general notation.

1. $\cos X = 0.8290$
   Solution: 34°

2. $\cos X = 0.6691$
   Solution: 48°

3. $\sin X = 0.9205$
   Solution: 67°

4. $\sin X = 0.8910$
   Solution: 63°

5. $\tan X = -0.2126$
   Solution: 168°

6. $\tan X = -7.1154$
   Solution: 98°

Solve for X. Assume that $0° \leq X < 360°$.

7. $\sin X = \dfrac{1}{2}$

8. $\sin X = \dfrac{\sqrt{2}}{2}$

9. $\cos X = -\dfrac{\sqrt{3}}{2}$

10. $\cos X = -\dfrac{1}{2}$

11. $\tan X = \sqrt{3}$

12. $\tan X = -1$

13. $2 \sin^2 X = 1$

14. $2 \cos^2 X = 1$

15. $\tan^2 X = 1$

16. $\tan^2 X = 3$

17. $\cos X \tan X = 0$

18. $\sin X \cos X = 0$

19. $(1 - \sin X)(1 + \sin X) = 0$

20. $(\cos X - 1)(\cos X + 1) = 0$

21. $3 \tan^2 X - 1 = 0$

22. $\tan^2 X - 3 = 0$

 23. $2 \sin^2 X - 3 \sin X + 1 = 0$

24. $2 \cos^2 X - 3 \cos X + 1 = 0$

25. $\sin 2X + \sin X = 0$

26. $\sin 2X + \cos X = 0$

27. $\cos 2X + \sin^2 X = 1$

28. $\cos 2X + \cos X = 0$

29. $\cos 2X - \sin X = 0$

30. $\cot X = \sqrt{3}$

C **31.** $6 \sin^2 X - 5 \sin X + 1 = 0$

32. $6 \sin^2 X + \sin X - 1 = 0$

33. $12 \cos^2 X + \cos X - 6 = 0$

34. $12 \cos^2 X - \cos X - 6 = 0$

35. $\tan^2 X - 5 \tan X + 6 = 0$

36. $\tan^2 X - 5 \tan X - 6 = 0$

37. $\sin X + \cos X = 2$

38. $\sec^2 X - \tan^2 X = 1$

EVIEW EXERCISES

1. Use a table or a calculator to evaluate $\cos 40°$. [17-1]

2. In triangle ABC, angle C is a right angle, angle A has a measure of 20°, and the hypotenuse has length 10 cm. What is the length of side a? [17-2]

3. A lighthouse is 100 ft high, and the angle observed in a boat from the base of the lighthouse to the top is 2°. How far is the boat from the lighthouse? [17-3]

4. In triangle ABC, angle A measures 100°, angle B measures 50°, and side a measures 100 ft. What is the length of side b? [17-4]

5. In triangle RST, side $r = 30$ cm, side $s = 40$ cm, and the measure of angle T is 60°. What is the length of side t? [17-5]

CALCULATOR EXTENSION   Trigonometric Equations

A calculator and the strategy of systematic trials can be used to solve some trigonometric equations. Solve each of the following equations for the domain $0° \leqslant X \leqslant 360°$.

1. $\sin 2X - \sin X = 0$

2. $\dfrac{\sin 2X}{\cos X} - 2 \sin X = 0$

3. $\sin 2X + \cos X = 0$

4. $\cos 2X + \sin X = 1$

5. Is any of the equations above an identity?

CHAPTER SUMMARY

▶ Basic Trigonometric Identities   [18-1]

For all angle measures X for which the functions are defined,

1. $\tan X = \dfrac{\sin X}{\cos X}$ **2.** $\cot X = \dfrac{\cos X}{\sin X}$ **3.** $\sec X = \dfrac{1}{\cos X}$

4. $\csc X = \dfrac{1}{\sin X}$ **5.** $\cot X = \dfrac{1}{\tan X}$ **6.** $\sin^2 X + \cos^2 X = 1$

7. $1 + \tan^2 X = \sec^2 X$ **8.** $1 + \cot^2 X = \csc^2 X$

▶ For all angles with measures X and Y,   [18-2, 18-3]

$$\cos (X - Y) = \cos X \cos Y + \sin X \sin Y$$
$$\cos (X + Y) = \cos X \cos Y - \sin X \sin Y$$

$$\sin (X + Y) = \sin X \cos Y + \cos X \sin Y$$
$$\sin (X - Y) = \sin X \cos Y - \cos X \sin Y$$

▶ Reduction Formulas   [18-2]

For all angles X, $\cos (90° + X) = -\sin X$ $\cos (90° - X) = \sin X$
                $\cos (180° + X) = -\cos X$ $\cos (180° - X) = -\cos X$
                $\sin (90° + X) = \cos X$ $\sin (90° - X) = \cos X$
                $\sin (180° + X) = -\sin X$ $\sin (180° - X) = \sin X$

▶ Double-Angle Formulas   [18-4]

For all angles X, $\cos 2X = \cos^2 X - \sin^2 X$ $\sin 2X = 2 \sin X \cos X$
                         $= 1 - 2 \sin^2 X$
                         $= 2 \cos^2 X - 1$

▶ Half-Angle Formulas   [18-4]

For all angles X, $\sin \dfrac{X}{2} = \pm \sqrt{\dfrac{1 - \cos X}{2}}$ $\cos \dfrac{X}{2} = \pm \sqrt{\dfrac{1 + \cos X}{2}}.$

 **HAPTER REVIEW**

18-1 **Objective:** To prove trigonometric identities.

Prove each identity.

1. $\dfrac{\sin X + \cot X}{\cos X} = \tan X + \csc X$

2. $\dfrac{\csc X - 1}{1 - \sin X} = \csc X$

3. $\dfrac{\sin X + \tan X \sin X + \cos X}{\sec X} = 1 + \sin X \cos X$

18-2 **Objectives:** To apply the formulas for the cosine of a sum or difference to simplify expressions.

To use reduction formulas to write cosine expressions as cosines or sines of angle measures X, $0° \leq X \leq 90°$.

Use radicals to express the numbers exactly.

4. $\cos 105°$

5. $\cos 255°$

6. $\cos 75°$

Write as the cosine of an angle X, $0° \leq X \leq 90°$.

7. $\cos 330°$

8. $\cos 505°$

18-3 **Objectives:** To apply the formulas for the sine of a sum or difference to simplify expressions.

To use reduction formulas to write sine expressions as sines or cosines of an angle X, $0° \leq X \leq 90°$.

Use radicals to express the numbers exactly.

9. $\sin 15°$

10. $\sin 75°$

11. $\sin 195°$

Let $\sin A = \dfrac{1}{4}$ and $0° < A < 90°$. Simplify.

12. $\sin (A - 90°)$

13. $\sin (540° + A)$

Write as the sine or cosine of an angle between $0°$ and $45°$.

14. $\sin (-134°)$

15. $\sin 257°$

18-4 **Objective:** To apply the double-angle and half-angle formulas for the sine and cosine to simplify expressions.

Suppose that $0 < X < 90°$ and $\sin X = \dfrac{8}{17}$. Find the following.

16. $\sin 2X$

17. $\cos 2X$

Suppose $180° < X < 270°$ and $\cos X = -\dfrac{1}{8}$. Find the following.

18. $\cos \dfrac{X}{2}$

19. $\sin \dfrac{X}{2}$

Simplify by writing as a single trigonometric term.

20. $1 - 2 \sin^2 27°$

21. $\sqrt{\dfrac{1 + \cos 36°}{2}}$

18-5 **Objective:** To solve trigonometric equations.

Solve for $0° \leq X < 360°$.

22. $\tan X + 1 = 0$

23. $4 \sin^2 X - 3 = 0$

24. $2 \sec X + 1 = \cos X$

25. $\sin X \cos X = \dfrac{1}{2}$

$\mathcal{C}$HAPTER 18 SELF-TEST

18-1 **Prove each identity.**

1. $\dfrac{\sin X + \tan X}{\sin X} = 1 + \sec X$ **2.** $\dfrac{\tan^2 X}{1 + \tan^2 X} = \sin^2 X$ **3.** $\dfrac{\csc X - \sin X}{\cos X} = \cot X$

18-2, **Write as equivalent expressions in terms of sin 15°, cos 15°, sin 35°, and**
18-3, **cos 35°.**
18-4

4. $\sin 50°$ **5.** $\cos 20°$ **6.** $\cos 7.5°$ **7.** $\sin 70°$

Write as the sine or cosine of an angle between 0° and 90°.

8. $\sin 240°$ **9.** $\cos - 22.5°$ **10.** $\sin 330°$

True or false for all angle measures X and Y?

11. $\sin X = \pm \sqrt{\dfrac{1 - \cos^2 X}{2}}$ **12.** $\cos (X + 270°) = \cos X$

13. $\cos (X - Y) = \cos X - \cos Y$ **14.** $\sin 4X = 2 \sin 2X \cos 2X$

Simplify by writing as a single trigonometric term.

15. $\sin 38° \cos 12° - \cos 38° \sin 12°$ **16.** $\cos 20° \cos 60° + \sin 20° \sin 60°$

18-5 **Solve for $0° \leq X < 360°$.**

17. $3 \cot^2 X = 1$ **18.** $\sin^2 X = 2$ **19.** $\tan^2 X - \sec X = 1$

$\mathcal{P}$RACTICE FOR COLLEGE ENTRANCE TESTS

Choose the best answer.

1. The value of $x - y = \underline{\quad ? \quad}$.

   A. 40   **B.** 50   **C.** 80   **D.** 100   **E.** 130

2. $(\cos Y - 1)(\cos Y + 1) + (\sin Y - 1)(\sin Y + 1) = \underline{\quad ? \quad}$.

   A. -2 **B.** -1 **C.** 0   **D.** 1   **E.** 2

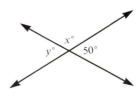

3. Where defined, $\tan X \csc X = $ __?__.

   A. $\sec X$　　　**B.** $\cot X$　　　**C.** $\dfrac{\cos X}{\sin^2 X}$　　　**D.** $\dfrac{\sin X}{1 - \sin^2 X}$　　**E.** 1

4. Which of the following is *not* an identity?

   A. $\sin\left(\dfrac{\pi}{2} - x\right) = \cos x$　**B.** $\cos\left(\dfrac{\pi}{2} - x\right) = \sin x$　**C.** $\cos\left(x - \dfrac{\pi}{2}\right) = \sin x$

   D. $\sin\left(\dfrac{\pi}{2} + x\right) = \cos x$　**E.** $\cos\left(\dfrac{\pi}{2} + x\right) = \sin x$

5. If $0 \le x \le \pi$ and $\sin x = -\cos x$, then $x = $ __?__.

   A. 0　　　**B.** $\dfrac{\pi}{4}$　　　**C.** $\dfrac{\pi}{2}$　　　**D.** $\dfrac{3\pi}{4}$　　　**E.** π

6. If $\cos A = \dfrac{1}{2}$, then $\cos 2A = $ __?__.

   A. $-\dfrac{\sqrt{3}}{2}$　　　**B.** $-\dfrac{1}{2}$　　　**C.** 0　　　**D.** $\dfrac{1}{2}$　　　**E.** $\dfrac{\sqrt{3}}{2}$

7. Given that $\cos(A - B) = \cos A \cos B + \sin A \sin B$, then $\cos(A + B) = $ __?__.

   A. $\cos A \cos B - \sin A \sin B$　　　　**B.** $\sin A \sin B - \cos A \sin B$

   C. $\cos^2 A - \sin^2 B$　　　**D.** $-\cos^2 A + \sin^2 B$　　　**E.** $2\cos A \sin B$

8. What is the area of the shaded region between the arc and the line?

   A. $\pi - 1$　　　**B.** $\dfrac{\pi}{2} - \dfrac{1}{2}$　　　**C.** $\dfrac{\pi}{2} - 1$

   D. $\dfrac{\pi}{4} - \dfrac{1}{4}$　　　**E.** $\dfrac{\pi}{4} - \dfrac{1}{2}$

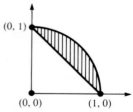

9. What is the range of the function defined by $y = \sin(2x) + 2$?

   A. $\{y: -2 \le y \le 2\}$　　　**B.** $\{y: 0 \le y \le 2\}$　　　**C.** $\{y: 0 \le y \le 4\}$

   D. $\{y: 1 \le y \le 3\}$　　　**E.** $\{y: 1 \le y \le 5\}$

10. If two fair dice are tossed, what is the probability that the product of the numbers on the top faces of the two dice will equal 12?

    A. $\dfrac{1}{18}$　　　**B.** $\dfrac{1}{12}$　　　**C.** $\dfrac{1}{9}$　　　**D.** $\dfrac{1}{6}$　　　**E.** $\dfrac{1}{4}$

11. If $0° \le X < 180°$ and $\tan X = -\sqrt{3}$, then $X = $ __?__.

    A. 150°　　　**B.** 120°　　　**C.** 90°　　　**D.** 60°　　　**E.** 30°

12. The graph of $y = \sin x$ reflected about the y-axis is the same as

    I. $y = \sin x$　　　**II.** $y = \sin(-x)$　　　**III.** $y = \sin(x + \pi)$

    A. I only　　　**B.** II only　　　**C.** III only　　　**D.** I and II only
    E. II and III only

$\mathcal{C}$UMULATIVE REVIEW (CHAPTERS 16–18)

16-1   **In which quadrant is each of the following points?**

     1. $W\left(\dfrac{7\pi}{6}\right)$ **2.** $W(\pi + 1)$

16-2   **Evaluate.**

     3. $\sin\left(2\pi + \dfrac{\pi}{2}\right)$ **4.** $\cos\left(-\dfrac{\pi}{2}\right)$

16-3   **5.** $\cos\dfrac{\pi}{6}$ **6.** $\sin\dfrac{5\pi}{4}$

     Solve for $0 \leqslant x \leqslant 2\,\pi$.

     7. $\sin x = \dfrac{1}{2}$ **8.** $\cos x = -\dfrac{\sqrt{3}}{2}$

16-4   **9.** What are the maximum and minimum values of $f(x) = -2 + \sin x$?

16-4,   **Sketch the graph for $-\pi \leqslant x \leqslant \pi$.**
16-5   **10.** $y = \sin x$ **11.** $y = 1 + \cos x$ **12.** $y = 2\cos x$

     13. $y = \cos 2x$ **14.** $y = \sin\dfrac{1}{2}x$

16-5   **State the period and amplitude.**

     15. $y = 4\sin x$ **16.** $y = \sin 4x$

16-6   **Evaluate.**

     17. $\cot\dfrac{\pi}{4}$ **18.** $\csc\dfrac{5\pi}{6}$

     19. Sketch the graph of $y = \tan x$ for $0 \leqslant x \leqslant 2\,\pi$.

     20. Evaluate $\cos 30°$.

16-7   **Evaluate.**

     21. $\mathrm{Cos}^{-1}\dfrac{1}{2}$ **22.** $\mathrm{Arctan}\ -1$ **23.** $\mathrm{Arcsin}\ -\dfrac{\sqrt{2}}{2}$

     24. $\sin(\mathrm{Sin}^{-1}\,0.5)$ **25.** $\cos(\mathrm{Tan}^{-1}\,-1)$ **26.** $\sin(\mathrm{Cos}^{-1}\,0.5)$

16-8   **27.** Express $\dfrac{11\pi}{15}$ in degree measure.

     28. Express $70°$ in radian measure.

17-1   **Evaluate.**

     29. $\sin A$ **30.** $\tan B$

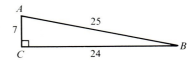

Use the given information about right triangle *ABC*, angle *C* = 90°, to solve.

31. $\tan A = \sqrt{5}$
$a = 5$
$b = ?$

32. $\sin B = \dfrac{1}{4}$
$c = 8$
$a = ?$

17-2   **33.** Determine sides *b* and *c* of this right triangle.

Solve.

34. A supporting cable is attached to a TV antenna 25 ft above the base. How long must the cable be in order to make an angle of 55° with the ground?

35. An airplane flying at 5000 ft begins its glide path 1.5 mi from the airport. At what angle does the plane descend?

17-3   **36.** Find the area of triangle *ABC* given *b* = 13 cm, *c* = 15 cm, and *A* = 40°.

37. If $\sin E = 0.7$, find *D*.

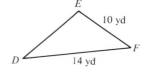

38. A rotten tree fell across a wall breaking as shown and forming angles of 40° and 60° with the ground. If the distance from *A* to *B* is 55 ft, how tall was the tree?

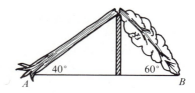

17-4   **39.** Draw a sketch to show that two triangles *ABC* are possible from this information: *A* = 58°, *c* = 14, *a* = 12.

40. Find angle *G* in triangle *GHJ*, given *H* = 30°, *h* = 6, and *j* = 5.

41. State the law of cosines in terms of a, b, c, and C for triangle ABC.

42. Find angle B for this triangle.

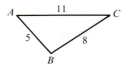

43. Find the length of the shorter diagonal of a parallelogram if the angle between sides of 4 cm and 6 cm is 50°.

18-1 **Complete these basic trigonometric identities.**

    44. $1 + \cot^2 X = $ _____?_____ .

    45. $\sec X = $ _____?_____ .

    46. Use basic identities to simplify: $\dfrac{\sin^2 X}{1 - \cos X}$.

    47. Prove this identity: $\tan X(\csc X + \cot X) = \sec X + 1$.

18-2 **48.** Evaluate $\cos 105°$ as $\cos(45° + 60°)$.

    49. Express $\cos 250°$ as a sine or cosine of an angle between 0° and 45°.

18-2, **Simplify.**
18-3

    50. $\cos(90° + X)$ **51.** $\cos(X - 180°)$

    52. $\sin(X + 270°)$ **53.** $\sin(90° - X)$

18-3 **Write as a single trigonometric function.**

    54. $\sin 44° \cos 20° + \cos 44° \sin 20°$

18-4 **55.** Evaluate $\sin 120°$ as $\sin(2 \cdot 60°)$.

    56. If $\sin X = \dfrac{1}{4}$ and $0° < X < 45°$, find $\sin 2X$.

Write as a single trigonometric function.

    57. $\sqrt{\dfrac{1 - \cos 38°}{2}}$ **58.** $2 \cos^2 48° - 1$

18-5 **Solve for $0° \leqslant X \leqslant 180°$.**

    59. $\sin 2X = \dfrac{\sqrt{3}}{2}$ **60.** $\sin X \cot X = 0$

    61. $\sin^2 X - 3 \sin X + 2 = 0$ **62.** $\cos 2X + \cos X = 0$

Squares, Square Roots, Cubes, and Cube Roots

n	n^2	$\sqrt{n}$	$\sqrt[3]{n}$	$\sqrt[3]{10n}$	$\sqrt[3]{100n}$	n^3	$\sqrt{10n}$
1.0	1.00	1.000	1.000	2.154	4.642	1.000	3.162
1.1	1.21	1.049	1.032	2.224	4.791	1.331	3.317
1.2	1.44	1.095	1.063	2.289	4.932	1.728	3.464
1.3	1.69	1.140	1.091	2.351	5.066	2.197	3.606
1.4	1.96	1.183	1.119	2.410	5.192	2.744	3.742
1.5	2.25	1.225	1.145	2.466	5.313	3.375	3.873
1.6	2.56	1.265	1.170	2.520	5.429	4.096	4.000
1.7	2.89	1.304	1.193	2.571	5.540	4.913	4.123
1.8	3.24	1.342	1.216	2.621	5.646	5.832	4.243
1.9	3.61	1.378	1.239	2.668	5.749	6.859	4.359
2.0	4.00	1.414	1.260	2.714	5.848	8.000	4.472
2.1	4.41	1.449	1.281	2.759	5.944	9.261	4.583
2.2	4.84	1.483	1.301	2.802	6.037	10.648	4.690
2.3	5.29	1.517	1.320	2.844	6.127	12.167	4.796
2.4	5.76	1.549	1.339	2.884	6.214	13.824	4.899
2.5	6.25	1.581	1.357	2.924	6.300	15.625	5.000
2.6	6.76	1.612	1.375	2.962	6.383	17.576	5.099
2.7	7.29	1.643	1.392	3.000	6.463	19.683	5.196
2.8	7.84	1.673	1.409	3.037	6.542	21.952	5.292
2.9	8.41	1.703	1.426	3.072	6.619	24.389	5.385
3.0	9.00	1.732	1.442	3.107	6.694	27.000	5.477
3.1	9.61	1.761	1.458	3.141	6.768	29.791	5.568
3.2	10.24	1.789	1.474	3.175	6.840	32.768	5.657
3.3	10.89	1.817	1.489	3.208	6.910	35.937	5.745
3.4	11.56	1.844	1.504	3.240	6.980	39.304	5.831
3.5	12.25	1.871	1.518	3.271	7.047	42.875	5.916
3.6	12.96	1.897	1.533	3.302	7.114	46.656	6.000
3.7	13.69	1.924	1.547	3.332	7.179	50.653	6.083
3.8	14.44	1.949	1.560	3.362	7.243	54.872	6.164
3.9	15.21	1.975	1.574	3.391	7.306	59.319	6.245
4.0	16.00	2.000	1.587	3.420	7.368	64.000	6.325
4.1	16.81	2.025	1.601	3.448	7.429	68.921	6.403
4.2	17.64	2.049	1.613	3.476	7.489	74.088	6.481
4.3	18.49	2.074	1.626	3.503	7.548	79.507	6.557
4.4	19.36	2.098	1.639	3.530	7.606	85.184	6.633
4.5	20.25	2.121	1.651	3.557	7.663	91.125	6.708
4.6	21.16	2.145	1.663	3.583	7.719	97.336	6.782
4.7	22.09	2.168	1.675	3.609	7.775	103.823	6.856
4.8	23.04	2.191	1.687	3.634	7.830	110.592	6.928
4.9	24.01	2.214	1.698	3.659	7.884	117.649	7.000
5.0	25.00	2.236	1.710	3.684	7.937	125.000	7.071
5.1	26.01	2.258	1.721	3.708	7.990	132.651	7.141
5.2	27.04	2.280	1.732	3.733	8.041	140.608	7.211
5.3	28.09	2.302	1.744	3.756	8.093	148.877	7.280
5.4	29.16	2.324	1.754	3.780	8.143	157.464	7.348
5.5	30.25	2.345	1.765	3.803	8.193	166.375	7.416

n	n^2	$\sqrt{n}$	$\sqrt[3]{n}$	$\sqrt[3]{10n}$	$\sqrt[3]{100n}$	n^3	$\sqrt{10n}$
5.5	30.25	2.345	1.765	3.803	8.193	166.375	7.416
5.6	31.36	2.366	1.776	3.826	8.243	175.616	7.483
5.7	32.49	2.387	1.786	3.849	8.291	185.193	7.550
5.8	33.64	2.408	1.797	3.871	8.340	195.112	7.616
5.9	34.81	2.429	1.807	3.893	8.387	205.379	7.681
6.0	36.00	2.449	1.817	3.915	8.434	216.000	7.746
6.1	37.21	2.470	1.827	3.936	8.481	226.981	7.810
6.2	38.44	2.490	1.837	3.958	8.527	238.328	7.874
6.3	39.69	2.510	1.847	3.979	8.573	250.047	7.937
6.4	40.96	2.530	1.857	4.000	8.618	262.144	8.000
6.5	42.25	2.550	1.866	4.021	8.662	274.625	8.062
6.6	43.56	2.569	1.876	4.041	8.707	287.496	8.124
6.7	44.89	2.588	1.885	4.062	8.750	300.763	8.185
6.8	46.24	2.608	1.895	4.082	8.794	314.432	8.246
6.9	47.61	2.627	1.904	4.102	8.837	328.509	8.307
7.0	49.00	2.646	1.913	4.121	8.879	343.000	8.367
7.1	50.41	2.665	1.922	4.141	8.921	357.911	8.426
7.2	51.84	2.683	1.931	4.160	8.963	373.248	8.485
7.3	53.29	2.702	1.940	4.179	9.004	389.017	8.544
7.4	54.76	2.720	1.949	4.198	9.045	405.224	8.602
7.5	56.25	2.739	1.957	4.217	9.086	421.875	8.660
7.6	57.76	2.757	1.966	4.236	9.126	438.976	8.718
7.7	59.29	2.775	1.975	4.254	9.166	456.533	8.775
7.8	60.84	2.793	1.983	4.273	9.205	474.552	8.832
7.9	62.41	2.811	1.992	4.291	9.244	493.039	8.888
8.0	64.00	2.828	2.000	4.309	9.283	512.000	8.944
8.1	65.61	2.846	2.008	4.327	9.322	531.441	9.000
8.2	67.24	2.864	2.017	4.344	9.360	551.368	9.055
8.3	68.89	2.881	2.025	4.362	9.398	571.787	9.110
8.4	70.56	2.898	2.033	4.380	9.435	592.704	9.165
8.5	72.25	2.915	2.041	4.397	9.473	614.125	9.220
8.6	73.96	2.933	2.049	4.414	9.510	636.056	9.274
8.7	75.69	2.950	2.057	4.431	9.546	658.503	9.327
8.8	77.44	2.966	2.065	4.448	9.583	681.472	9.381
8.9	79.21	2.983	2.072	4.465	9.619	704.969	9.434
9.0	81.00	3.000	2.080	4.481	9.655	729.000	9.487
9.1	82.81	3.017	2.088	4.498	9.691	753.571	9.539
9.2	84.64	3.033	2.095	4.514	9.726	778.688	9.592
9.3	86.49	3.050	2.103	4.531	9.761	804.357	9.644
9.4	88.36	3.066	2.110	4.547	9.796	830.584	9.695
9.5	90.25	3.082	2.118	4.563	9.830	857.375	9.747
9.6	92.16	3.098	2.125	4.579	9.865	884.736	9.798
9.7	94.09	3.114	2.133	4.595	9.899	912.673	9.849
9.8	96.04	3.130	2.140	4.610	9.933	941.192	9.899
9.9	98.01	3.146	2.147	4.626	9.967	970.299	9.950
10	100.00	3.162	2.154	4.642	10.000	1000.000	10.000

Common Logarithms

N	0	1	2	3	4	5	6	7	8	9
10	0000	0043	0086	0128	0170	0212	0253	0294	0334	0374
11	0414	0453	0492	0531	0569	0607	0645	0682	0719	0755
12	0792	0828	0864	0899	0934	0969	1004	1038	1072	1106
13	1139	1173	1206	1239	1271	1303	1335	1367	1399	1430
14	1461	1492	1523	1553	1584	1614	1644	1673	1703	1732
15	1761	1790	1818	1847	1875	1903	1931	1959	1987	2014
16	2041	2068	2095	2122	2148	2175	2201	2227	2253	2279
17	2304	2330	2355	2380	2405	2430	2455	2480	2504	2529
18	2553	2577	2601	2625	2648	2672	2695	2718	2742	2765
19	2788	2810	2833	2856	2878	2900	2923	2945	2967	2989
20	3010	3032	3054	3075	3096	3118	3139	3160	3181	3201
21	3222	3243	3263	3284	3304	3324	3345	3365	3385	3404
22	3424	3444	3464	3483	3502	3522	3541	3560	3579	3598
23	3617	3636	3655	3674	3692	3711	3729	3747	3766	3784
24	3802	3820	3838	3856	3874	3892	3909	3927	3945	3962
25	3979	3997	4014	4031	4048	4065	4082	4099	4116	4133
26	4150	4166	4183	4200	4216	4232	4249	4265	4281	4298
27	4314	4330	4346	4362	4378	4393	4409	4425	4440	4456
28	4472	4487	4502	4518	4533	4548	4564	4579	4594	4609
29	4624	4639	4654	4669	4683	4698	4713	4728	4742	4757
30	4771	4786	4800	4814	4829	4843	4857	4871	4886	4900
31	4914	4928	4942	4955	4969	4983	4997	5011	5024	5038
32	5051	5065	5079	5092	5105	5119	5132	5145	5159	5172
33	5185	5198	5211	5224	5237	5250	5263	5276	5289	5302
34	5315	5328	5340	5353	5366	5378	5391	5403	5416	5428
35	5441	5453	5465	5478	5490	5502	5514	5527	5539	5551
36	5563	5575	5587	5599	5611	5623	5635	5647	5658	5670
37	5682	5694	5705	5717	5729	5740	5752	5763	5775	5786
38	5798	5809	5821	5832	5843	5855	5866	5877	5888	5899
39	5911	5922	5933	5944	5955	5966	5977	5988	5999	6010
40	6021	6031	6042	6053	6064	6075	6085	6096	6107	6117
41	6128	6138	6149	6160	6170	6180	6191	6201	6212	6222
42	6232	6243	6253	6263	6274	6284	6294	6304	6314	6325
43	6335	6345	6355	6365	6375	6385	6395	6405	6415	6425
44	6435	6444	6454	6464	6474	6484	6493	6503	6513	6522
45	6532	6542	6551	6561	6571	6580	6590	6599	6609	6618
46	6628	6637	6646	6656	6665	6675	6684	6693	6702	6712
47	6721	6730	6739	6749	6758	6767	6776	6785	6794	6803
48	6812	6821	6830	6839	6848	6857	6866	6875	6884	6893
49	6902	6911	6920	6928	6937	6946	6955	6964	6972	6981
50	6990	6998	7007	7016	7024	7033	7042	7050	7059	7067
51	7076	7084	7093	7101	7110	7118	7126	7135	7143	7152
52	7160	7168	7177	7185	7193	7202	7210	7218	7226	7235
53	7243	7251	7259	7267	7275	7284	7292	7300	7308	7316
54	7324	7332	7340	7348	7356	7364	7372	7380	7388	7396
55	7404	7412	7419	7427	7435	7443	7451	7459	7466	7474
56	7482	7490	7497	7505	7513	7520	7528	7536	7543	7551
57	7559	7566	7574	7582	7589	7597	7604	7612	7619	7627
58	7634	7642	7649	7657	7664	7672	7679	7686	7694	7701
59	7709	7716	7723	7731	7738	7745	7752	7760	7767	7774
60	7782	7789	7796	7803	7810	7818	7825	7832	7839	7846
61	7853	7860	7868	7875	7882	7889	7896	7903	7910	7917
62	7924	7931	7938	7945	7952	7959	7966	7973	7980	7987
63	7993	8000	8007	8014	8021	8028	8035	8041	8048	8055
64	8062	8069	8075	8082	8089	8096	8102	8109	8116	8122
65	8129	8136	8142	8149	8156	8162	8169	8176	8182	8189
66	8195	8202	8209	8215	8222	8228	8235	8241	8248	8254
67	8261	8267	8274	8280	8287	8293	8299	8306	8312	8319
68	8325	8331	8338	8344	8351	8357	8363	8370	8376	8382
69	8388	8395	8401	8407	8414	8420	8426	8432	8439	8445
70	8451	8457	8463	8470	8476	8482	8488	8494	8500	8506
71	8513	8519	8525	8531	8537	8543	8549	8555	8561	8567
72	8573	8579	8585	8591	8597	8603	8609	8615	8621	8627
73	8633	8639	8645	8651	8657	8663	8669	8675	8681	8686
74	8692	8698	8704	8710	8716	8722	8727	8733	8739	8745
75	8751	8756	8762	8768	8774	8779	8785	8791	8797	8802
76	8808	8814	8820	8825	8831	8837	8842	8848	8854	8859
77	8865	8871	8876	8882	8887	8893	8899	8904	8910	8915
78	8921	8927	8932	8938	8943	8949	8954	8960	8965	8971
79	8976	8982	8987	8993	8998	9004	9009	9015	9020	9025
80	9031	9036	9042	9047	9053	9058	9063	9069	9074	9079
81	9085	9090	9096	9101	9106	9112	9117	9122	9128	9133
82	9138	9143	9149	9154	9159	9165	9170	9175	9180	9186
83	9191	9196	9201	9206	9212	9217	9222	9227	9232	9238
84	9243	9248	9253	9258	9263	9269	9274	9279	9284	9289
85	9294	9299	9304	9309	9315	9320	9325	9330	9335	9340
86	9345	9350	9355	9360	9365	9370	9375	9380	9385	9390
87	9395	9400	9405	9410	9415	9420	9425	9430	9435	9440
88	9445	9450	9455	9460	9465	9469	9474	9479	9484	9489
89	9494	9499	9504	9509	9513	9518	9523	9528	9533	9538
90	9542	9547	9552	9557	9562	9566	9571	9576	9581	9586
91	9590	9595	9600	9605	9609	9614	9619	9624	9628	9633
92	9638	9643	9647	9652	9657	9661	9666	9671	9675	9680
93	9685	9689	9694	9699	9703	9708	9713	9717	9722	9727
94	9731	9736	9741	9745	9750	9754	9759	9763	9768	9773
95	9777	9782	9786	9791	9795	9800	9805	9809	9814	9818
96	9823	9827	9832	9836	9841	9845	9850	9854	9859	9863
97	9868	9872	9877	9881	9886	9890	9894	9899	9903	9908
98	9912	9917	9921	9926	9930	9934	9939	9943	9948	9952
99	9956	9961	9965	9969	9974	9978	9983	9987	9991	9996

Natural Logarithms

N	0	1	2	3	4	5	6	7	8	9
5.5	1.7047	7066	7084	7102	7120	7138	7156	7174	7192	7210
5.6	7228	7246	7263	7281	7299	7317	7334	7352	7370	7387
5.7	7405	7422	7440	7457	7475	7492	7509	7527	7544	7561
5.8	7579	7596	7613	7630	7647	7664	7681	7699	7716	7733
5.9	7750	7766	7783	7800	7817	7834	7851	7867	7884	7901
6.0	1.7918	7934	7951	7967	7984	8001	8017	8034	8050	8066
6.1	8083	8099	8116	8132	8148	8165	8181	8197	8213	8229
6.2	8245	8262	8278	8294	8310	8326	8342	8358	8374	8390
6.3	8405	8421	8437	8453	8469	8485	8500	8516	8532	8547
6.4	8563	8579	8594	8610	8625	8641	8656	8672	8687	8703
6.5	1.8718	8733	8749	8764	8779	8795	8810	8825	8840	8856
6.6	8871	8886	8901	8916	8931	8946	8961	8976	8991	9006
6.7	9021	9036	9051	9066	9081	9095	9110	9125	9140	9155
6.8	9169	9184	9199	9213	9228	9242	9257	9272	9286	9301
6.9	9315	9330	9344	9359	9373	9387	9402	9416	9430	9445
7.0	1.9459	9473	9488	9502	9516	9530	9544	9559	9573	9587
7.1	9601	9615	9629	9643	9657	9671	9685	9699	9713	9727
7.2	9741	9755	9769	9782	9796	9810	9824	9838	9851	9865
7.3	9879	9892	9906	9920	9933	9947	9961	9974	9988	2.0001
7.4	2.0015	0028	0042	0055	0069	0082	0096	0109	0122	0136
7.5	2.0149	0162	0176	0189	0202	0215	0229	0242	0255	0268
7.6	0281	0295	0308	0321	0334	0347	0360	0373	0386	0399
7.7	0412	0425	0438	0451	0464	0477	0490	0503	0516	0528
7.8	0541	0554	0567	0580	0592	0605	0618	0630	0643	0656
7.9	0669	0681	0694	0707	0719	0732	0744	0757	0769	0782
8.0	2.0794	0807	0819	0832	0844	0857	0869	0882	0894	0906
8.1	0919	0931	0943	0956	0968	0980	0992	1005	1017	1029
8.2	1041	1054	1066	1078	1090	1102	1114	1126	1138	1150
8.3	1163	1175	1187	1199	1211	1223	1235	1247	1258	1270
8.4	1282	1294	1306	1318	1330	1342	1353	1365	1377	1389
8.5	2.1401	1412	1424	1436	1448	1459	1471	1483	1494	1506
8.6	1518	1529	1541	1552	1564	1576	1587	1599	1610	1622
8.7	1633	1645	1656	1668	1679	1691	1702	1713	1725	1736
8.8	1748	1759	1770	1782	1793	1804	1815	1827	1838	1849
8.9	1861	1872	1883	1894	1905	1917	1928	1939	1950	1961
9.0	2.1972	1983	1994	2006	2017	2028	2039	2050	2061	2072
9.1	2083	2094	2105	2116	2127	2138	2148	2159	2170	2181
9.2	2192	2203	2214	2225	2235	2246	2257	2268	2279	2289
9.3	2300	2311	2322	2332	2343	2354	2364	2375	2386	2396
9.4	2407	2418	2428	2439	2450	2460	2471	2481	2492	2502
9.5	2.2513	2523	2534	2544	2555	2565	2576	2586	2597	2607
9.6	2618	2628	2638	2649	2659	2670	2680	2690	2701	2711
9.7	2721	2732	2742	2752	2762	2773	2783	2793	2803	2814
9.8	2824	2834	2844	2854	2865	2875	2885	2895	2905	2915
9.9	2925	2935	2946	2956	2966	2976	2986	2996	3006	3016

Natural Logarithms

N	0	1	2	3	4	5	6	7	8	9
1.0	0.0000	0100	0198	0296	0392	0488	0583	0677	0770	0862
1.1	0953	1044	1133	1222	1310	1398	1484	1570	1655	1740
1.2	1823	1906	1989	2070	2151	2231	2311	2390	2469	2546
1.3	2624	2700	2776	2852	2927	3001	3075	3148	3221	3293
1.4	3365	3436	3507	3577	3646	3716	3784	3853	3920	3988
1.5	4055	4121	4187	4253	4318	4383	4447	4511	4574	4637
1.6	4700	4762	4824	4886	4947	5008	5068	5128	5188	5247
1.7	5306	5365	5423	5481	5539	5596	5653	5710	5766	5822
1.8	5878	5933	5988	6043	6098	6152	6206	6259	6313	6366
1.9	6419	6471	6523	6575	6627	6678	6729	6780	6831	6881
2.0	6931	6981	7031	7080	7129	7178	7227	7275	7324	7372
2.1	7419	7467	7514	7561	7608	7655	7701	7747	7793	7839
2.2	7885	7930	7975	8020	8065	8109	8154	8198	8242	8286
2.3	8329	8372	8416	8459	8502	8544	8587	8629	8671	8713
2.4	8755	8796	8838	8879	8920	8961	9002	9042	9083	9123
2.5	9163	9203	9243	9282	9322	9361	9400	9439	9478	9517
2.6	9555	9594	9632	9670	9708	9746	9783	9821	9858	9895
2.7	9933	9969	1.0006	0043	0080	0116	0152	0188	0225	0260
2.8	1.0296	0332	0367	0403	0438	0473	0508	0543	0578	0613
2.9	0647	0682	0716	0750	0784	0818	0852	0886	0919	0953
3.0	1.0986	1019	1053	1086	1119	1151	1184	1217	1249	1282
3.1	1314	1346	1378	1410	1442	1474	1506	1537	1569	1600
3.2	1632	1663	1694	1725	1756	1787	1817	1848	1878	1909
3.3	1939	1969	2000	2030	2060	2090	2119	2149	2179	2208
3.4	2238	2267	2296	2326	2355	2384	2413	2442	2470	2499
3.5	1.2528	2556	2585	2613	2641	2669	2698	2726	2754	2782
3.6	2809	2837	2865	2892	2920	2947	2975	3002	3029	3056
3.7	3083	3110	3137	3164	3191	3218	3244	3271	3297	3324
3.8	3350	3376	3403	3429	3455	3481	3507	3533	3558	3584
3.9	3610	3635	3661	3686	3712	3737	3762	3788	3813	3838
4.0	1.3863	3888	3913	3938	3962	3987	4012	4036	4061	4085
4.1	4110	4134	4159	4183	4207	4231	4255	4279	4303	4327
4.2	4351	4375	4398	4422	4446	4469	4493	4516	4540	4563
4.3	4586	4609	4633	4656	4679	4702	4725	4748	4770	4793
4.4	4816	4839	4861	4884	4907	4929	4951	4974	4996	5019
4.5	1.5041	5063	5085	5107	5129	5151	5173	5195	5217	5239
4.6	5261	5282	5304	5326	5347	5369	5390	5412	5433	5454
4.7	5476	5497	5518	5539	5560	5581	5602	5623	5644	5665
4.8	5686	5707	5728	5748	5769	5790	5810	5831	5851	5872
4.9	5892	5913	5933	5953	5974	5994	6014	6034	6054	6074
5.0	1.6094	6114	6134	6154	6174	6194	6214	6233	6253	6273
5.1	6292	6312	6332	6351	6371	6390	6409	6429	6448	6467
5.2	6487	6506	6525	6544	6563	6582	6601	6620	6639	6658
5.3	6677	6696	6715	6734	6752	6771	6790	6808	6827	6845
5.4	6864	6882	6901	6919	6938	6956	6974	6993	7011	7029

Trigonometric Functions

Angle	sin	cos	tan	cot	sec	csc	Angle
0.0°	0.0000	1.000	0.0000	undefined	1.000	undefined	90.0°
0.1°	0.0017	1.000	0.0017	573.0	1.000	573.0	89.9°
0.2°	0.0035	1.000	0.0035	286.5	1.000	286.5	89.8°
0.3°	0.0052	1.000	0.0052	191.0	1.000	191.0	89.7°
0.4°	0.0070	1.000	0.0070	143.2	1.000	143.2	89.6°
0.5°	0.0087	1.000	0.0087	114.6	1.000	114.6	89.5°
0.6°	0.0105	0.9999	0.0105	95.49	1.000	95.49	89.4°
0.7°	0.0122	0.9999	0.0122	81.85	1.000	81.85	89.3°
0.8°	0.0140	0.9999	0.0140	71.62	1.000	71.62	89.2°
0.9°	0.0157	0.9999	0.0157	63.66	1.000	63.66	89.1°
1.0°	0.0175	0.9998	0.0175	57.29	1.000	57.30	89.0°
1.1°	0.0192	0.9998	0.0192	52.08	1.000	52.09	88.9°
1.2°	0.0209	0.9998	0.0209	47.74	1.000	47.75	88.8°
1.3°	0.0227	0.9997	0.0227	44.07	1.000	44.08	88.7°
1.4°	0.0244	0.9997	0.0244	40.92	1.000	40.93	88.6°
1.5°	0.0262	0.9997	0.0262	38.19	1.000	38.20	88.5°
1.6°	0.0279	0.9996	0.0279	35.80	1.000	35.81	88.4°
1.7°	0.0297	0.9996	0.0297	33.69	1.000	33.71	88.3°
1.8°	0.0314	0.9995	0.0314	31.82	1.000	31.84	88.2°
1.9°	0.0332	0.9995	0.0332	30.14	1.001	30.16	88.1°
2.0°	0.0349	0.9994	0.0349	28.64	1.001	28.65	88.0°
2.1°	0.0366	0.9993	0.0367	27.27	1.001	27.29	87.9°
2.2°	0.0384	0.9993	0.0384	26.03	1.001	26.05	87.8°
2.3°	0.0401	0.9992	0.0402	24.90	1.001	24.92	87.7°
2.4°	0.0419	0.9991	0.0419	23.86	1.001	23.88	87.6°
2.5°	0.0436	0.9990	0.0437	22.90	1.001	22.93	87.5°
2.6°	0.0454	0.9990	0.0454	22.02	1.001	22.04	87.4°
2.7°	0.0471	0.9989	0.0472	21.20	1.001	21.23	87.3°
2.8°	0.0488	0.9988	0.0489	20.45	1.001	20.47	87.2°
2.9°	0.0506	0.9987	0.0507	19.74	1.001	19.77	87.1°
3.0°	0.0523	0.9986	0.0524	19.08	1.001	19.11	87.0°
3.1°	0.0541	0.9985	0.0542	18.46	1.001	18.49	86.9°
3.2°	0.0558	0.9984	0.0559	17.89	1.002	17.91	86.8°
3.3°	0.0576	0.9983	0.0577	17.34	1.002	17.37	86.7°
3.4°	0.0593	0.9982	0.0594	16.83	1.002	16.86	86.6°
3.5°	0.0610	0.9981	0.0612	16.35	1.002	16.38	86.5°
3.6°	0.0628	0.9980	0.0629	15.89	1.002	15.93	86.4°
3.7°	0.0645	0.9979	0.0647	15.46	1.002	15.50	86.3°
3.8°	0.0663	0.9978	0.0664	15.06	1.002	15.09	86.2°
3.9°	0.0680	0.9977	0.0682	14.67	1.002	14.70	86.1°
4.0°	0.0698	0.9976	0.0699	14.30	1.002	14.34	86.0°
4.1°	0.0715	0.9974	0.0717	13.95	1.003	13.99	85.9°
4.2°	0.0732	0.9973	0.0734	13.62	1.003	13.65	85.8°
4.3°	0.0750	0.9972	0.0752	13.30	1.003	13.34	85.7°
4.4°	0.0767	0.9971	0.0769	13.00	1.003	13.03	85.6°
4.5°	0.0785	0.9969	0.0787	12.71	1.003	12.75	85.5°
	cos	sin	cot	tan	csc	sec	Angle

Trigonometric Functions

Angle	sin	cos	tan	cot	sec	csc	Angle
4.5°	0.0785	0.9969	0.0787	12.71	1.003	12.75	85.5°
4.6°	0.0802	0.9968	0.0805	12.43	1.003	12.47	85.4°
4.7°	0.0819	0.9966	0.0822	12.16	1.003	12.20	85.3°
4.8°	0.0837	0.9965	0.0840	11.91	1.004	11.95	85.2°
4.9°	0.0854	0.9963	0.0857	11.66	1.004	11.71	85.1°
5.0°	0.0872	0.9962	0.0875	11.43	1.004	11.47	85.0°
5.1°	0.0889	0.9960	0.0892	11.20	1.004	11.25	84.9°
5.2°	0.0906	0.9959	0.0910	10.99	1.004	11.03	84.8°
5.3°	0.0924	0.9957	0.0928	10.78	1.004	10.83	84.7°
5.4°	0.0941	0.9956	0.0945	10.58	1.004	10.63	84.6°
5.5°	0.0958	0.9954	0.0963	10.39	1.005	10.43	84.5°
5.6°	0.0976	0.9952	0.0981	10.20	1.005	10.25	84.4°
5.7°	0.0993	0.9951	0.0998	10.02	1.005	10.07	84.3°
5.8°	0.1011	0.9949	0.1016	9.845	1.005	9.895	84.2°
5.9°	0.1028	0.9947	0.1033	9.677	1.005	9.728	84.1°
6.0°	0.1045	0.9945	0.1051	9.514	1.006	9.567	84.0°
6.1°	0.1063	0.9943	0.1069	9.357	1.006	9.411	83.9°
6.2°	0.1080	0.9942	0.1086	9.205	1.006	9.259	83.8°
6.3°	0.1097	0.9940	0.1104	9.058	1.006	9.113	83.7°
6.4°	0.1115	0.9938	0.1122	8.915	1.006	8.971	83.6°
6.5°	0.1132	0.9936	0.1139	8.777	1.006	8.834	83.5°
6.6°	0.1149	0.9934	0.1157	8.643	1.007	8.700	83.4°
6.7°	0.1167	0.9932	0.1175	8.513	1.007	8.571	83.3°
6.8°	0.1184	0.9930	0.1192	8.386	1.007	8.446	83.2°
6.9°	0.1201	0.9928	0.1210	8.264	1.007	8.324	83.1°
7.0°	0.1219	0.9925	0.1228	8.144	1.008	8.206	83.0°
7.1°	0.1236	0.9923	0.1246	8.028	1.008	8.091	82.9°
7.2°	0.1253	0.9921	0.1263	7.916	1.008	7.979	82.8°
7.3°	0.1271	0.9919	0.1281	7.806	1.008	7.870	82.7°
7.4°	0.1288	0.9917	0.1299	7.700	1.008	7.764	82.6°
7.5°	0.1305	0.9914	0.1317	7.596	1.009	7.661	82.5°
7.6°	0.1323	0.9912	0.1334	7.495	1.009	7.561	82.4°
7.7°	0.1340	0.9910	0.1352	7.396	1.009	7.463	82.3°
7.8°	0.1357	0.9907	0.1370	7.300	1.009	7.368	82.2°
7.9°	0.1374	0.9905	0.1388	7.207	1.010	7.276	82.1°
8.0°	0.1392	0.9903	0.1405	7.115	1.010	7.185	82.0°
8.1°	0.1409	0.9900	0.1423	7.026	1.010	7.097	81.9°
8.2°	0.1426	0.9898	0.1441	6.940	1.010	7.011	81.8°
8.3°	0.1444	0.9895	0.1459	6.855	1.011	6.927	81.7°
8.4°	0.1461	0.9893	0.1477	6.772	1.011	6.845	81.6°
8.5°	0.1478	0.9890	0.1495	6.691	1.011	6.765	81.5°
8.6°	0.1495	0.9888	0.1512	6.612	1.011	6.687	81.4°
8.7°	0.1513	0.9885	0.1530	6.535	1.012	6.611	81.3°
8.8°	0.1530	0.9882	0.1548	6.460	1.012	6.537	81.2°
8.9°	0.1547	0.9880	0.1566	6.386	1.012	6.464	81.1°
9.0°	0.1564	0.9877	0.1584	6.314	1.012	6.392	81.0°
	cos	sin	cot	tan	csc	sec	Angle

TABLES

Trigonometric Functions

Angle	sin	cos	tan	cot	sec	csc	Angle
9.0°	0.1564	0.9877	0.1584	6.314	1.012	6.392	81.0°
9.1°	0.1582	0.9874	0.1602	6.243	1.013	6.323	80.9°
9.2°	0.1599	0.9871	0.1620	6.174	1.013	6.255	80.8°
9.3°	0.1616	0.9869	0.1638	6.107	1.013	6.188	80.7°
9.4°	0.1633	0.9866	0.1655	6.041	1.014	6.123	80.6°
9.5°	0.1650	0.9863	0.1673	5.976	1.014	6.059	80.5°
9.6°	0.1668	0.9860	0.1691	5.912	1.014	5.996	80.4°
9.7°	0.1685	0.9857	0.1709	5.850	1.015	5.935	80.3°
9.8°	0.1702	0.9854	0.1727	5.789	1.015	5.875	80.2°
9.9°	0.1719	0.9851	0.1745	5.730	1.015	5.816	80.1°
10.0°	0.1736	0.9848	0.1763	5.671	1.015	5.759	80.0°
10.1°	0.1754	0.9845	0.1781	5.614	1.016	5.702	79.9°
10.2°	0.1771	0.9842	0.1799	5.558	1.016	5.647	79.8°
10.3°	0.1788	0.9839	0.1817	5.503	1.016	5.593	79.7°
10.4°	0.1805	0.9836	0.1835	5.449	1.017	5.540	79.6°
10.5°	0.1822	0.9833	0.1853	5.396	1.017	5.487	79.5°
10.6°	0.1840	0.9829	0.1871	5.343	1.017	5.436	79.4°
10.7°	0.1857	0.9826	0.1890	5.292	1.018	5.386	79.3°
10.8°	0.1874	0.9823	0.1908	5.242	1.018	5.337	79.2°
10.9°	0.1891	0.9820	0.1926	5.193	1.018	5.288	79.1°
11.0°	0.1908	0.9816	0.1944	5.145	1.019	5.241	79.0°
11.1°	0.1925	0.9813	0.1962	5.097	1.019	5.194	78.9°
11.2°	0.1942	0.9810	0.1980	5.050	1.019	5.148	78.8°
11.3°	0.1959	0.9806	0.1998	5.005	1.020	5.103	78.7°
11.4°	0.1977	0.9803	0.2016	4.959	1.020	5.059	78.6°
11.5°	0.1994	0.9799	0.2035	4.915	1.020	5.016	78.5°
11.6°	0.2011	0.9796	0.2053	4.872	1.021	4.973	78.4°
11.7°	0.2028	0.9792	0.2071	4.829	1.021	4.931	78.3°
11.8°	0.2045	0.9789	0.2089	4.787	1.022	4.890	78.2°
11.9°	0.2062	0.9785	0.2107	4.745	1.022	4.850	78.1°
12.0°	0.2079	0.9781	0.2126	4.705	1.022	4.810	78.0°
12.1°	0.2096	0.9778	0.2144	4.665	1.023	4.771	77.9°
12.2°	0.2113	0.9774	0.2162	4.625	1.023	4.732	77.8°
12.3°	0.2130	0.9770	0.2180	4.586	1.023	4.694	77.7°
12.4°	0.2147	0.9767	0.2199	4.548	1.024	4.657	77.6°
12.5°	0.2164	0.9763	0.2217	4.511	1.024	4.620	77.5°
12.6°	0.2181	0.9759	0.2235	4.474	1.025	4.584	77.4°
12.7°	0.2198	0.9755	0.2254	4.437	1.025	4.549	77.3°
12.8°	0.2215	0.9751	0.2272	4.402	1.025	4.514	77.2°
12.9°	0.2233	0.9748	0.2290	4.366	1.026	4.479	77.1°
13.0°	0.2250	0.9744	0.2309	4.331	1.026	4.445	77.0°
13.1°	0.2267	0.9740	0.2327	4.297	1.027	4.412	76.9°
13.2°	0.2284	0.9736	0.2345	4.264	1.027	4.379	76.8°
13.3°	0.2300	0.9732	0.2364	4.230	1.028	4.347	76.7°
13.4°	0.2317	0.9728	0.2382	4.198	1.028	4.315	76.6°
13.5°	0.2334	0.9724	0.2401	4.165	1.028	4.284	76.5°
	cos	sin	cot	tan	csc	sec	Angle

Trigonometric Functions

Angle	sin	cos	tan	cot	sec	csc	Angle
13.5°	0.2334	0.9724	0.2401	4.165	1.028	4.284	76.5°
13.6°	0.2351	0.9720	0.2419	4.134	1.029	4.253	76.4°
13.7°	0.2368	0.9715	0.2438	4.102	1.029	4.222	76.3°
13.8°	0.2385	0.9711	0.2456	4.071	1.030	4.192	76.2°
13.9°	0.2402	0.9707	0.2475	4.041	1.030	4.163	76.1°
14.0°	0.2419	0.9703	0.2493	4.011	1.031	4.134	76.0°
14.1°	0.2436	0.9699	0.2512	3.981	1.031	4.105	75.9°
14.2°	0.2453	0.9694	0.2530	3.952	1.032	4.077	75.8°
14.3°	0.2470	0.9690	0.2549	3.923	1.032	4.049	75.7°
14.4°	0.2487	0.9686	0.2568	3.895	1.032	4.021	75.6°
14.5°	0.2504	0.9681	0.2586	3.867	1.033	3.994	75.5°
14.6°	0.2521	0.9677	0.2605	3.839	1.033	3.967	75.4°
14.7°	0.2538	0.9673	0.2623	3.812	1.034	3.941	75.3°
14.8°	0.2554	0.9668	0.2642	3.785	1.034	3.915	75.2°
14.9°	0.2571	0.9664	0.2661	3.758	1.035	3.889	75.1°
15.0°	0.2588	0.9659	0.2679	3.732	1.035	3.864	75.0°
15.1°	0.2605	0.9655	0.2698	3.706	1.036	3.839	74.9°
15.2°	0.2622	0.9650	0.2717	3.681	1.036	3.814	74.8°
15.3°	0.2639	0.9646	0.2736	3.655	1.037	3.790	74.7°
15.4°	0.2656	0.9641	0.2754	3.630	1.037	3.766	74.6°
15.5°	0.2672	0.9636	0.2773	3.606	1.038	3.742	74.5°
15.6°	0.2689	0.9632	0.2792	3.582	1.038	3.719	74.4°
15.7°	0.2706	0.9627	0.2811	3.558	1.039	3.695	74.3°
15.8°	0.2723	0.9622	0.2830	3.534	1.039	3.673	74.2°
15.9°	0.2740	0.9617	0.2849	3.511	1.040	3.650	74.1°
16.0°	0.2756	0.9613	0.2867	3.487	1.040	3.628	74.0°
16.1°	0.2773	0.9608	0.2886	3.465	1.041	3.606	73.9°
16.2°	0.2790	0.9603	0.2905	3.442	1.041	3.584	73.8°
16.3°	0.2807	0.9598	0.2924	3.420	1.042	3.563	73.7°
16.4°	0.2823	0.9593	0.2943	3.398	1.042	3.542	73.6°
16.5°	0.2840	0.9588	0.2962	3.376	1.043	3.521	73.5°
16.6°	0.2857	0.9583	0.2981	3.354	1.043	3.500	73.4°
16.7°	0.2874	0.9578	0.3000	3.333	1.044	3.480	73.3°
16.8°	0.2890	0.9573	0.3019	3.312	1.045	3.460	73.2°
16.9°	0.2907	0.9568	0.3038	3.291	1.045	3.440	73.1°
17.0°	0.2924	0.9563	0.3057	3.271	1.046	3.420	73.0°
17.1°	0.2940	0.9558	0.3076	3.251	1.046	3.401	72.9°
17.2°	0.2957	0.9553	0.3096	3.230	1.047	3.382	72.8°
17.3°	0.2974	0.9548	0.3115	3.211	1.047	3.363	72.7°
17.4°	0.2990	0.9542	0.3134	3.191	1.048	3.344	72.6°
17.5°	0.3007	0.9537	0.3153	3.172	1.049	3.326	72.5°
17.6°	0.3024	0.9532	0.3172	3.152	1.049	3.307	72.4°
17.7°	0.3040	0.9527	0.3191	3.133	1.050	3.289	72.3°
17.8°	0.3057	0.9521	0.3211	3.115	1.050	3.271	72.2°
17.9°	0.3074	0.9516	0.3230	3.096	1.051	3.254	72.1°
18.0°	0.3090	0.9511	0.3249	3.078	1.051	3.236	72.0°
	cos	sin	cot	tan	csc	sec	Angle

Trigonometric Functions

Angle	sin	cos	tan	cot	sec	csc	Angle
18.0°	0.3090	0.9511	0.3249	3.078	1.051	3.236	72.0°
18.1°	0.3107	0.9505	0.3269	3.060	1.052	3.219	71.9°
18.2°	0.3123	0.9500	0.3288	3.042	1.053	3.202	71.8°
18.3°	0.3140	0.9494	0.3307	3.024	1.053	3.185	71.7°
18.4°	0.3156	0.9489	0.3327	3.006	1.054	3.168	71.6°
18.5°	0.3173	0.9483	0.3346	2.989	1.054	3.152	71.5°
18.6°	0.3190	0.9478	0.3365	2.971	1.055	3.135	71.4°
18.7°	0.3206	0.9472	0.3385	2.954	1.056	3.119	71.3°
18.8°	0.3223	0.9466	0.3404	2.937	1.056	3.103	71.2°
18.9°	0.3239	0.9461	0.3424	2.921	1.057	3.087	71.1°
19.0°	0.3256	0.9455	0.3443	2.904	1.058	3.072	71.0°
19.1°	0.3272	0.9449	0.3463	2.888	1.058	3.056	70.9°
19.2°	0.3289	0.9444	0.3482	2.872	1.059	3.041	70.8°
19.3°	0.3305	0.9438	0.3502	2.856	1.060	3.026	70.7°
19.4°	0.3322	0.9432	0.3522	2.840	1.060	3.011	70.6°
19.5°	0.3338	0.9426	0.3541	2.824	1.061	2.996	70.5°
19.6°	0.3355	0.9421	0.3561	2.808	1.062	2.981	70.4°
19.7°	0.3371	0.9415	0.3581	2.793	1.062	2.967	70.3°
19.8°	0.3387	0.9409	0.3600	2.778	1.063	2.952	70.2°
19.9°	0.3404	0.9403	0.3620	2.762	1.064	2.938	70.1°
20.0°	0.3420	0.9397	0.3640	2.747	1.064	2.924	70.0°
20.1°	0.3437	0.9391	0.3659	2.733	1.065	2.910	69.9°
20.2°	0.3453	0.9385	0.3679	2.718	1.066	2.896	69.8°
20.3°	0.3469	0.9379	0.3699	2.703	1.066	2.882	69.7°
20.4°	0.3486	0.9373	0.3719	2.689	1.067	2.869	69.6°
20.5°	0.3502	0.9367	0.3739	2.675	1.068	2.855	69.5°
20.6°	0.3518	0.9361	0.3759	2.660	1.068	2.842	69.4°
20.7°	0.3535	0.9354	0.3779	2.646	1.069	2.829	69.3°
20.8°	0.3551	0.9348	0.3799	2.633	1.070	2.816	69.2°
20.9°	0.3567	0.9342	0.3819	2.619	1.070	2.803	69.1°
21.0°	0.3584	0.9336	0.3839	2.605	1.071	2.790	69.0°
21.1°	0.3600	0.9330	0.3859	2.592	1.072	2.778	68.9°
21.2°	0.3616	0.9323	0.3879	2.578	1.073	2.765	68.8°
21.3°	0.3633	0.9317	0.3899	2.565	1.073	2.753	68.7°
21.4°	0.3649	0.9311	0.3919	2.552	1.074	2.741	68.6°
21.5°	0.3665	0.9304	0.3939	2.539	1.075	2.729	68.5°
21.6°	0.3681	0.9298	0.3959	2.526	1.076	2.716	68.4°
21.7°	0.3697	0.9291	0.3979	2.513	1.076	2.705	68.3°
21.8°	0.3714	0.9285	0.4000	2.500	1.077	2.693	68.2°
21.9°	0.3730	0.9278	0.4020	2.488	1.078	2.681	68.1°
22.0°	0.3746	0.9272	0.4040	2.475	1.079	2.669	68.0°
22.1°	0.3762	0.9265	0.4061	2.463	1.079	2.658	67.9°
22.2°	0.3778	0.9259	0.4081	2.450	1.080	2.647	67.8°
22.3°	0.3795	0.9252	0.4101	2.438	1.081	2.635	67.7°
22.4°	0.3811	0.9245	0.4122	2.426	1.082	2.624	67.6°
22.5°	0.3827	0.9239	0.4142	2.414	1.082	2.613	67.5°
	cos	sin	cot	tan	csc	sec	cos

Trigonometric Functions

Angle	sin	cos	tan	cot	sec	csc	Angle
22.5°	0.3827	0.9239	0.4142	2.414	1.082	2.613	67.5°
22.6°	0.3843	0.9232	0.4163	2.402	1.083	2.602	67.4°
22.7°	0.3859	0.9225	0.4183	2.391	1.084	2.591	67.3°
22.8°	0.3875	0.9219	0.4204	2.379	1.085	2.581	67.2°
22.9°	0.3891	0.9212	0.4224	2.367	1.086	2.570	67.1°
23.0°	0.3907	0.9205	0.4245	2.356	1.086	2.559	67.0°
23.1°	0.3923	0.9198	0.4265	2.344	1.087	2.549	66.9°
23.2°	0.3939	0.9191	0.4286	2.333	1.088	2.538	66.8°
23.3°	0.3955	0.9184	0.4307	2.322	1.089	2.528	66.7°
23.4°	0.3971	0.9178	0.4327	2.311	1.090	2.518	66.6°
23.5°	0.3987	0.9171	0.4348	2.300	1.090	2.508	66.5°
23.6°	0.4003	0.9164	0.4369	2.289	1.091	2.498	66.4°
23.7°	0.4019	0.9157	0.4390	2.278	1.092	2.488	66.3°
23.8°	0.4035	0.9150	0.4411	2.267	1.093	2.478	66.2°
23.9°	0.4051	0.9143	0.4431	2.257	1.094	2.468	66.1°
24.0°	0.4067	0.9135	0.4452	2.246	1.095	2.459	66.0°
24.1°	0.4083	0.9128	0.4473	2.236	1.095	2.449	65.9°
24.2°	0.4099	0.9121	0.4494	2.225	1.096	2.439	65.8°
24.3°	0.4115	0.9114	0.4515	2.215	1.097	2.430	65.7°
24.4°	0.4131	0.9107	0.4536	2.204	1.098	2.421	65.6°
24.5°	0.4147	0.9100	0.4557	2.194	1.099	2.411	65.5°
24.6°	0.4163	0.9092	0.4578	2.184	1.100	2.402	65.4°
24.7°	0.4179	0.9085	0.4599	2.174	1.101	2.393	65.3°
24.8°	0.4195	0.9078	0.4621	2.164	1.102	2.384	65.2°
24.9°	0.4210	0.9070	0.4642	2.154	1.102	2.375	65.1°
25.0°	0.4226	0.9063	0.4663	2.145	1.103	2.366	65.0°
25.1°	0.4242	0.9056	0.4684	2.135	1.104	2.357	64.9°
25.2°	0.4258	0.9048	0.4706	2.125	1.105	2.349	64.8°
25.3°	0.4274	0.9041	0.4727	2.116	1.106	2.340	64.7°
25.4°	0.4289	0.9033	0.4748	2.106	1.107	2.331	64.6°
25.5°	0.4305	0.9026	0.4770	2.097	1.108	2.323	64.5°
25.6°	0.4321	0.9018	0.4791	2.087	1.109	2.314	64.4°
25.7°	0.4337	0.9011	0.4813	2.078	1.110	2.306	64.3°
25.8°	0.4352	0.9003	0.4834	2.069	1.111	2.298	64.2°
25.9°	0.4368	0.8996	0.4856	2.059	1.112	2.289	64.1°
26.0°	0.4384	0.8988	0.4877	2.050	1.113	2.281	64.0°
26.1°	0.4399	0.8980	0.4899	2.041	1.114	2.273	63.9°
26.2°	0.4415	0.8973	0.4921	2.032	1.115	2.265	63.8°
26.3°	0.4431	0.8965	0.4942	2.023	1.115	2.257	63.7°
26.4°	0.4446	0.8957	0.4964	2.014	1.116	2.249	63.6°
26.5°	0.4462	0.8949	0.4986	2.006	1.117	2.241	63.5°
26.6°	0.4478	0.8942	0.5008	1.997	1.118	2.233	63.4°
26.7°	0.4493	0.8934	0.5029	1.988	1.119	2.226	63.3°
26.8°	0.4509	0.8926	0.5051	1.980	1.120	2.218	63.2°
26.9°	0.4524	0.8918	0.5073	1.971	1.121	2.210	63.1°
27.0°	0.4540	0.8910	0.5095	1.963	1.122	2.203	63.0°
	cos	sin	cot	tan	csc	sec	cos

Trigonometric Functions

Angle	sin	cos	tan	cot	sec	csc	Angle
27.0°	0.4540	0.8910	0.5095	1.963	1.122	2.203	63.0°
27.1°	0.4555	0.8902	0.5117	1.954	1.123	2.195	62.9°
27.2°	0.4571	0.8894	0.5139	1.946	1.124	2.188	62.8°
27.3°	0.4586	0.8886	0.5161	1.937	1.125	2.180	62.7°
27.4°	0.4602	0.8878	0.5184	1.929	1.126	2.173	62.6°
27.5°	0.4617	0.8870	0.5206	1.921	1.127	2.166	62.5°
27.6°	0.4633	0.8862	0.5228	1.913	1.128	2.158	62.4°
27.7°	0.4648	0.8854	0.5250	1.905	1.129	2.151	62.3°
27.8°	0.4664	0.8846	0.5272	1.897	1.130	2.144	62.2°
27.9°	0.4679	0.8838	0.5295	1.889	1.132	2.137	62.1°
28.0°	0.4695	0.8829	0.5317	1.881	1.133	2.130	62.0°
28.1°	0.4710	0.8821	0.5340	1.873	1.134	2.123	61.9°
28.2°	0.4726	0.8813	0.5362	1.865	1.135	2.116	61.8°
28.3°	0.4741	0.8805	0.5384	1.857	1.136	2.109	61.7°
28.4°	0.4756	0.8796	0.5407	1.849	1.137	2.103	61.6°
28.5°	0.4772	0.8788	0.5430	1.842	1.138	2.096	61.5°
28.6°	0.4787	0.8780	0.5452	1.834	1.139	2.089	61.4°
28.7°	0.4802	0.8771	0.5475	1.827	1.140	2.082	61.3°
28.8°	0.4818	0.8763	0.5498	1.819	1.141	2.076	61.2°
28.9°	0.4833	0.8755	0.5520	1.811	1.142	2.069	61.1°
29.0°	0.4848	0.8746	0.5543	1.804	1.143	2.063	61.0°
29.1°	0.4863	0.8738	0.5566	1.797	1.144	2.056	60.9°
29.2°	0.4879	0.8729	0.5589	1.789	1.146	2.050	60.8°
29.3°	0.4894	0.8721	0.5612	1.782	1.147	2.043	60.7°
29.4°	0.4909	0.8712	0.5635	1.775	1.148	2.037	60.6°
29.5°	0.4924	0.8704	0.5658	1.767	1.149	2.031	60.5°
29.6°	0.4939	0.8695	0.5681	1.760	1.150	2.025	60.4°
29.7°	0.4955	0.8686	0.5704	1.753	1.151	2.018	60.3°
29.8°	0.4970	0.8678	0.5727	1.746	1.152	2.012	60.2°
29.9°	0.4985	0.8669	0.5750	1.739	1.154	2.006	60.1°
30.0°	0.5000	0.8660	0.5774	1.732	1.155	2.000	60.0°
30.1°	0.5015	0.8652	0.5797	1.725	1.156	1.994	59.9°
30.2°	0.5030	0.8643	0.5820	1.718	1.157	1.988	59.8°
30.3°	0.5045	0.8634	0.5844	1.711	1.158	1.982	59.7°
30.4°	0.5060	0.8625	0.5867	1.704	1.159	1.976	59.6°
30.5°	0.5075	0.8616	0.5890	1.698	1.161	1.970	59.5°
30.6°	0.5090	0.8607	0.5914	1.691	1.162	1.964	59.4°
30.7°	0.5105	0.8599	0.5938	1.684	1.163	1.959	59.3°
30.8°	0.5120	0.8590	0.5961	1.678	1.164	1.953	59.2°
30.9°	0.5135	0.8581	0.5985	1.671	1.165	1.947	59.1°
31.0°	0.5150	0.8572	0.6009	1.664	1.167	1.942	59.0°
31.1°	0.5165	0.8563	0.6032	1.658	1.168	1.936	58.9°
31.2°	0.5180	0.8554	0.6056	1.651	1.169	1.930	58.8°
31.3°	0.5195	0.8545	0.6080	1.645	1.170	1.925	58.7°
31.4°	0.5210	0.8535	0.6104	1.638	1.172	1.919	58.6°
31.5°	0.5225	0.8526	0.6128	1.632	1.173	1.914	58.5°
	cos	sin	cot	tan	csc	sec	

Angle	sin	cos	tan	cot	sec	csc	Angle
31.5°	0.5225	0.8526	0.6128	1.632	1.173	1.914	58.5°
31.6°	0.5240	0.8517	0.6152	1.625	1.174	1.908	58.4°
31.7°	0.5255	0.8508	0.6176	1.619	1.175	1.903	58.3°
31.8°	0.5270	0.8499	0.6200	1.613	1.177	1.898	58.2°
31.9°	0.5284	0.8490	0.6224	1.607	1.178	1.892	58.1°
32.0°	0.5299	0.8480	0.6249	1.600	1.179	1.887	58.0°
32.1°	0.5314	0.8471	0.6273	1.594	1.180	1.882	57.9°
32.2°	0.5329	0.8462	0.6297	1.588	1.182	1.877	57.8°
32.3°	0.5344	0.8453	0.6322	1.582	1.183	1.871	57.7°
32.4°	0.5358	0.8443	0.6346	1.576	1.184	1.866	57.6°
32.5°	0.5373	0.8434	0.6371	1.570	1.186	1.861	57.5°
32.6°	0.5388	0.8425	0.6395	1.564	1.187	1.856	57.4°
32.7°	0.5402	0.8415	0.6420	1.558	1.188	1.851	57.3°
32.8°	0.5417	0.8406	0.6445	1.552	1.190	1.846	57.2°
32.9°	0.5432	0.8396	0.6469	1.546	1.191	1.841	57.1°
33.0°	0.5446	0.8387	0.6494	1.540	1.192	1.836	57.0°
33.1°	0.5461	0.8377	0.6519	1.534	1.194	1.831	56.9°
33.2°	0.5476	0.8368	0.6544	1.528	1.195	1.826	56.8°
33.3°	0.5490	0.8358	0.6569	1.522	1.196	1.821	56.7°
33.4°	0.5505	0.8348	0.6594	1.517	1.198	1.817	56.6°
33.5°	0.5519	0.8339	0.6619	1.511	1.199	1.812	56.5°
33.6°	0.5534	0.8329	0.6644	1.505	1.201	1.807	56.4°
33.7°	0.5548	0.8320	0.6669	1.499	1.202	1.802	56.3°
33.8°	0.5563	0.8310	0.6694	1.494	1.203	1.798	56.2°
33.9°	0.5577	0.8300	0.6720	1.488	1.205	1.793	56.1°
34.0°	0.5592	0.8290	0.6745	1.483	1.206	1.788	56.0°
34.1°	0.5606	0.8281	0.6771	1.477	1.208	1.784	55.9°
34.2°	0.5621	0.8271	0.6796	1.471	1.209	1.779	55.8°
34.3°	0.5635	0.8261	0.6822	1.466	1.211	1.775	55.7°
34.4°	0.5650	0.8251	0.6847	1.460	1.212	1.770	55.6°
34.5°	0.5664	0.8241	0.6873	1.455	1.213	1.766	55.5°
34.6°	0.5678	0.8231	0.6899	1.450	1.215	1.761	55.4°
34.7°	0.5693	0.8221	0.6924	1.444	1.216	1.757	55.3°
34.8°	0.5707	0.8211	0.6950	1.439	1.218	1.752	55.2°
34.9°	0.5721	0.8202	0.6976	1.433	1.219	1.748	55.1°
35.0°	0.5736	0.8192	0.7002	1.428	1.221	1.743	55.0°
35.1°	0.5750	0.8181	0.7028	1.423	1.222	1.739	54.9°
35.2°	0.5764	0.8171	0.7054	1.418	1.224	1.735	54.8°
35.3°	0.5779	0.8161	0.7080	1.412	1.225	1.731	54.7°
35.4°	0.5793	0.8151	0.7107	1.407	1.227	1.726	54.6°
35.5°	0.5807	0.8141	0.7133	1.402	1.228	1.722	54.5°
35.6°	0.5821	0.8131	0.7159	1.397	1.230	1.718	54.4°
35.7°	0.5835	0.8121	0.7186	1.392	1.231	1.714	54.3°
35.8°	0.5850	0.8111	0.7212	1.387	1.233	1.710	54.2°
35.9°	0.5864	0.8100	0.7239	1.381	1.235	1.705	54.1°
36.0°	0.5878	0.8090	0.7265	1.376	1.236	1.701	54.0°
	cos	sin	cot	tan	csc	sec	

Trigonometric Functions

Angle	sin	cos	tan	cot	sec	csc	Angle
36.0°	0.5878	0.8090	0.7265	1.376	1.236	1.701	54.0°
36.1°	0.5892	0.8080	0.7292	1.371	1.238	1.697	53.9°
36.2°	0.5906	0.8070	0.7319	1.366	1.239	1.693	53.8°
36.3°	0.5920	0.8059	0.7346	1.361	1.241	1.689	53.7°
36.4°	0.5934	0.8049	0.7373	1.356	1.242	1.685	53.6°
36.5°	0.5948	0.8039	0.7400	1.351	1.244	1.681	53.5°
36.6°	0.5962	0.8028	0.7427	1.347	1.246	1.677	53.4°
36.7°	0.5976	0.8018	0.7454	1.342	1.247	1.673	53.3°
36.8°	0.5990	0.8007	0.7481	1.337	1.249	1.669	53.2°
36.9°	0.6004	0.7997	0.7508	1.332	1.250	1.666	53.1°
37.0°	0.6018	0.7986	0.7536	1.327	1.252	1.662	53.0°
37.1°	0.6032	0.7976	0.7563	1.322	1.254	1.658	52.9°
37.2°	0.6046	0.7965	0.7590	1.317	1.255	1.654	52.8°
37.3°	0.6060	0.7955	0.7618	1.313	1.257	1.650	52.7°
37.4°	0.6074	0.7944	0.7646	1.308	1.259	1.646	52.6°
37.5°	0.6088	0.7934	0.7673	1.303	1.260	1.643	52.5°
37.6°	0.6101	0.7923	0.7701	1.299	1.262	1.639	52.4°
37.7°	0.6115	0.7912	0.7729	1.294	1.264	1.635	52.3°
37.8°	0.6129	0.7902	0.7757	1.289	1.266	1.632	52.2°
37.9°	0.6143	0.7891	0.7785	1.285	1.267	1.628	52.1°
38.0°	0.6157	0.7880	0.7813	1.280	1.269	1.624	52.0°
38.1°	0.6170	0.7869	0.7841	1.275	1.271	1.621	51.9°
38.2°	0.6184	0.7859	0.7869	1.271	1.272	1.617	51.8°
38.3°	0.6198	0.7848	0.7898	1.266	1.274	1.613	51.7°
38.4°	0.6211	0.7837	0.7926	1.262	1.276	1.610	51.6°
38.5°	0.6225	0.7826	0.7954	1.257	1.278	1.606	51.5°
38.6°	0.6239	0.7815	0.7983	1.253	1.280	1.603	51.4°
38.7°	0.6252	0.7804	0.8012	1.248	1.281	1.599	51.3°
38.8°	0.6266	0.7793	0.8040	1.244	1.283	1.596	51.2°
38.9°	0.6280	0.7782	0.8069	1.239	1.285	1.592	51.1°
39.0°	0.6293	0.7771	0.8098	1.235	1.287	1.589	51.0°
39.1°	0.6307	0.7760	0.8127	1.230	1.289	1.586	50.9°
39.2°	0.6320	0.7749	0.8156	1.226	1.290	1.582	50.8°
39.3°	0.6334	0.7738	0.8185	1.222	1.292	1.579	50.7°
39.4°	0.6347	0.7727	0.8214	1.217	1.294	1.575	50.6°
39.5°	0.6361	0.7716	0.8243	1.213	1.296	1.572	50.5°
39.6°	0.6374	0.7705	0.8273	1.209	1.298	1.569	50.4°
39.7°	0.6388	0.7694	0.8302	1.205	1.300	1.566	50.3°
39.8°	0.6401	0.7683	0.8332	1.200	1.302	1.562	50.2°
39.9°	0.6414	0.7672	0.8361	1.196	1.304	1.559	50.1°
40.0°	0.6428	0.7660	0.8391	1.192	1.305	1.556	50.0°
40.1°	0.6441	0.7649	0.8421	1.188	1.307	1.552	49.9°
40.2°	0.6455	0.7638	0.8451	1.183	1.309	1.549	49.8°
40.3°	0.6468	0.7627	0.8481	1.179	1.311	1.546	49.7°
40.4°	0.6481	0.7615	0.8511	1.175	1.313	1.543	49.6°
40.5°	0.6494	0.7604	0.8541	1.171	1.315	1.540	49.5°
	cos	sin	cot	tan	csc	sec	Angle

Trigonometric Functions

Angle	sin	cos	tan	cot	sec	csc	Angle
40.5°	0.6494	0.7604	0.8541	1.171	1.315	1.540	49.5°
40.6°	0.6508	0.7593	0.8571	1.167	1.317	1.537	49.4°
40.7°	0.6521	0.7581	0.8601	1.163	1.319	1.534	49.3°
40.8°	0.6534	0.7570	0.8632	1.159	1.321	1.530	49.2°
40.9°	0.6547	0.7559	0.8662	1.154	1.323	1.527	49.1°
41.0°	0.6561	0.7547	0.8693	1.150	1.325	1.524	49.0°
41.1°	0.6574	0.7536	0.8724	1.146	1.327	1.521	48.9°
41.2°	0.6587	0.7524	0.8754	1.142	1.329	1.518	48.8°
41.3°	0.6600	0.7513	0.8785	1.138	1.331	1.515	48.7°
41.4°	0.6613	0.7501	0.8816	1.134	1.333	1.512	48.6°
41.5°	0.6626	0.7490	0.8847	1.130	1.335	1.509	48.5°
41.6°	0.6639	0.7478	0.8878	1.126	1.337	1.506	48.4°
41.7°	0.6652	0.7466	0.8910	1.122	1.339	1.503	48.3°
41.8°	0.6665	0.7455	0.8941	1.118	1.341	1.500	48.2°
41.9°	0.6678	0.7443	0.8972	1.115	1.344	1.497	48.1°
42.0°	0.6691	0.7431	0.9004	1.111	1.346	1.494	48.0°
42.1°	0.6704	0.7420	0.9036	1.107	1.348	1.492	47.9°
42.2°	0.6717	0.7408	0.9067	1.103	1.350	1.489	47.8°
42.3°	0.6730	0.7396	0.9099	1.099	1.352	1.486	47.7°
42.4°	0.6743	0.7385	0.9131	1.095	1.354	1.483	47.6°
42.5°	0.6756	0.7373	0.9163	1.091	1.356	1.480	47.5°
42.6°	0.6769	0.7361	0.9195	1.087	1.359	1.477	47.4°
42.7°	0.6782	0.7349	0.9228	1.084	1.361	1.475	47.3°
42.8°	0.6794	0.7337	0.9260	1.080	1.363	1.472	47.2°
42.9°	0.6807	0.7325	0.9293	1.076	1.365	1.469	47.1°
43.0°	0.6820	0.7314	0.9325	1.072	1.367	1.466	47.0°
43.1°	0.6833	0.7302	0.9358	1.069	1.370	1.464	46.9°
43.2°	0.6845	0.7290	0.9391	1.065	1.372	1.461	46.8°
43.3°	0.6858	0.7278	0.9424	1.061	1.374	1.458	46.7°
43.4°	0.6871	0.7266	0.9457	1.057	1.376	1.455	46.6°
43.5°	0.6884	0.7254	0.9490	1.054	1.379	1.453	46.5°
43.6°	0.6896	0.7242	0.9523	1.050	1.381	1.450	46.4°
43.7°	0.6909	0.7230	0.9556	1.046	1.383	1.447	46.3°
43.8°	0.6921	0.7218	0.9590	1.043	1.386	1.445	46.2°
43.9°	0.6934	0.7206	0.9623	1.039	1.388	1.442	46.1°
44.0°	0.6947	0.7193	0.9657	1.036	1.390	1.440	46.0°
44.1°	0.6959	0.7181	0.9691	1.032	1.393	1.437	45.9°
44.2°	0.6972	0.7169	0.9725	1.028	1.395	1.434	45.8°
44.3°	0.6984	0.7157	0.9759	1.025	1.397	1.432	45.7°
44.4°	0.6997	0.7145	0.9793	1.021	1.400	1.429	45.6°
44.5°	0.7009	0.7133	0.9827	1.018	1.402	1.427	45.5°
44.6°	0.7022	0.7120	0.9861	1.014	1.404	1.424	45.4°
44.7°	0.7034	0.7108	0.9896	1.011	1.407	1.422	45.3°
44.8°	0.7046	0.7096	0.9930	1.007	1.409	1.419	45.2°
44.9°	0.7059	0.7083	0.9965	1.003	1.412	1.417	45.1°
45.0°	0.7071	0.7071	1.0000	1.000	1.414	1.414	45.0°
	cos	sin	cot	tan	csc	sec	Angle

TABLES

GLOSSARY

absolute value (p. 68) The distance from the origin to the coordinate x.

absolute value of a complex number (p. 234) The absolute value of a complex number $a + bi$ is
$$|a + bi| = \sqrt{a^2 + b^2}$$

absolute-value inequality properties (p. 68) For all real numbers a and x, $a > 0$,
$|x| \le a$ is equivalent to $-a \le x \le a$;
$|x| \ge a$ is equivalent to $x \le -a$ or $x \ge a$

additive inverses (p. 19) Pairs of real numbers that have the sum 0.

additive inverse of a matrix (p. 622) For each matrix $A_{m \times n}$ there is a matrix $-A_{m \times n}$ (the additive inverse of A), such that $A + (-A) = Z$.

algebraic expressions (p. 5) Expressions that are made up of variables, numbers, grouping symbols, operation signs, and exponents.

amplitude (p. 669) Half the difference between the maximum and minimum values of a periodic function.

angle of depression (p. 712) An angle that measures between 0° and 90° formed by a horizontal ray and a ray from the observer to the object observed below.

angle of elevation (p. 712) An angle that measures between 0° and 90° formed by a horizontal ray and a ray from the observer to the object observed above.

Arcosine X (p. 686) A number between 0 and π whose cosine is X.

Arcsine X (p. 686) A number between $-\frac{\pi}{2}$ and $+\frac{\pi}{2}$ whose sine is X.

Arctan X (p. 687) A number between $-\frac{\pi}{2}$ and $+\frac{\pi}{2}$ whose tangent is X.

arithmetic mean (pp. 4, 239) The sum of the numbers in a set divided by the number of numbers in the given set.

arithmetic means (p. 488) Terms of an arithmetic sequence that are between two given terms.

arithmetic sequence (p. 488) For each positive integer n, the sequence with the first term a_1 and nth term a_n is an arithmetic sequence if and only if $a_n = a_1 + (n - 1)d$.

arithmetic series (p. 500) The indicated sum of the terms of an arithmetic sequence.

asymptotes (of a hyperbola) (p. 382) The lines within which the branches of the hyperbola lie, and which are approached by the branches as $|x|$ increases.

augmented matrix (p. 637) The coefficient matrix for a system of linear equations with a final column included for the constants of the equations.

axis of symmetry (p. 367) A line in the plane of a graph such that the part of the graph on one side of the line is a reflection of the part on the other side.

base of an exponential or logarithmic function (p. 441, 446) The positive number b, $b \ne 1$, in $y = b^x$ or in $y = \log_b x$.

biased sample (p. 596) A sample that is not random.

binomial (p. 191) A polynomial with two terms.

boundary condition (p. 74) An extreme value in an inequality problem. Solutions will be less than or greater than that value.

center of a circle (p. 361) The point in a circle from which the distance to any point on the circle is a constant.

center of an ellipse (p. 375) The intersection of the axes of symmetry.

central tendency of a set of numbers (p. 575) A number considered to be the most typical or representative of that set.

circle (p. 361) The set of all points in a plane such that the distance (radius) from a given point (center of the circle) is constant.

circular functions (p. 680) Periodic functions related to the unit circle.

closure (p. 18) A set of numbers is closed under an operation if combining any two elements in the set by that operation yields a number in the set.

coefficient (p. 185) The constant factor of a monomial.

coefficient determinant (p. 156) A determinant D that expresses the denominators of the roots in the general solution of a system of equations.

coefficient matrix (p. 632) The matrix
$\begin{bmatrix} a & b \\ d & e \end{bmatrix}$ for a system of equations

$$ax + by = c$$
$$dx + ey = f$$

cofunctions (p. 706) The pairs of functions sine and cosine, tangent and cotangent, secant and cosecant.

collinear (p. 109) Points on the same line.

column matrix (p. 610) A matrix with one column.

combination (p. 538) A selection of objects considered without regard to their order.

combining like terms (p. 15) Simplifying terms containing the same variable factors.

common difference (d) (p. 488) The constant difference between successive terms in an arithmetic sequence.

common factor (of two monomials) (p. 201) A monomial that is a factor of each monomial.

common logarithm (p. 455) Base-10 logarithm.

common ratio (p. 493) The ratio of any term to the

preceding term in a geometric sequence. The common ratio is a constant.

complement of an event (p. 543) Event A is a complement of event B with respect to sample space S if and only if A and B include all outcomes of S, and A and B have no outcomes in common.

completing the square (p. 313) A method used to solve a quadratic equation in which a number is added to both sides of the equation so that one side is a perfect square.

complex conjugates (p. 322) For all real numbers a and b, $a + bi$ and $a - bi$ are complex conjugates.

complex fraction (p. 230) A fraction that has fractions in either the numerator or the denominator or both.

complex number (p. 317) A number of the form $a + bi$, where a and b are real numbers and i is the imaginary unit.

components of an ordered pair (p. 83) The individual numbers in an ordered pair.

compound inequality (p. 63) A sentence linking two conditions with "and" or "or". At least one of the conditions is an inequality.

conic section (p. 361, 389) A curve that has a second-degree equation and is defined in terms of the distance of its points from fixed points and/or lines. This includes circles, parabolas, ellipses and hyperbolas.

conjugates (p. 282, 418) Two binomials of the form $(a + \sqrt{b})$ and $(a - \sqrt{b})$, where a and b are rational numbers.

consistent system of equations (p. 138) A system that has at least one solution.

constant (p. 333, 407) A number or a polynomial of degree 0.

constant difference (*d*) (p. 488) The difference between successive terms in a sequence.

constant of inverse variation (p. 252) The number k in the inverse variation $y = \dfrac{k}{x}$.

constant linear function (p. 97) A function whose equation can be written in the form $y = b$ and whose graph is a horizontal line.

constant term of a polynomial (p. 407) The term a_0 which can be considered the coefficient of x^0.

constant term of a quadratic equation (p. 333) The term c in the form $y = ax^2 + bx + c$.

constant of variation (p. 113, 259) The number k in the direct variation $y = kx$ or in the inverse variation $y = \dfrac{k}{x}$.

continuous (p. 423) A polynomial function whose graph is smooth without "jumps".

converge (p. 513) If there is a real number that is the value of the infinite series, the series converges.

convex polygonal region (p. 172) A region that has a polygon with no "indentations" as a boundary.

coordinate (pp. 9, 83) The number associated with a particular point on a number line.

coordinate axes (p. 83) Two perpendicular lines selected in a plane.

coordinates of a point (p. 83) The numbers of an ordered pair.

correlation coefficient (p. 587) A number between -1 and $+1$ which is a measure of the dispersion of data points about a regression line.

corresponding elements of matrices (p. 610) For two matrices with the same dimensions, the elements in the same row and the same column.

cosecant function (p. 680) $\csc X = \dfrac{1}{\sin X}$ for all values of X for which the denominator is not zero.

cosine function (p. 655) For each real number X, let $P(j, k)$ be the point that is X units from $(1, 0)$ in the counterclockwise direction along the circle $j^2 + k^2 = 1$. The cosine is the function such that $\cos X = j$.

cotangent function (p. 680) $\cot X = \dfrac{\cos X}{\sin X}$ for all values of X for which the denominator is not 0.

cube root (p. 273) $\sqrt[3]{64} = 4$ since $4 \times 4 \times 4 = 64$.

cubic polynomial (p. 407) A polynomial of degree 3.

cycle (p. 663) The graph of a periodic function through one fundamental period.

decreasing function (p. 441) A function such that for any numbers a and b in the domain, if $a > b$, then $f(a) < f(b)$.

degree of a monomial (p. 185) The sum of the exponents of the variables.

degree of a polynomial (pp. 191, 407) The degree of the term (or terms) of highest degree.

dependent events (p. 549) Two events A and B are dependent if and only if $P(A \text{ and then } B) \neq P(A) \cdot P(B)$.

dependent system (p. 138) A system whose graphs coincide and that has infinitely many solutions.

dependent variable (p. 118) If the value of a depends on the value of b, or if a is usually defined in terms of b, a is called the dependent variable, and it is graphed on the vertical axis.

depressed equation (p. 419) The equation $Q(x) = 0$, where $Q(x)$ is the quotient when a polynomial has been divided by a factor $(x - r)$.

descending order (p. 193) A polynomial is written in descending order when the term with highest degree is written first, followed by the term with next highest degree second, and so on.

determinant (p. 155) A real number represented by a square array of numbers.

determinant of a matrix (p. 633) The determinant of a matrix is the determinant with the same corresponding elements.

dimensions of a matrix (p. 609) The number of rows and the number of columns.

direct variation (p. 111) Two variables are said to vary directly if and only if there is a constant of variation or (constant of proportionality) k, $k \neq 0$, such that $y = kx$.

directed network (p. 627) A network that indicates the direction of flow on each arc.

directrix (p. 366, 379, 387) A line used in the definition of a conic section.

discriminant (p. 329) The expression $b^2 - 4ac$ of the quadratic formula that determines several characteristics of the roots of a quadratic equation.

dispersion (p. 153) A measure of how closely a set of data are clustered about the mean.

distance formula (p. 287) For points $P_1(x_1, y_1)$ and $P_2(x_2, y_2)$
$$P_1P_2 = \sqrt{(x_2 - x_1)^2 + (y_2 - y_1)^2}.$$

diverge (p. 513) If there is no real number that is the value of an infinite series, the series diverges.

domain of a relation (p. 84) The set of first components of the ordered pairs in the relation.

double root (p. 329) Two roots that are alike.

eccentricity (p. 379, 387) A ratio used in some definitions of conic sections.

ellipse (p. 374) The set of all points in a plane such that the sum of the distances (focal radii) from two given points (foci) is constant.

ellipsis (p. 487) "..." A symbol indicating that the pattern continues in a sequence.

equal matrices (p. 611) For any $m \times n$ matrices A and B, $A = B$ if and only if $a_{ij} = b_{ij}$ for all $i \leq m$ and $j \leq n$.

equivalent transformation (p. 241) A transformation that results in an equation equivalent to the original.

event (p. 542) A subset of a sample space.

explicit definition (p. 488) A definition used to state the relationship between a term t_n of a sequence and the number n of that term.

exponential decay (p. 474) A decay that begins rapidly but decreases slowly with time and is represented by the equation
$$P = P_0e^{kt}, k < 0.$$

exponential equation (p. 442) An equation with the variable in an exponent.

exponential function (p. 441) For all real numbers x and for all positive numbers b, $b \neq 1$, the equation $y = b^x$ defines an exponential function with base b.

exponential growth (p. 474) Growth that begins slowly but increases rapidly with time and is represented by the equation
$$P = P_0e^{kt}, k > 0.$$

factorial notation (p. 533) For each positive integer n, $n! = n(n - 1)(n - 2)...3 \times 2 \times 1$. Also, $0! = 1$.

field (p. 29) A set of numbers with two operations that has the closure, commutative, associative, identity, and inverse properties for addition and multiplication and distributive for multiplication over addition.

finite sequence (p. 487) A sequence that has a last term.

fitted line (p. 585) The line that best approximates the graph of the relationship between two variables, if that relationship is nearly linear.

focus (p. 366, 374, 379, 381, 387) The fixed point or points (foci) used to define a conic section.

fractional equation (p. 241) An equation with a variable in the denominator of a fraction.

function (p. 90) A relation in which each element of the domain is paired with exactly one element of the range.

function notation (p. 122) Representing any number in the range of the function f as $f(x)$, in which x is the corresponding number in the domain.

fundamental period (p. 651) The smallest value of p (of a periodic function) such that $f(x + p) = f(x)$.

geometric mean (p. 270) The square root of the product of two numbers. It is also called the mean proportional.

geometric means (p. 494) The terms of a geometric sequence between two given terms.

geometric sequence (p. 493) For each positive integer n, and for each real number r, $r \neq 0$, the sequence with the first term a_1 and nth term a_n is a geometric sequence if and only if $a_n = a_1r^{n-1}$.

geometric series (p. 500) The indicated sum of the terms of a geometric sequence.

greatest common factor (**GFC**) (p. 201) The common factor that is a multiple of each common factor.

greatest integer function (p. 117) A step function that pairs a real number with the greatest integer that is less than or equal to the real number.

half life (p. 475) The length of time it takes half of an amount of radioactive material to decay.

harmonic mean (p. 240) In a set of n numbers, n divided by the sum of the reciprocals of the numbers.

hyperbola (p. 381) The set of all points in a plane such that the absolute value of the difference of the distances (focal radii) from two given points (foci) is constant.

hypotenuse (p. 705) The longest side of a right triangle. It is opposite the right angle.

identity (p. 741) An equation that is true for all elements of its domain.

identity element (p. 18) A number which added to or multiplied times any number in a set yields that same number in the set.

identity properties (p. 18) There are real numbers 0 and 1 such that for each real number a, $a + 0 = 0 + a = a$ and $a \times 1 = 1 \times a = a$.

imaginary number (p. 317) A complex number that is not real.

inconsistent system of equations (p. 138) A system with no solution.

increasing function (p. 441) A function such that for any numbers a and b in the domain, if $a > b$, then $f(a) > f(b)$.

independent events (p. 549) Two events not affected by each other. Two events A and B are independent if and only if $P(A$ and then $B) = P(A) \times P(B)$.

independent variable (p. 118) If the value of a depends upon the value of b, or if a is usually defined in terms of b, b is called the independent variable, and it is graphed on the horizontal axis.

index (p. 267) The number represented by n in $\sqrt[n]{b}$.

index of summation (p. 500) The variable used in sigma notation.

infinite geometric series (p. 513) A geometric series with an infinitely large number of terms.

infinite sequence (p. 487) A sequence that does not have a last term.

interquartile range (p. 576) The difference between the upper and lower quartiles of a set of numbers.

inverse of an ordered pair (p. 272) The inverse of (a, b) is (b, a).

inverse functions (p. 431) Functions f and g are inverse functions if and only if $f(g(x)) = g(f(x)) = x$ for all numbers x in the domains of both f and g.

inverse of a 2 × 2 matrix (p. 634) If $A = \begin{bmatrix} a_1 & b_1 \\ a_2 & b_2 \end{bmatrix}$,

then $A^{-1} = \dfrac{1}{\det A} \begin{bmatrix} b_2 & -b_1 \\ -a_2 & a_1 \end{bmatrix}$, where $\det A \neq 0$.

inverse of a relation (p. 272) Relation B is the inverse of relation A if it consists of the inverses of the individual ordered pairs in relation A.

inverse variation (p. 252) Two quantities x and y vary inversely if and only if there is a constant k, $k \neq 0$, such that $y = \dfrac{k}{x}$.

irrational number (p. 1) A real number that is not a rational number, i.e. cannot be expressed as the quotient of two integers.

latus chord (p. 367) A segment whose endpoints are on a parabola, which passes through the focus, and is parallel to the directrix.

leading coefficient (p. 407) The coefficient of the term of a polynomial with the highest degree.

like terms (p. 15) Terms that contain identical variables with identical exponents.

linear combination (p. 148) An equation that is formed by adding multiples of two equations together.

linear equation in two variables (p. 97) An equation of the form $y = mx + b$.

linear function (p. 97) A function is a linear function if and only if its domain is the set of all real numbers and its equation can be written in the form $y = mx + b$.

linear polynomial (p. 407) A polynomial of degree 1.

linear programming (p. 172) A branch of mathematics based on the maximum-minimum property.

linear term of a quadratic equation (p. 333) The term bx in an equation of the form $y = ax^2 + bx + c$.

literal equation (p. 47) An equation in which constants are represented by letters.

logarithmic equation (p. 470) An equation involving logarithms of expressions containing variables.

logarithmic function (log) (p. 447) For all positive real numbers x and b, $b \neq 1$, there is a real number y such that $y = \log_b x$ if and only if $x = b^y$.

lowest terms (simplest form) (p. 228) A fraction is expressed in lowest terms when its numerator and denominator have no common factors other than 1 or -1.

main diagonal of a square matrix (p. 624) The diagonal from the upper left to the lower right.

major axis (p. 375) The longer axis of an ellipse.

mapping (p. 89) An association from the elements of the domain to the elements of the range.

matrix (matrices) (p. 609) A rectangular array of numbers arranged in rows and columns.

maximum value (p. 346) The y-coordinate of the vertex of the graph of a quadratic function that opens downward.

mean (p. 579) The sum of a set of numbers divided by the number of numbers in the set.

mean absolute deviation (p. 579) The average absolute deviation from the mean for a set of numbers.

mean proportional (p. 494) The geometric mean between two numbers. (See *geometric mean*.)

median (p. 575) The middle number in a set of numbers arranged in order.

midpoint (p. 287) The point on a segment that is equidistant from the endpoints.

midpoint formula (p. 288) If the coordinates of point A are (x_1, y_1) and the coordinates of point B are (x_2, y_2), then the coordinates of the midpoint of segment AB are

$$\left(\frac{x_1 + x_2}{2}, \frac{y_1 + y_2}{2} \right)$$

minimum value (p. 346) The y-coordinate of the vertex of the graph of a quadratic function that opens upward.

minor of an element (p. 160) The determinant that remains after the row and column containing the element have been deleted.

minor axis (p. 375) The shorter axis of an ellipse.

mode (p. 569) The number that occurs most often in a set of numbers.

monomial (p. 185) A constant (a number), a variable, or a product of constants and/or variables.

multiplicative inverses (or reciprocals) (p. 19) Pairs of real numbers that have the product 1.

multiplicative identity matrix (p. 624) A square matrix with 1's on the main diagonal (upper left to lower right) and other entries 0.

mutually exclusive events (p. 544) Two events A and B are mutually exclusive if and only if they have no outcomes in common.

nth root (p. 267) If $a^n = b$ with a and b real numbers and n a positive integer, then a is the nth root of b.

natural logarithms (p. 460) Base-e logarithms.

negative exponents (p. 223) For each nonzero number a and for each positive integer n,

$$a^{-n} = \frac{1}{a^n}$$

negative reciprocals (p. 104) Two numbers having a product of -1.

negative square root (p. 267) The negative of the principal square root.

negative square root function (p. 272) The function with the equation $y = -\sqrt{x}$.

network (p. 627) A set of points (vertices) connected by arcs.

nonequivalent transformation (p. 241) A transformation that results in an equation not equivalent to the original.

nonlinear system (p. 393) A system of two or more equations at least one of which is nonlinear.

normal distribution (p. 591) A specific bell-shaped algebraic function approximated by many frequency distributions.

one-to-one function (p. 91) A function in which each element of the domain is associated with a unique element of the range, and each element of the range is associated with a unique element of the domain.

opposites (p. 19) Two numbers whose sum is zero. Also called additive inverses.

ordered pair (p. 83) A pair of numbers that identifies the location of a particular point on a graph.

ordered triples (x, y, z) (p. 162) The set that is the solution of an equation in three variables.

origin (on a graph) (p. 83) The point of intersection of the coordinate axes. It is designated (0, 0).

origin (on a number line) (p. 9) The point on the number line associated with zero.

outcome (p. 542) The result of an experiment.

parabola (pp. 333, 366) The set of all points in a plane that are the same distance from a point (focus) as they are from a given line (directrix). It is the graph of a quadratic function having a U shape.

parallel lines (p. 104) Lines that have equal slopes.

partial sum of a series (p. 513) The sum of a finite number of terms of the series.

Pascal's triangle (p. 196) A triangular arrangement of numbers in which each number is the sum of the two numbers above it in the preceding row.

perfect square trinomial (p. 210) The square of a binomial, with the form $a^2 \pm 2ab + b^2$.

periodic function (p. 651) A function $y = f(x)$ is periodic if and only if there is a real number p such that for each x in the domain of f, $f(x + p) = f(x)$

permutation (p. 532) An arrangement of a number of objects in a definite order.

perpendicular lines (p. 104) Lines with slopes that are negative reciprocals.

point matrix (p. 628) A 2×1 matrix whose elements are the coordinates of a point.

point-slope form (p. 106) If (x_1, y_1) is a point on the line $y = mx + b$, then $y - y_1 = m(x - x_1)$ is the point-slope form of the equation.

polynomial (p. 191) A monomial or the sum of monomials.

polynomial function (p. 408) A function P whose values are defined by a polynomial. $P(x) = a_n x^n + a_{n-1} x^{n-1} + \ldots + a_2 x^2 + a_1 x + a_0$.

power function (p. 272) Functions with equations of the form $y = x^n$, with n a positive integer.

prime factorization (p. 201) A representation of a number as the product of its prime factors.

principal cube root (p. 267) the one real-number cube root of a real number.

$$\sqrt[3]{64} = 4; \sqrt[3]{-64} = -4$$

principal square root (p. 267) The positive square root, denoted by $\sqrt{}$.

$$\sqrt{25} = 5$$

principle square root function (p. 272) The function with the equation $y = \sqrt{x}$.

probability of an event (p. 542) The ratio of the number of outcomes in the event to the number of outcomes in the sample space.

pure imaginary number (p. 316) Any number of the form ai, where a is real, $a \neq 0$.

pure quadratic equation (p. 309) A quadratic equation with no x-term.

Pythagorean theorem (p. 286) If a and b are the lengths of the legs of a right triangle and c is the length of the hypotenuse, then $a^2 + b^2 = c^2$.

quadrants (p. 84) The four regions in the plane formed by the axes.

quadratic equation (pp. 212, 309) An equation that can be expressed in the form $P(x) = 0$, where $P(x)$ is a quadratic polynomial in x. It can be written in the form $ax^2 + bx + c = 0$

quadratic formula (p. 311) The roots of $ax^2 + bx + c = 0$, $a \neq 0$, are
$$\frac{-b + \sqrt{b^2 - 4ac}}{2a} \text{ and } \frac{-b - \sqrt{b^2 - 4ac}}{2a}$$

quadratic function (p. 333) A function whose equation can be written in the form $y = ax^2 + bx + c$, where a, b, and c are real numbers and $a \neq 0$.

quadratic polynomial (pp. 212, 407) A polynomial of degree 2.

quadratic term (of a quadratic equation) (p. 333) The term ax^2 in the equation $y = ax^2 + bx + c$.

quartiles (p. 575) The upper and lower quartiles are numbers which, together with the mean, divide an ordered set of numbers into approximately equal quarters.

radian (p. 682) If a central angle of a circle with radius r intercepts an arc of length s, the measure of the angle is $\frac{s}{r}$ radians.

radical (p. 267) The symbol $\sqrt[n]{b}$ (read $\sqrt[n]{b}$ as "the nth root of b") used to indicate the principal nth root of b.

radical equation (p. 291) An equation with radicands that contain variables.

radicand (p. 267) The expression under a radical sign.

radius (p. 361) The distance from the center to a point on the circle.

random sample (p. 596) A sample of a population that has exactly the same probability of being selected as every other sample of its size.

range of a relation (p. 84) The set of second components of the ordered pairs.

range of a set of numbers (p. 576) The difference between the largest and smallest numbers in a set.

rational algebraic expression (or rational expression) (p. 228) The quotient of two polynomials.

rational approximation (p. 268) A rational number used in place of a nearly equal irrational number.

rational exponents (p. 295) For all positive integers m and n, and all real numbers a for which the radical represents a real number, $a^{\frac{m}{n}} = (\sqrt[n]{a})^m = \sqrt[n]{a^m}$

rational number (p. 1) A number that can be expressed as the quotient of two integers. (Division by zero is not defined.)

rationalizing the denominator (p. 281) The process of changing an irrational denominator to a rational one.

real numbers (p. 1) The set of all rational and irrational numbers.

reciprocals (p. 19) Pairs of real numbers that have the product 1. Also known as *multiplicative inverses*.

regression line (p. 587) A fitted line determined by a specific algebraic technique.

relation (p. 84) A set of ordered pairs.

repeating decimal (p. 1) A decimal in which a digit or a group of digits repeats forever, e.g. $0.66666 \ldots$ or $0.846846846 \ldots$.

repetend (p. 2) The portion of a repeating decimal that repeats.

restrictions (p. 273) The set of possible values for the variables for which an expression is real, or for which it is defined.

resultant (p. 733) The sum of two vectors.

row matrix (p. 610) A matrix with one row.

sample space (p. 542) The set of all possible outcomes of an experiment.

scalar (p. 615) The real number that is a factor in scalar multiplication.

scalar multiplication (p. 615) For any scalar c, a real number, and any $m \times n$ matrix A with elements a_{ij}, the product of c and A is the $m \times n$ matrix whose elements are ca_{ij}.

scientific notation (p. 187) The product of a power of 10 and a number greater than or equal to 1 and less than 10.

secant function (p. 680) $\sec X = \dfrac{1}{\cos X}$ for all values of X for which the denominator is not 0.

second-order determinant (p. 155) A determinant with two rows and two columns.

sequence (p. 487) A function defined on the positive integers or a subset of consecutive positive integers starting with 1.

series (p. 499) The indicated sum of the terms of a sequence.

set-builder notation (pp. 10, 84) A mathematical sentence that "builds" the set by selecting the elements that belong to the set.

sigma (Σ) notation (p. 500) Expresses the sum of a series.

sine function (p. 655) For each number X, let $P(j, k)$ be the point that is X units from $(1, 0)$ in the counterclockwise direction along the circle $j^2 + k^2 = 1$. Then the sine is the function such that $\sin X = k$.

slope of a line (p. 98) The ratio of the change in y (Δy) to the change in x (Δx), ($\Delta x \neq 0$). Or, if $x_1 \neq x_2$, the slope of the line through (x_1, y_1) and (x_2, y_2) is the ratio

$$\frac{\Delta y}{\Delta x} = \frac{y_2 - y_1}{x_2 - x_1} = \frac{y_1 - y_2}{x_1 - x_2}$$

slope-intercept form (p. 99) The form $y = mx + b$ of a linear equation in two variables. The slope is m and the y-intercept is b.

solving a triangle (p. 711) Finding all the unknown measures of a triangle.

square matrix of order n (p. 610) A matrix with n rows and n columns.

square root (p. 267) If $x^2 = y$, then x is a square root of y.

standard form of a polynomial (p. 407)
$$a_n x^n + a_{n-1} x^{n-1} + \ldots + a_2 x^2 + a_1 x + a_0$$

standard form of a quadratic equation (in one variable) (pp. 212, 309) $ax^2 + bx + c = 0, a \neq 0$.

standard form of a quadratic function (p. 333) $y = ax^2 + bx + c$

step function (p. 117) A function whose graph resembles a staircase.

subset (p. 11) A set all of whose elements are elements in a larger set.

standard scores (or z-scores) (p. 592) An expression for each value in a frequency distribution in terms of the number of standard deviations it is above or below the mean.

substitution (p. 142) A method of solving systems of equations by replacing one variable with another variable or variable expression that is equal to it.

system (p. 137) A set of equations having the same variables.

tangent function (p. 680) $\tan X = \dfrac{\sin X}{\cos X}$ for all values of X for which the denominator is not 0.

terms of a sequence (p. 487) The numbers in a sequence.

theorem (p. 29) A statement that has been proven to be true.

third-order determinant (p. 160) A determinant with three rows and three columns.

transformation matrix (p. 628) A matrix used for multiplying a point matrix to give a new point matrix.

translation (p. 363) A transformation made by substitutions that shift each point of a given graph to a different location without changing the shape of the graph.

trinomial (p. 191) A polynomial with three terms.

unit circle (p. 649) A circle with center at the origin and with a radius of one unit.

value of a series (p. 499) The simplified sum of a series.

variable (p. 5) A symbol, usually a letter, that represents, and may be replaced by, any number from a particular set of numbers.

vectors (p. 610) Matrices with either one row or one column.

vertex of a parabola (p. 366) The point on a parabola midway between the focus and the directrix.

vertical-line test (p. 91) If no vertical line intersects a graph of a relation more than once, then the relation is a function.

vertices of an ellipse (p. 375) The endpoints of the major and minor axes.

vertices of a hyperbola (p. 382) The two points in which a hyperbola is intersected by the line through the two focus points.

vinculum (p. 267) The bar over the radicand.

wrapping function (p. 649) The function that maps the real numbers onto the points of the unit circle.

x-axis (p. 84) The horizontal axis.

y-axis (p. 84) The vertical axis.

y-intercept of a graph (p. 98) The y-coordinate of the point at which a line crosses the y-axis.

zero matrix (p. 622) An $m \times n$ matrix whose elements are all zero. It is denoted $Z_{m \times n}$ or just Z.

Symbols

{ }	Set		Z	Zero matrix
$\emptyset$	Empty set		$\mathscr{R}$	Set of real numbers
$=$	Is equal to		$^\circ$	Degree
$\approx$	Is approximately equal to		$-a$	Opposite or additive inverse of a
$\neq$	Is not equal to		$\|a\|$	Absolute value of a
$>$	Is greater than		a^n	nth power of a
$<$	Is less than		$\sqrt{a}$	Principal or positive square root of a

Set { }
Empty set $\emptyset$

$=$ Is equal to
$\approx$ Is approximately equal to
$\neq$ Is not equal to
$>$ Is greater than
$<$ Is less than
$\geq$ Is greater than or equal to
$\leq$ Is less than or equal to

(x, y) Ordered pair x, y
$P(x, y)$ Point P with coordinates x, y
Δx Delta x; the change in x

$P(x)$ Polynomial with variable x;
$$P(x) = a_n x^n + a_{n-1} x^{n-1} + \cdots + a_1 x^1 + a_0, a_n \neq 0$$

i Imaginary number whose square $= -1$; $i^2 = -1$, $i = \sqrt{-1}$

$a + bi$ Standard form of a complex number
$P(a + bi)$ Point P with coordinates (a, b) in the complex plane
$\bar{z}$ Conjugate of complex number z
a_n nth term of an arithmetic or geometric sequence
S_n Sum of n terms of a sequence; the value of a series with n terms
S The value of an infinite series
Σ Sigma, the summation symbol
$\displaystyle\sum_{k=1}^{n} x_k$ The sum, or series, $x_1 + x_2 + \cdots + x_n$
$\displaystyle\sum_{k=1}^{\infty} x_k$ The infinite series $x_1 + x_2 + x_3 + \cdots$

A^{-1} Inverse of square matrix A
$A_{2 \times 3}$ Matrix A with 2 rows and 3 columns
a_{ij} Matrix element in the ith row, jth column
$\det A$ Determinant of square matrix A
I The square identity matrix

Z Zero matrix
$\mathscr{R}$ Set of real numbers
$^\circ$ Degree
$-a$ Opposite or additive inverse of a
$\|a\|$ Absolute value of a
a^n nth power of a
$\sqrt{a}$ Principal or positive square root of a
$\pm\sqrt{5}$ Positive or negative $\sqrt{5}$
$3 \pm \sqrt{5}$ 3 plus or minus $\sqrt{5}$
$\sqrt[n]{a}$ Positive nth root of a
$f(x)$ Result of applying function f to x
f^{-1} Inverse of function f
$[x]$ Greatest integer function of x
b^x Exponential function of x (base b)
$\log_b x$ Logarithmic function of x (base b)
$\log x$ Common logarithmic function of x (base 10)
$\ln x$ Natural logarithmic function of x (base e)
e An irrational number equal to 2.7182818 ... (the base of natural logarithms)
$\bar{A}$ Complement of event A
$P(A)$ Probability of event A
$n!$ n factorial; the product $n(n - 1)(n - 2) \cdot \ldots \cdot 3 \cdot 2 \cdot 1$
$_nP_r$ Number of permutations of n things taken r at a time
$_nC_r$ Number of combinations of n things taken r at a time
$\sin x$ Sine function of x
$\cos x$ Cosine function of x
$\tan x$ Tangent function of x
$\cot x$ Cotangent function of x
$\sec x$ Secant function of x
$\csc x$ Cosecant function of x

Metric System

1 kilometer (km) = 1000 meters (m)
1 centimeter (cm) = 0.01 meter
1 millimeter (mm) = 0.001 meter

1 kilogram (kg) = 1000 grams (g)
1 milligram (mg) = 0.001 gram

1 kiloliter (kL) = 1000 liters (L)
1 milliliter (mL) = 0.001 liter

km/h Kilometers per hour
m/s   Meters per second
°C   Degrees Celsius
m^2 Square meter
cm^2 Square centimeter
m^3 Cubic meter
cm^3 Cubic centimeter

$\mathcal{S}$ELECTED ANSWERS

Chapter 1

Page 3, Classroom Exercises
1. Rational **2.** Rational **3.** Irrational **4.** Rational
5. 0.625 **6.** $0.\overline{428571}$ **7.** $\frac{7}{20}$ **8.** $\frac{69}{25}$ **9.** $\frac{2}{9}$

Pages 3–4, Written Exercises
1. Rational **3.** Rational **5.** Rational **7.** Rational
9. Irrational **11.** Rational **13.** Irrational
15. Irrational **17.** $0.8\overline{3}$ **19.** $0.\overline{2}$ **21.** 0.1875
23. 0.488 **25.** $\frac{16}{25}$ **27.** $\frac{911}{200}$ **29.** $\frac{41}{9}$ **31.** $\frac{25}{33}$
33. F **35.** F **37.** T **39.** $0.\overline{142857}$, $0.\overline{285714}$, $0.\overline{428571}$, $0.\overline{571428}$; Multiply the numerator of the fraction by $0.\overline{142857}$. **41.** $\frac{7}{16}$; $\frac{6}{16}, \frac{7}{16}, \frac{8}{16}$
43. $\frac{9}{4}$; $\frac{8}{4}, \frac{9}{4}, \frac{10}{4}$ **45.** T **47.** T **49.** T **51.** T
53. $\frac{78}{275}$

Page 4, Review Exercises
1. 5 **2.** -24 **3.** -2.68 **4.** -73.2 **5.** $-7\frac{3}{4}$ **6.** $9\frac{3}{8}$
7. 20 **8.** -8 **9.** 2.45 **10.** $3\frac{1}{3}$ **11.** -32 **12.** -11

Page 7, Classroom Exercises
1. 20 **2.** 20 **3.** 28 **4.** 28 **5.** 35 **6.** 2

Pages 7–8, Written Exercises
1. 6 **3.** 17 **5.** 100 **7.** -46 **9.** 16 **11.** -28
13. 58 **15.** 29 **17.** 6 **19.** -9 **21.** -2 **23.** 66
25. -48 **27.** -1 **29.** 8 **31.** 1 **33.** -5 **35.** 5
37. 2 **39.** 16 **41.** -207 **43.** -72 **45.** 78 **47.** 12
49. Yes **51.** No **53.** No **55.** Yes **57.** No

Page 8, Review Exercises
1. 20 **2.** $\sqrt{2}$ **3.** $\sqrt{3}$ **4.** 35

Page 8, Calculator Extension
1. $0.\overline{739130434782608695652}1$
2. $0.\overline{176470588235294}1$ **3.** $0.\overline{157894736842105263}$

Page 11, Classroom Exercises
1. $\frac{3}{4}$ **2.** $\frac{13}{18}$ **3.** $\{x{:}x > -3\}$ **4.** $\{x{:}x$ is an integer and $x < 3\}$ **5.** $\{x{:}x < -1\}$ **6.** $\{x{:}x > 0.5\}$
7.

Pages 11–13, Written Exercises
1. $\frac{1}{10}, \frac{1}{8}, \frac{1}{6}$ **3.** 0.806, 0.81, 0.860 **5.** $-\frac{3}{8}, -0.37$
7. $-\sqrt{2}, -1.4$ **9.** 0.63, $\frac{7}{11}$ **11.** $\frac{\sqrt{5}}{3}, \frac{\sqrt{14}}{5}$
13. $\{x{:}x > 12.5\}$ **15.** $\{x{:}x < -\pi\}$ **17.** $\{x{:}x$ is an integer $> 99\}$ **19.** $\{x{:}x$ is an integer $< 3\}$
21. $\{x{:}x > 2\}$ **23.** $\{x{:}x < -1\}$
25.
27.
29.
31. $\sqrt{0.6}, \frac{4}{5}, \frac{17}{5}$ **33.** $\frac{5}{6}, \frac{\sqrt{26}}{6}, \frac{\sqrt{3}}{2}$
35. $\frac{3}{8}, \frac{3}{7}, \frac{4}{9}$ **37.** $\{x{:}x$ is an integer $> -\pi\}$
39. $\{x{:}x$ is an integer $> -1\}$ **41.** $\left\{x{:}x > \frac{1}{2}\right\}$
43.
45. T **47.** F **49.** $\sqrt{2}$ **51.** o

Page 13, Review Exercises
1. -0.41 **2.** -7.45 **3.** 420 **4.** -0.37 **5.** -0.028
6. 4.5 **7.** 0.66 **8.** 0.02 **9.** 32,000 **10.** $\frac{7}{10}$ **11.** $-\frac{1}{6}$
12. 6.2

Page 13, Self-Quiz 1
1. $0.\overline{692307}$ **2.** 0.175 **3.** $\frac{31}{200}$ **4.** $\frac{14}{33}$ **5.** $\frac{13}{3}$
6. $\frac{15}{14}$ **7.** 0 **8.** $\frac{121}{9}$ **9.** $\frac{\sqrt{5}}{3}$
10. $\{x{:}x$ is an integer and $x > 9\}$ **11.** $(x{:}x > -3.5)$

Page 15, Classroom Exercises
1. Assoc. (add.) **2.** Distributive **3.** Comm. (add.)
4. Assoc. (mult.) **5.** $9x^2 + 10x$ **6.** $42x - 5$
7. Distributive; Assoc. (add.); Distributive; Computation

Pages 16–17, Written Exercises
1. Assoc. (add.) **3.** Comm. (add.) **5.** Comm. (add.)
7. Assoc. (mult.) **9.** Distributive **11.** Distributive

13. Distributive; Computation   **15.** Assoc. (add.);
Comm. (add.); Assoc. (add.); Distributive; Computa-
tion   **17.** $11a + 8b$ **19.** $7x^2 + 7y$ **21.** $15x + 59$
23. $x^2 + 10x + 25$ **25.** $5x^2 + 13x + 2$ **27.** F   **29.** T
31. F   **33.** Distributive; Distributive; Comm. (add.);
Assoc. (add.); Computation   **35.** Think of 999 as
$(1000 - 1)$.   **37.** Think of 996 as $(1000 - 4)$; 997 as
$(1000 - 3)$; and 998 as $(1000 - 2)$.
39. $a(b + c + d)$
   $= a(b + c) + ad$ Distributive
   $= ab + ac + ad$ Distributive
41. $(a + b)^2 - b^2$
   $= (a + b)(a + b) - b^2$ Def. of exponent
   $= (a + b)a + (a + b)b - b^2$ Distributive
   $= a^2 + ba + ab + b^2 - b^2$ Distributive
   $= a^2 + ab + ab + b^2 - b^2$ Comm. (add.)
   $= a^2 + 1ab + 1ab + 1b^2 - 1b^2$ Identity for mult.
   $= a^2 + (1 + 1)ab + (1 - 1)b^2$ Distributive
   $= a^2 + 2ab + 0b^2$ Computation
   $= a^2 + 2ab$ Identity for add.
   $= a(a + 2b)$ Distributive

Page 17, Review Exercises

1. $-\dfrac{9}{8}$ **2.** $-1\dfrac{7}{12}$ **3.** $\dfrac{9}{20}$ **4.** $-\dfrac{21}{8}$ **5.** -0.036
6. 470   **7.** 5   **8.** -3 **9.** $P = 32$ cm; $A = 60$ cm^2
10. $\{x{:}x > -2\}$

Page 21, Classroom Exercises
1. T   **2.** F   **3.** F   **4.** T   **5.** F   **6.** T   **7.** Closure
property   **8.** Subt. of real numbers   **9.** Identity for mult.
11. $3x - 3y$ **13.** $28a - 21b + 7$ **15.** $2a^2 - 7ab - 15b^2$

Pages 21–23, Written Exercises
1. Add. identity   **3.** Closure   **5.** Closure   **7.** Add.
inverse   **9.** Mult. inverse   **11.** T   **13.** T   **15.** T
17. F   **19.** T   **21.** $5x + 15y - 10$
23. $-2x + 3y - 2$ **25.** $2a^2 + 5ab + 2b^2$
27. $a^2 + 6a + 9$ **29.** $n^2 - 4n + 4$ **31.** $9x + 6$
33. $-4w - 9$ **35.** $10x - 8$ **37.** $7c + 7$
39. $a + 10$ **41.** $b - 44$ **43.** $-4.8a$ **45.** $\dfrac{5}{6}r - \dfrac{1}{2}$
47. $4.5w - 1$ **49.** $\dfrac{1}{10}x - \dfrac{9}{10}$ **51.** T   **53.** F   **55.** F
57. F   **59.** $-\dfrac{b}{2}$ **61.** Assoc. (add.); Comm. (add.);
Assoc. (add.); Mult. identity prop.; Distributive;
Computation

Page 23, Review Exercises
1. -2 **2.** $P = 40$ in.; $A = 100$ in.^{2} **3.** $P = 48$ cm;
$A = 96$ cm^2 **4.** $P = 56$ cm; $A = 144$ cm^2

Page 25, Classroom Exercises
1. 20, 26, 33   **2.** $Q = 5n + 5$ **3.** $4n - 2$

Pages 26–27, Written Exercises
1. 19, 23, 27   **3.** 25, 31, 38   **5.** 48, 96, 192   **7.** $\dfrac{5}{6}, \dfrac{6}{7},$
$\dfrac{7}{8}$ **9.** 0.0004, 0.00005, 0.000006   **11.** 25, 36, 49
13. $Q = n(n + 1)$; 420   **15.** $Q = n(n - 1)^2$; 361
17. $Q = n(n + 3)$; 460   **19.** $2n$ **21.** n^2 **23.** $\dfrac{n - 1}{n}$
25. $10n + 5$ **27.** $100n + 88$ **29.** $2n$ **31.** $n(n + 1)$
33a. 4950   **33b.** $\dfrac{n(n - 1)}{2}$
35. $n^2 + n(n + 1) = n^2 + n^2 + n = 2n^2 + n$;
$\dfrac{2n(2n + 1)}{2} = n(2n + 1) = 2n^2 + n$
37. Each of n teams plays one game with each of
$(n - 1)$ remaining teams. Each of n lines intersects
each of $(n - 1)$ remaining lines in one point. The situations are mathematically identical.

Page 28, Review Exercises
1. 2   **2.** 6100   **3.** -14.6 **4.** $-1\dfrac{2}{3}$ **5.** $2\dfrac{1}{3}$ **6.** $\dfrac{7}{15}$
7. $P = 100$ cm; $A = 480$ cm^2 **8.** $C = 10\pi$ in.;
$A = 25\pi$ in.^{2} **9.** $C = 20\pi$ m; $A = 100\pi$ m^2

Page 28, Self-Quiz 2
1. Closure (add.)   **2.** Mult. inverse   **3.** Assoc. (add.)
4. Comm. (add.)   **5.** Distributive   **6.** $46 + 8x$
7. $2b^2 + 5ab + ac$ **8.** $-\dfrac{2}{2}$ and $\dfrac{2}{2}$ **9.** $\dfrac{0}{2}$ **10.** $-\dfrac{3}{2}$ and
$-\dfrac{2}{3}$ **11.** $Q = \dfrac{n}{n + 2}$ **12.** $Q = n^3 - 1$

Page 32, Classroom Exercises
1. Mult. identity; Def. of subtraction; Distributive;
Computation   **2.** Let $2n$ and $2m$ be even numbers,
where n and m are integers. $2n \cdot 2m = 2(2nm)$. Since
the set of integers is closed with respect to multiplication, the product $2nm$ is an integer, which we call p.
Therefore, $2n \cdot 2m = 2p$, an even number. Thus the
product of any two even numbers is an even number.

Pages 32–33, Written Exercises
1. Additive identity; Additive inverse; Assoc. (add.);
Mult. identity; Distributive; Additive identity; Mult.
identity; Additive inverse   **3.** Def. of subtraction; Mult.
identity; Distributive; Computation
5. Let $2n + 1$ and $2m$ represent an odd and an even
number; n and m are integers.
$2n + 1 + 2m = 2n + 2m + 1$
$\qquad\qquad\quad = 2(n + m) + 1$

$(n + m)$ is some integer, p, because of the closure property of addition. $2n + 1 + 2m = 2p + 1$, an odd number.

7. Let $2n$ be an even number, where n is an integer. $(2n)^2 = (2n)(2n)$, an even number.
In Classroom Exercise 2, it was shown that the product of two even numbers is an even number.

9. Let $(2n + 1)$ represent an odd number; n is an integer. $(2n + 1)^2 = (2n)^2 + 2(2n) + 1$
$(2n)^2$ is some even number by Exercise 7. $2(2n)$ is some even number because of the closure property of multiplication. The sum $(2n)^2 + 2(2n)$ is some even number by Exercise 6. The Sum $(2n)^2 + 2(2n) + 1$ is odd by the definition of odd number.

11. For all real numbers a and b,
$(-a) + (-b) = -(a + b)$
$$(-a) + (-b) = (-1a) + (-1b) \text{ Mult. identity}$$
$$= (-1)(a + b) \text{ Distributive}$$
$$= -(a + b) \text{ Proved in Exercise 2}$$

13. For all real numbers a, b, and c, $a(b - c) = ab - ac$
$$a(b - c) = a(b + (-c)) \text{ Def. of subtraction}$$
$$= ab + a \cdot (-c) \text{ Distributive}$$
$$= ab + a \cdot (-1c) \text{ Mult. identity}$$
$$= ab + (a \cdot -1)c \text{ Assoc. (mult.)}$$
$$= ab + (-1 \cdot a)c \text{ Comm. (mult.)}$$
$$= ab + -1(ac) \text{ Assoc. (mult.)}$$
$$= ab + -ac \text{ Proved in Exercise 2}$$
$$= ab - ac \text{ Def. of subtraction}$$

15. 6

Page 33, Review Exercises

1. $P = 52$ cm; $A = 136$ cm^2 **2.** 75% **3.** $\frac{9}{20}$

4. 0.06 **5.** 15%

Page 33, Extension

1. No; there is none. **2.** Yes **3.** No

Pages 36–37, Chapter Review

1. Rational **3.** Rational **5.** 15 **7.** 400 **9.** $\{x : x < 3\}$
11.

13. Assoc. (mult.) **15a.** Yes **15b.** No **17.** $x^2 - x - 6$
19. 36 **21.** $2(n + 4)$ **23.** Mult. identity; Distributive

Pages 37–38, Chapter 1 Self-Test

1a. $0.5\overline{4}$ **b.** 0.0875 **2a.** Rational **b.** Irrational
3a. F **b.** T **4.** -4 **5.** 7 **6a.** $0.\overline{6}$ **b.** $\sqrt{11}$
7.

8. $\{x : x < \sqrt{7}\}$ **9a.** $4s + \frac{8t}{3}$ **b.** $4 - 2x$ **10a.** Assoc.

(mult.) **b.** Distributive **11a.** T **b.** T **12a.** Mult.

identity **b.** Additive identity **13a.** 24 **b.** $\frac{7}{8}$

14a. $Q = 2n + 1$ **b.** $Q = 2n^2$ **15.** Comm. (add.);
Assoc. (add.); Mult. identity; Distributive; Computation;
Distributive **16.** Let $5n$ and $5m$ be multiples of 5; n
and m are integers.
$5n \cdot 5m = 5(5nm)$
$5nm$ is an integer, p, by the closure property of
multiplication. So $5n \cdot 5m = 5p$, a multiple of 5.

Page 39, Practice for College Entrance Tests

1. D **2.** C **3.** C **4.** A **5.** C **6.** C **7.** A **8.** E
9. B **10.** A **11.** B

Chapter 2

Pages 42–43, Classroom Exercises

1. $\{12\}$ **2.** $\{9\}$ **3.** $\{24\}$ **4.** $\left\{\frac{11}{3}\right\}$ **5.** $\left\{\frac{45}{2}\right\}$ **6.** $\{-4\}$

7. $\left\{-\frac{27}{2}\right\}$ **8.** $\left\{\frac{41}{3}\right\}$ **9.** $\left\{\frac{19}{4}\right\}$ **10.** 3.5

Pages 43–46, Written Exercises

1. $\{7\}$ **3.** $\{1.4\}$ **5.** $\{80\}$ **7.** $\left\{\frac{13}{2}\right\}$ **9.** $\left\{\frac{7}{2}\right\}$ **11.** $\{3\}$

13. $\{6\}$ **15.** $\{7\}$ **17.** $\{2\}$ **19.** $\{-3\}$ **21.** $\{-1\}$
23. $\{3\}$ **25.** 12 **27.** \$8000 **29.** 28 lb/in^2

31. $\left\{\frac{17}{9}\right\}$ **33.** $\{2\}$ **35.** $\{-4\}$ **37.** $\{-3.5\}$ **39.** $\{5\}$

41. 1.2 ft **43.** 55°F **45.** $\{5.7\}$ **47.** $\{2\}$ **49.** $\{1.6\}$
51. 410 cycles per second; 350 cycles per second **53.** 28

Page 46, Review Exercises

1. 36 cm; 54 cm^2 **2.** 628 m; 31,400 m^2 **3.** 40 cm;

60 cm^2 **4.** 60% **5.** 0.35 **6.** 8% **7.** $\frac{11}{10}$

8. $x(a - c)$ **9.** $x(m + 3)$

Page 48, Classroom Exercises

1. $x = \frac{c + b}{a}$ **2.** $x = -ab$ **3.** $x = \frac{d}{a + b}$

4. $x = \frac{by - y}{1 + b}$ **5.** $x = \frac{ac}{b} - y$ **6.** $x = \frac{b_2 y - b_1 y}{a_1 - a_2}$

7. $h = \frac{2A}{b_1 + b_2}$

Pages 48–50, Written Exercises

1a. $x = \frac{5}{2}$ **b.** $x = \frac{c - b}{a}$ **32a.** $x = \frac{11}{7}$ **b.** $x = \frac{m + k}{j}$

5a. $x = \frac{3}{2}$ **b.** $x = \frac{t - rs}{r}$ **7.** $r = st$ **9.** $r = \frac{w}{s + t}$

11. $r = k(j + h)$ **13.** $w = \dfrac{d - ab}{c}$ **15.** $t = \dfrac{f}{c} - e$

17. $x = wz - y$ **19.** $x = \dfrac{c - by}{a}$ **21.** $x = \dfrac{bc}{d}$

23. $b_1 = \dfrac{2A}{h} - b_2$ **25.** $b = \dfrac{2A}{h}$ **27.** $\pi = \dfrac{C}{d}$

29. $p = \dfrac{i}{rt}$ **31a.** $C = \dfrac{Vn}{n - t}$ **b.** $t = \dfrac{n(C - V)}{C}$

33a. $L = \dfrac{I}{0.000012(T - t)}$ **33b.** $T = \dfrac{I}{0.000012L} + t$

33c. $t = T - \dfrac{I}{0.000012L}$ **35a.** $V_2 = \dfrac{P_1 V_1 T_2}{T_1 P_2}$

35b. $P_2 = \dfrac{P_1 V_1 T_2}{T_1 V_2}$ **35c.** $T_2 = \dfrac{P_2 V_2 T_1}{P_1 V_1}$ **37.** $m_1 = \dfrac{Fd^2}{km_2}$;

$d^2 = \dfrac{km_1 m_2}{F}$ **39.** $E = I(R + nr)$; $R = \dfrac{E}{I} - nr$,

$r = \dfrac{1}{n}\left(\dfrac{E}{I} - R\right)$

Page 50, Review Exercises
1. -10 **2.** 0 **3.** -24 **4.** 345 **5.** 5 **6.** 3 **7.** 1.25
8. 0.0003 **9.** $\dfrac{9}{20}$ **10.** $\dfrac{23}{20}$ **11.** 150 **12.** 150 **13.** 0.445
14. 294.91 **15.** 60% **16.** $1.\overline{6}\%$ **17.** $\approx 44.23\%$
18. $\approx 226.09\%$ **19.** 125 **20.** 80 **21.** 87%

Pages 54–55, Classroom Exercises
1. $n + (n + 1) + (n + 2) = 120$; 39, 40, 41
2. $g + 2g + g + 100 = 900$; 1st—200 gadgets; 2nd—400 gadgets; 3rd—300 gadgets

3.

	Cost in dollars	Tickets sold	Total cost in dollars
Students	2	x	$2x$
Adults	4	$250 - x$	$4(250 - x)$

100 student; 150 adult

Pages 55–57, Written Exercises
1. $x + (x + 1) + (x + 2) + (x + 3) + (x + 4) = 65$; 15
3. $b + 2(b + 5) = 100$; 35 cm, 30 cm
5. $\dfrac{75 + 80 + 95 + x}{4} = 85$; 90
7. $(x + 500) + (x + 250) = 5500$; 2875 gal
9. $\dfrac{x}{10} + \dfrac{x}{8} = 1$; $4\dfrac{4}{9}$ h

11.

	Rate (km/h)	Time (h)	Distance (km)
Walking	x	2	$2x$
Running	$2x$	$\dfrac{1}{2}$	$2x\left(\dfrac{1}{2}\right)$ or x

6 km/h

13.

	Rate (km/h)	Time (h)	Distance (km)
Premley to Quimton	85	x	$85x$
Quimton to Ramsburg	75	$x + 1$	$75(x + 1)$

5 hours

15.

	Rate (parts per hour)	Time (hours)	Work (parts produced)
Machine R	50	x	$50x$
Machine S	80	$x - 3$	$80(x - 3)$

Machine R: $7\dfrac{1}{2}$ h; machine S: $4\dfrac{1}{2}$ h

17. 30 min   **19.** $1\dfrac{1}{3}$ h   **21.** 21 h   **23.** 5:10 P.M.

Page 57, Review Exercises
1. $3\dfrac{4}{33}$ **2.** $0.\overline{18}$ **3.** 2   **4.** $\dfrac{1}{5}$ **5.** $1500

6.

7.

Page 57, Self-Quiz 1
1a. $\left\{\dfrac{13}{8}\right\}$ **b.** $\left\{6\dfrac{2}{3}\right\}$ **c.** $\{-1\}$ **2.** 35.4 ft

3a. $r = \dfrac{A - p}{pt}$ **b.** $r = \dfrac{L}{\pi + 6}$ **4.** $\dfrac{25}{11}$ h

Page 61, Classroom Exercises
1. $\{x : x < 5\}$

2. $\{x : x < 6\}$

3. $\{x : x > 3.75\}$

4. $\{x : x > 11\}$

5. A minimum of 313 people

Pages 61–62, Written Exercises
1. $\left\{x : x > 4\dfrac{1}{2}\right\}$

3. $\{m : m < 2\}$

5. $\{a : a > 9\}$

7. $\{r : r > 4\}$

9. $\{q : q < 5\}$

11. $\{y : y > 2\}$

13. Sales > \$1200   **15.** Less than $3\frac{1}{2}$ hours

17. $\left\{x : x > -\dfrac{57}{2}\right\}$

19. $\left\{T : T > \dfrac{10}{3}\right\}$

21. $\left\{b : b > -\dfrac{5}{8}\right\}$

23. $\{t : t > -3\}$

25. $\{r : r < 5\}$

27. $\{k : k < 2\}$

29. Less than 3.1 hours
31. If $c < d$, then $c - d$ is a negative number. If $a < b$, then $a(c - d) > b(c - d)$, because multiplication by a negative number $(c - d)$ reverses the sense of the inequality.   **33.** $\dfrac{1}{a} < \dfrac{1}{b}; \dfrac{1}{a} > \dfrac{1}{b}$

Page 62, Review Exercises
1. Comm. (add.)   **2.** Add. inverse   **3.** Assoc. (mult.)
4. Mult. identity   **5.** $7a + 8b$ **6.** $-18 - 3a$
7. $6x^2 - 8x + 5$ **8.** $4a^2 - 12ab + 9b^2$ **9.** $10x^2 - x - 3$

Page 62, Extension
1. Set 1:13; Set 2:26   **2.** Set 2

Page 65, Classroom Exercises
1. $2m > 13$ or $2m = 13$ **2.** $-2 < 3x$ and $3x < 6$
3. $2 < y < 3$ **4.** $4w \leqslant -8$

5.

6.

7. $\{t : -1 < t < 4\}$

8. $\{n : n \leqslant -4\}$

Pages 65–67, Written Exercises
1. $x \leqslant -2$ **3.** $y \leqslant \dfrac{1}{2}$ **5.** $-5 < a < 0$

7.

9.

11.

15.

17.

19. $(n : n \leqslant 1)$

21. $\{w : -2 < w < 3\}$

23. $\{x : 2 \leqslant x \leqslant 5\}$

25. $\{r : -2 < r < -1\}$

27. $\{m : < m \leqslant 6\}$

29. $\{a : a \leqslant 1\}$

31. $-1 \leqslant x \leqslant 3$ **33.** $x < -1$ or $x > 3$ **35.** $x \geqslant -1$ and $x \neq 2$ **37.** $\left\{q : q \geqslant -\dfrac{5}{3}\right\}$ **39.** $\left\{b : b \geqslant \dfrac{14}{11}\right\}$
41. all real numbers   **43.** $\left\{x : x < -\dfrac{1}{2} \text{ or } x > 0\right\}$
45. $\emptyset$ **47.** More than 30   **49.** For $x < 4$, $y > 7$. For $x \geqslant 4$, $y \geqslant 7$.   **51.** $1 < x < 4$
53a.

53b. $x < 2$
55a–b.

$a = b$; distributive

Page 67, Review Exercises
1. 130   **2.** 65   **3.** 115   **4.** 0.25   **5.** 1.125   **6.** 0.21

7. $-\dfrac{5}{9}$ **8.** $\dfrac{15}{8}$ **9.** $\dfrac{3}{5}$ **10.** $Q = n^2$ **11.** $Q = 2^n$
12. $Q = 3n + 4$

Page 70, Classroom Exercises

1. $\{x: -2 \le x \le 2\}$

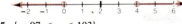

2. $\{x:x > 1 \text{ or } x < -1\}$

3. $\{x:x < 1 \text{ or } x > 3\}$

4. $\{x: -5 < x < -1\}$ **5.** $\{x:x \le -\dfrac{1}{3} \text{ or } x \ge 1\}$

6. $\left\{x:x \ne -\dfrac{3}{2}\right\}$ **7.** $|x| \le 2$ **8.** $|x| > 2$ **9.** $|x - 1| < 2$

Pages 70–72, Written Exercises

1. More, 2, 0 **3.** Less, 3, 2 **5.** $|3 - (-2)|$
7. $|x + 2| < 2$ **9.** $|x| < 1$ **11.** $|x| \ge 2$ **13.** $|x - 2| < 1$
15. $|x + 1| \ge 1$
17. $\{-5, 5\}$

19. $\{7, -1\}$

21. $\{x: -2 < x < 2\}$

23. $\{x:x < 0 \text{ or } x > 4\}$

25. $\{p: 97 < p < 103\}$

27. $\{y: -1 < y < 5\}$

29. $\{b:b < -5 \text{ or } b > 1\}$

31. $\{t: \dfrac{-5}{2} < t < \dfrac{1}{2}\}$

33. $\{d: 1 < d < 5\}$

35. $x: -14 < x < 10$ **37.** 0
39. $\{x:x \ge 15 \text{ or } x \le -3\}$ **41.** $\{x:x < 0\}$
43. $\{x:x < 2\}$ **45.** $\{x: 1 < x < 3 \text{ or } 5 < x < 7\}$

age 72, Review Exercises
1. $3n$ **2.** $10n + 90$ **3.** $\dfrac{n}{2^n}$ **4.** $\dfrac{13[11(7n)] - n}{1000} = n$

Page 75, Self-Quiz 2
1. a. $\{x:x > 2\}$

b. $\{y:y > 48\}$

2. The minimum attendance must be 546.

3a. $\left\{n:n \ge \dfrac{17}{4}\right\}$ **3b.** $\{x: -4 < x \le 4\}$

4a.

4b.

5. $x > -4$ and $x < 2$

6. $\left\{y:y \le -\dfrac{2}{3} \text{ or } y \ge 2\right\}$

7. $|x - 1| < 1$

Page 75, Classroom Exercises
1. length ≤ 30 m

2. $4(x - 2(1.25)) + 8(x - 1.25) = 16(12)$; $17\dfrac{2}{3}$ in.

Pages 75–76, Written Exercises
1. $2(6e) + 6(2e) = 2(30)$;

edge: $2\dfrac{1}{2}$ in.; height: 5 in.

3. $4e + 4(2e) = 90$;
base edges are 7.5 cm;
sloping edges are 15 cm

5. $x + (x + 2) + (x + 4) + (x + 6) + (x + 8) = 100$;
16 cm; 18 cm; 20 cm;
22 cm; 24 cm

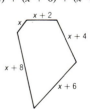

7. $8\left(t + \dfrac{1}{4}\right) = 12t;$

<table>
<tr><td>Anne</td><td>$\dfrac{8 \text{ km/h}}{\left(t + \frac{1}{4}\right) \text{ h}}$</td></tr>
<tr><td>Althea</td><td>$\dfrac{12 \text{ km/h}}{t \text{ h}}$</td></tr>
</table>

30 min or $\dfrac{1}{2}$h

9. $\dfrac{120.5}{\pi + 4}$ in. ≈ 16.87 in.   **11.** 9 cm

13. 3.6 in. by 4.8 in.

15. $4(x - 2.5) + 4x + 4(x - 2.5) + 1.25 \leqslant 192;$

$17\dfrac{9}{16}$ in.

Page 76, Review Exercises

1. 35   **2.** 120   **3.** 120

4. Let $2m + 1$ and $2n + 1$ represent two odd integers where m and n are integers.
$(2m + 1) + (2n + 1) = 2m + 2n + 2 = 2(m + n + 1)$
Since the set of integers is closed with respect to addition, $(m + n + 1)$ is an integer. Therefore, its double is even.

5. Let $7m$ and $7n$ represent multiples of 7 where m and n are integers. Then $(7m)(7n) = 7(7mn)$. Since the set of integers is closed with respect to multiplication, $(7mn)$ is an integer. Therefore, $7(7mn)$ is a multiple of 7.

Pages 78–79, Chapter Review

1. $\{70\}$ **3.** 3   **5.** $w = \dfrac{P - 2l}{2}$

7. $2(w + 20) + 2w = 160$ **9.** 250 widgets

11. $\{x : x > 3\}$

13. $(x : x \leqslant -3\}$

15. $\{x : 2 < x < 5\}$

17. $\{x : -3 < x < -1\}$

19. $0 < A \leqslant \dfrac{1}{2}(10)(5)$

Pages 79–80, Chapter Self-Test

1. $\left\{\dfrac{1}{6}\right\}$ **2.** $\left\{\dfrac{9}{2}\right\}$ **3.** -175 **4.** $t = \dfrac{m - k}{c}$

5. $w = \dfrac{z + b}{ab}$ **6.** $x + (x + 2) + (x + 4) = 204; 66$

7. $\dfrac{75 + 90 + 82 + x}{4} = 85; 93$ **8.** $\left\{m : m > \dfrac{7}{3}\right\}$

9. $\{y : y > -3\}$ **10.** $\left\{x : x < \dfrac{61}{11}\right\}$ **11.** $\left\{t : t < \dfrac{48}{5}\right\}$

12. $\{k : k \leqslant 7\}$

13. $\{y : -1 < y < 3\}$

14. $\{x : -2 < x < 2\}$

15. $|x| \geqslant 2$ **16.** $\left\{w : w < -\dfrac{7}{2} \text{ or } w > -\dfrac{5}{2}\right\}$

17. $\{x : -1 \leqslant x \leqslant 2\}$

18. $h \leqslant 80$ in.

Pages 80–81, Practice for College Entrance Tests

1. B   **2.** C   **3.** B   **4.** C   **5.** D   **6.** B   **7.** D   **8.** A
9. C   **10.** A   **11.** A   **12.** C   **13.** D   **14.** B   **15.** A

Chapter 3

Page 86, Classroom Exercises

1. C   **2.** F   **3.** E   **4.** (3, 1)   **5.** $(-2, 0)$ **6.** (0, 3)
7. I   **8.** I   **9.** IV   **10.** x-axis   **11.** y-axis
12. $\{-3, 1, 3\}; \{-2, 0, 2, 4\}$ **13.** Reals; $\{y : y \geqslant 0\}$
14. $\{2\}; \{-5\}$ **15.** Reals; Reals

16. $\{x : x \geqslant 0\}$; Reals

Pages 86–87, Written Exercises

1. B   **3.** D   **5.** A   **7.** (1, 4)   **9.** $(-1, -4)$ **11.** (2, 0)
13. II   **15.** y-axis   **17.** III   **19.** y-axis   **21.** $\{0, 1\}$;
$\{3, 5, 7\}$ **23.** $\{-3, -2, -1\}; \{5\}$ **25.** $\{0, 2, 4\}$
27. $\{0, 0.1, 0.2\}$ **29.** $\{10, 9, 8\}$

31.

33.

35.

37.

39. {x:x ≥ 0}; Reals   **41.** Reals; Reals

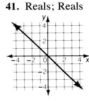

43. {0}; {y:y ≠ 0}   **45.** Reals; Reals

47. Reals; {y:y ≥ 4}   **49.** {(0, 0), (1, 1), (16, 2),
(81, 3), (256, 4), (1, −1),
(16, −2), (81, −3), (256, −4)};
{0, 1, 16, 81, 256};
{0, 1, 2, 3, 4, −1, −2, −3, −4}

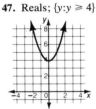

51. {(1, 1), (1, 2), (1, 3), (1, 4), (2, 2), (2,6)}; {1, 2}; {1, 2, 3, 4, 6}

53.

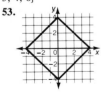

55.

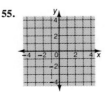

57.

59.

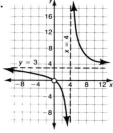

Page 88, Review Exercises

1. 25   **2.** 27   **3.** 26   **4.** 12.31   **5.** 31,400

6. 1331   **7.** 2, $2\frac{1}{3}$, $2\frac{2}{3}$, 3, $3\frac{1}{3}$, $3\frac{2}{3}$, 4   **8.** 9, 4, 1, 0, 1, 4, 9

Page 88, Extension

1. Mean ≈ 35.54; median ≈ 35.5; mode = 36

Pages 92–93, Classroom Exercises

1. {(−2, −2), (1, 1), (2, 1), (3, −1), (3, −2)}; Not a function   **2.** {(−3, 1), (−1, −1), (1, 3), (2, 4), (3, 3), (4, −1)}; Function   **3.** {0, 4}; {0, 2, −2}; not a function
4. {0, 2, −2}; {0, 4}; function, not 1-1   **5.** {3, −2, 5}; {7, 8}; function not 1-1   **6.** {−2, −1}; {5, 8, 9}; not a function   **7.** Reals; reals; function; 1-1   **8.** {x:x ≥ 0}; reals; not a function.   **9.** {x:x ≠ 0}; {y:y ≠ 0}; function; 1-1
10. {2}; reals; not a function
11. {x: −2 ≤ x ≤ 2};
{y: −2 ≤ y ≤ 2}; not a function
12. Reals; reals; function; 1-1

Pages 93–95, Written Exercises

1. {(−2, 16), (0, 0), (2, 16)}; function   **3.** {(81, −3), (81, 3), (256, −4), (256, 4)}; not a function
5. {(−3, 3), (−2, 2), (−1, 1), (0, 0), (1, 1), (2, 2), (3, 3)}; function   **7.** {2, 3, 4}; {3, 4, 5}; function **9.** {2}; {3, 4, 5}; not a function   **11.** {0, 2, 3, 6}; {−5, −1, 0, 3, 4}; not a function   **13.** {56, 75, 85, 93}; {−2, 4, 8, 12, 17}; not a function   **15.** {−6, −1, 4, 7, 50}; {−92, −6, 0, 10, 20}; function   **17.** {−2, 0, 1, 2, 3}; {1, 3, 4, 5, 6}; function   **19.** {(−2, 1), (−1, 1), (0, 1), (1, 2)}; {−2, −1, 0, 1}; {1, 2}; function   **21.** {(−2, 1), (−2, −1), (1, 2), (1, −2)}; {−2, 1}; {−2, −1, 1, 2}; not a function
23. 1-1 function   **25.** 1-1 function

27. 1-1 function

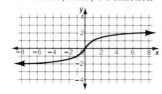

29. Reals; reals; 1-1 function

31. {3}; reals; not a function

Ordered pairs will vary for Exercises 33 and 35.
33. Function **35.** Function
37. Function   **39.** Function

  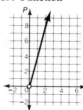

41. $a = b$ **43.** $p = q$

Page 95, Review Exercises

1. $6\frac{1}{6}$ **2.** $2\frac{5}{6}$ **3.** $7\frac{1}{2}$ **4.** $2\frac{7}{10}$ **5.** $17\frac{17}{36}$ **6.** -3

7. $2\sqrt{10}$ **8.** $y = \dfrac{7 - 2x}{3}$ **9.** $y = \dfrac{c - ax}{b}$

Page 100, Classroom Exercises

1. Yes   **2.** No
3. Yes   **4.** No

5. $1; -5$ **6.** $y = -x + 3; -1; 3$ **7.** $y = \dfrac{5}{2}x + 3; \dfrac{5}{2};$

3 **8.** -2 **9.** $\dfrac{7}{4}$ **10.** $2; -5$ **11.** $-1; 3$ **12.** $1; 1$

13. $0; 0$

Pages 100–102, Written Exercises

1. No **3.** No **5.** Yes **7.** Yes **9.** Yes **11.** No

13. No **15.** No **17.** No **19.** $3; -6$ **21.** $0; 7$

23. $-\dfrac{1}{2}; 2$ **25.** $\dfrac{4}{3}; -4$ **27.** $-\dfrac{1}{5}; 0$ **29.** $\dfrac{2}{3}; -\dfrac{5}{3}$

31. No **33.** Yes **35** Yes **37.** Yes **39.** $\dfrac{3}{2}, -\dfrac{3}{2}$

41. $m; -mx_0 + y_0$ **43a.** 0, 4, 16, 36 **43b.** $\dfrac{4 - 0}{2 - 0} = 2;$

$\dfrac{16 - 4}{4 - 2} = 6;$ $\dfrac{36 - 16}{6 - 4} = 10$ **45.** $\dfrac{9}{2}; -1$ **47.** No

49. Yes

51. $y = x + 2$ if $x \geqslant -2$;
       $y = -x - 2$ if $x > -2$

53. $(x_1, mx_1 + b); (x_2, mx_2 + b); \dfrac{\Delta y}{\Delta x} = \dfrac{(y_2 - y_1)}{(x_2 - x_1)} =$

$\dfrac{(mx_2 + b) - (mx_1 + b)}{x_2 - x_1} = \dfrac{mx_2 - mx_1}{x_2 - x_1} = \dfrac{m(x_2 - x_1)}{(x_2 - x_1)} = m$

Therefore, the slope is independent of x and y.
55. $q - ap$

Page 102, Review Exercises

1. Yes **2.** No **3.** $\dfrac{17}{99}$ **4.** $10\dfrac{1}{4}$ **5.** $-\dfrac{7}{9}$ **6.** -24

7. -48 **8.** 0 **9.** -273 **10.** $\dfrac{a + b - 30}{5}$

Page 103, Self-Quiz 1

1. $\{-0.1, 0, \pi, 4\}; \left\{-1, \dfrac{1}{2}, \sqrt{2}, 10\right\}$

2.   **3.**

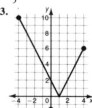

4. Function; $\left\{-2, -\dfrac{1}{2}, 0, 3\right\}; \left\{0, \dfrac{1}{4}, 4\right\}$ **5.** Not a

function; $\{x{:}x \geqslant 1\}$; reals **6.** Function;
$\{x{:} -3 \leqslant x \leqslant 3\}; \{y{:} -3 \leqslant y \leqslant 1\}$ **7.** Not a function;
$\{x{:} -2 \leqslant x \leqslant 2\}; \{y{:} -2 \leqslant y \leqslant 2\}$ **8.** $\dfrac{3}{2}; -6$

9. $0; -\dfrac{1}{2}$ **10.** $\dfrac{4}{5}; -2$

Page 103, Extension

1. The mean increases by 10. **2.** The mean is doubled.

Page 107, Classroom Exercises

1. Parallel **2.** Perpendicular **3.** Perpendicular
4. Perpendicular **5.** Neither **6.** Perpendicular

7. $y = -\dfrac{1}{2}x$ **8.** $y = -\dfrac{3}{2}x$ **9.** $y + 1 = -\dfrac{1}{4}(x - 3)$

10. $y = \dfrac{1}{7}x + \dfrac{39}{7}$

Pages 107–109, Written Exercises

1. $y = \dfrac{1}{2}x$ **3.** $y = 2x$ **5.** $y = -2x$ **7.** $y = \dfrac{3}{2}x$

9. $y = \dfrac{3}{2}x$ **11.** $y = -\dfrac{3}{4}x + 9$ **13.** $y = -\dfrac{3}{2}x + 12$

15. $y = \dfrac{2}{3}x + \dfrac{10}{3}$ **17.** $y = -2x + 8$ **19.** $y = \dfrac{2}{3}x - 5$

21. $y = 3$ **23.** Slope of $\overline{AB} = \dfrac{1}{2}$; slope of $\overline{CD} = -2$;

$\dfrac{1}{2}(-2) = -1$ **25.** Slope $\overline{EF} = \dfrac{1}{2}$ = slope $\overline{GH}$

27. $y = -\dfrac{3}{4}x - 1$ **29.** $y = -\dfrac{4}{3}x + 5$

31. $y = -\dfrac{3}{2}x + \dfrac{17}{2}$

33. $y = 3x + 9$ **35.** $y = -\dfrac{4}{3}x$ **37.** $x = 4$ **39.** Right

triangle **41.** Slope through (3, 3) and $(-1, 2)$: $\dfrac{5}{4}$; slope

through $(-2, 1)$ and (5, 0): $-\dfrac{1}{7}$; diagonals are not perpen-

dicular **43.** $\dfrac{3}{4}; \dfrac{3}{4}$; collinear **45.** 7; 7; collinear

47. Linear; $R = \dfrac{2}{3}S + 5$ **49.** Linear; $C = K - 273$

51. 2 **53.** 1

55. 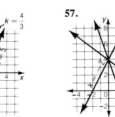 **57.**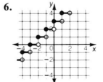

Page 110, Review Exercises

1.

2.

3. $\{x:x < 1\}$ **4.** Mult. identity **5.** Distributive
6. $4x - 10$ **7.** $2x^2 - 2x + 7$ **8.** $6x^2 - x - 15$
9. $x^2 - 81y^2$

Page 110, Extension

1. 88 **2.** 88 **3.** ≈ 88.37 **4.** 20; 16.5; 17

Page 114, Classroom Exercises

1. No **2.** Yes; π **3.** Yes; 200 **4.** No **5.** No

6. Yes **7.** $\dfrac{49}{3}$ **8.** 400 lb

Pages 114–116, Written Exercises

1. Yes **3.** No **5.** d **7.** r^2 **9.** $\sqrt{A}$ **11.** The
volume of a sphere (V) varies directly as the cube of its

radius (r); $\dfrac{4}{3}\pi$ **13.** 15 **15.** 12 **17.** 165 **19.** 6π

21. 54 **23.** 6 **25.** $3\sqrt{3}$ **27.** 6 or -6 **29.** 54 cm^2
31. Direct variation; 6 **33.** Not direct
35. 16; $d = 16t^2$; 10s **37.** 108; $f = 108\sqrt{T}$; 64 lb

39a. **39b.**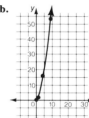

39c.

39d. c **39e.** 2 **39f.** $y = 2x^3$

Page 116, Review Exercises

1. 25 **2.** 160 **3.** 48 cm^2; 28 cm **4.** 24 cm^2; 24 cm
5. 144 in.^{2}; 56 in. **6.** 100π cm^2; 20π cm **7.** $\sqrt{5}$ cm

Page 119, Classroom Exercises

1. 3 **2.** 6 **3.** -5 **4.** -5 **5.** 6
6. **7.** F
8. Either

Pages 119–120, Written Exercises

1. 2 **3.** 0 **5.** 10 **7.** -8 **9.** -3 **11.** 2

13.

15.

17.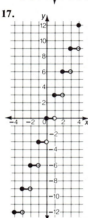

19.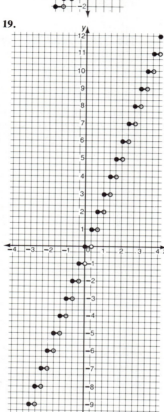

21. 12   **23.** 0   **25.** -37 **27.** 15   **29.** $A = [a]$
31. $S; I = 500 + 0.055$ **33.** $h; R = 25 + 15h$ **35.** T
37. F   **39.** F   **41.** T

43.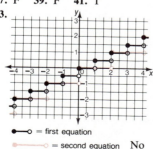

45.

● ─○ = first equation

○ ─○ = second equation   No

No

47. $n = 0.5$
49. $100 * \text{INT}(X/100 + 0.5)$

Page 121, Review Exercises
1. $97 + 3n$ **2.** 2^n **3.** Comm. (add.); Assoc. (add.);
Computation   **4.** Assoc. (add.); Add. inverse; Add.
identity   **5.** Let m and n be integers; $2m$ and $2n$ are
even numbers; $(2m)(2n) = 4mn$, where mn is some
integer and $4mn$ is a multiple of 4.   **6.** $\sqrt{2}$ **7.** $\sqrt{3}$

Page 121, Self-Quiz 2
1. $y = 3x + 5$ **2.** $y = \frac{4}{3}x - 4$ **3.** $\frac{48}{7}$ **4.** $S = 6e^2$
5. -4 **6.** 4

7.

8. $P = \dfrac{d}{33}$

Page 124, Classroom Exercises
1. -3 **2.** 4.3   **3.** 2.3   **4.** $-3a + 1$ **5.** $5|a|$
6. $-2x + 1$ **7.** 0   **8.** 6   **9.** 0   **10.** $[-3a + 2]$
11. $|-2a + 1|$ **12.** -4 **13.** F

Page 124–125, Written Exercises
1. 81   **3.** 16   **5.** $\frac{1}{4}$ **7.** 3   **9.** 8   **11.** 0   **13.** -12
15. $-\frac{5}{3}$ **17.** $\{6\}$ **19.** $\left\{-\frac{6}{5}\right\}$ **21.** $\{5, -5\}$
23. $\{\sqrt{11}, -\sqrt{11}\}$ **25a.** 18   **b.** 6   **27a.** 10   **b.** 30
29a. 13   **b.** 13   **31a.** $a + 3$ **b.** $a + 3$ **33a.** 0
b. -12 **35a.** $4(-a + 4)$ **b.** $-4a + 4$ **37.** $-5, 3$
39. -1 **41.** $f(g(x)) = 3(4x) = 12x$;
$g(f(x)) = 4(3x) = 12x$ **43.** $f(g(x)) = 5|2x| = 10|x|$;
$g(f(x)) = |2 \cdot 5x| = |10x| = 10|x|$ **45.** $g(x) = \frac{1}{2}x + 3$
47. $j(x) = -\frac{2}{3}x + 8$ **49.** $\frac{x-2}{3}$ **51.** $\{y : y \neq -2\}$
53. $g(a) \cdot g(b) = a^n b^n$; $g(ab) = (ab)^n = a^n b^n$

Page 125, Review Exercises
1. $\{x : x < 3\}$

2. $\{x : x > -4\}$

3. $\{x : 5 \leqslant x \leqslant 10\}$

4. $\{x : -18 \leqslant x \leqslant -8\}$

5. $\{x: -2 \leqslant x \leqslant 4\}$

6. $\{x: x \geqslant -2 \text{ or } x \leqslant -4\}$

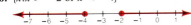

7. $|x - 1| > 2$

Pages 127–128, Chapter Review

1a. II **b.** I **c.** IV **d.** y-axis

3. Reals; $\{y: y \geqslant -1\}$

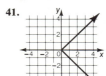

5. Not a function

7. 1-1 function

9. -1

11. $y = \dfrac{2}{3}x$

13. $y = -x - 1$

15. 18

17. -4

19. 40 **21.** 50 **23.** 52

Page 129, Chapter 3 Self-Test

1. $\{-2, 0, 3, 4\}$ **2a.** T **b.** F **c.** T **d.** T

3a. $y = -\dfrac{1}{2}x + 2$ **b.** $y = 2x - 10$ **4.** $-\dfrac{3}{2}; \dfrac{15}{2}$

5a. $-\dfrac{5}{2}$ **b.** $\dfrac{2}{5}$ **6.** $x = 4$ **7.** $\dfrac{\pi}{2}$ **8.** 48

9. $\{-3, -2, -1, 0, 1\}$

10.

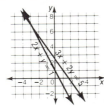

11. $c = 2 + 0.5p$

12a. -6 **b.** 17 **c.** 6

d. $3[4x + 2]$

Pages 130–132, Practice College Tests

1. A **2.** C **3.** B **4.** D **5.** C **6.** D **7.** B **8.** A
9. C **10.** A **11.** C **12.** D **13.** C **14.** B **15.** C
16. C **17.** A **18.** A **19.** D **20.** B **21.** A
22. B **23.** A **24.** D

Pages 132–135, Cumulative Review (Chapters 1–3)

1a. Rational **b.** Rational **c.** Rational

d. Irrational **3.** $\dfrac{5}{3}$ **5.** $\dfrac{12}{5}$ **7.** $\dfrac{1}{8}, \dfrac{1}{6}, \dfrac{1}{3}$

9.

11. Distributive **13.** Add. inverse **15.** $5w + 3$

17. 33, 65, 129 **19.** $\dfrac{n}{n + 2}$ **21.** $(2n)^2 = 4n^2 = 2(2n^2)$

23. $\left\{\dfrac{3}{2}\right\}$ **25.** \$30,000 **27.** $h = \dfrac{A - 2s^2}{4s}$

29. 75 parts/h and 125 parts/h

31. $\{x: x > -4\}$

33. $\{x: -1 < x < 3\}$

35. $\{y: -3 < y < 5\}$

37. $|x| < 4$ **39.** 11 ft by 22 ft

41.

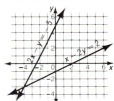

43. Yes **47.** $y = -\dfrac{3}{2}x + 1$

49. No **51.** $\dfrac{9}{2}$

53.

55. S;

57. $-2a$ **59.** -2

Chapter 4

Page 139, Classroom Exercises

1. $\{(-3, 7)\}$ **2.** $\{(-4, -3)\}$

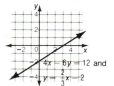

3. Inconsistent **4.** $\{(x, y): y = \dfrac{2}{3}x - 2\}$

$y = 2x + 1$; $y = 2x - 3$

$4x - 6y = 12$ and $y = \dfrac{2}{3}x - 2$

5. 7 quarters, 12 dimes

Pages 139–141, Written Exercises

1. $\{(2, 6)\}$

3. $\{(1, 2)\}$

5. $\{(2, -1)\}$

7. Inconsistent

9. $\{(2, 3)\}$

11. $\{(x, y): x + 2y = 6\}$

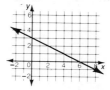

13. $d = 2g;$
$d = 6 + g;$ 12

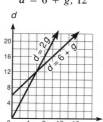

15. $t + f = 28;$
$f = t + 10;$ 19

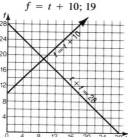

17. $b = p + 6;$ $1b + 3p = 38;$ 14 loaves of bread, 8 pies

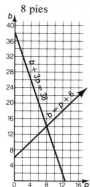

19. $P = \frac{5}{2}Q;$ $P + Q = 14;$ 10 gal of P, 4 gal of Q

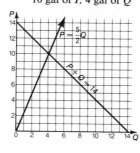

21. T **23.** F **25.** F **27.** 4 **29.** Any real number
31. -4
33.

35. $x = 6$

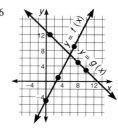

Page 141, Review Exercises

1a. 0.1875 **16.** $0.\overline{15}$ **2a.** $\frac{163}{100}$ **2b.** N $= \frac{41}{99}$ **3.** $-\frac{7}{3}$
4. $-\frac{4}{3}$ **5.** 10 **6.** $\frac{6}{11}, \frac{7}{12}, \frac{8}{13}$ **7.** $\{x:x > \sqrt{2}\}$
8. $x: x$ is an integer and $x > 9\}$

Page 145, Classroom Exercises

1. $\{(4, 1)\}$ **2.** $\left\{\left(-\frac{7}{4}, -\frac{1}{8}\right)\right\}$ **3.** $\emptyset$ **4.** 210 adult, 240 student

Pages 145–147, Written Exercises

1. $\{(-2, 5)\}$ **3.** $\{(7, 4)\}$ **5.** $\{(x, y): y = 2x - 3\}$
7. $\left\{\left(\frac{6}{5}, 6\right)\right\}$ **9.** $\emptyset$ **11.** $\{(-2, -3)\}$ **13.** $\left\{\left(4, -\frac{3}{2}\right)\right\}$
15. $\left\{\left(\frac{3}{2}, -\frac{1}{2}\right)\right\}$ **17.** $\left\{\left(5, \frac{4}{3}\right)\right\}$ **19.** $2(p + w) = 360;$
$3(p - w) = 360;$ 30 mph, 150 mph **21.** $l = w + 3$ and $2(l + w) = 41;$ 11.75 cm, 8.75 cm **23.** $4.75
25. 48 **27.** 7 mph **29.** $\{(20, 20)\}$ **31.** $\{(15, 6)\}$
33. $\left\{\left(\frac{3}{8}, \frac{5}{6}\right)\right\}$ **35.** $\left\{\left(\frac{ac}{a + b}, \frac{bc}{a + b}\right)\right\}$ **37.** $\left\{\left(-\frac{1}{9}, 6\right)\right\}$
39. $\left\{\left(4, \frac{1}{2}\right)\right\}$

Page 147, Review Exercises

1. Mult. identity **2.** Comm. (add.) **3.** Distributive
4. Assoc. (add.) **5.** Mult. inverse **6.** Closure (mult.)
7. $\frac{5}{32}, \frac{6}{64}, \frac{7}{128}$ **8.** Q $= n^2 - 1$ **9.** $5n$ **10.** $101n$

Page 150, Classroom Exercises

1. $7x = 28; \{(4, 1)\}$ **2.** $8x = -14; \left\{\left(-\frac{7}{4}, -\frac{1}{8}\right)\right\}$

3. $18y = 0$; $\{(2, 0)\}$ **4.** $y = 11$; $\left\{\left(-\dfrac{13}{2}, 11\right)\right\}$
5. 1700 pages/h, 2100 pages /h

Pages 151–152, Written Exercises
1. $\{(2, 2)\}$ **3.** $\{(4, 1)\}$ **5.** $\{(12, 8)\}$ **7.** $\{(5, -3)\}$
9. $\{(3, -1)\}$ **11.** $\{(-2, 4)\}$ **13.** $\left\{\left(\dfrac{2}{3}, \dfrac{3}{2}\right)\right\}$
15. $\left\{\left(-\dfrac{2}{3}, -\dfrac{3}{4}\right)\right\}$ **17.** 65 and 35   **19.** 7
21. $\left\{\left(\dfrac{5}{2}, \dfrac{15}{4}\right)\right\}$ **23.** $\{(-1, 2)\}$ **25.** $\left\{\left(\dfrac{1}{2}, -2\right)\right\}$
27. Machine P: 4.5 h;   machine Q: 2.5 h   **29.** 0.5 h
31. $\dfrac{32}{3}$ and $\dfrac{40}{3}$ **33.** 9000   **35.** 32 lb of 32% alloy, 48 lb
of 12% alloy   **37.** $\{(-3, 2, 5)\}$ **39.** $\left\{\left(2, \dfrac{1}{2}, -3\right)\right\}$

Page 152, Review Exercises
1. $\{24\}$ **2.** $\{6\}$ **3.** $\{-5\}$ **4.** $h = \dfrac{2A}{b}$
5. $y = \dfrac{-c - ax}{b}$ **6.** $L = N\left(1 - \dfrac{V}{c}\right)$
7. $n + (n + 1) + (n + 2) = 147$; 48, 49, 50

Page 153, Self-Quiz 1
1. $\{(2, -4)\}$ **2.** $R + T = 20$; $R = T + 6$; 13

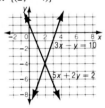

3. $\{(-1, 1)\}$ **4.** 3.5 mph   **5.** $\{(2, -1)\}$
6. 50 mL of 30%, 150 mL of 70%

Page 153, Extension
1. Set A: Set B:
    65   77   84   90   64   72   82   92
    66   92   77   84
    69   93   79   86

Set C: **2.** A   **3.** C   **4.** A
66   72   83   90
67   76   88   94

Page 158, Classroom Exercises
1. -7 **2.** 4   **3.** 1   **4.** $\left\{\left(\dfrac{13}{5}, \dfrac{7}{5}\right)\right\}$ **5.** $\{(-3, -2)\}$

Pages 158–159, Written Exercises
1. -7 **3.** 7   **5.** 7   **7.** 40   **9.** 3; 58; -19

11. 31; 45; -13 **13.** -2; -18; 1   **15.** $\left\{\left(\dfrac{13}{31}, \dfrac{1}{31}\right)\right\}$
17. $\left\{\left(-11, \dfrac{29}{4}\right)\right\}$ **19.** $\left\{\left(\dfrac{385}{31}, \dfrac{30}{31}\right)\right\}$ **21.** $\left\{\left(\dfrac{59}{31}, -\dfrac{33}{31}\right)\right\}$
23. $\left\{\left(\dfrac{75}{2}, \dfrac{93}{2}\right)\right\}$ **25.** $\left\{\left(\dfrac{3}{2}, -\dfrac{2}{3}\right)\right\}$ **27.** $\left\{\dfrac{3}{2}\right\}$ **29.** $\{5\}$
31. $\{-2\}$ **33.** $50; $3.50   **35.** $20; $.35   **37.** $D = 0$;
$Dx \neq 0$; $D_y \neq 0$

Page 159, Review Exercises
1. $\{x : x < 4\}$
2. $\{x : x \geq 8\}$
3. $\{x : \dfrac{1}{2} \leq x \leq 3\}$
4. $\left\{x : -10 < x < \dfrac{5}{2}\right\}$
5. $\left\{x : \dfrac{5}{2} < x < \dfrac{7}{2}\right\}$
6. $\{x : x < -1 \text{ or } x > 2\}$
7. $|x - 1| < 2$

Pages 162–163, Classroom Exercises
1. $\begin{vmatrix} 1 & 0 \\ 2 & -6 \end{vmatrix}$ **2.** $\begin{vmatrix} 3 & 4 \\ 1 & 0 \end{vmatrix}$ **3.** $\begin{vmatrix} 4 & -2 \\ 0 & 0 \end{vmatrix}$ **4.** -4
5. Second row   **6.** -20 **7.** 0   **8.** 1

Pages 163–164, Written Exercises
1. -24 **3.** -20 **5.** -11 **7.** $-\dfrac{41}{2}$ **9.** 6   **11.** 10
13. -84 **15.** $\{(1, 3, -2)\}$ **17.** $\{(-2, -4, 5)\}$
19. $\{(2, 0, -3)\}$ **21.** $\{5\}$ **23.** $\left\{\dfrac{4}{3}\right\}$ **25.** 417
27. $E = 3 - 3x + 4x^2$; $5,500,000   **29.** 44

Page 165, Review Exercises
1. Def. of subtraction; Distributive prop.; Mult. identity   **2.** $5x + 5y = 5(x + y)$
3. $2x + 2(x + 10) = 100$ 20 cm and 30 cm

4. $\frac{1}{6}$ h; cyclist: $3\frac{1}{3}$ km; runner: $1\frac{2}{3}$ km

5.   **6.**

Page 168, Classroom Exercises

1. 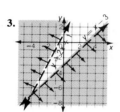   **2.**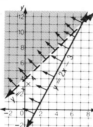

3.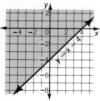

Pages 168–169, Written Exercises

1. Yes **3.** No **5.** Yes **7.** Yes **9.** No **11.** No
13. Dashed **15.** Solid

17.   **19.**

21.   **23.**

25. **27.**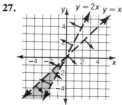

29.   **31.**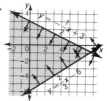

33.   **35.**

37.   **39.**

41. 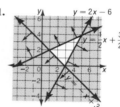 **43.**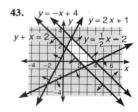

45. 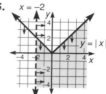 **47.**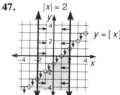

49. 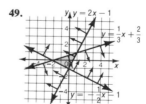 **51.**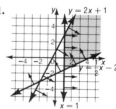

53. $k < 2$ **55.** $k < 2$

Page 170, Review Exercises

1. Not a function **2.** Function; not 1-1. **3.** 1-1
function **4.** No **5.** $m = -\frac{3}{4}$; $b = 3$ **6.** Slope $= \frac{1}{4}$;

798 Selected Answers

y intercept $= \dfrac{5}{2}$ **7.** $y = 2x - 2$ **8.** $y = \dfrac{2}{3}x + 8$

9. $y = -\dfrac{1}{2}x - 5$

Page 170, Self-Quiz 2

1. 21   **2.** $\left\{\left(\dfrac{7}{5}, \dfrac{12}{5}\right)\right\}$ **3.** $\{5\}$

4. $-4\begin{vmatrix} -1 & 2 \\ 7 & 1 \end{vmatrix} - 3\begin{vmatrix} 9 & -1 \\ -5 & 7 \end{vmatrix}$

5. 26   **6.** $\{(1, 3, -2)\}$

7. 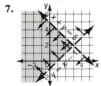   **8.**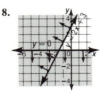

Page 173, Classroom Exercises

1. No   **2.** Yes   **3.** No   **4.** (4, 7)   **5.** $-7; (-1, 1)$

Pages 174–176, Written Exercises

1. Yes   **3.** No   **5.** 32; (8, 0)   **7.** 58; (4, 10)   **9.** 18;
(3, 4)   **11.** 16; (0, 8)   **13.** 640; (40, 20)   **15.** 60; (10, 0)
17. 1.2; (0, -4)   **19a.** $x + 2y \le 10$ **b.** $2x + y \le 14$
c. x and y must be counting numbers
d.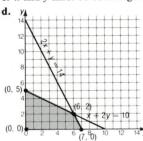

e. $R = 2x + 3y$ **f.** 60 of A and 20 of B   **21a.** 200
cord and 100 cordless   **b.** 200 cord and 100 cordless
c. 200 cord and 100 cordless, or 300 cord; yes

Page 176, Review Exercises

1. 40   **2.** 500   **4.** -3 **5.** Yes

3. 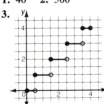   **6.**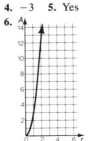

7. 47   **8.** 49   **9.** -17

Pages 178–180, Chapter Review

1. None   **3.** Infinite number   **5.** {(1, 5)}   **7.** Wind:
25 mph; plane: 175 mph   **9.** {(4, -8)}   **11.** 92
13. -14 **15.** $\begin{vmatrix} 2 & -9 \\ -6 & 1 \end{vmatrix}$; yes   **17.** {3}

19.   **21.**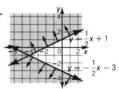

23. 28

Pages 180–181, Chapter 4 Self-Test

1a. Infinite number   **b.** None   **2.** Consistent and
independent   **3.** {(3, 0)}   **4.** $\left\{\left(\dfrac{1}{2}, -\dfrac{3}{2}\right)\right\}$ **5.** {(-1, 3)}
6. $7 - 3y$ **7.** {(5, 16)}   **8.** {(2, 1)}   **9.** The graph will
go through the point of intersection of the given lines.

10. -17 **11.** $\left\{\dfrac{4}{11}\right\}$ **12.** $\left\{\left(\dfrac{5}{2}, -4\right)\right\}$ **13.** 83

14. $\begin{vmatrix} 1 & -4 \\ 3 & 12 \end{vmatrix}$ **15.** 16

16.   **17.**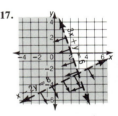

18. 47; (3, 7)   **19.** 30   **20.** 240 mph; 60 mph   **21.** $4;
$7.50

Pages 182–183, Practice for College Entrance Tests

1. C   **2.** B   **3.** D   **4.** A   **5.** A   **6.** B   **7.** C   **8.** A
9. C   **10.** C   **11.** B   **12.** B   **13.** D   **14.** D   **15.** D
16. B   **17.** A   **18.** D   **19.** C   **20.** B   **21.** B
22. A   **23.** A   **24.** B

Chapter 5

Page 188, Classroom Exercises

1. 3; 4   **2.** -12; 0   **3.** -2; 6   **4.** x^8 **5.** a^5
6. $6a^3b^5$ **7.** x^{12} **8.** $125x^6$ **9.** $8a^6b^9$ **10.** 30,400
11. $9.87 \cdot 10^4$ **12.** $3.456 \cdot 10^9$ **13.** $3.564 \cdot 10^{12}$

Pages 188–190, Written Exercises

1. Yes   **3.** No   **5.** Yes   **7.** Yes   **9.** No   **11.** No
13. -3; 2   **15.** 1; 7   **17.** 17; 1   **19.** 5; 0   **21.** 2; 7
23. -1; 3   **25.** x^6 **27.** w^8 **29.** a^8b^{12} **31.** $-63y^5$

33. $72n^5$ **35.** $72m^5$ **37.** 3^{3a} **39.** x^{m+2} **41.** x^{2m}
43. 2^{a+4} **45.** $x^{3a}y^3$ **47.** $-42a^{2x}$ **49.** $63{,}200$
51. $50{,}000{,}000{,}000$ **53.** $2 \cdot 10^2$ **55.** $1.9 \cdot 10^5$
57. $5.13 \cdot 10^{13}$ **59.** $9.6 \cdot 10^{13}$ **61.** $3.3 \cdot 10^{21}$
63. $1.68 \cdot 10^{13}$ **65.** Negative **67.** Negative
69. Negative **71.** Positive **73.** The product of an even number of negative factors is positive, of an odd number is negative. **75.** $12ab^2$ cm^3 **77.** $-x^{14}$ **79.** $-48m^4n^5$
81. $-15r^{10}s^4t^2$ **83.** $2.16 \cdot 10^{14}$ **85a.** $1.1666 \cdot 10^{25}$ lb
85b. $5.2497 \cdot 10^{27}$ g **87a.** $1.3104 \cdot 10^{21}$ m^3
87b. $1.04832 \cdot 10^{31}$

Page 190, Review Exercises

1.

2. $(x{:}x > -1)$ **3.** Comm. addition **4.** Assoc. mult.
5. $Q = 2n + 8$

Page 192, Classroom Exercises

1. Yes **2.** No **3.** Yes **4.** No **5.** $2; -5$ **6.** $3; 7$
7. $2a^2 - 8a + 4$ **8.** $7xy^2$ **9.** $-8y^2 + y + 6$
10. $-4b + 10c$ **11.** $2x^2 - 12x + 18$
12. $6x^3 - 4x^2y + 2x^2$ **13.** $6a^4b^2 - 6a^3b^3$

Pages 192–194, Written Exercises

1. Yes; binomial **3.** No **5.** No **7.** Yes; monomial
9. Yes; trinomial **11.** No **13.** Yes; other **15.** 2
17. 0 **19.** 3 **21.** 6 **23.** $a^3 + ab + 5b$
25. $-x^3 + x^2 - 5x + 5$ **27.** $4a^2 + a$
29. $a^3 + a^2 + 2$ **31.** $3x^2 + 4x - 2$ **33.** $-11x + 2$
35. $x^3 + xy^2 + 4y^3$ **37.** $-a^2 + 5ab - 2b^2$
39. $4x^2 + x^2y + 7xy + 4xy^2$ **41.** $-a^2b - 6ab^2$
43. $ab - a + b + 4$ **45.** $2x^5 - 6x^3$ **47.** $3x^3 - 6x^2 + 3x$
49. $-x^4 + 2x^2$ **51.** $3a^4 - 4a^2$ **53.** $6a^2 - 2ab$
55. $2x^3 + 3x^2y$ **57.** $14x^2 - 2xy$ **59.** $14x^3 + 4x^2y$
61. $-ab^3 + a^2b^2 - 10ab$ **63.** True **65.** True
67. True **69.** True **71.** $y^{j+2} - 3y^{j+k}$ **73.** $r^j + r^{2+j}$
75. 10 **77.** 4 **79.** $10x^2 + 12xy$

Page 195, Review Exercises

1. $-\dfrac{1}{32}$ **2.** $5(n + 1)$ **3.** $10 \cdot 2^n$ **4.** 2 **5.** Mult. identity
6. Assoc. (add.); Comm. (add.); Assoc. (add.); Distributive; Computation

Page 195, Extension

1a. Defective **b.** Perfect **c.** Defective **d.** Perfect
e. Abundant **f.** Defective **g.** Abundant **2a.** 6; 28; 496 **b.** 8128

Page 198, Classroom Exercises

1. $6a^2 + 2a - 20$ **2.** $6m^2 - 13mn + 6n^2$
3. $x^3 - x^2 - 5x + 2$

4. $x^6 + 6x^5y + 15x^4y^2 + 20x^3y^3 + 15x^2y^4 + 6xy^5 + y^6$
5. $8a^3 + 48a^2 + 96a + 64$
6. $16x^4 - 32x^3y + 24x^2y^2 - 8xy^3 + y^4$

Pages 198–199, Written Exercises

1. $8x^2 - 2x - 15$ **3.** $3x^2 - 26xy + 16y^2$
5. $8ac - 10ad - 12bc + 15bd$
7. $a^3 + 5a^2 + 10a + 12$ **9.** $x^2y^3 + x^2y^2 + xy^2 + xy$
11. $x^2 - x - y^2 + 5y - 6$ **13.** $9a^2 - b^2$ **15.** $x^3 - 8$
17. $a^4 + 4a^3b + 6a^2b^2 + 4ab^3 + b^4$
19. $a^6 + 6a^5b + 15a^4b^2 + 20a^3b^3 + 15a^2b^4 + 6ab^5 + b^6$
21. $x^4 + 12x^3 + 54x^2 + 108x + 81$
23. $t^3 - 15t^2 + 75t - 125$
25. $81 - 108s + 54s^2 - 12s^3 + s^4$ **27.** $2x^2 + x - 1$
29. $3x^2 - 5x + 2$ **31.** $3x^2 - 11x + 10$
33. $x^3 - 6x^2 + 12x - 8$ **35.** $27x^3 + 54x^2 + 36x + 8$
37. The last number is the sum of the previous numbers; 35
39. The last term is the sum of the other terms; 21.
41. $y^8 - 16y^7x + 112y^6x^2 - 448y^5x^3 + 1120y^4x^4 - 1792y^3x^5 + 1792y^2x^6 - 1024yx^7 + 256x^8$
43. $x^7 + 21x^6b + 189x^5b^2 + 945x^4b^3 + 2835x^3b^4 + 5103x^2b^5 + 5103xb^6 + 2187b^7$ **45.** $243a^5 - 810a^4b + 1080a^3b^2 - 720a^2b^3 + 240ab^4 - 32b^5$ **47.** $531{,}441$
49. $1024a^5 + 2560a^4b + 2560a^3b^2 + 1280a^2b^3 + 320ab^4 + 32b^5$ **51.** $19{,}487{,}171$ **53a.** r **53b.** 2 **53c.** 2

Page 200, Review Exercises

1. $\{5\}$ **2.** $\left\{-\dfrac{3}{2}\right\}$ **3.** $\{4\}$ **4.** $h = \dfrac{2V}{\pi r^2}$
5. $h = \dfrac{s}{2\pi r} - r$ **6.** $y = \dfrac{c - ax}{b}$
7. $10x = \dfrac{1}{2}(x - 10) + 100$; 10
8. $\{x{:}x > -3\}$
9. $\{x{:}x < 2\}$
10. $\{x{:} 2 \le x \le 4\}$
11. $\{x{:}x > 3 \text{ or } x < 2\}$
12. $\{x{:} -2 \le x \le 4\}$
13. $|x| \le 2$

Page 200, Self-Quiz 1

1. No **2.** Yes **3.** No **4.** Yes **5.** 2 **6.** 5 **7.** 4
8. $-6xy^2$ **9.** $6 \cdot 10^7$ **10.** $20a^3b^4$ **11.** 4 **12.** 3
13. $-5x + 13$ **14.** $14x^3 - 14x$ **15.** $6a^2b - 10ab^3$
16. $7x^2 - 9xy - 10y^2$ **17.** $28a^3 - 43a^2 + 17a^2 - 2$
18. $27x^3 - 27x^2y + 9xy^2 - y^3$

Page 202, Classroom Exercises

1. 7 **2.** 13 **3.** $5xy$ **4.** $3a^2b$ **5.** $5xy(x^2 + 2y)$
6. $b(3a^4 - 5c^3)$ **7.** $5u(3tu - 4)$ **8.** $3x^3yz(2x + 5y)$

Pages 202–204, Written Exercises

1. $\{1, 2, 4, 17, 34, 68\}$ **3.** $\{1, 5, 7, 25, 35, 175\}$
5. $\{-21, -7, -3, -1, 1, 3, 7, 21\}$ **7.** $\{-28, -14, -7,$
$-4, -2, -1, 1, 2, 4, 7, 14, 28\}$ **9.** $2 \cdot 3 \cdot 7$
11. $2 \cdot 3^2 \cdot 5$ **13.** $9x$ **15.** $2xz$ **17.** $2a$ **19.** $5(x + 2y)$
21. $x(7x - 3)$ **23.** $5x(x + 1)$ **25.** $6xy(3y - 2x)$
27. $6b(-5ac + 4c - 3a^2)$ **29.** $3tu(5u + 7t - 1)$
31. $ab^2(7ab 5 + 3a)$ **33.** $4a^2b^2c^3 (2bc - 3a)$
35. $\dfrac{3x(x - 2)}{4y(2x + 3)}$ **37.** $\dfrac{7a^2b(2b - 3)}{3c(2b - 3)}$ **39.** $4r^2 - \pi r^2$;

$r^2(4 - \pi)$ **41.** $\dfrac{1}{2}\pi r^2 - r^2; r^2\left(\dfrac{1}{2}\pi - 1\right)$ **43.** F; 10 has 4,

20 has 6 **45.** T **47.** T **49.** F; 2 has 2, 6 has 4 **51.** T

53. GCF $= ab$ **55.** GCF $= 3xy$ **57.** $r^2\left(2 - \dfrac{1}{2}\pi\right)$

59. $4r^2$

Page 204, Review Exercises

1. Domain: Reals;
Range: $\{y : y \geq 0\}$

2. Function; no 1-1
3. 1-1 function
4. Yes
5. No
6. $y = \dfrac{1}{3}x + 3$
7. 3

Page 206, Classroom Exercises

1. $(x + 3y)(x - 3y)$ **2.** $\left(\dfrac{2a}{3} - b\right)\left(\dfrac{2a}{3} + b\right)$
3. $(c + 2d)(c^2 - 2cd + 4d^2)$
4. $(3a - b)(9a^2 + 3ab + b^2)$ **5.** $3a(x - y^2)(x + y^2)$
6. $2m(2m + 3n)(2m - 3n)$ **7.** $(2a + 1)(3b - 4)$
8. $4xy(x - 2)(y - 4)$

Pages 206–207, Written Exercises

1. $(3p + q)(3p - q)$ **3.** $(4r + 5s)(4r - 5s)$
5. $\left(\dfrac{2}{5}x + \dfrac{3}{4}y\right)\left(\dfrac{2}{5}x - \dfrac{3}{4}y\right)$ **7.** $(a^3 + b)(a^3 - b)$
9. $3p(p + 2q)(p - 2q)$ **11.** $11a^2(3 + b)(3 - b)$
13. $(3 - p)(9 + 3p + p^2)$ **15.** $(2r - 1)(4r^2 + 2r + 1)$
17. Simplest form **19.** $5(x - 1)(x^2 + x + 1)$
21. $3(a - 3b)(a^2 + 3ab + 9b^2)$
23. $(x + 4)(x^2 - 4x + 16)$ **25.** Simplest form
27. $(3a + 2)(9a^2 - 6a + 4)$
29. $a(5b + 1)(25b^2 - 5b + 1)$
31. $2a(x + 2)(x^2 - 2x + 4)$ **33.** $(b + 2)(a + 3)$
35. $(b + 5)(a - 4)$ **37.** $(x + y)(x + 5)$

39. $(y + 3)(x + 4y)$ **41.** $c(b - 6)(a + 3)$
43. $b(a + c)(a + 3b)$ **45.** $(2p + 1)(p - 2q)$
47. $3(x + 2)(x - y)$ **49.** $(a^2 + 4)(a - 2)(a + 2)$
51. $(b + 3)(b - 5)(b + 5)$ **53.** $R(R + 2)(R^2 - 2R + 4)$
55. $(x + 2)(x^2 - 2x + 4)(x - 2)(x^2 + 2x + 4)$
57. $a(a + 3)(a + 4)(a - 4)$ **59.** $a - b$ **61.** $a + b$
63. $(a - b)(a + b)$

Page 207, Review Exercises

1. r^2 **2.** 300 **3.** -10 **5.** 100 **6.** a
4.

Page 210, Classroom Exercises

1. $(x + 3)(x - 1)$ **2.** $(y + 3)(y + 4)$
3. $(x - 5)(x - 2)$ **4.** $(5 - x)(3 + x)$
5. $(2a - 1)(a + 4)$ **6.** $(3b - 5)(2b - 1)$
7. $(2a + 3)^2$ **8.** $3a(a + 2)^2$

Pages 210–211, Written Exercises

1. $(x + 5)(x + 2)$ **3.** $(x - 6)(x + 3)$
5. $(w + 8)(w - 3)$ **7.** $(x - 6)(x - 8)$
9. $(t + 24)(t - 24)$ **11.** Simplest form
13. $(3 - x)(7 - x)$ **15.** $(1 + z)(2 - z)$
17. $(2x + 1)(x + 3)$ **19.** $(5x - 2)(x + 3)$ **21.** Simplest
form **23.** $(2y + 1)(2y + 3)$ **25.** $(4x + 1)(x - 3)$
27. $(5 - x)(5 + x)$ **29.** Simplest form
31. $(2x + 1)(2x + 9)$ **33.** $y(y + 6)(y - 2)$
35. $(3x + 2)(2x - 5)$ **37.** $x(6x - y)(x + 10y)$
39. $2xz(5x - 2)^2$ **41.** $3xy^2(3x - 5)^2$
43. $(8x - 9y)(6x - y)$ **45.** $(2x^3 - 3)(x^3 + 2)$
47. $(3x^n - 4)(x^n + 6)$ **49.** $(4x^{3n} + 3)(2x^{3n} - 3)$
51. $(x + 1)(x - 1)^2(x^2 + x + 1)$
53. $(x^n + y^m)(x^n - y^m)$
$(x^{2n} + x^ny^m + y^{2m})(x^{2n} - x^ny^n + y^{2m})$

Page 211, Review Exercises

1. $\{(4, 6)\}$

2. $\{(2, 6)\}$ **3.** $\{(3, 2)\}$
4. $\{(4, -1)\}$

Page 211, Self-Quiz 2

1. 24 **2.** $7xy$ **3.** $3x(9 - x)$ **4.** $2ab(ab^2 - 4a^2 + 6b)$
5. $(3x - 2y)(3x + 2y)$ **6.** $(a - 3)(a + 2b)$

7. $(4x - 1)(16x^2 + 4x + 1)$ **8.** $3(r^2 + s^2)(r + s)(r - s)$
9. $(x - 14)(x + 2)$ **10.** $(4 + x)(3 - x)$
11. $(5y - 2)(y + 3)$ **12.** $7y(x + 3)^2$
13. $x(x - 8)(x + 2)$ **14.** $(x + 2y)(x - y)$

Page 213, Classroom Exercises
1. $x^2 + 5x + 4 = 0$ **2.** No   **3.** $\{-2, 3\}$ **4.** $\{-3, -2\}$
5. $\left\{-\dfrac{2}{3}, \dfrac{3}{2}\right\}$ **6.** $\left\{-1, \dfrac{3}{4}\right\}$ **7.** $\{-1, 3\}$ **8.** $\left\{-\dfrac{1}{2}, 4\right\}$

Pages 214–215, Written Exercises
1. $x^2 + 2x - 3 = 0$ **3.** $x^2 + 5x + 6 = 0$
5. $x^2 + 6x + 8 = 0$ **7.** Yes   **9.** No   **11.** Yes
13. $\left\{-2, \dfrac{5}{2}\right\}$ **15.** $\left\{-\dfrac{7}{4}, -\dfrac{2}{3}\right\}$ **17.** $\{-2, 8\}$ **19.** $\{2, 8\}$
21. $\{-6, -2\}$ **23.** $\{-9, 2\}$ **25.** $\left\{-\dfrac{7}{6}, 0\right\}$
27. $\{-3, -2\}$ **29.** $\{-1, 5\}$ **31.** $x(x + 7) = 60$;
$\{-12, 5\}$; 5 ft   **33.** $x(x + 13) = -36$; $\{-9, -4\}$; $-9, 4$;
$-4, 9$ **35.** $x^2 + (x + 7)^2 = (x + 8)^2$; 5, 12, 13
37. $\left\{-\dfrac{1}{6}, \dfrac{3}{2}\right\}$ **39.** $\{6, 10\}$ **41.** $\left\{\dfrac{2}{3}, \dfrac{4}{3}\right\}$ **43.** $\{-9, 2\}$
45. $\left\{-\dfrac{7}{3}, \dfrac{5}{4}\right\}$ **47.** 13   **49.** 20 rods by 10 rods
51. 5 ft   **53.** $\{-1, 1, 4\}$ **55.** The domain of a variable
may include zero, and you cannot divide by zero.

Pages 215–216, Review Exercises
1. -52 **2.** $\{(3, 2, 7)\}$ **3.** $(8, 0)$ **4.** $(0, 8)$

Page 216, Extension
1. $\{x: -2 < x < 3\}$

2. $\{y: y < 2 \text{ or } y > 5\}$

3. $\{x: -8 \leqslant x \leqslant -2\}$

4. $\{r: r \leqslant -5 \text{ or } r \geqslant 3\}$

5. $\{x: x < 0 \text{ or } x > 5\}$

6. $\{x: x = 3\}$

7. Length < 4 units

Pages 218–219, Chapter Review
1a. No   **b.** Yes   **c.** No   **d.** No   **e.** Yes   **3a.** $45x^4$
b. $1.23 \cdot 10^{34}$ **5.** 6   **7a.** $3a^2 + 2ab - 8b^2$

b. $x^4 + 8x^3y + 24x^2y^2 + 32xy^3 + 16y^4$ **9.** $2rs^2$
11. $(3p + q)(3p - q)$ **13.** $2(m^2 + 2n^2)(m^2 - 2n^2)$
15. $(x + 1)(5x - 4)$ **17.** $x(9y + z)(2y + z)$
19. $\left\{-3, \dfrac{1}{2}\right\}$

Pages 219–220, Chapter 5 Self-Test
1. Monomial; 6   **2.** No   **3.** $135x^5y^3$ **4.** $2.12 \cdot 10^{21}$
5. 4   **6.** $-3xy^2 + 11x^2y$ **7.** $-19a^2b - 15ab^2$
8. $2x^3 - 12x^2y + 18xy^2$ **9.** $r^4 - 8r^3s + 24r^2s^2 -$
$32rs^3 + 16s^4$ **10.** $54a^2 - 36ab + 6b^2$
11. $7xy(1 - 6y)$ **12.** $5a^2b(4 - 3ab)$
13. $(3x + t)(3x - t)$ **14.** $(2a - 1)(b^2 + 3)$
15. $2(y - 2)(y^2 + 2y + 4)$ **16.** $(2x - 3y)(x - y)$
17. $\{-3, 12\}$ **18.** $\{-7, 1\}$ **19.** $\{12, 13\}$ **20.** 15 in.;
20 in.; 25 in.

Pages 220–221, Practice for College Entrance Tests
1. C   **2.** E   **3.** B   **4.** A   **5.** C   **6.** E   **7.** C   **8.** B
9. E   **10.** B   **11.** A   **12.** D   **13** C   **14.** A   **15.** E
16. A   **17.** D   **18.** E

Chapter 6

Page 225, Classroom Exercises
1. $\dfrac{1}{8}$ **2.** $\dfrac{1}{100,000}$ **3.** $\dfrac{1}{256}$ **4.** 9   **5.** $\dfrac{1}{36}$ **6.** 27
7. 16   **8.** $\dfrac{1}{81}$ **9.** $\dfrac{1}{1000}$ **10.** 64   **11.** $\dfrac{1}{x^3}$ **12.** $\dfrac{x}{y^2}$
13. a^4 **14.** $\dfrac{b^3}{a}$ **15.** x^{-2} **16.** $3^{-1}y^{-4}$ **17.** a^3b^{-12}
18. xy^{-2} **19.** $6.7 \cdot 10^{-5}$ **20.** $3.14 \cdot 10^{-7}$
21. $1.2 \cdot 10^{-10}$ **22.** $6 \cdot 10^{-7}$

Pages 225–227, Written Exercises
1. $\dfrac{1}{16}$ **3.** 1   **5.** $\dfrac{27}{8}$ **7.** 64   **9.** -8 **11.** $\dfrac{1}{6}$ **13.** $\dfrac{9}{8}$
15. 25   **17.** $\dfrac{1}{64}$ **19.** $\dfrac{1}{27}$ **21.** $\dfrac{1}{10,000}$
23. $1,000,000,000,000$ **25.** $\dfrac{1}{a^7}$ **27.** $\dfrac{a^2}{b^3}$ **29.** $\dfrac{xz^2}{y}$
31. xy^2 **33.** x^3y^{-3} **35.** $4x^{-2}y^{-3}$ **37.** a^6b^2
39. $4b^{-1}$ **41.** $6.2 \cdot 10^{-4}$ **43.** $2 \cdot 10^{-13}$
45. $1.7 \cdot 10^{-4}$ **47.** $4 \cdot 10^{-4}$ **49.** $1.45 \cdot 10^{-13}$
51. $2.2 \cdot 10^{-7}$ **53.** 5.0×10^1 kg
55. $7 \cdot 10^{-7}$ kg/cm^3 **57.** $x > 4$ **59.** $x = 0$
61. $x > -3$ **63.** $x > -1$ **65.** $x \leqslant -3$
67. $-3 \leqslant x \leqslant 3$

Page 227, Review Exercises
1. $4x^2 + 17x + 10$ **2.** Comm. (mult.)   **3.** Mult.
inverse   **4.** $2x^2 + 13x + 15$ **5.** $Q = 2n - 1$

6. $R = 3 - 2m$ **7.** $\dfrac{6}{32}$ **8.** $3n - 2$ **9.** $n(n + 1)$

10. Let m and n be whole numbers. Then $2m$ and $2n$ are both even numbers. $(2m)(2n) = 2(mn)$ By the closure property of multiplication, mn is a whole number, p. $2p$ is an even number.

Page 230, Classroom Exercises

1. $\dfrac{3a}{2b}$; $a \neq 0$, $b \neq 0$ **2.** $\dfrac{1}{3}y - \dfrac{2}{3}x$; $x \neq 0$, $y \neq 0$

3. $x - 3$; $x \neq -2$ **4.** $x + 3$; $x \neq 3$ **5.** $-\dfrac{1}{2 + y}$; $y \neq 3$,

$y \neq -2$ **6.** $-x - 4$; $x \neq 5$

Pages 230–231, Written Exercises

1a. $2xy$ **b.** $x \neq 0$, $y \neq 0$ **c.** $\dfrac{3x^2}{2y^4}$ **3a.** b **b.** $b \neq 0$

c. $\dfrac{a + b}{3}$ **5a.** ab **b.** $a \neq 0$, $b \neq 0$ **c.** $\dfrac{ab + b}{a}$

7a. $a + 3$ **b.** $a \neq -3$, $a \neq -2$ **c.** $\dfrac{a - 2}{a + 2}$ **9.** $\dfrac{x + 3y}{2x}$

11. -1 **13.** 2 **15.** 1 **17.** $\dfrac{x - 4}{x - 8}$ **19.** $x - 4$

21. $\dfrac{1}{x + 2}$ **23.** $\dfrac{w}{w + 1}$ **25.** $\dfrac{-1}{1 + 2x}$ **27.** -1

29. $-2x - 3$ **31.** $x - 7$ **33.** Equivalent   **35a.** $x = 3$
35b. $x = -8$, $x = -2$ **37a.** $x = 6$ **37b.** $x = -4$,
$x = 8$ **39a.** $x = -4$ **39b.** $x = -2$, $x = 1$
41a. $b = 2$ **41b.** $b = 3$, $b = -2$ **43a.** $d = 3$;
$d = 2$ **43b.** $d = -3$, $d = -2$ **45a.** $a = 0$

45b. $a = 4$, $a = 3$ **47a.** $x = -\dfrac{1}{3}$ **47b.** $x = 1$, $x = -1$

49a. None   **49b.** $x = y$ or $x = -y$ **51.** $\dfrac{b - a}{b + a}$ **53.** $\dfrac{5}{13}$

55. $\dfrac{1}{x}$ **57.** $\dfrac{y - x}{y + x}$ **59.** $\dfrac{ab}{b - a}$ **61.** -1

63. They are alike except at $x = 0$, where y is undefined for the first equation and $y = 0$ for the second equation.
65. They are alike except at $x = 2$ where y is undefined for the first equation and $y = -1$ for the second equation.

Page 232, Review Exercises

1. $a = \dfrac{v - v_0}{t}$ **2.** $b_2 = \dfrac{2A}{h} - b_1$ **3.** 4   **4** 16 and 4

5. $\{x : x > -5\}$

6. $\{x : -2 \leq x \leq 4\}$

7. $\{x : -1 < x < 3\}$

8. $\{x : x < -1 \text{ or } x > 3\}$

9. $|x + 2| \leq 1$

Page 234, Classroom Exercises

1. $\dfrac{2x^2}{3}$; $y \neq 0$ **2.** $\dfrac{2x^2}{3}$; $x \neq 0$, $y \neq 0$ **3.** $2(x + y)$;

$x \neq y$, $x \neq -y$ **4.** $2(x + y)$; $x \neq y$, $x \neq -y$

Pages 234–235, Written Exercises

1. $\dfrac{wy}{xz}$; $x \neq 0$, $z \neq 0$ **3.** $\dfrac{wz}{xy}$; $x \neq 0$, $z \neq 0$, $y \neq 0$

5. $\dfrac{4xy^3}{27}$; $y \neq 0$, $x \neq 0$ **7.** $\dfrac{4}{27x^2}$; $x \neq 0$, $y \neq 0$

9. $\dfrac{x}{x + 2}$; $x \neq 2$, $x \neq -2$ **11.** $\dfrac{3(x + 2)}{2(x - 2)}$; $x \neq 0$, $x \neq 2$

13. $\dfrac{10(x + 2y)}{3x + 14y}$; $x \neq 2y$, $x \neq -\dfrac{14}{3}y$ **15.** $\dfrac{a^2}{b^2}$; $a \neq -b$,

$a \neq 0$, $b \neq 0$ **17.** $(a + b)^2$; $a \neq 0$, $b \neq 0$

19a. a **19b.** $\dfrac{b}{b + 2}$ **19c.** $\dfrac{c}{c + 3}$ **21a.** $\dfrac{x + 1}{x + 2}$

21b. $\dfrac{x - 1}{x + 2}$ **21c.** $\dfrac{x + 2}{x + 4}$ **21d.** $\dfrac{x + 1}{x - 2}$

23. $\dfrac{x^2 - 9}{x^2 - 16}$; $x \neq -4$, $x \neq -2$, $x \neq 3$, $x \neq 4$

25. $\dfrac{x^2 + 3x + 2}{x^2 - 4x + 3}$; $x \neq -5$, $x \neq -1$, $x \neq 1$, $x \neq 3$, $x \neq 4$

27. $\dfrac{ad}{c^2}$; $b \neq 0$, $c \neq 0$, $d \neq 0$ **29.** $\dfrac{ad}{b^2}$; $b \neq 0$, $c \neq 0$,

$d \neq 0$ **31.** Never

Page 236, Review Exercises

1a. I   **b.** IV   **c.** III   **d.** II
2. Reals; $\{y : y \geq 1\}$

3. Function; not 1-1
4. Not a function   **5.** Yes

6. Slope: $\dfrac{2}{3}$; y-intercept: -8

7. -2 **8.** $y = 2x + 5$
9. 900

Page 236, Self-Quiz 1

1. $\dfrac{4}{3}$ **2.** $\dfrac{y^2}{x^3}$ **3.** $\dfrac{b^4}{a^5 c^2}$ **4.** $x^{-1}y^3$ **5.** $2n^2$ **6.** $6 \cdot 10^7$

7. $\dfrac{x + 4y}{2xy}$ **8.** $-(a + b)$ **9.** $\dfrac{x - 2y}{x + y}$ **10.** $\dfrac{2x}{3}$

11. $\dfrac{3m^2 n^2}{4}$ **12.** $2(x - 2)$

Page 238, Classroom Exercises

1. $12x^2 y^2$ **2.** $2x(x + 2)$ **3.** $x^3(x + 1)^2$

4. $\dfrac{5}{6x}$; $x \neq 0$ **5.** $\dfrac{5a^3 + 3b}{a^2b^2}$; $a \neq 0, b \neq 0$

6. $\dfrac{a + 1}{a}$; $a \neq 0, a \neq 1$

Pages 239–240, Written Exercises

1. $12ab^2$ **3.** $x(x + 2)$ **5.** $(x + 4)(x - 3)$

7. $\dfrac{5b + 3a}{ab}$; $a \neq 0, b \neq 0$ **9.** $\dfrac{b^2 - a^2}{ab}$; $a \neq 0, b \neq 0$

11. $\dfrac{5a + 3b}{a^2b^2}$; $a \neq 0, b \neq 0$ **13.** $\dfrac{5x + 21}{x(x + 3)}$; $x \neq 0$,

$x \neq -3$ **15.** $\dfrac{11x - 10}{(x + 2)(x - 2)}$; $x \neq -2, x \neq 2$

17. $\dfrac{x}{(x + 2)(x + 3)}$; $x = -2, x - 3$

19. $\dfrac{2x^2 - 7x + 4}{(x - 4)(x - 3)}$; $x \neq 4, x \neq 3$

21. $\dfrac{4 - ab}{ab}$; $a \neq 0, b \neq 0$ **23.** $\dfrac{9}{9 - x}$; $x \neq 9$

25. $\dfrac{1}{n}$; $n \neq 0, n \neq -1$ **27.** $\dfrac{1}{n}$; $n \neq 0, n \neq 1$

29. $\dfrac{(a + b)^2}{ab}$; $a \neq 0, b \neq 0$ **31.** $\dfrac{2a^2 + 6a + 3}{(1 + a)(1 + 2a)}$;

$a \neq 1, a \neq -\dfrac{1}{2}$ **33.** $\dfrac{a^2}{a^2 + 4}$; $a \neq -4$

35. $\dfrac{-w}{(2w + 1)(w - 1)}$; $w \neq \dfrac{-1}{2}, w \neq 1$ **37.** 3 **39.** $\dfrac{7}{24}$

41. $\dfrac{a^2 + 1}{2a}$ **43.** $\dfrac{8}{3}$ **45.** $\dfrac{1}{3}$ **47.** $\dfrac{3abc}{ab + ac + bc}$

49. $H = \dfrac{2}{\dfrac{1}{m} + \dfrac{1}{n}}$ $A = \dfrac{m + n}{2}$ If $\dfrac{2}{\dfrac{1}{m} + \dfrac{1}{n}} > \dfrac{m + n}{2}$,

then $\dfrac{2}{\dfrac{m + n}{mn}} > \dfrac{m + n}{2}$.

$\dfrac{2mn}{m + n} > \dfrac{m + n}{2}$

$\dfrac{4mn}{2(m + n)} > \dfrac{(m + n)(m + n)}{2(m + n)}$

$4mn > (m + n)(m + n)$

$4mn > m^2 + 2mn + n^2$

$0 > m^2 - 2mn + n^2$

$0 > (m - n)^2$

Since $(m - n)^2$ must be positive, this inequality cannot be true and $H \leq A$ for $m > 0, n > 0$.

Page 240, Review Exercises

1. -12

2.

3. -375

4. 525

5. One

6. $\{(6, 2)\}$

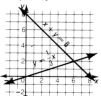

7. $\{(-1, 3)\}$

8. $\{(3, 0)\}$

Page 242, Classroom Exercises

1. $\{12\}$ **2.** $\{1\}$ **3.** $\left\{\dfrac{5}{3}\right\}$ **4.** $\emptyset$ **5.** $\left\{-\dfrac{5}{3}, 1\right\}$ **6.** $\{-1\}$

Page 243, Written Exercises

1. 20 **3.** $4n^2$ **5.** $x^2 - 9$

7. No, -1 cannot be a solution because it will make two of the denominators equal to 0. **9.** $\{8\}$ **11.** $\left\{\dfrac{4}{3}\right\}$

13. $\left\{\dfrac{2}{7}\right\}$ **15.** $\{-9\}$ **17.** $\left\{\dfrac{2}{3}\right\}$ **19.** $\{-4\}$

21. $\{-5, 1\}$ **23.** $\{-4\}$ **25.** $\{1, 5\}$ **27.** $\{4\}$ **29.** $\{0\}$

31. $\emptyset$ **33.** $\{x{:}x \neq -1, x \neq 1\}$ **35.** $\{3, -2\}$

37. $\{x{:}x \neq -1, x \neq 3\}$ **39.** $\{x{:}x = 2a\}$

Page 244, Review Exercises

1. 4

2. $D = \begin{vmatrix} 1 & 1 & -1 \\ 1 & -1 & 0 \\ 2 & 0 & 4 \end{vmatrix}$ $D_x = \begin{vmatrix} 4 & 1 & -1 \\ -3 & -1 & 0 \\ -12 & 0 & 4 \end{vmatrix}$

$D_y = \begin{vmatrix} 1 & 4 & -1 \\ 1 & -3 & 0 \\ 2 & -12 & 4 \end{vmatrix}$ $D_z = \begin{vmatrix} 1 & 1 & 4 \\ 1 & -1 & -3 \\ 2 & 0 & -12 \end{vmatrix}$

3.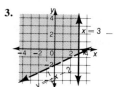

4.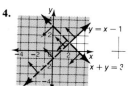

5. -5 **6.** 10

Page 247, Classroom Exercises

1. 60 **2.** $\dfrac{1}{60}$ **3.** $\dfrac{1}{t}$ **4.** $\dfrac{24}{60}; \dfrac{24}{t}$ **5.** $\dfrac{24}{60} + \dfrac{24}{t} = 1$; 40 min

Pages 248–250, Written Exercises

1. $\dfrac{100}{r}; \dfrac{60}{1.2r}; \dfrac{100}{r} + \dfrac{60}{1.2r} = 3$

3. $\dfrac{200}{r}$; $\dfrac{400}{r}$; $\dfrac{200}{r} + \dfrac{400}{r} = 4$ 5. \$2; \$4 7. 4.8 h
9. Carol: 30 words/min; Doug: 33 words/min 11. 3 ohms;
6 ohms 13. 40 km/h 15. 1800 rpm; 2.5 min
17. 4 ohms, 6 ohms, 12 ohms 19. 40, 10, 8

Page 251, Review Exercises
1. $2.6 \cdot 10^{13}$ 2. $75x^4$ 3. $3x^2 + 7x - 2$
4. $x^2 - 3x - 4$ 5. $2x^2 + x - 15$
6. $x^4 + 4x^3y + 6x^2y^2 + 4xy^3 + y^4$ 7. $3a^2bc$
8. $3x(2x^2 - 3x + 5)$

Page 251, Self-Quiz
1. 4 2. $-\dfrac{b}{2a}$ 3. $\dfrac{3y+7}{y^2-1}$ 4. $\left\{-\dfrac{12}{5}\right\}$ 5. $\{-5, 3\}$
6. $\{1\}$ 7. 170 transmissions per hour

Page 255, Classroom Exercises
1. Yes 2. No 3. $\left\{\dfrac{7}{3}\right\}$ 4. $\left\{\dfrac{7}{9}\right\}$ 5. $6\dfrac{2}{3}$ h

Pages 255–257, Written Exercises
1. Yes 3. No 5. No 7. Yes 9. 20 11. $\dfrac{1}{8}$
13. $\dfrac{3}{2}$ 15. 9 17. 0.01 19. 3 21. $\dfrac{9}{4}$ 23. $\dfrac{9}{25}$
25. $\dfrac{20}{15} = \dfrac{y}{45}$; 60 min 27. $\dfrac{10}{12} = \dfrac{y}{36}$; 30 cm 29. 4 cm
31. 0.04 cm 33. 180 mph 35. 10 cm
37. 17 kg rock is 5 cm; 5 kg rock is 17 cm 39. 10
41. 36 43. 5,771,088,000,000 miles per year
45. ± 3 47. $\dfrac{a}{4}$ 49. $\pm \dfrac{b}{4}$

Page 258, Review Exercises
1. $2(x + 3)(x - 3)$ 2. $(x + 2)(x^2 - 2x + 4)$
3. $2x(x - 3)(x^2 + 3x + 9)$ 4. $(x - 6)(x + 3)$
5. $(2x - 1)(x + 5)$ 6. $(3 - x)(1 + x)$ 7. $\{3\}$
8. $\{-7, 4\}$ 9. $\left\{-\dfrac{1}{3}, 1\right\}$ 10. $\{-7, 2\}$ 11. $\left\{1, \dfrac{5}{2}\right\}$
12. $\left\{1, \dfrac{3}{2}\right\}$ 13. $\left\{\dfrac{4}{3}, -2\right\}$ 14. $\left\{4, -\dfrac{2}{3}\right\}$
15. $\left\{\dfrac{5}{2}, -\dfrac{3}{2}\right\}$ 16. $\left\{\dfrac{7}{2}, -\dfrac{3}{2}\right\}$

Page 260, Chapter Review
1. $\dfrac{3y}{x^2}$ 3. $-4m^{-1}n$ 5. $3 \cdot 10^2$ 7. $\dfrac{y-x}{2}$; $x \neq 0$,
$y \neq 0$ 9. $\dfrac{x-1}{x+1}$; $x \neq 0$, $x \neq -1$ 11. $\dfrac{c}{2b}$; $a \neq 0$, $b \neq 0$,
$c \neq 0$ 13. $2w$; $w \neq -1$, $w \neq 0$, $w \neq -4$ 15. $\dfrac{5x(x-2y)}{2x^2y^2}$
$x \neq 0$, $y \neq 0$ 17. $\left\{\dfrac{11}{2}\right\}$ 19. $\{3, -2\}$ 21. 30 ohms;
60 ohms 23. 144

Page 261, Chapter 6 Self-Test
1. $\dfrac{1}{64}$ 2. $\dfrac{1}{16}$ 3. $7 \cdot 10^{-13}$ 4. $\dfrac{b^2}{a^4}$ 5. $\dfrac{st^3}{3r^2}$ 6. $5x^{-4}$
7. $-4b^{-1}c^{-3}$ 8. $1 + 2y$ 9. $y + 6$ 10. $\dfrac{a+6}{a}$
11. $\dfrac{35x}{y}$; $x \neq 0$, $y \neq 0$ 12. $\dfrac{ab}{a+b}$; $a \neq 0$,
$a \neq -b$ 13. $\dfrac{3}{x}$; $x \neq 0$, $x \neq -2$ 14. $\dfrac{2x+2}{x(x-1)}$;
$x \neq 0$, $x \neq 1$ 15. $\dfrac{9b + 10a}{2ab^2}$; $a \neq 0$, $b \neq 0$
16. $\dfrac{3y-2}{y+4}$; $y \neq -4$ 17. $\{-1\}$ 18. $\{2\}$
19. $\{1, -4\}$ 20. 5 km/s 21. 4 22. 1 h 30 min

Pages 262–263, Practice for College Entrance Tests
1. E 2. A 3. B 4. A 5. C 6. D 7. C 8. B
9. E 10. D 11. B 12. D

Pages 263–265, Cumulative Review
1a. Infinite number 1b. One 1c. None
3. $x = 2y + 1$ 5. $\{(1, 1)\}$ 7. 34 9. $\begin{vmatrix} 2 & -7 \\ 3 & 5 \end{vmatrix}$
11. $\left\{\left(\dfrac{3}{2}, 2, -\dfrac{1}{2}\right)\right\}$
13. 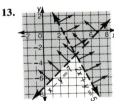 15. w^{10} 17. $27x^6$
19. $7x^2 - 10x + 11$ 21. $z^3 + 64$ 23. $2a^2b$
25. $5mn(n + 6m - 2)$ 27. $a(a + 8)(a - 8)$
29. $(2x - 3)^2$ 31. $\{6, -5\}$ 33. $\dfrac{1}{64}$ 35. $a^{-2}b^{-1}$
37. $\dfrac{x}{x-1}$; $x \neq -5$, $x \neq 1$ 39. $\dfrac{b}{3}$; $a \neq 0$, $b \neq 0$
41. $\dfrac{3}{16}$; $m \neq -\dfrac{1}{2}n$, $m \neq \dfrac{1}{2}n$ 43. $\dfrac{b+1}{b}$; $b \neq 0$, $b \neq 1$
45. $\{-7\}$ 47. $\{3\}$ 49. 4

Chapter 7

Pages 268–269, Classroom Exercises
1. T 2. F 3. F 4. T 5. F 6. T 7. T 8. T
9. T 10. 6 11. -8 12. Not real 13. 2 14. -2
15. 9.6

Pages 269–271, Written Exercises

1. Yes **3.** Yes **5.** No **7.** Yes **9.** Yes **11.** Yes
13. Rational **15.** Irrational **17.** Irrational **19.** Rational **21.** Irrational **23.** Irrational **25.** F **27.** F
29. T **31.** T **33.** 9 **35.** $-\dfrac{2}{5}$ **37.** $-\dfrac{1}{2}$ **39.** $-\dfrac{2}{3}$
41. 3 **43.** -2 **45.** -8.4 **47.** 2.7 **49.** 8.375; 64; 70.140625 **51.** 0.8 s **53.** 5.5 s **55.** 100 cm
57. 26 mi **59.** 12 **61.** $\sqrt{15}$ **63.** F; $x = -\sqrt{2}$
65. F; $\dfrac{1}{4} < \sqrt{\dfrac{1}{4}}$ **67.** T **69.** $\sqrt[6]{7}$ **71.** $\sqrt[6]{5}$ **73.** $\sqrt{6}$

Page 271, Review Exercises

1a. Rational **1b.** Irrational **1c.** Rational **1d.** Irrational **2.** 5 **3.** $7\sqrt{3}$ **4.** 3 **5.** $\dfrac{n}{2^n}$

Page 271, Calculator Extension

2.6; Yes

Page 275, Classroom Exercises

1. $5\sqrt{2}$ **2.** $4\sqrt{3}$ **3.** $2\sqrt[3]{2}$ **4.** $2\sqrt[4]{6}$ **5.** $|a|$ **6.** $-b^2$
7. $|x|y\sqrt{y}$; $y \geq 0$ **8.** $|a|b^2\sqrt{-a}$; $a \leq 0$ **9.** $a^2 b\sqrt[3]{b}$
10. $3x^2\sqrt{2x}$; $x \geq 0$ **11.** $2a^2\sqrt{6ab}$; $a \geq 0, b \geq 0$
12. $-x^2$

Pages 275–276, Written Exercises

1. $a \geq 0$ **3.** None **5.** $b \neq 0$ **7.** $b \geq 0$ **9.** $2\sqrt{5}$
11. $2\sqrt[3]{3}$ **13.** Simplest form **15.** $-3\sqrt[3]{2}$ **17.** $|a|b\sqrt{b}$
19. $b\sqrt[3]{a^2}$ **21.** Simplest form **23.** $p^5 q^6\sqrt[3]{p^2}$ **25.** $\dfrac{x^2}{y-2}$;
$y \neq 2$ **27.** $\dfrac{y^3\sqrt{y}}{2x}$; $y \geq 0, x \neq 0$ **29.** $4x\sqrt{3}$; $x \geq 0$
31. $2c^2\sqrt{2c}$; $c \geq 0$ **33.** $6a^5\sqrt{5a}$; $a \geq 0$ **35.** $5xy^3\sqrt{6y}$;
$x \geq 0, y \geq 0$ **37.** $|r|t^4\sqrt{6}$; $t \geq 0$ **39.** $|a+2|$ **41.** $x \geq 0$,
$y \leq 0$ or $x \leq 0, y \geq 0$ **43.** $t \leq 5$ **45.** $-\sqrt{5} \leq t \leq \sqrt{5}$
47. None **49.** $x = \pm 6\sqrt{2}$ **51.** $x = +3|b|\sqrt{10a}$, $a \geq 0$
53. $a\sqrt[n]{a^2}$ **55.** $b\sqrt[n]{b^{-2}}$ **57.** $x = 1 \pm 2m\sqrt{n}$; $n \geq 0$
59. $3 + 2\sqrt{2}$

Page 276, Review Exercises

1. $\{12\}$ **2.** $r = \sqrt{\dfrac{a}{\pi}}$ **3.** $\left\{x : x > -\dfrac{3}{2}\right\}$
4. $\{x : -1 \leq x \leq 4\}$ **5.** $\{x : 2 < x < 4\}$
6. $\{x : x > -1 \text{ or } x < -3\}$

Pages 276–277, Self-Quiz

1. T **2.** T **3.** T **4.** -4 **5.** $-\dfrac{1}{5}$ **6.** $4\sqrt{3}$
7. $3a\sqrt[3]{2a}$ **8.** $|x|y^2$ **9.** $a^2 b^4\sqrt[3]{4a^2}$ **10.** $\dfrac{-r\sqrt{2}}{4}$; $r \neq 0$
11. $2ab\sqrt[4]{2a}$; $a \geq 0, b \geq 0$

Page 283, Classroom Exercises

1. $\dfrac{\sqrt{3}}{3}$ **2.** $\dfrac{5\sqrt[3]{4}}{2}$ **3.** $\dfrac{\sqrt[3]{4}}{2}$ **4.** $\dfrac{\sqrt{a}}{a^3}$; $a > 0$ **5.** $3x\sqrt{x}$;
$x > 0$ **6.** $\dfrac{1-\sqrt{3}}{-2}$ **7.** $\dfrac{\sqrt{3}}{2}$ **8.** $\dfrac{\sqrt{a}}{a}$; $a > 0$ **9.** $\dfrac{\sqrt[3]{98}}{7}$
10. $\dfrac{\sqrt[3]{y^2}}{y}$; $y \neq 0$

Page 277, Calculator Extension

1. -1.06 **2.** 5.43 **3.** 2.27 **4.** 15.6 **5.** -0.40
6. Yes **7.** No **8.** Yes **9.** Yes

Page 279, Classroom Exercises

1. $-\sqrt{7}$ **2.** $1 + 4\sqrt{5}$ **3.** $16 - 24\sqrt{3}$ **4.** 7
5. $2 - 2\sqrt{3} + \sqrt{5} - \sqrt{15}$

Pages 279–280, Written Exercises

1. $3\sqrt{3}$ **3.** $3\sqrt{5} + \sqrt{10}$ **5.** $7\sqrt{3}$ **7.** $6\sqrt{5} + \sqrt{10}$
9. Simplest form **11.** $2\sqrt[3]{5} + 2\sqrt[3]{3}$
13. $6 + \sqrt{3} + \sqrt{5}$ **15.** $7 + 2\sqrt[3]{6}$ **17.** $\sqrt{6}$ **19.** 2
21. $2 + \sqrt{6}$ **23.** $2\sqrt{15} + 3\sqrt{14}$
25. $5 + 2\sqrt{3} + \sqrt{10} + \sqrt{30}$
27. $2 + 5\sqrt{2} + 2\sqrt{5} + \sqrt{10}$ **29.** $8 + 5\sqrt{2}$ **31.** 6
33. $15 - 4\sqrt{14}$ **35.** $x^2 - 7$ **37.** Yes **39.** Yes
41. No **43.** $x^2 - 8x + 13$ **45.** $4 - 4\sqrt{a}$
47. $(x - 1)\sqrt[3]{xy} + 2\sqrt{xy}$ **49.** $a^2 - a\sqrt{6} - 12$
51.
$$(\sqrt{48} - 1)^2 + (4 + \sqrt{3})^2 \overset{?}{=} (\sqrt{68})^2$$
$$48 - 2\sqrt{48} + 1 + 16 + 8\sqrt{3} + 3 \overset{?}{=} 68$$
$$48 - 2\sqrt{16 \cdot 3} + 1 + 16 + 8\sqrt{3} + 3 \overset{?}{=} 68$$
$$48 - 8\sqrt{3} + 1 + 16 + 8\sqrt{3} + 3 \overset{?}{=} 68$$
$$68 = 68 \quad \text{It checks.}$$
53.
$$(1 + \sqrt{2})^3 - 5(1 + \sqrt{2})^2 + 5(1 + \sqrt{2}) + 3 \overset{?}{=} 0$$
$$(3 + 2\sqrt{2})(1 + \sqrt{2}) - 5(3 + 2\sqrt{2}) + 5(1 + \sqrt{2}) + 3 \overset{?}{=} 0$$
$$7 + 5\sqrt{2} - 15 - 10\sqrt{2} + 5 + 5\sqrt{2} + 3 \overset{?}{=} 0$$
$$\text{It checks.} \quad 0 = 0$$
55. $\sqrt[3]{\sqrt{b}} \cdot \sqrt{\sqrt[3]{b}} = \sqrt{\sqrt[3]{b}} \cdot \sqrt{\sqrt[3]{b}}$ (See Ex. 54) $=$
$(\sqrt{\sqrt[3]{b}})^2 = \sqrt[3]{b}$, $b \geq 0$

Page 280, Review Exercises

1a. Yes **b.** No **c.** Yes **2.** $-\dfrac{3}{2}$; 6 **3.** a
4. $y = -\dfrac{2}{3}x$ **5.** $y = -2x + 5$ **6.** 27 **7.** 36
8. 49 **9.** 47

Pages 283–285, Written Exercises

1. $\sqrt{2}$ **3.** $\dfrac{\sqrt{3}}{3}$ **5.** $\dfrac{\sqrt{30}}{6}$ **7.** $\dfrac{\sqrt{5}}{3}$ **9.** $\dfrac{4\sqrt{3}}{3}$
11. $\dfrac{\sqrt{15}}{6}$ **13.** $\dfrac{\sqrt[3]{6}}{2}$ **15.** $\dfrac{\sqrt[3]{15}}{4}$ **17.** $\dfrac{\sqrt[3]{3}}{3}$ **19.** $\dfrac{5\sqrt[3]{2}}{2}$

21. $\sqrt[3]{2}$ **23.** $\dfrac{15 + 5\sqrt{2}}{7}$ **25.** $\dfrac{\sqrt[4]{6}}{2}$ **27.** $\dfrac{\sqrt[5]{60}}{3}$

29. $\dfrac{\sqrt[4]{9}}{3}$ **31.** $\dfrac{4\sqrt{x}}{x^4}; x > 0$ **33.** $\dfrac{4x\sqrt{y}}{|x|}; x \neq 0, y > 0$

35. $\dfrac{2x\sqrt{5x}}{y^2}; y \neq 0, x > 0$ **37.** $\dfrac{\sqrt{5x}}{x}; x > 0$ **39.** $\dfrac{\sqrt{5x}}{5};$

$x \geq 0$ **41.** $\dfrac{\sqrt[3]{xy^2}}{y}; y \neq 0$ **43.** $\dfrac{\sqrt[3]{75x^2y^2}}{5y^2}; y \neq 0$

45. $\dfrac{\sqrt[4]{xy^2}}{|y|}; x \geq 0, y \neq 0$ **47.** $\dfrac{\sqrt[5]{x^4y^4}}{y^2}; y \neq 0$

49. $\dfrac{2 + \sqrt{x}}{4 - x}; x \neq 4, x \geq 0$ **51.** $\sqrt{x} + \sqrt{y}; x \neq y, x \geq 0,$

$y \geq 0$ **53.** $\dfrac{\sqrt{56 + x - x^2}}{7 + x}; -7 < x \leq 8$

55. $\{9 + 3\sqrt{7}\}$ **57.** $\{4\sqrt{7} + 8\}$

59. $\left\{\dfrac{5 + \sqrt{7}}{3}\right\}$ **61.** $\{4\sqrt{5} + 4\sqrt{3}\}$ **63.** $\left\{\dfrac{\sqrt{42} + 3\sqrt{2}}{4}\right\}$

65. To rationalize $\sqrt{x} - y$, multiply $\sqrt{x} - y$ by itself. To rationalize $\sqrt{x} - \sqrt{y}$, multiply $\sqrt{x} - \sqrt{y}$ by its conjugate, $\sqrt{x} + \sqrt{y}$.   **67.** $\sqrt[4]{2}$ **69.** $\sqrt[3]{a}; a \geq 0$

71. The order makes no difference (assuming $a \geq 0$).

Page 285, Review Exercises

1. $\{(-18, -31)\}$ **2.** $\{(2, 4)\}$ **3.** 25 dimes and 10

quarters   **4.** $D = \begin{vmatrix} 4 & 1 \\ 3 & -5 \end{vmatrix} D_x = \begin{vmatrix} 10 & 1 \\ 0 & -5 \end{vmatrix} D_y = \begin{vmatrix} 4 & 10 \\ 3 & 0 \end{vmatrix}$

5.

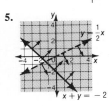

$x + y = -2$

Page 285, Self-Quiz 2

1. $4\sqrt{2}$ **2.** $1 - 7\sqrt[3]{3}$ **3.** $28 - 10\sqrt{3}$ **4.** Yes

5. $\dfrac{\sqrt[3]{6}}{3}$ **6.** $2 + \sqrt{2} + \sqrt{6} + \sqrt{3}$ **7.** $-\dfrac{3\sqrt{7}}{7}$

8. $\dfrac{a\sqrt[3]{2a^2b^2}}{2b}; b \neq 0$ **9.** $\left\{\dfrac{3 - \sqrt{2}}{7}\right\}$

Pages 288, Classroom Exercises

1. $3\sqrt{13}$ **2.** $2\sqrt{10}$ **3.** $|y_2 - y_1|$ **4.** $\left\{\dfrac{1}{2}, -\dfrac{1}{2}\right\}$ **5.** $(16, 8)$

Pages 289–290, Written Exercises

1. 6   **3.** 12   **5.** 6   **7.** 13   **9.** $2\sqrt{10}$ **11.** $\sqrt{61}$

13. $\sqrt{13}$ **15.** 25   **17.** 15   **19.** 0.5   **21.** Yes

23. No   **25.** $\left(2\dfrac{1}{2}, 2\right)$ **27.** $(0, -1)$ **29.** $(-1, 0)$

31. $y = -x + 7$ **33.** $y = -\dfrac{1}{2}x + \dfrac{3}{2}$ **35a.** $2\sqrt{10};$

$2\sqrt{13}; 2\sqrt{17}$ **37.** $\sqrt{10}; \sqrt{10}$ **39.** $\sqrt{13}; \sqrt{13}$

41. It is half.   **43.** $(6, 4)$ **45.** $\dfrac{5\sqrt{5}}{2}$

47. Pythagorean theorem: If $a^2 + b^2 = c^2$, then it is a right triangle. Or find the slopes of the lines containing the vertices: If two lines have slopes that are negative reciprocals, the lines are perpendicular and the triangle is a right triangle.

49. $D = \left(\dfrac{x_1 + x_2}{2}, \dfrac{y_1 + y_2}{2}\right)$

$E = \left(\dfrac{x_2 + x_3}{2}, \dfrac{y_2 + y_3}{2}\right)$

$\left(\dfrac{x_2 + x_3}{2} - \dfrac{x_1 + x_2}{2}\right) = \left(\dfrac{x_3 - x_1}{2}\right)$

$\left(\dfrac{y_2 + y_3}{2} - \dfrac{y_1 + y_2}{2}\right) = \left(\dfrac{y_3 - y_1}{2}\right)$

$d(DE) = \sqrt{\left(\dfrac{x_3 - x_1}{2}\right)^2 + \left(\dfrac{y_3 - y_1}{2}\right)^2}$

$= \dfrac{\sqrt{(x_3 - x_1)^2 + (y_3 - y_1)^2}}{2}$

$d(AC) = \sqrt{(x_3 - x_1)^2 + (y_3 - y_1)^2}$

$\dfrac{1}{2}d(AC) = \dfrac{\sqrt{(x_3 - x_1)^2 + (y_3 - y_1)^2}}{2}$

$d(DE) = \dfrac{1}{2}d(AC)$

Page 290, Review Exercises

1. 48   **2.** $1.26 \cdot 10^{16}$ **3.** $x^2 - 10x + 5$

4. $2a^2 + ab - 15b^2$ **5.** $2ab(a + 3 + 4b)$

6. $(a + 2)(b + 3)$ **7.** $(2x + 3)(2x - 3)$

8. $5(a + b)(a - b)$ **9.** $(x - 8)(x + 3)$

10. $(2x + 3)(x + 1)$ **11.** $\{6\}$ **12.** $\{-3, 4\}$

Page 292, Classroom Exercises

1. $\emptyset$ **2.** $\{1\}$ **3.** $\{12\}$ **4.** $\{3\}$

Pages 293–294, Written Exercises

1. $\{11\}$ **3.** $\left\{\dfrac{13}{2}\right\}$ **5.** $\{3$ **7.** $\emptyset$ **9.** $\{1, 3\}$ **11.** $\{3\}$

13. $\{34\}$ **15.** $\emptyset$ **17.** $\{1\}$ **19.** $\{4\}$ **21.** $\{-21\}$

23. $\{-2\}$ **25.** $\{1\}$ **27.** $\{9\}$ **29.** $\{5, 8\}$ **31.** $(9, 2)$ and

$(-1, 2)$ **33.** $(6, -6)$ and $(-8, 8)$ **35.** $\{4\}$ **37.** $\left\{\dfrac{1}{2}\right\}$

39a. $y = 5$

39b. The equation of the line containing $(2, 3)$ and $(2, 7)$ is $x = 2$. The midpoint of the segment is $(2, 5)$. $y = 5$ is the equation of the line perpendicular to $x = 2$ and passes through (2, 5). Therefore, $y = 2$ is the equation of the line which is the perpendicular bisector of the segment joining the two points. **41.** $\dfrac{15\sqrt{2}}{2}$ g **43.** $\dfrac{50}{3}$ g

45. 10.05 g; 10.61 g; 11.55 g; 16.67 g; 70.89 g

Page 294, Review Exercises

1. $\dfrac{3}{xy^2}$; $x \neq 0$, $y \neq 0$ **2.** $3a^{-1}b^2c^{-2}$ **3.** $\dfrac{x}{3} - 1$

4. $a + b$ **5.** $\dfrac{3bc}{2}$ **6.** $\dfrac{8a^2}{9bc}$ **7.** $\dfrac{3y + 4x}{xy}$ **8.** $\dfrac{x^2 - 2x - 1}{x^2}$

Page 294, Self-Quiz 3

1. $PA = 2\sqrt{34}$ and $PB = \sqrt{34}$. Therefore, $PA = 2\,PB$.

2. $AB = BC = AC = 4\sqrt{2}$ **3.** $\left\{\left(\dfrac{13}{2}, -2\right)\right\}$

4. $\left\{\dfrac{1 + 2\sqrt{5}}{6}\right\}$ **5.** $\{2 + \sqrt{7}\}$ **6.** $\left\{\dfrac{19}{2}\right\}$ **7.** $\{3\}$

8. $\{5\}$ **9.** $\emptyset$

Page 297, Classroom Exercises

1. $3^{\frac{1}{2}}$ **2.** $a^{\frac{1}{3}}$ **3.** $6^{\frac{2}{3}}$ **4.** $\sqrt[5]{2}$ **5.** $-2\sqrt[4]{2}$ **6.** $x\sqrt[3]{x}$

Pages 297–298, Written Exercises

1. $2^{\frac{1}{3}}$ **3.** $2^{\frac{3}{2}}$ **5.** $2^{-\frac{1}{2}}$ **7.** $2^{-\frac{13}{7}}$ **9.** $3^{\frac{1}{4}}$ **11.** $(-5)^{\frac{1}{3}}$

13. $13^{\frac{3}{5}}$ **15.** $3^{-\frac{4}{5}}$ **17.** $\sqrt{3}$ **19.** 4 **21.** $\dfrac{\sqrt[4]{7^3}}{7}$

23. $-\dfrac{\sqrt[3]{4}}{2}$ **25.** $x\sqrt[3]{x}$ **27.** $3x^2\sqrt{x}$ **29.** $2\sqrt{y}$

31. $2a\sqrt[3]{a}$ **33.** 8 **35.** 27 **37.** 9 **39.** $\dfrac{1}{2}$ **41.** $5\sqrt[4]{5}$

43. $7\sqrt[5]{49}$ **45.** $5^{\frac{7}{2}}$ **47.** $5^{\frac{2}{3}}$ **49.** 5^{-1} **51.** $5^{-\frac{1}{2}}$

53. $\sqrt[3]{x}$ **55.** $x^3\sqrt{x}$; $x \geq 0$ **57.** $25x\sqrt{x}$; $x \geq 0$

59. $\dfrac{\sqrt{2x}}{4}$; $x > 0$ **61.** $\sqrt{2 - x}$; $x \leq 2$

63. $\sqrt[4]{1 - 2x}$; $x \leq \dfrac{1}{2}$ **65.** $\sqrt{3}$ **67.** $\sqrt{x} + 6$, $x \neq 36$

Page 298, Review Exercises

1. $\left\{\dfrac{5}{2}\right\}$ **2.** $\{10\}$ **3.** 125 ohms **4.** $3\dfrac{3}{7}$ h **5.** 6 **6.** 25

Pages 300–301, Chapter Review

1a. No **b.** Yes **c.** No **3a.** 7.7 **b.** 2.7

5. $2|x|y\sqrt{y}$; $y \geq 0$ **7.** $5x\sqrt{21y}$; $x \geq 0$, $y \geq 0$

9. $10\sqrt[3]{2} - 3$ **11.** Yes **13.** $\dfrac{3ab^2\sqrt{2ab}}{|a||b|} = \dfrac{3a|b|\sqrt{2ab}}{|a|}$

15. $\dfrac{\sqrt[3]{6}}{2}$ **17.** $\{-(2 + \sqrt{3})\}$ **19.** $\sqrt{73}$ **21.** $\left(-2, 3\dfrac{1}{2}\right)$

23. $\{24\}$ **25.** $5 \cdot 6^{-\frac{1}{5}}$ **27.** $7x^{\frac{1}{2}}y^{\frac{3}{2}}$ **29.** $2\sqrt[3]{18}$

Pages 301–302, Chapter 7 Self-Test

1a. Rational **b.** Not real **c.** Irrational **2.** 3.1

3. $2\sqrt[3]{3}$ **4.** $-5\sqrt{2}$ **5.** Simplest form **6.** $a^4b^3\sqrt[3]{a^2}$

7. $6x^2\sqrt{2}$; $x \geq 0$ **8.** $\sqrt[3]{2} + 3\sqrt{2}$ **9.** $24 - 12\sqrt{6}$

10. Yes **11.** $-\dfrac{\sqrt{2}}{2}$ **12.** $3\sqrt[3]{5y^2}$; $x \neq 0$, $y \neq 0$

13. $-\dfrac{\sqrt[5]{4a^2}}{2a}$; $a \neq 0$ **14.** $x\left(\dfrac{\sqrt{3(x-1)}}{x - 1}\right)$; $x > 1$

15. $5\sqrt{5}$ **16.** $\left(-\dfrac{1}{2}, 2\right)$ **17.** $\left\{\dfrac{\sqrt{15} - \sqrt{3}}{4}\right\}$

18. $\{\pm 2\sqrt{2}\}$ **19.** $\emptyset$ **20.** $7^{-\frac{2}{3}}$ **21.** $(x + 1)\sqrt[3]{(x + 1)}$

22. $4\sqrt[4]{2}$ **23.** 9

Pages 302–303, Practice for College Entrance Tests

1. A **2.** C **3.** D **4.** B **5.** B **6.** A **7.** C **8.** B

9. D **10.** C **11.** C **12.** B **13.** C **14.** B

15. C **16.** C

Chapter 8

Page 307, Classroom Exercises

1. Yes **2.** No **3.** $\{\pm\sqrt{3}\}$ **4.** $\{2 \pm 2\sqrt{2}\}$

5. $\{-3 \pm \sqrt{14}\}$ **6.** $\left\{\dfrac{1 \pm \sqrt{19}}{3}\right\}$

7. Width: 9 m; length: 13 m

Pages 307–309, Written Exercises

1. $0x^2 + 8x + 8 = 0$; no **3.** $2x^2 + 12x + 6 = 0$; yes

5. $x^2 + 0x - 5 = 0$; yes **7.** $3r^2 + 10r + 8 = 0$; yes

9. $(x + 3)^2 = 0$ **11.** $(x + 4)^2 = 21$ **13.** $(x - 2)^2 = 2$

15. $(x - 2)^2 = 0$ **17.** $\left\{\dfrac{-1 \pm \sqrt{29}}{2}\right\}$ **19.** $\{\pm\sqrt{7}\}$

21. $\{2 \pm \sqrt{5}\}$ **23.** $\emptyset$ **25.** $\{-5 \pm \sqrt{10}$ **27.** $\emptyset$

29. $\{-3 \pm 2\sqrt{5}\}$ **31.** $\left\{\dfrac{9 \pm \sqrt{53}}{2}\right\}$ **33.** $\left\{\dfrac{-7 \pm \sqrt{33}}{2}\right\}$

35. $x(x + 4) = 6$; width: $(-2 + \sqrt{10})$ m;

length: $(2 - \sqrt{10})$ m **37.** $\dfrac{1}{2}h[(h + 5) + (h + 11)] = 3$;

$(1 + \sqrt{19})$ cm and $(7 + \sqrt{19})$ cm **39.** $\left\{\dfrac{-5 \pm \sqrt{33}}{2}\right\}$

41. $\left\{-1, -\dfrac{2}{5}\right\}$ **43.** $\left\{\dfrac{-3 \pm \sqrt{15}}{2}\right\}$ **45.** $\left\{\dfrac{-5 \pm \sqrt{13}}{6}\right\}$

47. $\left\{\dfrac{3 \pm 2\sqrt{11}}{7}\right\}$ **49.** $\{-1 \pm \sqrt{13}\}$ **51.** $\dfrac{1}{2}x(x + 2) = 5$;

$(1 + \sqrt{11})$ cm **53.** $(x - 35)^2 + x^2 = (x + 10)^2$;

40 cm, 75 cm, 85 cm **55.** 28 ft/s **57.** 42 ft/s **59.** No

Page 309, Review Exercises

1. $\dfrac{14}{99}$ **2.** Assoc. (mult.) **3.** Comm. (add.)

4. Distributive **5.** Identity (mult.) **6.** Add. inverse

7. $Q = 3x + 2$ **8.** $(-1)^n$
9. Comm. (add.); Assoc. (add.)

Page 312, Classroom Exercises
1. $2x^2 + 6x - 5 = 0$; $a = 2, b = 6, c = -5$
2. $2x^2 - 7x - 4 = 0$; $a = 2, b = -7, c = -4$
3. $a = 1, b = -1, c = -2$ **4.** $6y^2 - 15y - 7 = 0$;
$a = 6, b = -15, c = -7$ **5.** $\left\{\dfrac{-3 \pm 3\sqrt{5}}{2}\right\}$
6. $\left\{\dfrac{5 \pm \sqrt{41}}{2}\right\}$ **7.** $\left\{\dfrac{7 \pm \sqrt{73}}{4}\right\}$ **8.** $\left\{\dfrac{7 \pm \sqrt{69}}{2}\right\}$

Pages 313–314, Written Exercises
1. $a = 1, b = 2.5, c = -3$ **3.** $a = 1, b = 5, c = 16$
5. $a = 1, b = -20, c = 4$ **7.** $a = 1, b = 11, c = 32$
9. $\left\{-2, -\dfrac{3}{2}\right\}$ **11.** $\left\{\dfrac{-5 \pm \sqrt{21}}{2}\right\}$ **13.** $\{3 \pm \sqrt{13}\}$
15. $\{2 \pm \sqrt{6}\}$ **17.** $\{4 \pm \sqrt{22}\}$ **19.** $\left\{\dfrac{-5 \pm \sqrt{61}}{6}\right\}$
21. $\emptyset$ **23.** $\left\{\dfrac{1}{6}, -4\right\}$ **25.** $\emptyset$ **27.** $\left\{\dfrac{-3 \pm \sqrt{33}}{4}\right\}$
29. $\emptyset$ **31.** $\left\{\dfrac{3 \pm \sqrt{33}}{4}\right\}$ **33.** $\{-2 \pm \sqrt{10}\}$
35. $\left\{-3 \pm \sqrt{11}\right\}$ **37.** $\left\{\dfrac{-\sqrt{15} \pm \sqrt{3}}{6}\right\}$ **39.** $4 + 2\sqrt{14}$;
$7 + 2\sqrt{14}$; $11 + 2\sqrt{14}$ **41.** $1 + 2\sqrt{2}$; $4 + 2\sqrt{2}$; $5 + 2\sqrt{2}$
43. 40 m by 80 m **45.** \$80 **47.** 6 s **49.** $(6 \pm 2\sqrt{6})$ s
51. 5 mph **53.** 20 mph **55.** T **57.** T

59. $\left(\dfrac{-b + \sqrt{b^2 - 4ac}}{2a}\right) + \left(\dfrac{-b - \sqrt{b^2 - 4ac}}{2a}\right)$
$= \dfrac{-b + \sqrt{b^2 - 4ac} - b - \sqrt{b^2 - 4ac}}{2a}$
$= -\dfrac{2b}{2a} = -\dfrac{b}{a}, a \neq 0$

61. $\dfrac{2a}{-b + \sqrt{b^2 - 4ac}} + \dfrac{2a}{-b - \sqrt{b^2 - 4ac}}$
$= \dfrac{2a(-b - \sqrt{b^2 - 4ac}) + 2a(-b + \sqrt{b^2 - 4ac})}{(-b + \sqrt{b^2 - 4ac})(-b - \sqrt{b^2 - 4ac})}$
$= \dfrac{-2a - 2a\sqrt{b^2 - 4ac} - 2ab + 2a\sqrt{b^2 - 4ac}}{b^2 - (b^2 - 4ac)}$
$= \dfrac{-4ab}{4ac} = -\dfrac{b}{c}, c \neq 0$

63. about $\{-2.54, 0.94\}$ **65.** about $\{-1.48, 0.94\}$

Page 315, Review Exercises
1. $r = \sqrt[3]{\dfrac{3V}{4\pi}}$ or $\dfrac{\sqrt[3]{6\pi^2 V}}{2\pi}$ **2.** $x + 5 = 2(x - 10)$; 25
3. $x + (x + 2) + (x + 4) = 120$; 38 cm, 40 cm, 42 cm
4. $\{x : x < -3\}$

5. $\{x : -3 \leq x \leq 5\}$

6. $\{x : x > 3 \text{ or } x < -1\}$

7. 24 cm, 48 cm, 14 cm, 14 cm **8.** $\dfrac{1}{2}$

Pages 318–319, Classroom Exercises
1. $\sqrt{2}i$ **2.** $\dfrac{2}{3}i$ **3.** -2 **4.** $-\sqrt{15}$ **5.** -15 **6.** $-i$
7. -1 **8.** i **9.** $-2 + 5i$ **10.** $0 + (-4)i$
11. $3 + 0i$ **12.** $\sqrt{29}$ **13.** $\sqrt{29}$ **14.** 6
15. $\left\{-1 \pm \sqrt{7}i\right\}$ **16.** $\left\{-\dfrac{3}{4} \pm \dfrac{\sqrt{47}}{4}i\right\}$

Pages 319–320, Written Exercises
1. $\sqrt{5}i$ **3.** $-10i$ **5.** -4 **7.** $10i$ **9.** $\sqrt{6}i$
11. $-\dfrac{\sqrt{5}}{5}$ **13.** -20 **15.** $-8i$ **17.** -9 **19.** 35
21. $2 + (-3)i$ **23.** $0 + 2i$ **25.** $7 + 0i$
27. $0 + \sqrt{5}i$ **29.** 13 **31.** 5 **33.** 2 **35.** $\sqrt{13}$
37. $\left\{-\dfrac{3}{2} \pm \dfrac{\sqrt{7}}{2}i\right\}$ **39.** $\left\{-\dfrac{1}{4} \pm \dfrac{\sqrt{23}}{4}i\right\}$ **41.** $\left\{\dfrac{2}{5} \pm \dfrac{1}{5}i\right\}$
43. $\{1 \pm 2i\}$ **45.** $-\sqrt{ab}$ **47.** $-a$ **49.** $-36\sqrt{ab}$
51. $\sqrt[3]{ab}$ **53.** i **55.** 1 **57.** i **59.** -1 **61.** T
63. F **65.** $x = 3\sqrt{2}$; $y = 3\sqrt{2}$ **67.** $-i$ **69.** 1
71. $-i$ **73.** $|a + bi| = \sqrt{a^2 + b^2}$. If $b = 0$,
$\sqrt{a^2 + b^2} = \sqrt{a^2} = |a|$

Page 320, Review Exercises
1. Domain = $\{x : x \geq 0\}$, range = reals **2.** It is not.
3. Slope: $\dfrac{3}{2}$, y-intercept: -5 **4.** It is not.
5. $y = -\dfrac{1}{2}x$ **6.** 15 **7.** r^2 **8.** -6 **9.** 144 **10.** 6

Page 320, Self-Quiz 1
1. $(x - 6)^2 = 33$ **2.** $\left(x + \dfrac{5}{2}\right)^2 = \dfrac{29}{4}$ **3.** $\{1, -4\}$
4. $\{-2 \pm 2\sqrt{3}\}$ **5.** $\emptyset$ **6.** -8 **7.** -16 **8.** 25
9. $-4 + 3i$ **10.** $8 + 0i$ **11.** $0 + 2i$ **12.** $\{2 \pm i\}$
13. $\left\{\dfrac{1}{5} \pm \dfrac{7}{5}i\right\}$

Page 323, Classroom Exercises
1. $9 - 5i$ **2.** $-1 + 3i$ **3.** 10 **4.** $-6i$ **5.** $8 + i$
6. $-1 - 2\sqrt{2}i$ **7.** $3 - 7i$ **8.** $4 + 2i$ **9.** 8
10. $-3i$ **11.** $12 + 15i = 12 + 15i$

Pages 323–324, Written Exercises

1. $12 + 12i$ **3.** $2 - 5i$ **5.** 24 **7.** $2\pi + 2\sqrt{2}i$
9. $15 + 3\sqrt{10}i$ **11.** $-2 + 3i$ **13.** $2 - 10i$
15. $-5i$ **17.** $\dfrac{2}{3}$ **19.** $8 + 9i$ **21.** $3 + 7i$
23. $-3 - 3i$ **25.** $-2 - 3i$ **27.** $-\sqrt{6} - 2\sqrt{5}i$
29. $2 + 3i$ **31.** $-2 - 10i$ **33.** 7 **35.** $\sqrt{2}i$
37. $(a + bi) - (c + di)$, where a, b, c, and d are real;
$(a + bi) - (c + di) = (a - c) + (b - d)i$. Since the
real numbers are closed with respect to subtraction,
$(a - c)$ and $(b - d)$ are some real numbers e and f. So
$(a + bi) - (c + di) = e + fi$, a complex number.
39. 5 ohms **41a.** $15 - 8i$ **41b.** 17 ohms **43.** They
are equal.

Page 324, Review Exercises

1. Infinitely many **2.** $\{(4, -1)\}$ **3.** $\{(12, 0)\}$ **4.** 4
5.
$$D = \begin{vmatrix} 1 & 1 & 1 \\ 1 & -1 & 0 \\ 2 & 0 & -3 \end{vmatrix} \quad D_x = \begin{vmatrix} 12 & 1 & 1 \\ 10 & -1 & 0 \\ 0 & 0 & -3 \end{vmatrix}$$
$$D_y = \begin{vmatrix} 1 & 12 & 1 \\ 1 & 10 & 0 \\ 2 & 0 & -3 \end{vmatrix} \quad D_z = \begin{vmatrix} 1 & 1 & 12 \\ 1 & -1 & 10 \\ 2 & 0 & 0 \end{vmatrix}$$

6.

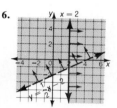

Page 327, Classroom Exercises

1. $36 + 8i$ **2.** $12 - 24i$ **3.** $\dfrac{3}{5} + \dfrac{4}{5}i$ **4.** $\dfrac{16}{13} + \dfrac{15}{13}i$
5. $(a + bi)(c + di) \overset{?}{=} (c + di)(a + bi)$
$(a + bi)(c + di) = (ac - bd) + (ad + bc)i$
$\qquad = (ca - db) + (da + cb)i$
$\qquad = (c + di)(a + bi)$

Pages 327–328, Written Exercises

1. $2 + 23i$ **3.** $43 + 18i$ **5.** $1 + 5i$ **7.** $-5 + 40i$
9. $24 - 36i$ **11.** $6 + 8i$ **13.** 61 **15.** -101
17. $-45 + 28i$ **19.** $\dfrac{3}{13} - \dfrac{2}{13}i$ **21.** $\dfrac{5}{26} + \dfrac{1}{26}i$
23. $\dfrac{1}{2} + 0i$ **25.** $0 - \dfrac{1}{10}i$ **27.** $-\dfrac{1}{10} + \dfrac{13}{10}i$
29. $\dfrac{3}{4} + \dfrac{1}{4}i$ **31.** $\dfrac{8}{29} - \dfrac{20}{29}i$ **33.** $-\dfrac{5}{2} + \dfrac{5}{2}i$ **35.** $0 - \dfrac{5}{3}i$
37. $-\dfrac{4}{5} - \dfrac{1}{5}i$ **39.** $(a + bi)(a - bi) = a^2 + b^2$

41. Let $(a + bi)$ and $(c + di)$ be complex numbers,
where a, b, c, and d are real and $c \neq 0$, $d \neq 0$.
$$\frac{a + bi}{(c + di)} = \frac{a + bi}{(c + di)} \cdot \frac{(c - di)}{(c - di)}$$
$$= \frac{(a + bi)(c - di)}{c^2 + d^2}$$
$$= \frac{(ac + bd) + (-ad + bc)i}{c^2 + d^2}$$
$(ac + bd)$ is some real number j, $(-ad + bc)$ is some
real number k, and $(c^2 + d^2)$ is some real number m,
since the real numbers are closed with respect to addition, subtraction, and multiplication. Therefore,
$$\frac{a + bi}{c + di} = \frac{j + ki}{m}$$
$$= \frac{j}{m} + \frac{k}{m}i$$
Since $m \neq 0$ (because $c \neq 0$, $d \neq 0$), $\dfrac{j}{m}$ is some real
number p and $\dfrac{k}{m}$ is some real number q, because the
real numbers are closed with respect to division
(divisor not equal to 0).
Therefore, $\dfrac{a + bi}{c + di} = p + qi$, a complex number.
43. $\{-3\}$ **45.** $\{5\}$ **47.** $\{(-9, 40)\}$ **49.** $\{-6\}$
51. $\dfrac{\sqrt{2}}{2} - \dfrac{\sqrt{2}}{2}i, \; -\dfrac{\sqrt{2}}{2} + \dfrac{\sqrt{2}}{2}i$
53. Let $z_1 = (a + bi)$ and $z_2 = (c + di)$, then
$\bar{z}_1 = (a - bi)$ and $\bar{z}_2 = (c - di)$.
Then $\quad z_1 \cdot z_2 = (a + bi)(c + di)$
$\qquad\qquad = (ac - bd) + (ad + bc)i$
and $\quad \overline{z_1 \cdot z_2} \; (ac - bd) - (ad + bc)i$
$\overline{z_1 \cdot z_2} \overset{?}{=} \bar{z}_1 \cdot \bar{z}_2$
$(a - bi)(c - di) \overset{?}{=} (ac - bd) - (ad + bc)i$
$(a - bi)(c - di)$
$= [ac - (-b)(-d)] + [a(-d) + (-b)c]i$
$= (ac - bd) + (-ad - bc)i$
$= (ac - bd) - (ad + bc)i$
Therefore, $\overline{z_1 \cdot z_2} = \bar{z}_1 \cdot \bar{z}_2$

Page 328, Review Exercises

1. $20a^2b^3$ **2.** $1.35 \cdot 10^{16}$ **3.** $-7x + 8$
4. $2x^2 - 7x - 15$ **5.** $a^3 + 3a^2b + 3ab^2 + b^3$
6. $x^4 - 8x^3 + 24x^2 - 32x + 16$ **7.** $a^3 + b^3$
8. $2a^2 + ab - 10b^2$ **9.** $3x(x^2 - 4x + 2)$

Page 328, Extension

1–2. Pure imaginary axis

3. $AO = BC = \sqrt{5}$;
$AC = OB = \sqrt{10}$
4. It is the same.

Page 331, Classroom Exercises

1. 1 rational   **2.** 2 rational   **3.** 2 imaginary

4. $k \geq -\dfrac{27}{4}$ **5.** $y = x^2$; $y^2 - 5y + 4 = 0$

6. $y = x^2$; $y^2 - 4y = 0$

7. $y = \sqrt{x}$; $y^2 - 9y + 8 = 0$

8. $y = x^{\frac{1}{3}}$, $y^2 + 5y + 6 = 0$ **9.** $\{-2, -1, 1, 2\}$

10. $\{-2, 0, 2\}$ **11.** $\{1, 64\}$ **12.** $\{-27, -8\}$

Pages 331–332, Written Exercises

1. -3; 2 imaginary   **3.** -3; 2 imaginary   **5.** 0;
1 rational   **7.** 361; 2 rational   **9.** 1.45; 2 irrational

11. $\dfrac{31}{9}$; 2 irrational   **13.** $y = h^2$; $y^2 - 2y + 1 = 0$

15. $y = \sqrt{x}$; $y^2 - 9y + 14 = 0$ **17.** $y = \sqrt[4]{x}$;
$y^2 - 6y + 8 = 0$ **19.** $y = k^4$; $y^2 - 17y + 16 = 0$

21. $y = x^{\frac{1}{3}}$; $y^2 - y - 2 = 0$ **23.** $\{-2, -1, 1, 2\}$
25. $\{4, 49\}$ **27.** $\{16, 256\}$

29. $\{-2, -1, 1, 2, -2i, -i, i, 2i\}$ **31.** $\{-1, 8\}$

33. $k = 9$ **35.** $k < 9$ **37.** False, $x^2 + 1 = 0$

39. True   **41.** False, $x^2 - 1 = 0$

43. $\left\{-4, -1, \dfrac{3}{2} \pm \dfrac{\sqrt{31}}{2}i\right\}$ **45.** $\left\{\dfrac{1}{4}, \dfrac{1}{9}\right\}$ **47.** $\{-8, -27\}$

49. $\left\{\dfrac{3}{2}\right\}$

51. If $x^2 + bx + c = 0$ has a double root, then
$b^2 - 4c = 0$; $b^2 = 4c$. If b is an even number, then it is
of the form $(2k)$. Since $b^2 = 4c$, it is a multiple of 4.
So b must be a multiple of 2 and even.   **53.** $\{\sqrt{2}$

55. $\{5i, -2i\}$ **57.** $\{0, 6i\}$

Page 332, Review Exercises

1. $(x - 2)(x^2 + 2x + 4)$ **2.** $(a - b)(c + d)$
3. $2(x + 2)(x - 2)$ **4.** $4(a + 2b)(a - 2b)$
5. $(7 - x)(2 + x)$ **6.** $(x - 5)(x + 4)$ **7.** $(5, 7)$

8. $\left\{\dfrac{1}{3}, -7\right\}$ **9.** $\left\{\dfrac{3}{2}, 2\right\}$

Page 332, Self-Quiz 2

1. $5 + 5i$ **2.** $-\dfrac{7}{4} - 5i$ **3.** $7 + 11i$ **4.** $-5 + 12i$

5. $-1 + 4i$ **6.** $2 - 2i$ **7.** -1 **8.** 2, imaginary
9. 2, irrational   **10.** $k > 4$ or $k < -4$
11. $\{3, -3, 2i, -2i\}$

Page 334, Classroom Exercises

1. $y = -2x^2 - 3x + 6$ **2.** $y = 3x^2 - 12x + 12$
3. $y = 0x^2 - 4x - 5$ **4.** $y = 0x^2 - 4x - 5$ **5.** Yes
6. Yes   **7.** No   **8.** Yes   **9.** $(0, 0)$; $x = 0$
10a. Yes   **b.** No   **c.** No   **d.** Yes

Pages 335–336, Written Exercises

1. Yes; $y = 1x^2 + 5x + 0$
3. Yes; $y = 2x^2 - 1x + 3$ **5.** No

7. 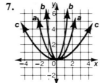   **9.**

11. $(0, 0)$; $x = 0$ **13.** $(0, 0)$; $x = 0$ **15.** 1   **17.** 1
19. 2   **21.** 0   **23.** 1   **25.** 2   **27.** b
29. $P = -1x^2 + 26x + 0$ **31.** $S = 2x^2 + 10x + 25$
33. $A = -x^2 + 18x + 0$
35. $S = -150x^2 + 2000x + 320{,}000$
37. $\{y: 0 \leq y \leq 9\}$ **39.** $\{y: -18 \leq y \leq 0\}$
41. $\{x: -6\sqrt{2} \leq x \leq 6\sqrt{2}\}$

43. No, they intersect at $(0, 0)$ and $\left(\dfrac{m}{a}, \dfrac{m^2}{a}\right)$.

Page 336, Review Exercises

1. $\dfrac{3a}{bc^2}$ **2.** $-3xy^{-2}$ **3.** $\dfrac{ab}{a + b}$ **4.** $\dfrac{a - b}{2}$ **5.** $\dfrac{9x}{10}$

6. $\dfrac{2}{x}$ **7.** $\dfrac{1 - x}{x^2}$ **8.** $\dfrac{x}{x^2 - 1}$

Page 339, Classroom Exercises

1. $y = 2(x - 5)^2$, $a = 2$, $h = 5$ **2.** $y = 1(x + 3)^2$;
$a = 1$, $h = -3$ **3.** $y = 3(x - 5)^2$; $a = 3$, $h = 5$
4. $y = -1(x - 2)^2$; $a = -1$, $h = 2$
5. $(3, 0)$; $x = 3$;   **6.** $(-2, 0)$; $x = -2$;
upward   downward

   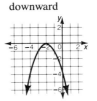

7. $(-4, 0)$; $x = -4$; upward

Pages 339–340, Written Exercises

1. $y = 1(x - 2)^2$ **3.** $y = 3(x + 10)^2$ **5.** $y = 1(x - 5)^2$
7. $y = 6(x + 1)^2$ **9.** $y = -1(x - 10)^2$
11. $y = 2(x + 3)^2$ **13.** $(6, 0)$; $x = 6$; upward
15. $(100, 0)$; $x = 100$; downward   **17.** $(-3, 0)$; $x = -3$;

upward   **19.** $(1, 0)$; $x = 1$; downward   **21.** $(1, 0)$;
$x = 1$; downward   **23.** $(-3, 0)$; $x = -3$; downward

25.
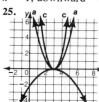
27.
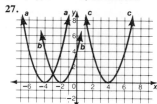

5.
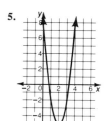

6.
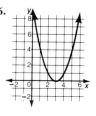

$(3, 0)$; $x = 3$; upward

$(2, -5)$; $x = 2$; upward

29. $y = 2(x + 3)^2$
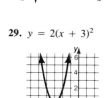

31. $y = \frac{1}{2}(x - 4)^2$
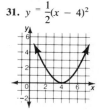

7.
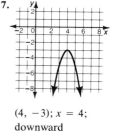

8.
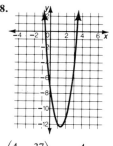

$(4, -3)$; $x = 4$;
downward

$\left(\frac{4}{3}, -\frac{37}{3}\right)$; $x = \frac{4}{3}$; upward

33. $y = -1(x - 1)^2$

35. $y = -\frac{1}{4}(x - 6)^2$
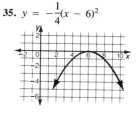

Pages 343–344, Written Exercises

1. $y + 3 = \frac{1}{2}(x + 2)^2$ **3.** $y - 9 = 3(x - 6)^2$

5. $y + 5 = 1(x + 2)^2$ **7.** $y - 6 = 2(x - 6)^2$

9. $y - 4 = -1(x + 0)^2$ **11.** $y + \frac{21}{4} = 1\left(x - \frac{5}{2}\right)^2$

13. $y + 19 = 4(x - 2)^2$ **15.** $y - 3 = 2(x + 1)^2$

17. $y + \frac{17}{2} = \frac{1}{2}(x + 5)^2$ **19.** $(12, 10)$; $x = 12$;

37. $y = -\frac{1}{2}(x - 4)^2$ **39.** True   **41.** True   **43.** True

45. True   **47.** $y = -3(x + 2)^2$ **49.** $y = \frac{1}{3}(x - 0)^2$ or
$y = 3(x - 4)^2$

downward   **21.** $(5, -2)$; $x = 5$; upward   **23.** $(1, 4)$;
$x = 1$; upward   **25.** $(-5, -3)$; $x = -5$; downward

27. $\left(-\frac{7}{2}, -4\right)$; $x = -\frac{7}{2}$; upward   **29.** $(3, 73)$; $x = 3$;
upward

Page 340, Review Exercises

1. $\frac{4 - x}{2x^2}$, $x \neq 0$ **2.** $\left\{\frac{1}{2}, -\frac{2}{3}\right\}$ **3.** 10 km/h   **4.** $66\frac{2}{3}$ h

5. 2500 cm³   **6.** 100

Page 343, Classroom Exercises

1. $y + 5 = 3(x - 2)^2$; $a = 3$, $h = 2$, $k = -5$

2. $y - 0 = 1(x - 3)^2$; $a = 1$, $h = 3$, $k = 0$

3. $y + 3 = -2(x - 4)^2$; $a = -2$, $h = 4$, $k = -3$

4. $y + \frac{37}{3} = 3\left(x - \frac{4}{3}\right)^2$; $a = 3$, $h = \frac{4}{3}$, $k = -\frac{37}{3}$

31.
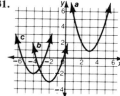

33.
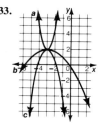

35. $y - 50 = \frac{-1}{10}(x - 100)^2$ **37.** $y - 6 = -1(x - 5)^2$

39. $y - 6 = \frac{1}{9}(x - 3)^2$ **41.** $k = 1$ or $k = -1$

43. $y - 3 = 1(x + 2)^2$　　**45.** $y - 4 = -\dfrac{1}{2}(x - 4)^2$

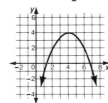

47. $y + 3 = -\dfrac{1}{4}(x + 2)^2$　　**49.** 0　　**51.** $k < 0$

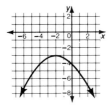

Page 345, Review Exercises

1. -12　　**2.** $-\dfrac{1}{3}$　　**3.** $6\sqrt{2}$　　**4.** $a^2|b|\sqrt{a};\ a \geq 0$　　**5.** 7

6. 0　　**7.** $\dfrac{3a\sqrt{b}}{|a|};\ a \neq 0,\ b > 0$　　**8.** $6 - 2\sqrt{3}$

Page 345, Self-Quiz 3

1. $y = 2x^2 - 6x + \dfrac{11}{2}$

2.

3a. Both　　**3b.** $y = -5x^2$

4. $y = 2(x + 5)^2;\ a = 2,$　$h = -5$

5. $(1, 0;\ x = 1;$ downward

6. $\left(-\dfrac{3}{2}, 0\right);\ x = -\dfrac{3}{2};$ upward

7. $\left(-\dfrac{5}{2}, 2\right);\ x = -\dfrac{5}{2};$ downward

8. $y - 3 = -2(x + 1)^2$　　**9.** $y - 2 = -1(x + 1)^2$

Page 348, Classroom Exercises

1. Minimum of 7 at $-\dfrac{3}{2}$　　**2.** Maximum of 12 at -3
3. 6 m by 6 m

Pages 349–351, Written Exercises

1. Minimum　　**3.** Maximum　　**5.** Maximum
7. Minimum　　**9.** Neither　　**11.** Both　　**13.** Minimum of
10 at -3　　**15.** Maximum of -12.3 at 5　　**17.** Maximum of
50.6 at 2.3　　**19.** Minimum of -6 at 4　　**21.** Minimum
of $-\dfrac{57}{4}$ at $-\dfrac{5}{2}$　　**23.** Minimum of 95 at -1　　**25.** Maximum

of 10 at 2　　**27a.** 196 ft　　**b.** $1\dfrac{1}{2}$　　**c.** 5　　**29.** 5 m by 10 m

31. \$12; \$72,000　　**33a.** 1.5　　**33b.** 202.5　　**35a.** 500
35b. 250,000　　**35c.** 0 and 1000　　**37a.** \$350　　**b.** \$55,950
39. 40; \$1600

c.

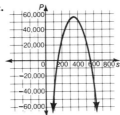

d. Loss of \$115,500 per month when no scales sold

41. Let x equal the length of a rectangle and $\left(\dfrac{p}{2} - x\right)$

equal the width. Then

$$A = \dfrac{p}{2}x - x^2$$

$$-A = x^2 - \dfrac{p}{2}x$$

$$-A + \dfrac{p^2}{16} = x^2 - \dfrac{p}{2}x + \dfrac{p^2}{16}$$

$$-A + \dfrac{p^2}{16} = \left(x - \dfrac{p}{4}\right)^2$$

$$A - \dfrac{p^2}{16} = -\left(x - \dfrac{p}{4}\right)^2$$

Maximum area of $\dfrac{p^2}{16}$ is at $x = \dfrac{p}{4}$. If $\dfrac{p}{4}$ is the length of

the rectangle, then $\left(\dfrac{p}{2} - \dfrac{p}{4}\right) = \dfrac{p}{4}$ is the width; so the

figure is a square side $\dfrac{p}{4}$.

Page 351, Review Exercises

1. $5\sqrt{2}$　　**2.** $\left(\dfrac{1}{2}, 3\right)$　　**3.** $\{1\}$　　**4.** $\{14\}$　　**5.** $\{126\}$

6. $\sqrt[3]{5^2}$ or $(\sqrt[3]{5})^2$　　**7.** $2^{-\frac{1}{3}}$

Page 352, Extension

1. D　　**2.** B and C　　**3.** They are reflections about the
real axis.　　**4.** C　　**5.** B and D　　**6.** They are reflections through the point $0 + 0i$.

Pages 354–356, Chapter Review

1. No　　**3.** $(x - 6)^2 = 6$　　**5.** $\left\{\dfrac{7}{3}, -\dfrac{1}{2}\right\}$　　**7.** $\left\{\dfrac{2}{3}\right\}$

9. $\dfrac{5}{3}i$　　**11.** $32i$　　**13.** $\{\pm 6\sqrt{2}i\}$　　**15.** $\sqrt{13}$　　**17.** $3 - 3i$

19. $26 + 13i$　　**21.** $\{-2\}$　　**23.** 2 imaginary
25. $\{\pm \sqrt{2}, \pm 2i\}$　　**27.** No

29.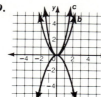

31. $(1, 0)$; $x = 1$, downward

33.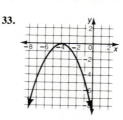

35. a and c   **37.** 17   **39.** 100 ft

Pages 356–358, Chapter 8 Self-Test

1. $-5x^2 + \frac{9}{2}x - \frac{3}{4} = 0$ **2.** $(x - 1)^2 = \frac{1}{2}$

3. $\{-7 \pm 2\sqrt{2}\}$ **4.** $\{\sqrt{2} \pm 3\}$ **5.** $\left\{\frac{3}{2}, \frac{5}{3}\right\}$ **6.** $-\sqrt{10}$

7. $8i$ **8.** -1 **9.** $x = -7, y = -\frac{8}{3}$

11. $\{-2 \pm \sqrt{2}i\}$ **12.** $\sqrt{10}$ **13.** -23 **14.** $\frac{4}{5} - \frac{8}{5}i$

15. 11   **16.** $-2i$

17.
$$x^2 - 6x + 13 = 0$$
$$(3 - 2i)^2 - 6(3 - 2i) + 13 = 0$$
$$9 - 12i + 4i^2 - 18 + 12i + 13 = 0$$
$$4 + 4i^2 = 0$$
$$4 + 4(-1) = 0$$
$$4 - 4 = 0$$

18. 1 rational   **19.** $k > \frac{9}{2}$ **20.** $\{64\}$

21. Yes, downward   **22.** Yes, downward

23. $|b| > |a|$ **24.** They have opposite signs.

25. $y = 2(x - 3)^2$

26.   **27.**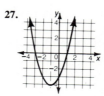

28. c   **29.** d   **30.** $y - 2 = 1(x + 1)^2$

31. Maximum of 3   **32.** 11,250 yd^2 **33.** $-\frac{1}{2}; -\frac{1}{4}$

Pages 358–359, Practice for College Entrance Tests
1. B   **2.** C   **3.** E   **4.** E   **5.** D   **6.** A   **7.** A
8. B   **9.** D   **10.** B   **11.** E   **12.** C

Chapter 9

Page 363, Classroom Exercises
1. $(0, 0)$; 9   **2.** $(-2, 5)$; 7   **3.** $(0, 4)$; 5
4. $(x - 3)^2 + (y - 4)^2 = 1$ **5.** $x^2 + (y - 6)^2 = 25$

6. $(x - 1)^2 + (y + 1)^2 = 4$

7. 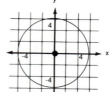   **8.**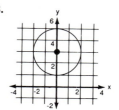

9. The graph is a circle with center $(-3, 0)$, radius 2, and the region outside it.

Pages 363–365, Written Exercises
1. $(x - 2)^2 + (y - 3)^2 = 16$
3. $(x + 3)^3 + (y - 4)^2 = 4$
5. $(x - 4)^2 + (y + 3)^2 = 2$ **7.** $x^2 + y^2 = 10$

9. 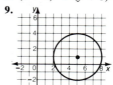   **11.**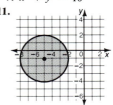

13. 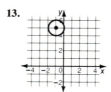   **15.**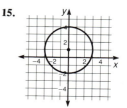

17. 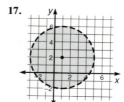   **19.**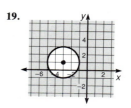

21. $(10, -6)$; 5   **23.** $(4, 15)$; $\sqrt{7}$ **25.** $(2, 0)$; 3
27. $x^2 + y^2 = 25$ **29.** $(x - 3)^2 + (y + 3)^2 = 9$
31. $x^2 + (y + 2)^2 > 9$

33. 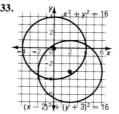   **35.**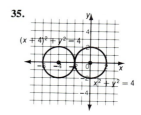

37.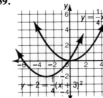
$y - 2 = (x - 3)^2$

39.

41.
$y - 3 = 2|x + 4|$

43a. $2\sqrt{5}$ **b.** $(x - 2)^2 + (y - 3)^2 = 20$ **c.** Inside
45. $(-3, 4)$; 7 **47.** $(10, 3)$; 1
49. $(x + 4)^2 + (y - 3)^2 = 16$

Page 365, Review Exercises

1. Infinitely many **2.** $\left\{\left(\dfrac{15}{7}, \dfrac{25}{7}\right)\right\}$ **3.** $\{(3, 4)\}$
4. $\{(2, 4)\}$ **5.** $y < 5 - x$ or $y < x - 2$

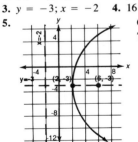

6. 4

Page 369, Classroom Exercises

1. $(2, -3)$; right **2.** 16; $(6, -3)$
3. $y = -3$; $x = -2$ **4.** 16
5.

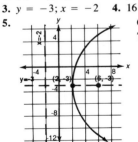

6. $(4, 2)$
7. $\sqrt{(x - 4)^2 + (y - 3)^2}$

8. $|y - 1|$ **9.** $y - 2 = \dfrac{1}{4}(x - 4)^2$

Pages 370–373, Written Exercises

1. $(8, -1)$; $x = 8$, $(8, 0)$; $y = -2$; opens upward
3. $(1, -2)$; $x = 1$; $\left(1, -\dfrac{23}{12}\right)$; $y = -\dfrac{25}{12}$; opens upward
5. $(3, 2)$; $x = 3$; $\left(3, \dfrac{1}{4}\right)$; $y = \dfrac{9}{4}$; opens downward

7. $y - 5 = \dfrac{1}{16}(x - 3)^2$; $x = 3$; $(3, 5)$
9. $y - 6 = \dfrac{1}{16}(x - 7)^2$; $x = 7$; $(7, 6)$
11. $x - 4 = \dfrac{1}{8}(y - 2)^2$; $y = 2$; $(4, 2)$
13. $x - 6 = -\dfrac{1}{8}(y - 3)^2$; $y = 3$; $(6, 3)$
15. $x - 7 = \dfrac{1}{12}(y - 10)^2$; $(7, 10)$; open to right
17. $x + 7 = -\dfrac{1}{12}(y + 10)^2$; $(-7, -10)$; opens to left
19. $y - 3 = \dfrac{1}{28}(x - 10)^2$; $(10, 3)$; opens upward

21.

23.

25. $x - 1 = \dfrac{1}{8}y^2$ **27.** $y - 4 = -\dfrac{1}{4}(x - 1)^2$
29. 5 cm **31a.** $y = \dfrac{16}{1875}x^2$ Answer varies with location
of vertex. **b.** 7.68 m; 11.52 m; 11.52 m; 7.68 m; 0 m
33. $y^2 = 2dx + d^2$
Divide both sides by $2d$, $d \ne 0$, to get an equation in
standard form.
$$\dfrac{1}{2d}y^2 = x + \dfrac{d}{2}$$
Focus is $\left(h + \dfrac{1}{4a}, k\right)$, where $h = -\dfrac{d}{2}$, $a = \dfrac{1}{2d}$, and
$k = 0$.
The focus is $(0, 0)$.
All equations of the form $y^2 = 2dx + d^2$ have the same
focus, since the focus $(0, 0)$ does not depend on the
value of d.
35. For the parabola $4py = x^2$, when $x = \pm 2p$, $y = p$.
Hence $(-2p, p)$ and $(2p, p)$ are the endpoints of
the latus chord. Thus the length of the latus chord is
$|2p - (-2p)| = |4p|$.

Page 373, Review Exercises

1. $18a^3b^2$ **2.** $3x^2 - 13x - 8$ **3.** $2x^2 + 7x - 15$
4. $6xy$ **5.** $(5x + 2)(5x - 2)$ **6.** $(3x - 2)(x + 3)$
7. $(3, 4)$ **8.** $\pi(r_2 + r_1)(r_2 - r_1)$

Page 373, Self-Quiz 1

1. $(x + 5)^2 + (y - 2)^2 = 36$
2. Region inside circle with center $(0, 1)$ and radius 2.
3. $x - 2$ for x, $y - 3$ for y

4. $(x + 1)^2 + (y - 10)^2 = 65$ **5.** $x - 1 = \frac{1}{12}(y - 2)^2$

6. $(-1, 2); x = -1; \left(-1, \frac{5}{2}\right); y = \frac{3}{2}$

7. Graph is parabola with vertex $(3, -1)$, axis of symmetry $x = 3$; opens upward.

Pages 376–377, Classroom Exercises

1.

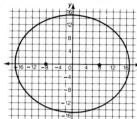

Foci:

$(-8, 0), (8, 0)$

3. $a = 5, b = 4, c = 3$;

$\frac{x^2}{25} + \frac{y^2}{16} = 1$ **3.** $a = 13$,

$b = 12, c = 5; \frac{y^2}{169} + \frac{x^2}{144} = 1$

Pages 377–380, Written Exercises

1. $\frac{x^2}{25} + \frac{y^2}{9} = 1$ **3.** $\frac{y^2}{36} + \frac{x^2}{4} = 1$ **5.** $\frac{x^2}{36} + \frac{y^2}{25} = 1$

7. $\frac{y^2}{225} + \frac{x^2}{9} = 1$ **9.** $\frac{y^2}{100} + \frac{x^2}{64} = 1$

11. $\frac{y^2}{100} + \frac{x^2}{36} = 1$ **13.** $\frac{x^2}{169} + \frac{y^2}{25} = 1$

15. $\frac{(y - 4)^2}{169} + \frac{(x - 3)^2}{144} = 1$

17. $\frac{(x + 2)^2}{25} + \frac{(y - 4)^2}{9} = 1$

19.

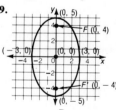

21.

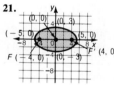

23.

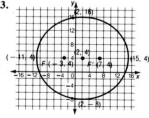

25.

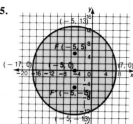

27.

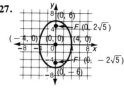

29.

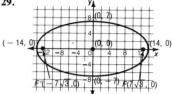

31. $y = \pm\sqrt{12 - (x - 1)^2}$ **33.** $y = 4(x + 2)^2$

35. $y = \pm\frac{3}{2}\sqrt{4 - x^2}$ **37.** 5.1 m   **39.** At least 10 ft.

41. $\frac{(x - 10)^2}{16} + \frac{(y - 6)^2}{12} = 1$ **43.** $\frac{x^2}{\frac{3}{2}} + \frac{\left(y + \frac{1}{4}\right)^2}{\frac{25}{16}} = 1$

45. $\pi ab - \pi b^2$; different approaches 0

Page 380, Review Exercises

1. $\frac{6c^2}{ab^2}$ **2.** $\frac{2 - 12xy}{3x}; x \neq 0, y \neq 0$ **3.** $\frac{27a^2}{50b^2}; a \neq 0$,

$b \neq 0$ **4.** $\frac{2}{1 - a}; a \neq 1$ **5.** $\{4\}$ **6.** $66\frac{2}{3}$ ohms   **7.** 1

Page 384, Classroom Exercises

1. $a = 4, b = 3, c = 5; \frac{x^2}{16} - \frac{y^2}{9} = 1$

2. $a = 4, b = 2\sqrt{5}, c = 6; \frac{y^2}{16} - \frac{x^2}{20} = 1$

3.

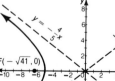

4.

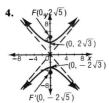

5.

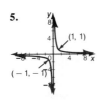

6.

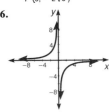

Pages 385–387, Written Exercises

1. $\dfrac{x^2}{4} - \dfrac{y^2}{4} = 1$ **3.** $\dfrac{y^2}{16} - \dfrac{x^2}{4} = 1$ **5.** $\dfrac{x^2}{16} - \dfrac{y^2}{9} = 1$

7. $\dfrac{y^2}{25} - \dfrac{x^2}{144} = 1$ **9.** Foci: $(-3\sqrt{5}, 0)$ and $(3\sqrt{5}, 0)$; asymptotes; $y = 2x$ and $y = -2x$; graph opens to the left and right with vertices $(-3, 0)$ and $(3, 0)$.

11. Foci: $(-\sqrt{29}, 0)$ and $(\sqrt{29}, 0)$; asymptotes: $y = \dfrac{2}{5}x$ and $y = -\dfrac{2}{5}x$; graph is the region inside the hyperbola with vertices $(-5, 0)$ and $(5, 0)$.

13. Foci: $(0, -10)$ and $(0, 10)$; asymptotes: $y = \dfrac{4}{3}x$ and $y = -\dfrac{4}{3}x$; graph is the hyperbola that opens upward and downward with vertices $(0, -8)$ and $(0, 8)$.

15. Foci: $(0, -4)$ and $(0, 4)$; asymptotes: $y = \dfrac{3\sqrt{7}}{7}x$ and $y = -\dfrac{3\sqrt{7}}{7}x$; graph is the region outside the hyperbola and the hyperbola with vertices $(0, -3)$, and $(0, 3)$.

17. Hyperbola is in the 1st and 3rd quadrants.

19. Hyperbola is in the 2nd and 4th quadrants.

21. $\dfrac{y^2}{16} - \dfrac{x^2}{20} = 1$ **23.** $\dfrac{x^2}{36} - \dfrac{y^2}{64} = 1$

25. Foci: $(-3\sqrt{5}, 0)$ and $(3\sqrt{5}, 0)$; asymptotes: $y = 2x$ and $y = -2x$; graph opens to the left and right with vertices $(-3, 0)$ and $(3, 0)$.   **27.** Foci: $(0, -5\sqrt{5})$ and $(0, 5\sqrt{5})$; asymptotes: $y = \dfrac{1}{2}x$ and $y = -\dfrac{1}{2}x$; graph opens upward and downward with vertices $(0, -5)$ and $(0, 5)$.

29. Foci: $(\sqrt{41}, 0)$ and $(-\sqrt{41}, 0)$; asymptotes: $y = \dfrac{5}{4}x$ and $y = -\dfrac{5}{4}x$; graph is the region outside the hyperbola with vertices $(4, 0)$ and $(-4, 0)$

31. Foci: $\left(0, \dfrac{3}{2}\sqrt{5}\right)$ and $\left(0, -\dfrac{3}{2}\sqrt{5}\right)$; asymptotes: $y = 2x$ and $y = -2x$; graph is the hyperbola that opens upward and downward with vertices $(0, 3)$ and $(0, -3)$.

33. Hyperbola is in the 1st and 3rd quadrants with the x and y axes as asymptotes.
35. Hyperbola is in the 2nd and 4th quadrants with the x and y axes as asymptotes.
37. Hyperbola is in the 1st and 3rd quadrants with the x and y axes as asymptotes.
39. Hyperbola is in the 1st and 3rd quadrants with center $(1, 0)$ and asymptotes $x = 1$ and $y = 0$.

41. $(y - 2)^2 - \dfrac{(x + 2)^2}{4} = 1$; asymptotes: $y = 3 + \dfrac{1}{2}x$ and $y = 1 - \dfrac{1}{2}x$ **43.** $\dfrac{(x - 5)^2}{25} - \dfrac{(y - 1)^2}{144} = 1$;

Asymptotes: $y = -11 + \dfrac{12}{5}x$ and $y = 13 - \dfrac{12}{5}x$

45. $3x^2 - y^2 - 48 = 0$ or $\dfrac{x^2}{16} - \dfrac{y^2}{48} = 1$

47. $9y^2 - 500y - 16x^2 + 2500 = 0$ or

$$\dfrac{\left(y - \dfrac{250}{9}\right)^2}{\dfrac{40,000}{81}} - \dfrac{x^2}{\dfrac{2500}{9}} = 1$$

Page 387, Review Exercises

1. $-\dfrac{2}{3}$ **2.** $2a\sqrt{3a},\ a \geq 0$ **3.** $\dfrac{\sqrt{10b}}{5b};\ b > 0$ **4.** $\dfrac{1}{4}$
5. 3   **6.** $-3 + 3\sqrt{2}$ **7.** $\sqrt{53}$ **8.** $\{-22\}$
9. 216 cm^2 **10.** $(3 - x)^{1/4}$ **11.a.** $-2\sqrt[4]{2}$ **b.** $6y\sqrt{y}$

Page 391, Classroom Exercises

1. Parabola   **2.** Hyperbola
3. $y - 1 = -1(x + 1)^2$ **4.** $(x + 2)^2 + (y + 3)^2 = 16$

Pages 391–392, Written Exercises

1. Hyperbola   **3.** Parabola   **5.** Parabola   **7.** Circle
9. Ellipse   **11.** Hyperbola
13. $x^2 + y^2 + 4x + 2y - 4 = 0$
15. $16x^2 + 9y^2 + 64x + 18y - 71 = 0$
17. $16x^2 - 9y^2 - 64x - 18y - 89 = 0$
19. $3x^2 + 0y^2 + 24x - 1y + 50 = 0$
21. Circle; $(x + 2)^2 + (y + 4)^2 = 3^2$; center $(-2, -4)$, radius 3.

23. Hyperbola: $\dfrac{(x - 3)^2}{4} - \dfrac{(y - 2)^2}{4} = 1$; center $(3, 2)$, vertices $(5, 2)$ and $(1, 2)$.   **25.** Hyperbola; $xy = 6$; in 1st and 3rd quad.

27. Ellipse; $\dfrac{x^2}{16} + \dfrac{(y - 3)^2}{4} = 1$; center $(0, 3)$, vertices $(-4, 3)$, $(4, 3)$, $(0, 5)$, and $(0, 1)$.
29. Parabola; $x - 3 = 3(y - 5)^2$; vertex $(3, 5)$, axis of symmetry $y = 5$, opening to right.   **31.** Hyperbola; $(x - 1)(y - 3) = 1$; center: $(1, 3)$; asymptotes: $x = 1$, $y = 3$

33. Hyperbola; $(x - 1)(y - 1) = 3$; center: $(1, 1)$; asymptotes: $x = 1$, $y = 1$ **35.** Graph is the region inside the ellipse with equation $\dfrac{(x + 2)^2}{1} + \dfrac{(y + 3)^2}{25} = 1$ and the ellipse itself.

37. Graph is the region outside the hyperbola with equation $\dfrac{x^2}{4} - \dfrac{y^2}{4} = 1$ and the hyperbola itself.

39. Graph is the region outside the hyperbola and the hyperbola itself.   **41.** Point, line, 2 intersecting lines, circle, ellipse, hyperbola, parabola

43.

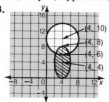

Page 392, Review Exercises

1. $\{3 \pm \sqrt{5}\}$ **2.** $\left\{\dfrac{3 \pm \sqrt{3}}{2}\right\}$ **3.** $-125i$ **4.** 5

5. $-4 + i$ **6.** $3 + 4i$ **7.** $\{2, -2, \sqrt{2}, -\sqrt{2}\}$

8. $\left\{\dfrac{5 \pm \sqrt{21}}{2}\right\}$

Page 392, Self-Quiz 2

1. $(-4, 0)$, $(4, 0)$, $(0, -6)$, $(0, 6)$; $(0, 2\sqrt{5})$, $(0, -2\sqrt{5})$
2. Graph has vertices $(-2, 0)$, $(2, 0)$, $(0, -5)$, $(0, 5)$ and foci $(0, \sqrt{21})$, $(0, -\sqrt{21})$ **3.** $\dfrac{x^2}{100} + \dfrac{y^2}{64} = 1$
4. Hyperbola has vertices $(-2, 0)$, $(2, 0)$ and foci $(\sqrt{13}, 0)$, $(-\sqrt{13}, 0)$ **5.** $\{(0, -5), (0, 5)$; $(0, \sqrt{41}), (0, -\sqrt{41})\}$ **6.** Hyperbola is in the 2nd and 4th quadrants.   **7a.** Hyperbola   **b.** Ellipse
c. Hyperbola   **d.** Circle   **8.** $(x - 1)^2 + (y + 2)^2 = 5$
9. Graph is the region inside ellipse and ellipse with vertices $(-4, 0)$, $(4, 0)$, $(0, -3)$, $(0, 3)$ and foci $(\sqrt{7}, 0)$ and $(-\sqrt{7}, 0)$.

Page 395, Classroom Exercises
1. $\emptyset$ **2.** $\emptyset$ **3.** $\{(0, 5), (0, -5)\}$

Pages 395–397, Written Exercises
1. $\{(3, 4), (-3, -4)\}$ **3.** $\{(2, 3), (-2, -3)\}$

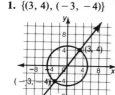   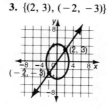

5. $\{(2, 3), (5, 6)\}$ **7.** $\{(2, 3), (-3, -2)\}$

9. $\left\{(-4, 0), \left(5, \dfrac{3}{2}\right)\right\}$ **11.** $\{(5, 3)\}$

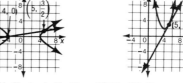

13. $\{(4, 3), (-4, 3), (0, -5)\}$ **15.** $\{(8, 0)\}$

17. $\{(10, 6), (10, -6),$ $(-10, 6), (-10, -6)\}$ **19.** $\{(1, 8), (-1, 3)\}$

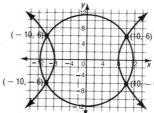

21. The graph is the circle with center $(0, 0)$ and radius 4, the circle with center $(0, 0)$ and radius 6, and the region between them.   **23.** The graph is the ellipse with center $(6, 2)$, vertices $(2, 2)$, $(10, 2)$, $(6, 5)$, $(6, -1)$, the circle with center $(6, 2)$ and radius 3, and the regions between them.

25. $\left(\dfrac{9}{2\pi} - 1\right)$ cm, $\left(\dfrac{9}{2\pi} + 1\right)$ cm   **27.** $\sqrt{10}$ cm by $\sqrt{10}$ cm

29. 12 and 9   **31.** $y = \dfrac{\sqrt{7}}{7}x + \dfrac{8\sqrt{7}}{7}$ **33.** $\sqrt{2}$

Page 397, Review Exercises
1a. Parabola with vertex $(0, 0)$ and axis of symmetry the y-axis; opens upward.   **b.** Parabola with vertex $(-3, 0)$ and axis of symmetry $x = -3$; opens downward.
c. Parabola with vertex $(3, 0)$ and axis of symmetry $x = 3$; opens downward.   **2.** $y - 2 = 3(x + 1)^2$
3. $(-3, -5)$ **4.** $x = -3$ **5.** Upward
6. Minimum; 5

818   Selected Answers

Pages 399–401, Chapter Review

1. $(x + 5)^2 + (y - 1)^2 = 4$

3. Graph is circle with center $(1, 3)$, radius 2, and the region inside.

5. $(y - 1)^2 = (x - 0)^2 + (y - 2)^2$ or $y - \dfrac{3}{2} = \dfrac{1}{2}x^2$

7. $(1, -3); x = 1; (1, -2); y = -4; 4;$ upward

9. Graph is ellipse with center : $(1, 0)$, vertices: $(4, 0)$, $(-2, 0), (1, 4), (1, -4)$. **11.** Graph is hyperbola with vertices: $(0, 2), (0, -2);$ asymptotes: $y = 2x, y = -2x;$ opens upward and downward. **13.** $\dfrac{x^2}{9} - \dfrac{y^2}{16} = 1$

15a. Hyperbola   **b.** parabola

   c. Ellipse   **d.** Circle

17. $\{(-6, -8), (2, 0)\}$ **19.** $\{(1, 0), (-1, 0)\}$

21. 4 cm; 7 cm

Page 401, Chapter 9 Self-Test

1. $(x + 1)^2 + (y - 2)^2 = 25$ **2.** Graph is circle with center $(0, 3)$, radius 3, and the region inside.   **3.** $x + 4$ for $x, y - 5$ for y **4.** $y = \dfrac{1}{4}(x + 3)^2$ **5.** Graph is a parabola with vertex $(-1, 4)$, axis of symmetry $x = -1$; opens upward   **6.** $\dfrac{x^2}{16} + \dfrac{y^2}{9} = 1$ **7.** $(2\sqrt{7}, 0)$, $(-2\sqrt{7}, 0)$ **8.** Graph is ellipse with center $(-2, 0)$; vertices $(-4, 0), (0, 0), (-2, 3), (-2, -3)$

9. $\dfrac{y^2}{25} - \dfrac{x^2}{11} = 1$ **10.** Graph is hyperbola in 2nd and 4th quadrants.   **11.** Graph is hyperbola with vertices $(4, 0)$, $(-4, 0)$; opens to the right and left.   **12.** Circle

13. Ellipse   **14.** Parabola   **15.** Hyperbola

16. $\dfrac{(x - 1)^2}{9} - \dfrac{(y + 2)^2}{81} = 1$ **17.** $\{(4, -2), (-2, 4)\}$

18. $\{(4, 2), (4, -2)\}$ **19.** 8 and 11   **20.** $-1, -2$

21. $-5, 2$

Pages 402–403, Practice for College Entrance Tests

1. C   **2.** D   **3.** A   **4.** B   **5.** D   **6.** B   **7.** A

8. E   **9.** B   **10.** C   **11.** C

Pages 403–405, Cumulative Review (Chapters 7–9)

1. True   **3.** 12   **5.** $2\sqrt{7}$ **7.** $2\sqrt{5}$ **9.** $\dfrac{\sqrt{10xy}}{6y}$

11. No   **13.** $\{3\}$ **15.** $\dfrac{\sqrt[3]{18}}{6}$ **17.** $\dfrac{5\sqrt{y}}{y}, y > 0$

19. $\{\pm 3\sqrt{2}\}$ **21.** $\left\{ \dfrac{7}{2}, -\dfrac{1}{2} \right\}$ **23.** 45   **25.** $2\sqrt{10}$

27. $3 - 7i$ **29.** $14 + 5i$ **31.** $-\dfrac{1}{3} - \dfrac{1}{3}i$

33. Two irrational roots   **35.** $\{-1, 1, 2i, -2i\}$

37. One at $(0, 0)$ **39.** Vertex: $(2, 0)$; axis of symmetry: $x = 2$; upward.

41.

43. Maximum; $(3, 5)$

45. $(x + 4)^2 + (y - 3)^2 = 36$

47. $y - 2 = \dfrac{1}{8}(x + 4)^2$

49.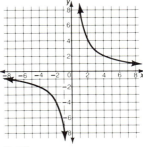

51. $\dfrac{x^2}{9} + \dfrac{y^2}{1} = 1$

53. $\dfrac{x^2}{16} - \dfrac{y^2}{9} = 1$

55.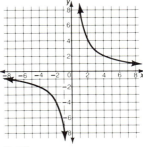

57. Ellipse   **59.** $\{(-2, 3), (3, 2)\}$

61. $\{(-2\sqrt{5}, -1), (-2\sqrt{5}, 1), (2\sqrt{5}, -1), (2\sqrt{5}, 1)\}$

Chapter 10

Page 410, Classroom Exercises

1. Yes   **2.** No   **3.** Yes   **4.** 5   **5.** 1   **6.** 2   **7.** 17

8. -118 **9.** -7 **10.** 478   **11.** -2 **12.** $-\dfrac{7}{16}$

Pages 410–411, Written Exercises

1. No   **3.** Yes   **5.** No   **7.** 3   **9.** 4   **11.** 1

13. $5x + 15$ **15.** $-x^2 + x + 3$ **17.** $-x$ **19.** 36

21. 1254   **23.** -36 **25.** 2   **27.** 11   **29.** 60

31.

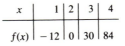

x	-4	-3	-2	-1	0
$f(x)$	-12	0	0	-6	-12

x	1	2	3	4
$f(x)$	-12	0	30	84

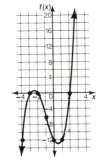

33. $-1, 0, 1$

35.

x	-4	-3	-2	-1	0
$h(x)$	280	72	0	-8	0

x	1	2	3	4
$h(x)$	0	-8	0	72

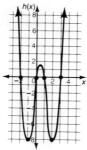

37.

x	-2	-1	0	1	2
$P(x)$	-105	-9	3	-9	15

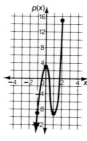

39.

x	-4	-3	-2	-1	0	1	2	3	4
$g(x)$	112	41	6	-5	-4	-3	-14	-49	-120

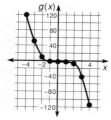

41.

x	-4	-3	-2	-1	0	1	2	3	4
$P(x)$	-10	-4	0	2	2	0	-4	-10	-18

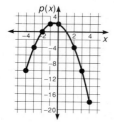

43. 0

45.

x	-5	-4	-3	-2	-1
$f(x)$	-5096	-1938	-600	-140	-24

x	0	1	2	3	4	5
$f(x)$	-6	-8	0	120	646	2184

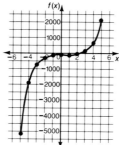

Page 411, Review Exercises
1. $1.35 \cdot 10^{15}$ **2.** $-8x + 10$
3. $x^3 + 6x^2 + 12x + 8$ **4.** $2x(x + 2y)$
5. $(a + b)(c + d)$ **6.** $2(a + 3b)(a - 3b)$
7. $(5x + 1)(x + 3)$ **8.** $\{1, -7\}$

Page 414, Classroom Exercises
1. $2x^3 + 3x^2 + 14x + 40$; 126   **2.** $4x^2 - 8x + 12$; -18
3. A factor   **4.** Not a factor

Pages 414–416, Written Exercises
1. $x^2 - 5x - 9$; -8 **3.** $2x^2 - 11x + 36$; -115
5. $5x^2 - 3x + 6$; -4 **7.** $2x^3 + 13x^2 + 60x + 240$;
960   **9.** $x^3 - 8$; 0   **11.** $x^4 + 3x^3 + 4x - 1$; 1
13. A factor   **15.** Not a factor   **17.** A factor
19. A factor   **21.** $x^3 + 2x^2 + 5$
23. $x^4 - 3x^3 + 5x + 1$ **25.** $x^4 - 12$
27. $(x - 2)(x^2 + 7x + 8) + 8$
29. $(x - 4)(5x^2 + 20x + 86) + 324$ **31.** 357
33. $a + b + c + d + e + f$ **35.** f **37.** 2   **39.** 8
41. 4   **43a.** $x + 2$, remainder 3   **b.** $x + 2 + \dfrac{3}{x + 1}$

c. $x + 2 + \dfrac{3}{x} - \dfrac{3}{x^2} + \dfrac{3}{x^3} - \dfrac{3}{x^4} \cdots$

45. $\dfrac{6x^3 - 9x^2 - 10x - 2}{2x + 1}$ is equivalent to

$\dfrac{3x^3 - \dfrac{9}{2}x^2 - 5x - 1}{x + \dfrac{1}{2}}$. To show that $(2x + 1)$ is a factor of

$6x^3 - 9x^2 - 10x - 2$, divide both the function and divisor by 2 (the leading coefficient).

$$
\begin{array}{r|rrrr}
-\dfrac{1}{2} & 3 & -\dfrac{9}{2} & -5 & -1 \\
& & -\dfrac{3}{2} & 3 & 1 \\
\hline
& 3 & -6 & -2 & 0
\end{array}
$$

Since the remainder is 0, $\left(x + \dfrac{1}{2}\right)$ is a factor of

$\left(3x^3 - \dfrac{9}{2}x^2 - 5x - 1\right)$, so $(2x + 1)$ is a factor of $(6x^3 - 9x^2 - 10x - 2)$.

Page 416, Review Exercises

1. $5a^{-1}bc^{-2}$ **2.** $\dfrac{ab}{a+b}$ **3.** $\dfrac{x}{6}$ **4.** $\dfrac{-2x^3 + 3}{3x^2}$

5. $\{1\}$ **6.** 66 h, 79.2 h **7.** 20

Page 416, Self-Quiz 1

1. $2x^3 - 19x^2 + 60x - 63; 3; 2$
2. $-3a^4 + 3a^3 - 25a^2 + 4a - 28; 4; -3$ **3.** 11 **4.** 17
5.

x	-2	-1	0	1	2
$f(x)$	4	-2	0	-2	4

6. $2x^2 - 2x - 2$, remainder -3 **7.** -1
8. $2x^5 + 5x^4 - 3x^3 - 4x^2 - 11x + 3 = (x + 3)(2x^4 - x^3 - 4x + 1)$

Page 419, Classroom Exercises

1. $x^4 - 6x^3 + 8x^2 + 6x - 9 = 0$ **2.** $\{2, 1 \pm 2i\}$
3. $\{-3, 1, 2\}$ **4.** $\{-2, 3, \pm\sqrt{2}i\}$

Pages 419–421, Written Exercises

1. $x^4 - 10x^2 + 9 = 0$ **3.** $x^4 + 2x^3 - x^2 - 2x = 0$
5. $x^4 + 10x^3 + 35x^2 + 50x + 24 = 0$
7. $(x + 3)(x - 1)^2(x - 4)^2 = 0$
9. $(2x - 1)(x + 1)^4 = 0$ **11.** $\{-3, -2, 2\}$
13. $\{-4, 2, 3\}$ **15.** $\{-4, -2, 2, 4\}$ **17.** $\{1, -2\}$
19. $\{2, 3 \pm \sqrt{5}\}$ **21.** $\{3, \pm 2\sqrt{2}\}$
23. $\left\{-3, \dfrac{-3 + \sqrt{5}}{2}\right\}$ **25.** $\{2, \pm 2i\}$ **27.** $\{1, 1 \pm \sqrt{3}i\}$
29. $\{-5, -1 \pm \sqrt{5}i\}$ **31.** False **33.** True
35. True **37.** $\pm 1, \pm 5, \pm\dfrac{1}{2}, \pm\dfrac{5}{2}$ **39.** $\left\{\dfrac{1}{2}, \dfrac{2}{3}, \dfrac{3}{2}\right\}$
41. $\left\{-\dfrac{1}{2}, \dfrac{3}{2}, \dfrac{5}{2}\right\}$

Page 421, Review Exercises

1. 1.6 **2.** $3|x|\sqrt{2}$ **3.** $\sqrt{2}$ **4.** $\sqrt[3]{x^2}, x \neq 0$ **5.** $\dfrac{\sqrt[3]{6}}{2}$
6. 16 **7.** $\{2\}$ **8.** -8

Page 426, Classroom Exercises

1. Four real roots **2.** Three real roots, one with multiplicity 2 **3.** One is between -2 and -1, one is between -1 and 0, one is between 0 and 1.
4. Between -3 and -2, 1 and 2, and 2 and 3

Pages 427–428, Written Exercises

1. Three real **3.** One real, two imaginary
5. Two real, one with multiplicity 2 **7.** Roots are between -3 and -2, -1 and 0, and 0 and 1. **9.** Roots

are between -1 and 0, and 0 and 1. **11.** Roots are between -1 and 0, 0 and 1, 1 and 2. **13.** Roots are between -2 and -1, -1 and 0, 1 and 2. **15.** There is a root between -1 and 0. **17.** Roots are between -2 and -1, 0 and 1, 1 and 2. **19.** There is a root between 0 and 1.

21.   **23.**

25. If the polynomial equation has a root with an odd-number multiplicity (3, 5, 7, etc.), then the root is not a point of tangency. For example, the function $(x - 1)^2(x + 3)^3 = 0$ has two multiple roots, 1 and -3. The multiple root 1 is a point of tangency, while at the multiple root -3 the graph crosses the x-axis.
27. $-1, 3, 4$ **29.** $-4, -2, 1, 2$ **31.** $-2, -1, 2$; two imaginary roots **33.** $\left\{-\dfrac{2}{3}, \dfrac{2}{3}, \dfrac{3}{2}\right\}$ **35.** $\left\{-\dfrac{1}{2}, \dfrac{1}{2}\right\}$

Page 428, Review Exercises

1. $\{3 \pm \sqrt{5}\}$ **2.** $\left\{\dfrac{2 \pm \sqrt{19}}{3}\right\}$ **3.** $-12i$ **4.** $4 + 9i$
5. $\dfrac{6 + 17i}{25}$ **6.** Two imaginary roots **7.** $\{\pm\sqrt{3}, \pm i\}$
8. $\{4, 100\}$ **9.** Yes; $y = x^2 - 8x + 19$

Page 429, Self-Quiz 2

1. $x^3 - 5x^2 + 3x + 9 = 0$ **2.** $x^2 - x - 2 = 0$; 2 and -1
3. $\{-1, \pm\sqrt{5}\}$ **6.**
4. Two real roots, a and j; two imaginary roots.
5. Between -3 and -2, -1 and 0, and 0 and 1

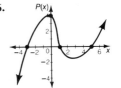

Page 429, Computer Extension

1. No **3.** $\{-1.5, 0.2, 0.3\}$

Pages 432–433, Classroom Exercises

1. Yes **2.** No **3.** $f^{-1}(x) = -\dfrac{1}{3}x + \dfrac{4}{3}$ **4.** No
5. Yes **6.** No **7.** No

Pages 433–434, Written Exercises

If $f(g(x)) = g(f(x)) = x$, then f and g are inverses.
1. $3\left(\dfrac{1}{3}x - 2\right) + 6 = \dfrac{1}{3}(3x + 6) - 2 = x$
3. $\dfrac{2}{3}\left(\dfrac{3}{2}x + 18\right) - 12 = \dfrac{3}{2}\left(\dfrac{2}{3}x - 12\right) + 18 = x$
5. $(\sqrt{x})^2 = \sqrt{x^2} = x, x \geq 0$ **7.** Yes **9.** No

11. Yes **13.** $f^{-1}(x) = \frac{1}{3}x - 5$ **15.** $f^{-1}(x) = 3x - 9$

17. $f^{-1}(x) = -\frac{1}{3}x - 6$ **19.** $f^{-1}(x) = -\frac{1}{6}x + \frac{4}{3}$

21. $f^{-1}(x) = x$ **23.** $f^{-1}(x) = \frac{1}{x}$, $x \neq 0$, $f^{-1}(x) \neq 0$

25. No **27.** Yes **29.** No

31a. $f^{-1} = \{(x, y): y = \frac{3}{2}x - 9\}$ **33a.** $f^{-1} = \{(x, y): y = \sqrt{x}, x \geq 0, y \geq 0\}$

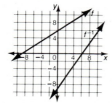

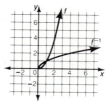

b. Yes   **b.** Yes

35a. $f^{-1} = \{(x, y): y = \frac{12}{x}, x \neq 0, y \neq 0\}$ **37a.** $f^{-1} = \{(x, y): y = -x\}$

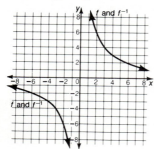

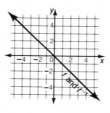

b. Yes   **b.** Yes

b. Yes   **39.** -3 **41.** 1

Pages 434–435, Review Exercises

1. $(x - 4)^2 + (y + 5)^2 = 9$

2. $y - 4 = \frac{1}{8}(x - 3)^2$; vertex: $(3, 4)$

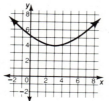

3. $\frac{(x - 5)^2}{9} + \frac{(y + 3)^2}{25} = 1$

4. Foci: $(5, 0)$, $(-5, 0)$; vertices: $(4, 0)$, $(-4, 0)$; asymptotes: $y = \frac{3}{4}x$, $y = -\frac{3}{4}x$

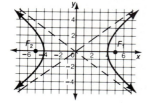

822   Selected Answers

5. Hyperbola: $\frac{(x + 2)^2}{1} - \frac{(y - 3)^2}{1} = 1$; center: $(-2, 3)$; vertices: $(-3, 3)$, $(-1, 3)$; foci $(-2 + \sqrt{2}, 3)$, $(-2 - \sqrt{2}, 3)$

Pages 436–437, Chapter Review

1. $-x^3 + 4x^2 + 2x - 7$; 3; -1 **3.** -14

5. $2x^3 - 3x^2 + 8x - 1$; -3 **7.** 8 **9.** $\{-3, -2, -1, 2\}$

11. Two real roots and two imaginary roots.

13. If f and g are inverses, then $f(g(x)) = g(f(x)) = x$.

$\frac{1}{3}(3x + 6) - 2 = 3\left(\frac{1}{3}x - 2\right) + 6 = x$

Pages 437–438, Chapter 10 Self-Test

1. $-a^4 - a^3 + 5a^2 + 4a - 4$; 4; -1 **2.** 18

3.

x	-3	-2	-1	0	1	2	3
$f(x)$	-16	0	4	2	0	4	20

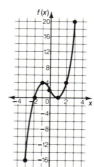

4. 16 **5.** -3

6. Because $f(1) = 0$. $(x - 1)$ is a factor.

7. $x^3 + 3x^2 - 4 = 0$

8. $\left\{-2, \frac{1 \pm \sqrt{3}i}{2}\right\}$

9. Between 1 and 2

10.

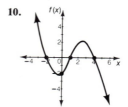

11. $f^{-1}(x) = \sqrt[3]{x}$

12. -1

13. Since $f(g(x)) = g(f(x)) = x$, the functions are inverses.

$\frac{1}{6}(6x - 5) + \frac{5}{6}$

$= 6\left(\frac{1}{6}x + \frac{5}{6}\right) - 5 = x$

Pages 438–439, Practice for College Entrance Tests

1. B **2.** C **3.** E **4.** D **5.** A **6.** E **7.** C

8. C **9.** A **10.** D **11.** E **12.** B

Chapter 11

Page 443, Classroom Exercises

1. a, because it does not contain the point $(0, 1)$; c, because it includes negative y-values. **2.** $\{4\}$

Pages 443–445, Written Exercises

1.

y	$\dfrac{1}{9}$	$\dfrac{\sqrt{3}}{9}$	$\dfrac{1}{3}$	$\dfrac{\sqrt{3}}{3}$	1	$\sqrt{3}$	$\sqrt[3]{9}$	3	$3\sqrt{3}$	9

3.

y	9	$3\sqrt{3}$	3	$\sqrt{3}$	1	$\dfrac{\sqrt{3}}{3}$	$\dfrac{\sqrt[3]{3}}{3}$	$\dfrac{1}{3}$	$\dfrac{\sqrt{3}}{9}$	$\dfrac{1}{9}$

5.

y	$\dfrac{4}{25}$	$\dfrac{2\sqrt{10}}{25}$	$\dfrac{2}{5}$	$\dfrac{\sqrt{10}}{5}$	1	$\dfrac{\sqrt{10}}{2}$	$\dfrac{\sqrt[3]{50}}{2}$	$\dfrac{5}{2}$	$\dfrac{5\sqrt{10}}{4}$	$\dfrac{25}{4}$

7 and 9. Graphs of (a) are all increasing functions. Graphs of (b) are all decreasing functions. The graphs of (a) and (b) intersect at point $(0, 1)$.   **11.** $\{1.2\}$
13. $\{0.7\}$ **15.** $\{1.6\}$ **17.** $\{-0.8\}$ **19.** $\{1.2\}$
21. $\left\{\dfrac{1}{2}\right\}$ **23.** $\{-2\}$ **25.** $\{1\}$ **27.** $\left\{-\dfrac{5}{2}\right\}$
29. $\{-3\}$ **31.** $\{-6\}$ **33.** $\left\{\dfrac{1}{5}\right\}$ **35.** $\left\{\dfrac{5}{2}\right\}$
37. $\{-4\}$ **39.** $\left\{\dfrac{3}{4}\right\}$ **41.** $\left\{\dfrac{6}{5}\right\}$

43. Graph (b) translates (a) 3 units left. Graph (c) translates (a) 1 unit right.
45. Graph (b) translates (a) 2 units up. Graph (c) translates (a) 2 units down.

47.

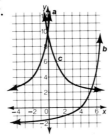

49. b; increasing   **51.** a; decreasing   **53.** Yes
55. Yes   **57.** Yes

Page 445, Review Exercises

1. $1.08 \cdot 10^{12}$ **2.** $x^2 - x - 9$ **3.** $a^3 + 6a^2 + 12a + 8$
4. $5ab(2b - c)$ **5.** $2(n + 3)(n - 3)$ **6.** $(3x + 4)(x - 1)$
7. $\{-6, 1\}$ **8.** $\dfrac{4}{3}\pi(r_2 - r_1)(r_2^2 + r_2 r_1 + r_1^2)$

Page 449, Classroom Exercises

1. $\log_6 216 = 3$ **2.** $\log_{25} 5 = \dfrac{1}{2}$ **3.** $3^4 = 81$
4. $16^{0.5} = 4$ **5.** 2   **6.** 5   **7.** 7   **8.** c

Pages 449–450, Written Exercises

1. $\log_2 32 = 5$ **3.** $\log_{10} 100{,}000{,}000 = 8$
5. $\log_7 2401 = 4$ **7.** $2^{10} = 1024$ **9.** $10^{0.845} \approx 7$
11. $7^{1.277} \approx 12$ **13.** $\{4\}$ **15.** $\{81\}$ **17.** $\{1\}$ **19.** $\{100\}$
21. $\{5\}$ **23.** $\{3\}$ **25.** $\left\{\dfrac{3}{2}\right\}$ **27.** $\{500\}$ **29.** $\left\{\dfrac{14}{3}\right\}$

31.

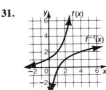

33.

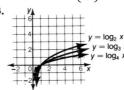

35.

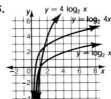

37. $\{\log_7 3\}$
39. $\{4 \log_3 6\}$
41. $\{20\}$ **43.** $\left\{\dfrac{1}{2}\right\}$

45. Let (i) $b^x = y$, $b > 1$. Then (ii) $\log_b y = x$, by definition of a logarithmic function. Substitute b^x for y in equation (ii). Then $\log_b b^x = x$, $b > 1$.

Page 450, Review Exercises

1. $\dfrac{3}{x^2 y}$ **2.** $\dfrac{a + b}{a - b}$; $a \neq \pm b$ **3.** $\dfrac{12}{x^2}$; $x \neq 0$, $y \neq 0$
4. $\dfrac{x^2 - x + 3}{3x^2}$; $x \neq 0$ **5.** $\left\{11\dfrac{1}{9}\right\}$ **6.** 120 ohms   **7.** 4

Page 450, Self-Quiz 1

1.

x	2	1	$\dfrac{1}{2}$	0	$-\dfrac{1}{2}$	-1
y	81	9	3	1	$\dfrac{1}{3}$	$\dfrac{1}{9}$

2. $\{2.6\}$ **3.** $\{-1.3\}$ **4.** $\left\{-\dfrac{1}{2}\right\}$ **5.** $\left\{\dfrac{1}{4}\right\}$
6a. $\log_5 625 = 4$ **6b.** $\log_{\frac{1}{2}} 8 = -3$ **7a.** $3^5 = 243$
7b. $10^{-4} = 0.0001$ **8.** $\left\{\dfrac{3}{2}\right\}$

Page 452, Classroom Exercises

1. 0.7781   **2.** 0.9542   **3.** 0.1761   **4.** 0.9030
5. $\log_b \pi + 2 \log_b r$ **6.** $\dfrac{1}{2}\log_2 a + \dfrac{1}{2}\log_2 b$ **7.** $\log_{10} Prt$
8. $\log_5 \dfrac{x^2}{y}$

Pages 453–454, Written Exercises

1. 1.27699   **3.** 1.65418   **5.** 0.47088   **7.** -0.82709
9. 0.46039   **11.** -0.47088 **13.** $\log_4 x + \log_4 y$
15. $\log_{10} M - \log_{10} N$ **17.** $\log_7 x + \log_7 y - \log_7 z$
19. $\dfrac{1}{5}\log_3 a$ **21.** $t \log_b 2 + 1$ **23.** $2 \log_6 x - 1$
25. $-2 - 2\log_4 y$ **27.** $-3 - 3\log_2 x$ **29.** $\log_5 \dfrac{x}{y}$
31. $\log_7 r^2 \pi$ **33.** $\log_c \dfrac{w^3}{v^2}$ **35.** $\log_{10} 10\sqrt{x}$
37. $\log_a \dfrac{\pi r^2 h}{3}$ **39.** True   **41.** True   **43.** True
45. True   **47.** True   **49.** $\{14\}$ **51.** $\{2\}$ **53.** $\{5\}$
55. $\{36\}$ **57.** $\{1.5\}$ **59.** $\{6\}$

61. Prove $\log_b\left(\dfrac{m}{n}\right) = \log_b m - \log_b n$

$m = b^{\log_b m}$ and $n = b^{\log_b n}$

$\log^b\left(\dfrac{m}{n}\right) = \log_b\left(\dfrac{b^{\log_b m}}{b^{\log_b n}}\right)$

$= \log_b(b^{\log_b m \,-\, \log_b n})$

$= \log_b m - \log_b n$

63. $\log_e i = \log_e I - \dfrac{Rt}{L}$

Rewrite $-\dfrac{Rt}{L}$ as a logarithm.

$\log_e i = \log_e I + \log_e e^{-\frac{Rt}{L}}$

Simplify.

$\log_e i = \log_e(Ie^{-\frac{Rt}{L}})$

$i = Ie^{-\frac{Rt}{L}}$

Page 454, Review Exercises

1. 3.2 **2.** $5|a|\sqrt{2}$ **3.** $5\sqrt{2}$ **4.** $2 - \sqrt{2}$ **5.** $\dfrac{5\sqrt[3]{3}}{3}$
6. 600 cm^2 **7.** $2\sqrt{5}$ **8.** {4} **9.** $2\sqrt[3]{2}$

Page 457, Classroom Exercises

1. 0.6355 **2.** 0.8129 **3.** 0.8451 **4.** 3.4771
5. $0.4771 - 2$ **6.** 0.7781 **7.** {3,000,000} **8.** {0.02}
9. {0.00003}

Pages 457–458, Written Exercises

1. 0.7126 **3.** 0.7782 **5.** 0.6042 **7.** 6.7782
9. 5.6042 **11.** -2.2218
13a. ≈ 0.3010 **b.** ≈ 0.3979 **c.** ≈ 0.6990
15a. ≈ 0.6021 **b.** ≈ 0.3010 **c.** ≈ 0.9031
17a. 2(0.4771) **b.** ≈ 0.9542 **19a.** 3(0.4771) **b.** ≈ 1.4314
21. {0.7945} **23.** {2.7945} **25.** {7.7945}
27. $\{-0.2055\}$ **29.** $\{-4.2055\}$ **31.** {4.91}
33. {491} **35.** {0.491} **37.** {0.00491} **39.** {2.58}
41. {2,580,000} **43.** {6.8506} **45.** $4a - b$
47. $x - 2b$ **49.** 2.3909 **51.** 0.8891 **53.** 2
55. $1 + 2\log x$ **57.** 63,095,734 **59.** 100,000,000,000

Page 459, Review Exercises

1. $\{-2 \pm \sqrt{10}\}$ **2.** $\left\{\dfrac{1 \pm \sqrt{15}}{2}\right\}$ **3.** $9i$ **4.** $\sqrt{13}$
5. $-3 + 5i$ **6.** $\dfrac{12 - 8i}{13}$ **7.** 2; irrational **8.** {100}
9. $y = 2x^2 - 2x + 2$
10. $(-5, 3); x = -5$; opens upward
11. $(1, -2); x = 1$; opens downward
12. Maximum of 4

Page 459, Extension

1. ≈ 1.780 **2.** ≈ 1.741 **3.** 0.3847 **4.** 3.3923

Page 462, Classroom Exercises

1. {0.3679} **2.** $\emptyset$ **3.** {2.0000} **4.** 2.2619

Pages 462–463, Written Exercises

1. 1.5728 **3.** 1.9879 **5.** 4.2711 **7.** -0.6733
9a. ≈ 1.0986 **b.** ≈ 1.3863 **c.** ≈ 2.4849
11a. ≈ 1.6094 **b.** ≈ 1.3863 **c.** ≈ 2.9957
13a. 3(0.6931) **b.** ≈ 2.0794 **15a.** 2(1.3863)
b. ≈ 2.7726 **17.** {0.9163} **19.** {1} **21.** {8.92}
23. {3.34} **25.** {4.5549} **27.** {54.2} **29.** 1.2925
31. 1.6826 **33.** 1.1606 **35.** $\ln C = \ln \pi + \ln d$
37. $\ln S = \ln 4 + \ln \pi + 2 \ln r$
39. $\ln V = -1.0986 + \ln b + \ln h$
41. $\ln t = \ln 2 + \ln \pi + \dfrac{1}{2}(\ln l - \ln g)$
43. 1.2528 **45.** 0.4055 **47.** 0.6931

Page 464, Review Exercises

1. $(x - 2)^2 + (y + 3)^2 = 16$
2. $(x + 5)^2 + (y - 4)^2 = 16$
3. $y^2 = x^2 + (y - 4)^2$ or $y - 2 = \dfrac{1}{8}x^2$
4. $(-3, 5); x = -3$ **5.** Graph has vertex $(0, -4)$; axis
of symmetry $x = 0$; opens upward **6.** $\dfrac{x^2}{25} + \dfrac{y^2}{9} = 1$

Page 464, Self-Quiz 2

1. 1.1631 **2.** -0.2365 **3.** 0.4421 **4.** $\dfrac{1}{2}(\log_a x - \log_a y)$
5. $\log_3\dfrac{x}{2y}$ **6.** $\log_7 a^3(\sqrt{b})$ **7.** 1.6042 **8.** -0.0269
9. {2.8768} **10.** {26.4} **11.** {0.360} **12.** {2.97}
13. 1.8083 **14.** 0.6419 **15.** {4.48} **16.** {2}
17. 2.0302

Page 467, Classroom Exercises

1. $x = \dfrac{\log 55}{\log 7}$ **2.** $\left\{\dfrac{12}{5}\right\}$

Pages 467–468, Written Exercises

1. {2.10} **3.** {1.59} **5.** {5.09} **7.** {1.71} **9.** {3.54}
11. {0.93} **13.** 10 years **15.** 9 years, 3 months
17. $\approx 4.7\%$ **19.** \$3966.44 **21.** (2.7, 6.5) **23.** (1.4, 0.7)
25. (2.27, 38.60) Form for answers for ex. 25–31 may
vary. **27.** $n = \dfrac{\log y - \log c}{\log x}$ **29.** $n = \dfrac{\log k - \log p}{\log V}$
31. $n = \dfrac{\log l - \log a + \log r}{\log r}$ **33.** $t = \dfrac{L}{R}(\ln I - \ln i)$
35. $\left\{\dfrac{10}{3}\right\}$ **37.** $\{-5\}$ **39.** $\{-1, 3\}$ **41.** $\dfrac{\log 45}{\log 15}$
43. $\dfrac{\log 7 \pm \sqrt{(\log 7)^2 + 8 \log 4 \log 7}}{2 \log 4}$

Page 468, Review Exercises

1. $\dfrac{x^2}{64} - \dfrac{y^2}{36} = 1$ **2.** Graph is in 1st and 3rd quadrants.
3. Graph has foci $(\sqrt{13}, 0)$, $(-\sqrt{13}, 0)$; vertices $(3, 0)$,
$(-3, 0)$; asymptotes $y = \dfrac{2}{3}x$, $y = -\dfrac{2}{3}x$ **4.** Hyperbola

5. $(x - 2)^2 + y^2 = 4$; circle with center $(2, 0)$, radius 2   **6.** $\{(0, 4), (-5, 9)\}$ **7.** $\{(0, 5), (-5, 0)\}$ **8.** 8 and 6 or -6 and -8

Page 471, Classroom Exercises
1. $\{8\}$ **2.** $\{5\}$ **3.** $\{3\}$ **4.** $\{10,000,000,000\}$

Pages 471–472, Written Exercises
1. $\{9\}$ **3.** $\left\{\dfrac{33}{2}\right\}$ **5.** $\left\{\dfrac{7}{2}\right\}$ **7.** $\{6\}$ **9.** $\{2, 4\}$
11. $\{2\}$ **13.** $\{10\}$ **15.** $\{1000\}$ **17.** 10^a **19.** $\dfrac{10^x}{2}$
21. $a10^d$ **23.** e^a **25.** e^{2+j} **27.** $n = \dfrac{r^4}{s}$
29. $A = 4\pi r^2$ **31.** \$604.14   **33.** \$704.14
35. \$800.43   **37.** \$732.22   **39.** No   **41.** $M = \dfrac{35.5}{W^{0.224}}$
43. ≈ 0.028 **45.** $t = 0.05$; equal to it   **47.** $\{0.01, 10\}$

Page 473, Review Exercises
1. $3x^2 + x - 10$ **2.** -2 **3.** $x^2 - 4x + 5$ **4.** It is.

Page 473, Self-Quiz 3
1. $\{-2.00, 2.00\}$ **2.** $\{3.16\}$ **3.** $\{-5, 1\}$ **4.** 9 years
5. $\{3\}$ **6.** $\{6\}$ **7.** $c = \dfrac{100}{t}$ **8.** 80

Page 473, Extension
$2^{216,091} - 1 \approx 7.461 \cdot 10^{65,049}$ This number has 65,050 digits.

Page 476, Classroom Exercises
1. 0.277   **2.** -0.277 **3.** Growth in 1, decay in 2

Pages 476–479, Written Exercises
1. \$1648.72   **3.** \$2718.28   **5.** \$2718.28   **7.** \$606.53
9. \$135.34   **11.** ≈ 8.7 **13.** ≈ 5.8 **15.** 0.0322
17. 0.00105   **19.** ≈ 6.6 **21.** ≈ 21.9 **23.** 18.4h
25. ≈ 300 s   **27.** 1980: 23,700,000; 1990: 28,084,500
29a. 137   **b.** 0.90   **c.** 103.90°C   **31.** $\approx 15,056.5$ years ago

Page 479, Review Exercises
1. Between -3 and -2, 0 and 1, 2 and 3
2.   **3.** Yes

Pages 481–483, Chapter Review
1.
$y = \left(\dfrac{1}{2}\right)^x$ $y = 2^x$
3a. $\{0.2\}$ **b.** $\{1.3\}$
5a. $\log_7 16,807 = 5$
b. $\log_{\frac{1}{3}} 81 = -4$
7. $\{81\}$ **9.** $\left\{\dfrac{1}{3}\right\}$
11. True   **13.** False
15. $\log_b x - \log_b y - \log_b z$ **17.** $\left\{\dfrac{1}{3}\right\}$ **19.** 2   **21.** $\{4.70\}$

23. $\{1.2238\}$ **25.** $\dfrac{\ln 25}{\ln 4}$ **27.** $\{2\}$ **29.** 7   **31.** $\emptyset$
33. ≈ 20.9

Pages 483–484, Chapter 11 Self-Test
1a. all real numbers; $\{y{:}y > 0\}$ **b.** Increasing
2.
3. 2 and 3
4. $\log_{64} 4 = \dfrac{1}{3}$
5. $6^{-2} = \dfrac{1}{36}$ **6.** $\{4\}$
7. $\{8\}$
8a. 0.4307   **b.** 1.3652
9. $\left\{\dfrac{1}{4}\right\}$
10. $\log_b x + \log_b y - 2\log_b z$ **11.** $\{2.6551\}$ **12.** $\{79.6\}$
13. 1.3646   **14.** $\dfrac{\log 24}{\log 8}$ **15.** $\{2\}$ **16.** 18
17. $x = e^{y-4}$ **18.** $\{8\}$ **19.** ≈ 7251 **20.** -0.231

Pages 484–485, Practice for College Entrance Tests
1. C   **2.** A   **3.** B   **4.** A   **5.** C   **6.** B   **7.** A
8. D   **9.** E   **10.** D   **11.** E   **12.** D   **13.** D

Chapter 12

Page 489, Classroom Exercises
1. 4; 46   **2.** 1; $\sqrt[15]{15}$ **3.** $\dfrac{1}{3}$; $\dfrac{15}{17}$ **4.** Yes; -2 **5.** No
6. Yes; 4   **7.** 53   **8.** $7\dfrac{1}{2}$, 10, $12\dfrac{1}{2}$

Pages 490–492, Written Exercises
1. 5; 50   **3.** 2; 200   **5.** 2; 20   **7.** 1; 100   **9.** No
11. Yes   **13.** No   **15.** Yes   **17.** 77   **19.** 15
21. 10   **23.** 104   **25.** 49   **27.** -21 **29.** $-5, -1, 3$
31. $-6, -8, -10$ **33.** 1   **35.** 65   **37.** 23, 26, 29
39. $-2\dfrac{1}{4}, -2\dfrac{1}{2}, -2\dfrac{3}{4}$ **41.** 1 point   **43a.** 0232   **b.** 0308
c. 94th   **d.** 726   **45.** $4n - 1$ **47a.** 604   **b.** 321st
c. 654th   **d.** $a_n = 3n + 4$ **49a.** $63\dfrac{1}{5}$ **b.** 93   **c.** 132
d. $a_n = \dfrac{1}{5}n + 63$ **51a.** $\dfrac{q}{p}$ **b.** $100 - 24\dfrac{q}{p}$
c. $a_n = \dfrac{q}{p}n + \left(100 - 25\dfrac{q}{p}\right)$ **d.** $100 + \dfrac{q}{p}$
53. $a_n = dn + (a_1 - d)$; slope: d; vertical-axis intercept: $a_1 - d$

Page 492, Review Exercises
1. $\{3 \pm \sqrt{5}\}$ **2.** $\{1 \pm \sqrt{6}\}$ **3.** $-8i$ **4.** 5
5. $-1 - 9i$ **6.** 20   **7.** i **8.** 2 irrational
9. $\{\pm \sqrt{3}, \pm i\}$

Page 492, Calculator Extension

1.–3. Answers will vary.

Page 495, Classroom Exercises

1. Yes, 2 **2.** No **3.** Yes, 3 **4.** 0.625 **5.** $-\dfrac{1}{8}$
6. 6 or -6

Pages 495–497, Written Exercises

1. Geometric **3.** Other **5.** Arithmetic
7. Arithmetic **9.** Geometric **11.** Other **13.** 648
15. 80 **17.** -486 **19.** -24.3 **21.** 10 or -10
23. $\dfrac{1}{4}$ or $-\dfrac{1}{4}$ **25.** 12 and 36 **27.** -12 and -48
29. 177.147 cm **31a.** 8.5% **b.** $10,000(1.085)^{20}$
33. $10,000(0.5)^{50}$ cm^2; $\approx 8.88 \times 10^{-12}$ cm^2
35. $\{\pm 2\sqrt{3}\}$ **37.** $\{5\dfrac{1}{3}\}$ **39.** about 6.3%

Page 497, Extension

1. 5, 20, 50, 110; other **2.** 256, 16, 4, 2; other
3. 256, 64, 16, 4; geometric **4.** $t_1 = 5; t_{n+1} = t_n - 3$;
$t_n = 8 - 3n$ **5.** $t_1 = 5; t_{n+1} = -3t_n; t_n = 5(-3)^{n-1}$

Page 498, Review Exercises

1.
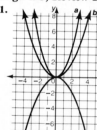
2.
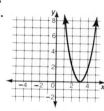

3. $y - 5 = -\dfrac{1}{4}(x - 4)^2$
4. $y + 4 = 2(x - 6)^2$

5. Minimum: 5 **6.** Maximum: 4

Page 498, Self-Quiz 1

1a. 1; -15 **b.** $\dfrac{1}{2}, \dfrac{9}{10}$ **2a.** 19 **b.** 72 **3.** 16, 13, 10
4. $\dfrac{2}{3}$ and $\dfrac{7}{3}$ **5a.** Other **b.** Geometric **c.** Arithmetic
6a. $\dfrac{81}{16}$ **b.** -27 **7.** 12 or -12 **8.** 22nd **9.** $4096

Page 501, Classroom Exercises

1. Geometric **2.** Other
3. $2 + 5 + 8 + 11 + 14 + 17 = 57$
4. $5 + 10 + 15 + 20 = 50$
5. $2^1 + 2^2 + 2^3 + 2^4 + 2^5 + 2^6 + 2^7 = 254$
6. $4 + 7 + 10 + 13 + 16 + 19 = 69$

Pages 501–502, Written Exercises

1. Other **3.** Arithmetic **5.** Geometric
7. $2 + 4 + 8 + 16 + 32 = 62$
9. $4 + 2 + 0 + (-2) + (-4) = 0$

826   Selected Answers

---

11. $1 + 2 + 3 + 1 + 2 = 9$ **13.** $6 + 12 + 18 = 36$
15. $1 + 0 + (-1) + (-2) = -2$
17. $4 \cdot 2^0 + 4 \cdot 2^1 + 4 \cdot 2^2 + 4 \cdot 2^3 = 60$ **19.** $\displaystyle\sum_{k=1}^{5} 2k$
21. $\displaystyle\sum_{k=1}^{5} 2^k$ **23.** $\displaystyle\sum_{k=1}^{5} 3_k$ **25.** $\displaystyle\sum_{k=1}^{48} 4 + 2k$ or $\displaystyle\sum_{k=3}^{50} 2k$
27. $\displaystyle\sum_{k=1}^{100} \dfrac{1}{k}$ **29.** Arithmetic **31.** Other
33. Geometric **35.** Arithmetic **37.** 16 **39.** $\dfrac{15}{16}$
41. False **43.** False
45. $\displaystyle\sum_{k=1}^{n} (a + k) = (a + 1) + (a + 2) + \cdots + (a + n)$

$= an + (1 + 2 + \cdots + n) = an + \displaystyle\sum_{k=1}^{n} k$

47. $\displaystyle\sum_{k=1}^{n-1} k(k + 1) = 1(1 + 1) + 2(2 + 1) + \cdots +$

$(n - 1)[(n - 1) + 1] = 1(2) + 2(3) + \cdots + n^2 - n =$

$2(2 - 1) + 3(3 - 1) + \cdots + n(n - 1) = \displaystyle\sum_{i=2}^{n} i(i - 1)$

Page 502, Review Exercises

1. $(x - 3)^2 + (y - 4)^2 = 25$ **2.** $x = \dfrac{1}{16}y^2$
3. $\dfrac{x^2}{25} + \dfrac{y^2}{9} = 1$ **4.** Foci: $(0, \sqrt{13}), (0, -\sqrt{13})$;

asymptotes: $y = \dfrac{3}{2}x, y = -\dfrac{3}{2}x$ **5.** Hyperbola

Page 505, Classroom Exercises

1. 56 **2.** 30 **3.** 111 **4.** 600 **5.** 420

Pages 505–507, Written Exercises

1. 108 **3.** 33 **5.** -1620 **7.** 8475 **9.** 5730
11. 9315 **13.** 820 **15.** 1905 **17.** $-\dfrac{725}{2}$ **19.** 45
21a. 2500 **b.** 2550 **c.** 1275 **23a.** 29 **b.** 390
25a. 75 b. 315 **27.** 85 **29a.** $814\dfrac{2}{7}$ **b.** $132\dfrac{8}{21}$
31a. 4 **b.** $6\dfrac{2}{3}$ **33a.** 36 **b.** 12 **35a.** 240 ft
b. 1296 ft **37.** $\{20\}$
39. Let $S_n = 1 + 3 + 5 + \ldots (2n - 3) + (2n - 1)$ be
the sum of the first n positive odd integers.

$$S_n = \frac{n(a_1 + a_n)}{2}$$
$$= \frac{n(1 + 2n - 1)}{2}$$
$$= \frac{n(2n)}{2}$$
$$= n^2$$

Page 507, Review Exercises

1. -5 **2.** $x^2 + 2x + 3$; 10
3. $(x + 1)(x - 1)(x - 3)(x - 3) = 0$

Page 510, Classroom Exercises

1. $\dfrac{1365}{4096}$ 2. $\dfrac{728}{81}$ 3. 255

Pages 510–511, Written Exercises

1. $6(2^{10} - 1)$ 3. $\dfrac{5}{2}(3^{21} - 1)$ 5. $16 - \left(\dfrac{1}{2}\right)^{45}$

7. $\dfrac{3}{4}(3^{24} - 1)$ 9. $5(2^6 - 1)$ 11. $\dfrac{128}{3}\left(1 - \left(\dfrac{1}{4}\right)^{15}\right)$

13. $\dfrac{2}{3}(1 - 2^{20})$ 15. $2\left(\left(\dfrac{1}{2}\right)^{100} - 1\right)$ 17. 7,777,770

19. 8420   21. $\dfrac{31}{32}$ 23. 42   25a. 2^{63} b. $\displaystyle\sum_{k=0}^{63} 2^k$

c. $2^{64} - 1$ 27. 1,594,322   29. $\dfrac{665}{729}$ 31. 2,097,151

33. 699,051   35. $-699,051$ 37. 20,971,500

39. 41,943,020   41. $-13,981,020$ 43. 6

Page 512, Review Exercises

1.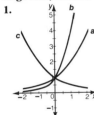

2. $\{-2\}$
3. $\log_2 16 = 4$
4. $\{8\}$
5. 0.9030
6. $\left\{\dfrac{8}{5}\right\}$
7. 1.9542
8. -0.9542

Page 512, Self-Quiz 2

1a. Arithmetic   b. Geometric

2. $-1 + (-2) + (-3) + (-4) = -10$ 3. $\displaystyle\sum_{k=1}^{11} \dfrac{5}{k}$

4. 5025   5. 2500   6a. 173   b. 5   7. $\dfrac{189}{16}$ 8. 378

Page 515, Classroom Exercises

1. Converges   2. Converges   3. $\dfrac{16}{3}$ 4. $\dfrac{10}{19}$

5. $0.5 + 0.05 + 0.005 + 0.0005 + \dots;\ \dfrac{5}{9}$

Pages 515–518, Written Exercises

1. Does not   3. Does   5. Does not   7. Does

9. 9   11. $\dfrac{1000}{9}$ 13. $\dfrac{3}{2}$ 15. 27   17. $\dfrac{2}{3}$ 19. 14

21. 10   23. $-\dfrac{10}{3}$ 25. $\dfrac{23}{99}$

27. $0.4 + 0.04 + 0.004 + \dots = \dfrac{4}{9}$

29. $0.9 + 0.09 + 0.009 + \dots = 1$

31. $0.23 + 0.0023 + 0.000023 + \dots = \dfrac{23}{99}$

33. $0.124 + 0.000124 + 0.000000124 + \dots = \dfrac{124}{999}$

35a. ≈ 0.005 cm   b. 3800 cm (2000 cm down and 1800 cm up)   37. 140 ft   39. Converges to 1.61803

41. $\dfrac{2}{3}$ 43a. 9×10^{-14} cm   b. 2^{50} c. ≈ 180 cm

d. ≈ 115 cm

Page 518, Review Exercises

1. $\{2\}$ 2. $\{1\}$ 3. $x = \dfrac{\log 2}{\log 1.08}$ or ≈ 9.0 4. ≈ 9.6
5. $\{22\}$ 6. $\{250\}$

Page 518, Computer Extension

1. 100   2. 10 FOR K = 1 TO 100; 10,000
3. 10 FOR K = 1 TO 30; 20 X = (1/2) ↑ K; 0.999999999

Pages 520–521, Chapter Review

1. 1; 255   3. It is not   5. 55   7. $3\dfrac{1}{2}, 5, 6\dfrac{1}{2}$

9. Geometric   11. Geometric   13. ≈ 5249

15. $5 + 8 + 11 + 14$ 17. $\dfrac{43}{30}$ 19. 55,450   21. 90

23. $\dfrac{50}{9}(10^4 - 1)$ 25. 40   27. Does not   29. 5

Pages 521–522, Chapter 12 Self-Test

1. 75   2. 104   3. Other   4. Geometric
5. Arithmetic   6. Arithmetic   7. $t_n = 2n + 6$
8. 5, 9, 13   9. 28 or -28 10. 27   11. 30
12. $-2 + (-4) + (-6) + (-8) + (-10)$ 13. 610
14. 15,150   15. 160   16. 14   17. $210\dfrac{7}{16}$ 18. 378
19. 12   20. $\dfrac{14}{33}$

Pages 522–523, Practice for College Entrance Tests
1. D   2. C   3. C   4. B   5. A   6. C   7. C
8. B   9. C   10. B   11. C

Pages 524–525, Cumulative Review (Chapters 10–12)
1. 337   3. 9   5. 8   7. $(x + 2)(x - 3)(x - 4)^2 = 0$
9. Roots between -2 and -1, 0 and 1, and 2 and 3.

11. $f^{-1}(x) = \dfrac{1}{5}x + \dfrac{1}{5}$ 13.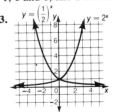

15. Decreasing   17. $\{1\}$
19. $\log_5 625 = 4$
21. $6^2 = 36$ 23. $2\log_3 x + \log_3 y$ 25. 2.6990
27. $\{50\}$ 29. $\{\approx 3.5264\}$ 31. $\{\approx 7.01\}$
33. $t = \dfrac{1}{r}\ln A$ 35. $\{3\}$ 37. 7; 255   39. 94
41. Arithmetic   43. $\dfrac{128}{2187}$
45. $5 + 3 + 1 + (-1) = 8$ 47. 380
49. $\dfrac{32}{3}\left(1 - \dfrac{1}{46}\right) = \dfrac{1365}{128}$ 51. $\dfrac{5}{33}$

Chapter 13

Page 528, Classroom Exercises
1. 4　**2.** 75　**3.** 36

Pages 528–530, Written Exercises
1. 18　**3.** 2688　**5.** 40　**7.** 180　**9.** 12　**11.** 2^{10}
13. 450　**15.** 96　**17.** 210　**19.** 150　**21.** 1024
23. 204　**25.** 17,576,000　**27.** 240　**29.** 255

Page 530, Review Exercises
1. -4　**2.** $2|a|b\sqrt{5b}; b \geq 0$　**3.** $7 + 4\sqrt{3}$　**4.** $\sqrt[3]{2}$
5. $1 + \sqrt{x}; x \neq 1, x \geq 0$　**6.** $2(\sqrt[3]{9x}); x \neq 0$　**7.** 13
8. $\{3, 4\}$　**9.** $2^{\frac{1}{2}} + 5^{\frac{1}{3}}$

Page 531, Extension

	1.	2.
Business	—	23.3%, 84°
Social Sciences	9.5%, 34°	3.6%, 13°
Health	6.5%, 23°	6.5%, 23°
Engineering	9.7%, 35°	7.5%, 27°
Education	8.8%, 32°	26.5%, 95°
Other fields	41.3%, 149°	32.7%, 118°

3. Answers will vary.

Page 535, Classroom Exercises
1. 720　**2.** 336　**3.** 840　**4.** 4　**5.** 3024; 6561　**6.** 3150

Pages 535–537, Written Exercises
1. 718　**3.** 120　**5.** 24　**7.** 56　**9.** 504　**11.** 120
13. 4032　**15.** 210　**17.** 120　**19.** 2520　**21.** 180
23. 125　**25.** 504　**27.** 362,880　**29.** 720　**31.** 72
33. 210; 100; 24　**35.** 5040　**37.** 12

Page 537, Review Exercises
1. $\{-3 \pm \sqrt{2}\}$　**2.** $\{-1 \pm \sqrt{5}\}$　**3.** $\{\pm 9i\}$
4. $-6 + i$　**5.** $\dfrac{3 - 4i}{5}$　**6.** $\{2, -2, 3i, -3i\}$　**7.** $\{4\}$
8. $y = 0x^2 - 6x - 6$; no　**9.**
10. 280; maximum, 6

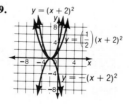

Page 539, Classroom Exercises
1. 15　**2.** 15　**3.** 56　**4.** Combinations　**5.** Permutations　**6.** Combinations　**7.** Permutations　**8.** $\dfrac{52!}{39!13!}$

Pages 539–541, Written Exercises
1. 35　**3.** 84　**5.** 18　**7.** 18,564　**9.** 1　**11.** 840
13. 192　**15.** 2520　**17.** 252　**19.** 10　**21.** 3136
23. 300　**25.** 36

27. A-A, A-B, A-O, A-AB,　**29.** 7920　**31.** 39
B-A, B-B, B-O, B-AB,
O-A, O-B, O-O, O-AB
AB-A, AB-B, AB-O,
AB-AB

33. $\displaystyle {}_nC_{n-r} = \frac{n!}{(n - (n - r))!(n - r)!}$
$$= \frac{n!}{r!(n - r)!}$$
$$= \frac{n!}{(n - r)!r!}$$
$$= {}_nC_r$$

Page 541, Review Exercises
1. $(x - 4)^2 + (y - 3)^2 = 25$　**2.** $\dfrac{x^2}{9} + \dfrac{y^2}{4} = 1$
3. Graph is hyperbola with vertices $(4, 0)$, $(-4, 0)$; asymptotes $y = x$, $y = -x$

Page 541, Self-Quiz 1
1. 11　**2.** 210　**3.** 120　**4.** 336　**5.** 792

Page 545, Classroom Exercises
1. 1　**2.** 0　**3.** $\dfrac{5}{8}$　**4.** $\dfrac{2}{9}$　**5.** $\dfrac{3}{91}$

Pages 545–547, Written Exercises
1. $\dfrac{4}{455}$　**3.** $\dfrac{12}{91}$　**5.** $\dfrac{24}{91}$　**7.** $\dfrac{1}{13}$　**9.** $\dfrac{1}{26}$　**11.** $\dfrac{11}{13}$
13. $\dfrac{3}{28}$　**15.** $\dfrac{15}{58}$　**17a.** $\dfrac{5}{6}$　**b.** $\dfrac{1}{4}$　**c.** $\dfrac{3}{4}$　**19.** $\dfrac{1}{2}$
21. $\dfrac{1}{16}$　**23.** $\dfrac{3}{8}$　**25.** $\dfrac{15}{16}$　**27.** Complementary events include all outcomes in the sample space; mutually exclusive events may not.　**29.** 0　**31.** $\dfrac{1}{18}$

Page 547, Review Exercises
1. $(x - 2)^2 + (y + 1)^2 = 9$　**2.** $(x + 1)^2 + y^2 \geq 4$
3. $(-1, -2); x = -1; (-1, -1); y = -3$

4. $(x - 12)^2 + (y - 5)^2 = 169$; Circle with center $(12, 5)$ and radius 13
5. $\{(4, -3), (-3, 4)\}$

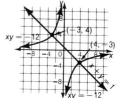

6. $\{(\sqrt{3}, 2), (\sqrt{3}, -2), (-\sqrt{3}, 2), (-\sqrt{3}, -2)\}$

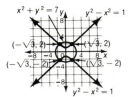

Page 550, Classroom Exercises

1. $\frac{1}{6}$ **2.** $\frac{1}{36}$

Pages 550–552, Written Exercises

1. 0.24 **3.** 0.10 **5.** 0.25 **7.** 0.00 **9.** $\frac{1}{12}$ **11.** $\frac{1}{4}$

13. $\frac{1}{6}$ **15.** $\frac{1}{4}$ **17.** $\frac{13}{204}$ **19.** $\frac{1}{17}$ **21.** $\frac{25}{102}$ **23.** $\frac{38}{245}$

25. $\frac{12}{49}$ **27.** 0.04 **29.** 0.16 **31.** 0.30 **33.** 0.027

35. 5:1 **37.** 2:1 **39.** $\frac{1}{8}$ **41.** $\frac{5}{6}$ **43.** $\frac{13}{48}$ **45.** 0.2

47. 0.4 **49.** 0.8 **51.** No **53.** $\frac{1}{216}$ **55.** $\frac{1}{72}$

57. ≈ 0.0271

Page 552, Review Exercises

1. 2 **2.** $2x^2 + 3; -1$ **3.** $\{1, -1, -6\}$
4. Single root at $(a, 0)$; double root at $(c, 0)$

5. $g^{-1}(x) = -\frac{x+3}{2}$ **6.** $f^{-1}(x) = \frac{1}{2}x + \frac{5}{2}$ **7.** No

Page 554, Classroom Exercises

1. $\frac{1}{6}$ **2.** $\frac{11}{36}$ **3.** $\frac{1}{18}$ **4.** $\frac{5}{12}$ **5.** $\frac{1}{4}$ **6.** $\frac{3}{4}$

Pages 555–556; Written Exercises

1. $\frac{1}{56}$ **3.** $\frac{9}{112}$ **5.** $\frac{19}{140}$ **7.** $\frac{1}{2}$ **9.** $\frac{1}{4}$ **11.** $\frac{2}{5}$ **13.** $\frac{1}{2}$

15. $\frac{2}{5}$ **17.** $\frac{3}{10}$ **19.** $\frac{2}{5}$ **21.** $\frac{1}{2}$ **23.** $\frac{20}{50}, \frac{15}{50}, \frac{5}{50}, \frac{10}{50}$

25. Yes; A or L is $a + b + c$; A is $a + b$, L is $b + c$ and A and L is b. **27.** A and B are independent and not mutually exclusive. **29.** 0.85

Page 556, Review Exercises

1.

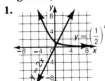

2. $\{6\}$ **3.** ≈ 0.9030
4. ≈ -0.1761
5. ≈ -1.0458
6. ≈ 1.5850 **7.** $a = be^2$

Page 556, Self-Quiz 2

1a. $\frac{2}{3}$ **b.** $\frac{8}{9}$ **2.** $\frac{13}{18}$ **3.** $\frac{1}{19}$ **4a.** No **b.** 0.1 **5.** $\frac{1}{2}$

6. $\frac{1}{5}$ **7.** $\frac{3}{5}$ **8.** $\frac{47}{100}$

Page 560, Classroom Exercises

1. $x^4 + 4x^3y + 6x^2y^2 + 4xy^3 + y^4$ **2.** $\frac{3}{8}$ **3.** No, the trials are not independent **4.** $10(0.2)^2(0.8)^3 \approx 0.20$

Pages 560–561, Written Exercises

1. $x^7 + 7x^6y + 21x^5y^2 + 35x^4y^3 + 35x^3y^4 + 21x^2y^5 + 7xy^6 + y^7$ **3.** $45a^8b^2$ **5.** $10ab^9$ **7.** $100a^{99}b$

9. $161,700a^3b^{97}$ **11.** $\frac{5}{16}$ **13.** $\frac{5}{32}$ **15.** $\frac{25}{72}$ **17.** $\frac{2}{27}$

19. $\frac{215}{216}$ **21.** $120\left(\frac{3}{4}\right)^7\left(\frac{1}{4}\right)^3$ **23.** $120\left(\frac{3}{4}\right)^7\left(\frac{1}{4}\right)^3 +$
$45\left(\frac{3}{4}\right)^8\left(\frac{1}{4}\right)^2 + 10\left(\frac{3}{4}\right)^9\left(\frac{1}{4}\right) + \left(\frac{3}{4}\right)^{10}$ **25.** $\left(\frac{1}{4}\right)^{10} +$
$10\left(\frac{3}{4}\right)\left(\frac{1}{4}\right)^9 + 45\left(\frac{3}{4}\right)^2\left(\frac{1}{4}\right)^8$ **27.** $\frac{100!}{70!30!}(0.3)^{30}(0.7)^{70}$

29. $\frac{100!}{0!100!}(0.3)^0(0.7)^{100} + \frac{100!}{99!1!}(0.3)(0.7)^{99} +$
$\frac{100!}{98!2!}(0.2)^2(0.7)^{98} + \frac{100!}{97!3!}(0.3)^3(0.7)^{97}$ **31.** ≈ 0.531

33. ≈ 0.886 **35.** More than 50 heads
37. All 5: $(0.2)^5$; At least 4: $(0.2)^5 + 5(0.2)^4(0.8)$; At least 3: $(0.2)^5 + 5(0.2)^4(0.8) + 10(0.2)^3(0.8)^2$; At least 2: $(0.2)^5 + 5(0.2)^4(0.8) + 10(0.2)^3(0.8)^2 + 10(0.2)^2(0.8)^3$; At least 1: $(0.2)^5 + 5(0.2)^4(0.8) + 10(0.2)^3(0.8)^2 + 10(0.2)^2(0.8)^3 + 5(0.2)(0.8)^4$; At least 0: $(0.2)^5 + 5(0.2)^4(0.8) + 10(0.2)^3(0.8)^2 + 10(0.2)^2(0.8)^3 + 5(0.2)(0.8)^4 + (0.8)^5$

Page 561, Review Exercises
1. 177,147 **2.** 910 **3.** $\frac{3}{2}$

Page 562, Extension

1.

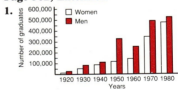

2. Answers may vary considerably.

	1920	1930	1940	1950	1960	1970	1980
Men	28%	28%	23%	71%	38%	36%	34%
Women	7%	13%	13%	18%	18%	25%	27%

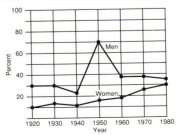

Pages 564–566, Chapter Review

1. 120 **3.** 15 **5.** $\frac{1}{90}$ **7.** 11 **9.** 83,160 **11.** 180

13. 16,744 **15.** $\frac{3}{4}$ **17.** Dependent **19.** 0.096 **21.** $\frac{1}{4}$

23. $\frac{992}{3125}$

Pages 566–567, Chapter 13 Self-Test

1. 540 **2.** 200 **3.** 336 **4.** 60 **5.** 720 **6.** 121

7. 15 **8.** 30,030 **9.** $\frac{1}{16}$ **10.** $\frac{2}{3}$ **11.** 0.36 **12.** $\frac{1}{6}$

13. $P(A) + P(B) = P(A \text{ or } B)$ **14.** $220x^9y^3$ **15.** $\frac{15}{64}$

Page 567, Practice for College Entrance Tests

1. C **2.** A **3.** E **4.** D **5.** D **6.** E **7.** C **8.** B

Chapter 14

Page 571, Classroom Exercises

1.

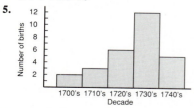

4	6 9
5	3 6 6 7 8
6	0 0 3 3 4 4 5 6 7 7 7 8
7	0 1 1 2 3 4 7 8 8 9
8	0 3 5 8
9	0 0

2. 67 **3.** Line graph **4.** Circle graph **5.** Bar graph
6. Circle graph **7.** Line graph **8.** Circle graph
9. Line graph

Pages 572–574, Written Exercises

1.

3. 170	6 7
171	1 3 6
172	2 4 6 6 7 9
173	0 1 2 4 4 5 5 6 7 7 7 9
174	1 2 3 4 6

5.

7.

9.

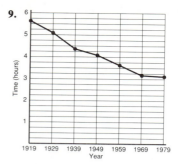

Winning time is decreasing; 3:00 and 3:30; The estimates are inaccurate because the segments do not represent actual data.

11.

13.

15.

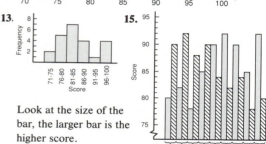

Look at the size of the bar, the larger bar is the higher score.

17. 53% **19.** $1414

Page 574; Review Exercises

1. $\{-12, 2\}$ **2.** $\left\{\frac{3 + \sqrt{29}}{2}\right\}$ **3.** $-8i$ **4.** 5

5. $-1 + 5i$ **6.** $\frac{3 - i}{2}$

Pages 576–577, Classroom Exercises

1a. 16 **b.** 13.5; 19 **c.** 5.5 **d.** 16 **2a.** 80.5
b. 75; 85.5 **c.** 10.5 **d.** 17
3.

Pages 577–578, Written Exercises

1. 15 **3.** 97 **5a.** 89 **b.** 82.5; 94.5 **c.** 15 **d.** 12
e.

7a. 66 **b.** 64; 66 **c.** 9 **d.** 2
e.

9a. 50.5 **b.** 48; 52 **c.** 4 **d.** 9 **11a.** 55
b. 51; 58 **c.** 7 **d.** 27
13a. 1731.5 **b.** 1726; 1739 **c.** 13.5 **d.** 43

15. Median: 41; lower quartile: 38; upper quartile: 46; range: 28

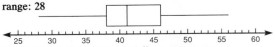

17. Both quartiles; interquartile range; range

19. All of them

Page 578, Review Exercises

1. 2 real rational roots   **2.** $(y - 1) = 2(x - 3)^2$

3. $(x - 4)^2 + (y + 3)^2 = 25$ **4.** $x - 1 = \frac{1}{4}y^2$

5. $\frac{x^2}{9} + \frac{y^2}{25} = 1$ **6.** $y = \frac{4}{5}x; y = -\frac{4}{5}x$

7. Ellipse; $\frac{(x - 2)^2}{9} + \frac{(y - 1)^2}{4} = 1$ **8.** $\{(2, 2)\}$

Page 580, Classroom Exercises

Mean: 14; mean absolute deviation: 2.57; variance: 14.86; standard deviation: 3.85

Page 581, Written Exercises

1. 15; 15; 1.7, 4; 2   **3.** 14; 12; 2.8; 1; 1

5. 22; 20; 4.5; 25; 5   **7.** 17   **9.** 6   **11.** 13   **13.** 9

15. Yes   **17.** Mean: 32; variance: ≈16; standard deviation: ≈4   **19.** Mean is increased by 5; standard deviation is unchanged.   **21.** Mean and standard deviation are divided by 2.   **23.** 1960–1964

25. 1920–1924

27.

	Mean	Standard deviation
1920–1924	47.6	7.6
1940–1944	34	5.02
1960–1964	48.6	6.95

Page 582, Review Exercises

1. -5 **2.** -6 **3.** $\{3, 1 \pm \sqrt{2}\}$

4. Between -2 and -1, 0 and 1, and 2 and 3   **5.** $-\frac{10}{3}$

Page 582, Self-Quiz 1

1.

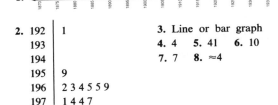

2.

192	1
193	
194	
195	9
196	2 3 4 5 5 9
197	1 4 4 7

3. Line or bar graph

4. 4   **5.** 41   **6.** 10

7. 7   **8.** ≈4

Page 583, Computer Extension

1a. 7; 2.236   **b.** 7; 2.236   **c.** 7; 2.646   **d.** 7; 1.732

2a. 10; 2; 1.414   **b.** 10; 8; 2.828   **c.** 10; 32; 5.657

d. 10; 50; 7.071   **3.** Answers will vary; $\{10, 20, 25, 30, 40\}$; $\{13.8, 13.84, 25, 36.16, 36.2\}$; etc.

Pages 587–588, Classroom Exercises

1. c   **2.** a   **3.** d   **4.** b

5.–6

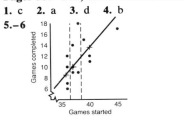

7. 14 games

Pages 588–590, Written Exercises

1a.–b.

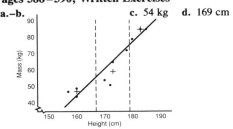

c. 54 kg   **d.** 169 cm

3a.–b.

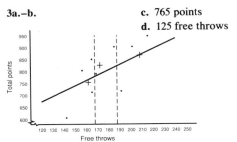

c. 765 points   **d.** 125 free throws

5. a   **7.** b

9a.–b.

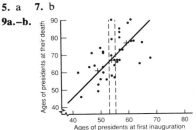

c. Positive; near 0

d. Only fair

11a.–b.

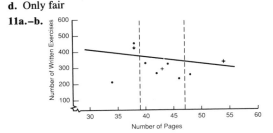

c. 355 pages

13. Answers vary; height and weight
15. Answers vary; distance from school and age

Page 590, Review Exercises
1. $\{-5\}$ **2.** $10^3 = 1000$ **3.** 2.097 **4.** 0.66
5. $\dfrac{\log 25}{\log e}$ **6.** ≈ 9 years **7.** $x = a \cdot 10^b$ **8.** ≈ 13.4

Page 593, Classroom Exercises
1. Greater than 3.7 **2.** -0.6 **3.** 0.84

Pages 593–594, Written Exercises
1. 50% **3.** 2.5% **5.** 68% **7.** 13.5% **9.** 32%
11. More than 2 standard deviations below mean.
13. More than 1 standard deviation above the mean.
15. Above the mean or less than 1 standard deviation below the mean **17.** More than 2 standard deviations from the mean. **19.** 1 **21.** 0.5 **23.** 3 **25.** 3 **27.** 0.34 **29.** 0.135 **31.** 0.84 **33.** 0.68 **35.** 0.975 **37.** 0.5 **39.** 0 **41.** -0.3 **43.** Line OK **45.** Check line **47.** To judge whether other nurps manufactured at the same time are defective **49.** The original cost may be great enough to cover the replacements based on the number of miles that original owners are expected to drive. **51.** The original cost may be great enough to cover the cost of replacing half of them.

Page 594, Review Exercises
1. 37 **2.** 20,000,000 **3.** $\sum_{i=1}^{11} (2i - 1)$ **4.** 235
5. $\dfrac{1}{4}(1 - (-3)^8)$ **6.** $\dfrac{3}{2}$

Page 595, Self-Quiz 2
1.–2.

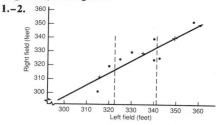

3. 328 ft **4.** 1.5 **5.** 68%

Page 598, Classroom Exercises
1. No, the sampling was not random. **2.** Answers will vary. Pick every tenth girl who enters the school.
3. Answers will vary. Choose 10 numbers, each number represents a coin toss. Let even numbers represent heads and odd numbers represent tails.

Pages 599–600, Written Exercises
1. 980, 186, 191 **3.** 241, 848, 633 **5.** 839, 821, 382

7. 91, 03, 61, 17, 24, 16, 69, 77, 18, 45; 0.3
9. 32, 91, 21, 87, 64, 17, 33, 89, 02, 55; 0.2 **11.** No
13. 6 **15.** 3 **17.** 2 **19.** 6 **21.** Fairly good. The average of the samples is 3.88. **23.** 21, 09, 74, 77, 25, 73, 35, 95, 02, 05; 0.5 **25.** 50, 39, 35, 22, 84, 42, 57, 90, 05, 66; 0.3 **27.** 0.37 **29.** 0.25 **31.** Answers will vary.

Page 601, Review Exercises
1. 64 **2.** 120 **3.** 15 **4.** $\dfrac{1}{3}$ **5.** $\dfrac{4}{15}$ **6.** $\dfrac{7}{8}$ **7.** $\dfrac{5}{16}$

Pages 603–604, Chapter Review
1.

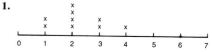

3. 2 **5.** 26 **7.** 14 **9.** 42 **11.** 17.6 **13.** 9
15.

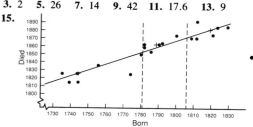

17. 1887 **19.**

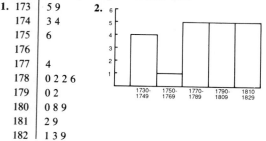

21. 2.5% **23.** 81, 14, 73, 70, 83 **25.** 3, 3, 0, 7, 8, 5, 8, 9, 8, 3; 4 heads

Pages 605–606, Chapter 14 Self-Test
1.

173	5 9
174	3 4
175	6
176	
177	4
178	0 2 2 6
179	0 2
180	0 8 9
181	2 9
182	1 3 9

2.

	1730–1749	1750–1769	1770–1789	1790–1809	1810–1829
6					
5			▇	▇	▇
4	▇				
3					
2					
1		▇			

3. 1788 **4.** 1862
5. 1831, 1875 **6.** 79
7.

8. 20 **9.** 25 **10.** 5 **11.** 25 **12.** 0.5

13.–14.

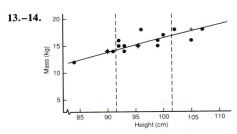

Mass (kg) vs Height (cm)

15. 15 kg **16.** 100 cm **17.** Well below average
18. 55 **19.** 68% **20.** 76–100 **21.** −1.5 **22.** 85
23. 7, 3, 21 **24.** 21, 6, 23 **25.** 5 **26.** 5

Pages 606–607, Practice for College Entrance Tests
1. B **2.** C **3.** A **4.** A **5.** E **6.** D **7.** C
8. C **9.** E **10.** B **11.** C **12.** E

Chapter 15

Pages 611–612, Classroom Exercises
1. −3 **2.** 4 **3.** a_{23} **4.** a_{32} **5.** a_{14} **6.** a_{21}
7. 3×4 **8.** $x = 2, y = -2$ **9.** $\begin{bmatrix} 7 & -5 & 0 \\ 0 & 2 & 7 \end{bmatrix}$

Pages 612–614, Written Exercises
1. 0 **3.** 2 **5.** −3 **7.** b_{31} **9.** b_{32} **11.** b_{21}
13. 3×3 **15.** 3×2 **17.** 1×3 **19.** $\frac{3}{3} \times 4$

21. $x = -3, y = \frac{3}{2}, z = -1$ **23.** $x = -\frac{3}{2}, y = 2, z = \frac{3}{5}$

25. $\begin{bmatrix} -3 & 0 & 1 \\ 10 & -4 & 5 \end{bmatrix}$ **27.** $\begin{bmatrix} 10 & 0 \\ 4\frac{1}{4} & -4 \\ 1 & 3\frac{1}{2} \end{bmatrix}$ **29.** 500

31. 50 **33.** 760 **35.** $\begin{bmatrix} 180 & 80 \\ 940 & 600 \end{bmatrix}$ **37.** 280

39. chairs **41.** $\begin{bmatrix} 6.8 & 1.5 \\ 2.9 & 0.7 \\ 0.4 & 0 \end{bmatrix} = Y$

43. $X + Y = \begin{bmatrix} 3.2 & 1.2 \\ 2.9 & 1.0 \\ 0.7 & 0.2 \end{bmatrix} + \begin{bmatrix} 6.8 & 1.5 \\ 2.9 & 0.7 \\ 0.4 & 0 \end{bmatrix} = \begin{bmatrix} 10 & 2.7 \\ 5.8 & 1.7 \\ 1.1 & 0.2 \end{bmatrix} = Z$

45. $P + Q = \begin{bmatrix} 0 & -7 & 2 \\ 9 & 1 & 0 \end{bmatrix}; Q + P = \begin{bmatrix} 0 & -7 & 2 \\ 9 & 1 & 0 \end{bmatrix};$
So, $P + Q = Q + P$
47. If $A = \begin{bmatrix} a_{11} & a_{12} \\ a_{21} & a_{22} \end{bmatrix}$ and $B = \begin{bmatrix} b_{11} & b_{12} \\ b_{21} & b_{22} \end{bmatrix}$,

then $A + B = \begin{bmatrix} a_{11} + b_{11} & a_{12} + b_{12} \\ a_{21} + b_{21} & a_{22} + b_{22} \end{bmatrix}$

and $B + A = \begin{bmatrix} b_{11} + a_{11} & b_{12} + a_{12} \\ b_{21} + a_{21} & b_{22} + a_{22} \end{bmatrix}$.

Since a_{ij} and b_{ij} are real numbers and real numbers are commutative, $a_{ij} + b_{ij} = b_{ij} + a_{ij}$. Therefore,
$\begin{bmatrix} a_{11} + b_{11} & a_{12} + b_{12} \\ a_{21} + b_{21} & a_{22} + b_{22} \end{bmatrix} = \begin{bmatrix} b_{11} + a_{11} & b_{12} + a_{12} \\ b_{21} + a_{21} & b_{22} + a_{22} \end{bmatrix}$

Page 614, Review Exercises
1. −7 **2.** $3x^2 - 10x + 20$; −28 **3.** $\{1, 2, -5\}$
4. Between −2 and −3, 1 and 2, 2 and 3
5. $f^{-1}(x) = \dfrac{10 - x}{2}$

Page 617, Classroom Exercises
1. $\begin{bmatrix} -6 & -3 \\ 15 & 0 \end{bmatrix}$ **2.** [14] **3.** $\begin{bmatrix} -1 & 4 & 5 \\ -14 & 21 & 16 \end{bmatrix}$ **4.** −1

Pages 618–620, Written Exercises
1. Yes **3.** Yes **5.** No **7.** Yes **9.** Yes **11.** Yes
13. $\begin{bmatrix} 4 & 8 \\ 12 & 16 \end{bmatrix}$ **15.** $\begin{bmatrix} 1 & 4 \\ -3 & -5 \end{bmatrix}$ **17.** [10] **19.** $\begin{bmatrix} 4 \\ -4 \end{bmatrix}$

21. $\begin{bmatrix} 1 & -1 \\ -18 & 20 \end{bmatrix}$ **23a.** $D = \begin{bmatrix} 0.8 & 0.3 & 0.2 \\ 0.2 & 0.1 & 0.05 \end{bmatrix}$

b. $W = \begin{bmatrix} 7.2 & 2.7 & 1.8 \\ 1.8 & 0.9 & 0.45 \end{bmatrix}$ **25a.** $Y = \begin{bmatrix} 10 & 20 & 25 & 6 \\ 8 & 15 & 20 & 10 \end{bmatrix}$

b. $L = \begin{bmatrix} 140 \\ 120 \\ 350 \\ 450 \end{bmatrix}$ **c.** $\begin{bmatrix} 15,250 \\ 14,420 \end{bmatrix}$

27a. [500 1000 3000 4000]
b. 50,000 units of wood; 53,000 units of filler; 102,500 units of fabric; 68,000 units of springs **c.** $\begin{bmatrix} 5 \\ 6 \\ 3 \\ 4 \end{bmatrix}$
d. Style A: $77, Style B: $126, Style C: $117, Style D: $158
e. $1,147,500 **29.** $x = -1, y = 3$

Page 620, Review Exercises
1. $\left\{ -\dfrac{1}{2} \right\}$ **2.** $10^5 = 100,000$ **3.** 0.1761 **4.** 1.7781

5. 1.5850 **6.** ≈5.9 **7.** $a = \dfrac{10^c}{b}$ **8.** ≈5.8

Page 621, Self-Quiz 1
1a. 0 **b.** 9 **c.** −4 **2a.** b_{22} **b.** b_{23} **c.** b_{31}

3. 3×2 **4a.** $\begin{bmatrix} 1 & -4 & -2 \\ 0 & -3 & 8 \\ -6 & -7 & -5 \end{bmatrix}$ **b.** Not defined

5. −2 **6a.** $\begin{bmatrix} 9 & 3 \\ 3 & -27 \\ -5 & 5 \end{bmatrix}$ **b.** Not defined

c. $\begin{bmatrix} -18 & -7 \\ -12 & 49 \\ -16 & 50 \end{bmatrix}$

1–6.

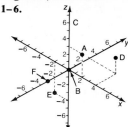

7. The plane containing the three points $(5, 0, 0)$, $(0, 5, 0)$, and $(0, 0, 5)$.

17. $\begin{bmatrix} 39 & 23 \\ 2 & 0 \end{bmatrix}$ **19.** $\begin{bmatrix} 69 & 40 \\ 50 & 29 \end{bmatrix}$ **21.** $\begin{bmatrix} 8 & 20 \\ 24 & -32 \end{bmatrix}$

23. $\begin{bmatrix} 34 & -30 \\ -36 & 94 \end{bmatrix}$ **25.** True **27.** True **29.** False

31. True **33.** False **35.** False **37.** If $A + C = B + C$, then $a_{ij} + c_{ij} = b_{ij} + c_{ij}$ and $a_{ij} = b_{ij}$. Therefore $A = B$

39. $\begin{bmatrix} -3 \\ 11 \\ 12 \end{bmatrix}$ **41.** $\begin{bmatrix} 6 & 2 \\ 16 & 10 \\ 12 & 18 \end{bmatrix}$ **43.** Undefined
45. Undefined

47. $\begin{bmatrix} 4 & 8 & -12 \\ 12 & -8 & 4 \\ 0 & 16 & 24 \end{bmatrix}$ **49.** $\begin{bmatrix} -32 & 36 \\ -48 & -44 \end{bmatrix}$

51. $x = 7, y = -\dfrac{11}{3}, z = \dfrac{7}{4}$ **53.** $x = 0, y = -8, z = -1$
For answer to number **55.**, see below.

Page 625, Classroom Exercises

1. $x = \begin{bmatrix} 1 & 5 \\ -2 & 9 \\ 1 & -6 \end{bmatrix}$ **2a.** A **b.** Z **c.** Z **3.** Let a_{ij} and b_{ij} be corresponding elements in $m \times n$ matrices A and B respectively. The corresponding elements of $k(A + B)$ and $kA + kB$ are $k(a_{ij} + b_{ij})$ and $ka_{ij} + kb_{ij}$ respectively. Since k, a_{ij}, and b_{ij} are real numbers and multiplication of real numbers is distributive over addition, $k(a_{ij} + b_{ij}) = ka_{ij} + kb_{ij}$. Since corresponding elements of $k(A + B)$ and $kA + kB$ are equal, $k(A + B) = kA + kB$. Therefore, scalar multiplication is distributive over the sum of two $m \times n$ matrices.

Page 626, Review Exercises

1. 25, 30, 35, 40, 45 **2.** 3, -6, 12, -24, 48
3. $\sum\limits_{t=1}^{7} t^2$ **4.** 30 **5.** 1950 **6.** 0.333333 **7.** 5

Page 629, Classroom Exercises

1. $\begin{bmatrix} 0 & 1 & 1 & 1 \\ 1 & 1 & 1 & 1 \\ 1 & 1 & 0 & 1 \\ 1 & 1 & 1 & 1 \end{bmatrix}$ **2.** $(1, -3), (5, 2),$ and $(-2, 6)$

Pages 625–626, Written Exercises

1. $\begin{bmatrix} -2 & -5 \\ -6 & 8 \end{bmatrix}$ **3.** $\begin{bmatrix} -5 & 1 \\ 1 & -11 \end{bmatrix}$ **5.** $\begin{bmatrix} 0 & 0 \\ 0 & 0 \end{bmatrix}$ **7.** $\begin{bmatrix} 7 & 4 \\ 5 & 3 \end{bmatrix}$

9. $\begin{bmatrix} 2 & 5 \\ 6 & -8 \end{bmatrix}$ **11.** $\begin{bmatrix} 2 & 5 \\ 6 & -8 \end{bmatrix}$ **13.** $\begin{bmatrix} 0 & 0 \\ 0 & 0 \end{bmatrix}$ **15.** $\begin{bmatrix} 1 & 0 \\ 0 & 1 \end{bmatrix}$

Pages 629–630, Written Exercises

1. $\begin{bmatrix} 0 & 1 & 1 \\ 1 & 0 & 0 \\ 0 & 1 & 0 \end{bmatrix}$ **3.** $\begin{bmatrix} 1 & 1 & 0 & 2 \\ 0 & 0 & 1 & 0 \\ 0 & 0 & 0 & 1 \\ 1 & 0 & 0 & 0 \end{bmatrix}$ **5.** $\begin{bmatrix} 5 \\ 2 \end{bmatrix}$ **7.** $\begin{bmatrix} -4 \\ 0 \end{bmatrix}$

---

55. Let $A = \begin{bmatrix} a_{11} & a_{12} \\ a_{21} & a_{22} \end{bmatrix}$, $B = \begin{bmatrix} b_{11} & b_{12} \\ b_{21} & b_{22} \end{bmatrix}$, and $C = \begin{bmatrix} c_{11} & c_{12} \\ c_{21} & c_{22} \end{bmatrix}$.

$(A \cdot B) \cdot C = \begin{bmatrix} a_{11}b_{11} + a_{12}b_{21} & a_{11}b_{12} + a_{12}b_{22} \\ a_{21}b_{11} + a_{22}b_{21} & a_{21}b_{12} + a_{22}b_{22} \end{bmatrix} \begin{bmatrix} c_{11} & c_{12} \\ c_{21} & c_{22} \end{bmatrix}$

$= \begin{bmatrix} c_{11}(a_{11}b_{11} + a_{12}b_{21}) + c_{21}(a_{11}b_{12} + a_{12}b_{22}) & c_{12}(a_{11}b_{11} + a_{12}b_{21}) + c_{22}(a_{11}b_{12} + a_{12}b_{22}) \\ c_{11}(a_{21}b_{11} + a_{22}b_{21}) + c_{21}(a_{21}b_{12} + a_{22}b_{22}) & c_{12}(a_{21}b_{11} + a_{22}b_{21}) + c_{22}(a_{21}b_{12} + a_{22}b_{22}) \end{bmatrix}$

$= \begin{bmatrix} a_{11}b_{11}c_{11} + a_{12}b_{21}c_{11} + a_{11}b_{12}c_{21} + a_{12}b_{22}c_{21} & a_{11}b_{11}c_{12} + a_{12}b_{21}c_{12} + a_{11}b_{12}c_{22} + a_{12}b_{22}c_{22} \\ a_{21}b_{11}c_{11} + a_{22}b_{21}c_{11} + a_{21}b_{12}c_{21} + a_{22}b_{22}c_{21} & a_{21}b_{11}c_{12} + a_{22}b_{21}c_{12} + a_{21}b_{12}c_{22} + a_{22}b_{22}c_{22} \end{bmatrix}$

$A \cdot (B \cdot C) = \begin{bmatrix} a_{11} & a_{12} \\ a_{21} & a_{22} \end{bmatrix} \begin{bmatrix} b_{11}c_{11} + b_{12}c_{21} & b_{11}c_{12} + b_{12}c_{22} \\ b_{21}c_{11} + b_{22}c_{21} & b_{21}c_{12} + b_{22}c_{22} \end{bmatrix}$

$= \begin{bmatrix} a_{11}(b_{11}c_{11} + b_{12}c_{21}) + a_{12}(b_{21}c_{11} + b_{22}c_{21}) & a_{11}(b_{11}c_{12} + b_{12}c_{22}) + a_{12}(b_{21}c_{12} + b_{22}c_{22}) \\ a_{21}(b_{11}c_{11} + b_{12}c_{21}) + a_{22}(b_{21}c_{11} + b_{22}c_{21}) & a_{21}(b_{11}c_{12} + b_{12}c_{22}) + a_{22}(b_{21}c_{12} + b_{22}c_{22}) \end{bmatrix}$

$= \begin{bmatrix} a_{11}b_{11}c_{11} + a_{11}b_{12}c_{21} + a_{12}b_{21}c_{11} + a_{12}b_{22}c_{21} & a_{11}b_{11}c_{12} + a_{11}b_{12}c_{22} + a_{12}b_{21}c_{12} + a_{12}b_{22}c_{22} \\ a_{21}b_{11}c_{11} + a_{21}b_{12}c_{21} + a_{22}b_{21}c_{11} + a_{22}b_{22}c_{21} & a_{21}b_{11}c_{12} + a_{21}b_{12}c_{22} + a_{22}b_{21}c_{12} + a_{22}b_{22}c_{22} \end{bmatrix}$

Since a_{ij}, b_{ij}, and c_{ij} are real numbers, the distributive property and commutative property of addition hold. Therefore, corresponding elements of $(A \cdot B) \cdot C = A(B \cdot C)$. Therefore, $(A \cdot B) \cdot C = A \cdot (B \cdot C)$ for all 2×2 matrices.

9.

11. $x = y$

13.

15.

17.

19. $\begin{bmatrix} 1 & 0 & 1 \\ 1 & 0 & 0 \\ 0 & 1 & 1 \end{bmatrix}$

21. Number of ways of getting from one point to another by following either one or two arcs.

Page 630, Review Exercises

1. 450   **2.** 720   **3.** 56   **4.** $\dfrac{1}{18}$ **5.** 0.21   **6.** $\dfrac{3}{4}$ **7.** $\dfrac{3}{16}$

Page 633, Classroom Exercises

1. Yes   **2.** $\begin{bmatrix} \dfrac{3}{2} & 2 \\ \dfrac{1}{2} & 1 \end{bmatrix}$ **3.** $\left\{\left(\dfrac{66}{7}, -\dfrac{57}{7}\right)\right\}$

Pages 634–635, Written Exercises

1. Yes   **3.** Yes   **5.** No   **7.** $\begin{bmatrix} 3 & -2 \\ -1 & 1 \end{bmatrix}$ **9.** $\begin{bmatrix} 2 & 8 \\ 3 & 1 \end{bmatrix}$

11. 0; no   **13.** 0; no   **15.** $\left\{\left(\dfrac{1}{2}, -\dfrac{1}{3}\right)\right\}$ **17.** $\{(3, -8)\}$

19. $\{(5, -3)\}$ **21.** $\begin{bmatrix} 1 & 0 \\ 0 & \dfrac{1}{k} \end{bmatrix}$

23. $\begin{bmatrix} 0 & \dfrac{1}{k} \\ \dfrac{1}{k} & 0 \end{bmatrix}$ **25.** $\begin{bmatrix} 0 & 1 \\ 1 & -k \end{bmatrix}$ **27.** $\begin{bmatrix} \dfrac{k}{k^2-1} & \dfrac{-1}{k^2-1} \\ \dfrac{-1}{k^2-1} & \dfrac{k}{k^2-1} \end{bmatrix}$

29. Yes

Page 635, Review Exercises

1.

177	7 8 9 9
178	5
179	0 0 0 1 1 3 4 4 5 7 7 9
180	2 3 9
181	1 3 4
182	0 1 6 6
183	2

2. 19; 13.5; 30; 16.5; 30   **3.** 10; 2.6; 8.8; 2.97

4a.–b.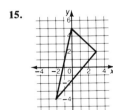

c. 25 points

5a. 0.68   **b.** 0.025
c. 0.475   **d.** 0.16
6a. 60%   **b.** 25%

Page 636, Self-Quiz 2

1. $2A = \begin{bmatrix} 2 & -4 \\ 6 & 8 \end{bmatrix}$, $AB = \begin{bmatrix} -10 & 3 \\ 20 & -1 \end{bmatrix}$, $(2A)B = 2(AB)$

$= \begin{bmatrix} -20 & 6 \\ 40 & -2 \end{bmatrix}$ **2.** $AC = \begin{bmatrix} 1 & 0 \\ 0 & 1 \end{bmatrix} = I$ **3.** False

4. True   **5.** False   **6.** True   **7.** $\begin{bmatrix} 1 & 1 & 1 \\ 0 & 0 & 2 \\ 1 & 1 & 0 \end{bmatrix}$

8. $(2, 3), (0, -1), (-3, -3)$ **9.** No   **10.** Yes

11. $\begin{bmatrix} \dfrac{1}{10} & \dfrac{1}{10} \\ -\dfrac{1}{10} & \dfrac{1}{10} \end{bmatrix}$ **12.** $\begin{bmatrix} \dfrac{3}{5} & -\dfrac{1}{2} \\ -\dfrac{2}{5} & \dfrac{1}{2} \end{bmatrix}$ **13.** $\begin{bmatrix} 2 & 3 \\ 5 & 5 \end{bmatrix}$

14. $\{(3, -4)\}$ **15.** $\{(-3, 6)\}$

Page 638, Classroom Exercises

1. $\{(-2, 3)\}$ **2.** $\{(-1, 3)\}$

Pages 638–639, Written Exercises

1. $\{(5, 3)\}$ **3.** $\{(1, -1)\}$ **5.** $\{(6, 2)\}$ **7.** $\{(2, -1, 3)\}$
9. $\{(1, 0, 3)\}$ **11.** $\{(2, 1, -1)\}$ **13.** $\{(1, 3, -1)\}$
15. $\{(8, -6, 5)\}$ **17.** $\{(2, -3, 4, 2)\}$

Page 639, Review Exercises

1. 55; 82; 37; 45; 66   **2a.** Greater than 157
b. Less than 125   **3a.** 2 below   **b.** 0.5 above
4a. -0.5 **b.** 1.5   **5a.** 85   **b.** 145

Pages 641–642, Chapter Review

1. C   **3.** 4×1 **5a.** b_{12} **b.** b_{11} **c.** b_{22}

7. $\begin{bmatrix} -21 & -3 \\ 9 & -12 \\ 0 & -6 \end{bmatrix}$ **9a.** 4×2 **b.** Not defined

11a. $\begin{bmatrix} 1 & 0 \\ 0 & 1 \end{bmatrix}$ **b.** $\begin{bmatrix} 0 & 0 \\ 0 & 0 \end{bmatrix}$ **13a.** $-A$ **b.** B **c.** Z
d. I

15.

17. $x + 2y = 3$
$2x - y = 10$
19. $\{(-8, 13, -5)\}$

1. 2×3 **2.** $[b_{11} \ b_{12} \ b_{13} \ b_{14}]$ **3.** $-8, 5$

4. $\begin{bmatrix} 6 & -9 & 4 \\ 2 & 9 & -1 \end{bmatrix}$ **5.** $\begin{bmatrix} 6 & 12 \\ -18 & 30 \end{bmatrix}$ **6.** 2×3

7. $\begin{bmatrix} 1 & 0 & 0 \\ 3 & -2 & -1 \\ -5 & 10 & 5 \end{bmatrix}$ **8.** $\begin{bmatrix} 0 & 24 & 4 \\ -25 & -9 & -16 \end{bmatrix}$

9. $\begin{bmatrix} 1 & 0 & 0 \\ 0 & 1 & 0 \\ 0 & 0 & 1 \end{bmatrix}$ **10.** $x = 2, y = 3, z = 10$

11. $Y = [5 \ \ 1 \ \ -4]$ **12a.** AB **b.** $B - I$

13. $\begin{bmatrix} 0 & 1 & 0 & 0 \\ 1 & 0 & 1 & 0 \\ 0 & 2 & 0 & 1 \\ 2 & 0 & 0 & 1 \end{bmatrix}$ **14.** $\begin{bmatrix} -1 \\ 1 \end{bmatrix}$ **15.** $\begin{bmatrix} -\frac{1}{8} & \frac{1}{4} \\ \frac{1}{2} & 0 \end{bmatrix}$

16. $\begin{bmatrix} 2 & -3 \\ 4 & 2 \end{bmatrix}\begin{bmatrix} x \\ y \end{bmatrix} = \begin{bmatrix} 6 \\ 7 \end{bmatrix}$ **17.** $\{(11, 6)\}$ **18.** $\{(1, 2)\}$

Page 644, Practice for College Entrance Tests

1. A **2.** E **3.** B **4.** E **5.** C **6.** B **7.** A
8. D **9.** D **10.** B **11.** B

Pages 645–647, Cumulative Review (Chapters 13–15)

1. 500 **3.** 120 **5.** 11,880 **7.** 90 **9.** 66 **11a.** $\frac{1}{13}$
b. $\frac{12}{13}$ **13.** $\frac{1}{6}$ **15.** $\frac{7}{13}$ **17.** $56a^3b^5$

19.

187	0 6 8
188	1 3 5 7
189	0 2 3 4 9 9
190	4 6 7
191	7 8
192	3
193	
194	9

21. 23 **23.** 13

25.

27. -1.25 **29.** $\begin{bmatrix} -3 & 0 & 12 \\ 1 & 5 & 11 \end{bmatrix}$ **31a.** 12 **b.** 0

33. -3 **35.** $[8008]$ **37.** $\begin{bmatrix} 7 & -7 \\ -6 & 8 \end{bmatrix}$

39. $\begin{bmatrix} 0 & 1 & 0 \\ 1 & 0 & 0 \\ 0 & 0 & 1 \end{bmatrix}$ **41.** $\begin{bmatrix} 4 & -6 & 0 \\ -1 & 4 & -5 \end{bmatrix}$

43. $\begin{bmatrix} 4 & -3 \\ 5 & 2 \end{bmatrix} \cdot \begin{bmatrix} x \\ y \end{bmatrix} = \begin{bmatrix} 2 \\ 14 \end{bmatrix}; \{(2, 2)\}$

Chapter 16

Page 652, Classroom Exercises

1. First **2.** Fourth **3.** Second **4.** Fourth
5. $\left(-\frac{\sqrt{2}}{2}, \frac{\sqrt{2}}{2}\right)$ **6.** $\left(\frac{\sqrt{2}}{2}, -\frac{\sqrt{2}}{2}\right)$ **7.** $\left(-\frac{\sqrt{2}}{2}, -\frac{\sqrt{2}}{2}\right)$
8. Answers vary. $(1 + 2\pi), (1 + 4\pi), (1 + 6\pi)$
9. Answers vary. $(1 - 2\pi), (1 - 4\pi), (1 - 6\pi)$

Pages 652–653, Written Exercises

1. First **3.** Third **5.** Second **7.** Third
9. Third **11.** Vertical **13a.** $\left(\frac{3}{5}, \frac{4}{5}\right)$ **b.** $\left(\frac{3}{5}, -\frac{4}{5}\right)$
c. $\left(-\frac{3}{5}, -\frac{4}{5}\right)$ **d.** $\left(-\frac{3}{5}, \frac{4}{5}\right)$ **15a.** $\frac{2\pi}{3}$ **b.** $\frac{4\pi}{3}$
17. $3 + 2\pi, 3 + 4\pi, 3 + 6\pi, 3 + 8\pi, \ldots$
19. $-1 - 2\pi, -1 - 4\pi, -1 - 6\pi, -1 - 8\pi, \ldots$
21. Yes; 2 **23.** No **25.** (1, 1) **27.** (-1, 1)
29. (-1, -0.5) **31.** (0.7, 1) **33.** Yes; 8

Page 654, Review Exercises

1. $2|a|b\sqrt{3b}, b \geq 0$ **2.** $\sqrt{2}$ **3.** $2\sqrt{a} + |b|\sqrt{2}, a \geq 0$
4. $\frac{\sqrt{10y}}{2}, x > 0, y \geq 0$ **5.** $3|x|y^2$
6. $3\sqrt{xy} - 3x, x \geq 0, y \geq 0$ **7.** $\{8\}$ **8.** $\{7\}$
9. $5^{\frac{1}{3}} + 6^{-\frac{1}{2}}$ **10.** $12\sqrt{10}$ **11.** 20

Page 658, Classroom Exercises

1. $-1, 0$ **2.** $\pm\frac{2\sqrt{2}}{3}$ **3.** 0.23 **4.** -0.23 **5.** -0.23
6. 0.23 **7.** -0.55 **8.** 0.55 **9.** -0.55 **10.** 0.55

Pages 658–659, Written Exercises

1. Positive **3.** Negative **5.** Negative **7.** Negative
9. Positive **11.** Positive **13.** Negative **15.** $-\frac{1}{2}$
17. $\frac{1}{2}$ **19.** $\frac{1}{2}$ **21.** $\frac{1}{2}$ **23.** $-\frac{\sqrt{3}}{2}$ **25.** $-\frac{\sqrt{3}}{2}$
27. $-\frac{\sqrt{3}}{2}$ **29.** $-\frac{\sqrt{3}}{2}$ **31.** ±0.8 **33.** $\pm\frac{5}{13}$
35. $\pm\frac{\sqrt{5}}{3}$ **37.** $\pm\frac{1}{4}$ **39.** F; $\sin \frac{\pi}{2} = 1$, $\sin\left(-\frac{\pi}{2}\right) = -1$
41. F; $\cos(-\pi) = -1$, $-\cos \pi = 1$ **43.** T
45. F; $\sin\left(\frac{\pi}{2} + \frac{\pi}{2}\right) = 0$, $\sin \frac{\pi}{2} + \sin \frac{\pi}{2} = 2$ **47.** F;
$\sin a = 1$, $a = \frac{\pi}{2} + 2\pi$ **49.** $\{x:x = 2 + k2\pi \text{ or } x = (\pi - 2) + k2\pi, k \text{ an integer}\}$ **51.** $\{x:x = 2 + k2\pi \text{ or } x = -2 + k2\pi, k \text{ an integer}\}$ **53.** $\emptyset$ **55a.** f is periodic **b.** a and b are the period or multiples of the period **c.** $f(a + b) = f(a) = f(b)$

Pages 659–660, Review Exercises

1. Graph is circle center $(-1, 2)$, radius 3, and region inside. **2.** $(3, -4); x = 3; \left(3, -4\frac{1}{2}\right); y = -3\frac{1}{2}$; opens downward **3.** $\frac{x^2}{10} + \frac{y^2}{1} = 1$ **4.** Graph has vertices $(-\sqrt{2}, 0)$, $(\sqrt{2}, 0)$ and asymptotes $y = \pm 2x$.
5a. Ellipse; $\frac{(x + 2)^2}{9} + \frac{(y + 1)^2}{16} = 1$ **b.** Hyperbola; $\frac{(x - 2)^2}{9} - \frac{(y + 1)^2}{16} = 1$ **6.** $\emptyset$ **7.** $\{(-6, -3)(9, 2)\}$
8. $\{(-4, 0), (4, 0)\}$

Page 664, Classroom Exercises

1. $\dfrac{1}{2}$ **2.** $-\dfrac{1}{2}$ **3.** $\dfrac{\sqrt{3}}{2}$ **4.** $\{x : x = k2\pi,\ k \text{ an integer}\}$

Pages 664–665, Written Exercises

1. $0, \dfrac{1}{2}, \dfrac{\sqrt{2}}{2}, \dfrac{\sqrt{3}}{2}, 1, \dfrac{\sqrt{3}}{2}, \dfrac{\sqrt{2}}{2}, \dfrac{1}{2}, 0$ **3.** $-\dfrac{1}{2}, -\dfrac{\sqrt{2}}{2}, -\dfrac{\sqrt{3}}{2},$
$-1, -\dfrac{\sqrt{3}}{2}, -\dfrac{\sqrt{2}}{2}, -\dfrac{1}{2}, 0, \dfrac{1}{2}$ **5.** $\left\{-\dfrac{1}{2}\right\}$ **7.** $\left\{\dfrac{\sqrt{3}}{2}\right\}$ **9.** $\left\{\dfrac{1}{2}\right\}$

11. $\left\{x : x = \dfrac{\pi}{6} + k2\pi \text{ or } x = \dfrac{5\pi}{6} + k2\pi,\ k \text{ an integer}\right\}$

13. $\left\{x : x = \dfrac{\pi}{4} + k2\pi \text{ or } x = \dfrac{7\pi}{4} + k2\pi,\ k \text{ an integer}\right\}$

15. $\left\{x : x = \dfrac{5\pi}{6} + k2\pi \text{ or } x = \dfrac{7\pi}{6} + k2\pi,\ k \text{ an integer}\right\}$

17. $\left\{x : \dfrac{\pi}{6} \le x \le \dfrac{5\pi}{6}\right\}$ **19.** $\left\{x : \dfrac{\pi}{6} \le x \le \dfrac{11\pi}{6}\right\}$

21. $\left\{x : \dfrac{2\pi}{3} \le x \le \dfrac{4\pi}{3}\right\}$ **23.** $\left\{\dfrac{\pi}{3}, \dfrac{5\pi}{3}\right\}$ **25.** $\left\{\dfrac{\pi}{6}, \dfrac{11\pi}{6}\right\}$

27. $\left\{\dfrac{5\pi}{6}, \dfrac{7\pi}{6}\right\}$ **29.** $\left\{x : x \ge \dfrac{1}{2}\right\}$ **31.** $\{x : x \le 0\}$

33. $\left\{x : x \ge -\dfrac{\sqrt{2}}{2}\right\}$ **35.** 0 **37.** $\dfrac{\sqrt{2}}{2}$ **39.** $-\dfrac{\sqrt{2}}{2}$ **41.** $4\sqrt{2}$

Page 666, Review Exercises

1. $x^2 - x - 2$ **2.** -6 **3.** No **4.** $y = \pm\dfrac{\sqrt{3}}{2}$
5. $x = \pm\dfrac{1}{2}$

Page 666, Self-Quiz 1

1. 2π **2a.** $(0, 1)$ **b.** $(0, -1)$ **3a.** Second
b. First **4.** 2π **5.** Reals **6.** $\{y : -1 \le y \le 1\}$
7a. $-\dfrac{\sqrt{2}}{2}$ **b.** $-\dfrac{\sqrt{2}}{2}$

8.

x	$\dfrac{\pi}{6}$	$\dfrac{\pi}{4}$	$\dfrac{\pi}{3}$	$\dfrac{3\pi}{4}$
$\sin x$	$\dfrac{1}{2}$	$\dfrac{\sqrt{2}}{2}$	$\dfrac{\sqrt{3}}{2}$	$\dfrac{\sqrt{2}}{2}$
$\cos x$	$\dfrac{\sqrt{3}}{2}$	$\dfrac{\sqrt{2}}{2}$	$\dfrac{1}{2}$	$-\dfrac{\sqrt{2}}{2}$

x	$\dfrac{5\pi}{6}$	$\dfrac{4\pi}{3}$	$\dfrac{11\pi}{6}$
$\sin x$	$\dfrac{1}{2}$	$-\dfrac{\sqrt{3}}{2}$	$-\dfrac{1}{2}$
$\cos x$	$-\dfrac{\sqrt{3}}{2}$	$-\dfrac{1}{2}$	$\dfrac{\sqrt{3}}{2}$

9a. $\left\{\dfrac{7\pi}{6}, \dfrac{11\pi}{6}\right\}$ **b.** $\left\{\dfrac{\pi}{6}, \dfrac{11\pi}{6}\right\}$

Page 670, Classroom Exercises

1. 4; 2 **2.** 2; $1 + 4k$ **3.** Graph is graph of $f(x)$
translated up 1 unit; 4; 2 **4.** Graph's points have 2nd
coordinates that are twice the 2nd coordinates of points
on graph of $f(x)$; 4; 4

Pages 671–673, Written Exercises

1a. $(-2\pi, 0), (-\pi, 0), (0, 0), (\pi, 0), (2\pi, 0)$ **b.** $(0, 0)$
c. $\left(-\dfrac{3\pi}{2}, 1\right), \left(\dfrac{\pi}{2}, 1\right)$ **d.** $\left(-\dfrac{\pi}{2}, -1\right), \left(\dfrac{3\pi}{2}, -1\right)$

3a. None **b.** $(0, 3)$ **c.** $\left(-\dfrac{3\pi}{2}, 4\right), \left(\dfrac{\pi}{2}, 4\right)$ **d.** $\left(-\dfrac{\pi}{2}, 2\right),$
$\left(\dfrac{3\pi}{2}, 2\right)$ **5.** None **b.** $(0, -2)$ **c.** $\left(-\dfrac{3\pi}{2}, -1\right),$
$\left(\dfrac{\pi}{2}, -1\right)$ **d.** $\left(-\dfrac{\pi}{2}, -3\right), \left(\dfrac{3\pi}{2}, -3\right)$ **7a.** None
b. $(0, 6)$ **c.** $\left(-\dfrac{3\pi}{2}, 7\right), \left(\dfrac{\pi}{2}, 7\right)$ **d.** $\left(-\dfrac{\pi}{2}, 5\right), \left(\dfrac{3\pi}{2}, 5\right)$

For Exercises 9–13, *k an integer. **9.** $x = k2\pi$, *
11. $x = k2\pi$, * **13.** $x = k2\pi$, * **15.** 9; 7; 1 **17.** -7;
-9; 1 **19.** 6; 4; 1 **21.** -11; -13; 1 **23.** 6
25. $x = 2 + 6k$, k an integer **27.** $x = 3 + 6k$, k an
integer **29.** $\{-2 \le g(x) \le 3\}$ **31.** Graph is graph of
g translated down 3 units **33.** 3; -1 **35.** $x = 4 + 6k$,
k an integer **37.** $(0, 0)$ **39.** 0 **41.** 2
43. $\{x : x = 2 + 6k$ or $x = 3.5 + 6k$ or $x = 4.25 + 6k$,
k an integer$\}$ **45.** Translation of f up 1 unit.
47. Translation of f down 2 units.
49.

Graph:

51. 1 **53.** 1 **55.** $\left(\sqrt{2} + k2\sqrt{2}, 0\right)$, k an integer

57.

n	0	$\dfrac{\sqrt{2}}{2}$	$\sqrt{2}$	$3\dfrac{\sqrt{2}}{2}$	$2\sqrt{2}$	$5\dfrac{\sqrt{2}}{2}$	$3\sqrt{2}$	$4\sqrt{2}$	$5\sqrt{2}$	$6\sqrt{2}$
$s(n)$	0	$\dfrac{1}{2}$	1	$\dfrac{1}{2}$	0	$-\dfrac{1}{2}$	-1	0	1	0

Period $= 4\sqrt{2}$; Maximum value of $s = 1$; Minimum
value of $s = -1$; Amplitude of $s = 1$; The $s(n)$-intercept
of $s = (0, 0)$; The n-intercept $= \left(\sqrt{2} + k2\sqrt{2}, 0\right)$, k an
integer; The graph of $s + 3$ is a translation of s up 3 units.

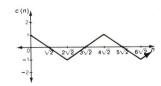

Page 673, Review Exercises

1. $x^3 - 3x + 2 = 0$ **2.** $\{-2, 1, 3\}$

3.

4. 2 real roots:
$x = -2$ (multiplicity 2) and
$x = 1\frac{1}{2}$ **5.** $f^{-1} = \frac{1}{2}x + \frac{3}{2}$ **6.** 4

Page 673, Extension

$y = |\sin x|$, period: π; amplitude: $\frac{1}{2}$

$y = [\sin x]$, period: 2π; amplitude: 1

$y = [|\sin x|]$, period: π; amplitude: $\frac{1}{2}$

$y = |[\sin x]|$, period: 2π; amplitude: $\frac{1}{2}$

Page 677, Classroom Exercises

1a. 2π **b.** 3 **c.** 3; -3 **d.** $x = 0, x = 2\pi; x = \pi$

2a. $\frac{2\pi}{3}$ **b.** 1 **c.** 1; -1 **d.** $x = 0, x = \frac{2\pi}{3}; x = \frac{\pi}{3}$

3a. 2π **b.** 4 **c.** 4; -4 **d.** $x = \frac{3\pi}{2}; x = \frac{\pi}{2}$

4a. $\frac{\pi}{2}$ **b.** 1 **c.** 1; -1 **d.** $x = \frac{3\pi}{8}; x = \frac{\pi}{8}$

5a. 2π **b.** 1 **c.** 1; -1 **d.** $x = \frac{3\pi}{2}; x = \frac{\pi}{2}$

6a. 2π **b.** 1 **c.** 1; -1 **d.** $x = \frac{\pi}{2}; x = \frac{3\pi}{2}$

Pages 677–679, Written Exercises

1a. 2π **b.** 4 **c.** 4; -4 **d.** $x = 0, x = 2\pi; x = \pi$

3a. 2π **b.** $\frac{1}{2}$ **c.** $\frac{1}{2}; -\frac{1}{2}$ **d.** $x = \frac{\pi}{2}; x = \frac{3\pi}{2}$ **5a.** π

b. 1 **c.** 1; -1 **d.** $x = 0, x = \pi; x = \frac{\pi}{2}$ **7a.** -1;

$x = 3\pi$ **b.** $(0, 0); (2\pi, 0), (4\pi, 0)$ **9a.** $-1; x = \pi$

b. $(0, 1); \left(\frac{\pi}{2}, 0\right), \left(\frac{3\pi}{2}, 0\right)$ **11a.** $-2; x = 0, x = 2\pi$

b. $(0, -2); \left(\frac{\pi}{2}, 0\right), \left(\frac{3\pi}{2}, 0\right)$ **13.** $y = 4 \cos x$

15. $y = -\sin x$ or $y = \sin(-x)$ **17.** $y = \sin 3x$

19a. 2π **b.** 3 **c.** 5; -1 **d.** Max: $x = \frac{\pi}{2}$;

Min: $x = \frac{3\pi}{2}$ **e.** $(0, 2)$ **21a.** 2π **b.** 3 **c.** 5; -1

d. Max: $x = \frac{3\pi}{2}$; Min: $x = \frac{\pi}{2}$ **e.** $(0, 2)$ **23a.** 4π

b. 2 **c.** 2; -2 **d.** Max: $x = 0, x = 4\pi$; Min: $x = 2\pi$

e. $(0, 2)$ **25a.** π **b.** 3 **c.** 4; -2 **d.** Max: $x = \frac{\pi}{4}$;

Min: $x = \frac{3\pi}{4}$ **e.** $(0, 1)$ **27a.** π **b.** 2 **c.** 4; 0

d. Max: $x = 0, x = \pi$; Min: $x = \frac{\pi}{2}$ **e.** $(0, 4)$

29. For each y, the x-coordinate of $y = g(2x)$ is $\frac{1}{2}$ the
x-coordinate of $y = g(x)$. **31.** The graph of $y = g(-x)$

838 Selected Answers

---

is the reflection of the graph of $y = g(x)$ about the
y-axis.

33.

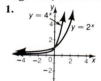

35. $\frac{4\pi}{3}$

37. $\pi \leqslant t \leqslant \frac{4\pi}{3}$,

$\frac{7\pi}{3} \leqslant t \leqslant \frac{8\pi}{3}$,

and $\frac{11\pi}{3} \leqslant t \leqslant 4\pi$

Page 679, Review Exercises

1.

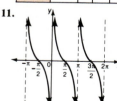

2. $x \approx 1.6$

3. $x \approx -1.6$

4. $x = 1.5$

5. $x \approx -1.5$

6. $\log_3 81 = 4$

7. $\log_{\frac{1}{4}} 16 = -2$

8. $2^4 = 16$ **9.** $7^3 = 343$ **10.** $\{5\}$ **11.** $\{32\}$

Page 683, Classroom Exercises

1. -1 **2.** 1 **3.** -1 **4.** $\frac{\sqrt{3}}{3}$

5. $\{x:x = k\pi, k \text{ an integer}\}$ **6.** π

Pages 683–684, Written Exercises

1. $\frac{3}{4}$ **3.** $\frac{5}{4}$ **5.** $-\frac{13}{5}$ **7.** $-\frac{12}{5}$

9.

x	0	$\frac{\pi}{6}$	$\frac{\pi}{4}$	$\frac{\pi}{3}$	$\frac{\pi}{2}$	$\frac{2\pi}{3}$	$\frac{3\pi}{4}$
$\cot x$	$\emptyset$	$\sqrt{3}$	1	$\frac{\sqrt{3}}{3}$	0	$-\frac{\sqrt{3}}{3}$	-1

x	$\frac{5\pi}{6}$	π	$\frac{7\pi}{6}$	$\frac{5\pi}{4}$	$\frac{4\pi}{3}$	$\frac{3\pi}{2}$
$\cot x$	$-\sqrt{3}$	$\emptyset$	$\sqrt{3}$	1	$\frac{\sqrt{3}}{3}$	0

11.

13. π **15.** Reals

17. $\frac{4}{5}; \frac{3}{5}; \frac{4}{3}; \frac{3}{4}; \frac{5}{3}; \frac{5}{4}$

19. $\frac{5}{13}; \frac{12}{13}; \frac{5}{12}; \frac{12}{5}; \frac{13}{12}; \frac{13}{5}$

21. $-\frac{20}{20}; \frac{21}{29}; \frac{20}{21}; \frac{21}{20}; -\frac{29}{21}; -\frac{29}{20}$

23. $-\frac{24}{25}; \frac{7}{25}; \frac{24}{7}; \frac{7}{24}; -\frac{25}{7}; -\frac{25}{24}$

25. False; $\tan \pi = 0$ **27.** True **29.** True

31. False; $\tan x = -\frac{12}{5}, \cot x = -\frac{5}{12}$

33. False; $\sin \frac{2\pi}{3} = \frac{\sqrt{3}}{2}$; $\cot \frac{2\pi}{3} = -\frac{\sqrt{3}}{3}$ **35.** $\tan x$

37. $2 \tan x$ **39.** 1

Page 684, Review Exercises

1.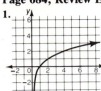

2. 4.322 **3.** {36}
4. 0.60206
5. −3.1549 **6.** 1.792
7. $\ln 2 \approx 0.6931$
$\underline{+\ln 5 \approx 1.6094}$
$\ln 10 \approx 2.3025$

Page 687, Classroom Exercises

1. 0 **2.** $\dfrac{\pi}{4}$ **3.** $\dfrac{\pi}{6}$ **4.** $-\dfrac{\pi}{4}$ **5.** $-\dfrac{\pi}{2}$ **6.** $\dfrac{\pi}{2}$

Pages 687–688, Written Exercises

1. $x = \sin y,\ -\dfrac{\pi}{2} \le x \le \dfrac{\pi}{2}$ **3.** $x = \tan y,\ -\dfrac{\pi}{2} < x < \dfrac{\pi}{2}$

5. $x = \sin y,\ -\dfrac{\pi}{2} \le x \le \dfrac{\pi}{2}$ **7.** $\dfrac{\pi}{3}$

9. π **11.** $-\dfrac{\pi}{6}$ **13.** $-\dfrac{\pi}{4}$ **15.** $\dfrac{5\pi}{6}$ **17.** False; by

definition **19.** False; $-\dfrac{\pi}{2} \le x \le \dfrac{\pi}{2}$ **21.** 0.4 **23.** $\dfrac{\sqrt{3}}{2}$

25. $\dfrac{\sqrt{3}}{2}$ **27.** 6 **29.** 0.75 **31.** 1 **33.** $\{x: -1 \le x \le 1\}$;

Reals **35.** No **37.**

39.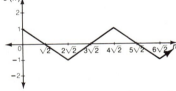

41.   **43.**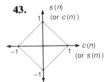

45. $(n, s(n))$ and $(s(n), n)$, $(s(n), c(n))$ and $(c(n), s(n))$

Page 689, Review Exercises

1.

2. $x \approx 9.966$ **3.** {35}
4. $k = e^{\frac{a}{2}}$ **5.** $\approx \$1822$
6. $k \approx 0.0069$

Page 689, Self-Quiz 2

1. 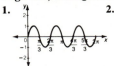 **2.** 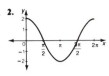 **3.** 2
4. $\dfrac{2\pi}{3}$

5.

x	$\dfrac{\pi}{4}$	$\dfrac{\pi}{3}$	$\dfrac{5\pi}{6}$	$\dfrac{5\pi}{4}$	$\dfrac{5\pi}{3}$
$\tan x$	1	$\sqrt{3}$	$-\dfrac{\sqrt{3}}{3}$	1	$-\sqrt{3}$
$\cot x$	1	$\dfrac{\sqrt{3}}{3}$	$-\sqrt{3}$	1	$-\dfrac{\sqrt{3}}{3}$
$\sec x$	$\sqrt{2}$	2	$-\dfrac{2\sqrt{3}}{3}$	$-\sqrt{2}$	2
$\cos x$	$\sqrt{2}$	$\dfrac{2\sqrt{3}}{3}$	2	$-\sqrt{2}$	$-\dfrac{2\sqrt{3}}{3}$

6a. π **b.** 2π **7a.** $-\dfrac{\pi}{4}$ **b.** $\dfrac{\sqrt{3}}{2}$

Page 693, Classroom Exercises

1. 0 **2.** 0 **3.** $-\dfrac{\sqrt{2}}{2}$ **4.** $\dfrac{1}{2}$ **5.** $\dfrac{3}{2}$ **6.** $\dfrac{\pi}{3}$ **7.** $\dfrac{\pi}{4}$

8. $\dfrac{3\pi}{20}$ **9.** 30 **10.** 135 **11.** $\dfrac{360}{\pi}$ **12.** $\dfrac{\pi}{90}$

Pages 694–696, Written Exercises

1. $\dfrac{1}{2}$ **3.** $\dfrac{\sqrt{2}}{2}$ **5.** Undefined **7.** $\dfrac{\sqrt{3}}{2}$

9.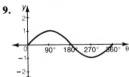

11. 2.29 **13.** 1.4 **15.** 30°
17. 0.3° **19.** −90°
21. 540° **23.** $\left(\dfrac{360}{\pi}\right)^{\circ}$
25. $\left(\dfrac{36}{\pi}\right)^{\circ}$ **27.** $\dfrac{\pi}{18}$
29. $\dfrac{\pi^2}{180}$ **31.** $\dfrac{20\pi}{9}$

33. $-\dfrac{2\pi}{9}$ **35.** 2 **37.** $\dfrac{d\pi}{180}$ **39.** * k an integer

a. $(k180°*, 0)$ **b.** $\theta = 90° + k360°*$
c. $\theta = 270° + k360°*$ **d.** $\theta = 30° + k360°*$ and
$\theta = 150° + k360°*$
e.

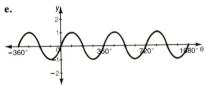

41. *k an integer **a.** $(k180°*, 0)$ **b.** 180°
c. $\theta = 90° + k180°*$

d.

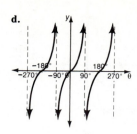

Note: k is an integer for exercises 43–57.
43a. 360°   **b.** $(k180°, 0)$
c. $\theta = 90° + k360°$
d. 3   **e.** $(0, 0)$ **45a.** 120°
b. $(k60°, 0)$
c. $\theta = 30° + k120°$
d. 1   **e.** $(0, 0)$ **47a.** 2°
b. $(0.5 + k°, 0)$
c. $\theta = k2°$ **d.** 1   **e.** $(0, 1)$
49a. 3.6°   **b.** $(0.9° + k1.8°, 0)$ **c.** $\theta = 1.8° + k3.6°$
d. 4   **e.** $(0, -4)$ **51a.** 1°   **b.** None
c. $\theta = 0.25° + k°$ **d.** *1*   **e.** $(0, 3)$ **53a.** 120°
b. None   **c.** $\theta = 90° + k120°$ **d.** 1   **e.** $(0, 2)$
55a. 4°   **b.** $(k2°, 0)$ **c.** $\theta = 3° + k4°$ **d.** 300
e. $(0, 0)$ **57a.** 3600°   **b.** $(k1800°, 0)$
c. $\theta = 900° + k3600°$ **d.** 0.01   **e.** $(0, 0)$
59. ≈866,000 miles Answers may vary slightly.
61. ≈2793 miles

Page 696, Review Exercises

1. 14, 18, 22, 26   **2.** $\dfrac{1}{8}$ **3.** $S_{10} = \displaystyle\sum_{k=1}^{10} 3 \cdot 2^{k-1}$

4. 100   **5.** 280   **6.** 390   **7.** $S_9 = \dfrac{3^9 - 1}{2 \cdot 3^8}$ **8.** 2

Page 696, Calculator Extension

1. ≈0.6109   **2.** ≈57.296°   **3.** ≈114.592°

Pages 698–701, Chapter Review

1a. $(0, 1)$ **1b.** $(1, 0)$ **3.** 2π **5.** $\dfrac{4}{5}$ **7.** $-\dfrac{4}{5}$

9. $\pm\dfrac{\sqrt{21}}{5}$ **11a.** $\left\{\dfrac{\pi}{3}, \dfrac{5\pi}{3}\right\}$

11b. $\left\{x: 0 \le x \le \dfrac{\pi}{4} \text{ or } \dfrac{3\pi}{4} \le x \le 2\pi\right\}$ **13.** 2π; 1

15.

17. $y = 2\cos\left(\dfrac{x}{2}\right)$

19a. $-\dfrac{7}{24}$ **b.** $-\dfrac{24}{7}$

c. $-\dfrac{25}{24}$ **d.** $\dfrac{25}{7}$ **21.** π

23. $-\dfrac{\pi}{3}$ **25.** $\dfrac{\sqrt{2}}{2}$ **27.** $-1 \le x \le 1$ **29.** $\dfrac{\sqrt{3}}{2}$

31. $\dfrac{\sqrt{3}}{2}$ **33.** $-120°$ **35.** $-\dfrac{5\pi}{18}$ **37.** ≈12.566 ft

Pages 701–702, Chapter 16 Self-Test

1a. Positive   **b.** Positive   **2a.** 0.91   **b.** 0.41   **3.** $-\dfrac{1}{2}$

4. True   **5.** True   **6.** $\left\{\dfrac{3\pi}{4}, \dfrac{5\pi}{4}\right\}$ **7.** $\left\{\dfrac{\pi}{3}, \dfrac{2\pi}{3}\right\}$

8. $\left\{\dfrac{\pi}{3}, \dfrac{2\pi}{3}\right\}$ **9.** 5   **10.** $\dfrac{\pi}{2}$ **11.** 2

12.

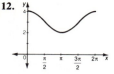

13.

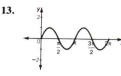

14.

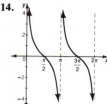

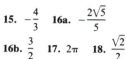

15. $-\dfrac{4}{3}$ **16a.** $-\dfrac{2\sqrt{5}}{5}$

16b. $\dfrac{3}{2}$ **17.** 2π **18.** $\dfrac{\sqrt{2}}{2}$

19. $-\dfrac{\sqrt{3}}{2}$ **20.** $\dfrac{\pi}{2}$ **21.** $-\dfrac{\pi}{6}$

22. 135°   **23.** ≈114.6°

24. $\dfrac{4\pi}{3}$ **25.** $-\dfrac{7\pi}{36}$ **26.** $\dfrac{5\pi}{2}$ ft ≈ 7.9 ft

Pages 702–703, Practice for College Entrance Tests

1. A   **2.** B   **3.** C   **4.** E   **5.** C   **6.** B   **7.** D   **8.** A
9. C   **10.** D   **11.** C   **12.** B

Chapter 17

Page 708, Classroom Exercises

1. 53.1°   **2.** 36.9°   **3.** 0.3846   **4.** 2.400

Pages 708–710, Written Exercises

1. $\sin A \approx 0.6522$, $\cos A \approx 0.7609$, $\tan A \approx 0.8571$, $\csc A \approx 1.5333$, $\sec A \approx 1.3143$, $\cot A \approx 1.1667$
3. $\sin R \approx 0.4167$, $\cos R \approx 0.8333$, $\tan R \approx 0.5000$, $\csc R \approx 2.4000$, $\sec R \approx 1.2000$, $\cot R \approx 2.0000$
5. $\sin D \approx 0.8800$, $\cos D \approx 0.4800$, $\tan D \approx 1.8333$, $\csc D \approx 1.1364$, $\sec D \approx 2.0833$, $\cot D \approx 0.5455$
7. $\sin L \approx 0.8000$, $\cos L \approx 0.6000$, $\tan L \approx 1.3333$, $\csc L \approx 1.2500$, $\sec L \approx 1.6667$, $\cot L \approx 0.7500$
9. $\sin P \approx 0.9487$, $\cos P \approx 0.3162$, $\tan P \approx 3.0000$, $\csc P \approx 1.0541$, $\sec P \approx 3.1623$, $\cot P \approx 0.3333$
11. $\sin X \approx 0.5000$, $\cos X \approx 0.8660$, $\tan X \approx 0.5774$, $\csc X \approx 2.0000$, $\sec X \approx 1.1547$, $\cot X \approx 1.7321$

13. $\dfrac{2\sqrt{13}}{13}, \dfrac{3\sqrt{13}}{13}$ **15.** $\dfrac{4}{5}, \dfrac{3}{5}$ **17.** $\dfrac{\sqrt{3}}{2}, \dfrac{1}{2}$ **19.** 0.2079
21. 0.1736   **23.** 3.732   **25.** -1.035 **27.** 1.068
29. 1.929   **31.** 58.3°   **33.** 22.7°   **35.** 36.7°
37. 162.2°   **39.** 147.8°   **41.** 97.5°   **43.** $5\sqrt{2}$

45. $\dfrac{10}{7}$ **47.** $\dfrac{15}{2}$ **49.** $\cot 23° = \dfrac{q}{p}$; $\cot 67° = \dfrac{p}{q}$

51. $\cos 17° = \dfrac{1}{p}$; $\csc 73° = p$ **53.** $\tan 7° = \dfrac{p}{q}$;
$\cot 7° = \dfrac{q}{p}$ **55.** $\sin 42° = \sqrt{1 - t^2}$; $\sin 48° = t$;
$\cos 48° = \sqrt{1 - t^2}$; $\tan 48° = \dfrac{t\sqrt{1 - t^2}}{|1 - t^2|}$ **57.** $\csc 84° = u$;
$\sin 84° = \dfrac{1}{u}$; $\cos 84° = \dfrac{\sqrt{u^2 - 1}}{u}$; $\tan 84° = \dfrac{\sqrt{u^2 - 1}}{|u^2 - 1|}$

Page 710, Review Exercises

1. -20 2. $x^2 - 4x$; 6   3. 2   4. $x^3 - 3x + 2 = 0$
5. $\{-3, 1, 2\}$ 6. 4, 0 with multiplicity 2
7. $f^{-1}(x) = -x + 6$

Page 713, Classroom Exercises

1. $AB \approx 7.5$, $BC \approx 4.5$, $B \approx 53°$ 2. ≈ 1700 ft

Pages 713–717, Written Exercises

1. $A \approx 53.1°$, $B \approx 36.9°$, $BC \approx 16$ 3. $A \approx 53.1°$,
$B \approx 36.9°$, $BC \approx 32$ 5. $AC \approx 7.7$, $BC \approx 6.4$,
$B \approx 50°$ 7. ≈ 4.7 9. ≈ 6.9 11. $\approx 48.0°$
13a. ≈ 4.8 mi   b. ≈ 6.2 mi   15. ≈ 42 ft   17. ≈ 549 ft
19a. ≈ 24 cm   b. ≈ 26 cm   21. ≈ 6969 m   23. ≈ 34.0 ft
25. $\approx 36.9°$ and $\approx 53.1°$ 27. ≈ 0.7 29. $\approx 8°$ 31a. $\approx 31°$
b. $\approx 50°$ 33. ≈ 7.8 m   35. ≈ 2800 km   37. ≈ 4000 km
39. $\approx 114°$

Page 717, Review Exercises

1.

	-2	-1	0	1	2
2^x	0.25	0.5	1	2	4
$\left(\dfrac{1}{2}\right)^x$	4	2	1	0.5	0.25

2. $\log_{10} 10{,}000 = 4$ 3. $\{200\}$ 4. 0.9030   5. $\{10\}$

Page 717, Self-Quiz 1

1. $\sin \theta = \dfrac{2\sqrt{2}}{3}$; $\cos \theta = \dfrac{1}{3}$; $\tan \theta = 2\sqrt{2}$; $\csc \theta = \dfrac{3\sqrt{2}}{4}$;
$\sec \theta = 3$; $\cot \theta = \dfrac{\sqrt{2}}{4}$ 2a. 1.376   b. 0.9681
3. $\approx 24.7°$ 4. $PR \approx 13$, $P \approx 48°$, $R \approx 42°$ 5. ≈ 212 ft

Page 720, Classroom Exercises

1. ≈ 59 cm^2 2. ≈ 6.2

Pages 721–722, Written Exercises

Answers may vary slightly.

1. ≈ 9 m^2 3. 9 in.^{2} 5. 40 cm^2 7. ≈ 29 m^2
9. $B \approx 80.6°$, $C \approx 29.4°$, $c \approx 1.0$ cm   11. $B \approx 26.9°$,
$A \approx 38.1°$, $a \approx 6.8$ m   13. $C = 20°$, $a = 10.0$ ft,
$c \approx 3.9$ ft   15. $B = 70°$, $a \approx 10.5$ cm, $c \approx 5.3$ cm
17. ≈ 4.5 km   19. ≈ 2.8 km   21. ≈ 32 m
23a. ≈ 31.1 cm, ≈ 31.1 cm   b. ≈ 23.8 cm   c. $20°$
d. 8.7 cm, 11.3 cm   e. No
25.

$$\dfrac{a}{\sin A} = \dfrac{c}{\sin C} \qquad \dfrac{b}{\sin B} = \dfrac{c}{\sin C}$$
$$c \sin A = a \sin C \qquad c \sin B = b \sin C$$
$$c \sin A - a \sin C = 0 \qquad c \sin B - b \sin C = 0$$
$$c \sin A - a \sin C = c \sin B - b \sin C$$
$$c \sin A - c \sin B = a \sin C - b \sin C$$
$$c(\sin A - \sin B) = \sin C(a - b)$$
$$\dfrac{\sin A - \sin B}{a - b} = \dfrac{\sin C}{c}$$

Page 723, Review Exercises

1. 2.9542   2. $\dfrac{2}{\log 5} \approx 2.86$ 3. ≈ 9.9 4. $\{10\}$
5. $a = \dfrac{10^c}{b}$ 6. \$1229.80   7. 0.0462

Page 723, Extension

1. 35 N   2. ≈ 71 N   3a. 171 mph   b. 470 mph
4. 400 N

Page 725, Classroom Exercises

1. None   2. 2   3. 1   4. 2

Pages 726–727, Written Exercises

Answers may vary slightly.

1. $B \approx 27.4°$, $C \approx 22.6°$, $c \approx 5$ 3. No solutions
5. $M \approx 40°$, $W \approx 110°$, $w \approx 13.2$ or $M \approx 140°$,
$W \approx 10°$, $w \approx 2.4$ 7. $\approx 34.2°$ or $\approx 145.8°$ 9. $\approx 8.1°$
or $\approx 140.9°$ 11. ≈ 11.4 or ≈ 61.6 13. 2   15. 1
17. $Q \approx 62.4°$, $R \approx 37.6°$, $r \approx 18.6$ 19a. $90°$
b. $2\sqrt{7}$ cm   21a. ≈ 197 m   b. ≈ 102 m
c. ≈ 168 m   23. $\approx 37.83 < a < 48$

Page 727, Review Exercises

1. 0, 7, 26   2. 10, 1, $\dfrac{1}{10}$ 3. Yes   4. 126   5. 64
6. 8 or -8 7. $\displaystyle\sum_{k=1}^{8} 2k - 1$

Page 728, Self-Quiz 2

1. ≈ 96 ft^2 2. $a \approx 5.5$, $b \approx 7.6$, $B = 66°$
3. $5 \tan 50° \approx 5.96$, $\dfrac{5 \sin 50°}{\sin 40°} \approx 5.96$
4. $S \approx 43.6°$, $T \approx 84.4°$, $t \approx 10.1$ 5. None

Page 728, Calculator Extension

$\sin \dfrac{\pi}{6} \approx 0.499999$; $\sin \dfrac{\pi}{6} = 0.5$

Page 731, Classroom Exercises

1. 16.5   2. 40.5°

Pages 731–732, Written Exercises

1. ≈ 12.4 3. ≈ 29.2 5. ≈ 13.5 7. $\approx 44°$ 9. 90°
11. $\approx 27°$ 13. $\sqrt{5}$ 15. $3\sqrt{5}$ 17. $5\sqrt{5}$
19. $\cos W = 0.875$, $\cos X = 0.6875$, $\cos Y = -0.25$
21. $\cos B = 0.6$, $\cos D = 0.6$, $\cos F = 0.28$
23. $\cos K \approx 0.2195$, $\cos M = 0$, $\cos P \approx 0.9756$
25. ≈ 5.1 27a. $\approx 63°$, $\approx 63°$, $\approx 117°$, $\approx 117°$
b. ≈ 7.5 cm   29a. 8.7 cm, 13.2 cm   b. 43.3 cm^2
31. ≈ 1136 km   33. ≈ 61.2 cm   35. ≈ 496 km

Pages 732–733, Review Exercises

1. 325   2. 1050   3. 260   4. $\dfrac{27}{2}\left(1 - \left(\dfrac{1}{3}\right)^9\right)$
5. 0.33333333   6. $\dfrac{3}{2}$

1. 130 mph, 22.6° east of north   **2.** 86.6 N, 30° north of east

Pages 735–737, Chapter Review

1. $\sin A = \dfrac{5}{6}$; $\cos A = \dfrac{5}{9}$; $\tan A = \dfrac{3}{2}$; $\csc A = \dfrac{6}{5}$;

$\sec A = \dfrac{9}{5}$; $\cot A = \dfrac{2}{3}$ **3a.** 23.8°   **b.** 62.5°   **5.** ≈ 5.9

7. $b = a \tan B$ **9.** ≈ 22 m^2 **11.** ≈ 1.4 km
13. $Z = 127.8°$, $X = 15.2°$, $x = 7.0$; or $Z = 52.2°$, $X = 90.8°$, $x = 26.6$ **15.** ≈ 8.5 in.

Pages 737–738, Chapter 17 Self-Test

1. Cosine   **2.** Cosecant   **3.** 2.904   **4.** 0.9438
5. $\approx 50.5°$ **6.** ≈ 6.4 **7.** ≈ 4.9 **8.** $\approx 35.7°$ **9.** 610 ft
10. $\approx 35°$ **11.** ≈ 19 **12.** $e = \dfrac{7 \sin 55°}{\sin 34°}$ **13.** None
14. 70.5° or 109.5°   **15.** ≈ 2.9 **16.** 14 cm

Pages 738–739, Practice for College Entrance Tests

1. C   **2.** A   **3.** E   **4.** D   **5.** C   **6.** B   **7.** D   **8.** B
9. B   **10.** E   **11.** B   **12.** A

Chapter 18

Page 743, Classroom Exercises

1. $\csc X - \sin X = \dfrac{1}{\sin X} - \sin X = \dfrac{1 - \sin^2 X}{\sin X}$
$= \dfrac{\cos^2 X}{\sin X} = \cos X \cot X$

2. $\dfrac{\sin X}{1 - \cos X} = \dfrac{\sin X(1 + \cos X)}{(1 - \cos X)(1 + \cos X)}$
$= \dfrac{\sin X(1 + \cos X)}{1 - \cos^2 X} = \dfrac{\sin X(1 + \cos X)}{\sin^2 X}$
$= \dfrac{1 + \cos X}{\sin X}$

Page 743, Written Exercises

1. $\tan X = \dfrac{\sin X}{\cos X} = \tan X + \tan X = 2 \tan X$

3. $(\sin X + \cos X)^2 = \sin^2 X + \cos^2 X + 2 \sin X \cos X$
$= 1 + 2 \sin X \cos X$

5. $\sin X (\csc X - \sin X) = \sin X \csc X - \sin^2 X$
$= 1 - \sin^2 X = \cos^2 X$

7. $\dfrac{1 + \cot^2 X}{1 + \tan^2 X} = \dfrac{\csc^2 X}{\sec^2 X} = \dfrac{1}{\sin^2 X} \cdot \dfrac{\cos^2 X}{1} = \dfrac{\cos^2 X}{\sin^2 X}$
$= \cot^2 X$ **9.** $\sin^2 X = 1 - \cos^2 X = 1 - \dfrac{1}{\sec^2 X}$

11. $\sin X \csc X - \cos^2 X = \sin X \cdot \dfrac{1}{\sin x} - \cos^2 X$
$= 1 - \cos^2 X = \sin^2 X$

13. $\dfrac{\sin^2 X}{\csc X} + \dfrac{\cos^2 X}{\csc X} = \dfrac{1}{\csc X} = \sin X$

---

15. $\tan X \cos X = \dfrac{\sin X}{\cos X} \cdot \cos X = \sin X$

17. $\tan X(\cot X + \tan X) = \tan X \cot X + \tan^2 X$
$= 1 + \tan^2 X = \sec^2 X$

19. $\dfrac{\cos X}{1 - \sin X} + \dfrac{\cos X}{1 + \sin X}$
$= \dfrac{\cos X(1 + \sin X) + \cos X(1 - \sin X)}{1 - \sin^2 X}$
$= \dfrac{\cos X(1 + \sin X + 1 - \sin X)}{\cos^2 X} = \dfrac{2 \cos X}{\cos^2 X} = 2 \sec X$

21. $\sin X \cos X \tan X = \sin X \cos X \cdot \dfrac{\sin X}{\cos X}$
$= \sin^2 X = 1 - \cos^2 X$

23. $\sec X \cos X + \dfrac{\tan X}{\cot X} = \dfrac{1}{\cos X} \cdot \cos X + \tan X\left(\dfrac{\tan X}{1}\right)$
$= 1 + \tan^2 X = \sec^2 X$

25. $\dfrac{\sin X}{1 - \csc X} - \dfrac{\sin X}{1 + \csc X}$
$= \dfrac{\sin X(1 + \csc X) - \sin X(1 - \csc X)}{(1 - \csc X)(1 + \csc X)}$
$= \dfrac{\sin X(1 + \csc X - 1 + \csc X)}{1 - \csc^2 X} = \dfrac{2 \sin X \csc X}{1 - \csc^2 X}$
$= -\dfrac{2}{\cot^2 X} = -2 \tan^2 X$

Page 743, Review Exercises

1. 12   **2.** $x^2 - 7x + 5$; 7   **4,**
3. $x^3 + 2x^2 + x = 0$
5. $f^{-1}(x) = 2x + 5$

Page 747, Classroom Exercises

1. $\dfrac{\sqrt{2} + \sqrt{6}}{4}$ **2.** $\sin X$ **3.** $-\sin 15°$ or $-\cos 75°$

4. $\dfrac{\sqrt{2} - \sqrt{6}}{4}$

Pages 747–748, Written Exercises

1. $\dfrac{\sqrt{6} - \sqrt{2}}{4}$ **3.** $\dfrac{-\sqrt{2} - \sqrt{6}}{4}$ **5.** $\dfrac{\sqrt{2} + \sqrt{6}}{4}$

7. $\dfrac{\sqrt{6} - \sqrt{2}}{4}$ **9.** $\dfrac{\sqrt{2} + \sqrt{6}}{4}$ **11.** $\cos X$ **13.** $\cos X$

15. $\cos X$ **17.** $-\sin X$ **19.** $\sin X$ **21.** $\sin X$
23. $-\cos 12°$ **25.** $\cos 12°$ **27.** $\sin 12°$ **29.** $-\sin 12°$
31. False   **33.** True   **35.** False   **37.** True
39. $\dfrac{\sqrt{2} - \sqrt{6}}{4}$ **41.** $\dfrac{\sqrt{2} - \sqrt{6}}{4}$ **43.** $\cos \dfrac{\pi}{10}$ **45.** $-\cos \dfrac{3\pi}{10}$

47. $\sin \dfrac{\pi}{10}$ **49.** $-\sin \dfrac{\pi}{10}$ **51.** $1 + \tan x_1 \tan x_2$
53. $\cot X_1 - \tan X_2$ **55.** $\cos 39°$ **57.** $\cos 90°$ or 0

Page 748, Review Exercises

1.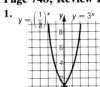
$y = \left(\frac{1}{3}\right)^x$ $y = 3^x$

2. {8}
3. {4}
4. {4}
5. ≈ 12
6. 500
7. $2054.43

Page 748, Self-Quiz 1

1. $\sec X - \dfrac{\tan X}{\csc X} = \dfrac{1}{\cos X} - \dfrac{\sin X}{\cos X} \cdot \dfrac{\sin X}{1} = \dfrac{1 - \sin^2 X}{\cos X}$

$= \dfrac{\cos^2 X}{\cos X} = \cos X$

2. $\dfrac{\sin X}{1 + \cos X} + \dfrac{1 + \cos X}{\sin X} = \dfrac{\sin^2 X + 1 + 2\cos X + \cos^2 X}{\sin X (1 + \cos X)}$

$= \dfrac{(\sin^2 X + \cos^2 X) + 1 + 2\cos X}{\sin X (1 + \cos X)} = \dfrac{2(1 + \cos X)}{\sin X (1 + \cos X)}$

$= \dfrac{2}{\sin X} = 2 \csc X$ **3.** $\dfrac{\sqrt{2}}{2}$ **4.** $\dfrac{-\sqrt{2} - \sqrt{6}}{4}$ **5.** $\cos 70°$

or $\sin 20°$ **6.** $-\cos 25°$ or $-\sin 65°$

Page 751, CLassroom Exercises

1. -0.3314 **2.** -0.1258 **3.** $-\sin 70°$ or $-\cos 20°$
4. $\dfrac{\sqrt{6} + \sqrt{2}}{4}$

Pages 751–752, Written Exercises

1. $\dfrac{\sqrt{6} - \sqrt{2}}{4}$ **3.** $\dfrac{-\sqrt{6} - \sqrt{2}}{4}$ **5.** $\dfrac{-\sqrt{6} - \sqrt{2}}{4}$

7. $\dfrac{\sqrt{2} - \sqrt{6}}{4}$ **9.** $\dfrac{-\sqrt{6} + \sqrt{2}}{4}$ **11.** $-\sin X$

13. $-\sin X$ **15.** $-\sin X$ **17.** $-\cos X$ **19.** $\cos X$
21. $-\cos X$ **23.** $-\sin 7°$ **25.** $\sin 7°$ **27.** $\cos 7°$
29. $-\sin 7°$ **31.** $\cos 10°$ **33.** $-\cos 2°$ **35.** $-\sin 2°$
37. $-\cos 5°$ **39.** $-\dfrac{4}{5}$ **41.** $-\dfrac{4}{5}$ **43.** $\dfrac{3}{5}$ **45.** $-\dfrac{3}{5}$
47. $\dfrac{\sqrt{6} + \sqrt{2}}{4}$ **49.** $\dfrac{-\sqrt{2} - \sqrt{6}}{4}$ **51.** $-\sin \dfrac{\pi}{14}$
53. $-\cos \dfrac{\pi}{7}$ **55.** $-\cos \dfrac{\pi}{6}$ **57.** $-\cos \dfrac{\pi}{8}$
59. $\cot X_2 - \cot X_1$ **61.** $\tan X_1 + \tan X_2$ **63.** $\sin 22°$
65. $-\sin 33°$
67. $\tan (X + Y) = \dfrac{\sin (X + Y)}{\cos (X + Y)} = \dfrac{\sin X \cos Y + \cos X \sin Y}{\cos X \cos Y - \sin X \sin Y}$

$= \dfrac{\dfrac{\sin X \cos Y + \cos X \sin Y}{\cos X \cos Y}}{\dfrac{\cos X \cos Y - \sin X \sin Y}{\cos X \cos Y}} = \dfrac{\tan X + \tan Y}{1 - \tan X \tan Y}$

Page 752, Review Exercises

1. 10, 50, 250, 1250   **2.** 43   **3.** 100 or -100
4. $\displaystyle\sum_{k=1}^{11} 2k - 1$ **5.** 120   **6.** 0.66666666   **7.** $\dfrac{4}{3}$

Page 755, Classroom Exercises

1. $\sin 36°$ **2.** $\cos 45°$ **3.** $\sin 70°$ **4.** $\cos 160°$
5. $2b^2 - 1$ **6.** $\sqrt{\dfrac{1 - b}{2}}$ **7.** $2ab$

Pages 755–756, Written Exercises

1. $\dfrac{24}{25}; \dfrac{7}{25}$ **3.** $\dfrac{4\sqrt{2}}{9}; -\dfrac{7}{9}$ **5.** $\dfrac{5\sqrt{11}}{18}; -\dfrac{7}{18}$

7. $-\dfrac{120}{169}; \dfrac{119}{169}$ **9.** $\dfrac{\sqrt{3}}{2}; \dfrac{1}{2}$ **11.** $\dfrac{4\sqrt{5}}{9}; -\dfrac{1}{9}$ **13.** $\dfrac{4}{5}; \dfrac{3}{5}$

15. $\dfrac{2\sqrt{2}}{3}; \dfrac{1}{3}$ **17.** $\dfrac{2\sqrt{13}}{13}; \dfrac{2\sqrt{13}}{13}$ **19.** $\dfrac{\sqrt{7}}{4}; \dfrac{3}{4}$

21. $-0.20; 0.98$ **23.** $-0.57; -0.82$ **25.** $\cos 16°$
27. $\sin 20°$ **29.** $\cos 248°$ **31.** $\sin 35°$ **33.** $\cos 56°$
35. $\cos 2°$ **37a.** $\dfrac{\sqrt{6} + \sqrt{2}}{4}$ **b.** $\dfrac{\sqrt{2} + \sqrt{3}}{2}$

c. $\left(\dfrac{\sqrt{6} + \sqrt{2}}{4}\right)^2 = \left(\dfrac{\sqrt{2} + \sqrt{3}}{2}\right)^2$ **39a.** $\dfrac{\sqrt{6} + \sqrt{2}}{4}$

b. $\dfrac{\sqrt{2} + \sqrt{3}}{2}$ **c.** $\left(\dfrac{\sqrt{6} + \sqrt{2}}{4}\right)^2 = \left(\dfrac{\sqrt{2} + \sqrt{3}}{2}\right)^2$

41a. $-\dfrac{5\sqrt{11}}{18}$ **b.** $-\dfrac{7}{18}$

c. $\left(-\dfrac{5\sqrt{11}}{18}\right)^2 + \left(-\dfrac{7}{18}\right)^2 = \dfrac{275}{324} + \dfrac{49}{324} = 1$

43.

$\cos X = 1 - 2\sin^2\left(\dfrac{X}{2}\right)$ $\cos X = 2\cos^2\left(\dfrac{X}{2}\right) - 1$

$\cos X - 1 = -2\sin^2\left(\dfrac{X}{2}\right)$ $\cos X + 1 = 2\cos^2\left(\dfrac{X}{2}\right)$

$\dfrac{1 - \cos X}{2} = \sin^2\left(\dfrac{X}{2}\right)$ $\dfrac{\cos X + 1}{2} = \cos^2\left(\dfrac{X}{2}\right)$

$\pm\sqrt{\dfrac{1 - \cos X}{2}} = \sin\left(\dfrac{X}{2}\right)$ $\pm\sqrt{\dfrac{\cos X + 1}{2}} = \cos\left(\dfrac{X}{2}\right)$

Pages 756–757, Review Exercises

1. 0   **2.** $\dfrac{1}{2}$ **3.** 2π **4.** 2   **5.** $2; -2$ **6.** $-2\pi, 0, 2\pi;$
$-\pi, \pi$ **7.** $\cos a = \dfrac{4}{5}, \tan a = \dfrac{3}{4}, \cot a = \dfrac{4}{3}, \sec a = \dfrac{5}{4},$
$\csc a = \dfrac{5}{3}$ **8.** $\sin a = \dfrac{1}{2}, \cos a = \dfrac{\sqrt{3}}{2}, \tan a = \dfrac{\sqrt{3}}{3},$
$\cot a = \sqrt{3}, \sec a = \dfrac{2\sqrt{3}}{3}$ **9.** $60°$ **10.** $\dfrac{3\pi}{4}$

Page 757, Self-Quiz 2

1. $-\dfrac{\sqrt{2}}{2}$ **2.** $\dfrac{\sqrt{6} - \sqrt{2}}{4}$ **2.** $\sin 24°$ **4.** $-\sin 30°$
5. $\dfrac{24}{25}$ **6.** $\dfrac{3\sqrt{10}}{10}$ **7.** $\cos 30°$ **8.** $\sin 35°$

Page 757, Calculator Extension

1. Answers will vary.   **2.** 90°N, 90°S; 0°

Page 759, Classroom Exercises

1. {180°}   **2.** {45°, 225°}   **3.** {45°, 135°, 225°, 315°}
4. ∅

Page 760, Written Exercises

1.–5. k an integer.

1. $\{X:X = 34° + k360°$ or $X = 326° + k360°\}$

3. $\{X:X = 67° + k360°$ or $X = 113° + k360°\}$

5. $\{X:X = 168° + k360°$ or $X = 348° + k360°\}$

7. $\{30°, 150°\}$ **9.** $\{150°, 210°\}$ **11.** $\{60°, 240°\}$

13. $\{45°, 135°, 225°, 315°\}$ **15.** $\{45°, 135°, 225°, 315°\}$

17. $\{0°, 180°\}$ **19.** $\{90°, 270°\}$ **21.** $\{30°, 150°, 210°, 330°\}$

23. $\{30°, 90°, 150°\}$ **25.** $\{0°, 120°, 180°, 240°\}$

27. $\{0°, 180°\}$ **29.** $\{30°, 150°, 270°\}$

31. $\{19.5°, 30°, 150°, 160.5°\}$

33. $\{48.2°, 138.6°, 221.4°, 311.8°\}$

35. $\{63.4°, 71.6°, 243.4°, 251.6°\}$ **37.** $\emptyset$

Page 760, Review Exercises

1. 0.7660 **2.** ≈ 3.4 cm   **3.** ≈ 2860 ft   **4.** ≈ 78 ft

5. ≈ 36.1 cm

Page 761, Calculator Extension

1. $\{0°, 60°, 180°, 300°, 360°\}$ **2.** $\{X: 0° \le X \le 360°,$
$X \ne 90°, X \ne 270°\}$ **3.** $\{90°, 210°, 270°, 330°\}$

4. $\{0°, 30°, 150°, 180°\}$ **5.** Yes, equation 2

Pages 762–763, Chapter Review

1. $\dfrac{\sin X + \cot X}{\cos X} = \dfrac{\sin X}{\cos X} + \dfrac{\cot X}{\cos X}$

$= \tan X + \dfrac{\cos X}{\sin X}\left(\dfrac{1}{\cos X}\right) = \tan X + \csc X$

3. $\dfrac{\sin X + \tan X \sin X + \cos X}{\sec X}$

$= \cos X(\sin X + \tan X \sin X + \cos X)$

$= \cos X\left(\sin X + \dfrac{\sin X}{\cos X} \cdot \sin X + \cos X\right)$

$= \cos X\left(\dfrac{\sin X \cos X + \sin^2 X + \cos^2 X}{\cos X}\right)$

$= \sin X \cos X + 1$

5. $\dfrac{\sqrt{2} - \sqrt{6}}{4}$ **7.** $\cos 30°$ **9.** $\dfrac{\sqrt{6} - \sqrt{2}}{4}$ **11.** $\dfrac{\sqrt{2} - \sqrt{6}}{4}$

13. $-\dfrac{1}{4}$ **15.** $-\cos 13°$ **17.** $\dfrac{161}{289}$ **19.** $\dfrac{3}{4}$ **21.** $\cos 18°$

23. $\{60°, 120°, 240°, 300°\}$ **25.** $\{45°, 225°\}$

Page 763, Chapter 18 Self-Test

1. $\dfrac{\sin X + \tan X}{\sin X} = 1 + \dfrac{\tan X}{\sin X} = 1 + \dfrac{1}{\cos X} = 1 + \sec X$

2. $\dfrac{\tan^2 X}{1 + \tan^2 X} = \dfrac{\tan^2 X}{\sec^2 X} = \dfrac{\sin^2 X}{\cos^2 X} \cdot \dfrac{\cos^2 X}{1} = \sin^2 X$

3. $\dfrac{\csc X - \sin X}{\cos X} = \dfrac{\dfrac{1}{\sin X} - \sin X}{\cos X} = \dfrac{\dfrac{1 - \sin^2 X}{\sin X}}{\cos X} = \dfrac{\cos^2 X}{\sin X \cos X}$

$= \cot X$

4. $\sin 15° \cos 35° + \cos 15° \sin 35°$

5. $\cos 35° \cos 15° + \sin 35° \sin 15°$

6. $\pm \sqrt{\dfrac{1 + \cos 15°}{2}}$ **7.** $2 \sin 35° \cos 35°$

8. $-\sin 60°$ or $-\cos 30°$ **9.** $\cos 22.5°$

10. $-\sin 30°$ **11.** False   **12.** False   **13.** False

14. True   **15.** $\sin 26°$ **16.** $\cos 40°$ **17.** $\{60°, 120°, 240°, 300°\}$ **18.** $\emptyset$ **19.** $\{60°, 180°, 300°\}$

Pages 763–764, Practice for College Entrance Tests

1. C   **2.** B   **3.** A   **4.** E   **5.** D   **6.** B   **7.** A   **8.** E

9. D   **10.** C   **11.** B   **12.** E

Pages 765–767, Cumulative Review (Chapters 16–18)

1. Third   **3.** 1   **5.** $\dfrac{\sqrt{3}}{2}$ **7.** $\left\{\dfrac{\pi}{6}, \dfrac{5\pi}{6}\right\}$ **9.** -1 and -3

11.   **13.**

15. $2\pi, 4$ **17.** 1   **19.**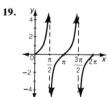

21. $\dfrac{\pi}{3}$ **23.** $-\dfrac{\pi}{4}$ **25.** $\dfrac{\sqrt{2}}{2}$ **27.** $132°$ **29.** $\dfrac{24}{25}$

31. $\sqrt{5}$ **33.** $b \approx 28.7$ cm; $c \approx 31.9$ cm   **35.** $\approx 32.3°$

37. $30°$ **39.**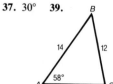

41. $c^2 = a^2 + b^2 - 2ab \cos C$ **43.** ≈ 4.6 cm

45. $\dfrac{1}{\cos X}$

47. $\tan X (\csc X + \cot X) = \tan X \csc X + \tan X \cot X$

$= \dfrac{\sin X}{\cos X} \cdot \dfrac{1}{\sin X} + \tan X \cdot \dfrac{1}{\tan X} = \dfrac{1}{\cos X} + 1 =$
$\sec X + 1$

49. $\cos 250° = -\sin 20°$ **51.** $-\cos X$ **53.** $\text{Cos } X$

55. $\dfrac{\sqrt{3}}{2}$ **57.** $\sin 19°$ **59.** $\{30°, 60°\}$ **61.** $\{90°\}$

INDEX

INDEX

CREDITS

Design Assistants: Julia M. Fair, Leslie Hartwell, DeNee Skipper and Denise Wallace

Cover Design: Uldis Purins, Sheaff Design Inc.

Photo Research: Barbara J. Goodchild

Cover Photos: (*from left to right*): Dan McCoy (Rainbow); © Art Matrix; Photo Researchers, Inc.

Chapter One: xii: Dan McCoy (Rainbow). **5:** Steve McCutcheon (Alaska Pictorial Service). **23:** Culver Pictures.

Chapter Two: 40: Yoav (Phototake). **43:** Ann McQueen (Stock/Boston). **44:** S. Silverman (Gamma-Liaison). **45:** Pro Pix (Monkmeyer Press). **51:** Mark Stevenson (Nawrocki Stock Photo). **52:** Kirk Schlea (Berg & Associates). **56:** David Madison (Bruce Coleman, Inc.). **58:** Ellis Herwig (The Picture Cube). **62:** Norman Owen Tomalin (Bruce Coleman, Inc.). **66:** Paolo Koch (Photo Researchers, Inc.). **68:** Charles M. Falco (Photo Researchers, Inc.).

Chapter Three: 82: E. R. Degginger (Bruce Coleman, Inc.). **83:** Eric Roth (The Picture Cube). **89:** George A. Dillon (Stock/Boston). **111:** Kevin Horan (Stock/Boston). **120:** Mark Antman (The Image Works, Inc.).

Chapter Four: 136: Steve McCutcheon (Alaska Pictorial Service). **140:** Miro Vintoniv (The Picture Cube). **146:** Keith Gunnar (Bruce Coleman, Inc.). **154:** Photo Researchers, Inc. **164:** Ron Sherman (Bruce Coleman, Inc.). **165:** The Bettmann Archive. **175:** Walter Chandoha.

Chapter Five: 184: Cameron Davidson (Bruce Coleman, Inc.). **190:** Science Photo Library (Taurus Photos, Inc.). **193:** Michael Markiw (Bruce Coleman, Inc.). **194:** Susan Van Etten (The Picture Cube). **198:** Martine Gilchrist (Photo Researchers, Inc.). **199:** Dan McCoy (Rainbow). **204:** The Computer Museum. **213, 215:** Alex S. MacLean (Landslides).

Chapter Six: 222: Courtesy of Bausch and Lomb. **226:** Betsy Cole (The Picture Cube). **232:** Geoffrey C. Clifford (Wheeler Pictures). **241:** Mark Sherman (Bruce Coleman, Inc.) **244:** The British Museum (Michael Holford). **245:** Pat F. Jones (Berg & Associates). **249, 250:** William Leatherman/© D. C. Heath. **252:** Susan Van Etten (The Picture Cube). **257:** Dave Schaefer (The Picture Cube). **258:** David Madison (Bruce Coleman, Inc.)

Chapter Seven: 266: © Michael Melford (Peter Arnold, Inc.). **267:** E. R. Degginger. **270:** *l* Copyright by Rand McNally & Co., R.L. 86GP61; *r* NASA. **277:** Courtesy of Tom Lehrer. **293:** Richard Megna (Fundamental Photographs).

Chapter Eight: 304: © Art Matrix. **309:** Mark Antman (The Image Works, Inc.). **314:** Richard Megna (Fundamental Photographs). **315:** Christopher Barker. **337:** Bob Burch (Bruce Coleman, Inc.). **345:** The Granger Collection. **349:** Kodansha. **350:** Thomas Hovland (Grant Heilman Photography, Inc.).

Chapter Nine: 360: Esa (Phototake). **361, 371:** Dan McCoy (Rainbow). **380:** The Bettmann Archive. **381:** Paul Johnson/© D. C. Heath. **388:** Alec Duncan (Taurus Photos, Inc.). **393:** Harry Hartman (Bruce Coleman, Inc.). **397:** Cary Wolinsky (Stock/Boston).

Chapter Ten: 406: Dan McCoy (Rainbow). **421:** The Bettmann Archive. **422:** Robert Schoen/© D. C. Heath. **430:** Fundamental Photographs.

Chapter Eleven: 440: Fred J. Maroon (Photo Researchers, Inc.). **445:** The Granger Collection. **454:** The Bettmann Archive. **458:** Yoav (Phototake). **467:** James Simon (The Picture Cube). **469:** Walter Chandoha. **472:** Kim Steele (Wheeler Pictures). **477:** Harriet Newman-Brown (Monkmeyer Press). **478:** Van Bucher (Photo Researchers, Inc.). **479:** Phil Degginger (Bruce Coleman, Inc.).

Chapter Twelve: 486: Runk/Schoenberger (Grant Heilman Photography, Inc.). **487:** Jane Burton (Bruce Coleman, Inc.). **491:** William Leatherman/D. C. Heath. **496:** Kodansha, Courtesy of Russ Lappa. **499:** David Madison (Bruce Coleman, Inc.). **507:** *t* William Leatherman/© D. C. Heath. *b* Courtesy of Mary Ellen Rudin. **508:** Norman Owen Tomalin (Bruce Coleman, Inc.). **511:** Stephen Dalton (Animals Animals). **513:** J. C. Carton (Bruce Coleman, Inc.). **517:** © Brent Jones. **522:** William Leatherman/© D. C. Heath.

Chapter Thirteen: 526: Phototake. **529:** Margaret C. Berg (Berg & Associates). **530:** Claudia Parks (The Stock Market). **531:** Bob Daemmrich (The Image Works, Inc.). **535:** Lewis Portnoy (Spectra Action, Inc.). **537:** William Leatherman/© D. C. Heath. **541:** Jonathan Weston (Photo Researchers, Inc.). **547:** Carol Palmer. **551:** Bob Higbee (Berg & Associates). **554:** J. A. Dichello, Jr. **560:** Robert Tringal; Jr. (Sportschrome, Inc.). Arnie Feinberg. **561:** Walter Chandoha.

Chapter Fourteen: 568: Dirck Halstead (Gamma Liaison). **575:** Chip Henderson (West Light). **584:** Michael Ponzini (Focus on Sports, Inc.). **596:** E. R. Degginger.

Chapter Fifteen: 608: Hayne Palmour (Berg & Associates). **613:** Hank Morgan (Rainbow). **615:** Robert Lightfoot (Nawrocki Stock Photo).

Chapter Sixteen: 648: E. R. Degginger (Bruce Coleman, Inc.). **664:** Micheal Simpson. **660:** Jerry Schad (Photo Researchers, Inc.). **667:** Richard Megna (Fundamental Photographs). **695:** Gerhard Gscheidle (Peter Arnold, Inc.).

Chapter Seventeen: 704: Grant Heilman Photography, Inc. **705:** Bruce Rosenblum (The Picture Cube). **714:** Robert Frerck (Odyssey Productions). **721:** Bohdan Hrynewych (Stock/Boston). **725:** Peter L. Chapman. **727:** David Ellis (The Picture Cube). **728:** Rob Crandall. **734:** Courtesy of Bryn Mawr College.

Chapter Eighteen: 740: NASA (Photo Researchers, Inc.). **766:** Tom Stack & Associates.